N
W
E
S
Duluth
Portland
Milwaukee
New York
Chicago
Philadelphia
Washington
Kansas City
St. Louis
Atlanta
Jacksonville
New Orleans
Legend
FORESTED AREA
NATIONAL FOREST
SHELTERBELT ZONE
U. S. HIGHWAY
Rudolph Wendelin

# THE YEARBOOK OF AGRICULTURE

# 1949

81ST CONGRESS, 1ST SESSION

HOUSE DOCUMENT NUMBER 29

# TREES

## The Yearbook of Agriculture

1949

UNITED STATES DEPARTMENT OF AGRICULTURE

*U.S. Government Printing Office* - Washington, D.C.

# The Yearbook Committee

F. C. CRAIGHEAD, *Bureau of Entomology and Plant Quarantine*

L. S. GROSS, *Forest Service*

L. M. HUTCHINS, *Bureau of Plant Industry, Soils, and Agricultural Engineering*

W. H. LARRIMER, *Forest Service*

C. B. MANIFOLD, *Soil Conservation Service*

CURTIS MAY, *Bureau of Plant Industry, Soils, and Agricultural Engineering*

JOHN M. MILLER, *Bureau of Entomology and Plant Quarantine*

DANA PARKINSON, *Forest Service, Chairman*

ARTHUR M. SOWDER, *Extension Service*

ARTHUR SPILLERS, *Forest Service*

ALFRED STEFFERUD, *Office of Information, Editor*

# Foreword

BY THE SECRETARY OF AGRICULTURE

I WISH, for several reasons, that every American might have the opportunity to read this book about trees. First, the book underscores the importance of forests to our national and individual prosperity, security, and happiness. Of all the figures and facts marshalled here in proof of this importance the most striking to me is that our drain of saw timber is one and one-half times its rate of growth. Other proof is close at hand—the wooden pencil with which I write, the chair I sit in, my desk, and the doors of my office.

If that is not enough evidence of the everyday importance of our forests, I have only to look out my windows at the stately trees that landscape architects planted to temper the summer heat, to join building and earth and sky in harmony, and to give pleasure to everybody.

These city trees bring to mind the watersheds, shelterbelts, groves, national forests, farm woodlands, community parks, and commercial forests between the eastern seaboard and the West, where I grew up. Truly, our woods and forests are one, in our lives, with soil, water, animals, and food. Soil and water conservation, flood control, permanent abundance, prosperity on the land—the very goals we work toward—involve the proper use of forests.

We all know what happened to the forests the first settlers saw. Most of our virgin timber has disappeared through exploitation, waste, destruction, or use and removal to meet the tremendous needs of a fast-growing Nation.

However, the genius of American democracy can yet restore our forests, rebuild our ghost towns, redeem our watersheds, and find new ways to fight fire and forest pests. Much remains to be learned; we are not yet of one mind about ways and purposes of protection. But the history of what we have done to correct a fault—another reason why I wish every American might read this book—is a lesson we can apply to other parts of our national life.

Most heartening and reassuring is the fact that our forestry achievements have come through democratic processes. Those with the most at stake—the men who needed grazing lands, for example, or those whose livelihood depended on irrigation, lumber, or wildlife—have opportunities to express their views. The guiding precept of the greatest good for the greatest number prevails.

All this embraces the conviction that a basic resource is a national trust. It also embraces faith in people and their leaders and faith in our country. We in the Department of Agriculture who are responsible for national forest lands try constantly to act with the humility and wisdom that befits custodians of such a great trust.

CHARLES F. BRANNAN.

# The Editor to the Reader

IN THE LIBRARY of the United States Department of Agriculture are 11,350-odd publications about trees and forests. Among the oldest of these volumes is the 120-page *Sylva, or a discourse of forest-trees, and the propagation of timber in His Majesties dominions. . . .* The English patriot and philosopher John Evelyn published it in 1664. It is full of warnings and advice: "Men seldom plant trees till they begin to be wise, that is, till they grow old, and find, by experience, the prudence and necessity of it."

One of the latest books in the library is *Breaking New Ground,* by the late American patriot and philosopher Gifford Pinchot. It is an autobiographical account of a pioneer forester's work for conservation of forests, soil, and water supplies.

To that goodly company, an average of 406 books, pamphlets, and articles about timber and its products is added each month. To that growing number also we are adding this Yearbook of Agriculture. An explanation of why we do so seems to be called for.

We have tried here to put into clearer perspective some items of history, importance, administration, and outlook that so far have been in scattered form. We have tried to explain another broad segment of the Department's work. We have tried to tell the essentials of choosing, planting, and growing trees as a farm crop, as a renewable national treasure, as a necessary part of country and city life. We have tried to make a book that is practical and useful for all Americans and interesting and inspiring for those who are unaware of the beauty and delight of the woods. We have tried to tell how and why to plant trees and care for them, and to offer a sort of forum to persons of divergent viewpoints, with all of which we do not necessarily agree.

Several hundred persons cooperated to produce this book. The names of many of them appear elsewhere. To many others in the Government Printing Office, the Department of Agriculture, and the Congress, grateful acknowledgment is made.

For help and loyalty beyond the terms of their job descriptions, thanks are due to Margaret V. Loyd, the editor's assistant, and Catherine F. George, of the Yearbook staff.

The drawings and charts were made by Rudolph A. Wendelin, Miss Leta Hughey, Linn A. Forrest, and Harry Rossoll, of the Forest Service; Sidney H. Horn, of Ames, Iowa; and Joseph H. Stevenson, of the Office of Information. Mr. Wendelin also made the end-paper maps, and Mr. Horn drew many of the illustrations at the heads of the chapters.

Leland J. Prater, of the Forest Service, supervised the taking of many of the photographs. Working with him were the following members of the Forest Service: Ross Angle, Herbert Armstrong, F. S. Baker, Paul S. Bieler, F. M. Cossitt, Duncan Dunning, Frank Flack, George Griffiths, P. Freeman Heim, Antonio A. Hernandez, Jay Higgins, Ashbel F. Hough, Roger Huff, C. R. Hursh, Wallace I. Hutchinson, Bluford W. Muir, Frederick Simmons, Harry Sperling, C. W. Straus, and Paul J. Zehngraff. Others whose photographs appear are Wilfred J. Mead, of the Bureau of Plant Industry, Soils, and Agricultural Engineering; Bob Branstead, B. C. McLean, and Hermann Postlethwaite, of the Soil Conservation Service; H. Miller Cowling, Russell B. Clapper, H. J. MacAloney, John M. Miller, and J. E. Patterson, of the Bureau of Entomology and Plant Quarantine; Ralph E. Lawrence, of Washington, and Dr. Curtis May and Edwin S. Menninger, who took the unusual pictures of tree flowers.

A word about the organization of the material in the Yearbook. We consider first the tree as a unit, a living thing; next, the tree as a member of a small group—in cities and around homes; finally, trees growing together in wood lots, groves, and forests, large and small. The main section of the book ends with chapters on specific problems and values—insects, fire, recreation, wildlife, forestry, and economic importance.

The last part is intended to furnish additional help—lists, charts, tables, a glossary of unusual terms, and references for reading—for those who wish to pursue the subject further. For many persons the fourth section will be the most useful of all.

ALFRED STEFFERUD.

# Contents

## FORESTS AND MEN

### *Trees Living Together*



### *What Do We Plant?*



### *The Small Woodland*

## *Fire, Friend and Enemy*



## *Fun in the Forests*



## *Forests and Wildlife*

## LISTS AND OTHER AIDS

### *To Know the Trees*



### *A Vacation Guide*

# THE TREE

*Live oak near Hahnville in Louisiana: "I am the gift of God and friend of man."*

# Trees and Men

## A TREE IS A LIVING THING

N. T. MIROV

FROM THE SEED that in the autumn falls to the ground and is covered with leaves and soil, a tree is born. The seed is a thing to marvel at.

Pick up a pine nut; crack it open. The rich kernel, called endosperm, is packed with starch, fat, and proteins. Inside the kernel is cradled the ivory rod that is an embryo pine, a baby tree. On one end of the miniature stem is a tuft of pale leaves; the tapering opposite end of the rod will develop into a root.

Cut open a mellow acorn. In it the baby tree does not rest inside rich, nutritional tissue. The starch and fat and proteins are packed in the two seed leaves of the embryo, which are plump and round like the two halves of a peanut. The whole acorn inside the shell is an embryo.

In the spring, when the soil gets warm enough and moisture is abundant, deep changes begin to take place in the dormant seed, already conditioned by the low winter temperatures. The embryo tree awakens from its sleep and begins to grow. What causes this awakening of life is not exactly known, and what is known is complicated, indeed. The growth hormone is activated; the enzymes, whose part is to direct and hasten living processes, start their work feverishly. The insoluble stored fats and starch begin to break down to soluble sugars, mainly dextrose. The stored proteins are split by the enzymes into some 20 soluble compounds called amino acids. Both sugars and amino acids are rushed to the growing points, where still different enzymes rearrange them into building

*Pictured above is the famous Logan Elm, in southern Ohio. State-owned, it antedates the Revolution. In 1939, the tree was 70 feet high and had a crown spread of 148 feet.*

802062°—49——2

material to be used by the germinating embryo. Proteins are formed again from the amino acids, and dextrose is partly used for building the body of the tree and partly burned up to provide necessary energy for the process.

The embryo grows fast. Soon the seed shell becomes too small and splits open. The newly born tree emerges above the ground. Its shoot begins to grow straight up and its roots straight down. The root has important work to do; it provides water for the young seedling. As soon as the little root of a seedling penetrates the ground, the tree is permanently anchored, for better or for worse, to the place where, unless it is transplanted, it has to stay all its life. From now on the tree has to depend on the nutrients available in that particular place and to develop under climatic conditions found there, which cannot be changed. In nature, however, a seedling generally begins its life in a place where its ancestors have been growing for a long time, so the little tree is well adapted to the existing conditions.

As it emerges from the ground, a young tree seedling is as tender as a blade of grass. Its seed leaves may remain in the shell below the ground, as in oak, or they may be carried above the ground, as in maple. In pine, the seed leaves pull themselves out from the endosperm and spread above the seedling like the crown of a miniature palm tree. On the tip of the little stem, tucked between the seed leaves, is the growing point or terminal bud that gives origin to the shoot; its growth continues as long as the tree lives.

Besides the root and stem tips, another important growing region is soon established in the seedling. It is called the cambium layer and is found between the wood and the bark. It makes the tree grow in girth. The cambium consists of a single layer of cells that retain their capacity to divide throughout the life of the tree. This single layer of cells has a peculiar property in that it gives origin both to the wood and to the bark. In the spring, when the cambium layer becomes active, it begins to split off rows of wood cells to the inside and rows of bark cells to the outside. Generally speaking, the bark part of the tree is much thinner than the woody part, or the stem. Bark continuously sloughs off, while the wood accumulates. In the soft inner bark, or bast, are formed sieve tubes, through which manufactured sugar dissolved in water flows from the foliage to storage tissues in stem and root.

The wood formed in the spring consists of light-colored, thin-walled cells; toward the end of the season smaller cells are formed—their walls are heavier and darker, and thus summer wood is formed. This alternation of spring wood and summer wood causes the concentric structure of the tree trunk known as annual rings; they are seen clearly on the cross section of a tree. By counting the annual rings of a tree, one can determine fairly closely its age. When growth conditions are favorable and food and water are abundant, the rings are wide. When drought occurs, the growth slows down and the rings are narrow. By reading a cross section of an old tree, one can determine what growth conditions prevailed during any particular year of the past.

In the cross section of the hardwood trees there may be seen numerous dots. These are canals, so-called vessels, that serve for conducting water along the trunk. In the conifers, like pines or firs, there are no vessels and water moves painstakingly up the trunk through minute holes from one cell to another.

Sixty percent of the wood of a tree is cellulose—by far the most important ingredient. The structure of cellulose is well understood and is rather simple: Molecules of dextrose are linked in pairs to form a more complex sugar, cellobiose, and these units are hooked up to form long chains of cellulose molecules. This structure of cellulose may be easily changed by action of even a weak acid; cellulose then falls apart into the original dextrose molecules, providing an enormous source of sugar that can be used for many purposes, from fattening hogs to production of industrial alcohol. Most of the cellulose used at present, however, is converted into pulp and paper.

The rest of the wood consists mostly of lignin, which is a binding material composed, like the cellulose, of carbon, oxygen, and hydrogen, but of an entirely different and more complicated chemical structure than cellulose. Lignin is not so useful as cellulose at present, but there is little doubt that valuable products will be made from it.

Besides cellulose and lignin, wood contains a small quantity of different substances—starch, fats, sugar, resins, tannins, and many others—and is literally saturated with water.

About 10 percent of the wood mass of a tree is found underground in the form of roots. The root system of a large tree is enormous. The total length of all roots of a big spreading oak tree amounts to many hundreds of miles. The function of the root is to provide water and minerals for the tree and to anchor it securely to the ground. It is important to keep in mind that the roots are part of a living organism and that they need air, food, and water for growing. Mistreatment of roots, such as tramping the soil above them, flooding them for long periods of time, or burying them too deeply, will affect the welfare of the whole tree.

The tree comes of age. Our tree gradually becomes taller and broader, and in the course of time it reaches maturity. The complicated mechanism functions with the precision of a machine, and its many vital processes are well coordinated. Some of the processes, such as respiration or digestion of fats, are strikingly similar in both plants and animals. Others, as mineral nutrition, are found only in the plants.

Let us consider first the process of photosynthesis—that is, the building with the energy of light. In this process, organic matter is formed literally from thin air and water. The air contains minute amounts of carbon dioxide (0.03 percent by volume or three parts in 10,000 parts of air). Through millions of small pores, or stomata, on the leaf surfaces, air penetrates the leaves and gives up about 10 percent of its meager supply of precious carbon dioxide to the tree. In the leaf cells are found small particles called chloroplasts; these contain a green substance, chlorophyll, similar in structure to the hemoglobin of the blood. In fact, in reflected light chlorophyll appears not green but blood red.

Carbon dioxide unites with the chlorophyll and in a chain of reactions, regulated by the enzymes, it combines with oxygen and hydrogen of water to form sugar. An excess of oxygen is released in this process. The energy that is needed for transformation of carbon dioxide and water into the organic substance (sugar) is supplied by sunlight. Only about 1 percent of the solar energy that falls on a leaf is used for photosynthesis. The sugar formed in the process of photosynthesis is dextrose. From it 95 percent of the body of the tree is ultimately made by a series of complicated reactions. Dextrose may be converted into other sugars or it may be combined with nitrogen to form the amino acids, the building blocks from which proteins are made and on which all life, both plant and animal, depends. Part of the dextrose is also used for other purposes, such as conversion into starch, fats, and other substances.

The most favorable conditions for photosynthesis are mild temperatures (about 70° F.) and diffused, moderate light. On hot, bright, summer days the efficiency of photosynthesis goes down. An ample supply of water is essential. When the soil is dry and not enough water is delivered to the crown, the rate of photosynthesis declines. Fertility of the soil is also important, for the building of the tree body requires an ample supply of mineral elements.

Respiration is another life process. Like other living organisms, a tree must respire. The process of respiration consists of oxidizing (burning at low temperature) dextrose sugar; although some energy is lost as heat, most of the energy released during the process is used by the organism for its vital processes. Thus sugar is a source of energy for a tree just as it is for a football player. The chemical reaction of respiration is a reversal of the chemical reaction of photosynthesis, as seen from the following scheme:

PHOTOSYNTHESIS: Carbon dioxide + water + energy expended→dextrose + oxygen;

RESPIRATION: Dextrose + oxygen→ carbon dioxide + water + energy released.

In daytime both photosynthesis and respiration occur at the same time.

Oxygen liberated in photosynthesis is used for respiration, while the carbon dioxide exhaled by the tree is used in photosynthesis. As photosynthesis is a more intensive process than respiration, during a normal day an excess of oxygen is eliminated and an excess of carbon dioxide is absorbed by the tree. When, under adverse conditions, daytime respiration is more intensive than the body-building photosynthesis, the tree loses weight instead of gaining. At night, because of the absence of light, photosynthesis is at a standstill, but respiration continues—just as in humans, oxygen is taken in and carbon dioxide is eliminated. Respiration is going on at all times in all living cells, in the leaves, the roots, and in the stem and bark.

While photosynthesis has its optimum in cool days and decreases when the weather becomes too hot, respiration does not have such an optimum. The warmer it gets, the more intense is the respiration. Respiration is less sensitive to the lack of water than photosynthesis; that is why during droughts, when photosynthesis stops, respiration still continues and causes great harm to the tree. Inside temperatures of 120° to 130° F. are deadly.

NITROGEN is needed by a tree for making its proteins. Without proteins a cell cannot grow and cannot divide. Generally speaking, an abundance of nitrogen promotes vegetative growth of a tree. Animals have no capacity for producing proteins from nitrogen; they depend on plants for the needed proteins.

A tree has the capacity to absorb inorganic nitrogen and with it to make its own proteins. Although four-fifths of the air consists of nitrogen, less than 1 percent of the element is found in the wood of a tree. And to get that little bit of nitrogen is an extremely difficult task for a tree. Nitrogen as found in the atmosphere cannot be used by the tree; it has to be converted into ammonia or into nitrates and only in this form (mostly as nitrates) can nitrogen be absorbed by the roots. Let us see how a tree manages its nitrogen economy.

Traces of ammonia are found in the air, and some of the nitrogen oxide is formed there, especially after thunderstorms. These substances are carried by the rain to the soil, but their quantity is altogether too meager to contribute much to the nitrogen nutrition. A few trees, such as the locust or alder, have on their roots nodules formed by bacteria that are capable of assimilating nitrogen from the air and converting it into nitrates, but most trees have no nitrogen-fixing nodules. There are free bacteria that live in the soil and can use atmospheric nitrogen. But these bacteria are not abundant and they like warmth, so that in cooler climates they are not active. Fallen leaves, if not burned, contain some proteins. These proteins are gradually decomposed into amino acids, ammonia, and eventually into nitrates. But fallen leaves contain only about 1 percent of nitrogen—slightly more in the hardwood leaves and slightly less in pine needles.

Animals waste a great deal of nitrogen, which they obtain from the plants. Fur, hair, nails, and skin, being made of proteins, contain nitrogen that cannot be used again by the organism. Large amounts of nitrogen are eliminated by the animals as waste.

Trees, however, are frugal with their nitrogen. They do not waste it, but use it over and over. A tree that is well supplied with nitrogen has lush, dark-green foliage, and its growth is luxuriant—a tree deprived of nitrogen is stunted and its leaves are pale green. An overdose of nitrogen is also bad for a tree. Conditions of nitrogen excess are extremely rare in nature, but might occur occasionally, for instance, in a tree grown in a chickenyard where supply of nitrogen is in excess.

How can you help a tree in its nitrogen nutrition? Growing nitrogen-fixing legumes, such as clover, near your trees will enrich the soil with nitrogen. The addition of leafmold to the soil would serve the same purpose. Remember, too, that removing or burning fallen leaves from around the trees deprives the trees of the much-needed nitrogen. If burning or removing must be done, it is wise to replace the loss by applying some nitrogen fertilizer. One word of caution in feeding trees with nitrogen. Nitrate fertilizers are leached rapidly from the soil; they are not absorbed by the soil as readily as, say, the phosphates. It is advisable therefore to add nitrates in small quantity and often, rather than to apply a large quantity at one time.

In applying fertilizer one should keep in mind that trees do not grow so fast as field crops, and thus their demand for nitrogen and for other nutrients is comparatively small.

Besides oxygen, hydrogen, carbon, and nitrogen, which are obtained from water and air, for proper functioning a tree needs several other elements, which it obtains from the minerals found in the soil.

Some of these mineral elements—potassium, phosphorus, and calcium—are needed in relatively large amounts. Other elements—magnesium, sulfur, and iron—are needed in relatively smaller quantities. Still others, called trace elements—such as manganese, copper, zinc, boron, or molybdenum—are necessary only in minute quantities. The need even of major elements is very small indeed. The total amount of the mineral elements in dry wood is less than one-half of 1 percent, and the need for the trace elements is so small that generally they are found in sufficient quantity in any soil.

Occasionally there may be a complete absence or too small a supply of the trace elements in a particular soil. In that case, a tree will not grow properly unless the lacking element is introduced. Great care should be exercised not to apply too much of the trace elements, lest great damage be done to the tree. For instance, while potash or phosphorus may be added to soil at the rate of, say, 1,000 pounds an acre, about 5 or 10 pounds an acre of a trace element is enough. More than that might be harmful to the trees. A specialist should be consulted before any trace element is added to the soil.

When wood is burned, all these and many other elements are found in the ashes, but some sulfur and phosphorus and all nitrogen are lost in smoke. Twenty-seven elements, including silver, titanium, and nickel, are found in the ashes of white pine. That does not mean that all these elements are necessary for the life of the tree. Some minerals that may be found in a tree, such as common salt, apparently are not needed for its proper functioning. These are absorbed by the roots simply because they happened to be in the soil; the tree has no way of telling the useful minerals from the useless or even harmful ones. For example, arsenic, though very poisonous to the tree, is as readily absorbed as phosphorus.

Mineral elements are needed by a tree to perform various vital functions. Phosphorus is found in some plant proteins; seeds and growing points are especially rich in phosphorus. Lack of phosphorus often manifests itself in purpling or bronzing of foliage, which is easy to detect. Sulfur also enters into the building of certain proteins. It is well distributed throughout the plant. Calcium apparently is somehow involved in the carbohydrate translocation. It enters into the construction of the cell wall; crystals of calcium oxalate are found often in the tissues of plants. Magnesium is a constituent of the chlorophyll molecule. It is also probably related to fat formation and to the synthesis of some proteins. Potassium is especially abundant in young growing parts of the tree; it has something to do with synthesis and translocation of sugars; in the absence of potassium, cells do not divide. Iron is needed to keep the tree green. Iron is not a part of the chlorophyll molecule, but without it chlorophyll cannot be formed. Iron is also needed in respiration. Generally, there is enough iron in any soil, but sometimes in alkaline soils it is found in an insoluble state. Iron-deficient trees lack the healthy color.

The physiological role of minor elements is little known, but symptoms of their deficiency are pronounced. At present our concept of the physiology of plant nutrition is in the process of revision. With the recent advances of nuclear physics, it is possible to prepare radioactive mineral salts. "Tagged" radioactive phosphorus or potassium can be followed as soon as it is absorbed by a plant; it can be traced to its destination and its function in plant life can be determined.

WATER IS CONTAINED in all tissues of a tree, both dead and alive. Young leaves or tips of roots contain up to 90 percent of water; tree trunks contain as much as 50 percent. Water is indispensable to the tree. All living processes take place in water. Sugars are built from carbon dioxide and water. Mineral nutrients are carried from the soil to the top of the tree in a stream of water. In the spring the organic materials in the form of sugars and amino acids are rushed in a stream of water from their places of winter storage to the bursting buds.

And there is the dramatic process called transpiration. In that process, water is absorbed by the roots, pushed into the sapwood, and then pulled up to the leaves (as high as 350 feet in redwood) above the ground. The energy needed for transpiration, as for photosynthesis, is supplied by the sun. About one-half of the solar energy falling on a leaf is used for transpiration. Through the same openings (the stomata) that admit carbon dioxide to the inner tissues of the leaf, the water is evaporated to the atmosphere, and this evaporation creates a tremendous pull on the minute, continuous strands of water in the sapwood and thereby causes a movement of water from the roots to the treetop. There is no such process in the tree as circulation of the sap similar to circulation of the blood in animals. Only a trifle of water is transported from the crown downward and comparatively little is retained by the tissues. The terms "the sap is up" and "the sap is down" are not correct and are misleading.

The formation of 100 grams of cellulose requires 55 grams of water. But while a tree increases its weight by 100 grams, it loses in transpiration nearly 100,000 grams (that is, 1,000 times more) of water.

Transpiration brings water from the soil to the leaves so that photosynthesis can be carried on. To enter through the cell walls, carbon dioxide must be dissolved in water. The surface of the chlorophyll containing cells must be moist at all times.

The leaves have a water-regulated mechanism that permits a tree to shut off the stomata and thus prevent loss of water. But the very same stomata have to be open in order to admit carbon dioxide for the photosynthesis. When stomata are open, the tree loses water; when they are closed, the tree cannot assimilate carbon dioxide. A balance between the two processes must be maintained by the tree.

The stomata open their little shutters early in the morning. At noon they begin to close, and just before sunset they are closed tight for the night. In some trees, stomata may open at night. During excessively hot and dry days the stomata are open only for a short time in the early morning and then close for the rest of the day. Under these conditions the tree cannot make much sugar from the carbon dioxide.

What can a man do to help a tree in its water economy? Not more than to supply it with water by irrigation, by preserving the natural mulch on the ground and thus reducing evaporation from the soil, and by not planting trees too close to each other or exposing the shade-loving trees to full sunlight.

THE PHYSIOLOGY OF GROWTH is this: Through the process of photosynthesis and with the help of nitrogen and the mineral elements, the tree builds up its body. In some trees, such as the giant sequoias, as much as 50,000 cubic feet of organic matter, mostly wood, may accumulate in this way. But the growth of a tree is not merely an accumulation of organic matter. Growth is an involved physiological process, in which the use of building materials is regulated by the growth substances or hormones.

Growth of a tree is retarded if mineral nutrition is held at a minimum and water is withheld. This is the method used by the Japanese in dwarfing trees; some of their dwarf trees, grown in small pots, may be several hundred years old. In fact, any pot-bound young tree is checked in its growth and thus is more or less dwarfed.

Growth of the tree depends not only on the correlation of its physiological functions but also on external factors like temperature, light, and moisture. Within a certain range, an increase of temperature of 18° F. nearly doubles the rate of growth of plants; but when temperatures are either too low or too high for a proper functioning of the organism, many disturbances may occur in the tree. In that case the growth of the tree is retarded, and although life may still continue there is no coordination between the different vital functions. The tree ceases to grow. The optimum temperature for growth is not necessarily the same as the optimum temperature for general development of the plant. Many trees need a low temperature period for their normal development; when this cold period is eliminated, they do not grow.

Light must also be available in the proper amount and quality. When light is lacking, the tree cannot manufacture organic matter and will eventually die. Light also retards the growth of the tree. In the dark, the shoots grow faster than in the light. In yellow and red light, the plant can assimilate carbon dioxide very well, but the plant does not develop normally—it behaves as if it were growing in the dark. For normal development a tree needs, besides yellow and red light, the blue, violet, and ultraviolet rays of the sun. Those rays are not needed for photosynthesis, and their action on the growth is that of retardation. The blue end of the spectrum is needed by a tree for formative purposes.

When a tree is bent by some mechanical force, such as the wind, its normal growth is disturbed. On the upward side of the tree, the newly formed cells of the sapwood are stretched; on the lower side, they are compressed. This distortion of the wood structure, due to pressure, is often noticed in our conifers. Where a pressure is applied, there is formed so-called compression wood, which lowers the quality of lumber manufactured from such wood.

In a temperate climate, trees show an annual periodicity of growth. The annual shoot completes its growth early in the season, say at the end of June. By that time, in many forest trees, all cell division for the next year's growth is completed in the bud. This means that the next year's growth pattern of a tree is determined almost a year before—all microscopic flower buds are set; all microscopic leaf buds are formed. The next season the growth takes place mostly by elongation of the bud cells prefabricated in the previous year. Growth in diameter takes place throughout the summer by division and enlargement of cambium cells.

A long time before cold weather sets in, the tree has already completed its seasonal growth; it prepares for the winter. Evergreen trees retain their foliage for winter, but deciduous trees act differently. They remove much of the nutrient material from the leaves; then a peculiar physiological process (abscission) of the leafstalks causes the leaves to drop. The tree is in a deep rest now and can withstand a great deal of cold. An unusual warm spell in late winter or early spring, however, may cause buds to open—subsequent cold may kill them. Sometimes a northern tree transplanted in the South might open its buds too early in the spring and suffer from a later frost.

Reproduction is possible when the tree reaches its physical maturity. The sexual reproduction of trees is basically similar to that of animals. In plants, reproduction manifests itself by the appearance of male and female flowers, which may be borne either on separate trees, as in cottonwood, or on the same tree, as in pine, or even combined into a perfect flower, as in the magnolia.

Pollen of the male flower fertilizes the ovule of a female flower, which then develops into the seed. The whole process of reproduction involves setting of flower buds, development of the male and female flowers, pollination, and development of the seed and fruit. Each process depends on internal as well as external conditions.

In annual plants, the reproductive stage means subsequent death; the plant dies as soon as the seed is matured. In trees, production of seed is continued for many years. In a tree there is a delicate balance between vegetative growth and reproduction. If a tree grows too fast, it will not produce much fruit or seed. The reproductive stage is generally reached when a tree begins to slow down its most vigorous height growth.

The accumulation of carbohydrates is conducive to the flowering, while the abundance of the minerals, especially nitrogen, promotes growth at the expense of reproduction. The proper balance between organic and mineral nutrition and the possible formation of flowering hormones occurs in the tree only after a certain stage of maturity has been reached. After that, a tree begins to produce seed, but not necessarily every year. Seed bearing is a taxing process. Much material and much energy are required for it. Many trees have periodicity of seed years, and the intervals between the good seed years vary in the different trees. Again, this periodicity apparently depends on a definite combination of nutritional and external factors. As the flower buds are set during the previous summer, the weather conditions of the last year have a lot to do with the flowering. Dry, warm weather generally is favorable for setting flower buds. Weather conditions prevailing during pollination and the development of pollen grains are also of importance. A great deal of light is needed for flowering. Trees grown in the open produce flowers and seed in profusion and much earlier than trees that are grown in the shade. Abundant sunshine at the time of setting flowering buds also contributes to the seed crop the next year.

The effect of photoperiod, or day length, discovered in 1920 by W. W. Garner and H. A. Allard of the United States Department of Agriculture, is of great importance in flowering of trees. Some trees flower only when the days are short, while others bloom when the days are long. A northern tree that was growing under the long-day conditions may not bloom if moved to the South, because the summer days of the new home are too short for it. If, say, a street lamp provides that extra needed light, a northern tree may burst into bloom even in a short-day country.

Certain chemical substances, such as ethylene, are known to break the dormancy of plants. If your lilac bush unexpectedly bursts into bloom earlier than usual, it might be because you had burned some fallen leaves or clippings nearby and the smoke supplied enough ethylene to awaken the dormant flower buds.

Sexual reproduction of trees plays an important part in the development of the diversity of our trees. By combining characters of the pollen parent with those of the seed parent, new combinations are formed, some of which may be very valuable. But sexual reproduction is not absolutely necessary for trees; many of them can be reproduced by vegetative means—cuttings, grafting, and budding.

OLD AGE comes to trees, as to all other living organisms. The span of life of a tree is specific. Gray birch is old at 40. The sugar maple lives longer, up to 500 years. Some oaks may live 1,500 years, junipers 2,000 years. Some of the giant sequoias are believed to be about 4,000 years old. Old trees are like old people—the infirmities of age are upon them. They have difficulty with respiration (its rate in old plants is much lower than in young plants); the annual shoots are not so vigorous as they once were, and the weakening cambium activity is reflected in the formation of fewer and fewer wood cells. Hence, the annual rings become narrower. As the rate of growth of the tree decreases, dead branches appear in ever-increasing numbers. The recuperative capacity of an old tree is impaired, and its wounds do not heal over so easily as before. The leaves become smaller; their moisture content decreases; the tree finds it more and more difficult to provide water for its vital functions; the inflow of food to the growing points drops; and the growth hormones probably cannot be transported in large enough quantity to the places where they are needed.

Causes of death of a tree may be numerous and are often difficult to diagnose. When a tree is broken by snowfall or uprooted by wind or killed by fire, the cause of death is evident. But often the cause is rather obscure. Sometimes lack of water may cause death of the tree, and again trees weakened by drought may fall prey to an insect or fungus attack.

Fire is an archenemy of trees. Its direct effect on trees is obvious enough. But there is also an indirect effect: Heat may injure patches of succulent inner bark of the tree trunk. Fermentation may easily start in these places and attract insects. The smoke of a fire contains some physiologically active gases—ethylene, for example, or acetylene. The gases may cause the opening of the dormant buds prematurely, thus exposing them to frost damage and contributing to the general weakening of the tree.

When a tree dies, its death almost always can be traced to some external cause—cold, fire, drought, insects, fungi, or malnutrition. Some of these causes are beyond our control. Others can be prevented. By taking good care of the tree, one can prolong its life. The tree should be well provided with water and light and be well nourished, or at least not deprived of nutritive substances. A healthy tree will resist attacks of insects and diseases; it will develop a large crown and a strong root system; and it will withstand the action of the wind.

If a tree is treated as a living organism, with an understanding of its vital functions, it will be a constant source of profit and pleasure to men.

N. T. MIROV *is plant physiologist of the Institute of Forest Genetics, which is a branch of the California Forest and Range Experiment Station, maintained by the Forest Service in cooperation with the University of California, in Berkeley. He holds a master's degree in forestry and a doctor's degree in plant physiology from the University of California.*

*The attention of the reader is directed particularly to later chapters and sections that relate to Dr. Mirov's subject, including the bibliography (For Further Reference) at the end of the book; Pointers on Planting, by T. E. Maki; First the Seed, Then the Tree, by Paul O. Rudolf; Direct Seeding of Trees, by W. E. McQuilkin; The Community of Trees, by Jesse H. Buell.*

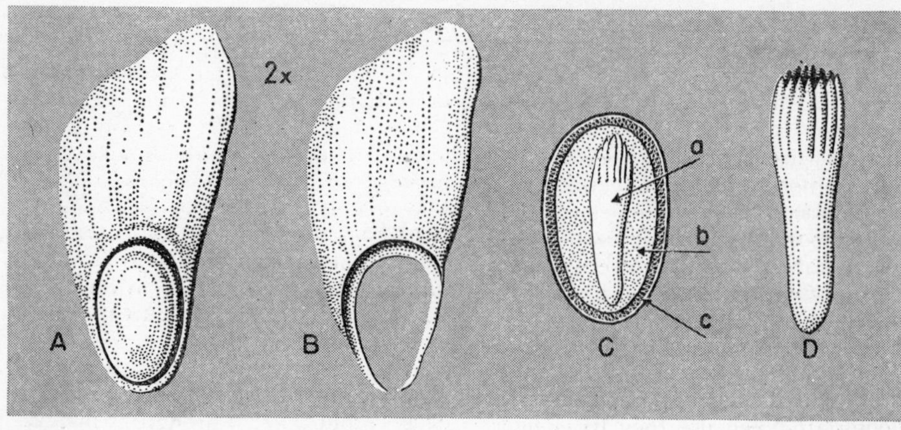


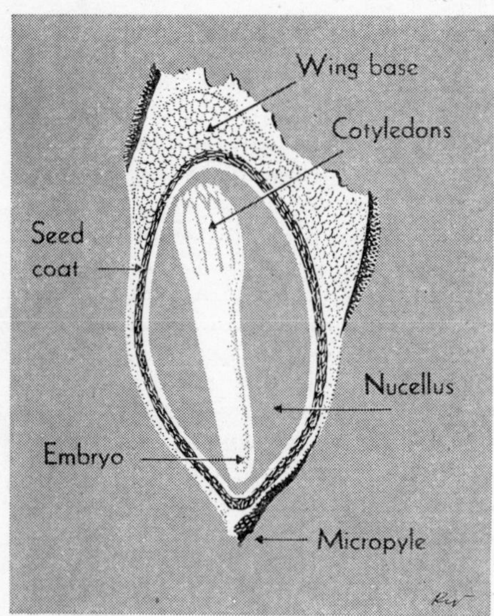


## DETAILS OF SEEDS

Above: A pine seed: *A,* seed with wing; *B,* detached wing; *C,* cross section of a seed showing embryo (*a*) surrounded by an endosperm (*b*), which is filled with storage food, and in turn surrounded by the seed coat (*c*); *D,* excised embryo with a tuft of seed leaves.

Opposite: A dewinged Douglas-fir seed in cross section.

Below: Seeds of several types: *A,* white fir, dewinged seed, borne in cones; *B,* silk-tree, seeds borne in pods; *C,* common spicebush, seeds borne in fleshy drupes; *D,* common buttonbush, 2 to 4 nutlets borne in dry, podlike fruits.

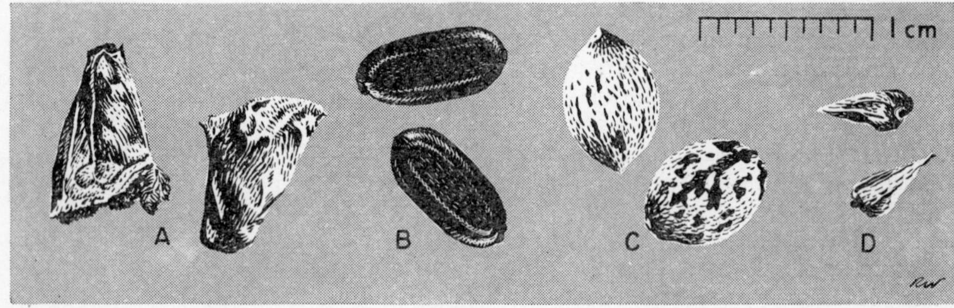

# SOME TREES ARE FAMOUS

CHARLES E. RANDALL

Some trees, like some persons, become famous. In every section there are trees that have the esteem of local people because of their associations with notable persons or events or because of their great size or age. Some of the trees that figured prominently in the early history of our Nation have become national shrines.

Trees are natural landmarks and memorials. Because they have more than the allotted life span of man, they carry their associations through generation after generation. There are trees still living that were planted by the first President of the United States. There are trees that have been immortalized by poets and artists. There are trees with special religious, esthetic, or sentimental associations. There are trees that are respected as the oldest living things on earth.

Almost as numerous as the places where George Washington is reputed to have slept are the trees associated with him. Living trees planted by Washington or under his direction at Mount Vernon include some tuliptrees, buckeyes, elms, pecans, hollies, lindens, hemlocks, and mulberries. Two pecan trees on the lawn near the mansion at Mount Vernon, grown from nuts given to Washington by Thomas Jefferson in 1775, are said to be the oldest trees now standing on the estate. Washington and Jefferson were kindred spirits in their love for trees, and the "Jefferson Pecans" are a living illustration of this congeniality.

The Washington Elm near the Senate wing of the United States Capitol in the District of Columbia survived until 1948. Under it, the first President was said to have watched the construction of the Capitol.

The Washington Friendship Tree, a horsechestnut, at Bath, Pa., is said to be a memorial to the friendship existing between Washington and Gen. Robert Brown in Revolutionary days. On one of General Brown's visits to Mount Vernon, when peace had come, Washington dug from his garden two young horsechestnuts and presented them to his friend, who carried them on horseback into the hills of Pennsylvania and planted them at his home at Bath. One of the trees still lives.

Charleston, in South Carolina, has its Washington Live Oak. The story goes that when George Washington visited Charleston in 1791 he was a breakfast guest in the beautiful plantation home of the Pinckney family. He heard the mistress of the household order her gardener to cut down the oak tree that obstructed the view from the new portico. Washington, the tree lover, expressed the wish that the tree should be spared. It was.

There were many other "Washington trees." One of the most famous was the Washington Elm in Cambridge, Mass., under which the leader of the American Revolutionary Forces assumed command in 1775. The tree is now dead, but its true descendants are growing on the campus of the University of Washington in Seattle and in the Arnold Arboretum at Jamaica Plain in Massachusetts. (Incidentally, some supposedly pedigreed cions of the Cambridge elm have been planted that were found to have a bar sinister on their escutcheon. When a forester inspected them a few years ago, all proved to be either English or Scotch elms and not the native American elm, and so could not be descendants of the historic tree. Somebody distributed, at fancy prices, plants or seed that were misrepresented as being from the original Washington Elm.)

And the John Quincy Adams Elm, planted on the White House grounds during the administration of President Adams, the great beech and other fine old trees on the estate of President

James Buchanan near Lancaster, Pa., the Grant Elm planted by President Grant in 1870 on the lawn in front of Woodstock Academy in Connecticut, the six tall hickories flanking the tomb of Andrew Jackson and his good wife, Rachel, at the Hermitage near Nashville, Tenn., and the Lincoln Oak at Lincoln's birthplace at Hodgenville, Ky., are examples of the many trees associated with Presidents of the Nation.

Many other trees have been associated with notable persons: The ancient oak at Crockett, Tex., under which David Crockett was said to have camped during his journey from the States to help Texas in its struggle for freedom from Mexican rule; the Buffalo Bill Elm, near Le Claire, Iowa, under which William F. Cody played when a boy; the giant hemlocks in Germantown, Pa., which, according to tradition, were planted by William Penn; and the horsechestnut at Stratford-on-the-Potomac, Va., mentioned in Gen. Robert E. Lee's diary as having been planted by his mother, Anne Carter Lee.

The lovely Charter Oak, in Hartford, Conn., was a famous historical shrine in earlier days. The charter of the Connecticut Colony, granted by King Charles II in 1662, was supposed to have been hidden in the oak by a patriot when Sir Edmund Andros demanded its surrender in 1687, at the command of King James II. The charter served Connecticut as a constitution from 1662 to 1816 and conveyed to the Colony all the land "from the said Narragansett Bay on the east to the South Sea on the west." When the tree blew down in 1856, the hole that concealed the charter had been enlarged enough to hold 25 men, so it was said. Pieces of the wood were made into gavels, picture frames, and chairs; one of the chairs stands in the senate chamber of the State capitol.

A number of Indian trail trees may still be found at various places in the Mississippi Valley. The trees were bent over when they were small saplings to mark an Indian trail, and for that reason often have several upright branches growing from the horizontal trunk. A good example of an Indian trail tree has been preserved and marked by the Daughters of the American Revolution in Evanston, Ill.

Many trees are famous in literature. The Evangeline Oak at St. Martinville, La., marks the place where the Acadians, driven from Nova Scotia, landed in 1758. It was immortalized by Longfellow's famous poem. Under the boughs of the Lanier Oak at Brunswick, Ga., the southern poet, Sidney Lanier, was inspired to write "The Marshes of Glynn." A tree since known as "Whittier's Pine Tree," near Sunset Hill, N. H., was named the "Wood Giant" by Whittier. The "Great Elm of Concord" in Massachusetts was beloved of Emerson, Hawthorne, and Thoreau. A tree in Wise County, Va., was made famous by John Fox, Jr., in his novel, *The Trail of the Lonesome Pine.* The tree in Tuolumne County, Calif., under which Mark Twain wrote *The Jumping Frog of Calaveras County,* which made him famous overnight, was known as the "Mark Twain Oak" until it was felled in 1929. Many other trees can be found that are associated with American authors, or that have a place in American literature.

Many trees of historical or sentimental interest have been destroyed or have suffered from neglect. Many others have been preserved through the efforts of civic organizations or interested local citizens.

In Norfolk, Va., Memorial Oak, a tree that is believed to antedate the city itself, was purchased jointly by the city and the Garden Club of Norfolk in 1923 and dedicated as a memorial to the sons of Norfolk who died in the First World War.

In McAlester, Okla., a lone pine stands in the middle of a wide street, protected by fence and concrete curbing. It is an example of the many favorite trees that a tree lover or civic-minded group saved by changing road locations or building plans.

**An Indian trail tree, a white oak in Highland Park, Ill. The tree took root at a point of secondary contact with the ground and continued to grow with two sets of roots.**

In Athens, Ga., was the "Oak that Owned Itself"—"for and in consideration of the great love I bear this tree," its owner, William H. Jackson, willed to it entire possession of itself and of all land within 8 feet of the tree on all sides. The deed, dated 1820, is recorded in the office of the town clerk.

There are freak trees, interesting as curiosities, such as the old elm in Hamburg, Conn., that grew around a gravestone; the G-trees of Biloxi, Miss.; the Lyre Tree, an elm of freak growth in Livingston, N. J.; the Cannibal Tree, a Douglas-fir that entirely enclosed an oak in Oregon; and the trees that started from seed and grew for many years on the top of the courthouse tower in Greensburg, Ind.

Dane County Village, near Madison, in Wisconsin, has a Forest of Fame, in which trees have been transplanted from the homes of many Presidents of the United States, famous generals, and personages associated with religion, science, music, and commerce, and from historic places such as Sherwood Forest in England. The Forest of Fame was started by John S. Donald, a professor in the University of Wisconsin. The first trees, from George Washington's home at Mount Vernon, were planted by Professor Donald on Arbor Day, 1916.

Among the trees that are of special interest to many tourists are the Japanese cherry trees in Washington, D. C., and the Mile of Christmas Trees in Pasadena, Calif. The awe-inspiring coastal redwoods and the giant sequoias of the California Sierra are visited by people from all parts of the world.

I have written about only a few of the notable trees, living and dead, for which Americans have a special fondness. Still to be mentioned are the trees for which I (and millions of Americans like me) have a particular affection, although they have no connections with Presidents or history and it is only our neighbors and friends that come to admire them. They are the trees in our own yards. For us they are reminders of how close trees are to our lives, of the words that I am told appear on a sign at the entrance to a public park in Portugal:

"Ye who would pass by and raise your hand against me, harken ere you harm me. I am the heat of your hearth on the cold winter nights; the friendly shade screening you from the summer sun; and my fruits are refreshing draughts quenching your thirst as you journey on. I am the beam that holds your house, the board of your table, the bed on which you lie, and the timber that builds your boat. I am the handle of your hoe, the door of your homestead, the wood of your cradle, and the shell of your coffin. I am the gift of God and friend of man."

CHARLES E. RANDALL *is a native of California and a graduate of Stanford University and George Washington University. After teaching in Oregon State College, work on ranches, newspaper work, and participation in a tree-disease survey in western forests, he joined the Bureau of Plant Industry, Soils, and Agricultural Engineering as a junior forest pathologist. In 1927 he entered the Forest Service as an editor and writer.*

*The General Sherman Bigtree in the Sequoia National Park, California*

# TREES REMEMBERED AND REMEMBERING

G. HARRIS COLLINGWOOD

Long before Maine became known as the Pine Tree State, before the men who accompanied De Soto complained of Florida as "cumbersome with woods and bogs," before Columbus and his intrepid crew from three little wooden ships knelt in reverent thankfulness on the shores of San Salvador Island in the Caribbean Sea, before Leif Ericson and his Norsemen set sail from the North Atlantic coast of an uncharted continent with a cargo of timbers for Greenland, there were, among the seemingly limitless forests of what is now known as North America, many of the same giant sequoias that now tower above their giant associates in isolated areas of the western slopes of the continent. Today, after more than three centuries of exploitation and development, few other trees are standing that may be said to "remember" any of those adventurous explorers. The sequoias could recall them all.

Were Columbus and his crew to return to see what has happened to the new land they discovered 457 years ago, they might find among perhaps a dozen varieties of trees some individuals that were standing when the discovery was reported to their royal patrons. These are the hardy, long-lived ones of more than a thousand tree species that inhabit this country.

Along the east coast a few of the original southern cypress or the bald-cypress still stand—but very few. Some of the biggest eastern hemlock could probably look that far back, as could also a few of the Carolina hemlock, in isolated coves of the Great Smoky Mountains. This is the tree that the late Charles Sprague Sargent described as America's most beautiful conifer. Among the broadleaved hardwoods they would find early companions only among the white oaks and post oaks, with possibly a rare old sassafras tree. Beyond the Great Plains, of whose existence those explorers had not the slightest shadow of information, they would find a larger variety and many more individual trees.

Extensive forests of Douglas-fir in Washington and Oregon include trees whose size in 1492 exceeded that of many present-day trees whose trunks are harvested and hauled to a sawmill. Among them, extending in more or less pure stands through British Columbia to the Alaskan coast, are larch, Engelmann spruce, noble fir, western redcedar, Sitka spruce, and Alaska-cedar, whose size and growth rings attest their age. But the biggest trees then, as well as now, were two varieties of sequoia: *Sequoia gigantea,* the bigtree or giant sequoia of California's high Sierra, and *Sequoia sempervirens,* the coast redwood, whose magnificent fluted columns rise high into the Pacific fog near the coast of northern California and southwestern Oregon.

Those trees, and more particularly the two sequoias with their associates, are part of an amazing heritage that has contributed immeasurably to the economy, political structure, and spiritual outlook of this Nation. The extent to which they and all other forest trees can continue to help support the national welfare depends on the foresight and efforts of the men and women who now inhabit this broad land.

During four centuries and more, while man has pressed with accelerating force upon the natural resources of the continent, forests that seemed a cumbersome burden to the early pioneers have become an asset whose contribution is only beginning to be fully recognized. As men and women journeyed across the land, broke the soil, and built towns, political needs made necessary division of the country into States, each with an identifying name.

Each State has characteristics, peculiarities, and resources that give rise to local pride, yet all have ideals in common and all bear allegiance to a central government. The struggles and strife that resulted in this common allegiance revealed increasing dependence upon trees. A few States early identified themselves by some of the trees that were characteristic of their area. Eventually, there developed a Nation-wide movement to designate a typical tree for each State—a mascot, as it were.

Maine was early dubbed the Pine Tree State, yet no single species of the pine has been officially recognized. That was perhaps too obvious since it could have been none other than the eastern white pine, whose clean, straight boles had early been selected by the King's men to serve as masts and spars for the British Navy and so had borne the blaze of the Broad Arrow.

Remembering her contributions to the development of the great agricultural and industrial Midwest during the turn of the century, Minnesota chose the same white pine for her emblem. Idaho chose the taller western white pine and has been vigorously vociferous in claiming for that tree the official name of Idaho white pine.

Two Southern States bear witness to the fecundity of forests and the economic importance of pines in their development. Alabama designated as her tree the slash pine, a dual-purpose tree. On it and the longleaf pine, a native also of Georgia, depends the naval stores industry which, until the recent age of chemistry, was the source of all our turpentine and rosin. Arkansas chose the shortleaf pine, her most numerous of these southern lumber producers.

Moving to the west, we find Montana has recognized the potential possibilities of the versatile ponderosa pine, whose easily worked wood long struggled under the name of western yellow pine. Wyoming memorialized the home-making efforts of her Indians and accepted the lodgepole pine. Other tribes of Indians were a strong influence upon the selection of New Mexico and of Nevada. New Mexico designated the pinyon pine and Nevada the singleleaf pinyon, whose nutlike seeds formed an important item in the Indian diet.

Recalling the Gothic arch under which General Washington reviewed the Colonial troops at Cambridge, and similar trees that grace her village streets and country highways, Massachusetts honored herself by singling out the American elm.

The Charter Oak, whose cavity played so significant and also so romantic a part in early Colonial history, was a white oak. So history may be said to have made the decision for Connecticut. White oak is also the choice of Maryland, whose Wye Oak, standing on her Eastern Shore, is said to be America's largest oak tree. Neighboring West Virginia, remembering that many families and industries depend on her heavy stands of hardwood forest, also chose the white oak. The settlers who trekked west found counterparts of those trees in the oak openings of the prairies, and Illinois chose the "native oak," the most common being the bur oak.

A sweet tooth and pride in the special quality of a product for which Vermont has long laid claim made the maple her natural choice. To designate this sugar maple, hard maple, or white maple is of little consequence, for all are names for the same tree. Whether New York chose the same tree because of its annual crop of sirup and sugar is a question. The children of Wisconsin, by vote, have asked their legislature to name the sugar maple as their State tree, also. These States may as logically have given weight to the hard, firm, white wood, whose uses range from shoe trees to flooring, and to the symmetry of the leaves and the brilliant autumn foliage.

The straight-grained, lightweight, easily cleaved, and durable eastern redcedar was cut and split into rails and posts for many southern pioneer fences. The first three of these qualities later singled out the wood as peculiarly adapted for the wooden casings of pencils, and the spicy odor added to its desirability. But with these qualities recognized, it was the durability of the wood that permitted pencil makers to use fence rails that had stood in place for a generation or more. As a result, many a Tennessee hill farmer paid off the mortgage on his farm with the cedar rails his father had cut. Small wonder, then, that Tennessee citizens voted to make eastern redcedar their State tree.

From southern New England to the Gulf coast and west into the Mississippi Valley grows a glossy-leafed giant known variously as yellow-poplar and whitewood, for its soft, even-grained wood, and as tuliptree, for its orange and yellow blossoms. The lumber is sought by cabinetmakers as well as carpenters, and it has contributed to homes and barns in the Middle West, as it now contributes to many woodworking industries. So it is the natural choice of Indiana and of Kentucky.

Utility may have vied with romance when Louisiana and Mississippi chose southern magnolia. The lumber from magnolia contributes to the need for even-grained, soft, easily worked hardwood, but the white blossoms against the shiny green leaves are a lasting memory of all who have enjoyed life in the South.

Some of the same love of beauty and romantic fervor attributed to the South may have influenced the people of Virginia and North Carolina in their choice of the flowering dogwood as their State tree. Similarly, the people of Oklahoma singled out the eastern redbud or Judas-tree, those of Missouri selected the Engelmann hawthorn or the red haw, and Delaware chose the American holly.

History records that the Southern soldiers were influenced in their campaign against Gettysburg by the hope they would get shoes in that area. Few may have realized that the shoemakers had established themselves in Pennsylvania because of the seemingly inexhaustible forests of hemlock, whose bark yielded tannin with which to make leather tough for shoe soles. But Pennsylvania knew it and has since named the eastern hemlock as her State tree. Farther west, the bigger variety, western hemlock, has been selected by Washington.

Long before the movement for State trees, Ohio was known as the Buckeye State, but not all of her present citizens have ever seen the *Aesculus glabra,* or Ohio buckeye.

Strangely enough, despite the wide range of growth of our American black walnut, it was left to Iowa to accept this tree, whose lumber is the most costly of all common American woods. Perhaps Iowa's choice was partly for lack of a wide choice of native trees. It was still more likely that Kansas, Nebraska, and South Dakota for the same reason picked the cottonwood, the tree which the early settlers cut for wood for their homes and fuel for their fires and the one they planted to give solace to their souls. Likewise, North Dakota looked to her watercourses and shelterbelts to find the green ash and claim it for her own.

In the Southwest, two States chose trees that furnish food as well as wood. Texas chose the pecan, whose nut crop fattens hogs and helps fill the candy bars of the Nation and whose lumber is increasingly chosen for furniture, flooring, and a host of uses for which a hard, resilient wood is needed. Farther west, Arizona accepted the honey mesquite, whose flowers are an important source of honey, whose bean pods are eaten by cattle, and whose wood is now directed to other uses than to feed a sheepherder's campfire.

Utah and Colorado went into high mountains and chose the blue spruce.

The sea-faring side of New Jersey may have influenced her acceptance of Atlantic white-cedar whose light, durable wood is prized by boat builders.

New Hampshire accepted the aromatic yellow birch, but Michigan, with a long list of beautiful native trees whose lumber supported much of her early economy, chose the apple. The

802062°—49——3

*". . . part of an amazing heritage . . ."*

apple is the only State tree not indigenous to the United States, but it is so widely planted and so important to the prosperity of Michigan as to seem natural to much of her landscape.

Florida and South Carolina chose trees of a comparatively unusual order. In Florida, it is the cabbagepalm, and in South Carolina, it is the same, but they call it the cabbage palmetto.

The two tallest trees in America grow on the Pacific coast and fortunately are given recognition. Oregon has selected the Douglas-fir and California the redwood. Each is a giant. Each is of great economic importance to the State that has selected it. Each has a great future as management of the stands of Douglas-fir and redwood is directed by forestry.

Many of these State trees played important roles in the building of America. That this country has more than a thousand other tree species from which choices might have been made indicates the wealth of our forest heritage. Other choices may yet be made, and some States may change their selections. Such recognition fosters the growing realization of man's dependence on trees. It is good that it has been encouraged.

G. Harris Collingwood *is the author (with Warren D. Brush) of the book, Knowing Your Trees.*

# QUESTIONS AND ANSWERS

W. W. BERGOFFEN

*What is the difference between trees and shrubs?*

There is no clear-cut distinction. However, a tree is commonly defined as a woody plant that reaches a height of at least 10 feet, has a single stem, and has a definite crown shape. A shrub usually is less than 10 feet tall and has several stems without a definite crown shape. Some specimens of plant species may take the form of a tree while others of the same species may take the form of a shrub—sumac and willows, for example.

*How many different kinds of forest trees are there in the United States?*

Precisely 1,182.

*What is the largest genus of forest trees?*

Hawthorns; the genus *Crataegus* comprises about 165 species.

*What is the largest genus of commercial forest trees?*

Oaks—about 60 species, not counting many hybrids and varieties.

*What section has the most kinds of trees?*

The Southeast—Virginia, North Carolina, South Carolina, Alabama, Georgia, Tennessee, Florida, Kentucky, Mississippi—has at least half of all the species in the country.

*What State has the largest number of different kinds of trees?*

Florida has 314 species of native and naturalized trees. Texas, Georgia, and California follow in that order.

*What State has the least number of different kinds of trees?*

North Dakota is almost treeless except, for example, cottonwoods and willows that grow along the streams. That is no aspersion, however, against that beautiful, happy State; North Dakota is a "grass" region; North Dakotans are as interested as anybody in trees.

*What is a "softwood"?*

A name in general use for trees of the pine family—the conifers, or cone bearers.

*What is a "hardwood"?*

A name in general use for trees belonging to families other than the conifers—such as the oaks, maples, hickories, and other broadleaf trees.

*What is our most important commercial forest tree?*

In terms of volume of standing timber and value of products cut, Douglas-fir is considered the most important commercial tree.

*In what kinds of trees in the United States are males and females separated?*

The holly, persimmon, ash, juniper, most maples, yew, and several of the less familiar trees. In those cases it is essential that both sexes be present to obtain well-developed fruit and seed.

*Can any trees reproduce without fertilization?*

Yes; asexual reproduction has been found to occur in several birches and perhaps in other species.

*What is the biggest living tree in the world?*

The General Sherman Bigtree in the Sequoia National Park in California. It is nearly 115 feet in circumference and 273 feet in height; its volume is 600,120 board feet.

*What is the world's tallest known standing tree?*

Founders Tree, a redwood in the

Humboldt State Redwood Park near Dyerville in California. It was 364 feet tall in 1947.

*Are any living trees direct descendants of fossil ancestors?*

Yes; most familiar example is ginkgo, a native of China that is now cultivated in the United States. The recently discovered "Dawn Redwood" (*Metasequoia*), also of China, was at first believed to be a "living fossil" but recent indications are that it may be a "surviving ancestor" of the well-known American coast redwood. In 1948, Dr. Ralph Chaney, of the University of California, headed an expedition into China to study the Dawn Redwood and bring back specimens and seed of it. Seedlings and transplants from China are growing at the University of California as a result of his effort. A league for the protection and preservation of these trees in China has been founded and is being encouraged and assisted by the "Save the Redwoods League" of the west coast.

*What is the oldest tree?*

The oldest tree is probably one of the big giant sequoias in California, variously estimated to be between 3,000 and 4,000 years old. The "Dragon Tree" of the Canary Islands, which was blown over in 1868, was estimated to have been as old as the Great Pyramid Cheops in Egypt—about 4,000 years old.

*Do tree seeds all weigh the same?*

Seed from conifers range from a half thousand seeds up to nearly a half million to the pound. White pine seed averages 27,000 a pound, for example; red pine, approximately 52,000; black spruce, 400,000; and Atlantic white-cedar, 460,000 to the pound. Torrey pine has about 500 seeds to the pound.

*How large do pine cones grow?*

The sugar pine of the Pacific Coast States produces the longest of pine cones, some exceeding 20 inches in length. The Mugho pine of Europe produces cones from less than 1 inch to 2 inches long.

*What is the difference between a bigtree, or giant sequoia, and a redwood?*

These trees are different species of the same family and genus. Botanically, the giant sequoia is known as *Sequoia gigantea,* and the redwood is known as *Sequoia sempervirens.* They grow in different places. The giant sequoia is found only on the middle slopes of the Sierra Nevada in California. The redwood grows only along the Pacific coast, within reach of the ocean fogs, from Monterey County northward to the Oregon line. The redwood has needlelike leaves; the giant sequoia has scalelike leaves.

*Is it a good practice to plant a new tree for every one cut?*

No. The use of a method of cutting that will assure renewal of the woods by natural reproduction is generally more economical and satisfactory. Nature usually plants many times as many trees as man cuts, if man helps nature by providing proper conditions on the cut-over areas.

*What kind of trees should I plant on my land?*

The safest rule is to plant trees that grow naturally in your neighborhood, because they are adapted to the local climate and soils. Before planting any exotic—foreign or introduced—species, consult your local forester or nurseryman to find out if it will grow on your soil.

*Can I get trees from the Government to plant on my land?*

The Federal Government does not distribute trees free of charge. It does, however, cooperate with the various State forestry agencies in producing and distributing trees for planting on private lands. Applications to buy trees should be made to the State forester. Trees grown in the State nurseries are sold at approximate cost of production.

Ornamental trees, of course, can be purchased from private nurseries.

*How can we start a community forest?*

Because community forests are publicly owned, the first step is to get the support of local authorities who must obtain title to the land—for a county forest, the county board; for a municipal forest, the mayor and his governing body; for a school forest, the school superintendent. Enlist also the support of other interested public-service organizations. Work up a plan of operation to cover the sort of forest desired as well as the type of development and use. Appoint a forest board to develop and manage the property. Seek expert advice on forest management from your local forester.

*In planting, do the roots need special care?*

John Burroughs, the eminent naturalist, wrote to the principal of a school in Pennsylvania:

"I am glad to hear that your pupils are going to keep Arbor Day; if you can teach them to love and to cherish trees, you will teach them a very valuable lesson. . . . Give the tree roots plenty of room and a soft, deep bed to rest in; tuck it up carefully with your hands. The roots of the tree are much more soft and tender than its branches and cannot be handled too gently. It is as important to know how to dig up a tree as how to plant it. A friend of mine brings quite large hemlocks from the woods and plants them on his grounds and has no trouble to make them live. He does much of the work with his hands, follows the roots along and lifts them gently from the soil, and never allows them to dry. The real feeders of the tree are very small, mere threads; the bulky, muscular roots are for strength; its life is in the rootlets that fringe them, and to let these delicate feeders dry, even by an hour's exposure to a drying air, is to endanger the vitality of the tree. By the way, in your planting do not forget the hemlock. It is a clean, healthy, handsome tree. Do not forget the ash, either, if only for the beautiful plum-colored foliage in autumn. Above all, do not forget the linden or basswood, a tree generally overlooked by our arborists. It is as pleasing as maple in form and foliage, and then it is such a friend of the honey bee. What a harvest they get from it, and just when other sources of honey supply begin to fail.

"I have somewhere said that when you bait your hook with your heart the fish always bite, and I will now say that when you plant a tree with love it always lives; you do it with such care and thoroughness."

*How successful are shelterbelt plantings in the Prairie States?*

Those plantings are generally successful. They directly affect the agricultural welfare of the region. They reduce excessive evaporation and the blowing of soil, and are a protective screen against the burning winds of summer and freezing winds of winter.

*What trees are most commonly used for Christmas trees?*

The greatest demand has been for balsam fir and Douglas-fir. Other popular Christmas trees, in order of their production, are black spruce, redcedar, white spruce, Scotch pine and southern pine, red spruce, Virginia pine, white fir, Norway spruce.

*How many Christmas trees are produced in the United States each year?*

About 21,000,000 trees; 87 percent are produced on private forest lands; about a million are harvested on the national forests. About 100,000 acres of woodland (most of it owned by farmers) are devoted solely to growing Christmas trees.

*How can I keep my Chirstmas tree fresh and green?*

Try to obtain a tree that has been harvested recently. Store it in a cool place; place the butt in water; sprinkle the branches daily. When you take the tree indoors, cut the butt diagonally about an inch above the original cut and keep the tree in a stand that contains water.

*What does a farm forester do?*

Upon request, he helps the owner of a small woodland work out a specific management plan right on the ground. He recommends the proper protection and cutting methods; assists the owner in marking the trees to be cut; helps measure the volume; and advises him in the marketing of the products. Surveys indicate that 2,000 farm foresters are needed to assist the country's 4.25 million small-woodland owners; there are now fewer than 200 on the job.

*How can I get advice and in-the-woods assistance in handling my own woodland right?*

Write your State forester at the State capital or your extension forester at the State agricultural college; or get in touch with your county agent, soil conservation district supervisor, or the local Forest Service representative. Any one of them will put you in touch with the nearest farm forester, who will work with you.

*What Government agency actually gives demonstrations on growing timber as a crop?*

The State extension forester (usually located at the State college of agriculture) works with the local county agent in staging such demonstrations.

*What are the Norris-Doxey woodland-management projects?*

They are the projects set up, under Federal law, to give on-the-ground woodland-management advice and assistance to farmers and other owners of small woodlands. In 1948, farm foresters worked with small-woodland owners in 650 counties. The farm forests are employed by the individual States with the Federal Government sharing in the cost and administration of the various projects.

*Is it profitable for a farmer himself to do the necessary work of improvement cutting in his woodland?*

It is possible for a farmer to make a dollar or more an hour by doing his own work in the farm woods.

*What is silviculture?*

Silviculture is the science and art of establishing and tending forests to get the best timber products. It is analogous to the planting, weeding, and other culture necessary to grow food crops.

*What are liberation or improvement cuttings?*

The removal of the bent, forked, or knotty trees, and diseased, rotted, insect-infested trees, and the broken and fire-damaged trees.

*Why do you prune young timber trees?*

By removing the knot-forming lower branches, pruning makes it possible to get clear wood earlier.

*What is sustained-yield timber management?*

A basic objective in timber management is to fix a rate of cutting that can be maintained at approximately the same rate in perpetuity through growth replacement of the volume harvested. Control over the rate of cutting for this objective is sustained-yield management.

*Is national forest timber ever sold?*

Yes. It is being sold currently at a rate of approximately 4 billion board feet a year. It is sold to supply needed fuel and other products for domestic use, to supply raw material for lumber industries, to provide employment and stability to towns or communities, and to harvest the timber crop that is continuously being produced on our national forest lands.

*How is national forest timber sold?*

More than 25,000 sales are made each year. About 90 percent of all the sales are made to small producers of fuel wood, pulpwood, posts, sawlogs, or other forest products. Sales under $500 in value may be made to individuals or companies by local forest officers without advertisement if competition for the timber is lacking. Sales in excess of $500 are advertised and sold to the highest acceptable bidder. In no case is national forest timber sold at less than its appraised market value. It must be paid for in advance of cutting; permits or contracts make adequate provision for protection and preservation of the soil, water, and remaining stand of timber.

*Can national forest timber be obtained free of cost?*

Free use of timber may be granted to bona fide settlers, miners, rural residents, and prospectors—for firewood, fencing, building, other domestic purposes, mining, and prospecting. Usually not more than $20 worth of timber is granted to any one person a year. Transients may take dead timber for their campfires and for similar uses without written permits.

*Why cannot foresters increase timber production through the use of hybrids as farmers have increased corn production?*

They can, but it takes time. Trees cannot be grown in a single season like corn. Promising hybrids of pine and hybrids of poplar are being tested.

*What is the age of the virgin fir timber now being harvested in the Pacific Northwest?*

The individual trees are 300 to 500 years old.

*How long does it take to grow a marketable crop of sawlog timber?*

In the South, 30 to 40 years (pine); Lake States and Northeast, 60 to 70 years (pine), 100 years (spruce), 100 to 120 years (hardwoods); west coast, 100 years (fir and hemlock); Rocky Mountain area, 150 to 180 years (western pine).

*How many man-days of labor does it normally take to convert 1,000 board feet of standing timber to 1,000 board feet of lumber?*

Two to three.

*What causes rot in trees?*

Rot or decay, sometimes termed dote or peckiness, is caused by the action on the wood by fungi, low forms of life related to the mushrooms. The fungus threads penetrate the wood and break it down.

*How many uses of wood are there?*

Somebody once counted 4,500 uses, but he did not guarantee that his tabulation was complete.

*Why should houses be built of dry lumber?*

Because wet lumber, and the seasoning of wood in place, result in unequal shrinkage, which causes plaster cracks, distortion of door and window openings, and uneven floors. Shrinkage also may cause air leakage around chimney and window openings. In floorings, it may cause unsightly cracks between the floor boards and may cause creaking floors.

*How long can wood houses last?*

Many American homes, which date from Colonial times, are still in excellent condition. Mount Vernon is one of them.

*Does paint preserve wood?*

No; paint does not preserve wood from deterioration due to decay. Paint prevents the weathering of wood; its main value is for decoration.

*Should wet or green lumber be painted?*

No. Paint does not adhere well to wet wood and is likely to peel off.

*Why does wood remain the leading material for houses?*

Wood is economical to use and easy to shape and work. It is excellent insulation material and it will give long service with moderate care. A house built of wood can be altered easily.

*How is wood used chemically?*

To make charcoal, wood alcohol, acetone, ethyl alcohol, wood-sugar molasses, fodder yeast, synthetic fibers, photographic films, and other molded articles, modified wood products such as compreg and impreg and staypak, many specialized products of wood pulp and paper, and a host of other chemical products.

*Is it true that most of the paper that we use today is made from wood?*

Yes. Only small quantities of paper are now made from linen or other cloth rags—the reverse of 150 years ago, when little, if any, paper was made from wood.

*How much wood is used for fuel?*

It is estimated that 63,000,000 cords of wood are annually used for fuel—about one-eighth of all the wood used in the United States.

*What major improvement has been made in recent years in the use of wood for shipbuilding?*

Ship keels and other long, heavy, or curved members can now be laminated from relatively small pieces of wood by the use of waterproof glues. Such laminated members often are superior to the solid pieces formerly used.

*How many cross ties are required for a mile of railway track?*

Three thousand cross ties are used in the average mile of railway track.

*How many cross ties are there in railway tracks throughout the United States?*

More than one billion.

*How many cross ties do the railroads install in a year?*

An average of about 50 million. Approximately 80 percent of the cross ties installed in replacements in recent years have been treated—that is, saturated with creosote, zinc chloride, or other preservatives to prevent decay or destruction by insects. The treatment more than doubles the service life of the ties. Bridge timbers, piling, poles, and other woods are also treated in this manner before use.

*Why is black walnut the outstanding wood for gun stocks?*

It is one of our best shock-resistant woods, it keeps its shape, attaches well to metal, and is durable. Black walnut also makes excellent furniture wood—it has a beautiful grain, is easy to work into any desired shape, and takes a good finish.

*How many wooden fence posts do American farmers use?*

About 500 million a year.

*What wooden shipping container is used today in much the same form as in the days of antiquity?*

The common barrel or cask; coopering is one of the oldest known crafts.

*What is the hardest American wood, in terms of density?*

Black ironwood, of a little-known species found in southern Florida, has a specific gravity of 1.04. It is so heavy it sinks in water.

*What is the softest American wood, in terms of density?*

Corkbark fir, found in parts of Arizona and New Mexico, has a specific gravity of 0.28.

*What are the main causes of forest fires?*

There are seven: Those caused by smokers' matches or by burning tobacco in any form; campfires; debris burning—fires which are originally set for clearing land or disposing of rubbish, stubble, and such and which get beyond control; incendiary, which are deliberately started with the intention of burning over the land or damaging property owned by someone else; lightning; lumbering; fires resulting from maintenance of right-of-ways or construction or operation of railroads.

*What is considered the worst forest fire in American history?*

The Peshtigo Fire in Wisconsin in October 1871—when 1,280,000 acres were burned over; homes, towns, and settlements were swept away, and 1,500 persons perished.

*What are the different types of forest fires?*

Crown—a fire that burns through the tops of trees, brush, chaparral, or that consumes all or a large part of the upper branches or foliage; ground—a fire confined to the materials composing the forest floor or beneath the surface, as in peat beds; surface—a fire that runs over the forest floor and burns only the surface litter, the loose debris, and the smaller vegetation or ground cover.

*What are the different parts of a forest fire?*

The fingers—these are the long, narrow tongues of a fire that project from the main body; the flanks—the parts of the edge of a fire between the head and the rear; the head—the part of the edge of a fire on which rate of spread is most rapid; the rear—the part of the edge of a fire on the windward or downhill side.

*What section has the greatest unprotected area of forest land?*

The South. In 1947, 11 Southern States had organized protection against fire on 92 million acres of private forest land; 82 million acres were without such protection.

*What are the principal causes of forest fires in the different sections?*

In the Lake States and New England, fires are mostly man-caused; careless smokers head the list. In the Eastern and Southern States, also, they are mostly man-caused; careless brush and field burners and (in the South) intentional fire setters head the list. In the Rocky Mountain area, more than 70 percent are started by lightning; the others result from carelessness while smoking. In the Northwest, about half the fires start with lightning; careless smokers and campers (who abandon campfires) are serious offenders. In California, lightning starts about 23 percent, careless smokers and campers most of the others.

*When is the danger of forest fires greatest?*

Generally speaking, the worst fire seasons in the eastern half of the country are in the spring and fall; in the West, late summer. But at no time of the year is every section of the United States completely free of the danger.

*How does one fight a forest fire?*

The first essential is to deprive the fire of its fuel by making a fire line or barrier down to mineral soil, all around the fire. After one has stopped the fire from spreading, he then extinguishes all the burning material within the fire area. This applies to all small forest or woods fires. For a small grass fire, the first action is to beat out the flames if possible. One should not try to put out a big fire alone.

*What is a smokejumper?*

He is a parachute fire fighter, especially trained and equipped to drop to forest fires in remote forest areas and put the fires out while they are still small.

*Are there many smokejumpers?*

The Forest Service employs more than 200 smokejumpers to help control fires in the roadless national forest areas of Idaho, Montana, Washington, Oregon, and California. This type of fire fighting is being extended to other States as well. Canada recently organized a smokejumper group in British Columbia.

*Are smokejumpers effective?*

Yes. They reduce forest fire losses. In 2 hours they can reach fires in roadless areas that formerly took 24 hours of foot travel. That 22-hour gain in time often spells the difference between using two men to put out a little fire and having to employ large forces of men to put out a big one.

*What are some of the precautionary measures against fire?*

Clean up logging slash; build fire breaks or fire lanes to divide the woods into small blocks; keep fire-fighting tools handy and in good condition; know the location of the local forest fire warden or forest protection officer; line up the fire-fighting manpower in the neighborhood in advance.

*What do foresters mean by "burning period"?*

Normally the "burning period" is the "heat of the day," from about 10 a. m. to just before sundown. Unusual weather or other conditions may prolong the "burning period" and even may create a severe "burning period" at night.

*What is a "backfire"?*

A fire intentionally set on the fire side of a control line as a part of the process of controlling a fire. Using such a fire when the control line is close to the fire edge is sometimes called burning out or clean burning.

*What is a "fire dispatcher"?*

He is a member of the forest fire-control organization who receives reports of the recovery and status of fires, determines the locations of fires, and sends the men and the supplies and equipment that are needed to suppress fires.

*How does the United States Weather Bureau cooperate with fire-control agencies?*

The Weather Bureau prepares special fire-weather forecasts for use by forest fire-control agencies. Three types are issued: A "general outlook" for 2 to 3 days; a "daily forecast" for the ensuing 36 to 48 hours; and, upon request, "special localized forecasts" for short periods of 3 to 12 hours.

*Why are man-caused fires usually worse than lightning fires?*

Lightning usually strikes on the tops of ridges and starts a small fire, which spreads slowly, especially if the lightning storm is accompanied by rain. Man-caused fires most frequently start along roads, trails, and streams, in canyons, or on the lower slopes of the hills; they spread rapidly uphill and often become conflagrations. Fires intentionally set, that is, incendiary fires, nearly always occur in periods of high fire hazard.

*What is the best way to dispose of burning matches and tobacco in the forest?*

Break your match in two and hold it in your hand until you are sure it is out. Put the burned end back in the box or in your pocket. Cigarettes and cigars should be put out by wetting the end with saliva, throwing them in water, or clearing a spot of inflammable material down to mineral soil, and grinding the fire out with the foot. Pipe heels, which are a particularly dangerous source of forest fire, should be ground out in mineral soil. Mechanical lighters for the pocket and ash containers for automobiles are recommended for all persons who travel in forests. It is well to refrain from smoking when the woods are dry.

*Will burning things thrown from airplanes in flight start fires?*

Several fires have occurred that were believed to have originated from burning material thrown from airplanes. We cannot give a categorical answer, but that the practice is dangerous seems obvious.

*Why did the Indians start fires in the forests?*

Tradition says that they did so to drive out game, but we have no positive proof that they did this as a regular custom over any large areas. The Indians had no matches and they used small campfires that they tended carefully; so, it is improbable that they set many fires. But with the coming of the white man, and the cutting and clearing of timber, fires became more numerous and widespread.

*What shall I do if I discover a fire?*

Try to put it out at once. If that is impossible, report it by telephone or in person to the nearest Federal or State ranger, ranger station, fire warden, or the forest officer. Remember: Minutes count in reporting fires.

*Is our concern about fire a purely modern worry?*

No; Ezekiel xx: 47: "Behold, I will kindle a fire in thee, and it shall devour every green tree in thee, and every dry tree: the flaming flame shall not be quenched, and all faces from the south to the north shall be burned therein." Exodus xxii: 6: "If fire break out, and catch in thorns, so that the stacks of corn, or the standing corn, or the field, be consumed therewith; he that kindled the fire shall surely make restitution."

*What is the most destructive agent of our forests, other than man?*

Forest insects and diseases account for more than double the losses each year than does fire.

*What is the most desirable forest environment for wildlife in general?*

It is the forest or woodland in which there is a mixture of food-bearing and cover-producing plants (from trees to grass), plus water and escape areas, all within the daily travel range of the wildlife. Contrary to a general belief, such conditions do not always exist in mature forests.

*Do deer compete with domestic livestock for forage on the forest range?*

If the numbers of deer and livestock are adjusted to the available food supply, there will be no conflict. Generally speaking, deer feed on browse; cattle and sheep prefer grasses and weeds. Competition exists only where livestock and deer, or both, are present in excessive numbers.

*What is meant by a "buck law"?*

A buck law is a hunting regulation that permits the killing of only antler-bearing males. It is desirable when the goal is to reestablish a herd. When herds are already established and in a healthy condition, however, the buck law is unnecessary, and its continued use complicates proper management.

*Can one tell the age of a buck deer by the number of points on its antlers?*

The points are not a reliable guide. A fully developed set of antlers usually indicates good health and maturity. Old deer often carry fewer points than young, growing bucks.

*Do I have to have a Federal permit to hunt or fish on a national forest?*

The State fish and game laws usually govern hunting and fishing on the national forests.

*What forest creatures are most to be feared?*

The common ticks. They may carry the Rocky Mountain spotted fever, a disease dreaded over a large part of the United States. In tick areas, inspect your body and clothing twice a day. If you find a tick attached to your body, remove it carefully to prevent infection through skin abrasions or cuts. Use tweezers if available. Be sure to remove the head of the tick. Paint the spot where the tick was attached with iodine or alcohol. The best protection against possible infection is inoculation with the tick shots developed by the Public Health Service.

*What poisonous snakes are in the forests of the United States?*

The rattlesnake is the most widely distributed poisonous reptile. The others are the cottonmouth or water moccasin, copperhead, and coral snake.

The best precaution against snake bites is alertness. Avoid coming into close quarters with the reptiles. Contrary to popular belief, snakes do not go out of their way to attack human beings. It is a good idea to carry a snake-bite kit when you are vacationing or working in snake-infested areas.

*How many Rocky Mountain goats are left?*

We estimate that there are 14,000 Rocky Mountain goats in the continental United States. Most of them are in the wilderness areas of the national forests in Washington, Idaho, and Montana. Goats are also found in Alaska. They may be hunted under special permit and in accordance with State laws.

*How many deer, elk, and black bear are there?*

Of the estimated 6,300,000 deer in the United States, a third are on the national forests. There are nearly 200,000 elk, of which about three-fourths spend all or part of their time on the national forests. About one-half of the estimated 150,000 black bear are on the national forests.

*What are the most important forms of forest game?*

Deer, elk, grouse, tree squirrels, turkey, and bear.

*How do caribou differ from their relatives, the deer, moose, and elk?*

The caribou are unique in that females, as well as males, bear antlers.

*Which predatory animals live in big forests?*

Coyote, lynx, wild cat, mountain lion.

*How do forest fires harm game animals, birds, and fish?*

Fire destroys the natural feeding and breeding grounds of the wild animals; severe fires may also kill deer and the smaller animals. The nests and young of birds are destroyed by fire; streams are filled with silt and ashes which can be injurious to the fish. Under some conditions, as in the longleaf pine, however, regulated fire can be used as a tool to improve the wildlife habitat.

*Is grazing by livestock harmful to hardwood forests?*

It certainly is. Hardwood forests should be protected from grazing, because livestock browse the young trees to the point of destruction.

*What is the place of grazing in the administration of the national forests?*

The use of national forest range by livestock is an essential part of the multiple-use principle that governs the administration of the national forests. Use of the range is an important part of the welfare of many communities and individuals, especially in the West. The Forest Service has expended approximately 16 million dollars for fence construction, water development, and artificial reseeding to make the range more usable by livestock. Besides, holders of grazing permits have invested about one-half billion dollars in livestock and ranches.

*Is "burning-off" injurious to the range?*

In certain pine types of the southern Coastal Plains and in certain sagebrush areas in the West, prescribed burning may be helpful. Uncontrolled or promiscuous use of fire on the range results in great damage to both soil and forage.

*Is it true that all that is needed to bring back a range is plenty of rain?*

Rain cannot bring back range plants that have been killed by overgrazing. A good rain can help restore the growth and vigor of range plants that drought has kept back.

*What does one mean by the grazing capacity of a range?*

The term applies to the maximum number of livestock that can be grazed on a given area for a given period of time without injury to the soil, the forage plants, the tree growth, or the watershed, with due provision for the game, recreation, and other land uses.

*What are the main objectives in range management on the national forests?*

There are three: Perpetuation of the water, soil, and forage resources through wise use, protection, and development; the permanent good of the livestock industry, through proper care and improvement of the grazing lands, under principles of practical operation; the protection of the established ranch owner against unfair competition in the use of the range.

*Does a grazing permit give any legal right to a national forest?*

No. Legal rights do not accrue in the use of national forest range. There can be no exclusive, no private vested right on lands owned by all the people.

*Does the forest influence the melting of snow as well as the disposition of rainfall?*

Yes. In the sections of the country where there is much snow, the influence of forests in retarding snow melt is more important than its effect on the disposition of rainfall. The snow-melting period may last several weeks longer in the forests than on open ground. Moreover, as the forest soil is likely to freeze less deeply than soil in the open, it absorbs more of the snow water. Spring freshets from melting snow on bare slopes are an important source of river floods. By delaying the melting of snow and feeding part of the snow water into the soil, forests prolong the period of runoff, reduce flood crests to that extent, and equalize stream flow in the rivers fed by snow melt.

*What is a watershed?*

A watershed, or drainage basin, is an area of land from which a stream gets its supply of water. It may be as small as a farm or as large as several States. It is more than a combination of hills and valleys and streams, forests, grass, farm crops, and the soil beneath. It may also include cities, roads, people, and animals. For there is an interrelation among all things, animate and inanimate, on a watershed that bears heavily on the yield of water from the land.

*How can one tell when a watershed is in good condition?*

On a good watershed, the ground is well covered with vegetation (grass, shrubs, trees); litter or duff (leaves, twigs, dried grasses) covers the forest floor; the streams are clear and clean; there are no gullies or erosion; and the banks of streams are stable.

*How do forests function in a storm?*

The forest acts in two ways during a storm. First, the canopy of leaves and branches breaks the impact of rain falling upon the earth. Even during a heavy rain one has the sense of the dripping of water from the treetops rather than a deluge from the sky. The second is in the effect of the layer of ground litter and humus, which act as a sponge cushion to absorb the water and reduce surface runoff. Much more significant than its spongelike absorption of water, however, is the action of the litter and the humus in keeping the soil mellow, porous, and more permeable and in preventing the sealing up of the seepage channels into the substratum, where the great supply of earth water is stored. Much of the earth water appears again at the surface in the form of springs and stream flow. The action is effective, and it continues regardless of the intensity or duration of the precipitation received.

*Do forests influence climate?*

Forests do not materially affect the climate over a large region. In the larger sense, climate is controlled by major factors of tremendous air movement around the earth and by latitude, altitude, and the relation of a given locality to oceans and land masses—such as the direction, the distance, height, and character of mountain ranges. Forests are the results (rather than the cause) of climate in this sense. Forests do materially affect the climate of the immediate locality which they occupy, however. That effect is due, among other things, to the crowns of the trees, which enclose the land much as roof and walls enclose a house. The forest is both cooler in summer and warmer in winter than open places are. The same holds true of daily extremes. Within the forest the air is more moist than outside, because the force of the wind is broken and less evaporation occurs. In the winter, the soil of the forest is less subject to frost than in the open because of the insulating effect of the litter and humus. Snow tends to lie longer in the forest than in the open.

*How can I find out where to camp and picnic on the national forests?*

For general information on vacationing in the national forests, write to the United States Department of Agriculture, Forest Service, Washington 25, D. C. Information about specific areas may be obtained from the regional foresters located at Missoula, Mont.; Denver, Colo.; Albuquerque, N. Mex.; Ogden, Utah; San Francisco, Calif.; Portland, Oreg.; Philadelphia, Pa.; Atlanta, Ga.; Milwaukee, Wis.; Juneau, Alaska.

*Is there a charge for camping and picnicking on the national forests?*

Generally there are no charges for camping and picnicking on the national forests. At some of the large recreational areas, concessioners furnish wood, operate bathhouses, and give other special services at a nominal charge. In 1948, a few large camp grounds were placed under permit and a charge of 50 cents a night for a group in an automobile (of not more than six persons) was authorized. The plan was an experiment, and may or may not be continued. In any event, most camping and picknicking areas on national forests will remain free.

*Are there cabins for rent on the national forests?*

The Forest Service does not operate rental cabins on the national forests nor maintain lists of available cabins. There are many cabins for rent on private lands within the national forests and privately owned cabins on national forest land. For information about such cabins write to the chamber of commerce in the locality to which you plan to go.

*Are trailers permitted on national forest camp grounds?*

Yes; on most of them. A few exceptions are made because of steep roads on which trailers are not practical. None of the usual trailer facilities (electricity, water, and sewerage connections) are available on national forest camp grounds.

*How many people use the national forests for recreation?*

In 1947, 21 million persons visited the national forests for recreation, among them 9 million campers and picnickers, 1¾ million who participated in winter sports, and hunters, fishermen, children at organization camps, guests at private resorts, people at summer homes, travelers in wilderness areas.

*What are the wilderness areas?*

They are roadless tracts in a number of national forests. In them the natural, primitive conditions are preserved. There are 77 wilderness areas in all, mostly in the Western States; they cover 14 million acres. Hunting and fishing are permitted.

*Where can one engage horses for wildnerness trips?*

Local dude ranches have horses, guides, and pack outfits available.

*What are trail rider trips?*

They are expeditions sponsored by the American Forestry Association, 919 Seventeenth Street NW., Washington 6, D. C. The Association, a nonprofit organization, arranges and conducts "Trail-riders of the Wilderness" trips into some of the wilderness areas. The American Forestry Association will send full information on request.

*How can I build a safe campfire?*

The safest way to build a campfire is to scrape away the inflammable material down to the mineral soil from an area 6 feet in diameter. Keep your fire small. Never build it against trees or logs. When you are through with it, soak the coals until no more smoke arises. Be sure your fire is dead out when you leave the campfire area.

*Where can I get a permit to build a campfire?*

From any Forest Service officer or State ranger. Although permits are not required at most developed camp and picnic areas (California excepted), persons should check with the local officials.

*Does the Forest Service rent sites on the national forests for summer homes?*

Yes. Sites for summer homes may be rented from the Forest Service on most national forests. Information regarding available summer-home tracts may be had from the forest supervisor of the national forest concerned.

*What are the rules for keeping a camp ground clean and sanitary?*

Burn or bury all garbage, refuse, and cans. Use camp toilets where provided; help keep them clean. If none is available, dig a trench at least 100 yards from the camp and the nearest stream, lake, or living spring; heap the earth to one side and fill the trench as it is used. Leave the camp neat and clean.

*What is the Appalachian Trail?*

It is a 2,000-mile trail from Maine to Georgia, 900 miles of which traverse eight national forests and two national parks along the crest of the Appalachian Mountains. There are open shelters for hikers at convenient intervals along the trail as well as closed shelters which may be reserved through local Appalachian Trail clubs. The trail is maintained and marked cooperatively by the Forest Service, the National Park Service, and the member clubs of the Appalachian Trail Conference. Excellent guide books and maps of the route may be obtained from the Appalachian Trail Conference, 1916 Sunderland Place NW., Washington 6, D. C.

*When was the first national forest in the United States created?*

The first forest reserve—the Yellowstone Park Timberland Reserve—was created by President Harrison on September 16, 1891. The land included within this reserve now forms parts of several national forests in Montana, Idaho, and Wyoming, adjacent to the Yellowstone National Park.

*When and why was the name "national forests" adopted?*

On March 4, 1907, the name "forest reserves" was changed to "national forests" to indicate that the forests and their resources were not reserved or locked up but were for immediate as well as future use.

*Who administers national forests?*

The Forest Service, a bureau of the United States Department of Agriculture, created February 1, 1905, by the merging of the former Division of Forestry of the General Land Office, Department of the Interior, and the Bureau of Forestry of the Department of Agriculture. The transfer to the Department of Agriculture was the result of recommendation by Secretary of Interior Hitchcock, the American Forestry Congress of 1905, and President Theodore Roosevelt.

*What becomes of the money received from the sale and use of national forest resources?*

All receipts from the national forests are deposited in the United States

Treasury. Under Federal law, 25 percent of these receipts is turned over to the States in which the national forests are located. The State in turn apportions this fund to the counties, each county receiving as its share a proportion of the receipts from the national forest or forests located within the county, based on the acreage of the national forest land within the county. This fund is used by the county for school and road purposes. The Federal law also requires that an additional 10 percent of all receipts from the national forests be expended by the Forest Service for trails and roads located entirely within the forests in the States from which the receipts are obtained.

*What are the duties of a forest ranger?*

Every national forest is divided into ranger districts with a forest ranger in charge of each. Sometimes he has an assistant ranger. A ranger district, the smallest administrative unit of the national forests, varies in size from 100,000 to 400,000 acres. The ranger's work involves supervision of timber sales, grazing, recreational and other uses of the forest. He helps build roads, trails, bridges, telephone lines, and other permanent improvements. He trains and inspects forest guards and temporary employees. He must know his district well enough to be able to conduct Forest Service business in any part of it, and he must know how to fight fire. He has routine reports to make, but he is primarily a field man rather than an office worker. His overall responsibility is to manage the forest as a renewable resource.

*What is the difference between a national forest and a national park?*

They are both Federal areas, and each has an important place in the conservation picture of the United States. However, the principle of use of resources is the vital distinction between them. Essentially, national parks are maintained for the *preservation* of outstanding features; national forests are for the *production* of the resources.

National forests are administered for the protection, development, and use of timber, water, range, and other resources in the public interest. A basic purpose is the protection of watersheds, to safeguard water supplies and prevent floods. Timber resources are managed to contribute toward a permanent supply of lumber and other forest products, and to serve as demonstration areas of forest management for the benefit of private timber owners and operators. National forest ranges are managed to provide a sustained supply of forage for the grazing of livestock. The forests are managed also to preserve their beauty and attractiveness for the recreational enjoyment of the people; to maintain a favorable habitat for wildlife; and in other ways to make their resources contribute to the economic stability and the welfare of the Nation.

National parks are dedicated to the primary purpose of preserving, for public enjoyment, superlative examples of the scenic and the majestic in nature, though they serve other important purposes such as wildlife conservation and the regulation of stream flow through watershed protection. As a rule, only lands containing outstanding scenic, geologic, or other natural wonders are included. The law requires that they be administered to provide for public enjoyment "in such manner and by such means as will leave them unimpaired for the enjoyment of future generations." National parks are thus, in a sense, great outdoor museums. The national parks are administered by the Park Service, a bureau of the United States Department of the Interior.

*Who owns the land in the United States that produces or can produce timber of commercial quality and quantity? On how much of it are cutting practices good? Fair? Poor? How much timber shall we need in 1955?—and 50 years hence?*

The information is given in the tables on pages 33 and 34.

OWNERSHIP OF COMMERCIAL FOREST LAND OF THE UNITED STATES, BY REGION[1]

| Region | All ownerships | Federally owned or managed: Total | Federally owned or managed: National forest | Federally owned or managed: Other | State, county, and municipal | Private: Total | Private: Farm | Private: Industrial and other |
|---|---|---|---|---|---|---|---|---|
| | *1,000 acres* | *1,000 acres* | *1,000 acres* | *1,000 acres* | *1,000 acres* | *1,000 acres* | *1,000 acres* | *1,000 acres* |
| New England | 30,851 | 891 | 822 | 69 | 666 | 29,294 | 6,477 | 22,817 |
| Middle Atlantic | 41,586 | 1,476 | 1,265 | 211 | 3,613 | 36,497 | 11,854 | 24,643 |
| Lake | 50,345 | 6,495 | 5,455 | 1,040 | 14,805 | 29,045 | 13,930 | 15,115 |
| Central | 44,213 | 2,117 | 1,951 | 166 | 326 | 41,770 | 25,789 | 15,981 |
| Plains | 3,326 | 332 | 30 | 302 | 4 | 2,990 | 2,960 | 30 |
| North | 170,321 | 11,311 | 9,523 | 1,788 | 19,414 | 139,596 | 61,010 | 78,586 |
| South Atlantic | 42,923 | 3,485 | 2,775 | 710 | 536 | 38,902 | 23,377 | 15,525 |
| Southeast | 89,390 | 5,909 | 3,802 | 2,107 | 1,216 | 82,265 | 33,134 | 49,131 |
| West Gulf | 50,953 | 4,684 | 3,561 | 1,123 | 408 | 45,861 | 12,549 | 33,312 |
| South | 183,266 | 14,078 | 10,138 | 3,940 | 2,160 | 167,028 | 69,060 | 97,968 |
| Pacific Northwest: | | | | | | | | |
| Douglas-fir subregion | 26,027 | 10,201 | 7,682 | 2,519 | 2,616 | 13,210 | 1,951 | 11,259 |
| Pine subregion | 20,177 | 12,811 | 9,659 | 3,152 | 819 | 6,547 | 1,383 | 5,164 |
| Total | 46,204 | 23,012 | 17,341 | 5,671 | 3,435 | 19,757 | 3,334 | 16,423 |
| California | 16,405 | 8,099 | 7,684 | 415 | 23 | 8,283 | 1,309 | 6,974 |
| North Rocky Mountain | 29,066 | 20,012 | 18,061 | 1,951 | 1,702 | 7,352 | 2,847 | 4,505 |
| South Rocky Mountain | 15,782 | 12,445 | 10,765 | 1,680 | 380 | 2,957 | 1,498 | 1,459 |
| West | 107,457 | 63,568 | 53,851 | 9,717 | 5,540 | 38,349 | 8,988 | 29,361 |
| All regions | 461,044 | 88,957 | 73,512 | 15,445 | 27,114 | 344,973 | 139,058 | 205,915 |

[1] Prepared by Forest Service, United States Department of Agriculture. Includes land capable of producing timber of commercial quantity and quality, and available now or prospectively for commercial use. Status beginning of 1945.

---

CHARACTER OF TIMBER CUTTING PRACTICES ON PRIVATE AND ON PUBLIC FOREST LANDS, UNITED STATES, 1945

| Ownership class | Commercial area | Percentage of operating acreage in properties or working circles being cut under practices that rate—: High order | Good | Fair | Poor | Destructive |
|---|---|---|---|---|---|---|
| | *Mil. acres* | *Percent* | *Percent* | *Percent* | *Percent* | *Percent* |
| Private | 345 | 1 | 7 | 28 | 56 | 8 |
| Public | 116 | 8 | 59 | 19 | 13 | 1 |
| Total | 461 | 3 | 20 | 25 | 46 | 6 |

SUMMARY OF ESTIMATED POTENTIAL ANNUAL REQUIREMENTS FOR TIMBER PRODUCTS IN THE UNITED STATES AND THE DRAIN ON DOMESTIC TIMBER

| | *1950–55* | | | | *50 years hence* | | |
|---|---|---|---|---|---|---|---|
| | | *Estimated drain* | | | | *Estimated drain* | |
| | *Potential requirement* | *From trees of all sizes* [1] | *From trees of saw-timber size only* [2] | | *Potential requirement* | *From trees of all sizes* [1] | *From trees of saw-timber size only* [2] |
| | *Million* | *Million cu. ft.* | *Percent* | *Million bd. ft.* | *Million* | *Million cu. ft.* | *Million bd. ft.* |
| Major timber products utilized in the primary form: | | | | | | | |
| Fuel wood.................. cord.. | [3]63 | 1,836 | 37.6 | 3,066 | [4]50 | 1,700 | 2,839 |
| Poles...................... pole.. | 5.7 | 91 | 90.0 | 318 | 5 | 80 | 279 |
| Piling................linear foot.. | 38 | 29 | 100.0 | 114 | 23 | 17 | 69 |
| Fence posts................ post.. | [5]600 | 480 | 25.7 | 492 | [5]600 | 480 | 492 |
| Mine timbers, hewed or round cubic foot . | 220 | 220 | 35.6 | 312 | 220 | 220 | 312 |
| Railroad ties, hewed..........tie.. | 22 | 238 | 98.5 | 1,084 | 18 | 194 | 887 |
| Major timber products that are further processed: | | | | | | | |
| In the manufacture of wooden products— | | | | | | | |
| Saw logs for lumber board foot [7].. | 42,500 | 8,670 | 98.9 | 44,345 | 39,000 | 7,956 | 40,692 |
| Logs and bolts for veneer board foot [8].. | 2,400 | 566 | 98.5 | 2,837 | 2,400 | 566 | 2,837 |
| Cooperage stock.......do.[8].... | 775 | 183 | 98.8 | 919 | 700 | 165 | 830 |
| In the manufacture of chemical products— | | | | | | | |
| Pulpwood............. cord.. | [6]29 | 1,660 | 70.2 | 5,784 | 40 | 3,320 | 10,678 |
| Wood for hardwood distillation cord.. | 0.5 | 34 | 35.0 | 53 | 0.5 | 34 | 53 |
| Logs and bolts for all other uses board foot [8].. | 1,000 | 236 | 100.0 | 1,200 | 1,500 | 354 | 1,800 |
| Cordwood for all other uses...... cord.. | 5 | 350 | 35.0 | 529 | 7 | 490 | 740 |
| Total....................... | ...... | 14,593 | 82.7 | 61,053 | ...... | 15,576 | 62,508 |

[1] All trees above 5 inches in diameter at breast height.

[2] Saw-timber sizes vary by regions but nowhere is it less than 9 inches.

[3] Estimated that 27 million cords might be cut from sound, living trees.

[4] Estimated that 25 million cords might be cut from sound, living trees.

[5] Estimated that 480 million posts might be cut from sound, living trees.

[6] Estimated that equivalent of 9 million cords may be imported as paper, wood pulp, and pulpwood.

[7] Measured in lumber tally.

[8] Measured in log scale.

This table was prepared by A. C. Cline; see p. 731.

*What is Arbor Day and how did it originate?*

It is a day set aside by law in most States for encouraging the planting of shade and forest trees, shrubs, and vines about homes, along highways, and about public grounds of the State, thus contributing to the wealth and comforts of the people. In some States, the law specifies the date on which Arbor Day will be observed, while in others the date is specified by the Governor or another official. The observance of Arbor Day by schools, civic organizations, and clubs usually includes programs designed to stress the importance of trees and their effect in improving the appearance of school grounds, streets, parks, and highways and to encourage the planting, protection, and preservation of the trees and shrubs and an acquaintance with the best methods for the conservation and use of our natural resources.

Arbor Day was first observed, as such, in Nebraska in 1872. The plan was conceived and the name "Arbor Day" proposed by J. Sterling Morton, then a member of the State Board of Agriculture, and later United States Secretary of Agriculture. At a meeting of the State Board of Agriculture of Nebraska, held at Lincoln, January 4, 1872, he introduced a resolution to the effect that Wednesday, the 10th day of April 1872, be especially set apart and consecrated to tree planting in the State of Nebraska and named Arbor Day. The resolution was adopted. Wide publicity was given to the plan, and more than a million trees were planted on the first Arbor Day.

*Who was Paul Bunyan?*

Paul Bunyan was a legendary lumberjack of early American logging days. In the North Woods men still embellish the stories about this boss logger, a fabulous giant who invented the lumber industry, dug Puget Sound, and built Niagara Falls so he could have a shower bath. One account says that Bunyan was born near the headwaters of the St. Lawrence River. Some say his parents were French-Canadians. Others say they were Scandinavians. When he was 2 weeks old he caught a full-grown grizzly with his bare hands. He fell into a river one day and caught 17 beaver in his beard, which he had from birth. At 3 months he had outgrown his parents' cabin and, because of damage he was doing to fences and barns as he played among the neighboring farms, said good-by to his parents and betook himself to a cave in the hills. There, as he grew up, he invented hunting and fishing.

In the Winter of the Blue Snow, Paul Bunyan found Babe, the Blue Ox, an animal that grew so big in his care that the distance between his eyes was measured by 17 ax handles, 3 cans of tomatoes, and a plug of chewing tobacco laid end to end. Among the many who have set down the lumberjack's mighty tales of Paul and Babe are James Stevens, R. D. Handy, and Glen Rounds. So big was Paul Bunyan's logging camp and so hearty his men that batter for their flapjacks was mixed in cement mixers and the griddles were greased by men who skated on them with slabs of bacon tied to their feet. Paul made Pike's Peak by piling rocks around a pike pole. He sharpened his ax on boulders rolling down mountainsides. He moved his camp 3,000 miles in a day by hitching Babe to it. When he was deepening the Mississippi, he built the Rocky Mountains with the dirt he threw to one side. In a few hours he logged off the Upside Down Mountain and, in a terrific fight with Hels Helsen, his foreman, so changed it that it became the Black Hills of South Dakota. He and his men and Babe cleared off whole townships between sunup and sunset. He cut down miles of trees to make a desert. He used young pine trees for toothpicks. He logged off the Dakotas with an axhead tied to a rope. He made a good start toward logging off Michigan, Wisconsin, and Minnesota.

The only one to get the better of Paul Bunyan, according to another legend, was an Indian chief. Grant Utley, of Cass Lake, a Minnesota community that is a rival of nearby Bemidji, whose civic-minded citizens have erected an heroic monument to Paul Bunyan, tells about Nanabushu, whom he calls "an even greater figure in the history of the Upper Midwest."

"It was Nanabushu," Mr. Utley writes, "who met Paul Bunyan about 9 miles east of Cass Lake, and gave him the first licking that he ever had, and sent him back where he belonged. For 40 days and 40 nights these two giants battled, but at last Paul, battered and bleeding, retired and left Nanabushu to rule over the million and a half acres, which later was to be called the Chippewa National Forest. Over this village hovers the spirit of Nanabushu, who long ago realized that if you take care of the forest, the forest will take care of you."

*Can molasses be made economically from wood?*

Research scientists of the Forest Products Laboratory have perfected wood molasses to the pilot plant stage of development. Funds provided by the Research and Marketing Act made possible the production of a sufficient quantity to permit several agricultural experiment stations to make practical tests of the wood molasses. Pilot plant operations indicated that costs can be kept low enough to make waste wood molasses attractive to livestock growers as a source of high-energy stock feed. In the first tests, wood molasses has compared favorably with blackstrap molasses for several purposes.

In making molasses, wood waste is treated with acid to convert it into a weak solution of sugar from which excess water is evaporated to produce a 50-percent solution of wood sugar. Wood sugar molasses is being tested as a preservative for grass silage at Washington, Oregon, and Wisconsin experiment stations. Montana experimenters are using wood molasses in preparing mixed feeds and mixed-feed pellets to use as a supplemental feed for sheep and cattle wintering on the range. This station found it possible to substitute molasses from lodgepole pine and larch for one-sixth of the grain ration for lambs.

At the Southern Forest Experiment Station a cooperating farmer found that up to 30 percent of oak molasses added to a mixture of cottonseed meal and hulls was palatable to older cattle, but that calves did not relish so much molasses.

Alternative ways of utilizing wood sugar are to grow feed yeast or produce ethyl alcohol.

*Why do foresters say on a forest and not in a forest?*

To foresters, a forest is an area that might include mountains, canyons, streams, open places, buildings, and other elements besides trees; they do not, therefore, consider themselves necessarily among trees or under trees or in a grove of trees, in the way a person thinks he has a picnic or hike, say, in the woods. A similar usage is *on the table* or *on the football field* or *on the page*.

*How much pulpwood does a newspaper use?*

Robson Black, the president of the Canadian Forestry Association, is authority for the statement that the Sunday edition of the New York Times has a weekly consumption of 800 cords of pulpwood, the product of 80 acres, and that a perpetual supply of newsprint for the Sunday Times requires a timber stand of 416,000 acres that is worked on a rotation of 80 years.

W. W. BERGOFFEN *is in charge of radio and television activities in the Division of Information and Education of the Forest Service. He joined the Forest Service in 1933 and worked as forest ranger on the Chattahoochee National Forest in Georgia and the DeSoto and Bienville National Forests in Mississippi prior to his assignment in Washington. Mr. Bergoffen is a graduate of the New York State College of Forestry at Syracuse University.*

# TREES AND HOMES

*Pecan trees—"Mississippi hickories"—were planted by George Washington at his Mount Vernon estate in Virginia. The nuts were given him by Thomas Jefferson.*

# Every Tree For Its Use

## TREES FOR THE COUNTRY HOME

W. H. LARRIMER

FOR TREES, as with people, an ideal place to grow up is in the country. There they find conditions of the soil, moisture, air, and sunshine that make for their best development.

Many farms lack the beauty as well as the practical advantages that result from the carefully planned selection and arrangement of trees around the farmstead. Too many have the wrong kind of trees; too many have trees that are misshapen and neglected; too many have trees that are located by chance where the seed happened to fall; too many, alas, have no trees at all.

An important feature in the general plan for the development of the farmstead is the intelligent and artistic use of trees and shrubs. The time, effort, and reasonable expense involved in carrying out such a plan is well repaid in the resulting years of contentment and pleasure, as well as the practical and monetary value they add to a farm. Although by proper selection and skill in arrangement trees can be made to fit into almost any requirement of a good farmstead plan, their full consideration should be included from the very beginning as an integral part of any such plan. Full advantage should be taken also of the opportunity to utilize adequate space available on the farm, as contrasted with the usually closely grouped plantings around the city or suburban homes.

*Above: The Wethersfield Elm in Connecticut, which was 201 years old in 1949, but doomed by the Dutch elm disease.*

Careful planning pays big dividends

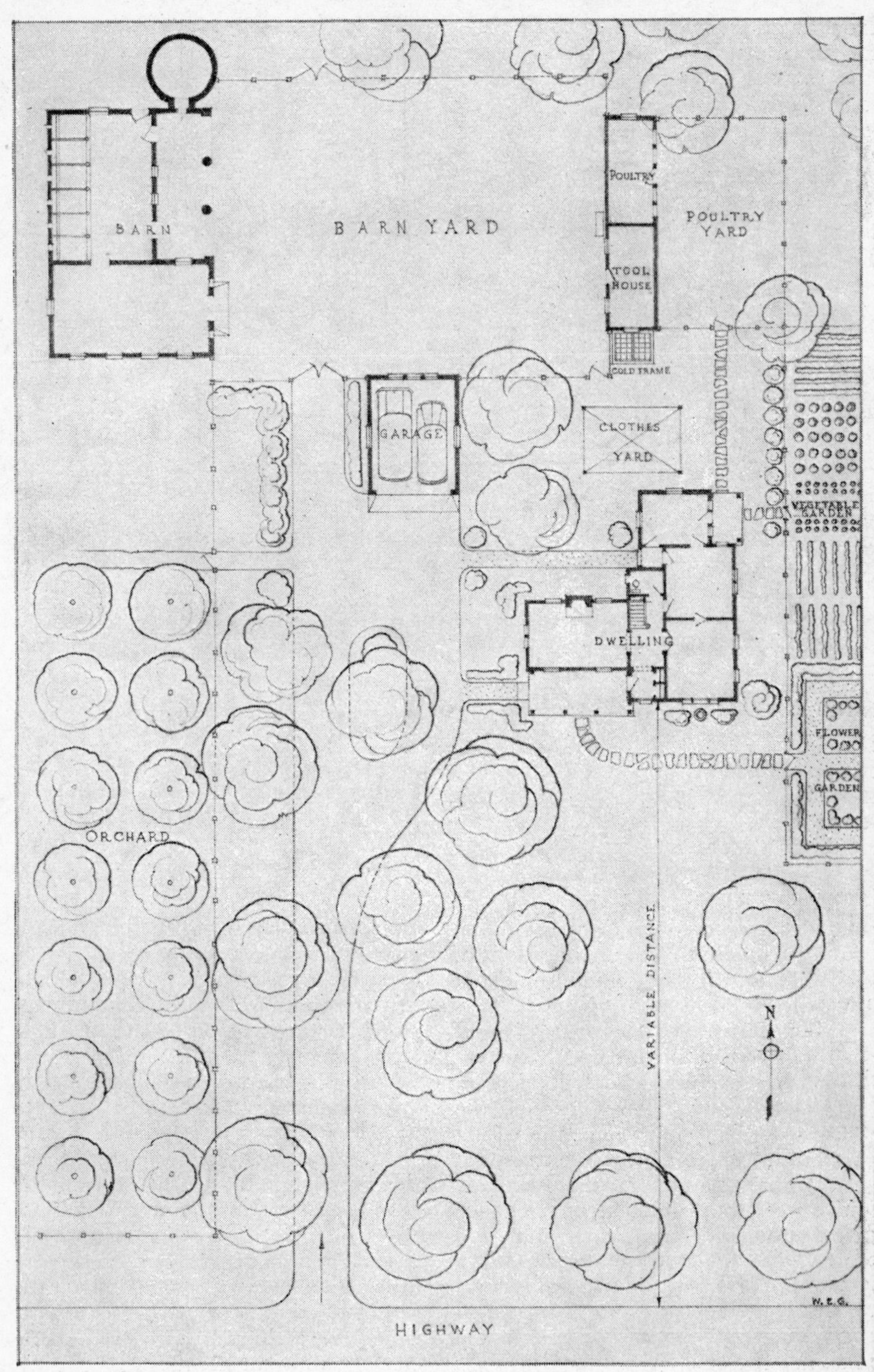


A good landscape plan shows the location and full-grown size of trees and shrubs.

The artistic use of trees enhances the beauty and value of a well-designed farmstead.

in planting trees around the farmstead. This use of trees in farmstead development is so important that it justifies the preparation of a separate site map to show the proposed tree locations. After the general features, such as roads, buildings, orchard, garden, lawns, and service yard, have been blocked in to scale, the map is ready for the trees and shrubs.

First, consideration should be given to attractiveness and ornamental effects. A house becomes a picture when framed by appropriate trees. Next comes planting for shade, protection, border, and background. Impatience at this stage may be costly. It is a simple matter to move a tree from one place to another on the map. Once a tree is planted and allowed to grow for a few years, however, it is a chore to move it. When the matter is called to your attention, you will be surprised how fast trees can grow. Take time to consult a landscape architect if one is available, or seek the advice of a reliable nurseryman. Make sure that they understand that you want the simplicity and informality appropriate for landscaping a farm home. Observe other farmsteads and adopt those features that are pleasing or otherwise desirable.

Also, look for things not to do. It is sad but true that most of our farmsteads show no evidence whatever of planning. Try not to make similar mistakes. Consult the available literature on the subject—articles in the farm journals or other magazines. All such preliminary study is worth your while.

The kind of trees to plant is closely related to the conditions of the place in which the trees are to be planted and the care and attention to be given them after planting.

Lists of trees that are adapted to different parts of the country are given elsewhere in this book. Weigh the merits and handicaps of each variety recommended and select those which fit your personal preference, as well as your particular needs and conditions.

The location and size of the trees and shrubs when they are full-grown should now be sketched in on your map, to scale. Rigidly resist the urge to plant too many trees or to interplant with temporary specimens. You become attached to these and their removal at the right time—or ever—is just out of the question.

Look out for the telephone lines. Trees and telephone, light, or power lines—each has its place, but they are not the same place. Try to avoid competition. If a conflict does occur and must be resolved in favor of the light or power lines, the outright removal of the trees is frequently more desirable than the mutilations often seen in such cases. Such problems may well be kept in mind in drawing up the original plans.

WITH THE PLAN COMPLETED, you are ready to begin planting. This does not mean that the plan cannot be revised.

Obvious changes can and should be made, but with discretion and confined mostly to the unplanted part of the plan. Keep in mind your ultimate objective and make only those revisions that will keep the development headed toward that objective. It should always be emphasized that a little extra care in planting may mean the difference between the loss of a favorite specimen tree or its survival and growth.

Just as soon as possible you should learn to know your trees as individuals. That includes recognition of the general characteristics that indicate their names without reference to a technical key.

One of the principal sources of satisfaction in really knowing trees is this flash recognition. It marks a stage in the friendship with trees that corresponds to the comfortable stage of friendship between people when they call each other by their first names.

W. H. LARRIMER *is a forester in the Branch of Research, Forest Service, Washington, D. C. He grew up on an Ohio farm, and received degrees from Purdue University and Ohio State University.*

# CITY TREES

IRVING C. ROOT, CHARLES C. ROBINSON

We rate a tree in a forest as potential lumber according to the texture of its wood and clean bole, its rapidity of growth, market value, and availability. City trees have price tags on them, of course (perhaps as much as $20 per inch of trunk diameter), but we appraise them largely on intangible values of shade and beauty. We judge the city tree by the shape of its canopy, its habit of growing tall and slender or small and spreading, its spring bloom or fall color, the shape and size of its leaves, and its evergreen or deciduous nature. Important, too, is whether it has any tendency to break in storms, whether it is a clean tree or a dirty one, its susceptibility to insect pests and disease, and its ability to adapt itself to the artificial conditions of cities.

No single item distinguishes a city more than its green areas, and probably our first reaction to a community is to its abundance or lack of trees. The shade they give from the sun makes the summer heat more tolerable, and filters for grateful eyes the dazzling reflection from masonry and concrete. A city of monumental buildings, like Washington, particularly needs trees to interrupt the reflected light. The landscape architect uses trees to soften hard building lines and accentuate vertical or horzontal details.

The home owner plants trees to give scale and proportion to desired features and to delight his family and neighbors with spring bloom and fragrance, green coolness in summer, color in autumn, and interesting branch-and-twig patterns in winter.

Trees form vistas, frame views, and define park areas. They can screen out undesirable sights, and separate active from passive recreation. They border our city lakes and streams and cast their reflections in our pools. Groups of trees are a back drop, a cyclorama.

For all their beauty, city trees are no weaklings. It is sometimes surprising how they can survive the artificial and adverse conditions under which they grow. Smoke and gases, physical injuries, the disrupted water table, hard-packed soil, lack of humus renewal and mulch, inadequate root space, reflected heat from pavements and buildings, and glacial blasts of air through the wind tunnel formed by street and buildings, all make their lot hard.

Because trees manufacture their food by the action of sunlight on elements in the leaf, any substantial accumulation of soot or residual oil from the air will screen out sunlight and retard this process of photosynthesis, resulting in a weakening of the tree from starvation. Trees such as ailanthus, horsechestnut, hackberry, American ash, ginkgo, poplars, sycamores, willows, lindens, and elms are all tolerant of soot and smoke. Others, like the sugar maple, sourgum, sweetgum, and honeylocust, can grow well only if the air is unpolluted.

No one seems prepared to say why one tree and not another can stand smoke and soot. It may be related to the effect of smoke and soot-impregnated soil on the mycorrhiza and their relation to root growth and feeding. Why some trees are more affected than others might be a fertile field for research. Perhaps investigation would show us how to grow sugar maples in smoky, soot-laden air where now they cannot survive. Perhaps some simple treatment of the soil or tree may some day make this possible.

Another factor that seems to affect the ability of a tree to withstand smoke and gases is the nature of its leaf surface. A rough, heavy, or sticky leaf will accumulate more soot and residual oil than a smooth or waxy one, and the latter is more easily cleaned off by rainfall and wind.

City trees are subject to physical injuries from many sources. Seldom is a sewer, drainage, or utility line put in on a tree-lined street but that some damage is done to the roots. Because the health of a tree is in direct proportion to the extent and effectiveness of its feeder roots, great care should be exercised that a minimum of damage be done to the tree roots during construction. This damage might not kill the tree, but it might so debilitate it that it would become easy prey to insects and disease.

The power and telephone companies used to expect their line-clearing crews to hack off the tops and sides of trees for line clearance. The branches exposed to the sun by the sudden removal of the protecting canopy were vulnerable to sunscald, which cracked the tender bark and permitted the inroads of disease and insect pests. Fortunately such butchering is on the wane, and few cities permit it today. More and more underground conduits are used; they eliminate unsightly poles and wires and do away with the necessity for any type of drastic tree pruning. Many trees are killed annually by illuminating gas from underground gas lines. One should be suspicious of chlorosis or yellowing of leaves and of any other signs of the unexplained declining health of a tree when it is located near an underground gas line.

Additional hazards of city trees are the bumps and splintering from vehicular accidents, the thoughtlessness of the boy who breaks off branches and gouges with his new knife or ax, and girdling by squirrels in a small park.

A mower in the hands of a careless maintenance man can severely damage the bark and cambium layer at the base of trees; those cuts and bruises can become immediate focal points for infectious diseases like verticillium wilt and canker stain of our sycamores. Indeed, there are several instances on record where injuries by lawn mowers were responsible for the spread of canker stain and the subsequent loss of rows of fine old sycamores.

Another disadvantage under which city trees live is the lack of humus build-up provided by the decay of fallen leaves. Humus or duff, formed by decayed leaves, is nature's food for the tree and her protection for its feeding roots from the sun and drying wind. When we remove this humus or do not permit its manufacture, we are disturbing one of nature's processes for tree growth and vigor.

In large city parks like Fairmount Park in Philadelphia and Rock Creek Park in the District of Columbia, much of the total area is left naturalized and the fallen leaves are allowed to remain, decay, and form the humus that provides much of the tree's natural food and its mulch for moisture retention. Public opinion demands, however, that the small park square, the quadrangle, and parking space along the street be kept free of fallen leaves and other debris. As a practical matter, it would be almost impossible, even if desired, to allow a build-up of fallen and decaying leaves. Clogged gutters and drain pipes, fire hazard, dangerously slippery streets, to name only a few, make necessary their prompt removal along streets and in most parks.

In their natural habitat trees usually grow in soils and moisture conditions that are best suited to them. Thus (in New England, Middle Atlantic, and Midwestern States to which this discussion pertains) we find elms, pin oaks, and sweetgums in low-lying land along the streams and even in swamps. Tuliptrees seem to like the mountain valleys from which they spread to the low-lying ridges. Red and white oaks and sourgums, on the other hand, may be found on higher mountains where their roots have to go deep for water.

Too often in city planting, particularly along the streets, we put in elms, oaks, and honeylocusts, with but little regard to their preference of soil and moisture conditions. Trees that in their native environment search deeply for water are planted alongside those with shallow roots. It is a tribute to nature's adaptability that elms can thrive alongside the deep-rooted white or red oaks.

Were it not for this amazing adaptability, the selection of trees for urban use would be even more complex. It is true, though, that the nearer we can duplicate natural conditions of the soil and the water table, the better we can expect our tree to thrive.

The runoff of rainfall is high in cities—almost 100 percent from paved areas. The ground has no chance to absorb and store up the moisture for future needs; most of the rainfall, rather, is immediately carried off into gutters and drains. Trees in sizable city parks seldom suffer from lack of moisture in periods of normal rainfall, but the street tree in a narrow parking never gets a fair share of water and cannot absorb the little it receives. An oak tree gives off some 120 tons of water in only one season through its leaves—water that must be replenished from the soil—and it seems almost miraculous that our street trees survive at all. An interesting observation is that in times of drought, street trees, which are conditioned to a constant substandard amount of moisture, fare better than those accustomed to adequate rainfall.

How can these adverse conditions be improved?

First, we must see that the tree we select for planting has a sufficiently large tree pit filled with good soil to accommodate potential roots for some years to come. The hole must have natural or artificial drainage to insure against wet feet and root suffocation. The variety selected should be environmentally suited to the designated site from the standpoint of exposure, elevation, and purity of air. It should be planted where physical hazards are few. If natural moisture is lacking, particularly during periods of drought, it must be watered. If it shows signs of starvation, it must be fed with inorganic fertilizer or organics like manure, tobacco stems, sludge, or tankage.

Use determines whether a tree is desirable or undesirable for city planting. A broad-spreading, low-hanging Chinese magnolia may be ideal as a specimen in a small city park or on home grounds but impossible as a street tree. A fastigiate English oak may be perfect for a narrow street but of limited use in the large park. Individual peculiarities may make certain trees undesirable for any urban use—the female ginkgo, whose fruit has a bad odor, for example, or the silver maple, which breaks easily in wind and snow, or the boxelder, which has rapid but unsightly growth. Lombardy and Carolina poplars are out of favor because their roots fill sewer lines.

For street use, species or varieties should be avoided that are subject to disease and insect pests. Just as a contagious disease will tend to spread rapidly through a family whose members are in close contact with one another, so the Dutch elm disease, for instance, will spread rapidly through a concentrated group of city elms unless strong preventive measures are taken.

Dutch elm disease and phloem necrosis of elm and the canker stain of sycamores make unwise their widespread planting, particularly for cities.

The Dutch elm disease, disseminated principally by the elm bark beetle, has spread quite rapidly and is difficult to control. The control of the carrier by spraying and a rigorous sanitation program, involving the immediate removal and destruction of all dead and dying wood, are at present the only effective means of dealing with this serious threat to our elms. This control is difficult because of the inaccessibility to spray machines of scattered infected trees. Canker stain of sycamores seems to be carried largely by man's own activities. Bruises made by lawn mowers and particularly pruning operations seem to be the chief means by which this canker stain is spread. For districts where canker stain is established, there are several primary control measures to be taken: Remove all diseased sycamores or diseased portions of them, and avoid all unnecessary mutilation. In zone 4 (New York and Philadelphia) prune the sycamore only between December 1 and February 15, and avoid asphalt tree paints during that period; disinfect all pruning tools before use on healthy sycamores between February 16 and November 30. Denatured alcohol used as a dip or swab is a satisfactory disinfectant. If wound dressing is necessary, use a gilsonite-varnish paint into which 0.2 percent phenylmercury nitrate has been mixed. For districts where the disease is not established, observe these precautions: Disinfect all of the pruning equipment thoroughly before the work begins; use new paint brushes and pots.

Most of the authorities are pessimistic about our ability to check entirely the Dutch elm disease or phloem necrosis, and at the moment we can only try to isolate them and to slow down their spread. The canker stain of sycamores, while serious enough, offers greater hope of checking and perhaps even eventual eradication or isolation.

We have listed the principal epidemic tree diseases which we are fighting today, but we must be alert for others which might appear at any time and alert to diseases which are chronic now but which might become epidemic.

In planting trees on the home grounds, in the squares and circles, the parkways, and large city parks, the determination of varieties hinges on the effects desired and factors of natural elevation and exposure that the trees require. There are several signposts to guide one in making the selections for those sites.

A good street tree is one that provides shade and ornamentation, keeps within the bounds required of its growth, does not interfere with vehicular or pedestrian traffic, and stays healthy.

Streets of different widths require trees of different shapes and sizes. A narrow, pyramidal, or columnar tree is indicated for the narrow street with a limited building set-back; a narrow street cannot accommodate a broad specimen red oak or sycamore, but Lombardy and bolleana poplars are well adapted to this type of planting if their roots do not interfere with sewers. Those poplars are softwooded and have a tendency to break in storms, but they are sometimes useful where others cannot be grown. The pyramidal English oak, the fastigiate form of the ginkgo, as well as the pyramid tuliptree, which are tolerant of smoke and soot, are admirably suited to this use. Where polluted air is not a factor, the columnar sugar maple, the pyramidal red maple, and perhaps the sweetgum will serve the purpose, although the sweetgum is sometimes objectionable because of its falling fruit in autumn.

The wider streets can be planted to American ash, Norway maple, tuliptree, sycamore, or the lindens, all of which resist damage from smoke and fumes. Again, if smoke is not prevalent, such trees as scarlet oak, willow oak, pin oak, sugar maple, thornless honeylocust, blackgum or sourgum, and Scotch elm can be used effectively.

On the broadest avenues and boulevards there is opportunity to use large, massive tree types. Unfortunately, most of these broadheaded varieties are susceptible to the gases, smoke, and soot. The patriarch red oak, white oak, black oak, willows, and even the larger pines, spruces, and firs can be effective in the wide parking along such thoroughfares.

The limitations of space imposed by streets do not apply in our selection of trees for large city parks and parkways, institutions, or residence grounds. There we have an opportunity to plant the more common, better-known species as well as add greatly to the interest and variety of the landscape by the use of the rarer and more unusual sorts.

Many trees of outstanding beauty are too sparingly used simply because one does not know them. Pink and white dogwoods are unsurpassed of their sort, but how many people know and use the Chinese and the Kousa dogwood, whose blooms come after the foliage has appeared? Most of us know the redbud, or Judas-tree, but how many are familiar with the beautiful white form of this spring bloomer?

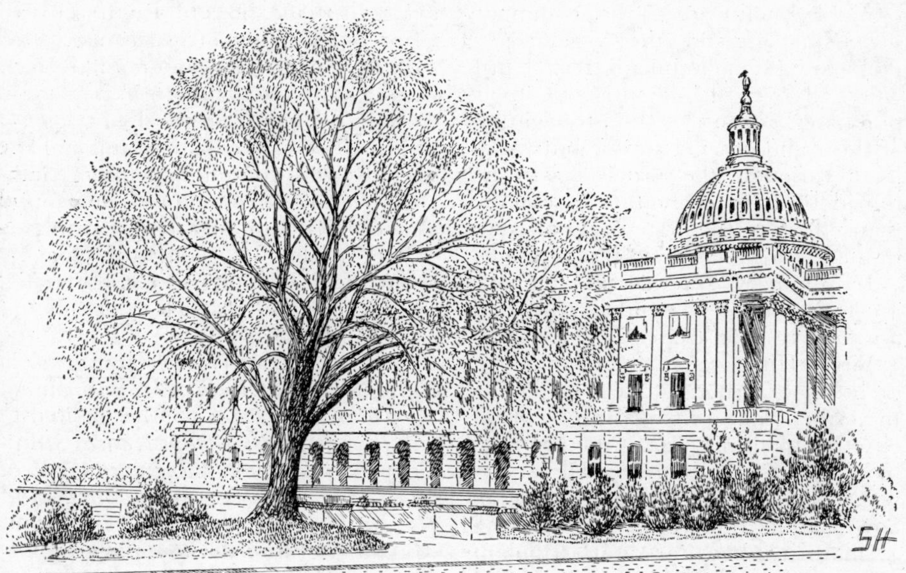

**"A city of monumental buildings, like Washington, particularly needs trees . . ."**

*Magnolia soulangeana,* the saucer magnolia, gets the spotlight, but the equally deserving star magnolia, *M. stellata,* and some of the *soulangeana* varieties remain relatively obscure. There is an encouraging trend toward the planting of more varieties of Japanese cherries, but several of the finest, Akebono, Mt. Fuji, and rosea, are still seldom seen. Among the flowering crab apples, *sargenti, theifera,* and Oekonomierat Echtermeyer are a few that deserve wider recognition.

Yellow is a relatively rare color among our flowering trees, and the yellow-blooming things, such as cornelian-cherry, goldenchain, and goldenrain-tree, can show up beautifully against a foil of green.

A number of other flowering trees, too little used, deserve mention: The red horsechestnut, *Aesculus carnea*; the fringetree, *Chionanthus virginica;* snowball, *Styrax japonica*; the silverbells, *Halesia tetraptera* and *monticola;* and various hawthorns, *Crataegus cordata, punctata, oxyacantha* and its varieties.

These flowering trees can be planted as single specimens, in groups, or in great drifts to enrich park and parkway plantings and add greatly to the interest of home grounds.

Chinese scholartree, *Sophora japonica,* and the zelkova are examples of outstanding shade trees that are little used. Both of these shade trees have the reputation of being trouble-free and long-lived. The scholartree gives additional dividends in its long white bloom panicles in August. The Kentucky coffeetree, too, offers great possibilities for more extensive use.

Most of us can visualize the spruces, firs, and pines at maturity, but not many, perhaps, think of the little conical sheared cypress or cedar, bought from the nurseryman, in terms of its ultimate magnificence in size and contour. Groups or specimens of Deodar cedar, cryptomeria, baldcypress, Lawson cypress, and umbrella-pine acquire character as they grow, and only when these less common trees have a chance to develop naturally do they attain their full picturesqueness.

City officials can do much to foster the propagation and development of good city tree types—for example, the pyramidal type of tuliptree, the pyramidal English oak, the columnar sugar maple, and the vegetatively propagated male ginkgo tree. Until cities all over the country, by their purchases, encourage the propagation of these and other desirable but little-used varieties, the growers will be forced by hard economics to confine their efforts to the more common and, in many cases, less desirable kinds.

In summary, several fundamentals are to be borne in mind if our cities are to have good trees.

First: Hire a competent landscape architect or arborist, one who knows the esthetic and practical problems of city tree planting. He is the key man in a successful program: He knows what varieties will or will not grow in any given location, how they will look at maturity, how far apart to plant the trees, and what soils will sustain them. He will use tree forms to create the desired effect.

Second: Select only those varieties adapted to your local conditions.

Third: Buy only the best obtainable materials; cheap, substandard trees are usually expensive in the end.

Fourth: Insist on proper planting to rigid specifications under the supervision of a competent plantsman.

Fifth: Spray, feed, water, and prune whenever necessary; perform these operations according to the latest scientific methods. Adequate maintenance is vital to the continuing survival and good health of trees and is as necessary as good original design and planting.

Sixth: Keep in sight the goal—beauty and livability. A city of trees is a better place in which to live.

IRVING C. ROOT *is superintendent of National Capital Parks, Department of the Interior. He has degrees in horticulture and forestry from Kansas State College and in landscape architecture from Massachusetts State University. He was formerly chief engineer for the Maryland National Capital Park and Planning Commission.*

CHARLES C. ROBINSON *is a graduate in landscape architecture of Pennsylvania State College and has devoted 20 years to the practice of his profession. He has specialized in the development of home grounds. He is a landscape architect with National Capital Parks in Washington.*

## SHADE TREES FOR THE NORTHEAST

ALMA M. WATERMAN, R. U. SWINGLE, CLAYTON S. MOSES

Throughout the Northeastern States, the maples, the elms, and the oaks have long been preferred for shade trees. The elms in this region, however, are threatened by two serious diseases. In the northwestern part a wilt disease impairs the value of red oaks for shade-tree planting. Fortunately, there are still many kinds of beautiful native trees and some introduced kinds that make satisfactory shade trees.

Some of the outstanding deciduous shade trees that can be recommended for residential and suburban sections, primarily because of their tolerance of city conditions, are: Sugar maple, Norway maple, red maple, white oak, pin oak, northern red oak, scarlet oak, Texas oak or Shumard oak, thornless common honeylocust, sweetgum, ginkgo, American sycamore, London planetree, common hackberry, black tupelo, green ash, silver linden, littleleaf linden, Kentucky coffeetree, yellow-poplar or tuliptree, the American yellowwood, Japanese pagodatree, and Amur corktree.

In heavily congested and industrial areas the following species may be used: The ginkgo, the thornless common honeylocust, London planetree, ailanthus or tree-of-Heaven, and the Amur corktree.

In the Northeastern States, a large

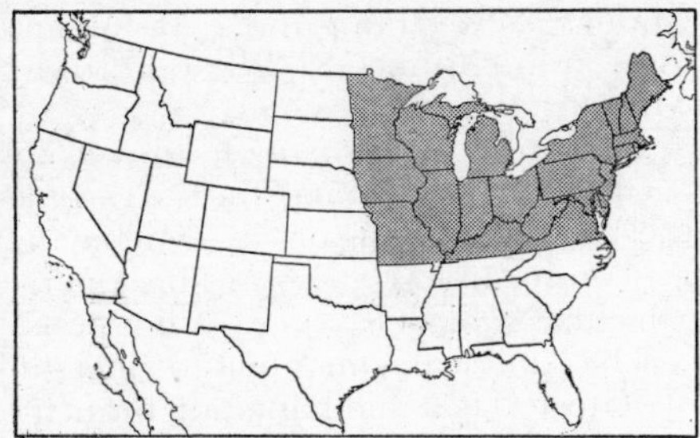

area, the climate and other conditions vary so much that not all the recommended kinds of shade trees will grow equally well throughout the region. The elevation above sea level, rainfall, the proximity of large bodies of water, river valleys, and other factors modify the natural distribution of plants and affect the growth of shade trees. For best growth, some kinds will be limited to the more northern or to the more southern sections. Some kinds that will grow in the southern border zone of the area may not grow at all in the most northerly parts. Some kinds of shade trees that grow best in New England may do well in the southern Appalachians, but very poorly on the Coastal Plain. On the other hand, some predominantly southern species may extend far north along the Atlantic coast.

THE MAPLES are widely planted as shade trees in the Northeast, but most of the native species are not entirely satisfactory for this purpose. They are short-lived, are subject to windbreak, and require moist, rich soil.

The Norway maple, introduced from Europe, and our native sugar maple are considered the most satisfactory for streets and lawns.

Sugar maple is one of the most common and attractive trees throughout the Northeast. It is a large tree, 50 to 90 feet in height. When it is grown in the open as a shade tree, it has a short trunk with a broadly egg-shaped or round-topped crown of stout, ascending branches. Horticultural varieties that have a narrow columnar head are especially adapted for planting along narrow streets. The leaves of the sugar maple are thin, bright, rich green, and in the North usually develop in May together with a profusion of yellowish-green flowers, from which bees obtain pollen and nectar. In the autumn the brilliant yellow, orange, and scarlet coloration of its foliage is attractive.

Sugar maple is readily transplanted, its rate of growth is moderate, and it is relatively long-lived, with a possible life span of more than 100 years. It is injured by city smoke and gas fumes and therefore is not suitable for planting in industrial or congested residential areas. It is valuable, however, on lawns, along suburban streets, or on farmsteads. It attains its best development when it is grown in well-drained, moist, rich soil, but it will survive in less favorable sites in gravelly soil. It is the source of maple sugar.

A wilt disease is sometimes serious, and several leaf diseases caused by fungi are common on sugar maple. Brown dead areas in or along the edge of the leaf blade often develop when drying winds or bright sunlight and high temperatures immediately follow a period of moist weather.

Norway maple is grown extensively from central New England and New York southward. It is usually about 30 to 60 feet tall at maturity, with a short trunk and numerous stout, ascending branches that form a low, round, spreading head. The greenish-yellow flowers appear in abundance in April and May before the leaves develop. The leaves are slightly larger than those of the sugar maple, deeper green, and firmer in texture. The dense foliage remains on the tree late in autumn and the leaves turn bright yellow before falling. Norway maple is easily transplanted, its rate of growth is moderate, and it tolerates a wide range of soil conditions. It stands unfavorable soil and atmospheric conditions in cities and therefore is widely used as a street tree. Its low, dense head, however, requires considerable pruning to adjust it to street conditions, and it is not adapted for planting along narrow streets.

802062°—49——5

A horticultural variety with a narrower, more upright crown is sometimes grown successfully under such conditions. Because the thick shade and mass of fine feeding roots of the Norway maple make it hard for grass to grow under the tree, Norway maple frequently is considered undesirable as a lawn tree.

The Schwedler maple, a variety of Norway maple, has a similar type of growth. When young, it has bright-red leaves that change to dark red and finally to green. It is planted on lawns and sometimes along suburban streets for ornament and for shade.

The Norway maple is subject to about the same pests as the sugar maple, but is less subject to leaf scorch.

Red maple, a native, is less desirable for a shade tree than either the sugar maple or the Norway maple. It can be used when a fast-growing tree is needed. The red maple develops a conical or broad, rounded crown, with bright-green leaves that assume brilliant shades of orange, red, and scarlet in autumn. The foliage casts a moderately dense shade. In the spring, masses of red flowers make it attractive.

Red maple is easily transplanted. The wood is somewhat weak and subject to storm damage, and its roots often enter and clog sewers.

THE ELMS are outstanding trees, but unfortunately the American elm cannot be recommended now except for limited planting, because of phloem necrosis and the Dutch elm disease, both of which are spreading rapidly and causing heavy losses. New public plantings of American elm should be delayed therefore until satisfactory control measures for the diseases have been developed, and the home owner will do well to consider carefully whether some other kind of shade tree cannot be planted instead.

In the Northeast, the Dutch elm disease extends from the Atlantic seaboard westward to Indiana. An isolated outbreak has been found in Colorado. It has not been found in Maine, New Hampshire, Michigan, Wisconsin, Minnesota, Illinois, Iowa, Missouri, or Arkansas.

Phloem necrosis is not known to occur in Pennsylvania, States east of the Appalachians, or in Michigan, Wisconsin, and Minnesota. The American elm is subject to several other pests.

The American elm grows to a height of 50 to 100 feet and has a tall, branching trunk. It develops numerous ascending or drooping branches that form various types of crowns, such as the typical vase or umbrella forms. The beauty of its various forms of growth and the arching of its branches above the streets of New England towns have made the American elm an outstanding characteristic of the landscape. None of the many introduced species of elm can equal it for ornament or shade. The greenish flowers appear in drooping clusters in April or May before the leaf buds open. The leaves are 4 to 6 inches long, rough, dark green, unequally rounded at the base; they turn yellow in autumn and usually fall rather early.

The American elm is easily transplanted, grows rapidly, and often lives between 70 and 100 years under city conditions. The American elm is tolerant of a wide range of soil conditions, except dry, sandy locations, but its best growth is developed in moist, well-drained soils. In its natural habitat it is found along streams or in low, moist ground. It grows well on streets and in yards. The growth habit of the branches is such that the crotches of old trees often have to be braced in order to withstand heavy wind or ice storms.

The rock elm might be used more for streets and lawns, as it is a large, strong, narrow-headed tree. This elm is more suited to the northern than to the southern part of the region, and should be considered particularly for the Lake States. Rock elm grows more slowly than American elm.

In this region two European species of elm are grown sometimes as shade trees. They are susceptible to the Dutch elm disease and also are frequently affected by the elm leaf beetle.

The English elm (*Ulmus procera*) is a large tree, sometimes reaching 100 feet in height. It has a straight trunk that extends into the tree crown, and branches that spread or ascend to form an oblong, rounded crown more like the oaks than the American elm. The leaves, 2 to 3 inches long, remain on the tree later in the autumn than those of the American elm. The English elm can be transplanted quite easily and is adaptable to the same types of soils as the American elm. It has the tendency to produce numerous shoots or suckers from the roots.

For that reason, another European species, the Scotch or Wych elm, which is similar to the English elm in form and growth habit but does not produce suckers, has often been preferred, both for lawn and street planting. The leaves of the Scotch elm are about 3 to 6 inches long. Several horticultural varieties of both these species are in cultivation.

The Chinese elm (*Ulmus parvifolia*) has small leaves, which turn bright yellow in the autumn before they fall. Its flowers are formed in August or September. It is easily transplanted and grows rapidly. It is hardy in southern parts of the region. The Morris Arboretum in Philadelphia has a beautiful, large specimen of this tree.

The Siberian elm is resistant to the Dutch elm disease, but it is subject to canker and leaf diseases. It is not recommended except for locations where better trees will not grow or for places where quick effects are wanted while the more durable species are getting started. It lives 25 to 40 years.

THE OAKS are hardy and long-lived, and have beautiful foliage in summer and autumn. Some of the species that are native to the Northeast are well adapted for use as shade trees on lawns and along streets.

In southern Wisconsin, northern Illinois, and northeastern Iowa, and down the Mississippi River to St. Louis, oak wilt threatens the red and black oaks particularly. The disease is spreading, and no control is now known for it. The red and black oaks therefore should not be planted as street trees in the infected area at present, and the home owner should realize that he runs a risk in planting them. In areas near the infected zone it would be prudent to use red and black oaks cautiously until more is known about the disease.

Pin oak in this region usually reaches 40 to 80 feet in height at maturity. It makes a satisfactory shade tree in southern Maine, eastern Massachusetts, Rhode Island, Connecticut, central and western New York, central Pennsylvania, and southward. The straight trunk extends into the crown. Its numerous slender branches, long, horizontal or ascending above, shorter and drooping below, form a broadly pyramidal head. The branches bear many short, upright, and pinlike twigs. The leaves are 4 to 6 inches long, deeply cut with five to seven bristle-tipped lobes, and are thin, firm, dark green, and glossy. They turn dark red in the autumn and sometimes remain on the trees during the winter. The pin oak blooms in May when the leaves are about one-third grown. It is particularly adapted for use as a shade tree, even on city streets, because of its narrow symmetrical form, the ease of transplanting, and rapidity of growth. It is tolerant of a wide range of soil conditions and of city smoke. Pruning the lower drooping branches is necessary, particularly for trees planted along streets.

Pin oak is subject to a leaf yellowing—chlorosis—if alkaline soil conditions prevent the trees from obtaining sufficient iron, but the injured trees will usually respond to soil treatment, injections, or sprays. The fungus diseases common to many species of oak, such as the cankers and wood rots, may occur on pin oaks, but otherwise the species is free from serious diseases.

The northern red oak is among the largest of the northeastern oaks. It grows well along the Atlantic coast close to the ocean, as well as inland in northern localities. It attains a height of 50 to 85 feet, occasionally up to 150 feet. The trunk is usually short. The widespreading branches form a broad, open, symmetrical crown. The leaves are 5 to 9 inches long, thin, firm, dull dark green, 7- to 11-lobed, with bristles at the tips of the lobes. The northern red oak is rather slow in leafing in the spring but retains its leaves late in the autumn, when they turn a brilliant red. Its inconspicuous light-green flowers appear late in May or early in June when the leaves are about one-half developed. It is relatively easy to transplant in early spring. The tree is of moderately rapid growth. It sometimes reaches a height of 18 feet in 10 years, and 50 to 75 feet in 50 years. It may live two or three centuries. It grows well in any well-drained soil, particularly in gravelly or sandy loam. It is intolerant of shade and wet soils. Because of its spreading crown, it requires a relatively large area for its best development, and therefore it is adapted for planting on lawns and along wide streets. It is moderately tolerant of smoke and soot and may be used on wide streets in suburban and moderately congested districts.

The northern red oak is susceptible to the fungus disease, Strumella canker, which may attack shade trees but is much more serious in the forest. Like most of our northern oaks, northern red oak may be severely attacked by wound-decay fungi. Its most serious enemy at present is oak wilt disease.

The scarlet oak is native throughout most of the area and makes an excellent shade tree except in northern New England, the northern half of the upper Lake States, the edge of the Plains, and the Coastal Plain in Virginia. In the most northern part of the region it is of medium height, 30 to 50 feet, but under more favorable growing conditions southward it may grow to 60 or 80 feet. The trunk is tapering and usually continuous into the crown. The lateral branches are ascending above, horizontal and spreading below, and form an open, narrow, irregular, or rounded head. The leaves are 3 to 6 inches long, with five to nine bristle-tipped lobes, thin, firm, glossy, and dark green. They turn dark red to bright scarlet in autumn. The flowers develop in May and early June when the leaves are about one-half grown.

The scarlet oak is quite readily transplanted, grows rapidly, and prefers dry, sandy soil, but it is more tolerant of moist soils than the red oak. It is adapted for planting on lawns and the wide streets in suburban areas, for it requires slightly less room for development than the northern red oak. It also endures city conditions and resists drought and smoke, but it is subject to rot by wound-decay fungi and therefore may suffer from wind breakage. It is subject to oak wilt.

White oak is one of our best shade trees for lawn planting. It is native to all parts of the region except a small area in the northern part of Michigan and northern and western Minnesota. It is a slow-growing, sturdy tree that grows 60 to 90 feet tall and develops a broad, rounded, open crown. It bears light-green leaves that turn brown in autumn and cling to the twigs through the winter. Its large size makes it unsuitable for planting along most streets. Young white oaks can be transplanted readily if carefully handled, but large specimens are difficult to transplant successfully. White oak trees often live more than a century. White oak is affected by oak wilt but is said to be less severely injured by the disease than are red or black oaks.

The Texas, or Shumard, oak is an attractive tree not often seen in most parts of the Northeast. It is hardy in southern Illinois and Indiana, western Ohio, southeastern Iowa, and the Coastal Plain of Virginia. It is not native in the Appalachians or north of Maryland. It grows 50 to 75 feet high, develops an open crown, and has foliage like that of the scarlet oak.

Willow oak develops into a handsome, large tree, and is useful along streets and in lawns. The leaves are an attractive light green and resemble willow leaves in shape. It is native in the Coastal Plain from Virginia to New York City and in the small area surrounding the junction of the Ohio and the Mississippi Rivers. In planting, 60 feet should be allowed between trees for full development.

THE GINKGO was introduced into America from China and Japan, where it has been grown for centuries in temple gardens. It has long been cultivated in northeastern United States as an ornamental and shade tree, particularly for street planting. It is hardy northward to southern Maine and may be grown near the seacoast. It reaches a height of 60 to 80 feet and has a single erect trunk continuous into the crown. The straight, slender branches are slightly ascending and form a broadly conical or pyramidal head.

The flowers appear in May; the male and female flowers are borne on separate trees. The female flowers develop into a stone fruit with a malodorous, fleshy outer layer, which, when the fruit falls, makes pavements slippery and disagreeable. For that reason, only trees that bear male flowers should be planted. The fan-shaped leaves, about 2 to 4 inches broad, resemble a leaflet of the maidenhair fern. In autumn they turn bright yellow and fall from the tree within a few days.

The ginkgo tolerates unfavorable city conditions and a wide range of soil conditions. It is relatively easy to transplant. It withstands wind and ice storms and is free from serious pests.

TULIPTREE, also called yellow-poplar, is native in Indiana and southern Michigan south of a line that extends eastward along the south shore of Lake Ontario, eastward to Massachusetts, and then southeastward diagonally to Rhode Island. It is native also in the southern tip of Illinois and in southeastern Missouri. It is grown as a shade tree as far north as central Vermont.

It reaches a height of 50 to 70 feet, with a tall, straight trunk that is continuous into the crown. The branches are ascending at the top and horizontal or slightly drooping at the base, but they have upcurved tips that form a low-branched, compact and pyramidal head when young. As the tree matures it develops an oblong and open crown. The leaves are light green, glossy, 5 to 6 inches long, and four-lobed, with petioles or stems as long as the leaves. They turn bright yellow before falling in the autumn. The large, tuliplike flowers are greenish yellow, 1½ to 2 inches deep, and 2 to 5 inches wide; they appear on older trees in May or June after the leaves develop.

The tuliptree is not easily transplanted, and its young fleshy roots must be carefully protected from drying during transplanting, which should be done in early spring. It requires a rather moist, well-drained soil and, once established, its growth is fairly rapid. In the forest it reaches maturity in about 200 years.

When soil conditions are favorable it may be used as a shade tree along wide streets in suburban areas. Its brittle wood, however, makes it rather susceptible to storm and ice damage and therefore it is sometimes considered undesirable for street planting. It is relatively free from fungus diseases, but a slight early leaf fall may occur as a result of dry summer weather. It is most satisfactory for planting in parks and around the home, where its attractive foliage and flowers make it valuable both for shade and ornament.

SWEETGUM is native to the southern part of this region. Its northern range extends diagonally from southeastern Missouri to southern Connecticut. It has been used successfully in more northern locations but has not proved hardy in some localities of the Lake States. It usually attains a height of 50 to 75 feet and its straight trunk is continuous into the crown. The slender ascending or spreading branches form a narrow pyramidal or broad, rounded, and open crown. The leaves are 3 to 5 inches long, broader than long, star-shaped with five lobes, thin, smooth, bright green, and glossy. They turn bright red or dark red or scarlet in the autumn; the foliage is attractive and ornamental in summer and autumn. The greenish and rather inconspicuous flower clusters appear in April or May when the leaves are about one-third grown. The fruit ripens in the autumn in ball-like, tough, spiny heads about 1 to 1½ inches in diameter, which remain on the tree into the winter.

Sweetgum is not very readily transplanted in heavy soils and in its more northern limits, but otherwise it will become easily adjusted to a wide range of soil conditions. All through New England it should be transplanted in early spring. It prefers a moist, well-drained soil, has a moderate growth rate, and will thrive near the seacoast. It reaches maturity in 200 to 300 years in the forest. Sweetgum is adapted to planting in suburban areas both as a street and a lawn tree. It is relatively resistant to fungus diseases as well as to damage from wind or ice storms.

THE AMERICAN LINDEN, or basswood, has been grown to some extent as a shade tree along roadsides, particularly in the suburban areas. Some of the European lindens, however, are usually preferred as lawn or street trees, because of their more ornamental, compact growth.

American linden is native throughout the Northeast, from the seacoast to altitudes of 1,000 feet. It may attain a height of 50 to 75 feet, sometimes even more than 100 feet, with a straight trunk that is continuous into the crown. The numerous and slender branches are ascending at the top, but tend to be slightly drooping below. They form a dense, broad, rounded crown. The leaves are unequal, heart-shaped, 5 or 6 inches long and almost as wide, thick and firm, dull dark green, and coarsely toothed along the margin. They remain on the trees late in the autumn and turn yellow before falling. The yellowish-white flowers, produced in loose clusters in late June or July after the leaves have developed, are well supplied with a fragrant nectar that attracts bees.

American linden is easily transplanted, comparatively fast growing, and in the forest reaches maturity in 90 to 140 years. It may be relatively short-lived on streets. It prefers a rich, well-drained, and loamy soil, and, like most species of linden, it is intolerant of dry locations or dry climate. It may be used as a shade tree on lawns or along wide streets in suburban areas, provided soil conditions are favorable.

American linden is susceptible to several leaf diseases but none is usually serious enough to cause lasting injury. A trunk rot, however, which occurs rather frequently, starts near the ground level and advances slowly upward. Affected trees are subject to breakage in windstorms and may become unsightly at an early age.

Several species of European linden have proved to be desirable and hardy shade trees in the Northeast. One, the European linden (*Tilia europaea,* sometimes sold under the name of *T. vulgaris*), forms a dense, pyramidal head, and its leaves are slightly smaller than those of the American linden. It is widely planted as a shade tree on lawns and along city streets and is relatively tolerant of city conditions. It is susceptible to trunk rot, which makes it subject to wind breakage.

Another species of similar growth habit is the littleleaf linden, whose leaves are 1½ to 2½ inches long and sometimes broader than long. It also grows successfully as a lawn or street tree in suburban areas.

The silver linden is considered one of the most satisfactory trees for street and lawn planting and is hardy from western Massachusetts and central New York southward. It may reach a height of 100 feet and has upright branches that form a dense, broad, pyramidal head. The leaves, about 2 to 4 inches long and almost as broad, are dark green on the upper surface and silvery white below. The small, fragrant, cream-colored flowers appear in July or August and are said to be poisonous to bees. The silver linden tolerates heat and drought and therefore is suitable for planting along wide city streets. It may also be grown successfully near the seacoast.

The pendent, or silverpendent, linden has leaves like those of the silver linden, but it has slender, drooping branches and is adapted to planting as an ornamental shade tree on lawns. Well grown, it may reach 80 feet.

THE AMERICAN SYCAMORE, or the planetree, is native in the region except in northern New England, northern Wisconsin, most of Minnesota, and northwestern Iowa. This tree has been planted rather extensively as a shade tree in its native range. It is susceptible to anthracnose, a fungus disease that attacks and kills the leaves when they are developing in the spring and also infects twigs, causing a disfiguring dieback. Therefore, it is not recommended for street or lawn planting.

THE LONDON PLANETREE, which is more resistant to anthracnose, has been grown successfully along wide streets and around suburban homes. This species is considered a hybrid between the American sycamore and the Oriental planetree, and is hardy in the southern parts of Maine, New Hampshire, Vermont, in central New York, and southward.

In the past few years it has proved susceptible to canker stain, a disease caused by a fungus that may kill large branches and entire trees. The disease may be controlled by using certain precautionary methods in pruning and in the treatment of cut surfaces and wounds. Detailed information about the disease and its control can be obtained by writing to the Division of Forest Pathology, Plant Industry Station, Beltsville, Md.

The London planetree may attain a height of 100 feet. Usually it has a short trunk that divides into several stout ascending secondary trunks. Its head is irregularly rounded or pyramidal. The bark resembles that of the American planetree, except that it is slightly cream-colored. The brownish bark peels off in rather large, thin patches, and exposes the yellowish or greenish innermost bark. The leaves, which have three to five lobes, are bright green, glossy on the upper surface, broader than long, and 4 to 10 inches wide. The rather inconspicuous reddish-green flowers appear in May when the leaves are partly developed. The fruit matures in September or October in greenish-brown, bristly balls, about an inch in diameter. The balls hang on the trees during winter.

The London planetree is easily transplanted, grows rather rapidly, and prefers a rich, moist, well-drained soil. It is tolerant of a wide range of soil conditions, however, and may be planted as a lawn or street tree where there is enough room for the spread of its branches. It endures city fumes.

AMERICAN YELLOWWOOD is native in the Southeastern States, but is hardy as a shade tree southward from eastern Massachusetts, Rhode Island and Connecticut, and southern New York. It is a small tree, usually not exceeding 30 to 45 feet, with a short trunk and several ascending or slightly spreading branches that form a broad, rounded head. The bark of the trunk is light gray or brown, usually smooth and attractive. The leaves are composed of seven to nine leaflets, bright green, smooth and firm, each leaflet 3 or 4 inches long. The leaves turn bright yellow in the autumn before they fall. In June, after the leaves have developed, the fragrant white flowers appear in loosely branched, drooping clusters, 10 to 16 inches long. In August or September, the fruit matures in pods about 4 inches long.

American yellowwood should be transplanted in the spring; it becomes established rather slowly. It prefers rich, moist, well-drained soil, but it is drought-resistant. The slender twigs are rather brittle and may break in severe windstorms. It is free from any serious fungus disease but its low head makes it suitable for planting as a street tree only in suburban areas along wide streets. The falling of the mature pods may be objectionable in some locations. Its attractive flowers and bark are ornamental on the home grounds, and its abundant foliage provides adequate but open shade.

European beech, an introduced species, is 40 to 65 feet high at maturity. It has a compact, oval crown and glossy, dark-green foilage. It prefers fertile, well-drained soil; it cannot stand soil compaction. The several good horticultural varieties that are available offer variation in growth habit, form, and color of foliage.

The thornless common honeylocust has gained favor for use on streets and lawns. Its small leaflets cast a light shade that does not prevent good growth of grass beneath it. It is high-rectangular or round-topped. This tree is long-lived and a rapid grower. The large, purplish-black fruit pods of the thornless common honeylocust may be interesting—or just a nuisance when they fall to the ground.

The common hackberry is a slow-growing tree of widespreading form that may reach 50 to 70 feet. Opinions differ on its desirability, but it seems to be gaining in popularity. Birds feed on the fruit. The interesting bark is formed into warts or narrow ridges. The leaves are a light green, and the foliage casts a moderately dense shade. It is easily transplanted.

In many places it is susceptible to a disease that causes an excessive production of small twigs, called brooms. This does not seem to be especially detrimental to the tree, however. During the growing season the brooms are inconspicuous; in winter they give a more massive effect to the tree. In habit it is something like the American elm, although not so graceful. It dislikes smoke and soot.

Trees of limited use include several species that are good in many situations or for special purposes.

The American mountain-ash is a small to medium tree, with a somewhat open to round-topped crown. It is short-lived, fairly slow in growth, and subject to attack by several pests. The white flowers in the spring and the bright-red fruits, which remain over winter and are eaten by birds, make it an attractive tree for suitable yard locations. In New England many beautiful specimens brighten the landscape.

The magnolias are not usually considered as shade trees, but the native cucumbertree magnolia has the necessary qualifications. It grows best in well-drained soil. It is native in the region from Pennsylvania southwestward in the mountains and in Ohio, Indiana, and Kentucky. The wide pyramidal crown reaches 50 to 90 feet in the forest. Its red fruits are conspicuous in the autumn. Its large leaves turn yellow before they fall. The sweetbay and the southern magnolia are sometimes used for shade in the southeastern part of the Northeast.

The black tupelo is native in all States in the region, except Minnesota, Wisconsin, and Iowa, and the most northern parts of New England, Michigan, and Missouri. It grows 50 to 70 feet tall and develops a pyramidal but irregular crown. The leaves, which are scarlet in autumn, are oval, leathery, and dark green. Black tupelo casts a moderately light shade. Large trees are difficult to transplant. The fruits are eaten by birds. Squirrels often cut off many young twigs in the spring. The black tupelo grows best in rich, moist soil.

Amur corktree, introduced from Asia, forms a low-branched, spreading, rounded crown, which may reach 40 to 50 feet in height. The leaflets are a shiny dark green above and light green below. The foliage casts light shade. It develops an attractive, corky bark. The low-branching habit limits its use on streets, but it is recommended for parks and lawns. It is smoke-tolerant and it can be transplanted readily.

Panicled goldenrain-tree, another Asiatic species, deserves consideration when some flowering tree of relatively quick growth is needed. It is hardy in central Ohio and in southern New England. The beautiful yellow panicles of flowers are produced in July.

The Japanese pagodatree, introduced from Asia, reaches 50 to 65 feet in height and has a rounded, spreading crown. The leaves are glossy and dark green on the upper surface and soft, hairy, and pale green on the lower surface. The tree has an intermediate rate of growth and casts light shade. The attractive, small, yellowish-white flowers are produced in loose, open clusters in midsummer. As far north as Ohio and southern New England the young trees are subject to winter injury but are hardy when mature.

The paper birch grows rapidly into a medium-sized tree, which is pyramidal in form at first and later becomes irregularly round. It is a fast grower. Its life expectancy in the forest is about 80 years, but it may be much less under shade-tree conditions. It is not adapted to street planting although it has been successfully used in parks. It is subject to attack by the bronze birch borer, which limits its use in some localities.

Silver maple is a large, widespreading tree of rapid growth. The leaves are whitish underneath, and when the pendulous branches sway in the breeze the tree has a flowing, silvery appearance. The wood is brittle and easily broken, and its roots often clog drain pipes. The silver maple is not recommended except for quick effects or for places where better trees will not grow.

Green ash is a tall, fairly narrow tree of rapid growth. It gives moderate shade. In the Lake States it is a fairly reliable tree that lends variety along streets or on lawns.

Kentucky coffeetree grows 40 to 60 feet tall. The shiny and pale-green leaflets turn clear yellow and fall in early autumn. The large brown seed pods hang on the tree through the winter. It is native from western New York southward in the Appalachians to Tennessee and westward to southern Minnesota. It also can be grown successfully as a shade tree in central and southern New England.

Several other deciduous shade trees are grown in this region but are not so common as those we have described.

Eastern black walnut is difficult to transplant. Some of the new varieties produce nuts that crack easily.

Bolleana poplar is a narrow upright tree that can be used for special effects. Most poplars are too short-lived to be a good investment, but this species is better than the Lombardy poplar.

Golden weeping willow, a pendulous variety, can be used effectively. American hornbeam is a good small tree to supplement larger ones.

Ohio buckeye and common horsechestnut have good forms and attractive flowers, but are prey to leaf blotch.

THE NARROW-LEAVED EVERGREENS, or conifers as they are more commonly called, are not suitable generally for planting along streets, but they are valuable as shade trees around the home, particularly in suburban areas, and are ornamental all the year.

Although the needles may persist for several years and the older parts of the twigs are bare of foliage, once the needles are lost from a conifer they are never replaced as are the leaves of deciduous trees.

The transplanting of some kinds of large evergreens is difficult, losses sometimes running as high as 10 or 20 percent for the larger trees.

EASTERN HEMLOCK is one of the most satisfactory evergreens for home planting throughout New England and southward in the highlands. It is a native and sometimes is called Canada hemlock. It is a large tree, 50 to 80 feet tall, with long, slender, horizontal branches, which ascend above and droop at the base, forming a broad, pyramidal head. The lowest branches very often extend to the ground. The terminal shoot of the straight trunk is flexible, and the small twigs and foliage are arranged in graceful sprays. The inconspicuous flowers appear in May and cones develop in the summer and autumn. The latter are formed at the tips of the small twigs; they are about one-half to three-fourths of an inch long, green at first, gradually turning reddish to brown.

In planting hemlock, the site should be carefully selected so that the young tree may be sheltered from any drying winds. The hemlock grows slowly and prefers a shady or sheltered location with moist soil. It may be grown in various types of soil, however, but will not be successful in an exposed site with dry, poor soil.

Red pine is native in northern New England and in the Lake States. It is also grown extensively in the area as a shade or ornamental tree. It may attain a height of 50 to 75 feet. The trunk is erect and continuous into the crown. The branches are stout, spreading, and slightly pendulous at the base of the tree. The tips of the branches usually turn upward. On young trees the branches extend to the ground and form a broad, pyramidal head. The bark of the trunk is reddish brown. The needle-shaped leaves are dark green, from 5 to 6 inches long, slender, brittle, and have sharply pointed tips. There are two in a cluster, in long, flexible tufts. They remain on the trees four or five seasons. The cones, about 2 inches long, are green when young; they gradually turn light brown and reach maturity the second autumn.

Red pine will grow best in light and sandy soil in sunny locations. It will not thrive in shady sites or in poorly drained soils. It is not readily transplanted but, when it is once established under favorable conditions, young trees will grow rapidly. The lifespan of the red pine in the forest is about 350 years.

The species is susceptible to a number of fungus diseases, including leaf diseases, cankers, and wood rots, but when grown in the open as a shade tree it is usually free from these diseases.

Eastern white pine, a native in much of the region, is valued highly both for shade and ornament. It may attain a height of 50 to 80 feet. Its straight and tapering trunk normally is continuous into the crown. The branches are widespreading and horizontal and generally are arranged in whorls of five. In the young trees they extend to the ground and form a broad-based and pyramidal or conical head. The leaves are three-sided, in clusters of five, and are bluish green, soft, slender, flexible, and about 3 to 5 inches long. They usually remain on the twigs for two seasons. White pine will grow in almost any location but nevertheless it likes best a rich, well-drained soil.

Under favorable conditions, white pine grows rapidly and reaches maturity in about 200 years, and in the forest its lifespan is about 450 years. As a shade tree it often becomes ragged after 40 to 60 years, particularly at low elevations or in the hotter and drier parts of the region.

Many fungus diseases attack the leaves, twigs, and trunk of the eastern white pine, but most of them cause only slight weakening or injury. Blister rust, a fungus disease, produces serious cankers on branches or trunk and may result in the death of the tree. Precautionary measures can usually be taken to prevent ornamental white pines from becoming infected.

White fir is native in the western part of the United States but is extensively and successfully grown as a shade or ornamental tree in the Northeast. It is hardy as far north as central Maine. It may attain a height of 60 to 70 feet. Its straight, tapering trunk and whorled, spreading branches usually extend to the ground and form a broad-based, pyramidal head. The leaves are narrow, flat, about 2 inches long, bluish green or silvery; they spread outward and curve upward from the twigs. They remain on the twigs for several years.

White fir will grow in a wide range

of soil conditions, but it is rather slow in becoming adjusted after it has been transplanted. It prefers a rich, moist, well-drained, gravelly or sandy loam. Even under the most favorable soil conditions, however, the growth of young trees is rather slow. Maturity is reached in 300 years in the forests.

White fir stands heat and drought well, but in the northern parts of the area late-spring frosts sometimes kill the tender new growth. A disease caused by a fungus that is native on northern balsam fir sometimes kills back the new growth and may seriously weaken the trees. For that reason it is usually inadvisable to plant the white fir near the balsam fir.

Nikko fir, native in Japan, is one of the most satisfactory firs for shade or ornament and is hardy in central and southern New England. It may reach a height of 50 to 60 feet. It has a straight and tapering trunk—with whorled, spreading branches, continuous to the ground. The leaves are narrow, flat, and about an inch long; closely set on the twigs, they spread outward and upward. They are shining, dark green on the upper surface and have two broad white bands on the lower surface, and remain on the twigs for several years.

Nikko fir may be rather slow in its growth for a few years after transplanting, but usually is slightly more rapid than the white fir. Although it prefers a rich, moist, and well-drained soil, it will also grow successfully in drier locations and is relatively tolerant of heat and drought.

No fungus diseases have been reported on Nikko fir in this country.

Oriental spruce is native in Asia Minor and is hardy in the central part of the region. It makes a graceful and attractive shade tree with a rather narrow, pyramidal head. The trunk, which may reach a height of 50 to 80 feet, is erect and tapering. It has dense and spreading branches, in whorls, horizontal or even slightly ascending above, somewhat pendulous below, and continuous to the ground. The leaves are from one-fourth to one-half inch long, closely set on the twigs, four-sided, shining dark green, and blunt at the tip. They remain on the twigs several years.

The Oriental spruce is slow growing and is most successful in rich, moist, well-drained soil. It is susceptible to a fungus disease that first attacks the lowest branches of old trees and gradually progresses upward. Cankers and dieback of these lowest branches sometimes disfigure the trees.

Colorado blue spruce, native in the western United States, is very well known as a lawn tree throughout the Northeast. It grows 50 to 80 feet in height. Its stout, horizontal branches extend the entire length of the straight, tapering trunk, and form a symmetrical, pyramidal head. The leaves are four-sided, sharp-pointed, and rigid and spread out from the twigs. They are about an inch long and vary from dull green to bluish green or silvery white. They remain on the twigs for several years, but they tend to lose their silvery color as they age.

The Colorado blue spruce is slow growing and is tolerant of a wide range of soil conditions. Most satisfactory growth is obtained in rich, moist, well-drained soil.

The lowest branches of older trees may be seriously injured by the previously mentioned fungus disease on Oriental spruce. The Colorado blue spruce is particularly susceptible to this disease, which causes large resinous cankers and dieback.

The native white spruce is most satisfactory for shade and ornament in the northern parts of the region. It develops into a symmetrical, pyramidal tree 50 to 60 feet tall, with dense, horizontal, spreading branches that extend to the ground. The leaves are about three-fourths of an inch long, four-sided, crowded on the twigs, slightly curved, light bluish green, and remain on the twigs for several seasons.

They give off a disagreeable, pungent odor when they are crushed.

The growth rate of white spruce is much slower in dry locations than in moist, well-drained soil. Its life span in the forest is 200 to 300 years.

It is slightly susceptible to the Oriental spruce fungus disease, but usually is not seriously injured.

Black Hills white spruce is compact and slow in growth, and is generally useful in the northern Lake States.

The common Douglas-fir is a large, pyramidal specimen, with branches growing well down to the ground.

MANY OTHER kinds of trees, both deciduous and evergreen, might have been mentioned here. This list tends to be conservative; it is based on the experience of many men who plant and take care of trees. But we compiled it with the thought that it could be a springboard from which you might take a deep plunge into the fascinating hobby of planting and growing shade trees around your home or develop an interest in the trees of your city streets and parks.

ALMA M. WATERMAN *is a forest and shade-tree pathologist in the Bureau of Plant Industry, Soils, and Agricultural Engineering. She is stationed in New Haven, Conn., where she has studied trees and their diseases for more than 25 years. Dr. Waterman is a graduate of Brown University.*

R. U. SWINGLE *is a forest pathologist and is in charge of the field headquarters of the Division of Forest Pathology in Columbus, Ohio. He is at present investigating phloem necrosis, an epidemic virus disease of American elm. Mr. Swingle is a graduate of Ohio State University.*

CLAYTON S. MOSES, *a graduate of Pennsylvania State College, is a forest pathologist in the Bureau of Plant Industry, Soils, and Agricultural Engineering and is stationed in Madison, Wis. In recent years he has investigated the epidemic dying of oak in Wisconsin and adjoining States.*

## SHADE TREES FOR THE SOUTHEAST

RALPH M. LINDGREN, R. P. TRUE, E. RICHARD TOOLE

Residents of the Southeastern States have a wide choice of trees for shade and ornamental purposes. They also have a difficulty in making their selection, for their section has variables in climate and altitude and other conditions that do affect tree growth. (Florida alone, for example, can be subdivided into at least three distinct zones in which climate and commonly used plants are likely to differ a good deal from each other.)

Furthermore, certain local conditions may sometimes prevent the successful use of a species within the recognized geographic range of the Southeast. For these reasons, the list of trees we present is not expected to be entirely acceptable throughout the region or adequate for specific localities.

THE LIVE OAK, a tree of history and beauty, is long-lived and rather slow growing. It attains tremendous size with age. It branches low into massive and widespreading limbs, and forms a broad, dense, round-topped crown of dark, glossy, evergreen leaves. It resists storm damage, insects, and diseases; the costs of care and maintenance therefore are relatively low.

Propagation from seed or transplants is not difficult. The live oak is used widely where enough space is available on lawns and along driveways and roads. Severe freezes injure it, but it is considered satisfactory in such inland cities as Shreveport.

SOUTHERN MAGNOLIA, with its beautiful flowers and evergreen foliage, is

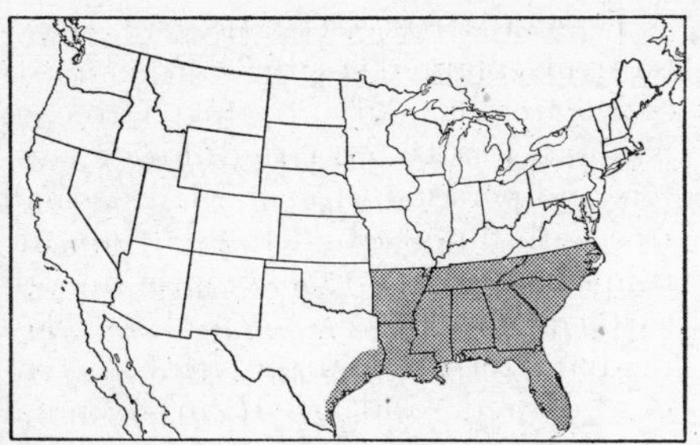

a popular shade and ornamental tree. Rather large at maturity, it forms a broad, conical crown of pleasing symmetry. The thick, leathery leaves are dark, shining green above and rusty brown below. Large, fragrant, creamy-white flowers, mostly produced before July but sometimes continuing until November, are followed by purplish, conelike fruits. The tree is rather slow growing and long-lived, relatively free of pests, and tolerant of varying conditions except poor drainage. It usually is propagated from seed or pot-grown transplants. Adequate space is needed for best development, and it is often used singly on lawns. In the mountainous regions, severely cold weather may kill much of the foliage.

THE CAMPHOR-TREE is frequently planted in lawns and parks and along streets in many localities. It is a medium-sized, stout evergreen that forms a handsome, dense-topped crown. The leaves, shiny green above and silvery blue below, are strongly aromatic when crushed. The fruit, a small bluish-black drupe, often is abundant and occasionally is considered a nuisance. The tree is hardy but prefers a well-drained soil, and, except for thrips and scale, has few damaging pests.

It is propagated usually from seed or pot-grown transplants. Well-established trees resist temperatures of 15° F. without a great deal of injury.

THE WILLOW OAK is a rather large, long-lived, and fast-growing deciduous tree that develops a fairly short trunk in the open. It has a dense oval or round-topped crown. Slender branches with light-green, willowlike leaves give the tree a graceful appearance. Although growth is best in moist soils, it also thrives satisfactorily in rather dry situations.

It is easily transplanted, moderately storm-resistant, and, except for gall insects on branches and a leaf rust disease, is relatively free of pests. The leaf rust is seldom disfiguring, but it is the alternate stage of a serious canker disease of southern pines. Willow oak is used extensively as an attractive shade tree for wide streets and large lawns.

THE RED MAPLE has brilliant scarlet to orange autumnal coloring, which adds greatly to its ornamental value. It is medium to fairly large in size. Its branches develop low on the trunk to form a dense, narrow, oblong head. Conspicuous reddish flowers appear in early spring and are followed by scarlet fruits and attractive foliage.

The tree grows rapidly, is relatively short-lived, thrives satisfactorily on fairly varied sites, and is rather easily propagated and moderately resistant to pests. Although grown less often than many other trees, the red maple is not uncommon in the Southeast.

THE FLOWERING DOGWOOD is a native tree that is grown widely for its attractive flowers, red berries, and pleasing crown. It attains 40 feet and has spreading branches that form a low, fairly dense, rounded head. The small greenish-yellow flowers, produced in April, May, or June, are surrounded by four large, white bracts; pink forms occur also. Red fruit and autumnal leaf coloration add ornamental value.

The tree, rather slow growing and long-lived, is propagated with some difficulty from seed and cuttings. It has relatively few pests. It thrives in shaded or exposed places but prefers well-drained and fairly light soils. While not always easily established, it is useful around many homes.

THE SWEETGUM is a large and fast-growing tree with a pyramidal or oblong crown. The star-shaped, deciduous leaves develop brilliant autumn colors that range from yellow through orange to red and deep bronze. Corky ridges on some of the branches and the persistent spiny, fruiting balls are characteristically present. The tree is fairly long-lived, tolerant of different sites excepting poorly drained ones, and moderately free of pests.

Transplanting is fairly easy in light but rather difficult in heavy soils. Its woody fruits are somewhat objectionable at times, and a top dieback in some localities has been noted.

The American holly may become a moderate-sized tree 40 feet in height. It has both shade and ornamental value. Its pyramidal crown of glossy evergreen leaves and its brilliant red berries lend beauty throughout the year. Certain individuals and varieties bear fruit much more abundantly than others, so that selections are desirable or necessary. The tree is fairly slow growing, long-lived, and rather resistant to insects and diseases.

Propagation with well-kept transplants is more successful than with wild seedlings. The tree is rather exacting in soil requirements but grows satisfactorily when established in acid soils. Although it is not particularly adaptable, the beauty of the American holly justifies listing it for suitable sites.

The American beech is a medium-tall tree, which branches close to the ground and has a large, open-spreading crown. It gives a good, dense shade. Unbroken light-gray bark, maintained throughout its life, is a distinctive characteristic. The tree thrives best on rich, well-drained soils in the mountains or bottom lands and is relatively free of pests.

A number of ornamental varieties of the European beech includes those forms with bronze-purple foliage, weeping branches, and cut leaves. Use of the beech for shade purposes is most common in the Carolinas and more mountainous parts of the region.

The common crapemyrtle is extensively planted in the warmer parts of the region. An introduced tree, it is noted for its attractive flower clusters and persistent foliage. It is a small tree with fluted trunk from which the thin bark peels off, leaving a smooth surface. The flowers, 1 to 1.5 inches in diameter, are purple, pink, lavender, or red, and occur in terminal panicles from June to September. The tree is fairly long-lived and slow growing, and is easily cultivated.

It prefers moist conditions during the growing season. In moist soils, it is subject to uprooting by severe storms. It is particularly useful if space is limited and a decorative tree is desired.

The eastern redbud is a rather small tree that is extensively favored for ornamental purposes. It usually branches 10 to 15 feet from the ground and forms a narrow erect, or spreading, flattened, or rounded head. Masses of attractive small light-pink to purple flowers appear from late in February to April.

The redbud grows fairly rapidly, is rather free of pests, and is propagated from seed or young transplants. Although moderately hardy, it prefers rich and fairly moist sandy loam soils. Special care in establishing and maintaining the tree may be required in some localities.

The water oak is a large tree that is grown extensively on wide streets and large lawns. It grows fast in early life and provides quick shade. It is tall and rather slender, with a round-topped, fairly symmetrical crown of ascending branches. Although it is not an evergreen, the leaves often persist until Christmas or after.

It is easily propagated, tolerant of varying conditions, rather short-lived, and somewhat more subject to mistletoe and storm damage than willow oak. Since it provides early shade, is easily handled, and has pleasing symmetry, the water oak is grown widely where adequate space is available.

The mimosa, or silktree albizia, is a rather small tree that is widely cultivated in the Southeast as an ornamental. It grows rapidly under a variety of conditions of soil and has graceful and fernlike leaves and striking colorful flowers. The flowers, pink in color and in clusters at the ends of the branches, usually come in May and June. The seed is produced in large quantities and propagation from seed is easy. A vascular wilt disease has been highly destructive to mimosa, but we hope resistant varieties can be bred.

The winged elm is medium in size, usually from 40 to 50 feet in height. It develops a short bole, with branches ascending into a fairly open round-topped crown. It is of pleasing proportions and has a somewhat lacy and drooping habit; the branchlets often are corky-winged. The tree grows fairly rapidly. It is moderately long-lived, and does well on dry as well as on rich, moist soils. Propagation from seed or transplants is not difficult. Although relatively resistant to pests, a destructive virus disease is known to attack it. The winged elm lacks some of the graceful qualities of the American elm, but is liked in many places.

The American elm, a highly prized shade tree, is planted extensively only in the more northern part of this region. It is described fully on page 50.

A supplemental list: The following trees are grown somewhat less extensively than those described, or, if widely used, have certain limiting features, which, however, may be considered minor in specific places.

Sugarberry, or the sugar hackberry. Fairly large and widely used for quick shade; not exacting in requirements; propagates easily, but tends to split in storms; subject to some mistletoe disfigurement; not very clean.

Pecan. Medium to rather large; is widely cultivated for nuts and to some extent for shade; fairly exacting in requirements; rather susceptible to diseases, insects, and mistletoes; nuts often lead to branch breakage.

Eastern redcedar. Medium-sized pyramidal conifer commonly used as an ornamental; it tolerates various soils; often subject to a complex of pest and environmental troubles that may require attention.

Panicled goldenrain-tree. Small to medium-sized introduced hardy, deciduous tree with sparse branching, fernlike leaves, large terminal panicles of yellow flowers in summer followed by attractively colored capsules; it is not widely tested but merits consideration for late-summer and fall coloring.

Yellow-poplar, or tuliptree. Large in size and grown to some extent for shade and ornamental purposes, its pleasing form, and floral characteristics; somewhat exacting in requirements; rather subject to breakage from storms.

Canary date. Massive, spreading ornamental planted widely in Florida and to some extent along coastal area; tolerant of soil conditions; subject to freezing in some parts of region; used chiefly as ornamental.

American sycamore. Extensively used, massive, spreading deciduous tree; grows rapidly; provides early shade; tolerates varied site conditions; propagates fairly easily; needs 60-foot spread space; subject to a number of pests; shedding of leaves, fruit, and twigs sometimes objectionable.

Carolina laurel-cherry. Small to medium evergreen cultivated somewhat for ornament and shade; grows rapidly; produces small white flowers in numerous short racemes; not very exacting; useful for limited space; not long-lived; leaves contain prussic acid poisonous to stock.

White oak. This is a large tree with a broad crown and spreading limbs; rather long-lived and fairly tolerant of varied sites; somewhat slow in growth and cultivated less extensively than several other oaks for shade.

Scarlet oak. Medium to fairly large with widespreading irregular crown; rather fast growing; brilliant scarlet fall coloring; it is short-lived; the dead

"A tree of history and beauty"—the Lafitte live oak in Louisiana.

branches may be common; mostly grown in northern part of region.

Laurel oak. Fairly large in size and commonly grown in the Southeast; pleasing form and semievergreen foliage; similar in many qualities to willow oak but somewhat shorter-lived and more subject to storm damage.

Pin oak. Rather tall, with broad, extensively branched crown; fairly fast growing; pleasing fall coloring; not long-lived; may bear numerous dead branches; cultivated mostly in northern part of region.

Cabbage palmetto. Tall, erect palm widely used along avenues in coastal regions of the Southeast particularly; greenish-white to yellow flower clusters in June, July, and August and small black berries in the fall; tolerant of varied sites; primarily an ornamental.

Weeping willow. Medium-sized, introduced, deciduous tree with graceful drooping branchlets; rather widely cultivated throughout region; damaged by pests in some sections; used largely as ornamental.

Eastern arborvitae. A medium-sized conifer with dense, narrow pyramidal crown; rather commonly used in northern part of region; fairly subject to disease, insect, and some environmental troubles; chief value is ornamental.

SOUTHERN FLORIDA is distinct from the rest of the region in climate and vegetation. Selected trees that are widely used for shade and ornamental purposes in southern Florida are listed.

Oxhorn bucida. Medium-tall, small-leaved evergreen for windbreak, beach, driveway, and home planting.

Horsetail beefwood, or Australian-pine. A medium-tall, evergreen shade tree for driveway, windbreak, and hedge planting in central Florida also.

Coconut. Tall palm with large leaves and nuts, for large landscape ornamental and beach planting.

Royal poinciana, or the flamboyant-tree. Large, spreading, deciduous tree with showy flowers, for large landscape ornamental.

Benjamin fig. Large, spreading evergreen for driveway planting and as ornamental shade tree.

Mango. Tall, broad evergreen for ornamental shade and, where selected strains are used, for fruit also.

Cajeput-tree. Medium-tall, yellow-flowered, slender evergreen for windbreak, beach, driveway, ornamental shade.

Cuban royalpalm. Tall palm with decorative, smooth trunk, for driveway and as large landscape ornamental on moist soils.

African tuliptree, or Bell flambeau-tree. Tall, rapid-growing, semideciduous, conspicuously flowered tree for ornamental and shade.

West Indies mahogany. Tall, slender evergreen that gives light shade for lawn, driveway, and general planting.

*The authors are forest pathologists in the Bureau of Plant Industry, Soils, and Agricultural Engineering of the Department of Agriculture.*

Ralph M. Lindgren *is in charge of the field headquarters of the Division of Forest Pathology in New Orleans. Dr. Lindgren is a graduate of the University of Minnesota.*

R. P. True *is stationed in Lake City, Fla. Dr. True is a graduate of the University of Pennsylvania.*

E. Richard Toole *is stationed in Asheville, N. C. He has been working for several years on mimosa wilt and other diseases of shade trees. Dr. Toole is a graduate of Duke University.*

## SHADE TREES FOR THE PLAINS

ERNEST WRIGHT, T. W. BRETZ

Good care is doubly important for shade trees in the Plains States.

Trees planted on shallow soil underlain with clay or other hardpans have little chance of survival unless watered artificially and, even then, growth is generally unsatisfactory. The best and deepest soil available should be chosen so tree roots can develop unhindered.

Cultivation, following planting, is necessary to help the trees compete with prairie grasses and other native vegetation. Cultivation should be shallow to avoid unnecessary injury to tree roots near the surface. After the crowns of the trees are well developed, particularly in group plantings, they tend to shade out competing vegetation, and cultivation may no longer be necessary. The tree also must be protected from injury by livestock and sometimes from damage by rodents.

At best, most of the trees planted in the Plains States are relatively short-lived as compared to the same species growing in more favorable regions.

Coarse and droughty gravels, claypan soils, the undrained alkaline basins (buffalo wallows), and shale-derived upland soils generally are unsuited for trees. Furthermore, the western third of the Plains States, from Texas to the Dakotas, have areas where the soil is deficient in iron or where iron or other essential nutrients are unavailable to growing trees.

Unavailability of iron causes chlorosis, or yellowing, of the leaves of some tree species, reduces growth, and frequently brings on premature death. Also, in Texas and Oklahoma along the Red River and southward east of the high plains, certain large areas are infested with the cotton root rot fungus, an indigenous soil fungus that infects the roots of many kinds of trees and eventually kills them. A few species, however, are highly resistant to the disease and will usually survive satisfactorily. The susceptibility of several of the more important tree species to cotton root rot is indicated later.

Adequate artificial watering of the shade and street trees is frequently not practicable in the Plains. In such cases their survival depends largely on rain

802062°—49——6

and snow. Furthermore, isolated individual shade trees do not have the advantage of gaining additional moisture by stopping drifting snow, as do shelterbelt or block plantings. Because of the reduction in annual precipitation from east to west in the midcontinental section of the United States, there is a corresponding reduction in the choice of usable tree species. Survival and growth are usually poor, even for the hardiest species, where annual precipitation is less than 16 inches in the extreme northern part and 20 inches in the more southern part of the Plains States.

Low winter temperatures can likewise endanger the survival of trees. Even worse are freezes in early fall and late spring. Consequently, the choice of species becomes more restricted the farther north one goes.

In the following discussion of trees for the Great Plains, we have separated broadleaf species from the conifers and describe in greater detail the trees that can be used in all parts of the Plains.

The broadleaf species include the ash, cottonwood, elms, oaks, birch, poplars, and others.

Green ash, a native species, develops spreading branches and makes a medium-sized, round-topped tree up to 50 feet in height. Its trunk may grow 1½ feet thick. It makes a moderate growth and the light-green foliage, turning golden yellow in autumn, gives dense shade. The greenish flowers develop in late spring. Green ash develops best in deep, rich, lowland soil, but it also does well on heavier upland soil. It is one of the best broadleaf trees for streets and yards in the Plains States. It is moderately drought-resistant, but it will stand wet as well as dry sites. Borers damage it, especially on droughty sites. Several relatively unimportant leaf spot diseases and a rust affect it. Green ash is moderately susceptible to cotton root rot.

White, blue, or red ash are important locally, principally on the extreme eastern edge of the Plains.

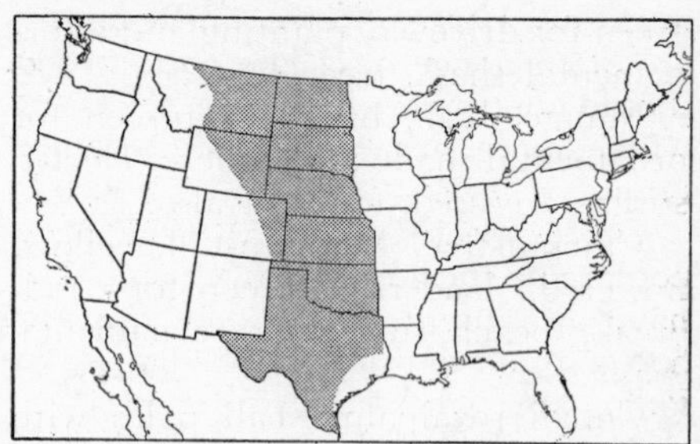

The plains cottonwood was widely planted by early settlers. This native tree quickly develops an open crown and it reaches a height of 80 or 90 feet. The trunk gets to be as large as 6 feet in diameter at the base. It affords light shade. Flower catkins appear in early spring before the leaves. The leaves become a colorful yellow in autumn. The trees may attain an age of 60 years or more on the better sites. Although they prefer rich, moist soil and thrive particularly well in the lowlands, they will also grow in drier, sandier locations of the uplands. They do poorly on soils with clay hardpan near the surface, and should not be planted on sand dunes. The life of the plains cottonwood on such soil is short, usually 10 years or less. The tree is susceptible to borers, especially on the drier sites.

Poplars and cottonwoods are highly susceptible to cotton root rot. Bacterial limb galls, not uncommon, cause considerable branch dying in older trees. Fungus stem cankers are destructive to young trees, especially on unfavorable sites where growth is slow. Leaf rusts are common but of little consequence to thrifty trees. Cottonwoods are subject to attack by gall insects, which make them unsightly but cause little harm. They are moderately drought-resistant when well established on good upland sites. They are also susceptible to chlorosis and grow poorly on alkaline soils. They are mainly usable as farmstead trees. When used for street plantings, only male trees should be selected, to avoid the nuisance from cottony seed. Roots of the cottonwood often clog sewer and drain pipes. The wood is weak and subject to breaking in storms. Large, old trees near houses are often dangerous. The cottonwood should not be planted on streets, except where more suitable species will not grow.

Other species, such as Lombardy poplar and the hybrid Carolina poplar, have also been used widely but are better suited to the eastern edge of the Plains area where rainfall is greatest.

THE AMERICAN ELM, perhaps the most beautiful broadleaf tree, sometimes reaches 90 feet in this region. This elm has a symmetrical, vase-shaped crown that frequently attains a width of 60 feet or more. It lives to an age of 75 to 100 years on the better sites, provides moderately dense shade, and grows moderately fast. Its small, brown flowers appear in early spring before the tree leafs out. It prefers deep, rich, moist loam, but it will stand adverse soil and weather conditions and does fairly well even on sandy exposed sites.

In the Plains States, American elm is often seriously attacked by the elm leaf beetle and European elm scale. The elm sawfly causes defoliation at times. The wooly elm aphid is also abundantly present, especially during wet seasons. A fungus leaf spot disease is common. Phloem necrosis has been found in eastern Nebraska, Kansas, and Oklahoma and is a serious menace to the existence of the American elm throughout the Plains. We fear that phloem necrosis will progress rapidly westward; until a method of control is discovered for this destructive disease, we advise against planting the American elm. Trunk rot due to a fungus is fairly common in planted street trees. American elm is susceptible to cotton root rot and should not be planted on soils infested by this fungus. Rabbits are another enemy.

THE SIBERIAN ELM, often sold under the name of Chinese elm, has been planted perhaps more widely than any of the other introduced species. It grows rapidly to a height of 50 to 60 feet. The main branches tend to grow upward and form sharp crotches that are easily broken by wind. Slime flux commonly develops in such wounds. The species provides moderately dense shade. Small purplish flowers appear in early spring before the leaves show. It does best on sandy loam soils, but it will also grow on sandy sites of low fertility. It lives about 50 years or less. It is drought-hardy, but, because it develops its leaves early in the spring and retains them later than most trees in the fall, it is in constant danger of severe damage by unseasonable freezes. Cytospora fungus cankers cause further damage to frost-injured trees. Siberian elm is highly susceptible to cotton root rot and cannot be used on soil infested by the fungus. Rabbits often damage it severely. This species is used for both street and yard planting, but is now in general disfavor because of its susceptibility to frost damage.

COMMON HACKBERRY makes a moderate growth up to 50 to 70 feet, and develops a large, rounded crown. Its spreading branches provide moderate shade. The small, greenish flowers appear in late spring. It prefers a rich, moist, and well-drained soil, but it will grow successfully on practically all types. The common hackberry is frost-hardy and withstands heat well. It attains an age of 60 to 70 years.

Webworms commonly cause defoliation, especially of young trees. This species is subject to rabbit damage. Witches' brooms are a distinguishing feature of older trees and are regarded as undesirable, but they do not seriously affect the health of the trees. Several minor leaf diseases occur on this species. It resists cotton root rot, and is drought-hardy when once established. It will not stand extensive flooding.

The common hackberry is a good street tree and should be used more extensively in this region.

THE BUR OAK, a large, slow-growing native tree, reaches a height of 80 feet on the best sites. Its life expectancy is 75 years or more. It has a short trunk and a broad, massive top that gives moderately dense shade. The slender flower catkins and the leaves appear in midspring. The bur oak does well on many soils but prefers rich bottom lands. Drought-resistant and frost-hardy, it should be planted more extensively despite its slow growth.

Twig galls are common, but few insects attack the tree. Leaf rollers are observed frequently and red spider occurs in dry years. Foliage diseases usually are not serious. Powdery mildew and leaf scorch sometimes do damage. Cronartium rust is common on oak leaves in some localities. Rabbit damage is severe to the young seedlings in the western part of the area. Bur oak is susceptible to the cotton root rot fungus.

Other species more limited in use are pin oak, black oak, and the chinquapin oak. In the uplands of Nebraska, the trunks of pin oaks often have vertical cracks that are the result of freezing injury.

Several broadleaf species have a more restricted use.

Ailanthus, or tree-of-Heaven, can be planted in the eastern part of the central and southern Plains. It grows rapidly, gives moderate shade, and lives 30 to 50 years. It develops best in light, moist soil but tolerates fairly heavy soils. It stands smoke and dust better than most trees and it is, therefore, adapted to street planting in factory districts. Only the female plants should be used, because the flowers of the male trees have a disagreeable odor and the pollen is said to cause catarrhal troubles. The brown seeds hang on the trees until late winter. Some persons may consider them unsightly. Ailanthus suckers so readily that it is objectionable in some locations. Webworms frequently defoliate the young trees. Ailanthus is moderately resistant to cotton root rot. Moderately drought-hardy, it does not stand flooding, and it is subject to wind damage.

European white birch, which has drooping branches, can be used in the easternmost part of the northern Plains. This widely used ornamental has several horticultural varieties. It gives moderate shade, prefers moist soil, and is not frost-hardy on dry soil sites. On favorable sites its life expectancy is 25 to 35 years. It is not drought-resistant. Bronze birch borer causes serious injury and is perhaps the main factor that limits survival. The young trees sunscald readily.

Yellow birch is better suited to dry sites. The best use for the birch species is as ornamentals.

The boxelder, a native, is mainly a yard tree in the northern and central Plains. It develops best on deep, rich, moist soil but survives surprisingly well on the dry and droughty sites. It gives moderate shade. It is short-lived, 20 to 40 years, depending on site quality. All in all, it deserves wider use in this zone.

One reason why it is in disfavor for planting near dwellings is that the boxelder bug, which breeds on the female trees, enters houses or cellars in search of hibernating places. Because the insect lays its eggs on the fruit, only male trees should be planted as a yard tree in the northern and central Plains.

Northern catalpa can be planted in the eastern part of the central and southern Plains. It commonly lives 35 to 40 years and is not especially drought-hardy. The large leaves are frequently affected by a Phyllosticta leaf spot disease, which, however, is not ordinarily serious. An insect known as a midge causes a leaf scorch. Decay fungi commonly invade the wood through wounds; the rot often advances rapidly and shortens the life of the tree. The species is not resistant to cotton root rot but it is moderately frost-hardy. The leaves sometimes turn yellow because of iron deficiency. Catalpa is not particularly popular because its blooms and seed pods can be a nuisance. Rabbits damage it.

KENTUCKY COFFEETREE, a native, is used as a street or yard tree in the central and southern Plains. It prefers a deep, moist soil but adapts itself to drier sites as well. The trees may grow as tall as 50 feet and may live 40 to 50 years. The leaves give light shade and are said to possess an ingredient poisonous to flies. The coffeetree is susceptible to cotton root rot and should not be used on infested soils.

THE CHINESE ELM has much the same habit of growth as the Siberian elm, but the flowers open late in the summer. It is small and half-evergreen from Oklahoma southward. It is like the Siberian elm in adaptation to soil conditions.

Other species of elm, such as the Scotch elm and English elm, and such native species as rock elm and slippery elm, can be used especially in the eastern part of the Plains. The first two, however, are almost as readily susceptible to frost injury as Siberian elm, and the latter two are considerably less drought-resistant. None of these has been widely used as street trees.

SUGARBERRY, or sugar hackberry, a native tree, is useful in the southern Plains. It is a smaller tree than the common hackberry but grows up to 25 feet tall. It is not so frost-hardy as common hackberry. It will grow on dry soil and is drought-resistant. It is not widely used.

Netleaf hackberry, also a native, is not widely planted. It grows up to 35 feet in height. It is drought-hardy but not especially frost-hardy. It grows naturally on rocky or gravelly soil.

THE BLACK LOCUST is suitable for parks and lawns in the central and southern Plains. A native, it does well on sandy soils and is moderately frost-hardy and drought-resistant, and long-lived, 40 to 60 years. The trunk is commonly attacked by wood-rotting fungi that follow borer injury. The wood rots materially reduce the length of life of the tree and are especially common in the southern Plains. Black locust is highly susceptible to chlorosis and to cotton root rot. The wood makes good fence posts.

COMMON HONEYLOCUST is valuable in the central and southern parts of the Plains. It grows well in most kinds of soils but prefers deep and rich loam. It lives 40 to 50 years. It is not so subject to borer injury as black locust, but trees on droughty soils are commonly attacked. Twig girdlers are common on this native species in the southern localities. It is susceptible to cotton root rot, but is drought-resistant and frost-hardy. It is less susceptible to chlorosis than the black locust. Its seed pods make good cattle feed. It grows well in street or yard plantings; in fact, it is one of the best trees for the central West.

A thornless variety of the common honeylocust is gaining favor. It has most of the desirable characteristics of the common honeylocust.

SILVER MAPLE can be used in the eastern part of the northern and central Plains, but is not recommended where better trees will grow. Under most favorable conditions this native tree may reach an age of 70 years. Not particularly drought-hardy, it prefers rich bottom-land soil but will do fairly well on fertile upland soil. Silver maple is subject to a number of insect attacks, mostly foliage destroyers such as bagworm, green worm, and bladder gall mites. Foliage is frequently infected with various leaf spot fungi, which are generally of minor importance. Twig borers are also common and may cause considerable damage. Trunk rots are common but occur most frequently in drought-weakened trees. A fungus disease, Verticillium wilt, occurs occasionally and sometimes kills the trees. Silver maple is susceptible to chlorosis, which is caused by lack of iron. It is best suited to growth in the eastern third of the area but will grow farther west when it is artificially watered. It often is subject to wind damage, but it is commonly used as a shade and street tree. Its roots commonly plug drain pipes.

Other species—sugar maple, Norway maple, black maple, red maple—are usable only in the extreme eastern border of the Plains area where rainfall is heaviest.

The Russian-olive, an introduction from southern Russia, usually attains less than 30 feet in height. It survives well on many sites, from sandy to alkaline soils, but prefers moist, rich soil in open sunlight. It is drought-hardy and moderately frost-resistant. The dry, cast-off leaves sometimes are eaten by sheep, goats, and cattle. Although it is but little troubled with insect or fungus attacks, it is susceptible to cotton root rot.

The Russian-olive merits wide use, especially in the drier and more alkali sections from the Dakotas southward. It is not especially desirable as a street tree, but if it is used in streets the lower branches should be pruned when the tree is young.

The American sycamore prefers rich, moist soil, but it can adapt itself to drier sites. It is not frost-hardy enough for planting in the northern Plains, but can be used in the eastern part of the central and southern Plains. Leaf blight, a fungus disease, is often prevalent and causes considerable defoliation, disfigurement, and reduction in growth. It is moderately resistant to cotton root rot, and is the best of the fast-growing tall trees for use on soil infested with the disease. It is susceptible to chlorosis, however, on alkaline sites. It is recommended for street planting in places free of blight. The American sycamore is widely planted as an ornamental.

The London planetree is less susceptible than the American sycamore to leaf blight, but is more restricted in range. It is best suited to the extreme eastern edge of the Plains where rainfall is highest. It is excellent in parks.

The eastern black walnut grows moderately fast and reaches a height of 60 feet or more. On favorable sites it will live 75 years. It thrives best on moderately friable soil that has good fertility and moisture. It will stand some flooding but will not live long on the swampy sites. Because its leaves and fruit hulls contain tannic acid and stain objects with which they come in contact, the tree should not be planted too close to walks or clotheslines. Several insects attack the leaves and fruit but do not endanger the health of the tree. Fungus diseases are also of little consequence. It is susceptible to cotton root rot and is not drought-hardy. It is used as a street and shade tree, but the fruits are objectionable on streets.

Weeping willow and black willow are sometimes used as shade trees. The European white willow appears to be more drought-resistant than the other species, but it should not be planted on dry sites.

The willows are all fairly short-lived and subject to insect damage and fungus diseases.

Desertwillow, native to the Southwest, develops into a small tree 20 to 30 feet high under favorable conditions. Often, however, it is shrublike, especially in hedge plantings. It is extremely drought-hardy and prefers a sandy soil. It will not tolerate flooding and is short-lived—probably about 20 years—but withal it is an excellent tree that can well be planted more widely in the Southwest. Its principal advantage over other species there is its high resistance to cotton root rot.

Other broadleaf species of local importance that do well on sandy soils and are usable principally in the southern parts of the Plains are the western soapberry (which is resistant to cotton root rot), and Osage-orange and eastern redbud, both of which are prey to cotton root rot.

The principal value of evergreens on the Plains is as ornamentals and for protection from wind. They do provide much shade, particularly when they are in groups. The most desirable species are eastern redcedar, Rocky Mountain juniper, ponderosa pine, common Douglas-fir, and some spruces.

THE EASTERN REDCEDAR, a medium-sized tree, forms a pyramidal or conical crown, grows 30 to 40 feet tall, and reaches an age of 100 years or more. Flowers are produced in small cones in midspring. It prefers loamy soil in open sunlight, but it will grow successfully on almost any soil. It is drought-resistant and frost-hardy but will not stand flooding. It is sometimes damaged by grasshoppers and hail, but it makes rapid recovery. It is subject to attack by red spider. The main objection to its use is that it is a bridging host for a rust that also attacks apple and related trees. Eastern redcedar should not be grown where apples are grown commercially, because of the possibility of damage by the rust. The rust galls cause relatively minor damage to the cedar except when infections are numerous on young trees.

Ornamental eastern redcedar is also damaged by a needle blight. It is the best evergreen for use on soil infested with the cotton root rot because it is highly resistant to the disease. Mice often damage young plants.

Rocky Mountain juniper resembles eastern redcedar, but it is perhaps even more drought-hardy. It is particularly suited for the western Plains area.

PONDEROSA PINE, a native, can be used in the Black Hills and vicinity. It grows slowly to a height of 50 to 75 feet. The broad, conical crown gives moderate shade. It is long-lived. It does well on various upland soils in full sunlight but it will not stand permanent shading. Ponderosa pine is susceptible to cotton root rot but it is frost-resistant and drought-hardy. It is used mainly as an ornamental and occasionally in street planting.

THE DOUGLAS-FIR: The Rocky Mountain strain of the common Douglas-fir makes a particularly good ornamental shade tree for the eastern part of the northern Plains. It is best adapted to a moist, deep, porous soil but it is moderately drought-hardy and fairly long-lived.

Common Douglas-fir here is practically free of serious pests. It is not recommended for use in the central part of the area, but it does fairly well in eastern Colorado and Wyoming. The common Douglas-fir grown from Pacific coast seed should not be used in any part of the Plains area.

WHITE FIR is one of the most beautiful of the coniferous ornamentals. It is about as drought-hardy as the Rocky Mountain Douglas-fir and does surprisingly well even on poor to dry, shallow sites after it has become well established.

AUSTRIAN PINE is similar to ponderosa pine but less adapted to poorer sites. It is subject to a fungus twig blight that causes some dieback of branches and is less drought-resistant than ponderosa pine.

SCOTCH PINE is a widespreading tree with somewhat scant foliage. It is well adapted to upland soil but less drought-hardy than either ponderosa pine or Austrian pine.

Several other pines also are useful in the region. Among them are jack pine, in the north-central part, on the lighter soils; loblolly pine and shortleaf pine, which can be grown in the southern parts, but are susceptible to cotton root rot; and the eastern white pine, which frequently makes an excellent tree in the eastern central Plains.

THE SPRUCES: Several species of spruces can be grown, particularly in the northern Plains. Colorado blue spruce, black spruce, and western white spruce are examples. As a class the spruces are fairly drought-resistant and frost-hardy. The spruces are somewhat shorter-lived than the pines, but are fine ornamental shade trees.

In the southern Plains the Arizona cypress is of limited value.

Ernest Wright *worked in the Great Plains region 7 years before he was transferred to the field headquarters of the Division of Forest Pathology in Portland, Oreg. In his work on the Great Plains, Dr. Wright studied the survival of trees in relation to climate and disease.*

T. W. Bretz, *a forest pathologist, conducts investigations on methods of controlling the phloem necrosis of elm in Missouri and nearby States. Dr. Bretz' experience includes searching for plant diseases in Iowa and Missouri on the Emergency Plant Disease Survey and teaching and research work in Texas, where he became familiar with conditions in the southern part of the Great Plains.*

# SHADE TREES FOR THE ROCKIES

LAKE S. GILL

Getting trees to grow along with the settlements and cities of the southern Rocky Mountain region has been all the more impressive because trees are naturally absent from most of the area.

The region—Arizona, Colorado, New Mexico, and Utah—is largely a high plateau 4,000 to 8,000 feet in elevation and broken by mountain ranges that often exceed 10,000 feet. In southern Arizona and southwestern New Mexico, roughly the area drained by the Gila River and its tributaries, the plateau is 1,000 to 4,000 feet in altitude. The plateau is largely treeless, although a few species occur along stream banks, and usually the foothills support an open woodland forest of low pinyons and junipers. Coniferous forests, broken occasionally by stands of quaking aspen, cover the sides of the mountains.

Normal precipitation is less than 16 inches a year, only about half of which falls during the growing season. In the Gila Basin the average annual rainfall is less than 12 inches, although there is proportionally more rain in the winter than in other parts of the region below 8,000 feet elevation. Precipitation is 20 to 30 inches in the mountains. Cold winters and hot summers are the rule except in the Gila drainage, where winter temperatures are usually mild. Wide changes in daily temperatures occur throughout the region, especially during the winter months. Late frosts are the rule. Searing winds are common. Most of the soil is alkaline; much of it is low in nitrogen and poor in physical characteristics. Often an impervious layer of hardpan lies close to the surface.

Under such conditions, the early settlers deserve great credit for introducing new trees. Today Salt Lake City, Denver, and Phoenix are outstanding examples of large cities that have been beautified by shade trees despite natural odds against them.

At first the plains poplar and the common hackberry, both native, were commonly planted. More recently, the plains poplar has lost favor because of its space requirements, its expansive and high water-consuming root system, and its untidy habit of shedding "cotton." The common hackberry is still widely used in difficult locations.

The black locust and boxelder were among the first introductions to survive the vicissitudes of climate and soil with minimum care. Later the Siberian elm joined them. These three cannot be surpassed in their ability to produce quick shade, stand abuse, and endure unusually unfavorable climatic and soil conditions.

Today the list of shade trees that can be grown successfully in the southern Rocky Mountains is indeed impressive. Most of them require supplemental ir-

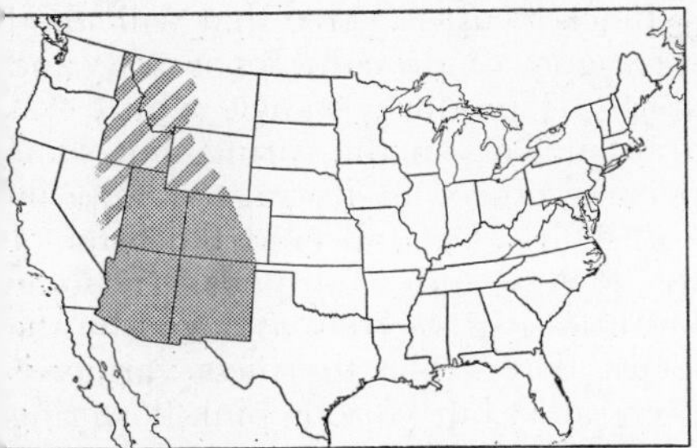

rigation. Sometimes the soil in which they are planted must be carefully selected or specially prepared, either with a view toward reducing alkalinity or of penetrating underlying hardpan to permit better drainage and root growth. Under the most severe conditions only the hardier kinds will live, but even in the northern part in protected locations a number of the more tender species that cannot be recommended for the whole region can be grown.

Following are brief descriptions and supplemental notes of the more common trees that have been successfully planted in the region. Most of the broadleaved evergreens suitable only for the extremely mild winters of the Gila River Basin have been omitted.

THE DECIDUOUS trees are listed first.

The tree-of-Heaven ailanthus, often called simply ailanthus, is an aggressive tree that can thrive where many other kinds would perish. It grows rapidly with some care, but it is relatively short-lived and provides little shade from its thin, loose crown. It is recommended as a street tree where low moisture, poor soil, and excessive heat preclude the use of more attractive species. It is almost immune to smoke and soot injury but is easily broken by snow and high wind. Only seed-bearing trees should be planted, as the pollen-bearing form, the male, has an offensive odor when it blooms. It may be planted throughout the region except in the high mountains or parts of the plateau where winter temperatures are low.

Green ash, although smaller than white ash, is the preferred street tree. It has darker foliage, is more resistant to drought, and seems to have fewer enemies. It is suitable for the plateau but it is not recommended for the mountains.

Velvet ash, especially the smooth or Arizona form, is well adapted to the Gila drainage area. It will not stand protracted cold, but it resists drought and can grow in strongly alkaline soil.

White ash has a rather oval crown and light-green and moderately dense foliage. It will stand abuse but is sensitive to drought. The oystershell scale often attacks it. It is not recommended for the mountains or the Gila Basin.

Boxelder develops into a tree with a ragged crown of fairly light-green foliage. Although the boxelder is extremely drought-resistant and able to withstand abuse, it is recommended only for places where more desirable trees will not grow. It is the breeding place of the boxelder bug, which in some years becomes objectionable in the houses nearby. Aphids commonly attack boxelder, and in the cities the honeydew that drops from them is objectionable on pavements. It will grow anywhere in the region. The Arizona form is best adapted to the Gila River drainage.

Northern catalpa, a relatively small tree, possesses a globe-shaped crown of large, heart-shaped leaves. It stands drought fairly well but not cold. Its flowers are large and attractive, but some persons object to it as a street tree because of the litter of the fallen flowers in early summer and the seed pods in autumn. It may be planted throughout the plateau, although it is not recommended for the extreme northern parts or for elevations above 5,000 feet.

American elm has been planted extensively on the plateau for many years. It is not very tolerant of alkali and should have plenty of irrigation to thrive. It is heavily attacked by the European elm scale. It is subject also to two serious epidemic diseases, the Dutch elm disease, which recently was found in Denver, and phloem necrosis, a killing virus disease that has not yet been found in the region. American elm should be used sparingly until controls are available for the diseases.

Siberian elm, which was introduced as Chinese elm and is still often called that, can persist despite drought, poor soil, and abuse, and at the same time provide shade and greenery. It is naturally scrubby in habit, but it can be trained while young into a fairly attractive street tree. It has been overplanted in some cities. Its root system is prone to invade tile sewers and to heave pavements and curbs. It produces seed profusely and the seedlings may become extremely noxious weeds in nearby gardens. It is not subject to the epidemic diseases described for American elm but is highly susceptible to the cotton or Ozonium root rot. Often the European elm scale attacks it.

The common hackberry is usually a small tree with a spreading, flat crown of dense, light-green foliage. It is excellent for use under adverse growing conditions in hot, dry climates. The foliage does not tend to turn yellow in alkaline soils. It is recommended for all parts of the region except in the mountains.

Thornless honeylocust forms a thin, irregular crown that provides light shade. It is one of the last trees to leaf out in the spring and one of the first to lose its foliage in the fall—a distinct shortcoming in a region of long, hot summers. But it is drought-resistant, hardy, and capable of withstanding abuse once it is established. It is not recommended for the mountains.

Linden is not extensively planted here, although it is recommended as a good street tree in some of the larger cities for places where it will receive fertilization and irrigation. It is subject to sunscald following transplanting. American linden and the littleleaf linden are the two preferred species for the high plateau. Local authorities should be consulted regarding suitability of linden in parts of northwestern Colorado.

Black locust is a tree that will stand the rigors of drought, poor soil, and abuse. It produces showy, white, fragrant flowers in the spring, but some persons object to its ragged appearance, early leaf fall, and the litter of its flowers and seed pods. In some localities it is severely attacked by the locust borer. The thornless variety is preferable, but various pink-flowering forms are gaining in popularity.

Norway maple is a handsome tree with a dense, globelike crown of dark-green foliage. It is favored as a street tree in the larger cities in places where irrigation and fertilization are possible and space is ample for root development. It is less subject to snow damage than silver maple and is moderately resistant to smoke injury. The Schwedler variety has bright red leaves in the spring, which later turn deep green. This variety is less likely to suffer from yellow foliage in alkaline soil than other maples. Norway maple is subject to sunscorch or leafscald, especially when the root system has not sufficient room to develop properly. It is best suited to the high plateau and is not recommended for the Gila River drainage. It is best to consult local authorities regarding the use of Norway maple and its varieties, as the species has proved to be tender in some localities.

Red mulberry is a somewhat larger tree than Russian mulberry but is less resistant to drought and cold.

Russian mulberry develops a crown of dense, dark-green foliage. It is fairly resistant to drought but is subject to winter injury. The fruits attract birds but also make a litter on walks and streets. The male, or staminate, trees do not produce fruit. This tree should not be planted in the mountains or in the colder parts of the high plateau.

Oak may be grown successfully in a few restricted areas in the region, notably in the foothills of northern Colorado. The limiting factor is soil alkalinity, which, besides giving the foliage a yellow cast, inhibits normal development for a naturally slow-growing tree.

Bur oak appears to be best adapted

to the plateau as a whole, but even with the best of care and conditions it grows slowly.

London planetree, a slow-growing but attractive tree, has a crown of deep-green leaves on a grayish-white, smooth stem. It makes a fine street tree where it can be planted in rich soil with ample irrigation. It is not recommended for the mountains or the cold plateaus of northwestern Colorado.

The closely related sycamore has much the same characteristics and requirements but is less desirable because of its susceptibility to a seriously disfiguring leaf blight.

Lanceleaf poplar is a clean-looking tree with moderately dense, light-green foliage and smooth, greenish bark. It is recommended for mountain areas only.

Narrowleaf poplar resembles lanceleaf poplar but is better adapted to lower elevations. With some care it makes a good street tree at altitudes of 5,000 feet or more. It is subject to attack by several borers, which, if not controlled, will ruin its apearance and shorten its life.

Lombardy poplar has a narrow columnlike crown of thin, almost upright, branches. It is better adapted to roadside than street planting. It seldom remains attractive more than 20 years, and is commonly killed about that age by an uncontrollable disease. It is not recommended for the mountain areas.

Plains poplar is a distinctive native tree with a low, spreading, irregular crown. It may be used anywhere on the plateau but should be planted only where it will have ample room to develop and where there is plenty of moisture. Stock from male, or staminate, trees is preferred as it does not produce the bothersome "cotton." This tree is rapidly losing popularity in the cities because it takes so much space, and in the agricultural areas it is being cut as a water conservation measure.

Russian-olive is a small tree with an irregular-shaped crown of silvery-gray foliage. It has a tendency to assume a shrubby habit but can be trained into an attractive tree. It is excellent for color contrast in group plantings. This tree is especially adapted to the high plateau. It is highly resistant to drought and tolerant of alkali.

Tamarisk has an irregular outline, thin, feathery, gray-green foliage, and white to pink flowers. It is well adapted to dry alkaline soils and will thrive with little care. It should not be used at elevations above 5,000 feet or in unusually cold locations, as found in some parts of northwestern Colorado.

EVERGREENS are worth particular attention.

Arizona cypress and its relative, the smooth Arizona cypress, have conical crowns of grayish-green foliage. They grow rapidly with irrigation and are especially adapted to the Gila River Basin or the lower elevations—below 5,000 feet—of the high plateau. They will not stand severe, protracted cold. Twig-girdling insects sometimes attack them in force.

Eucalyptus can be grown only at the lower elevations of the Gila River Basin—and even there they may be killed or damaged in the relatively severe winters that sometimes occur. Of the several species that have been extensively planted in southern Arizona, the horncap eucalyptus is most tolerant of alkali and hardpan so prevalent in the area.

Rocky Mountain juniper, another native of the plateau, frequently is found growing with Colorado pinyon pine. It is a small evergreen tree with a conical crown of greenish to greenish-gray cast. The branchlets often droop and have a weeping effect. This tree can be used effectively as a specimen in formal planting, or in seminatural groupings, as for example, with pinyon. In Denver, with irrigation, it develops into an attractive tree of moderate size.

Aleppo pine is used extensively in the Gila River Basin as an ornamental or specimen tree but will not grow elsewhere in the region where winters are more severe.

Austrian pine makes a fine specimen tree anywhere in the region. It develops a cone-shaped crown of deep-green foliage, which is little affected by hot, dry winds. Some irrigation is necessary on the plateau.

Canary pine, useful as a specimen tree, has light-green foliage of medium density. It will not stand long periods of cold weather, and therefore it can be planted with success only in the Gila River Basin; even there it should receive irrigation.

Colorado pinyon pine, also native to much of the plateau, does well under cultivation. It grows slowly into a low, scrubby tree too small for shade but good for group plantings in full sunlight. It will respond to some irrigation, but constant heavy watering is detrimental.

Ponderosa pine is a native tree with much the same appearance as Austrian pine, but usually it is slower in growth. Growth is extremely slow the first 10 years or so. Later it can grow a foot or more annually even in severe locations provided it receives some irrigation.

Scotch pine resembles Austrian and ponderosa pines in ruggedness but is less regular in shape.

Colorado spruce, often called Colorado blue spruce, is similar to Engelmann spruce except that the foliage is always gray green or bluish green. At elevations below 8,000 feet it tends to become scraggly with age and for that reason is less suitable than Engelmann spruce on the plateau. With watering it makes a beautiful, ornamental tree.

Engelmann spruce, with its tall, cone-shaped crown of green to gray-green foliage, is well suited to lawn planting and for use as an outdoor Christmas tree. It will thrive in both mountain and plateau areas if provided with fairly rich soil and given some protection from high winds.

FOR THE NORTHERN Rocky Mountain region, resistance to cold is a paramount consideration in the selection of shade trees. Suitable species are Norway maple, cutleaf birch, basswood, white poplar (alba), green ash, hackberry, American elms, Austrian pine, Scotch pine, Black Hills spruce, Colorado blue spruce, and Norway spruce. Russian-olive and the Siberian pea-tree may also be used where a smaller type of tree is desired.

LAKE S. GILL *is a forest pathologist of the Bureau of Plant Industry, Soils, and Agricultural Engineering. He is stationed in Albuquerque, N. Mex. He has investigated many aspects of forest- and shade-tree problems in the Southwest. Dr. Gill is a graduate of Yale School of Forestry.*

---

*What do we plant when we plant the tree?*
*We plant the ship, which will cross the sea.*
*We plant the mast to carry the sails;*
*We plant the planks to withstand the gales—*
*The keel, the keelson, the beam, the knee;*
*We plant the ship when we plant the tree.*

*What do we plant when we plant the tree?*
*We plant the houses for you and me.*
*We plant the rafters, the shingles, the floors,*
*We plant the studding, the lath, the doors,*
*The beams, the siding, all parts that be;*
*We plant the house when we plant the tree.*

*What do we plant when we plant the tree?*
*A thousand things that we daily see;*
*We plant the spire that out-towers the crag,*
*We plant the staff for our country's flag,*
*We plant the shade, from the hot sun free;*
*We plant all these when we plant the tree.*

HENRY ABBEY

# SHADE TREES FOR CALIFORNIA

W. W. WAGENER

Climate is the key to the trees that can be grown in a region. On the Pacific coast, the key to the climate is the Pacific Ocean, which imparts its relatively mild temperatures and its characteristic summer droughty period. The region embraces more than 16° of latitude and extends inland about 120 miles to the high barrier formed by the Sierra and Cascade Mountain chains. East of the barrier, the climate is arid or semiarid and has a much greater yearly range in temperatures. Eastern Washington, eastern Oregon, and a part of eastern California share this interior type of climate. This article discusses shade trees in California; the next article is about trees in the northern Pacific area—the western parts of Washington and Oregon.

No part of the United States presents a greater diversity in climate, topography, and soils than California. Relatively mild winter temperatures and a long summer dry season are common to all parts of the State except the higher mountains, but in other respects even a few miles may bring wide differences in the conditions that govern tree growth.

Few trees, consequently, have sufficient adaptability to be satisfactory in all parts of the region, and the planter must make his choice on the basis of the conditions prevailing in his own neighborhood. An important consideration in inland districts is whether the tree is to receive supplemental irrigation, directly or indirectly, or whether it must depend on moisture provided by the winter rains. Another is whether the ground contains appreciable quantities of soluble salts, commonly known as alkali. If so, the choice should be species known to be alkali-tolerant.

From the thousands of trees that will grow successfully in California, or parts of it, I shall discuss here a limited number that are generally suitable for shade and ornament or have specific qualities that fit them for use under conditions that are unfavorable for most species. In general, I omit trees used primarily for accent or specimen planting, the palms, nearly all of the eucalypts, and a few species of other types that once were popular but are not recommended now because of insects, diseases, or undesirable qualities. Among the last are the elms, Monterey cypress, and the black acacia.

Besides the trees here described, the owner who is considering planting around the home should not overlook the ornamental and shade value of our fruit and nut trees. The apricot, avocado, cherry, orange, kaki persimmon, mission fig, Persian walnut, and many another often serve a double utility.

THE CALIFORNIA LIVE OAK is a rather evenly rounded tree when it is young; it spreads broadly with age. It grows up to 30 to 75 feet—rather slowly at first but faster when it is well established and supplied with moderate amounts of water in summer. Its leaves are small and oval, dark green and glossy above, paler below, and rather dense. It casts a fairly dense shade unless the crown is thinned by pruning. For yards, streets, and roadways it is satisfactory in the coastal districts, where it is native, and also in the less hot and dry parts of the interior. In some districts it is subject to defoliation by the larvae of the California oak moth which never kill the tree and are readily controlled by sprays. Some trees suffer from mildew in the coastal districts that have summer fogs. Because heavy pruning and heavy summer watering favor the development of mildew, the tree should not be planted on lawns or other areas that are constantly irrigated. Despite these disadvantages, the merits of the tree make it good for many districts.

SOUTHERN MAGNOLIA is a medium-sized or tall (25 to 60 feet), round-topped or pyramidal evergreen with large, thick, glossy, dark-green leaves and rust-colored branchlets and buds. It is slow of growth, moderately long-lived, and relatively few insects and diseases bother it. The large, white, showy, fragrant flowers come in late summer and fall. It is hardy throughout the region except in the higher mountains, but does not tolerate alkali. Altogether, it is a satisfactory ornamental for home and street. It should be given additional moisture in summer in most parts of the region.

CAMPHOR-TREE is a handsome, compact, medium-sized and oval-crowned, evergreen tree, 20 to 40 feet in height when mature, with dense, glossy, light-green foliage, bronze-tinged in spring. The leaves, which have an odor of camphor when crushed, cast a fairly dense shade. The flowers are small, yellow, and inconspicuous; the growth rate is moderate, and the length of life is average. The trunk is rather heavy and enlarged at the base. Camphor-tree is satisfactory for planting around the home and as a street tree if parkways are wide enough. It is hardy in most of the region, including the central valleys, but it needs access to additional moisture in the drier situations in summer. It is fairly tolerant of alkali.

RED IRONBARK, a slender and open, medium-sized, evergreen tree of the eucalyptus family, eventually grows to 50 to 60 feet in height. It has rough, furrowed, dark, and persistent bark and small, gray-green leaves. The flowers are deep pink and are produced in profusion in late winter, spring, and into June. Its growth rate is moderate and its longevity is average. It is hardy to about 15° F. and stands drought well. Thus it is adapted to both coastal and inland situations. Moderately alkali-tolerant, it is a satisfactory tree for roadsides as well as for backgrounds or screen planting around the home.

THE CALIFORNIA PEPPERTREE is a medium to large and broadly round-topped, evergreen tree, and 30 to 50 feet high when mature. Its finely cut, light-green and drooping foliage casts a light shade. The small and yellowish-white flowers come in many-branched clusters and are followed in fall by pendent bunches of small, rose-colored fruits that persist through the winter. It grows fast and is of average longevity. It is somewhat tender, but it can stand temperatures of about 18° F.; consequently, it is usable in most of southern California and the milder parts of central and northern California. Although it is drought-resistant and somewhat tolerant of alkali, it has the reputation of harboring black scale and therefore is in disfavor among many citrus growers. It is also susceptible to Armillaria root rot, better known in the region as oak root fungus, and for that reason is uncertain on land formerly occupied by oak woodlands. It used to be planted often as a street tree, but for that purpose it has several faults. Nevertheless, the peppertree is so firmly identified with California, so attractive when it is properly used around the home, and fits so well with California architecture that it will remain popular.

CAPE CHESTNUT is a medium-sized, round-headed tree, 50 to 60 feet high when mature. Its medium-sized, elongated, somewhat sparse leaves cast a light shade. Growth rate is moderate; it is fairly long-lived. It is cultivated chiefly for its panicles of showy, lavender-rose flowers that appear in late May and June. Hardy in most of southern California and in warmer situations elsewhere in the region, it can endure temperatures to about 15° F. In the colder locations it is partly deciduous. It is suitable for planting around the home and as a street tree, but it requires watering in the summer.

THE GINKGO, an erect, rounded, and pyramidal tree, becomes somewhat spreading with age. The ginkgo is long-lived and rather slow growing to an ultimate height of 40 to 50 feet in California. The unique leaves are medium-sized, fan-shaped, and a clear green in color, changing to yellow in autumn. Because it is hardy and has practically no pests, it is useful both as an ornamental and shade tree, but it needs extra summer moisture in the drier places. Only male trees should be planted, because the fallen, mature fruits of the female tree have a disagreeable odor.

THE NORWAY MAPLE is a medium-sized, round-headed, spreading, deciduous tree, 25 to 60 feet high. It has moderately large, light-green leaves that form a dense crown and cast a rather heavy shade. It is relatively fast growing, of average length of life, and hardy. It has proved satisfactory as a lawn and street tree in the interior and mountain valleys of the region, except for a tendency of the roots to raise sidewalks. It is moderately tolerant of alkaline soils.

The silver maple is fast growing, large, spreading, and 60 to 100 feet in height. Its large leaves, bright green above and silvery below, form a rather open crown, which casts a medium to light shade. The flowers, greenish and in clusters, appear before the leaves. It is hardy, and its useful life is about average. It is similar to the Norway maple in uses and districts to which it is best adapted. Its roots sometimes raise sidewalks.

THE LONDON PLANETREE is rounded and pyramidal in habit, but becomes spreading with age. It grows to 30 to 70 feet, and has large, broad, lobed, green leaves that form a rather open crown and cast a light shade. Its growth rate is rapid; its longevity is about average. Its light-colored bark peels in thin plates. The brown, globular fruiting heads, about an inch in diameter, disintegrate when mature.

It is hardy throughout the region, but it is subject to the sycamore blight, which attacks the leaves, and the sycamore scale. Some strains of the tree are practically immune to the blight and resistant to the scale. It is a satisfactory shade and street tree, especially for inland valleys, when propagated from parent stock selected for freedom from blight and pests. The London planetree is alkali-tolerant.

THE SWEETGUM forms a rounded pyramidal tree, usually reaching not over 50 feet in height in California, with deeply furrowed bark and medium-large, deeply lobed, dark-green leaves, paler on the under side. These turn to a crimson or wine purple in the fall. The seeds are borne in spherical heads—which are about an inch in diameter and rather prickly on the outside. The tree grows at a moderate rate and it produces a compact head, which casts a medium-dense shade. It is hardy and relatively long-lived, but not tolerant of alkali. The sweetgum is satisfactory as a street tree and for home planting in all parts of the region, except on alkaline soils. It is not adapted to locations exposed to dry winds, and it requires extra summer moisture in the drier localities.

OF THE VELVET ASH, the Modesto or Montebello forms make a spreading but rather compact tree, 30 to 40 feet high when mature. The willow-like, deep-green leaves cast a medium-dense shade. Fast in growth, it is hardy except at high elevations in the region. In longevity it is about average. It is drought-resistant, moderately tolerant of alkali, and more resistant to the red spider type of mite than the regular form. It is subject to occasional defoliation by insects in some districts, but these pests can be controlled readily by sprays. A popular shade and street tree for the interior valleys, it stands drying winds well and succeeds with little moisture. Recently a leaf disease has appeared in parts of the region which may make it less desirable as a shade tree in the future.

THE CAROLINA POPLAR, a tall, upright tree from 40 to 100 feet in height, is pyramidal to columnar in form and is fast growing. The medium-sized and rounded, bright-green leaves cast a medium shade. Of average longevity, it is hardy and slightly tolerant of alkali. It grows best in moist sites. Only the male trees should be used in order to avoid the disagreeable fuzz that is shed from the blooms of the female.

This and the other more spreading types of poplar are especially adapted as shade or roadside trees in mountain valleys or around irrigated pastures in the lower inland valleys. Suckers are sometimes troublesome. Poplars should not be planted close to sewer lines because of the penetrating roots.

PIN OAK forms a rounded, pyramidal tree when young but tends to become irregular at maturity, with a height of 50 to 80 feet. The deeply cut, glossy, dark-green leaves cast a medium-dense shade and turn an attractive scarlet in the late fall. The tree grows at a moderate rate and is hardy and long-lived but not tolerant of alkali nor resistant to drought. In California, pin oak is a desirable street and shade tree for both inland and coastal districts where extra moisture can be supplied during the summer.

SOUTHERN RED OAK is a round-topped tree with spreading branches, 50 to 70 feet high at maturity. The leaves are medium large, incised, dark green above and pale below, and dark red in late fall. It casts a medium shade. Its growth rate is relatively rapid. It is fairly long-lived, but is not drought-resistant or tolerant of alkali. It resembles pin oak in uses as well as in its range of suitability.

THE CALIFORNIA BLACK WALNUT, a large, irregularly rounded tree that is 50 or more feet high at maturity, usually is taller than broad and branches from the trunk rather high above the ground. Its bark is furrowed. The dark-green leaves are divided into many leaflets and cast a medium-dense shade. Growth rate is rapid. It is long-lived, fairly tolerant of alkali, and drought-resistant. The hard, rounded nuts are borne in a green husk and mature in late fall. It is a desirable roadside and shade tree for coastal and interior valleys in locations where the falling nuts are not objectionable. It stands dry winds well.

THE CHINESE PISTACHE is a round-topped, fairly long-lived tree, 40 to 60 feet high when mature. Its growth rate is moderately rapid. Its attractive, divided foliage becomes highly colored in late fall. The flowers are inconspicuous. The female trees bear pendent, open sprays of small fruits that are scarlet in late summer and purplish in fall. It is hardy everywhere in the region except at high altitudes. It is moderately alkali-tolerant and is especially adapted to dry climates for shade or roadside planting. It is not desirable as a street tree because of the many fruits of the female trees.

THE PANICLED GOLDENRAIN-TREE is a rather low, widespreading, round-headed, deciduous tree, 20 to 30 feet high at maturity and somewhat open in habit. It casts a light to medium shade. The leaves, composed of many fine leaflets, are dark green above and paler beneath, and give a soft, fernlike appearance. The profuse yellow flowers are borne in large clusters in late summer. The fruit is a papery-walled capsule and remains on the tree until fall. The growth rate is fairly rapid. It is hardy and its length of life is about average. The tree is drought-resistant and will tolerate alkali, including black alkali, to a greater extent than almost any tree known. It is therefore especially adapted to difficult situations in the drier portion of the region where few other species will succeed, but it will grow well in more favored locations. It deserves to be more widely planted.

OF THE WHITE MULBERRY, the Kingan fruitless variety is a fast growing, broadly, round-topped, deciduous tree,

30 to 40 feet high when mature. Its medium-sized, broadly oval, thin, light-green leaves cast a rather dense shade. It stands heat, drought, and alkali exceptionally well, and will give a quick shade under conditions where most trees would fail. The branches are somewhat brittle and eventually are subject to wind breakage in windy situations unless they are carefully pruned back when necessary.

This fruitless variety overcomes the objection to falling fruits common to most other mulberries. It is not recommended for locations where other trees of better types will do well, but it is unexcelled for unfavorable places where a quick, nonpermanent tree is needed.

The canary pine is tall, slender, and fast growing when it is young, but ultimately becomes rather broad and round-topped. It reaches 60 to 80 feet in height, with long, grayish-green, drooping foliage and rather slender cones 4 to 8 inches long. The bark is reddish brown and lightly fissured. It is hardy in most of the region below an elevation of 2,000 feet, and endures temperatures down to about 10° F. It is moderately long-lived. It casts a light-to medium-dense shade. A handsome tree, the canary pine is especially useful for background and screen planting.

The Coulter pine is a stout, thrifty, roundly pyramidal native conifer with rather long, stiff, dark-green needles and fissured dark-brown to blackish bark, Coulter pine is 50 to 80 feet high when mature, moderately long-lived, and hardy in nearly all parts of the region. Its cones are large, decorative, 9 to 14 inches long, and composed of stout, sharp-pointed scales. It is especially adapted as a specimen or background tree in hill or valley situations where little or no supplementary moisture can be supplied. Because the heavy, prickly cones may fall after the tree becomes older and offer a hazard, it should not be planted where it will overhang buildings or walks.

802062°—49——7

The Lawson cypress, a narrow to broadly pyramidal tree, is native to the coast of southwestern Oregon and northern California. It reaches a height of 75 to 100 feet in cultivation. Its growth rate is moderate. The foliage is bright green or bluish and hangs in broad, flat, drooping, fernlike sprays. Its shade is dense. It is hardy throughout the region and is long-lived under favorable conditions. It is an excellent specimen or background tree for the coastal districts and the cooler portions of interior valleys and foothills where alkali is absent. It needs additional summer moisture, except in the coastal belt which is subject to summer fogs.

Nurserymen offer a number of horticultural forms of the species that differ from the parent type in color of foliage and growth habit.

The California incense-cedar is a native conifer, broadly pyramidal when young if it is not crowded. It is narrowly columnar to broadly and irregularly pyramidal in later life. Its mature height is 80 to 100 feet. The tapering trunk is broad at the base, with deeply ridged, reddish to cinnamon-brown, fibrous bark. The deep-green foliage grows in pliant, flattish sprays and casts shade of medium to heavy density. Growth is moderately rapid and the species is long-lived. It is fairly free of pests.

The California incense-cedar is hardy anywhere in California and usually will succeed except on alkaline soils. It requires supplemental moisture during the summer in the drier parts. It is excellent as a specimen tree or for background planting. It will also succeed as a roadside tree in moister localities if it is given enough room to grow properly.

The Deodar cedar is a graceful tree, broadly pyramidal in form at the base and narrowing to a thin spire at the top in younger trees. It is irregularly pyramidal and spreading when mature and 50 to 100 feet high. The lower branches persist to old age. The foliage of short needles, in clusters on pendulous branchlets, is green or glaucous-green in color. This cedar is relatively fast growing and long-lived. Deservedly it is the most popular conifer for planting in the region, for it is almost free of insects and diseases and successful in coastal and interior districts. It requires added summer moisture in the drier parts of the interior. It is adapted both to home and roadside planting if space is ample.

W. W. WAGENER, *a forest pathologist in the Bureau of Plant Industry, Soils, and Agricultural Engineering, is in charge of the field headquarters of the Division of Forest Pathology in San Francisco. Dr. Wagener is a graduate of Yale University.*

# SHADE TREES FOR THE NORTH PACIFIC AREA

T. W. CHILDS

The northern part—western Washington and Oregon—of the Pacific coast region resembles the southern part in several respects, but three differences greatly influence the kinds of shade trees that can be used in the two areas. In western Washington and Oregon, precipitation is greater and more frequent than farther south, average temperatures are lower, and the summer dry season is much shorter. The Pacific coast itself, a long, narrow strip to the west of the barrier ranges, is divided naturally into the northern and southern (that is, California) subdivisions by the main summit of the Siskiyou Mountains.

The unusually favorable climate in western Washington and Oregon permits the use of a wide range of tree species, both native and introduced.

East of the Cascade Range, environmental conditions are ordinarily much less favorable, and the species listed are not generally suitable for that area.

COMMON HACKBERRY develops here into a round-topped tree with a mature height of 40 to 60 feet. Its growth is moderately rapid and it is moderately long-lived. Its shade is of medium density; leaves appear in late April or early May. It resists drought, cold, and wind; twig brooming (witches'-broom) is not serious. Although inferior to American elm in some respects, common hackberry should be a good yard and street tree in many localities east of the Cascade Range. Its smaller size and relative resistance to pests make it a desirable substitute for elm along narrow streets and in places where the elm leaf beetle is destructive.

THE AMERICAN YELLOWWOOD is a widespreading tree, 50 to 60 feet high when mature. Growth is moderately rapid and it is moderately long-lived. Its small white flowers in long clusters appear in early June. The leaves turn bright yellow in late fall. It is resistant to cold. It is fairly resistant to drought, and relatively free from insect and fungus pests. American yellowwood has not been planted extensively, but it deserves to become more popular as a street tree and as a yard tree. It is well adapted to the territory west of the Cascade Range and should also do well in the Columbia River Valley and on the Snake River Plain if it is watered occasionally.

SWEETGUM, a rounded, pyramidal tree, has a mature height of 80 to 120 feet. It is moderately rapid in growth, long-lived, fairly resistant to cold and relatively free from pests, but it is susceptible to injury by drought and by wind. Its star-shaped leaves, about 6 inches across, turn crimson or wine purple in the fall. The bark is deeply furrowed. It casts a moderately dense shade and makes rather heavy demands on soil fertility and moisture, so that water and fertilizer must be generously applied if a good lawn is to be maintained. Sweetgum is an excellent street and yard tree. It has attractive form and brilliant fall color.

THE YELLOW-POPLAR, or tuliptree, is narrowly pyramidal to broadly spreading and grows rapidly to 100 to 160 feet. It is long-lived and fairly resistant to cold, but it is intolerant of drought and city smoke. It is relatively free from pests. The yellow flowers, about 2 inches in diameter, beautiful but not showy, appear in early June. The leaves are keystone-shaped and turn yellow in the fall. The tree requires moist, fertile soil and has a tendency to rob lawns of moisture and nutrients. This handsome tree unfortunately is not well suited to most city locations and is generally undesirable as a street tree. It is recommended for use on larger suburban and country properties for shade and ornament.

THE NORTHERN RED OAK is broadly round-topped. Its growth is moderately rapid, and it may attain a height of 60 to 90 feet. It is moderately long-lived. The shade is of medium density. It resists cold but not drought and is susceptible to root rot. The leaves turn dark red or orange to brown in early fall. It requires considerable space and fertile soil for good development. This oak has proved to be an excellent street tree in the Eastern States and should be equally satisfactory in the Pacific Northwest. If given enough water, the northern red oak may prove to be a valuable shade tree in many localities east of the Cascade Range.

THE OREGON WHITE OAK grows slowly but is very long-lived. Its mature height is 60 to 80 feet. This tree is broadly round-topped and its shade is rather sparse to moderately dense. Old trees frequently are infected with mistletoe and sometimes with wood rots. It requires moderate moisture and soil fertility for good growth, but does not compete seriously with lawns. It adds neither grace nor brilliant color to the landscape, but those lacks are far outweighed by its restful form and air of tranquil permanence. Notwithstanding its slow growth, this fine native should be more extensively used as a yard tree on lots of medium and large size and as a street tree where space is available for its development.

THE PIN OAK may be pyramidal to rounded and irregular, and 50 to 80 feet high at maturity. Its growth is moderately rapid and it is moderately long-lived. Its shade is of medium density. It is fairly resistant to cold but is not resistant to drought. The leaves appear in late spring, turn deep scarlet in late fall, and often remain on the twigs during most of the winter, particularly on young trees. It prefers rich and moderately moist soil, and is more easily transplanted than either northern red oak or the Oregon white oak. It does well in city environments and can be used to advantage along streets.

THE BIGLEAF MAPLE is broadly and compactly round-topped. Its mature height is 60 to 80 feet. Growth is rapid. It is moderately long-lived. Shade is dense. It is susceptible to a wilt disease and often is attacked by insects, which cause "honey-dew" to drip from the leaves. It makes heavy demands on soil fertility and moisture, so that maintenance of a lawn under it is difficult. A disease of unknown cause that affects the leaves and kills the twigs has been observed recently in parts of California. This handsome native has been widely used, and even more widely misused, west of the Cascade Range. It is not a desirable street tree because its roots heave sidewalks badly and its dense growth necessitates frequent and drastic pruning by line-clearing crews. It has also proved unsatisfactory in most city yards because of its space requirements, litter, and its injurious effect on lawns. These failures have more or less obscured the suitability of bigleaf maple for planting along rural roads and around the country homes.

Norway maple is slightly smaller and grows a little less rapidly than bigleaf maple, but is not otherwise preferable.

THE AMERICAN ELM cannot be recommended unqualifiedly for use in the Pacific Northwest. Elm leaf beetle is often serious, and spraying is necessary to control this pest.

PACIFIC MADRONE, a narrowly oblong to broadly round-topped, broadleaf evergreen, has a mature height of 60 to 80 feet. Its growth is moderately rapid and it is long-lived. It gives sparse to medium shade and is resistant to drought but not to severe cold or wind. The small white flowers appear in showy clusters from March to May; the fruits are orange red in late fall. The leaves are oval, 3 to 5 inches long, glossy dark green above and pale below. The bark is thin and pea green or orange to reddish brown. This unusually colorful native is well suited for use as a yard tree west of the Cascade Range, in the Columbia River Valley of central Washington, and perhaps also in favorable localities elsewhere in this region. It is less satisfactory as a street tree, because it scars easily and its smooth bark is a constant temptation to small boys with jackknives. Its appearance is occasionally impaired for a short time by leaf-spotting fungi, but pests seldom cause any permanent harm.

A FEW ADDITIONAL SPECIES are valuable for special situations.

For windy sites in western Washington and northwestern Oregon, the California sycamore is useful.

Rock elm, European linden, and eastern black walnut can be used in the mountains and valleys of eastern Oregon and Washington where conditions are not too severe.

Green ash is satisfactory for the arid plateaus east of the Cascade Range.

CONIFERS RECOMMENDED for western Washington and Oregon include several species of cedar, cypress, and pines.

ATLAS CEDAR is pyramidal and 90 to 100 feet high when mature. Its growth is moderately rapid and it is long-lived. Its shade is sparse to medium. It is fairly resistant to cold and pests. Foliage is bluish green or silvery blue in one popular variety—blue Atlas cedar. It requires fairly rich soil and moderate moisture.

Atlas cedar and its close relatives, the Deodar cedar and cedar-of-Lebanon, must be given considerable space for good development and for proper display of their attractive forms. They have been successfully used sometimes for street trees. If given an adequate water supply, they should do well in many localities east of the Cascades.

LAWSON CYPRESS has been widely planted because of its rapid growth, the blue-green color of its foliage, and its slender form. It is hardy throughout the region and is long-lived under favorable conditions. Unfortunately, in the Northwest a root disease has killed many fine specimens.

THE CALIFORNIA INCENSE-CEDAR is broadly pyramidal when young, but later it tends to become narrowly columnar to broadly and irregularly pyramidal. Its mature height is 80 to 100 feet. Growth is moderately rapid and it is long-lived. The deep-green, frondlike foliage casts shade of medium to heavy density. The fibrous bark is deeply ridged and reddish to cinnamon brown. The trunk is broad at the base and tapers rapidly. It is fairly resistant to drought, cold, and pests. The ability of California incense-cedar to thrive in city environments is questionable, but it will undoubtedly prove to be valuable for both shade and ornament in large suburban and country yards. It is native to the eastern slope of the Cascade Range as far north as Mount Hood, and should do well in the Columbia River Valley and on the Snake River Plain.

HIMALAYAN PINE is a broadly pyramidal tree that reaches a height of 120 to 150 feet. It grows rapidly and is moderately long-lived. It is fairly resistant to cold and drought. It is susceptible to a fungus twig canker but highly resistant to white pine blister rust. The rather sparse foliage is grayish green. A handsome tree for large yards, the Himalayan pine is not suitable for street planting.

COMMON DOUGLAS-FIR grows moderately fast to a height of 160 to 180 feet, and is long-lived. Its shade is of medium density. It is fairly resistant to cold and drought but not to wind. In some localities, exposure to city conditions has resulted in the slow decline and eventual death of many trees of this species. Douglas-fir is more tolerant of such unfavorable environments when exposed to them from the seedling stage; however, this species seems generally to be more suitable for country than for city use. Seed of local origin should be used east of the Cascade Range, where climatic extremes are much greater than in the coastal region and are likely to result in injury to planting stock of nonlocal origin.

Shore pine is valuable for windy situations in western Washington and northwestern Oregon.

T. W. CHILDS *conducts research on problems of forest and shade trees. He is a member of the Bureau of Plant Industry, Soils, and Agricultural Engineering, and is stationed in Portland.*

# POINTERS ON PLANTING

T. E. MAKI

No home owner is too poor or busy or inexperienced to let his yard go treeless. Poor?—he can use small trees, which cost little, or he can dig up wildings in the woods. Busy?—he can learn easily the techniques of planting trees rapidly. Inexperienced?—he can do a satisfactory job with a little study and observation.

He should first know something about choosing a tree.

ABOUT SIZE: Small trees recover so quickly from transplanting that in a few years they provide shade, effective screening, windbreak, and modification of vistas. No expenditure on the home grounds increases the value of the property so quickly and easily as landscaping with young trees; they are an investment rather than an expense.

We are here concerned with these small specimens, that is, seedlings and trees up to about 3 inches in diameter of trunk, or up to about 15 feet in total height. Practically all the steps in planting small trees apply to both shrubs and large trees, but the latter take special equipment and skill and usually cost more than owners care to spend.

Next, trees must be adapted to the climate and the soil of their new situation and be in harmony with the purpose of the planting.

For screens and windbreaks, it is best to plant evergreens like the spruce, hemlock, fir, cedar, juniper, holly, and similar species that retain live branches close to the base throughout their life.

For shade in the yard, deciduous trees (like birch, elm, mulberry, red oak, sycamore, and willow) or evergreens (like Norway spruce; live oak; Douglas-fir; white, ponderosa, pitch, and loblolly pines) are suitable. In the open, these species develop spreading limbs and may be pruned from below sufficiently to give good clearance.

In places where species that attain heights of only 40 to 50 feet at maturity are adequate, it is unwise to choose those that grow into giants of 100 feet or more. Later damage from limb breakage and windthrow can largely be avoided by proper selection and location of trees at planting time.

It is better not to plant species like maples and elms directly on lawns. These and some others form a mat of surface roots and are voracious feeders. Much extra watering and fertilizing is required to keep the lawn under such trees green and healthy.

Some trees, like the American elm, have a forking habit of growth that may require bracing later. Others, like silver maple and yellow-poplar, have brittle branches that break easily in wind and ice storms. Pin oak, blackgum, green ash, shipmast locust, redgum, and similar species have an erect habit of growth, require less space, and withstand wind and ice storms better.

Some species are rapid growers but are intolerant of shade. Frequently that quality characterizes the relatively short-lived species, like aspen, cottonwood, and some of the other poplars. The Carolina poplar, which has been widely used in landscaping, is a poor choice around homes because of its short life and its tendency to clog up sewer lines with its roots.

Do not mix rapid and slow growers in the same grove or windbreak, or else be sure that the slow growers do well under shade.

The trees one selects should be healthy and vigorous. Trees grown in a well-established local nursery are preferable to wild ones or to nursery stock shipped in from great distances. Native species are preferable to the exotic—introduced—ones, but exotics of proved adaptation may be used freely. Some home owners believe that individuality and beauty require exotic species, but that is not so. A little time spent in observation and inquiry on successfully landscaped grounds in one's own community may be invaluable in getting the right start.

If one does choose wilding stock, open-grown specimens are hardier and easier to dig than stock in dense woods.

Season of planting: Experts can plant trees successfully at almost any time of the year, but the novice should plant only in the fall, winter, or early spring, when most trees are more or less dormant. In some localities, fall planting is as successful as spring planting; in others, it may be either somewhat better or decidedly worse.

In the Eastern States south of a line from Boston to Buffalo, Chicago, and Kansas City, and east of a line from Topeka to Corpus Christi, deciduous trees can be moved from the time leaves turn in the autumn until buds burst in the spring, except when temperatures are below freezing. The same holds for the humid coastal region on the Pacific, from northern California to British Columbia.

Within those zones, evergreens may be planted from late summer till late spring, provided they are moved with a ball of earth around the roots.

North and west of the indicated lines, spring planting is recommended for both evergreens and the deciduous plants because severe freezes or dry winds harm the newly reset plants. Exceptions are the peninsula of Florida and the interior and southern parts of California. In those places, evergreens can be transplanted whenever soil moisture is abundant; deciduous trees can be transplanted when they are as nearly dormant as they are likely to become there.

Spacing: In working out the space requirements of the trees, it is well to draw a sketch to scale, showing buildings, roads, driveways, walks, courts, shrubs, flower beds, and whatever else will influence the placement of trees. On this sketch one should plot the areas the trees will need when they are mature.

Common mistakes are to plant too close in an effort to get quick screening effects, to set small trees under windows, to crowd the walls of buildings, and to plant trees where they will eventually block vistas that should remain open. The oft-quoted rule, "plant thick and thin quick," is no good unless one is aiming at natural grove effects, a goal mainly sought only in windbreak plantings.

Some trees, like white oak, live oak, black walnut, and elm, need 50 to 60 feet between the trunks at maturity. Smaller trees, like willow, dogwood, and holly, need about 20 feet. Redcedar, fir, hemlock, and spruce need 20 to 30 feet, but if they are used for windbreaks they may be planted as close as 8 to 10 feet. Columnar varieties like juniper, Lombardy poplar, and arborvitae frequently need only 6 to 8 feet. A Sunday afternoon's stroll through a park or an open grove in the country will yield enough information on bole size and crown area of mature trees of several species. The basic point to remember is to plant far enough from buildings, walks, and driveways to obviate costly moving or much pruning when the trees are big.

Preparation of the site: The usual advice is to transplant a tree in soil at least as good as the soil in which it previously grew. That advice is sound enough where it can be applied, but planting stock frequently comes from rich, well-drained nursery sites and has to be reset in inferior soil. In such instances, some site preparation is essential.

Drainage is of first importance. Sometimes heavy clay soil or hardpan is encountered at the bottom of the planting hole, but is fortunately underlain by sand or gravel. If so, puncture the compacted layer several times with a large soil auger, post-hole digger, or similar tool and fill the resulting holes with gravel. This will permit water to percolate downward into the pervious sand or gravel layer beneath. For small seedling stock, a 3- to 5-inch layer of gravel at the bottom of the hole is all that is needed.

If the soil is especially tight and is not underlain by a sand or gravel layer, the use of agricultural tile is recommended. A single line of 3- or 4-inch tile laid across the bottom of the hole and barely covered by a layer of crushed rock or coarse gravel will help drainage. The bottom of the hole should slope toward the tile, which should be carried to a suitable outlet.

In digging the hole, the good topsoil should be set aside and saved for backfilling. Since the soil dug out of holes is often infertile and either too heavy or too light, it is advisable to mix material into it to improve texture and fertility. In heavy soils, a mixture of one-third topsoil, one-third sand or weathered cinders that are screened to remove large chunks, and one-third mixture of equal parts of peat moss and subsoil is recommended. Well-rotted manure, finely chopped sod, leafmold, or weed compost may be substituted for peat moss. In light soils, the recommended mixture for backfilling is one-third topsoil, one-third peat moss, rotted manure, leafmold, compost, or finely chopped sod, and one-third mixture of equal parts of subsoil and sand or cinders. Turn over these mixtures three or four times with a shovel, separating out all stones, the larger woody root fragments, and other trash.

On the more unsatisfactory sites, as beach sands or where grading or erosion has exposed a gravelly, cemented subsoil, it is advisable to dig out entire bed areas or enlarged holes and fill them in with friable, fertile new soil.

Temptation is ever present to add mineral fertilizers in preparing the site for planting. The wise man will subdue this urge. He will just see that the soil is well drained, has abundant moisture, and is of proper tilth to permit good aeration.

Digging bare-root stock: Until they are 15 to 20 feet high, deciduous species (like pin oak, sycamore, locust, elm, maple, willow, ash, yellow-poplar, and basswood) that shed their leaves each autumn and remain leafless over winter can be easily moved with bare roots. Other deciduous species (like white oak, blackgum, persimmon, hickory, walnut, dogwood, and birch) can also be moved bare-rooted, but they recover more slowly and require more care to insure survival.

The first step in digging up a tree for transplanting is to make a circular trench around the outside spread of the roots of the tree. A tree with a 1-inch trunk diameter (measured a foot above the ground) should have a trench with at least a 10-inch radius. The trench radius should be increased about 10 inches for each inch of increase in trunk diameter. Depth of trench should be at least 18 inches, except in situations where the roots are especially shallow. Cut small roots with a spade and larger ones with an ax.

Second, remove the soil from the roots by carefully working inward from the edge of the trench, using a narrow-tine spading fork to comb the roots. Continue combing until most of the roots are exposed. For large trees that require more time to dig, cover exposed roots with wet burlap.

Third, tip the tree carefully to loosen it further after all lateral roots are uncovered. Avoid strain on any roots that escaped cutting. If a strong taproot is encountered, dig deeper to obtain at least 20 to 30 inches of taproot, depending on the size of the tree.

Fourth, cover all roots temporarily with damp burlap, moist soil, leaves, or other material to keep them from drying after the tree has been lifted. Whenever possible, move trees on calm, cloudy days to reduce root drying.

Trees should be planted as soon as possible after lifting. Where delay is unavoidable, trees may be maintained without deterioration by setting them in easily worked, well-drained soil.

DIGGING BALLED STOCK: All evergreens are best moved with a ball of soil that keeps a central core of the sensitive roots intact and reduces the transplanting shock. Deciduous trees may also be moved with balled roots, but the need is not so great as with evergreens. The width of the ball varies with the size of the plant, as shown in the first table.

To dig balled stock:

First, mark a circle on the ground around the tree, making the radius of the circle somewhat larger than the width of the ball.

Second, dig a vertical trench just outside the marked circle, going down below the zone of abundant fibrous roots. The depth of the ball varies with the size of the tree, as in the second table.

Third, cut any lateral roots flush with the inside face of the trench. To avoid jarring the soil loose, use pruning shears or a saw instead of an ax for the larger roots.

Fourth, pare off all the surplus soil with the back of the spade toward the ball. Trim the sides to slope inward so that the diameter at the bottom of the ball is a few inches less than that at the top, and the surface of the ball is smooth.

Fifth, if the ball is not more than 18

RECOMMENDED MINIMUM BALL DIAMETERS FOR DIFFERENT SIZES OF SHRUBS AND TREES

| *Shrubs and small trees* | | *Larger trees* | |
|---|---|---|---|
| *Height of plant* | *Diameter of ball* | *Tree diameter 1 foot above ground* | *Diameter of ball* |
| *Feet* | *Inches* | *Inches* | *Inches* |
| 1½- 2 | 11 | 1¼-1½ | 18 |
| 2 - 3 | 12 | 1½-1¾ | 20 |
| 3 - 4 | 14 | 1¾-2 | 22 |
| 4 - 5 | 16 | 2 -2½ | 24 |
| 5 - 6 | 18 | 2½-3 | 28 |
| 6 - 7 | 20 | 3 -3½ | 33 |
| 7 - 8 | 22 | 3½-4 | 38 |
| 8 - 9 | 24 | 4 -4½ | 43 |
| 9 -10 | 26 | 4½-5 | 48 |
| 10 -12 | 29 | 5 -5½ | 53 |
| 12 -14 | 32 | 5½-6 | 58 |
| 14 -16 | 36 | 6 -7 | 65 |

RECOMMENDED DEPTHS TO DIG FOR DIFFERENT BALL SIZES

| *Diameter of ball* | *Depth of ball* |
|---|---|
| *Inches* | *Inches* |
| 10 | 8 |
| 20 | 15 |
| 30 | 20 |
| 48 | 30 |

inches in diameter and the soil is compact, adhering firmly, simply undercut the ball and tip it over on a square of burlap. Then lift the ball from the hole. Next, draw burlap tight around the ball and pin it in place with nails. If the soil is loose or the ball diameter exceeds 18 inches, reinforce the pinning with heavy cord, net fencing, or light rope drawn around the ball. The pinning and roping should be completed in the hole before lifting. Digging is easier and balls hold together better if the soil is fresh. Take advantage of periods immediately following rains to move trees.

Balls too large to lift by direct manpower require the use of platforms and rollers. Trees requiring ball diameters of 4 feet or greater are best moved with special machinery. Moving large trees is a job for experts, not one that the average home owner should attempt on his own. But it is well to remember that large trees can be moved successfully and that throughout the country there are arborists equipped to undertake such jobs—which are often difficult and cost accordingly.

Planting: Schedule the planting job so that all soil preparation is completed and all holes dug before the plants are brought in. This will reduce the length of time the trees need to be out of the ground.

The steps in planting bare-rooted and balled stock are somewhat different.

For bare-rooted stock:

First, inspect the hole to see that it has a flat bottom and is deep enough and wide enough to accommodate the roots freely without any cramping.

Second, shovel 3 to 4 inches of topsoil or prepared soil into the bottom of the hole. Heap up a mound in the center of the hole at the spot where the base of the trunk will rest. The mound should be large enough to prevent formation of air pockets as the soil packs and recedes.

Third, inspect the roots and prune off any ragged ends. Insert tree and fill in the earth to hold the tree at about the depth it had in its former location.

Fourth, spread out the roots to approximately their original position, and shovel in backfill of topsoil or prepared soil to hold them in place. Trample the soil carefully around the trunk and roots to prevent excessive settling of soil away from the roots, taking care not to scuff any bark from the roots or base of trunk.

Fifth, when the hole is nearly filled, pour in several gallons of water. Water will cause rapid settling of soil and bring it into close contact with the roots. After free water has disappeared, fill in the hole level with the adjoining ground. Add more filling later if the soil continues to settle. To reduce runoff during subsequent watering, build up a small ridge around the hole.

For trees planted with a ball of soil:

First, see that the hole is at least a foot wider than the ball diameter and about 5 inches deeper than the ball.

Second, heap up a low mound in the center of the hole. Measure the depth of the ball as accurately as it is possible, then adjust mound height to insure leaving the tree at the same level it held in its former location. Lower the tree into the hole, then shovel in enough soil at the base of the ball to hold it in place.

Third, remove the burlap and shovel in topsoil or prepared soil until the hole is about half full. Tramp down to reduce air pockets.

Fourth, fill the hole with water, and when this has soaked away, fill with soil up to ground level.

Fifth, build up a 3- to 4-inch ridge around the outer edge of the ball to reduce runoff from watering. If the ball is compact, of heavy texture, and much drier than adjoining backfill, examine the ball to see whether it is absorbing water. The tendency is for water to percolate downward and outward into the looser, lighter textured adjoining soil, leaving the ball dry. If this is happening, take special precautions to see that the ball is adequately moistened at the start.

PRUNING: Enough leaf-bearing surface of newly transplanted deciduous trees should be thinned out by pruning to balance the loss of roots. Prune only lateral branches, removing from one-half to two-thirds of them. The main leader and any short branches growing out directly from the leader or the main trunk should be left undisturbed. Most evergreen trees require little, if any, pruning, except to remove broken or injured branches.

Wounds from pruning or other injury, if more than a square inch in area, should be dressed with special asphalt-base tree paint, shellac, or other suitable wound dressing to hasten healing and reduce the possibility of decay. High-quality roofing asphalt may be used (as a substitute) if prepared dressings are not obtainable. Tree-wound dressing compounds and paints are available at arborists' supply houses and also in most well-stocked hardware and paint stores.

AFTER-CARE: The work does not end after the tree has been set in the ground, has been given a preliminary watering, and has been properly pruned.

If the tree is more than 7 feet tall and in a situation exposed to winds, it needs support. A single stake, long enough to reach up into the lower part of the crown after being driven down to solid soil about 1 foot from the base of the trunk, will do for trees up to 2 inches in trunk diameter. The tree is fastened to the stake with wire, which is run through a piece of old garden hose to keep it from cutting into the bark. If wire and hose are not available, burlap and sash cord or light rope will do.

Trees that are 2 to 4 inches in diameter require two or three such stakes. Trees larger than 4 inches in diameter should be guyed down with three or more guys. Use wire or cable run through old garden hose or attached to the tree by means of a lag hook, and fasten the lower ends to 2-inch by 4-inch by 4-foot stakes or to deadmen.

Another point to remember is mulching. A 2- to 3-inch layer of peat moss, leaves, straw, hay, shredded corn stalks, bagasse, wood shavings, or similar material laid down in a circle over the root area is definitely advisable. This mulch will reduce evaporation, prevent early freezing, and keep down weeds. On deciduous trees a mulch layer is not necessary after the first 2 years, but on evergreens, particularly broadleaf types, a continuous mulch layer is desirable. Where rodents are numerous, the mulch layer should be pulled away from the base of the trunk to reduce possibilities of girdling injury.

To the newly planted tree, proper watering is the most important of all measures. The soil should be kept fresh at all times and occasionally be well-saturated to make sure that roots have not dried out. But waterlogging should definitely be avoided. Excess water will kill some species faster than drought.

Exposed trunks of newly planted trees are sometimes injured by sunscald. To prevent this injury, wrap the trunk and lower limbs with strips of burlap or with special horticultural crepe paper, which comes in strips 4 to 6 inches wide. The wrapping should remain on at least a year. Inquire among local nurserymen or experienced tree planters to determine which species, if any, require wrapping.

No fertilizing is advised at planting time, but when the tree is established, say 6 months to a year after planting, moderate fertilizing is recommended. The kinds and amounts of fertilizers and the season of application depend on the local soil and climate. Advice on this matter can usually be obtained from the county agent, State experiment station, or any local nurseryman.

T. E. MAKI *is in charge of the Gulf-coast Branch of the Southern Forest Experiment Station, Gulfport, Miss. A graduate of the University of Minnesota, where he majored in forestry and soils, he has had experience in landscape plantings in the Lake States, Idaho, Maryland, and Mississippi.*

# KEEPING SHADE TREES HEALTHY

CURTIS MAY

The formula for keeping shade trees healthy has three parts: Selecting kinds of trees that are adapted to your locality; planting them in good soil; and following a program of soil maintenance, watering, pruning, and treatment for diseases and insects.

The kinds of shade trees that will grow well in the different regions are discussed in preceding articles. A few general considerations need to be repeated here: Generally speaking, the species that grow naturally in any region are adapted to the climate of the region and can cope with native pests. If they also can withstand the artificial conditions imposed when they are planted for shade trees, it is advisable to use them, provided they are of the proper form and size. Some trees grow satisfactorily outside their natural range, it is true, and many species introduced from other continents succeed well in various parts of the United States. Before one makes extensive plantings of the introduced species, he will do well to check their usefulness, hardiness, and values. On those points, other sections of this book, aboretums, experiment stations, nurserymen, and garden publications give a wealth of information.

Your properly chosen tree has been planted—how does it grow?

If it grows well, leave it alone. If it does poorly, one or several remedies may be needed. Some of the symptoms of disease and decline in trees are so specific that the cause can be diagnosed accurately and easily. Other symptoms can develop from a number of causes. Five early warnings that all is not well are sparse foliage; leaves that are paler green than normal; dieback of the tips of the twigs; drying and loosening of the bark; and abnormally slow growth.

Look first to the soil—its fertility, drainage, aeration, and moisture. The trouble might be that the roots are not developing as they should because the soil is heavy clay, airless and poorly drained, such as the soil often is that is excavated in the construction of a basement. If so, fertilizer, organic matter, and loosening of the soil are needed.

Most of the roots of trees do not grow deeply into the earth. Unless the soil is gravelly or sandy, the bulk of the roots of most kinds of trees is likely to be found in the upper 3 feet; commonly they penetrate even less deeply. When the minerals in the soil mass in which the roots are growing become inadequate to maintain good growth, the tree begins to show signs of decline. Annual depletion of the mineral elements by taking away all grass clippings and fallen leaves may not affect the tree for several decades of its early life, but after 30 to 50 years signs of mineral depletion often are evident. Street trees are even more likely to decline from lack of soil fertility than lawn trees, because the soil mass in which their roots can develop well is likely to be even more restricted than it is for lawn trees. The need for additional minerals in the soil can be corrected by applications of fertilizer.

The fertilizer should be applied regularly, preferably in the spring, just about the time growth begins. It can be applied safely until about the middle of the summer in most parts of the country—even later in the Deep South. Or, the fertilizer can be put on in the fall after the trees have lost their leaves. Evergreens, however, should not be fertilized in the late fall.

The amount of fertilizer to be used without danger of causing injury varies somewhat with the kind of tree, the condition of the soil, and the time of application. A safe dosage is 2 pounds for each inch in diameter of the trunk 3 feet above the ground line. Wherever possible, it should be put into the ground to a depth of 15 to 24 inches to encourage deeper root growth.

When fertilizer is spread on the surface over a period of several years, the tree tends to develop roots at the surface of the soil, which interferes with mowing the lawn, and during drought periods cannot obtain sufficient water.

Maples and elms tend to produce many roots near the surface even under the best conditions, and fertilizer on the soil encourages the habit.

If a chemical fertilizer is used, it should be thoroughly soaked deep into the soil; otherwise it might cause some burning of plants, and the roots, which take up nutrients only in solution, will be able to get it slowly or not at all.

The practice of raking and burning the fallen leaves each autumn and removing all grass clippings eventually reduces the fertility of the soil to such a low point that trees may not get enough of the mineral elements they need. In the forest the decaying fallen leaves provide a protective mulch that conserves natural moisture and tempers summer's heat and winter's cold. They return to the soil the mineral elements necessary for tree growth. Grass under trees may rob them of needed minerals. Top dressing the lawn does not meet the requirements of the tree, but a heavy application of well-rotted manure over the root area of the tree is usually beneficial.

A SECOND FACTOR that sometimes affects the growth of shade trees is the lack of aeration of the soil. Clay soils that bake hard in summer and that are heavy and sticky when wet are not favorable for good tree-root growth. Such soils can be made looser by the addition of sand or some other suitable material and organic substances, such as manure, peat, compost, thoroughly rotten sawdust, decayed leaves, and so on. The materials can be worked into the top 4 to 6 inches of soil. Ordinarily for that purpose it is better to use a fork than a shovel, because a fork injures the roots less. A surface mulch of organic material is often helpful; it helps to conserve water and provides insulation against overheating.

For the decomposition of newly fallen leaves and sawdust, additional nitrogen is required. Unless nitrogen is added, the addition to the soil of fresh leaves or sawdust may actually reduce the amount of the essential nitrogen available to the tree roots. Moreover, fresh manure, newly fallen leaves, and similar materials mixed into the soil or buried in it may release, during decomposition, injurious substances that are poisonous to the trees. However, leaves and sawdust can be used as surface mulches.

Trees often get too little water: Many street trees grow in places where the area of soil exposed to rainfall is small; lawn trees have to compete for water with grass and other plants. Moreover, the drain pipes that honeycomb the soil in cities remove from it, every day, thousands of gallons of water and might lower the soil water table so much that established trees cannot get enough water.

Heavy watering will prevent damage from this cause. Light sprinkling merely moistens the ground for only a few inches and does not benefit the trees. A thorough soaking of the ground for several hours once a week is much better than sprinkling each evening.

A COMMON CAUSE of the decline of established trees in residential areas is damage done to them when the houses were built and streets laid out.

Soil piled on the ground over the root area of a tree can kill it within a few weeks or after a score of years, depending upon the depth of the fill, the sensitivity of the species, and other factors. A few inches of earth fill over its roots can kill the American beech. The American elm will often withstand several feet of earth fill.

If the earth fill happens to be gravel or has a large amount of decomposed organic matter in it, the effects may not be evident until 15 to 30 years later. Gradual compaction of the filled-in soil and the complete decomposition of the organic material slowly reduces permeability of the soil to air and the roots die slowly from suffocation. Eventually the tops of trees with damaging earth fills over their roots begin to die back. Often they blow over in storms—the stubs might have rotted below the soil line and for some distance above it; oxygen starvation of the roots combined with wood decay has finally killed the tree.

How can one tell whether an earth fill has been made over the root area of a tree? Normally the base of a tree at the ground line and just above it is greater in diameter than the main trunk a few feet above the ground. A buttress or flaring of the trunk just above the ground line indicates that it has grown normally at that soil level. However, if the trunk enters the ground without expanding, flaring, or buttressing, one should be suspicious that an earth fill has been placed over the roots. The soil around the base of the trunk should then be removed to determine if a fill has been made.

The bad effects of a fill can often be prevented or overcome by installing drain tiles in the soil. The tiles should be placed at the old soil level. They should open into a well built around the base of the tree. This well can either be left open or can be filled with coarse stones. The tiles may be installed either in a radiating pattern or be laid in parallel lines. In either case they will provide both aeration and a place to introduce water during drought.

MANY DISEASES of shade trees are caused by parasitic fungi and bacteria. Some virulent parasites will attack and disfigure or kill trees even though they are growing under the best possible conditions. Many weak parasitic organisms, however, that do practically no damage when trees are growing well can destroy trees that grow under poor conditions.

To avoid the attacks of many kinds of twig blights and trunk and branch cankers caused by weakly parasitic organisms, give your trees the best possible growing conditions—keep them well fertilized, provide organic material in the soil, make certain that the soil is permeable to air, and water adequately during droughts.

Many of the virulent fungus parasites can be controlled by the application of fungicides, but for others no means of control are yet available. Some diseases can be prevented by controlling the insects that spread them.

Most leaf diseases (which do their damage by reducing the ability of the leaves to make sugars and other foods needed for growth and other normal functions) can be controlled by spraying with fungicides. Sycamore anthracnose, a destructive fungus disease, will respond to pruning of the cankered branches and spraying with a fungicide two or three times in summer.

Bordeaux mixture is the commonly recommended fungicide. For this work power sprayers are usually necessary.

Leaf spots of elm, maple, horsechestnut, ash, and many other kinds of trees can be controlled by spraying.

Many leaf diseases are not sufficiently serious to warrant spraying for them. They ordinarily will not kill a tree in one season, but if the attack is serious year after year, great damage may result.

The fungi that cause cankers of the limbs and branches can often be controlled by removing the diseased branches or by cutting out the cankered tissues. When cankers are excised, the wounds should be painted with an

---

**Illustrated on the next two pages are the form and comparative size of commonly planted shade trees. They are drawn to scale; the distance between the horizontal lines is 10 feet. Another point brought out is one that home owners often overlook—a young tree, 2 or 3 feet high when it is planted, may in time grow into a giant, and therefore should not be planted too close to a house. The drawings were made by Rudolph A. Wendelin; the original silhouettes were prepared by Marguerite M. McCormick, under the direction of Curtis May, of the Bureau of Plant Industry, Soils, and Agricultural Engineering.**

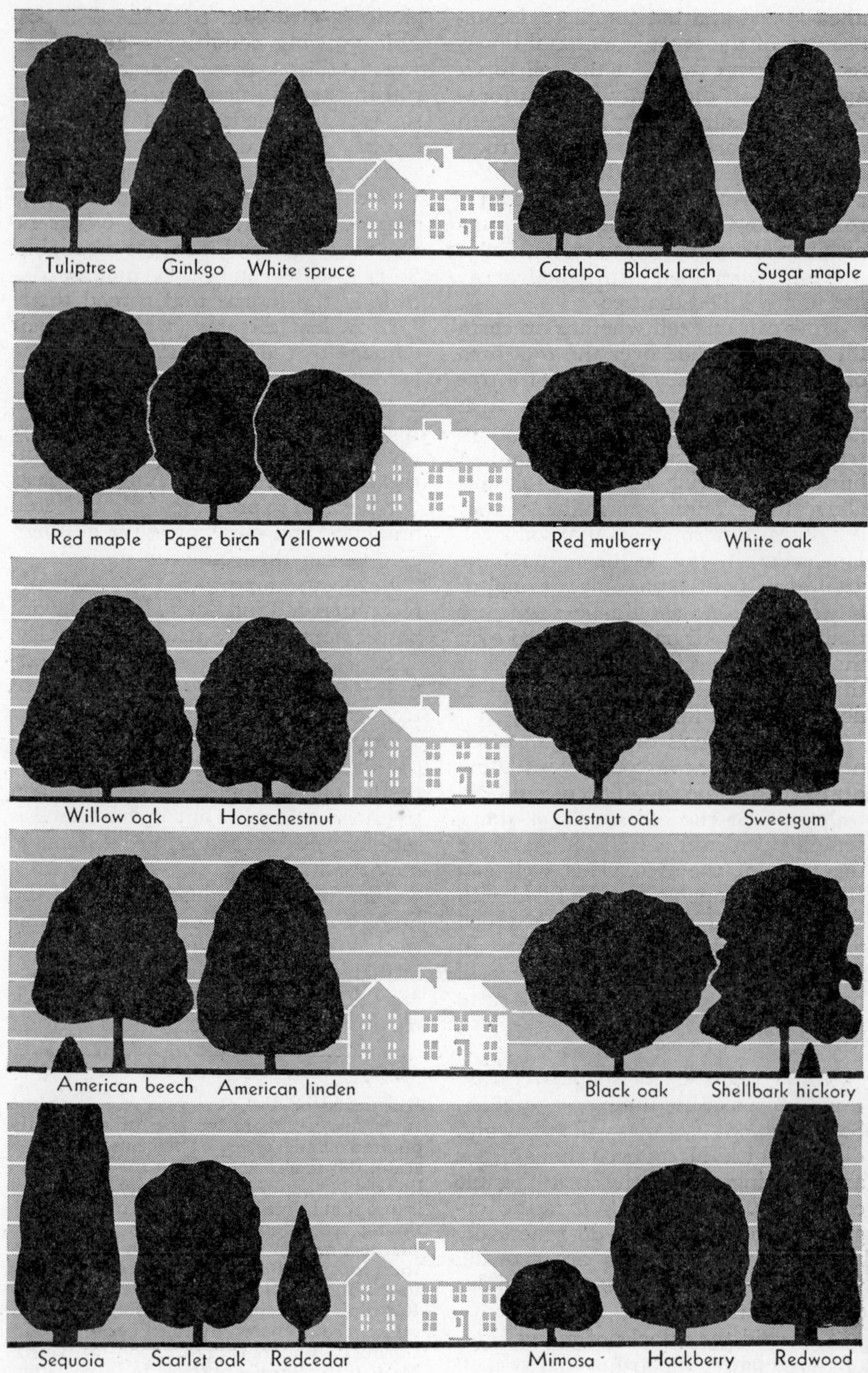
Tuliptree
Ginkgo
White spruce
Catalpa
Black larch
Sugar maple
Red maple
Paper birch
Yellowwood
Red mulberry
White oak
Willow oak
Horsechestnut
Chestnut oak
Sweetgum
American beech
American linden
Black oak
Shellbark hickory
Sequoia
Scarlet oak
Redcedar
Mimosa
Hackberry
Redwood

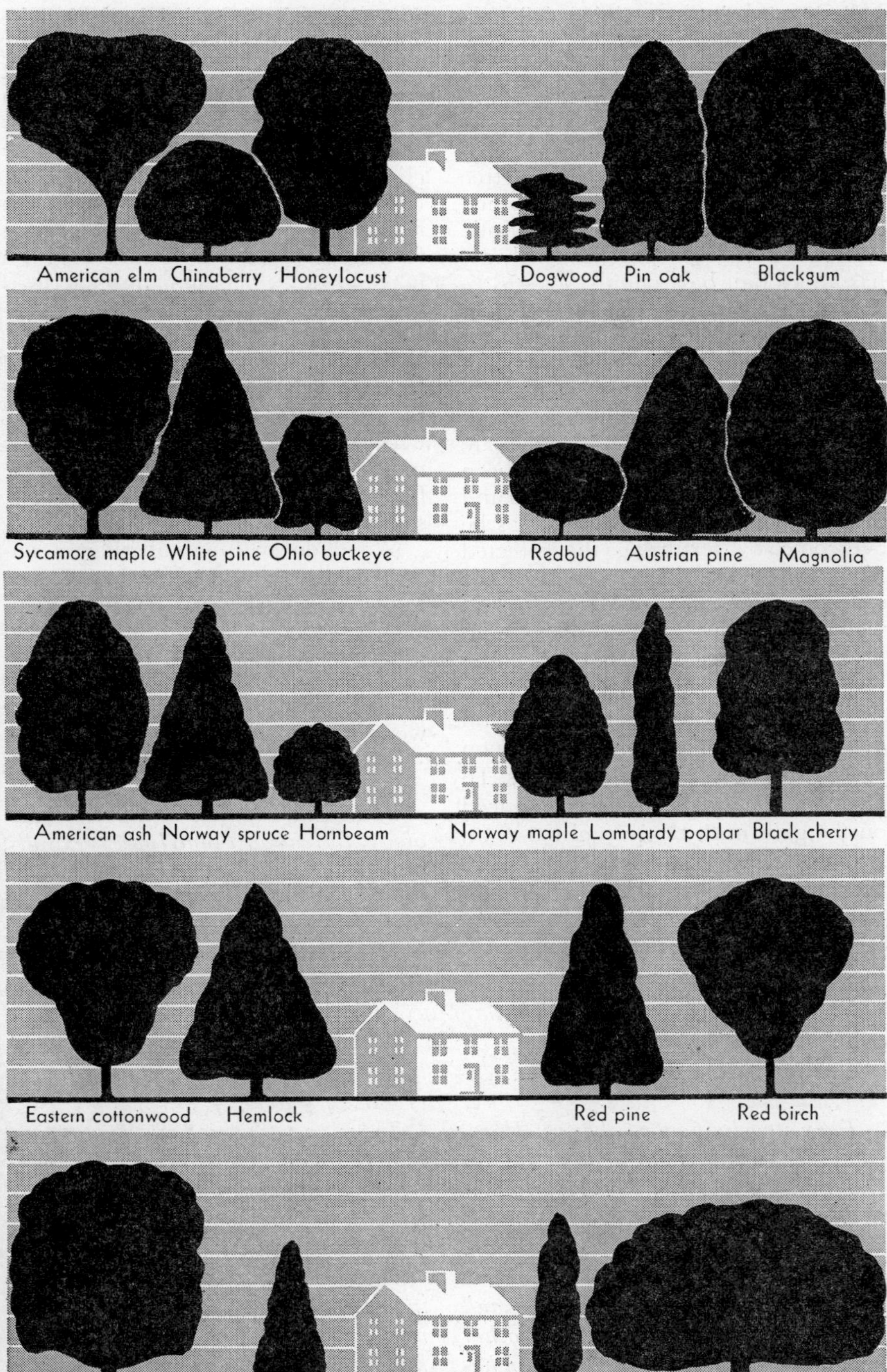
American elm
Chinaberry
Honeylocust
Dogwood
Pin oak
Blackgum
Sycamore maple
White pine
Ohio buckeye
Redbud
Austrian pine
Magnolia
American ash
Norway spruce
Hornbeam
Norway maple
Lombardy poplar
Black cherry
Eastern cottonwood
Hemlock
Red pine
Red birch
Madrone
American holly
Arborvitae
Live oak

asphaltum paint containing 0.2 percent phenol-mercury nitrate, a powerful fungicide.

One might want to treat the wound caused by pruning dead and undesirable branches from a tree. Many hardware stores and paint stores sell tree paint or tree wound dressing, which usually is obtainable in either plastic or liquid form and practically always has an asphalt-base paint.

Ordinary asphalt roofing paint is satisfactory, but it is not antiseptic.

Some fungi develop in the wood of living trees and cause wilt and dieback of the tops. They are difficult to control; for the most part, no adequate means of combating them have been developed. Verticillium wilt of elm and of maple, however, can sometimes be overcome by fertilizing the affected trees, improving the condition of the soil in which they are rooted, and watering heavily during dry spells.

Some kinds of fungi require more than one kind of plant to complete their life cycle. For example, one kind of gall that develops on the common redcedar is caused by a rust fungus. To develop, the fungus spores produced on the galls must be transmitted to an apple or closely related tree, on which they cause leaf and fruit spot. The spores are then carried back, by the winds or otherwise, to redcedars, which they infect. The rust fungi that have such a life history generally can be controlled by spraying, but sometimes one can avoid such diseases by eliminating one of the host plants.

Along the northeastern seaboard, ash rust sometimes becomes epidemic; the fungus that causes it develops on marshgrass, which sometimes is used as a mulch in orchards.

Decay of the wood of limbs and trunk can be combated by removing the affected parts or removal of the decayed wood. Sometimes the cavities made in removing decayed wood are filled with concrete or other materials; sometimes they are left open.

Wood decay fungi often gain entrance through wounds that expose sapwood or heartwood. Avoidance, insofar as possible, of wounding and painting of accidental wounds and pruning cuts over 1½ inches in diameter will assist in the prevention of wood decay.

Curtis May *is a principal pathologist in the Division of Forest Pathology, Bureau of Plant Industry, Soils, and Agricultural Engineering, United States Department of Agriculture.*

---

*THE PHOTOGRAPHS in the next section were chosen to summarize the main points in this book and to awaken interest in the purposes and pleasures of trees and forests:*

*Our forests are diverse in types, extent, and uses.*

*They are a living part of every American's life, whether he lives in Puerto Rico, North Dakota, Alaska, whether in Maine or Hawaii.*

*They provide paper, recreation, furniture, foods, feeds, protection from wind and flood, homes for birds and other wildlife, and so many other products and comforts that no man has counted them all.*

*Forests protect hillsides and mountainsides and make on them living reservoirs of water.*

*Trees and forests, however, are not something only on a far mountain. The trees at our own doors are neighbors, friends, and helpers.*

*These trees, these forests, need care.*

*We are making great strides in caring for our trees and forests. We have new machines, uses, cutting methods, knowledge of breeding trees, improvements in watershed practices, fire fighting, planting, marketing, and more.*

A forest is more than trees. Here in the Rogue River National Forest in Oregon where a ranger (above) and his pack train paused on an inspection tour, there are lodgepole pine and alpine fir; mountains, which store the snow and rain for the plains below; and a tree-girt lake, a link in the natural water-supply system. Or like Big Flat (below), which faces City Creek Peak in the Fishlake National Forest in Utah, a forest may include mountain meadows on which graze cattle, sheep, and deer that bulk large in the Nation's supply of meat and wool. The grass and the alpine fir beyond are vital in the protection of the watersheds.

In Tongass National Forest in Alaska (above), a raft of Sitka spruce and western hemlock sawlogs is abuilding on Hood Bay. It will be towed to a sawmill in Sitka. Dense coastal forests of Alaska can support huge pulp mills besides other timber-using industries. Below: Vacationists on a trail-rider wilderness trip portage across Curtain Falls, Superior National Forest in Minnesota. Across the stream is Canada. This wilderness area is in the proposed Quetico-Superior International Peace Memorial Forest. Scores of folk take horseback and canoe trips; to other millions, forests afford opportunities for picnicking, camping, skiing, fishing, hunting, hiking.

Here are contrasts in forests, methods, uses. Above: A father-son team uses a gasoline-powered saw to cut ponderosa pine in Kootenai National Forest, Montana. Some saws are driven by electricity—a departure from logging that relies on saws, axes, hard muscle. America has plenty of forest land—but saw-timber supply is declining; drain is 50 percent greater than growth. Also, quality of saw timber is deteriorating. Below: Pitsawing tabonuco into lumber for furniture, in Luquillo Mountains, Caribbean National Forest, Puerto Rico. Pitsawing developed into vertical saws driven by water power; later came modern circular and band saws.

In a plant in Rothschild, Wis., lignin, precipitated from waste liquor of the sulfite pulping process, is extracted by a vacuum filter (above). Mixed with soda and cooked, lignin yields vanillin, source of "vanilla" flavoring, and desulfonated lignin, base for plastic and molding resins. Waste sulfite liquors also contain wood sugars which may be converted into ethyl alcohol and high-protein yeast and molasses for livestock feed. Below: A large pulp and paper company's yard at Luke, Md., where 20,000 cords of all kinds of hardwoods (except black locust and walnut) are kept always on hand for making all sorts of paper, particularly fine stock for books.

Soon after this small mill started operations in second-growth pine in California, bark beetles began competing with it for trees. The red-brown trees in the background are infested and dying; some can be sawn into lumber, but blue stains will lower their value. Spread of the beetles can be checked by burning the bark and using toxic oils and proper disposal of slash. Below: To protect a new crop of western white pine in St. Joe National Forest, Idaho, from blister rust, a crew grubs out ribes—gooseberries and currants—which are the hosts of blister spores. The crew works in lanes marked by string to assure complete coverage of the area.

Smokejumpers, who parachute from airplanes to rugged and remote fastnesses not easily accessible to men afoot, form our newest fire-fighting force. Above: Two young, trained, daring jumpers have landed and with streamers signal the pilot: "Landed O. K. Can handle fire alone. Drop tools here." Such action saves precious time and valuable forests. Below: Fire that swept through Engelmann spruce in Arapaho National Forest, Colorado, 50-odd years ago left desolation that time has not healed. The flames killed all seed, all seed trees; only replanting can return the tract to production. Fire destroys today's forests as well as tomorrow's lumber.

Poor cutting increases the waste of our forests. Above: Stumps cut high leave valuable timber in the woods. Removal of all the choice trees greatly degrades the forest; and often it is 50 to 100 years before such areas can produce saw timber. Below: The New York farmer who owns this white pine sold the trees for a lump sum to a mill operator, who cut everything that would make a two-by-four, and left ruin that it will take years to repair. A farm forester could have advised the farmer on management and sales, suggested a fair selling price and proper cutting practice, and saved the sturdy young trees for regular harvests in the future.

Here are two examples of good cutting. Above: In Columbia National Forest, Washington, between French Butte and Mt. Rainier, 60- to 100-acre patches of Douglas-fir (instead of whole mountainsides) are clean-cut, with regard to location of seed trees, prevailing winds, slopes, ease of logging, roads. New growth will start soon; then other blocks will be cut. Below: A farm wood lot in Chemung County, New York, after cutting but before logs are removed. The tract was carefully cut: Low stumps, healthy young trees left for later harvests, standing trees undamaged. Such a wood lot can return steady income in cash sales, posts, and fuel for home use.

Research has disclosed better ways to care for trees and forests. Above, left: An entomologist inspects hybrid of Jeffrey and Coulter pines exposed in cage to a weevil that is particularly destructive to young Coulter pines. The cage allows him to assess results quickly. Above, right: At Pike Bay Experimental Forest in Minnesota a geneticist finds that Scotch pines grown from seed from northern Europe resist cold better than stock from central Europe. Below: The Coweeta weirs, Southeastern Forest Experiment Station in North Carolina, yield useful facts on stream flows from watersheds on which different amounts of vegetation have been removed.

Foresters believe that millions of acres in the United States should be planted to trees. Nurseries throughout the country produce seedlings for public and private forests. In a Georgia nursery, above, longleaf pine seedbeds are being sprayed with bordeaux mixture to control brown spot disease. Below: Tree-planting machine in Bienville Parish, Louisiana, can plant up to 10,000 seedlings a day. A colter wheel slices the sod; a trencher opens the cut; the operator spots seedlings at the right depth and spacing; finally, wheels behind pack the seedlings. Hand planting, though much slower, still must be used on areas of rough and rocky terrain.

Above: The forest of a large paper company in Maine. Cut in 1935 to a 12-inch stump diameter limit, the stand was opened up to allow white pine and spruce advance reproduction to get established. That is good forestry; it saves loss of revenue from cutting undersized stock, insures a nurse crop that prevents sunscald, provides intermediate cuts for periodic sales, assures greater ultimate returns, steadies employment. Below: The Otsego Forest Products Cooperative Association's sawmill in Cooperstown, N. Y.—an example of a way in which owners of woodlands cooperate in meeting problems of cutting and selling timber and keeping wood lots producing.

On watch over forests are rangers, scientists, lookouts, loggers, work crews. Modern equipment multiplies their effectiveness and cuts costs. Above: Using portable power equipment to spray insect-infested lodgepole pine in Teton National Forest, Wyoming. Below: Pilot Carl Nelson and District Ranger William J. Trygg land their amphibious plane on Thomas Lake in Superior National Forest to get data on fire hazard—rainfall, humidity, dryness of vegetation. Planes supplement regular lookouts when visibility is low and fire danger is high. Nelson and Trygg cover in hours an area that old-time rangers in canoes and afoot took months to survey.

# PROTECTING SHADE TREES FROM INSECTS

R. A. ST. GEORGE

Many kinds of insects attack shade trees. Some of the worst infest the trunk or the branches or the leaves. Some merely mar the appearance of the part attacked. Others cause severe injury. But of all of them it can be said that they have specific habits whereby they and their damage can be identified, assessed, and used to determine the need for applying control measures. It is convenient to separate the more important insect enemies of shade trees into two groups, those that attack weakened and dying trees and those that infest the more healthy ones.

The first group includes many species of bark-infesting and wood-boring beetles. They can detect trees that have reached a decadent stage long before a man can see the changes associated with decadence.

The ambrosia beetles frequently are among the first insects to attack weakened trees. Their presence can be detected by the strings or piles of white, powdery frass that they push to the bark surface as they extend their tunnels deep into the wood. It is a positive indication that the tree is dying. If the infestation is confined to a small area on one side of the trunk, the tree might be saved by taking measures to revitalize it—fertilizing and watering, and by applying a protective chemical spray to the stem of the tree. But if the attack extends entirely around the trunk, the processes of decadence are likely to have progressed so far that the tree will die, and the expenditure of large sums of money to save it is questionable. Often it is more practical to dispose of such a tree than to try to save it.

Certain of the roundheaded beetles attack dying trees. The females of some species of the roundheaded beetle make slits or pits in the bark and deposit their eggs in them. After the larvae have worked beneath the bark and into the wood their presence can be detected by the noise they make while cutting their tunnels and also by the coarse, shredded wood fibers that are pushed to the bark surface.

Many bark beetles attack weakened trees. They work between the bark and the wood. They make small shot holes in the bark and push their granular borings to the surface. Their color, which is similar to that of the bark, helps one to distinguish between the bark borers and wood borers. Certain species, known as turpentine beetles, are much larger than the rest of the bark beetles and confine their attacks to the bases of trees. A large, reddish pitch tube is formed at each point of entry. In the eastern and southern sections of the country, their attacks are mostly unsuccessful, but in the western pine regions turpentine beetles can sometimes kill slow-growing and injured trees and cause considerable concern to owners of mountain homes.

The obvious way to combat these insects is to keep the trees healthy—to remove the factors responsible for the weakening of shade trees. Among the factors causing the most damage are prolonged droughts; earth fills; sunscald and whipping of the stems, due to severe thinnings around trees left for natural shade; mechanical injury to the trunks and roots of trees made by heavy equipment while cutting roads and grading the soil around new homes; poor drainage; transplanting at the wrong time of year; and not using due caution in handling the trees or caring for them sufficiently until they are well established.

The second group includes those insects that attack healthy trees. All parts of the tree are subject to infestation.

The stem borers include many kinds

802062°—49——8

of beetles and moths. Their larvae cause injury by tunneling into the sapwood and heartwood of the trunks. The locust borer, which attacks black locust, is a good example of this group.

The twig borers and girdlers consist principally of certain roundheaded beetles, the larvae of which mine or girdle the terminal shoots. Sometimes the girdled terminals are not entirely broken off by the wind; then dangling dead branches become conspicuous, especially on hickory and oak trees.

The white-pine weevil attacks and kills the leaders of white pines.

A moth causes similar injury to the terminal shoots of the red and Scotch pines.

The elm bark beetles feed in the crotches of the smaller branches of the elm tree and, in doing so, transmit the spores of the destructive Dutch elm disease.

Certain sucking insects, known as chermids, attack the terminal shoots of white pines and frequently cause a marked drooping of the branches or their death.

The buds of several species of pines are subject to attack by tip moths.

The gall-making insects consist for the most part of tiny flies, certain plant lice, small wasps, and some mites. Most of them are relatively unimportant.

The leaf feeders include nearly all types of insects and their close relatives, the mites; the chewing insects destroy the foliage and the sucking insects remove the juices. Some mine the leaves; others work on the surface.

The elm leaf beetle and the Japanese beetle are good examples of the leaf-eating type. They skeletonize the foliage and cause the leaves to turn brown and drop to the ground. Repeated defoliations weaken elms and may cause their death.

Of these two insects, the Japanese beetle is by far the more important economically. Unchecked by its natural enemies and supplied with an abundance of its natural food plants, it soon spread over much of the eastern United States. Serious infestations now occur from Connecticut to North Carolina. The beetles appear during June and remain active until the latter part of August in the vicinity of Washington, D. C. They cause most extensive injury during the first 2 or 3 weeks, when they attack the upper and outer parts of trees and shrubs exposed to sunlight. The beetles also can seriously injure flowers, fruits, vegetables, and the grubs destroy the roots of grass and other plants.

The catalpa worm, or sphinx, is an example of the kind of insect that eats the entire leaf and frequently all the leaves of a tree.

The bagworms attack many kinds of trees. Their favorite host is arborvitae. Their presence can be detected by the cases or bags on the trees.

The locust leaf miner is a small, brownish beetle that deposits its eggs on the leaf surface. The new-hatched larva penetrates the leaf and mines the interior. Severe injury disfigures the leaves and may kill them.

Spider mites and such insects as the aphids, chermids, and scales suck the juices from the foliage of many kinds of shade trees. One leafhopper that feeds on elm leaves has been found to transmit the elm virus disease, which kills the trees more quickly than the Dutch elm disease.

General precautionary measures can do much to prevent such insect damage to shade trees. Some, which do not require the use of chemicals, are aimed at safeguarding the trees from the weakening influences to which they are frequently subjected during and following new construction.

Trees that are being left to provide shade about new residences, after thinnings have been made among the remaining trees, should have their trunks wrapped with burlap or other suitable material to prevent sunscald in hot weather.

Isolated tall trees of small diameter should be anchored by guide wires to keep them from being whipped by the wind.

Trees cut in thinnings made during the fall months should be removed from the property before spring to avoid attracting insects; if they are cut in summer, they should be disposed of at once.

The lower part of the trunks should be boxed to protect the bark from mechanical injury while heavy equipment is being used about the property.

Changes in grade level around trees should be avoided wherever possible. If it is necessary to raise the grade more than about 6 inches, injury to the trees can be reduced by installing a system of tiles and a well about the trunk of each of the trees so that air can reach the roots. (Details are given in Department of Agriculture Farmers' Bulletin No. 1967, *Reducing Damage to Trees From Construction Work.*)

Good drainage away from the building and the trees is needed. In transplanting, one should choose the right time of year to move the particular species. The ball of earth about the roots should be as large as possible. The tree needs plenty of water for a considerable period after it is placed in a new location.

During a drought, all trees should be watered as much as practical.

Sometimes it is wise to apply commercial fertilizer to the soil around trees to help maintain or improve their vigor.

Toxic chemicals, applied to the bark, can often protect trees against insects that attack the main stem and limbs. Such chemical protection is especially desirable where summer homes are built in wooded areas. A chemical like DDT, which acts as a contact insecticide as well as a stomach poison, is suitable. It will help to prevent attack even by many of the insects that are attracted to the trunks of weakened trees.

Applications of DDT in the form of emulsions or wettable powders have prevented attack by many insects that infest the buds and foliage of various kinds of shade trees. However, DDT is not a cure-all, and certain insects, such as bagworms, some of the aphids, scales, and the spider mites, are not readily controlled by this chemical.

Other newer chemicals that have recently appeared on the market and show promise for killing some of these insects and mites are methoxychlor, hexaethyl tetraphosphate, tetraethyl pyrophosphate, and parathion. Methoxychlor is reported to be only slightly toxic, while the other chemicals are regarded as being highly toxic to humans and warm-blooded animals, so considerable care must be taken in handling them. Because of this hazard and until further experimentation has been conducted to determine the tolerance of various plants to these chemicals, they are not recommended at this time for general use.

Several controls are now available. Trees that have become infested by insects despite precautionary measures should be examined carefully to determine whether the trees are dying, whether they should be disposed of so as not to menace the remaining trees, or whether they can be saved by the application of a toxic chemical.

Dying trees—in their bark and wood—usually contain broods of insects that can damage nearby living trees if they are allowed to develop and emerge.

Bark beetles, usually the most important of these insects, can be destroyed either by burning the infested bark or by applying chemicals. It is important that any contemplated control measures be carried out promptly before the insects can mature and emerge, preferably at the first sign of change of color in the foliage.

All types of bark-boring insects can be killed by felling the trees and thoroughly spraying the bark with a solution composed of one part orthodichlorobenzene to six parts of fuel oil. Placing the tree trunks in the sun will help to increase penetration of the spray. The log sections should be turned at least once in order to treat thoroughly the entire bark surface. Care must be taken in applying this spray to avoid getting it on living trees, shrubs, or flowers, as it will injure or kill them. Precautions must be taken also to keep the spray from coming in contact with the skin and especially from reaching the eyes of the operator.

Borers that tunnel the main trunks of shade trees are difficult to control. The method usually employed consists of injecting into the burrow some fumigant, such as carbon bisulfide, and then closing the opening with putty or its equivalent, so as to confine the gas.

If the insect is of the type that works mainly beneath the bark, like the dogwood borer, a mixture of paradichlorobenzene and cottonseed oil daubed on the parts attacked is often effective in killing the insects. A DDT emulsion sprayed on the bark should be beneficial in preventing further attack, and the application of fertilizers and water will increase the vitality while the trees are overcoming the infestation.

Damage to pine trees caused by turpentine beetles can be checked either by cutting out the attacking beetles as soon as the pitch exudations are observed or by injecting carbon bisulfide into their galleries.

Infested terminals of trees attacked by twig borers and twig girdlers should be removed and burned.

A good control for scale insects and mites consists of applying a dormant-strength miscible oil spray in the spring just before new growth begins. These and other sucking insects, like aphids, that are present on the terminal shoots in summer should be sprayed with a contact insecticide, such as an emulsion of nicotine sulfate, soap, white oil.

Damage by tip moths can be checked by spraying the terminal growth of pines with a DDT emulsion or wettable powder. For best results, the spray has to be put on as the eggs hatch.

Many of the leaf feeders are controlled with applications of lead arsenate, which is more effective than DDT in controlling certain insects, such as the bagworm. In general, however, DDT is the more valuable material because it is effective a long time and because it kills insects when they crawl over sprayed surfaces, as well as when they eat it or are touched by it.

Various kinds of spraying equipment are available for applying insecticides to shade trees. The simple 3-gallon type is suitable for spraying a few low trees about a home. Large power sprayers and the new mist blowers are used for treating large trees on residential, city, or park areas.

If an insect outbreak affects the trees over a wide territory, it is best for all concerned to cooperate in planning a control program. United action can reduce the insect population more quickly and more effectively than if each person acts independently. Furthermore, where tall trees are concerned, community action will make practical the use of high-power spraying equipment, such as hydraulic machines or the more modern mist blowers. It is not necessary to go into detail on an important point like this—a point that every home owner appreciates. He knows how difficult and costly it is to replace trees that have died, how precious are his shade trees, how close his friendship with them can become—quite beyond measurement in dollars and cents. But if such a measure is needed, we have one by J. A. Hyslop, formerly of the Department of Agriculture. He has estimated that the losses due to insects in shade trees total 87 million dollars a year in the United States. Home owners, alone and together, can stop the insects.

R. A. St. George *is an entomologist in the Bureau of Entomology and Plant Quarantine, and is stationed at the Agricultural Research Center at Beltsville. He is a graduate of the Massachusetts Agricultural College and George Washington University. He has been associated with the Division of Forest Insect Investigations since 1918 and has specialized in research problems concerning insects that affect forest and shade trees.*

# FORESTS AND MEN

*A juniper centuries old: "A man does not plant a tree for himself, he plants it for posterity."*

# Trees Living Together

## THE COMMUNITY OF TREES

JESSE H. BUELL

AS ONE gets farther and farther beyond the centers of population he comes finally to the forests that human activities have not changed—to virgin forests. In them, one can see better what man has done to forests and how he can more wisely mold them to his benefit. In these manless forests, also, a person comes to understand that a forest is a changing, living community, subject always to the forces of inanimate nature—earth, air, sunshine, and rain; to the interaction within them of plants and the animals; to the changes that forests themselves can effect in their environment.

Green plants are the engines for the manufacture of the carbohydrates—the basic stuff that all vegetable matter comes from, all animals live on, and by which, ultimately, all of us are fed, clothed, sheltered, and kept warm. A forest is a vast battery of such engines. In a single growing season an acre well stocked with vigorous trees may produce 3 or 4 tons of useful wood, not counting the additional unmeasured pounds of the new growth on branches and roots and in leaves, buds, flowers, and seeds. The raw materials are carbon dioxide from the air, water and mineral nutrients from the soil, and warmth and energy from the sun. Of these, only water and warmth are likely anywhere on earth to be too scarce for forest growth. Carbon dioxide makes up only 3 parts in 10,000 parts of the atmosphere, but unlimited fresh supplies are continually brought by air currents. Mineral nutrients, although indispensable, are needed in such small quantities—they make up only a small fraction of the dry weight of trees—that they are abundant enough almost everywhere to keep forests growing.

But forests use up vast quantities of water. To make a summer's growth, the roots of the acre of healthy forest that grew 3 or 4 tons of wood may take up from the soil 4,000 tons of water. Much of this water, passing up from the roots through the trunk, branches, and leaves, escapes into the surround-

*The drawing at the top of the page is of a scene among the redwoods in California.*

ing air. Its chief usefulness to the tree is to carry nutrients from the soil and organic materials from storage places in the trunk and roots to the leaves and the growing twigs. Although the water that is transpired into the air never goes into the building of woody tissue or leaves, trees cannot live without it. Such quantities are required that the climate over large areas of the earth is too dry to supply them.

And the circumpolar regions are too cold for tree growth. No plant can thrive where monthly mean temperatures are below freezing the year around. Just a few days in midsummer, warm enough to melt the snow and thaw out the soil to a depth of an inch or two, may bring into bloom tiny alpine plants on the bleak north shore of Greenland within 350 miles of the Pole. But so short a growing season would give a tree no chance to store up food for another season's burst of growth and it could not withstand the intense cold of the arctic winter.

So it was that before man began to use the forests their distribution over the continents was determined by the climatic pattern of the earth. Drought and cold are the barriers that limit tree growth, but the effect of each depends upon the other. It is the combination of temperature and rainfall that counts: A rainfall sufficient for vigorous tree growth in the Temperate Zone, to give an instance, might be inadequate in the Tropics, where water evaporates more rapidly from the soil and plants transpire faster, and would be useless in the polar regions, where temperatures are below freezing most of the time.

In general, forests occur only where the annual precipitation is more than 15 or 20 inches a year and where the frost-free period is at least 14 or 16 weeks long. In regions too dry for forests, grasses grow or they give way to desert; where it is too cold, tundras and icefields spread. The broad forest zones of the earth are the coniferous forests that stretch around the world above about 45° north latitude, follow the mountains farther south, and (in North America) extend down the Pacific coast and then reappear in the southeastern United States; the broadleaf, Temperate Zone forests of eastern North America, western Europe, and eastern Asia; the scrub or woodland forests that border the desert areas of all the continents; and the tropical forests of Africa and South America.

We in the United States are fortunate in our present and past climates, for they have given us the richest and most varied forests to be found anywhere in the Temperate Zones. In Maine or Michigan the forests are spruce and fir. In the South they are longleaf and loblolly pines; in between they are birch, maple, white pine, and hemlock toward the north, and oaks, hickory, and yellow-poplar toward the south. In parts of California are giant redwoods; in other parts are scrub chapparal and woodland that border dry lands where cacti are as big as trees; they, in turn, give way to deserts where almost nothing grows. West of the Cascade Mountains in Oregon and Washington are Douglas-fir forests; eastward to the far edge of the Rockies are ponderosa and lodgepole pines where the rainfall is sufficient, with spruce and fir showing up in the places where the mountains go high enough to reach the alpine cold. In the wide belt stretching from the base of the Rockies toward the Mississippi, the only trees you will find are cottonwoods and willows along the creeks or planted shelterbelts around the farms, for this is the great domain of the grasses. Within the broad pattern there are innumerable variations.

But neither the broad pattern nor the local variations are standing still.

In the first place, climates are continually shifting. Geological revolutions, such as inundations, mountain uprisings, and ice ages, can profoundly alter weather and vegetation. We do not need to go into details, but one example is especially interesting. When the icecap moved slowly down from the polar regions, Temperate Zone trees, which at one time grew almost to the Pole itself, migrated southward ahead of the freezing weather. In Europe the trees finally came to the Alps, which made an east-to-west barrier directly across their path. The climate of the mountains was already cold, and, because none of the scattering seeds lodged where they could grow, many species disappeared; only a few were left to repopulate the land when the glacier receded. Today Europe has only a few native kinds of trees. In our country, the mountains run north and south, and none lay in the way of the trees that were retreating before the ice. Consequently a rich variety survived the ice age and gave us our present wealth of species.

The second source of change is the forest itself. It is a living community of trees; through its own internal workings it is constantly adjusting itself. Within the community, plants and animals live, grow old, and die; sometimes they help their own kind to inherit their places; more often they hinder them from doing so; always, however, they alter the environment, and, through that alteration, change the forest itself.

On any tract of land, these continuing adjustments bring about a natural development of the vegetation that resembles the evolutionary development of an animal or plant. Early plant communities give way to more advanced forms in a succession of infancy, youth, and maturity that, while the climate stays unchanged, is regular and predictable. These regular and predictable changes are of utmost importance: We can modify them by the way we treat the forest; we can speed up natural succession or delay it, depending on the kind of forest most useful to us.

Let us, then, take a closer look at natural forest succession, and consider ways in which we can modify it.

Every forest area began once as a stretch of bare rock or of water. If it was a lake, algae and other floating plants first appeared. As they died and sank they made the lake more shallow, and plants could grow that must have their roots in the bottom and their leaves above the water. The remains of these in time built the land still higher, making the area less suitable for floating and rooting acquatic plants and more favorable for land plants. These, in turn, took over and helped to build up the ground with decaying leaves and stems and to dry it out by transpiring quantities of water. Herbs gave way to bushes and they to forests, because climate was favorable.

If the forest area began as bare rock, lichens first got a toehold in the crevices that could catch a few drops of moisture. Gradually, as one generation after another added its substance to the fragments of rock broken away by weathering or the corrosive action of the lichen juices, a thin layer of soil was built up in which mosses could take root and the process continued. As each type of plant spread its shade and added more humus, the air near the ground was made cooler so that evaporation was lessened, and the soil became more spongy and could hold more rain water. The soil deepened and got more moist, the shade increased, and new plants were favored over those already there. Finally again, because the climate permitted, a forest resulted.

None of us in his lifetime can see all these stages over a single area. The whole process may take hundreds or thousands of years, and some of the steps may change so slowly that they seem interminable. But in one spot we can find lichens helping the slow disintegration of rock, in another polypody ferns growing on soil so thinly spread over a ledge that they dry to tinder during drought, and in another blueberry bushes where the soil is a few inches deep. Elsewhere we can find pitch pines and scrub oaks in dry situations and a forest of maple and beech in a deep, moist cove. By going from one place to another we can picture the slow process of succession.

Or, in a favorable situation, it may be moving so fast that we can apprehend its progress in a few years. Take an abandoned farm in southern Connecticut. The summer after cultivation stops, tall weeds grow in the fields. Next year, there may be a little grass beneath the weeds, and blackberry seedlings will have started. At the end of 5 years, the field will be a tangle of briars. Here and there clumps of gray birch will have started from seed blown in by the wind, and junipers will be dotted about where birds have lighted and have gotten rid of the seeds of the juniper berries they have been eating. In 10 years, the old field is a young forest of birch and juniper higher than your head; in 20 years, oaks and maples will be coming in in the shade; in 40, the birches will be dying out, some of the oaks that got an early start will be crowding the junipers, and the place will begin to look like the wood lot that never was plowed.

Meanwhile, around the edges of the millpond down the slope, the pickerelweed and waterlilies will have grown farther and farther out into the water. The shore line will have been pushed out with a tangle of buttonbushes, and at the upper end of the pond, where 40 years ago one could push a rowboat, there may be a forest of red maples with oaks coming in along the drier edges.

Both in the old field and the millpond, as in all vegetational succession, progress is toward median moisture. Dry areas become less dry, and the wet areas less wet.

The important lesson to be gained from a study of natural plant succession is that, wherever the climate is suitable for forests, the trend is toward them. Fire may destroy them, insects or diseases decimate them, or winds blow them down; but, given time, they will build back again. Furthermore, once the process of succession is understood for a region, the steps can be predicted. The trend is not only toward a forest but toward a particular type of forests, the forest that can use most efficiently the rainfall and the temperatures that prevail. It will be made up of trees whose seedlings can grow in the shade of their parents. Such a forest perpetuates itself. It is the climax, and does not change unless the climate changes or it is disturbed.

Of all the disturbers of forests, man is first. Because trees grow in climates comfortable for him and favorable to agriculture, he has destroyed them to make room for his cities and his farms. He has needed wood, and to satisfy that need has used up or cut into forests on vast acreages of land that he did not intend to use for anything else. When the first settlers came to this country there were 1,072 million acres of forests within the 1,905-odd million acres that now make up the United States. Only 624 million acres remain; of them, only 45 million are at all comparable to the original forests. The forest land most suitable for farming has already been cleared. The trend is now the other way; large areas once farmed have been abandoned.

Forestry is the handling of forest lands to satisfy the needs of man, just as farming is the management of farm lands to serve his purposes. As agriculture is the science underlying farming, so silviculture underlies forestry. Both deal with plants. The basis of both is botany. Their difference is of degree rather than kind.

Forestry generally sticks closer to nature than farming does, following the natural progress of plant succession almost exactly if the kinds of trees in the climax forest furnish the most useful wood products. The farmer had to get rid of the original forest and often felled the trees and burned them. The crops he raises are different from the climax forest. Trees cut in the virgin forest are themselves the first crop in forestry, and the successive crops are much like the one that grew naturally.

In farming, new crops are started by plowing and planting seed. That is not often done in forestry. Instead, natural seeding from trees left standing is depended upon. When small trees grown in nurseries are planted in forests, it is usually to correct some mistake in land management, such as the clearing for farms of land not suitable for farming or the accidental burning over of forests; or it is done to alter drastically the type of forest that grew naturally.

Agriculture tends the growing crop by tilling the ground to reduce the competition of weeds. In forestry, tillage is almost never used except during the earliest stages when trees are raised in nurseries and planted in the forest. Rather, the weed trees are cut. Sometimes they can be used. The weeds a farmer pulls are rarely useful.

Agricultural crops are mostly annual; the forest crops, almost never. In agriculture, one crop is removed with comparatively little thought of the one to follow. In forestry, there is emphatic need to consider the next crop. It is the chief duty of silviculture to devise methods for harvesting forests in such a way that a new crop will be assured—so that plenty of seed of the wanted species will be shed on the ground and conditions will be right for their germination and the growth of the seedlings.

The tools of silviculture are the ax and fire-fighting equipment—the ax to modify natural succession to man's needs, and the fire-fighting equipment to keep forest fires in their places.

In order to understand more intimately what silviculture is and to get its relation to natural forest succession clearer, let us go back to the community of trees. And to make it easier let us consider specific forests.

First, a tract of loblolly pine in the Carolina Piedmont. A great deal of loblolly pine grows in this region, but we have evidence that it is not the climax forest. Loblolly is intolerant of shade, and the new seedlings cannot grow beneath the old trees, which change the environment by shading the ground and by adding moisture-holding humus to it. Shady, cool, moist, humus-covered ground is a hard place for loblolly seedlings to get started. Those conditions favor the shade-enduring hardwoods, oaks, gums, and hickories. A little study of surrounding areas will show that loblolly is a pioneer species on abandoned fields and burned-over areas. Its seeds are light and winged, and mature trees can seed large areas in a single season. Consequently all trees in a stand of loblolly are likely to be about the same age. These facts indicate that loblolly forests are the result of disturbances in the natural succession. Further proof comes from the forests along the creeks where fields have never been cultivated and where fires burn less readily. These forests are hardwoods.

Hardwoods are evidently the climax type in the Carolina Piedmont, or at any rate they are a higher stage in succession than loblolly pine. But hardwoods are not what we want to grow there. Pine is better suited to a greater number of products than hardwood, and it grows faster. So the job of silviculture is to devise a method of harvesting our tract of loblolly to get another crop of the same species started.

That can be done by clear cutting the stand except for the trees necessary to produce the seed for the next crop. Clear cutting will lay the ground open to the hot sun. It will dry out. Much of the moisture-holding humus will disappear and again conditions favorable to pine seedlings will prevail. It is true that to perpetuate loblolly pine we must push nature backward a step. But consider how much further back we would go to raise a crop of tobacco: To do that, every vestige of natural growth would be removed first and later kept out by tillage.

Another example: An acreage of northern hardwoods in Michigan—the sugar maple, yellow birch, beech. Seedlings of those species can grow in the shade cast by their parents, and all ages of trees, from seedlings to veterans, grow together. Remnants of the original forests evidently undisturbed for many tree generations are of this type. We must suppose that northern hardwoods are one of the climaxes here and that the forest would perpetuate itself if it were left undisturbed.

The problem of silviculture in this case is to harvest the crop with as little disturbance as possible. The procedure is therefore to imitate the way individual trees die in the natural forest and cut a mature tree here and there.

To round out the picture, consider land that has been abandoned for agriculture in an area once covered with forests. Eventually this land will revert to forests. But if there are no seed trees nearby of pioneer species that can start on dry, shadeless land, it may take a thousand years. Natural succession can be hurried along by planting such abandoned fields to pine.

All of these examples are oversimplified. But more details of silvicultural methods are given in later articles.

Real simplification of silviculture can come only with more knowledge of how forest communities behave. The very richness of the forests in these United States multiplies the problems of the silviculturist. For many forest associations, we know little about natural succession; for some, we can only guess at the climax type toward which the association tends. So much of our original forests has been destroyed or cut over that it is hard or impossible to find undisturbed areas of many types. Belatedly we are establishing, on the national forests and elsewhere, natural areas in the few remaining virgin-forest communities. These areas are to be protected from all cutting and other artificial alterations so that we can learn from them the nature of our climax or near-climax forests.

Most bothersome of unsolved silvicultural problems are those that deal with the effects of modifications that must necessarily be made when the tree crops are harvested. To work in the direction of natural succession is usually easy and inexpensive. To work against it is harder and may be costly. For instance: Will it be possible continuously to keep back the hardwoods in the Carolina Piedmont and raise pine without eventually having to fertilize the soil artificially? Can we manage to tolerate just enough of the soil-enriching hardwoods without letting them get the upper hand? Or will we have to go to the expense of plowing and planting trees if we insist on raising pine? Such questions probe deeply into the underlying laws of ecology.

We seek ever the best balance between the ways of nature and our wants. To make the forests yield useful products while maintaining and improving their natural vigor requires continuous, painstaking research.

Foresters must be forward-looking. A single tree crop may require 200 years to mature. But the single crop is not the only concern; there must be provision for successions of them. Furthermore, we cannot wait a century or two between harvests. Things must be arranged so that some trees can be harvested each year or every few years. That requires foresight and planning, and leads to another branch of forestry—forest regulation.

The basic rule of forest regulation is to cut each year a volume of timber no greater than the volume that grew during the year. If the layers of wood added to the trees on an acre of northern hardwood forest in Michigan total, say, 250 board feet each year, then trees with a volume of 250 board feet or less can be removed from the acre annually without reducing the growth capacity of the forest. Thus yield can be sustained indefinitely.

But sustained yield of our forests depends on more than making plans. It depends on how well we are able to work with nature and get her to work with us. Wherever this cooperation is attained, communities of men and communities of trees are in harmony.

Jesse H. Buell *is assistant chief of the Division of Forest Management Research in the Forest Service. He was formerly engaged in research in silviculture at the Southeastern Forest Experiment Station.*

# FOREST TYPES OF THE UNITED STATES

WILLIAM A. DAYTON

Because of the size of the United States, the diversity of its conditions, and the wealth of its vegetation (we have about four times as many tree species as does Europe) and because of differences in terminology and of opinions on classification, climaxes, and such, it is not surprising that ideas about the forest types of the United States are still somewhat controversial.

Dr. James Graham Cooper (1830–1902), Army surgeon, explorer, and naturalist, seems to have been the first to publish a vegetative-type map of North America. It appeared in 1859 in his paper *On the Distribution of the Forests and Trees of North America, with Notes on its Physical Geography.* Overleaf is reproduced the United States part of Dr. Cooper's map; the original letters for his regions are retained, but hachures have been added to make their differentiation clearer to the eye. It will be observed that four of Dr. Cooper's regions are in the Eastern seaboard, three are in the Appalachians, six are in the Plains States, five are in the Rocky Mountain areas, three are in the Intermountain area, and two on the Pacific coast. Most of them are forested areas, at least in part.

Dr. Cooper was a link between ancient students of the subject and the modern investigators, who have added a great deal to our ken of botany.

Theophrastus of Eresus (372–287 B. C.) by the will of Aristotle became heir to the great philosopher's celebrated library, guardian of his children, and his successor as head of the Lyceum at Athens. Theophrastus has been called "primus verorum botanicorum"—the first real botanist. He was perhaps the first to emphasize the relation of trees and other plants to their environment, and may rightly be regarded as the father of the concepts of ecological and vegetative types.

Nearly two centuries ago, Linnaeus, in his *Philosophia Botanica,* had a chapter on plant distribution correlated with the geographic regions, climate, soils, and the other factors of habitat.

Henry Solon Graves, who published *Practical Forestry in the Adirondacks* in 1899, is generally credited with the introduction of the term "forest type" in this country. The late Dr. Frederic E. Clements, a distinguished ecologist and author of *Plant Formations and Forest Types,* published in 1909, calls Professor Graves' types "plant (or forest) formations." He separates formations into associations, associations into societies, societies into communities (with two or more principal or secondary species), and communities into families (defined as groups of cospecific individuals).

The Ecological Society of America tentatively suggested this definition of "forest types" in 1934: "A forest stand essentially similar throughout its extent as regards composition and development under essentially similar conditions, i. e., essentially similar throughout as regards floristic composition, physiognomy, and ecological structure."

Ten years later the Committee on Forestry Terminology of the Society of American Foresters defined forest type thus: "A descriptive term used to group stands of similar character as regards composition and development due to certain ecological factors, by which they may be differentiated from other groups of stands. The term suggests repetition of the same character under similar conditions. A type is *temporary* if its character is due to passing influences such as logging or fire; *permanent* if no appreciable change is expected and the character is due to ecological factors alone; *climax* if it is the ultimate stage of a succession of temporary types. A *cover*

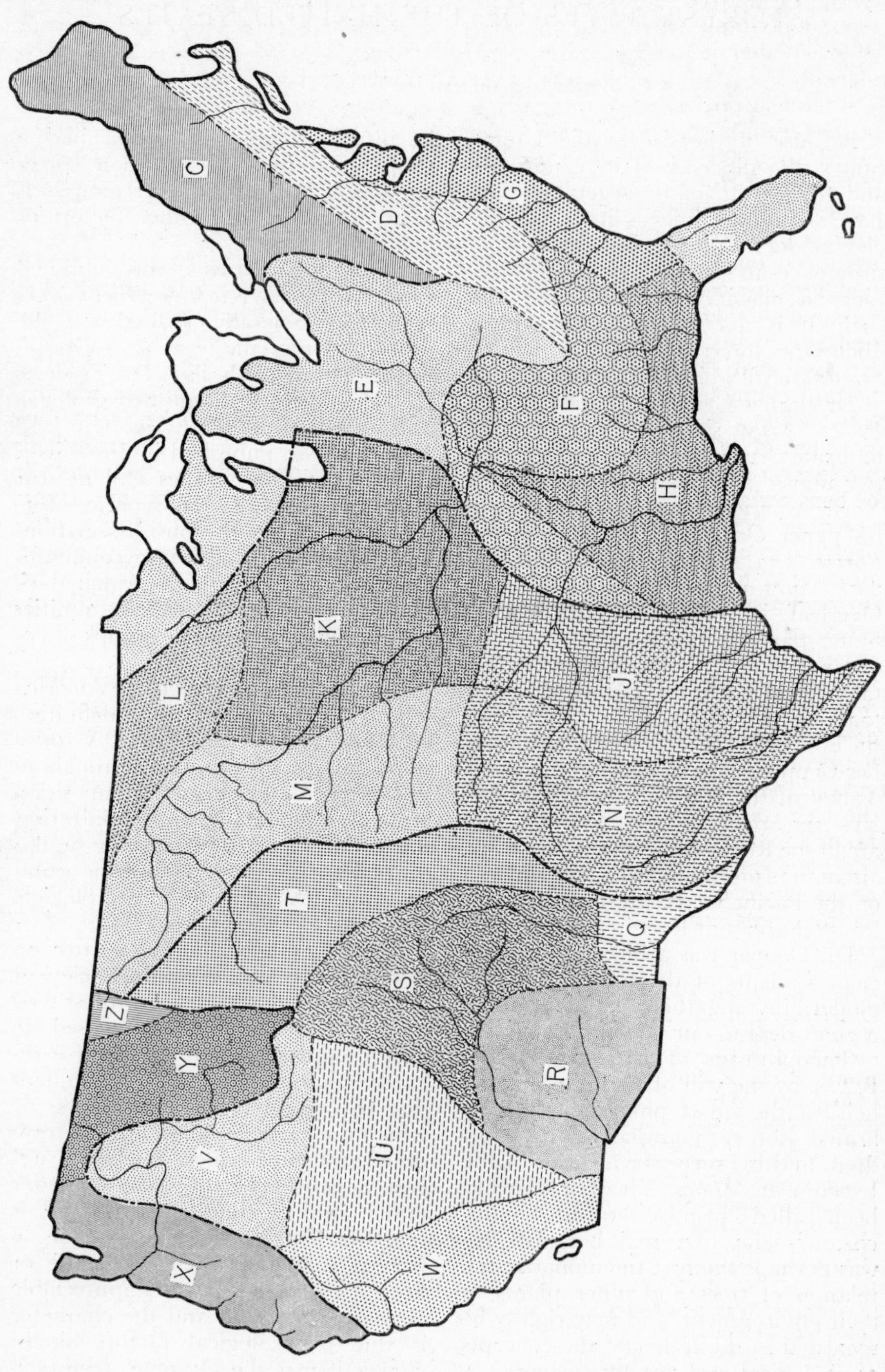
C
D
G
I
E
F
H
K
J
L
M
N
T
Q
S
R
Z
Y
V
U
X
W

type is a forest type now occupying the ground, no implication being conveyed as to whether it is temporary or permanent."

Raphael Zon, in *Principles Involved in Determining Forest Types*, published in 1906, emphasizes the importance of forest types in silvical studies of individual species, and sets forth a philosophy basic to determining forest types. The main considerations are physical conditions of climate, soil, and the like; man and his operations; accidents, such as fire and wind. He says that "one of the most important characteristics of a forest type is its *stability,* its resistance to invasion by other forms," and adds that the reproduction of the forest must always be considered.

Arthur W. Sampson (*The Stability of Aspen as a Type,* 1916) believes that aspen is a temporary type, replaced, slowly but surely, by conifers.

Carlos G. Bates, in *Forest Types in the Central Rocky Mountains as Affected by Climate and Soil,* 1924, states that, in a general way, the forest zones of that region correspond with air-temperature zones. He adds that a review of the facts leaves little doubt that the tree species of the central Rocky Mountains are controlled in their distribution almost wholly by the degree of insolation of the site, with the resultant temperatures, and by the closely related surface conditions of moisture.

A distinguished Finnish forester and ecologist, Aimo K. Cajander, places forest typification on a combined ecological and biological basis (*The Theory of Forest Types,* English translation revised by Mr. M. L. Anderson, 1926). He recognizes two kinds, in principle, of forest classification, according to quality and site. He says: "The features of a plant association are generally determined by those species which are present in the greatest abundance and frequency. Those species, however, which are present at a lesser rate of abundance, but are, nevertheless, always or nearly always present, are also, of course, equally characteristic of the association. Finally those species, which, though they may be more or less rare, are met with, however, almost exclusively in the association in question, are also characteristic of that association. On the other hand, of course, the absence of certain plant species is also a very important feature in the delineation of a plant association, although the definite establishment of absence is more difficult."

Arthur Freiherr von Kruedener, who published *Waldtypen—Klassifikation und ihre volkswirtschaftlich Bedeutung* in 1927, based scientific classification of forest types on three factors: Climate, soil, and plant associates: "Was wir unter Waldtypen verstehen, sowie von den Faktoren—Klima, Boden-Untergrund und Pflanzengemeinschaft, welche drei in ihrer Verbindung uns erst den Begriff des Waldtyps geben."

Gustaf A. Pearson, in *Forest Types in the Southwest as Determined by Climate and Soil,* 1931, distinguishes seven broad zones with four forest types: Woodland, ponderosa ("western yellow") pine, Douglas-fir, and Engelmann spruce. The soil differences, he says, appear to be due more to physical than to chemical differences, the more porous soils being best suited to tree growth, the upper altitudinal range determined by ability to withstand low temperatures and the

**◄ Adapted from Dr. James G. Cooper's *Distribution of the Forests and Trees of North America* (1859). The letters indicate: C, Lacustrine Province (Canadian Region); D, E, F, G, Apalachian Province (Alleghany, Ohio, Tennessean, Carolinian Regions, respectively); H, Mississippian Region; I, Floridian Region (part of West Indian Province); J, K, L, M, N, Campestrian Province: (1) Prairies, J (Texan Region), K (Illinois Region), L (Saskatchewan Region), (2) Arid Plains, M (Dacotah Region), N (Comanche Region); Q, Mexican Province (Chihuahian Region); R, S, T, U, V, Rocky Mountain Province (Arizonian, Wasatch, Padoucan, Utah, and Shoshone Regions, respectively); W, X, Y, Z, Nevadian Province (Californian, Oregonian, Kootanic, and Yukon Regions, respectively).**

lower altitudinal range to drought endurance. The soil, except locally, rarely acts as a limiting factor. He does not regard light as a limiting factor in the range of trees, but it may affect the composition of stands.

Marinus Westveld (*Type Definitions Based on Statistics of Stand Composition,* 1934) gives type definitions of the red spruce-yellow birch (with yellow birch subtype) as well as the red spruce-sugar maple-beech (with sugar maple subtype) types. In the red spruce-yellow birch type, the conifers usually make up more than 40 percent of the stand, with spruce and the balsam fir in about equal numbers, the yellow birch composing between 25 and 50 percent, and sugar maple seldom more than 5 percent of the total stand. In the red spruce-sugar maple-beech type, the conifers make up 25 to 45 percent of the stand, spruce usually being more abundant than fir. Sugar maples generally make up more than 10 percent of the stand and, combined with beech, usually considerably exceed the yellow birch in number.

Again, in the field of forest classification systems and their terminology, there is a large literature and differences in viewpoint.

The eminent German forester Heinrich von Cotta in 1804 listed forest lands in 100 quality classes, "0" being absolutely barren land incapable of producing wood of any sort, and "100," the best imaginable land.

W. Schütze, who wrote *Beziehungen zwischen chemischer Zusammensetzung und Ertragsfähigkeit des Waldbodens* in 1871, classified six areas of German forest land on the basis of determining in a surface layer 5¾ feet deep the percentage of mineral matter soluble in hydrochloric acid. This is a refinement in the methodology of forest typification which obviously it has not been practical to utilize in this country on any large scale.

The late John W. Harshberger, in his *Phytogeographic Survey of North America,* 1913, divides the part of North America lying within the United States into two zones, temperate and subtropical. These zones, so far as forests are concerned, are again divided into 9 regions, 24 districts, and 16 areas. Under these forest areas, forest and other plant formations are recognized.

Jesse B. Mowry (*The Nature and Development of Forest Types,* 1920) recognizes two classifications of the term "forest type": Where type means (1) locality, and (2) composition. He believes that, for the present at least, forest types should be designated by terms indicating both concepts. He emphasizes the importance of moisture in tree growth, their tissues consisting of from 65 to 95 percent of water, and quotes Ebermeyer to the effect that conifers require less potash, lime, and phosphate than do deciduous trees.

Although published a quarter of a century ago, still the best available map of the vegetation of the United States is that by Homer L. Shantz and Raphael Zon (*Natural Vegetation,* Section E, *Atlas of American Agriculture,* U. S. Department of Agriculture, Bureau of Agricultural Economics, Part I—*The Physical Basis of Agriculture,* 29 pages, Washington. 1924). This map is reproduced on the next page, on a smaller scale and with hatching replacing the original colors. It will be observed that the forested and woodland areas are classified in it under 18 divisions.

A booklet of the Forest Service, *Instructions for Making Timber Surveys in the National Forests,* 1925, has a chapter, "Standard Classification of Forest Types," covering 7 treeless land types and 52 woodland and forest-land types.

The Committee on Forest Types of the Society of American Foresters in 1940 recognized and defined 97 forest types in the eastern United States. "Eastern United States" is interpreted to include "the eastern forests which are separated from the western forests by a broad zone of relatively treeless or desert country. The territory covered by the committee extends in some places to the westward of the eastern

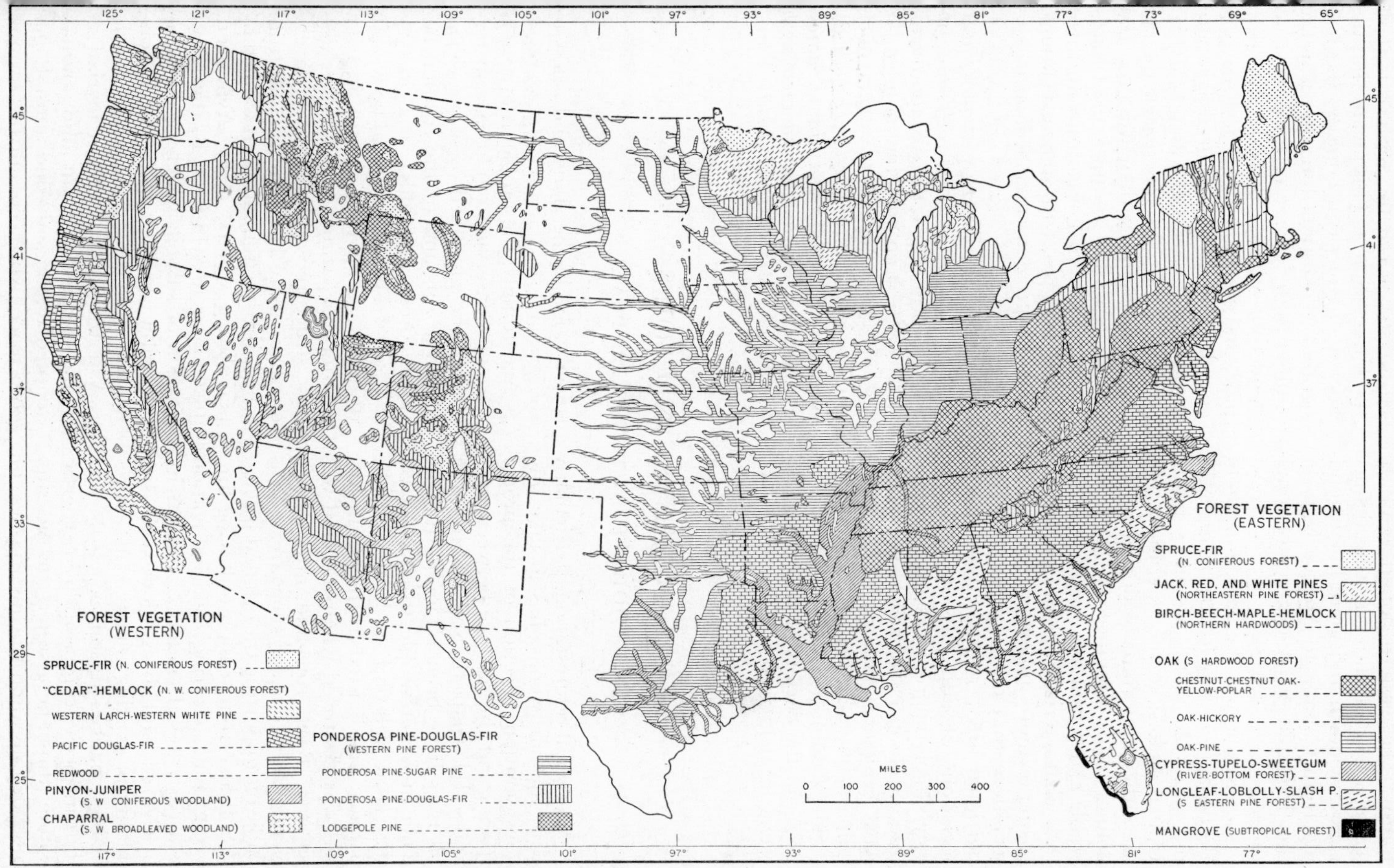
FOREST VEGETATION (WESTERN)
SPRUCE-FIR (N. CONIFEROUS FOREST)
"CEDAR"-HEMLOCK (N. W. CONIFEROUS FOREST)
WESTERN LARCH-WESTERN WHITE PINE
PACIFIC DOUGLAS-FIR
REDWOOD
PINYON-JUNIPER (S. W CONIFEROUS WOODLAND)
CHAPARRAL (S. W BROADLEAVED WOODLAND)
PONDEROSA PINE-DOUGLAS-FIR (WESTERN PINE FOREST)
PONDEROSA PINE-SUGAR PINE
PONDEROSA PINE-DOUGLAS-FIR
LODGEPOLE PINE
MILES
0 100 200 300 400
FOREST VEGETATION (EASTERN)
SPRUCE-FIR (N. CONIFEROUS FOREST)
JACK, RED, AND WHITE PINES (NORTHEASTERN PINE FOREST)
BIRCH-BEECH-MAPLE-HEMLOCK (NORTHERN HARDWOODS)
OAK (S HARDWOOD FOREST)
CHESTNUT-CHESTNUT OAK-YELLOW-POPLAR
OAK-HICKORY
OAK-PINE
CYPRESS-TUPELO-SWEETGUM (RIVER-BOTTOM FOREST)
LONGLEAF-LOBLOLLY-SLASH P. (S EASTERN PINE FOREST)
MANGROVE (SUBTROPICAL FOREST)

802062°—49——9

forests. The western boundary of the 'eastern United States' as thus defined is a wavy north and south line extending from Canada to Mexico between the 97th and 101st degrees of longitude."

Lee R. Dice, in the book *The Biotic Provinces of North America,* 1943, recognizes 20 biotic provinces in the United States, in 17 of which trees are either important or dominant. He defines biotic province as "a considerable and continuous geographic area . . . characterized by the occurrence of one or more important ecologic associations that differ, at least in proportional area covered, from the associations of adjacent provinces. In general, biotic provinces are characterized also by peculiarities of vegetation type, ecological climax, flora, fauna, climate, physiography, and soil."

The Committee on Western Forest Types of the Society of American Foresters in 1945 recognized and defined 50 forest types in the western part of the United States. This means that the Society of American Foresters has recognized 147 distinct forest types in the United States. Some of these, such as ponderosa pine, redwood, lodgepole pine, and Engelmann spruce, may occupy large areas in pure or almost pure stands. Most of the types, however, are mixed. In general, eastern types are more complex than western, and conifer types less complex than hardwood forests. In going from north to south, the types, with some exceptions, tend to a greater number of species.

WILLIAM A. DAYTON *is in charge of dendrology and range-forage investigations of the United States Forest Service. He is probably best known for his publications on native range plants and is joint editor, with Harlan P. Kelsey, of Standardized Plant Names. Mr. Dayton has been connected with the Forest Service since 1911.*

# FORESTS AND SOILS

JOHN T. AUTEN, T. B. PLAIR

Successful reforestation, particularly with the hardwoods, has to take into consideration selection of the proper species and the balance between trees and soil. Perhaps the soil has eroded or all trees have been removed from it: Then it is not simple to choose trees that grow well on bare land; also, the balance that existed in the virgin forests was destroyed when the land was cleared. Basic soil and atmospheric changes often make such areas incapable of supporting the original species.

Soil loss from erosion following fire, overgrazing, clearing, and cultivation is a basic loss. It reduces productivity of cleared land; it also lowers the site quality in existing forests. Any appreciable change in soil necessitates a shift in species composition in order to obtain those best suited to the site. Site deterioration means species of lower value in the stand and a loss to the owner.

Accordingly, the problems of restoring and conserving our trees and forests will be simplified by a knowledge of forest soils and of the relation between forests and soils.

A soil is a natural mineral body with distinct features that identify it, even in widely separated areas. It has definite structure with horizons or layers, one over the other. The topsoil, from which the fine soil has been washed by percolating waters, is the A horizon. Just under it is horizon B, the heavy horizon or subsoil, which receives the fine soil washed out of A. The C horizon is the parent soil material below B.

A fertile soil contains a myriad of living organisms, plant and animal, adapted to the soil conditions. It has pore space, which contains water and air. To some degree, like a living body, it absorbs oxygen and releases carbon dioxide. A soil has characteristic parts in harmony with its environment. Its productivity depends on all of its parts.

The formation of a soil, a slow process, doubtless began on the first crust of the earth, when heating and cooling and wetting and drying cracked the surface rocks, made little patches of loose rubble, and caused little pockets of mineral crystals to settle in crannies and depressions, and allowed lichens, mosses, and other simple plants to grow in the thin soil and on porous rocks. Rain dissolved the softer parts of the rocks and made soluble minerals available to plant roots.

As the soil mantle grew deeper, the soil grains became finer. Water percolated through the soil mass, carried fine particles from the surface layer downward, and deposited them at lower depths to form subsoil. Plant debris fell on the surface and the micro-organic life appeared. Larger and more complex plants appeared until finally trees and forests, as we know them today, emerged with their characteristic soils.

Each forest soil developed its orderly arrangement of horizons, its porous and absorptive structure, and its balanced and active population of bacteria, molds, fungi, worms, insects, and animals. Roots of the trees anchored the soil in place; the leaves provided a protective cover of litter and added fertility yearly.

Soils differ broadly among climatic provinces. Basic differences occur because rainfall, temperature, and rocks are different. Any part of the earth having a characteristic climate and parent-rock material has its special kinds of soil: The gray, desert sagebrush soils of southern Wyoming; the subhumid, chestnut-colored prairie soils of western Nebraska; the black, tall-grass prairie soils of Iowa and Illinois; the gray-brown, hardwood-covered soils of Indiana and Illinois; the gray, leached, pine-covered podzol soils of Maine; and the rich-brown, humid, forest soils of the Northwest.

Even within a climatic province, many differences occur among soils, chiefly because of differences in vegetation, degree of slope, and the nature of the parent rock. Vegetation alters the surface of soils, but the primary local difference is permeability of the soil to water. Permeability is altered according to changes in coarseness of the soil and is controlled largely by the nature of parent rocks and by the subsoil density associated with topography. A basic factor in soil formation is the relation of topography to subsoil.

Rain falling anywhere on bare soil puddles it with muddy water. Such muddy water contains colloidal soil—exceedingly small soil particles, some of them almost molecular in size. If the soil surface is sloping, much of the muddy water runs off. If the surface is flat, much of the water seeps into the lower soil, where the colloidal particles are deposited, forming a part of the B horizon. This horizon forms in the lower soil at depths usually ranging from 8 up to 36 inches, depending on height of the water table during the formative period. The thickness of this zone depends on the rate of internal drainage and fluctuation of the water table during the rainy season. Density of the B horizon is affected by the flatness of the terrain. In general, the flatter the terrain the denser the B horizon. This horizon—sometimes called the subsoil, or where very dense, a claypan—is the key to drainage.

Soils in any one area are affected by differences in parent-rock material. Coarse sands from sandstone do not puddle as much as clay from shales; hence subsoil formation is less pronounced in sandstone- than in shale-derived soils. Differences in the rock composition do not alter the basic soil-forming process, but do affect the rate of soil formation.

Soils affect the trees principally through soil air and soil moisture. Seasonal available soil moisture commonly determines what species grow in any forest and their rate of growth.

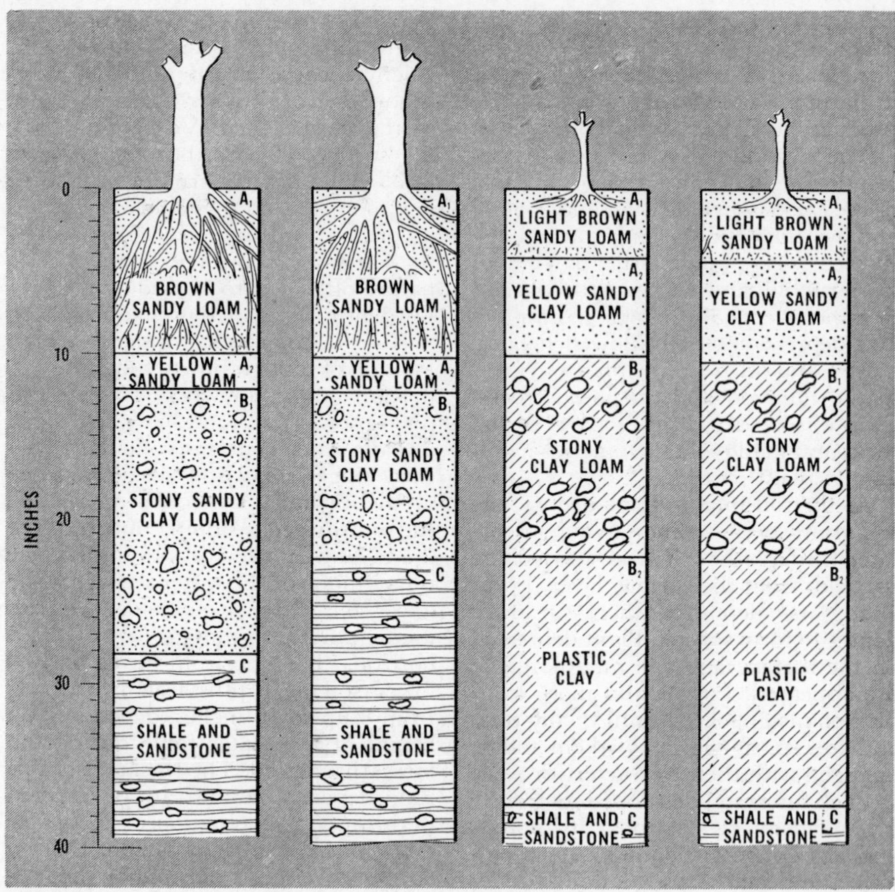


**Graphic relation between equal-aged yellow-poplar and subsoil in the same planting.**

Soils affect forests much as soils affect any other crop. Dry soils in the hardwood belt are likely to have dry-site oaks, like scrub oak, blackjack, and scarlet oak. Moist soils support such species as yellow-poplar, beech, maple, black walnut, and red and white oaks. Wet soils are more favorable for sycamore, cottonwood, redgum, pin oak, and willow.

Four general soil conditions influence forests through their effects on available soil moisture: Surface porosity, subsoil density, aspect, and depth. The first affects rate of water absorption; the second, free movement of water in the soil; the third, surface evaporation rate; and the fourth, the volume of water available. Surface porosity is an ever-present and indispensable attribute of the forest soils. A forest soil always develops porosity under a protective litter cover. This porous surface facilitates absorption.

Water movement is governed by subsoil density: The denser the subsoil, the slower the movement of water through it. Furthermore, the shallower the A horizon above a tight subsoil, the less rainfall the soil absorbs because of the smaller volume of porous surface soil.

Aspect and exposure influence available soil moisture by affecting the rate of evaporation. South- and west-facing slopes normally have less soil moisture than north and east. In hilly or mountainous country, the quantity of moisture available to a tree varies with its position on the slope. Trees on lower slopes normally have more available moisture than trees on otherwise similar upper slopes. Deep soils that have adequate water-holding capacities keep trees growing at maximum rates—if other factors are not limiting—whereas shallow soils not having adequate water-holding capacity do not.

Some tree species grow well under many soil conditions, others do not. Black locust, for instance, can grow on deep or shallow, moist or dry soils. True, it does not grow equally well on all situations, but it does persist. Other species, such as yellow-poplar, occur on only a few deep moist soils and usually do not become established on shallow dry soils or on tight claypan soils. Segregation of species within their ranges is therefore often due to differences in soils.

Forest types or associations of tree species depend somewhat upon relative tolerance of the several associated species to shade. Some stand more shade than others. For instance, ponderosa pine, cottonwood, and black locust are less tolerant of shade than yellow-poplar, white oak, beech, and hemlock. Some species appear to be more tolerant under some soil conditions than under others. Two factors, then, chiefly determine forest types in any climatic province: First, the inherent capacity of a species to withstand the shade and, second, the soil conditions.

FORESTS AFFECT THE SOIL most of all through litter. Litter breaks the impact of rain, retards runoff, and filters rain water into the soil without disturbing soil structure. In dry weather, litter reduces surface evaporation. When litter decays, it provides mineral elements for tree growth. It shelters microbiotic life, which breaks down many kinds of complex substances into simple forms, and it shelters worms that help to keep the soil granular and mellow. In extremely cold weather, the forest litter acts as a blanket through which the heat from the soil cannot escape rapidly. Litter therefore reduces the depth of freezing of forest soils. When a forest soil does freeze, it tends to honeycomb and is therefore permeable to sudden rains that may come in late spring.

Litter is the source of the humus horizon of a forest soil, and the humus layer is the part of a forest soil that distinguishes it from an agricultural soil. Cultivated soils contain humus, too, but it chiefly comes from a humus layer previously formed under grass or forest. The humus of a farmed soil is maintained only by extraordinary methods of crop rotation and fertilizing, whereas the humus layer of a forested soil is maintained by the yearly leaf fall. When bare fields are planted to trees the humus layer increases in thickness. This increase is a good index of site recovery.

Forests help prevent peak floods through their effect on the soil. A porous, permeable soil absorbs rainfall faster than a cultivated soil. A soil covered with litter, brush, and tree stems retards runoff of much surface water that may not be absorbed quickly. Experiments show that from a 40- to 50-inch rainfall in Ohio, forests store about 6 inches more water than fields in cultivated row crops.

The forest intercepts much of the force of wind-driven rain, and thus prevents beating of the protective litter and soil. It protects the soil from excessive heat, light, and drying winds. Its roots hold the soil in place. They have grown, died, and decayed through centuries, and have made the soil more and more porous and permeable. As they decay, they leave deep channels through which water may percolate and air may move.

Rain water dissolves salts of calcium, potassium, and magnesium from the soil, causing it to become sour, but in the hardwood region these bases, replenished in the litter, tend to preserve a "sweet" soil. These elements, together with organic matter, keep the

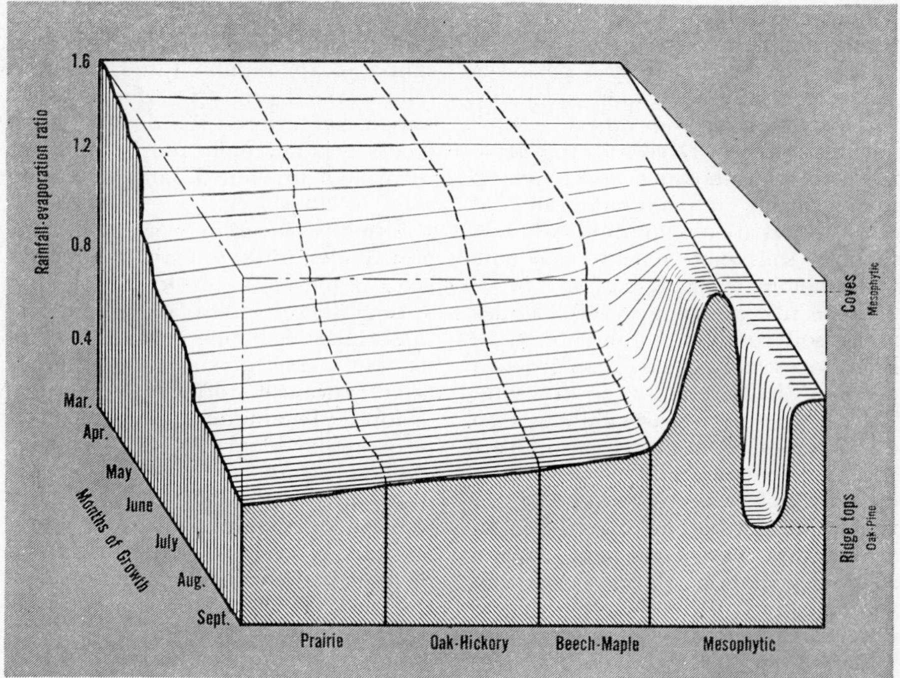


**GOVERNING EFFECT OF RAINFALL-EVAPORATION RATIO ON VEGETATION**

**Each vertical plane cutting the figure from front to back locates a geographic position between the prairie of western Iowa (left) and the Appalachian Mountains of West Virginia (right) with its rainfall-evaporation ratio by months. The undulations at the right represent contrasting evaporation rates on Appalachian ridges and coves.**

upper hardwood-forest soil mellow and granular. The forest absorbs mineral elements from the soil, and in turn largely replaces them in the yearly leaf fall. If the forest dropped more leaves than decayed each year, it would eventually bury itself in its litter; and if the rate of organic-matter decay were greater than the rate of organic accumulation, the soil would at intervals be totally devoid of organic matter. Such conditions never occur; a balance short of them is maintained.

OF THE FACTORS that adversely affect forest soils, burning alone usually does not seriously influence a hardwood-covered soil. It destroys the litter, which protects the mineral soil, but subsequent erosion does the real damage. Fire in a coniferous forest is frequently more serious since shallow soils over bedrock are more common.

Overgrazing is injurious to any kind of forest. In wet weather trampling compacts the soil and makes it hard and harsh when it dries. Trampling breaks up the litter cover, thereby exposing mineral soil to excessive drying in summer. Heavy grazing destroys forest soil structure, and eventually lowers its site quality.

Since soils are formed slowly, their loss through accelerated erosion is especially serious. Erosion is more damaging to some soils than to others. Many of the hardwood lands of southern Illinois grew only a few good crops after the trees were removed. The porous, organic-rich loess mantle disappeared quickly when the protective litter was plowed under.

Aspect and degree of slope greatly affect the rate of site deterioration due to erosion. Any disturbance of site by erosion is much worse on dry south

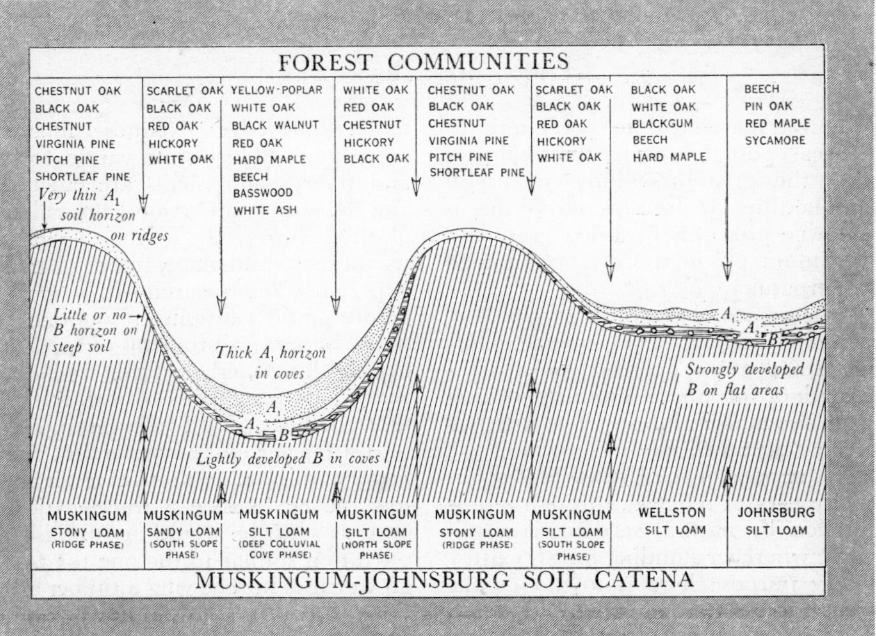


**Soil, topography, and tree species become adjusted in natural stands.**

slopes and ridges than on moist north slopes because the dry sites are already nearer the critical soil moisture level.

Cultivation of forest soil immediately reduces its natural porosity and destroys its protective litter. Erosion then attacks the body of the soil.

Experiments conducted by the Central States Forest Experiment Station and reported in 1945 show that site quality for black locust, black walnut, and yellow-poplar may be predicted on the basis of easily recognizable soil properties, such as permeability to water, depth to subsoil, and slope, position, and aspect. Studies by the Soil Conservation Service in the Pacific Northwest show that growth rates of Douglas-fir and ponderosa pine may be predicted on the basis of the same soil properties.

Agreement on the relationship between the same set of general soil properties and tree growth in such widely separated and different regions suggests that soil-tree relationships are basic and applicable to many more forest regions. Predictions of tree suitability to, and rate of growth on, bare land help to set values on land intended for reforestation. These soil-tree relationships provide some basis for predicting the eventual site quality of deteriorated land. They assist also in choosing the best tree species for degraded sites and in managing stands to maintain a composition of more desirable species.

JOHN T. AUTEN, *a soil scientist in the Forest Service, has been engaged in forest-soil investigations since 1929. He was once soil analyst for the Iowa soil survey and professor of chemistry and soils in Pennsylvania State College. He is a graduate of the University of Illinois and of Iowa State College.*

T. B. PLAIR *is chief of the Regional Forestry Division, Soil Conservation Service, Pacific Coast Region, and has been primarily concerned with planning forest land use since 1935. He is a graduate of Mississippi State College and the University of California School of Forestry.*

# FOREST RENEWAL

LEONARD I. BARRETT

Forestry attempts to perpetuate at the least cost the species that will provide the greatest volume of useful commodities. In forestry, harvesting is followed promptly by a new crop, and maximum productivity is maintained in perpetuity.

The means of establishing new forest crops are few. They include planting small trees or seed, securing a growth of sprouts, and natural seeding from the mature forest. The first two are important locally in several of the forest regions of the United States, but prompt forest renewal, through reproduction by natural seeding, is applicable wherever standing forests exist.

My purpose here is to discuss the basic factors that must be considered in seeking natural forest renewal and the methods that are finding success in the United States.

The methods of renewing forests were born at least 700 years ago, when the feudal lords and communal forest owners of central Europe felt the pinch of short wood supplies and vanishing game habitats and, through edicts and restrictions, sought to perpetuate forest resources. At first, the methods were based on the observations and folklore of huntsmen and did not begin to receive the benefit of systematic and scientific scrutiny until about the middle of the eighteenth century. From then on, progress was comparatively fast; within 100 years European foresters developed well-defined and effective ways to get continued productivity of forests. The practice of forestry was elevated from a folklore or speculative status to that of applied science.

The beginning of a conservation movement in the United States about 50 years ago saw many attempts—in teaching, research, and practice—to transplant the European prescriptions to American forests. They did not succeed too well. Gradually, as our own basic knowledge expands, methods more applicable to our varied forests and their requirements are emerging and creating an American science of silviculture. The science is still in its infancy, and many more years of experience and research will be needed before sound solutions are obtained to many important problems of forest renewal. But American foresters believe that modern methods of research will shorten this period of development.

If a farmer, in one operation, could harvest this year's crop of grain and sow the next, using a fraction of the crop as seed, he would accomplish an operation similar to the one the forest grower uses in renewing a timber crop. For farm crops it would not work, because the life processes of the plants require intense culture and care if the yield is to be worth while. The farm manager approaches his job with the viewpoint of comparatively complete control of the crop environment that is needed to meet the demanding requirements of specific plants. He has learned that it pays to modify the weather; he controls moisture by irrigation and frost by smudge pots.

Trees also are demanding in their requirements for germination, early survival, and best growth. The cultural measures necessary to meet these requirements, however, are generally quite different from those needed to meet the requirements of farm crops. The intensity of culture used in farming would be wasteful and sometimes inimical to successful forest renewal. Another article in this book discusses the biology of the forest, and shows how natural trends over long periods change the species in a forest. It indicates also that forests respond to the natural variations in the factors that affect tree growth by a change in species or in rate of growth and thrift.

The biological basis of successful

forest regeneration is a knowledge of these long-time trends, of the natural factors and their variations that affect tree growth, and of how the variations meet the basic requirements of the trees for best development. Thus the manager of woodlands must have as fully developed a knowledge of plants and the specific environments with which he is dealing as the farmer. But the woodland manager necessarily seeks his objective by guiding and modifying these natural trends and factors, rather than by attempting such complete environmental control as the farmer. His methods are less obvious therefore than those of farming and often may not be apparent to the untrained eye.

THE BASIC REQUIREMENTS of trees are light, heat, moisture, and wind—particularly in the early stages of seed production and dissemination, germination, and survival. When a tree is beyond its first stages, the texture and chemical composition of the soil must be added. Because a man cannot change the requirements of trees, success in securing natural regeneration depends upon how well he can change and modify the natural factors to meet the requirements of the tree.

Reactions of tree species to changes in these factors vary widely. I. T. Haig learned from experiments in Montana that only 8 percent of lowland white fir seedlings on mineral soil survived in full sunlight, whereas about 90 percent survived under intensities of 24 percent and less of full sunlight. At the same locality, less than 15 percent of western larch seedlings survived under either full sunlight or almost complete shade, while more than 80 percent survived under one-fourth of full sunlight.

George P. Burns at the Vermont Agricultural Experiment Station found that sugar maple seedlings required only about 2 percent of full sunlight.

Paul J. Kramer at Duke University discovered that loblolly pine seedlings required nearly full sunlight for best development. At the same time he discovered that the life processes of eastern red oak could be fully satisfied under about one-third of full sunlight.

Working in the Lake States, Hardy L. Shirley showed that, under unmodified conditions with only the amount of light varied, the dry weight of 2-year-old jack pines in 80-percent light was four times that of those in 23 percent light. Within those variations of light, white spruce showed no significant difference in dry weight.

Similar variations in requirements between species could be cited for the other factors that affect tree growth. The important point to keep in mind is that trees vary widely in the conditions under which they develop well, and the creation of those conditions is vital to successful forest renewal.

Because these factors are all interrelated, a modification of one affects another. For example, light is one of the most easily controlled. That is accomplished by cutting that changes the density of the forest canopy and allows light to enter the stand in proportion to intensity of the cut. A change in the amount of light reaching the forest floor affects soil temperature. Soil moisture also is affected, because the trees that are removed no longer draw upon it.

Light is so important and (more than any other single factor) is so closely correlated with other factors that species of forest trees are often classified on the basis of their apparent tolerance or intolerance to shade. This concept of tolerance is really an expression not only of the shade-enduring capacity of a species but also of its ability to develop well under the complex of all factors associated with various degrees of light. The concept is imperfect in several respects and is unsatisfactory if it is universally applied to the exclusion of other considerations, but it provides a useful working principle in devising methods of forest renewal.

Under this concept, tolerant species are those that can become established and develop well as an understory in a well-stocked stand of larger trees, while intolerant trees are those that cannot survive such a subordinate position.

From the examples I have cited, it is apparent that species such as sugar maple, white spruce, and the lowland white fir are very tolerant of shade, jack pine and loblolly pine are rather intolerant, and western larch and eastern red oak have intermediate ratings in the scale of tolerance.

Seeding characteristics of trees are also important in arriving at workable methods of forest renewal.

The means of natural dissemination of seed are key factors and can be divided into two major groups. The largest group is the light-seeded species whose seed can be disseminated by the wind. Seed of these species are attached to wings, downy material, or other structures that aid in distribution by the wind. In this group are the pines, spruces, and firs, and many important broadleaved species such as the yellow-poplar, the ashes, maples, birches, elms, poplars, and others. The second group consists of heavy-seeded species whose seed is distributed only by gravity, with some rather ineffective aid by birds and animals. This class includes the oaks, walnut, hickories. Obviously with these there can be little lateral distribution from the parent tree by wind. Hence, with this group, the trees chosen to reseed an area must be more closely spaced than with the group whose seed is wind-borne.

Seed-producing capacity is another important characteristic to be considered. It may be poor because the intervals between the good seed years may amount to as much as 6 or 7 years (with species such as red pine, longleaf pine, and beech) or because not much seed is produced, as is the case with chestnut oak. Other species (such as Virginia pine and scarlet oak) bear good crops every year or two.

Many other seeding characteristics are of importance. One is the time over which seed is dispersed. Some species, like white pine and the firs, spread their seed within a few days or weeks. Others, such as loblolly pine, spread a considerable portion within a few weeks, but continue to shed significant quantities of seed for several months after the cones open. Still others, such as jack pine, lodgepole pine, and pond pine, retain seed in persistent cones for several years, shedding few or none until opened either by the heat of a fire or by exposure, after felling, to the high temperatures that exist near the soil surface in midsummer.

As in basic requirements, seeding characteristics vary widely between the species, and knowledge of them is needed by anyone who wants to accomplish forest renewal.

As to cutting: I mentioned earlier that forest renewal is an integral part of the harvesting process and how readily light and associated factors can be modified by cutting. Seeding characteristics, too, can be taken advantage of by cutting, because relatively few trees are needed for regeneration purposes where species produce good crops of wind-borne seed.

The knowledge of a species and its requirements, coupled with the tools of logging, are the basic equipment for successful forest renewal.

A forest composed of the tolerant species, that is, those that develop well in an understory position, if they are protected from fire and grazing, will contain on a single acre trees of many sizes and ages. To the layman it may present an unkempt appearance, and his first reaction may be a desire to clear away the underbrush. The woodland manager who deals with such a forest feels fortunate, because his problems of forest renewal are relatively simple and almost automatic. In this type of forest, the scattered individual mature trees or small groups of them are removed at intervals along with the deformed, diseased, overcrowded, or otherwise unneeded trees. The rate of such cutting is prescribed by a branch of forestry called management or regulation, which determines the rate of growth and allowable cut so that continuous production from a single property is assured, provided the renewal phases are properly handled in harvesting.

Such an all-aged forest is known as a selection forest, and the harvest and renewal method applicable to it as the selection system. No particular provision is needed for differences in seeding characteristics of species, because many trees of seed-producing age are always standing on an acre. Also present are smaller trees ready to take advantage of and fill in the high openings created by the harvest of the large, mature individuals or groups. Natural renewal under the selection system therefore is constantly under way and, unlike some of the other systems, is not limited to any particular period in the life history of the forest.

Too much emphasis cannot be placed, however, on the greatest controlling factor respecting the applicability of the selection system: It works well as a method of forest renewal only where the chosen species are capable of germination, survival, and satisfactory development in the shade of a productive stand of older and larger trees. Some species native to the United States that fall in this category are sugar maple, beech, some of the firs and spruces, and several more tolerant hardwoods or broadleaved species.

For species that will not thrive in an intimate mixture of all ages and sizes, methods aimed at eventual complete removal of the mature crop must be adopted. Although a number of such methods have been developed, they all have their origins in two broad, basic systems; each has the ultimate objective of producing stands in which there is relatively little variation in the age of individual trees.

One of the basic systems consists of a series of partial cuttings as the stand approaches maturity and terminates in a final cut that removes the last of the crop. Two or more cuttings may be spaced over a period of 10 to 30 years, or more, if the situation is particularly difficult.

Early cuttings of the series have several objectives. They harvest the poorer trees that may not survive until later cuts as well as improve the growth rate of the better trees that are left. They may also harvest trees suitable for specific products that have an unusually good demand at the time. From the viewpoint of forest renewal, however, they open the stand enough to stimulate production of seed and provide light so that new seedlings may start. Later cuttings continue the harvest features and gradually provide more light and other conditions favoring the continued establishment of the new crop and its development.

When a satisfactory stand of young trees has become established, the final cut of mature trees is made; it frees the new crop of all competition with the old. The number of cuttings, their intensity, and the periods between the cuttings vary widely with the species and other conditions, but all these variations are covered in the shelterwood system. In the partial-cutting stages, it may closely resemble or even be confused with the selection system. Where such confusion exists, the forest manager must seek reorientation in a knowledge of the basic requirements of the species or the mixture of species with which he is dealing.

The shelterwood system is designed to meet the requirements of species that require partial shade during establishment and early life, or of those that tolerate some shade but are poor seed producers, or of those that are heavy-seeded. Red pine is an outstanding example of a species whose requirements are met by this system. Ponderosa pine, the southern pines, and the less tolerant oaks (such as black oak and scarlet oak) also seem well adapted to renewal by the shelterwood system.

This system has an important feature in the opportunity it provides for the control of competing brush. In many localities, too heavy a cut in the maturing forest creates conditions favoring the invasion of shrubs or other undesired plants, which may offer such serious competition to seedlings of the desired species that they can later be established only by expensive artificial measures, such as the removal of brush followed by planting. In many areas where such a threat is present, careful attention to the timing and intensity of cutting can control brush and favor establishment of valuable tree species.

THE OTHER BASIC SYSTEM is substantially a single cutting that removes all or nearly all of the mature crop. It is primarily a clear-cutting system, but its use in forestry is accompanied by the concept of small cutting areas so located with reference to seed sources that a plentiful supply of seed can be promptly disseminated over the cutting locality. The methods developed under this system take many forms. In shape, they conform more or less to the clear-cut strips, blocks, wedges, or spots. After new growth is established in the clear-cut areas, another series of cuttings in adjoining mature timber is made. In the United States, where much forest renewal must be accomplished in forests that have been unmanaged in the past, a single series of cuttings may consist of a diverse pattern of irregularly shaped areas on which mature timber stood at the time management was started.

If renewal is to be prompt and adequate, the size of such clear cuttings must be held to a safe minimum. That is usually smaller than many persons suppose, and is dictated by the effective seeding distance of the adjoining uncut timber. For many species (like the southern pines) such a distance is usually not more than 400 or 500 feet. For others (such as red spruce or Douglas-fir) it may be three or four times that distance. Winds often carry seed for many miles, but the distance over which enough seed will reach the ground to produce a satisfactory stocking of young growth is usually rather short.

The location of cutting areas downwind from seed sources is sometimes important. For species that shed an entire seed crop in a few days or weeks, a wise precaution is to locate cutting strips at right angles to the direction of prevailing winds during the time of year when seed is shed. The location of other types of clear-cut areas can be similarly directed with reference to desirable seed sources and prevailing winds during the time of seed fall. Mountainous terrain and its effect on wind currents may be fully as important as the direction of prevailing winds, and local knowledge of these characteristics of wind is useful. For species that shed seed slowly in the fall and winter months, the location of the cutting areas with respect to wind currents is of less importance. The variations in wind direction over a long period are enough to accomplish the necessary dissemination.

Of greater importance than wind is the quantity of seed necessary to produce an established crop of seedlings. The difference between the number of seed reaching the ground and the number of resulting seedlings is tremendous. The difference has not been measured for all species and localities in the United States, but study thus far indicates that 200 to 400 seed reach the ground for every seedling that becomes successfully established.

Satisfactory renewal, therefore, requires that several hundred thousand seed an acre reach the ground within a few years after cutting.

The reasons for this difference are many. Forest-tree seed are important as food for wild birds and animals and, where heavy populations of wildlife exist, all or most of a seed crop may be consumed. Many seed fall on inhospitable spots for germination, and many seedlings succumb during their first season to the competition of other plants or adverse weather. The practical importance of this difference be-

**Gullying of forest land is healed in time by tree growth.**

tween amount of seed produced and the seedlings established is that abundant sources of seed must be kept available. Often that means the necessary seed source must consist of well-stocked blocks, strips, or other bodies of mature trees. The jack pine, Douglas-fir, and lodgepole pine are typical species for which block methods of clear cutting are providing satisfactory conditions for forest renewal.

Some species produce such copious crops of seed at short intervals that renewal can be accomplished by leaving individual trees well distributed over the cutting area. For these, a modified clear-cutting method called the seed-tree system, has proved suitable. Sufficient seed for necessary renewal is produced by a dozen or more mature trees an acre. If maturity is judged on the basis of small-sized products such as pulpwood, which can be produced from young trees, seed production may not yet have reached a very high level and the method may fail because of the lack of sufficient seed. The lack may be offset by leaving more seed trees per acre, in which case the method approaches and may actually become the shelterwood system. Such a tendency toward the shelterwood is also characteristic of species that demand full light for good development, but are poor producers of seed. The seed-tree method is often effective with such wind-firm species as the Virginia pine, the slash pine, and loblolly pine, although the shelterwood method is favored by many for the last two.

WITH MANY of the various methods aimed at the production of even-aged stands, additional measures designed to make more efficient use of the seed will pay dividends. Since most wind-borne seed germinate best in contact with mineral soil, some form of rough cultivation, either immediately before or after seed fall, is effective. This operation is usually accomplished by a heavy tractor and disk combination and is necessarily limited to rather smooth ground. It is particularly effective where winter logging on snow or the logging equipment does not accomplish much scarification of the forest floor and exposure of mineral soil. It is also recommended following the cutting of species with persistent cones that open best at high temperatures. In the process of disking, the cone-bearing limbs of cut trees are broken and forced close to the soil; there the high surface temperatures slowly open the cones and release the seed.

THE REACTION OF MATURE stands to partial cuttings of the selection and the shelterwood systems is adverse for some species. That reaction takes the form of increased death of trees left in the cutting area for future growth and for seed sources. So far, we can give only theoretical explanations for this increased death rate. One explanation is that temperature and soil moisture are suddenly changed by the cutting, so that new conditions are created to which the older trees cannot adapt themselves. Freed wind movement may increase the rate at which water is evaporated from leaves and needles, thus upsetting physiological processes in the tree. Mechanical injury to roots from severe bending as falling trees strike some of their neighbors is another possible contributor to the increased death rate.

Except for the particularly sheltered areas, the reaction frequently takes place in the older stands of both eastern and western hemlock, Douglas-fir, the yellow birch, and some species of spruce. Other species may show the same reactions to lesser degrees. Thus we find that the tolerant hemlocks which should respond well to the selection system have other characteristics that require clear-cutting methods in many localities.

SHALLOW SOILS over the bedrock may make the selection or shelterwood systems dangerous, because a partial cutting removes some mutual mechanical support and permits increased wind velocity. Loss from windthrow may be serious. An inherent lack of windfirmness due to typical shallow-root systems also results in windthrow. Engelmann spruce is a species that requires clear cutting in spots because of a lack of wind firmness.

ADAM SCHWAPPACH, a distinguished European forester of the past century, cites an experience that carries an important message for all who seek success in forest renewal. In tracing the development of European forestry, he related:

"An important step in the progress of sylviculture was the evolution of the so-called Selection System, introduced at the end of the eighteenth century. By it, single trees or small groups in the forest are chosen and felled, according as their state of maturity suggests, and the necessity for younger growth requires. Originally adopted for the utilisation and regeneration of deciduous species, particularly Beech, the system met with the commendation of those pioneers in scientific forestry, G. L. Hartig and Heinrich von Cotta. Upon the selection method being applied to the Scots Pine—the species least suited to this treatment—failure resulted, which caused a sudden reaction in favour of clear-felling with subsequent planting. Both the selection and the clear-felling systems have their peculiar advantages under particular circumstances; but the indiscriminate use of either leads naturally enough to disappointments."

LEONARD I. BARRETT *is chief of the Division of Forest Management Research of the Forest Service. Before taking that position in 1945, he was director of the Central States Forest Experiment Station in Columbus, Ohio; chief of the Division of Forest Management Research in the Southeastern Forest Experiment Station in Asheville, N. C.; junior forester and assistant silviculturist in the Central States and Southern Forest Experiment Stations. Before entering on his research career in 1926, Mr. Barrett served 2 years as a fire lookout, surveyor, and timber estimator on various national forests in the Pacific Northwest and Alaska.*

# What Do We Plant?

## FIRST THE SEED, THEN THE TREE

PAUL O. RUDOLF

IN THE United States more than 600 species of woody plants are useful for conservation planting, and some 75 million acres are in need of reforestation. For that, more than 100,000 tons of forest seeds will be needed. We should therefore know all we can about forest seeds—where they are borne, how often good crops come, when seeds are ripe, when is the best time to collect, how to clean them, how to store them, how to obtain prompt germination, how good they are, and what their origins are.

SEEDS DEVELOP from flowers. The floral organs are the stamens and the pistils, which produce the sperm, or male cells, and the egg, or female cells, which, when united, produce the seed. Some trees and shrubs have bisexual, or perfect flowers. Many, however, have stamens and pistils borne in separate flowers, either on the same plant or on separate plants. Others have both perfect and unisexual flowers on the same plant. A knowledge of these habits helps the seed collector to know what trees are likely to produce seeds and also what crop to expect from the abundance of blossoms.

*Above: A onetime Navy plane is used to seed white pine on burned-over forest lands in Maine.*

A typical tree seed consists of an embryo, usually embedded within an endosperm (sometimes very thin or even absent), all enclosed in one or two seed coats. The embryo is a complete plant in miniature. The endosperm contains food reserves that become available for germination and early growth. The seed coat protects the embryo from injury before germination.

Tree seeds range in size from the powderlike rhododendron seeds to the large black walnuts. They differ greatly also in shape, color, and other characteristics. From the standpoint of collection and extraction, however, seeds fall into three groups:

1. True seeds readily extracted from dry fruits. Included in this group are trees whose seeds are borne in cones (fir, hemlock, larch, pine) or in fruits that split open, such as pods (honeylocust, locust, yellowwood), or in capsules (e. g., the fremontia, poplar, willow). Commercial seed is almost always the true seed.

2. Dry fruits with seeds surrounded by a tightly adhering fruit wall. Included are species whose seeds are borne in achenes (clematis, cliffrose, eriogonum), the nuts (chestnut, filbert, oak), and samaras, or key fruits (ash, elm, maple). Because it is hard to do so, seeds of this group are seldom extracted from the fruits. For all practical purposes the entire fruit is the seed.

3. Seeds of fleshy fruits. Included are species whose seeds are borne in accessory fruits (buffaloberry, wintergreen), aggregate fruits (raspberry), the berries (barberry, currant, honeysuckle), the drupes (cherry, dogwood, plum, walnut), multiple, or collective fruits (mulberry, Osage-orange), or pomes (apple, pear).

To SUPPLY the needs of the seed trade and reforestation, large quantities of tree seeds must be collected, extracted, and stored every year.

In scouting out supplies, the seed collector should keep eight points in mind:

1. The parent plants should be of desirable form and development.

2. Trees whose crowns receive light from above and the sides usually produce the bulk of the seed crop.

3. The flowering habit determines which trees will produce seeds and the part of the crown in which they are borne.

4. Estimates based on actual count of fruits on representative trees or on small sample plots well distributed over the collecting area are most reliable.

5. "Tree seed farms," set aside in mature stands of particularly good development or plantations of known good seed source, which produce seed in reasonable abundance, will provide desirable local collecting areas.

6. The tree seed-crop reporting services, available in some regions, tell the collector where good local crops are.

7. The soundness of seeds in individual localities, or even on individual plants, should be tested.

8. Next year's potential crop can be estimated from the number of first-year fruits for such trees as the pines, black oaks, and others which require 2 years to mature their fruits.

RIPENESS of the seed and the length of time it may remain on the plant or on the ground without deterioration or injury determine the time of collection. Collectors usually judge the ripeness of fruits by their general appearance, color, degree of "milkiness" of the seed, hardness of the seed coat, their attractiveness to animals, or some combination of these factors. For some pines, ripeness can be determined more accurately by the floatability of freshly picked cones in motor oil, kerosene, or other liquids.

The exact time for starting seed gathering must be determined for each species in each locality each year. However, the general season in which to make collections is known for a great many species, some of which are:

Spring: Berlandier ash, river birch, cottonwoods, elms (except Chinese), red maple and silver maple, poplars, and the willows.

Summer: Bigcone-spruce, cherries, Douglas-fir, elders, alpine larch, magnolias, red maple, mulberries, Siberian pea-shrub, plums, serviceberries, California sycamore.

Fall: The ashes (except Berlandier), beeches, bigcone-spruce, birches (except river birch), boxelder, catalpas, cherries, Douglas-fir, Chinese elm, firs, hickories, junipers, the larches (except alpine), magnolias, maples (except the red and silver), oleasters, Osage-orange, pecan, most pines, plums, spruces, sycamores, walnuts.

Winter: Ashes (except Berlandier), yellow birch, the boxelders, catalpas, Osage-orange, black spruce, Norway spruce, sycamores, walnuts.

Any season: Aleppo pine, bishop pine, jack pine, lodgepole pine, Monterey pine, pond pine, sand pine.

Forest seeds commonly are collected from standing trees. Most tall trees must be climbed and the fruits or seeds detached by hand picking, by cutting them off, or by knocking them off. In hand picking, the fruits usually are placed in containers. If the fruits are cut or knocked off, they are usually caught in sheets spread below. Seeds usually are hand-picked or flailed from small trees or shrubs without climbing them.

It is usually cheaper to collect seeds from felled rather than from standing trees. The collector must, however, gather seeds only from trees cut after the fruits have begun to ripen.

Twenty or thirty years ago conifer cones frequently were gathered from squirrel hoards in the Lake States and the West. This is still done to some extent. However, seed collection from rodent caches is of limited usefulness because the parent trees are unknown, hoards are difficult to find consistently, and few species are included. Some successful collectors gather squirrel-cut cones from the ground.

Seeds or fruits are gathered from water surfaces or from drifts along the shores for a few tree species, such as baldcypress and some of the willows.

Fruits should be taken to the extraction point soon after collection. Fleshy fruits should neither be crushed nor dried for very long. Others should be spread out and dried partially before shipment.

To PREVENT spoilage, to conserve space and weight in the shipment and storage, and to facilitate handling and sowing, seeds of many species must be separated from the fruits and cleaned of fruit parts and debris.

Seeds are separated from the fruits by drying, threshing, depulping, or cleaning procedures such as fanning and sieving.

The simplest method of drying is to spread the fruits in shallow layers so that there is free circulation of air across and around each fruit. Where the climate is damp, or the quantities of fruit great, drying is usually done under a roof.

Artificial heat is necessary to open some cones readily. Artificial drying ordinarily is done in special kilns which aim to provide the highest dry heat that the seeds can stand without injury. Two general types of kilns are used for extracting seeds from cones: The simple convection and the forced-air. The former has long been in use; the latter has been developed since 1934. Newly developed in Canada is a kiln using batteries of infrared lamps.

Convection kilns depend upon the natural rise of heated air through cones spread on trays placed directly above the source of heat. Forced-air kilns are more complicated. Heat and humidification are supplied by steam, and fans provide forced circulation of the warm air. Temperature and the humidity are controlled automatically by an electrically operated recorder-controller. Forced-air kilns are more efficient than convection kilns. For example, it takes from 24 to 72 hours to extract seeds from red pine cones in convection kilns as compared to 5 hours in forced-air kilns. However, forced-air kilns are more expensive and require skilled men to install and operate them. The infrared kilns give promise of efficiency and relative cheapness and ease of operation.

Upon their removal from the kiln, cones are run through tumblers—revolving boxes or drums with screened sides—to shake out the seeds.

The seeds of many dry fruits must be separated from the bunches, pods, or capsules in which they grow. The simplest methods are flailing or treading under foot. Sometimes agricultural machinery can be used. Frequently, however, special apparatus is necessary for fully efficient extraction. Two

802062°—49——10

types have proved widely useful, a macerator developed by the Forest Service, and a hammer mill. Either can produce several hundred pounds of clean seeds a day.

Some small fleshy fruits are dried whole. However, the seeds of most fleshy or pulpy fruits must be extracted promptly to prevent spoilage. Small lots can be cleaned by hand, by treading in tubs, or by rubbing through hardware cloth with hand brushes and water from a hose. Food choppers, concrete mixers, feed grinders, cider mills, wine presses, and restaurant potato peelers have been used for removing seeds from fleshy fruits, but none of these are as widely applicable as the Forest Service macerator or the hammer mill. Mulberries, chokecherries, or Osage-orange fruits, which require mashing and soaking before they can be run through the macerator, should not be allowed to ferment.

Seeds of several species, such as elm, maple, and oak, require no extraction, but need merely to be freed of chaff or trash. Often dried, without extraction, are some of the small fleshy fruits such as the chokecherries, elders, hollies, manzanitas, mountain-ashes, Russian-olives, and viburnums.

Methods of seed extraction commonly used for several species are:

Air or kiln drying: The arborvitaes, baldcypress, bigcone-spruce, ceanothuses, chamaecyparises, chestnut, chinquapins, cypresses, Douglas-fir, elms, eucalyptus, firs, hemlocks, California incense-cedar, larches, pines, poplars, common prickly-ash, redwood, spruces, sweetgum, willows.

Kilns necessary: The Aleppo pine, bishop pine, jack pine, lodgepole pine, Monterey pine, pond pine, sand pine. (The cones remain unopened on the trees for several years in all these species.)

Threshing or screening: Acacias, alders, baccharises, beeches, catalpas, Kentucky coffeetree, filberts, fremontias, hickories, honeylocusts, American hornbeam, common lilac, locusts, Siberian pea-shrub, eastern redbud, the rhododendrons, silktree, sourwood, sumacs, walnuts, witch-hazel.

Depulping: Apples, aralias, barberries, blackberries, buffaloberries, lilac chaste-tree, the cherries, cotoneasters, creepers, elders, grapes, hollies, honeysuckles, black huckleberry, common jujube, junipers, red mahonia, manzanitas, mountain-ashes, the mulberries, Osage-orange, common pear, common persimmon, plums, European privet, raspberries, meadow rose, sassafras, common sea-buckthorn, serviceberries, silverberry, snowberries, western soapberry, common spicebush, tupelos, viburnums, yews.

Cleaning methods: Apache-plume, ashes, birches, antelope bitterbrush, the elms, hackberries, eastern hophornbeam, common hoptree, the lindens, mountain-mahoganies, oaks, Carolina silverbell, tanoak, common winterfat, yellow-poplar.

Cleaning is sometimes necessary. For better storage and handling, seeds of many species must be cleaned of chaff, trash, adhering fruit parts, or empty seeds, after separation from the fruits. Sometimes cleaning is combined with extraction and often a combination of methods is required to clean the seeds. Most of the conifer seeds, for example, must be both dewinged and fanned.

Conifer seeds may be dewinged by hand rubbing, beating or trampling in sacks, or moistening and raking. Large-scale dewinging is usually done in machines, which tumble the seeds against stiff brushes, or in a macerator. Such machines must be used and adjusted carefully or much of the seed will be injured.

Often seeds can be cleaned satisfactorily by running them through screens, either dry or with running water. Often two screens are used in series, one with a mesh large enough to pass the seeds but hold back larger objects, and a second with a mesh small enough to hold the seeds but to pass smaller material.

Fanning is the principal means of removing wings or light chaff from many kinds of seeds. Sometimes empty seeds also are fanned out. Small lots can be cleaned by passing them from one container to another in the wind or in front of a fan. Large lots usually are run through standard agricultural seed fanning or cleaning mills. Unless fanning is done skillfully, either too much debris will remain or too many good seeds will be blown out.

Seeds of most pulpy or fleshy fruits can be cleaned most effectively by flotation in water. Sound seeds usually sink, whereas poor seeds, skins, and pulp either float or sink more slowly. Freshly gathered acorns often are separated from the cups and weeviled fruits by flotation in water. Loblolly pine seeds can be cleaned better by flotation in water than by fanning. Prompt drying after such wetting is essential.

To determine the amount of fruit needed for specific sowing or market requirements, it is necessary to know the extraction factor.

The amount of cleaned seeds produced per 100 pounds of fruit as usually collected ranges from 30 to 50 pounds for many species, and may range from 1 to nearly 100 pounds, as shown below:

One to five pounds: Apples, arborvitaes, red chokeberry, cucumbertree, golden currant, Douglas-fir, firs, hemlocks, honeysuckles, black huckleberry, California incense-cedar, inkberry, the larches, common lilac, mountain-ashes, the mulberries, Osage-orange, common pear, pines, raspberries, serviceberries, common snowberry, spruces, mahogany sumac.

Six to ten pounds: Glossy buckthorn, silver buffaloberry, black chokeberry, the elders, firs, honeysuckle, mountain-holly, western snowberry, skunkbush sumac, sweetfern, sweetgum, American sycamore, yellow-poplar.

Eleven to twenty pounds: Japanese barberry, bearberry, chamaecyparises, cherries, devils-walkingstick, elders, euonymuses, riverbank grape, shellbark hickory, pawpaw, Siberian peashrub, common persimmon, plums, redwood, Russian-olive, common sea-buckthorn, common spicebush, sugar sumac, common winterberry.

Twenty-one to forty pounds: Ailanthus, apricot, Japanese barberry, American beech, boxelder, most buckthorns, butternut, the gum bumelia, catalpas, cherries, Kentucky coffeetree, Virginia creeper, desertwillow, dogwoods, American filbert, fringetree, shagbark hickory, shellbark hickory, American holly, honeylocust, eastern hophornbeam, junipers, common jujube, locusts, mountain-mahoganies, common persimmon, eastern redbud, Russian-olive, common sea-buckthorn, silktree, western soapberry, smooth sumac, staghorn sumac.

Forty-one to sixty pounds: Ailanthus, indigobush amorpha, baldcypress, boxelder, Kentucky coffeetree, desertwillow, elms, European filbert, mockernut hickory, Norway maple, sugar maple, oaks, pecan, Fremont silktassel, smooth sumac, black walnut, little walnut, southern waxmyrtle.

Sixty-one to eighty pounds: Ailanthus, ashes, boxelder, lilac chaste-tree, bitternut hickory, mockernut hickory, pignut hickory, lindens, sugar maple, Tatarian maple, oaks, pecan.

Eighty-one to one hundred pounds: Ailanthus, bitternut hickory, pignut hickory, black maple, red maple, sugar maple, oaks, laurel sumac.

Storage varies considerably. Forest seeds seldom are sown immediately after extraction and cleaning. Commonly they are extracted in the fall and held over winter. Often, too, they must be held for several years because some species produce good crops infrequently. In either case the seeds should be stored so as to maintain high viability. For some species this is a simple matter; for others it is quite difficult, and for many, suitable storage practices are not yet known.

The simplest and oldest method of storage is to hold the seeds at air temperatures either in sacks or, preferably, in sealed containers. Storage may be at room temperatures, in cool cellars, or frequently in special seed-storage sheds. Seeds of many species can be kept for one or more years in such sheds, but for longer periods cold storage is necessary.

Seeds of many woody plants keep well at temperatures between 33° and 50° F. Before storage, seeds of most conifers should be dried to a moisture content below 10 percent of oven-dry weight. Seeds of the oaks, hickories, and silver maple, however, should be kept above 35-percent moisture content, and those of southern magnolia should not be allowed to dry at all. Proper cold storage requires a refrigerator or cold room in which temperatures can be held nearly constant. Sealed containers maintain the right moisture content and are best for such storage.

Many of the nuts and some other seeds often can be stored for a few months by mixing them with one to three times their volume of moist peat moss, sand, or chopped sphagnum moss, and placing them in a refrigerator or holding them over winter in the ground under a mulch. Sometimes fall sowing is used instead.

The short-lived seeds of the poplars can be kept fairly well for several months in sealed containers from which much of the air has been exhausted by suction pumps, or in which the relative humidity of the air is less than 20 percent. So far, however, vacuum storage has been attempted on a laboratory scale only.

Under proper storage, seeds of most trees can be kept viable for 5 to 10 years and that of some species has been kept for several decades. The best storage methods known for several species follow:

Dry, cold storage in sealed containers: Apples, arborvitaes, ashes, barberries, bigcone-spruce, birches, antelope bitterbrush, blackberries, silver buffaloberry, ceanothuses, lilac chastetree, the cypresses, Douglas-fir, elders, elms, firs, riverbank grape, hackberries, hemlocks, honeylocusts, common hoptree, black huckleberry, junipers, larches, black locust, maples (other than silver), the mountain-ashes, oleasters, Osage-orange, pines, some poplars, common prickly-ash, raspberries, eastern redbud, redwood, sassafras, giant sequoia, the snowberries, spruces, sumacs, sweetgum, witch-hazel, yellow-poplar.

Moist, cold storage: Beeches, buckeyes, chestnut, chinquapins, filberts, hickories, silver maple, oaks, tanoak, walnuts, yews.

At air temperatures: Acacias, Kentucky coffeetree, eucalyptus, fremontias, common lilac, lindens, common pear, the Siberian pea-shrub, European privet, meadow rose, fourwing saltbush, the common sea-buckthorn, common winterfat.

Under partial vacuum: Some poplars.

Pretreatment is sometimes required. Seeds of some trees and shrubs germinate quite promptly. Those of many, however, often fail to sprout even when exposed to suitable conditions of temperature, moisture, oxygen, and light. Such seeds are called dormant, and special treatment is required to induce germination.

There are two main causes of seed dormancy: (1) An impermeable or hard seed coat which prevents water and oxygen from reaching the embryo, or sometimes prevents the embryo from breaking through even though water has entered; and (2) internal conditions of the embryo or stored food. Many kinds of seeds have only one kind of dormancy, but there are many others which have double dormancy.

To overcome seed-coat dormancy, seeds usually are subjected to one of the following pretreatments: (1) Soaking in concentrated sulfuric acid (usually from 15 to 60 minutes); (2) scarifying the seed coats with abrasives; or (3) soaking in hot water (usually at a temperature of 170° to 212° F.) for about 12 hours as it gradually cools.

Treatments used to break internal dormancy are: (1) Cold stratification, in which the seeds are placed in moist sand, acid granular peat, or chopped sphagnum moss and held at 32° to 41° F. for 1 to 4 months; and (2) chemical treatment, in which the seeds are soaked in such materials as thiourea or exposed to fumes of such substances as ethylene chlorhydrin. The chemical treatments have been largely confined to experimental use.

To overcome double dormancy, the seed coat must be made permeable and the embryo or stored food induced to undergo the changes necessary for germination. Sometimes cold stratification is sufficient, but more often soaking in hot water, acid treatment, scarification followed by cold stratification, or warm followed by cold stratification is necessary. Double dormancy can often be broken by sowing the seed soon after collection in the late summer and early fall.

Out of 444 species of tree and shrub seeds studied, 33 percent were nondormant, 7 percent had seed-coat dormancy, 43 percent had internal dormancy, and 17 percent had double dormancy. A single species may have both dormant and nondormant seeds, or more than one kind of dormancy.

Typical species with dormant seeds:

Seed coat dormancy: Acacias, amorphas, Dahurian buckthorn, feltleaf ceanothus, the hairy ceanothus, Monterey ceanothus, Kentucky coffeetree, honeylocusts, black huckleberry, locusts, mesquite, common persimmon, silktree, western soapberry, sumacs (except skunkbush).

Internal dormancy: Alders (except European), the ailanthus, apples, most ashes, baldcypress, barberries, beeches, bigcone-spruce, birches (except river), antelope bitterbrush, American bittersweet, buckeyes (except California), alder buckthorn, glossy buckthorn, cascara buckthorn, buffaloberries, lilac chaste-tree, cherries, American chestnut, chokeberries, creepers, currants, flowered dogwood, devils-walkingstick, Douglas-fir, euonymuses, filberts, firs, fringetree, gooseberries (except roundleaf), riverbank grape, hackberries, hemlocks, hickories, hollies, honeysuckles, eastern hophornbeam, common hoptree, American hornbeam, junipers, most larches, common lilac, Pacific madrone, magnolias, most of the maples, the European mountain-ash, mountain-laurel, the mulberries, bitter nightshade, black oaks, oleasters, pawpaw, common pear, most pines, plums, common prickly-ash, European privet, sassafras, serviceberries, common sea-buckthorn, Fremont silktassel, Carolina silverbell, common spicebush, spruces (except the western white), sweetgum, sycamores, common trumpetcreeper, tupelos, viburnums, walnuts, southern waxmyrtle, checkerberry wintergreen, yellow-poplar.

Double dormancy: Bristly aralia, black ash, blue ash, European ash, bearberry, most ceanothuses, cotoneasters, most dogwoods, elders, fremontia, the panicled goldenrain-tree, downy hawthorn, black jetbead, some junipers, common jujube, the lindens, manzanita, Amur maple, American mountain-ashes, the mountain-holly, Osage-orange, Digger pine, Swiss stone pine, whitebark pine, raspberries, eastern redbud, meadow rose, wild-sarsaparilla, snowberries, skunkbush sumac, witch-hazel, yellowwood, yews.

Seed quality largely governs the rate at which seeds should be sown to produce a certain number of good seedlings. Tests can disclose several of the fundamental characteristics of quality: Genuineness, purity, number of seeds to the pound, moisture content, and viability.

The sample tested should be truly representative of the entire lot. Representative sampling can be attained either by thorough mixing of the entire seed lot before sampling, or by drawing a number of small subsamples of equal size at random from different parts of the lot in proportion to the quantity of seeds in each part. The number of seeds required for a germination test seldom should be less than 400, tested separately in four equal parts. For lots larger than 100 pounds, from 800 to 1,000 seeds should be used.

Genuineness is determined by comparing a representative sample of the seed lot under test with samples of known identity. Purity commonly is expressed as the percentage by weight of clean whole seeds true to species in a sample containing seeds and mixed impurities. The number of seeds per pound is obtained by careful weighing of a counted number of seeds. It is usually expressed in two ways: The number of clean seeds per pound of the sample as received and the number of clean seeds per pound of pure seeds. Moisture content usually is expressed as a percentage of the oven-dry weight of the seeds after commercial cleaning, but not on a pure seed basis.

Viability, or the percentage of seeds capable of germinating when exposed to the most favorable conditions, is determined directly by germination tests or indirectly by cutting tests, the growth of excised embryos, flotation, biochemical staining of embryos, or measurements of enzyme activity. The indirect methods give quicker results, but they are seldom as reliable as direct germination tests.

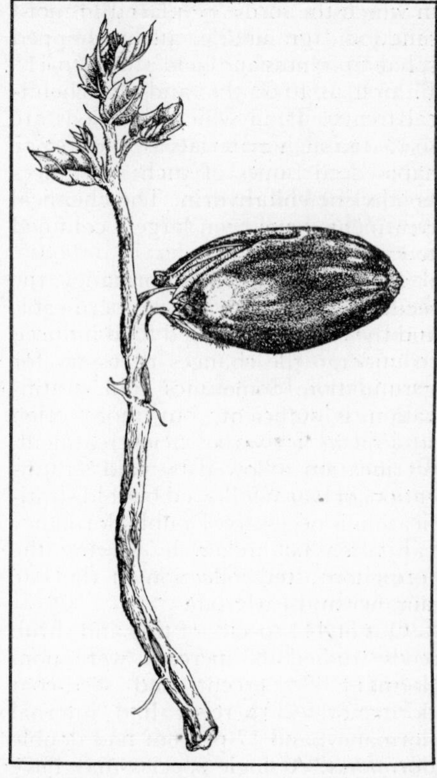

**Oak seedling. The two plump seed leaves packed with food remain inside the acorn.**

Germination tests usually are made in flats, porous clay pots, or greenhouse benches filled with fine sand, acid peat (sometimes used as compressed mats), or sphagnum moss; or in germinators on porous plates, blotters, filter paper, or agar. Sand, peat, or sphagnum moss are preferred as giving results closer to germination in the nursery. Carefully counted numbers of seeds, pretreated where necessary, are sown on the surface of peat mats or at controlled depths in sand, moss, or peat flats. Small seeds are sown shallow; larger seeds deeper, as a rule.

The sand, peat, or other medium must be kept at a fairly constant moisture level. Air temperatures should be controlled closely. Many species germinate well at temperatures fluctuating from 68° F. at night to 86° during the day; some do just as well at constant temperatures of 70° or 75°; others need temperatures that fluctuate from 50° (night) to 77° (day); and some germinate best at temperatures between 40° and 50°. The needs of each species must be known and supplied for best results. Light is not necessary for germination of most tree seeds, but aids that of some southern pines. Germination tests ordinarily are run for 30 to 60 days. Counts should be made every 2 or 3 days, and systematic records of results should be kept and made available to the seed user. Promptness of germination is almost as important to nurserymen as amount.

NURSERYMEN DETERMINE the rate of sowing from the laboratory tests as modified on the basis of their own experience. Nursery germination of tree seeds commonly is from 50 to 80 percent of laboratory germination. Since further losses normally occur after germination, the usable seedlings produced by a number of species usually run from 10 to 60 percent of the viable seeds sown. The following produce 10 to 15 usable seedlings for every 100 viable seed sown: European white birch, silver buffaloberry, Siberian crab apple, desertwillow, elms, Tatarian honeysuckle, European larch, common lilac, and Russian mulberry. Lilac chaste-tree, Japanese larch, and redwood yield 16 to 20 usable seedlings; Dahurian buckthorn, hackberries, Siberian larch, black locust, and nannyberry produce 21 to 30; the common jujube and Siberian pea-shrub, 31 to 40; and the baldcypress, pines, and spruces, 41 to 60.

THE SOURCE OF SEED is important. Forest trees and shrubs have evolved races within species. Each race is specially adapted to thrive under the conditions in which it has developed. Unless seeds of proper origin are used in forest planting, trees undesirable in vigor, form, or hardiness may result even though the right species has been used.

Studies started more than 100 years ago in Europe and about 35 years ago in the United States have shown that there are climatic races in about 30 North American and 35 foreign tree species. Doubtless many other trees and shrubs also have developed races. Comprehensive information is available for only five trees: Ponderosa pine and Douglas-fir from North America; and Scotch pine, Norway spruce, and European larch from Europe. Within these species the various races differ in rate of growth, stem form, leaf length, and color; the time that growth starts and stops; resistance to frost, drought, diseases, and insects; fruit and seed size; and wood quality.

Some forest trees, within areas of uniform climate, have even developed races particularly adapted to local site conditions. Furthermore, trees of the same species within an individual stand may display much hereditary variation in all the characteristics listed under climatic races. For these reasons seed collectors should use extreme care in selecting the stands and even individual trees from which they obtain seeds. They should try to have stands of desirable trees set aside as tree-seed farms to provide a continuous source of high-quality seeds.

In most countries of northern and central Europe rigid laws have been enacted to enforce the use of forest-tree seeds of suitable origin. In the United States no Federal legislation has yet been passed, but some dealers have provided information as to seed origin. The United States Department of Agriculture in 1939 adopted a forest-seed policy, stressing the use of local seeds, and some other agencies have followed suit.

ON THE BASIS of present knowledge, there are three general requirements that should be enforced either by voluntary action or regulation:

Seed collectors should be required to label their seeds accurately and adequately as to species, time of collection, and place of collection.

Seed dealers should be required to purchase only properly labeled seeds from collectors who are known to be reliable.

Users of seed or nursery stock should demand adequate information as to seed origin and should use only seeds of local origin or of proven adaptability to local conditions, or stock grown from such seeds.

PAUL O. RUDOLF *is silviculturist at the Lake States Forest Experiment Station, maintained by the Department of Agriculture in cooperation with the University of Minnesota. He has been doing research in forest-planting, forest-seed, and nursery problems in the Lake States since 1931 and is author of numerous publications on those phases of forestry. Mr. Rudolf holds degrees in forestry from the University of Minnesota and Cornell University.*

# DIRECT SEEDING OF TREES

W. E. MCQUILKIN

Growing tree seedlings in a nursery and transplanting them later to the field is the standard artificial means for establishing forest plantations. On good sites and poor, in wet years and dry, the use of nursery stock, properly grown and properly planted, has proved more likely to succeed than any other artificial method.

Direct seeding, which means sowing seeds in the field where the trees are to grow, thus bypassing the nursery and transplanting operations, under some conditions may be a simpler, faster, and less expensive reforestation method. Because of certain inherent drawbacks, however, direct seeding is not regarded as a method to replace planting on a wide scale, but rather as a useful adjunct to it by which, in selected situations, reforestation can be speeded up and costs reduced.

By conservative estimates, we now have in this country at least 30 million acres of land in need of artificial restocking. Obviously, any procedure that will facilitate getting this land back into forest production should be fully utilized.

ADVANTAGES AND DISADVANTAGES will first be considered. With proper procedures on selected sites, direct seeding may be done successfully at lower cost than for planting nursery stock. Furthermore, since direct seeding is not dependent upon maintenance of a nursery and the starting of stock 1 to 4 years in advance, it permits a degree of flexibility in reforestation programs according to availability of labor, allotments of funds, and the press of other jobs that is impossible with planting. If curtailment is necessary, seeds can be held over a year or so more easily than growing nursery stock; with expansion, seed usually can be procured upon shorter notice and with less advance planning. Also, seeding can be done over a considerably longer season.

Growth direct from seed in the field permits normal development of root systems. Transplanting at best entails mutilation of roots and a set-back in growth. Although most species seem to suffer no lasting damage when properly handled, many cases of poor growth and disease in forest plantations are believed to be caused by malformed root systems that result from improper or careless planting. Some strongly taprooted species seem by nature poorly adapted to withstand transplanting—they typically suffer high mortality, and many of the survivors fail to regain the vigor of natural, undisturbed trees. With direct seeding, all depressive after-effects of transplanting are avoided.

On very stony areas, direct seeding is especially advantageous. Successful planting at reasonable cost on such sites may be almost impossible because of difficulty in digging holes to required depth and in finding enough rock-free soil to make a proper refill around the roots. Trees starting from seed in such ground are able to extend their roots around and between the stones, and may make excellent growth.

Opposed to these advantages is one major disadvantage that relegates direct seeding to a secondary place; namely, that with a few possible exceptions (such as on extremely stony ground) direct seeding almost always entails greater risks of failure than planting nursery stock.

Greater risks are inherent in the method. Because of greater palatability to wildlife, greater susceptibility to certain types of insect injury and diseases, smaller size, undeveloped root systems, and generally greater fragility, seeds and newly germinated seedlings in the field almost unavoidably are more vulnerable to injury and death or destruction by all the natural obstacles to plant establishment than are transplanted nursery stock. In the nursery, seeds and seedlings are given intensive care and protection during the highly vulnerable early growth period; such care cannot practicably be given in the field.

The natural obstacles most likely to interfere more in direct seeding than in planting are the rodents and birds, drought, competition or smothering by the surrounding vegetation, injuriously high surface-soil temperatures, frost heaving, insect pests, as well as the seedling diseases.

Of these, rodent and bird depredations upon the seed, and direct-heat injury from high soil temperatures are problems practically unique to direct seeding. Planters of nursery stock ordinarily escape them entirely, and nurserymen can feasibly institute control measures if required. In certain sections, throughout the Western States particularly, seeding without some form of rodent control generally is futile; in other sections, notably the southern Gulf Coast States, birds are the major problem.

Direct-heat injury and mortality (independent of drought effects) may occur among tender, newly germinated seedlings if the surface-soil temperature rises above 120° F. Such temperatures are not unusual on bare ground in full sun; considerably higher temperatures sometimes develop on black soil surfaces or south-facing slopes. In extreme cases, even transplanted nursery stock may be damaged.

Both seedings and plantings are affected by the other obstacles named, but in general seedings are more sensitive and more likely to fail as any factor or condition becomes increasingly unfavorable. Little trees starting from seed in the field are more subject to the damaging effects of drought, root competition from other plants, and frost heaving because of their less well-developed root systems; they are more subject to smothering by other plants because of their handicap in height. Certain insect pests, like cutworms and white grubs, sometimes are highly destructive to the tender young plants but ordinarily do not seriously damage the 1- or 2-year-old seedlings. Likewise, serious damage from certain of the diseases, notably damping-off, is largely restricted to the period during and immediately after germination.

Other lesser disadvantages of direct seeding as compared to planting are that it requires a good deal more seed per reforested acre—seed that may sometimes be difficult to obtain—and that it is a somewhat more painstaking type of work, especially with small-seeded species like most conifers, which germinate poorly unless the depth of coverage is carefully controlled.

With recognition that direct field seedings are inherently more sensitive to adverse factors than plantings, the art of successful seeding can be characterized as, first, the discernment and the utilization of the combinations of species, site conditions, and the seasons where natural obstacles to plant establishment are relatively few or present in mild degree; and, second, application of such treatments as are necessary and economically feasible for lessening the obstacles or modifying the factors most likely to cause failure.

Several principles and methods: Direct seeding generally should be restricted to the more favorable sites. These sites usually are characterized by fairly deep, mellow, loamy, and well-drained soils situated on lower slopes and benches with northern or eastern exposures, in coves, or on bottom lands.

Site selection is more important in dry climates than in the moister ones. In the Lake States, for instance, which average rather dry among the forest climates, direct seeding generally is an uncertain undertaking except on the lower lying parts of the areas known as sand plains. Extensive acreages of this formation are found in Wisconsin. Seeding tests in the sand plains have indicated good chances for success where the ground-water table lies between 2 and 5 feet from the soil surface, but increasingly greater risks of failure as the water table gets deeper.

Besides good soil and moisture conditions, sites favorable for seeding are characterized by relatively thin and open plant cover. This points to recent burns on forest land and to recently abandoned farm lands as being among the most likely situations for satisfying direct-seeding requirements.

Seeding can be done any time that field conditions permit from late fall to early spring—roughly October through April in the North, with a somewhat shorter spring season in the South. Fall sowing generally is best because it allows the seed to afterripen naturally on the ground and germinate as soon as the weather is favorable in the spring. With spring sowing, seeds that require afterripening must have been previously stratified at near freezing temperatures for one to three months. When no positive rodent-control measures are planned, spring sowing sometimes is advisable because of the shorter period during which the seeds are exposed to the foraging of the animals.

All experience indicates that direct seeding with most species in the western forest regions is futile without some form of rodent control. Effective control measures are of two types: Hardware cloth covers placed over the seeded spots, and poisoning the area before seeding.

Covers or "screens" of hardware cloth (3 or 4 meshes to the inch) are effective but relatively costly and inconvenient. They are made usually in a conical or dome shape to permit nesting for carrying and storage. At prewar prices, covers 6 inches in diameter could be made for about 4 cents each, and with reasonable care were expected to serve about 10 seasons. Thus, where seeding might be done year after year, the prorated cost per spot for screens could be reduced to less than one-half cent. Even at that rate, the cost runs around $5 an acre of 1,000 to 1,200 spots; to this must be added the labor cost of placing them on the spots, lifting them later, and storage. Obviously, seeding with screens offers little chance for reducing reforestation costs below those that are needed for planting. Their use clearly is out of the question for a private landowner with a small, one-season job.

The prepoisoning for rodents, before seeding, seems to offer the best promise of effective control at reasonable cost. Experimental trials of this method, as developed at the Northern Rocky Mountain Forest and Range Experiment Station in cooperation with the Fish and Wildlife Service, were interrupted by the war and have not been resumed there. However, the prepoisoning technique has been employed successfully since the war in the Pacific Northwest.

The procedure at the Northern Rocky Mountain Station was to place about a tablespoon of poisoned bait (hulled sunflower seed treated with thallium sulfate) at 20-foot intervals over the seeding area a week before sowing the seed. Four experimental field trials of 10 to 50 acres each were made on cut-over and burned forest land in the western white pine type, seeding with western white pine. After 5 years, from 67 to 79 percent of the seeded spots on these areas were stocked. Subsequently a 97-acre tract was seeded as a reforestation job by CCC labor without the painstaking care exercised in the earlier experiments. After 5 years this tract showed 62 percent of its spots stocked. Some of the spot failures here were attributed to too-deep coverage of the seeds by careless workmen rather than to rodents. Other tests showed that treating the tree seeds with poison failed to give adequate rodent control where the area had not been prepoisoned. When prepoisoning was used, treating the seed did not increase the stocking enough to justify the added costs.

Cost of the bait used in the prepoisoning was about 25 cents an acre, and the labor required to spread it was about 2 man-hours.

Repellents for rodent and bird control have been tried, applied both on the seed and on or around the seeded spots. No substance thus far tested has given effective control.

Species with relatively small seed sometimes can be direct-seeded successfully even in areas of high rodent pressure, without specific control measures. Apparently the animals simply do not find all the seed in these instances. In tests with western redcedar and Engelmann spruce, seeded without protection at the Northern Rocky Mountain Forest and Range Experiment Station, most of the spots showed some germination, and where sites were favorable and ground cover fairly open, 64 to 97 percent of the spots were stocked 5 years later. Where failures occurred, they were generally attributable to drought or overgrowth by other plants, rather than to damage by rodents.

In the Eastern States, direct seeding often can be done without special treatments to control rodents. Mice, which here are the most common offenders, typically are most numerous in heavier types of cover where seeding generally would be inadvisable because of plant competition. Choicer seeding areas, like recently cultivated fields or fresh burns with scant cover, harbor relatively few mice, and seedings on them usually will not be seriously molested. In moderately heavy cover where furrowing or clearing of spots normally would be required in preparation for seeding, it has been found helpful to do this work several weeks in advance of sowing. The animals investigate immediately; if they find nothing of interest they apparently pass by the spots or furrows thereafter without close examination. Thus a delayed sowing may largely escape molestation.

In some localities where studies have been made, mouse populations are known to fluctuate from high to low on about a 4-year cycle. Probably this is true of mouse populations generally. Obviously, seedings made during the low of a cycle will be less likely to be seriously molested. Information on mouse cycles can be obtained from the Fish and Wildlife Service or, in some States, from the State biologist or State forester.

Prepoisoning entire seeding areas as has been done in the northern Rocky Mountain region is not generally recommended in the East because of the denser human population and greater danger of accidental consumption of the poisons by domestic livestock, pets, desirable forms of wildlife, or unsuspecting people. Some States prohibit such poisoning by law, or control it by requiring the landowner to show cause for use of poison and obtain a permit from State or local authorities.

In the Southern and the Gulf Coast States, trials of direct seeding mostly have been unsuccessful because of depredations by birds. No effective controls short of the costly screening method have been found, and seeding, therefore, is not now generally advocated in that region.

Ground preparation of some sort usually is required for success in seeding unless the existing plant cover is sparse and open. Where they are feasible, furrows plowed on the contour are probably the cheapest effective procedure. Spacing between furrows should be 6 to 8 feet, the depth should be no greater than is required for good turning action by the plow, the furrow slices should all be thrown down slope, and the work preferably should be done several weeks before seeding. Where plowing cannot be done, seed spots 1 to 2 feet in diameter are prepared by scalping off the vegetation with a mattock or hazel hoe. Deep digging of the spots to loosen the soil is not necessary. Where the cover is sufficiently open to allow location of seed spots at satisfactory spacing on bare soil between clumps of vegetation, ground preparation may be omitted. The omission should be recognized, however, as an acceptable increase in risk taken for the sake of lower labor costs.

In seeding new burns without furrowing or scalping, ashes should be raked or brushed aside before sowing. Fresh ashes in contact with the seed have been found to inhibit root growth and may cause many seedlings to fail immediately after germination.

Rates of sowing should be governed by percentages of viable seed, which for most tree seed runs far below 100 percent. On large operations that involve considerable investment, seed quality should be ascertained by germination tests. For the small operator such tests often are inconvenient to make, especially with the species whose seed require cold stratification. A reasonably dependable substitute is to determine the percentage of soundness by cutting each seed in a sample with a knife or mashing with a hammer.

For the sowing operation, the fastest and cheapest hand method on clean ground or after furrowing is to use a garden-type mechanical seeder, which a man can push along without undue effort. Relatively small-seeded species like pines should be sown to average two to three sound seeds to the lineal foot of row. Covering may be done by use of the shoe attachment furnished with most seeders, or by a brush drag drawn along the furrow after the seed are dropped. With fall sowing in furrows, covering often is not necessary, as the seed will be covered anyhow by rain and frost action. However, immediate covering may be of some value in concealing the seed from birds and rodents. Guard carefully against excessive coverage; small seeds, like pine and spruce, should not be planted more than a quarter inch deep.

In the spot seeding of small seeds, sow about 10 sound ones on a spot. Covering may be accomplished by light raking or, better, by sowing in two or three little trenches made with the finger, a pointed stick, or any convenient small tool. Fill the trenches level over the seeds with soil and firm gently with the hand or foot.

Recently a tool has been designed for spot seeding consisting of a blade for scarifying the soil, a seed chamber, and a spring mechanism which can be adjusted to deliver a definite amount of seed. On areas requiring little or no preparation of the spots, it is reported that one man with this tool can seed 2 to 3 acres a day. The tool is not at present available on the market, but construction is fairly simple. Specifications can be obtained from the Oregon State Department of Forestry, at Salem.

Though application of supplemental treatments means more labor time and shrinkage or elimination of any cost differential in favor of seeding, extra treatments or refinements in technique are in some situations almost prerequisite to success. Mulching, for instance, will markedly increase the amount of successful germination in regions such as the southern Piedmont, where hot, dry conditions often develop during the early spring. Especially on the heavy soils that have little natural cover to shade the surface and retard drying, mulch is practically a requirement in that region. On such sites, mulch also greatly reduces losses from frost heaving. Costs for mulching vary greatly according to availability of suitable material. On grassy fields where material can be raked directly into the furrows or on to the seed spots, costs usually will not be prohibitive. Hauling mulch to the seeding site involves greater expense, but may be feasible if pine litter or other material can be picked up easily in the vicinity. Seed should not be covered with soil if mulch is used, as that covers them too deep; when used, the mulch must be spread lightly with all entangled mats and chunks broken apart. Inexperienced labor almost invariably tends to spread mulch too thickly; ideally, it should nowhere exceed one-half inch when settled.

Another instance of need for special treatment occurs when seeding openings among the hardwood trees and sprouts where considerable leaf litter is cast each fall. Experience with spot seeding in situations of this sort at the

Central States Forest Experiment Station has shown the necessity for raising each spot an inch or so above the surrounding level to escape the lodging of leaves and smothering of the young plants. With spots properly located away from the natural obstacles where litter collects, this slight elevation causes most leaves to slide off or be carried on by the next gust of wind.

Where screen covers are used, they should be placed on the spots immediately as sown; delay of a few hours or overnight may be too late. Though they may be lifted anytime after germination is completed, screens usually are left in place until fall or the following spring. Leaving them through the first summer is desirable in that they cast a light shade which measurably reduces soil temperatures and evaporation, and thereby tends to increase seedling growth.

Nut seeds, such as walnuts or acorns, produce a more robust seedling from the start than smaller seeds like pine or the yellow-poplar. Early mortality is lower, and, consequently, fewer seeds need to be sown. The usual practice with good-quality nuts is to sow two to the seed spot, placing them several inches apart so that, if both grow, one can be removed later without injuring the other. In furrows, single nuts are planted at intervals of 2 to 3 feet. Depth of planting should be 1 to 2 inches, or about twice the thickness of the seed.

Inasmuch as nut seeds are especially subject to rodent depredations, spring seeding, with its much shorter period of exposure, often is preferable to fall seeding. However, nuts held overwinter require careful storage. For most species they should be stratified in moist sand or peat moss either in a refrigerated room or in an outdoor pit on a well-drained site. Pits should be deep enough to prevent solid, winter-long freezing. Germination will start in pits as soon as ground temperatures begin to rise in March or early April, at which time the nuts should be removed and planted without delay. Acorns of the white oak group require no afterripening and may be held overwinter without stratification in an unheated cave or humid, cold room.

The foregoing discussion has dealt only with hand methods, sometimes aided by common machines, such as plows and mechanical seeders. Those are the methods on which we can pass some measure of judgment based on results, but even here the background of experiment and experience is too scant to warrant final conclusions. Furthermore, these methods have all embodied the idea of spot or row seeding often with more or less ground preparation. Broadcast seeding, after numerous unsuccessful trials on the national forests 35 to 40 years ago, was abandoned as a futile effort.

Now, HOWEVER, A NEW TECHNIQUE is stirring the imagination of many foresters—seeding from airplanes. With the great impetus given to aviation by the war, and the increasing awareness of our dwindling timber resource accentuated by the war, it was natural that the idea of rapid reforestation by airplane should emerge and demand trial. The airplane has been adapted with phenomenal success to the dispersal of insecticides and fungicides over field, orchard, and forest. It has been used successfully in the West to seed herbaceous species for watershed protection after fires, to seed rice fields, and has found some use in range reseeding. Why not use airplanes to reseed the forest?

Several tests of airplane seeding of forest trees are now under way. One of the first was 600 acres seeded in the spring of 1946 by the Oregon State Board of Forestry. The Crown Zellerbach Corporation in Oregon seeded 1,100 acres by air in 1947, and 2,600 acres more in 1948, the latter by helicopter. The Central States Forest Experiment Station tried airplane seeding of trees in 1948 on spoils left after strip mining bituminous coal, and the Northeastern Forest Experiment Station seeded about 2,500 acres in Maine on land burned-over in the fall of 1947. The Department of Lands and Forests of Ontario, Canada, also has been experimenting with airplane seeding.

The degree of success to follow from these experiments remains to be determined. Preliminary inspections of the area seeded in Maine indicate a poor catch of seedlings there. Of the other areas mentioned, reports on degree of stocking have been received only for the 1946 seeding in Oregon. On a recently burned part of that area which was seeded to Douglas-fir and Port-Orford-cedar (1/4 pound of seed of each an acre), examination of 166 4-milacre circular line plots in the fall of 1947 showed 52 percent of the plots stocked. Plots of this size (about 14.9 feet in diameter) give perhaps an unduly favorable picture of stocking density. When tallied by milacre plots, the percent of stocked plots on the same area was only 22. Though this amount of seedling catch leaves much to be desired, the Oregon investigators feel the results are satisfactory and plan to continue their airplane seeding.

At this early stage in developments, the ultimate usefulness of the airplane in forest seeding cannot be foretold. Rapid coverage of ground is its chief attraction. Compared to 1, or at best, 2 or 3 acres a man-day by hand methods, or even several times those amounts by use of simple machines like garden seeders, the ability of the plane to spread seed on 100 acres in a matter of minutes opens vistas of reforestation that heretofore have been only conservationists' dreams. And the cost factor is favorable; present indications are that airplane seeding can be done for from $3 to $6 an acre—cheaper than the most efficient hand or simple machine methods.

The airplane method, however, has several shortcomings, chief of which is that it represents a return to broadcast seeding—a procedure that has been rather thoroughly tried in the past and found wanting.

In 1937, after extensive seeding studies in the Lake States, Hardy L. Shirley expressed the prevailing philosophy regarding broadcast seeding in these words: "There seems to be no more certain way of wasting a large amount of seed and accomplishing nothing than to broadcast it on unprepared soil in the Lake States."

Though Shirley restricted his statement to the Lake States, it would have found ready acceptance among foresters had it been broadened to include the entire country. Practically all forest-seeding experience supported it. In view of this bit of history, what is the outlook for airplane seeding, which is nothing more than the adaptation of a new machine to a discarded method?

Airplane seeding offers promise of limited successful use because of two developments in the last decade: (1) A greater appreciation among foresters of the importance of proper site selection for direct seeding; and (2) with special reference to the West, the development of practicable methods of rodent control by mass prepoisoning prior to seeding.

Suitable sites for airplane seeding will be those which, in addition to meeting other requirements, have undergone recent denudation, either by large, hot fires or disturbances of the soil. There the seed will find the mineral soil that many species, especially the conifers, require for effective establishment of seedlings, the young plants will encounter a minimum of competition, and animal population will be at low ebb. The main problem is to get the seeds planted, that is, covered sufficiently to promote germination. To accomplish that, the seed is dispersed in the winter, preferably on soft snow, so that it will become embedded before germination time by the physical action of melting down of the snow, frost movements, and spring rains. As the natural plant cover returns to an area following denudation, the area rapidly declines as a broadcast seeding site. Some measure of ground preparation becomes increasingly necessary, and sooner or later a stage is reached where

again broadcasting would waste seed.

Seeding from the air involves the same basic procedures as spreading insecticides and fungicides, except that flight strips must be narrower because seeds fall more sharply than mists or dusts. On the experiment in Maine, flight strips were 50 feet wide, with the plane flying 50 to 75 feet above the treetops. Ground crews must precede the plane to erect flags and wind-socks at corners and along boundaries as guides for the pilot. Distributing devices are whatever an ingenious mechanic can devise to fit the plane and the job. On the Maine job the plane used was a converted N3N Navy training biplane with equipment originally designed for spreading poisoned bran grasshopper bait. The hopper held about 17 bushels. Material flowed from the bottom of the hopper through a slot into a pan under the fuselage from which it was blown out by the slip stream through four fanwise diverging channels. Agitators in the hopper were operated by a small gear box and shaft mounted on one wing and driven by wind vanes. With this distributing apparatus, the flow of pure pine seed could not be regulated satisfactorily; consequently, the seed was mixed with sawdust. By trial and error, proportions of 12 of sawdust to 1 of seed and 6 of sawdust to 1 of seed, by volume, were found to give the 2 desired density rates of approximately 4,000 and 8,000 seeds an acre. These rather low rates were necessitated by the limited amount of seed available. Only white pine was sown; original plans called for red pine also, but seed could not be had.

These details on the Maine seeding are cited merely as one example. With other kinds of seed and distributing equipment, the procedures might vary considerably. The Ontario investigators, for instance, devised a mechanism for distributing undiluted seed through the camera hatch of a Cessna Crane plane. They also have worked with coated or pelleted seed, which increases seed weight by about six times, thus causing the seed to strike the ground with greater force and embed themselves to some degree in the surface soil or litter. The partial embedding, plus the coating of diatomaceous earth and the fly ash, provide more or less coverage for the seed and thereby promote better germination and higher survival. Fungicides, fertilizers, and rodent repellents have been incorporated into the seed coatings, but with no significant benefits except possibly from fungicides in reducing losses from damping-off.

As for costs: That direct seeding can be done at lower cost than planting has been amply demonstrated by experiments and early administrative experience—the latter mostly prior to 1913—on the western national forests. Most of those pre-1913 seedings failed, however, which points up the highly significant fact that lower operating costs an acre mean little unless percentages of successful stocking by seeding and by planting are consistently about the same, or, if not, that the costs for seeding are enough lower to compensate for the larger margin of failures.

We have no cost records for the more recently developed seeding techniques that are sufficiently comprehensive in acreage and years to provide real comparisons with planting in terms of successfully stocked acres. We have only the evidence from relatively small-scale experimental trials which strongly indicates, but does not conclusively demonstrate, that seeding can be done on selected sites in various sections of the country at lower, or at least no higher, costs per successfully stocked acre than planting.

In the northern Rocky Mountain tests before the war, seeding western white pine, exclusive of poisoning, cost approximately the same as planting 2–0 stock (about 1 man-day of labor plus $3.34 for seed or $3.60 for stock for an acre of 800 spots), and $3.86 less than for 2–2 stock, which is the grade usually recommended for planting in that region. Prepoisoning, which required 2 man-hours and 25 cents for bait an acre, brought seeding charges slightly above those for planting 2–0 stock, but still well below those for 2–2 stock. On suitable sites, fully as good stocking usually was achieved with seeding as with planting. The cost for ponderosa pine seed, for 2–0 seedlings, and for the usually preferred 1–2 transplants were $3.64, $3.20, and $5.60, respectively. Though this leaves a margin in favor of seeding as compared with transplant stock, it is an appreciably narrower margin than for white pine. Seeding costs for Engelmann spruce and western redcedar, on the other hand, run far below planting costs because with these species nursery stock is rather expensive to produce, whereas seed costs are low on an acre basis because of the large number of seed to the pound. C. S. Schopmeyer and A. E. Helmers estimate costs for seed well under 50 cents, while the nursery stock would cost at least $7 or $8 an acre.

Tests in Oregon, using the seeding tool mentioned on a preceding page, show that under favorable conditions of weather, terrain, and accessibility, burned-over Douglas-fir land can be prepoisoned for rodents and then spot-seeded at 1946 wage rates for about $6 an acre, approximately $4 of which is for labor. With less favorable conditions, costs will run from $7 to $8 an acre. No direct comparisons with planting have been reported; however, seeding (mostly with Douglas-fir) has reportedly given good results on northern slopes and some fair catches on southern slopes. Planting the same type of terrain undoubtedly would cost at least twice as much—perhaps more.

In the sand plains of the Lake States, on old fields in Ohio and the Atlantic Piedmont region, and on depleted forest areas in the Missouri Ozarks, successful seeding of pines has been done for approximately half the usual costs for planting—in round numbers, about $5 versus $10 an acre or per 1,000 spots. Those are the prewar figures; at present wage rates the costs would be higher but the relationships probably would be about the same. No rodent-control measures were employed. The above costs were based on use of a mechanical seeder in furrows at the Lake States and Piedmont locations, and spot seeding in Ohio and the Ozarks. Spot seeding in the Piedmont, using mulch over the spots, cost about the same as planting. Planting costs are based on local practices, typically 1-0 or 2-0 stock, the species being principally the jack pine in the Lake States, loblolly pine in the Piedmont, and shortleaf pine in Ohio and the Ozarks. In all probability, seeding can be done throughout much of the eastern forest region by similar methods and at about the same relative costs as in those experiments. The approximately 50-percent lower operating costs for seeding appear adequate to compensate for the greater risks involved, and indicate that the method might well be more widely used as a supplement to planting.

Costs for airplane seeding will not mean much until more evidence is available on the degree of success to be expected. If a fair percentage of airplane seedings do succeed, the cost aspects of the method are especially attractive. The previously cited job in Maine was done for about $3.50 an acre. This figure does not include any rental or depreciation charge for the plane; however, a private concern offered to do the flying for 50 cents an acre. The Oregon State Board of Forestry reports costs of $5.13 an acre for their 1946 job, which costs included prepoisoning for rodent control and some snag felling. On the latter job, mixtures of Douglas-fir, Port-Orford-cedar, western hemlock, and Sitka spruce seed were used at the rate of one-half pound an acre.

Flying costs will be influenced appreciably by size and shape of the seeding areas. Situations that permit flight strips of a mile or more will go much faster than those where strips are shorter, thus requiring more time to be spent in turns. Probably the helicopter will prove to be better suited and more economical than the conventional-type planes for working smaller tracts.

RECOMMENDATIONS: Since direct seeding, even though it has several advantages over planting, has the major drawback of generally being more subject to failure, one may ask where or under what circumstances it can be used to best advantage.

The statements to follow refer to the tested hand methods or simple machine methods. No recommendations regarding airplane seeding are warranted now, except that developments be watched with a critical but open mind.

First, seeding can be advocated in those localities and on those classes of sites where experiments have shown that it has a good chance to succeed. Among these are cut-over and burned moist slopes and benches in the northern Rocky Mountain white pine type; the similar areas in the northwestern Douglas-fir region; the low-lying sand plains in the Lake States; the better old-field sites in the East Central States and Atlantic Piedmont; the better cut-over forest sites in the Missouri Ozarks. Its use might well be extended, on a small scale at first, to other sections or localities having conditions similar to any of the above areas. No curtailment of planting in favor of seeding is proposed; rather the planting should be pushed with full vigor during the proper season, but sites deemed suitable for seeding should be bypassed. Then as conditions permit at other times, seed the selected areas.

Second, seeding can be advocated on certain classes of sites, notably very stony areas, where good planting is difficult, expensive, or impossible.

Third, seeding is admirably suited for filling in fail spots in natural reproduction or plantations and other small or out-of-the-way places that hardly would justify taking in a planting crew. Such places can be seeded during the off season for planting by a few men at relatively small expense. If the seedings are successful, the gain is definitely worth while; if they fail, little is lost.

Fourth, seeding can be suggested for special consideration in the establishment of any species that is difficult to handle or tends to react unfavorably to the usual nursery and transplanting procedures. For instance, some strongly taprooted nut species, like black walnut, preferably should be direct seeded where the method is at all feasible.

Finally, seeding appeals to many farmers for starting or restocking a few acres of wood lot, partly because it can be done intermittently at odd times, partly because many men derive satisfaction in growing their trees from seed of their own collection from a favor-

802062°—49——11

able source, while saving the price of nursery stock in the process. Establishing a wood lot is an excellent project for farm boys and many, like their fathers, derive satisfaction and good experience by starting with seed collection rather than purchased nursery stock.

W. E. McQuilkin *is a forester at the Northeastern Forest Experiment Station. From 1938 to 1942 he was engaged in direct-seeding studies at the Southeastern Forest Experiment Station. Dr. McQuilkin is a graduate of Doane College and the Universities of Nebraska and Pennsylvania.*

---

CROSSES AMONG THE WHITE PINES ATTEMPTED BETWEEN 1939 AND 1948 AT THE INSTITUTE OF FOREST GENETICS, PLACERVILLE, CALIF.[1]

| Seed parent[2] | *Pollen parent* | | | | | | | | | | | | | | | | | | |
|---|---|---|---|---|---|---|---|---|---|---|---|---|---|---|---|---|---|---|---|
| | *Pinus koraiensis* | *cembra* | *albicaulis* | *flexilis* | *armandi* | *ayacahuite* | *lambertiana* | *parviflora* | *peuce* | *peuce × strobus* | *excelsa* | *monticola* | *strobus* | *cembroides* | *monophylla* | *edulis* | *bungeana* | *balfouriana* | *aristata* |
| *Pinus—* | | | | | | | | | | | | | | | | | | | |
| *koraiensis* | | | | | | | | | | | | | | | | | | | |
| *cembra* | | | | | | | | | | | | | | | | | | | |
| *albicaulis* | U | U | | | | | | | | | | | | | | | | | |
| *flexilis* | | | | | U | | U | | | | | | U | | | | | | |
| *armandi* | | | | | | | | | | | | | | | | | | | |
| *ayacahuite* | | | | | | | | | | | | | | | | | | | |
| *lambertiana* | U | | | F | F | F | | U | U | | | F | F | | | | | | F |
| *parviflora* | | | | | | | | | | | | | | | | | | | |
| *peuce* | | | | | | | | | | | | | | | | | | | |
| *peuce × strobus* | | | | | | | | | | | | | | | | | | | |
| *excelsa* | | | | U | | | U | | | | | U | U | | | | | | |
| *monticola* | U | | | | U | H | F | U | U | H | H | | H | | | | | | F |
| *strobus* | | | | | F | | F | | | | H | U | | | | | | | |
| *cembroides* | | | | | | | | | | | | | | | U | | | | |
| *monophylla* | | | | | | | | | | | | | | | | | | | |
| *edulis* | | | | | | | | | | | | | | | U | | | | |
| *bungeana* | | | | | | | | | | | | | F | | | | | | |
| *balfouriana* | | | | U | | | | | | | | F | | | | | | | U |
| *aristata* | | | | U | | | | | | | | F | | | | | | U | |

[1] F—failure. This does not mean that the cross cannot be made but that the attempts to date have failed.

U—unknown results. These represent recent crossing attempts of which the seeds have not yet matured or have not yet been planted.

H—hybrids secured from the cross.

[2] Only those white pines are listed that have been used for crossing. Cones mature approximately 15 months after pollination; the success of a cross is not known until the third year, when planted seed from the attempted cross have germinated.

# PINE BREEDING IN THE UNITED STATES

J. W. DUFFIELD, PALMER STOCKWELL

Trees fit into the general rule that the plants and animals which nature gave us have not been considered quite good enough. For millions of years, it is true, nature has developed a breathtaking variety of forms, each wonderfully adapted to its surroundings. Changes in climate or the conformation of the earth's surface have caused the extinction of some forms and the development and migration of others. But during the long development of civilization man has learned to alter some of the myriad forms of life about him, making them better suited to his needs.

Centuries of breeding have developed livestock and plants that have special value, but only recently has man applied his knowledge of breeding to the development of better forest trees. Much of this work has been done with pines because of their wide distribution and their value for many wood products. Today pine-breeding research has progressed to the point that promising pine hybrids exist for each of the major timber-producing regions in the United States.

How has this point been reached? And what are the results now ready for trial?

As long as man used only an occasional tree he was not concerned with replacing it. But when he began to fell sizable sections of the forest, he observed that the succeeding cover was often different from the one he had removed. To insure another tree crop of the type harvested, he often found it necessary to sow seeds or plant young trees. This practice foreshadowed the beginning of forest-tree improvement, perhaps 500 years ago. In his early planting operations, the forester soon learned that certain local races of trees surpassed the average.

American foresters, influenced in their early work by European forestry, were quick to import one of Europe's leading timber trees, the Scotch pine, a species that, despite its name, extends from the British Isles into Siberia and from the Arctic Circle as far as southern Austria and the Iberian Peninsula. Foresters in New York State found that Scotch pine from the shores of the Baltic Sea made a respectable tree in their plantations, while the same species grown from south German seed produced gigantic corkscrews and other bizarre and useless forms. Foresters in almost every European country have studied Scotch pine from various sources and have come to recognize an almost limitless number of local races, each fitted by natural selection into the mold of the local climatic and soil conditions.

In the past few years, several workers in the Forest Service, notably R. H. Weidman, T. T. Munger, and W. G. Morris, have completed studies of local races of ponderosa pine and Douglas-fir, two of our most widespread and important western conifers. An interesting study of altitudinal races of ponderosa pine in the Sierra Nevada of California was initiated by L. Austin, also of the Forest Service. Work of this kind has led foresters to the realization that careful comparative studies of climate and soils and of the growth of local races should enable them to proceed with more certainty in their work of reforestation.

In recent years most spectacular results have been achieved by this analytical approach in parts of Italy, South Africa, Australia, and New Zealand—regions that have rather meager native conifer forests and only moderate rainfall, most of which falls in the winter. Such a climate resembles that of coastal California, where a few small patches of natural Monterey pine survive. The fossil record shows that this pine once occupied a much larger area, but because of increasing dryness along the coast it was squeezed into a smaller and smaller area. There it was making its last stand when the botanists found it. Given a fresh start in Australia, New Zealand, Italy, and South Africa, this almost extinct pine delighted foresters by its rapid growth and good form. In places where it was a complete stranger, it found just the conditions of soil and climate it needed.

These examples show the effectiveness of natural selection in shaping the heredity of trees so as to fit them for growth in specific types of environment. It would be surprising, however, if men were content with a process so slow that it can only be seen in the unfolding of the fossil record. Foresters have turned to artificial selection or sought some other man-made device to speed up the remodeling of forest trees.

Biologists generally agree that certain features of species are especially important to survival of the race. The features have to do with the survival of the individual and perpetuation of the species. Furthermore, infancy is the period in the individual's life during which the balance between survival and death is most precarious. Thus the features most strongly molded by natural selection, the so-called adaptive features, have to do largely with the start of life of the individual. The forester, however, is largely concerned with the characteristics of mature or young-mature trees. His selection has been aimed at the development of trees especially suited to producing usable products such as clear lumber, smooth veneer, or strong paper in the greatest possible quantities per acre per year. His selection therefore must take quite a different direction from the one practiced by nature.

Before our knowledge of the science of genetics was developed, selection was practiced in the woods. Seed trees of good form were left and misshapen wolf trees were cut, or, if plantings were needed, seed was collected only from the best-formed trees. With the recognition of Gregor Mendel's work at the turn of the century, some foresters realized that well-formed seed trees might carry in a recessive or concealed condition certain hereditary factors that could cause some of their offspring to be of an inferior quality. Other early work by geneticists showed that many characteristics of plants and animals—such as size, quality, and resistance to unfavorable environmental influences—were determined by many hereditary factors. So, for a tree to have the maximum growth rate or a certain form, it had to have just the right combination of a large number of hereditary factors. That fact revealed the relative ineffectiveness of selection practiced in the woods as a method of improving the heredity of a forest and eventually led to deliberate efforts to develop superior types of forest trees by genetic methods.

It is always difficult to point with certainty to the originator of an idea, and we hope to be forgiven if we unwittingly slight the "father of tree breeding." Klotzsch, in Germany, attempted to cross Scotch pine with Austrian pine in 1845. His statement that he planted the hybrid seed the spring following pollination is at variance with the facts, because 2 years are required for the formation of seed of those species. Nils Sylven in 1909 undertook to investigate the heritability of certain well-recognized crown types in Norway spruce and Scotch pine growing in Sweden. This he did by making self-pollinations to determine whether the various crown types would breed true. From 1912 to 1924, Augustine Henry, in England, and several Americans, including Helge Ness, A. B. Stout, E. J. Schreiner, and others, began controlled pollination work, the foundation stone of tree breeding.

In 1925, James G. Eddy, after seeking the advice of Luther Burbank, established the Eddy Tree Breeding Station at Placerville, in northern California. The station was later deeded to the United States, to be managed by the Forest Service as the Institute of Forest Genetics. The Institute soon narrowed the scope of its work to the genetic improvement of the timber pines. John Barnes, W. C. Cumming, and W. G. Wahlenberg pioneered in the development of pollination techniques. F. I. Righter joined the station staff in 1931 and, with W. C. Cumming, perfected the techniques and used them to demonstrate the great possibilities for genetic improvement that could be realized through species hybridization in the pines. At about this time, Philip C. Wakeley, also of the Forest Service, made a number of crosses between the timber-pine species of the Southeastern States.

Much of the pioneer work in pine breeding thus is behind us.

Three general methods are available to the tree breeder today. Two of them—selection and hybridization—consist of using and recombining hereditary variations already existing among trees. The third method can be used to create hereditary variations through physical or chemical treatments.

Selection becomes much more effective when it is combined with other techniques, such as progeny testing, vegetative propagation, or hybridization. Progeny tests of self-pollinated plants help determine which parents to select for the best offspring. But since the pines are predominantly cross-pollinated, a progeny test in which only the seed parent is known tells only half of the story. Vegetative propagation, which is used by fruit growers to multiply selected trees, has not yet reached a stage of development for pines which would permit economical propagation of forest planting stock except in New Zealand, where it is practiced with Monterey pine. Great progress has been made, however, by workers in South Africa and Australia; by K. W. Dorman and his associates, who have been working with turpentine pines in the southeastern part of the United States; and by N. T. Mirov, of the Institute of Forest Genetics in California.

This work has resulted in techniques by which the clones from selected pines may be vegetatively propagated for research purposes or for establishment of seed-producing plantations. Members of a clone are merely parts of a single tree, made to produce roots and become self-supporting or supplied with roots by grafting. Numerous experiments have shown that pines and many other forest trees can produce few seed as a result of self-pollination; usually the few seedlings so produced are weak. Pollination between members of the same clone is equivalent to self-pollination. For that reason, mixing several clones in a seed-producing plantation is necessary to insure cross-pollination and satisfactory seed production. Such plantations in Sweden contain from 6 to 12 selected clones, all from a single local race to insure adaptability. When two selected trees or clones are cross-pollinated, there is no certainty that the offspring will be better than the average for the species, but when half a dozen or more selected clones are allowed to interpollinate the chance for average superiority of the offspring is increased. Only by controlled pollination can it be determined which pairs of clones will consistently produce superior offspring. Perhaps the most promising field for selection work with pines is the search for trees resistant to disease and insect attack.

The methods and benefits of pine hybridization were discussed in an article on hybrid forest trees in the 1943-1947 Yearbook of Agriculture.

Briefly, the benefits to be expected are hybrid vigor, the combination of desirable characters in a single plant, and the uncovering by hybrid segregation of hitherto unsuspected characters in the offspring derived from breeding within a hybrid population. Naturally, hybridization can be expected to be most effective if the parents are selected rather carefully.

As to the third method available to tree breeders, most of the techniques for initiating new hereditary variations are barely out of the laboratory and as yet cannot be consciously directed—they might more appropriately be called shotgun methods in their present state of development. They include the induction of gene mutations and chromosome rearrangements by X-ray and other types of radiation, heat treatments, and cold shocks. The doubling of chromosome numbers by treatment of seeds or growing points with colchicine, acenaphthene, or other chemicals was once regarded as promising for making pine hybrids true-breeders. This hope has faded somewhat in the face of a number of failures of this type of experimentation, and at present such work is placed in the category of pure research, which, given sufficient time and effort, may yet produce valuable tools for the practical tree breeder.

What has been accomplished by these methods and how and where can the accomplishments be put to use?

Perhaps the best way to answer is to make a tour of the forest regions of this country, stopping long enough in each to see what the breeders have to offer.

In the Northeastern States, the eastern white pine is most interesting to the tree breeder because of its great commercial value and because of the challenge offered by its susceptibility to the attacks of two major pests, the white-pine weevil and the white pine blister rust. This pine belongs to a group of closely related species, which includes the western white pine of the northern Rockies as well as the Pacific Northwest, Himalayan white pine, and the Balkan pine of Yugoslavia and Greece. The last two pines are of particular interest because they exhibit some resistance to blister rust.

Several pine breeders have made hybrids within this group. Workers at the Arnold Arboretum of Harvard University and at the Institute of Forest Genetics have found that hybrids between eastern white pine and western white pine, between western white pine and Himalayan white pine, and between Himalayan white pine and eastern white pine are all more vigorous than the parent species. During the first 7 years of growth, the hybrid just about doubles the height growth of the parents.

L. P. V. Johnson and C. Heimburger of Canada have crossed eastern white pine with the Balkan pine. C. Syrach-Larsen in Denmark also has made this cross and has grown hybrid seedlings that are already producing pollen.

Some of this pollen has been used in crosses with the western white pine at the Institute of Forest Genetics. By this means we hope to introduce the blister rust resistance of the Balkan and Himalayan pines into a cross that exhibits hybrid vigor. The work of A. J. Riker and associates at the University of Wisconsin has shown that in areas heavily infected with blister rust a rare tree may be found to have a high degree of resistance. These trees are now being used to produce stock that can be tested for resistance to blister rust. Dr. C. Heimburger is emphasizing both blister rust resistance and resistance to white-pine weevil attack in his breeding work with the white pines.

The practical value of all hybrids depends on their adaptation to the climate in which they are planted.

Some of the hybrids mentioned are of unknown hardiness in the Northeast, but we can be confident that others will thrive because both parent species are known to be hardy. This applies especially to the eastern-western white pine hybrid and to a less certain degree to the hybrids involving the Balkan white pine. The Himalayan pine is known to be hardy in Philadelphia, and therefore hybrids involving this species should thrive at least that far north.

Pitch pine, which is currently of minor importance in the Northeast because of its poor form and slow growth, has been successfully crossed with loblolly and shortleaf pines to yield hybrids that surpass pitch pine in form and rate of growth. The hardiness of these hybrids has not yet been tested in the more northerly region inhabited by pitch pine, but it is reasonable to expect that the hybrids will be at least intermediate in cold resistance.

THE SOUTHEASTERN AND SOUTHERN STATES have four principal timber pines—all used in hybridization work. None of the crosses so far made have resulted in conspicuous hybrid vigor comparable to that found in the white pine crosses, but some of them combine desirable properties of the parent species in such a way as to be of great interest to timber growers. The cross between shortleaf and loblolly pines is generally superior to shortleaf pine in form and growth rate and gives some promise of growing in areas outside the natural range of loblolly pine, notably in eastern Texas and Arkansas.

Loblolly and shortleaf pines have both been crossed with slash pine, perhaps the most productive pine in the region for both timber and naval stores. Slash pine would contribute much more to the economy of the South if it were not comparatively restricted in its distribution; it is to be expected that crosses with loblolly and shortleaf pines can be made that will considerably extend the range of slash pine without sacrificing productivity. The natural hybrid between longleaf and loblolly pines has been known for some time, and a number of second-generation hybrids have been tested at the Institute of Forest Genetics. Some of these show strikingly good form and rapid growth under conditions wholly unfavorable to longleaf pine.

FOR THE LAKE STATES two important timber pines have been used in crosses, which have shown remarkable vigor. The first of these, eastern white pine, has already been discussed under the northeastern region. The second, jack pine, has been crossed with lodgepole pine of western United States to give a hybrid as vigorous as jack pine and as much as 79 percent taller than lodgepole pine of the same age. So far, this cross has been made only with the lodgepole pine of the high Sierra Nevada, which is a relatively slow-growing tree at medium to low altitudes.

It is quite possible that lodgepole pine from lower elevations in the Pacific Northwest or in the Rocky Mountains may be used with a selected local race of jack pine to produce even better hybrids. This cross should have great appeal to the pulpwood growers and is comparatively easy to produce.

Preliminary experiments at the Institute of Forest Genetics have shown that jack pine cuttings can be rooted rather easily, thus opening up the possibility of establishing clonal seed-parent blocks of this species that can be mass-pollinated with lodgepole pine pollen to produce hybrids at relatively low cost. The scheme is especially practicable for jack pine, which normally produces sound seeds at an earlier age than most other pine species.

WESTWARD, in the northern Rocky Mountain and Pacific Northwest regions, the same hybrids that show promise in the Lake States are likely to succeed. Recent work by T. T. Munger shows that at the Wind River Arboretum in southern Washington, eastern white pine equals the western white pine in growth and form. Thus it is reasonable to expect that hybrids that have shown superior growth in tests in California and Massachusetts will thrive in the Northwest. Although neither of the parent species is generally resistant to blister rust, it is believed that resistance can eventually be introduced from resistant species such as Balkan and Himalayan pines or from resistant individuals of eastern white pine. No doubt some resistant trees of western white pine will eventually be found and brought into the breeding program.

For the central and southern Rocky Mountains, the Southwestern States, and California, a number of the hybrids have been produced. Monterey pine of the mild California coast has been crossed with knobcone pine, which is generally found in locations with much lower winter temperatures and more extreme summer drought than occur in locations where Monterey pine has survived. It is a typical combination hybrid that brings together the greater drought and frost resistance of the knobcone pine and the rapid growth and good form of Monterey pine. Studies under way at the Institute of Forest Genetics suggest that practical methods of vegetative propagation may be found to establish plantations made up of superior clones of this hybrid.

California's infant paper industry may in time derive much of its raw material from plantations of this and similar hybrids in the foothills surrounding the great Central Valley, at the lower border of the pine belt. Although the area is known to favor excellent growth of ponderosa pine, it has produced little pine timber in recent years because of frequent fires and rainfall conditions that are not often favorable to the natural establishment of ponderosa pine seedlings.

Both Monterey and knobcone pines carry their own fire insurance in the form of cones that open after fires and shower the burned-off areas with millions of seeds. The hybrid between these species is highly fertile and has "fire cones," which are produced abundantly when the trees are little more than 5 years old.

Several hybrids between the so-called yellow pines show great promise for the semiarid West, although no certain cases of hybrid vigor have been found. Ponderosa pine of the Pacific slope is known to grow more rapidly than the Rocky Mountain ponderosa pine, but the ability of the coastal variety to thrive in the Rocky Mountain region or in the Southwest is open to serious question. In tests in California, however, the hybrids of these two have caught up to ponderosa pine in height growth at 5 years. A distinct possibility is thereby offered to the forest planters in the Rocky Mountain region and the Southwest. An even more promising hybrid has been made by crossing ponderosa pine with Apache pine, a close relative from Arizona. The hybrid is remarkable for its rapid root penetration and diameter growth, both of which greatly exceed those of ponderosa pine, and for the fact that it equals ponderosa pine in height growth.

Jeffrey pine, a native of California, Oregon, Nevada, and Mexico, and long thought to be closely related to ponderosa pine, is generally of excellent form but of slower growth than ponderosa. A few years ago Jeffrey pine was found to have crossed, in several parts of its range, with Coulter pine, a species found only in California and Mexico.

Coulter pine, under California conditions, is one of the fastest growing pines although it is limby and relatively short-lived. Pollen from the natural hybrid between these pines, applied to flowers of Jeffrey pine, produced an abundant crop of backcross hybrids. In repeated tests these hybrids have grown almost as fast as Coulter pine, and have exhibited as good crown and stem form as Jeffrey or ponderosa pine. Elsewhere in this Yearbook, an account is given of insect resistance of this interesting hybrid, which may yet offer stiff competition to pondersa pine, heretofore the undisputed king of the western pines.

THESE RESULTS of research are encouraging. The principles and techniques of pine breeding are reasonably well worked out. Hybrids and strains of superior growth rate, hardiness, insect resistance, gum yield, and other qualities have been produced with trees from widely separated localities. The superior forms so far produced should be very useful, but they cannot be expected to grow equally well under all climatic and soil conditions. As with other crops, it will be necessary to breed pines to fit the major climatic regions and in some cases particular sites within a region.

The present status of pine breeding might be likened to that of corn breeding in the early 1930's. The principles and techniques had been pretty well worked out by various research workers, and a number of high-yielding corn strains had been produced. The next step was to make hybrid seed available to the farmers. When this was done, the planting of new strains spread amazingly; during the next 6 years hybrid corn came to occupy more than 80 percent of the land planted to corn in the Corn Belt, with an increased yield averaging about 20 percent. Although existing hybrid pines may be expected to increase the yield on plantation sites to which they are adapted, no seed of these superior tree strains is now available for general distribution. Devising means for production and distribution of those hybrids that seem worthy of trial in the various regions is the next step needed to capitalize on the results of pine-breeding research.

J. W. DUFFIELD, *a geneticist, joined the staff of the Institute of Forest Genetics in 1946. A graduate of Cornell and Harvard Universities, he worked as a forester for the Forest Service in Michigan and as a tree breeder for the Northeastern Forest Experiment Station.*

PALMER STOCKWELL *is geneticist in charge, Institute of Forest Genetics, a branch of the California Forest and Range Experiment Station, maintained by the Forest Service in cooperation with the University of California, in Berkeley. He has served with the Boyce Thompson Southwestern Arboretum in Arizona, the Carnegie Institution in California, the Soil Conservation Service in New Mexico, and, since 1937, the Forest Service. He is a graduate of the University of Arizona and holds the doctor's degree from the Stanford University.*

# POPLARS CAN BE BRED TO ORDER

ERNST J. SCHREINER

Scientific breeding has given us the hybrid poplars that grow faster than our native species and resist better the inroads of insects and disease. New hybrids now can be practically bred to order.

Poplars offer outstanding possibilities for rapid improvement through scientific breeding for several reasons. First of all, nature has provided a wide diversity of germ plasm, the stuff that controls inheritance; there are a large number of relatively rapid-growing species and varieties that extend over a wide climatic range. Because poplar species hybrids are reasonably fertile, one can create new types that combine the best characteristics of many species and varieties. Breeding is simplified because branches cut from mature trees can be made to flower and fruit in the greenhouse. Most poplars can be reproduced easily from stem cuttings. Thus inherently excellent trees can be utilized almost at once without continued breeding for many generations to get the type true from seed; a new and improved hybrid can be multiplied by cuttings with the assurance that every tree will be exactly like the selected individual.

The painstaking, patient work of improving forest trees began in Germany in 1845, when Johann Klotzsch crossed two species each of pine, oak, elm, and alder, and observed that after 8 years his hybrids averaged one-third taller than the parent species. In the following 60 years scientists accumulated additional evidence on the occurrence of hybrid vigor in crosses between tree species and varieties, but there was no effort to create better forest trees by scientific breeding. Augustine Henry, professor of forestry in the Royal College of Science, Dublin, was the first forester to do something about it and to urge strongly that the artificial production of trees by crossing was a new and important field of forest research.

"In countries like our own," he said

in 1910, "the only hope of salvation for forestry is in growing timber rapidly. . . . We are ourselves making some experiments in cross-fertilization this year; but more workers are required in this field. Hitherto, nothing whatever has been done to improve the breeds of forest trees; and foresters have never even thought of the possibilities in this direction, though gardeners and farmers have shown the way for centuries."

Four years later he described several hybrids he had made, including a vigorous poplar hybrid (×*Populus generosa*), and again directed attention to certain first-generation hybrid trees that, as in other plants, "are remarkable for their size, rapid growth, early and free flowering, longer period of life, the ease with which they can be multiplied, and in all probability their comparative immunity from disease."

In the United States, suggestions on breeding forest trees began to appear in the reports of the American Breeders Association in the early 1900's. But hybridizing poplars so as to produce fast-growing trees for reforesting cut-over pulpwood lands was first advocated in 1916 by Ralph H. McKee, then head of the Paper and Pulp School in the University of Maine.

Dr. McKee, convinced of the practical possibilities by Augustine Henry's hybridization results, turned for help and advice on a breeding program to A. B. Stout, plant breeder and director of laboratories at the New York Botanical Garden. The Oxford Paper Co., in Maine, agreed to finance the program, and in April 1924 the work was started in cooperation with the New York Botanical Garden. Botanists and foresters had laid the ground work; the persistence of Dr. McKee, a research chemist, brought the financial support for large-scale hybridization.

The project had headquarters at the New York Botanical Garden under the supervision of Dr. Stout, who was directly and solely responsible for the planning and direction of the poplar breeding. The most complete collection in the country of poplar species and varieties of blooming age was in Highland Park, Rochester, N. Y. Within 2 years the breeding work at the New York Botanical Garden and Highland Park had produced thousands of new hybrids; the hybrid seedlings in pots filled two entire greenhouses. Late in 1926 the Oxford Paper Co. established near Rumford Falls, Maine, a nursery devoted entirely to the propagation of the best of those hybrids. There, more than 13,000 seedlings, which represent 99 cross-combinations among 34 types of poplars, were set out in forest plantations in 1927 and 1928. Those seedlings represent thousands of new combinations of germ plasm.

Sixty-nine of the most promising hybrids were being propagated for large-scale reforestation planting in 1932, when a change in pulpwood utilization practically eliminated the Oxford Paper Co.'s need for poplar pulpwood; research chemists had adapted the soda process to the utilization of birch, beech, and maple. Previously, only aspen wood, the native poplar, was used for soda pulp to provide the short-fibered stock necessary for the manufacture of most high-grade papers. Birch, beech, and maple grow abundantly near Rumford, and good business dictated their use. Nevertheless, the company continued to maintain the hybrids because of their potential value for reforestation. During the depression years the project was on a bare maintenance basis and it was not possible to establish test plantations of the best hybrids.

Congress appropriated funds for research in tree breeding in the Northeast in 1936, and the Oxford Paper Co. transferred the new hybrids and its breeding records to the Northeastern Forest Experiment Station. It took several years to propagate stocks of the selected hybrids, and then, just when planting stock in sufficient quantity for large-scale field tests was available, the war stopped the work, and it went back again to a maintenance basis.

In 1947 we started once more to build up our growing stock of 200 selected hybrids for comprehensive forestation tests throughout the Northeast. We hope this time to be able to complete the job. Research with living trees cannot be slowed down, stopped, and started again, without loss of results out of all proportion to the length of the inactive period. Nature keeps her steady pace without regard for depressions and wars; trees that can be transplanted this spring will be too large next year; trees that are dying this month can provide symptoms of their malady if they are examined in time, but next month may be too late; a thinning in hybrid poplar delayed a year can result in more than merely retarded growth—it can start the entire stand on the road to degeneration.

DURING OUR YEARS of work with it, we have thought of the hybrid poplar as the farmer's tree—a tree that can provide a forest income for many farmers, with marginal land and depleted wood lots, earlier than the slow-growing species can.

The rapid growth of the hybrids has been demonstrated in the original plantations in western Maine, where the growing season is relatively short. They were planted 6 by 6 feet apart on farm land abandoned about 60 years ago. They were never thinned (contrary to good practice) because we wanted to let natural selection eliminate the weak.

Judging from the growth of the selected hybrids in the unthinned plantations, we can predict that with good forestry methods the poplar hybrids will produce at least 40 cords of wood an acre in 15 years. The prediction is based on the actual growth of individual hybrids whose equally vigorous neighbors gave them far greater competition than would be permitted under good forestry. At the prewar roadside price of $8 a cord, we figure a gross income of $320 for 40 cords an acre over 15 years—10 cords an acre from thinnings between the eighth and tenth years, and 30 cords an acre at 15 years. Properly thinned stands need not be cut in 15 years; in 20 to 25 years they would produce logs for veneer or lumber.

As for net income, a farmer would calculate the amount of work he would have to do on his plantation. Each newly planted acre will require approximately 10 days of work from planting to harvest, of which all but the planting and cultivation in the first year can be done during slack seasons. The work of the first year (preparation of land, planting, and cultivation, which would take 4 man-days an acre) would be required only once—when the timber is harvested the hybrid poplars will regenerate themselves from root suckers. In the third or fourth year, thinning the trees would take 1 man-day an acre. Between the eighth and tenth year, thinning would require approximately 5 man-days an acre. Besides work required to grow the crop, there will be the harvest labor, which can also be handled as a winter or off-season job. If the farmer does the work himself, he simply transfers the difference between gross and net income from one pocket to the other; if the work is done by hired labor, the net income will compare favorably with that from many other farm crops.

These estimates are based on growth in Maine, where the growing season is short. With a longer growing season, the hybrids will grow faster. Dormant cuttings (12-inch lengths of 1-year-old stems without roots) of 102 different hybrids were planted at the Agricultural Research Center in Maryland in the spring of 1947. Fifty of them grew to an average height of 6 to 8 feet in a year. In 1 year from cuttings, the same hybrids would grow only 2½ to 3 feet in Maine and 4 to 5 feet in western Massachusetts.

OTHER CHARACTERISTICS than rapid growth have been considered in making the selections. The hybrids were selected for resistance to poplar diseases present in the Maine plantations, and they now are being subjected to direct inoculation tests. The variation among the new hybrids in susceptibility to damage by Japanese beetles has been observed for several years in Connecticut, Pennsylvania, and Maryland. Only a few have so far been found susceptible to the insect.

The ability to root from cuttings is another major point in selecting the hybrids for further testing. All of the selected hybrids grow practically 100 percent from cuttings planted directly in the field on properly prepared ground. The branching habit has also been considered; sometimes it has been possible to select hybrids with few and small-diameter branches. The largest branches on some of these sparsely branched hybrids, trees 60 to 70 feet tall, are less than 3 inches in diameter. Trees with few and small branches will require a minimum of labor for limbing-out, and will provide lumber or veneer logs with a minimum of small knots.

For other sections of the United States, the hybrids are promising. A few of the earliest selections that were tested on a small scale in the Pacific Northwest have been reported to be better than the native cottonwoods in rate of growth and resistance to disease. Evidence on this point is not yet conclusive.

One should remember that the original purpose of the poplar-breeding project was to develop fast-growing trees for pulpwood forestation in Maine and New England. The hybrids were planted in western Maine, where the growing season is short and winter temperatures drop far below zero. Hundreds of seedlings failed to survive this rigorous test—many because they continued to grow too late into the fall, others because they started to grow too early in the spring. Some of the nonhardy hybrids that were lost in Maine might have done exceptionally well in a warmer climate. Although many of our new hybrids, selected for disease resistance, will be valuable over large areas outside the Northeast, I believe additional breeding is necessary to produce the best adapted and fastest growing hybrids possible for the warmer regions of the country. Such breeding should include the native southern and western poplars and the best of our disease-resistant hybrids.

Research with varieties and hybrids of poplars is going on now in Canada, Europe, Great Britain, Scandinavia, the Soviet Union, South America, South Africa, and Australia. The research in several countries is on a much larger scale than in the United States. Poplars are so important to the forest economy of Europe that before the war their culture and improvement was studied in practically every European country. Since the war, the interest of European foresters in poplars has greatly increased. The International Poplar Commission, established in 1947, has sponsored two international conferences on poplar, in Paris in 1947 and in Rome in 1948.

In this country, poplars for reforestation have not come fully into their own because of two handicaps. They are susceptible to diseases that, under certain conditions, can wipe out an entire plantation, and they require considerable care in planting and are highly intolerant of both top and root competition. They cannot be planted and forgotten on abandoned fields or brush land; the ground must be prepared properly before planting, and the plantation has to be kept free of grass and weeds for at least the first year. Later the trees must be thinned before mutual competition begins to interfere with their growth. On the credit side, the hybrid poplars respond quickly to good care, and their rapid growth will pay a profit on the labor involved. Carefully selected hybrids will largely eliminate the disease hazard.

The future is bright for fast-growing, disease-resistant poplar hybrids. Poplar wood in this country is used for paper pulp, boxes, veneer for fruit and vegetable containers, excelsior, and for minor uses. Recent advances in the use of wood promise an expanded market in the future. New physical and chemical treatments can endow poplar wood with properties capable of bringing it into competition with many hardwoods and conifers. The increasing use of plastics is bound to favor the growing of a tree, like hybrid poplar, that can produce cellulose and lignin rapidly.

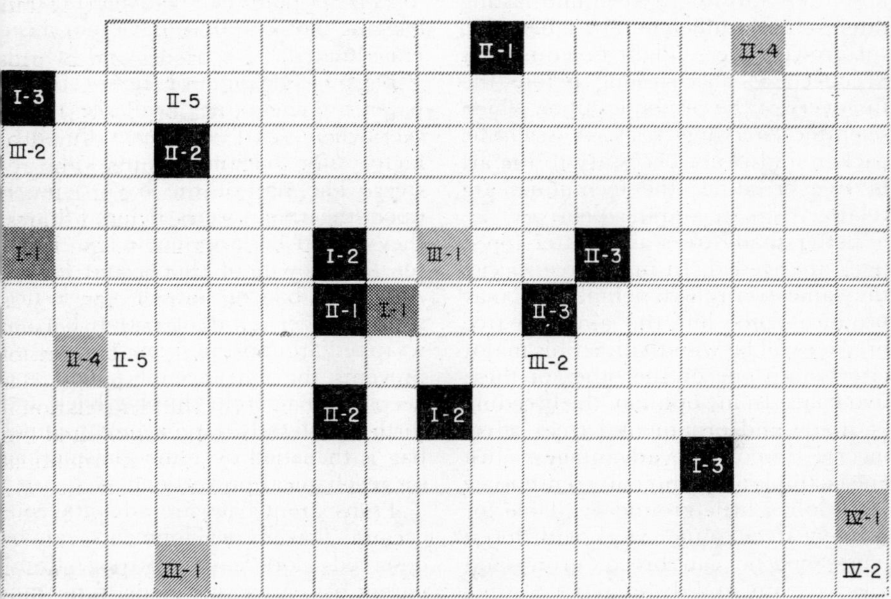


Each square represents a 20- by 20-foot plot containing 50 trees of a poplar hybrid.

No feeding during the entire infestation.

Light feeding. Up to 25 percent of leaves damaged on 20 percent to 100 percent of the trees.

Medium feeding. About 50 percent of leaves damaged on 80 percent to 90 percent of the trees.

Heavy feeding. More than 75 percent of leaves damaged on 100 percent of the trees.

**This diagram shows the random planting arrangement of 102 poplar hybrids, which represent 30 different parentages. Japanese beetle infestation was heavy in 1947; as late as September 9 beetles were as numerous as 10–12 per leaf on the most susceptible plants. Although the insects were feeding everywhere on the sparsely scattered weeds growing under the hybrids, beetle feeding was found on only nine hybrids representing four parentages. Three of these parentages include hybrids that were entirely free of beetle feeding during the entire infestation.**

**Parentage No. I (*Populus charkowiensis*×*P. balsamifera virginiana*). Hybrids No. I–1, I–2, I–3 were all susceptible.**

**Parentage No. II (*Populus charkowiensis*×*P. caudina*). Hybrids No. II–1, II–2, II–3, II–4 were susceptible. Hybrid No. II–5 was nonsusceptible.**

**Parentage No. III (*Populus charkowiensis*×*P. berolinensis*). Hybrid No. III–1 was susceptible. Hybrid No. III—2 was nonsusceptible.**

**Parentage No. IV (*Populus simonii*×*P. berolinensis*). Hybrid No. IV–1 was susceptible. Hybrid No. IV–2 was nonsusceptible.**

**The extremely wide variation in susceptibility among individual hybrids of the same parent trees is of great significance to forest-tree breeding. Such differences were hardly expected for an insect like the Japanese beetle which feeds on many species of plants. If the 1947 results are confirmed during the next few years, it will justify intensive breeding for resistance to other forest insects, such as the spruce budworm.**

# AMATEUR TREE BREEDERS? WHY NOT?

ERNST J. SCHREINER

The amateur can find ample scope for a creative interest in breeding and hybridizing trees. There are only two absolute requisites, a keen and lasting interest and sufficient available land for growing trees. Plant breeding was practiced as an art long before the discovery of the principles upon which scientific breeding rests. A scientific background is not necessary to the art of tree breeding; the techniques are relatively simple and inexpensive.

Better shade trees and better forest trees are needed. In many tree species the same controlled pollinations may produce both, but the amateur tree breeder will be wise to direct his major efforts into one or the other of these two fields. In my opinion, the breeding of shade and ornamental trees offers several important advantages. Just one example: The breeding enthusiast with only a little ground available for growing trees cannot work with forest types, but he can breed, grow, and select ornamental dwarf types.

Tree-breeding methods are much the same as those used by the breeder of the agricultural and horticultural plants. Controlled breeding requires protection of the female flowers from chance pollination both before and after the desired pollination has been made. That usually is accomplished by covering the unopened flower buds with bags of paper, vegetable parchment, light canvas, or cloth. Bags made from cellulose sausage casings, which are available in a fair range of sizes, are excellent for many kinds of trees.

For trees that produce separate male and female flowers on the same twigs (for example, birch, hickory, oak), one must remove the male flowers from the part of the branch that is to be bagged. If the tree bears perfect flowers (male and female parts in the same flower), the stamens, which produce the pollen, must be carefully removed before they mature. Such emascula- tion is not necessary if the tree doe not set viable seed to its own pollen This latter point can be determined b bagging flowers that have not bee emasculated.

Bags of glassine or heavy brow paper are cheap, are available almos everywhere, and are generally satis- factory for bagging many kinds o trees. The size of the bags depend upon the tree species being worked they should be large enough to allow for the growth of shoots and leaves A glassine bag of suitable size is tied securely over a bit of cotton batting wrapped around the stem. The cotton prevents the entrance of pollen and keeps the bag from slipping back and forth. A slightly larger brown-paper bag is then tied over the glassine bag for mechanical protection.

Transparent bags are advantageous because flower developments can be observed more easily. Strong, trans- parent bags are easily made from com- mercial sausage casings, which come in cylindrical strips of various diameters and lengths. Strips cut into suitable lengths can be made into pollination bags in several ways; one easy way is to gather and tie one end of the casing over a small cotton plug.

When the female flowers under the bags are fully open and receptive, they must be dusted with pollen from the selected male parent. For some insect-pollinated species it is safe to remove the bags and to apply the pollen directly with a small cotton swab, but the wind-pollinated trees (such as the oaks, hickories, and poplars) should be pollinated without removing the bags. With such species a tiny puncture is made in the glassine bag and the pollen is blown into the bag with an ordinary glass medicine dropper. The small puncture in the bag is then immediately covered with scotch tape, or second glassine bag may be tied over the original. The heavy paper bag is then replaced and the bags are left in position until the flowers are past bloom. Sausage-casing bags may be punctured for pollination, or the tip of the bag may be opened carefully, just enough to admit the dropper.

The medicine droppers work best if the ends are drawn out to a relatively fine point in the heat of a gas flame. A loose wad of absorbent cotton inserted in the dropper, just below the rubber bulb, will conserve pollen by keeping it out of the bulb. Such droppers are cheap enough to be used for one kind of pollen and then discarded.

Pollen can be collected directly from the tree selected as the male parent, but there is less danger of contamination if flowering branches are cut and kept indoors, in water, until the pollen is shed. Special care must be taken to prevent any mixing of pollen from different trees. Pollen can be handled most conveniently in small vials stoppered with plugs of absorbent cotton. Most pollen will remain viable for at least several days, if the cotton-stoppered vials are kept in a tight jar and stored in a refrigerator.

Accurate records are essential; flowers, pollen, seeds, and seedlings should be labeled to provide a detailed record of the parentage of all progenies produced by controlled breeding. The amateur breeder should record such information as location and description of parent trees, dates of bagging, pollen collection, pollination, removal of bags, collection of seed, storage of seed, and date of planting. Such records are necessary for planning future breeding work, especially breeding directed toward the improvement of particular characters or qualities.

The tree breeder also should collect seed, matured to natural pollination, from both parents of his successful crosses. The seedlings and trees grown from such open-pollinated seed can be used as a "yardstick" to determine how much the control-bred seedlings differ from their parental types.

Seed can be planted in pots, in flats, or in carefully prepared seedbeds; the essential thing is to maintain the identity of each seed lot from the time the seed is collected until the seedlings are planted in a permanent location. The final planting location of the seedling progenies is best recorded on a map.

The study of his progeny trees can keep the amateur breeder occupied for many years. From frequent observations during every month of the growing season, by literally living with his trees, the amateur will soon recognize differences between trees of even the same parentage. Where "yardstick trees" of the parent types are included in the plantation, they will provide a good measure for estimating improvement in the progenies derived from controlled breeding.

Ernst J. Schreiner *has done research in tree breeding since 1924, when he left the New York State College of Forestry at Syracuse University shortly before graduation to work on poplars. His first work with hybrid poplars was as research forester with the Oxford Paper Company from 1924 to 1935. After a year with the Tennessee Valley Authority as associate tree-crop specialist, he joined the staff of the Northeastern Forest Experiment Station as forest geneticist. He holds degrees from the New York State College of Forestry at Syracuse (1926) and from Columbia University.*

---

*Many a tree is found in the wood*
*And every tree for its use is good:*
*Some for the strength of the gnarled root,*
*Some for the sweetness of flowering fruit;*
*Some for a shelter against the storm,*
*And some to keep the hearthstone warm;*
*Some for the roof, and some for the beam . . .*

HENRY VAN DYKE

# PRODUCTION OF PLANTING STOCK

FLOYD M. COSSITT, C. A. RINDT, HARRY A. GUNNING

To produce the millions of treelings that are needed for reforestation and for planting on farm woodlands, wildlife areas, stream banks, windbreaks, and erosion-control projects in the United States, nurserymen grow more than 40 coniferous species of trees and shrubs and fifty-odd hardwood species. To get the quality, quantity, and variety needed, the growers have to observe most carefully, in exact sequence, a number of well-defined procedures. Their work embraces the attention to detail that the grower of orchids must have, the cycles of seed-time and harvest that govern the farmer's work, the long view of things that the parent takes in rearing children. Nurserymen must have practical knowledge of a half dozen sciences—genetics, botany, entomology, soils, dendrology, pathology. Patience, too.

From the time they sow the seed in the nursery until the trees are ready to be shipped to the planting site, the men must care for the seedlings scientifically to make them strong enough to stand the hardships they will encounter in their permanent home. The nursery soil must contain certain plant nutrients in the right amounts necessary for healthy growth. The nursery stock must be protected from many diseases, weeds, as well as insects. Cold hardiness, shade requirement, tolerance to sun, and other factors must be observed. Too much water makes the trees soft and weak; too little retards their growth. Some species must remain in the nursery as long as 5 years, maybe more, before they are ready to be planted in the field; others are ready in a year. All can better live and populate a new forest if they have had proper care in the nursery.

Every State in the United States has some form of planting program that requires nursery stock. The Forest Service operates nurseries to produce planting stock for reforestation on national forests and for a few States tha have cooperative programs with farmers. The Soil Conservation Service ha nurseries to produce trees for farms i the organized soil conservation districts. Other federal agencies, amon them the Fish and Wildlife Service, o the Department of the Interior, and th Tennessee Valley Authority, conduc planting programs on land they administer. The State nurseries, which provide planting stock for use on State owned land and for use by farmers, ar increasing in number and quantity o production. Many private lumber companies, paper-pulp companies, and soi conservation districts are establishin nurseries to get stock for their own forestry programs. Some private individuals, too, are finding pleasure an profit in operating small nurseries.

This discussion deals with large-scal nursery operations, but the man wh wants to grow his own stock might fin in it many helpful suggestions.

Nursery-grown trees were planted o 181,000 acres in the United States i 1947. Approximately 217 million tree were used. To date, in the Unite States, nearly 6,700,000 acres hav been planted with more than 8 billio trees and shrubs that started life i nurseries.

SELECTING A GOOD SITE is of first importance in successful nursery management. Its topography, location, fertility, soil texture, drainage, and availability of water affect markedly the cos and quality of the stock. One rarel finds an area that has all the desirabl features of an ideal nursery site; compromises usually are necessary, but th extent and number of the exception determine the desirability of the site

The acreage required depends o the age and the species of trees to b grown. Approximately 1,000,000 coni fer seedlings can be produced on an acre with seedbed densities of 30 plants to the square foot. Correspondingly greater acreage production can be had under densities of 90 to 100 plants to the square foot. Transplanted conifers in beds with 6-inch row spacing will approximate 400,000 plants an acre. Row-planted deciduous trees will produce 150,000 usable plants an acre.

In the Southern States, most of the species used for reforestation will attain field-planting size in a single growing season. In the Northern States, because of a shorter season and slower-growing species, from 2 to 5 years are needed to produce satisfactory field-planting stock. The acreage of nursery land required to meet an annual production quota, therefore, is a matter of arithmetic that takes into account species, season, and proper consideration of the fact that enough land must be provided to permit rotations of trees and soiling crops.

The ideal nursery site is most likely to be a smooth, flat, moderately sandy soil on a stream terrace. The site should have a uniform slope, preferably in one direction in order to facilitate surface drainage. Terraces are needed where the nursery is on an erosive soil with a slope in excess of 2 percent. In coniferous nurseries, Nichols-type terraces are considered best so that tractor-drawn cultivating equipment can cross them. Broadleaf trees usually are grown in drill rows spaced 16 to 42 inches apart. A hilly or irregular surface adds materially to the cost of operations; it is poor economy to begin production on anything but the best available site, even though the initial investment may seem high.

Serious consideration also should be given to the hazards of flooding; the lateness of spring frosts and the earliness of fall frosts; the season at which digging can be started and its relationship to the planting area; accessibility to the nursery on all-weather roads; availability of public utilities—electric power, telephone, telegraph, and railroads and other shipping facilities.

TEXTURE OF SOIL bears importantly on all cultural operations of a nursery. It must be friable to permit working in the fall and winter and earlier in the spring than one does with ordinary farm crops. Sandy loam soils are considered best. They should have a silt and clay content of 15 to 25 percent, and an alkalinity range of 5.5 to 6.5 pH. Extremely sandy soils are unsuitable because leaching removes plant nutrients at a rapid rate. On the other hand, heavy soils demand greater care in nearly all cultural operations and are subject to frost heaving in the colder climates.

If the topsoil is a fertile, porous, sandy loam that is underlaid with a retentive subsoil, it is ideal for producing nursery stock. A subsoil with a hardpan should be avoided because it prevents good drainage. Seedlings grow vigorously with well-developed roots in a deep soil of good quality; they develop a ramifying root system with few fibrous roots where the soil is poor.

THE SPECIES of the stock to be produced has some bearing on the selection of the nursery site, but it is not of first importance. It is wise, however, to locate the nursery within the planting region. Many nurseries produce both conifer species and deciduous species. The deciduous species generally are tolerant of a wider variety of soil conditions. Conifers do best in soils with an alkalinity range of from 5.0 to 6.0 pH. Soils with a higher alkalinity are more favorable to fungi, which cause mortality in young coniferous seedlings.

Seasonal laborers are required in nursery work, particularly for 2 or 3 months in the spring and early summer and in the fall. The nursery should be located where labor is available and where the minimum amount of time is required to go to and from work.

The first step in developing a nursery site is to bring the soil into good physical condition. Then suitable facilities—buildings for storage and equipment—must be built to meet the

802062°—49——12

needs of the program. A soil conservation plan is needed so as to retain and improve fertility and prevent erosion. Terraces and drainage should be put in where necessary. It is wise to make several maps and keep them up to date: A topographic and soil map of the nursery; a plan that shows all permanent features; and a map, to be prepared each year, that shows the current use of each unit or part of a unit, including treatment of the soil, species of nursery stock on it, and age class. The maps serve as a record of stock produced and are a year-to-year record of soil management. Permanent roads that divide the plots into workable units should be established.

BUILDINGS vary in number, kind, and character with the climate and location of the nursery in relation to labor and other services.

In some climates, trees can be graded and packed for shipment as they are dug.

Where the digging season is short or the weather is unfavorable, stock must be graded and packed under shelter. In some climates, where the planting seasons do not coincide with the nursery seasons, cold storage is needed to hold nursery stock when it is out of the ground, and a well-designed building that has facilities for sorting, packing, and storage of nursery stock is essential. In mild climates, a simple shelter and a temporary heeling-in bed usually are enough.

The superintendent, or nursery foreman, should reside on the grounds so as to be always within reach. On a large nursery, houses may be desirable for other yearlong personnel. The operations of a nursery demand 24-hour attention; neglect at critical periods may mean loss of trees. Sometimes a dormitory and mess hall are necessary for laborers. Besides the quarters for personnel, buildings are needed for office, laboratory, storage of equipment, seed extracting and cleaning, and for repair work. The repair shop should be designed to handle all but major repairs to equipment. Usually the office and laboratory can be in one building which should be placed so that visitors will go there first for a proper welcome and an introduction to the work that is being carried on in the nursery.

IRRIGATION is necessary to the production of good plants in most nurseries, although some species can be grown without irrigation in regions where precipitation is adequate for farm crops.

Ordinarily, an overhead sprinkler system is used for the irrigation of conifers. Usually this consists of runs of 1- to 1½-inch pipe up to 500 feet in length and 50 feet apart, with spray nozzles at 3-foot intervals, and supported on posts 2 to 6 feet above the ground. Water coverage on both sides of each pipe is obtained as the pipe is rotated from side to side by a water motor or oscillator. Other systems employ revolving sprinkler heads on upright pipes at intervals of 40 to 60 feet. The installations may be fed by permanent underground or portable surface pipes.

The quantity of water and the methods of applying it (especially to coniferous seedlings) strongly influence the quality of the stock. During the germination period, the seedbed must be kept moist but not saturated. An even distribution of water during the growing season results in a uniform growth of plants throughout the seedbed. The quantity of water needed varies with the soil, climate, and age class of the stock being grown. Under similar climatic conditions, a light, sandy soil demands more water than a heavier soil. First-year seedlings require more frequent light waterings than older stock.

LAND cannot be cropped repeatedly without measures to maintain its productivity. Nursery stock returns nothing to the soil because the trees are removed, root and branch. Nutrients are taken from the soil faster than they become available naturally. Nursery stock can be grown satisfactorily for several years on exceptionally good land, but the application of fertilizers becomes necessary sooner or later.

The use of soiling crops, in rotation with tree crops and supplemented by heavy applications of compost, is a good way to maintain an acceptable level of fertility and soil structure. The application of the plant nutrients that are deficient in the soil without regard to the physical condition of the soil will seldom suffice.

Much can be done to maintain good physical condition in both heavy and light soils by adding organic matter. Many kinds of rotted vegetable matter can be used: Rice, oat, and wheat straw; hardwood sawdust, which needs extra nitrogen for decomposition; pine needles and leaves, which are used in limited amounts; and other like materials. Nurseries located near peat bogs make extensive use of peat as a source of humus. About 3 percent of organic matter in the top 6 inches of soil is desirable. Compost is commonly applied at the rate of 2 to 5 tons an acre every 2 or 3 years. From 200 to 600 pounds an acre of chemical fertilizer is applied.

The principal supplements needed in nurseries are nitrogen, phosphorous, and potash. Occasionally lime, and, rarely, minor (or trace) elements are added. The three major elements must be available in sufficient amounts to supply the heavy demands made by the tree crops—it has been calculated that a crop of 2-year-old untransplanted white pine (at a density of 100 to the square foot) removed 94.6 pounds of nitrogen, 31.8 pounds of phosphoric acid, and 41.6 pounds of potash an acre. Nurserymen make repeated soil analyses to determine the amounts of chemical fertilizers and compost to add.

Fertilizers of animal and vegetable origin are preferred but are sometimes impossible to get in the quantities needed, and the fertilizers of mineral origin must be used. Experiments show that better results are had when the mineral fertilizers are added through soiling crops and fortified composts, rather than when they are applied directly in liquid or solid form to the tree crops. On the lighter soils it frequently is necessary to apply fertilizers as a side dressing to correct chlorosis and to keep the crops healthy. The most desirable amount of fertilizer can best be determined by local experimentation. The quantity depends not only on the kind of soil but also on the species of trees being produced. The condition and quality of the trees indicates whether or not adequate fertilizer is being applied.

As for seed and sowing: Where trees and shrubs native to the region are being used, the use of seed from the nearest possible source will best guarantee the hardiness and vigor that are required in the field plantings. If one cannot get seed nearby, he should obtain it from localities of similar climate and altitude. The use of northern seed in the South is likely to produce trees of slow growth and poor development, which may eventually succumb to drought and heat. Southern seed used too far north may produce trees that lack the hardiness to withstand the northern winters. It is safest to use seed from native trees that are adapted to the climate of the region and from well-formed, vigorous specimens.

The quality of the seed collected depends largely on the collector's good judgment. Immature seed definitely has poor keeping quality and lower germination capacity than well-ripened seed. The color of the seed coat usually can be considered a reliable indicator of seed maturity. Simple cutting tests will give a rough estimate of the potential germinating capacity of the seed in question. This is a common-sense economy measure to prevent collection of the immature, weeviled, hollow, or otherwise defective seed.

Sowing the tree seed, an exacting operation, must be controlled carefully to obtain the maximum germination and the desired density. The seed of some species must be sown in the fall, others in the early spring, and some as late as July. Some may be sown either in the spring or fall; early fall sowing and immediate germination are desired for others. Each species must be given individual consideration to secure the desired size and development. Seed of some species sown in the fall does not germinate until warm weather comes in the spring.

Some of the species that require fall sowing or stratification are white pine, spruce, redcedar, juniper, and the nut and stone species of the broadleaf trees. Longleaf pine seed is sown in October; it germinates promptly and by mid-December the seedlings are well established. Jack pine and shortleaf pine are sometimes sown in late June for transplanting the following spring or are left in place for another year. In the South, shortleaf, loblolly, and slash pines are sown in March and early April. Farther north, spring sowing is done in April and May. Hard-seeded species are sown in the fall for early spring germination, or they are stratified or otherwise treated to induce germination and sown in the spring. Cottonwood seed must be sown shortly after it is collected, otherwise it will suffer serious losses in germinative capacity.

Presowing treatment to break dormancy is necessary for some species. Stratification consists of placing the seed in a moist medium, such as peat moss, sand, or sawdust, and keeping it at temperatures ranging from 32° to 41° F., for periods varying from 2 weeks to 2 months. This treatment is substituted for fall sowing. A method used to break dormancy of species with impervious seed coats is to remove a portion of the outer coat with acid. Black locust, honeylocust, soapberry, and coffeetree are sometimes treated in this manner. Scarification, that is, the reducing of the thickness of the seed coat by mechanical means, is sometimes used in place of the acid treatment. Ash, mulberry, Osage-orange, and catalpa respond to soaking in water before they are sown.

As far as possible, all seed is sown by tractor-drawn seeding machines. Some seeds are so irregular in shape or size (because of out-growth and appendages) that they cannot be sown with a machine and must be sown by hand. All conifer and many broadleaf species are sown mechanically. Cottonwood, oak, walnut, and ash are some of the seed sown by hand.

The seed cover for the germination period varies with the type of soil, climatic conditions, and the species. In the northern regions, sand is used to cover conifer seed where the soil contains a high percentage of clay, otherwise native soil is used. In the South, burlap is used extensively for cover during the germination period. Pine needles or straw may be substituted for burlap with good results. Mulching to prevent frost heaving is a requirement for fall-sown seedbeds in the northern nurseries; straw held in place with wide mesh wire is commonly used. Where the frost heaving is severe, the older seedlings and some transplants must be covered.

Hardwood seedlings, with few exceptions, are grown without mulching. In the heavier soils where crusting is serious, the seed is covered slightly deeper and, when germination starts, the excess soil and crust is removed to permit the seedlings to emerge normally. A light mulch cover of straw, pine needles, or leaves is sometimes used to keep the soil surface moist and prevent the formation of a crust.

The density of seedlings in seedbeds varies from 4 to 100 to the square foot. Those to be shipped as seedlings are given sufficient space for optimum development. The seedlings to be transplanted after 1, 2, or 3 years are grown at greater densities to reduce their cost. Broadleaf species usually are shipped as 1-year-old seedlings, but most conifers must be left in the nursery for 2 to 5 years.

Great care is taken to obtain proper density. Germinating a large enough sample of each lot of seed is standard practice to determine the number of seed to sow. Seed changes in germinative capacity while in storage; consequently, tests must precede the sowing of any seed lot regardless of previous tests. Low germination results in shortage of stock and irregular waste of valuable seed. Moreover, the resulting stock usually has an unfavorable top-root ratio.

Protection of seedlings from disease, insects, birds, rodents, ants, and weather begins before the seed is sown and goes on until the stock is shipped.

Where damping-off is common, the soil must be treated before sowing. Sulfuric acid, aluminum sulfate, formaldehyde, or ferrous sulfate are used in various concentrations, depending on the acidity of the soil, buffer action, and the severity of the disease. Some soils require one-fourth ounce or less of aluminum sulfate, while others require 1½ ounces to the square foot. Sulfuric acid is applied in a 1- to 2-percent solution at the rate of 6 gallons to 100 square feet. Formaldehyde is applied at the rate of one-fourth ounce to the square foot where the acidity of the soil should not be changed.

Protection from birds sometimes is necessary, particularly during the germination period. Some nurseries are located on flyways where the number of birds is much greater than in other nurseries. Repellents are used to some extent but usually are ineffective. Where the seedbed area is small, wire screen over the beds is cheaper. Ants, moles, crayfish, and field mice are a source of trouble in certain localities. Poison bait and carbon disulfide or other fumigants are used for them.

Transplanting is necessary for certain species. It is done to improve the quality of the stock, making it better fitted to survive on adverse sites. Root systems of the transplants develop a greater amount of small fibrous roots, and height growth is retarded; consequently, a better top-root ratio is secured. Transplanting is done in the fall or spring. Spring is preferable because of the danger of losses in winter.

Transplant beds are 4 to 6 feet wide with rows across or lengthwise. Where the trenches are made with a tractor-drawn trencher, the rows run lengthwise; when opened by hand, they usually run crosswise. Two-year-old transplants usually are spaced 2 inches apart; younger trees may need only 1⅓ inches. The distance between the rows is from 6 to 8 inches, to permit multiple row cultivation.

The use of transplant boards enables the planting at one time of a large number of seedlings. The boards are filled with seedlings in small portable shelters, then they are carried to the bed, the trees planted, and the board returned to the shelter for refilling. Throughout the entire operation, the roots must be kept moist.

A machine patterned after a celery transplanter is frequently used to transplant mechanically. When a mechanical transplanter is used, individual seedlings are inserted into the machine by an operator riding a self-propelled or tractor-drawn unit, or multiple units. The machine opens and closes the trench for the seedling. The rows are lengthwise of the bed.

Transplanting broadleaf species usually is confined to small trees that are intermingled with larger trees. They are used as liners, or transplant stock, when this method is cheaper than to discard them and grow the same number from seed.

Cultural operations, among them weeding, watering, and the protection from insects, disease, and other damage, require a crew of men during most of the growing season. The labor peak is reached when growth is the fastest, because of the weeding job. Summer rains interfere with virtually all of the work and, in prolonged rainy seasons, additional manpower is needed to do the various jobs in season. It is good practice to keep the soiling crops and areas around the nursery free of weeds to prevent maturing of weed seed.

The conifer seedbeds are weeded by hand until all the seedlings are large enough to be cultivated mechanically. In southern nurseries, machines can be used 2 to 3 weeks after germination. In northern nurseries, where initial growth is slower, machine weeding is supplemented by hand weeding the first year and, for some species, the second and third year. Transplants sometimes are hoed or cultivated to remove the greater part of the weeds, and the rest of the weeding is done by hand.

Drill-sown hardwoods are cultivated with ordinary farm-tractor cultivators in about the same manner as farm row crops. Cultivating tools should not go deeper than 2 inches. Timeliness is important to keep weeds from interfering with normal development of the trees.

In areas of high summer rainfall and longer growing season, the weeding job is greater than in drier areas or colder climates. Normally, about one-half man-day to 1,000 trees is necessary in the South and about half that in northern sections.

Recent developments indicate that costs of weeding conifers can be reduced appreciably by the use of a petroleum product known as Stoddard's Solvent, or mineral spirits. When applied under certain temperature and soil-moisture conditions, conifers are unaffected, but most of the weeds and grasses are killed. This promises to reduce weeding costs, particularly in the South, to about 5 or 10 cents per thousand trees. Other chemicals such as 2,4–D and ammonium sulfamate are being used to some extent.

Some species need shade during the first year. Tolerant trees, such as the spruce, hemlock, balsam fir, and white-cedar require 50 percent cover. In some localities where growth is slow, shade is necessary for 2 and sometimes 3 years. Other species, such as white pine and Douglas-fir, can be grown in some localities without shade but require it in others. Generally, hardwoods are grown without shade except for a small amount during the germination period. Sugar maple must be kept under shade during the first year. Care must be exercised in using shade because of the tendency of all species to develop large, succulent tops susceptible to frost damage or other injury. Winter mulches of straw, pine needles, or seed-free hay are needed in nurseries where frost heaving is serious, particularly on shallow-rooted seedlings and transplants. Where frost heaving occurs throughout the winter, mulch is applied in the late fall before snowfall. If confined to the spring period, it is applied after the snow has melted.

Lifting, grading, and packing of trees for shipment to planting sites is commonly termed "stock distribution." In the Deep South the work may start around December 1 and end in late February. Northward, spring planting begins in February and continues to April, interrupted only by inclement weather. Farther north, spring planting may not begin until late April and extend to mid-May or later. Fall planting starts in October and continues until frost or snow.

Most deciduous stock is dug during the fall months, counted, graded, and held in storage or in heeling-in beds until planted.

It is essential to have a current inventory of trees in the nursery according to species and age classes. It is obtained by counting a series of random samples. The intensity of the sampling varies from 0.5 percent for beds with uniform density and size to 5 percent for those with high variability. The average density is obtained from the random samples and is used in computing the total number on hand. A smaller number of samples is dug and graded; from them is obtained the cull percentage, which is used as a factor in computing the total number of plantable trees. The sampling unit is either 6 inches or 1 foot wide, extending across the bed. Deciduous trees in rows are inventoried by a series of 1-foot random samples, amounting to 0.5 to 1 percent of the total stand.

Care must be taken to get accurate inventory data. The samples must be representative, the counts accurate, and the grading specifications the same as those to be used in culling at the time of shipping. Inventories should not vary more than 5 percent from the shipping count.

Trees are loosened in the soil by mechanical lifters, which are connected directly to tractors that straddle the bed, or are pulled by cable and winch mounted on a tractor at the end of the bed. They are then gathered by hand, bunched, and transported to the packing shed. Digging forks are used as supplemental lifting tools in the heavier soils to retain all the fine rootlets, because stock that is stripped in lifting is inferior.

Fine rootlets must be kept moist from the time lifting starts until the trees are planted. To do this, the roots are covered with soil or wet burlap as soon as they are taken from the ground. Conifers are especially sensitive to injury of this nature. Lifting should not be done when air temperatures are below freezing. Bare roots of plants suffer damage if they freeze.

Grading and packing is done in temporary field shelters or in permanent packing sheds. Where weather conditions permit, the stock is graded and packed in the nursery near the seedbeds as it is removed from them. Where permanent packing sheds are used, the stock is taken from the fields in baskets or boxes to the sheds where it is graded and packed. Here, better control may be exercised over the graders, and the trees are better protected from sun and drying winds. For shipment, the stock is packed in crates or bales with the roots in wet sphagnum moss or shingletow. It is necessary to have an accurate count of the stock shipped, particularly where small orders are sent to farmers. Grading tables with moving belts are used to facilitate counting and packing. Graders place a specified number of trees in each compartment on the belt as it moves forward. These are dropped at the end, ready to be tied in bunches of 25 to 100, depending on the size of the stock.

It is unnecessary to tie or count accurately the stock shipped in large orders. The crates or bales are uniform in size and a random sample count is made to obtain an estimate of their contents. A 5-percent sample is usually within 3 percent of the actual count.

In normal operations, stock is lifted, packed, and shipped without delay, but that procedure is not always possible during adverse weather conditions. Nursery storage is necessary until the trees are called for. Heel-in beds under shelter can be used as temporary storage. Cold storage, with temperature between 33° and 35° F., is used at some nurseries. In late spring, cold storage is effective for holding stock dormant, when normally growth would start in the nursery beds, until it is needed at the planting site. Where heavy freezing occurs, broadleaf species are usually dug in the fall and stored in cellars. With good aeration and temperatures between 30° and 34°, it can be kept in good condition for several months.

Defining a plantable tree is an extremely difficult task. Size is not the complete answer. It has been demonstrated that trees forced with water or fertilizer have a lower survival than unforced trees of equal size. Trees with a greater number of fibrous roots have a higher survival than those with only large tap and long lateral roots. Acceptable stock must assure reasonably high survival on the area where it is planted. Critical soil-moisture and climatic conditions on the planting site may require special nursery practices to produce stock of required quality or age class. Younger, less sturdy stock of the same species will do equally well under more favorable site conditions.

Coniferous stock should have a ratio of top to root, by weight, between 1 to 1 and 3 to 1. Those with higher values than 3 top to 1 root do not survive well except in favorable years and locations.

Other factors that are used to grade coniferous stock are height, length of root, stem diameter at ground line, and development of winter buds. Height varies from 2½ inches for some species to upwards of 10 inches for others. Longleaf pine is unique because it does not develop a stem in the nursery. Roots of all species are generally cut to 8 inches because it is difficult to plant longer ones. Trees stripped of laterals and the smaller rootlets are not considered plantable grade.

STEM DIAMETER or caliper is a good indicator of grade. Small, spindly stock, resulting from overcrowding in the seedbed, may meet the requirements as to height and root length but is unplantable because of the small, weak stem. Generally, conifers should be three thirty-seconds of an inch or more in diameter. Extremely large stock with a caliper of more than one-half inch is inferior to smaller and better balanced trees.

If the desired size and other characteristics are not obtained the first year, the seedlings remain in the nursery for a year or more. If they do not develop a well-balanced system of roots in the seedbed, they are lifted and transplanted in the nursery. The age class is designated by the number of years they remain in the seedbeds and transplant beds. Thus, 1–0 indicates 1-year seedlings; 1–1 indicates 2-year-old trees, 1 year in the seedbed and 1 year in the transplant bed; and 2–1 indicates 3-year-old trees that have remained 2 years in the seedbed and 1 year in transplant bed. This system provides a ready designation of age and cultural practice.

Hardwood species have a lower ratio of top to root than conifers, averaging less than 1 to 1. Total green weight and caliper are a better basis for determining their quality. Generally, those with diameters ranging from two-sixteenths to six-sixteenths of an inch and heights of 8 to 36 inches survive better than smaller trees.

MAINTENANCE of nursery buildings, grounds, and the equipment is ordinarily scheduled for the slack season. Nurseries accessible to the general public have many visitors and the impression they receive is influenced greatly by the condition of the facilities. Neat, well-maintained buildings and grounds add much to the working conditions, and properly maintained tools and motor equipment is an incentive for safe, efficient work. A regular maintenance program reduces time lost when nursery work is in progress.

The trend toward mechanization increases the investment in equipment and overhead costs. Salaries have increased sharply, and unless offset by greater production the indirect charges become excessive. The technical problems encountered in nursery work require specialized training and experience. A small nursery operated as a part-time job and with a minimum of equipment usually is less efficient than the larger nurseries with a full complement of equipment and a full-time nurseryman. Smaller nurseries near the planting area are more economical because the cost of transporting stock from larger nurseries may offset the savings of large-scale production.

THE DEVELOPMENT of new machinery and techniques is an important feature of all nursery work. Cultivating seedlings with machinery results in substantial savings over hand labor. Treating seedbeds with a selective herbicide before sowing helps cut weeding costs.

Much nursery work is now done by women. Threading transplant boards, hand weeding, and grading are a few of the jobs performed by them.

Cold storage for seed and stratification facilities are being installed at the larger nurseries.

The amount of planting stock grown in the United States is increasing. During the war years many nurseries were closed but have since reopened. New nurseries are being established and old ones expanded. Now that field-planting machines are being used more extensively, landowners, both large and small, are planting their forest lands and abandoned fields to trees at an increasing rate.

The first important factor in any reforestation job is the production of high-quality nursery stock in the quantity needed for the planting job. It is like the foundation of a building. The plantations and the planting job can be no better than the nursery stock on which they depend.

FLOYD M. COSSITT *is a graduate in forestry of the University of Idaho. From 1921 to 1933, he was forest ranger and junior forester in the Northern Rocky Mountain Region of the Forest Service. He worked on the Prairie States Forestry project from 1934 to 1936; since then he has been in charge of planting and nurseries in the Southern Region.*

C. A. RINDT *is in charge of planting, disease control, and timber-stand improvement in the Division of Timber Management in the North Pacific Region of the Forest Service. His assignments have included work on the Manistee Purchase Unit, the Emergency Rubber Project, and the Nicolet National Forest. Mr. Rindt is a graduate in forestry of Iowa State College.*

HARRY A. GUNNING *is the assistant director of the United States National Arboretum in Washington, D. C. From 1919 to 1935 he was in the Division of Plant Exploration and Introduction of the Bureau of Plant Industry, Soils, and Agricultural Engineering. From 1935 to 1948 he was chief of the Nursery Division, Soil Conservation Service. Mr. Gunning is a graduate in horticulture from Kansas State Agricultural College.*

# THE WIND RIVER EXPERIMENTAL FOREST

LEO A. ISAAC, WILLIAM E. BULLARD

An experimental forest is an outdoor laboratory, an area set aside for research in the reproduction, growing, and harvesting of forest crops. It covers 40 acres, or 20,000 acres, enough land so that one can conduct fundamental studies and extend the results to a commercial or pilot-plant scale. New findings and time-tested methods are tried out side by side, and the results compared as the forest develops and time passes.

One of these outdoor workshops—the Wind River Experimental Forest in the Douglas-fir region—is in the heart of the Cascade Mountains. It forms part of the upper reaches of a hanging valley that empties into the Columbia Gorge near Carson, Wash.

The Wind River locality is the cradle of forest research in the northwestern part of the United States. There, as early as 1910, some of the first cutting was done on a national forest. A year or two later the first Forest Service nursery was established, the first arboretum started, and the first natural area in the region was set aside there in 1925 to maintain in perpetuity virgin-forest conditions.

Early work in forest research was done in the nursery and on nearby Columbia National Forest land. Then, in 1932, some 10,000 acres surrounding this center was set aside as the Wind River Experimental Forest.

The tract is typical of a vast forested area at the middle elevations in the Cascade Mountains, where the soil and topography are such that the area will probably be kept forever in forest production and not diverted for grazing or other agricultural uses. It is a good timber-growing site—not the best, but about equal to the average in the region. Physical features of the experimental forest are similar to those of the surrounding country. The underlying rocks are basalts, the peaks are old lava vents, and some lava flows are still exposed. The soils are mostly red-brown shot loams, very porous, heavily leached, and often containing a high percentage of broken rock. Elevations range from 1,000 to 3,500 feet above sea level. The climate, typical of the lower western slopes of the Cascade Mountains, is wet, except for the summer months. Rainfall averages 87 inches a year, of which 13 inches falls as snow. Nearly every night of the year relative humidity approaches 100 percent. Temperature extremes vary from below zero to over 100° F., and the frost-free season is short. During the dry, windy summers, the fire hazard is great. Forest trees grow well, but field crops do not.

The experimental forest consists of many age classes of timber grown up after old burns in the original forest and after some recent cuttings. There are approximately 4,000 acres of old-growth Douglas-fir and hemlock within the boundaries. An additional 2,500 acres of the area was burned by the great Yacolt forest fire of 1902. Part of that area now supports some small patches of old growth, some scattered large old-growth trees, and a wide variety of stands of natural regeneration—some well-stocked stands that followed promptly after the burn, some partially stocked areas, and some areas consisting mostly of brush with occasional young trees growing in it. About 600 acres of this area was reburned by the forest fires of 1927 and 1929; about 500 acres of that was promptly replanted and now supports a 20-year-old plantation of Douglas-fir, which will soon be large enough for the cultural-cutting operations. A few miles away from the main area lies a 3,500-acre watershed of 100-year-old Douglas-fir. The forest here is approaching maturity, and is representative of the vast, older second-growth stands in the region.

Timber types vary by age and composition. The young forest which seeded in naturally after the great fire of 1902 is mostly Douglas-fir, but there is a scattering of the western hemlock, western white pine, western redcedar, and balsam firs. Likewise, the 100-year-old stand is practically pure Douglas-fir, with hemlock and cedar beginning to show up in the understory. The old-growth forest is now in the process of transition from the intolerant even-aged Douglas-fir to the tolerant climax forest of hemlock and other shade-loving species. The Douglas-firs are old, but the other species are of all ages; in addition to hemlock, they include Pacific silver fir, grand fir, western white pine, western redcedar, and Pacific yew. Where the timber is of merchantable size, volumes range from 20,000 to 100,000 board feet an acre.

One of the important features of the experimental forest is the Wind River natural area. This block of 1,200 acres of the old-growth area was set aside to preserve in an undisturbed state for scientific observation and study an example of the virgin timber of the region. Most of the stand is Douglas-fir 300 to 460 years old; the largest trees are more than 6 feet in diameter and 200 feet tall. Parts of the stand are still practically pure even-aged Douglas-fir, while other parts are in various stages of transition from Douglas-fir to the climax forest of the shade-tolerant species. In places the Douglas-fir has entirely disappeared and hemlock is the dominant tree. This tract serves as an undisturbed check area for adjoining stands that are being placed under management. It is systematically covered with permanent sample plots on which timber growth, mortality, and other ecological changes are recorded.

Many forest-research projects have been completed on the experimental forest and many are under way. They vary from single observations or sample plots to commercial-size forest cutting operations. Early Douglas-fir nursery and planting techniques were worked out there, and many fundamental studies have been made that have shaped the silviculture of the region.

Seed of Douglas-fir and its associates, once thought to live years in the forest floor, was found to germinate or die mostly within a year after it falls. Forests that supposedly grew from this duff-stored seed following logging and slash burning were found to come from seed brought in considerable distances by the wind. Measurements of the seed flight of Douglas-fir and its associates, made by releasing seed at tree heights from a box kite over snow fields and also by catching the natural seed fall in seed traps, still stand as the most accurate and complete records ever made of tree-seed flight.

Fire studies made there on weather and fuel relationships, slash disposal, and so on have formed much of the background for the fire-protection system in this forest region.

Meteorological and biological studies that disclosed surface temperatures lethal to seedlings (both from heat and frost) and the seedling losses from excessive drought, lack of cover, competition, and rodent damage explained why seedlings came in thickly on some areas, while others refused to restock. These were supplemented by cone-crop records, which showed that several years elapsed between medium and heavy seed crops.

Thirty years of life history, recorded on sample plots after early cutting and burning, shows the gradual decrease in rate of restocking as the distance from the seed source of uncut timber increases. Ten years was required to stock adequately the first cut-over quarter of a mile from green timber, and 20 years for the second on cool, favorable northerly exposures; the hot southerly exposures and flat bottoms, where brush and grass competition was heavy, are still irregularly stocked or nonstocked.

A measure of the second period in the life history of Douglas-fir stands consists of 35 years of records on permanent growth plots in young stands; these show an average annual net growth of 645 board feet an acre despite an annual loss of half that amount that occurs as these stands approach and attain commercial size and maturity. Studies now indicate that most of the annual loss can be saved by light improvement cuts.

Pruning studies showed that 25- to 30-year old stands could be pruned to clear the first 18-foot log of knot-producing branches with no reduction of growth rate or entrance of decay resulting from the operations. The difference in value between a pruned and an unpruned tree, when projected 50 years into the future, was calculated to equal several times the cost of pruning plus 3-percent compound interest.

Spacing-test plantations of 23-year-old Douglas-fir show volume growth, stem-quality development, and fire hazard for spacings from 4 by 4 feet to 12 by 12 feet. They indicate that 6 by 6 feet to 8 by 8 feet spacing should give the most satisfactory combination of quality and volume growth. The widest spacing had the largest trees, but those large trees also had the largest limbs, which makes the largest knots in lumber.

Heredity plantations of Douglas-fir, now 35 years old, show a 33-percent variation in growth rate between the best and the poorest of 13 selected strains of stock and indicate that local strains may not be the best unless seed is taken from good trees in good stands.

A similar plantation of ponderosa pine, produced from seed from various parts of the Western States, shows that trees of the best strains are nearly double the size of the poorest, and also that young trees from limby, crooked parent stock or tall, clean-boled parent stock retain these parental characteristics when planted side by side in test plantations.

Light stand-improvement cuts in 100-year-old stands reduced mortality losses, increased net growth, and made possible the salvage of trees attacked by bark beetles and *Poria weirii*—a serious root rot that complicates the production of timber crops.

Experimental partial cuts in over-mature old-growth stands have indicated that in most cases concentrations of old-growth trees might better be clear-cut. In stands having an understory of trees below commercial size, it was possible sometimes to remove the large old trees and allow the younger element to continue growth with little loss or damage until it reached a size that could be harvested. However, injury to the reserve stand must be avoided. Studies at Wind River showed that top, bole, or base injury from logging or sunscald resulted in serious decay entrance within 10 years with nonresinous species, such as hemlock and the balsam firs.

These method-of-cutting studies are being continued on a larger scale in both young- and old-growth stands. The new work will include tests of measures to reduce loss from windfall, insects, and disease, to retard brush invasion, speed up restocking, and control species composition. With the increase in the demand for wood, studies are developing in the more complete utilization of wood in logging operations and in the salvage of waste for pulp and other special uses.

One of the most highly valued features of the experimental forest is the arboretum. It is the oldest proving ground in the region for the conifers of the world and now has growing groups of more than 135 species—practically all that will survive in that climate. There students are able to study species growing side by side and collect seed and specimens.

LEO A. ISAAC *obtained his forestry training at the University of Minnesota. He has spent 4 years in administrative work on the national forests and 24 years in forest research in the Pacific Northwest. His chief interest has been in silvicultural research, and he is the author of several publications in that field. At present he is in charge of silvicultural research at the Pacific Northwest Forest and Range Experiment Station in Portland, Oreg.*

WILLIAM E. BULLARD *was graduated from the University of California in 1935 with a degree in forestry. Since then his chief interest has been the correlation of watershed management with forest management. He spent 6 years in silvicultural and flood-control research in California and Washington, D. C., 4 war years on the Guayule Rubber Project in California, and 2 years in forest-management work as officer in charge of the Wind River Experimental Forest.*

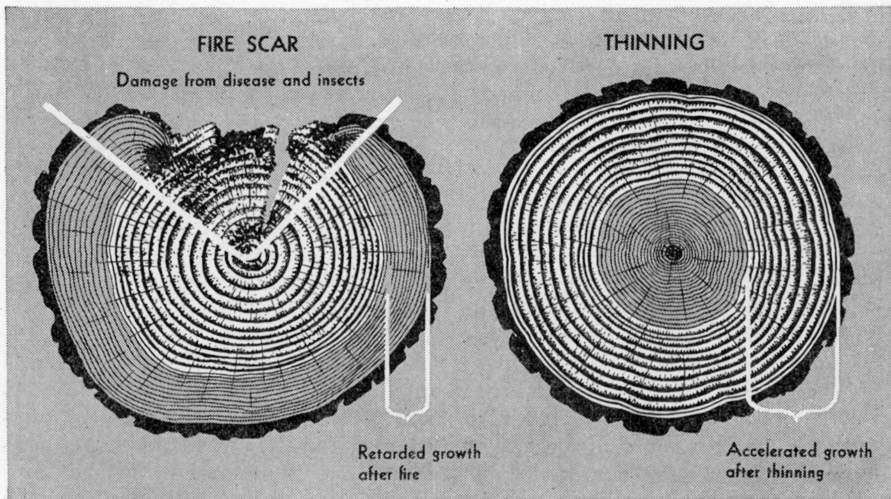


How fire and thinning influence the growth of trees.

# The Small Woodland

## CASH CROPS FROM SMALL FORESTS

R. E. McARDLE

A FARMER in Louisiana was offered $500 for all the timber in his wood lot. To him it seemed a good price, and he needed the money. But after consultation with his county agricultural agent the farmer had a forester examine the wood lot. As a result of this examination, he decided not to sell all of the timber in the tract. But, instead, with the help of the forester, the farmer made thinnings to release the crowded trees for faster growth, and he made an improvement cut to get rid of defective trees and weed species that were taking up space needed by high-value species. In that way he sold about a third of his timber, and he got $1,700 for it. Moreover, 5 years hence he will be able to make another sale. If present plans are carried out, the wood lot will become more and more productive and bring him a regular income from sale of products.

An Oregon farmer was offered $1,500 for his timber provided no restrictions were imposed on cutting all trees the operator wanted to take. On advice of a forester, the owner had the timber cruised and marked for a partial cut. As a result he obtained $7,500, and still has an excellent forest, which will soon produce enough wood for another cut.

In Michigan, the owner of a small stand of oak thought it had no value until he was offered $800 for all the timber on the tract. After analyzing his opportunities, he sold a small part of the timber for $950, and at the same time put his forest into condition to yield another income in a few years.

A small woodland in Missouri has furnished the extra cash needed to put one of the owner's daughters through the State university; another daughter is in the university now, and four boys are in line for similar education.

In Kentucky, a landowner was offered $7,000 for 310 trees selected by the buyer. On advice of a forester, however, only 199 trees were marked as mature and ready for harvest. Bids were invited and those 199 trees were sold for $12,600. Equally important

*Above: One value of woodlands is that they add to the enjoyment of farm life.*

was the fact that adequate growing stock of the more valuable species, properly spaced to obtain maximum growth, was left on the land with an eye to future values.

In South Carolina, the owner of a farm woodland was tempted to sell the entire tract for $2,500. With a forester's help, he sold part of the timber for $7,460 and has half of his trees, the best ones for future growth, still at work on the land growing more wood for another harvest.

These few examples illustrate how a small but ever-increasing number of farmers and other owners of small woodlands are obtaining cash crops.

Most owners of small forest tracts do not usually think of these properties as having possibilities for a regular income; to them, the trees in their woodlands might have no particular value except possibly for fuel wood and fence posts. An offer of a few hundred dollars for all the timber in a small tract probably would strike most such owners as an unexpected bit of good fortune. Yet a small forest, even one of only 50 or 60 acres, can be made to yield its owner good financial returns at regular intervals of 5 or 10 years, sometimes more frequently.

The key to forest profits is, of course, good forest management. Good management happily is within the reach of most owners of small forest properties. Many, however, will need technical assistance in getting started in profitable woodland management because few owners of small forests now earn their living, or even a small part of it, solely by growing timber. Timber production, if engaged in at all, is definitely a side issue to farming, teaching school, selling hardware, banking, or some other full-time job. Timber growing to the great majority of small-forest owners is a new business.

The need for technical help is further emphasized by the unfortunate fact that far too many forest properties have been allowed to deteriorate. Sometimes the cream has been skimmed from the forest crop so often that there are left only the less desirable species, the defective trees and those too small to yield a salable product. Technical knowledge is required to turn such deteriorated properties into fast-growing forests well stocked with high-value trees. Experience with other crops is, of course, helpful in forest management. But many aspects of timber production and harvesting and marketing are entirely different from those of other crops.

In the past 5 or 6 years substantial—although still far from adequate—progress has been made in providing small-forest owners with technical assistance in woodland management. Public agencies furnish most of the assistance now available. This publicly sponsored forestry assistance is handled by State agencies in cooperation with the Department of Agriculture. It is intended for small-forest owners who plan to do their own forestry work and includes two closely related but distinct types of assistance: Education in the techniques of forest management and marketing and in-the-woods technical advice and service to individual forest owners.

State forestry departments and extension services, the Federal Government, and a number of private organizations sponsor educational programs that direct attention to the prominent part small forests have in the Nation's wood supply and to the profitableness of timber as a cash crop. Valuable as mass educational activity of this kind may be, it cannot, of course, furnish detailed and specific instruction in the techniques of woodland management. Such instruction, however, is included in the cooperative Federal-State program. This important aspect of education is under the immediate supervision of 67 State extension foresters, who work through the county agricultural agents in 45 States. Instruction in management of woodlands is thus coordinated with existing public educational facilities and with other nonresident teaching in agriculture.

Extension foresters carry on their

educational work through meetings, usually held in a farm woodland, of fairly large groups of farmers. This group instruction includes demonstrations of good cutting practices, thinning, pruning, tree planting, log scaling, forest-fire prevention, fence-post preservation, farm use of forest products, and other aspects of timber growing and use. Bulletins and leaflets are used to supplement the field work.

Every forest property, however, has peculiarities that are key factors in determining the specific requirements of forest management. This is particularly true of small woodlands, most of which have been culled over so often that uniformity of forest conditions is the exception rather than the rule. In this important respect, tree crops are totally unlike other crops with which the landowner can begin with bare land every year or two. The forest owner, however, must start with what he happens to have and must make the desired changes gradually over a period of years. When, therefore, a landowner finds that conditions in his own woodland differ appreciably from those in the example used by the instructor, he often has difficulty in applying what he has learned. It is also a common experience to encounter problems not included or not yet reached in the course of instruction. It is then that the individual landowner needs competent technical help in getting his forestry activities headed in the right direction so as to avoid making mistakes that perhaps cannot be remedied for many years. Effective assistance can be given only after examining the woodland itself.

Such service to individual small-forest owners is the other part of the cooperative Federal-State program. It is provided by State foresters in 40 States. In some States, the State foresters also are able to furnish timber-cruising and timber-marking services for a moderate fee if the landowner wants additional help beyond the day or so that can be given without charge. This type of service fits in well with other operational work of State forestry departments in forest-fire control, insect and disease control, production of forest planting stock, and the like. Assistance of this kind is provided individual forest owners through 173 cooperatively employed farm foresters, each of whom is assigned to a group of 3 or 4 counties. The 650 counties now having this service are about a third of the total number that need it.

When assistance is requested, the farm forester visits the woodland with the owner. Together they discuss the owner's plans for the area, taking into account his need for additional cleared land, the desirability of reforesting the run-down or eroding fields, the owner's immediate financial requirements or need of forest products for home use. The farm forester then uses his technical knowledge and experience to size up the opportunities for the woodland management on that particular area. He makes a simple management plan that outlines timber cutting, planting, thinnings, and protection of the forest from fire, insects, and grazing. If the landowner has timber ready for harvest, the forester can recommend a method of cutting, helps the owner to mark the trees to be cut, helps estimate their volume, and advises the owner on marketing. Sometimes, when the job justifies employment of a forester for several weeks, the farm forester suggests the names of qualified consulting foresters. An important aspect of the farm forester's work is to make a later check-up visit to see how the owner is getting along. Through the State forester, or directly, the farm foresters keep in touch with the State extension forester so that individual assistance and group instruction can be coordinated effectively.

As might be expected, numerous owners of small woodlands do not live on the area or for some other reason will not do their own woods work. Relatively little public assistance is at present available to these absentee owners. Unfortunately, also, few private foresters are either experienced in small-owner problems or are willing to take over the management of small properties on a part-time basis. Many of those now engaged in this work claim that they cannot afford to work with owners of fewer than about 500 acres. Then, too, there is the understandable reluctance of landowners to pay a fee for the services of even a part-time technician until they have proof—on their own lands—that the cost of competent technical services is fully justified. But in time there will be more private foresters specializing in management of small forest properties, and absentee owners, convinced by results obtained on nearby properties, will be willing to pay a reasonable fee for technical service. Public foresters encourage such developments.

Important as small forest holdings are—or can be—to their owners in yielding a substantial extra income, these small forests are even more important to the Nation. Much of our present output of forest products comes from small woodlands. As remaining virgin forests, mostly in large holdings, are cut, the Nation's dependence on small woodlands will increase.

All of the forest land in public ownership and all of the land held by large sawmill and pulp and paper companies, even if managed for continuous timber production, will not yield enough timber to meet future national needs. Less than half of the country's total acreage of commercial forest land is in those ownership classes; the rest is in small holdings. The outstanding importance of small forests in the private-forestry picture cannot be overemphasized; nearly 3 of every 4 acres in private ownership is in individual holdings of less than 100 acres. Furthermore, despite many exceptions, those small woodlands are not being managed for continuous forest production. Only 4 percent of the present cutting on small woodlands is good enough to insure adequate future timber crops. Still more disturbing is the fact that on 71 of every 100 acres of small woodland recently cut over, no plan was made for another timber crop. That is a challenge to all of us.

R. E. McArdle *is an assistant chief of the Forest Service, in charge of cooperative work in State and private forestry. His early life was spent in Kentucky and Virginia. He is a graduate in forestry of the University of Michigan. Among his positions have been assignments in the Forest Service in the Pacific Northwest, a term as dean of the School of Forestry at the University of Idaho, director of the Rocky Mountain Forest and Range Experiment Station, and director of the Appalachian Forest Experiment Station.*

## ROOTS AND STEMS AND DOGWOOD BOLTS

A. G. HALL

Good advice to the owner of a small tract of woodland is: "Stop, look, and know before you go into the woods with your ax."

A Florida farmer thought he had 60 acres of quite worthless woods—spindly pines and dogwood trees—because he had not taken the time to find out that sound dogwood bolts were in demand by manufacturers of shuttle blocks for the textile industry. He consulted a farm forester, fortunately, before he cleared his "worthless" land for pasture. Instead of being a liability, the trees netted him $40 a cord. Today that farmer is in the business of raising dogwood for shuttle blocks.

Similarly, individual walnut trees, sometimes worth from $50 to several hundred dollars each, are often saved from the fuel-wood pile by the timely advice of a county agent, extension forester, farm forester, or buyer of walnut veneer logs.

Very often the landowner has to be reminded that the plants of the forest—all plants, not just the trees—are composed of many parts into which nature has placed special properties or substances. The key to successful utilization of these many plants is to determine to what economic uses their special attributes are best adapted for the greatest return. A man also needs to know the markets and the best means of producing and harvesting the products for continuous crops. The owner of large tracts can concentrate on one or two products, like sawlogs and pulpwood, but the owner of a small property often must supplement the income from his main product with the income from several minor products.

The best sources of information are the State and Federal agricultural agencies and the trade associations, because they are in the business of discovering new and improved uses of forest products.

Roots and stems of plants may yield food, fiber, fuel, drugs, dyes, gums and resins, and wood specialties.

Leaves may contain oils and dyes or special fibers for special uses. They may have decorative value, or they may be ideal for composting.

The bark may be a source of cork, tannins, drugs, fiber, fuel.

Flowers, besides their decorative value, may also produce oils.

The fruits are important for food or oils. They might be marketed for their seed or for use as decorations.

The forest-land owner, therefore, loses nothing by taking the time to find out the full possibilities of his land, but he stands to lose present and future values if he makes a hasty move.

Planning for maximum use of a wooded area requires, first, a complete inventory, not only of the trees and woody plants but also of the small herbs and other vegetation that form the forest understory.

Few are the woodland products that do not have some utility.

802062°—49——13

From the roots come quite a number of products.

Recently I received a request from a New Jersey florist for a supply of Osmunda fern, a fairly common plant in the swamps and wet woods of the East and Northeast. The florist was seeking a source of the plant because he wanted to use its roots in the making of compost for growing orchids.

Ginseng, another plant of the forest floor, occurs in shady, well-drained locations in the hardwood forests from Maine to Minnesota and southward into the mountains of the Carolinas and Georgia. An export trade in ginseng has existed in this country for more than a century; the average annual value of the ginseng root for the Oriental market is about one million dollars. Ginseng is now cultivated, but the wild product found in the woodlands is highly favored in the trade and brings the highest prices. Forest plantings of ginseng, while slower growing than those in artificial shade, are less expensive to establish and require less attention.

Sassafras root finds a limited sale at roadside stands to persons to whom the use of a tonic of sassafras tea is traditional. This is a pin-money product. But both the root and the stem are used for the extraction of oils for the flavoring of root beers and some proprietary medicines. The oil is used also to produce an artificial "heliotrope" for the manufacture of perfumes.

The pitch-laden wood of the roots of some of the southern pines, because of their high inflammability, reach the market as "lighter knots" or "lighter" wood. Sure to blaze when they are exposed to flame, they are ideal for use in fireplaces.

Stumps and roots of the resinous species have also found a market by the ton in the South. A special process has been developed for extracting the resin. And owners of "worked out" turpentine stands have been able to realize a profit from clearing out the dead and dying trees.

During the Second World War, the

impossibility of importing the foreign briar into this country for the manufacture of smoking pipes led to a revival of an old southern industry. In North Carolina and Tennessee, pipe blocks were made from laurel and rhododendron burls, the large, abnormal growths of hard wood that appear at the root collar of the shrubs. At that time, the burls were sold for 10 to 12 dollars a ton.

Similarly, the heavy burl growth at the root collar of the western manzanita was developed into pipe materials. The market for those products fell off after the war, but burl growth, because of its intricate design and generally hard wood, has a limited market for specialty items.

THE STEMS yield items that many of us are not aware of.

Many trees, often individuals of a species rather than a whole stand, have special uses worth investigating before the tree is consigned to the sawmill or pile of fuel wood. The veneer industry is particularly interested in these special uses. Frequently the butt log of an old, sound walnut tree will be worth many times for veneer what it would bring as a sawlog. The prices sometimes realized—running into a thousand dollars or more for one tree—warrant investigation.

Other hardwoods may also find a veneer market—oak, yellow-poplar, redgum, maple, and the cottonwood, among them.

To bring the highest prices, veneer logs or bolts should be straight, symmetrical, large, and free of defects.

Likewise in demand is eastern redcedar, the tree from which pencils, cedar lining for chests, and some insect repellents are made. Large redcedar is eagerly sought by manufacturers of cedar chests; and small stock—of the fence-post variety—will be purchased by the pencil-block companies. Even the sawdust of the tree, if produced in quantity, is the source of cedar oil.

Baseball bats are made from young, second-growth white ash; wood from old trees is usually too fine-grained and brittle for the purpose. Hence the owner of a stand of young ash may often realize a considerably greater income from the sale of ash bolts than from logs for lumber. Before cutting his ash into the short 40-inch bolts required by bat manufacturers, he should check with the buyers to determine whether his wood meets specifications. About 750,000 board feet of ash is used annually to keep baseball teams supplied.

A somewhat similar market is the one for handle stock. Good handles for striking and lifting tools require qualities not often found in sawed boards. Consequently they are produced from bolts or short logs of hickory and ash. Samples should be sent to the manufacturers before extensive harvesting is undertaken.

Excelsior bolts cut from aspen, basswood, cottonwood, white pine, buckeye, and some other woods find a ready market as packing material. In Michigan alone, chiefly in the Upper Peninsula, 49,554 cords of excelsior bolts were marketed in 1946. For the Lake States, the total was 95,463 cords, twice the amount in 1936.

American farmers use an estimated 500 million wooden fence posts annually, but probably fewer than 5 percent of them are given preservative treatment to lengthen their useful life. For untreated posts, the more decay-resistant woods must be used, but their life can be considerably extended by simple treating methods. For the less resistant species, treatment is necessary if satisfactory use is to be obtained. The woodland owner, then, will do well to establish his fence-post business on a quality basis.

Small poles, likewise, are a marketable item in farming areas. And where vegetable gardening is carried on in areas with limited wood supply, the woodland owner may also find a market for small but straight material for bean poles.

Sound, clear white oak is the source of tight cooperage, the barrels used to hold liquids. The supply of this material has reached an all-time low, and consequently the prices for good cooperage stock are at an all-time high. While other types of containers have taken the place of wooden ones for some liquids, there are still others, notably whiskey, for which a suitable substitute for wood has not yet been found. The owner of any of the various species of white oak should investigate this market.

Another little-known product of the woodland is basket willow. The American green willow, a tree of the clay loam soils of the East and South, often grows where few other commercial products will grow—in lands subject to flooding and on the borders of lakes, streams, and rivers. The marketable product is the rods, or young shoots, that spring from well-established rootstocks or stumps. Willow may be propagated by setting out cuttings about 10 inches long in the early spring. The cuttings root easily in the moist earth and within a few years have developed well-rooted stock from which rods can be harvested each year. Peeled willow brings the highest prices in the basket market. Before undertaking any extensive propagation, the owner should be sure a local market exists, however; the industry is diminishing in this country.

The California-laurel, or the Oregon-myrtle, neither a laurel nor a myrtle, belongs to a family that includes the eastern sassafras and the "loblolly bays" of the South. It grows from southwestern Oregon to the southern border of California. Its beautiful grain makes it valuable for cabinet and finishing work. The wood, therefore, becomes a specialty item that brings a better price for special uses than it does as lumber.

Many farmers use 15 to 20 cords of wood each year; as a home-use product, therefore, fuel wood stands high on the list. For the market it may be a profitable source of income. With good roads and easy transportation, woodland owners find it profitable to haul fuel wood 15 miles or more to the city markets. In most large cities, fireplace wood is a luxury item that sells at luxury prices. Where the woodland produces more fuel wood than the farmer can use himself, the fuel-wood market provides an outlet for the wood which might otherwise be wasted. In such cases, it is well for him to establish a steady year-round market and to service that market with sound, high-calorie wood.

Too few wood sellers make a point of marketing quality wood. Those who do are assured of a group of satisfied customers. The fuel value of wood varies considerably; generally, it is highest in the heavier woods. One standard cord of such wood as oak, maple, hickory, and beech is equal to roughly a ton of coal in heat value; the heat value of lighter woods such as cedar, spruce, soft pine, poplar, and basswood is about half as much. Local custom and uses determine the sizes into which the fuel wood should be cut, but there is one unalterable standard—the wood must be thoroughly dry. Hence, the owner must plan his work so that the wood is cut several months before he intends to sell it.

Cutting fuel wood, if done wisely, can be a way to improve a poor timber stand. Trees that should be cut because they will never make good timber or are interfering with the growth of others may make excellent fuel. Tops and heavy limbs of trees cut for other purposes often can be converted into cordwood for the market or home use. Slabs, edgings, and sawmill trimmings also may have fuel value.

Among the other stem products are those derived from the sap or liquids in the trees. Chief among them is the resin or gum of the longleaf and slash pines of the South. Operating a turpentine orchard is often a major enterprise, but it also is a minor enterprise on thousands of woodlands. If good turpentining practices are followed on the small holdings, as on the large ones, the producing life of the tree can be extended, and after the tree has been worked out it will still yield valuable products in the form of pulpwood, fence posts, cross ties, or sawlogs.

A little-known gum product is that produced by the sweetgum or redgum tree, one of the most common hardwoods of the South, although few farmers or landowners have much use for it. Farmers in Clarke County, Ala., however, have developed a $200,000 business in the sweet gum from the tree. Known as "storax," the gum is gathered much as is the gum of the naval stores pines and, processed, is used for adhesives, salves, incense, and perfume.

The production of maple sirup and sugar is confined mostly to New England, New York, Pennsylvania, Ohio, Maryland, and the Lake States. The sugar maple tree is the best producer, although red and silver maples, which yield about one-half the sugar content of the sugar maple, can also be used. For commercial operations, it is desirable to have at least 500 to 1,000 trees that can be tapped. Owners of smaller numbers of sugar trees, however, can combine their output for processing. Mature trees are excellent sap producers as long as they remain vigorous, even though their rate of growth may be slow. A seasonal operation, the making of maple sirup employs farm labor profitably for 2 to 5 weeks each year when the sap begins to flow, generally from February 15 to April 15. Drawing off the sap does little harm to the trees. Trees that have been tapped for years still can yield good sawlogs and other wood products. The sugar stock must be protected from fire and grazing.

Minor markets are also found for the resin of the balsam fir and the bark and twigs of the black birch, from which medicinal products are derived.

Often stem products involve the whole plant. For example, in many parts of the country farmers and others supplement their incomes by selling large fern fronds and attractive weed plants to florists for use in bouquets.

Sphagnum moss, because of its good water-holding ability—it is much more absorbent than cotton—often finds a ready market at forest nurseries and gardeners' supply houses. It is ideal for packing seedlings for shipment and as a medium for seed germination. It is a long-stemmed moss that is harvested in commercial quantities in Wisconsin and New Jersey. Harvesting is done by taking the massed moss from the water and permitting it to dry in the sun.

Spanish moss, that sombre, dull-green decoration found on trees in the lowlands of the South, is also a marketable item. The moss clings to the tree only for support and does the tree no harm unless it covers it so completely that it prevents development of leaves and buds. It derives its living from the air. Easily gathered, it finds a market as packing material.

The cork oak is a native of the shores of the western Mediterranean, but it has been found to thrive if planted in the United States in regions where the mean annual temperature ranges from 50° to 70° F. The tree has several uses. Being evergreen, it makes a desirable ornamental tree; its acorns make good feed for hogs; its bark yields cork, which can be stripped from healthy trees without injury to the trees. The tree is adaptable to many types of soil if drainage is good. It may be grown from acorns or from nursery stock. The cork harvest can begin when trees are 13 to 20 years old. The markets for cork are good, and the cork-using industry in this country is encouraging the establishment of plantations.

The bark of western buckthorn, or cascara sagrada, which ranges from Puget Sound southward into Lower California, is used for its medicinal value. In Oregon and Washington, collection of the bark is often an important local industry. Cut stumps generally sprout vigorously, yielding additional crops if conservatively managed. The wood is of no commercial value.

Among the leaf products we can include Christmas trees, because their evergreen leaves or needles are of most importance in their sale and use. Christmas trees in quantity are rarely the products of a small woodland. More and more, the Christmas-tree market is being served by owners of plantations who have set the trees out for the express purpose of growing Christmas trees. A large number also come from thinnings in plantations established for other purposes. The Christmas-tree industry is discussed in other articles in this book. It is well here, however, to remind the small landowner that the Christmas-tree market often is an attractive one for the disposal of small evergreens from crowded plantations and from overstocked natural seeding of fields. If evergreen timber harvesting is done at the right time of the year, well-formed tops may be dressed up for the Christmas-tree market.

Branches of evergreen trees, notably those of the longleaf pine of the South, are eagerly sought for Christmas decoration. To a lesser degree other evergreen boughs likewise find a place in the Christmas market.

Needles of pine, spruce, and fir have a fragrance that helps create a specialty market for balsam pillows. While the market is limited, it can provide more than pin money for persons living near resorts where such pillows are purchased for souvenirs and gifts.

In the mountain industries of the South, pine needles are used along with raffia and other weaving materials for baskets and small hand-woven articles and novelties.

The leaves of the wintergreen plant, found growing in the woods of the East and North, is one of the sources of wintergreen flavor, similar to that of the black birch inner bark. Most of the wintergreen flavoring is now produced synthetically, but the natural-plant extract is used to a limited extent.

The eucalyptus tree, several species of which have been introduced on the west coast, is a multipurpose tree suitable for fuel wood and lumber in about 25 years. Oil from its leaves is used in making medicines and perfumes.

Leaves of the eastern white-cedar likewise produce marketable oils.

When no other use can be found for them, hardwood leaves may be utilized in nature's own fashion for compost. The compost pit or pile may also find a market, especially if the landowner is near a city where flower and vegetable gardeners create a demand for it.

Galax is an attractive evergreen herb which grows in the open woods from Virginia to Georgia. Its leaves are used by florists for decoration. Often overlooked by woodland owners, it can be a cash crop if harvested conservatively. Its creeping rootstocks make it relatively easy to propagate and retain on woodland soils.

FRUIT CROPS, for our purpose here, range from cones to mushrooms.

Boys and girls of the 4–H Clubs in Emanuel County, in Georgia, earned $1,000 in 1948 by collecting 1,000 bushels of longleaf pine cones. The cones were sold to the State Department of Forestry for seed for the forest nursery. Seed, particularly that of conifers, is in great demand by forest-tree nurseries throughout the country. As planting programs expand, the demand will grow. Markets are found not only at the State nurseries but among the private nurseries and others. The woodland owner with a good seed crop should look to these markets, learn the specifications for collecting, storing, and shipping cones and other fruit that may be in demand. The markets may not be found locally, but the State forester or extension forester will be able to say where they are.

Cones also can be sold for decorative purposes and for use in the manufacture of novelties. Small cones, such as those of the hemlock, are tied into wreaths of evergreen material or artificial greenery for Christmas use. Larger cones, in groups of three to five, become wall decorations. Others may be painted, dyed, or otherwise ornamented for use as Christmas-tree trimmings and window hangings or desk and table novelties. Craft shops are the markets for such materials, but the woodland owner or his family may develop a winter-evening pastime into a paying proposition.

Tree fruits for human food are products of such trees as the hazel, hickories, pecans, walnuts, and, to a limited degree, the pines. When available in quantity, they constitute marketable items, but even the yield from an individual tree often provides food for the landowner.

In the Tennessee Valley, the harvesting of black walnuts for the market is a major enterprise each fall. Around 700,000 pounds of walnut kernels are produced annually by farmers in six counties in southwestern Virginia and in eastern Tennessee. While efforts are being made to have landowners plant and cultivate varieties of black walnuts of higher yield, the market for wild walnuts continues to exist. Walnuts may be sold in the shells to shelling plants or the meats can be extracted by farm labor.

The persimmon and pawpaw generally find no market, but are ideal for home consumption.

Other fruits for home consumption and occasionally for the market are mulberries, wild blueberries, huckleberries, raspberries, blackberries, and (in the Northeast and Lake States) wild cranberries. A large amount of blueberries as well as huckleberries come from wild plants, in the Northern and New England States chiefly, but also from the Middle Atlantic, Appalachian, and Southern States.

Wild grapes and wild cherries seldom find a market as such, but those fruits provide the sources for homemade jams and jellies and wines. The jams and jellies make good items for roadside markets.

Mistletoes are flowering parasites. The dwarf mistletoe of the West is very destructive of the host pines on which it grows, but the larger mistletoe, used for Christmas decorations and common in the South, is less damaging to the hardwoods on which it grows. The whole plant is harvested—stems and leaves, with or without the flowers or fruit. Sprigs with fruit on them generally bring the higher prices.

Holly, a favorite Christmas green, provides a seasonal livelihood for many woodland owners. An attractive forest or ornamental tree, it can be ruined by overzealous cutting, although it is a hardy tree—in its adapted range—and has few insect and disease enemies. For commercial cuttings, special care must be taken to prune individual trees lightly. The crops should be harvested with tree trimmers—not an ax, saw, or corn knife. Cuts should be made at junctions of main and lateral branches; the cuts should be smooth and clean. Generally, trees do not produce berries until they are about 10 years old, and then only the female ones. A special warning about holly: Country people should cut holly only on their property; city people should buy holly branches from reputable dealers who can give assurance that no vandalism was involved in gathering them.

Mushrooms are classified as a fruit crop because the stem and cap, which are harvested and eaten, are really the fruiting body of a ground fungus. Mushrooms are exceedingly rapid in growth; they spring up overnight following a spring or fall rain. If they are not picked within 24 hours, they generally start to decay. When they occur in small quantities, they provide food for the landowner's table. In greater amounts, they may be sold to local markets or provide another item for the roadside stand. It is important that the harvester learn to identify the poisonous and nonpoisonous varieties.

We have seen (mostly by example, for there are many other salable forest products) how wide a scope a small forest presents. By proper husbandry, its yields and values can be increased.

No plant in the forest is too small to be considered; no part of the plant is too insignificant to find an attractive market or home use. The secret of success in the management of small woodlands may be summed up as follows: Find out what the land is growing and is capable of growing; discover or develop a use and market for it; learn what the plant needs for its best development; and practice intelligent husbandry and conservative harvesting, so that continuing crops may be assured.

A. G. Hall *is forester for the American Forestry Association and associate editor of the magazine, American Forests. Beginning in 1933, he was employed with the Forest Service and with the States of Pennsylvania and New Jersey and, during the war, with the War Production Board on problems of lumber and lumber products. Since 1945, with the American Forestry Association, he has conducted a department in American Forests dealing with the problems of small-woodland management.*

# COOPERATIVES AND SMALL WOODLANDS

ALLEN W. BRATTON

Seventy-six cooperatives in 26 States have attempted to solve some or all of the problems of growing, harvesting, processing, marketing, and purchasing forest products. Mostly they have been small, local organizations. Thirty have handled forest products as the major part of their business. Pulpwood, logs, fence posts, fuel wood, and Christmas trees are the products most frequently handled. Two cooperatives have processed and marketed maple products exclusively, and one has dealt with naval stores.

Not all of the 76 cooperatives are now in existence. Several failed. Not more than one in every four is active and is following its original objectives. A few, established to serve a special and temporary service, have done the job and wound up their businesses. Several are inactive; their services may be less important now to their members than when markets were harder for individuals to find.

Some of the forest-product cooperatives, the pioneers, have contributed to better forest practices. They are establishing invaluable patterns for future organizations that are bound to spring up. In that they are marketing or purchasing or service groups, they follow generally the pattern of agricultural cooperatives, which, it is estimated, handle about one-fifth of the products sold by farmers and about one-sixth of the farmers' expenditures for supplies and equipment, and which number more than 10,000, have more than 5 million members, and do a volume of business of over 6 billion dollars a year.

The problems that the forest cooperatives have tried to solve develop from the smallness of the small woodland, which, as a rule, produces only a part of its owner's income. It is usually cut-over at long intervals when there happens to be a chance for a cash sale. Most of the owners have acquired no real knowledge of forest management. They tend to assume that the growth of trees, like the succession of the seasons, is something they can do nothing about. The woodland now does not produce enough income to justify much effort in trying to find out how to manage it. Owners have cut whatever happened to grow on the land whenever they needed money or considered the woodland ready to cut—once or twice in a lifetime. More and more of their time has gone elsewhere, and many of them have lost the skills of the woodsman. Much antiquated equipment is still in use because modern logging devices are too expensive for small owners to buy and operate for their small logging jobs.

Nearly all woodland owners are occasionally faced with the problem of marketing products from their lands. Though they may cut timber for posts, poles, fuel wood, and lumber, it is rare that surpluses do not develop, especially in the managed woodlands. Hardwoods may be abundant where softwoods are needed, or only fuelwood material where sawlogs are needed for lumber. Specialized knowledge and training are required to market well the products of the forest.

The very fact that small quantities are produced places the seller at a disadvantage, particularly in producing sawlogs and pulpwood that are normally marketed in large volume. The owner whose woodlands represent a relatively minor factor in his total business cannot be an expert in marketing forest products. If the highly useful service of local sawmills in custom sawing special items is not available, the woodland owner must sell his logs and purchase the needed lumber or other products at retail. To farmers, this is not an unusual experience, for they have long purchased supplies at retail and sold products at wholesale. Agricultural cooperatives have been making changes in practices, however.

The forest-products cooperatives generally may be grouped as branches and subsidiaries of large agricultural cooperatives, cooperative stores, marketing associations, processing cooperatives, special-purpose cooperatives, and organizations that function as cooperatives.

SEVERAL LARGE agricultural cooperatives handle forest products. Most of them are purchasing organizations that supply farmers with lumber, posts, boxes, and crates for agricultural products. Large-scale purchasing and in some cases manufacture of agricultural containers by the cooperative mean savings to members.

The large cooperatives should be able to contribute much toward the advancement of forestry. They can short-cut many difficulties faced by small local cooperatives because of their financial stability, established educational programs, wide geographic coverage, lower management costs, and simplified organization procedures. Those characteristics strongly favor the larger, established cooperatives; many of the small independent forest cooperatives have failed for want of them.

Branches and subsidiaries of large cooperatives have some disadvantages. Forest management, to be scientific and entirely practical, requires special training and experience. That is not always given proper consideration by those responsible for the policies and business of large cooperatives concerned only in a minor way with forest products. Not all of the members of the large agricultural cooperatives are likely to be forest-land owners and directly interested in that part of the business—the dilution of interest on the part of both management and members weakens the forestry program.

Most cooperatives have not had a firm policy in regard to conservative cutting practices. The result has been to continue and even accelerate the usual short-sighted methods of exploitation where good markets develop.

A large agricultural cooperative that has made progress toward improving forest practices is the Farmer's Federation of Asheville, N. C. It is a dual-purpose marketing and purchasing cooperative. In 1930, it established a forest-products department and then opened a log yard at each of its 17 warehouses. It has marketed as much as 1,000 carloads of forest products a year. The three objectives of its forest program are: To obtain agreement from all landowner-operators to give full cooperation to State and National agencies in fire prevention and suppression and to adopt cutting practices based on sustained annual yields; to get the same agreement with operators who are not the landowners (often financed and otherwise assisted by the association); and to introduce improved methods of cutting, logging, and manufacture of timber products to obtain the maximum utilization.

The forest-products department has handled logs, posts, pulpwood, tannin-extract wood, chemical wood, cross ties, poles, and lumber. Concentration yards make possible the accumulation of truck and carload units for market.

The Farmer's Federation has been successful in its program of forest-management education. It has worked closely with public foresters and has sponsored forward-looking programs.

Cooperative stores are independent associations that, incidentally to other business, sell forest products for members and, at times, for nonmembers. They have not concerned themselves with the methods used in harvesting forest products. They have obtained better prices for members than individuals could command, but the results have been overcutting and liquidation of the forest resource.

The Rock Cooperative Co., Inc., of Rock, Mich., was organized in 1913 to sell agricultural products and to buy merchandise. Later the cooperative also undertook to market forest products and to do processing. The venture was successful in marketing agricultural products. The forest products were marketed satisfactorily, but because no plan was made to provide for sustained-yield management, the cooperative has virtually cut itself out of forest products. The cooperative sold $265,613 worth of logs and pulpwood in 1930, but sales in 1943, a war year, were only $21,000.

The independent marketing cooperative is the type most frequently organized. Such cooperatives have been formed primarily for collective marketing of the forest products produced by members who are encouraged to follow approved logging and forestry practices.

They have enjoyed a degree of success in getting forestry practiced by members. The degree has been limited because none of the cooperatives has reached an impressive proportion of the woodland owners in the area it serves. Such a cooperative has the advantage of low cost of organization and operation. Members usually have a unity of purpose as a local organization, dealing with a few similar products and problems.

The small independent forest cooperatives have found the going rough in times of good markets for stumpage. In such periods, the strong stimulus of a marketing service has been needed less. Because they are small, they often lack financial stability and cannot afford the services of a skilled, full-time manager. They find it difficult to maintain interest of members during periods between timber harvests. Several have been organized without adequate preparation. Not all of the small associations that are now inactive have failed. Several have suspended operations during the period when markets are good enough to make this service of less current interest. These dormant associations expect to operate again "when times are right."

This type of cooperative will probably continue to be the most popular in this country. It should be pointed out, however, that the success of the small forest cooperative is sensitive to the degree of knowledge its members have of its objectives and their appreciation of the value of sound forest management; and it depends on their willingness to participate actively in the work of the cooperative.

The West Virginia Forest Products Association, for example, was established in 1937 to furnish complete forest-management service to its members, many of whom are nonresidents. The association has tried to relieve owners of the many responsibilities of forest-land ownership, and especially the technical aspects of managing forest lands. The services offered include inventorying, marking and selling timber, and supervising cutting operations. Intensive management practices are followed and cutting is based upon sustained-yield principles. The association has made a healthy growth. During the year ended October 1945, the cooperative managed 30,000 acres of forest land bearing 100 million board feet of timber. It sold more than a million feet of saw timber at a fee of about $1 per thousand. Plans for the future include the ownership of some manufacturing equipment—a trend also noted in other marketing cooperatives that have established themselves.

Few attempts have been made to organize cooperative associations that would provide the members with processing facilities as well as with technical forestry service and assistance in marketing. Such, however, are the services offered by the largest and oldest forest cooperative.

Processing cooperatives have several advantages. The ownership of a plant and equipment provides a focal point of interest. Manufacturing profits that usually go to an independent processor are retained by the association. Scaling and grading practices, designed to give members a fair return for products, can be easily adopted. The volume of business makes the use of modern equipment possible with the result that high-quality products can be manufactured efficiently. Members find it possible to buy materials they need for their own use readily and at savings. Raw products can be exchanged for needed materials and the development of markets for all sizes and qualities of material results in better forest use.

Processing cooperatives are faced with more problems of financing and management than are the simpler forms of associations. Considerable capital must be raised to get started. This usually means borrowing money and meeting payments of interest and principal. Management is more complicated; besides the technical problems of running a cooperative, there are also the problems of forest management, business operation, processing, and selling.

The Otsego Forest Products Cooperative Association, Inc., of Cooperstown, N. Y., is an example of a forest cooperative that offers its members services ranging from forest management through the marketing of finished products. Organized in 1935, the cooperative was assisted through loans from the Federal Government for the construction of a modern sawmill complete with dry kilns, planer, resaw, and other equipment. It has nearly 1,000 members, mostly farmers, who own 31,000 acres of woodland, which bears 50 million board feet of timber.

The Otsego association manufactures and markets more than 2 million feet of lumber a year. Cutting is on a sustained-yield basis. A substantial part of the production, especially the softwood products, goes back to members for use on their farms.

The adoption of forest management, scientific log scaling and grading, modern processing, and efficient marketing characterizes the association. Through these services it is offering the essentials of a sound forestry business not previously available in the Cooperstown area.

Special-purpose cooperatives have been useful on occasions when large numbers of producers, acting as individuals, have found themselves at a disadvantage.

An illustration was the situation created by the hurricane in New England in 1938. Hundreds of woodland owners suddenly found they would have to dispose of timber that they had not intended to sell for some time. A special-purpose cooperative organized in central Massachusetts, the Petersham Forest Products Cooperative, did a good job of disposing of windthrown timber for its members in an orderly and financially satisfactory way.

Another type of cooperative is one organized to market special products. There are at least two that deal in maple-sugar products and one that handles naval stores.

During the war, the demand for special products, such as black walnut for gunstocks, brought about the formation of small local pools in the Central States. They helped manufacturers locate critically needed stumpage and logs and helped members get substantially better prices for their trees than they could get as individuals.

Local circumstances dictate the organization of special-purpose cooperatives. Usually an urgent, temporary situation has stimulated organization. They are relatively easy to organize. Often they can be a strong influence in getting better management practices into the woods. Frequently, however, the situation that stimulated the formation of the association has not been identified by members with a demand for technical guidance in forest practices.

Two organizations that have come into being in the Northeast in the past few years are organized for the purpose of stimulating better forestry. One functions primarily as a marketing group, the other provides technical services in growing and harvesting forest products. Neither is legally constituted as a true cooperative, but both function much the same as cooperatives. They are carrying forward their objectives in forestry and for that reason are of special interest.

Because the laws of Pennsylvania do not recognize forest products under the agricultural cooperative laws, a recently formed association in that State has organized as a corporation. In so doing, the organization has foregone some of the advantages afforded by agricultural cooperatives. The organization is a true cooperative, however, as it follows all the principles in its relations with patrons that distinguish a cooperative from a simple business corporation.

The New England Forestry Foundation, organized and incorporated in 1944, is a unique organization that had its origin in a need expressed by woodland owners for forest-management services. It has a nonprofit basis, partly endowed and partly financed from the income from its operations. It operates through management centers in charge of foresters. Six such centers, each embracing about 200,000 acres, were in operation in 1948.

The services of the Foundation include drawing up management plans, marking timber, and providing assistance in arranging logging and marketing of timber products. Of increasing importance is the work of training logging crews because the Foundation has found, as have others, that management plans are more likely to be put into effect if work crews that are trained to do the work in accordance with cutting plans can be furnished the owners. Thus far, the New England Forestry Foundation has undertaken work on 58,000 acres for 172 clients, who own 118 million board feet of timber that is valued at $866,000. The Foundation has marketed more than 5 million feet of timber for owners.

Associations that function as cooperatives, yet are not legally organized as such, have an advantage because they do not have to follow a number of the rigid requirements demanded of cooperatives. Their responsibilities to stockholders are different, and the accounting is simpler. The manager's responsibilities are restricted to a comparatively small group, and greater flexibility is possible.

On the other hand, the groups do not have certain important advantages of cooperatives. The interest of the members is apt to be less than when each member has an equal vote in the affairs of the organization. The chances for joining into federations to influence forest practices over wider areas may not be as good as in the case of cooperatives.

Many problems, not all of which have been solved, have been encountered by the pioneer forest cooperatives.

The problem overshadowing all the others has been in getting the volume of business needed in the early operating period to carry a minimum but necessary overhead. Failure to obtain such a volume has resulted from several causes: Inadequate and inaccurate initial surveys of timber available to the cooperative; inadequate initial financing; lack of qualified management; and lack of a thorough understanding among organizers and early members of cooperative principles and sustained-yield forestry.

The record of the forest cooperatives might have been different had not general economic conditions taken a sharp upturn as a result of the Second World War. The market conditions that brought about their organization changed rapidly, and the chief problem and reason for organizing, that of marketing, was wiped out. Improved markets for farm products and a short labor supply found many small timberland owners spending less of their efforts on harvesting forest crops. The important benefit of supplementing incomes by getting a labor return (as well as stumpage) from the wood lots was lost. Lost also was the sustaining interest of the members.

THE BASIC PRINCIPLES of the successful organization and operation have been learned from the long and successful record of farm cooperatives.

The experience records of forest cooperatives, though short by comparison, clearly show that the same principles are just as applicable and important to success. They boil down to a few fundamentals:

Membership must be open to all who will actively participate in the organization, and active leaders must be found who are able and willing to contribute to the benefits of all members.

There should be a common interest among members in the services offered and products handled.

The principle of "one member, one vote" and general equality among the members should be followed.

Cooperatives are in themselves nonprofit undertakings and must pursue a course that will render services to members at cost.

Because success depends on the use members make of their organization, savings should be distributed to members on the basis of their patronage.

Cooperatives should operate in a conservative manner and assume no unusual risks. Safe reserves must be carried, and expansion or new ventures by the cooperative should be carefully explored.

Partisan and sectarian differences have no place in cooperatives. Harmony in obtaining objectives is a critical issue and the organization should be viewed strictly as a business venture for mutual economic benefit.

There is little chance for success if the cooperative does not carry on a sustained and vigorous program of education. Goals should be kept constantly before the members and efforts made to teach better practices in producing and harvesting forest products. Only well-informed members can be good members.

The cooperative must develop adequate marketing facilities if it is to render full service to members.

To warrant organization, a cooperative, like any other business, must have a sufficient volume of business. The long-time social and economic benefits that can be derived from forest conservation may be considered as desirable byproducts of the forest-management programs of forest cooperatives, but immediate economic considerations will determine the success of the cooperative as a business.

Before organization is undertaken, investigation should be made to determine the existence of satisfactory local markets. Do local plants adequately utilize the forest products to be marketed? Do they follow practices that assure a fair return to producers and encourage better forest management? Is there a surplus of material over and above that which can be satisfactorily handled through established market outlets? If not, could a cooperative fill the gaps?

An inventory of forest resources in the area is of great importance. Specific information needed is where the timber is located, species available and proportion of each, condition of timber, and whether there is a surplus beyond the needs of the individual owners. Techniques using aerial photographs are now available that will provide much of this information accurately and inexpensively.

It is equally important to study the

attitude of woodland owners toward forest management, cooperatives, and marketing problems. Experience has demonstrated that a poll of woodland owners' attitudes can supply useful information. Such a poll can also shed light on the availability of the forest resources of the area. A surprising proportion of the resource has generally been found in such small individual holdings that operations would be impractical for anyone except an owner who can spend his own time in harvesting the few products. Timber in estates, tied up by legal restrictions and timber reserved for recreational use and for other special purposes may not be available. Some owners may not be interested in forest management or may be antagonistic toward cooperatives.

The preliminary surveys will show whether a marketing organization is really needed and wanted, and whether adequate timber and a sufficient volume of business are in prospect to make a go of it.

In most cases of record, groups interested in the formation of forest cooperatives have found public assistance available in making the necessary preliminary surveys. The Department of Agriculture has given help.

No categorical answer can be given to the question of the type of cooperative to organize. The preliminary surveys will indicate the type needed. Financial and legal limitations will further influence a choice.

Several cooperatives in the past have been able to get loans from Federal agencies. Such loans have been supplemented by local financing through the sale of stock. Several cooperatives have had only local financing.

The legal steps and organizational procedures are well understood and much has been written on the subject. Most States have agricultural cooperative-marketing laws that apply to forest products.

The minimum size of organization that should be considered is one that would support one full-time forester-manager. Cooperatives that have tried to operate below this minimum have had little success. There is probably a practical limit as to the size that a cooperative might eventually reach, but the best advice seems to be to start small and grow as much as possible.

Opinions have differed about the ownership of processing equipment. It seems this is a matter governed by local conditions and what is needed to make the forestry program work. If equipment is needed and it is the only answer to the problem, then it should be planned for. Where satisfactory processing facilities are already available, fair-pricing practices are followed, and the type of cooperation can be had that will promote better forestry on the lands of members, then it may be that the cooperative need only supply technical and marketing services.

The continued development of forest cooperatives is warranted, I believe, because they have demonstrated enough success in obtaining better markets and in stimulating interest in better woodland management. Interest now is reviving in areas where cooperatives were being considered just before the war, and a number of new groups are studying the prospects of organizing.

The experience records cover a wide enough variety of types of forest cooperatives to meet the situation in most areas where there are problems pertaining to ownership of small woodlands. Experiences of those already working with cooperatives can prevent those venturing into the field from making many of the same mistakes if they will but seek advice and help.

Forest cooperatives should not be looked upon as a solution to small wood-lot management problems as a whole, or even to all of the wood-lot problems in an area where a successful cooperative operates. Under the most favorable conditions, it is improbable that more than 25 percent of the owners in any one area will become members of a forest cooperative. With encouragement, most members will improve their management practices. The activities of members will also favorably influence the management of woodland by nonmembers.

Cooperatives do not offer much to owners of nonproductive and depleted woodlands. Strong organizations may be able to afford such owners some help, but there is a limit to the amount of help a cooperative can give that does not contribute to keeping the organization financially strong.

Forest cooperatives have unrealized potentialities for improving forest conditions generally. The opportunities for success will increase as landowners and cooperative managers gain experience and as woodlands are made more productive under good management. Their influence extends beyond their members alone, for a strong minority of owners can set the pace for price levels, manufacturing practices, grading and scaling practices, and for forest practices in any area. Hand in hand with such influences go stabilized employment, increased income, and a strengthening of the rural economy.

ALLEN W. BRATTON *received his bachelor's degree in forestry from the University of Maine in 1932 and did graduate work at the University of Massachusetts. He entered the Forest Service in 1933 and served 5 years on the White Mountain and Cumberland National Forests. In 1940 he joined the staff of the Northeastern Forest Experiment Station; from 1942 to 1948 he worked on the problems of organization and operation of forest cooperatives, and was stationed in Cooperstown, N. Y. In 1948 he entered private practice as a consulting forester.*

# WINDBREAKS AND SHELTERBELTS

JOSEPH H. STOECKELER, ROSS A. WILLIAMS

In an effort to determine the value of adequate windbreaks on American farms, 508 farmers in South Dakota and Nebraska were asked for their opinions. They placed the annual savings in their fuel bill alone at $15.85.

In another measure of the value, the Lake States Forest Experiment Station conducted an experiment at Holdrege, Nebr. Exact fuel requirements were recorded in identical test houses. One was protected from winds; the other was exposed to the full sweep of the wind. From the experimental data it was possible to calculate the savings to be expected under various prevailing conditions, if a constant house temperature of 70° F. were maintained. The amount of fuel used was reduced by 22.9 percent.

Also the average of the savings for houses protected on the north in Holdrege and three other localities in the Great Plains—Huron, S. Dak., Dodge City, Kans., and Fargo, N. Dak.—was 20.2 percent. Assuming a 10-ton annual consumption of coal, this represents a saving of 2 tons of coal a year. Under good protection, on three sides of a house, the fuel saving may run as high as 30 percent.

Dairymen, livestock feeders, and breeders have rather positive ideas of how the protection afforded by trees reduces their feed bills and increases their calf crops. Eighty-six livestock feeders in Nebraska and South Dakota placed this average annual saving at more than $800; 62 livestock breeders reported that their savings amounted to more than $500 annually; 53 dairymen placed their savings at $600.

Further study of the subject was made at the Montana Agricultural Experiment Station at Havre. Two herds of cattle were wintered on the same rations—one in the protection of trees and shrubs, the other in an open lot with some protection from a shed. The tree-protected animals gained 34.9 more pounds each during a mild winter, and lost 10.6 pounds less during a severe winter, than the unprotected herd.

Another experiment conducted by V. I. Clark, superintendent of the experiment station at Ardmore, S. Dak., involved the weighing of two herds of cattle in different pastures—one protected by the natural tree and shrub growth along a stream, the other without protection. They were reweighed after a 3-day blizzard. The animals that had some protection each lost an average of 30 pounds less than those in the exposed pasture.

Farm families depend upon gardens for much of their subsistence, and most of them are aware of the influence of a windbreak in increasing the quality and quantity of vegetables and fruit from gardens and orchards. In the opinions of farmers interviewed, the increase was $67.15 on 323 farms in Nebraska and $84.43 on 260 farms in South Dakota. A few farmers believed the windbreaks did not increase the production of their gardens.

W. P. Baird, horticulturist in charge of fruit and vegetable investigations at the Northern Great Plains Field Station at Mandan, N. Dak., says that "a windbreak is on duty protecting the fruit gardens at all seasons of the year, and it is almost useless to consider growing fruit on the Plains without such protection."

So far we have discussed windbreaks, which are the shorter and more blocky plantings about farmsteads. Much like them, but more extensive, are the shelterbelts, a term used to denote comparatively narrow strip plantings—sometimes single rows of trees—that are designed to protect fields.

EXPERIENCE with systematic plantings of shelterbelts to protect fields goes back to 1789, when a group of German Mennonites, who emigrated to the Russian Steppes, began the shelterbelts that since have been extended to thousands of miles. The term "shelterbelt" was used as early as 1833, so it is apparent that some thought for controlling wind erosion by use of trees was in existence over a century ago. Since the days of the shelterbelt project, initiated in the Great Plains some 14 years ago, the term has become part of the everyday language of farmers on the Plains.

Few tree planters were among the earliest settlers of the United States. They came when the westward migration started to the prairies of Illinois and the Great Plains; those pioneers realized that it was going to take more than a sod house to give them the protection to which they had been accustomed in the wooded East. It was not surprising, therefore, that a plantation of trees often shared with the garden the first patch of sod that was broken. Wildings collected along nearby streams comprised their planting stock. We have records of some of these plantings in Nebraska Territory as early as 1854; many are still alive, monuments to the courage of the pioneers and evidence of the desirability of using hardy, native planting stock. Later immigrants from Europe often brought tree seeds with them from their old homes.

The passage of the Homestead Law in 1862 brought more settlers to the Great Plains and the need for more tree planting. Kansas was the first, in 1865, to provide a tree-bounty law in efforts to encourage more planting. This was followed in 1869 by Nebraska and the Dakota Territory which passed tax-exemption laws that favored tree planting. J. Sterling Morton, third Secretary of Agriculture, founded Arbor Day and saw its first official celebration in his home State of Nebraska in 1872. It was primarily through his encouragement that the Timber Culture Act was passed by Congress in 1873. Although it helped to stimulate tree planting, probably fewer than one-third of the trees established during the time the act was in force can be attributed directly to it.

It has been the history of tree planting throughout the world that the establishment of windbreaks and shelterbelts has not progressed fast enough to keep pace with the needs without some assistance by the Government. The thousands of miles of shelterbelts that now protect millions of acres of farm lands in Russia; the mile after mile of tree strips in Jutland, without which farming would be impossible; similar planting in Hungary; the 18,510 miles of tree belts planted in the Great Plains shelterbelt from North Dakota to Texas; and the 211 million trees planted to shelterbelts and windbreaks in the Prairie Provinces of Canada—all owe their success to sound Government policies put into effect through well-administered and Government-assisted projects.

There was a period in the United States after the repeal of the Timber Culture Act in 1891 when little public encouragement was given to tree planters. A renewal of interest was shown in 1904 with the passage of the Kincaid Act and later, in 1916, by the inclusion of the demonstrational tree planting in the program of the Northern Great Plains Field Station near Mandan, N. Dak.

The available records through January 1, 1948, indicate that some 123,191 miles of windbreaks and shelterbelts have been planted since the middle of the past century. Of 96,596 miles planted through private initiative, 39,400 are accounted for by single row Osage-orange hedges planted between 1865 and 1939 by farmers of Kansas, encouraged by a State bounty.

The shelterbelt project, sometimes referred to as the Prairie States Forestry Project, was established in 1934, a time of serious drought, dust storms, and depression. Its purpose was to plant badly needed shelterbelts and at the same time provide work for people in the drought-stricken Great Plains.

In the Great Plains between 1935 and 1942, 18,510 miles of field shelterbelts, not counting those on farmsteads, were planted by the Forest Service. The Soil Conservation Service of the Department of Agriculture (to which the work was transferred in 1942) planted 8,363 miles between 1934 and 1949 in its program on soil conservation districts. The Wisconsin State Conservation Department furnished stock and, with the Extension Service, was responsible for establishing 5,942 miles of shelterbelts. In California, the fruit-tree growers planted 2,000 miles of belts to protect citrus orchards and vineyards. In Indiana, truck gardeners have planted 100 miles on muck land. Many more miles of shelterbelts for which no published records are available probably have been planted in other States.

The farm plantings before 1935 did not include the large numbers that could also be classified as shelterbelts, but landowners who were fortunate enough to have them in the droughty 1930's had proof of their benefits. Pioneer planters of shelterbelts and windbreaks in the Great Plains had little knowledge of how to make trees live and only a meager knowledge of the growth habits of the trees they had to use. It is surprising, in view of those handicaps, that even moderate success was attained.

Progressive farmers and orchardists plant shelterbelts for two primary purposes—to control soil blowing and to protect crops. Some southern Great Plains cotton planters find it necessary to replant two and three times on the unprotected fields. Sugar-beet farmers on sandy, irrigated fields in the West frequently have a crop cut off by drifting sand as it emerges from the ground. The small-grain and corn farmers have had similar experiences. From the time that crops are well established until they are ready for harvest, they are constantly subjected to damage or to destruction by soil drifting, blow-down, firing by hot winds, loss of soil moisture, or damage from frost and sleet. Orchards are subjected to the same damages, but the greatest benefits are realized from protecting the trees during the pollination stage and preventing wind damage to the ripening fruit.

Besides, properly located and arranged shelterbelts can do much to beautify the landscape and act as snow fences in winter, thus helping to keep open highways and rural roads.

Thomas T. Wilson, of the Manitoba Department of Public Works, said that planted snow traps can be considerably cheaper than the usual slat-wire snow fence. His data, based on 201.6 miles of caragana hedge, indicates a prorated cost per mile for a year of about $100, assuming an average effective life of 25 years for the planting. Prorated costs of slat-wire snow fences were about $225 per mile for a year, assuming an average life of 20 years for this type of fence. Hence, the cost of the planted hedges is less than half that of slat-wire snow fence. The comparison, of course, does not consider the possible rental cost of the land the caragana hedge may occupy, but in places where a 200-foot right-of-way is owned, this question is resolved.

The effects on field crops are less distinct. A survey among Nebraska farmers showed that 29 farmers rated high the value of field shelterbelts, although 18 had been unable to observe benefits. The average estimated gain in production amounted to $43 a year. In South Dakota, 27 farmers said the crop gain was $60 a year per farm.

A mistake made by some observers is to note only that corn or small grains growing at the edge of a field protected by the belt is usually inferior to that growing a few rods out in the field, where, in fact, the greatest benefit nearly always occurs. A fair comparison can be made only between both of these zones and the distant part of the field that has no protection. But a large number of systematic measurements throughout entire fields has shown that sound comparison could easily lead to differences of opinion,

802062°—49——14

because the ground near the belt may be substantially better or poorer than that far out in the field. A farmer with a shelterbelt 40 years old may not remember how the different parts of the field varied in productivity before there was a shelterbelt there.

This variability of production within fields has made so difficult the determination of average shelterbelt gains in the fields measured from 1935 to 1941 by the Lake States Forest Experiment Station that the entire mass of data is being restudied. Predictions as to what will be shown by analyses not previously tried may be erroneous.

In general, however, it appears that a field protected by a single-row shelterbelt, equivalent to the Osage-orange hedge so common in Nebraska and Kansas, will show a net gain in yield equivalent to the crop on an area as long as the belt and as wide as its height, after allowance for shading and sapping. Any belt of greater width will be profitable for protective purposes alone, then, provided its width between the outside stems does not exceed its height.

While it seems apparent that wider belts add somewhat to the benefits, it is probable that the narrow belt yields the greatest return on the land occupied, if the value of the timber products is low. Benefits arise from several different causes, and in consequence are unlikely to be the same in all directions from north-south and east-west belts. Areas west of belts possibly benefit less than those in other directions; in northern parts of the Plains, where the snowfall is heavier, greater benefits apparently are produced than in the central or southern areas.

Winter grains and other early crops may benefit more from the snow held on the field, near the belt, than from other causes, while corn possibly benefits most by protection from hot, drying winds. The final results may be somewhat different from these predictions, and in any case they apply only in the area from the Dakotas to Kansas, and not to the drier portions of those States or to better-watered regions. Except for 1936, when only a few measurements were made, the period does not include any years of serious drought.

OTHER CROPS besides wheat and corn show good response to shelterbelt protection. An investigation of eight cottonfields in western Oklahoma and northern Texas showed an increase of 17.4 percent above normal between 0 and 5H, and 7.9 percent increase between 5H and 10H (with H representing a horizontal distance of one tree height from the edge of the belt). The normal yield of cotton grown beyond the zone of tree protection was 288.6 pounds of lint to the acre.

In California, one- and two-row eucalyptus windbreaks are said to be effective in protecting citrus fruits from bruising and dropping for a total distance of 5 to 7 times the average height of the trees. The trees easily attain heights of 60 to 80 feet within 10 to 20 years after planting.

H. E. Wahlberg, of Orange County, Calif., reports returns from 20 citrus groves grown under windbreak protection as averaging $445.48 an acre. On 20 unprotected citrus groves, the return was only $271.34 an acre. According to those figures, a grower could use 1 acre of trees on a 10-acre plot for windbreak purposes and still get $1,295.92 more return on the remaining 9 acres than on the unprotected 10.

Dale Bumstead, an orchardist near Phoenix, Ariz., reported that shelterbelts of eucalyptus are important in reducing cullage in his citrus fruit. His 1946 crop had a cullage of 18.5 percent, and cullage averaged 19 percent for a 3-year period. The citrus industry reports that the average cullage is about 50 percent.

Dr. Arvil L. Stark, secretary of the Utah Horticultural Society, is authority for the statement that fruit will not set on the windward side of trees when windy conditions prevail, because bees will not work in the wind. Shelterbelts, by reducing winds, thus can create

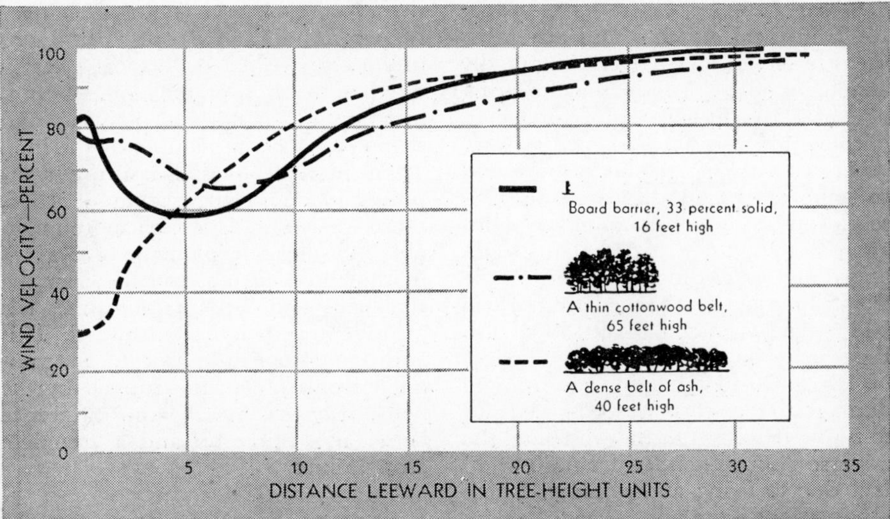


**Wind velocity at instrument stations 16 inches above the ground in 15-mile-per-hour wind blowing at right angles to three types of windbreaks: (1) A 16-foot high board fence of 33 percent density; (2) a dense belt of green ash, 290 feet wide; (3) a thin, rather open cottonwood belt, 165 feet wide. The velocities are given in percentages of wind velocities in an open field nearby.**

more favorable conditions in orchards for pollination by bees.

Another benefit of windbreaks was cited by F. L. Overly, superintendent of the Tree Fruit Branch Experiment Station near Wenatchee, Wash. He pointed out that spraying for insect control results in more even and complete coverage in protected areas because of lower wind velocities. Moreover, protected orchard trees do not develop as much lean or become as lopsided as those in exposed areas.

Anyone who has stood in the protection of a belt of trees on a windy day has observed that the wind was considerably reduced near the trees. How much is this reduction in wind velocity, and how far does it extend?

The zone of influence is most easily shown graphically. The chart shows what this effect is for a 15-mile-an-hour wind for several different types of barriers. In this study, distances were expressed in terms of windbreak heights, in order to provide a convenient comparison of zones of influence for the tree belts of different heights; for instance, the term 3H refers to a horizontal distance equal to three times the height of a tree belt.

It is seen that the wind velocity near a dense wide belt of ash may be reduced to as low as 30 percent of that in the open; for a thin cottonwood belt, it is about 66 percent of normal velocity; for a board barrier, it is about 58 percent. All three windbreaks show some effect out to about 30 times their height, but the effect beyond 20H is rather minor.

The results are substantiated by studies made in other parts of the United States.

Pioneer tree planters, especially in Nebraska, planted east-west shelterbelts for protection of fields against south winds. It has often been reported that such protection may reduce the drying power of winds, and may at times prevent the firing of crops when the temperature of southwesterly winds is excessive.

Observation by Alba Briggs in July 1939, in York County and adjoining areas in Nebraska, showed a markedly beneficial effect in reducing the firing of corn—the drying up of foliage in hot, windy weather. Benefits were greatest on the north side of belts and to some extent on the east side. Observations on 8 fields showed no damage out to 11 to 40 tree heights, with an average of 23 times the height of the trees. Tree heights ranged from 18 to 50 feet and averaged about 35 feet. On the south side of Osage-orange hedges of 18- to 20-foot height, accentuated damage to the corn was observed out to 5 tree heights. On the west side, the adverse effect extended from 30 to 40 feet due to firing and sapping. These observations were not carried through to assess values in terms of actual final crop yields, but they show a similarity to many of the yield measurements.

An 8-year-old shelterbelt near Norfolk, Nebr., played an important part in helping its owner, Ernest Fuhram, to win the 1947 corn-yield contest for his county. His 10-acre test plot made 106 bushels of corn an acre. Mr. Fuhram said, " I had 90 acres of corn north of the shelterbelt, including the 10-acre test plot, and it was quite evident that the protection the trees gave the field made a lot of difference last year. The best corn was near the shelterbelt and the yield tapered off as the distance from the trees was increased."

In irrigated areas, shelterbelts can be of considerable value in reducing water loss from evaporation. From Scotts Bluff County, Nebr., it is reported that in growing alfalfa an irrigated field protected by shelterbelts required one less irrigation a season than unprotected fields on nearby farms.

Tree belts trap snow and hold it on agricultural land, especially in the northern and central Great Plains. Hence, some measure of moisture conservation is attained, because in unprotected areas much of the snow is blown into gulches, low spots, and road ditches, where it is of no direct benefit to the crop. Good agronomic practices, such as leaving tall stubble over winter, standing strips of cornstalks, or unmowed sweetclover, can also retain much of the snow on the land. A combination of shelterbelt planting and strip cropping is undoubtedly the best. In a number of soil-moisture samplings made in the spring of 1936, there was about 4 percent more available moisture (or 2.5 inches of water) in the top 4 feet of soil between the tree belts and a point four times the average tree height to leeward. This additional moisture, largely accumulated from snowdrifts trapped by the belts, may at times be the difference between a fair crop and a complete crop failure.

In developing a shelterbelt, the present-day tree planter can progress with a great deal of assurance, especially if he will seek the assistance of his local State or Federal forester, county agent, or district conservationist.

Although many details involved in the successful establishment of a windbreak or shelterbelt must be worked out to meet local needs, a number of fundamental principles contribute to success, irrespective of the locality or conditions under which windbreaks or shelterbelts may be planted.

Careful preparation of the site, good planting with hardy stock, and thorough cultivation are three factors that go hand in hand. When all three are well done, the results are sometimes spectacular, but one cannot slight one of them and hope to make up for it by intensive application of the others.

Good site preparation means thorough tillage and, if the soil is weedy or dry, summer fallowing for a season. Some sites call for subsoiling, others terracing, contour planting, or, in the drier regions, diking and building of water-diversion structures.

It is extremely important that the planting stock be grown from seed produced in the general locality in which the trees are to be planted. This is one of the principal contributing factors to the unusual success of the shelterbelt planted in the Great Plains during one of the Nation's most severe droughts.

Although hand planting is still common and will probably continue to be used for small and rough areas, most windbreaks and shelterbelts will be planted with machines in the future. One type of mechanical tree planter may be constructed by the farmer or his local blacksmith for as little as $175. Others, capable of planting as many as 1,000 trees an hour, are available through purchase from manufacturers, or loan by the soil conservation districts or other agencies.

If hand planting is done, we recommend a long-handled, straight-shanked shovel, such as is common on farms in irrigated areas. The planting job is best if done on well-prepared, reasonably moist ground. On sandy loam or heavy soils, a subsoiler run down the row before planting will loosen the soil and speed up planting. Trees are carried in a metal or wood carrying tray or in a large bucket, and kept covered with wet burlap and some shingle tow or moss.

In using the shovel, the loose, dry soil is scraped off, and the shovel blade is sunk vertically to full depth with the concave side toward the planter; the handle is pushed forward to break out the soil and the shovel pulled toward the planter with the handle inclined slightly toward the planter; the backwall, away from the planter, is made vertical by a second cut and the shovel again drawn back and held to keep the soil from rolling into the hole; a tree is inserted with roots dangling downward, the hole is then half filled and tamped with the heel, then completely filled and tamped again. One man can plant from 50 to 120 trees an hour by this method, depending on the condition of the soil.

In moist soil, planting can also be done in deep, freshly opened furrows. In this method, the tree is held against the vertical side of the furrow without curling the roots and enough soil is scraped with the foot against the roots to hold the tree in place. Then another furrow is plowed against the trees and the soil packed in with the foot or by running the tractor tires over the second furrow-slice and very close to the trees. A crew of one with a tractor, assisted by two helpers, can plant about 350 to 500 trees an hour.

Planting by machine saves labor and time. The planting machines consist of a tractor-drawn trenching device which is mounted on a unicarrier or chassis and which opens a narrow V-shaped trench about 12 inches deep, 4 inches wide on top, and about 1½ inches wide at the bottom. Two men usually ride the machine and place the trees in the open trench, which is then mechanically closed and firmed by packing wheels—all in the same operation. A production of 1,000 to 1,200 trees an hour is generally attained by such machines.

There is a wide range of climate, elevation, and soils in various parts of the United States where windbreaks and shelterbelts are desirable. These factors govern the choice of trees and shrubs selected for planting. Some of the better species mentioned here are used in areas where this type of tree planting is desirable.

The most promising species for the Great Plains include the Chinese elm, green ash, hackberry, honeylocust, cottonwood, white and golden willow, the American elm, boxelder, chokecherry, Tatarian honeysuckle, caragana, eastern and Rocky Mountain redcedar, and ponderosa pine. The adaptability of these and other species in the various Prairie and Plains States is set forth in tables in the last section of this book.

For northwestern United States, including Idaho and the dry-farming areas of eastern Washington and Oregon, the species that have given best results in farm windbreaks and shelterbelts are green ash, black locust, honeylocust, the Chinese elm, caragana, the boxelder, ponderosa pine, Austrian pine, and Colorado blue spruce. On the sites with better moisture conditions, as in low spots or irrigated areas, the golden willow, silver poplar, and the native cottonwoods do well.

In the Corn Belt region of north-central United States, the trees that have proved adaptable are green ash, American elm, black locust, honey-locust, hardy catalpa, black walnut, the Russian-olive, redbud, honeysuckle, Norway spruce, white spruce, Black Hills spruce, red pine, and white pine. In areas with considerable moisture, the golden willow, green willow, and native cottonwoods are recommended.

In southwestern United States, the citrus-growing sections of Arizona, New Mexico, and California, eucalyptus (sometimes known as bluegum) has been used most satisfactorily to protect citrus groves. In California, Monterey cypress has been used to some extent, while in Arizona and New Mexico, the Arizona cypress is planted occasionally with success.

In the New England States, New York, and Pennsylvania, the planting is usually confined to the farmstead windbreaks, and conifers are favored, including Norway and white spruce, white pine, and red pine.

In the southeastern part of the United States from Georgia westward to eastern Texas, there is occasionally an area of sandy soil that requires protection from wind erosion. Under such conditions the native pine species, especially loblolly pine, makes a satisfactory quick-growing shelterbelt.

Good composition in a shelterbelt, like good structural engineering in a bridge or barn, improves its appearance and increases its effectiveness.

For an all-purpose principal shelterbelt in the drier parts of the United States, one of the most important requirements for good composition is a tight row of shrubs on the windward side.

Shrubs should be combined with conifers, low, medium, and tall trees to produce a compact barrier. Five rows represent the minimum that should be used when maximum protection is needed; seven rows are better.

The protection afforded by the principal shelterbelt may be carried entirely across the farm with one-, two-, and three-row supplemental belts at intervals of 10 rods to 20 rods or more depending upon the protection that is needed.

In the citrus-growing sections of California and the Southwest, one- or two-row plantings of eucalyptus or cedar give good results. In areas of better rainfall or where experience has shown that narrow belts will survive (for example, on muck soils of Indiana) single-row plantings of willow are satisfactory.

On the sandy soils of central Wisconsin, three-row belts, preferably of red and jack pine, are recommended.

THOROUGH CULTIVATION is necessary during the first 3 to 5 years of the life of the plantation. No amount of careful site preparation and good planting will compensate for neglect. In most cases, the regular farm equipment can be used in caring for the belts. If the equipment is too wide, some modification can be made by the farmer or his local blacksmith. Usually a spacing of 12 feet between rows will require a cultivation period of 5 years or more, depending on how fast the trees grow. A closer spacing will considerably shorten this period. As soon as the crowns of the trees come together enough to shade out grass and weeds, cultivation can be discontinued, except in dry areas where rainfall is so scant that continued cultivation is necessary.

Two great enemies of trees are fire and livestock. When fire occurs, it is usually sudden and its destruction is complete; it brings to naught the years of care. The damage caused by livestock is as sure as fire in destroying eventually the windbreak or shelterbelt. Browsing of shrubs and the lower branches of trees and young reproduction opens up the stand to the drying effect of the winds, allows the snow to blow through, and generally reduces the effectiveness of the planting. Constant trampling by stock so compacts the soil that it puddles and seals the surface, and a smaller portion of the precipitation reaches the tree roots; moreover, the trampling may injure the roots or result in breakage or other damage to the stem of the tree.

Tree plantings, if adequately protected, do not demand frequent attention, but the comparatively simple measures that are needed do require timely application.

Pruning of shelterbelts should ordinarily be confined to the removal of dead or diseased trees or broken limbs. Some thinning may be desirable in thickly planted stands or other special circumstances.

After a planting has reached maturity and small openings begin to appear in the crowns, underplanting is important and will fill in the gaps. Usually only very tolerant trees, such as redcedar, will succeed among the older trees.

Joseph H. Stoeckeler *is in charge of the Northern Lakes Forest Research Center at Rhinelander, Wis., a branch of the Lake States Forest Experiment Station. He has been engaged in research in the Forest Service since 1931. From 1935 to 1942, when the Prairie States Forestry Project was pushing extensive shelterbelt planting in the Great Plains, he participated in the investigations that provided the technical standards for that project.*

Ross A. Williams *has been chief of the Division of Forestry for the Northern Great Plains Region of the Soil Conservation Service at Lincoln, Nebr., since 1935. Previously he served with the Forest Service and taught at the Ranger School of the New York State College of Forestry and at Montana State University.*

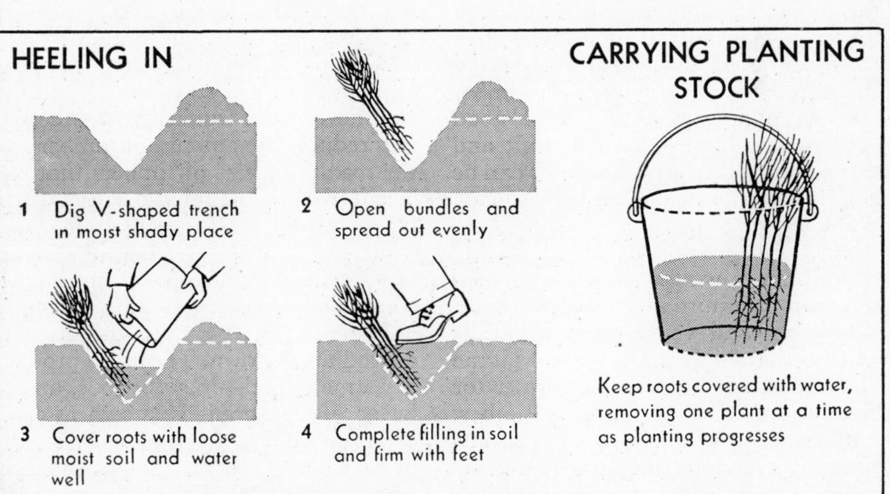

# GROWING BETTER TIMBER

ARTHUR KOEHLER

The man who grows trees for timber will do well to remember that as the twig is bent the tree is inclined. He will find that he can guide natural processes and improve on them. With a purpose like the one watchful parents and teachers have with young people, he can straighten out deficiencies in tree growth by his proper management of young stands of timber, which, if left to follow their bent, make inferior wood.

He knows less about the possibilities of improving on nature in growing timber than he does about agricultural crops. But because many of the present second-growth stands still are in the formative stage and all future stands will be so, his opportunities for improving the quality of the wood in such stands are many. As a rule, second-growth forests (that is, young forests that develop after the old, virgin growth is removed) are smaller when they are cut, have more taper, produce a smaller proportion of knot-free wood, furnish little quarter-sawed lumber, and their individual boards vary more in width and density than old-growth timber.

Furthermore, although intensive cultural methods to improve the quality of the crop may not be so well justified for forest as for agricultural products, the difference in value between timber of poor quality and timber of good quality is so large that net profit and the usefulness of forest products can be enhanced by judicious timber-growing practices.

The first question is: What quality of timber are we going to want when the crop is mature in 25 to 100 years?

Sawlogs and veneer logs generally will be the chief products, in volume and value, of commercial forests for generations to come, because timber, lumber, and veneer have certain outstanding characteristics unequaled by other materials — comparatively low cost of manufacture, ease of working, ease of fastening with nails, screws, and glues, light weight coupled with adequate strength in appropriate sizes for many uses. It is likely that coarse-fiber products (insulating boards, sheathing boards, hard boards, and papers for fiberboard-box manufacture) will find a wider future use than now; for them, however, we should be able to get a large part of the raw material from thinnings, forest residues, low-quality wood, secondary species, and offal from the major wood-utilization processes. Timber, ties, poles, and most lumber and veneer products will still require natural wood of good quality.

What kind of trees do we want for timbers, lumber, and veneer?

In the first place, they must have adequate size in order to be converted and used profitably. In the future, that size probably will be somewhere between 12 and 24 inches in diameter. It may not be profitable to grow trees 4 feet in diameter on a commercial basis because it takes too long. But size is only one consideration. Fully as important are the form of the tree trunk and the defects and quality of the clear wood that it contains.

A valuable quality in trees for sawlogs and veneer is straightness and uprightness of the trunk. Crookedness in logs reduces the amount of lumber and the maximum size of timbers that can be cut from them and also causes warping of sawed products in drying, difficulty in getting a smooth surface, and, because of the cross grain that accompanies crookedness—low strength.

Leaning tree trunks usually are curved up or down. They also produce abnormal wood—in softwoods, on the lower side, where it is known as compression wood; in hardwoods, on the upper side, where it is known as tension wood. M. Y. Pillow, in his investigations at the Forest Products Laboratory, found that both types of abnormal wood shrink excessively and unevenly along the grain in drying, so that large and small pieces alike are crooked, and that they have unreliable strength properties. Compression wood becomes more pronounced the farther the tree trunk leans and the faster it grows. In rapidly growing, second-growth softwood stands it is especially important to eliminate trees that lean 5° or more. Less is known about tension wood in hardwoods.

It is not practical to straighten small trees that are crooked or leaning. Deformed and inclined trees should be removed while young; they will not produce high-grade wood.

Excessive taper also is objectionable, for obvious reasons, in logs for veneer, electric-wire poles, piling, railway ties, and fence posts.

Taper is governed by the ratio of diameter to height growth.

Annual growth in height is determined principally by the quality of the site, that is, climatic and soil conditions. The density of the stand influences the height growth only slightly.

Growth in diameter is determined by the quality of the site and the density of the stand. On a given site the ratio of diameter to height growth, or the amount of taper, is determined by the growing space of a tree. The faster trees grow in diameter, the more taper they will have. Open-grown trees have too much taper for many uses. As will be seen later, growing space also influences the size and persistence of the lower limbs, hence taper also is an index of the character of the hidden knots in a tree trunk; that is, the greater the taper, the larger the knots.

Even when trees grow straight and vertical, the grain in them—that is, the direction of the fibers—often is not parallel with the axis of the stem. Various types of distortions of the fibers, some of them detrimental and some advantageous, may occur. Spiral grain, which is an inclined growth of the fibers that gives the trunks a twisted appearance, may occur in individual trees of any species. The twist may be to the right or to the left; usually it is more pronounced in wood the farther it is from the center of the trunk. This is a point in favor of second-growth, because the trees are smaller when harvested than are old-growth trees and consequently the maximum slope of spiral grain should average less in second-growth timber.

Spiral grain is consistently objectionable. It causes poles, timbers, ties, and lumber to twist during drying. It has a weakening effect when the slope is greater than 1 in 20. It causes chipping and roughness when lumber is planed against the grain.

We do not know the cause of spiral grain, but we do know that it is not caused by actual twisting of the tree trunk by the wind or otherwise. Opinions differ as to whether spiral grain is due to heredity or environment. It seems to be more severe in trees that grow slowly under adverse conditions, as at timber line; it may be that slow growth brings out more strongly any hereditary tendencies toward spiral grain that may be present.

To be on the safe side, seed for forest planting should not be collected from trees that have spiral grain. Young trees with spiral grain should be removed from a forest as soon as convenient after they are discovered. In trees with stringy outer bark, such as the cedars, cypress, sequoias, and willows, the direction of the grain in the wood can be gaged by the direction of the fibers in the bark or by bark ridges. Even in such trees as pine, Douglas-fir, white oak, elm, ash, and the basswood, which have scaly bark with pronounced fissures and ridges after they have passed the young stage, spiral grain can be detected by the direction of the ridges in the bark. In many kinds of young trees with smooth bark, unfortunately, spiral grain cannot be detected by any simple means.

Interlocked grain, that is, spiral grain that reverses in direction from right to left and back every few years, is hereditary, because it occurs almost universally in certain species, notably sweetgum, black tupelo, and many of the tropical species. It produces a beautiful ribbon figure in quarter-sawed lumber and quarter-sliced veneer, especially in species in which the wood has a high natural luster, such as mahogany, Philippine lauan, and African sapele. But it also causes lumber, especially plain-sawed boards, to warp in drying, and makes planing difficult, because the knives must cut against the grain in part of the board no matter which way it is planed. Wood with interlocked grain is difficult to split, although for driveway planking and large rollers, such as those used for house moving, that is an advantage.

Other types of distorted grain that occur in occasional trees are wavy, curly, and bird's-eye grain, all of which are considered ornamental and increase the value of the trees in which they are found. Unfortunately, they cannot be detected easily without mutilating the young trees, although a limited amount of research indicates that, if the outer bark is removed over a small area of the stem, the pattern of the grain is revealed by the fibers in the inner bark, which follow the same course as the wood fibers. Cutting into but not through the inner bark in spots does not damage the tree.

The profits from growing trees certainly could be increased if wood of desirable types of figure could be produced at will. Apparently successful experiments are being made in Finland in growing figured birch. If, as in the case of walnut, a delicious nut with a thin shell could be produced in addition to figured wood, there need be little question as to whether the financial outcome of growing such timber would be plus or minus. Problems of that kind require a great deal of special study for a long period, but, like all research, it need not be repeated once it is done thoroughly.

Knots, the most common defects in lumber, are the bases of live and dead branches imbedded in the growing tree trunk. They affect the appearance, smoothness, strength, tightness, finishing, and other properties of lumber and veneer. Lumber without knots is worth three or four times as much as knotty lumber, except where the knots are such that they are considered ornamental. The parts of knots that are produced by limbs while green, known as intergrown knots, are not so detrimental as those produced by limbs that persist after death, which often are discolored, even partly decayed, and loose.

The development of knots in trees can be reduced in two ways. One way is to maintain stand conditions crowded enough while the trees are young that the lower branches will die and break off while they and the tree trunk are still small in diameter. In such trees the knots in the lower part of the trunk, especially the intergrown parts, as a rule will be shorter.

The dead branches often persist for an extraordinarily long time in some species, notably eastern and western white pines, sugar pine, red pine, ponderosa pine, Douglas-fir, and Engelmann spruce. They may hang on after death for 50 to 150 years or more before they break off, leaving longer dead knots than intergrown knots in the lower portion of tree trunks from stands that are fairly well-stocked. In such species, practically no knot-free lumber can be produced naturally in a commercially reasonable length of time, 75 to 125 years.

A better way to produce knot-free lumber is to prune young timber trees. Whether it pays to prune forest trees depends on the market value of different grades of lumber of a particular species when the wood is harvested and on the original cost of pruning and the number of years over which the cost must be carried. But because the difference in value of knot-free and knotty lumber from virgin timber is large and unpruned second-growth timber will have less knot-free lumber than old-growth timber, it is reasonable to expect that clear, second-growth lumber will be at a high premium. If forest trees are pruned, the stand can be kept more open without danger of the trees becoming too limby, and hence individual trees will grow faster and produce merchantable timber in a shorter time.

Less is known about the advisability of pruning hardwood trees. Decay seems to enter the trees through the cut branches more readily, especially in some species, or new sprouts may develop along the trunk. More research is needed on this subject, but for both softwoods and hardwoods the trees should be pruned while small because the cost of pruning is less, small branch stubs will heal over more rapidly, small knots do not degrade lumber so much as large knots, and more knot-free lumber will be produced. Pruning is of most value for trees that are left to grow to sawlog size. Although pruning of trees grown for poles and pulpwood also would be advantageous from a utility standpoint, its over-all economic benefits are more questionable.

An interesting result of the study of the knots in Douglas-fir at the Forest Products Laboratory was that the trees growing on one of the poorer sites in Oregon, where growth in height and diameter was at a comparatively slow rate, had smaller, albeit more numerous, knots than trees growing on one of the better sites. Because size of knots is a more important factor than number in the commercial grading of common lumber, the poorer site produced a higher grade of lumber on the average than did the better site. On the other hand, in the manufacture of ponderosa pine box veneer and shooks, some mills make a practice of cutting out clear bolts between knot whorls. In that case, trees from the better sites, which grow faster in height and therefore have a longer distance between knot whorls, have the advantage over trees from poor sites.

The apparent inconsistency that better wood sometimes is produced on the poorer sites is explained by the fact that sites are classified on the basis of the volume of wood they can produce per acre per year, regardless of quality.

Even in straight, vertical, straight-grained trees, the quality of the clear wood of each species may vary considerably, in accordance with the conditions under which the trees grew.

Slowness or rapidity of growth of a tree influences greatly the properties and usefulness of the wood produced by it. In general, when softwood trees grow rapidly or slowly they produce lighter and weaker wood than when the rate of growth is more moderate. This does not necessarily mean inferior wood, because wood of light weight may have advantages where strength is not essential. Hardwood trees also usually produce light and weak wood when growing slowly, but rapid growth, as a general rule, results in heavier and stronger wood than does a more moderate growth.

In second-growth timber that has come up on cut-over or burned-over lands and in most plantations, the trees grow rapidly while young because they have abundant growing space. Later, as they become larger and crowd each other, they slow down. Consequently, the annual rings of growth are wide at the center and narrow near the bark. Such uneven rate of growth is objectionable from several standpoints, especially for lumber from small trees in which the narrow and wide-ringed parts cannot be easily segregated on account of their small size. The inner wide-ringed wood and the outer narrow-ringed wood may differ in density and strength. When used for flooring, they wear unevenly; they have different machining and gluing properties; even their pulping characteristics are different.

Wood of rapid growth in some of the pines shrinks excessively along the grain. The result is crooking of lumber and dimension stock when it is combined with wood of slower growth.

That, however, does not seem to be the case in Douglas-fir, much of which is wide-ringed at the center because of having come up in the open after fire, storm, or cutting.

Benson H. Paul, who is working at the Forest Products Laboratory on the relation of growth conditions to wood quality, found that a reduction in growth is particularly objectionable in hardwoods used for purposes where strength is essential, as with hickory and ash for tool handles. If the rate of growth is slowed down from, say, 5 to 17 rings an inch from youth to maturity, the outer, slowly grown part is apt to be exceptionally low in toughness—in fact, more so than if the rate of growth had not been rapid in youth.

A tree of more uniform rate of growth is more desirable for most lumber uses than one that shows wide variation in width of annual rings.

Old-growth Appalachian oak and yellow-poplar have a reputation for being soft-textured because of their slow or moderate growth rates in dense stands and under soil and climatic conditions not so conducive for rapid growth as in the Mississippi Delta. The indications are that second-growth oak and yellow-poplar from the same region, because of their more rapid growth, will not be so soft-textured.

Some species of trees, when grown in swamps that are under water much of the year, as in the lower Mississippi Valley, usually have enlarged butts that extend 6 to 10 feet above ground and contain wood that is much softer than the normal wood higher in the trunk. This swell-butted material is of inferior quality, but it occupies a relatively large percentage of the volume of the trunk in water tupelo, ash, and baldcypress. On the other hand, some species of oaks and cedar elm, which grow well under the same conditions, do not produce swelled butts having lightweight wood. This is an important point to consider in reforesting such bottom lands.

Observations on pines growing in the sands of western Florida and Nebraska show that strong, dense wood will not be produced in trees that have inadequate soil moisture during the summer when the strength-giving summer wood is formed. The light wood produced in trees growing under such conditions has advantages, however, for uses that do not require high strength because the wood is easily handled, easily worked, and does not shrink and swell so much as denser wood of the same species. It is important to know, however, that dense and strong yellow pine cannot be produced under adverse growing conditions in summer.

Experience and laboratory tests have shown large variations in wood quality in each species of timber. Considering the differences that may occur even in the same tree, it is evident that environment is responsible for much of the variation.

Heredity also has an important role. There are indications that straightness of trunk, limbiness, straight grain, figured wood, and rapid growth are hereditary, as well as resistance to disease, cold, and drought. Therefore, in order to get the largest return from timber growing, seed trees should be selected with an eye to quality; young trees of inferior quality should be eliminated early in a growing stand, and trees retained for the final crop should be given cultural treatment that will insure wood of desirable characteristics as far as is economically feasible.

A compromise must usually be made between quantity and quality. The highest returns often are not obtained by growing trees either as quickly as possible in fairly open stands or at a slow and uniform rate in dense stands to produce wood of better quality. The peak in profits usually lies somewhere between the two extremes of growth. Nor may it be economical to eliminate all the defective trees and plant pedigreed seedlings in their place. Quality, however, should always be kept in mind in managing forests for wood production.

To SUMMARIZE: The owner or manager of a tract of young timber can do certain things to improve its value and usefulness when merchantable, but obviously it is not practical to cultivate, fertilize, irrigate, and graft forest trees, as is done with horticultural and agricultural crops.

A forester can control several factors, by means of which he can straighten out his forest so that it will produce greater returns than if left alone.

The more important of these factors are:

1. Choice of species. The growth of the more desirable species can be encouraged by planting them and eliminating the less desirable ones. The choice must be based on what will grow well in the area concerned and what the probable future value will be for the kind, quantity, and quality of timber he expects to produce. The usefulness of a species should not be based entirely on the reputation of the old-growth timber, because second-growth may be materially different in some respects.

2. Density of stand. By maintaining fully stocked stands as far as possible, the maximum volume of wood will be produced on an acre each year, but the forester still has some leeway in the matter. In a moderately dense stand, there will be fewer trees to the acre, but the trees will grow faster and mature earlier than in a dense stand. The wood, however, may be of poorer or better quality, depending on the kind and the purpose for which it is to be used. Ash wood grown for handles, for example, will be stronger the more open the stand, but oak grown for furniture will be softer and more stable in the denser stands.

3. Improvement cutting. The poor and defective trees should be cut as soon as they interfere with the growth of trees of better form and values.

4. Tree injuries. Injuries to trees by fire, disease, insects, man, and beast should be kept at a minimum.

5. Pruning. The crop trees should be pruned while young.

As the old-growth timber becomes scarcer and the second-growth occupies more and more land and as people invest more money in forest land with the expectation of reaping profits some years hence, the incentive to grow better timber will increase. It is too bad that so little is known as yet as to the effect different sites and different types of forest management have on the quality of the wood in different species. But some progress is being made. Unlike agricultural crops, it often takes many years to get usable results in experimenting with forest trees. Foresters are asking for information we should have started 20 years ago to get.

One thing is sure: The best kind of timber that it is economically practical to produce in second-growth stands will not be had unless man tends the forests properly, just as he has learned to do with his fields and gardens.

ARTHUR KOEHLER *was graduated from the University of Michigan forestry school in 1911. He has the master of science degree from the University of Wisconsin. He has carried on research in wood structure and identification of wood at the Forest Products Laboratory since 1911, and was in charge of the Division of Silvicultural Relations from 1927 to 1948.*

# THE JOB OF PLANTING TREES: A SURVEY

PHILIP C. WAKELEY, G. WILLARD JONES

The planting of forests has been going on for a long time in Europe, India, South Africa, Australia, and New Zealand. In the United States, the first few scattered plantations were started 60 to 70 years ago in New England, New York, and Pennsylvania. The first large plantings date from about 1900, but for a generation thereafter planting went slowly. By the end of 1934, the total planted area was only about 2⅓ million acres.

The establishment of the Tennessee Valley Authority, the Prairie States Forestry Project, and the Soil Conservation Service and the expansion of the national forest and State nursery and planting programs extended public and farm planting from 1935 on, except during the war years.

By the end of 1948, nearly 5 million acres had been planted successfully in the United States—46 percent of it by farmers and private landowners, 7 percent by industrial organizations, 19 percent by States, counties, and municipalities, and 28 percent by Federal agencies. Planting has been most extensive in the Lake States, the South, New York, Nebraska, Pennsylvania, Iowa, and Kansas. Only Rhode Island, Delaware, Arizona, Nevada, and Wyoming—which are either small or relatively dry-climate States—report fewer than 10,000 acres each as successfully planted. In 1948 the demand on State and industrial nurseries exceeded all records.

Many individuals have been working on seed, nursery, and planting problems: T. E. Maki, a forester, perfected a method of testing pine cones for ripeness by floating them in oil, thus saving thousands of dollars formerly wasted on immature cones. Raymond C. Rietz, a heating engineer, designed cone-drying kilns and worked out safe kiln schedules for extracting pine seed from the cones. Lela V. Barton, a botanist, made important discoveries having to do with storing tree seed and increasing and speeding up its germination in the nursery. S. A. Wilde, a soil scientist, developed special fertilizer and compost treatments for forest nurseries in the Lake States. Carl Hartley, a forest pathologist, developed methods for preventing nursery seedlings from damping-off. Joseph H. Stoeckeler, E. J. Eliason, and Floyd M. Cossitt, foresters, evolved a highly economical way to weed seedbeds of pine by spraying them with dry-cleaning fluid.

The planting bar most widely used in the South was designed by three foresters, a ranger, a tool-company official, and a boy in the Civilian Conservation Corps. Professional foresters, implement manufacturers, and State forestry and pulp-company technicians have developed practicable tree-planting machines. Hundreds of others also have made contributions.

The techniques of planting are still advancing rapidly. Today persons who want to grow trees have a better chance of success than ever before.

Successful planting depends on sound information, good judgment, and careful work. Indeed, a conspicuous aspect of planting in America has been the outstanding success of many beginners who have observed local conditions carefully, compared information and suggestions from several sources, and intelligently chosen methods to fit their particular needs.

A FUNDAMENTAL PRINCIPLE is that, on any given site, native species do better than those brought in from another country or region. When species are planted out of their natural range, they are more susceptible to disease, insects, and damage from frost and ice than are native species. Douglas-fir, when planted in northwestern Oregon where it is native, for example, attains 18 inches in diameter and 50 to 60 feet in height in 35 years. In the Lake States, it does not grow nearly so high.

Special purposes sometimes justify exceptions to the rule of native species.

Scotch pine, which is native to western Europe, can be planted confidently in Indiana or Ohio for Christmas trees, and white spruce makes a good ornamental or windbreak in North Dakota.

The species planted vary with regions. On the national forests, for example, slash and longleaf pines are most widely planted in the Gulf States; loblolly pine in the Central Atlantic Coast States; shortleaf pine in the Ozarks; red, white, and jack pines and white spruce in the Lake States and the Northeast; Douglas-fir, Port-Orford-cedar, and ponderosa pine in the Pacific Northwest; ponderosa pine and the western white pine in the Rocky Mountains; and ponderosa pine and Jeffrey pine in California. The same species are generally planted on similar State, municipal, and private lands.

In the Great Plains region, eastern redcedar and Rocky Mountain juniper are the favored conifers. The boxelder, green ash, American elm, hackberry, the black locust, Siberian elm, honeylocust, and catalpa are the most-favored hardwoods.

In the Northeast, eastern white pine and red pine are favored species, supplemented by some Scotch pine, Norway spruce, white spruce, and jack pine, and small quantities of European larch and several hardwoods.

People often ask why conifers are usually planted on worn-out and abandoned farm land that once supported fine hardwood forests. The answer is that cropping and fires have destroyed the humus that covered the old forest floor, lowered soil fertility and moisture-holding capacity, and compacted the subsoil. Hence, it is usually necessary to make the first crop conifers, which build up the soil until the native hardwoods gradually reestablish themselves, often from seeds brought in by birds, rodents, or the wind.

Most plantations are made with nursery-grown seedlings. The rapid first-year growth of southern pines makes it possible to use seedlings 10 to 15 months old and as they come from the beds in which they were sown. Hardwoods are also planted as 1-year-old seedlings, especially in the Central States and the Great Plains. Use of such young stock helps keep down the planting costs.

Jack pine 2 years in the nursery bed is favored in the Lake States and 2-year-old Douglas-fir and Port-Orford-cedar in Oregon.

Most other conifers are transplanted at least once before they leave the nursery. Transplanting is the most expensive of all nursery operations, but it greatly improves hardiness and root system of the seedling and thus gives it a better chance to survive when planted out.

The digging, packing, and transporting of wilding seedlings usually involves considerable expense, quite often more than the cost of an equal number of nursery-grown seedlings. The mortality sustained in transplanted wildings is quite frequently severe. For those reasons, we do not recommend the use of wildings for planting. Experience has proved that the premium stock produced under controlled nursery conditions to meet approved specifications is usually less expensive than seedlings secured from areas near to the plantation.

To give planted trees their best chance to live and grow, some kind of tilling is usually needed to remove sod and brush from the planting site.

The several kinds include scalping the spots at proper intervals with a mattock, plowing shallow furrows 6 to 8 feet apart, or using a heavy disk to eliminate brush and churn up and expose mineral soil. On the Great Plains, thorough summer fallowing of the soil has been found necessary before planting of shelterbelt trees. In planting for erosion control, gully banks must sometimes be plowed in, gully channels dammed, and slopes mulched. Open sand plains, however, and much of the cut-over longleaf pine lands require no preparation; on other longleaf pine lands a single burn a year before planting may be enough.

Tilling is important, particularly when planting wild lands in the north where the planting sites are usually overgrown with heavy sod and dense brush. By removing this vegetation, competition for the young trees for moisture, light, and soil nutrients is greatly reduced. The cost of preparing the site will vary with density of the vegetation and the kind of tilling that is done. For large plantations double-buster plows drawn by crawler-type tractors are frequently used. Furrows in which the trees are to be planted are plowed at intervals to give desired spacing of the trees. This type of site preparation is efficient and economical. Heavy tractor-drawn disks have proved to be effective in preparing difficult sites of heavy brush, but the cost is correspondingly greater. For small or wood-lot plantations, scalping spots with a mattock or grub hoe, although laborious, is more practical than plowing or disking because it does not require heavy and expensive equipment.

The most frequently used hand planting tool is probably the grub hoe or mattock. On some sites it is used to make a slit just large enough for the roots. Where transplants or especially well-rooted seedlings are used, however, it is usually better (even though slower and more expensive) to dig a hole in which the roots can be well spread.

Throughout most of the South where the soil is sandy loam and relatively free from stones and where slit planting is successful, a planting bar with a 10-inch wedge-shaped blade is used for 1-year-old stock. The same is true for seedling stock in parts of the Lake States. Technique with these bars was brought to a high peak of efficiency by the Civilian Conservation Corps planting crews. Crack planting teams had no trouble in setting 300 trees a man-hour; even average crews set about 160 a man-hour. A man planting in holes with a mattock does well to plant 65 to 80 trees an hour.

Planting machines have now been improved and are in use to reduce costs, labor, and time. Two or three men (one on the tractor and one on the planter, or two alternating as planter and follow-up man to replant trees set too high) can set 1,250 to 1,750 trees an hour. Different machines have been developed for the sand plains of the Lake States and the bunchgrass-covered, shallow, sandy loams with stiff subsoils of the southern pine region. Some of the machines work well in fairly heavy brush. None has yet been adapted to hilly or rocky land, however, or to areas cluttered with logs and tops.

Machine planting is becoming popular in the Lake States region among farmers who have small fields which they desire to plant to a productive crop. The areas usually include worn-out fields that have been cropped for many years and require a minimum of tilling to place them in shape for planting trees. Planting by machine is a relatively simple operation. It involves making a deep narrow slit in the soil in which the tree is inserted as the machine moves forward. The opening is closed and the soil firmly packed around the roots of the tree by small rolling packing wheels, which follow closely behind the trencher.

How closely to space the trees depends on the purpose of the plantation. The closer the spacing, the more trees are needed to the acre and the more they cost to produce, transport, and plant. Closely spaced trees must be thinned early, or they will crowd each other severely and fall off in growth rate. These facts have led to the use of wide spacings, with trees 8, 10, 16, or even 20 feet apart each way. Trees so spaced reach merchantable size at the earliest possible age, although their quality and their total volume per acre in the early years are often low.

On the other hand, closely spaced

trees use the ground more fully during the early years of the plantation, stop erosion sooner, produce more wood on an acre, allow higher mortality without the need of replanting, shed their lower branches sooner, and permit a wider choice of trees in thinning. Many costs of growing timber, such as fire protection and taxes, are incurred by the acre, but practically all profits accrue by the tree. Therefore, within limits, the more trees to the acre the better.

A spacing of 6 by 6 feet (1,210 trees an acre) has always been popular. Spacings of 5 by 6, 5 by 5 (1,742 trees an acre), and 4 by 6 are increasing in use, especially with larger markets for small products and the development of machine planting. At these spacings, trees generally grow well until some can be thinned out and sold for pulpwood, fence posts, or small poles, or used for fuel. The rest are left to grow until they again become crowded, when more are sold. Except for special purposes, however, spacings closer than 4 by 6 feet cannot be recommended. Costs are too high, and growth may fall off too soon.

Some of the earlier plantations are now old enough to show that planted forests are economically sound. Earnings of $24.60 an acre are reported from thinnings on a 30-year-old red pine plantation established in northern Wisconsin by the State in 1913. The sale of Christmas trees from thinnings in 6- to 9-year-old red and jack pine plantations in the Lower Peninsula of Michigan brought an average of $80 an acre—and as high as $122 an acre (200 trees an acre at 61 cents each).

A paper company in Wisconsin has planted 18,000 acres, and each year plants several thousand acres more. Seven other forest industries in Wisconsin had planted 18,700,000 trees on 18,600 acres, as of April 22, 1947, and had dedicated 300,625 acres to permanent forests. In the Pacific Northwest, extensive planted areas are already under management in a tree-farm movement, which is growing rapidly.

About 75 million acres of forest land in the United States were classified in 1946 as poorly stocked seedling or sapling areas, or as deforested. Forest restoration on such idle lands commonly requires planting, although under fire protection a portion will gradually restock naturally. Several million acres more of partly stocked land will give larger and quicker returns if interplanted; additional millions of acres of submarginal farm land should be planted to trees.

How much of this area Government agencies, industry, and farm and other private owners will manage to plant is hard to predict. Certain it is that the job needs to be tackled on a far larger scale than in the past.

One goal might be for small owners to do their part of the job by planting a billion trees a year, or 20 million acres in 20 years; planting on large private holdings and on public lands might add 10 million acres to this goal. We believe, however, that the goal might well be much higher—90 million to 100 million.

However we gage the job ahead, it represents a tremendous undertaking, neither technically simple nor cheap. It is, however, a constructive effort, one in which many individuals can contribute to the lightening of the general load at profit to themselves.

Philip C. Wakeley, *a native of New Jersey, has degrees in forestry from Cornell University. He has been employed by the Southern Forest Experiment Station since 1924, and has been in charge of seed, nursery, and planting research. He has written several technical publications on aspects of forest regeneration.*

G. Willard Jones, *a forester in the Forest Service, is in charge of reforestation in the Lake States region. For the past 32 years he has been engaged in nursery production and field-planting work in the Northern Rocky Mountain and Lake States regions.*

802062°—49——15

NUMBER OF PRIVATE OWNERS OF COMMERCIAL FOREST LAND IN THE UNITED STATES AND THE AVERAGE SIZE OF HOLDING BY SIZE OF OWNERSHIP,[1] BY REGION, 1945

[Farm [2] and nonfarm combined]

| Region | *All owners* | | | *Small (under 5,000 A.)* | | | *Medium (5,000 to 50,000 A.)* | | | *Large (over 50,000 A.)* | | |
|---|---|---|---|---|---|---|---|---|---|---|---|---|
| | *Number* | *Total area* | *Average size* | *Number* | *Total area* | *Average size* | *Number* | *Total area* | *Average size* | *Number* | *Total area* | *Average size* |
| | | *1,000 acres* | *Acres* | | *1,000 acres* | *Acres* | | *1,000 acres* | *Acres* | | *1,000 acres* | *Acres* |
| New England | 243, 958 | 29, 294 | 120 | 243, 719 | 17, 661 | 72 | 194 | 2, 150 | 11, 082 | 45 | 9, 483 | 210, 733 |
| Middle Atlantic | 514, 908 | 36, 497 | 71 | 514, 768 | 32, 702 | 64 | 115 | 1, 722 | 14, 974 | 25 | 2, 073 | 82, 920 |
| Lake States | 586, 472 | 29, 045 | 50 | 586, 347 | 24, 545 | 42 | 91 | 1, 260 | 13, 846 | 34 | 3, 240 | 95, 294 |
| Central States | 987, 445 | 41, 770 | 42 | 987, 353 | 40, 068 | 41 | 85 | 1, 185 | 13, 941 | 7 | 517 | 73, 857 |
| Plains | 121, 607 | 2, 990 | 25 | 121, 607 | 2, 990 | 25 | ........ | ........ | ...... | ........ | ........ | ...... |
| North | 2, 454, 390 | 139, 596 | 57 | 2, 453, 794 | 117, 966 | 48 | 485 | 6, 317 | 13, 025 | 111 | 15, 313 | 137, 955 |
| South Atlantic | 526, 056 | 38, 902 | 74 | 525, 706 | 33, 068 | 63 | 312 | 2, 938 | 9, 417 | 38 | 2, 896 | 76, 211 |
| Southeast | 679, 306 | 82, 265 | 121 | 677, 750 | 58, 227 | 86 | 1, 456 | 13, 799 | 9, 477 | 100 | 10, 239 | 102, 390 |
| West Gulf | 446, 564 | 45, 861 | 103 | 446, 000 | 30, 771 | 69 | 483 | 4, 766 | 9, 867 | 81 | 10, 324 | 127, 457 |
| South | 1, 651, 926 | 167, 028 | 101 | 1, 649, 456 | 122, 066 | 74 | 2, 251 | 21, 503 | 9, 553 | 219 | 23, 459 | 107, 119 |
| North Rocky Mountain | 20, 967 | 7, 352 | 351 | 20, 930 | 3, 868 | 185 | 27 | 318 | 11, 778 | 10 | 3, 166 | 316, 600 |
| South Rocky Mountain | 7, 486 | 2, 957 | 395 | 7, 383 | 1, 766 | 239 | 96 | 838 | 8, 729 | 7 | 353 | 50, 429 |
| Pacific Northwest | 72, 586 | 19, 757 | 272 | 72, 390 | 11, 735 | 162 | 163 | 2, 526 | 15, 497 | 33 | 5, 496 | 166, 545 |
| California | 18, 351 | 8, 283 | 451 | 18, 184 | 3, 984 | 219 | 149 | 1, 414 | 9, 490 | 18 | 2, 885 | 160, 278 |
| West | 119, 390 | 38, 349 | 321 | 118, 887 | 21, 353 | 180 | 435 | 5, 096 | 11, 715 | 68 | 11, 900 | 175, 000 |
| All regions | 4, 225, 706 | 344, 973 | 82 | 4, 222, 137 | 261, 385 | 62 | 3, 171 | 32, 916 | 10, 380 | 398 | 50, 672 | 127, 317 |

[1] In the northern and southern regions, 70 percent of the small farm and nonfarm owners have woodlands which do not exceed 50 acres each; 16 percent have holdings which vary in size from 50 to 100 acres, 12 percent vary from 100 to 500, and only 2 percent of the small owners have holdings exceeding 500 acres each.

[2] The average size of *farm woodlands* is 43 acres. About 900 farm woodlands are in the medium size group.

# PLANTING A SMALL SOUTHERN WOODLAND

W. R. HINE

The man who wants to plant a small woodland in the South should first make up his mind on several points. Growing timber is a long-time project. It requires good judgment in weighing the several factors. It requires careful long-range planning and a disposition to abide by decisions made. It is well to reach sound conclusions at the start.

Wise land management dictates that each field should be devoted to the purpose for which it is best suited. Land suited to the production of food crops normally should be used for such crops. Similarly, pasture land should be devoted to growing livestock, and land that is better suited to growing trees, including worn-out and eroded land, might properly be devoted to growing a timber crop.

Common sense suggests that planting be done only on land that will not restock satisfactorily within a reasonable time. Many forest acres, though bare of seed trees, will reseed naturally from the surrounding woods, and the young trees will grow if protected from fire, trampling, or grazing as may be necessary. A good stand of loblolly pine, for example, will adequately reseed the surrounding area to a distance of 400 feet or more. Many landowners have planted, only to find in 3 to 5 years that seedlings from nearby trees restocked the area, rendering planting unnecessary.

Potential forest land that is not restocking to trees adequately or in a reasonable length of time should be planted. Adequate stocking means at least 500 commercially valuable seedlings, fairly well distributed per acre. Young trees in stands with fewer than 500 an acre at the start often grow up excessively limby and produce only low-grade products. Poorly stocked stands grow less volume for a given area than well-stocked stands. A reasonable length of time to wait for natural reseeding depends on the cost of planting and the value of the annual growth of forest products. If, for example, it costs $8 to plant an acre of loblolly pine, which will grow at the rate of 1½ cords an acre a year, worth, say, $3 a cord, then an owner would be better off financially if he planted in preference to waiting more than 3 years for nature to reseed.

An owner will want to consider what kind of trees to plant and this involves a number of factors. A point of first importance will be the market value of products grown.

While nearly any sound tree of good form is marketable when timber is in urgent demand, some species are difficult to market when demand falls off. Pines are generally in demand. They are closely utilized, bring good prices, and grow more volume per acre than hardwoods. Slash pine and longleaf pine, in addition to their general usefulness for wood products, also produce turpentine and rosin. Hardwoods present more of a marketing problem. They are more limited in their usefulness and hence may not sell so readily. Some species, as the hickories, are often difficult to market. An occasional species, such as blackjack oak, is seldom marketable at all. This difference in utility is the basis for one of the South's most difficult forest-management problems. Everywhere pines are cut heavily, and the less productive, less valuable hardwoods are left in possession of the soil. Most planters prefer pine or other softwoods.

Some owners may plant for a special product, as fence posts. For that purpose they want such durable species as black locust, or redcedar, Osage-orange, or catalpa.

The ability of a species to ward off the hazards of a locality is a point for consideration in selection. Fire has been the scourge of southern forests.

Longleaf pine develops a skirt of needles, which protects the bud and growing tissue inside the bark. Longleaf will survive fires that kill other pines and hardwoods. Shortleaf has the rare quality among pines of being able to sprout after its top has been killed back by fire.

Seedling diseases are also important. Longleaf is highly susceptible to brown spot needle disease (*Scirrhia acicola*), which in some localities may prevent seedlings from attaining height growth. Slash pine or loblolly pine may be substituted. Each within its range, and on the suitable sites, will grow up without any serious interference from brown spot. Shortleaf pine in the western Gulf States is severely stunted by the LeConte sawfly (*Neodiprion LeContei*), but loblolly is relatively uninjured by this insect. Shortleaf pine suffers heavy losses over part of its range from a disease called littleleaf. Loblolly, on similar sites, is relatively free of this disease. Longleaf may prove an even better substitute.

A longleaf plantation may be wiped out by native hogs which graze on the roots. While other pines may be killed by hog grazing, the damage is not usually serious. Hardwood seedlings may be injured by grazing and trampling by cattle. Pine seedlings suffer less than hardwoods, but neither will survive heavy grazing.

Trees for planting should be native to the locality. Exotic trees or strains of trees from distant sources have no place in the small woodland until proved by public agencies. Species from distant sources almost invariably prove less successful than local trees. For example, slash pine is an excellent species in its native range along the Coastal Plain of the Southeastern States, but it suffers breakage from snow and ice when planted north of its range. Strains of loblolly pine planted 100 or more miles from the parent trees sometimes suffer a higher rate of infection with stem canker (*Cronartium fusiform*) than the local trees that belong to the same species.

Species should be adapted to soil and moisture conditions of the area to be planted. Longleaf pine will grow on the most difficult dry, deep sandy ridges within the natural range and make excellent timber. Loblolly pine on the same site is often so heavily infected with stem canker that the trees must be salvaged early for pulpwood or be lost through decay and death. Some pine will serve for almost any dry, eroded, or less fertile area. Loblolly pine, within its natural range, is especially effective in reclaiming eroded soils and gradually rebuilding them. Pines grow well in good soil, too.

Hardwoods generally require the more fertile, well-watered soils with good drainage. Black locust, for example, will grow rapidly on good, well-watered soils, but will fail completely on poor soil or dry sites. Commercially valuable hardwoods, such as white oak, walnut, black cherry, and yellow-poplar, likewise require soils equal in fertility to those on good agricultural lands, but occasionally a landowner has an odd corner of such land that will make a better return with a crop of good hardwood trees than with annual crops.

The discussion thus far suggests that the tree planter will encounter many problems on which he may need the counsel of an expert. Each planting area presents its own special set of conditions and problems. Many of them require decisions on a technical basis. Technical help is available for those who wish it. The State forester, the local forester for any public agency, or the county agent will gladly give advice on request. The forester will go over the property with the owner and discuss whatever questions may arise. He will explain why species succeed or fail under varying conditions. He will discuss the relative values of different species and present facts on rate of timber growth, markets, and cash returns. The owner may then weigh the facts he has obtained from his own observations, from the forester, and from others, and reach his own conclusions.

Spacings vary from as close as 3 by 3 feet to 10 by 10 feet, and even wider.

Narrower spacings, say 5 by 5 feet and closer, are usually intended for erosion-control purposes or Christmas-tree culture. The primary objective is to get the ground protected from rain and washing as soon as practicable.

Intermediate spacings, 6 by 6 feet to 8 by 8 feet, are primarily for timber production.

Wide spacings, 10 by 10 feet and wider, are sometimes used for the production of naval stores.

Close spacings grow more wood per unit of area than wide spacings because trees use the soil moisture and sunlight more completely.

C. H. Coulter, the State forester of Florida, reported a growth of 34.8 cords to the acre on a 13-year-old slash pine plantation spaced 8 by 8 feet, and 20.2 cords for one planted 12 by 12.

Closely planted trees, however, must be kept thinned so as to retain a third or more of the length of the stem in green crown; otherwise, the production of wood will slow down. Many planters who desire to grow wood products space the trees so that the first thinning will be made when a substantial proportion of the trees reach the size for the product desired. Thus an owner in the South who plans to make his first thinning for a pulpwood market might plant on a 6- by 6-foot spacing or thereabouts. His first thinning would be made at the end of 15 to 25 years, depending on the soil.

Men of the Forest Service planted 2 acres on an abandoned field on the Apalachicola National Forest in Florida on a 6- by 6-foot spacing using 3-year-old wild slash pine seedlings. Pulpwood was the first in the series of expected products. Exceptionally rapid growth made it necessary to thin the planted stand 11 years after planting. The cut on a selective basis removed 16 cords an acre and left 22 cords an acre. Numerous plantings at that spacing have been thinned profitably at 15 and 20 years of age.

An owner who plans to make his first thinning for saw timber would choose a wider spacing, say 8 by 8 feet, and expect to thin at 30 to 40 years. The first sawlogs from planted stands in the South have not yet been cut, although Jim Fowler, M. L. Shaw, and others have some trees of sawlog size in stands 20 years of age.

A naval stores operator who plants slash or longleaf pine might prefer a wide spacing so as to produce long, large, green crowns for the maximum production of gum. C. W. Sinclair, of Madison County, Fla., was able to turpentine 90 trees an acre, all 9 inches or larger in diameter, at 13 years on a 12- by 18-foot spacing. Most foresters recommend a moderately close spacing to assure fairly complete utilization of the site and also to assure the natural pruning of branches. The products such as pulpwood, naval stores, poles, and sawlogs would be harvested as they became available.

Planting on lands that have been cultivated is usually done without special preparation of the planting site. Plantings on cut-over forest land may likewise be made without prior preparation of the site, other than perhaps burning off the accumulated grass, weeds, and brush. Removal of such trash exposes the bare soil and makes the planting operations more convenient. Competition for the young trees is reduced, and the fire hazard is temporarily eliminated. Loosening the soil in cut-over forest land likewise aids seedling growth. Seedlings almost invariably grow better in loosened soil—as evidenced by their growth along road banks. Mr. Coulter found that seedlings on an old field grew substantially better than trees on adjacent unbroken forest soil. Earl Porter, of the International Paper Co., found that woods soils, broken with a heavy harrow 3 months before planting, produced trees that at the end of 4½ years were 70 percent taller than those on soils not harrowed.

At least three ways of planting deserve consideration. They are direct seeding, planting with wild seedlings, and planting with nursery seedlings.

It is possible to reforest by sowing or planting seed directly on prepared ground, and there are examples of satisfactory stands obtained by this method. T. J. Fountain, of Taylor County, Ga., prepared a 100-acre field as if he were going to plant watermelons. He sowed it to longleaf pine seed. Each seed was planted by hand, deep enough to cover the seed, but with the wing sticking out in the breeze. Contrary to the customary habit of waiting several years before starting height growth, many of Mr. Fountain's longleaf seedlings grew several inches the first season. He now has a near-perfect 15-year-old longleaf stand with trees 35 feet tall and 6 to 7 inches in diameter at breast height. On the other hand, many capable people have failed in their efforts to obtain a stand by direct seeding. Until sure-fire methods for successful direct seeding are worked out, it is cheaper in the long run to plant high-grade, nursery-grown seedlings.

Plantings may be made with wild seedlings, which grow naturally in old fields or along road banks or borrow pits. Wild seedlings 6 inches to 12 inches tall can be lifted and transplanted during the dormant season—late fall and winter.

One notable planting with wild stock was made in 1928 by M. L. Shaw, on worn-out farm land in Clinch County, Ga. With help from his father and hired hands, he planted 72 acres with wild slash pine seedlings dug up in the forest. He used a 10 by 10 spacing. He replanted the fail places in 1929 and 1930. His pines, thinned for pulpwood in 1942, yielded 8.6 cords an acre, or $20 an acre, at the end of 14 years. In 1947, he started turpentining 5,000 trees on a selective basis, chipping only crowded trees and those of poor form. He cut the turpentined trees in 1948, and they yielded 500 cords of pulpwood. Prior to the cutting in 1948, the stand had 28 cords to the acre and about 275 trees 7 to 13 inches in diameter. Total growth for 20 years was 36 cords an acre. The land, originally worth $2 an acre, has already produced $44 worth of pulpwood and now has a well-stocked stand of saw-timber trees.

The wild seedlings are recommended only in exceptional cases. They are rarely available close by in the quantity needed and of the right size for transplanting. They are generally not so well developed in root and top as nursery-grown stock, and hence would not be so uniformly successful where equivalent care was given. Expert and careful handling is required in lifting and transporting wild seedlings. The cost might easily exceed the cost of nursery-grown stock, and an inexperienced planter might have greater losses with wild stock than with nursery-grown stock. Nevertheless, if a man knows how to handle wild seedlings and takes all the necessary care, they should prove satisfactory.

Planting should be done in the dormant season, after the hardwood leaves drop in the fall and before new growth shows in the spring. Trees should not be planted in frozen ground. Seedlings showing new growth are likely to fail under ordinary handling. Of course, it is possible with small seedlings, excellent care, and plenty of rain, to transplant at any season of the year when the ground is not frozen.

The solution for most small-woodland owners is to purchase nursery-grown seedlings from a State forest-tree nursery. Any publicly employed forester, State or Federal, or any county agent will assist a landowner to place his order and get any information he may need about planting. Trees from the State nursery are grown to the size that gives the best success when transplanted, and only healthy, vigorous, well-developed trees are sold. Trees come properly wrapped and ready for planting. If the trees are handled carefully and planted properly, according to directions received with the seedlings, an owner should be rewarded with a successful plantation, provided rainfall is adequate.

Woodland owners will do well to order their seedlings well in advance of the time of planting. State forest nurseries strive to raise enough seedlings to supply the demand. Sound public financing suggests that they plan to grow no more than they sell. In the South, about 20 months elapses from the time plans are laid and seed collected until the seedlings are lifted from the nursery. Seedlings may not be held over in southern nurseries through a second growing season because they become too large for economical transplanting. The State can therefore do a better job of nursery-production planning if orders are placed about 1½ years ahead of the date when the owner wishes to plant. Of course, the State may be able to fill small orders placed only a few months ahead of the date of planting.

Planning ahead is sound business for the planter also. It enables him to take proper care of the seedlings, make adequate preparation of the planting site, and arrange for the necessary labor.

Seedlings should be planted promptly after receipt from the nursery. If planting is necessarily delayed for a day or two, seedlings may be stored in a cool, dry place in the package as received from the State nursery. If seedlings are received unwrapped, as in a truckload shipment, or if the delay in planting may extend to several days, seedlings should be heeled-in. The heel-in site should be cool, well-drained, and shaded from the sun.

Trees are heeled-in in long trenches. The trench made with a shovel or spade is dug deep enough to accommodate the full length of the tree roots. One side of the trench, the upper side, if on an incline, is sloped. Trees are spaced out on the sloped side thinly so that some roots of each tree touch the slope. Loose dirt is shoveled over the roots, all of which should be covered. Soil is then firmed lightly and the trees are watered. Trees are lifted from the heel-in bed as needed; the remaining trees are kept well watered until planted.

Tree roots must be kept moist and sheltered from the sun and the wind. Seedlings are transported in a bucket or another watertight container. Wet moss or sawdust should cover the roots at all times, and the trees should be taken from the container one at a time as needed and promptly planted.

Tools used in hand planting are simple and inexpensive. The mattock and spade are still used where the soil is thin; with them, special care is necessary to provide enough dirt to cover the roots properly.

Newer tools have been designed for use where the soil is loose and deep. One, the planting dibble, is a long, wedge-shaped bar that is fastened to a handle. It is used to make a slit in the ground deep enough to take the roots without doubling them back. The seedling is placed in the hole. Its roots are spread as much as possible to insure individual contact with the soil. The tree is set in the soil at the approximate depth that it grew in the nursery. After proper setting, the seedling is firmed in, and the hole closed with the same tool. Distance between rows is measured off and the end of the row is marked with a flag as a guide to the planter. Spacing along the rows is measured by pacing.

For larger plantations, planting machines drawn by tractors are now used. One type of planting machine opens a narrow slit in the soil with a trencher plow. The slit is held open by two parallel iron runners long enough to permit the insertion of a seedling. After that, the slit is closed and firmed about the seedling roots by two rolling wheels, which press the soil from either side. Other types work similarly with slight variations.

Planting costs may vary, and average estimates have little value for a given prospective planting.

Pine seedlings from State nurseries in the South cost $2 to $3.50 a thousand; hardwoods cost $3 to $10. Elsewhere seedlings may sell for as much as $25 or more, depending on the cost of production.

Costs for planting in the field likewise vary with wage scales and the ease or difficulty of planting. Planting pine seedlings on average abandoned fields or on cut-over forests with reasonably loose soil should require approximately 1½ man-days an acre. This estimate is based on planting 908 trees on a 6- by 8-foot spacing and assumes planting at the rate of 600 seedlings per man-day, which is not difficult for experienced planters.

Planting with the recently developed planting machines is much faster. Two men with a track-type tractor and a planting machine can plant, in clay soils and light oak stands, 12,000 to 15,000 trees in an 8-hour day. In sandy soils, a farm-type wheel tractor and machine can do as well. The same number of seedlings an acre can be planted by machine at one-third to one-half the cost of hand planting.

Although planting by hand will continue to be more practical for most small owners for some time to come, custom-machine planting is already available. In some localities public-spirited citizens or institutions will lend planting machines free to planters. Machines offer important possibilities for an expanded program of planting.

Satisfactory survival and growth in planted stands are relatively easy to obtain if good judgment is used in the selection of species and areas to be planted and if proper care is given in planting and protecting the plantation.

Thousands of farmers who had never planted trees before have obtained a satisfactory survival. Donald Brewster, a consulting forester, reported successful survival of 91 percent of 1.4 million slash pine trees from the Florida State Nursery that farmers planted during a 10-year period. General observations over the South indicate that this is not too high to expect for slash, loblolly, and the shortleaf pines if due care is exercised.

But planting as a business venture is not without its hazards. An extended period of dry weather in the first year of planting may kill the seedlings before they become established. Such losses are not uncommon, particularly west of the Mississippi River. It may be repeated that little can be done about the weather, but the woodland owner with many acres to plant can arrange to spread the job over several years. The loss for a dry year will thus not be so great as if he had planted the entire area in that one year.

A more serious threat to plantations is fire. Most planted trees are easily killed by fire in their early years. Even longleaf pine may be killed by repeated severe fires. Many owners burn over the planting site before planting. This eliminates the accumulated fuel and the chances for a serious fire at least until the following fall. The careful owner will plow firebreaks 6 feet or wider, cleared of all inflammable material down into the bare soil, around the plantation. If the plantation is large, it should be broken up into blocks of 20 or 40 acres with additional firebreaks. Some owners burn their southern pine plantations as an insurance against disastrous losses. Burning must be done under carefully controlled conditions or the fire set by the owner may be as disastrous as wildfire.

If trees are killed by fire before they reach merchantable size, there is, of course, nothing to salvage. However, Mrs. Hugh Mayes, of Leon County, Fla., had a severe fire in a 53-acre field of 10-year-old slash pine. About one-half the trees were killed. She sold the fire-killed pine trees as pulpwood for enough to pay all planting and carrying costs. The remaining trees, though temporarily slowed down in growth, recovered in 3 or 4 years and are now growing nicely.

Grazing by domestic stock provides a definite hazard to planted trees. Cattle graze closely such hardwood trees as white oak, yellow-poplar, and ash, which are frequently used in plantings. Trampling by cattle packs clay soils and makes both seedling survival and growth difficult. Cattle often ride down young trees to graze on them or brush off the flies. Light grazing by cattle in pine stands may not do great harm, but it will not help the plantation. Sheep seriously interfere with the growth of young longleaf seedlings by nipping the buds. Hogs will destroy a plantation of longleaf by grazing the roots. The plantation should be protected, as necessary, from livestock by fencing.

Planted trees are susceptible to the same diseases and attacks by insects as are trees in natural stands of the same species. Longleaf pine that is held back from making height growth by brown spot may be released by careful burning. The flames check the spread of the disease for a year or two, allowing the longleaf pine to make height growth and get above the zone of dangerous infection. Loblolly pine and slash pine are especially susceptible to stem canker. Careful culling of seedlings at the nurseries has greatly reduced the chances that the planter will receive infected trees. However, infection may occur on the growing tips of trees of any size when the pollen is flying in the spring. About the only known practical remedy in planted stands is to thin out the infected trees. They are easily recognized by the masses of orange spots in the spring and by the swollen, distorted trunk and limbs. Thinning is usually delayed until the cut products may be used on the place or sold. Hardwood trees are subject to various rots which enter from an injury, as from fire or logging damage. Diseased trees should be removed.

Pine plantations suffer somewhat from insect attacks. Occasionally these are serious, but, over the South as a whole, insects do relatively little damage to plantations. This is probably because the trees in plantations are usually well spaced, affording each room for healthy development.

Some loss to plantations results from the southern pine beetles. Losses occur when the trees are severely injured as by lightning, fire, or extended dry weather. Pink pitch tubes building up on the bark, small black beetles working in the cambium layer just under the bark, and yellowing or browning needles in the dying trees give warning of the presence of the southern pine beetle. The remedy is to remove and utilize or burn the trees that show evidence of beetle activity. Rain in normal quantity will restore the ability of the trees to drown out the insects with resin if the insect damage has not progressed too far. It also serves to check the spread of infestations.

The LeConte sawfly sometimes strips needles from the young pines. Damage is especially severe in southern Arkansas and northern Louisiana, where shortleaf trees may be held back for several years. Many trees are killed. The tip moth (*Rhyacionia frustraus*) damages both shortleaf and loblolly by tunnelling in and killing the young, tender growing tips.

It is hardly practical to attempt to kill the insects in small plantations. DDT would probably prove effective if it could be applied economically. The extent and severity of attacks vary from year to year, and in time the stands grow to a height (usually about 7 feet) above which injury from either insect is of little consequence.

Planters attempt to minimize the possibility of loss by using two or more species. The severity of attack usually varies with different species and hence two species assure a better chance of success. Close spacing allows for some loss of trees.

Plantings by the small owners have been fairly successful despite natural hazards and normal run of human failings. Coulter, who kept careful records for 15 years on plantings with seedlings from the Florida State Nursery, reports 80 percent of all plantings successful. Other State foresters throughout the country report success in 75 percent of all plantings under the Federal-State cooperative program.

Mrs. A. M. E. Brown, of Columbia County, Fla., was 56 years old in 1930 when she planted her first pine trees. Her 42-acre field had failed repeatedly when it was planted to the usual crops of cotton and corn. The county agent suggested she try a tree crop, and the forester from the State forester's office recommended slash pine, native to her farm. When Mrs. Brown reached 70 years of age and the trees were 14 years old, she had one-third of them cut for pulpwood. The trees had grown at the rate of 2 cords an acre a year. Receipts from the sale of pulpwood repaid all expenditures on the plantation and gave her a net return of $900. The plantation is ready for a second thinning in 1949, with an expected yield of another 10 cords an acre.

Mrs. Brown and her 42 acres of planted woodland are important because they are representative of 1,600,000 woodland owners throughout the South and the 122,000,000 acres that they own; their average holding is 74 acres of woodland. Among these small ownerships are some 20 million acres in need of planting, or roughly 11 percent of the total commercial forest area.

Another example is James Fowler, a farmer in Treutlen County, Ga., who has "culled" his farm lands for more than 20 years. As parts of his fields failed to produce satisfactory crops under cultivation, he planted them to trees. He had 5,200 acres in planted stands in 1949. He began turpentining in 1937, when his earliest planted trees were 11 years old. Those trees, with the first turpentine faces worked out, now have the second or back face in operation. He has 150,000 planted pine trees that are being worked for turpentine and 300,000 more of proper size.

Distribution of planting stock to small owners by State forest nurseries has increased from 630,000 seedlings in 1926 to 96 million in 1947. A grand total of approximately 800,000 acres has been successfully planted by southern small-woodland owners in the past two decades. Many thousands of owners have proved to themselves and their neighbors that tree planting is practical and profitable. Many more landowners are interested and ready to plant when the seedlings are available. The two State forest-tree nurseries in Georgia grew 18 million trees in 1947; the landowners applied for 34 million seedlings.

The South is making but little actual headway on its goal of replanting the millions of acres in small private woodlands that need replanting. In 1947, some 40,000 acres in farm and other small holdings were planted. At any such rate, hundreds of years will be required to plant the idle or partially restocked potentially productive forest land of the South. As a matter of fact, to the area that needs replanting, many thousand acres are added each year through erosion and soil depletion in crop and pasture lands and through overcutting and fire in forest lands.

Congress recognized the importance of the problem when it passed the Clarke-McNary Act and the Norris-Doxey Act, which provide for Federal assistance to State forestry agencies in the production and distribution to farm-woodland owners of forest-tree planting stock. All Southern States cooperate in this work with the Federal Government. The total annual Federal appropriation to twelve Southern States under the two acts for production and distribution of planting stock amounts to $33,600. The program is supervised in each State by the State forest service. The States produce seedlings and sell them to woodland owners at the approximate cost of production. State workers also furnish advice on planting. While the Federal participation is limited to farmers, the States serve farm and nonfarm, large and small owner alike, assuming the extra cost for nonfarmers from State funds.

W. R. Hine *is in charge of the Division of Information and Education of the Southern Region of the Forest Service.*

# HOW TO CARE FOR YOUR SMALL FOREST

M. M. BRYAN

To care for your small forest, know first your goal.

A good small forest has needles, leaves, twigs, and small branches on the ground, a mat that absorbs water and keeps the soil from washing away. Under the litter is a layer of humus, usually dark-colored and rich looking.

A good woodland has no damaged and diseased trees. Poorly formed and overripe trees have been cut out, so that good ones have room to grow. Remaining are well-formed trees that are suited to the locality, the soil, and the climate, and that will make high-quality products.

The forest floor has little sunlight: If all trees are the same age, grass and young trees cannot grow under them because there is no sunlight; in a mixed-age forest, there will be little trees just sprouting, seedlings of various sizes, and large, mature, or nearly mature, trees. If your forest is in the West or South, it may be more open, and may even have some grass or plants under the trees.

The good forest has enough good trees, neither too many nor too few. If your goal is to grow Christmas trees, the ground will be covered. If you are a turpentine farmer, a few hundred trees per acre are right.

No matter what forest product is being grown, the crowns of the trees will be full and healthy; about a third of the total height of each tree will have branches and leaves. If the trees are all about the same age, the canopy will be closed in the form of a ceiling. If the trees are of all ages, there will be no continuous ceiling of foliage.

Trees close together usually grow tall and straight. They are trying to get light. Lack of sunlight on the lower branches causes them to die and break off. Thus, a healthy tree prunes itself and produces clean and straight logs, without too much difference in size between the butt and the top of the last log.

Wildfire and grazing animals have no place in a good forest. In some western and southern forests, a little grazing is possible. Hogs are kept out.

Several rules of good management will help you grow good trees.

1. *Make improvement cuttings;* remove the undesirable trees so that the better ones can grow faster. Usually several improvement cuttings are made before the final product is harvested.

Often the products removed will pay: Fuel wood can be cut from the poorer trees, railroad ties from short, forked trees, and even some sawlogs for home use. The good trees that are left are called the crop trees.

If each acre is adequately covered or fully stocked with the better hardwood trees, the forest should grow from ½ to 1 cord of wood a year on each acre. In the small forest of good pine, growth will average from 1 to 2 cords an acre a year—perhaps more in the South.

2. *Thinnings* should be made whenever the tops of the trees become crowded or when many dying branches appear—an indication that the trees want more room to grow. Often young seedlings become crowded; when they are thinned, firewood, pulpwood, bean and tobacco poles, and fence posts can be removed. In a few years another thinning can be made to yield mine timbers, small poles, pulpwood, railroad ties, more fence posts, and a few sawlogs.

Weed trees should be cut. Blackgum, chokecherry, scrub oak, or other less valuable trees may crowd out better trees.

Thinning also removes the excess of young trees; often the unwanted small trees can be cut about halfway down and the tops bent over. They continue to live and, by shading the ground, make the better trees grow tall and straight.

*When to thin* is important. Usually thinning is needed:

(*a*) In young, fully stocked stands when about 15 to 20 years old;

(*b*) in the young stands that have stopped growing or become stagnated;

(*c*) when the crowns of young trees are crowded and many dead branches occur;

(*d*) when an interval of 5 to 10 years has passed between thinnings and the trees again crowd each other.

*How to thin* is sometimes more difficult than knowing when to thin.

A single thinning should not remove more than one-quarter of the volume in a stand.

Yellow-poplar, cottonwood, sweetgum, loblolly pine, slash pine, and any fast-growing trees can be thinned more heavily than trees such as white oak, basswood, and ash.

For southern pines and hardwoods the rule of thumb called D+6 is often used. For example, the diameter at breast height of one healthy tree is 10 inches and the diameter of the other healthy tree is 6 inches. Added together and divided by 2, the average diameter of the two crop trees is 8 inches; 8 inches considered as 8 feet, plus 6, equals 14 feet, the proper spacing between crop trees of this size.

In the West, the rule D+4 can be used for spacing crop trees of ponderosa pine. Other species may require different spacing and local advice may be needed in such cases.

Good sense is needed in thinning the small forest. Following a rule may result in thinning a clump of 6 to 10 good trees to only 2 or 3, when actually it might be better to cut only 2 or 3 trees, which will give the clump plenty of room to grow.

When a fast-growing young tree is directly under a mature tree that is soon to be cut, the young tree should be left for a future cutting.

Consider each tree individually and determine its chances of growing into good timber.

3. *Liberation and salvage cuttings* are part of the care. Wolf trees—large, branchy individuals with spreading crowns—often keep down the more desirable little trees that should be growing for the future. Forked, knotty, crooked, and other poorly formed trees also take up space needed by better seedlings and saplings. Diseased, rotting, as well as insect-infested trees will probably die before they can be cut into fuel wood or fence posts; they should be removed by poisoning or by girdling with an ax.

The undesirable hardwood trees and sprouts can be poisoned successfully with Ammate (the trade name for ammonium sulfamate). This poison can be applied close to the base of the tree. Chip out small cups in the tree trunk with an ax at 6-inch intervals around the tree. Place 2 level tablespoonfuls of Ammate crystals in each cup for trees 4 inches in diameter and over. For trees under 4 inches in diameter, 1 tablespoonful a cut is enough. Leave the trees to die; they should not be girdled or cut down because sprouting might occur. After a year, it is generally safe to cut the tree down if you want to. Use the poison in late summer or early fall. A 32.5-percent water solution of Ammate sprayed on green leaves will kill small trees and sprouts of undesirable species, such as blackjack oak.

Other poisons, obtainable from seed houses, are used for killing undesirable trees and shrubs like the persimmon, blackgum, and sweetgum.

Vines growing on trees kill them by shading or bending. Protect the crop trees by cutting the vines off at the ground.

Usually it is best to make a liberation cutting in early summer; sprouts from fresh stumps are less likely to appear then; and, it is easier to see which trees to cut.

Salvage cutting means removing the overripe trees that are growing too slowly to be profitable. Overripe trees are usually recognized by their light-colored bark, flattened crowns, and thin foliage. They should be cut and made into useful products before they are attacked by insects, disease, or are otherwise damaged. The thrifty, fast-growing trees that are damaged by fire, insects, disease, winds, or lightning should be salvaged while the wood is still usable.

4. *Pruning* the trees frequently increases their value.

In considering whether to prune, you should determine whether or not better prices will be received for the product to be harvested.

Local advice may be helpful and certainly is needed if any question arises as to the best time for pruning and how to go about it.

Prune only the vigorous and healthy crop trees.

Select about 200 to 225 such trees on each acre.

Prune trees the first time when they are from 4 to 6 inches in diameter. Cuts heal rapidly on these young trees and the knots will be small.

Prune in early spring just before the growing season begins.

Make clean cuts close to the trunk of the tree. A long stub may rot and later cause the tree to decay or be attacked by insects.

At any one pruning, remove no more than the lower third of the branches that make up the live crown of the tree.

Removal of too many live limbs will slow down the growth of the tree for several years.

After the trees have grown larger, another pruning up to 16 feet in height or for two clear logs may be desirable.

The best tool to use is a pruning saw with a 12- to 18-inch blade, 3½ to 5½ points to the inch. A ladder and hand saw can be used for the high branches. Some prefer a pruning saw fastened to a long pole. Do not use an ax.

Work safely; a falling limb is dangerous; ladders should be firmly placed against the tree.

HARVEST CUTTINGS are made to get cash from sales of products or to get material for home use. The way harvest cuttings are made determines whether the small forest is to provide continuous crops of trees, either annually or at intervals of 5, 10, 15 years or longer.

There are four types of harvest cuttings.

1. *Clear cutting* is the removal of everything of any value.

The small forest should not be cut in the way unless it is being cleared for pasture or crops. Many years will elapse before clear-cut land will provide cash returns or a crop of timber that can provide products for home needs. Sometimes undesirable trees seed in on the cleared land and the next crop of trees is less salable or has no value at all. Often the cleared woodland must be planted—usually a costly matter. Generally, the long-time cash income from woodland that has been clear-cut will be smaller than under any other method.

Some species of trees that grow in even-aged stands are best harvested by clear cutting. The area can then be replanted with the same type of trees that were cut and a new stand obtained.

Local advice should be sought before clear cutting a small forest of a particular species.

2. *The seed-tree method* is adaptable to certain even-aged small forests. By this method, at least 10 healthy, vigorous trees that average 10 to 12 inches in diameter at breast height should be left on each acre. The only advantage of seed-tree cutting over clear cutting is that the area may not need to be planted. If this method is used, it is usually best to leave the seed trees in groups. Often strips of trees are left standing to provide seed. Cutting in strips, however, is usually practiced in large forest areas.

3. *The diameter-limit method* is often used in the harvest cutting. All trees above a certain diameter at breast height, 10 to 12 inches in pine and 16 to 18 inches in hardwood, may be cut. This method has the fault that all the poorly formed, weak, diseased, and slow-growing trees under the desired

diameter limit are left in the woods to take up room. Also, all healthy, fast-growing trees above the diameter limit are cut at a time when they are producing the greatest amount of high-quality wood.

The method should be used only when the owner of the small forest has little time to spend in supervising the harvest of his forest.

These three methods—clear cutting, seed-tree cutting, and diameter-limit cutting—are of little use in the management of the small forest. They may be recommended for particular forests, but generally they will ruin the productive capacity of the small forest for many years.

4. *Selective cutting,* the best method of harvesting woodland products in a mixed-aged forest, is a combination of stand-improvement cutting and harvest cutting; it has many advantages also in even-aged stands.

Selective cutting should be made whenever there are trees that are ready for harvest. The following are guides to help the owner in the selection of trees for cutting:

(*a*) Cut the mature trees; they are ripe and have stopped growing.

(*b*) Select the less desirable species and any damaged, crooked, limby, or diseased trees; this gives the better trees more room to develop.

(*c*) If there are too many young, healthy trees in parts of the small forest, cut several of them so that the others can grow faster.

All trees selected for cutting should be marked: Paint is the best; it is easy to see; it can be removed in case of an error; it does not injure the tree. (An ax or hatchet blaze may cause blue stain or open the tree to insect attack.) An old paint brush on a long stick makes the marking easy. Medium-blue, yellow, and white paint show up well in the woods. Whitewash can also be used, but both whitewash and paint should be worked into the bark so that the mark will remain on the tree for the longest possible time. Often an old sock filled with lime will make a good mark if the cutting is to follow in a short time. If paint is used in a spray gun, it should be thinned with kerosene. It is often economical to use surplus paint that collects around the farm for marking timber.

Put at least two marks on each tree to be cut. One should be at breast height and the other just above the ground line; the mark on the stump is used to check the cutting after it has been completed. Put both marks on the same side of the tree and mark the trees on the side where the cutters or buyers usually enter the forest—it saves time that would be spent running around hunting the marked trees.

A defective or cull tree should be marked differently from the trees to be cut for salable products. An X mark or two dots or some other symbol will indicate that it is to be cut for fuel wood, just girdled, or poisoned and left there to die. The young, thrifty, straight, vigorous, full-crowned crop trees to be left for a future cut should have no marks at all on them.

An owner of a small woodland who is practicing selective cutting for the first time may find it difficult at first to mark the trees to be cut. A careful study of individual trees, advice or assistance from the local forester, and practice will make the job progressively easier.

Perpetuation of the small forest is usually taken care of by nature if the owner protects it from fire, grazing, and other damage.

If the trees are of mixed age, the older ones produce seed and the spaces opened up by selective cutting will be covered in a few years with small seedlings.

Trees that are all the same age and about the same size can be harvested in a series of three cuttings.

The first cutting will take out the larger trees, the ones that are mature and ready for harvest, and any others that need to be cut. Open spaces occur where the trees have been removed; the material on the forest floor rots faster and the mineral soil is sometimes exposed. The remaining crop trees, the larger ones, develop larger crowns and produce more seed.

The second cutting removes a few more trees during the winter and just after a heavy seed crop. The open spaces seed in with a heavy crop of seedlings, and the forest is on its way to adequate restocking.

Both of the cuttings should be light enough so that grass and weeds will not come in on the open spaces.

After the seedlings become established and can get along without the protection of the older trees, the last of the old trees can be cut.

This method of harvesting an even-aged small forest takes advantage of natural seeding and should result in a crop of young trees of the species desired.

There are particular kinds of trees in even-aged stands that can best be harvested by the seed-tree method. If yours is an even-aged forest, and a local forester advises clear cutting so that the species you have can again be grown in the area, 2 or 3 years can be saved by replanting the cut-over area with trees from the State nursery.

Often a small forest that has been heavily burned or pastured will reseed itself if livestock and fire are kept out after the young seedlings start growing. If the ground has been packed or is covered with a heavy sod, hogs may be turned in before the seeds fall. The hogs will root up the ground and prepare a seedbed. After the seeds fall or are blown in on the area, all grazing should be restricted until the young seedlings become well established.

The small forest can sometimes be perpetuated from sprouts from uninjured clean stumps that remain after cutting. Most of the hardwoods, except basswood, do not sprout satisfactorily after the tree has reached 60 years. Most of the cone-bearing trees do not sprout; exceptions are young shortleaf and pitch pines. Trees cut during winter or early in the spring usually produce the best sprouts, and there is less likelihood of any injury the following winter. Sprouts from trees that have been cut in the summer often are killed by the next winter's frost.

Where to plant trees is important. Planting is often desirable as a means for perpetuating small forests or of starting a new forest, and trees of a useful variety successfully started on the right land are almost sure to return a profit.

1. Plant trees on land that has little or no other use on the farm. Areas that are too small for growing crops are often used to grow a few trees that will be valuable for home use.

2. Understocked or sick forest areas that are not reseeding naturally can be planted.

3. Small forests that have been cut over and that are not reseeding satisfactorily should be planted.

4. If land has been cut up or ruined by erosion, the forest-tree seedlings will often hold it in place and produce a valuable crop in years to come.

5. If a small forest is filled with trees of no value, such as scrub oak or other worthless varieties, it can be torn up with land-clearing equipment and planted with trees that will have a future value.

6. Often the worn-out, rocky, or hilly land on a farm can be planted to trees, not only for the protection they afford the land, but to provide a home for wildlife, to beautify the farm, and to grow a few fence posts or timbers for home use.

It is well to remember that land that has been abandoned or considered useless will often grow a crop of trees.

What to plant: Look around the community or general area where your land is located; see what kinds of trees are growing best and plant that type on your land. It is also good business to plant species of trees that grow fast and develop salable products in a few years; however, a fast-growing tree that will not produce a salable product should not be planted.

Hardwoods usually require better soils than conifers. Hardwoods need plenty of water and if the soil is of a type that absorbs water readily so the tree roots can get it without difficulty, a hardwood plantation is usually successful. Hardwoods grow best in a deep, loose, crumbly type of soil, where the roots have plenty of room to develop and where the subsoil is of the type that permits good root development.

Conifers often will grow in soils that are unsuitable for the hardwoods and where the available water is less than that required by hardwood seedlings. Generally they will grow even if not cultivated after planting. The roots are often shorter—another reason for better survival. For these reasons conifers are often the best species for worn-out, heavily gullied fields, abandoned pastures that are to be converted to woodland, the sandy areas, and areas where the soil is heavy or has a tendency to be cloddy or has a hardpan underneath.

Some general suggestions on the important species to plant if your land is in the South:

1. White pine at most elevations in the mountains.

2. Loblolly pine on most soils at lower elevations.

3. Shortleaf pine in the same areas as loblolly pine, except on drier soils.

4. Slash pine on the sandy loam soils with plenty of moisture. Longleaf pine grows best on dry, sandy soil, on sandy ridges, and on sandy loam soils.

5. Walnut on good soils and on rich bottoms. Other hardwoods, such as the locusts, that are planted for fence posts grew best if planted on the better soils.

6. Yellow-poplar on good soils. In parts of Virginia, North Carolina, and South Carolina, particularly the Piedmont area, Virginia pine is sometimes planted on the poorest soils. Loblolly pine, shortleaf pine, and redcedar are also desirable species to plant on poor to moderate soils.

In the Southern Appalachian Mountain region, these species can be planted:

1. Virginia pine, redcedar, shortleaf pine, and pitch pine on poor soil

2. White pine on moderate soils.

3. White ash, yellow-poplar, and th black locust on still better soils.

4. Black walnut on the best lanc

A number of different species shoul be considered if you live in the Centra States:

1. Jack pine on the poorest soil Shortleaf and pitch pine can also b planted on some of the worst loca tions. On medium soils, Norway spruce red pine, white pine, red oak, cotton wood, and white ash will grow.

2. Black walnut and yellow-popla on the best land, and black locust o land not quite so good.

If you land is in the Lake States o New England, the following species ar often planted:

1. Jack pine or Scotch pine on th worst land.

2. White spruce, Norway spruce and white pine on fairly good soil

3. Yellow-poplar, white ash, red an white oak are suitable for the bes soils.

Seedlings generally are more satis factory than seed for starting a plan tation or in regenerating forest areas Birds and rodents often cause a direc seeding of conifers to fail. Tree seed do not germinate in extremely dr years. A few of the pines will grow fron seed if they are planted within thei natural ranges. Walnut, oak, hickory and other nut trees are often startec from seed. The nuts should be plantec in holes and covered firmly with soil tc a depth of about the width of the seed Walnuts, hickory nuts, and acorns ca be planted in the spring after th ground has become soft enough tc work or after the frost has disappeared Generally, it is better to plant thes seeds in the fall, even though there is a danger that hogs or rodents will di them up for food during the winter

In small plantings it is unwise tc broadcast tree seed. Instead, a numbe of seeds can be planted in a small spo that has been cleaned of grass or othe litter. Ten to fifteen seeds can be distributed over this small area and then covered with about one-eighth inch of soil. The cleared patches for seeding can be 4 to 6 inches in size. If there is danger of erosion, a light mulch can be placed over the seeded spots, in which case the seeds do not need to be covered with soil. Seeds of pine should be sown in the fall for best results.

IN PLANTING THE SEEDLINGS, these points may be helpful:

1. Seedlings planted in the fall before frost usually get a good start. If there is danger of frost-heaving, the seedlings may be planted in the spring just after the frost is out of the ground.

2. Seedlings should not be planted if they are still growing, that is, late in the spring or in summer.

3. Some State nurseries send out trees for planting that have been kept dormant in cold storage. If this practice has proved successful in your locality, you can plant seedlings at times when other work is not pressing.

4. Seedlings are planted, as a rule, with the spacing of 6 by 6 feet or 8 by 8 feet. Some seedlings that tolerate shade do best if planted close together. Others require more room. Approximately 1,000 trees to the acre is a satisfactory stocking once the plantation has become established.

5. Trees that grow rapidly can be spaced more widely than slow-growing species. If the soil is poor, more trees can be planted to allow for loss.

6. Sometimes the tree seedlings are planted in furrows to conserve moisture and prevent erosion.

The number of trees to the acre for specific spacings is: 5 by 5 feet, 1,742 trees; 6 by 6 feet, 1,210 trees; 6 by 8 feet, 908 trees; 8 by 8 feet, 680 trees.

Often it is desirable to plant several species in the same plantation to insure against damage by insects or disease, against failure of one species on the particular soil, and against the possibility that one species will grow into a crop of no value. Trees that stand much shade can be grown with those that require much sunlight.

802062°—49——16

It is not advisable to plant any fast-growing seedlings in a mixture that grows slowly.

Seedlings for planting on the farm and in the small forest can be obtained from the State forest-tree nurseries, which sell tree seedlings at cost or less; county agents and local foresters have the order blanks. Orders for the seedlings should be placed early.

Ordinarily it is not wise to plant tree seedlings that have been obtained from great distances.

Many seedlings die because they are improperly handled after they have been received from the nursery.

If the time, labor, and money invested in planting seedlings are not to be lost:

1. Keep the tree seedlings moist, particularly the roots.

2. Keep in the shade until planted.

3. A cool, well-ventilated place for storage is important.

4. Place the roots of the seedlings in moist soil or sand if planting is delayed for several days.

Of the several methods of planting, the one most suitable for the particular soil or area involved should be determined before the seedlings are taken from the heel-in bed or from their place of storage.

Slit planting means placing the seedling in the soil in a slit that has been made by a grub hoe, mattock, or spade. Planting bars, a special tool for making the slits, work well in light or medium soils where there is little debris or other trash on the land.

On rocky or trashy land, a hole can be dug and the tree seedling planted ¼ to ½ inch deeper than it grew in the nursery. Usually there is a mark on the stem that shows how deep it grew. The roots should be carefully placed so that they are not bent or crowded. If the hole is shallow and the seedling roots are doubled back or restricted in any way, the seedling might die. The soil should be firmly packed around the roots of the seedling—not too tightly but enough to remove the air pockets.

Where the soil is dry, watering often means the difference between success or failure of a planting.

Tree-planting machines are available in many States. In some localities they can be rented from the State forestry agencies or private owners; in other places they are available on loan from soil conservation districts, or other local organizations.

It is often profitable to cultivate tree seedlings, particularly for the first 2 or 3 years after planting.

Seeds and grass often kill hardwood seedlings and, in the Plain States (on the prairies), the shelterbelts or windbreaks must be cultivated to insure their establishment. Some pines, notably slash and loblolly, however, react unfavorably to cultivation and are more subject to disease if cultivated.

THE ENEMIES OF THE SMALL FOREST are many. Some of them can be highly destructive.

A wildfire, in a few minutes, can destroy the work of a lifetime in building up a stand of valuable timber; each year owners of small forests lose more than 15 million dollars because of fire. Most of these fires are man-made.

Get in touch with the nearest forester promptly if there is any indication that insects or disease are in your forest. Improvement cuttings, the removal of infested trees when a selective cutting is made, and the application of the best principles of forest management are enough in most cases to keep the small forest in a healthy condition and prevent serious damage, unless a general epidemic hits the locality.

About grazing the small-forest, the owner should remember:

1. High-quality timber should be grown on land maintained for that purpose.

2. Good cattle and good pasture go together. A fence between the forest land and the pasture land insures that neither the trees nor the cattle will suffer from interference by the other.

Many well-managed small forests are damaged during a logging operation—the falling trees may be thrown against the crop trees or careless skidding may tear the bark from their trunks.

The skid trails should be carefully located. A skid trail or road running up and down hill in a small forest often develops into a large gully and pours water into fields below. With some species, a border of trees should be left around the small forest after a cutting operation to protect it from heavy winds.

Often crop trees are exposed to excessive breakage from ice and snow—a sign that cutting has been too heavy and that trees should be left in clumps until they become wind-firm or are removed.

AN ACCURATE MEASUREMENT of the timber one has for sale must be made before a profitable sale can be made.

Knowing how much one has to sell from the small forest is just as important as knowing what to sell.

The owner should know the general specifications of the different timber products so that the returns from one product can be compared with the value of another.

Integrated use assures greater returns. Each tree should be carefully considered and cut into products that will bring the greatest return. A mature tree might yield two valuable sawlogs from the butt, several cross ties above that part cut for sawlogs, some pulpwood from the larger limbs, and firewood from the top. Nothing is wasted if this integrated utilization method is used in sizing up each tree before it is cut.

It may be more profitable for the owner to do his own cutting when integrated utilization is involved, because many timber operators do not handle more than one product at a single cutting.

Some advantages of integrated utilization are:

1. Care can be exercised so that each tree will be cut properly.

2. The owner or his employees can

closely supervise the cutting operation.

3. Each tree can be sized up before it is cut and the particular products can be determined.

4. The numerous products which result from integrated cutting will return greater profits. Pulpwood can be sold to pulpwood contractors, sawlogs to a local sawmill, and, in many localities, fuel wood brings a good price.

5. The owner can make several cuttings, taking out specific products each time. Poles and piling can be removed from the pine forest, after which sawlogs can be cut. The last cutting can consist of pulpwood from the tops and smaller trees that are marked. The same is true if hardwoods are being cut. Sawlogs or veneer bolts come first, cross ties next, and perhaps a sizable cutting of fuel wood from the tops.

If repeated cuttings are being made, care should be exercised or the small forest may be cut too heavily. Also, the high-quality products may be creamed off and the value of the forest for future harvests greatly reduced.

The various products cut from the small forest are measured differently.

Firewood is usually sold by the cord or rick.

Pulpwood is measured in cords, pens, or units.

Poles, piling, and mine timbers are measured by the running foot of length.

Fence posts, ties, and small poles are sold by the piece or unit.

Sawlogs are sold by board feet measure. A piece of lumber 1 inch thick, 12 inches wide, and 12 inches long is a board foot (a square foot of lumber 1 inch thick).

Measuring the board-foot content of a log is not difficult:

1. Secure a log-scale stick from your county agent or local forester. This stick has the board-foot contents of various sized logs marked upon it. By holding the stick at the small end of the log across the average diameter, the contents can be read direct.

If a log-scale stick is not available, three steps can be followed in measuring a log:

(*a*) Using a ruler or a yardstick, measure the average diameter of the log inside the bark at the small end. If the log is not round, measure the shortest and the longest diameter, add them together, and divide by two; this will give the average for the log being measured.

(*b*) Measure the length of the log to the nearest foot. Allow 2 or 3 inches for trimming off the battered ends at the time it is sawed into some product.

(*c*) From a log-scale table, determine the board feet in a log of the diameter and length that you have measured.

Three tables are in wide use for determining the scale of logs. The Doyle (which is used almost exclusively, particularly in the South), the International, and the Scribner decimal C. It is best to scale logs from the small forest according to whichever rule is legal in your State or has been generally accepted by buyer and seller.

If many small logs are to be sold, the International scale is considered the most accurate. The Doyle rule gives too low a measurement for logs under 28 inches in diameter. The Scribner decimal C rule is used in national forests and in many localities throughout the country.

If the logs have many defects, some deduction should be made from the scale. Common defects are rot, cat faces, ingrown bark, worm holes, check, shake, and pitch ring. Also, crooked or twisted logs resulting from spiral grain reduce the value of logs intended for high-quality lumber. First-grade logs have few or no defects; the number and kind of defects and the size of the log determine the other grades. An owner can learn a great deal by watching logs being sawed up at the mill. Certain defects or flaws soon become apparent. In scaling, then, he can estimate how much wood is wasted by the defect and deduct it from the board feet shown in the log table.

As yet there are no uniform log

grade rules; grading methods or systems are different throughout the country. Individual mills often have grading rules of their own. Prices, of course, depend on grades, and a top-grade sawlog always has a higher value than a lower-grade log.

Selling logs by grade is more profitable than selling them ungraded, but grading is so difficult for some products, particularly sawlogs, that advice of a forester is generally necessary if advantage is to be taken of this practice.

Estimating standing timber requires training and practice. It is easier to find the board feet in a sawlog than in a tree before it is cut. If the small-woodland owner is going to sell his trees on the stump or ask for bids for his standing timber, he must measure the trees to determine how much he has to sell.

The owner should also have a measurement of his trees for comparison with the measurement that a timber operator or timber buyer may have made at some different time. The chances of losing money on a timber sale are much less if the owner makes his own estimate of the amount and kind of products he has to sell.

Three steps to follow in measuring a tree are:

1. With home-made calipers, a carpenter's square, or a yardstick, measure the diameter of the tree in inches at breast height—4½ feet above the ground.

2. Stand back from the tree and estimate how many usable 16-foot logs can be cut from it. A pole 17 feet high (having a 1-foot allowance for stump height) will be helpful in deciding the number of 16-foot logs.

3. Using the tree-scale tables, find the volume of the tree in board feet. If the tree is 18 inches in diameter and 2½ merchantable logs can be cut from it, there will be 206 board feet in the tree by the Doyle rule, or 292 board feet by the International rule. As in scaling logs, the Doyle rule gives a lower volume than the International. These tables are made up from averages from the actual measurements of many trees. The local forester can advise the landowner on the proper table to use in his area and will have copies of it. (See also pages 851–853.)

Tree-measuring sticks may also be available from the county agent, the local forester, or the State extension forester. The tree-measurement stick will save time, and the volume of the tree in board feet according to the number of 16-foot usable logs can be read direct.

On the small forests of 50 to 100 acres, all the trees that are to be sold should be counted and marked. As the trees are marked and counted, the volume of every tenth tree should be measured. After all the trees have been counted, add the volume of all the trees that have been measured, multiply this total volume by 10, and you will have the estimated volume of your entire stand.

If the woodland is small, the best way to get a good estimate of the volume of the standing trees is to measure every tree. The sum of these measurements is the estimate of the number of board feet in that part of the stand that is to be cut, or in the entire forest if all of the trees are measured.

In the larger forests, one can estimate the volume of the entire stand by measuring only sample plots. It is important in making such an estimate to obtain a fair sampling, or the samples should represent the average in the best or worst part of the woodland. Usually samples of a quarter or a fifth of an acre in size are easier to work with. Sometimes 1-acre plots are used (1 acre is a 208-foot square). One-quarter of an acre is a 104-foot square, or 118 feet in diameter, if round. Round plots are easier to measure and to use in timber estimating than square plots.

Time will be saved if the trees are marked for cutting at the same time they are measured for board-feet content. Foresters sometimes recommend a timber cruise, which provides volume, growth data, and other information that is used in preparing a plan for the small forest.

Pulpwood is measured differently from sawlogs or standing trees. The local pulpwood buyer, county agent, or local forester will have specifications or know where to get them. Since different mills have different requirements as to length, it is always wise to get complete information before cutting begins or a sale is made.

PULPWOOD MAY BE SOLD from your small woodland in a number of ways:

1. Pulpwood trees can be sold on the stump and harvested by local contractors or agents of a company.

2. The owner can cut the pulpwood and sell it to the same individuals.

3. Pulpwood also can be cut by the owner, and hauled and loaded on the railroad car for shipment to the pulp mill. In this way, the pulpwood is measured on the car after it is delivered to the plant. Some owners cut and deliver pulpwood to the railroad siding, where it is measured while still on the truck or after it is piled.

The standard cord is the most common unit of measurement for pulpwood, but it is also measured in pens or units. A standard cord is a stack of pulpwood 4 feet high, 4 feet wide, and 8 feet long. It equals 128 cubic feet. It contains about 90 cubic feet of solid wood and bark, the remainder of the stack being air spaces. Freshly cut pulpwood is often piled 3 to 4 inches higher than the required 4 feet to allow for shrinkage when the wood dries.

Pens are hollow cribs of pulpwood about 6 feet high.

The unit is often called the long cord, and results from the practice of many mills wanting wood in lengths varying from 4½ feet up to 8 feet. A stack of pulpwood, in any of these lengths, 4 feet high and 8 feet across the front is called a unit. In any one unit the sticks should all be the same length. Since the units are made up of longer sticks than the 4-foot wood in a standard cord, the units contain a greater volume of solid wood. A standard cord of 4-foot pulpwood contains 90 cubic feet of solid wood; a unit of 5-foot pulpwood contains 113 cubic feet of solid wood. A unit of 6-foot pulpwood contains 136 cubic feet of solid wood.

You should be familiar with these various units of measure for pulpwood so that you do not by mistake sell a unit of wood for the price of a standard cord.

Often you will lose if you sell your pulpwood in pens, because the pens are usually built up with sticks of pulpwood of varying sizes. Buyers generally require five pens of wood for a standard cord or one unit. Five pens of pulpwood that have been cut 4 feet long and in which the sticks are all 6 inches in diameter will equal a standard cord, or approximately one unit of 5-foot wood. But five pens of pulpwood 12 inches in diameter equals 2 cords or 2 units. A woodland owner in this second case will lose a cord or a unit of wood if the buyer takes five pens.

Always measure pulpwood in cords or units, and sell it in the same way.

SOME OF THE OTHER PRODUCTS that the small-forest owner can sell are:

*Railroad ties.*—Because most ties are now treated with chemicals to prevent decay, practically all tree species in the small forest can be cut for ties.

*Poles and piling* are cut from southern pines, eastern white-cedar, Douglas-fir, and oak. Usually only the best trees will yield high-grade poles and piling. Specifications vary, and nothing should be cut until the owner knows what sizes he can sell and how to cut them. The local buyer or forester will have this information.

*Veneer logs* are used to make crates, boxes, and baskets, and the fancy veneer logs or bolts are used in making fine furniture. Black walnut, basswood, black cherry, the yellow birch, maple, yellow-poplar, the sycamore, sweetgum, blackgum, tupelo, beech, elm, and cottonwood in the small forest often yield veneer logs. Specifications differ for the individual plants and no cutting should be done until the specifications are known. Valuable timber can be wasted and left in the woods by improper cutting of this product.

*Mine timbers* include props, lagging caps, sills, and ties. Specifications differ for each and it is best to see the buyer before cutting any type of mine timbers.

*Bolts and billets* are short lengths of logs used for making handles, spokes, cooperage, excelsior, woodenware, and many other small products. Ash, hickory, beech, birch, maple, and oak are used for ax, hammer, hoe, rake, and shovel handles. Aspen, cottonwood, basswood, willow, yellow-poplar, and southern pines are used for excelsior. Whiskey barrel staves are made from white oak bolts. Other barrels are made from staves of ash, beech, birch, maple, basswood, elm, and sweetgum. Each plant has its own specifications. The forest owner should find out what the plant will buy and how the product is measured—whether in cords, board measure, pieces, or the running foot.

*Fuel wood* has value for home use because a standard cord of longleaf pine, hickory, oak, beech, rock elm, hard maple, the black locust, or sweet birch, if dry, will give as much heat as 200 gallons of fuel oil or a ton of the best coal. The heavier woods will weigh about 2 tons a cord. Two cords of the lighter woods (the white pine, spruce, cedar, redwood, poplar, cypress, basswood) will give as much heat as a ton of hard coal. Heat value is increased if the fuel wood has been cut early and allowed to dry. Fuel wood can be cut from trees that are unsuitable for any other use and from limbs of trees that have been removed for other purposes.

Sell your forest products for a profit. That is the reward for good forest management.

Each time the management practices are improved on the small forest, each time a better method of selling is practiced, the owner receives more cash.

Four principles to help in making profitable sales are:

1. Sell only measured amounts of timber. Other products from farm and industry are sold by exact measurement: Bushels of corn, pounds of beef tons of coal, and gallons of oil. When the forest owner sells his timber on the stump for a lump sum to the first buyer who comes along with an offer, the sale usually returns a large profit to the buyer.

Intelligent selling is based on knowing what one has to sell, both as to the amount and quality. It requires thought, care, and experience. Advice from a forester may be needed until the woodland owner is confident he can go it alone.

2. Harvest your own timber if it is possible.

If cutting and selling the converted products such as sawlogs, pulpwood, veneer logs, poles, and so forth, is a possibility, a little rough figuring will determine whether or not it will be profitable:

(*a*) Estimate the sale value of the timber on the stump.

(*b*) Determine harvesting costs—cutting, logging, hauling the product to market, and so on. The purchase of saws, tools, miscellaneous supplies, a truck, and other operating equipment, loss by depreciation, and the wages of hired help and labor all are harvesting costs.

(*c*) Estimate the sale value of the forest products you plan to cut.

(*d*) From the sale value, subtract the stumpage value and the harvesting costs.

(*e*) What remains is the owner's wages and profit.

Generally there is a profit in harvesting one's own timber. Also, greater care can be exercised in protecting the remaining crop trees from damage.

3. Find the most profitable market, both for sale of the trees on the stump and the converted products.

A little effort often uncovers numerous outlets for forest products:

(*a*) Ask your neighbors; they may have just made a sale.

(*b*) The county agent often will know.

(*c*) The local forester will have a list of markets and prices and often knows of markets elsewhere.

(*d*) Look for advertisements in your local paper or get a copy of a lumber trade journal.

(*e*) You may run an advertisement locally or in a metropolitan paper or trade journal.

(*f*) Write several of the wood-using industries. They furnish specifications and prices, and often their buyer will call if requested.

Fuel wood is needed by packing houses, bakeries, lime-kilns, brickmakers, and tobacco growers. Highway departments use piling, bridge timbers, and posts. Railroads need ties and heavy timbers. Mining companies and telegraph companies want poles. Paper companies buy pulpwood. Veneer logs, sawlogs, and bolts and billets can be sold to woodworking plants. Plants that make wine and whiskey barrels are ever on the lookout for high-grade white oak.

4. Marketing converted products brings the greatest profit.

Long, high-quality logs can be sold to mills that cut large timbers on special order. Lower-quality, short logs can be taken to a small mill that cuts lumber. Good white oak often will produce valuable stave bolts from the butt cuts, while the rest of the tree can be sold as sawlogs. Large, high-grade logs of other species such as sweetgum, yellow-poplar, walnut, and so on, can be sold separately as veneer logs for a high price. Tall, straight trees can be cut into poles or piling and sold at a premium.

Always before creaming-off the best trees in a small forest for the products that bring the highest prices, be sure you can sell for a fair price the less valuable trees that need to be cut. Often a small forest is high-graded and then no one will buy the lower-quality timber that remains.

The owner of a small forest who sells converted products must use skill and care in turning them out. All profit may be lost if many logs, poles, posts, timbers, or piling are rejected by the buyer.

If the owner does the cutting himself, greater care can be exercised. If a contractor is hired to do the work, the owner should personally supervise the cutting operation.

GETTING BIDS ON STANDING TIMBER or converted forest products is good business.

*The points to tell the prospective bidder about your standing timber are:*

The location and size of the woodland in acres.

The estimated amount for sale in board feet, cords, or other measurements.

The kinds of trees for sale.

The quality of the timber and its size range in diameter and height.

Whether logging will be hard or easy due to rough ground, hills, or deep ravines.

Accessibility to roads, railroads, and paved highways.

Whether the trees are old growth or second growth.

Whether the trees are forest grown or came in on old fields.

*Prospective bidders on products you have cut will want to know:*

Kind of product.

Amount for sale, such as number of cross ties, poles, posts, and so on.

Quality of the converted products.

Grade—if possible.

Lengths, and other sizes needed to explain the product.

Location of products.

Kinds of timber in the products: Hickory, walnut, oak.

*General items to include in all letters asking for bids, on stumpage or converted products, are:*

Owner's name and address.

Conditions of sale as to payment, and so on.

When the timber or converted products may be examined.

The right to reject any and all bids.

Generally the highest bid is the one to accept, but if the market is distant and transportation costs high, a lower bid from a nearer market may be more profitable. Grading rules must be considered. Also, liberal scaling under a low-value rule may offset high prices under a precise rule. The reliability of the buyer must be considered.

Sales contracts are good insurance. A written agreement setting forth details of a sale of stumpage or converted products, signed by the buyer and the seller, will avoid misunderstanding.

*In every agreement covering the sale of stumpage, either verbal or written, the following items should be specified precisely:*

Description of the sale area.

Estimate of amount of timber to be cut.

Kind of trees and approximate sizes.

Sale price and provisions for payment before and during cutting.

Guarantee of title to timber.

What trees are to be cut—those marked with paint or blazed, the diameter limit, and so on.

Definition of merchantable trees.

Time limit sale is to run; when cutting and removal of timber will stop.

Place and method of measuring—log rule to use.

Protection of forest from fire and logging damage.

Right of entrance and exit to the forest.

Payment of taxes.

Method for settlement of any disagreements that may arise.

A performance bond, particularly in larger sales.

When converted products are sold, all agreements, written or oral, should state the method of measuring and grading, quantity to be delivered, merchantability limits, rate of delivery to a specified point such as a railroad siding, loaded on car, and so on, time limit for delivery or to fulfill contract and the time and method of payment.

A timber-sale agreement takes little time and effort and will result in accord between buyer and seller.

Future sales are easier where past sales have been satisfactory to both parties.

M. M. Bryan *grew up in Pennsylvania, where his grandfather and his great-grandfather had been active in logging, lumbering, and sawmilling. He is a graduate in forestry of Pennsylvania State College. His work in the Forest Service has included timber-stand-improvement work, timber surveys on the national forests, land acquisition, assignments as ranger and forest supervisor, flood-control surveys, and State and private forestry. He now is chief of the Woodland Management Section in the Division of Cooperative Forest Management. Much of the information in this article is based on a bulletin, Managing the Small Forest, by Mr. Bryan and other men in the Department of Agriculture.*

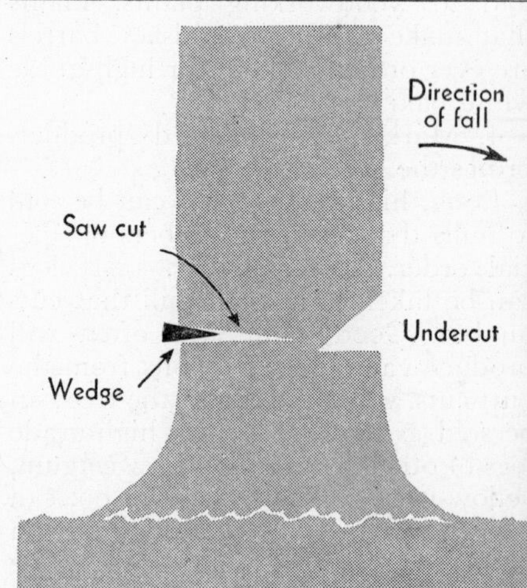


**This diagram illustrates the felling of a tree. Two cuts are made on opposite sides of the tree; the undercut guides the direction of fall. (See page 241.)**

**The drawings on the following pages show some of the methods and tools used in forest operations.**

## DIBBLE PLANTING

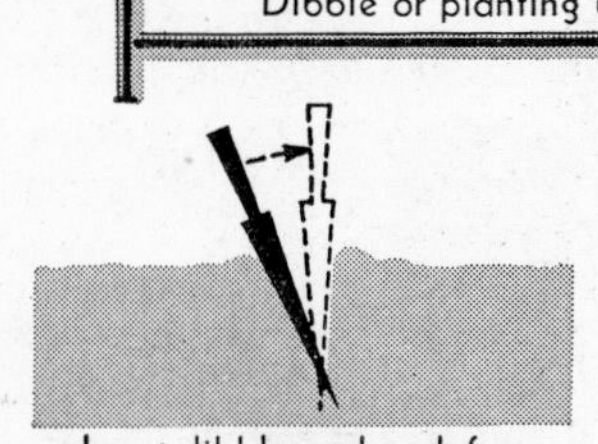


Insert dibble and push forward to upright position.

Remove dibble and place seedling with root collar at ground level.

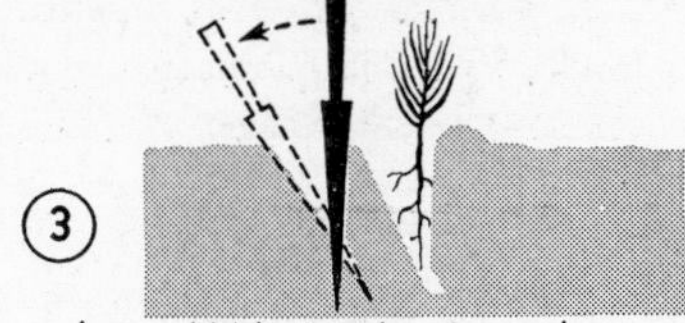


Insert dibble 2 inches from plant—pull back .to firm soil at bottom of roots.

Push dibble forward to firm soil at top of roots.

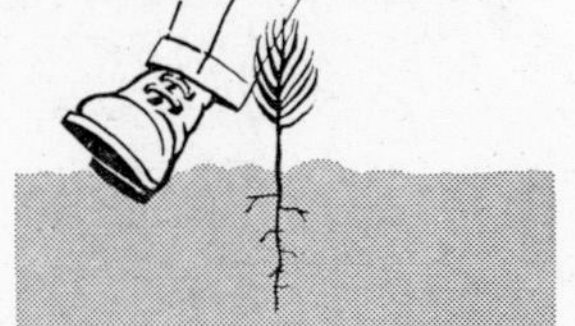


Fill in last hole by scraping soil with shoe.

Pack soil firmly around seedling.

## MATTOCK PLANTING

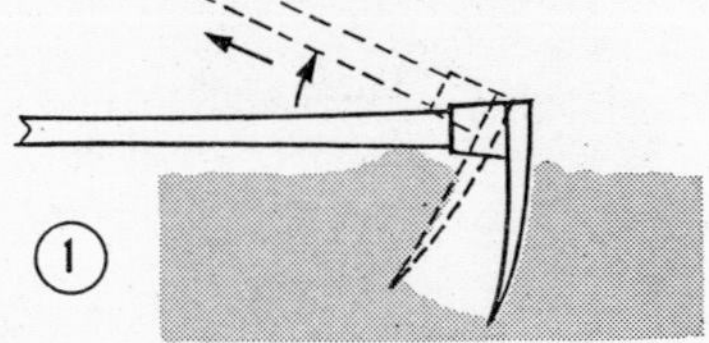


Insert mattock—lift handle and pull back.

Place seedling at correct depth, packing roots with moist soil.

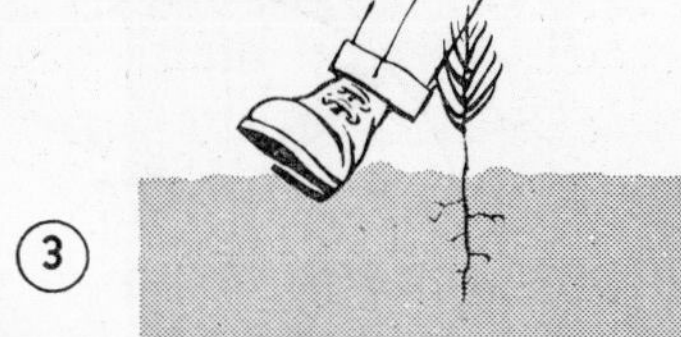


Fill in around seedling by scraping soil with shoe.

Pack soil firmly around seedling.

HOW THINNING UNDESIRABLE TREES IMPROVES THE FOREST

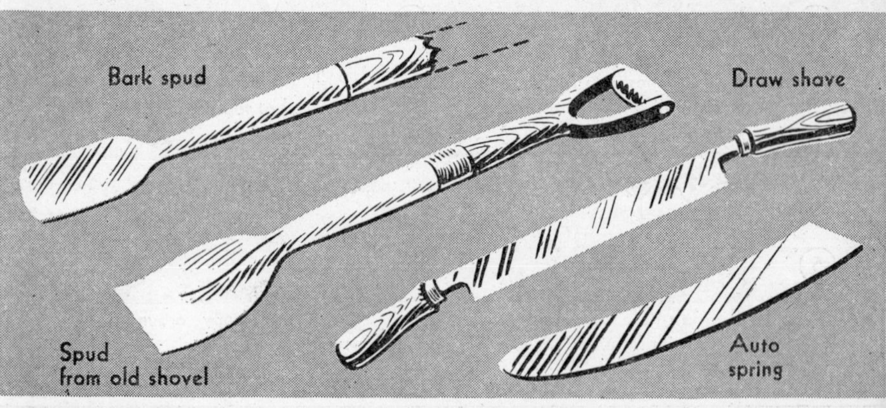

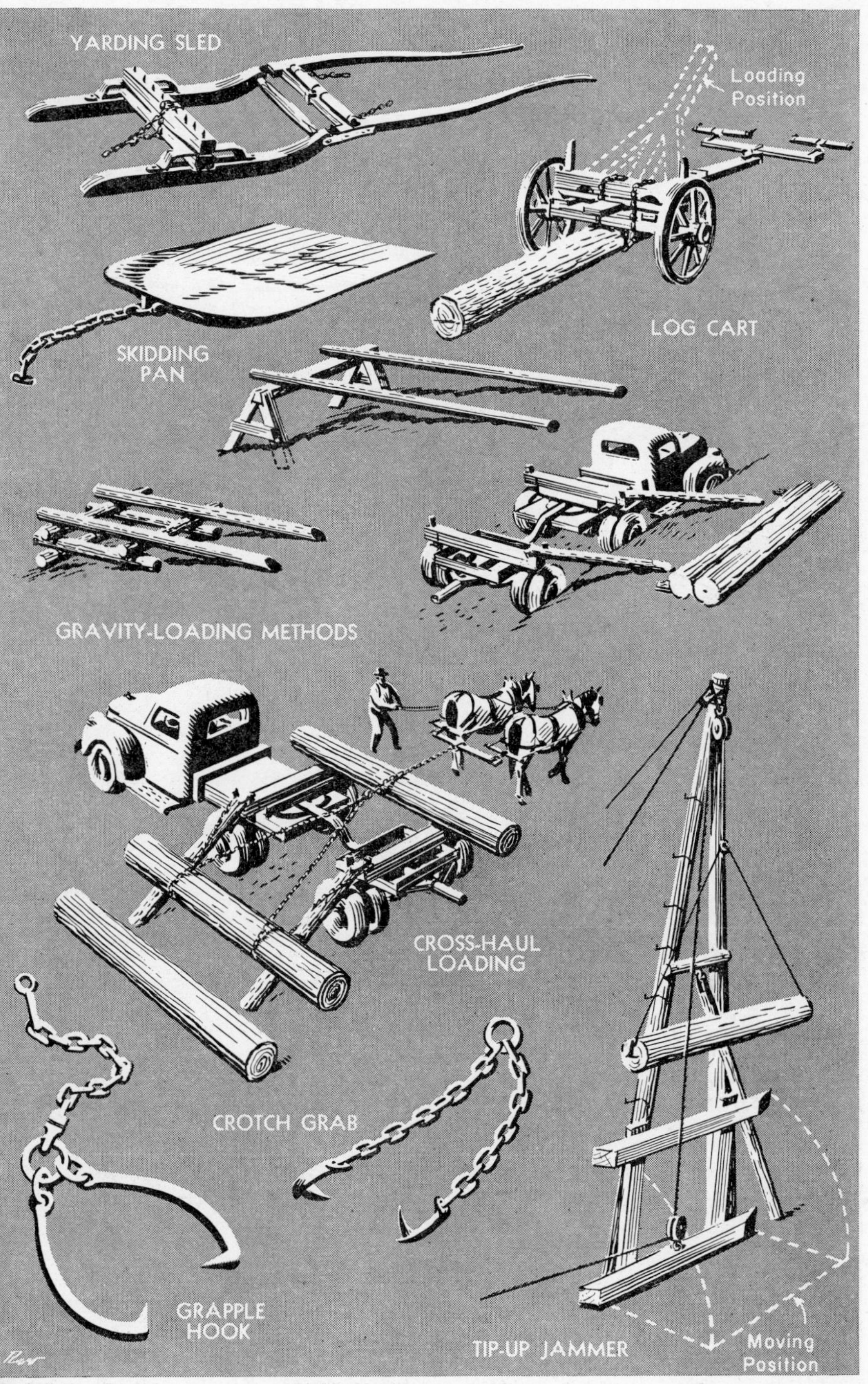
YARDING SLED
Loading Position
SKIDDING PAN
LOG CART
GRAVITY-LOADING METHODS
CROSS-HAUL LOADING
CROTCH GRAB
GRAPPLE HOOK
TIP-UP JAMMER
Moving Position

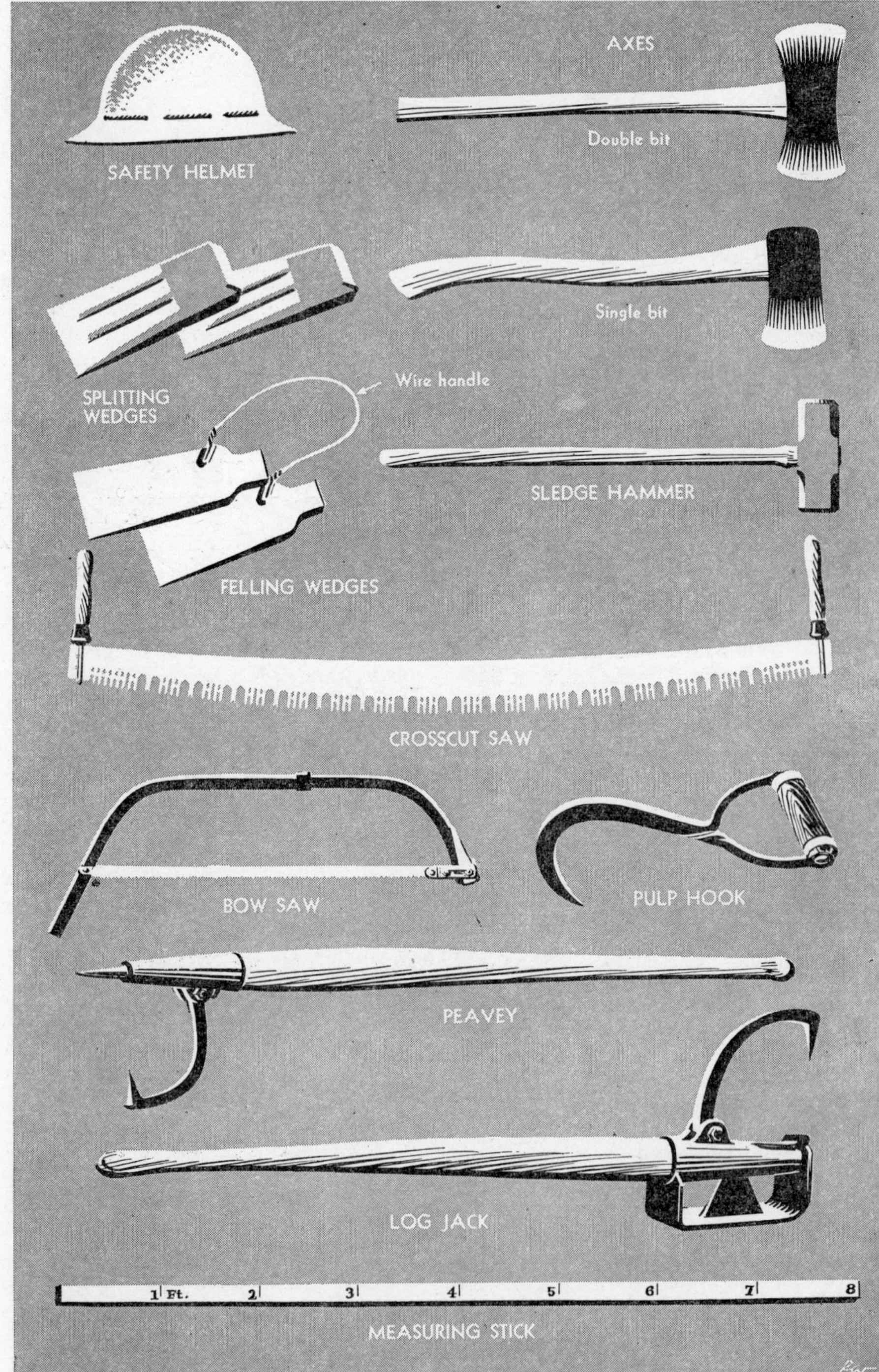
SAFETY HELMET
AXES
Double bit
Single bit
SPLITTING WEDGES
Wire handle
SLEDGE HAMMER
FELLING WEDGES
CROSSCUT SAW
BOW SAW
PULP HOOK
PEAVEY
LOG JACK
1 Ft. 2 3 4 5 6 7 8
MEASURING STICK

# HARVESTING THE SMALL FOREST

ARTHUR M. SOWDER

Harvesting the woodland crop, or logging, is the last stage in the production of the crop. It is like the final step in producing potatoes or doing farm chores, such as milking. A farmer does not sell his potatoes while they are in the ground or the milk while it is in the cow. By doing his own harvesting or chores, he is selling his services.

In the South, for instance, about one-half the value of some harvested forest products, such as sawlogs, is represented by the standing tree—hence one-half comes about through logging and hauling. In other words, harvesting doubles the sawlog returns from the woodlands.

Owners of small woods who do their own logging are apt to practice good forestry. When one does his own logging according to a sound plan, he will exercise more care to get better utilization, avoid damage to future crop trees, leave the area in better shape for forthcoming operations, and—more than likely—protect his woodland from fire, insects, and diseases.

Logging generally can be done in slack seasons. Often it is a welcome change from other farm work. It can fit in nicely with a balanced farm program. Usually winter is the best season for the woods work: Snow, frost, and frozen ground facilitate skidding and hauling, although they increase the accident rate and, for products that must be peeled, cold is a handicap.

Logging is hard work, but it is surprising how some jobs can be made easier by planning, how quickly experience makes one more efficient in the use of tools and equipment, and how much effort is saved by keeping tools sharp. In fact, farmers often say that after a day or two in the woods they enjoy the work. The hardest part is to get started—and, after starting, to remember that experienced woods workers usually take breathers, or rest periods, equal to 5 percent of the workday.

Before he starts his tree harvest, the owner should know the outlets for the crop. If they are to be marketed, the products should be contracted for by written agreement. It is worth while to inquire about the products in demand, and study the logging of those products as to quantity and quality, with the equipment available. Also, before starting, it is well to mark the trees to be cut with paint, crayon, or lime spots. In marking, the owner should bear in mind that it usually costs more per cord or per thousand board feet to log small trees than it does large ones, but in time the owner will learn which are the profitable tree sizes and species and how long it takes trees to grow to a profitable logging size. It is a good idea likewise to consult a local forester or the county agent. They will know local conditions and markets and be able to advise on the practicability of doing the logging one's self or letting it out on contract. If any help is to be hired, they can give good advice on the going wages, the phases of the work that have been declared too hazardous for under-age workers, and the workmen's compensation requirements.

Mechanical equipment, such as power saws, wood splitters, and tree planters, has helped make some of the work easier.

As with other types of farm work, scarcity of help has led to increased mechanization in woodland operations in order to maintain production. In logging, however, mechanization has not materially lowered the production costs on the smaller operations.

Many small operators have abandoned the use of the power chain saw, because they have found it more expensive than hand tools. The two-man gas saw is too costly to use on intermittent, low-production jobs in the small timber. To be economical, it requires enough timber to keep a crew of three to five men busy. One-man power chain saws, now on the market, promise to be better suited to use on small jobs in small timber. If one owner of a small woodland cannot afford to buy mechanized equipment, he might go in with other owners and purchase it jointly. Or, equipment is available sometimes on a custom basis, the same as threshing machines and corn pickers. Another possibility is to trade labor or arrange through a service type of logging ring, operated on a fee basis not unlike the spray rings employed in horticulture, for some of the work.

But even with ordinary tools, the work is made easier by using one's head, keeping the tools sharp and in safe working condition, planning the logging work and lay-out, and taking advantage of gravity.

Three steps are involved in logging, but the ways of doing the work in the suggested steps will vary according to the woodland and the product harvested. The steps are:

1. Felling (or falling) the tree and preparing the products, which includes:
   - *a.* Limbing the tree;
   - *b.* Bucking it into product size;
   - *c.* Peeling, splitting, and hewing the products, when required;
   - *d.* Slash disposal, if necessary.

The essential tools and equipment for this step are:

Fiberboard safety helmet.
Ax.
Saw.
Wedge.
Hammer.
Measuring stick.
Coal oil.
Saw file.
Whetstone.

The optional tools are:

Peavey, or cant hook.
Log jack.
Pulp hook.
Peeling tools.
Tie-making tools.
Wood splitters.

2. Skidding products from stump to skidway, landing, or assembly point.

The essential tools and equipment are:

Skidding chain.
Peavey.
Power (animal or machine).
Rigging.
Ax.

The optional tools and equipment are:

Tongs or grapple hooks.
Skid sled.
Skid pan, etc.
Extra rigging.
Wagon.
Log cart.

3. Loading the products on wagon or truck (and perhaps unloading at the destination).

The essential tools and equipment are:

Peavey, or cant hook.
Cross-haul line.
Pole skids.
Power (animal or machine).
Rigging.
Wagon or truck or sled.

The optional tools and equipment are:

Loader or jammer.
Pulp hook.
Block and tackle.

One should be careful, so as to avoid accidents. The most common accidents in the woods are due to axes, saws, suspended broken branches, and being on the downhill side of rolling logs. Even in lifting there is a right and wrong way. Properly done, the arms and back are kept straight and the legs bent, so that the lifting is done with the leg muscles. Wherever possible, direct lifting should be avoided and use made of a peavey or pole. A fiberboard safety helmet, a part of the essential equipment, protects the head from falling limbs, or, in woods language, the widow makers.

THE AX is probably the most important of all logging tools. It is in use about one-half of the woodsman's working time. For that reason, if any choice is possible, one should give careful consideration to its selection—to fit the ax to the work contemplated.

Of a hundred patterns and sizes, a few pointers to consider are:

The wider blades are better suited for softwoods (the evergreens) and the narrower blades for hardwoods.

The handle should be of straight grain, smooth, free of defects, and lined up in the same plane as the cutting edge of the head, with the head well down on the shoulder. Rough handles raise blisters.

The weight, single or double bit, and hang will vary according to preference and use. An ax weighing from 3 to 4 pounds is about the right weight.

Properly forged and tempered steel axheads are usually found in the better axes.

For productive and safe work, the ax should be kept sharp. The user must have good footing with a firm grip on the handle. Room is needed to swing the ax. The most common obstructions, low limbs and brush, should be removed.

The ax should be carried at one's side, with the hand just behind the axhead. One-fourth of the accidents in the woods are attributed to ax cuts. A single-bitted ax is somewhat less dangerous to use than a double-bitted one.

The ax should be kept in a safe place when not in use—such as standing against a tree or stump, with the handle up. It is unwise to use the side of an ax for a sledge hammer in wedging; a sledge hammer or mall should be used for wedging.

A SAW is used about a third of a woodsman's working time. The one- and two-man crosscut saws in 5½- to 6-foot lengths are the most common.

The bow saw, 3 to 4 feet long, with a tapered saw blade held under tension, and easily operated by one man, is well adapted for timber up to a foot in diameter, such as pulpwood, fuel wood, fence posts, poles, and the smaller sawlogs.

A smaller bow saw is handy for severing limbs, treetops, and working in post-size material.

For large timber, the length of the saw should be about twice the diameter of the largest material to be cut, so that one can use long, straight strokes and bring out the accumulated sawdust in the gullets.

The tooth pattern varies with the species of wood to be cut and condition of the wood, its seasoning, whether it is frozen, and so on. A narrow, curved crosscut saw is better suited to wedging in smaller timber than the wide, straight-backed type.

A properly sharpened saw makes shavings, not sawdust. As with the ax, there is no substitute for practice, either in using the saw or in fitting it.

It is best to carry the crosscut saw with only one handle attached. The blade should be over the shoulder with the teeth out. One should be sure no one is following close behind. If necessary to carry the saw at one's side, the teeth should be kept up so the saw can be thrown aside in case of a fall. The bow saw can be slung over the shoulder, teeth to the rear. Either type can be protected by a piece of garden or fire hose, slit lengthwise, and tied over the teeth. Burlap offers some protection. The saw should be kept in a safe place when it is not in use. Sawtooth injuries are usually serious.

Power saws are finding a place in larger operations and on a custom basis on small jobs. Plans for home-made types of crosscut power saws suitable for bucking logs will be sent by the Department of Agriculture on request.

METAL WEDGES, preferably of untempered steel, are useful for falling, bucking, and splitting. They should be driven with a sledge hammer or mall, not with the side of an ax. They are of various sizes and shapes. They are cumbersome to carry around and easily misplaced, but are indispensable. A wedge with a badly mushroomed head is dangerous, because metal fragments may fly off when it is struck.

Steel wedges are not recommended

for use with a power saw—rather, wooden or specially made wedges of soft metals, aluminum or magnesium.

Wedges made of shock-resistant, seasoned woods, such as ash, beech, birch, dogwood, gum, hickory, ironwood, maple, oak, or persimmon, are satisfactory and often can be made locally—even on the logging job. Satisfactory dimensions of wedges are 4 inches wide and 7 inches long, with a thickness and taper comparable to that of metal wedges.

Explosive wedges sometimes are very helpful for splitting large logs, but only an experienced person should use them.

A hammer weighing 4 or 5 pounds is recommended for driving wedges. A large nail driven into the eye of the hammerhead, and sharpened spikelike, permits the hammer to be stuck into a log, so that one can keep track of it.

For pitchy woods, such as pine and spruce, coal oil is essential for cleaning the saw blade to prevent sticking. It is best applied from a flat bottle, a size convenient to carry in a trouser pocket.

Another essential tool is an 8-foot, straight, measuring stick made from a board or a sapling, with 1-foot markings plainly indicated. It saves time in measuring off the proper lengths of felled trees. A hook on one end facilitates its use. The specified trimming allowance (3 or 4 inches for most sawlogs) may be added by eye, but one should be careful not to cut off the end of the measuring stick when making a mark with the ax. An inch or two short may place the log into the next shorter length class, thus wasting wood and lowering the selling price.

A good file with a handle is easy to carry in the woods and can be used to sharpen tools during rest periods. Some woodsmen prefer to use a whetstone for sharpening their axes.

THE OPTIONAL EQUIPMENT includes the peavey, or cant hook, which is cumbersome to carry about the woods but is helpful in rolling or prying logs, ties, and bolts, and in bucking, skidding, loading, and unloading.

It takes no special skill to use the peavey for prying, but there is a knack in using it for loading, unloading, and rolling logs. The beginner should first learn to use the peavey from behind the log or bolt.

A log jack—an adaptation of the cant hook—is a tool used in raising the log being sawed a few inches off the ground so as to avoid sawing into the ground, or to keep the saw from binding.

A handy tool for getting hold of short bolts or pulpwood is the pulp hook, which resembles the common hay hook. Injuries while using the pulp hook usually come from missing the wood and striking the leg instead.

A half dozen hand tools and several types of machines for removing the bark of forest products are on the market. The common hand tools are timber shaves, peeling spuds, a garden spade, or merely an automobile spring leaf. The type to be used depends chiefly on the size of timber, the species, and the season of the year. For peeling timber the size of pulpwood and posts, a support, or shaving "horse," can be conveniently made.

There are several mechanical peeling machines. Some shave the bark off with revolving cutter heads; others knock the bark off with a fast-revolving, short-chain length or hammers.

The broadax is of standard design. It is used in hewing building logs and ties. Skill in handling it comes through practice. It is heavy and hazardous to use.

Farm-made machines for splitting wood have proved successful in the Lake States and North Central States. There are two general types. One uses a fly wheel, 3 or 4 feet in diameter, to which a splitting wedge is attached. The other has a wedge welded to a moving piston head. The first seems to be the more versatile; splitting a cord of stove wood an hour with it is not unusual. More than 300 machines of this type are in use by farmers in North Dakota.

So much for the kinds of tools and

equipment used in the first step of logging—felling the trees. Some suggestions about the operation follow.

FELLING TREES is hazardous and difficult. More men lose their lives while felling trees than on any other woods job, because tree fallers have a tendency to take chances instead of precautions. A beginner would profit by working with an experienced faller.

The tools best adapted to a particular felling job depend on the species, size, and character of the timber. A two-man crew works to good advantage for timber of average size.

In felling, a common logging waste occurs by leaving high stumps, for usually the best grade of lumber is cut from the stump portion of the tree. Low stumps save wood and mean less obstructions in the skidding operations to follow. For trees up to 20 inches in diameter, stump heights should be kept to 8 inches or less, and 12 inches for larger trees.

To determine the direction of fall for a tree, one must consider the lean of the tree; wind movement; slope of the ground, and subsequent skidding; openings on the ground; possible damage to other trees, including future crops; soundness of the tree at the cut; and the ground cover (rocks and logs). Felling should be done with a thought to skidding. The object is to fell the tree without breaking it or damaging other trees and to drop it in a spot from where it can be easily skidded.

Brush and limbs that interfere with use of the tools should be removed first. A quick get-away route should be determined before the tree starts to fall. Trees dropped uphill on steep slopes are especially dangerous, for they are apt to slide.

IN FELLING, two cuts are made on opposite sides of the tree, the undercut and the main saw cut. The undercut is made with a saw on the side the tree will fall, and into about one-third the diameter. A wedge-shaped section is then chopped out to form the undercut. Properly done, the undercut guides the direction of fall. The main saw cut is then made on the opposite side of the tree, slightly above the base of the undercut. When the saw begins to bind, it is time to use a wedge. Before the final cut is completed, sound plenty of warning to all in the vicinity by yelling "t-i-m-b-e-r." Sometimes a 15- to 20-foot pry pole (never an ax) against the tree is an aid in felling it. As the tree starts to the ground, withdraw the saw and quickly move to a safe distance; stand facing the falling tree and watch the top, preferably from behind a large tree. Do not try to carry tools, but be on the lookout for widow makers. Trees with unbalanced crowns, with excessive lean and defective trunks, and so on, often give difficulty and occasionally get hung up in neighboring trees. Then one must use his ingenuity to free them and, in doing so, the utmost in care and alertness is demanded.

LIMBING AND BUCKING is done when the tree is down. To facilitate handling and skidding, the limbs should be cut flush with the stem.

Limbing is done mostly with an ax; that, too, can be a dangerous job if the ax is used improperly. As a precaution against injury when swinging an ax, overhead branches should be removed. The chopper should work with his feet on the ground (not standing on a log or limb) and cut the branches on the opposite side, thus swinging the ax away from the body.

Bucking—that is, cutting up—the tree is an exacting job. In bucking, the logger largely determines the grade of each product by separating the high-value sections from those of low value. Proper bucking permits cutting out defects, eliminating crooked portions, and the like. The entire merchantable tree length should be considered and measured carefully, and allowances made for any necessary trimming.

Bucking trees into sawlogs and veneer logs is more difficult and more involved than making pulpwood or

802062°—49——17

fuel wood. Bucking usually requires from one-tenth to one-fifth of a logger's time.

In the woods, the under limbs often are left on to furnish support in bucking. Blocking may be necessary to prop ends of the logs to avoid pinching the saw or to keep the wood from splitting. Such a prop is called a "dutchman." Sometimes sawing is done on the under side to avoid pinching the saw. A peavey, or log jack, comes in handy to put the pieces into sawing positions. Working alone, the bucker should work on the upper side of logs, or block them to prevent rolling.

When the main tree stem is to be made into a variety of products (sawlogs, pulpwood, piling, fuel wood, and posts) according to the utilization and markets, the terms "integrated logging" or "integrated utilization" are used. That is often accomplished by skidding the entire merchantable length to the skidway, landing, or assembly point, and doing the bucking there.

It is helpful to have the stem off the ground during bucking; that is done at the skidway or the landing by rolling the material on skid poles.

If the log has to be peeled, the bark is most easily removed in spring and early summer, immediately after felling. Some of the products from which bark is removed are fence posts, poles, piling, ties, building logs, and, sometimes, pulpwood. The type of peeling tool to be used depends on the species of wood, size of timber, and season of year. Some of the peeling machines now available are rather costly and are not adapted to small jobs. Occasionally peeling is done to recover the bark for industrial uses.

Splitting is usually necessary for fuel wood, stave bolts, large fence posts, and the like. Splitting mauls, wedges, and hammers are used. For stove-length fuel wood, portable splitting machines, previously mentioned, are efficient. Outlets and markets for products to be split should be well known or contracted for before performing the work.

Railroad ties made in the woods are usually fashioned with a broadax and cut to specification.

The slash—limbs, tops, and debris—accumulated from the felling and limbing operations may have to be gotten out of the way of the skidding operations. They should be left so as not to be a serious fire hazard or a handicap to the remaining trees or seedlings. In general, slash should be chopped to lie flat on the ground so it will decay more rapidly. Under certain conditions, it should be piled and burned.

THE SKIDDING EQUIPMENT needed to move products from the stump to an assembly point depends on the size, length of product, skidding distance, lay of the land, soil conditions, season of year, and how the logs were felled.

Animals or machines supply the draft power needed to move the products from the stump to skidding terminal—skidway, landing, or the assembly point. Often a horse or a mule can handle small products economically over short distances of several hundred feet. Large material and longer hauls require a team or tractor.

A peavey, to pry and lift log ends and roll the products at the skidway, landing, or assembly point, makes the lifting work easier.

A 12- to 15-foot skidding chain or wire-rope choker (with a slip hook to circle and hold the log and attach the free end to the rigging of the draft power) makes up the necessary skidding outfit. Log tongs and grapple hooks can be considered optional.

Extra items, which it may pay to buy, include various skidding aids such as skidding pans, the yarding sleds, wheeled bummers, the logging scoots, wagons, and log carts.

SKIDDING, OR YARDING, is the first movement of products from the stump. Usually they are dragged over the ground to the skidway, landing, or assembly point.

It pays to give considerable thought to skidding in order to do the job economically and with little damage to the future woods crop. Careful planning means less delay. Under normal operations it has been estimated that delay time takes up 40 percent of the working day. Poorly constructed skid roads account for 15 percent of this. Battered rocks, mud holes, as well as broomed stumps are unnecessary obstructions in the skid trail. Obviously skid trails should be wide enough for the draft power and products to clear on curves. Strategic location of skidway sites and skidway construction also are important to loading and hauling.

Dragging over the ground is called ground skidding. Teamsters should always work on the uphill side of the log and never attempt to ride a log being skidded. There is danger of being struck or crushed by the logs as they are dragged through the woods. The danger is greatest when curves and roughness of the skid trail may cause the logs to roll or swing unexpectedly.

For pulpwood, posts, and fuel wood (where roads are suitable), it is often practicable to load right on the means of final transportation and eliminate the skidway stop. This is called "hot" logging.

For ground skidding small logs and poles, where a single horse or mule with harness and rigging is the draft power, a skidding chain with a slip hook is about all that is needed. For large timber that requires a team of horses or tractor, some additional equipment is needed: Skidding tongs, grab chains or "dogs," and a hammer to drive the "dogs" or hooks into the wood and remove them at the destination.

Pulling logs by the small ends and beveling or nosing them with an ax helps in skidding. Maintaining skid trails and roads in good shape usually reduces skidding costs. Especially for animal skidding the trails should be arranged to take advantage of gentle slopes. Large logs that slide too fast can be snubbed by wrapping chains around them.

The construction of the skidding terminals, the skidways, rollways, and landings, affects the output of skidding and later loading out of the products. At least two long, straight logs or skids, strong enough to support the logs, poles, and piling, are necessary. They are slightly inclined to make the rolling toward the loading point easy. When it is necessary, the logs, poles, and other products can be piled or decked on skidways by using skid poles and peaveys. Care must be taken to prevent the pieces from rolling and injuring the workers.

If the volume of timber, ground conditions, and skidding distance warrant, equipment might well be provided for raising the front end of the log off the ground. A sled, known as the go-devil, or even a wooden crotch, is used for the purpose. They can be made in the workshop.

Another handy device to prevent logs from nosing in the ground is a pan, which can be made of boiler plate. The front end of the log rests on the pan. Yarding sleds, drays, logging scoots, log carts, and wheeled bummers are other types of equipment for more distant skidding to keep the front ends of logs off the ground. Plans for making all these can be had from the Department of Agriculture. Equipment for skidding large timber over greater distances usually includes factory-made mechanical or hydraulic log carts, arches, and logging sulkies; all of them require the high-powered tractors. The jeep has also been put into service for logging small tracts. A logger in Indiana put an A-frame arch skidding-unit trailer mounted on dual wheels on his jeep, attached a crosscut-saw rack on the left rear fender, and installed a rack for a power chain saw over the right front fender.

Some savings in logging costs are realized by skidding long logs, even the entire tree length to a merchantable top. That requires rather straight skid trails, more power, and generally uniform ground conditions. At the skidway, roadside, or mill, the long pieces are cut into proper lengths more advantageously and economically than in the woods. Also, power saws are more effective under such situations.

For loading and unloading, the third step, the essential tools and equipment include the peavey, cross-haul line, pole skids, draft power, rigging, and the conveyance. The draft power, animal or machine, has been mentioned; so has the peavey.

A cross-haul line is a 3/8-inch chain, or chain and cable combination, 30 to 40 feet long, usually crotched and with grab hooks in the free ends. Pole skids are made on the job from pole-size material. Loading requires little more in the way of tools and equipment than is necessary for skidding.

Loaders or jammers are of various designs, some of which can be made in the home workshop. Plans for a simple one, easily moved, call for a substantial skid base and an **A**-frame boom structure of timbers, the necessary cable, blocks, guy lines, and hooks.

Three methods are economically suited for loading out skidways of logs, poles, piling, and comparable round material on small jobs. They are rolling by hand, cross hauling, and moving with loader or jammer. The latter two require draft power. A loading crew usually consists of two or three men.

The simplest loading possible is from a skidway so located as to permit gravity loading onto the conveyance. Two skid poles, readily fashioned on the job, are set to permit rolling the round pieces onto the truck, wagon, or sled. Round pieces, if they are not too large, can also be rolled up by hand on skids from the ground level, but the job is easier with draft power and cross-haul line.

The **A**-frame jammer is worth making if there is much loading out to be done from the ground level. With this method there is less chance that rolling logs will injure workmen.

Conveyor-type loaders, not unlike those built to raise bales of hay from the ground to a wagon, can be used to good advantage for small forest products. Load capacity is reduced if pieces are not piled on the vehicle. Special types of loaders have been made to handle products in bundles or packages. Such package loading of pulpwood has cut down loading costs on larger operations. The loaders are operated by a hydraulic lift arrangement, or the package is raised by a crane. Unloading is usually done likewise.

Special loading devices have been made according to the products, such as end loading of a truck for long poles and piling. Other types of loaders and unloaders, using booms and cranes, both swing and fixed, are designed for handling large volumes.

Wagons, trucks, and sleds, depending on available equipment and season of year, are the usual types of conveyances for moving timber. Trucks are generally used for long distances. The average wagon is not built to transport heavy logs, nor for distances greater than a quarter-mile. A tractor-trailer combination, such as might be available on some farms, is satisfactory. The load must be properly blocked, balanced, and securely wrapped with chains to keep it intact during transit.

It is not unusual for an owner of a small woodland tract to sell his forest products at the skidway or roadside and thus eliminate the loading and hauling. It hardly pays to buy special equipment and conveyances for the purpose, and the ordinary vehicles found on the farm are usually too light for sawlogs, poles, and piling. As mentioned, many products, such as pulpwood, fuel wood, distillation wood, fence posts, and stave bolts are loaded by hand at the stump or landing. This limits the size of the sticks. A pulp hook is an aid to loading such small pieces.

Most unloading of short pieces is still done by hand. A dump truck sometimes is used. Sawlogs, poles, and piling are often removed from conveyances by quick release devices so that the load readily rolls off.

Arthur M. Sowder *is an extension forester in the Department of Agriculture.*

# Christmas Trees

## THE TRADITION

ARTHUR M. SOWDER

TRIMMED Christmas trees were first used in the United States apparently during the American Revolution, when Hessian soldiers softened their homesickness with them. In a description of Christmas festivities at Fort Dearborn, Ill., in 1804 mention is made of a Christmas tree.

The idea and the tradition spread widely through the young land: We read that people in Cambridge, Mass., put up Christmas trees in 1832; in Philadelphia, 2 years later; Cincinnati, in 1835; Rochester, N. Y., 1840; Richmond and Williamsburg, in Virginia, 1846; Wooster, Ohio, 1847; and Cleveland, 1851.

At first, the trimmings, if any, consisted mostly of small tufts of cotton and strings of popcorn and cranberries. Other decorations were flowers, replicas of foodstuffs, paper ornaments, and the like—no factory-made ornaments, tinsel, electric lights, or baubles.

Some historians trace the custom of lighting the Christmas tree to Martin Luther (1483–1546). The story is told that he was strolling through the countryside alone one Christmas Eve under a brilliant starlit sky, and his thoughts turned to the nativity of the Christ Child. He was awed by the beauty of the heavens and the wintry landscape: The blue light on the low hills outside Weimar, and on the evergreens, the snow flakes sparkling in the moonlight. Returning home, he told his family about it and attempted to reproduce the glory of the outdoors. To a small evergreen tree he attached some lighted candles so as to portray the reflection of the starry heaven.

Apparently candles did not come into wide use at once. Mention of the Christmas-tree custom in Strasbourg a century later did not include lights. In fact, at first, the use of lights on a tree was considered ridiculous and referred to as "child's play." For two centuries following Luther, the Christ-

*The illustration above, drawn from a photograph, shows an aspect of the Christmas-tree harvest.*

mas-tree custom appears to have been confined to the Rhine River district. From 1700 on, when the lights were accepted as part of the decorations, the Christmas tree was well on its way to becoming an accepted custom in Germany, and during the Revolution the tradition of the Christmas tree bridged the Atlantic.

Finland is said to have accepted the custom in about 1800, Denmark 1810, Sweden 1820, and Norway about 1830. From the Scandinavian countries the custom spread to France and England about 1840. Records show that 35,000 Christmas trees were sold in Paris in 1890.

Some persons trace the origin of the Christmas tree to an earlier period. Even before the Christian era, trees and boughs were used for ceremonials. Egyptians, when they observed the winter solstice, brought green date palms into their homes as a symbol of "life triumphant over death." When the Romans observed the feast of Saturn, a part of the ceremony was to raise an evergreen bough. The early Scandinavians are said to have done homage to the fir tree. To the Druids, sprigs of evergreen in the house meant eternal life; to the Norsemen, they symbolized the revival of the sun god Balder. To the superstitious, the branches of evergreens placed over the door would keep out witches, ghosts, and the evil spirits.

This does not mean that our present Christmas-tree custom might perforce have evolved from paganism, any more than did some of the present-day use of greenery in rituals. Trees and branches can be made purposeful as well as symbolic. The decorated Christmas tree has become an accepted tradition during yuletide, and Christmas would be incomplete without it.

Through the years the tradition has become so well established that two-thirds of all American homes now follow the custom. The Christmas tree is a symbol of a living Christmas spirit and brings into our lives the fragrance and freshness of the forest.

Just how Christmas-tree decorations other than lights developed is vague. It may be that tufts of cotton and strings of popcorn were used on the branches as a substitute for snow in the manner Martin Luther used candles to represent lights on the snow-flecked evergreens. Fruit, such as apples, was easy to attach to the trees and provided color, as did strings of cranberries. Pictures or models of foodstuffs, such as hams and bacons, were once used as substitutes for the real items too heavy for slender branches.

The suggestion has been made that the idea of decorating trees is an outgrowth of a practice adopted by early dwellers of the forest. Certain foodstuffs were hung in trees to get them out of reach of prowling animals. On the other hand, trees were worshiped by many, and gifts of food were often hung in the branches as offerings or sacrifices to the deities. Such giving was a Christian trait; thus the gifts were hung in "Christian trees"— or Christmas trees.

The fir seems to be the tree most commonly mentioned in reviewing the evolution of the Christmas tree. The fact that the twigs of the balsam fir resemble crosses more than do other evergreens may have had something to do with it. On the other hand, it may be that the word "fir" was used to designate a number of evergreens before botanical nomenclature was well known, for even today many people, unable to identify the various evergreens, speak of them as "firs."

Also, it seems that extracts from the fir, especially balsam fir, were used for medicinal purposes; probably for that reason it was widely sought after and used. Certainly the perfume of the balsam is one of its outstanding features. At any rate, if the fir tree predominated as the early Christmas tree, then our forefathers selected wisely, for the fir is the favorite of today.

Many people are troubled about cutting evergreens for Christmas trees. President Theodore Roosevelt, as a conservationist, felt so keenly about the matter, for example, that he used to forbid their use in the White House. He called it wasteful. One year, however, his sons Archie and Quentin smuggled one in and set it up in Archie's room. The President's friend and advisor on conservation measures, Gifford Pinchot, assured him that the supervised and proper harvesting of Christmas trees was good for the forests. From then on the White House had a tree.

Those who object to the cutting of Christmas trees might well remember that forestry looks not only to the perpetuation but also to the wise use of woodlands. By careful selection of trees to be cut, it is possible to obtain evergreen trees without harming the forest—often, indeed, with positive benefit to it, just as it is possible to thin out stands of young trees for fuel and obtain faster growth and greater returns in saw timber from the remaining trees. Actually, if properly directed, there is no reason why the joy associated with the Christmas evergreen may not be a means of arousing in the minds of children an appreciation of the beauty and usefulness of trees; and keen appreciation of the beauty and usefulness of trees is a long step toward the will to plant and care for them.

LIVING CHRISTMAS TREES, fittingly decorated and lighted, can become the center of outdoor community interest and seasonal celebrations. Smaller spruces, firs, or hemlocks planted in tubs or similar containers make excellent living Christmas trees for homes. They especially appeal to children and, because they remain alive, keep the fire hazard to a minimum. Then the planting of the live Christmas tree near the home on New Year's Day (if weather and soil permit) serves as a fitting ceremony to end the holiday week. If kept watered and reasonable care is taken in transplanting, the tree is almost sure to grow. In fact, the same tree may be used for two or more successive Christmases before it grows too large to be easily handled.

WHEN ITS PURPOSE IS SERVED, the tree should be disposed of properly. A Twelfth Night ceremony, in which the Christmas trees, wreaths, and boughs are collected from the several homes and burned in a blaze of glory, is observed in some American cities—a fitting end for a tree of tradition and sentiment and much better than discarding it on a backyard trash heap.

The basis for the custom may derive from the time when the early Christians celebrated the feast of the Nativity of Christ for 12 days, placing special emphasis on the last or Twelfth Day.

The community burning of the trees, which appears to have originated in Germany, was instituted to commemorate the light of the Star of Bethlehem, which guided the Three Wise Men to where the infant Christ lay in the manger. Through the centuries various peoples have observed the custom in various ways; often rites to insure better crops were involved.

ARTHUR M. SOWDER, *after graduation from the University of Idaho, School of Forestry, was employed as a logging engineer and logging-camp foreman. Before joining the Department of Agriculture as an extension forester, he taught forestry subjects, including logging, at the University of Idaho.*

# CHRISTMAS TREES—THE INDUSTRY

ARTHUR M. SOWDER

Nearly all species of evergreens are used for Christmas trees. Availability, cost, and sentiment are among the points that most people have in mind when they buy Christmas trees. Other attributes that make a tree desirable are its retention of needles or foliage after it is cut, especially when it is placed indoors; its pyramidal, compact shape; ample nonprickly, deep-green foliage; limb strength sufficient to support the ornaments and electric lights; pliable branches (so that they can be tied compactly for shipment); and fragrance.

The States bordering Canada, except North Dakota, produce most of our Christmas trees.

Recent estimates of the cut of the Christmas trees in 11 Northeastern and Middle Atlantic States were 6,428,000; 3 Lake States, 5,200,000; the 5 Central States, 207,500; 14 Southern States, 3,163,500; 4 Prairie States, 5,000; 6 southern Rocky Mountain States, 150,000; 5 Pacific Coast and Northwest States, 6,296,400—a total of 21,450,400 trees.

Montana, the only State to report production figures over a period of years, in one season shipped trees to 31 States, among them Illinois, 545,000 trees; Iowa, 285,000; Kansas, 180,000; Missouri, 175,000; Texas, 150,000; Nebraska, 145,000; Minnesota, 135,000; Oklahoma, 110,000; Washington, 100,000; California, 90,000; New York and Maryland, 5,000 each. Even Cuba received a supply of Montana-grown evergreens. Under normal conditions, Montana can probably maintain an annual output of 3 million trees, which it reached in 1943, 1946, and 1948.

Most of the 21,450,400 trees harvested came from privately owned lands. About 13 percent were cut from public lands—Federal, State, and county. Of the 87 percent from private lands, the numbers of trees from farm woodland and from nonfarm or industrial lands are about equally divided. In Montana, during a recent year, 83 percent of the trees were cut from privately owned woodlands, 10 percent from Federal lands, and 7 percent from State lands. In the Northeastern States, most of the trees are taken from naturally forested areas or from pasture lands upon which the trees encroached.

Of the 13 percent from public lands, about 1 million trees come from national forests, 1.5 million from State and county lands, and a small number from other Federal lands. Established plantations yield approximately 1.5 million trees a year.

More than 5 million trees are imported annually. In 1947, the figure was 6,808,158 trees, valued at $1,909,167. Nearly all of the trees are shipped in from Canada, but a few have been imported from Newfoundland, Labrador, and the Dominican Republic. Some tree dealers in the United States own or lease forested areas in Canada for cutting Christmas trees.

Thus the total number of Christmas trees distributed in the United States is about 28 million.

About half the trees are shipped by rail and half by highway. A few are moved over water—even fewer are shipped by air.

The most common size of tree is 5 to 7 feet, for homes; but the trees range from a foot or two, for tables, to those 20 feet or more tall, which are used in schools, churches, business houses, hotels, and so on. One of the largest Christmas trees ever brought in from the forest was placed in Pershing Square in Los Angeles for Christmas 1948. It was a 67-year-old white fir that measured 96 feet, 2 inches tall.

Trees 30 to 70 feet high can be "made" by attaching short sections of water pipes, spoke fashion, to a telephone pole and fitting small trees into the pipes. The pipes are welded to heavy metal bands; the bands, in turn, are bolted to the pole at intervals.

Supply and demand, the species, and the degree to which the trees possess the desired characteristics determine prices. On the basis of prices reported in various sections of the country, the trees produced in a recent year would make a 20- to 50-million dollar industry, according to whether values are based on the wholesale or retail prices quoted. An estimate of 6 million dollars has been placed on the value of the trees at the roadside or the railroad siding. A carload of trees on a rail siding in Montana represents an estimated 80 to 100 man-hours of work.

The 3 months before Christmas are the busy ones in the industry. In summer and early fall, the trees are located, the contracts are let, the markets canvassed to obtain estimates on demand, woods labor hired, and plans laid for transportation. The trees later are selected, cut, moved to the woods concentration yard, and then sorted, graded, often tagged, bundled, butt-trimmed, hauled to a shipping center, and then transported to markets.

A typical large operation will find the harvesting crews in the woods by October, and occasionally even earlier. Ax, hatchet, or pruning saw are the common tools used to sever the stems. The trees are carried or dragged by hand (or occasionally hauled by horse or tractor) to the concentration yard in the woods. One man can cut and yard about 200 trees a day. A wooden frame is used to hold the trees while they are tied into bundles to aid shipping and to prevent excessive drying. A bundle may contain 10 or 12 trees of 4 feet or less, or one large tree. In the rack, the butt ends of the trees are squared to present a neat appearance, facilitate handling, and make the ends ready for use in stands. After cutting and before leaving the woods, the trees are kept as cool and damp as possible, but they must be hauled out before deep snow becomes a handicap. An operator in Minnesota harvests almost the year around by placing the trees in cold storage as soon as possible after cutting and processing.

From the concentration yards, the bundles of trees are loaded on trucks or sleds for their journey from the woods to the rail- or truck-shipping points. The trees shipped by rail are usually loaded into boxcars or flat cars. A carload varies from 1,000 to 4,000 trees. A 3-ton truck can haul from 500 to 1,200 trees.

Farmers contribute trees and labor to the industry. In Montana, the sale of wild-grown Christmas trees adds nearly a million dollars annually to the farm income. Farmers favor this forest crop because of the good returns for their labor, short rotation, low capital investment, and the fact that the harvest season interferes little with other farming activities. Farmers who cannot market their own trees often sell them to contractors at roadside or rail siding.

Several Christmas-tree companies handle most of the cut and distribution of Christmas trees. Company representatives contract with woodland owners or growers for roadside or railroad-siding delivery.

Problems of marketing include the impermanence of some operators and trespass by irresponsible persons who, in years when the venture looks profitable, remove trees without permission. Some States now have rigid trespass laws. Another problem: Christmas trees sometimes are not cut according to good forest practices. Indiscriminate cutting leaves trees of poor quality.

In some States an effort has been made to develop standardized grade classifications with graduated prices. Careful grading could result in utilizing trees that are not perfectly symmetrical. For example, a tree to be placed against a wall or in a corner need not be full on all sides.

Trees cut from national forests may bear a tag with the following statement: "This tree brings a Christmas message from the great outdoors. Its

THE ESTIMATED ANNUAL PRODUCTION OF CHRISTMAS TREES BY SPECIES, UNITED STATES

| *Species* | *Estimated production* | *Percentage of total* |
|---|---|---|
| | *Number* | *Percent* |
| Balsam fir | 6,435,000 | 30 |
| Douglas-fir | 5,830,500 | 27 |
| Black spruce | 2,363,000 | 11 |
| Redcedar | 2,128,545 | 10 |
| White spruce | 1,990,200 | 5 |
| Scotch pine | 806,925 | 3 |
| Southern pine | 652,550 | 3 |
| Red spruce | 594,160 | 3 |
| Virginia pine | 370,000 | 2 |
| White fir | 335,000 | 2 |
| Norway spruce | 303,400 | 1 |
| Red fir | 165,000 | (1) |
| Red pine | 156,000 | (1) |
| Alpine fir | 148,450 | (1) |
| White pine | 45,640 | (1) |
| Grand fir | 34,980 | (1) |
| Arizona cypress | 19,980 | (1) |
| Jack pine | 15,000 | (1) |
| Colorado blue spruce | 9,540 | (1) |
| Pinyon pine | 3,150 | (1) |
| Hemlock | 1,600 | (1) |
| Juniper | 810 | (1) |
| Engelmann spruce | 300 | (1) |
| Miscellaneous pines | 8,670 | (1) |
| Not identified | 32,000 | (1) |
| Total | 21,450,400 | ......... |

[1] Less than 1 percent.

cutting was not destructive but gave needed room for neighboring trees to grow faster and better. It was cut under the supervision of the U. S. Forest Service on the—National Forest."

Many Christmas-tree growers and producers attach tags to trees to indicate species and height class. This is a means also of identifying the places where the trees were grown and can be an aid in stamping out trespass and theft. Minnesota requires that a vender's tag be attached to every Christmas tree sold in the State.

Because the trees begin to lose moisture as soon as they are cut, no more time than necessary should elapse between cutting and use to avoid discoloring and falling of the needles. As soon as a tree is obtained, it should be stored in a cool, shady place with the butt end placed in water and the branches sprinkled daily. A fresh diagonal butt cut about an inch above the original cut will aid the absorption of water. It is surprising how much moisture an evergreen will absorb when the butt is placed in water. As the moisture evaporates through the foliage, the air becomes redolent of the forest. (Lighted candles or other open flames should never be used on or about Christmas trees. All possible precautions against fire are necessary, including the checking of electric lights and connections and avoiding combustible decorations and flammable reflectors for the colored lights. Overloading the electric circuits and accumulations of wrapping paper under the tree are other common fire hazards.)

Outdoor living Christmas trees are becoming increasingly popular for one can use such an evergreen as part of the home landscaping. Some communities encourage outdoor tree decorations by providing prizes for the best-decorated home tree. Probably the best-known outdoor living Christmas tree is the one lighted and dedicated annually by the President in Washington. This Christmas Eve program was first begun in 1923, and a living tree has been used since 1924. Throngs gather around an evergreen on the White House lawn to participate.

In the years in which there appears to be a surplus of Christmas trees on some markets of the country, the question is raised whether the tradition is not a wasteful one. It would be desirable to balance supply with demand, but that is difficult. In this respect the marketing of Christmas trees shares the same hazards as many other semiperishable commodities. Some of the larger dealers, when they find one city market oversupplied, quickly reship quantities to other markets reported in short supply.

A fully stocked timber stand may mature less than 100 trees an acre, all that are left of an original stand of 5,000 to 10,000 seedlings established by nature. These surplus seedlings are desirable to provide competition for the final crop trees. Such competition is nature's way of pruning side limbs and ultimately growing high-quality lumber, for knots in lumber are caused by limbs. A reasonably well-stocked stand of young Christmas trees established by nature can produce, under management, at least 50 trees an acre annually. Many young forest stands are so thick that thinnings are necessary to assure satisfactory growth of timber. Thinnings release the final crop of trees so they can make their best growth. Actually a properly supervised harvest of Christmas trees proves beneficial to the remaining stand.

Evergreens on the poorer forest soils grow more slowly. This slow growth usually produces good-quality Christmas trees—trees that are denser and more symmetrical. On many forested areas, the Christmas-tree crop is the only practicable one. On some such areas the trees grow satisfactorily for 15 to 25 years, then stagnate and, if they are not cut for Christmas trees, they likely will not be utilized at all. On certain State lands in Minnesota, up to 750,000 trees are cut annually under such a management plan.

Even though some trees grow larger than the usual Christmas-tree sizes, the utilization can be complete. For example, this is how a Michigan Christmas-tree grower markets trees a foot or more in diameter. The tops provide a well-shaped Christmas tree, often with a good cluster of cones, and such trees command a premium on the market. The main stem or trunk of the tree is made into a building log or timber, with the smaller cuts suitable for building rafters. The green foliage of the side limbs is tied into bundles and provides material for wreaths. Thus, usually the entire tree is utilized. On some operations the main stem may go into pulpwood.

# THE FARMER AND CHRISTMAS TREES

ARTHUR M. SOWDER

Many farmers are finding that Christmas trees are a profitable crop. A Christmas-tree plantation fits in well with good land utilization and aids in the conservation of soil and moisture—a good way to salvage an eroded hillside or gully or to make use of rocky land or an idle corner. Some plantations are only part of an acre in size.

Most of the Christmas trees used in the United States are cut from areas where the trees have grown naturally. However, the number of trees harvested from plantations is increasing annually. About 100,000 acres of plantations are now devoted to growing Christmas trees in this country. Two-thirds of the acreage is owned by farmers. Pennsylvania has nearly 40,000 acres in Christmas-tree production.

Each plantation-grown tree can be given plenty of space to grow into a symmetrical tree, in contrast to uncared for wild trees in crowded or dense stands. However, merely planting the tree and expecting to return in a few years and reap a harvest cannot be depended upon. A well-shaped tree, grown under adequate spacing conditions, with uniform distance between whorls or branches and fully shaped, will command the best price. Christmas trees respond to intensive management. Returns can normally be expected in 8 to 10 years after planting.

Things to consider in selecting a Christmas-tree planting site are value of the land, soil and climate, location of site with respect to market centers, accessibility, and the existing vegetative cover.

A prospective grower of Christmas trees should give careful consideration to the selection of species. While most evergreens are used for Christmas trees, yet some command better market prices than others. There appears to be no best all-around Christmas tree. Desirable characteristics are:

1. Retention of needles between the time of cutting and through the Christmas holidays.
2. Full, symmetrical shape.
3. Limb strength adequate to support ornaments and electric lights.
4. Sufficient nonprickly foliage with a healthy green color.
5. Fragrant odor.
6. Pliable branches that are not too brittle so they can be tied compactly for shipment, yet regain their shape when released.

Desirable species to be considered for farm plantings are: Norway spruce (*Picea excelsa*), Douglas-fir (*Pseudotsuga taxifolia*), Scotch pine (*Pinus sylvestris*), the balsam fir (*Abies balsamea*), white spruce (*Picea glauca*), red pine (*Pinus resinosa*), eastern redcedar (*Juniperus virginiana*), the Colorado blue spruce (*Picea pungens*), grand fir (*Abies concolor*), and Fraser fir (*Abies fraseri*).

First consideration should be given, however, to matching the species with the local climate and planting site—that is, soil, moisture, slope, and exposure. In the selection of species, a good guide is to observe what evergreens are growing satisfactorily in the vicinity of the proposed planting. Low ground could well be a frost pocket and may prove detrimental to new growth. Well-drained and relatively poor soils are satisfactory, provided they are not too thin. The soil should not be the best nor yet the poorest. Good soil may make the trees grow tall and spindly. Evergreens generally are not adapted to alkali soils. Avoid wet, heavy clays, coarse sands, and gravel. Christmas trees can be a profitable poor-field crop. If soil preparation is necessary, it should be done well in advance of planting.

The planting stock can usually be obtained from public and private nurseries, and names and addresses can be had from the Forest Service, United States Department of Agriculture, Washington 25, D. C.

Only good, healthy, graded seedlings and transplants are worth planting. Transplants may cost more but should reach marketable size a year or so earlier. The growing of planting stock from seed is not an easy undertaking and means a year or two of waiting. Some farmers obtain seedlings and line them out in transplant rows near the planting site for a year or two. Where wild evergreen seedlings, such as balsam fir, are available, they can often be used for planting stock.

Many Christmas-tree growers prefer a 4- by 4-foot spacing—that is, 4 feet between trees in the row and 4 feet between rows. It is practicable to plant evergreens with a 3- by 3-foot spacing with the expectation of removing every other one as the trees develop.

The tree sizes most in demand by the Christmas trade are those 6 to 8 feet high; that size is best grown when the trees have been thinned to about a 6-foot spacing.

| *Spacing in feet* | *Number of trees required per acre* |
|---|---|
| 3 by 3 | 4, 840 |
| 4 by 4 | 2, 720 |
| 5 by 5 | 1, 740 |
| 6 by 6 | 1, 210 |
| 7 by 7 | 890 |
| 8 by 8 | 680 |

If the growing of Christmas trees is to be tied in with the production of wood products such as fence posts, pulpwood, or sawlogs, then wider spacing is necessary as the trees develop.

Planting may be done in the spring or fall when the trees are dormant. Spring planting is usually more successful—just as soon as the frost is out of the ground and before growth starts.

In handling the small trees, the roots should never be allowed to dry out. The package of trees should be soaked with water as soon as received and the trees planted as soon as possible. If the trees are not planted promptly, they may be stored for a day or two in a cool, damp place with the package well soaked with water. If it is necessary to delay planting as much as 10 days, the small trees should be heeled-in by lining them out in a cool, moist, shady place; one should make sure the roots are thoroughly watered.

Two-man crews (or a man and a strong boy) are satisfactory for planting Christmas trees—one man digs the hole, preferably with a mattock or grub hoe, and fills in the soil, while the other carries the planting stock in a bucket of water and inserts the tree. It pays to use extra care in planting to insure a good stand and thus avoid replanting.

If some woody vegetation—such as brush—covers the planting site, it is imperative that it be removed before planting. The small trees should be set the same depth as they grew in the nursery with the roots well spread out in the planting holes. The roots should never be allowed to dry out, hence moist soil should be firmly packed about the roots at the time of planting. Air pockets about the roots should be avoided and firming the soil with the heel will prevent this.

An 80-percent survival is considered satisfactory. It may be necessary to replace any small trees that do not survive the first year or two. Where different species are planted on an area, it is not desirable to alternate rows by species; it is better to plant each species in a group or block.

Weeds, grass, and brush should not be allowed to handicap the small trees. In areas of limited rainfall during the growing season, two or three cultivations each summer may be necessary to eliminate competition of weeds and grasses. Weed growth around the trees may keep the lower branches from developing. Later on, weed removal by mowing is usually adequate and will not disturb the lateral tree roots near the surface.

Pruning Christmas trees to shape them is usually time well spent. It enhances the value of the trees and reduces the number of cull trees. Some growers plan to prune each tree several times before it is harvested. One man can prune about 50 trees an hour. A few pruning suggestions are:

1. Keep terminal growth to about a foot per year.
2. Keep the lower and the lateral branches pruned so that the tree will grow to a conical and uniform shape.
3. Begin pruning a tree just as soon as the leader develops a length out of proportion to the laterals, which may be when it is 2 or 3 years old.
4. For pines, pruning must be done in early summer. For short-needled evergreens, such as spruces and firs, pruning may be done at any time.
5. Sharp pruning shears do the best job.
6. Pruning usually should not be done the year that the tree is to be harvested.

A grower of Christmas trees is confronted with many hazards. Probably the greatest is fire—and most fires are due to carelessness. Other handicaps are tree and insect diseases; rodents and rabbits; brush and hardwood seedlings; adverse weather, such as drought, unseasonable frosts, hail, heavy snow, and wind; animals (both domestic and wild—by browsing, trampling, and occasionally rubbing); and thievery.

Among the many records of successful Christmas-tree enterprises is one from a grower in Ohio who planted 12,000 trees on 4 acres in 1927. Nine years later he began harvesting the crop. At the end of another 9 years he had cut 2,000 trees and received $1,200 for the stumpage, thus averaging 60 cents a tree, or $300 an acre. He reported that the Christmas trees alone yielded slightly more than 7-percent compound interest net, and that he has left a good stand of potential saw timber.

An annual average harvest of 600 trees from a 15-acre tract in New York State over a 15-year period has grossed the owner a total of $7,000 on a combination retail and wholesale basis. This grower estimates it costs him 30 cents per tree to plant, prune, harvest, and market, or a total of $2,700, leaving a net return of $4,300.

Evergreen trees are often planted primarily for soil protection, the returns from Christmas trees being incidental. In Ottawa County, Mich., for example, the sandy soil supported a fine stand of virgin pine timber in the 1880's. Logging operations and subsequent fires denuded the soil, and the sand started blowing to adjacent croplands. The county agricultural agent encouraged the farmers to plant trees to keep the sandy soil in place. Scotch pine, white spruce, and Norway spruce seedlings were supplied to farm cooperators at low cost and were planted at the rate of about 1,200 trees to the acre. In 4 to 8 years the trees found a ready market as Christmas trees. In one year, the farmers realized more than $50,000 from the sale of 70,000 evergreens. The next year more than 200,000 trees were removed, and the farmers received more than $100,000 for them. The 1948 returns totaled nearly $300,000. A dense growth of trees was left to prevent soil blowing, and more Christmas trees are in prospect. Later, as the trees grow larger, a pulpwood harvest will be made, the treetops to be sold for Christmas decorations. Still later as the remaining trees reach pulpwood and sawlog size, they will be converted into lumber.

A FAIRLY NEW PRACTICE in Christmas-tree farming, especially with the well-managed plantations, is stump culture. In general, this method is practicable before the stems get too large (up to 6 inches stump diameter) or trees become too old (up to 15 or 50 years). When Christmas trees are severed above live-branch whorls, the uppermost remaining limbs, or newly developed adventitious buds, form new leaders. Eliminating all but one, two, or possibly three such leaders, after at least one year's growth, may cause those left to grow into satisfactory Christmas trees called turn-ups. The root system of such a stump tree is usually adequate to produce suitable trees in a shorter period than the original crop tree. However, when trees are growing too close together, the understory trees may undergo severe root and crown competition from these stump trees, which then become wolf trees. Usually four or five individual trees can be grown in the space occupied by one such stump or wolf tree. Stump culture is best adapted for trees growing in openings. Careful pruning attention must be given to the trees produced through this rather exacting practice.

The appearance of a Christmas tree on the market is important. Best prices are paid for well-shaped, freshly cut trees. When cut, the butt should be trimmed off neatly. Many people like to obtain a freshly cut tree and like to make their own selection from among growing trees. This is an advantage for Christmas-tree plantations established close to market centers.

A curved pruning saw has been found to be an efficient tool for cutting Christmas trees. Trees not harvested one year can be held over to the next or left to grow into larger trees for forest products. A grower should not harvest large quantities of Christmas trees unless a market is assured; even better, the trees should be sold under written contract. Cooperative harvesting and marketing offers good possibilities. Branches trimmed to shape up harvested trees as well as those from culled trees usually find a ready market as wreaths or table and mantle decorations.

ARTHUR M. SOWDER *is an extension forester in the Department of Agriculture.*

# Company Forests

## LARGE PRIVATE HOLDINGS IN THE NORTH

HARDY L. SHIRLEY

FORESTRY on large private properties has made gratifying progress in the Northern States during the past two decades. The effect is becoming visible in the woods and mill, in the factory and office. Companies have doubled and trebled the number of foresters they employ; foresters themselves have risen to positions in which their opinions count on policies governing forest-land acquisitions, cutting practices, sustained-yield operations, wood processing, and the long-term plans for future timber supplies.

Change is entering the woods in other ways. The old-time lumberjack is slowly giving way to the mechanically skilled timber worker who can handle power chain saws, power skidders, bulldozers, mechanical loaders, trailer trucks, and new road-building equipment. The trained personnel now have demanded improved logging camps and better living standards for woods workers. Officials of companies that follow good practices on their own land have sought to spread good forest practices to all timberlands that furnish products to their mills.

The reasons for the better forestry are many. Outstanding has been the wartime shortages of saw timber, pulpwood, mine timbers, and other products. More important is the growing realization that intelligently applied forestry pays. Pulp companies particularly have been quick to react to their changed situation. Canada has placed restrictions on the export of pulpwood to the United States in order to safeguard supplies for her own mills. In New York State alone from 1917 to 1940 a total of 69 pulp- and paper-manufacturing plants closed. Twenty-one new high-capacity mills were established during the period to increase paper capacity from 5,022 to 6,487 tons a day, but pulp capacity declined. A

*Pictured above: Single tong loading with a mobile crane in the west coast fir region.*

net decrease of 39 paper mills and 56 pulp mills occurred. The New York State Department of Commerce attributes this decline primarily to the scarcity and high price of pulpwood.

Pulpwood is now being transported long distances. Some mills in the Lake States haul spruce from Colorado and Montana, Pennsylvania mills haul from New Brunswick and Virginia, and New York mills from Ontario, northern New Hampshire, and the Maritime Provinces of Canada. A mill in the southern White Mountains of New Hampshire recently purchased pulp lands along the northern boundary of Maine where the wood must be floated down the St. John River to a railhead, then hauled some 375 miles to their mill. Coal-mining companies also are concerned. To insure a permanent supply of mine timbers, companies are acquiring and managing forest land. Spool manufacturers, veneer makers, roofing-felt companies, as well as lumber companies, likewise are seeking dependable supplies of timber.

The beginnings of large-scale private forestry in the North date back more than 100 years to the large individual and family holdings built up as permanent timberland investment properties in Maine, New Hampshire, New York, and other Northern States. Management plans were seldom prepared, but agents for the owners sold cutting rights, collected the money, and distributed it among the several owners. Forestry entered the operation only in that the land was held permanently for timber crops rather than abandoned or sold after the first harvest; a few individual owners actually insisted on applying minimum-diameter cutting limits.

Other private forestry programs have been functioning for two decades or even more in the North. Outstanding successes and some discouraging failures have occurred. Obstacles that caused abandonment of past forestry programs still persist to plague future forest enterprise. The good and the bad must both be weighed before future trends can be predicted with assurance.

Much cause for optimism exists, but only a good beginning has been made. Scarcity is a dominant factor in spurring forestry action. So far, however, effort has been concentrated more on acquiring extensive holdings than on building up high-yielding capacity on the land. A few intensively managed properties are yielding timber volume and dollar profits at two to five times the average return per acre.

The North, as considered here, includes all States north of the southern boundaries of Maryland, West Virginia, Kentucky, and Missouri, and east of the western boundaries of Iowa and Minnesota. My discussion is confined primarily to large timberland holdings, those of 50,000 acres or more, but a few smaller holdings are mentioned to show important developments in private forestry. All types of ownerships are included—whether the land is held by milling companies for their supplies, by investors, or by those interested in subsurface rights.

Ownership of large forest holdings in the North is distributed among individual owners, families, investment companies, pulp and paper companies, lumber companies, mining companies, and some others.

The large private holdings are concentrated in Maine, which has 31 owners who control more than half the total area in large holdings in the North. Protection of forests against fire is good in almost all cases. The exceptions are the forests owned by coal-mining companies, where hazards are high, local interest low, and public cooperation in fire protection meager. The degree of protection attained, however, is determined more by the work of the State fire-control organizations than by special effort of individual owners. The companies that have their own fire-control organizations are the exception in the North.

The cutting practices currently applied over most of the large holdings leave much to be desired. Many properties that are operated on essentially a sustained-yield basis have cutting standards best designated as "chopper's choice." Some companies attempt to apply diameter limits and a few mark trees before cutting. Where only extensive management is practiced, marking of individual trees is not always essential—particularly in areas and stands that are subject to windthrow and among tree species, such as aspen and jack pine, that have relatively short lives. Yellow birch, although subject neither to windfall nor early decadence in a closed forest, declines in vigor on areas selectively logged. Over much of northern Maine, where roads are lacking, hardwoods are still unmerchantable. Serious losses are occurring from birch dieback and beech scale. The death of old trees will, however, release spruce and balsam fir that will produce a valuable crop.

Case studies of a few owners will be presented. Those selected are not the only ones with good forestry programs, nor have they necessarily the best programs. Some were selected because they have some distinctive feature in their program. Information has been gained from published articles, letters, interviews with company foresters, and conversations with other persons familiar with the programs.

The first group of examples includes the individual, family, and investment holdings.

That type of large forest holdings is found primarily in the unorganized towns of Maine, where the remoteness and lack of transportation restrict operations to extensive, rather than intensive, forestry.

The Coe and Pingree estate, built up in the late nineteenth century, at one time included more than a million acres. The founder, David Pingree, insisted on restricted cutting of spruce to trees 14 inches in diameter and larger. The practice was abandoned soon after the turn of the century, when pulpwood cutting came to the fore. The heirs still own a large area of the land. Management practices today are on an extensive basis, but the property continues to yield periodically a substantial income to its owners.

Gifford Pinchot and Henry S. Graves, among the first Americans to be trained scientifically as foresters, drew up management plans in 1898 for Nehasane Park and the Whitney Preserve, two Adirondack properties that were held primarily for recreation. The owners, however, early became interested in scientific forestry as a means of making the properties self-supporting.

Careful timber estimates were made, type maps were prepared, and contracts for cutting spruce trees to a 10-inch diameter limit were drawn up. The white pine, considered overmature, and cherry were cut without restrictions. Other hardwoods were not merchantable. Yield studies indicated that a cut of the same intensity could be had again at the end of 36 years. Nehasane Park was logged first in 1898 and 1899 and again in 1915 to 1930. A third cutting is now under way. It is difficult to make an accurate comparison between actual yields and anticipated yields. In the first place, the management plan as prepared by Mr. Graves was not fully carried out. The cutting intervals were shorter than he had expected and the diameter limits were lowered. Furthermore, defective hardwoods were not removed and they expanded following the removal of merchantable trees. The volume of softwood and the quality of hardwood declined because of logging practices.

Operations on the Whitney Preserve have always been somewhat more conservative, and the forest is somewhat better in quality. On the whole, both properties have fared better than average Adirondack land. Cutting policies have varied with markets, however, and the economic requirements of the owners more than they have with the silvicultural requirements of the forest. Neither property can be considered an ideal example of applied forest management, but the properties have

802062°—49——18

returned substantial incomes in the past and give every promise of continuing to do so in the years ahead. Because much of the hardwood timber is now merchantable for pulpwood and because prices of timber have increased decidedly during the 50 years, today's cash income from the property equals that of the past, even though the volumes being harvested now are considerably less.

THE DEAD RIVER CO. and the Eastern Corp., manufacturers of paper, recently concluded a 10-year renewable management agreement on a sizable acreage of land. It requires diameter cutting limits as follows: Balsam fir, 6 inches; spruce and hemlock, 10 inches; pine, 10 inches for pulpwood and 12 inches for sawlogs. Large pine and large hardwoods suitable for saw timber, veneer, and novelties are reserved by the Dead River Co. Cutting may not exceed three-fourths of the calculated growth over any 5-year period. Areas are selected for cutting with regard to maturity, protection of forests against fire, insects, and disease, and in a manner that will insure reasonable silvicultural control. Past management of the Dead River Co. holdings has been conservative, so that the properties cut over now contain more timber than when acquired.

The properties are to be developed intensively by building all-year gravel roads and encouraging industries that are necessary to get high returns from the properties. Complete utilization from the land is possible through markets for all commercial species that are growing on the land.

A FEW OTHER estate and investment holdings have access to diversified markets and the benefits of management by a trained forester. They are the exception rather than the rule. The general practice when the original owner died has been to divide the equity but leave the physical property intact.

Divided ownership spreads the risk from fire, insect damage, and other hazards, makes it possible for the group owners to enjoy income at short intervals, and enables them to draw up satisfactory contracts with companies interested in purchasing timber. On the other hand, as the equity of each individual diminishes because of increase in number of heirs, interest likewise diminishes. Diffused ownership makes agreement on one single-management policy difficult. In the long run, individual heirs interested in the greatest current income or interested in liquidating the property tend to make their weight count at the expense of those willing to manage the land as a long-time investment property.

Group owners have been obliged to place management responsibilities on a single individual who acted as agent for all. These agents were often lawyers, retired judges, real estate dealers, or individual members of the family, most of whom had no knowledge of forestry. Consequently, sales and cutting practices were left largely to the discretion of the buyer of timber. Before 1900, these were mostly lumbermen interested in spruce saw timber; cutting was therefore confined to saw-timber trees.

Thereafter, extensive pulp operations brought progressively more drastic cuttings. The removal of softwood without cutting hardwoods has led to serious deterioration. Investment properties have been particularly susceptible to such deterioration because they lay in the unorganized towns of Maine, where few roads have been built. Only timber that could be driven down the streams was merchantable.

Family-type holdings are gradually being acquired by pulp companies. A few of the larger holdings may persist for some decades to come, but they will be the exception rather than the rule. Stability of long-term management objectives appears to be out of the question for most such properties. Owners generally are unwilling to develop the properties intensively by building roads, erecting homes for forest workers, and encouraging such industries as are necessary to get high returns from the timber property. That may be due in part to reluctance to see organized towns develop that will undoubtedly increase the tax rate on the forest holdings. Special taxes have been levied in the unorganized towns to provide good protection against fire, but many owners have resisted attempts to open up the land for development.

As interest in forestry began to develop in the early 1900's, men with training in forestry offered their services to the owners on a consulting basis. A few firms of consulting foresters are well established and deal chiefly with family-type holdings. They have undoubtedly been a stabilizing influence in this type of ownership.

Family and investment holdings also played a considerable role in forest history in the Lake States, but there the speculators, lumber companies, and others who were interested more in short- than long-term management gained control. Because fires and other hazards were greater, and agricultural values more promising in the Lake States than in the Northeast, permanent holdings of the land for forest production was given little consideration. Throughout the other Northern States, permanent holdings of timberland in large blocks on strictly an investment basis was essentially unknown.

Lumber companies are one of the less important groups of large timberland holders in the North. The practice in the past was chiefly to cut the land clean of all timber of merchantable size and to sell the land to others, or allow it to revert to the public for taxes. Some areas stripped for saw timber were cut over immediately thereafter for pulpwood and chemical wood. Such a practice in western Pennsylvania caused extensive decline in forest productivity—especially if fire followed. Aspen, pin cherry, and gray birch that seeded in after fire produced no real values. Scrub oak was even less useful. All hindered valuable seedlings. On areas having poor air drainage, there developed permanent frost pockets covered with grass, ferns, or low brush.

Lumber companies, by and large, and certain other timber industries, have an indifferent record. When conditions are favorable, they may initiate progressive forestry measures, only to drop them later. Two large lumber companies recently dropped their programs entirely. Others that adopted selective cutting are not on the sustained-yield basis. In some companies, which do have good programs, only one or two persons in the management are convinced of its necessity. Indifference, conviction that forestry will not pay, even spirited opposition to selective logging for saw timber and veneer are still reported to be widespread in the industry.

An outstanding exception among the northern lumber companies is the Goodman Lumber Company, of Goodman, Wis. Organized about 1906, the company for 20 years made little effort to practice forestry. By 1920 it became evident that the land was not well suited to agriculture and the enactment of the Wisconsin Forest Crop Law, substituting a 10-percent severance tax for the annual property tax, turned Mr. Goodman's attention to forestry. State protection of forest land against fire also improved.

The company began its first cycle of selective cutting in 1927. Cutting was restricted to 35 to 55 percent of the merchantable volume; trees of medium size, but still capable of vigorous growth, were left. This first cycle of selective cutting was completed in 1944. Plans for the second cutting cycle were outlined by Robert Martin in an article published in the *Journal of Forestry* in 1945. The interval between cuts is being reduced from 17 to 10 years. The volume to be removed in the second cycle will be 10 to 20 percent, or a minimum of 2,000 board feet. An extensive road system and improved utilization has made this possible. Sustained yield is now the rule. Lands cut over in 1927 and later are increasing in the volume of products that can be harvested for chemical wood, pulpwood, veneer bolts, and sawlogs.

Today, after 37 years of operation, timber reserves are substantially equal to the initial forest capital with which the company was launched. With restriction of sawlogs cut, the company erected a wood-chemical plant, veneer mill, shingle mill, and pulp mill for roofing felt to use the wood in defective trees, treetops, and young trees cut in thinnings. In this way the work volume has been maintained. The better grades of lumber are kiln-dried for special uses.

Timber growth and yield is now determined on the basis of tree-vigor classes. Integrated utilization and marketing have been so coordinated that tree marking for best silviculture is identical with tree marking for financial return. Officials of the company are convinced that by selective cutting and integrated utilization, the income from operations during the past 20 years has been as high as the income would have been from the liquidation cutting. The property now, however, is valuable as a going enterprise and can continue indefinitely to yield current high returns in terms of output. Employment, good will, and the tax base also are permanent.

Much more efficient utilization has doubled the number of man-hours of work per unit of timber cut. The company is today a good example of integrated utilization for a relatively small operation. The company built a town with stores, schools, churches, and homes for its employees. A modern village with desirable living conditions is important, because skilled workers in forests and conversion plants are essential for the success of integrated utilization and good forestry practice. Good forest management has also developed on the farm woodlands adjacent to Goodman, because the owners are assured a continuing, nearby market for their forest products.

A few other lumber companies have tried to follow a forestry program.

The VonPlaten-Fox Co. of norther Michigan is one. Its ownership is les concentrated, and some difficulties hav been encountered in getting all owner to subscribe to a long-term management program.

The Patten Timber Company an the Ford Motor Company in Michigan and the Roddis Lumber and Veneer Company of Wisconsin also hav been practicing selective cutting.

Although it is not strictly a lumbe company, the Draper Corporation manufacturers of spools and textil machinery, have acquired substantia areas of forest land and are engaged i organizing it for sustained-yield forestry. Because many of the company' products are made from wood turnings, it is possible for them to use timbe in relatively small sizes. Their progran is still new, but promises to be one o the more intensive forestry efforts i the North.

Mining companies of necessity ow considerable areas of forest land t control subsurface rights. The averag company, however, owns considerabl fewer than 50,000 acres, and pays littl attention ordinarily to the timber th land supports. Timbers are essentia for deep-mining operations, but mos companies have chosen to buy fron others the timber they need for mine ties, props, lagging, and other purposes, rather than to grow it on company lands. As local props becom scarce, however, companies turn thei attention to their own forest lands Some employ foresters and hav started forestry programs. A few hav had programs of sorts under way fo 30 or 40 years, but have not followe them with vigor or steadfastness o purpose.

One West Virginia company tha has a large holding of coal land nov has a broad forestry program. Timbe is being leased separately from coal Diameter limits for cutting are specified and are varied to favor the specie that are best for mine props and lumber. Close utilization and concentra tion on defective materials is favored. The company's forester estimates that the program now under way will double the yield of timber on lands to which it applies. Land covered by old leases remain unaffected.

Other coal companies likewise have forestry programs, some of which have been under way for 5 years or more. Some include good cutting practices. Others have had desultory programs with little net results to show for their operations. The common picture is indifference toward surface values on the part of both companies and miners. Fires have been frequent and disastrous, and much of the land supports meager growth.

Copper- and iron-mining companies in the Lake States have forestry programs. One, the Cleveland Cliffs Iron Company, first became interested some 25 years ago and has gradually improved its practice since. The Copper Ranger Company in Michigan and the Oliver Iron Mining Company in Minnesota have adopted progressive programs.

Although they do not manage forest land as such and are not strictly mining companies, oil and natural gas companies influence forest practice in regions where they operate wells. Subsurface rights have been leased over extensive forest areas. Those rights permit the companies to enter the land, erect equipment, drill wells, and operate pumping stations and pipe lines. Timber is cleared from the vicinity of wells. In western Pennsylvania, where wells have long been operated, a system known as "five spotting" has been in use. Four wells are drilled in a square, with a fifth in the center. Water is pumped down the corner wells to help force oil from the center one. In many fields a regular pattern of wells occupies the land to the serious detriment of forestry operations. Both public and private forestry is impeded by "five spotting" on forest land.

Wood-chemical companies have had an unstable record. Started at the turn of the century primarily to manufacture charcoal, wood alcohol, and acetic acid, they grew to substantial importance during the First World War. They operated in New York, western Pennsylvania, the Lake States, the Appalachians, and other regions. New processes for making synthetic methanol and acetic acid and a declining demand for charcoal brought on hard times. During the late 1920's and 1930's, plant after plant dropped out. The few that remained enjoyed a new prosperity during the Second World War, but now are again on the decline. With such a background, it is small wonder that wood-chemical companies have shown little interest in forestry.

Certain companies, however, have been outstanding. One owns about enough land to supply its needs. It cuts over the property at about 30-year intervals and removes all material of chemical-wood size. Reproduction is prompt, and operations are essentially on a sustaining basis. The forest produces only chemical wood, most of it from sprout growth.

A second company, affiliated with a large chemical concern, employs foresters and operates essentially on a sustained-yield program. A vigorous research program has uncovered a number of derivatives from the crude wood tar that remains after removing wood alcohol and acetic acid. The outlook for the company's future forestry program is bright. Less promising is the outlook for a group of companies in western Pennsylvania, few of which have ever had a forestry program. In fact, the majority own no land and purchase chemical wood from jobbers and individual operators.

The Gray Chemical Company operated on a different pattern. Land sufficient to supply half the company's needs was acquired. Additional wood was purchased from local farmers and other landowners; the company was careful to provide them a steady market for their wood. A permanent labor force was built up of independent farmers, company loggers, and others who regularly cut timber for company use. The company bought run-down farms and fixed up homes for cutters and truckers who supplied wood for the plant. A sawmill was purchased to break down trunks from decadent trees into sizes suitable for use in the company retorts. Good logs were sawed into lumber. Research to diversify products was sponsored. Activated carbon and other high-priced products stabilized company income.

Company lands were initially clearcut at about 40 years of age. The practice was changed to partial cutting so as to increase yield and to favor saw timber that might further lend stability to operations. Stockholdings were distributed among company officials and others in an effort to build up community interest in the operation. During the peak of wartime activities, outside interests purchased the plant and five others in the vicinity. The new management has dropped the company's forestry program.

Among the railway companies, the Pennsylvania Railroad owns a substantial area of forest land in Pennsylvania, from which it obtains water for its engines. Lands to be cut are designated by the company forester and cut on a diameter-limit basis. Management is conservative.

The Western Maryland Railway has cooperated with the West Virginia Pulp and Paper Company in sponsoring a program of conservative selective cutting on company lands. The objective has been to increase returns from the timber, which is sold to the West Virginia Company, and to increase stability of employment for local residents. The companies join forces to convince local cutters that they can prolong their jobs by following good forestry practices. The program has been successful.

A few other railways, notably the New York Central and the Norfolk & Western Railway, engage in forest-land management through subsidiary coal companies.

Pulp and paper companies lead all others in forestry in the North. They control the largest area of land, employ the most foresters, and have the greatest financial stake in sustained-yield forestry. Their programs date from the turn of the century. Extensive forestry has characterized operations in remote areas of northern Maine, the Adirondacks, and the Lake States. Intensive forestry programs exist on some accessible lands.

George Amidon, of the Minnesota and Ontario Paper Company, at the 1947 meeting of the Society of American Foresters, reported substantial progress in forestry by the pulpwood industry in the Lake States, where there are 112 pulp and paper mills. Foresters were employed by 35 percent of the mills in 1937 and by 59 percent in 1947; 27 foresters were employed in 1937 and 130 in 1947. The total land owned was about a million acres in 1937 and 1,900,000 acres in 1947. Most of the mills reported that they are attempting to manage their lands on a sustained-yield basis. The pulpwood cut from the lands averages only one-twelfth of a cord annually. In time this might be increased to a third, or even one-half cord as the lands are restored to high productivity. About a third of the mills have planting programs under way that will help restore the lands. The mills are also carrying on other activities, such as research on little-used species, cooperation with State and Federal Governments in forest protection, and demonstrations of good forest practices among small owners.

The Great Northern Paper Company, in Maine, which began acquiring lands before 1900, has followed an extensive forestry program, which has involved special improvements along streams to facilitate driving and long cutting cycles on essentially a sustained-yield basis. Only spruce and fir have been cut on the remote lands. The company, experienced in river driving, probably drives more pulpwood than any other in the country.

The Brown Company owns large areas of land in the United States and Canada. Past operations, on an extensive basis, resembled those of other owners of remote areas. In 1940 or so, the company became concerned about its future timber supply. An aerial photo survey was made of its own lands and of other lands tributary to the mills at Berlin, N. H. Reassured by the results, the company built a new sulfate mill. Additional foresters were employed in the woodlands department, and mechanical skidders, logging arches, portable cut-off saws and pulpwood loaders, bulldozers, as well as mechanical road-building equipment were introduced. New portable camps were erected to provide greater comfort for loggers.

The company is committed to long-term sustained-yield operations. Improved cutting practices are being introduced. Foresters in key positions in the company have a high degree of authority over the timber-management policies. The Brown Company cooperates with other companies in the area in an effort to build up an over-all sustained-yield program that embraces all companies that purchase timber in the same area.

The Hollingsworth and Whitney Company owns large areas of land in Maine. A forestry program has been under way for a number of years. Recently the company made an aerial survey of its lands as a basis for a broad management plan. Forestry practices are being improved on present holdings and additional land is being acquired. By talks and motion pictures at schools and granges, good forestry is promoted among farmers and other small-woodland owners.

More than 20 years ago, the Oxford Paper Company was sponsor of a tree-breeding program to develop rapidly growing aspen hybrids for book paper. Fast-growing hybrids were produced, but the company learned that it could use native hardwoods in place of aspen. Pulp and paper and other northern companies have shown an interest in the aspen hybrids, however, and have set out plantations.

The Nekoosa-Edwards Paper Company, the Consolidated Water Power and Paper Company, and other firms in the vicinity of Wisconsin Rapids, Wis., have active forestry programs.

The Nekoosa-Edwards program, which dates from 1926, has featured plantings on abandoned farm land. The company operates its own nursery, in which operations are highly mechanized. Field planting by machine has reduced costs by one-half and has increased survival of seedlings. Every year for 20 years some planting has been done by the company. The planted area totals 17,000 acres, and is an outstanding venture in forest planting. The company's cutting practices are on a conservative basis. The company owns about 110,000 acres and is acquiring more land so that mill needs can be met entirely from its own holdings. Its own fire-control organization includes tank trucks, tool caches, and trained fire fighters. Fire losses since 1926 have been restricted to 137 acres.

The Consolidated Water Power and Paper Company owns and manages 160,000 acres. In the past 15 years it has planted 7,000 acres of open land, with varying success, and now has under way experiments with direct seeding. The company prefers to buy well-stocked lands and follows a diversified plan in procurement of raw material. Part of the needs is met from company lands, part from county forests and national forests, and part from local farmers and other owners of pulpwood.

The Finch-Pruyn Company in New York has pioneered in forestry in the Adirondacks. Spruce and fir are cut on company land and driven down the Hudson River to the company's mill at Glens Falls. The land has been under forest management for 37 years; the sustained-yield cutting budget was based on a growth rate of two-tenths cord an acre a year. For a long time, all trees to be cut were marked under the supervision of foresters, spruce to a variable limit of 8 to 9 inches in diameter and balsam fir to a limit of 6 to 7 inches.

Marking was abandoned during the war because their young foresters left for military service. The control of cutting was taken over by the operating superintendent and his staff. Since the war, the forestry and operating divisions have been closely integrated, and foresters are gradually replacing the old-style operators. Despite a considerable forestry effort, the company has found that growth has not come up to expectations; the average rate is estimated at just under one-tenth cord an acre a year. To arrest further liquidation of their own growing stock, the firm now buys pulpwood from other owners. Growth on special company study plots has averaged about one-half cord a year; that fact emphasizes the importance of proper stocking. Thought is now being given to methods to correct the slow recovery of mature stands following cutting and measures to improve rate of growth.

The New York and Pennsylvania Company, Inc., manufacturers of pulp and paper, and its subsidiary, the Armstrong Forest Company, for more than 50 years have managed their timberlands in Pennsylvania for continued growth of pulpwood. The first company forester was employed in 1907. Pulpwood has been produced with an eye always on the maintenance of forest growth. The company's forestry program includes planting of bare lands, an intensively developed primary and secondary road system to make possible frequent light cuts, integrated utilization of pulpwood and saw timber, a system of permanent cutting plots to furnish guides to better practice, a training program for wood cutters to improve the quality of their work, efforts to devise new logging techniques and equipment, and other activities deemed valuable in improving the output from company lands.

The West Virginia Pulp and Paper Company obtains the bulk of the wood used at its mills in New York, Pennsylvania, Maryland, and Virginia from farmers and other suppliers over wide areas. Recognizing that the mills cannot continue to produce and meet their heavy expenses unless the wood supply is secure, the company for many years has taken an active interest in protection of the forests from fire and has lent support to the efforts of public agencies to reduce the number and size of fires in the woods. The next natural step is to encourage improvement of woodlands through application of forestry principles by those who supply the wood. The company naturally wants to see the cutters handle the woodlands so they will produce year after year, with steady employment for themselves and their equipment. At some of the mills the company has distributed booklets that explain details of economical and safe production, care of roads, and simple methods of getting improved growth on the forest land. Since a profitable market is furnished for large quantities of wood that has no value for lumber, progress is being made toward establishment of full production on the areas where wood is being cut.

The Eastern Pulpwood Company has acquired large areas of forest land in Maine and New Brunswick. Originally the land was held as a timber reserve, while pulpwood was procured from outside sources. Company lands are now being cut on a conservative basis with sustained yield in mind. Balsam fir is cut to a lower diameter than spruce in an effort to reduce damage from spruce budworm, at present a serious threat to Maine softwoods.

The International Paper Company owns more than a million acres, acquired mostly about 1898, in New York, Vermont, New Hampshire, and Maine. Timber cut from the lands has furnished a large part of the company's pulp requirements; the rest comes from open-market purchases and from Canada. When a timber inventory and growth studies on the American holdings are completed, the company plans to draw up a management system to guide operations for many years to come. Lack of complete information on the company's forest capital and particularly on growth rate has precluded certainty as to sustained yield.

A special feature of the program is the Phillips Brook management area in northern New Hampshire—a 23,000-acre tract in a single-stream valley, on which an intensive forestry pilot operation is under way. From the demonstration area, on which every effort is being made to employ the best forestry practices, company officials hope to glean information to guide their own work and other forestry work in the Northeast.

Of special interest are the companies that make pulp for roofing felt, floor coverings, and wall boards. They became important users of wood pulp only after the other pulp and paper companies were well established. Because they can pulp small-sized wood with the bark on, they have a competitive advantage over companies that require peeled wood. Nevertheless, some of them have started a land-acquisition program. Their activities increase the opportunities for integrated utilization in the territory tributary to their mills.

Forestry programs are also under way on lands controlled by the Kimberley-Clark Corporation, Tomahawk Kraft Company, Mosinee Paper Company, Minnesota and Ontario Paper Company, Northwest Paper Company, the Mead Corporation, St. Regis Paper Company, Penobscot Development Company, and others. In fact, interest in management for continuous production is characteristic of most pulp and paper companies, regardless of whether they own and operate their own land or purchase timber from other owners.

Professional foresters own and operate a few fair-sized forest properties. The Luther forest in New York State and the Watson forest property in Michigan are examples.

The Luther property was acquired some 50 years ago by retaining lands after lumbering and by buying and planting abandoned farm land. Gradually, more than 6,000 acres were acquired. Bare land that made up half the area has been planted to pine, spruce, and other species. Some of the original lots have been logged three times, and the plantations have come into yield. The operation is probably the most intensive to be found on any medium- to large-sized forest property in the United States. Present operations are confined entirely to thinning plantations; some plantations have been thinned twice, and several have already returned in income far more than their original costs. A few show handsome profits above original costs, yet are just now entering the period of most rapid growth. All timber harvesting has paid its way. Some trees have been cut for fuel wood, some for pulpwood, some for lumber that has been sawed on the property, and a substantial amount has been sold in random lengths for cooperage.

The present owner, the son of the original owner, feels that he could not manage his property successfully without carrying on his own logging and marketing operations. Most of the timber he sells now and most of what he has sold in the past would have no stumpage value. It gains in value only as he finds an outlet for wood that will bring him a return above harvesting costs. The work is well organized, properly mechanized, and provides year-round employment for about 10 men. The property is a successful example of a profitable private forest that was started on bare land. The owner has kept a careful record of expenses and knows that the property is yielding him a fair interest on his investment above all expenditures and is accumulating forest capital that will make his future harvests progressively more valuable.

The Watson property, of 26,000 acres in upper Michigan, has been gradually built up over 25 years. Started originally as a partnership, it is now in the hands of one owner.

Most of it was cut-over land acquired from the county tax sales and outright purchases from lumber companies and others after it had been logged off. Swamp and swamp-border types predominate, running heavily to balsam fir, spruce, northern white-cedar, and aspen. To provide ample permanent employment for his 50 workmen while growing stock is being built up, stumpage is purchased from other landowners. A special effort is made to provide continuous yearlong employment by purchasing both upland and lowland and by having a good distribution of types and size classes. Current cutting is estimated to be about 25 percent less than the growth.

The example of these men should be of particular value to others interested in family or corporate holdings. Both have found it necessary to do their own logging. Both recognize that permanent markets are essential for continued operations. Both believe in relatively intensive forestry. Both wonder how they can maintain continuity of management beyond their own lifetimes. Inheritance taxes alone can destroy each property by wiping out working capital or forcing heavy cuts that upset sustained-yield operations and the year-round business that depends thereon. Dispersal of the property among heirs might prove equally disastrous. Their practice of accumulating capital in growing stock on the ground makes both operations highly vulnerable to inheritance taxes and division. Both are examples of the premise that foresters are exceptionally well equipped to own and manage timberland.

Foresters differ from most other owners of forest lands in their attitude toward capital investment. Foresters recognize that their investment can usually be built up most readily by cutting less than current growth and by saving the best-formed and most vigorous trees as growing stock. In this way yield per acre increases in volume and value without increasing the outlay for roads, protection, and maintenance. Other investors, not realizing the efficiency of such a program, are more likely to cut heavily and to invest their extra earnings in additional land and thus assume all the burdens that go with care of the land. Only foresters, in my opinion, seem to appreciate the need to balance purchases of new land against increased efforts on existing holdings.

Several other foresters are managing their own timberlands. Areas of 1,000 to 10,000 acres are owned by Ned Bryant, Harry Clark, John Kiernan, Sterling Wagner, and several others. The Wagner property is of special interest in that it combines saw-timber, fuel-wood, and mine-prop operations with a resort business in the forest.

OWNERSHIP of large forest properties in the North has changed appreciably during the past two decades. Pulp and paper companies are the strongest and most stable owners. The large investments in pulp and paper mills can be liquidated only over long periods of time and make necessary a continuous supply of timber. Many of the companies are enlarging their holdings. Others are attempting to stimulate good forest practices on the part of private owners who control land tributary to their mills.

BECAUSE FEW LUMBER COMPANIES were responsible owners of forest land in the past, few are important timber owners today. Lumber companies face several difficulties. They have last call on the timber. Fuel wood, chemical wood, pulpwood, mine timbers, posts, poles, ties, and many other products can all be cut from trees before they reach saw-timber size. Though the sawlogs bring a higher price than the smaller material, many owners sell when their timber first becomes marketable. Moreover, less than half the merchantable material harvestable throughout a rotation is likely to be of sawlog size. Unless a lumber company operates subsidiary plants to process small material, as the Goodman Lum-er Company has done, or develops an utside market, it does not enjoy the ull fruits of the land. Integrated use, ather than single use, is essential for fficient management.

Sawmill operations in the North are nostly small enterprises, often conlucted by men of limited experience n the lumber business. Few large sawimber tracts now exist. Small-sawnill operators have neither the capital nor stability to engage in long-time orestry ventures. Furthermore, the umber market fluctuates violently in orice levels. Sawmill men are particuarly vulnerable to business declines n periods of depression. Bulkiness and veight of the product further militates gainst building up a stable, long-term nterprise in a region of small land oldings and heavily exploited forests. The lumber companies that I menioned earlier that do have good forstry programs are exceptional rather han characteristic of the industry in general. It will be a long time before umber companies as such become an mportant factor in forest-land manigement in the North.

The wood-chemical companies have hown a high degree of variability with he changing times. I believe they cannot be looked to as important timberand owners of the future. Few of hem have shown the foresight to manige their forest properties for integrated yield of the forest products.

Mining companies, utility companies, and water companies in the long run should become stable owners and operators of forest land. They are obliged to own the land anyhow, they enjoy an income from their mining or other operations, and there is little reason, economic or otherwise, for them not to do a good job of forest management. That many of them have failed to do so in the past is attributed primarily to lack of interest rather than lack of financial ability.

Individual family ownerships and investment owners as a group tend to relinquish their property to pulp companies and others that have a greater stake in yield from forest lands. They are subjected to the vicissitudes of inheritance taxes, property taxes unadjusted to yield from the land, and to division of equity upon the death of the original owner. It seems almost impossible to expect, under the existing laws and economic forces, that any form of individual ownership can enjoy stability beyond the life of the owner. Without this stability it is impossible to maintain a permanently productive forest property.

Properties owned by individual foresters are new and, indeed, promising. But they are subject to the weaknesses of any other type of individual ownership. They are subject to overextension of credit and other financial difficulties that may force liquidation, and they are likely to be dismembered as a result of inheritance taxes or division of property after the original owner dies.

No type of private ownership in the United States at present is such that it guarantees permanently good forest practice on the land. Pulp companies, lumber companies, individual private owners, mining companies, and others have all started forestry programs and abandoned them later because of various circumstances. No private forestry program in the North can be considered permanent under existing economic conditions. The stronger corporations, on the whole, seem to be more responsible owners and the ones that are gradually getting control of more and more forest lands. Present economic trends point to an increasing concentration of timberland ownership in the hands of a few large companies and public agencies.

A CITIZEN may rightly ask how effectively the large private forest holdings meet the public interest in good protection of the land against fire, insects, and disease outbreaks, protect the watershed values, insure sustained yield and a steady employment, open lands to recreational use by the public, and spread economic opportunity.

The points are taken up one by one.

Large private-forest holders in the North appreciate the importance of good fire control and support State efforts to this end. A few have their own fire-control organizations. The critical 1947 fire season in Maine caused staggering losses in organized towns in southern Maine, where protection was under the supervision of local fire wardens. Lacking specific authority, and without time to organize the towns, the forest commissioner could give only limited help. When an appeal was made to him, he augmented local forces and helped bring in Federal aid. At the same time, the State organization protected all unorganized towns in northern Maine and losses were insignificant. Large landowners who had insisted on a good protective system deserve some of the credit for the efficient performance where the State was free to act.

Control of forest-insect pests and diseases has been largely a public function, but private landowners have cooperated by making their lands available for experimental use and by supporting public agencies in their control program.

The large forest holdings furnish relatively good watershed and soil protection. Throughout the North, fire control is one of the most effective methods of reducing flood runoff and protecting the soil. Local damage due to heavy cutting, downhill skidding, and mountain roads has resulted in erosion and some watershed deterioration, but that is a local rather than widespread condition.

More critical is clear cutting that results in serious frost damage. Such damage is not uncommon in the Allegheny plateau, sections of the Adirondacks, and other regions where clear cutting may expose land surfaces that are subject to poor air drainage. Once all the timber cover is removed, a frost pocket develops that may persist for decades before a forest cover can be reestablished. Weather records taken in frost pockets show that they are definitely cooler than surrounding lands on

TOTAL AREA OF LARGE FOREST HOLDING IN THE NORTH AND AVERAGE PERCENTAGE OF FOREST LAND BURNED EACH YEAR, BY STATES, 1941–45. DATA ARE BASED ON REAPPRAISAL OF THE FOREST SITUATION, 1946

| State | Land in large holdings | Total forest area burned annually |
|---|---|---|
| | *Acres* | *Percent* |
| Kentucky | 197,033 | 1.2[illegible] |
| Maine | 8,618,092 | .1[illegible] |
| Michigan | 2,371,353 | .1[illegible] |
| Minnesota | 335,128 | .2[illegible] |
| Missouri | 319,000 | 2.1[illegible] |
| New Hampshire | 484,689 | .2[illegible] |
| New York | 888,310 | .2[illegible] |
| Pennsylvania | 104,407 | .4[illegible] |
| Vermont | 278,254 | .0[illegible] |
| West Virginia | 445,672 | 1.4[illegible] |
| Wisconsin | 579,743 | .0[illegible] |
| Total | 14,621,681 | ........ |

clear nights when heat loss through earth radiation is rapid.

A number of large holdings are operated on an extensive sustained-yield basis. Sustained yield often is followed where cutting standards are far from the best that might be used, although companies that practice poor silviculture obviously are obliged to own and protect more land than they otherwise would require. Community sustained yield is a strong objective of pulp and paper companies that must protect large investments. It is also the objective of the Goodman Lumber Company, the Luther and Watson managements, and the Western Maryland Railway.

Relatively little progress has been made, however, toward building up community, county, and State sustained-yield forestry throughout the North. Beginnings are being made in Vermont, New Hampshire, and Wisconsin. Industries have taken the lead over public agencies in sponsoring such programs. Integrated sustained use of all products of the forest should be the objective, and vastly greater public leadership should be directed toward that end.

Most large private holdings in the North are open to public fishing, hunting, trapping, and camping. A property in the Pocono region of Pennsylvania is operated jointly for timber, fishing, hunting, and recreation. The owner of the 2,500-acre property has fenced it against trespass; he stocks the streams for fishing, and furnishes special hunting privileges to guests at his lodge. He operates his own sawmill and cuts enough timber to supply the needs of his resort and offers some timber for sale. It is one of the few forests operated by a forester to return income from each resource the property affords. A similar property in the Catskills is managed as a recreational area tributary to a large resort hotel. The timber is cut on a sustained-yield basis and the wood used primarily for fuel for the furnaces and fireplaces of the hotel.

Some of the owners in the Adirondacks are leasing hunting and trapping rights to game clubs and other sportsmen. The public generally opposes restrictions on hunting on large private properties lest the poor man be excluded. Many large companies appreciate that viewpoint, and have allowed use of their lands for recreation. Many require permits so they can regulate use to some extent, but most impose no restrictions. Perhaps, as pressure of population and hunting increase, more and more owners of large holdings will lease hunting and trapping rights.

Cherished by all Americans is the belief that our country is a land in which the energetic man with limited resources can build his own independent business enterprise. The rise of giant corporations in recent decades has restricted the fields of endeavor open to small business. The forest-products industries have occupied a big position in our small-business economy in the past. Has concentration of forest ownership in the North adversely affected opportunities for small business? Pulp and paper companies, to be sure, have acquired large holdings, but of the 170 million acres of commercial forest land in the North, large ownerships control but 15 million acres, 9 percent.

Ample opportunity still exists for anyone so minded to acquire and manage his own forest property, provided he have modest capital resources at his command. To the extent that large holdings stabilize industries and market outlets, the small owner is favorably served by their existence. Moreover, the policies of many large holders is to encourage good practice on the nearby lands. Large owners, as a rule, seek full development and use of their property, thereby expanding rather than restricting economic opportunity. Of course, to the extent that they condone poor cutting practices in their own lands and on the lands of others that they operate, resources to support additional forest industries are thereby diminished.

Special problems beset private owners of forests—taxes, fluctuating or inadequate markets, and depleted forests, among them.

The general property tax unquestionably works heavy hardship on some owners. Sometimes taxes are so high they absorb all income from the property in the form of timber growth. Rarely is the property tax adjusted to the income that might be expected from the land. Paul E. Malone, in a study of forest taxation in Hancock County, Maine, found that small properties tend to be taxed at a higher rate an acre than large properties; improvements on the land show a low rate of increase in tax with increase in value; assessment practices and local tax rates vary widely so that little relationship exists between timber yield and the tax.

In three towns in Hancock County, Maine, taxes per acre varied thus:

| | *Area* | |
|---|---|---|
| | *1 to 9 acres* | *More than 1,000 acres* |
| Amherst | $0.10 | $0.09 |
| Eastbrook | .21 | .11 |
| Franklin | .49 | .08 |

CHARACTER OF TIMBER CUTTING PRACTICES ON LARGE PRIVATE HOLDINGS IN THE NORTH. DATA ARE BASED ON REAPPRAISAL OF THE FOREST SITUATION, 1946

| *Ownership class* | *Land owned* | *Acreage in properties being cut under practices that rate—* Good | Fair | Poor |
|---|---|---|---|---|
| | *Acres* | *Percent* | *Percent* | *Percent* |
| Family and investment | 3,444,047 | 10 | 74 | 16 |
| Pulp companies | 7,625,932 | 9 | 76 | 15 |
| Lumber, veneer, and cooperage companies | 2,015,315 | 8 | 23 | 69 |
| Mining companies (coal) | 553,705 | ....... | 6 | 94 |
| Mining companies (iron) | 932,682 | 5 | 31 | 64 |
| Other | 114,000 | ....... | ...... | 100 |
| Total | 14,685,681 | 9 | 62 | 29 |

Few assessors make any attempt to adjust the assessment with changes in soil productivity or changes in the degree of timber stocking. These two differences alone determine whether a property can return income. In all organized towns of Maine, property taxes on forest land are considered to be so high as to preclude large timber holdings. Consequently, few of the large timberland holders own any appreciable acreage in the organized towns.

Several States, among them Minnesota, Wisconsin, Michigan, and New York, have adopted forest-crop laws that enable the landowner to defer the major part of his current tax and to pay the rest by yield tax when the timber is harvested. The total land area in the North under such classification probably does not exceed a million acres. In New York, only two large properties, the Luther property and the Fisher property, are under the yield-tax law. The Goodman property is a large one in Wisconsin under such a law. The fact that these laws have not been more widely used is an indication that many owners do not find the forest property tax too burdensome. The laws may act as a deterrent to excessive valuation by assessment officers.

The inheritance tax is a handicap to individual owners, especially when most of their capital is tied up in the standing timber on their land. When a private-forest owner builds up a valuable sustained-yield property, he naturally would like to have the property continued and would like his heirs to enjoy the benefits from it. An inheritance tax, which must be met in a single payment, can wreck such holdings. Distributing the period over which such payments may be made to 10 years or longer would enable a large number of such properties to be maintained. State and Federal Governments might well give consideration as to how this particular problem can be met.

The Federal income-tax law definitely favors the forest owner by making it possible for him to list timber harvested as a long-term capital gain. In this way his tax on timber growth need never exceed 25 percent however high his tax may be on current income. Few timberland owners appear to appreciate the investment opportunities such a tax law affords.

Another handicap is the relative lack of skilled woods workers, particularly workmen who will cut conservatively. Operators have sometimes been obliged to abandon conservative cutting methods because the wood choppers refused to cut trees on a selective basis. Cutters have refused to cut selectively (even though their own income on a piece-work basis would be higher if they did so) until they were given convincing demonstrations. Intensive training is needed to increase the worker's efficiency and his safety. The accident rate in logging and lumbering is high, but good safety programs and proper training can reduce the rate. Training in safety will pay worker and operator.

In certain States, notably New York, workmen's compensation insurance is considered a serious deterrent to good forest practices. The rate is about 14 percent of the pay roll; for those that have a serious accident, it is 37 percent. Obviously, operators who are obliged to pay that big a part of their pay roll in insurance are under an extreme handicap in all their work. Recently several adjustments have been made to reduce the burden, but correction can come only with accident reduction.

Poor growing stock is an outstanding difficulty. It takes time to convert a forest that has been repeatedly high-graded into a valuable timber-producing property. Weed species, defective or valueless trees, and worthless shrubs prevent the establishment of good second-growth timber on many areas. Even where second growth is well established, the merchantable stands are often too scattered to permit building up a property that can be managed efficiently. Until well-organized timber properties have a value considerably above their liquidation value, few landowners will make the effort required to build up high-yielding, well-managed forest properties. Only a few people seem to have the necessary vision and patience to invest their capital in building up such valuable forests.

Perhaps the greatest obstacle facing the private timberland owner in the North is disorganized and fluctuating markets. The statement appears paradoxical, because the North consumes far more wood than it grows. But timber depletion has led to a scarcity of dependable wood processors. Many owners are serviced only by small, inefficient, portable mill owners. Lacking experience and capital, they saw boards varying in thickness, realize a poor-grade outturn, improperly pile and season the lumber, and fail to get top prices. They are obliged therefore to buy their logs and stumpage cheaply. Trade channels also are poorly developed. From New York, small-dimension beech is shipped to Wisconsin for processing, and to Massachusetts for furniture squares, wood turnings, and cooperage. Yet New York imports a large amount of wood, and has local use for all that can be grown. Many owners have felt that they must acquire their own processing plants if they are to have a ready market for all products of the forest. This is true of at least one of the investment properties in Maine, the Luther forest holding, and others.

A NUMBER OF COOPERATIVES have been organized to improve markets. Outstanding is the Otsego Forest Products Cooperative Association, which handles logging, milling, seasoning, finishing, and lumber sales, and thereby gains the advantages that accrue from converting stumpage into more readily marketable commodities. A steady market has been maintained during periods when local sawmills hesitated to purchase timber. Other associations, organized on the cooperative principle but with more restricted fields of operation, service timberland owners of the section. Their influence on markets is only local, however, and for the North as a whole is minor. They do indicate one possible means of offsetting uncertain markets, nevertheless.

Two other types of associations have been formed to meet the specific marketing difficulties of private timberland owners. Connwood, with headquarters in New Haven, Conn., was organized to promote forestry by aiding owners in harvesting, marketing, and processing forest products. Any producer of forest products who makes sales through the corporation is a participating member, and those who have subscribed for stock are voting members. Each voting member has one vote. After setting aside legal reserves, dividends on stock may be up to 6 percent and the remainder of the surplus, if any, is distributed on the basis of patronage. The corporation has successfully developed new markets for Connecticut forest products and thereby has helped owners to sell timber. The company employs its own forester and manager. The management hopes to obtain exclusive contracts with good market outlets, so that it can be in a position to demand good forest practices from persons who use its services. Sustained yield is advocated. In 1947, the corporation handled more than $70,000 worth of business for its members.

The New England Forestry Foundation, with headquarters in Boston, represents another effort to get private forests under management. It is a nonprofit corporation set up to give complete forestry service to woodland owners at cost. Work is conducted through management centers, each in charge of a trained forester. Forestry crews are organized and trained to work as private operators under contract on the lands of its clients. These crews, called forestry companies, do all kinds of silvicultural work as well as logging. All operations are under the direct supervision of a management forester.

The foundation now has six management centers in three States, eight full-time foresters, and three crews. It has more than 70,000 acres under management, which contain well above a million dollars worth of stumpage. The organization is still in the formative stage, and must raise funds privately for training foresters and for the overhead of organizing centers. It estimates that it will be completely self-supporting when it has 20 or 25 centers.

Both organizations and several cooperatives have tried to fill the gap that exists between what is feasible to do on the land and what operators are willing to do. None is organized primarily to make money for the stockholders or for timber processors; their task, rather, is to promote good markets and, through them, good forestry.

The tree-farm movement, under the leadership of the American Forest Products Industries and the State forestry organizations, is getting started.

Wisconsin has seven tree farms that cover 420,476 acres. Called industrial forests, they include some of the best and most intensively managed forests in the country. Among them are those of the Goodman Lumber Company, Nekoosa-Edwards Company, and the National Container Corporation.

Agencies in Michigan and Minnesota are interested in joining this tree-growing endeavor.

In the Central States, Ohio has eight tree farms that total 1,563 acres. In Missouri, Illinois, Kentucky, and Indiana, arrangements are being made to undertake the program.

In the East, Pennsylvania (with 11 units and 1,563 acres) and New Jersey (with 7 units and 9,151 acres) have tree farms in operation. West Virginia and Massachusetts started tree-farm projects in 1948.

Several advantages can be listed as reasons why the northern section offers opportunities for forestry:

1. The wide variety of species that possess high technical qualities, among them the valuable hardwoods like yellow birch, black cherry, black walnut, white ash, yellow-poplar, sugar maple.

2. Some of the best softwood trees to be found anywhere in the United States—white pine, white spruce, red spruce, black spruce, red pine, and the less-valuable but prolific jack pine, Virginia pine, shortleaf pine, balsam fir, and hemlock.

3. An intensively industrialized section, which offers potential markets for all types and sizes of forest products.

4. A climate conducive to good forest management, and fire-control organizations that have good records.

5. Accessible forest land. Except in northern Maine and the Adirondacks, most of the northern forest land has

good primary and secondary roads; a high percentage of the timber that is grown can be marketed.

6. Land values in keeping with productivity. Probably forest land is as reasonably priced now in the North as in any other section of the country; it is possible therefore for owners seriously interested in undertaking intensive forestry to purchase forest lands at prices that are not excessive, in view of the income that may be expected.

7. Manageable insect and disease problems. The North has had several devastating attacks by forest-insect pests and diseases—the chestnut blight, the spruce budworm, larch sawfly, LeConte sawfly, forest tent caterpillar, white pine blister rust, gypsy moth, beech scale, birch dieback, white-pine weevil, and others. Only the chestnut blight has eliminated a species, and even in that case forest recovery was rapid through quick expansion of associated forest trees. Modern control techniques and good management can keep losses moderate, and easy access permits salvaging of damaged timber.

8. Forests that respond rapidly to good management. Only foresters of long experience in managing a specific forest area can fully appreciate the point. An outstanding example is the Pack Demonstration Forest at Warrensburg, N. Y.—a property built up of abandoned farms. For more than 20 years the forest has largely paid its own way through receipts from timber harvested and processed. Capital values in terms of stumpage meanwhile have been accruing annually at the rate of $2 an acre. The property now supports one family for each 200 acres of land, with only one-half the growth being harvested. Agriculture in much of New York can do little better.

9. High prices for timber. On record are prices for ash and oak stumpage as high as $35 and $65 a thousand board feet; white oak of stave quality has brought $100. The ordinary run of timber in the North normally sells for higher prices than comparable qualities in the West and South.

THE OUTLOOK for private forestry in the North appears bright, considering the progress of the past 10 or 15 years. Forest lands are gradually being consolidated into stronger and more permanent hands. Pulp and paper companies particularly are taking over large areas of the valuable timber-growing land tributary to their mills. A few progressive lumber companies and some private foresters and investors have undertaken intensive forestry programs on lands they hold. Foresters are achieving places of high prominence in the timber-operating companies of the North and they are encouraging their companies to practice good forestry on the land they own and on lands near their operations.

Difficulties exist, to be sure. Progress has not all been permanent. Companies and private individuals that started out bravely on a good forest program have abandoned it for one reason or another and have reverted to the indifferent practices of the past. The number of new operators that are taking up forestry, however, exceeds those that are dropping out. The movement is in the right direction. High-quality timber is scarce throughout the North. Operators pay high prices for it. The increased importance of veneers, wood turnings, and other novelty products that bring high prices and yet can be made from timber in relatively small sizes has improved potential market outlets for managed forests. Markets for pole-sized timber such as would be taken out in thinnings and for low-grade hardwoods that should be removed in improvement cuttings remain spotty. Until these can be stabilized in each important timber-producing locality, forestry is not on a secure basis.

The trends in forest-land ownership may or may not be considered desirable. Gradually forest land is drifting into the hands of large owners, primarily pulp and paper companies. A large volume of timber still exists in the hands of farmers and other small owners. These lands are mostly too

802062°—49——19

scattered for a large holder to consolidate them for profitable management.

Disorganized markets, difficulties in selling to responsible operators, heavy taxes, and workmen's compensation insurance militate against a small timberland owner in the North. Equally difficult is the lack of good-quality growing stock on the land.

The public has already taken many steps to encourage better forest practice in the North. Good fire control, forest tax laws, service to private owners in forest management and marketing have been introduced by many States. These have been supplemented by the educational and service programs promoted by the Federal Government through State foresters and extension foresters. Research aimed at helping private owners is being extended and broadened. Yet the public needs to go further than it has to encourage full development.

A few pioneers, such as Luther and Watson, are doing outstanding work. More should be encouraged and the difficulties that beset them minimized. It is most important that outstanding leaders in the North recognize the problems they must face. They are taking progressive steps to meet them. The progressive thinking that has led to State forest practice acts, to State aid in management and marketing, and to starting organizations such as Connwood, the New England Forestry Foundation, and programs of experimental and demonstration forests is perhaps the best guarantee of a bright future for private forestry in the North.

HARDY L. SHIRLEY *is assistant dean, the New York State College of Forestry at Syracuse University.*

*The following furnished material for his article: Herman Work and W. R. Gingerich, West Virginia Pulp and Paper Company; James G. McClellan, American Forest Products Industries, Inc.; Harris A. Reynolds, New England Forestry Foundation; Ralph C. Hawley, Connwood, Inc.; Russell Watson, Manistique, Mich.; F. G. Kilp, Nekoosa-Edwards Paper Company; Karl A. Swenning, Hollingsworth and Whitney Company; C. S. Herr, Brown Company; William Hilton, Great Northern Paper Company; Robert Lyman, formerly with the Gray Chemical Company; George T. Carlisle, Prentiss and Carlisle Company, Inc.; George C. Sawyer, Houlton, Maine; David H. Hanaburgh, consulting forester, Buchanan, N. Y.; Lyman A. Beeman, Finch Pruyn Paper Company; C. O. Brown, International Paper Company; L. J. Freedman, Penobscot Development Company; R. B. Goodman, Goodman Lumber Company; D. B. Demeritt, Dead River Company; E. O. Ehrhart, Armstrong Forest Company; T. F. Luther, The Luther Forest; D. B. Bonebreak, Pocahontas Land Corporation; E. B. Moore, New Jersey Department of Conservation; Harold Round, Pennsylvania Railroad; A. A. Maxwell, Ruberoid Company; George Amidon, Minnesota and Ontario Paper Company; and E. B. Hurst, Consolidated Water Power and Paper Co.*

**A blazed tree on an old military trail in Coeur d'Alene National Forest, Idaho.**

# PRIVATE FORESTRY IN THE WEST

CHAS. L. TEBBE, H. J. ANDREWS

One-third of all existing saw timber in the United States is in the western half of Oregon and Washington. The entire West, with only one-fourth of the commercial forest land, supports two-thirds of the saw-timber volume. Some of the implications are at once apparent.

First of all is the growing dependence on the West for national requirements of forest products. Western lumber production has increased nearly 50 percent since 1938. The number of sawmills has more than doubled. Pulp-mill capacities are being expanded. Hitherto inaccessible areas are being operated. The country is getting its quality products in increasing amount from the virgin old-growth timber of the West.

Heretofore the East has provided the bulk of the national production (55 to 60 percent since 1929), but it has done that at the expense of its growing stock, and the size of the timber harvested has steadily declined.

The cutting and management practices used in harvesting the old-growth timber in the West must be such as to insure that a new crop of trees will be grown to replace the old forest after it is cut.

Responsibility for continued productivity is shared by Federal, State, and county governments and private owners, because all of them own or control timberland. Nearly 40 percent of western commercial forest land and timber, however, is in private hands. Generally speaking, this includes the best and most accessible timber and the most productive sites. It is also the scene of the greatest logging activity. About 72 percent of the 14 billion feet produced in the West in 1946 came from private lands. The kind of forestry practiced there during the initial cutting will determine in large measure the character, the scale, and the value of the contribution western timberlands can make in the future.

THE FIRST MAJOR REQUIREMENT that must be met if we are to achieve sustained yield is to have a sufficient quantity of merchantable second-growth timber available to fill our needs by the time the virgin forests have been cut. That means we must keep the cut-over lands fully productive and budget the cut of old growth so that the timber supply in an area will not be exhausted before a new crop of trees has grown to usable size.

If it takes 100 years for trees to attain sawlog size, it is obvious that an owner must not remove more than one-hundredth of his timber inventory each year; otherwise there will come a time when sustained yield will be disrupted. For example, if he clear-cuts his entire forest property at the rate of one-fiftieth of his supply, at the end of 50 years he will have no trees older than 50 years; if he uses the individual-tree selection system, the reserved trees will have to be cut before they have had time to put on enough growth to offset the amount cut. Each year the owner will be decreasing his capital instead of operating on the interest.

Cutting practices that will maintain productivity of forest land are a second prerequisite to sustained yield and to stabilized industry and communities. Many years of research and experience have defined cutting practices for most timber types. They are relatively easy to put into practice, especially in the well-stocked stands in the West. A little effort before logging and during logging will save more young trees and insure more prompt regeneration than will many times the effort expended in planting or other rehabilitation measures taken after a destructive logging operation.

Finally, if we are going to grow trees and manage forests, we must protect them from fire, insects, disease.

Of the three requirements, volume control, to insure continuity of production, is now the greatest problem. In large measure the pattern is already set, for, despite the shorter history and large timber inventory of the West, the forest-products industry here is by no means in its infancy. Development of private lands has been rapid.

The largest sawmills in the world are here. In Oregon and Washington, 1,200 sawmills annually produce as much lumber as do 37,000 sawmills in the East and South. Amortization of large-plant investments usually necessitates a large annual production. Even where this is not the case, a mill that is designed to turn out 100, 200, or 300 thousand feet of lumber each day cannot be operated economically on much less. When a plant or group of plants is once installed, therefore, timber requirements become inflexible, except within narrow limits. If the aggregate plant capacity is not geared to the capacity of the tributary land to grow timber, an excessive rate of cutting, ultimate timber shortage, and curtailed production are inevitable. Excess installed capacity was the fault most commonly committed in the early days by many of the older plants.

More important for the future is the character of plant installation now being made in hitherto undeveloped areas, in southwest Oregon and northwest California, for example. If, somehow, the lessons learned from experience were brought to bear on the pattern of mill installation in the new areas, volume control, sustained yield, and stabilized communities and pay rolls would be assured. But that does not appear to be in prospect. We are in a fair way to repeat the mistake that led to transitory sawmills elsewhere.

An illustration is in Lane County, Oreg., where the wealth of timber was so great that the sustained-yield capacity was estimated a few years ago at 832 million board feet annually. In 1938 some 86 sawmills consumed about 376 million board feet of logs, a moderate cut in view of the allowable cut under sustained yield. By 1943 the number of plants had increased to 128, and they consumed 879 million board feet of logs, somewhat more than the sustained-yield limitations. In 1944 the cut was 875 million feet; in 1946, 204 mills cut 955 million feet of timber.

In other areas also the pressures to overdevelop are tremendous. Communities want to grow; usually they welcome all mills that can possibly get a foothold in the territory. Nearly always small holdings are available for purchase, and afford new operators a chance to start. New plants go up in the expectation of getting more private and Government timber, and before long the cutting exceeds the sustained-yield capacity.

In the absence of control over the volume of timber cut, everything possible should be done to minimize the shock of the impending timber shortage and to shorten its duration. Everything depends then on keeping lands fully productive and on adopting good practices in cutting and utilization.

Of the 12 Western States, California, Oregon, Washington, Idaho, and New Mexico have regulatory laws governing cutting practices on private lands. The laws vary in regard to forestry requirements and administration. They are more effective in some States than in others, and within States the requirements in some timber types are more satisfactory from the standpoint of assuring continued productivity than in other timber types. They establish minimum requirements—a floor below which operators may not go. They do not assure sustained yield. It takes volume control as well as good cutting practices to do that. A maximum forest productivity can only result from more intensive practices, which depend, to a large extent, on individual private initiative. Notable progress has been made, but universal adoption of the best cutting practices is hampered by several factors.

Probably the basic explanation is no different here than it is elsewhere—the adoption of forestry practices means a break with the traditional way of doing things. But a few factors are peculiar to the West: Western forest properties are characteristically mountainous and relatively inaccessible, larger, uninhabited, and valuable chiefly for growing trees. Usually the properties are owned by the operators—mill operators or logging contractors. The timber in the virgin forest is large, heavy equipment is required, and roads that cost $20,000 or more a mile sometimes must be built and maintained to move the timber. Such are the factors that have discouraged frequent returns to an area to make successive light cuts, to salvage dying trees, to recover the values in trees left for seed. The tendency has been to remove all possible value and volume at the time of the first cut (in order to reduce the fixed per-acre cost to a minimum) and be done with the area indefinitely.

Another difficulty stems from the fact that most operators do not own sufficient timber for the plants whose amortization and inflexible log requirements dictate high-level production. They cannot or will not curtail the cut sufficiently to prolong their life until their own and the neighboring cut-over lands produce another forest of usable size. If that were done, then the proper cutting practices, the leaving of enough reserve stands, and other forestry measures would be matters of immediate self-interest.

A survey in 1945 attempted to appraise the treatment that was accorded all forest land then being operated. If it were repeated now, it would doubtless show improvement, but in 1945 the results left little doubt as to the urgency of the need for better forestry practices. Five ratings were used: High order, good, fair, poor, and destructive. In each instance, the basis of ratings was productivity of the land after cutting. A high-order rating required the best type of cutting to assure quantity and quality yields consistent with the full productive capacity of the land. A destructive rating was applied to land without timber values and without means for natural reproduction.

The cutting practices on all western private timberlands rated good and better on 5 percent of the 28,340,000 acres; fair on 34 percent; poor on 50 percent; and destructive on 11 percent.

Under the rating system that was used, the 39 percent of operating area rated at least fair was a measure of definite accomplishment. It indicated that much of the area received forestry treatment about as intensive as was practicable, considering current economic feasibility. But because the criterion was productivity of the land after cutting, regardless of economic or other conditions, the fact that 61 percent of the cutting was in poor or destructive classifications was indicative of the job ahead.

Signs of progress, however, are at hand. Western operators have dealt successfully with the problems of harvesting big timber in inaccessible country far from market. They have forged ahead in the development of superb plants and facilities. Logging tractors, heavy-duty logging trucks, and road-building machinery have set the pace for other sections of the country. In the mills that account for most of the production, precision equipment and perfection of manufacturing processes produce products of high quality.

Efficiency of operation enables western operators to compete in eastern markets despite the higher wage and freight rates.

Also, there is a growing consciousness of the need for forestry and of the opportunities in that field. Only a few years ago forestry and its terminology were the stock in trade of a few professional foresters. Now nearly every logger knows about forestry.

In 1947 some 212 foresters were employed by the private timber companies in the Douglas-fir region; 44 private consulting forestry firms employed 75 foresters, who worked with companies that did not have their own professional help; more than 130 foresters were employed by the lumber industry in California, and a smaller but growing number of foresters worked in Idaho and other Western States.

Another indicator of better days ahead is the belated but nonetheless remarkable increase in many parts of the West in the selling price of young timber and reproducing lands. Only a few years ago such land was accorded little or no value. Hundreds of thousands of acres of it reverted to the States and counties for taxes. Whether bare or well stocked with reproduction or poles, it all brought the same price, practically nothing. So, owners were denied the incentive they might have had to keep their lands productive. Now that has changed. Many a tract that was abandoned for taxes has since been bought back (frequently by the original owner) for $4 to $12 or more an acre.

Protection against fire is being improved through Federal, State, and private cooperation. Almost all private forest land in the Western States is now under protection. While serious losses continue to be sustained, size and frequency of fires have been reduced.

Many lumber and pulp and paper companies are augmenting their holdings and are consolidating ownerships. They are buying virgin timber to prolong their life in old-growth timber and delay the day of their dependence on second growth. They are buying second-growth timber and reproducing lands to increase ultimate growth and to improve their distribution of age classes. This large-scale purchase of reproducing land is one of the best indications of the serious intent of some operators to practice forestry and to stay in business permanently.

A parallel movement is the growth and development of tree farming. The first tree farm was established in the West in 1941. It was the forerunner of what has become a national program.

A new development with great possibilities is the integration of the forest-products industry—the installation of a variety of wood-using plants in conjunction with the ordinary single-purpose sawmill. The availability of a sawmill to use sawlogs, a veneer plant for peeler logs, a pulp plant for pulp species, fiberboard mills, pressed-log plants, bark-conversion plants, and others to utilize waste, in an integrated type of industry, gives the forest manager an outlet for all that the forest grows. There is less compulsion to direct the plans and cutting of the woods department to conform to the particular sizes, grades, and species of lumber that are in big demand at the time. The forest manager can cut the trees and the areas that need to be cut for silvicultural reasons. Each product of the forest is put to its highest use, with resultant wider margins and increased funds with which to intensify forest practices. In at least one instance both the raw material and the various utilization processes are in one ownership. In others a single timber property supplies plants of diversified ownership.

CHAS. L. TEBBE *is director of the Northern Rocky Mountain Forest and Range Experiment Station. He entered the Forest Service in 1934 and became assistant regional forester of the North Pacific Region in 1940. After graduation in forestry from the University of California, he worked for a number of years in western forest industry and spent 2 years developing large forest properties in the Philippine Islands.*

H. J. ANDREWS *has worked in the North Pacific Region of the Forest Service for 11 years, first as assistant regional forester and since 1943 as regional forester. He was in charge of forest surveys conducted by the Pacific Northwest Forest Experiment Station from 1930 to 1938. Mr. Andrews has been employed by lumber companies in the South, by the Michigan Department of Conservation, and as a member of the forest school faculties of the University of Michigan and Iowa State College.*

# FORESTRY ON LARGE OWNERSHIPS IN THE SOUTH

J. HERBERT STONE, CHARLES F. EVANS, W. R. HINE

In few places and in few times has interest in growing trees as a commercial crop been greater than it is now among the owners of large private forests in the South.

The reasons for this upsurge are many. So are the evidences of it. Pulp companies, sawmill owners, investment corporations, and the larger woodland owners are aware that trees have great market value. Prices obtained are high and supplies are limited. Public forests have demonstrated over and over that timber is a crop that grows. Many forest industries are placing their holdings under good forest management; instead of trying to sell cut-over land, they are buying additional areas of forest land; they are teaching forest management to their employees and to small owners from whom they buy forest products. Businessmen in the other fields, educators, legislators, and leaders in thought and action generally are taking an interest in the movement; they also have learned that timber is one of the South's great resources.

Between the Potomac and the Gulf of Mexico, from the Atlantic to the prairies of Texas and Oklahoma are 183 million acres of forest and potential forest land—40 percent of the commercial forest land of the country. Soil and climate, except in limited areas, are favorable for tree growth.

FOUR MAJOR TOPOGRAPHIC REGIONS are recognized: The mountains, the Piedmont, the Coastal Plains, and the Delta.

In the mountains, the forests are made up principally of hardwood trees, oaks, yellow-poplar, cherry, and others. The white pine and hemlock occur, mixed with the better hardwoods in the moist coves. Spruce grows on some of the higher, colder ridges. Shortleaf pine and some other pines mix with the hardwood species on the lower mountain slopes. Rainfall ranges from 60 to 100 inches a year. The rough and steep topography makes for difficult and expensive logging.

A substantial part of the mountain forest area is in public ownership, acquired for the purpose of controlling the rain and snow that fall on the headwaters of the navigable streams. Some large areas remain in private ownership. The rest is in small ownerships, strips of forest land running from the crop and pasture land in the valley up the slope to the ridge. Relatively slow growth and higher costs of logging make the mountain region a little less attractive to private forest enterprise than the other regions.

The Piedmont forests are a mixture of southern pines and upland hardwoods. The more prolific light-seeded pines have reclaimed large areas abandoned by agriculture. At one time or another, 90 percent of the Piedmont has been under cultivation. Hardwoods, however, come in under the pines, and often with or without the help of man, reclaim the area. Therein lies one of the most difficult problems.

Rainfall in the Piedmont averages about 60 inches annually. The topography is rolling; logging is relatively easy and inexpensive. The heavy rainfall, frequently in severe downpours, and an erodible soil, require especial care in locating log and skid roads and drainage to avoid soil depletion and damage to the water resource. Forest holdings in the Piedmont are mostly small and held as part of the farm.

On the Coastal Plains, forests are predominantly pine, including the longleaf, slash, loblolly, and shortleaf. Also included are the bottom-land hardwoods along the many rivers and the cypress and tupelo in the swamps.

Rainfall is heavy—usually averaging about 60 inches along the Gulf coast but dropping off gradually from the Mississippi westward to the treeless prairies. Logging is relatively easy and inexpensive, except in the swamps and deeper river bottoms and except during periods of prolonged rain. Tree growth is generally rapid. The large private holdings of the South are mostly located in the Coastal Plains along the Atlantic Ocean and the Gulf of Mexico, and in the rolling uplands of Texas, Arkansas, Louisiana, and Mississippi. A warm climate, abundant rainfall, and a long growing season assure excellent conditions for both the establishment and growth of trees. Most soils are reasonably well drained and can store water and plant nutrients. Throughout the region, trees are the paying crop for 57 percent of the land. With proper attention, this could be one of the most productive timber regions anywhere.

The Delta province is that area of fertile flood plain lying along the Mississippi River and stretching from southern Missouri to the Gulf. It embraces about 32 million acres.

The forest is composed largely of hardwood species and growth is rapid. Annual floods are the rule in this area, but the water does not remain on the land long enough to affect adversely growth or the regeneration. The condition of annual floods is, however, an obstacle to logging. The logging must be done in the summer and early fall. Some years this period is shortened materially by the summer rains. The heavy, large-sized timber that is obtained from the Delta forests requires a heavier and more expensive type of logging equipment than is ordinarily needed in the pine forests of the South.

There are wide variations in the fertility of the Delta soils. Many of them, however, are quite fertile and clearing for agriculture has been going on in the past. There may be some additional clearing in the future for this purpose. However, it seems probable that 40 to 50 percent of the area will remain in forests. Ownerships are medium to large. There are a number of sawmills with ownerships in excess of 50,000 acres. Large farms or plantations are more typical of the area than small ownerships, and many of these plantations include forest areas in excess of 1,000 acres.

The Delta is a productive timber area and tree crops can be made an increasingly important part of the local economy with good management. From the standpoint of forest practices, it is an area where the forest is least understood by foresters, and yet forests can furnish substantial employment and income to the people and forest products to the Nation. This source of employment looms more important as the mechanization of cotton production on the farms increases.

Forest industries are second only to agriculture in their contribution to the economy of the South. With a product estimated to be worth more than 2 billion dollars annually, the industry serves every citizen. It provides nearly every owner, large or small, with a market for forest products. Wood cutters, truck drivers, railroad men, sawmill hands, and many others earn wages handling forest products. The butcher, the banker, and the doctor serve the people who handle the forest products. In nearly every community, operating units of the forest industry employ workers, buy products, pay taxes. The contribution is so general and so long-continued that most people assume it will always be with us, not realizing that the timber resources on which this vast industry depends might play out.

In the latter part of the nineteenth century, the South felt the effect of the Nation's expansion. Large mills were constructed. They mowed down the virgin timber on a liquidation basis. The financial arrangements of that day were predicated on the rapid and the complete removal of the standing trees; the concept of timber as a crop was neither understood nor accepted by the industry. Gradually, the original stands were cut over and, by 1935, the virgin timber had been cut.

Hundreds of big mills had to quit. Smaller mills that cut smaller trees and required less volume a day took over. They cut the remnants and the second growth that had reached merchantable size since the first operation. In 1944, we still had 18,000 sawmills, which cut 12.6 billion board feet, or 38 percent of the country's lumber for that year.

Most of them are quite small. Eighty-two percent of the mills produce less than 1 million board feet a year, 16 percent produce 1 to 5 million, 2 percent produce 5 million or more. The sawmill industry brings in 1½ billion dollars of the South's total income.

The gum naval stores is one of the oldest industries. At its peak in 1908–9, it produced nearly 2 million drums of gum rosin; in 1946–47, about a third that much was produced because other sources of turpentine and rosin had been developed through destructive distillation of longleaf pine stumps and the recovery from pulp-mill wastes.

The pulp industry is our newest large forest industry. The first permanent pulp mill in the South was built by the Carolina Fibre Co. at Hartsville, S. C., in 1891. Growth of the industry was slow until the early 1930's but has been rapid for the past 15 years. Today, one-half the pulp and one-third of the paper of the United States is produced in the South. Some 50 mills utilize 8 million cords of wood annually. The industry is still expanding.

Thus far, the industry has concentrated on production of kraft paper. The difficulty of obtaining pulp and the pulpwood for the manufacture of paper for newsprint and other light-colored papers, however, is causing the industry to consider the South's possibilities in those fields also. The first newsprint mill in the South, built by the Southland Paper Co. at Lufkin, Tex., started production in 1940. A second mill was started in 1948.

The pulp and paper industry has stimulated business in the South. Communities where pulp mills have been built have prospered. The industry has invested more than a billion dollars and manufactures products that add 500 million dollars to the income of the region. An estimated 100,000 persons are employed directly in the production, transportation, and manufacture of wood pulp.

Many other products are obtained from the forests and form an important part of the raw material for the forest industry—poles, piling, cross ties, fence posts, fuel wood, pipe bowls, handles, and furniture among them. Each is important: Fuel wood is the only heating material available to millions of southerners, and is especially important to many tobacco farmers, who use it to cure tobacco. More oil is being used for heating, but the trend may be halted by limitations in the oil supply and through improvements in wood-burning equipment. Mines must have wood props. Electric companies must have wooden poles. Railroads must have wooden cross ties. Chemistry is transforming wood into clothing, cattle feed, plastics, and many other new products. All point up the fact that the welfare of the cities of the South is closely keyed to the proper management of the timber resource; more wood products mean more industry, more industry means more pay rolls, more pay rolls mean more business for the cities.

Forest lands in the South require protection from uncontrolled fire. They should be so managed that succeeding cuts of forest products will maintain and build up the growing stock of trees for the production of continuous crops of forest products. A survey in 1945, made by State and Federal foresters, shows how the forest lands are being protected and managed. On large ownerships (holdings of more than 5,000 acres), fire protection was rated as adequate on 38 percent and inadequate or nonexistent on the rest; cutting practices were considered good on 32 percent, fair on 26 percent, and poor on 42 percent. On holdings of fewer than 5,000 acres, fire protection was rated as adequate on 42 percent and inadequate on the rest; cutting practices were good on 2 percent, only fair on 24 percent, and poor on 74 percent.

Although large holdings as a rule are more exposed to fire and the fires that start there are not so easily controlled, the owners of large holdings are doing about as well as the owners of small holdings in controlling fires. Large holdings likewise show a substantially better job in harvesting practices than the small private holdings.

Less than 25 years ago, thousands of forest fires annually burned millions of acres in the South. The risk of losing the accumulated growth of many years through a single fire kept prudent men from attempting to practice forest management. But with Federal and State help, under the Weeks Law and later under the Clarke-McNary Law, protection of the forest lands became feasible, and gradually the larger holdings were placed under organized protection under State supervision. Today 80 percent of the larger holdings are under organized protection, although as yet not all are adequately protected. Many of the larger owners, recognizing the need for more intensive protection, have supplemented the States' efforts with extra men, tools, tractors, plows.

Seventeen million acres of large private holdings were rated in 1944 as receiving adequate protection from forest fires. For areas in the loblolly-shortleaf-hardwood type, that means a burn of less than 1 percent annually over a 5-year period. While forest fires remain an ever-present threat, and continue to take a toll in wasted timber growth running into millions of dollars annually, the fire problem has been solved to the point where a large owner is reasonably sure that he can grow a paying forest crop, provided he pays the cost of protection, 5 to 10 cents an acre annually, and carries out the practices now recommended.

One-third of the larger owners followed good cutting practices in 1944—meaning that the owner selected the trees to be cut from his woods and left trees in adequate number to assure reasonable stocking and improved succeeding stands. More than 3 million acres on large ownerships showed a high order of forest-management practice.

The Crossett Lumber Co., of Crossett, Ark., illustrates how many ownerships follow sound cutting practices. The company is now cooperating with the Arkansas Forestry Commission in organized protection of its 500,000 acres under the Clarke-McNary Law. Besides the fire crews and equipment available throughout the regular State organization, the company provides extra crews and equipment, as needed, to the State's chief of fire control. The trees cut from the forest are closely utilized in an integrated set of plants that produce lumber, pulp, chemicals, and lesser products. Nonmerchantable trees are destroyed by girdling or poisoning. Bare and nonrestocking lands are replanted to trees. Foresters direct all woods operations; a forester is in charge of each block of 50,000 acres.

The more than 5 million acres that the pulp companies own in the South are under organized fire control; more than three-fourths are being cut according to good or better cutting practices, and the rest is cut so as to assure continuous crops of pulpwood.

THE PULP AND PAPER INDUSTRY uses less than 10 percent of the timber taken from the southern forests; the demand for wood has already brought the several pulp companies in competition with each other and with other segments of the forest industry. In order to assure adequate supplies of wood, all pulp companies have acquired a substantial portion of the necessary forest acreage. Some are undoubtedly in a position to grow their needs; others are not, and the pulp industry as a whole is not. Prices of forest lands have risen materially, and the remaining large blocks of forest land are strongly held. A large part of the forest land, particularly that included in the 61 million acres of farm ownership, is not available for purchase.

Several of the pulp companies are taking steps to bring all their acreage into full production. A new practice is to rid their lands of worthless trees by girdling in order to permit good young trees to grow. The process, which costs generally from $1 to $5 an acre, is less expensive than planting an equal area. The industry planted 19 million trees on fee lands in 1947–48, and furnished 7 million seedlings free to growers of pulpwood. Many companies are planting their idle lands as fast as seedlings can be grown in their own or in State nurseries. An example is the Gaylord Container Corp., which has more than 50,000 acres in plantations.

The pulp industry also encourages other private owners to put their forest lands under good management. For example, the Southern Kraft Division of the International Paper Co. employs in the South many foresters at the present time, some of whom supervise the cutting and forest-improvement operations on company lands, while the others assist private owners from whom the company buys pulpwood.

The Southern Pulpwood Conservation Association, whose membership includes the leading pulp companies of the South, carries on a campaign to promote good forest practice by its member mills and by the owners from whom the industry buys wood. The association employs three foresters to advise and assist pulpwood contractors and small-woodland owners in better cutting practices. Member mills now employ 18 foresters to promote better practices in their own territory.

The heavy demand for wood has worked in two ways. The favorable market for pulpwood, small sawlogs, and other small products has shortened the period an owner must wait for his returns and created a market for small trees. On the other hand, the market for such small material has led many owners to cut far more heavily than before. Where the owner does not cut conservatively, the net result is to reduce his over-all return and to reduce the total volume of wood products.

Large sawmill holdings are often under conservative forest management. About 90 percent of the holdings are under organized protection from forest fire and about one-half are managed according to good or better cutting practices. The Urania Lumber Co., which in the early 1900's pioneered in the practice of forestry, has succeeded so well in its management that its mill, instead of cutting out as did many of its contemporaries, must be materially enlarged to harvest its current annual growth. Other examples from all over the South could be cited; altogether, some 8 million acres of forest lands in sawmill ownership were reported as under good or better management in 1945; on several million acres more, practices have improved since 1945.

In the Delta hardwoods the Anderson Tully Lumber Company of Memphis owns more than 200,000 acres on which good forestry is being practiced. The company is looking to sustained operation.

But the sawmill industry as a whole is not so well off. On one-half of the sawmill ownership in 1945 cutting practice was fair or poor—an inadequate stand, or perhaps only seedlings and seed trees were left. The sawmill industry draws on the entire South for its timber. The South was obliged to cut 24.9 percent more timber of sawlog size in 1944 than it grew in that year. Standing saw-timber resources have been declining for many years. The sawmill industry and other industries that use trees 9 inches in diameter and larger at 4½ feet from the ground face a situation of declining timber supplies. Greater progress than we have thus far made is necessary if we are to continue to hold the industry on its present scale.

The naval stores industry likewise is making progress in the practice of better forest management. Seventy-nine percent of the industry, based on number of working faces, is cooperating under the Naval Stores Conservation Program, which requires conservative chipping practices. Many operators have adopted even more progressive measures than are required in the program and are chipping only a part of the operable stand, leaving some trees to grow to an even larger, more profitable size. Nonrestocking stands are now being planted.

There is a growing recognition of the interdependence of one industry on another. Certain pulp companies sell trees of sawlog size to the lumber industry. The lumber industry and the naval stores industry sell thinning and tops to the pulp industry, and the naval stores industry has an opportunity to turpentine a portion of the trees used by both the sawmills and pulp mills prior to harvest.

Nonforest-industry owners hold about 40 percent of the forest land in large holdings; they include investment holdings, mining companies, railroads, oil companies, game clubs, and individuals. Timber growing is a secondary interest for most of them. Ownership there is more likely to change than where the land is held by forest industries. As a result, policies affecting the timber resource vary greatly and, on the whole, the timber resource is less well protected and managed.

Even in this group there is progress in forest management. The increasing value of stumpage has brought added returns and established higher values for land. The Tennessee Coal & Iron Co., recognizing an increased value for the mine props and other products used in its mining operations, has had its land under protection and management for a number of years. The Atlantic Coast Line Railroad recently placed 100,000 acres of land in south Florida under protection and good management. Game clubs have found that, through a reasonable compromise, timber can be grown and harvested on lands devoted primarily to game. Investment companies have frequently found that the timber, long overlooked, has managed to produce a crop of real value, one that will require consideration in the future policy of management. Several investment companies have made agreements providing for orderly cutting.

The outlook for private forestry on large ownerships in the South is bright. Markets for forest products are strong and bid fair to continue so for some years. The South is entering a period of industrial expansion and needs much lumber for construction. The pulp industry, which already produces half the Nation's pulp from southern trees, is still expanding. Makers of furniture also are moving into the South. Not only must the South supply its own needs, it must continue to supply forest products for other users.

The South offers good prospects for timber growing as a business. A warm climate, long growing season, and ample rainfall assure excellent growth where soil and drainage are good. The species grown mostly are softwoods, which make up 90 percent of the wood in commerce. Logging is a relatively simple engineering operation and costs are low. The South has a good transportation system and the timber is readily accessible to world markets.

Some problems must be faced. The first is fire, but we think the day of fire control throughout the South will not long be delayed. State legislatures are increasing the appropriations for the work. Three of 12 Southern States have authorized State-wide fire control.

Another problem is regeneration of stands. Regeneration through natural seeding is generally well assured if ample seed trees of the right species are left, but over much of the loblolly-shortleaf-hardwood type, less desirable hardwoods often claim the soil after cutting, and tend to exclude the higher-yielding pines. That is especially true in the Piedmont area. Killing through girdling is a practical answer for a part of the region, but in some areas, the best answer has not yet been found. Meanwhile, good hardwoods make a desirable crop.

Again, hogs or sheep destroy all reproduction over large areas of longleaf pine lands. The problem has now been solved on some areas, with satisfactory returns to the owner, through fencing and planting.

Some areas have been so severely cut over as to preclude restocking from the remaining trees. Artificial reforestation with machines now does a satisfactory job at a reasonable cost. Several large owners, as well as many smaller ones, who planted 15 and 20 years ago have already harvested thinnings enough to repay all costs to date and have excellent stands for future growth.

Perhaps the most universal problem is to increase the stocking of high-quality trees. The timber stands today are second-growth. They have sprung up untended. They are a mixture of trees of good form and trees of poor form; crowded trees and trees with too much space for proper development; diseased or scarred trees and healthy, uninjured trees. The greatest single task is to improve those stands systematically. It will take several cuts over the years.

More skilled forest managers are needed. They can help landowners to increase average rates of about 150 board feet an acre a year to 400 board feet an acre on good land. Skilled management can be expected to increase the quality also.

While the prospect for improved forest management on large private ownerships is bright, there is no basis for complacency. No large segment of the forest industry owns enough land to supply its own needs for forest products. Currently, the South is cutting 25 percent more timber of sawlog size than is being grown. The sawmill industry, with less than 10 percent of the forest land, cannot hope to produce more than a fraction of its timber requirements, even if all its holdings were under intensive management. While individual mills or companies may be able to grow their own needs, the forest industry as a whole is dependent on the 122 million acres in small private holdings.

If the present trend of overcutting and deterioration continues, we may expect a pinching off of the industries using sawlog-size trees. It is possible that the same trend continued may curtail operations even for the industries using the smaller-sized trees. Certainly there will be much keener competition. Shortage of timber supplies and unreasonably high prices for forest products will lead to the use of substitutes. Both tend to reduce and curtail the forest industry and its services to the South and the Nation.

Large ownerships can serve their own interests and the interests of the areas from which they draw forest products by placing their own holdings under high-order protection and management. Through their work, they can lead others to an appreciation of good forest practices. Second, and perhaps of more significance, they should follow good forestry practices when cutting forest products from the lands of others. Finally, in the interest of assuring ample supplies of wood as a basic raw material, large-forest owners should support programs of education and service that are designed to help the 1,500,000 owners of the small-woodland tracts on which the industry depends for 75 percent of its raw forest products.

J. HERBERT STONE *is regional forester in charge of Forest Service activities, except research, in the Southern Region. He is a native of Connecticut and holds degrees in forestry from Yale University.*

CHARLES F. EVANS, *a native of Wisconsin, is assistant regional forester in charge of cooperative forestry work in the Southern Region of the Forest Service. Mr. Evans holds degrees from the University of Wisconsin and Yale University.*

W. R. HINE *is in charge of the Division of Information and Education of the Southern Region of the Forest Service. He is a native of New York and holds a degree in forestry from Cornell University.*

# NAVAL STORES: THE INDUSTRY

JAY WARD

Naval stores are the derivatives of the crude gum—oleoresin—that comes from living pine trees, pine stumps, and dead lightwood. Some are byproducts from sulfate pulp mills. The term is limited generally to turpentine and rosin, but it can be said to cover pine tar, pine oil, and rosin oils. In the trade, the product from living pine trees is known as gum naval stores; the product from stumps, lightwood, and pulp mills is called wood naval stores. In Colonial days, gum was cooked down to a thick tar and used to preserve the ropes and calk the seams of the ships—and from that we got the name "naval stores" for the products used now in a hundred ways unconnected with ships.

The gum naval stores industry, at its peak in 1908–9, produced 750,000 barrels (50 gallons each) of gum spirits of turpentine and 1,998,400 drums of gum rosin (520 pounds net weight each). The United States in normal times supplies the world with one-half its needs for turpentine and rosin. Since 1938, the production of gum naval stores has fallen off considerably. The industry in 1947–48 produced 294,028 barrels of turpentine and 828,128 drums of rosin, bringing a total return to the South of 39 million dollars.

The naval stores industry is rooted in antiquity. It antedates the Christian era in the Mediterranean countries. Early historians wrote of the process then used: How the natives gathered the resins or gums of the trees in that region and cooked them in open pots until a thick pitch was left in the bottom; how they stretched fleecy sheepskins over the tops of the pots to catch the oily vapors that arose from the boiling gum, and then wrung out the wet fleece to recover the oils; and how the oils were used in many products, one of which was for varnish for mummies. Genesis records that Noah was commanded by the Lord: "Make thee an ark of gopher wood; rooms shalt thou make in the ark, and shalt pitch it within and without with pitch."

When Columbus discovered America, the center of production in Europe extended from Scandinavia through the Baltic countries. From them came quantities of tar and pitch for use by the fleets of wooden sailing vessels of all the European nations. King Phillip of Spain drew from this source for his Spanish Armada. Queen Elizabeth drew from it for her British fleet. One of the basic commodities sought by the Europeans in the New World was a source of naval stores for their ships.

Turpentining is one of the oldest and most picturesque of American industries. The production of tar, pitch, rosin, and turpentine started when the first settlers landed on the Atlantic coast. The report of Sir Walter Raleigh's first expedition to America in 1584 referred to "the great forests of pine of species unknown to Europe until found in the New World." The report of the second expedition mentioned once again "the trees that yielded pitch, tar, rosin, and turpentine in great store."

In 1608 eight Dutchmen were sent to Virginia to make pitch, tar, soap, and rosin. Two years earlier, in 1606, the French were drawing turpentine gum from the trees of Nova Scotia. In *The Maine Woods,* Thoreau told about the tar burners of New England. One of the earliest acts of the Pilgrim Fathers was to request in 1628 that "men skylful in the making of pitch" be sent to them from England. The Plymouth and Massachusetts Bay Colonies produced great quantities of tar and pitch from their beginning as colonies, as did all the other North Atlantic colonies from Maine to New Jersey. The first tar burners in New England and later on in North Carolina used the dead and down wood, or, the dead down lightwood, which they found in large quantities in the virgin forests all about them.

Colonists began coming in large numbers to North Carolina about 1665, and tar burning, a practice which until then had been a New England monopoly, began to take hold quickly. The new settlers in North Carolina, moreover, soon discovered that the abundant growth of southern yellow, or longleaf, pine was a more prolific source of gum than the pitch pine of New England. By 1700 the production of naval stores was an important part of the economy of North Carolina. As in New England, gum, tar, and pitch became established as accepted media of exchange in the payment of rent and public dues.

So important did England consider her source of naval stores in the Colonies that bounties and premiums were paid to producers to stimulate production and improve the quality of the products. The bounties, which were designed to equalize the heavy freight costs across the Atlantic in competition with the Scandinavian and other European producers, continued to be paid until the beginning of the Revolutionary War. In 1728 the British Navigation Acts prohibited the Colonies from shipping direct to any foreign country pitch, tar, and the crude gum, along with other specified commodities. The laws required the routing of such commodities through English ports. Measures for the regulation of the industry and for the payment of bounties were introduced by the Royal Governor of North Carolina: In 1735, providing for inspection of the operations; in 1736, prohibiting the encroachment of tar burners on crown lands; and in 1764, regulating the quality and quantity of all tar, pitch, and turpentine barreled and sold, even requiring the producer's brand on all barrels.

When the Colonies became a Nation that was trying to establish itself in world affairs and build up trade with other nations, naval stores had a significant role in merchant shipping. Naval stores served as a tribute with which we bought partial safety for our vessels on the seas, especially in the Barbary States of North Africa. In 1815 the States, with force, overcame the pirates of Tripoli, Tunis, and Algiers, and ceased paying the tribute.

The area of production of gum naval stores has shifted through the years. The first change from New England southward came about when it was found that the longleaf pine trees were better yielders than the pitch pine of New England. In 1850, North Carolina and South Carolina accounted for more than 95 percent of the total American production. The Carolinas did not keep up this yield, and in 1947 they accounted for less than half of 1 percent of the total production. The shift was brought about by the clear cutting of the virgin stands in those States without leaving enough seed trees for reproduction. Such exploitation of the virgin forests continued southward and westward through all the South Atlantic and Gulf States into eastern Texas.

As late as 1920, it was generally thought and officially predicted that within another 10 years gum production in this country would be practically at an end. That belief, probably more than anything else, gave rise to the development of the wood naval stores industry. Nature, however, has confounded the experts; instead of the failure of reforestation in the deep South, second-growth longleaf and slash pines have abounded to an extent that indicates that the production of gum naval stores can continue indefinitely. The major part of our production the past several years has come from about 150 counties in South Carolina, Georgia, Florida, Alabama, Mississippi, and Louisiana. Southern Georgia and northern Florida produce more than 90 percent of the total.

During the seventeenth and eighteenth centuries, the crude gum was gathered in the woods, shipped to the eastern seaports of Wilmington, Philadelphia, and New York, and forwarded to England for distillation. The technique in the woods consisted in what is known as the "boxing" system. By that system, a cavity or "box" was cut into the base of the tree to catch and hold the crude gum as it flowed down the trunk of the tree after scarification or "chipping," which, then as now, was performed with a chipping tool or hack on each tree or "face" weekly from about March 15 until October or November. The boxing type of operation continued until the early part of the twentieth century. It was then found that, because of the smaller diameter of the second-growth pines, some improvements would have to be made.

Experiments conducted in 1901 and 1902 by Dr. Charles H. Herty led to the adoption of the cup and gutter system, which is still being used. Antedating the work of Dr. Herty, W. W. Ashe conducted experiments at Bladenboro, N. C., in 1894 in an effort to demonstrate the advantages of using cups and gutters over the practice of boxing the trees.

The crude cast-iron retorts that were used in the early distillation process gave a poor quality of product because of the reaction from the iron and because no water was added to the gum. About 1834 copper-pot stills were introduced. They were partly enclosed by brick work and the heat was applied directly from wood fires. Water was added to the gum; when heat was applied a separation of the gum took place. The condensed vapors produced the turpentine, and the residue in the still produced rosin. The turpentine, combined with water, was drawn off from the still and was passed through a simple dehydrator that contained rock salt. After this separation, the turpentine was run into barrels or tank cars for shipment, or into large tanks for storage. The melted rosin was then drawn off from the base of the still and passed through the wire strainers and layers of cotton batting attached to the wire screen. The rosin, still hot, was packed in barrels or drums, or in thick paper bags for marketing.

A naval stores experiment station under the supervision of the Department of Agriculture was established at Olustee, Fla., in 1932. The station has developed better gum-distillation methods and has done much to foster the establishment of large central distillation plants, an idea that originated with McGarvey Cline, a former director of the Forest Products Laboratory. The first central plant was completed by the Glidden Co., in 1934, in Jacksonville, Fla. In 1948 about 30 such plants, strategically located through the naval stores belt, processed more than 80 percent of all the gum. They have displaced all but about 100 of the small old-time backwoods fire stills, about 1,300 of which were scattered throughout the piney woods in 1933.

CENTRAL DISTILLATION means a more uniform product, better packaging, and improved facilities for distribution. The central plants, by providing a ready cash market, have opened the way for the smaller owner of timber to work his own timber rather than lease it to the old-time large commercial operators. The owner thus gets a better profit from this byproduct of his forest. Forest conservation is another result.

The change to central distillation has had a part also in breaking down the old factorage system of financing. Because working out a turpentine place took many years, an operator rarely could get credit from the commercial banks. Usually the large amounts of money required to set up and maintain a commercial turpentine operation were supplied by a few large quasi-banking institutions known as factors, who extended credit for the payment of leases on turpentine timber (usually for a minimum of 4 years), for the purchase of livestock, trucks, cups, tins, and for advances to pay wages.

Most of the factors also operated wholesale grocery and supply departments from which food, stock feed, clothing, and other supplies were furnished to the operator. In turn, the operator would set up his own commissary, from which he would dole out rations to his woods and still workers. The factors were protected by a blanket mortgage and usually by an insurance policy on the life of the operator. The operator had to deliver all the turpentine and rosin he produced to the factor as his selling agent. The deliveries were usually made to a storage yard, where the operator would get a warehouse receipt to be turned over to the factor.

Although the factor charged a liberal commission and initial storage and insurance charges, his services as sales agent were often simply paper transactions. Under this system the factors had a controlling influence on the entire gum naval stores industry. Their profits were large, but the risks they took were great and many bad-debt losses were incurred. This feudalistic pattern of financing was bitterly criticized, but it seemed to be the only system that could be devised under the circumstances; without it, the industry hardly could have survived.

Tar burning, which was practiced in New England, prevails in a few places in South Carolina, Florida, and Louisiana, the methods there being much the same as in Colonial times. Lightwood is stacked and covered with dirt (and sometimes with sheet iron) to make a kiln. A hole is dug in the firm ground, or, sometimes, a concrete base is provided for catching the pine tar that flows from the slowly burning timbers. A residue of charcoal is left.

The process has an improved, modern counterpart in destructive distillation, in which the wood—pine stumps and dead down lightwood—is placed in a retort. Heat applied to the retort gives both a light oil distillate and a heavy oil or pine tar oil distillate. The light oil distillate is refined to make DD wood turpentine, dipentene, and pine oil; the heavy oil distillate is refined to produce various types of oils to meet specific needs for insecticides, plasticizers, soaps, pharmaceuticals.

802062°—49——20

In the steam-solvent process, the stumps are hogged, or ground, and placed in heated digesters. Live steam is introduced and the more volatile components are carried off and condensed. Later they are refined by fractional distillation into steam-distilled wood turpentine and pine oil. The remaining shredded resinous wood is treated with a mineral-oil solvent, which dissolves the rosin and the high-boiling liquid products. The solution is clarified and the solvent is evaporated, leaving a residue of wood rosin. The extracted wood is used for fuel or paper pulp. A variation of the steam-solvent process consists of first extracting the turpentine, rosin, and pine oil with a suitable solvent, and then separating those products by fractional distillation with steam.

Sulfate wood turpentine is recovered by condensing the vapors that are released from the pulping digesters in the production of pulp from pine wood by the sulfate process of making paper. The crude byproduct is heavily contaminated with sulfur compounds, which are removed by chemical treatment and fractional distillation. The refined byproduct is marketed as sulfate wood turpentine. The spent cooking liquor obtained in this method of making paper pulp, commonly called black liquor, is treated to recover a mixture of fatty and resin acids known as tall oil or liquid rosin.

OF 10,000-ODD PRODUCERS of gum, more than 7,000 are small gum farmers who work less than one crop of turpentine faces on farm wood lots (a crop consists of 10,000 faces). Fewer than 2 percent are commercial operators who work more than 10 crops. In 1947 only 55 operated more than 20 crops.

The old-time commercial operator worked leased timber almost exclusively; sometimes in the past a turpentining operation would be made up of leased timber from as many as 300 or 400 separate owners. Most of these larger producers' operations are now confined to large corporately owned tracts. One of the largest of these tracts in the naval stores belt, for instance, is the Suwanee Forest of the Superior Pine Products Co., at Fargo, Ga. The tract contains 209,000 acres of timber, which has been efficiently managed for more than 20 years. The naval stores operations on the tract have been conducted by Harley Langdale, of Valdosta, Ga. Besides this acreage, Judge Langdale works other leased lands and fee-owned lands, and is regarded as the largest producer of gum naval stores.

More than 20 years ago the Sessoms Land & Lumber Co. acquired a tract of about 80,000 acres in Clinch and adjoining counties of Georgia. Among those who joined Alex K. Sessoms, of Cogdell, Ga., in establishing this timber-management unit was Austin Cary of the Department of Agriculture, to whom goes great credit for developing good forestry practices in the naval stores belt. The tract has been operated for naval stores by three brothers, Robert, Gordon, and Clarence Newton, who are the third generation of Newtons to engage in the industry, and who now operate three large units in Georgia and one in Mississippi.

Another large holding is that of the Tennessee Coal & Iron Co. in southern Alabama. For several years it has been operated on a lease basis by the Stallworth family of Mobile.

Another firm that has managed expertly large timber holdings is the Brunswick-Peninsula Corp., of Brunswick, Ga. It was founded by the late R. E. Benedict, a professional forester who had worked for the Forest Service and the Canadian Forestry Commission, and M. L. Rue, who is now the head of the enterprise. They purchased 110,000 acres of timberland 25 years ago in Glynn, Wayne, Brantley, Ware, and Clinch Counties in Georgia with the main aim of producing naval stores.

Among others who also have contributed toward improved conditions in the industry are W. B. Gillican, of Homerville, Ga., who, in a lifetime association with it, has exerted a wholesome influence on practically every phase of the industry; Turpentine and Rosin Factors, Inc., of Jacksonville, Fla., which for many years has been a large factorage house and which has since become a large distributor of turpentine in convenient and attractive containers; the factorage-dealer concerns of Taylor, Lowenstein & Co., of Mobile, Ala., and the Peninsula-Lurton Co., of Pensacola, Fla., which operate central distillation plants; the Columbia Naval Stores Co., of Savannah, Ga., which for many years was a large dealer organization and now operates several central distillation plants; James Fowler, of Soperton, Ga., who started planting forest trees on his 14,000-acre cropland plantation in 1925 and is now a foremost individual planter of tree seedlings; and the Gillis family, also of Soperton and among the pioneers in forest-tree planting.

Each of the pulp mills established in the South in the past several years has acquired large tracts of timber to insure a continuing supply of pulpwood. The holdings range from 50,000 to 600,000 acres. It is believed that the firms plan to lease the properties to experienced turpentine operators, who will manage them properly, before final harvesting. In that way the forests will serve the multiple purpose of providing naval stores, poles, piling, and lumber, besides pulpwood; complete utilization of the timberlands will lessen the waste that would result from their use as a single-crop operation.

The gum naval stores industry has always been generally classified as a low-wage industry. In public hearings in 1933 it was brought out that the average worker's income was less than $6 a week. As late as 1940, the average wage of chippers was $7.50 a week; in 1948 it was about $32.

Besides the increase in earnings, improvements have been made in the past several years in the living quarters furnished the turpentine woods workers. Instead of miserable cabins with only clapboard shutters for windows, many workers now live in better cabins that have glass windows and electricity.

Many of the improvements in the methods of production, processing, and marketing gum naval stores have resulted from experimental and research work in the Department of Agriculture. Besides the ones I have mentioned, better chipping methods have come from demonstrations that the narrower and lighter streaks will produce just as much gum and will help conserve timber. A method has been developed for the application of acid stimulants to freshly streaked turpentine faces to prolong the gum flow. With that development came a bark-chipping hack and a satisfactory device for the application of acid. Other experiments look to greater mechanization in turpentining practices. Another project now in progress seeks to develop a high-yielding strain of turpentine pines. Under Federal-State cooperation, nurseries have been established to provide planting stock; from the nurseries in the naval stores belt, many millions of seedlings have been supplied to owners of turpentine timber. Interest is increasing in the establishment of planted turpentine orchards.

Jay Ward, *a native of Tennessee, came to the Department of Agriculture as a marketing specialist with the Agricultural Adjustment Administration in 1933. From 1936 until his retirement in October 1948, he was in charge of the Naval Stores Conservation Program, which was set up in 1936 under the Soil Conservation and Domestic Allotment Act and administered by the Forest Service. A graduate of Benton College of Law at St. Louis, he practiced law in Missouri and engaged in various business enterprises before entering the employ of the Federal Government.*

# NAVAL STORES: THE FORESTS

CARL E. OSTROM, JOHN W. SQUIRES

The naval stores belt extends across the Coastal Plain from the Savannah River to the Mississippi. It is a favored section for growing forest crops. Each acre of pineland can produce wood products, gum naval stores, and forage. Although the soils in most of the area are relatively poor for field crops, the long growing season insures growth of trees. The level topography makes almost every acre of dry land accessible for the easy removal of products. Tree planting is cheaper and easier than elsewhere in the country.

Forests occupy nearly three-fourths of the land area in the belt. Forest activities dominate the lives of scores of counties and towns, especially in the continuous forest areas of the "flatwoods," or lower Coastal Plain near the coast. Rail and road traffic runs heavily to pulpwood, logs, poles, gum barrels, rosin drums, and stump wood. Agricultural crops mostly are of minor importance. A large proportion of the rural people work in the woods, and get much of their fuel and meat from them.

People in the area are especially aware of the importance of forests to the future of the South. Residents who have watched slash pine stands or plantations spring up under protection are convinced of the importance of pine forests to the future of their communities. Nevertheless, it is quite clear that these pine forests are producing less than half as much as they could. It is obvious that doubling the size of the forest industries is the biggest thing that could happen in sections where forests already provide the greatest source of income.

The first steps in doubling the forest production in the naval stores belt are the rather elementary ones of fire protection and tree planting. The size of that task is shown in figures for Florida, which contains half of the 44 million acres of forest land in the naval stores belt. In Florida, one-half of the land is still without fire protection and some 3 million acres are in need of planting. Fire protection and stocking are somewhat better in the naval stores section of Georgia, Alabama, and Mississippi.

Forest management in the region is of great complexity. The forester does not merely harvest ripe trees; he maintains the flow of a wide variety of products—naval stores, pulpwood, ties, logs, poles, piling, cattle. For localized areas in the southern pine region, particularly in the heavy rough of Florida, to get protection he usually must burn the underbrush every few years, and the burning, turpentining, timber cutting, and grazing all must be scheduled as to time and location so that the owner will realize the maximum net income from his forest property.

FOREST MANAGEMENT in the area is still dominated by naval stores but less than before. The first efforts at turpentining second-growth trees several decades ago were often ruinous. A description of an operation in 1911 says that trees as small as 5 inches in diameter were turpentined, as many "faces" were placed on each tree as the space would allow and the faces were started high enough to avoid any bending over, and the wounds or "streaks" were an inch in depth and height. After 5 years about half the trees were dead. The timber was cut and the area was abandoned.

Foresters and leaders of the naval stores industry, seriously alarmed over the threat to future timber supplies caused by the premature and careless turpentining, in 1924 sent a commission to France and Spain to study the methods used there.

This constructive attitude and technical improvements developed by early research workers brought considerable progress in conservation. Substitution of the cup for the "box" chopped in the base of the tree reduced windthrow and damage to the trees by surface fires. It also reduced waste of gum and improved its quality. Conversion of the industry to more conservative chipping practices gave higher sustained production of gum, lowered mortality and windthrow, and increased the working life of the surviving trees. The practices were demonstrated on a large scale in national forests in Florida, where provisions written into the leases required producers to use methods that reduced damage to the trees and also gave the highest yields of gum over a period of several years.

The Naval Stores Conservation Program established in 1936 provided for a conservation payment per face to producers who meet the standards of good practice established by foresters and representatives of the industry. It has been an effective instrument for the introduction of improved methods of turpentining, among them a provision to prohibit tapping of trees under 9 inches. Now only a small fraction of all trees tapped are smaller than the recommended size.

The improvements in woods practice went a long way toward remedying unnecessary wastefulness and destruction of individual trees. But one improvement only paves the way for others. There remain at least two major opportunities for improvement in turpentining practices—raising the low output per man in harvesting of crude gum and better integration of turpentining with timber production through systems of selective cupping in place of the diameter-limit system.

The output per man is considerably less than it was a century ago. In today's scattered stands, which average about 20 or 30 working trees to the acre, the turpentine laborer spends nearly two-thirds of his time walking from tree to tree and only one-third of his time in productive work. Each chipper now tends fewer faces than his predecessors did in the more fully stocked virgin forest. Furthermore, the average turpentined tree is only 10 or 11 inches in diameter; and the yield per tree is consequently much lower than from the larger, old-growth trees.

During the decades in which production per tree, per acre, and per man were declining in the turpentine woods, efficiency in the use of labor and introduction of mechanical devices were advancing steadily in the industries that compete with naval stores for markets and manpower. Those industries captured more and more of the gum naval stores market. Gum naval stores producers were unable to keep enough workers in the woods to meet production goals during the war and the industry may continue to lose ground in the postwar competition unless improvements in technique and equipment are successful in raising the efficiency of production. Since most of the labor is expended in producing raw gum in the woods and little is needed in processing it, more efficient methods of gum extraction and harvesting are obviously needed. For example, it is necessary in the traditional methods of turpentining to visit each tree 40 times a season to produce a yield of 8 or 9 pounds of crude gum or oleoresin.

Recent research has centered on several improvements that give promise of correcting as rapidly as possible the inefficiency of gum harvesting.

Application of acid to the streak to stimulate the flow of gum is the most promising new technique that has been developed since the introduction of the cup several decades ago. Experiments at the Lake City Branch of the Southeastern Forest Experiment Station have demonstrated that streaks sprayed with sulfuric acid yield 50 to 100 percent more gum than untreated streaks.

Treatment with sulfuric acid also extends the normal period of gum flow after chipping. As a result, the streaks chipped every 2 weeks and sprayed with acid produce as much gum per season as untreated streaks applied at the usual weekly interval. Although the additional work of spraying acid slows down the chipper to about 90 percent of his usual speed, the longer chipping interval permits him to work up to 80 percent more timber with no sacrifice in yield per tree. In that way a chipper can increase his production for the season by 80 percent. If the interval of chipping and acid treatment is increased to 3 weeks, the yield per tree is somewhat less, but the greater number of trees that are worked under this system enables a chipper approximately to double his output of gum for the year.

Chemical stimulation may also help to save a portion of the butt log for timber production. Doubling the customary chipping interval and applying acid provides approximately normal annual gum yields while proceeding only a little more than one-half as high up the tree. Or, in trees designated for thinning or harvest cutting, the usual total yield for the normal 5- or 6-year life of a face can be obtained in a shorter period of years by chipping at the customary interval but applying acid in addition. Although sulfuric acid has a greater effect on prolongation of gum flow than any chemical that has yet been tried, it is corrosive and must be handled with caution. Research men are bending every effort to find a gum-flow stimulant that will be nearly as easy to handle as water.

A new system of chipping involves cutting to the usual height of one-half inch but only to the depth of the outer surface of the wood. If acid is applied, the method gives just as much gum as does application of acid with the traditional method of chipping one-half inch into the wood. The new technique of "bark chipping" is now in its fifth year of use by selected cooperators in the industry. It requires less physical effort than the standard method, is easier to teach to new workers, and leaves the butt of the tree in better condition for utilization. The spread of this new method depends on the acceptance of chemical stimulation, for, without application of acid, the yield is less than for the traditional chipping.

A new type of tool, or hack, has been developed for bark chipping. This new method of taking off only the bark provides an excellent opportunity for equipment research to develop a mechanical hack. Although there is always room for improving the equipment used in bark chipping and acid treatment, the major drawback to use of the new techniques by untrained laborers is the shortage of men to show them how. Leaders of the industry are receptive, but the solitary chipper in the turpentine woods is the man who must be trained in the new methods of work.

Research on the equipment and mechanization has been started in response to a plea from industry. The mechanization of competing industries, such as the harvesting of pulpwood and of pine stumps for wood naval stores, has left the gum naval stores industry behind. Except for the introduction of bark chipping and acid treatment, the hand methods used in producing crude gum have been unchanged for decades.

The first step in the research was to meet the rather rigorous needs for a shatterproof, acidproof, one-hand spray device for applying sulfuric acid. This need appears to have been met for the present by the introduction of a sprayer having a bottle made of rubberlike plastic. A simple squeeze on the bottle delivers a spray with a minimum of manipulation. Research has been started on a combined chipping and spraying device that will add further to the simplicity of acid treatment of the faces.

The development of strains of pine of superior gum-yielding capacity, grown in adequately stocked plantations, is expected to bring the greatest improvement in the long run in efficiency of gum harvesting. The parallel between the possibilities of such plantations of southern pines and existing plantations of superior strains of rubber and fruit trees is evident.

Research on the selection, vegetative propagation, and selective breeding of high-yielding naval stores pines was started several years ago. Select strains thus far isolated promise to provide at least two times the present yield per tree; they could be grown in plantations containing 200 or more workable trees to the acre in place of the present average of 20 or 30 faces to the acre in wild stands. Improvements in growth rate and other tree characteristics can also be expected from research in this field.

In respect to the timber supplies and methods of processing and marketing, the industry is now in a favorable position to progress. The chief problems in the production phase are to raise the efficiency of gum harvesting by improvements of techniques, to grow adequately stocked forests, and to fit turpentining into its proper place in good forest management.

Progress in timber management has been spotty. By far the largest part of the original 58 million acres in the naval stores belt was covered with stands of longleaf pine, intermingled with slash pine in the ponds and low places. After the exploitation of the old growth, new stands in the eastern part of the belt had a great deal more slash pine and will have more and more as fire protection is extended. On the driest soils, where longleaf pine occurred with low-quality oaks, the oaks are now taking over. The longleaf pine was culled out of these stands, and often did not reproduce itself. On the better soils in the western part, longleaf pine is most at home and will continue to be the major crop.

The first logging, in the northeastern part of the belt, was not very close, and enough seed trees were usually left to provide for restocking. The western and southern parts were logged later with large equipment. They were cut much closer, were often burned, and vast areas did not reseed. They still present a tremendous planting job.

However, it is the wise management of the crop of second growth that is the major topic of this discussion.

Where fires are controlled and a seed source is present, slash pine seeds in at a surprisingly rapid rate. A dense young stand of slash pine usually benefits from early thinning when the trees are just an inch or two in diameter. If the stand is thinned to 600 to 800 trees an acre, the trees will reach cordwood size more rapidly, and entrance into the stand with trucks or pulpwood saws for thinning will be greatly facilitated. Thinning such stands mechanically with a heavy brush-cutting roller has been tried by the National Turpentine & Pulpwood Corp., of Jacksonville, Fla., but it is too early to assess the results.

Longleaf pine ordinarily seeds in less densely than slash pine, and also shows more graduation in size of tree, so that early thinnings are usually unnecessary.

When a good stand of turpentine pines gets to pulpwood size, the struggle for its diversion to one of many uses begins. In former days, when the average stand was perhaps 20 turpentine trees to the acre and there was no market for thinnings, there was not much point in turpentining only selected trees. Hence the custom arose of turpentining all the trees that were large enough to provide a reasonable flow of gum. The custom was also due to the circumstance that most naval stores producers then owned their own turpentine stills, and were chiefly interested in producing enough gum to keep these stills in operation.

The whole pattern of forestry has changed since the diameter-limit system came to be the custom. We now have many plantations and dense natural stands of slash pine. There will be many more in the future. We now have excellent markets for thinnings, so that there is no need to cut all or nothing. Furthermore, the recent conversion from hundreds of small direct-fire stills in the woods to a few dozen large central processing plants has provided a ready market for gum produced by independent operators and gum farmers. The latter usually own the land and have no compulsion to exploit their timber too heavily for naval stores.

All of these changes have made the time ripe for greater emphasis on good timber-management practices in the naval stores region. The most essential change is to get away from the custom of turpentining every tree in the stand as soon as it reaches 9 inches in diameter. Any properly stocked naval stores stand will need thinning or other silvicultural treatment at various times if it is not to be liquidated at an early age. In any such treatment, the trees to be cut are determined on the basis of spacing, form, and size. Diameter-limit cupping overlooks spacing and form and selects on a basis of entirely inadequate information the trees to be cupped and cut.

When a properly stocked naval stores forest is ready for cupping, a decision must be made on the type of management that will best suit the needs of the owner. The decision arrived at will depend on the owner's circumstances, but ordinarily he will be interested in maximum sustained income per acre from the integrated production of wood and gum.

An improvement cut is the first step. If the trees to come out in the improvement cut have already been turpentined, the cut is made immediately, for these "worked-out" trees do not pay their way in timber growth and should be removed.

If the improvement cut is in unturpentined trees, and if there are enough of them per acre, those large enough should be turpentined before they are removed. Crooked, forked, and excess trees to be removed in a thinning will yield just as much gum as the best timber trees that will usually be reserved for later turpentining.

Where the stand is in good condition the first cutting will be a thinning. The poorest quality trees in all crown classes are removed, plus the additional trees that should come out to provide best spacing of the remaining stand.

Since the trees (at least the larger ones) that are to come out in a thinning are ordinarily to be turpentined before removal, the selection of the trees must be done anywhere from 2 to 10 years in advance of the cutting. The length of this period should depend on the time at which the stand will need thinning. If no thinning will be required for 10 or 20 years, then two or even three faces can be worked one after another on each marked tree. On the other hand, if the stand is overcrowded and needs thinning soon, the trees can be turpentined heavily with the use of acid on one wide or two standard faces for 1 to 3 years before they are removed. The number of well-stocked natural and planted stands is increasing rapidly, and these new techniques for rapid turpentining in advance of thinning in crowded stands should become increasingly applicable.

The best guide to the need for thinning in a southern pine stand is the proportion of the total height of the tree that is occupied by live crown. The stand should be so managed as to keep this proportion between 30 and 40 percent for wood production and perhaps somewhat nearer 50 percent for maximum gum production.

The optimum density to be maintained under management in naval stores stands of different ages and on different soils has not yet been determined. A rule of thumb for selecting trees for cupping 3 to 5 years in advance of thinning is to leave between the reserved trees a space equal in feet to twice the average tree diameter in inches. Thus the space between an 8- and a 12-inch tree would be about 20 feet (10×2), which is also equal to the sum of the two diameters in inches.

Where selective cupping results in tapping a smaller number of trees per acre, it results in some increase in current production costs. However, a stand that is dense enough for a thinning will ordinarily provide an acceptable number of trees for turpentining, just as it would for selective cutting. If a loss of efficiency is occasioned by wider spacing in a given selective cupping, it should be repaid with interest in the second cupping cycle, when the next trees to be tapped will be considerably larger in diameter. A 12-inch tree yields 50 percent more gum than a 9-inch tree, although the increased cost of turpentining per tree is negligible. On the Osceola National Forest in northeastern Florida, the plan of management calls for three successive cycles of turpentining before the stand is removed. In each cycle, those trees are turpentined which a forester has marked to come out in the next thinning or other cutting.

In understocked stands, where thinning is not needed, the owner has a choice of deferring any turpentining until the trees are larger and denser, or cutting off the stand and replanting it, or marking it for a seed-tree cutting to get reproduction. The important precaution is that he should not simply cup every tree over 9 inches without knowing what his next step in stand management is to be.

The regeneration of the even-aged stands of slash pine is no problem as long as there is sufficient seed source. In longleaf pine, regeneration by natural means is a good deal less certain. In Florida the preference is toward leaving longleaf seed trees in groups. Longleaf pine seedlings need sizable openings wherein to become established.

Repeated and untimely fires are the worst enemy of reproduction, and many areas with a seed source restock rapidly as soon as they are brought under protection. Other areas may have so much vegetative growth that reproduction is facilitated by using carefully controlled fire to burn off the accumulated "rough" in advance of seedfall.

Improvements in planting machines and the shift to more intensive forestry will probably result in a great increase in forest planting in the naval stores belt. In the future the problem of "nonrestocking lands" ought to vanish.

Burning the woods to improve the forage is common practice in the naval stores area. In the open-range sections, where the law allows unrestricted grazing of unfenced land, the landowner either has to burn his land or expect others to burn it for him. If the land does go unburned for 10 or 15 years, the accumulated herbaceous and the shrubby fuels, draped with large quantities of dead pine needles, make an extremely hot and destructive fire.

The cheapest way to control this fire hazard is by carefully controlled or prescribed burning whenever it is needed. Such burning provides the necessary fire protection and forage and makes the area much more accessible and attractive to naval stores and timber operators. Deliberate burning is contrary to everything that foresters taught in the recent past, but the practice of prescribed burning has so many advantages in large portions of the region that a whole technique for it has been perfected and put into use in the past few years, particularly in the national forests of Florida in the flatwoods section. The technique is described in publications of the Southern Forest Experiment Station and in an article by John W. Squires in the *Journal of Forestry* for November 1947.

The chief purposes of prescribed burning are usually to reduce the fire hazard or to prepare the seedbed for longleaf pine, but it has several other uses. It may control disease (such as brown spot needle blight in longleaf pine), improve the range, or hold back undesirable vegetation.

The first step is to examine the tract and decide which places are to be burned in a given year. The purpose and type of burn should be clearly defined in advance, and, on large areas, maps should be prepared of the part to be burned. On a large tract, the blocks to be burned must be selected in such a way as to protect other areas from wildfires coming in from the outside. The burning should be planned so that it provides fresh forage where it is most needed in range management. It must also be made to fit in as well as possible with current naval stores operation. Burning should be done just before the installation of new faces. Otherwise raking of the litter away from the turpentined trees is usually essential to prevent burning of inflammable faces.

In slash pine areas particularly, it is important to postpone burning on reproducing areas until the young stand becomes well established. Even in larger stands, the interval between burns must be flexible if fire is to be integrated properly with other forest uses. Experience in the Florida flatwoods indicates that perhaps one-seventh of the gross acreage of a large tract will be burned in a given year.

After the selection of areas to be burned, fire lines are plowed at intervals of about 600 or 700 feet at right angles to the particular wind direction that is preferred for burning. The fire is set with a drip torch on the downwind side of the strip, so that the fire backs through the area against the wind. In Florida, the fires are usually set a day or two after a rain when there is a northerly wind of 3 to 10 miles an hour.

Burning always does some damage. The proper technique of prescribed burning results in the lowest sum of costs plus damages. On large areas this sum should amount to about 21 cents an acre for one burn, or perhaps 3 cents an acre a year when prorated to the gross acreage of the property.

Although the techniques of burning have been worked out, there is still much to be learned about fitting the burning into an integrated pattern of timber management, turpentining, and grazing.

Cattle grazing is more important in the rather open stands of the naval stores region than in any other forest region in the East. Florida, which contains most of the forest land in the naval stores region, has more beef cattle than any other southern State east of the Mississippi; many of the cattle graze on forest range. The cattle industry in Florida returns 48 million dollars annually—more than the gum naval stores industry brings to the whole naval stores belt.

It is recognized that cattle grazing ordinarily has no detrimental effects on timber production in the turpentine belt, and actually is helpful in reducing the fire hazard. As a practical matter of fact, if an owner does not graze cattle on his own land in the open range country, someone else will.

But despite the recognized place of grazing in the management of naval stores forests, a great deal remains to be learned about integrating grazing with other uses of the land. Present herd-management practice is rather primitive. The cattle are usually grazed yearlong on the forest range, whereas the forage in winter is not sufficiently nutritious to meet minimum needs of the animals. The results are small calf crops, low calf weights, and high death losses.

Research has shown the nutritive value of the forest range at each season of the year, and has indicated the kind, amount, and timing of supplemental feeding that is necessary for good health of cattle on Coastal Plain ranges. Research has also shown that forest range cattle need yearlong mineral supplements, especially phosphorus. This is provided by a mixture of 2 parts steamed bonemeal to 1 part salt.

Supplemental feeding may be provided in the form of concentrates, such as cottonseed meal, or by making improved pasture available at seasons when the nutrient content of the native forage is low.

Where feasible, good herd-management practices should be instituted to maintain the quality of the herd and to limit calving to the best time of the year. Cross fences are necessary for proper control of the herd and proper use of the range, but on poor land it may be difficult to demonstrate the soundness of such an investment.

THE PRESSURE OF DIFFERENT USES on the forest land here has been heavy. A decade or two ago the mortality and loss of growth resulting from turpentining was as great as the total amount of the pine lumber harvested. In Florida if it had not been for repeated forest fires—usually associated with grazing—which killed out the young growth and perpetuated understocked stands, the State could be producing twice as much timber as it now does.

In northeastern Florida, by far the best-timbered section of the State, the average growing stock is less than 5 cords an acre, and the growth is one-sixth cord an acre a year. The average saw-timber growth is 47 board feet an acre a year, and the saw-timber stand is being cut a good deal faster than it is growing.

The various pressures on the land for wood, grass, and gum cannot simply be removed. They must be integrated in sound systems of forest-land management. Turpentining must be done with a view to stand improvement and timber production. Grazing fires must be converted into systems of prescribed burning for forest protection. The whole complex must be worked into a management pattern that takes advantage of those pressures on the land for profit.

It is the multiple profit from wood, gum, and grass that Capt. I. F. Eldredge, a forester, had in mind when he said: "Nowhere in the United States are silvicultural and economic conditions more favorable for intensive industrial forestry management than in the naval stores belt of the Southeast."

CARL E. OSTROM *is in charge of the Lake City Branch of the Southeastern Forest Experiment Station. Since 1934 he has been employed at several of the regional forest experiment stations. His work has consisted of research in silviculture and regeneration in the Northeast and the Northwest and research in naval stores production in the Southeast.*

JOHN W. SQUIRES *is supervisor of national forests in Mississippi. As a boy he lived in Louisiana, and later, in the employ of the Forest Service, he was stationed in Georgia, Florida, and Mississippi. As supervisor of the national forests in Florida, he cooperated with the experiment station at Lake City on the correlation of prescribed burning, naval stores, and grazing activities.*

# The National Forests

## THE PEOPLE'S PROPERTY

C. M. GRANGER

THE PEOPLE of the United States own 180 million acres in national forests. A third of the Nation's commercial timber, a sixth of its commercial timberland, a large part of the summer ranges for western livestock, and 70 percent of the big game of the West are on that land—and nearly all the important sources of western water and most of the recreation areas.

There are national forests in 38 States, Alaska, and Puerto Rico; there are purchase units—the seeds of national forests—in two other States. Within the outer boundaries of the forests are nearly 230 million acres, of which the Nation owns 180 million.

The national forests are administered by the Forest Service under the general direction of the Secretary of Agriculture. Other bureaus in the Department of Agriculture and elsewhere in the Government furnish technical advice on special problems, such as the control of insects and tree diseases and forecasting of fire weather.

*The drawing at the top of this page shows the entrance to a national forest.*

Most of the national forest areas and resources are in the West, but the forests east of the Great Plains have great local and regional importance because of their resources and their value as demonstration areas for working out the solution to forest problems.

The national forests came into being in 1891 when the people of the United States decided to stop giving away the Nation's timberland as fast as they could and keep some of it permanently as the people's forests, and Congress adopted an act that empowered the President to set aside forest reserves for the purpose of "securing favorable conditions of waterflows, and to furnish a continuous supply of timber for the use and necessities of citizens of the United States."

Beginning with Benjamin Harrison, the various Presidents have established national forests by proclamation under the act, but most of the national forests were proclaimed by three Presidents—Harrison, Cleveland, and Theodore Roosevelt.

The only large areas of public land

left in 1891 were in the West. But the value of permanent Federal forests was recognized in the East, so in 1911 the Weeks Law was enacted to authorize purchase by the Federal Government of lands necessary to the protection of the flow of navigable streams. The Clarke-McNary Act of 1924 enlarged the policy of the Weeks Law to include the purchase of lands on the watersheds of navigable streams for timber production. Under those acts, most of the national forests east of the Mississippi have been established.

The national forests are truly national in both purpose and value. Many States do not produce enough timber or the right kind for their own needs, and the national forests help to supply them. Water for irrigation, power, and domestic purposes in many cases is supplied by streams that rise far away in national forests in other States. The lamb chop served in Chicago may have come from Wyoming's high ranges in the national forests. Many people from the Midwestern Plains spend their vacations in the cool national forests in the West. Twenty-five percent of the gross revenues from the sale of national forest timber and other commercial uses is paid to the States for distribution to the counties in which the national forests lie, to be used for roads and schools. The fund is a large part of the revenue of many counties. Another 10 percent is made available to the Forest Service to pay part of the cost of building and maintaining roads and trails in the national forests.

The forests yield a sizable income. For the fiscal year that ended in June 1948, it was more than 25 million dollars. The sum reflects the greater demand for timber from the national forests; in 1940 the income was $5,860,000. In that year, income was 48 percent of the fund appropriated for the protection and management of the national forests; in 1948 it was almost 100 percent.

The national forests are forests in the larger sense. They are not just areas covered with trees; they are a composite of trees, brush, grass, water, wildlife, scenery. Each of these elements has its own value; together they give the forest a value much greater than that of a producer of wood.

By direction of the Secretary of Agriculture, when the national forests were placed under his administration in 1905, "All land is to be devoted to its most productive use for the permanent good of the whole people, and not for the temporary benefit of individuals or companies . . . and where conflicting interests must be reconciled the question will always be decided from the standpoint of the greatest good of the greatest number in the long run."

The national forests are managed on the principle of multiple use, a simple enough concept that often is hard to apply because of the impact of one use on another and the striving of groups interested in one use to get priority for that one use. The essence of multiple-use management is to make each area yield the maximum number of benefits and to fit each use to the other. Exclusive right-of-way is given to one use only when that use is clearly dominant.

Thus, timber-cutting practices may have to be varied from those designed solely for wood production in order to increase water yield or stabilize water flows. Similar variations occur where recreation or scenic values are important. Some openings must be left or made in forests and forest plantations to benefit the wildlife. Grazing in the South may be fostered without hurting timber production by proper management. Grazing and wildlife use must here and there be adjusted to each other. And so on.

Public understanding and support of the multiple-use plan of management has grown in late years. When some stockmen proposed that lands used for grazing in the national forests be sold to the holders of grazing permits, many people protested and gave vigorous endorsement of the multiple value of the national forests.

No user of the national forest gets any vested right in the property. Each use has a limited duration. Privileges to use are just that—privileges, and not rights above those of all the people, who own the forests.

The national forests, exclusive of those in Alaska and Puerto Rico, contain 518,417 million board feet of timber, which is 32 percent of the Nation's total. The timber is managed on the basis of sustained yield—the cut is restricted to the sustained productive capacity of the management unit. The system gives stability of supply of forest products, employment, and tax base, or its equivalent.

The timber is sold to help supply the local, regional, and national needs. About 25,000 sales are made each year. They range from a few dollars' worth to large sales that involve 100 million board feet or more and are valued at hundreds of thousands of dollars. Timber for domestic use is granted free in small quantities to certain classes of local users, including farmers. Many farmers make an off-season business of buying and cutting stumpage and selling the products.

Timber cutting is now proceeding at the rate of nearly 4 billion feet a year, an increase from about 1¼ billion in 1939. The national forests now supply 10 percent or more of the national lumber cut, plus large quantities of poles, posts, mining timbers, railroad ties, pulpwood, fuel wood, and Christmas trees.

With the sharp reduction in private stumpage, the demand for national forest timber is steadily increasing. The policy is to make it available just as fast as possible, subject to sustained-yield limitations. Needed are an expanded system of access roads, better timber inventories, management plans to insure orderly sustained-yield marketing. That achieved, it is estimated that the annual cut could be increased to about 6 billion board feet. As forest management becomes more intensive, including reforestation of about 3¼ million acres of burned areas and blank spots, the annual cut can be further increased.

Of great potential importance is the national forest timber in southeastern Alaska—78 billion board feet, mostly hemlock and spruce, which is particularly suited to pulp and paper manufacture. It will support a cut of about a billion board feet a year, which, if converted into newsprint, would supply about one-fourth of the Nation's needs. Encouraging indications are at hand that large-scale pulp operations in Alaska may soon be initiated under favorable long-term contracts. A preliminary award of one such contract has already been made.

Puerto Rico has a small national forest. In that wood-hungry country, every tree in the national forest has great value, especially for charcoal, the universal fuel.

The Sustained-Yield Unit Act of March 29, 1944, which provides for cooperative sustained-yield units, affords a means of combining the management of private and public timber under certain conditions so as to insure good forestry and sustained-yield practice on areas of private forests where short-term liquidation or inadequate supply for sustained yield would otherwise jeopardize community stability. We are giving effect to this law as fast as practicable. One large unit has already been established under a 100-year cooperative agreement. About 100 applications, formal and informal, were on file for processing in 1948.

The existence of the national forests provides assurance of continuity of timber supply in varying measure to many communities and consumers. National forest timber cannot fully replace disappearing or curtailed private supplies of stumpage, but in many situations it can greatly reduce the adverse consequences of private liquidation.

Nearly the whole irrigated agricultural system in the West depends on water from streams that rise in the national forests, or from underground sources mainly fed from national forest watersheds. Almost every city in the mountain and coastal West derives its water supply from those streams, either direct or through underground sources. All power developments are on streams that rise in the national forests.

The national forests occupy less of the watershed area in the eastern half of the country, but do include some of the important watersheds.

Mismanaged forest and range land can and does have large adverse effect on water flows in the form of floods, erosion, and diminished supply. Some of the largest reservoirs in the West are silting up at a rate that will seriously diminish their storage capacity in less than two generations. This silting is due in considerable part to misuse of range lands outside the national forests. The obvious serious consequences of forest and range denudation gives complete validity to conservation policies in effect on the national forests—even if water alone were involved.

Some grazing of cattle, sheep, and horses is allowed on nearly every national forest, but it is in the West that this resource and its use assumes major proportions. The national forest range is mostly summer range and complements home ranches or ranges that provide pasturages the rest of the year. Some southwest ranges are yearlong.

National forest ranges in 1947 supported 1,247,000 cattle and horses (mostly cattle) and 3,409,000 sheep. There were 21,798 paid permits and 6,762 free permits, the latter for small numbers of milk cows or horses needed for domestic purposes. The average paid permit in the western forests was for 67 head of cattle and horses; that for sheep, 1,073 head. Most permits run for 10 years.

More than 800 local advisory boards, the representatives of permit holders, help fix policies and programs and give advice on range administration.

As with timber, the policy is to manage the ranges on a sustained-yield basis. Stocking must be adjusted to grazing capacity. Unfortunately many ranges are overstocked, for several reasons, in spite of substantial reductions over a long period. About half of the 10,000 range allotments require further adjustments. They range all the way from minor changes in methods of management to heavy reductions in the numbers of livestock and, in a few cases, total closure to grazing use.

Before reductions are made, it is the policy to discuss the matter with the permit holder, give him a chance to ride the range with the forest officer, and, if the cut is heavy, to spread it over several years.

Reliance is not placed on reductions alone to relieve the overgrazed ranges. Employed also is better management of the stock on the range, more range improvements to facilitate management (fences, water developments, and the like), reseeding, and the reduction of rodent damage and poisonous weeds, which prevent full use of some ranges.

The established fees for grazing use are based on a comparison of the value of national forest ranges with what stockmen pay for private and other publicly owned ranges, but with liberal discounts that bring the national forest fees well below those paid for other comparable ranges. Fees are adjusted each year according to the market price of livestock the preceding year in 11 Western States.

In earlier years, the policy was to encourage rather liberal redistribution of the grazing privilege to accommodate new applicants or increase the permits of those who were permitted numbers too small to make anything like a stable enterprise. In the interest of stability of established enterprise, the policy has been modified so that for many years there has been little redistribution, and none is contemplated during the 10-year permit period, that began in 1946, except such as may be possible through limited reductions in permits when an outfit sells out and the preference is transferred to a successor.

Wildlife is regarded as one of the major resources of the national forests, one that should be given the proper share of attention. In the West, this involves principally good management of game populations already existing; in the South, it is a matter of building up the resource.

Unfortunately, in many places in the West and in the national forests in the Lake States, populations of deer and elk have outgrown their food supplies, and the first job is to reduce the numbers to the carrying capacity of the range. Progress is being made as understanding grows that wildlife must be managed much like any other crop.

The primary interest of many millions of people in the national forests is related to opportunities for recreation.

So, more than 4,500 camps and picnic areas have been provided. Many places have been developed for swimming and boating. About 240 winter-sports areas have been fitted up. Resorts to accommodate transient visitors are permitted in many places. Organization camps to facilitate low-cost vacations are featured. About 12,000 summer homes are under permit.

Forest wildernesses are an important and unique feature of many national forests. Their purpose is to preserve wild land in its primitive condition, without roads or other man-made installations not absolutely essential to their protection.

The 77 wilderness areas range in size from 1,800,000 to 5,000 acres. Altogether they cover about 14 million acres. In them one can go afoot or on horseback, get far away from the usual evidences of civilization, and see country as it was when the white man came.

Interest in preserving the integrity of these wilderness areas has grown amazingly. For example: In 1940 a hearing was held on a proposal to make a reservoir (for irrigation) out of Lake Solitude in the Big Horn Mountains in Wyoming. Few seemed to care that the proposed reservoir would destroy the beauty of Lake Solitude. The plan was deferred because of the war, but was brought up again at another hearing in 1948. Then the preponderance of expressed sentiment favored leaving Lake Solitude in its primitive state as one of the outstanding features of the wilderness area.

The miscellaneous uses of the forests make an almost endless list. There are apiaries and fox farms; artificial fish ponds, where trout are raised for market; cabins for skiing clubs; mineral springs for the ailing; trappers' cabins; and branding corrals and counting pens used by the stockmen. Altogether, nearly 100 different sorts of uses are under permit—a total of 44,000 permits that cover more than 2 million acres and bring in around $700,000 each year to the Treasury.

Appropriations for the purchase of land for national forests have been made almost every year since the enactment of the Weeks Law in 1911. Congress enacted a general forest-exchange law, under which the Forest Service may acquire forest land within the forest boundaries by exchanging for it other national forest land or national forest timber.

A number of other bills authorize the use of part of the receipts from the national forests to acquire land within the boundaries. This type of legislation, as with the forest-exchange acts, is based on a desire to consolidate in public ownership most of the privately owned land within the national forest boundaries. To further the acquisition of such land, some counties forego their share of the so-called 25-percent fund from the part of the receipts that is used to buy the land. Some communities in Utah have established and financed a special organization to buy certain private lands on their watersheds and turn them over for administration as part of the national forests.

The principal purpose of acquisition by these various means is to place in Government ownership—that is, ownership by all citizens—the forest lands in or near the national forests that will not be given suitable treatment in private ownership or that would otherwise best promote the public interest by being publicly owned—vital watersheds, for instance, or lands needed to round out timber-management units.

EFFECTIVE PROTECTION of the forests against fire, insects, and tree diseases is mandatory. To that end, a highly developed fire-control organization in the national forests utilizes many devices to detect and suppress forest fires—airplanes, helicopters, parachutes, and many more that are less spectacular. We dare not sit back and feel secure because of them, however. Man-caused fires are the principal source of trouble for the whole country, and every citizen has a responsibility to help stamp out this kind of carelessness. It is the citizen's forests that burn. Tree-killing insects and diseases take a heavy toll of timber or young growth each year. Against them, too, we must organize forces and campaigns; they may strike here today and there tomorrow.

To protect and use the national forests, a network of roads, trails, telephone lines, radio channels, fire lookout towers, and other physical improvements is necessary. Much of it has been installed, but more is needed—particularly the additional roads needed to open up the remaining large areas of inaccessible timber. When that is done, the rate of cutting on the forests could be increased at least 50 percent.

A bulwark behind the national forests, as with other forests, is research, which has pointed the way to the best forestry practices in all important aspects of the undertaking. Research men in the Department of Agriculture and in other agencies of the Government have contributed fruitfully to the struggle to combat fires, insects, and diseases; to the techniques of managing the timber as a crop and in utilizing it most effectively; to the conservative use and renewal of forest ranges; to the safeguarding of watersheds; and in many other fields.

Much remains to be done before we can feel that the national forests—this "everyman's empire"—are handled most frugally and most fruitfully. To say that is not an admission of failure; it is a way of saying how great is the obligation to preserve, protect, and develop these properties that all American citizens own.

C. M. GRANGER *is assistant chief of the Forest Service, in charge of national forest administration. He is a native of Michigan and a graduate in forestry of Michigan Agricultural College. He entered the Forest Service in 1907, and has served successively as forest assistant, deputy supervisor, and forest supervisor on national forests in California, Colorado, and Wyoming, as assistant regional forester in the Rocky Mountain Region, and as regional forester for the Pacific Northwest.*

# APPALACHIAN COMEBACK

M. A. MATTOON

Like a strong backbone, the Appalachians extend southward from New England. They are America's oldest mountains, the home of sturdy people, the sites of some of the newer national forests. How the forests and the people are joined for mutual benefit is the theme of this article.

People first saw the forests in the early days when Britain, Holland, France, and Spain were sending colonists to our eastern seaboard, and intrepid men like Spottswood, Boone, and Sevier, lured by tales of opportunities in the great valley beyond the mountains, scaled the Blue Ridge and beheld range after range, hills and peaks, as far as eye could see. It was the domain of the Cherokee, the Seneca, the Catawba. In the blue haze, the forest stretched unbroken, chiefly hardwood, with great expanses of oak, chestnut, yellow-poplar, cherry, beech, maple, ash, white pine, hemlock, and, at higher elevations, spruce, and fir.

The forests were first used by the men who pushed on through the mountains and into the valley of the Ohio. As the little bands threaded the wilderness trails, some saw their opportunity en route and stayed behind. They made clearings in the rich bottom lands at the forks of streams and reared their families there. Later new homesteads were carved from the wilderness further "up the creek." The population grew, and people tended land, turned out stock, and hunted. Villages grew into towns that were built with wood from the forest. The great poplars, pines, and oaks within easy reach of mountain watercourses were rafted to distant sawmills for use by the growing Nation outside this fastness.

The big forest still stood in its silent grandeur, however; so far, there had been only a nibbling at its edges or a little hole here and there cleared for pasture or a deadening in which to grow corn for the family at the head of a creek. It was an immensely rich timber world that contained the finest hardwood that ever stood; a country of endless beauty, one in which its isolated folk passed on to their descendants of today words and songs little changed from those of Elizabethan England.

During and after the Civil War, the railroads began to string the little villages together. Railroads crept up the valleys slowly in search of the almost unlimited supplies of coal. Oil brought them into the Pennsylvania highlands. As the little balloon-stacked engines rocked over the slender rails, the whistle warned of approaching doom. With assured rail shipment to the outside, where an expanding Nation demanded and got what it needed, the stage was set for the coming of the big sawmills into the mountains. They came, slowly at first, and then with logging railroads of their own, like locusts. Handsome timber in increasing amounts fell to the ax, but there always seemed to be more. Sawmill towns sprang up in their temporary ugliness, thrived, and vanished as the cutting moved on. Fire raged on the heels of loggers, and devastation over large areas seemed certain. When Europe burst into the horror of warfare in 1914, demands on the forest mounted and reconstruction saw no let-up. So the large sawmills, accompanied by many little sawmills, marched across the face of the remaining Appalachian wilderness, and its big timber disappeared. Today, after the Second World War, a host of little mills is picking up the scraps and eating into thrifty young timber that will be needed in the future.

And the people in this mountain country? Little farms are strung along the stream bottoms and at the heads of the creeks. But the country has changed and young folk like to hear tell of the days that were. Most recognize that an enormous forest restoration task is ahead. Not so many realize that it has already been started.

Shortly after the turn of the century, a few far-seeing men in New England and the South noticed the disappearing forests, the damage to soil and young timber from fire, the effect on stream flow and the purity of water supplies. They saw that those things were not good. After years of work with an apathetic public, success crowned their efforts, and in 1911 the Congress enacted legislation whereby it became possible for the Federal Government to purchase areas of wild lands on the headwaters of the navigable rivers, and the chain of national forests in the Appalachians was born.

Purchase of land has been going on through the years until now there are about 6 million acres in public ownership under well-organized protection against fire, and managed so that the remaining resources can be conserved, improved, and made to serve the needs

802062°—49——21

of local people in greater abundance.

This, of course, cannot be done in completeness overnight. It is a long-time task that carries over several generations, because recovery of the damaged soil and the regrowth of the forest takes time. But there is much that skilled management can do to guide and aid nature in the restoration process, and even in its depleted condition the forest can contribute useful products by the removal of trees which will improve growing conditions for those left to comprise the new forest. The guiding policy in the management of the timber resource on these national forests, then, is one of improvement, of rebuilding the growing stock, of attaining a maximum production from the soil through wise use.

When the white man first came to this country, the forest was in virgin condition. Decay and mortality in old trees offset growth. Immense wealth was stored in the old timber, but the forest produced little. A productive forest is a growing forest and one in which the trees should be used as they reach maturity. Now that the country is settled and demands for wood increase, the new forest must become a wood-producing factory instead of the immense storehouse of timber first seen by the pioneers.

Forests are restored by growth. If depletion is to be gradually changed to full production, the drain upon the forest must be less than growth. In this process the national forest ranger is guided by the general concept that the trees that offer the best chance for rapid growth and high value shall be allowed to develop fully by removing those that are defective, of poor form, or with other undesirable qualities.

Many species of trees grow in the Appalachian national forests, and it is interesting to trace the uses into which some of them are processed.

The larger pines and hemlocks are turned into lumber that finds its way into farm-building construction and repair nearby. Tops and small trees go into pulpwood. Most of the chestnut is cut into cordwood and trucked to nearby mills that produce tanning extract; the spent chips are made into paper. Hemlock and chestnut oak bark is also a tanning agent. Locust is made into fence posts and some is turned into insulator pins for telephone and telegraph lines. Choice ash goes into ball bats, snow shoes, tennis rackets, and tool handles. The oaks are widely used for flooring, general construction, and furniture. Especially choice logs of the yellow-poplar, oak, beech, birch, and maple are turned for veneer. Dimension stock in great variety is made from most hardwoods. The chief outlet for spruce and fir is in pulpwood.

The raw materials for some of these products are sometimes shipped long distances, but usually the processing plants are within easy trucking distance of the forest by reason of good highways and the development of the forest road system. Many local industries derive a large part of their raw materials from the forests and, by and large, it is the people who live within them or nearby who furnish these raw materials.

Because of early indiscriminate cutting and fire, the forest is not suited to large-scale harvesting operations today. The volume of timber to the acre is too light to support the heavy investments necessary to large enterprises. Merchantable timber is scattered and often composed of remnants inaccessible to the big logging jobs of the past. Much of the area is in young timber in the sapling stage or of pole size. Consequently, sales of timber involve relatively small amounts in each transaction and are directed toward utilizing the remnants of overmature, decadent, old growth for sawlogs and veneer stock or into thinning or improvement-cutting operations in young timber for pulpwood, chemical wood, and other cordwood products. Successful management requires the execution of numerous small sales scattered over wide areas. Fortunately, this fits well into the pattern of local population, both as to location and financial ability.

The result is a system of small sales to many people with limited resources who can and prefer to become timber operators, each in his own right rather than leave the home and work for someone else. Such opportunity is in harmony with the ingrown independence and self-sufficiency of mountain folk. Many of those who live on their native acres farm during the growing season and get out timber from the forests after the crops are in. Consequently, there is a growing clientele of farmer-loggers who readily augment their cash income by timber work and still stay near their own firesides.

This interdependence is still further sealed by the fact that the protection of the forest from fire is not only the Government's business but the concern of local residents, and they automatically become the core of the fire-control organization. This works for close relationship between the local forest ranger and the people in his district. It is interesting that these purchasers of timber return again and again, and on some ranger districts as many as 500 small sales of timber are made in a single year. Often the ranger has a sizable waiting list. There are 45 ranger districts in the 11 national forests in the Appalachians.

The local small operator of national forest timber is not always a farmer. Many are in the wood-processing business as their major vocation. Some small lumber producers operate one or more small sawmills. Others log ties and mine timbers or cordwood for local markets on a year-round basis. Local residents get much of their fuel wood from dead material free of charge from the national forest.

The district ranger knows from his inventory of the timber the areas that need treatment for improvement of the forest, either through the harvesting of mature and decadent trees or the thinning of young stands so as to increase growth. His yearly plan of work includes the sale of the trees on such areas, and it is geared to the needs of his people. Within the allowable annual cut of his district, prescribed by the long-range timber-management plans and the limitations of the available administrative time and money, the annual sales program forms a large part of his work. While he may have some large sales of timber to the larger operating companies, much of his time and effort is taken up with the making and administration of small sales.

To ILLUSTRATE the handling of a sale and its place in the local economy, let us consider the case of the owner of a mountain farm that is near the Blue Ridge and almost surrounded by forest. The farmer and his boys had finished their fall work. He had a small sawmill, a tractor for power, and a truck. He needed lumber for repair of his buildings; a neighbor had spoken about building a new barn, the big yard in town would take any lumber he could bring in, and a paper mill not far away was buying pulpwood. The farmer had a market for all wood he could harvest; he knew of a patch of old-growth timber a mile above his house on the national forest and of a young stand of pole-sized trees that would make pulpwood.

He went to see the ranger, who consulted his maps and records, and then examined the timber. The ranger saw that some of the older trees were ready to be cut, and he laid out the boundary of the timber that could be sold. He selected the trees that should be cut and those that, by reason of thrift and quality, should be left for future growth. Those to be cut were marked, the volume of each was tallied, and the stumpage value was calculated, based on the difference between the sale value of the lumber and the cost of producing it, less a proper allowance to the farmer for profit and risk.

Because the amount due the Government was less than $500, no public advertisement was required, and the sale contract was drawn up at once. The farmer elected to pay for the trees in lump sum. He mailed his remittance and soon after signed the contract. Matters were cleared so he and the boys could start logging. The timber would not run his mill all winter, but he could keep it busy with the logs his neighbors brought in from their own lands or had purchased from forest property, as he had. Also, the ranger had told him of a larger tract of timber farther away; it would be advertised shortly, and the farmer planned to bid on that.

The stand of pole-sized timber had been marked when the ranger was working in the neighborhood. The marking was designed to thin out the area and give the best trees a better chance to grow. He estimated that 100 cords could be cut. The farmer's boys wanted to do it, but the stumpage would cost them about $200. Because they did not have the money to pay for it all at once, they paid $50 when they signed the contract and arranged to pay the rest in installments when 25 cords were cut and stacked for measurement by the ranger. A hundred cords meant 50 trips for the farm truck to the paper mill, where they got about $15 a cord.

Sometimes such sales to people in the locality are as small as a single tree, which can be split into shingles to cover a cow shed or a few stringers for a bridge. Sometimes the sales are for a few fence posts, sills, and various farm needs. Again, the sales might be up to 5 million board feet. For the seven Appalachian national forests from Virginia and Kentucky north, the average size of timber sales is fewer than 50,000 board feet and less than 60 acres in area.

For a given volume of timber to be cut annually on a sustained-production basis, the cost of administration per thousand board feet is higher when many small transactions comprise the annual cutting budget. Nevertheless, the small sale in the Appalachians helps the local people and is useful in the improvement of the forest itself. Much study has been given to techniques and methods of preparing and administering this type of timber sale to insure good forestry practice at the least cost and still meet the obligations to local forest users.

For example, the scaling of logs or the measurement of cordwood in small amounts as produced by many small operators scattered over a wide territory, whenever the producer needs such service, takes a great deal of time and travel. Through training and practice, forest rangers can accurately measure the amounts of usable products in the standing tree and at the same time mark the trees to be cut. The necessity for scaling after cutting at frequent intervals is eliminated, and considerable time is saved. In such sales, the operator is purchasing the merchantable contents of a specified number of standing trees estimated to contain a given number of thousands of board feet or cords of wood, as the case may be.

Purchasers prefer the tree-measurement method for several reasons, chief among which is the elimination of operating delays caused by the inability of a busy forest officer to scale or measure just when the purchaser is ready to saw the logs or haul the wood. The ranger frequently checks the accuracy of his tree measurement by comparing his estimate with the outturn from selected trees or with the purchaser's own measurement of what he has cut from a given sale.

Timber may be paid for in installments in advance of cutting, a practice that is universal for larger sales in order to reduce the part of the purchaser's operating capital that is tied up in uncut stumpage. For small sales it is practical to require payment for stumpage in lump sum, thereby reducing the cost connected with securing large numbers of small payments and the accounting work connected with them. Sales on a lump-sum payment basis are increasing in number, but in making small sales the forest officer takes into account the prospective purchaser's ability to pay.

Throughout the chain of Appalachian national forests, from Maine to

Georgia, between 50,000 and 10,000 of these small sales are made annually to local people. The total enterprise is far-reaching in its benefits. It will continue through the years. The contributions to the well-being of many country people and to the stabilization of local industries and communities are substantial. By the same token, those people working with their Government, but not for it, observe the gradual reclothing of the devastated slopes of their native mountains and the progress toward restoration of the basic resource that nature placed there in the beginning. They feel they have a part in the process. No other residents have a greater interest in the control of forest fires, in the rehabilitation of fish and game, or in other associated benefits of well-managed forest property than those who make all or a part of their living from the products harvested from it.

M. A. MATTOON *is the assistant regional forester in charge of timber, range, and wildlife management in the Eastern Region of the Forest Service. After 4 years as forester in the Pisgah National Forest in North Carolina, he was supervisor, successively, of the Cherokee National Forest in Tennessee and Georgia; Pisgah National Forest; and White Mountain National Forest in New Hampshire and Maine.*

# THE AU SABLE COOPERATIVE

JOHN E. FRANSON

The Huron National Forest is in the east-central part of the Lower Michigan Peninsula. It embraces some of the land that grew the famous Michigan white pine. The present annual cut in the forest consists largely of jack pine in scattered blocks of poor stocking and quality. The best blocks of this remaining timber were sold in the 1930's to large pulpwood operators. Between 1938 and 1940, several blocks of the remaining jack pine were advertised for sale on the Tawas District. But—for a significant reason that gives point to this article—no bids were received on those offers.

In an effort to harvest the mature timber and to establish a group of local experienced cutters who would receive the benefit of part-time employment to supplement their farm income, men in the Department of Agriculture considered the possibility of forming a cooperative. One was established in 1940, the AuSable Forest Products Association, a nonprofit organization, which was incorporated under the State laws as a timber-marketing cooperative and whose membership is restricted to residents within or near the Huron National Forest.

Before then, the timber had been sold by bid to contractors—the so-called "gyppo" operators. Those contractors had recruited transient labor, some with families, others single, who would move to the woods and there live in shacks or huts with poor sanitation and unsatisfactory social conditions. Wages paid to cutters were low; failure of the contractor to live up to the usual codes of conduct made local laborers refuse to work at pulpwood cutting; and county officials held the operations to be liabilities because of the added drain on their meager resources. When the work was finished, some cutters and their families remained to become public charges. Worse, the sales to large operators negated the previously favorable public relationship with local residents and authorities; the large advertised sales were more economical to administer, but citizens strongly objected to them and officials had to spend considerable time in attempting to justify them.

For those reasons, and others, no

bids had been received on the Tawas Ranger District, even though the minimum stumpage was only 75 cents a standard cord. Prospective bidders stated the timber was too scattered, of poor form, and too difficult to haul because of plantation furrows. Repeated sale offers brought no better response, but the job of disposing of 3,600 cords of jack pine a year remained.

On the other hand, many men in the intermingled small farming communities in the forest area needed more money. Also, to help them, work in the woods needed to be integrated with the spare time of the farm labor, rather than used at the will of the contractors.

This need for employment was recognized in the preliminary discussions, and it was thought a cooperative might be the solution: Individuals in a cooperative would not be too interested in the size of blocks of timber as long as a cord or two could be easily ricked together; a marketing agency could overcome the objections of the pulp companies, who would not deal with an operator who might have only 10 or 20 cords to sell, and wages would tend to be higher without a trader or contractor who would take his commission and profits and reduce unfairly the margin for cutting and stumpage. A marketing cooperative, moreover, would employ local labor; stumpage would be at an appraised rate, and any money remaining after expenses would be returned to the cutters as patronage refunds; and the serious objections of local governing bodies would be eliminated.

Three meetings were held in the communities to explain the workings of a cooperative and to determine the attitudes on such an organization. The men who attended the meetings expressed themselves in favor. The larger paper companies agreed to buy the output of the association. By-laws and articles of incorporation were drafted and approved and recorded by the Michigan Corporation and Securities Commission. The Farm Security Administration (now the Farmers Home Administration) of the Department of Agriculture approved a $3,000 unsecured loan.

Individuals then began cutting on a sale of $500 or less, the amount that is within the ranger's authorization. When one man's output was measured, the cooperative paid him the agreed price with money from the loan. The first year's cut amounted to 400 cords of peeled jack pine, valued at $3,200 on the railroad cars.

The cut in the second year, which amounted to about $15,000, consisted of jack pine pulp and sawbolts and aspen pulpwood. The third year's operation was reduced to about $1,000 because exceptionally heavy snow impeded winter operations. The fourth year, however, 100 participating members sold timber worth $40,000.

The first 3 years, the ranger was the elected secretary-treasurer of the cooperative, but when the volume of business reached $40,000, a part-time secretary-treasurer was hired by the board of directors to keep the accounts, bill freight cars, and do the general clerical work. The ranger still administered sales, scaling, and hiring of truckers. In 1946, a full-time secretary-treasurer, experienced in woods work, was hired to handle administration.

The cooperative now does an annual business of about $100,000, has retired the $3,000 loan, and has $20,000 in working capital of undeclared patronage dividends. About 25 cutters and 6 truckers depend upon the cooperative for most of their livelihood. About 75 part-time cutters and truckers earn supplemental income. A comparison of wages indicates the cooperative pays the highest wage rate for comparable jobs in the vicinity, and about 25 percent higher rates than pulp contractors. Deep snow, which once stopped work, is now plowed by county employees and paid for by the association at standard wages. Stumpage rates and the value of the product both have increased. Bad social conditions in the woods have been eliminated; objections and concern about conditions have given way to cooperation among residents in other phases of forest administration, such as forest-fire control.

Because most of the timber has been cut from national forest lands, encouragement is given to adding output from privately owned wood lots and other timberlands. Because the contracts require the use of good forest practices as a condition of marketing, productivity of the forested acreage is improving. A further requirement is that the participants cannot employ others to work for them; members of a family or neighbors, therefore, usually work together on a partnership basis, and nobody can form a group of undesirable "gyppo" operators that could circumvent the primary purpose.

The area is fortunate in that the only equipment necessary for cutting is an ax and a buck saw.

The AuSable Forest Products Association has proved to be good business for its members, companies that buy its products, and the public agencies whose work it furthers. Similar cooperatives possibly can be successful in places where the following conditions exist: The product to be harvested is of low value with little margin for profit and risk; the annual cut is relatively small, so that the total margin does not attract large operators; some agency is at hand to aid the organization during its formative years; local experienced wood cutters are available; only a small investment per person is required; and a local individual or organization is willing to lend money under strict supervision at 5 or 6 percent interest.

JOHN E. FRANSON *is forest ranger on the Lower Michigan National Forest, with headquarters at East Tawas.*

# EVOLUTION OF MANAGEMENT ON CHIPPEWA

H. BASIL WALES

The great pineries of the Lake States helped tremendously in the industrial and agricultural development of the Midwest. But because sawmills were operated on the basis of cut-out-and-quit, timber was harvested without thought of the future; stands were cut over and burned without giving heed to the new crop that otherwise would have followed. The sawmills on the pine stands in the Lake States were on their way out by 1900, with little prospects of future production of the prized pine construction lumber.

The story of the Chippewa National Forest illustrates what could have been done throughout the Lake States to insure future productivity and how the crude measures to secure a new forest developed into extensive management and then intensive management.

At the close of the nineteenth century some of the best pine timber that remained in the Lake States was on Indian reservations in Minnesota. Pressure by lumbermen for more timber to clear cut and the pressure by women's clubs and other organizations to save the timber by placing it in a national park finally led to a compromise. Congress instructed the Secretary of the Interior to sell timber on Indian reservations and hold the money for the benefit of the Indians.

The Morris Act of 1902 included a feature unique among land laws in that 5 percent of the timber stand on certain lands in north-central Minnesota was to be reserved from cutting and held for seed-tree purposes—as the pinelands were cut over, they were to be dedicated to forestry. Thus, one of the first large-scale efforts in forest management in this country was a harvest of virgin white pine and red pine, with a provision for regeneration of the stand. Nearly 200,000 acres of such forestry lands were to be selected and the timber sold. The law directed also that timber on the islands of Cass Lake and Leech Lake, and on Sugar Point and Pine Point that extend into Leech Lake, and on a unit equivalent to 10 sections of pine timber be reserved from sale.

The law was amended in 1908 to create the Minnesota National Forest within definite boundaries, including the forestry lands and all other lands except individual Indian allotments (which had already been made) and swampland which was claimed by the State of Minnesota under the acts of 1850 and 1860. The amendment raised the seed-tree reservation on the pine areas remaining to be sold to 10 percent of the stand.

Not all the land within the exterior boundaries of the Minnesota National Forest supported merchantable white pine and red pine. Areas of heavy soil carried mixed hardwoods—the sugar maple, basswood, yellow birch, oak, and others. There were also areas of aspen, with other species in mixture, and second-growth stands of jack pine and red pine. Those areas of second growth are probably explained in the accounts of aged Indians of the "fire of two summers," which burned in northern Minnesota and which, according to ring counts, occurred in the early 1860's. The second-growth pine was too small to be merchantable under the terms of the Interior Department sales; other species were small and valueless, besides.

Thus a new national forest was born. It was comprised of about 190,000 acres, which included some 10 sections of virgin white pine and red pine, about 3 townships of second growth (which followed the early fire), a township of hardwoods and other valueless species, and the cut-over land that had standing seed trees among the stumps.

Early records indicate that the seed trees were relatively wind-firm and stood up well despite some heavy winds. Post-logging decadence, induced by the sudden opening of the stand and consequent drying of the soil, was prominent and cumulative.

In 1930, seed trees, particularly of white pine, had all but disappeared from many parts of the cut-over area. Red pine seed trees were more prominent, especially in the part of the forest that was cut over in the later years of the harvest, but decadence was evident among them, too. Nevertheless, the red pine trees showed good diameter growth.

Many foresters have studied regeneration of the pine stand following cutting. All seem to agree that about two-thirds of the reproduction was present as small seedlings when cutting was done. Good seed yields occurred in 1904, 1910, 1914, 1917, and in 1920 within the cutting period, and since then in 1924, 1927, 1930, 1937, and 1943. There has been considerable seed fall, but apparently the conditions were not right for the successful establishment of pine.

For the successful establishment of a new forest of red pine or white pine, a good seed fall, exposed mineral soil obtained by summer logging, and favorable weather conditions for a year or two following germination of the seed seem to be required. If the seed finds a favorable seedbed, a hot, dry sun may kill the tender seedlings. The establishment of grass, weeds, bracken, brush, or low-value hardwoods is another deterrent.

Despite the adverse situations, possibly one-third of the established red pine second growth has come in as a result of the preservation of seed trees. On good white pine sites, white pine reproduction often is conspicuously absent. That does not mean that seedlings of white pine were not present at the time of logging or did not come in later, but, rather, that such seedlings generally could not survive. White pine sites are generally more moist and more fertile than those of red pine and hence are quickly reclothed by nature with dense competing vegetation. The white pine is relatively tolerant of shade, but dense shade will kill the young seedlings. White pine is a favorite food of the snowshoe hare, which builds up to tremendous populations at cyclic intervals. The hare is regarded as the final adverse factor in precluding the natural regeneration of white pine over most of this particular project area.

Under the terms of the timber-sale contract, slash had to be piled and burned. That was a new and rather onerous requirement to the purchasers, who had been accustomed to leaving slash as it fell. Much established reproduction, therefore, was lost by the careless burning of slash. The burned places usually came back to weeds, grass, or aspen, although if jack pine trees remained in the stand, the heat of the fires caused the serotinous cones to open and disperse seed; consequently, jack pine became established to a considerable extent along with red pine.

The seed-tree method of obtaining regeneration cannot be said to be fully successful. But that method—plus a reasonable success in fire protection and the fact that seedlings were already established when the logging was done—brought in a substantial acreage of second-growth red pine, considerable jack pine, and some white pine.

Upon completion of the logging and milling, the sawmill at Cass Lake, which had bought most of the merchantable timber, blew its whistle for the last time—another big mill had exhausted its accessible timber supply, just as hundreds of other mills had done; it had cut-out-and-quit.

That, however, was quite a different quitting. Not so much devastation was left behind. Slash had been disposed of to reduce the hazard of slash fires. Much of the area was covered with young seedlings. Other parts had reforested naturally to jack pine and aspen. There were older age classes of jack pine, aspen, and other hardwoods, even if nobody wanted to buy them.

After all the merchantable pine had been cut in 1923, the forest was largely on a custodial basis. Protection against fire was the main item, although the men in charge tried to develop new markets for the little-used aspen and the overmature jack pine. They established a forest-tree nursery that had an annual production of about a million 2-year seedlings, but planting was not eminently successful. A box mill came in to utilize jack pine lumber for box and crating production, but it did not last long. It was succeeded by a more adequately financed company, which produced box lumber for shipment to their main box plant at Cloquet, Minn. It put in a small box unit to furnish supplemental employment to a stranded people. A few other sales were made, and a couple of small portable mills were brought in to work in the hardwoods.

In cooperation with the University of Minnesota, the Lake States Forest Experiment Station was established in 1926 to investigate forestry problems in the Lake States. Raphael Zon, the director, recognized the opportunity and the necessity of solving the problems connected with the reestablishment of a new forest. He established plots for the study of release and thinning and, in the older stands, plots for the study of growth and reproduction.

Such was the situation in 1930 in the new national forest that now is called, through Presidential proclamation, the Chippewa National Forest.

It had been discovered that aspen, which has no odor to taint food products, was suitable for box lumber. The aspen that followed the fire of two summers had reached maturity, and a sale of some 40 million board feet, about two-thirds aspen, to be cut over a period of 12 years, was advertised. It was bid in at a dollar a thousand board feet; other species and products likewise were priced low. The purchaser contracted to deliver at least 3 million feet of aspen to the box mill at Cass Lake each winter.

Logging operations started in the fall with a crew large enough to deck the minimum required delivery by the middle of February. Hauling started as soon as the ground was frozen solid. The product was delivered in 100-inch and 200-inch lengths.

The long lengths were recut to 100 inches, and the bolts went up the bull chain through a circular saw, which split the logs in half. The halves were then sent through a horizontal band saw, which took off a board from the flat side. The slab was returned by moving chains for additional runs through the band. The mill procedure is mentioned because it is said to be the first mill built on that principle.

The sale of aspen opened a new market for a previously unused species that forest devastation and fire had made available in large volume throughout the Lake States. The sale also seemed to mark the transition point from a custodial and protective job to one of active management of the resource, extensive at first but gradually moving forward to a high degree of intensity. The logging operation continued throughout the depression, and, when the Cloquet sawmill closed because of timber exhaustion, the main box plant was moved to Cass Lake to augment facilities there. The mill now uses other species as well as aspen.

Although the use of aspen for box lumber augured well for the future, it was not possible to extend sales appreciably during the depression. Only low-value material was available, and most of it was relatively inaccessible. Markets and accessibility control the intensity of management which may be given a forest stand. Extensive management could be applied only on the areas where sales could be made.

Plans for the future could be developed, however. Timber surveys were made, and preliminary plans were developed for the management of the timber stand, particularly the hardwoods, aspen, and matured jack pine. Two experimental forests, the Pike Bay and Cut Foot, were established in the early 1930's for use by the Lake States Forest Experiment Station, and a resident forester was appointed to conduct research into the problems of silvicultural management in the forest. The causes of failure of the planting efforts were worked out, and silvicultural research was intensified.

Guiding data were thus at hand when the Civilian Conservation Corps was created in 1933 and when other emergency relief programs were inaugurated. There were seven 200-man CCC camps located in strategic work areas. The camps were primarily for the employment of young men, but because of widespread unemployment and the need of trained strawbosses, up to 10 percent of the enrollment was recruited from local people who had worked on various forest operations. The program enabled the foresters in charge to give cultural treatment to young stands and to develop physical improvements on the forest far beyond their hopes and anticipations.

Because of the studies that had been made in handling young stands, the CCC boys were put to work on stand improvement earlier and with greater assurance than elsewhere in the region. The continuance of the CCC's from 1933 to 1942, together with labor assigned from other relief programs, enabled foresters in charge to accomplish nearly all the noncommercial stand-improvement work that needed attention at the time. Seedling and sapling stands were given release from overtopping brush, aspen, and other low-value species. Dense stands of saplings were thinned, and about 300 potential final-crop trees an acre were given their first pruning. To a limited extent, some older stands that were approaching minimum commercial size were also given treatment by cutting out suppressed trees and trees of poor form. This left a stand of thrifty, well-formed trees with more room to grow. Fuel wood was salvaged for use in the camps, and some was sold in an extremely limited market. Young plantations were combed over to find the weak trees still living but suppressed by the heavy growth of brush; they were released to the full sunlight by cutting away the brush, and made a remarkable recovery.

The large, new Lydick Nursery, with a capacity of 10 to 12 million seedlings and transplants, was started in the spring of 1934 in order that the areas made unproductive by fire or the rapid invasion of brush might be planted. The physical development of the protective and administrative improvements was also under way. A better road system, that made accessible all parts of the forest, was planned and started. Old woods roads were cleared and improved to serve as fire ways and to enable work crews to be transported closer to the job.

In 1935 the Chippewa National Forest was enlarged by the establishment of the north and south Chippewa Purchase Units under the Clarke-McNary Law of 1924. That action added greatly to the job load, because many different problems were involved—land examination and appraisal and negotiations for purchase. The land within the purchase units had been largely cut over and repeatedly burned, although isolated areas protected by lakes and swamps had escaped fire. The original forest area appeared as an oasis of pine in a sea of forest devastation. Also, in the purchase units, many isolated settlers were struggling for a livelihood on land poorly adapted to agriculture. On areas of better soil were sparsely settled farm communities. Destruction of the forest had deprived the settlers of an opportunity of earning a supplemental income in the woods.

From the standpoint of forest management, one had to start from scratch to restore and build up forest productivity. The CCC program helped greatly. At first the job was one of establishing protection facilities—lookout towers, communication lines, and roads—for more rapid transportation for fire-fighting crews.

As land was purchased, the process of restoring the forest became a more important part of the program. By the time that title was established, suitable planting stock was available at the new nursery. Release, thinning, and pruning operations were also undertaken in the limited areas of purchased land, where sapling stands had survived fire. At the same time, other resource values were enhanced. The camp work plans included projects for the protection and the administration of the forest, recreational development, and better food and habitat for wildlife. Land use plans were prepared to strengthen the agricultural communities through the transfer of settlers from poor and isolated tracts.

By 1936 the need for experienced men in the camps was greatly reduced, because, with training and experience, the young men developed qualities of leadership. The local men were gradually released; unfortunately, they were thrown out of employment, so that most of the residents within or near the enlarged forest were again in distressing circumstances.

The upsurge of recovery in 1937, however, seemed to offer the opportunity for employment in the harvest of wood products from the forest. Good results came from a campaign to locate markets for the class of material available that could be removed on a stand-improvement and salvage basis. By 1939, according to the late C. E. Knutson, the forest supervisor, not a man within the forest area, able and willing to work, was on the county relief rolls. The markets, however, were rather far from the forest and the returns were somewhat less than they would otherwise have been.

In April 1940, a severe glaze storm wreaked havoc in some of the treated stands in the original forest area, with lesser damage over a larger area. In early August a 70-mile hurricane swept a patchy 20-mile swath across the unit. After each storm the CCC boys opened roads and repaired telephone lines. At about the same time an epidemic of the jack pine form of the spruce budworm appeared to be killing overmature jack pine in a large area.

Salvage of the material about to be lost made it necessary to find larger markets. Each forest officer fell to. Paper companies agreed to buy up to 10,000 cords of peeled pulpwood; the timber-sale purchasers had to be trained in the art of peeling. An owner of a chain of retail lumber yards was induced to bring in a portable sawmill. A number of other mills followed. In the next 2 years, some 35 million feet of sawlogs and 20,000 cords of pulpwood were salvaged. Intensive management required that the "holes" in the forest be made productive. The presence of a large labor supply in the remaining CCC camps, plus an abundance of trees in the nursery, made that possible. Now, 9 years after the two devastating storms, one hardly knows where the storms hit.

The war's heavy demands for wood products opened the markets for all classes of material, even material that had been unmerchantable. The forest was ready, and the men in charge made the most of the opportunity to make light, partial cuts that placed the forest in a better growing condition and at the same time supplied the wood urgently needed in the war. The best part is that the amount of growing stock has not been depleted; today the volume is larger than before the depression and even before the Second World War.

Intensive management—the application of silvicultural practice to the forest stand in full measure—includes cultural work in young stands below commercial size, planting of nonproductive areas, and improvement and harvest cuts on a commercial basis. Management within the original forest area has evolved to a high degree of intensity and is well on its way within the purchase-unit additions.

In the Chippewa National Forest, light commercial cuts are practicable as soon as the trees are 30 to 35 years old. Additional light cuts can be made at 10-year intervals; each time the area is left in a thrifty growing condition so that maximum productivity is assure

While the CCC is no longer avai able for work in young stands belo commercial size, the Knutson-Vander berg Law is something of a substitut The law authorizes the collection money, in addition to stumpage, place timber-sale areas in good produ tive condition. It is not practicable require the purchaser to do all the wor that should be done. He removes on trees which "have served their pu pose in the stand," and which will yiel merchantable products. Some fill-i planting may be needed on parts of th area to get full stocking. Trees belo commercial size may need thinning release. Other trees may need prunin so that they may produce clear lumbe

The sales of timber on the Chippew Forest show a steady upward tren Within or near the enlarged forest a 37 sawmills that depend to varyin degrees on national forest timber. Si additional sawmills, located at mor distant points, draw somewhat on th forest. The annual production of thos mills is about 30 million board fee About one-fourth of the raw materi comes from the national forest. A muc larger volume is shipped to more dis tant points for conversion.

A wide diversion of species as we as products comes out of the enlarge forest. Sawlogs, box bolts, and tie which go through the sawmills, ap proximate 7,714,000 board feet an nually. Other products represent a equivalent of about 15,000,000 fee more. We figure that the timber har vested in 1947 represents 115,000 man days of employment in the woods an in the primary milling process. It is no desirable as yet to cut the full annua growth. Growing stock must be buil up to a maximum. As this point i reached in different areas the annua cut can be increased.

In 1947 the counties in which th forest is located received 4 cents a acre for each acre of national fores land, under the act of May 23, 1908 which provides for the return of 2 percent of the total receipts on a na tional forest. An additional 1.6 cents an acre was returned to the Forest Service for road and trail construction.

Larger payments to the counties will be made in the future as the timber grows into more valuable products. In 30- to 40-year stands, light cuts of timber on a stand-improvement basis bring in relatively low returns, but they can be handled at a profit to the Government and to the purchaser as well. For example, in 1947, on a 37-acre tract of 40-year-old red pine mixed with 40- to 60-year-old jack pine, 33.03 cords of jack pine box bolts, 15.23 cords of pulpwood, and 2,500 board feet of red pine were cut to bring the Government an average stumpage return of $5.14 an acre; the operator made $8.23 a day after expenses for cutting, skidding, and hauling. A per acre average of only 1.25 cords and 67 board feet was harvested. Another sale in the same general locality averaged only 1.16 cords an acre and gave a stumpage return of $3.71 an acre. The lightly cut stands are now in a position to make maximum growth.

In contrast to those low returns from improvement cuts in young stands is the average per acre receipt from two sales made in 1945 in an 80-year-old red pine and jack pine stand. From an area of 252 acres, 422,000 board feet of jack pine, 36,500 board feet of red pine, 202 pieces of red pine piling, and 417.4 cords of mixed pine pulpwood, that had a total stumpage value of $6,880.13, were cut. Of this area, 150 acres had been given a light improvement cut 5 years before, at which time $1,158.12 was received for stumpage. The average return was $31.90 an acre. Stumpage values on the two sales in 1945 averaged $12 a thousand board feet for jack pine sawlogs, $13 a thousand board feet for red pine sawlogs, 7 to 14 cents a linear foot for piling, and $1.50 a cord for pulpwood. After the cutting, an average of 185 thrifty trees remained to the acre; their volume was 10,800 board feet and 4.4 cords of pulpwood. The trees will continue to grow in volume and value.

Truly, intensive management has evolved in the Chippewa Forest, especially in the original forest area. Timber can be harvested in increasing amounts at higher values. Yet the picture is not wholly bright. Only 589,117 acres out of a gross area of 1,313,656 acres are in Federal ownership and thus susceptible to intensive management as a part of the national forest. A considerable mileage of roads remains to be constructed or improved, particularly in the purchase-unit addition.

With the passing of CCC and other emergency programs, it has been necessary to discontinue most of the road construction as well as the noncommercial stand-improvement operations and to reduce the reforestation program to about 20 percent of what it should be. The large nursery investment at Cass Lake is wholly inactive. The production of seedlings for Chippewa Forest had to be concentrated at another nursery to reduce overhead costs to a minimum.

The Knutson-Vandenberg Act is helpful, because it provides funds for stand-betterment work, including fill-in planting on timber-sale areas. It does not, however, help any in bringing about a productive timber stand on areas where sales are not practicable.

That plantations will pay their way is shown by data taken more or less at random in the many plantations established in the forest. The figures used are average.

In the spring of 1937 one 178-acre plantation of jack and red pines was established with 1,564 trees to the acre, at a cost of $19.19 an acre. Ten years later 1,400 trees were making fine growth. The height of the dominant trees was 23 feet, and the trees were just reaching minimum pulpwood size. The stand contained 2.18 cords to the acre, worth $4. In another 10 years, the first partial cut can be made to give the best trees more growing space.

In the fall of 1934 an experimental plantation of jack pine was made in the Pike Bay Experimental Forest to determine the feasibility of converting brush and the low-value hardwoods to conifers. Two-year seedlings were used. The original spacing between trees was 5 feet by 6 feet (1,452 trees to the acre), but the plantation went through a severe drought in 1936 and 300 fence posts were harvested in 1945. In 1947, nevertheless, 1,176 trees were still growing on an acre. Because of the experimental nature of the plantation, the cost was high—$33 an acre. Already there are 6.7 cords of pulpwood, worth about $13, available, although half of the trees are still less than minimum pulpwood size. The next cut should be made about 1955 to thin the stand.

A 1923 red pine plantation, 6 feet by 6 feet in spacing, has 820 trees an acre left; the merchantable volume is 1,390 board feet and 24.2 cords, worth about $60 if clear-cut now. The density of the stand suggests the desirability of making a thinning that will yield box bolts and pulpwood. While the actual cost of establishment is missing, it would appear that a light cut would yield a stumpage return sufficient to pay the initial cost of establishment as well as the essential pruning of thrifty crop trees.

The market demand is steady for all products from pulpwood size up. A market must be developed for salvage material just under pulpwood size. The young stands that were given release and thinning in the early days of the depression period have now grown to a point where a commercial improvement cut is desirable to keep the stand growing steadily at an even rate. Much of the material which should be removed is too small for pulpwood.

An effort is being made to mechanize operations in the woods, so that the material can be handled economically as posts to supply a market in the Great Plains. A trial sale was made in 1947 on 16 acres of red pine, which had been thinned in 1934 at 23 years of age. The tract was marked on a strict improvement basis, and all thrifty well-formed trees were left with more room to grow. It yielded 2,500 posts, 26.1 cords of pulpwood, and 7.8 cords of box bolts. As the purchaser found the cost of hand peeling posts too high to allow fair profit, he crowded as much of the larger post material to pulpwood as he could.

The stumpage return to the Government averaged $6.80 an acre. The purchaser hired all the work of felling, peeling, skidding, and hauling, yet made $1.40 an hour for his own time in giving supervision to the operation. Had an adequate post-peeling machine been available, the production of posts probably would have been more economical. Such machines are being manufactured and the securing of several to be operated on a custom basis will be another advance in intensive management. Jack pine, aspen, and other species, as well as red pine, should be suitable for fence posts if treated.

The market for fence posts will be limited by the capacity of pressure-treating plants, which already have full schedules of railroad ties, poles, piling, and other timber. Additional treating capacity close to the forest is needed.

A semichemical plant for the production of boards and container material, and one that can use the small material of most species with the bark on, would be a welcome addition. Likewise, additional plants for processing and remanufacture will add much towards further intensity of management. The installation of a concentration yard and finishing plant at Deer River as a project of the Iron Range Resources and Rehabilitation Commission was undertaken in 1948.

When the present management plans were prepared in the early 1930's, they were based on rather crude data as to volume. Growth calculations failed to take into consideration the better growth resulting from stand-improvement work. Moreover, the allowable cut did not consider fully the market opportunities that have since developed, especially for the small material. The present prescribed allow-ble cut is believed to be too conserva-ive. To correct this, and to have a aore substantial basis for intensive ıanagement, a new inventory was tarted in 1948.

The entire forest was photographed :om the air in 1947. The mapping of ypes was subsequently begun, and the ıventory developed through an in-ensive system of sample plots on a tatistically accurate basis. Attention vas given to redetermining the growth ate. We believe that the new type of ıaps, inventory, and growth data will roduce a management plan that will rescribe a greatly increased allowable nnual cut. Further attention can then e given to market requirements and evelopment, and action can be taken o insure full employment and com-aunity stability.

The process of rebuilding a fully pro-uctive forest is not completed but is well under way. The value of good management has been demonstrated and will become even more apparent as the trees grow toward maturity.

H. Basil Wales *entered the Forest Service in 1911, immediately after graduation from Michigan State College. After 19 years in the Southwest in various capacities, he was promoted to his present position as chief of the Division of Timber Management in the North Central Region. Since 1930 he has guided forest rehabilitation on the 12 national forest administration units in that region and has developed preliminary management plans to direct stand-improvement and harvest cuts. He directed the establishment of more than 700,000 acres of successful plantations, some of which are now ready for the first thinning on a commercial basis.*

# FORESTRY IN THE BLACK HILLS

ARTHUR F. C. HOFFMAN, THEODORE KRUEGER

On the western edge of the Great 'lains, separated from the massive ℓocky Mountains by long stretches of rairie, lie two of our national forests, he Black Hills and the Harney.

Huddled along the State line be-ween Wyoming and South Dakota—vith all but a thumb in the southwest-rn quarter of South Dakota—this sland of timber extends about 40 miles rom east to west, and 120 miles from ıorth to south. Its gross area is 1,524,-'97 acres, all but 20 percent (311,756 ıcres) of which is owned by the Fed-ral Government.

Its altitude ranges from 3,500 to ,240 feet (at Harney Peak), but most f the forest exhibits a rolling topog-aphy. There are, however, some fairly leep canyons on the lower ends of the nain drainages and some plateaus that ıave precipitous sides. Its generally ıigh situation subjects the forest to ex-remes of weather—severe hail storms, unseasonable freezes, tornadoes, and heavy rains and snows. A favorable factor for tree and forage growth is that the period of heaviest precipitation is in May and June, when more than 15 inches of rain may fall, although the average is usually about 8 inches.

Fauna and flora of East and West meet on the Black Hills and Harney National Forests—more simply named the Black Hills National Forest or the Black Hills. The commercial timber stand is 95 percent ponderosa pine and about 5 percent western white spruce (*Picea glauca* var. *albertiana*). A small area contains lodgepole pine. The total stand of coniferous timber is estimated to be 2,346 million feet, board measure. The average tree contains about 250 board feet, and the average stand is a little over 5,000 board feet an acre. The few hardwoods here have rather low economic importance:

Paper birch, the boxelder, cottonwood, aspen, ironwood, and bur oak.

The spruce grows in the higher altitudes on the northern and western slopes and in the draws and gulches. A narrow stringer of grassland lies in the gulch bottoms. The remainder of the forest is the natural site for the pine.

Wherever seed trees exist, natural reproduction does occur rapidly and surely; planting and seeding are necessary only in places where fire completely killed the stand. The young growth invariably comes in so thick that it is called dog-hair stands, and must be thinned to relieve the overcrowded condition. Up to 1948, 266,000 acres had been thinned.

In settlement and use, the Black Hills area is new country. It was considered to be Sioux Indian land until the gold stampede to the southern hills began in 1875. Agitation followed to open the area to settlers. On February 28, 1877, President Grant signed an act that excluded the Black Hills from the Indian reservation and legally opened the country. Settlement and mining activities had already started, however, and most of the camps and towns were established by 1876.

Unregulated cutting of the timber started at once to provide material for buildings and mines at Lead, Deadwood, Rochford, Carbonate, Mystic, Galena, Sturgis, and Rapid City. Portable sawmills operated at most of these places, and a string of them extended along the eastern side of the forest from Sturgis to Black Hawk. Cutting was also done on Rapid Creek to supply Rapid City.

At first, utilization of the forest was poor. Little action was taken to prevent forest fires until a series of large fires convinced settlers and miners that the timber supply would have to be more wisely used. Utilization began to be somewhat closer, probably because within the decade a large demand had developed for mine timbers, ties, fuel, and for lumber and heavy timbers.

No consideration was given then to the future of the resource, however and clear cutting was the rule unti about the turn of the century.

By 1897, enough of the resident realized that better care of the timber lands was necessary to assure adequat future supplies of timber and forage and they petitioned the Governmen to make a forest reserve of the area. I 1897, President Cleveland withdrev all land in the Black Hills from entry on September 19, 1898, the Black Hil Forest Reserve was placed under administration. It was later divided int two units for administrative purpose and renamed the Black Hills Nationa Forest and Harney National Forest.

Applications to purchase timbe were received by the supervisor almos immediately. The first one was fron the Homestake Mining Company which for some time had been cuttin timber in this area. The resulting sale the first one made on any nationa forest in the United States, is familiarl known as Case 1. The company ha continued to be a heavy purchaser o national forest timber.

The conditions of sale and cuttin for Case 1, compared with those nov in effect, are of historic interest, a showing the initial step in the developing of silvicultural practices on th forest.

Offered in Case 1 were 15,519,30 board feet of saw timber and 5,10 cords of wood from the tops of liv trees, at a minimum of $1 a thousan board feet and 25 cents for a cord Standing dead timber was offered fo 50 cents a thousand feet and dow dead timber for 15 cents a cord. Th timber to be sold was called Norwa pine but was actually ponderosa pin In comparison, the advertised minimum stumpage price in the same locality had increased in 1948, in one cas at least, to $17.37 a thousand boar feet.

Eight contracts were let for the eigh sections of land comprising the sal area. Cutting started at Christmas i 1899. Cutting the first year was to strict 8-inch-diameter limit, which pro duced an average of about 5,000 board feet an acre. Later, at the request of the Forest Service, the method of cutting was modified so that not more than two of the larger trees were left on an acre for seed trees. One of the requirements of the contract was that the slash be piled by the operator after all tops had been made into cordwood. In general, however, the slash was poorly piled; on the less accessible places, where the cordwood was hard to get out, the purchaser's contractors followed the practice of covering the trimmed tops with slash.

Before the cutting was completed and the case closed in April 1908, four extensions of time had been granted. The total cut was less than the estimated volume by almost a million board feet, but, because of the removal of practically all of the reserve stand, the area will not be ready for a second cut for many more years.

A survey showed that actually an average stand of only 482 board feet had been left per acre when the cut was made. In 1924, the average stand per acre had increased to 2,611 board feet. This indicates how rapidly the volume increases when heavy cuttings are made, but is no argument for cutting as heavy as that originally done in the Case 1 area.

When the forest was established, it was thought that local demands would be sufficient to use the entire allowable cut. In the beginning, the lumbering and timber industry grew at the same rate as the mining industry developed. Actually, for many years, the size of the timber industry was limited by local demand.

The Homestake Mine is still the largest single user of local timber on the Black Hills National Forest. The company has purchased large holdings of timberland that were in private ownership to supplement timber available to them from the national forest.

Railroads also used a great deal of the Black Hills timber. The agricultural areas surrounding the national forest developed at about the same rate as the mining industry, which provided a market for the agricultural products; farmers, too, were users of the products of the timber.

A sawmill, now known as the Warren Lamb Mill, was established in Rapid City in 1907. The expanding lumber industry needed outside markets to absorb the production that exceeded local needs, but the ban on interstate shipping of any except fire- or insect-killed timber restricted the growth of the lumbering industry, until 1912. In that year it was lifted.

Thereafter the industry was free to expand and was limited only by the size of the allowable cut provided for by the management plans. The volume of timber cut varied in accordance with business conditions: It was up in good times and down in times of depression, but through the years more stability was evidenced in this industry than in some other industries, such as farming and livestock raising.

To date an estimated 2,800 million board feet of timber has been cut from the areas in the Black Hills. Of that amount, about 1½ billion feet were cut in the old mining days from 1876 to 1898, before the national forest was created. Between 1908 and 1948, the cut was 1,084,923,000 board feet.

The average annual cut of 40 million feet since 1942 has furnished 140,000 man-days of labor a year in woods and mills to local people.

BLACK HILLS TIMBER has always had a high cull factor (15 to 35 percent). The timber cuts out mostly low grades of lumber. Eventually, lumber from the Northwest was shipped into the Black Hills territory and competed strongly with local lumber. The larger mills developed new markets by becoming a supplier of special products that could be made from low-grade lumber—boxes and crates for the meat-packing industry, grain doors, table tops made by gluing together small pieces of lumber, and shipping crates for refrigerators. Utilization of a high percentage of the log became general.

802062°—49——22

When the forest was established and cutting of timber started under government supervision, it was not supervised by trained foresters. Young men who later occupied responsible positions in the Forest Service, however, started their early work and gained experience on this forest. The development of proper methods of cutting, slash disposal, and fire protection were started and gradually improved.

Before the establishment of the national forests, most of the timber cutting was in the accessible stands. The sawmill operators took as many or as few of the trees as they wanted and converted them into mine timbers, ties, lumber, or cordwood. They passed up the diseased, the deformed, and the limby trees, and those on steep or rocky slopes. Consequently, the stand was left in poor silvicultural condition, cluttered with slash, and extremely vulnerable to damage by fire. Poor trees occupied space needed for growing better trees.

Federal foresters imposed regulations that were intended to stop such wasteful cutting. Much experimental marking was done. Foresters developed a progressive intensification of cutting practices—from clear cutting to diameter limit, selection cutting, and the present shelterwood system. Records show that the latter system was originally advocated by some early-day foresters. More recently the tendency has been away from heavy cuts to light cuts at shorter intervals.

In the first rules for marking that were prepared for the forest, emphasis was placed on the need to insure natural reproduction in case of fire. As insurance, it was the policy to leave two, three, or four seed trees on an acre. The first marking rules apparently were based on the idea that a second cut would not be made within 80 years or more.

Clear cutting with seed trees is good under some conditions, but experience taught foresters that other methods were better in the Black Hills. By 1913 they could use a selection system by which, in certain areas, some trees with good growth possibilities could be left for a second cut. The interval between cuts thus could be shortened.

In the Black Hills, good progress has been made toward achieving the objective of forestry—to produce and use all the timber that the soil on the area will grow. The ideal never is reached in large areas of rough land, such as national forests; economic considerations have a powerful influence, and other uses of the forest must be coordinated with timber production. However, selective cutting has developed through the years. The demand for timber has continued. Better roads have been built. Logging methods and equipment have been improved. By 1926, forest practices had developed to the extent that the selection system was applied universally in the Black Hills. The initial cut in virgin stands was lighter. The more thrifty trees—amounting to 1,500 to 2,000 or more board feet an acre—were left for future cuts. Under those conditions, shorter intervals between cuts became practicable.

The establishment of reproduction in the Black Hills requires no special effort when proper cutting practices are followed. Present marking rules are based on the idea of harvesting the mature crop trees and the development of silvicultural conditions favorable to the maximum growth of the reserve stands. Cutting cycles are being shortened and cuts per acre are made lighter. This is possible through the development of the access-road system, by which the stands are made more accessible to cutting and to favorable markets for sawlogs and other timber products.

Present management plans are predicated upon cutting cycles of 30 to 35 years. They will be shorter in the future, however, as more intensive forestry becomes economically practicable. Subject to variations in existing mature stands, the aim is to leave reserve stands averaging 2,000 to 3,000 board feet, net scale, an acre. One of the basic principles of the present marking policy is that the rate of growth of a reserve tree depends on the amount of release that results from cutting adjacent trees and on the age and vigor of the individual tree that is left.

The preparation of plans for management of the timber resource was started soon after the forest was established, but the plans were incomplete and ineffective, due in part to the lack of definite information on rate of annual growth and amount of timber on the forest. By 1923, however, enough basic information was available to permit better planning.

The plan made in 1925 for the Nemo working circle was typical of all plans applied here until 1937 to 1948, when the plans were completely revised. The Nemo plan provided for a rotation of 140 years and 4 cutting cycles of 35 years each. It was thought that one could remove 70 percent of the volume of the stand in trees that were 10 inches or more in diameter at breast height.

Later timber surveys, which now cover the entire forest except a small part of the southern end, have made available more reliable information on volume and classes of timber. Subsequent research has provided better information on rates of growth. Consequently, it has been possible to prepare better and more effective timber-management plans. The most outstanding change in the latest plan is the shortening of the cutting cycle to 30 years.

Since 1898 there has been regulation of allowable cut of timber on the forest. In the beginning, because the information was lacking about total volume of timber and rate of growth, cutting budgets were based largely on guess. From the time they were first assigned to the Black Hills, foresters were aware of the need for instituting scientific forestry practices in the handling of the resources. They received support from most of the people, and eventually convinced at least the timber-using industries that regulation of cutting and protection of the timber stand were imperative if those industries were to survive. Heavy demand for the timber makes it possible to observe the principles of regulated cutting in that the amount to be cut, as well as the units that are to be cut, can be actually controlled.

The total annual, allowable sustained-yield cut for the two forests is 36 million board feet of saw timber. In addition, a large volume is available as cordwood, fence posts, poles, and so on, taken largely from thinnings.

Annual growth is now considered sufficient to justify an annual cut of that volume, and little change will be necessary unless insects, fires, or tornadoes cause heavy losses. The volume of timber cut each year may exceed or may not equal the allowable amount, but the volume must be in agreement with the allowable amount over a 10-year period.

The local timber operators are familiar with these important management plans, and know they must be observed. During the Second World War, some operators tried to get an increase in the allowable annual cut, with the understanding that, after the war, a corresponding reduction of cut would be made. They changed their minds, however, when they were shown that economic depression would result after the war if the normal activity of the timber industry were to be reduced substantially.

During the time of the Emergency Relief Administration, National Industrial Recovery Administration, and the Civilian Conservation Corps, thousands of acres of dense young stands were thinned and some pruning of crop trees was done. The work was expensive because only a small part of the material that was removed could be sold. During the war, the demand for fence-post material was heavy, and it became possible to get young post-size stands thinned without cost to the Government. Better yet, the material brought some revenue to the Treasury. The post industry has been rather well stabilized, and each year a sizable acreage is thinned by the post operators. The largest of these operators has a pressure-treating plant at Deadwood, which peels, treats, and ships up to 50 cars of treated posts monthly. Some thinning also is done annually on timber-sale areas under provisions of the Knutson-Vandenberg Law. Still, areas of natural reproduction will always exist and they will have to be thinned at the right time so that supply of post material will be assured. Research work is in progress to determine the allowable annual cut for post-timber stands.

When utilization of the timber in the Black Hills was started, the only method of hauling and skidding was by horse and oxen. Roads were poor and poorly drained. They deteriorated rapidly when maintenance was discontinued; the sections that were on steep grades soon became unusable.

When it was necessary to go farther back into the woods, railroads were built to haul logs and lumber. Then came motortrucks. The Homestake Mining Company used trucks that pulled two trailers; this combination could haul average loads of 14 thousand board feet of logs from the woods to the mill. The industry improved its transportation system as rapidly as the manufacturers of vehicles developed better trucks and tractors. All logs now are transported on trucks, and most of the skidding is done by tractors. The size of the trucks varies from 1½ tons to capacities of 7,000 board feet. Truck hauling is so efficient that it has entirely replaced railroad logging.

Better roads on the forest are necessary. Because the trend in management plans is to provide for shorter cutting cycles, more permanent roads are needed so that plans can be formulated for timber cutting on areas where cutting has to be done or where cutting should be done to salvage insect-infested or the windthrown trees. Also, it is more economical to have roads of a permanent type: They save cost of rebuilding each time an area is logged and make possible the hauling of larger loads or the use of smaller trucks.

The degree of utilization of timber that has been cut on the forest has varied usually with the general changes in economic conditions. In the early days there was close utilization because of the need for lumber, mine timbers, and fuel; later, the selling price of timber products determined largely how much of the tree could be used. Because there is such a large percentage of defect in the Black Hills timber and because the allowable cut has been less than the demand much of the time, foresters and efficient operators alike have concentrated on developing markets and uses for low-grade lumber and on methods for getting more out of each log. The necessary length of haul from the woods to the market caused costs of operation to go up; so, it became necessary either to leave more of the tree in the woods or to find a way to make a profit from all that was hauled to the market.

One way that the yield of the log was increased was by the use of resaws, which enabled the mills to get merchantable material from most of the slab. Markets were developed for short and narrow boards, which were glued together to make table tops. It became possible to dispose of small pieces for use in making boxes and crates, and a market was found for short-length moldings. There is still a good market for fuel, so little material now goes to the refuse burner.

The demand for Black Hills timber will apparently always be larger than the allowable cut. Unless future costs become excessive, even more intensive utilization than is obtained at present should be in order.

Intensive forestry in the Black Hills depends directly on the protection that can be given the forest.

It has suffered much damage from fires, four of which have burned over 80,000 acres. Damage by insects has been great in some years; from 1895 to 1909, approximately 1½ billion feet of timber on the western side of the forest was destroyed by the Black Hills beetle (*Dendroctonus ponderosae* Hopk.). Another large infestation of the beetle started in 1946, and it became necessary to initiate a large-scale control project, which in 1948 treated 46,000 insect-infested trees and for which Congress made a special appropriation of $235,000.

In 1893, fires destroyed the timber on large areas on the drainages of the Elk, Iron, and Polo Creeks. Other large fires were the McVey, in 1939, which burned 21,857 acres; the Rochford, in 1931, which burned 21,590 acres; and the Lost Gulch, Moskee, Buskala, Matt, Victoria, Black Fox, Beaver, and Bearlodge fires, each of which denuded large areas. Between 1909 and 1947, 92,760 acres of national forest land were burned over by 4,130 fires and about 28,000 acres of private land burned in the Black Hills.

We have to cut losses from fires. In this day of better methods of hauling men and equipment, better communication systems, and better fire equipment, the annual loss from fire should be much lower. A hopeful sign is that more and more people are becoming increasingly aware of how dangerous it is to be careless with matches in or near forests, and how close is the relationship between fire control and timber management on the Black Hills. If the protection job is ineffective, the resource-management plan is upset; so, also, are the plans of every operation that depends upon the forest for its raw material.

On the areas where the loss from insect damage occurred, natural reproduction took place so that artificial reforestation has been unnecessary. But many of the fires completely killed everything on large areas, and planting or seeding, or both, has been necessary to start another stand of timber.

The first reforestation work done on the Black Hills was in 1905, on what was called the Custer Peak Experiment Area. Forty acres were successfully established by the broadcast and the corn-planter methods. Since then, 10,946 acres have been planted; 9,570 acres more have been seeded. At the end of 1948, 13,472 acres had been reforested. The present plan is to plant a million trees a year for at least 10 years.

The care, protection, and utilization of the timber always will be the most important work of those who are in charge of the forest—activities that protect the watershed and provide a stable supply of raw material for the lumber and timber industry. But many people think more and oftener of the other uses that are made of the forest.

The Black Hills National Forest probably has as great a variety of uses as any in the Nation. It is all accessible and all used, and there is little friction among the various classes of users. South Dakotans have deep loyalty for the forest and have great and helpful interest in what is being done on it.

Grazing is one use. The average number of stock grazed under permit between 1943 and 1948 was 27,435 head of cattle and horses and 28,262 sheep. The stock graze mostly in the gulches and stream bottoms, on the stringers of bluegrass range, on old-burn areas, and on some of the exposed ridge tops. Most of the 682 holders of grazing permits live on small to medium-sized farms inside the forest boundaries. These men are deeply conscious of fire hazard; they are always the first to arrive at the fires that do start; they are the backbone of the first attack crews. They know they are protecting their own as well as public property.

The use of the forests for recreation is constantly increasing. A large industry has grown up to take care of tourists. The forest officers consider the recreation feature of the forest a resource in itself and actively protect it as such. Out-of-State visitors to the forests come mostly from the Middle West. Many others from more distant regions stop on their way to the Northwest. The chambers of commerce and other groups whose function is to serve the guests are aware of the value of the tourist business and the importance of keeping the forest in good shape.

On the forest are five camps for church organizations, camps for Boy Scouts and Girl Scouts, a YWCA camp, and health camps. Two Government-owned camps are used by 4-H Clubs and other groups of young people. Several colleges and universities conduct summer field work in the forest, which is an exceptionally good area for the study of geology, mining, botany, forestry, ornithology, and other sciences. Among the institutions that have done such work are Dartmouth College, Smith College, South Dakota School of Mines, Spearfish State Teachers College, and Princeton University.

The streams are not large or numerous and fishing is somewhat limited. The forests have many mule deer and whitetail deer, but only a few elk.

Mining is important in the region. The Homestake Mining Company's mine at Lead, established in 1876, is the largest producer of gold in the Western Hemisphere. The industry uses large volumes of timber products, and its employees make full use of the recreational facilities of the forest. The mining companies and their employees are also willing fire fighters and protectors of the forest.

Three hydroelectric power plants use water that originates on the forest.

The fiftieth anniversary of the establishment of the Black Hills National Forest was observed on September 19, 1948, on the place and date of the first timber sale. Much progress has been made in forestry since that date, but much remains to be done.

ARTHUR F. C. HOFFMAN, *a forester, joined the Forest Service in 1910 as field assistant on the White River National Forest in Colorado. Beginning in 1917, he was successively supervisor of the San Juan, Montezuma, and Rio Grande National Forests, all in Colorado, and supervisor of the Black Hills National Forest, with headquarters at Deadwood, S. Dak. He retired from the Forest Service in 1948.*

THEODORE KRUEGER *is staff assistant in timber management in the office of the regional forester in Denver. He was supervisor of the Black Hills National Forest from 1930 to 1938, when much of the work of improving the timber by thinning and opening the stands and building access roads was done.*

# TAMING A WILD FOREST

JOHN R. BRUCKART

The Douglas-fir region in the western part of Oregon and Washington covers some 55,000 square miles. Five-sixths of it is forest land and one-sixth is farm land. On the forest land stands one-third of the saw timber remaining in the United States. Two-fifths of that saw timber is in the national forests, which make up 16,000 square miles of the most isolated forest land in western Oregon and Washington. The saw timber is mainly Douglas-fir, with some hemlock, cedar, and true firs.

The Willamette National Forest, in west-central Oregon, is one of these Douglas-fir forests. Forest management on the Willamette has several unique aspects, but otherwise it typifies forest management on the other national forests of the Douglas-fir region.

In 1893, when President Grover Cleveland established the 4,883,000-acre Cascade Range Forest Reserve, he included within its boundaries the 1,819,483 acres that are now the Willamette National Forest. The forest was created in its present form in 1933, when the Santiam National Forest (created in 1911) and the Cascade National Forest (created as such in 1908) were combined.

At the time of President Cleveland's proclamation, and for 20 years thereafter, the territory was the real untamed, wild, virgin forest—practically as untouched by man as it had been in 1804 when Lewis and Clark first explored the Oregon country. Indeed, practically the only change had been the one inflicted by fires. Trees that had sprouted from seed at the time of William the Conqueror still flourished as primeval giants in the humid valleys and canyons; deer wandered over trails that Indians had always used for hunting and fishing; the white man's only marks on the wilderness were three wagon trails through Cascade Mountain passes and three small settlements.

As in the rest of the Douglas-fir region, the forest reached mile on mile across mountains and canyons. The mantle of trees was unbroken but for the ghosts of past fires. The stately Douglas-fir was king, and the king's girth was so large that a 10-foot measure would not cover the distance across a fallen giant's stump. Many of the trees were clear of branches to 150 feet above the ground. As the timber approached higher elevations at the Cascade summit, the Douglas-fir grew smaller in size and gradually merged with upper-slope and subalpine types—mountain hemlock, alpine and silver fir, and Engelmann spruce, which now are valuable chiefly for watershed protection and recreation and as a reservoir of pulp for the future.

So vast was the forest that the first national forest administrators themselves did not know how much resource had been put in their custody or what the growth habits of the trees were. Whatever was known in those days of the art of forest management could hardly apply to those forests. The techniques and doctrines of forest management had been devised for European forests, and seemingly no common denominator, whether economic or physical, was at hand for managing forests that differed as much as these did from European forests. The only logical thing that the early rangers and supervisors could do was to use their own judgment, and to wait and see what would happen.

Things did begin to happen. Timber claims and homestead entries brought people to the more accessible parts of the forest. Their activities and the dry summers and the lightning storms soon made it apparent that something would have to be done about forest fires or there would be no forest left to administer. It was apparent also that the bulk of the forest land was valuable principally for protecting the watersheds and for growing timber, but that streams and lakes should be preserved for fishing and recreation and the alpine meadows near the summit could be used for grazing cattle and sheep.

THE FIRST MANAGEMENT PROCEDURES developed on the Willamette National Forest were for fire protection. The reason was simple: If fire were not kept out of the forest, there would be no need to devise complicated sustained-yield plans. Fires here were endemic—a recurring phenomenon. Since the beginning of time, lightning had struck the high ridges and fires had burned unchecked until autumn rains put them out. In wet years, the fires were small. In dry years, the fires were catastrophic. In the high country, when fires did not occur naturally, the Indians set their own fires once in a while in the belief that old burns made the best grounds for hunting and huckleberry picking. Even the early miners and settlers considered it proper to touch off a few thousand acres of forest land if they thought any personal advantage would accrue.

In 1902 Forest Examiner Fred G. Plummer looked over the part of the reserve that is now the Willamette National Forest and said: "From all points on the . . . divide the views are grand. On a clear day the panorama extends from Mount St. Helens, in Washington, to Diamond Peak, and includes 10 snow-capped mountains, with hundreds of lesser peaks. The middle ground is of lakes, meadows, cinder cones, and rivers of lava, and the foreground would be in perfect keeping with the picture if it were not too frequently an unsightly burn."

He estimated that 10 percent of the area was covered by new burns and that probably 90 percent of the entire forest at some remote period had suffered from fires, of which traces still remained.

In the beginning men were lacking to do the job. Among the first supervisors were men like Cy Bingham, a westerner who combined the positions of county judge and sheriff with his Government work, and Tom Sherrard, a young easterner who had studied forestry in Europe. Each field man had about 500,000 acres to protect from fire or trespass. On such large areas one man could do little in serious fire situations except to put out small fires and report the acreage burned over by the larger fires.

The forests in the Douglas-fir region always have been uniquely susceptible to bad fires. The dry summers, the predominance of resinous trees, and the great volume of inflammable material on the ground create an acute hazard all through the summer. The increasing use of the forest by travelers, vacationers, loggers, and settlers has increased the chances of man-caused fires. Lightning storms can easily ignite the material; in critical fire weather, a spark from a logging donkey, a burning match, or the cigarette of a passerby can set off a conflagration.

Several bad fire years have occurred on the Willamette National Forest since it was created. One of the worst was in 1919, when several fires burned over about 31,000 acres.

Through the years a systematic fire-protection organization has been developed. The number of smokechasers was increased. Lookout cabins were built. The back country was made more accessible by new trails and roads. New fire-fighting tools were developed. Portable pumps and hose that could be carried by men or pack animals were used. Dropping men and supplies from airplanes was then tried. Agreements were made with hundreds of experienced loggers, sawmill workers, and other local cooperators for getting trained fire fighters in a hurry.

The effect of the organization is evident from the record for the 5 years from 1943 to 1948. During the period (when, it is true, the weather was favorable for fire fighting), 391 fires were started on the forest, practically all by lightning, but the area burned averaged only 139 acres each year.

Another step came in the techniques of burning logging slash. Fire experts agree that slash from logging is the most dangerous type of fuel. As a result of a series of large fires in slash, for many years the controlled burning of the slash was considered necessary. The early logger was not particularly skillful in his burning techniques, however; it was not unusual for a slash-burning fire to get out of control. Through experience, men learned that in this region slash could be burned safely only at certain periods of the year—usually after the first heavy fall rains—and then only by using careful burning procedures. It has become standard practice to postpone burning until fuel under the green timber is wet (usually after 2½ to 5 inches of rainfall); to start burning in the afternoons so that fires will die down during the night; to burn downhill on steep slopes. Thus fire hazard is reduced with a minimum of damage to the forest. Recently improved cutting practices, such as partial cutting or area selection, have tended to simplify the slash-burning problem by breaking up slash areas into small segments.

The headwaters of the Middle Fork Willamette, McKenzie, and Santiam Rivers are within the Willamette forest. All are major contributors to the flow of the Willamette River, whose waters are important to agriculture and industry in Oregon.

The management of the national forest is planned to safeguard the water yields, through maintenance of an adequate forest cover. Protection from fire, regulation of timber harvesting, and control of grazing help to maintain and improve watershed conditions.

THE SELLING of timber to private logging operators and sawmills started early in the history of the Willamette National Forest. The first sale was one for 14 million board feet to J. B. Hills of Oakridge, in 1905. Between 1905 and 1940 the timber business increased at a comparatively modest rate. Recreation and fire protection were still the main items of business. The average cut on the entire forest for the 35 years was about 33 million board feet a year, and was mostly on the accessible Oakridge-Westfir area on the southern end of the forest and on the Detroit-North Santiam area at the northern end of the forest. The first timber sales on three of the six ranger districts on the forest were not made until after 1940.

In the Willamette Valley logging has changed from a primitive form to a highly mechanized operation within the span of a single generation. Early-day bull teams gave way to steam donkey logging; steam donkeys, in turn, were supplanted by trucks and tractors. Old-timers now high in lumbering circles, like Faye Abrams of Springfield and H. J. Cox of Eugene, can remember when they logged with bull teams and horse teams and how they later switched to steam donkey, chutes, and skid roads.

Early logging in the Douglas-fir region was primitive. Bull teams, made famous by the legends of Paul Bunyan's Blue Ox, were the primary logging machines until nearly 1900. The early 1900's saw the coming of power logging—the emergence of the steam donkey as the principal logging machine. Several years later, high-lead logging was developed. In high-lead logging, a lumberjack had to cut off the top of a tall tree, called a spar tree. Logs were hauled to the landing by a long cable rigged to the top of the spar tree. By hauling in the cable, the donkey engine dragged the largest logs to a common pile, sometimes called a "cold deck," from which point the logs were skidded by another machine along a chute or a skid road to be loaded on the railroad or dumped into the river. River driving was common on the Willamette and McKenzie Rivers in the early 1900's.

The method was destructive to trees left standing. Any standing tree in the path of a load of logs on its way to the landing would promptly be knocked flat, for steam donkeys were powerful engines.

Despite the use of cheaper river driving close to rivers, the logging railroad reached its peak as a logging tool at about the same time as the steam donkey. The first large timber sales made on the Willamette were logged with donkey and railroad, a method so expensive that much of the timbered country was considered inoperable because of the rugged topography.

Because of its rough terrain and because a huge volume of privately owned timber was readily accessible to water transportation in the Puget Sound, Grays Harbor, and Columbia River territories, only a moderate amount of cutting of Willamette National Forest timber was made for nearly 40 years after the first timber sale was made.

The boom in truck and tractor logging in the late 1930's and the greater demand for lumber as war approached gave impetus to the spurt in timber sales that started in 1940 when 56 million board feet were cut and increased to 207 million in 1948.

Another advance came in 1933, when an analysis of the resources of the Douglas-fir region by the Pacific Northwest Forest and Range Experiment Station was finished. From it came more definite information about what was actually on the ground—an inventory of timber types and dependable estimates of board-foot volumes; a framework on which to base future plans for timber cutting and from which the allowable annual sustained-yield cut could be calculated. On the basis of forest-management formulas the allowable annual cut was determined to be 323 million board feet, the amount that the land could grow if it is kept fully productive.

With the allowable cut determined, still another problem remained—what methods of cutting would most effectively keep the lands productive.

The Forest Service always has reserved the right on its timber sales to require that, as a fire-prevention measure, the slash be burned; that no merchantable logs be left in the woods after logging; that stumps be cut low to keep from wasting timber; and that seed trees be left to reseed cut-over areas.

Until recently, however, extensive areas of clear cutting were common on national forest timber sales, with the provision that seed trees be left. The seed-tree method of providing for restocking of young trees left something to be desired, it was found, because lone Douglas-fir trees are easily blown down by strong winter winds that periodically buffet the Pacific coast. The cut-over land, with no seed source, consequently often grew up to brush instead of to young fir trees.

The development of truck and tractor logging made it possible to reduce the size of clear-cutting areas and still not make the logging cost too high to permit cutting.

Truck and tractor logging is a flexible mode of operation. It made possible sales to small operators, who could afford to log timber only where a limited capital investment in logging equipment and development was required. Tracts of timber not large enough to justify building an expensive logging railroad could be opened.

The first cruisers who had scouted the forest observed that most of the timber volume on the Willamette was in old-growth, overmature stands of Douglas-fir. Later cruises and the publication of the systematic resource survey confirmed their observations. True, in certain localities there were extensive stands of second-growth, the sequel to large fires that had devastated vast areas along the Cascades in the nineteenth century. But far the greater part of the volume was in overmature, stagnant stands—stands that were losing as many board feet each year from decay, disease, and windthrow as they were adding through new growth. The worst of it was that losses were in the slow-growing and high-quality "yellow fir," from which most of the valuable clear lumber and plywood is produced in this region. The first need, then, was to convert the overmature timber to a growing condition—to utilize the old trees and to harvest the trees that were likely to be windthrown.

To accomplish their purpose, foresters needed a logging system that would have four characteristics: It had to bypass growing parts of a stand but cut the overmature trees, so as to convert the stagnant forest into a growing forest in the shortest time. It had to extend the transportation system over the entire forest more quickly, so as to make possible the salvage of windfalls and the fire-killed or insect-killed trees, and the profitable thinning of young stands at a later date. It had to leave a large part of the timber as a reserve to provide for natural reproduction and preserve the values of watershed protection, recreation, and scenery. It had to avoid creating extensive areas of slash accumulation.

That ideal logging system is the one to use in converting forest management from a virgin-timber basis to a vigorously growing, second-growth basis in about 100 years—the rotation (that is, the number of years required to mature a crop of timber) in which Douglas-fir forests produce a maximum volume of wood.

A FOREST usually consists of trees of different sizes; sometimes the age of trees on a single acre can vary widely. Some trees are vigorous and fast growing; others are weak and may live only a short time. Foresters study the composition of timber stands and develop cutting practices to fit particular conditions.

Some forests—such as those composed chiefly of ponderosa pine—respond well to partial cutting, or selective logging. Trees marked for cutting are those that are economically ripe and those that are weakened by insects, disease, or fire. The younger, healthy trees are left for further growth. Thus, the poor-risk and mature trees are removed over the whole area; a full forest cover is left, with only small openings. In these, the young trees become established, and the production of future timber crops is uninterrupted.

Selective logging has been done in Douglas-fir forests. The results have not always been good. It is difficult to remove large trees from these dense stands without serious injury to some of the trees which it is planned to leave. Loss from windfall may be serious. On some stands, careful application will produce desirable results, but often it is not practicable to cut the old-growth Douglas-fir stands on the basis of selecting individual trees to be removed. That is very true on steep slopes.

Another key reason for not using the true selective-logging system in old-growth Douglas-fir hinges upon a characteristic of Douglas-fir seedlings: The young trees will not tolerate shade. Unless the openings made by logging are one-half acre or larger in size, Douglas-fir seedlings will not thrive and the Douglas-fir stand will not reproduce itself. And if enough trees are logged selectively to open the stand sufficiently to insure Douglas-fir reproduction, the danger of serious windfall becomes excessive.

Workers in the Douglas-fir region therefore turned to other means of accomplishing the same purposes—area selection, which also is termed patch cutting, logging by staggered settings, or clear cutting by small blocks. Whatever the name, the principle was the same—to clear-cut small areas of timber and to leave reserve or seed strips surrounding the cut-over areas. Leaving solid reserve strips seemed to eliminate most of the danger of windthrow. After the cutting units, as the blocks to be cut over were called, were clear-cut, enough light could get to the ground to favor the natural reseeding and survival of Douglas-fir seedlings rather than those of minor species. Patch cutting, or area selection, met the other requirements of the ideal Douglas-fir silvicultural system. It made less fire hazard. It tended to minimize damage to watersheds, scenic beauty, and wildlife. It favored salvage logging. The more they tried it, the better the foresters liked it.

As the patch-cutting idea developed, methods of laying out logging units improved. At first, no one knew what was the proper size for the cutting patches. Foresters laid out units as large as 120 to 200 acres, but patches of that size did not seem to reseed completely from green timber around the fringes; it has since been necessary to plant some of those cut-over areas in order to assure satisfactory stocking of new trees. The policy now is to have cutting patches that average from 40 to 100 acres each, with no part of the cut-over area further than 1,000 feet from green timber. With logging units this small, it seems that natural restocking will be assured in most cases.

As additional insurance, the timber-sale policy now is to assess a cooperative deposit, under the Knutson-Vandenberg Act, to provide for planting and stand-improvement work on the sale area after logging is completed. If a logged-over area has not restocked naturally after 5 years, it is replanted.

Under the area-selection system, the reserve timber—often designated as seed strips—is left standing until the cut-over patches are covered with trees and until those new trees are old enough to bear seed. Then the second and third cuts can be made to complete logging of the mature timber.

Patch cutting involves certain difficulties. Because it is essentially a clear-cutting system, the only way to get good forestry is in the lay-out of the logging plan. The designation of which timber is to be cut and which is to be left, the size and location of the cut-and-leave areas, and the location of roads and spar trees all limit the practices, good or bad, that will be used in logging. Improper lay-outs and poor road locations increase logging costs; the result is lower stumpage prices for the standing timber and a tendency toward poor forest practices.

The areas that will not be cut in the original patches should also be considered carefully since their lay-out, when they, in turn, are logged sometime in the future, also depends on the original location of roads and cutting areas. The men who do this planning must be good foresters and good practical logging engineers.

In order to lay out a system of patch cutting intelligently, a great deal of engineering work is needed before a timber sale is made. A road system over which the timber cut in the first cutting cycle can be hauled must be located, with the thought in mind that the same road might be used in making the second cut 20 or 40 years later and that salvage cuts may be made at other times.

To locate the road system and lay out the proposed cutting units in a logical and practical manner requires a good topographic map such as forest cruisers usually make when they measure standing timber to determine how many board feet of lumber can be cut from the timber. Also essential is a map that shows the kind of trees and kind of stand of timber that is on the ground.

Proper planning in advance is important because the lay-out determines to a large extent the cost of logging. For example, timber on gentle slopes ordinarily should be tractor-logged. In order to log with tractors, the truck roads that tap any cutting area must be located below the unit because it is much more economical for tractors to drag heavy loads downhill. On the other hand, high-lead logging on steep ground is most economical when the logs are pulled uphill, because the logs tend to hang up and become tangled with stumps when they are pulled downhill. Therefore, roads should be located above "high-lead shows" but below "cat shows."

The ideal now on the Willamette National Forest is to keep the work of cruising, mapping, and road location at least 5 years ahead of the logging operations. The use of aerial photographs—which show streams and ridges exactly as they are on the ground, or, if they are of large enough scale, even the individual trees on the ground—may eliminate much of the field work that is necessary in making logging plans.

Although the allowable annual cut of the Willamette National Forest under sustained-yield management has been set at 323 million board feet, the actual cut in 1940 was only 56 million board feet. By 1948, it had been increased to 207 million board feet, still more than 100 million feet short of the allowable goal. It is desirable to reach this goal quickly in order to convert all of the forest land that is available for cutting to a growing instead of a stagnant condition as soon as possible without impairing the sustained-yield capacity of the forest. Planners expect that by 1952 the Willamette will reach an annual cut of 323 million board feet and maintain that figure as a permanent annual cut—a production that will last as long as the forest lasts.

Timber on the Willamette National Forest is naturally tributary to three Oregon counties: Lane, Linn, and Marion. The greater part would go to Lane and Linn Counties, in each of which is cut annually an average of about a billion board feet of timber, mostly on private land.

Sustained-yield capacities of public and private lands have been estimated as about 400 million feet for Linn County and 800 million feet for Lane County. Private timber, which accounts for about 50 percent of the total supply, now is being cut two to three times as fast as it can grow anew.

As the supply of private timber is cut out, the Willamette timber will be called upon more and more to support a number of communities that depend on it, among them Eugene, Springfield, Sweet Home, and Lebanon. The fact that this public timber is being cut on a sustained-yield basis will be a factor in the stability of the communities.

It has been estimated that Willamette timber will provide employment directly for some 5,000 persons when cutting does reach the sustained-yield level; many thousands more will be supported indirectly. On the Willamette, the problem has not been to limit the cut but to increase it up to the allowable limit. The reason has been the remoteness and inaccessibility of the back country, in which much of the timber grows.

Orderly harvesting of the timber will require the development of a system of timber-access roads. Early completion of the system is needed in order to prevent steadily occurring losses from natural causes in overmature and decadent stands. Such a road system will also serve as an aid in protection of the timber against fire and insect attack and will permit salvage of material lost from such causes.

The road-building plan on the Willamette calls for the early construction of 31 miles of timber-access roads into four main drainages—the Fall Creek, South Fork McKenzie, Blue River, and Winberry.

Definite steps have been taken to safeguard and develop recreation on the Willamette. Two areas of magnificent scenic beauty, the Mount Jefferson Wild Area and the Three Sisters Wilderness Area, have been set aside to be kept free of logging roads or other marks of civilization. In them will be 210,000 acres of land ,to be preserved in its pristine glory, unchanged from its condition when the first pioneers and fur traders set foot on them in the early nineteenth century. Also to be reserved from cutting are scenic strips along all major highways, fishing streams, and lakes. Several natural areas are also planned, to remain forever untouched, even by trails, as evidence to future generations of what their forefathers found here and as laboratories for scientific study.

The Forest Service has built 173 forest camps and picnic areas on the Willamette National Forest. Fireplaces, benches, and tables are provided for campers. Shelters are available in the inaccessible regions for use in rainy weather. Two organization camps are available now to civic and welfare organizations and three winter-sports areas have been developed.

In many of the more accessible recreational areas, such as the Breitenbush Hot Springs, the McKenzie River, the Upper Willamette River, and the North and South Santiam Rivers, resorts and hotels are operated by private concessions under permit. All six ranger districts have plans for leasing sites for summer homes.

Practically all the recreational improvements on the Willamette were built by the workers of the Civilian Conservation Corps. The thousands of youths, housed in eight camps from 1933 to 1941, built the forest camps, picnic areas, organization camps, winter-sports areas, trails, and roads during the great opening-up period of the 1930's. Their work also in fighting forest fires, building protection roads and trails, and constructing lookout stations and guard stations was invaluable in preventing disastrous fires and raising fire-protection standards.

The use of the ski areas on the Willamette Pass and McKenzie Pass territory has grown very rapidly. An even greater development has been the Hoodoo Butte area on the Santiam Pass, where a winter-sports area accommodates—at little cost—1,500 skiers.

With four snow-capped peaks—Mount Jefferson, North, Middle, and South Sister—all over 10,000 feet in elevation, and numerous lesser peaks, including Mount Washington (7,802 feet) and Three Fingered Jack (7,848 feet) as a backdrop, the high part of the forest along the summit of the Cascade Range possesses a scenic grandeur all its own. Hundreds of mountain lakes, many of which furnish excellent fishing, dot the alpine-meadow country. The Oregon Skyline Trail, a mecca for beauty seekers, follows the Cascade summit along the eastern boundary and traverses much of the more beautiful portion of the forest. The trail crosses through the Mount Jefferson Wild Area past the Eight Lakes Basin, skirts Three Fingered Jack and Mount Washington, wanders across the Three Sisters Wilderness Area, and heads south past Diamond Lake toward Crater Lake National Park.

FISH AND WILDLIFE are another of the multiple values of the Willamette. Patch cutting helps protect the game, because the patches are quickly covered with tree seedlings and palatable browse and for 15 years or so the patches provide excellent feed for deer, elk, and small game. For this reason, the system of patch cutting should materially benefit the wildlife resources of the forest. The game census of 1947 estimated 540 elk, 860 bear, 7,400 deer, 100 cougar, and 1,100 beaver.

GRAZING is another forest use, although it is carried on to a limited extent only. The 22 grazing units are located mainly along the summit of the Cascade Range and in the most part consist of alpine-type meadows and old burns. As these areas are protected from fire, encroachment of conifer tree growth is gradually taking place and the net usable grazing area is constantly decreasing. It seems that grazing is destined never to be more than a minor use on the Douglas-fir forests west of the Cascades.

JOHN R. BRUCKART, *now supervisor of the Willamette National Forest, entered the Forest Service as a forest guard on the Snoqualmie National Forest in 1909. He has served since as district ranger, assistant forest supervisor, regional forest inspector, and forest supervisor in the Pacific Northwest. He has been associated with Douglas-fir management since early in his career, having done timber cruising, sale administration, and timber-appraisal work. He pioneered in the development of slash-disposal, fire-protection, and utilization techniques and the improvement of cutting practices. He received the Superior Service Award of the Department of Agriculture in 1947.*

# NEW SECURITY FOR FOREST COMMUNITIES

DAHL J. KIRKPATRICK

The Sustained-Yield Unit Act was designed to permit the Federal forest-management agencies to combine public and privately owned forest lands for joint sustained-yield operation. It also authorized the designation of dependent forest communities as the manufacturing points for Federal timber.

The need for such legislation as a measure to assure community stability was recognized on the Pacific coast a generation ago—when the ultimate result of excessively rapid private timber liquidation became apparent. The measure was enacted by the Seventy-eighth Congress on March 29, 1944, as Public Law 273 (58 Stat. 132; 16 U. S. C. 583–583i).

The law promises to be of considerable help to communities that depend on the forest industries for their economic support. It can assure sustained-yield management on large areas of the private forest lands that otherwise might be subjected to liquidation with the inevitable aftermath of community deterioration and ruin.

An example of how the legislation

works is illustrated by a review of the first case to which it was applied, the Shelton Cooperative Sustained-Yield Unit.

The Simpson Logging Co. started its operations in Shelton, the seat of Mason County, Wash., in 1895. At first, the company's operations were confined to logging. The entire output was sold on the log market of Puget Sound. The company grew and prospered with the new community. By the time the Sustained-Yield Unit Act was adopted, the frontier town of Shelton had become a flourishing town of 4,800 population, and the Simpson Logging Co. had matured into a substantial concern that operated two large sawmills and a Douglas-fir plywood plant at Shelton, as well as two outlying logging camps in the tributary forest area. The other important source of industrial support for the community was a pulp mill of an annual capacity of 75,000 tons.

During the first half century of timber operations in and about Shelton, the vast virgin forest, which had stretched back almost endlessly from the shores of Puget Sound, had shrunk to an alarming degree. Serious losses from forest fires in 1902 and active timber cutting by several large operators pushed back the forest frontier.

Then, one by one, as the virgin forest was depleted, the operating firms closed down or moved away. The last to reach the end of its holdings was the Henry McCleary Timber Co., which, besides its logging facilities, operated a sawmill at Shelton and a plywood plant and sash and door factory in the nearby company town of McCleary. The Simpson Logging Co. bought out the McCleary concern in 1942.

Unlike most of its contemporaries in the logging and lumbering business on Puget Sound, the Simpson Logging Co. did not let its cut-over forest lands revert to the counties for taxes, as was then customary. It kept its holdings and, as the opportunity permitted, extended its ownership of reproducing forest lands by buying the cut-over areas of other operating companies and by redeeming lands that the counties had acquired through tax foreclosure. Simpson pioneered in urging and securing the establishment of a forest fire-protection system in Washington. The firm's forest-land program was based upon a belief that forestry in western Washington would ultimately be a profitable business enterprise—that the ownership and protection of young growing forests would be the foundation on which such an enterprise would be built.

A few years after lumbering operations started near Shelton, the unappropriated public domain in the remote mountainous country, beyond what was then considered to be the economic limits of timber exploitation, was set aside as a part of the Olympic National Forest.

Little public notice was taken of the action; the reservation was largely beyond the zone of high-quality old-growth Douglas-fir, in rugged terrain where logging would be difficult and costly, and far from settlements and the Puget Sound log market. The values involved were so low that the withdrawal action was of little local concern.

During the time that the better and more accessible private timber in the lowlands was being used up, the national forest stumpage almost went begging. But with the development of transportation systems for harvesting the private forest zone and the introduction of improved logging equipment, the national forest resource became physically and economically accessible. It was no longer a remote area of low-grade timber in the back country; it became a valuable forest property whose management was vital to the well-being of the people in Shelton and McCleary.

When the Sustained-Yield Unit Act was passed, the Simpson Logging Co. owned 20,000 acres of virgin timberland that contained a billion board feet of timber. Simpson also had 140,000 acres of reproducing forest lands that supported young trees from 1 to 70 years old. The annual log requirements of Simpson's manufacturing facilities amounted to about 100 million board feet. About 7,400 persons depended for their livelihood on the continuation of the company's operations at that level of production. The national forest resource in the area tributary to the company's operations consisted of 110,000 acres of forest land, 89,000 acres of which were old-growth timber stands having a total volume of 4⅓ billion board feet.

Under sustained-yield harvesting, the cut from the national forest lands alone would have been 48 million board feet a year. Simpson's holdings could not practically have been subjected to sustained-yield management if anything approximating the current plant requirements were to be supplied. The company did not own enough mature timber. The 100 million board feet per year rate of cutting would have forced the company to liquidate its timber in 10 years; after that, production from company lands would have dropped to next to nothing for 30 years or so until the trees on the reproducing lands reached cutting size. During that period, production would have fallen to a level measured by the company's competitive purchases of national forest timber. It could not have exceeded 48 million a year. It might have been a great deal less. An extremely severe curtailment of industrial activity and a consequent economic crisis would have been inevitable in Shelton and McCleary.

The sustained-yield unit act permitted the Forest Service to join its timber resource with that of the company for unified management. The large reservoir of old-growth timber in national forest ownership thus could be used to bridge the production gap, pending the economic maturity of the company's young stands, and assurance could be given that the company's wood-using facilities in Shelton and McCleary would be maintained at approximately current levels. Within the limits of sustained-yield forest management, comparable stability for these communities could not otherwise be achieved. A combination like that for management purposes would guarantee that good forest practices and sustained yield would be applied to 268,000 acres of forest lands rather than to the 110,000 acres of national forest ownership alone. In consequence of these obvious public benefits, the Simpson Logging Co. and the Forest Service reached a sustained-yield agreement, effective January 1, 1947.

Advantages became apparent almost at once.

In the first year of operation under the agreement, the employment in the Simpson Logging Co. industries grew from 1,350 to 1,800 persons.

An insulation-board plant has been opened in Shelton. It employs 200 men on 3 shifts. Its raw material comes from wood formerly wasted or used as fuel for the generation of power at Shelton. It furnishes an outlet also for the small stuff from thinnings and the stand-improvement cuttings, which will be available in quantity from the reproducing stands within the unit.

A new and very modern community, Grisdale, was established as the seat of the company's logging operations at the railhead 48 miles west of Shelton. It provides houses for more than 400 persons and has recreational facilities, a school, and a community center.

The community of McCleary, which for a decade had been on the decline, has been revitalized. It is no longer a company town. The homes and business places have been sold to their occupants, civic improvements have been made, and a corporate form of government has been established. The company has modernized the plywood plant as well as the door factory. Employment and the production of finished products have increased. Other company plants have been modernized to some extent and the logging railroad and machine shops have been moved from the heart of the Shelton business district to an industrial site on the water front.

In addition to those improvements, private business and residential construction in and near the two towns has increased markedly. Now that the future security of the communities seems assured, further advances can be expected under the cooperative sustained-yield program as new processes are developed for the expanded and more complete utilization of the raw products grown on the lands of the unit. These new utilization facilities are expected also to provide a market for raw material from the young forests of the noncooperating landowners who are within the area.

THE ADMINISTRATION of the cooperative-unit phase of the Sustained-Yield Unit Act requires that private cooperators contribute substantially to the cooperative enterprise.

They must own considerable areas of productive forest lands and volumes of merchantable timber. They must agree to maintain the lands committed to management in a high state of productivity by carrying out advanced programs of forestry, protection, and development. They must agree to follow timber-cutting plans that are geared to the sustained productive capacity of the cooperating lands of the unit. They must keep abreast of advances made in manufacturing techniques, so as to assure fullest possible use of all available raw products and achieve maximum employment and community support.

In return for the public benefits that will accrue as a result of these commitments by the private cooperators, they are given the privilege of purchasing national forest timber within the cooperative unit at appraised prices without competitive bidding.

THE EXTENT to which programs of cooperative forest management ultimately can be applied in our national forest system depends on several factors. One is the willingness of qualified cooperators to assume the responsibilities that the Forest Service imposes to assure the fulfillment of the objectives of the act. Another is that the forest lands proposed for commitment to cooperative management be of relatively high productivity—otherwise, sustained-yield management on them might be poor business.

Because of the widely mixed nature of the ownership of private forest land throughout the country, many potential cooperators cannot meet the minimum qualifications of land and timber ownership. Sometimes the low productivity of some of our forest zones discourages long-term private-forest programs. These facts, plus the extent of private-forest depletion in some areas, make it seem unlikely that cooperative forest-management units will embrace very large proportions of the Nation-wide public-forest resource.

Present indications in the Pacific Northwest are that cooperative-management units will not involve more than 25 percent of the total sustained-yield cut allowed on national forests—maybe much less. In California there are only a few opportunities for the beneficial institution of cooperative-management programs.

In the northern Rocky Mountains, it is probable that cooperative-management units will be limited. In other national forest regions the extensive development of cooperative sustained-yield management programs does not at this time appear likely.

From a national standpoint, therefore, cooperative management is expected to have restricted application.

FURTHER AUTHORITY was extended by the Sustained-Yield Unit Act to agencies that administer Federal forests. By formal declaration they can establish sustained-yield units that comprise only Federal forest land. This aspect is designed to protect the stability of communities that depend primarily on the sale of Federal timber or other forest products. It is intended to

802062°—49——23

be used in situations where the stability of a community could not be assured under the usual procedures of selling timber. Units of this kind are called Federal sustained-yield units.

Timber sold from these dedicated areas must be given at least primary processing within the community that needs the support. In all instances an effort will be made to support local secondary wood-using industries in existence at the time the unit is established or to encourage the establishment of secondary utilization processes in communities that do not have them. The Federal-unit program thus can be made to contribute most to the accomplishment of the objectives of the act by broadening the employment base.

The law also permits the selection and designation of qualified operators in Federal units who will be allowed to purchase the national forest timber from the area without competitive bidding. In most communities that depend primarily on Federal timber, however, there are already more wood-processing plants than can be supported by the sustained allowable cut of the available public forest lands. Under such conditions there is no distinct advantage to the community in designating one of the plants as the exclusive beneficiary of the act. Consequently, in such situations it is planned that the timber will be offered for sale under regular bidding procedure with the stipulation that manufacturing take place in the community intended to be supported. Competition for the timber will be limited to purchasers who can meet the local processing requirements.

Only one Federal unit has been established so far under the authority of this phase of the act. It is known as the Vallecitos Sustained-Yield Unit and is situated on the Carson National Forest in New Mexico. The formal declaration establishing the unit was executed by the Chief of the Forest Service on January 21, 1948. Its purpose is to provide the incentive for the establishment of suitable milling and remanufacturing facilities to handle the small cut that the unit will yield in order to provide supplemental employment for the community of ranchers residing in and near the village of Vallecitos. Assurance of a stable supply of raw forest products was needed to induce the establishment of remanufacturing facilities and make the level of local employment more consistent with the needs of the people of the community.

As in the case of cooperative units, the extent to which the Federal-unit program may find application in the administration of the national forest system cannot be predicted. The opportunities for beneficial action seem to be wider than in the cooperative-unit field. Because the Federal-unit program does not require contracts with private forest-land owners, fewer conflicting interests need to be resolved. It is designed only to direct the ordinary management programs for Federal forest lands so as to give the greatest help to dependent communities.

In the Pacific Northwest region and California an estimated maximum of 30 percent of the total allowable annual cut from national forest lands may be dedicated ultimately to local dependent communities under the Federal-unit phase of the act. Extensive use of the plan in the northern Rocky Mountains does not seem likely. In the Southwest, the act may be applied beneficially in establishing Federal units for numerous small communities, as in Vallecitos. It should do good in situations in which national forest timber has been contributing nothing or less than it could to community stability.

But these two phases of the Sustained-Yield Unit Act—the cooperative unit authority and the Federal-unit program—can assure important public benefits. They can improve the practices of using and processing wood; they can steady employment; they can give benefits that flow from industrial and community stability. They are, above all, a new approach to one part of our forestry problem.

Dahl J. Kirkpatrick, *a native of the Pacific Northwest, is the son of a pioneer forest ranger. He was graduated from the College of Forestry of the University of Washington in 1929, and became a member of the Forest Service in 1930. He has served in various capacities in the Pacific Northwest since that time and is presently a member of the regional forester's staff in Portland, Oreg., handling activities connected with the administration of the Sustained-Yield Unit Act.*

# REBUILDING A SOUTHERN FOREST

FRANK A. ALBERT

The rebuilding of the Bienville National Forest began on June 15, 1936. It was then a sorry tract in the middle of Mississippi, about 45 miles east of Jackson. Severe logging and repeated wildfires had wasted it away.

The 175,375 acres in the forest should produce 10,000 board feet of timber to the acre. But, in 1936, only 89,455 acres were well enough stocked with timber to be considered salable; on that part, the average was only 569 board feet to the acre. The rest was even worse. The average stand for the whole forest was 298 board feet; it varied from 48 board feet to 4,011 in a few spots.

The bad economic conditions then reflected the exhaustion of the forest and the general depression. Between 50 and 75 percent of the land of the large lumber companies and 40 to 50 percent of the land of small owners was tax delinquent. Nearly all the sawmills in the area were losing money. The governments of Jasper, Newton, Scott, and Smith Counties, in which the forest lies, and the citizens were impoverished. Many of the people were sustained by the relief programs. This was the cut-over, burned-over, abused land that the Government bought in 1936. With the help of the Civilian Conservation Corps and the Works Progress Administration, work started.

The residents considered the area as wild land (laying out—not being used) and therefore subject to burning and trespass at will. The aims and methods of the national forest program were explained to them; they had thought the Government was buying the land as a boondoggle.

In the tasks of changing such thinking into something cooperative as well as constructive, the first item was fire prevention. Demonstrations were given of what good forestry would mean to the welfare of the communities. Results were almost immediate. In 1941, Bienville had only 46 fires that burned 1,655 acres.

To control fires and develop the resources, fire lookout towers, telephone lines, residences for fire lookouts, warehouses, repair shop, fences, and 172 miles of roads were constructed. The first fire-suppression work was done mainly with hand tools. Today the work is handled by small crews of three or four men equipped with mobile radio and fast, light tractor-plow outfits. Modern methods and equipment have greatly reduced the losses and costs.

After the protective measures of fire control were under way, constructive action was started to restore the wrecked stands and the large denuded areas. The removal of the pine timber from those areas had left too great a proportion of low-grade hardwoods, and the areas were covered now primarily with brush and the worthless species.

Work to improve the timber stand was carried on in pine reproductions. The work consisted of felling or girdling the overtopping, worthless hardwoods to release the pine. Good hardwoods were left; so were food and shelter trees for wildlife.

To help check the encroachment of brush on large areas that had insufficient seed trees, 12,000 acres were planted to loblolly pine and longleaf pine. From 500 to 700 loblolly pine seedlings per acre survived; their enemy was fusiform rust (*Cronartium fusiforme*). Brown spot disease and hogs and sheep destroyed some longleaf pine seedlings, but 400 to 500 survived per acre. (In some places natural loblolly reproduction now is encroaching into the longleaf pine and is causing some concern, because loblolly pine on poor sites is especially susceptible to fusiform rust disease.)

Already, after 13 years of protection and management, the results can be seen. People who visit the area now find it hard to believe that a few years ago the tract was almost worthless. It is stocked with a merchantable stand of about 3,000 board feet an acre—10 times the volume that existed when the land was purchased. A steady stream of sawlogs, pulpwood, railroad ties, fuel wood, and other products comes out of the forest. It has made a great change in the economic and community life of adjoining towns and villages.

At first, because of the poor stand, little timber was sold. From 1936 to 1942, only 756,000 board feet were cut. The annual cut since then has been: In 1942, 2,190,000 board feet; 1943, 3,048,000; 1944, 5,304,000; 1945, 5,133,000; 1946, 8,333,000; 1947, 15,072,000; and, in 1948, 25,296,000.

Rapid restocking and growth of timber under effective fire protection made possible this unusual, steady increase.

Today the timber stands and growth are estimated as follows: Present volume of saw timber, 330 million board feet, and 190 million of pulpwood; annual growth of saw timber, 35 million board feet, and 11 million of pulpwood.

The annual cut of saw timber in 1948–52 is put at 12 million board feet, and of pulpwood, 5 million. In 1952–57, the annual cut will be about 20 million board feet; the cut will increase gradually until it reaches a potential cut of approximately 70 million board feet a year by 1970 or so. The intention is to sell the sawlog timber first and then the pulpwood. After the sale of pulpwood will come whatever silvicultural work is needed, such as removing the unmerchantable hardwoods which overtop pine. Cutting will be regulated so that food and den trees are left for game.

Some of the areas are being cut for the second time in 13 years. The short cutting intervals—5 years for pulpwood, 10 years for sawlogs—are possible because of rapid growth and the good system of forest roads.

On one 20-acre parcel in Scott County, 2,585 board feet an acre were cut in 1941. The second cut, 2,300 board feet of logs and 4 cords of pulpwood an acre, was made in 1946; the grade of the second cut ran 20 percent better than the 1941 cut. It is estimated that the plot now has 10,000 board feet per acre of good saw timber.

Administration of the Bienville National Forest is made difficult because it is comprised of many small scattered tracts. It is not a large, solid block of Government-owned timberland, but its boundaries enclose 382,820 acres, of which only 46 percent is federally owned. Such scattered ownership increases the cost of all phases of administration and adds to the problems of management: Sometimes property lines are poorly marked and in dispute; matters of fire control and public relations are harder to handle.

Ivo W. Miller, the Bienville district ranger, recognized that situation when he returned from the war and took over. He determined on a dual aim: To make the forest contribute to the welfare of the neighboring farmers and others, and to secure their interest and cooperation in its protection and management. He believed they should take part in their own forestry program and should appreciate the values of forestry on their own forties. He initiated a plan to apply the principles of farm (or small-scale) forestry on the scattered Government tracts in his district, utilizing local people and small-scale operators for harvesting the timber.

He formed an advisory committee of leading citizens to help manage the forest, so that it would be operated smoothly and efficiently and with the maximum benefits to the local economy. Members of the committee met with the supervisors and Ranger Miller to discuss the problems and work out solutions. The program was effective.

THE FIRST EFFORT to place the scattered lands under intensive management was made through small timber sales to neighboring farmers. At once the problem came up of financing the farmers who did not have the money to buy and operate the timber. Ordinarily, they are financed by a sawmill or a larger operator, in which case their log market is limited to that particular mill. But in the Bienville forest, the small farmers got most of their credit from local bankers, who were enthusiastic over the prospect of developing this small, scattered logging industry. (Now, about 90 percent of the small operators are able to finance themselves.)

With the independent financing, the farmers could work their timber sales, which averaged 42,000 board feet, during their off season and could sell their timber products to the best financial advantage. From the start, this business developed into a cooperative project. Two or more farmers helped each other cut the timber and haul it. For example, on no one sale was there enough white ash to be hauled profitably to the Newton market. But when several men pooled their ash logs and hauled them to market on one truck, the logs could be sold at a premium price as white ash, rather than as "log-run" to the local sawmill at a much lower price. Likewise, high-value veneer logs, perhaps 2 or 3 veneer logs out of a 42,000-board-foot sale, were hauled to Jackson; white oak stave stock went to a stave mill; cross-tie logs were sold to a cross-tie mill, and so on. Sawlogs were decked along roads or at the farmer's home place to be sold when the market was good.

How such special markets were made available to the farmer-operators is exemplified in the development of a cross-tie market in the south end of the forest, where many scattered tracts have only "hill hardwoods" that are of low quality and suitable mostly for cross ties. No cross-tie market existed in that part of the forest. Roy Hughes, of the Bienville timber-marking crew, solved the problem by persuading the T. J. Moss Tie Co. to place a small mill in the area and buy the farmers' cross-tie cuts. In a year the farmers cut 18,000 cross ties.

The sales of timber to farmers amount to a considerable volume. In 1946, nearly 5 million board feet was sold to 141 small operators; in 1947, more than 11 million board feet was sold to 244 operators. Despite such a volume, the forest is not being overcut. Most of this timber is "hill hardwood" that is overtopping the pine reproduction, and is being removed in improvement cuts, rather than as a commercial undertaking. Hardwood stumpage prices are kept reasonably low as an inducement to keep the sales going while the market will absorb the low-grade hardwoods; at the same time the forest is being put in a good growing condition, because the removal of the low-grade hardwoods accelerates the growth of the remaining choice species of pine and hardwoods.

All the sales are handled on a tree-scale basis. The farmers participate in selecting and measuring the trees, and thereby get practical instruction in the woods by foresters as to why one tree is marked to be cut and another tree is left to grow. They also learn something about the use of tables to determine the volume of the trees they buy in the sales. They use the information in handling timber in the national forest as well as on their own wood lots.

At least 25 owners have given their own farm wood lots—which total 4,000 acres—this silvicultural treatment.

Another benefit is a sharp reduction in the number of fires on these scattered holdings. Reasons are: Under the timber-sale agreements, the farmer-operators are required to fight fire anywhere within a mile of their sale boundary; they have an opportunity in the woods to study the effect of fire; and they have come to feel that they have a personal stake in the forest.

THE LOCAL ECONOMY has improved. The Federal Government does not pay the counties any taxes for the lands owned by it in the national forests, but it does pay 25 percent of the receipts from the national forest to the counties in which a forest is located. The share of each county is in proportion to the amount of national forest acreage in the county. The average return to the counties under this arrangement in 1943–47 has been 18.7 cents an acre per year. The average land tax collected by the counties for similar lands has been 21.5 cents an acre. The gap between the tax rate and the annual payments is closing; in 1947, the return to the counties from Bienville National Forest timber-sale receipts was 20.5 cents an acre. In addition, the State of Mississippi collects its severance tax on all timber cut in the national forest.

Besides the direct monetary returns, the Bienville National Forest contributes to the local economy in several ways. The money for the improvements adds to local income; the improvements themselves help business and enhance local welfare; the yield of forest products creates opportunities for the local industry and employment. Since it will be a continuing yield, industries and jobs will continue.

FRANK A. ALBERT *joined the Forest Service immediately after he was graduated in forestry at Pennsylvania State College in 1926. He has served in national forests in New Hampshire, Virginia, West Virginia, Florida, North Carolina, and Mississippi. He now is assistant regional forester in the Division of Lands, Recreation, Wildlife, and Watershed Management.*

# PINYON-JUNIPER IN THE SOUTHWEST

QUINCY RANDLES

The short, scrubby growth of conifers that now covers some 40,000 square miles in Arizona and New Mexico has been used by man for probably 20,000 years. The growth is less conventional in form and of less obvious value than the forests at higher elevations, but it served the Indians for a long time. It also served the Europeans when they arrived some four centuries ago; they founded their first settlements in and near the woodland forest, which was more inviting as a site for homes than the colder, higher elevations or the hot, lower elevations.

The woodland forest is one of two broad classes in which forests in the Southwest are often placed.

One is called the saw-timber forest. The products from the three forest types that make up this class are used largely for the production of lumber and other sawn products. The three types are the ponderosa pine, Douglas-fir, and Engelmann spruce. They occur at elevations of 7,000 to 11,500 feet, the latter being timber line in Arizona and New Mexico.

The second class of forest, the woodland, gives products that have been used almost exclusively for fuel and posts. The woodland forest also comprises three types. One is the cypress type, composed of Arizona and smooth cypress, which grows in a limited area and has only local importance. The second one, the evergreen-oak type, is found mostly in Arizona at elevations of 4,500 to 6,000 feet, and is made up largely of Arizona and Emory oak; it is of considerable importance in its area. The third type is the pinyon-juniper, with which we are here concerned.

The pinyon-juniper type occupies an area in Arizona and New Mexico far in excess of all other forest types combined. The area is estimated at 17 percent of the total area of both States, or some 25 million acres. This forest is fairly well distributed over the two States, except in the eastern part of New Mexico and western and southern Arizona. The pinyon-juniper forest occurs below the ponderosa pine at elevations of about 5,000 to 7,000 feet. The lower elevation at which the forest occurs is determined by lack of moisture. Annual precipitation in the Southwest increases with increased elevation. The annual precipitation in the pinyon-juniper areas is from 12 inches at the lower edge to 18 inches at the upper limits. Some 50 to 60 percent of the moisture falls between May and September.

The moisture requirements place the pinyon-juniper type in a belt of varying widths around the mountains and on the mesas that are higher than 5,000 feet. The presence of forest and its type and density give the traveler in the Southwest a measure of the total precipitation at a given point. The open stands of pinyon-juniper indicate precipitation of 12 to 14 inches. The denser stands indicate 16 to 18 inches of rain and snow. The saw-timber forests of ponderosa pine and the others indicate a total of 19 to 25 inches.

Soils of all classes appear to be acceptable to pinyon and juniper, which grow on soils derived from both sedimentary and igneous rock. The Rocky Mountain juniper prefers soils derived from limestone.

Temperatures in the pinyon-juniper type of forest are about 5° lower than in the grassland zone below and about 6° higher than in the ponderosa pine zone immediately above. The mean maximum temperatures approximate 67°; mean minimum, 37°; and mean annual, 52°. The growing season is longer than in the ponderosa pine forest. Winters are not so severe, and snows do not get so deep.

The pinyon-juniper forest contains several species of pinyon and juniper in varying mixture.

Of the three species of pinyon in Arizona and New Mexico, by far the most abundant and most widely distributed is the *Pinus edulis,* commonly called pinyon. Its short needles, usually less than 2 inches long, occur two to the bundle. It produces most of the pinyon nuts collected locally for food and for sale.

The other species are of less importance. The one-needle pinyon (*Pinus monophylla*) has only one needle to the bundle. The Mexican pinyon (*Pinus cembroides*), also of limited occurrence, has two or three needles to the bundle.

The pinyons are relatively small trees, rarely more than 35 feet tall. They have short, quite limby boles. They are usually less than 2 feet in diameter.

Four species of juniper, locally called cedars, occur in various parts of the pinyon-juniper type.

The one-seed juniper (*Juniperus monosperma*) is a small, short-boled tree, which branches into a broad, spreading top almost from the ground level. It is usually found on the drier sites and at the lower edge of the type. Normally it is the first tree species that one sees as he goes from the lower to the higher elevations.

The Utah juniper (*Juniperus utahensis*), also short, rarely exceeds 20 feet in height and 2 feet in diameter. The trunk is fairly free of branches, which usually are less than 6 feet long.

The alligator juniper (*Juniperus pachyphloea*), so named because the bark on the mature tree is so broken that it resembles the back of an alligator, is the tallest of the local junipers. Sometimes it reaches a height of 60 feet. Specimens up to 5 feet in diameter are sometimes seen, but the average tree is shorter and smaller.

The Rocky Mountain juniper (*Juniperus scopulorum*) is of a more conventional tree form. Occasionally it grows 30 to 40 feet tall and up to 3 feet in diameter. It has a straight but rapidly tapering trunk.

The pinyon-juniper forest is usually open, and the openings among the trees are occupied by the grasses and shrubs. The short stems and broad crowns of the individual trees, usually of one species of pinyon and one or more species of juniper, give to the forest a pleasing appearance.

Explorations of early Indian habitations show that many were located in valleys, in or near the pinyon-juniper forest. The reasons why they selected those places are not known, but many factors favored them for home sites—an agreeable climate, a growing season long enough for farm crops, and an abundance of fuel for cooking and heating. The wood, especially juniper wood, was light to handle—an important detail because before Spanish exploration the Indians had no beasts of burden and had to carry things themselves. The wood was easy to work with the primitive stone axes and hammers or by hand.

The forest supplied pinyon nuts for food; archeologists have found pinyon nuts in ruins. Early Spanish explorers, Cabeza de Baca among them, noted the small pine trees, whose seed they considered better than those of Spain. The thin husks, he said, were beaten while green, made into balls, and eaten. The dry nuts were pounded in the husks and used as flour. Coronado told of the extensive areas of pines, which, he remarked, were only two or three times as high as a man before they sent out branches, and the great quantities of pine nuts they produced. He stated that the Indians collected and stored the nuts each year.

Fuel wood for cooking and heating was no doubt the forest product most valuable to the early Indians. They used some wood in constructing temporary shelter and permanent housing; some wood, found in ruins, was used for terracing logs, roof beams, and door lintels, and incorporated in masonry walls. Some material up to 14 feet long and 12 inches thick has been found—what a job they must have had in working sticks of that size with stone tools. The wood of all the junipers is fairly light and soft, however; that of the pinyon is also soft, but brittle.

The early Indians made some use of the juniper berry for food; the bark was used for cradles, sandals, torches, and similar products.

The early Indians also got much of their food from corn, beans, squash, and other cultivated crops; the pinyons, acorns, and seeds, which could be had for the taking; deer, antelope, elk, ground sloth, camel, and Taylor buffalo. Good forage for game was provided by the grasses and shrubs found in the openings in the pinyon-juniper forests; turkeys fattened on the pinyon nuts and juniper berries. All in all, therefore, the woodland forest provided most of the basic needs of the earliest inhabitants in the region; it may not have been absolutely essential, but it was of great value.

The same pattern of use continued after the coming of the Spanish. Their settlements were in the larger valleys, where irrigation water was available. They also depended on the forest for fuel and some building material. The Spaniards, besides, needed fences for their domestic stock, and that the pinyon-juniper amply provided. The burro and the horse that they brought with them saved human labor in getting those supplies. (The burro, with a pack load of fuel wood, remained a familiar sight for a long time throughout the Southwest.) Because the Spaniards had better tools for working wood, they made much wider use of the products of the forest.

So it is natural that the Spanish-Americans of the Southwest still have a high opinion of the value of the pinyon-juniper forest; the pinyon is their traditional Christmas tree, and they use the foliage of the pinyon and the juniper for decorations on special occasions.

The coming of the American to the Southwest in increasing numbers after 1840 added several new elements. To the usual demand for forest products were added new ones: Demand for more fencing materials to take care of the expanding herds of domestic livestock and more fuel to supply the growing population.

This demand for fuel continued heavy until the railroads reached the Southwest, coal mining increased, and oil and gas became available. Such changes have lowered the local consumption of wood fuel at many points and have reduced the demands on the pinyon-juniper forest, but have by no means eliminated the need.

In depression times, the use of wood is greatly increased, and many people get their supply directly from the forest; many rural families still depend entirely on wood, and many townspeople prefer wood for fuel. Woodyards in towns and cities still do a good business.

The demand for pinyon-juniper will continue, too, as long as people like a wood-burning fireplace, for which there is nothing quite like the heat of the pinyon and the fragance of burning juniper.

Over the years the products of the forest have been used largely for domestic purposes and near the forest. Some fuel and posts have been produced commercially to supply local demands and for shipment to other States. Also produced are pinyon charcoal, props and ties for coal mines, fuel for burning lime and for smelting ores, and fence posts. The posts bring the highest stumpage price of any product from the type; juniper is used for this purpose. The most serviceable post is one split from an old tree that has 3 inches or more of heartwood, but younger trees that have an appreciable amount of heartwood are excellent; the highly colored heartwood is the part that resists decay.

The pinyon nut has been handled commercially for the past 40 years. The value in relation to bulk makes shipment to distant points possible. Before 1940, nearly 1½ million pounds were shipped annually. In 1936, the shipments totaled 8 million pounds. Pickers have been paid as little as 5 cents a pound, and up to 60 cents in 1947 when the crop was almost a total failure. A fair crop in 1948 resulted in a price of 25 cents to 30 cents a pound.

When a good crop of nuts is produced, only a small percentage of the crop is gathered. Demand is normally below supply. The surplus is usually stored to meet needs during later years of crop failure. Crop failures are frequent and therefore it would probably be unprofitable to undertake any costly effort to encourage greater use. Most of the nuts shipped in the past went to New York City. Some are consumed locally, some are machine-shelled, and some, after shelling, are made into candy.

Only limited attempts have been made to exploit the products of the woodland forest for other than the conventional uses of fuels and posts. The small size, rapid taper, and low quality of the usual stem of both pinyon and juniper, with the consequent high expense of producing usable sawn material, have discouraged use. Only relatively small-sized, clear pieces can be cut, and waste is heavy. Pencil slats were produced experimentally from the Utah juniper. These were satisfactory, but too expensive to meet competition. Some sawn material has been cut from the Rocky Mountain juniper and used as closet lining, custom-built furniture, for inlays and cedar chests, and so forth. Costs are high, but the products are attractive. The colored heartwood has been used for carvings and novelties, but only on a small scale. The cones of the pinyon are being used to produce incense.

The area occupied by the type, due to low precipitation and heavy evaporation, is not a high-yielding watershed. The runoff per acre is lower than that for the saw-timber type, where total precipitation is greater and the winter precipitation is in the form of snow. Although the yield per unit of area is low, the total yield from the large area is of material value, especially because most farming is done under irrigation and water in the Southwest is most important.

The pinyon-juniper forest furnishes grazing for domestic livestock and game. Animals that spend the summer at higher elevations come in winter to the lower ground, where snows are not so deep as to cover the forage. Some livestock and game use the forage yearlong, but if such grazing is not properly regulated, the grass and the shrub cover essential to protect the soils from erosion is seriously reduced. Winter use alone is best suited to maintaining normal cover. The light stand of relatively sparse foliage trees of the type produces much less forest litter than do the saw-timber forests at higher elevations. The litter is effective in soil protection and in reducing runoff, but the grass and shrubs in the intervening nonforested areas must be maintained to insure soil stability. When this is overused, sheet and gully erosion result. The pinyon-juniper type, because of the heavy use by livestock and game, contributes appreciable quantities of silt to streams.

Only during the past 40 years, since the creation of the national forests, has any positive action been taken to give protection to the forest and to direct wood harvests in ways that would insure continuous yields of benefits and products. Fires once denuded large areas. The pinyon is susceptible to bark beetle attacks, and considerable losses have resulted from this cause. Mistletoe causes material losses in mature juniper. Destructively heavy cutting has practically denuded some areas; on others, cutting has severely reduced the stands. Recovery is slow.

The seeds of the pinyon and junipers are heavy and normally fall close to the parent tree. The spread of the type is slow unless the seeds can be spread by other means—for example, by birds, game, and domestic stock. The passage of the seeds through the digestive tract materially aids germination, and this method of seed dispersal by animals is important in aiding the extension of the type. This extension is especially noticeable along trails used by sheep in their travels from winter to summer ranges and return, and in the large natural openings, locally called parks, within the range of the species, and around the edges of the type.

After the national forests were established, adequate fire protection was given pinyon-juniper forests. Better roads were built and made easier the harvest of fuel and posts. Positive action was taken to initiate a system of cutting by which only trees above a fixed diameter or dead or diseased trees could be harvested. The aim was to insure an adequate seed supply and sufficient stand to maintain forest conditions. Since yield and prices of the product are low, any system followed must be selected with the end of balancing costs and results. Growth is slow—probably not more than a half inch in diameter a decade. Virgin stands approximate 200 years of age. The volume per acre measured in cords varies greatly, being lowest at the lower edge of the type where yields will not exceed 2 to 4 cords; better stands often yield 25 cords to the acre. The slow growth and low yields are the result of low precipitation.

In assessing the future of this forest area, of which some 20 percent is in national forests, one should remember that some of it has been heavily cut and has little chance for another crop for a long time; some of it has been lightly cut; some has only been high-graded for post material. Except for limited areas in the rather inaccessible places, only minor areas of so-called virgin stands remain. The growth and yields are low.

The products cut in the past have been low in price, and private owners therefore have had little incentive to take positive management action to maintain or increase productivity. Research on the public lands to determine potentialities has been limited. More data on sound management are needed; so is an effort to find new and profitable uses for the few high-grade products the area can furnish. The extensive area of the type would indicate adequate supplies of material to meet present and future needs. It should be the aim to keep this large land area producing successive crops of essential wood products, since the forest is, all things considered, the highest use of the area.

Quincy Randles, *formerly in charge of timber management in the Southwestern Region of the Forest Service, is now retired. He holds degrees from the College of Wooster in Ohio and the University of Michigan. He started work with the Forest Service in 1911.*

# PONDEROSA PINE IN THE SOUTHWEST

C. OTTO LINDH

From train or highway, the traveler in Arizona and New Mexico sees treeless mesas, deserts, some scattered woodlands, century-old habitations, the white gold of the sunshine, and the bright blue of the cloudless sky. He does not see, far back from the main routes, the plateaus, the high mesas, and the slopes that are clothed with valuable forests.

In Arizona and New Mexico are 6,280,000 acres of forest land from which trees can be harvested. About 4 million of these acres are in national forests, a million in other Federal ownership and the Indian reservations, and a million in the ownership of States and counties and individuals.

The most valuable tree in the Southwest is the ponderosa pine, which in volume accounts for 88 percent of the total of all commercial species and produces 90 percent of the 375 to 400 million board feet of lumber cut each year. Unbroken stands extend for miles.

Ponderosa pine grows where the annual precipitation is 18 to 24 inches—less water than any other large commercial tree requires. In the Southwest it grows at elevations of 6,500 to 8,000 feet, which correspond to the 18- to 24-inch precipitation zone. At lower elevations it is found in mixture with junipers, pinyons, and oaks. In its main range, pure stands are the rule. On cool, northern slopes and at upper elevations, it is mixed with Douglas-fir, spruce, limber pine, and white fir. Small aspen groves are not unusual throughout the type, except at the lower elevations. Disregarding extremes, ponderosa pine stands contain 5,000 to 15,000 board feet an acre. Over large areas, in the main range, stands average about 10,000 board feet an acre.

The virgin stands of ponderosa pine in the Southwest are unusually decadent or injured. Western red rot reduces gross volumes by 15 to 25 percent—or more on some rocky ridges. Mistletoe, the slow killer, is widespread. The Cronartium rust is found throughout the type on individual trees here and there. Bark beetles are not unusually serious and seldom reach epidemic proportions, except that several species of *Ips* and *Dendroctonus* make serious inroads in small areas during cycles of dry weather. Lightning causes the most damage and highest mortality. If it does not kill the struck tree outright, it leaves a long open wound, into which disease organisms enter easily. Abert squirrels and porcupines girdle the limbs and tops of trees, especially those of sapling and pole size. The girdled trees become deformed, and rot enters the wounds.

Ponderosa pine is a light-loving tree. It reproduces and grows best with some overhead and side light. It seldom reproduces in full shade. Because of the low annual precipitation, it needs plenty of space to reach its largest growth. At the same time, a dense stand is desirable, at least through the sapling and pole stage, in order to keep the lower limbs small and obtain natural pruning on the main bole.

The spring period in the Southwest is unusually dry and windy. Summer rains are the rule, but often are no more than showers. A combination of a good seed crop and early and heavy summer rains is needed to insure reproduction of ponderosa pine. Seldom does the combination occur. In 1918, the seed crop was heavy, the following spring was favorable for germination and establishment, and the summers of 1919 and 1920 were above average for continued seedling growth. As a result, large areas of reproduction and saplings are now common in most of the Southwest. Since then, only relatively few seedlings have become established each year.

History does not record how soon the Spanish erected the first sawmill in New Mexico after Oñate led the first settlers into the Valley of the Rio Grande del Norte in 1598. One of the first sawmills in northern Arizona was brought overland from the Salt Lake region by the Latter Day Saints and erected south of Flagstaff at Sawmill Springs in 1878.

Large-scale lumbering operations began with the construction of the first railroad (now the Atchison, Topeka & Santa Fé) through the timbered parts of the Southwest. Between 1878 and 1881, the forests near Las Vegas, Pecos, and Santa Fé, in New Mexico, were heavily cut for ties and construction material. In the 1880's the stands on the Colorado Plateau near Flagstaff and Williams, in Arizona, were extensively cut. Since then, the lumber industry has thrived and spread.

Early cutting of ponderosa pine was strictly on a basis of cut and use what you can. The usable trees in the most available areas were cut; the rest were usually burned, with no thought to conservation or forestry. Some of the scars are still noticeable, but most of the heavily cut areas are now partly clothed with forest growth, and many areas have fine stands of young ponderosa.

The largest lumbering operations are in the vast ponderosa pine stand on the Colorado Plateau, which extends unbroken from the Gila Wilderness Area in New Mexico almost 300 miles northwest toward the Grand Canyon.

A typical operation is the one that is centered at Flagstaff, in the heart of the Coconino National Forest. During the past 70 years the local mills have cut more than a billion board feet from 350,000 acres. The two large mills and several saw mills can continue to cut about 60 million board feet a year of national forest timber on a sustained basis. More than 40 million board feet of sawlogs a year are brought in 34 miles by a logging railroad from the virgin stands of ponderosa pine south of Flagstaff. Large trucks deliver logs to the railhead from as far away as the Mogollon Rim. Sawlogs cut near the established mills are trucked directly to the mills.

The lumber industry has a capital investment of about 3 million dollars in sawmills, box factories, cut-up plants, and power plants in the Flagstaff community. The industry depends almost wholly on timber from the national forest. It provides employment for about 750 persons. Wages paid amount to 1¾ million dollars a year. The Flagstaff community depends to a large extent on the maintenance of a stable forest-products industry.

North of Flagstaff and across the Grand Canyon is a unique island of commercial ponderosa pine timber—

1½ billion board feet on the 184,000 acres of national forest land on the Kaibab Plateau. For centuries only Indians used it. In the 1870's Mormons settled in the lowlands, 30 miles or so to the north near the Utah-Arizona line, and operated one or two small sawmills intermittently.

Highways first tapped the Kaibab Plateau soon after the Marble Canyon bridge was completed across the Colorado River in 1928. The plateau is the home of the famous Kaibab mule deer herd; there, also, Theodore Roosevelt hunted the mountain lion. It is an isolated region—from the center of the timber, the nearest railroad on the north is 140 miles away; on the south, 175 miles.

No wonder, then, that the large body of ponderosa pine on the Kaibab Plateau was relatively untouched until the Second World War. Good highways, good trucks, the scarcity of good timber, and high prices came together at about the same time. Timber was sold, mills were installed, and for the first time lumber moved to the outside world. Now lumber moves on large trucks over the Marble Canyon bridge, across the desert, past the wind-swept hogans of the Navajo Indians, and thence to markets over the Atchison, Topeka & Santa Fé. The closest mill to the Santa Fé Railroad is 165 miles; the farthest, 205 miles. The development is typical of the western pioneer days, but it happened in the early 1940's.

The future for the Kaibab Plateau timber looks bright. The opportunity is there for an integrated manufacturing and remanufacturing industry on a substantial and continuing scale. New highways will reduce the distance to the railroad. After 80 years, the local people are assured of employment opportunities in a basic manufacturing industry. At the same time, the other values of wildlife, recreation, water production, and grazing of livestock need not be impaired if the timber harvest is orderly and management of the forest is careful.

In much of central Arizona and in northern New Mexico the operations are small. Most of the sawmills have a circular head saw and annually cut ½ million to 5 million board feet of rough green lumber. They are located in interior forest communities, where the inhabitants depend on the local resources of water, forage, and the harvesting and manufacture of forest crops.

A TYPICAL CASE is the operation at Vallecitos, in the Carson National Forest in New Mexico. The established operator there cut annually a million board feet or less before 1948. Trucks hauled the rough green lumber 63 miles to the nearest railroad shipping point. Employment was furnished to 8 or 10 persons. The sawmill was poorly located in relation to the available timber and existing roads.

Technicians were called in to analyze the situation at Vallecitos. They decided the annual cut should be not less than 1½ million board feet. The operator said he would relocate the mill, install seasoning and finishing facilities, construct a small box factory or cut-up plant to utilize low-grade material, and continue to use local labor and furnish lumber at regular prices to people nearby if he were assured a stable supply of timber. If that were done, employment would be increased up to 400 percent, the annual wages would be increased by as much as $30,000, and the communities of Vallecitos, Canyon Plaza, and Petaca would be helped materially.

Accordingly, under section 3 of the Sustained-Yield Unit Act, steps were taken to establish a Federal Sustained-Yield Unit. At the required public hearing on the proposal, in December 1947, more than 100 residents attended to get information, ask questions, and make comments. They agreed that the unit would be a good thing.

On January 21, 1948, the Vallecitos Federal Sustained-Yield Unit was formally established, the first of its kind in the United States. In the year since, progress has been made in carrying out the declared policy for the unit: In 70 years, then, lumbering in the Southwest has progressed from logging with oxen and cutting ties for railroads to big wheels and logging railroads, to modern trucks and complete manufacturing facilities, and, finally, to the integrated plant in little Vallecitos, whose life and livelihood are actually determined by the life of the forest.

THE NATIONAL FORESTS, which embrace two-thirds of the commercial timberland in the Southwest, were established at the turn of the century.

At first, cutting was directed toward leaving thrifty seed trees and protecting the few poles and sparse reproduction. But with research, experience, improved fire protection and establishment of reproduction, and improvements in logging and transportation facilities, the cutting practices have gradually changed, and they have progressed through various steps—the cutting of selected groups of trees, the heavy cutting of selected individual trees, and light cutting of selected trees to improve the growth of the stand.

Much of the credit for the progress is due to almost 40 years of research at the Fort Valley Experimental Forest near Flagstaff. The late G. A. Pearson, a long-time employee of the Forest Service, was in charge of research for 35 years. He kept individual records of thousands of ponderosa pine trees, measured growth of residual trees, and studied results of many different types of cutting practices on large experimental plots. The findings give southwestern forest managers a wealth of material to use as a base for progressive forest practices.

Management is not static or necessarily uniform throughout the national forests in the Southwest. Management is by small units, or working circles, and management plans are made for each. The annual cut from each varies from 1 million to 60 million feet.

In the preparation of management plans for ponderosa pine, foresters are guided by the general objectives and policies established for all the national forests in the Southwest. They are:

1. To make the first harvest cut in all virgin stands within the next 20 years or less, in order to harvest quickly the dying trees, to begin the process of improving growth and quality, and to make all commercial timber stands accessible by a permanent road system.

2. To make the initial cut in virgin stands on a light improvement-selection basis, designed to remove from 30 to 50 percent of the gross volume, or 5 to 10 trees an acre.

3. Periodically, at least once a decade, to make a light intermediate cut in the old cut-overs to remove decadent trees and to thin the poorest trees from groups or dense stands where root or crown competition impairs net-quality growth.

4. To utilize, to the greatest extent possible and thereby improve the forest, all material that should be thinned from the sapling and pole stands and all material normally left in the woods in a sawlog operation.

In the initial harvest cut in virgin ponderosa pine stands, many trees are readily recognized as requiring removal. They are the decadent trees—those with mechanical injuries such as lightning streaks, those with heavy mistletoe, the bad leaners, the rough, limby trees, and the large, old trees of declining growth and thrift. It is not difficult for a trained or experienced marker to select those trees for removal. Special skill is involved in selecting the additional trees for removal, which will further improve the stand. The major considerations are spacing, quality, and thrift, so the marker looks for the poorest trees—those that are rough or crooked or have large limbs, or that have large, low crowns or slight mechanical injuries, particularly in the lower bole. Their removal will enhance the growth of the trees that are left in the stand. The isolated wolf tree, with large, low limbs, and the rough, limby tree are first sought for and marked.

In the intermediate cuts in old cut-overs, the objective is much the same as in the virgin stands, but special emphasis is placed on improving the stand so as to increase growth in the younger sawlog trees and the oncoming poles and saplings. Residual trees that have serious infections of mistletoe, have been struck by lightning, or have other mechanical injuries are marked for removal. Groups are thinned by the removal of the poorest and roughest trees. After their removal, net growth takes place on the best-quality stems.

One can make intermediate light improvement-selection cuts of 300 to 600 board feet an acre in the old cut-overs, because the stands have been made accessible by permanent roads. Logging is done by tractors or horses, portable loaders, and light trucks. As roads are improved and lighter mobile equipment is developed, it is expected that stands, from which the initial harvest cut has been made, will be cut over every few years. By so doing, mortality will be minimized, whether from wind, lightning, disease, or insects, and quality growth will increase. Within a few decades, even in areas that were heavily cut 30 to 70 years ago, the net harvestable growth should be at the rate of 150 board feet or more an acre each year. Foresters work toward that objective; if they reach the goal, they will be producing a large volume of excellent wood in a forest that has almost the characteristics of a desert in habitat and moisture requirements.

THE TREES OF THE FUTURE are the seedlings, saplings, and poles, all under 12 inches in diameter at breast height. They are found as individuals in openings, in open stands, in dense groups, or as an understory. In the Southwest, young ponderosa pines are usually limby if they are not growing in dense stands. To produce the maximum growth in quality trees for the future, special attention must be given to the trees of tomorrow. To that end, help is given by the Knutson-Vandenberg Act, under which a small part of the stumpage value of the trees that are being sold can be used to improve the timber stands. Based on an analysis of each area, a decision is made as to the need for improving the stand and its cost. The collection of funds is provided for in the timber-sale agreement. Most current collections vary from 25 cents to a dollar a thousand board feet.

Research experiments and tests have indicated that highest priority should be given to pruning trees of small sizes—usually 4 to 11 inches in diameter at breast height. The best saplings and small poles are selected as crop trees for pruning. All limbs are cut flush with the bark to a height of 9 to 17 feet, depending on the size of the stem. Not more than one-half of the live limbs are removed, because it is essential that a thrifty crown of adequate size be retained. Trees with dead limbs more than 1½ inches in diameter are seldom pruned because of the possibility of the entrance of western red rot in the large wounds. The most productive areas are selected first for pruning. They are the best growing sites and are free of mistletoe infections. By pruning now, while trees are small, clear lumber or veneer will be produced in the future, instead of low-value boards with knots.

Besides the periodic pruning of the best trees, worthless, unusable trees are removed by poisoning or cutting; they are the rough, limby, or deformed trees that occupy space and use moisture that should be made available for the good crop trees.

Young stands of ponderosa pine can be further improved by utilizing the small stems that should be cut in periodic thinnings. Little has been done so far with them, but they are worth attention. One possibility is to use the smallest stems, 4 to 10 inches, for posts and poles, which are used by the tens of thousands in the Southwest. They would have to be given a preservative treatment, because untreated ponderosa pine is not durable in contact with the ground. No custom treating plant exists now in the Southwest, but foresters are making an inventory of the raw material and analyzing the potential market, so as to determine the best location for a treating plant and to interest prospective operators.

Another possibility is to use the trees of small sawlog size (12 to 18 inches in diameter) in a log gang or small band mill that would be built especially to handle small logs economically. At several locations such an operation would be feasible.

Forest officers are working with mill operators to promote more efficient manufacture of lumber by small circular mills and the replacement of circular mills with band mills. They also advocate the further finishing and remanufacture of forest products and increased use of waste.

Such management devices in th Southwest will strengthen the econom of tomorrow and provide further en ployment opportunities for those i rural communities in and near th forests. They also will improve th forest, and, in turn, will increase wealt and employment.

C. Otto Lindh, *assistant regiona forester in the Division of Timbe Management, is stationed in Albu querque, N. Mex. Upon graduatio from Oregon State College in 1927, h joined the Forest Service, and ha held various positions, from assistan ranger to assistant regional foreste His work has been in the fields of fir control and timber management in th Northwest and Southwest.*

# PINE FORESTS OF CALIFORNIA

B. O. HUGHES, DUNCAN DUNNING

The national forests of California have 7.7 million acres of land suitable for growing timber as the primary crop. Of this total, 5.6 million acres bear virgin or old-growth forests unaffected by lumbering and 1.2 million acres have younger stands left in the first logging operation. The rest is not stocked with trees, mostly because of fires before the late 1890's.

In converting these three kinds of areas to well-ordered croplands, forest managers must reckon with a complex mixture of assets and liabilities. Generally speaking, the national forests are not the most favorably situated timberlands in the State. The more accessible, more productive lands passed to private ownership before the forests were established.

Five conifers make up more than 95 percent of the volume of the standing timber. Of these, ponderosa pine is the most generally useful and of widest occurrence. The fine-textured sugar pine commands the highest price, but constitutes only one-tenth of the volume. Both pines reach their best de velopment along the western slope o the Sierra Nevada.

Douglas-fir and white fir each mak up about one-third of the timber vol ume and are important component of the mixed forests of both the Sierr Nevada and Coast Range, sometime forming almost pure stands.

California incense-cedar occurs in termingled with the other species forming only one twenty-fifth of th volume. It is presently the world's mos important pencil wood and is prize for fence posts, rails, and other use requiring resistance to decay.

Native hardwood trees are of rela tively minor importance in California The introduction of valuable timbe hardwoods from the Eastern States o elsewhere has not been successful. No are any introduced conifers know that are more generally useful and tha could survive and grow better than th natives. Several promising hybrid pine are now being tested; some of thes may prove useful in certain localities

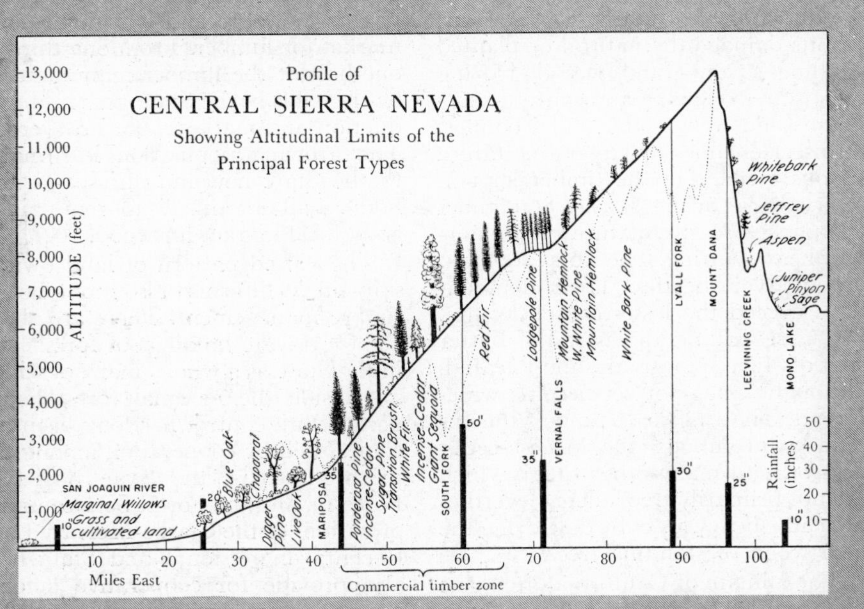


Ponderosa pine is the mainstay of the national forest management, with sugar pine the favored species in restricted, highly productive localities. By good management the proportion of these trees in the stands can be considerably increased and serious insect damage, diseases, and soil deterioration common in single-species forests can be avoided. But constant care is needed to keep these two valuable pines from being crowded out by the associated firs and cedar, which are more easily established by natural seeding.

All the five native conifers can grow rapidly and attain merchantable saw-timber dimensions of 18 to 50 inches in diameter in 75 to 150 years, according to quality of soil.

The problem of transforming the wild natural forests for more efficient timber growth has one highly favorable aspect: The high values stored in the large smooth stems of the old trees that occasionally exceed 600 years in age. Some of this reserve capital can be reinvested in the forest to correct the many deficiencies. Provision for this has been made through the Knutson-Vandenberg Act, which authorized the planting of fail-places, removal of undesirable trees and brush, pruning crop trees, and other stand improvement.

A notable deficiency of the virgin forest is that the land is now stocked with trees only to a little more than 60 percent of its capacity. Good management aims to increase stocking by about one-third. Accomplishing this is made difficult by an excess of old trees. The large, old trees contain from 60 to 95 percent of the stand's saw-timber volume. This is slow-growing or deteriorating timber ready for harvesting; it should be replaced. Thus, growing stocks must first be reduced before they can be built up by natural regeneration or planting into thriving forests that contain young trees for future harvests.

Reconstructing the stands by planting or seeding is made difficult by hosts of aggressive shrubs—manzanitas, ceanothus, and others—growing between the trees or waiting as seed to take possession of the soil when trees are cut.

802062°—49——24

Squirrels, chipmunks, and mice add to the difficulties by destroying tree seed; rabbits damage the natural or planted seedlings. Cone- and seed-destroying insects are serious pests, as are the cutworms and weevils that kill seedlings.

Insect enemies of larger trees are a serious menace to the timber kept in reserve as growing stocks. Sometimes the pests force premature or undesirably heavy cutting. The worst are bark, or engraver, beetles. Their depredations exceed the losses caused by fire.

Of tree-killing diseases, the blister rust of sugar pine is the most feared, although it has not yet become widespread. The ring scale fungus, the Indian paint fungus, the incense-cedar dry-rot, and many other fungi, which are not primarily tree killers, nevertheless cause heavy losses by destroying the heartwood of standing trees.

The climate of California often gets bad marks—perhaps unjustly—from forest managers. The long, warm, dry summers contribute to an excessive fire danger. As to tree growth, however, better understanding gained in recent years tends to discount the opinion that high summer temperatures and low growing-season rainfall are extremely adverse features. The trees are well adjusted to survive these normal rigors of their environment. Close observation has shown that most failures of planting and natural seeding resulted from crowding by weeds and shrubs, damage by rodents and insects, or faulty timing and methods. More knowledge and improved skill can overcome these obstacles.

With respect to topography and transportation, the national forests in California have disadvantages as compared with other forest regions. The bulk of the timber covers the manifold ridges and canyons of the western Sierra Nevada and northern inner Coast Range between altitudes of 3,000 and 7,000 feet. The Coast Range timber is least accessible by roads. Terrain of the northeastern volcanic plateau, with its extensive forests of ponderosa pine, is more favorable.

Offsetting the difficulties of transport is the large and expanding local market for lumber. From one-third to one-half of the lumber manufactured by the mills in the State goes into production and marketing of farm crops. The growing population is bringing to the State new industries and new home building likely to maintain a good local market for wood.

The varied pattern of land ownership in California also complicates timber management. There are about 18,300 private holdings of forest land in the State as a whole, many of which are inside the national forest boundaries. Fire control has long been accomplished by cooperation among the private owners, the State Board of Forestry, and the Forest Service under provisions of the Clarke-McNary Law. Recent congressional and State laws also provide for cooperative defense against insect enemies and tree diseases. Another recent congressional law—the Sustained-Yield Unit Act—authorizes cooperative management of the interdependent private and federal timber, but no agreements have yet been consummated. Problems arising from divided responsibility have been simplified in many instances by land exchanges.

The wood-growing capacity of the national forests of California under good management is estimated to be slightly more than a billion board feet a year. The allowable cut during the period of converting the old growth to thrifty and well-ordered stands is restricted to 972 million board feet. The volume actually logged has averaged much below the allowable cut and in 1947 was 555 million feet. The rate of cutting obviously can be increased by opening up inaccessible areas.

After cutting started in 1898, the proportion of the sawmill production in the State that came from the national forests rose gradually to about 10 percent in 1939. Thereafter the proportion has risen more rapidly, reaching 20 percent in 1947. Depletion of the more accessible private timber doubtless will continue this trend in cutting on the public forests. An era of accelerated use is at hand, presenting the opportunity to improve and intensify all management procedures.

The direction that such improvement should take is suggested by the lessons from 50 years of experience.

Naturally, the early years of administration were devoted to surveying boundaries, classifying the land, constructing improvements for administration and fire control, suppressing fires, inventorying the timbered areas to guide cutting and preparation of forest working plans, and directing timber cutting under sale contracts. These activities continue today, some of them expanded and intensified as better methods have been discovered by experience and research or as population and markets have increased.

Advancements in timber management depended largely on the market for old growth. There has been no appreciable outlet for the small trees that should be removed in thinnings to improve young stands on cut-over land. Lack of markets for young growth also has been a deterrent to reclamation of deforested areas by planting. Somewhat more than 300,000 acres of old growth have been cut over in timber sales; approximately 30,000 acres of young stands in cut-over land have been subjected to thinning and crop-tree pruning; and about 28,000 deforested acres have been planted.

The early timber-sale administrators were forced to begin cutting at a time when forestry was a mere word without local significance. They had no research and only limited experience to guide them. Tree growth and seeding habits, the behavior of competing brush, insect risks, and nearly all other important factors of forest management were subjects of conjecture.

Those early foresters were conservative, fortunately, and determined to leave on the land the best growing stock possible. They marked for cutting little more than half the stand volume, leaving a large share of ponderosa and sugar pines in the hope that natural seeding would increase the proportion of these species in the new stands. They reduced waste by requiring that stumps be cut low and small top logs be utilized. To reduce fire danger, they insisted that logging engines have spark arresters, that all logging slash be piled and burned, and that all dead trees be felled. They also originated and enforced many logging restrictions to prevent damage to seed trees and young growth. The early-day outlook on future markets being rather dim, the first sales were made on the assumption that second cuttings would not be feasible in fewer than 30 to 60 years.

To determine the effects of cutting procedures as well as to improve them, studies were begun almost with the first sales. Within 10 years the records showed that reserving heavy proportions of pine and drastically reducing the firs accomplished little or no improvement in the proportion of pines growing in young forests. It became evident, also, that the many large pines left uncut continued to grow at slow rates or suffered heavy losses from insect attacks, windthrow, and other agencies. Such information, and the good markets during the First World War and in the early 1920's, led to heavier cuttings that sometimes removed as much as 80 percent of the stand volume.

A trend towards the lighter cutting, which began about 1928, can be traced to three causes: The general depression in markets, already felt in the lumber industry; information from studies that showed that heavy financial losses resulted from cutting pines smaller than 18 to 22 inches, or firs smaller than 30 inches in diameter; and improved standards for selecting the trees least apt to die if left for seed and growth. The introduction of tractors also made logging more flexible and permitted lighter cuts and wider option in selecting the trees to harvest.

The revival of markets that began with the Second World War did not reverse—but accelerated, rather—the trend toward lighter cutting in the national forests. With good markets, it became profitable to log less accessible timber, lighter volumes, smaller and lower-quality trees, and less valuable species, and to make return cuts at shorter intervals. This opportunity has been seized to bring about a long-desired change in methods of converting the old, decadent forests to younger, thriftier ones.

The procedure now followed is to make a light initial cut that covers the old growth as rapidly as possible and utilizes the trees that would die if logging were delayed. A second cutting will follow in less than 30 years to open new areas for seeding, give the young, established seedlings room to grow, and harvest any additional trees that appear likely to die.

A critical factor in success of this procedure is the ability to identify the trees threatened with death. Effective rules for recognizing such high-risk trees have been formulated from many thousands of case histories of individual trees dating from 1910. Properly applied, those rules can reduce the volume of wood lost through mortality. Test cuttings in a 10,000-acre demonstration forest over a 10-year period reduced volume loss more than 80 percent. That was accomplished by removing as little as 15 percent of the total volume in the stand and cutting only the high-risk trees.

Such risk-tree selection is more effective in forests of ponderosa pine. In stands of other conifers it must be supplemented by salvaging trees that are actually dying or dead before the wood is stained or destroyed by fungi. Both high-risk and salvage logging require ready access by good roads.

Much remains to be done before the national forests can serve their many functions at full capacity. Three great jobs are ahead: Reclaiming nearly a million acres of deforested land by planting, increasing stocking on more than 500,000 acres of land cut over before acquisition, and converting in an orderly way the 5½ million acres of old growth to productive growing stands. The first two are the most difficult.

The planting job has been scarcely touched in the exploratory efforts that have been possible so far. Before rapid headway can be made, special heavy-duty machines must be developed for removing tough shrubs from steep, rocky land without excessive soil damage; cheaper, more lethal chemical methods for clearing brush must be perfected; and effective means of controlling destructive rodents must be found. Planting also is involved in building up stocking on the cut-over land from its present 26 percent of soil capacity to 75 or 80 percent.

Thinning and pruning overdense young stands and removal of large defective trees are most needed on the cut-over lands. Here, also, less expensive methods must be developed as the work is expanded.

Future cutting methods for the old-growth areas doubtless will advance beyond the tree-selection philosophy of today in the direction of detailed control of stocking on small areas. Logging must be more varied to fit stand conditions as they change from acre to acre. Cutting also must be closely coordinated in time and place with other supplementary measures, such as clearing and scarifying the soil to make favorable seedbeds, planting spots that fail to seed naturally, rodent control, blister rust control, and thinning and pruning in young-growth stands.

The years immediately following the logging are the most critical; frequently they determine whether the new plant cover will be pines, firs, or mere brush. Once the stand is opened, the conversion process must be continued until trees are reestablished. An error in timing, such as logging when there is no tree seed or omission of some necessary step (for example, not planting when seed crops fail), may mean loss of area to brush. That is more lastingly expensive than loss of trees. Once brush takes control, rec-

Tree classes for ponderosa pine, based on age, position, the length and width of crown, form of top, and vigor—factors that reflect growth, survival, and seeding capacities.

*Class 1.* Age class, young or thrifty mature; position, isolated or dominant (rarely codominant); crown length, 65 percent or more of the total height; crown width, average or wider; form of top, pointed; vigor, good. Trees of this class are rarely over 30 inches in diameter, even on good sites. The bark is dark brown and roughly fissured into ridges or small plates.

*Class 2.* Age class, young or thrifty mature; position, usually codominant (rarely isolated or dominant); crown length, less than 65 percent of the total height; crown width, average or narrower; form of top, pointed; vigor, good or moderate. Such trees are usually less than 24 inches in diameter. They are commonly the inside codominant trees of groups.

*Class 3.* Age class, mature; position, isolated or dominant (rarely codominant); crown length, 65 percent or more of total height; crown width, average or wider; form of top, round; vigor, moderate. These trees are ordinarily between 18 and 40 inches in diameter, depending on site quality. The bark is light brown or yellow, with moderately large, smooth plates.

*Class 4.* Age class, mature; position, usually codominant (rarely isolated or dominant); crown length, less than 65 percent of the total height; crown width, average or narrower; form of top, round; vigor, moderate or poor. These are commonly the inside or codominant trees of this age class. Except for their small poorly developed crowns and smaller size, they are similar to Class 3 trees.

*Class 5.* Age class, overmature; position, isolated or dominant (rarely codominant); crown of any size; form of top, flat; vigor, poor. These are usually the largest trees in the stand. The bark is light yellow in color, the plates often very wide, long, and smooth, especially near the base. The bark may be thin, having weathered more rapidly than it has grown. The foliage is usually rather pale green and very thin.

*Class 6.* Age class, young or thrifty mature; position, intermediate or suppressed; crown of any size, usually small; form of top, round or pointed; vigor, moderate or poor. These are understory trees, rarely over 12 to 14 inches in diameter. The bark is dark and rough.

*Class 7.* Age class, mature or overmature; position, intermediate or suppressed; crown of any size, usually small; form of top, flat; vigor, poor. These understory trees are rarely over 18 inches in diameter. The bark is light colored, thin, smooth.

lamation by clearing and planting becomes increasingly more difficult. Such intensive treatment depends heavily on the findings of research; it also requires detailed working plans, and, above all, well-planned and well-constructed logging roads. Establishing intensive management costs more, but it is cheapest in the long run. Timber growth and, ultimately, cutting can be increased to twice what they are now, and maintained at that level. That can be done without endangering California's vital water supply, harming the mountain soils, or jeopardizing recreation and other values.

B. O. HUGHES *has been chief of the Division of Timber Management in the California Region of the Forest Service since 1944. He began work with the Forest Service in 1923; his experience since that time includes assignments on the Eldorado, Shasta, and Lassen National Forests and timber-management work in the California and the Southern Regions. From 1940 to 1943 he was supervisor of the Mississippi national forests. He holds degrees from Cornell University and the University of California.*

DUNCAN DUNNING, *since 1927, has been in charge of forest-management research at the California Forest and Range Experiment Station. He began work with the Forest Service in 1916 on the Shasta National Forest and at the Feather River Experiment Station. He is a graduate of the University of California.*

# SMALL RANCHERS AND THE FORESTS

WILLIAM L. ROBB

From the 104 national forests near which they live in the West, operators of small ranches obtain many millions of board feet of timber products.

Practically all of this timber is obtained through small sales that involve a stumpage value of $500 or less. The number of such small sales made yearly in a typical period, from 1941 through 1945, ranged from 10,895 in 1943 to 15,938 in 1941.

The largest demand is for saw timber, followed in order by fuel wood, corral and fence poles, fence posts, and miscellaneous products such as house logs, derrick sets, and cellar poles.

The buyers use most of these timber products for maintaining and improving their own property, but many cut and sell lumber, poles, posts, and mine props during otherwise slack seasons.

In a typical case, the rancher or farmer applies to the local forest ranger for the type and amount of timber he wants. The ranger issues a sale permit to the applicant and, upon receipt of notice that payment for the timber has been made, marks the trees to be cut. The rancher then does the cutting; the ranger checks at intervals to see that terms of the permit are fulfilled. Under the sales agreement, the rancher must complete the cutting and removal of the timber within a given time; cut low stumps, and otherwise make the fullest use possible of each marked tree; dispose of limbs and tops so as to provide for the establishment of new growth of young trees and reduce the fire hazard; move the logs so as not to damage the young trees or cause soil erosion; and follow other operational requirements to assure the best use of the forest.

For some years the timber purchaser was required to assemble, or deck, his logs on the timber-sale area (or at some other agreed-upon location) for scaling or measurement by the forest officer before removal. The common practice now is to make small sales by what is known as the tree-measurement procedure. The volume of individual trees is determined at the time they are marked for cutting.

In the case of a sale for saw timber, the forest officer blazes each tree to be cut and numbers it, consecutively, on the blaze. He measures its diameter at a point 4½ feet above the ground with a diameter tape and its merchantable height with an Abney level or hypsometer. Diameter and height measurements are recorded for each tree as the marking and measuring go forward. From tables prepared for each tree species in the timber stand the volume of lumber that can be sawn from each marked tree is calculated and recorded. A sufficient number of trees are marked to produce a gross volume, as determined from the volume tables, somewhat in excess of the amount which the purchaser applies for.

Usually some of the trees marked contain defects in the form of rot, checks, or crooks, or are unavoidably broken when they are felled. To be sure the purchaser gets the full volume of the usable material desired, the gross volume, as determined from the volume tables, is reduced by the amount of such defect and unavoidable breakage as occurs. This deduction is arrived at by scaling a sample of felled trees to determine the difference between their gross and usable volume. This difference is then applied to the whole.

In order to handle most efficiently the great number of small sales made annually and to provide the most service to purchasers, units of timber are set aside on most national forests and ranger districts where small sales are concentrated. Such units are located, as far as practicable, close to communities from which most requests for timber are received. In them the forest officer usually marks and measures enough trees in the spring to take care of all the small sales he expects to have during the normal logging season.

As each application is received, previously marked and measured trees are assigned to the applicant and specified by number in his permit. The assignment, by number, of trees previously marked is done consecutively as applications are received. Each permit-holder is given directions on how to reach the area where the timber is located. Periodically the forest officer inspects the cutting area.

Many small ranchers in the West use national forest forage for their livestock in summer. The forage is managed, like timber, on a sustained-yield basis. The use of forest range is permitted on payment of a grazing fee based on the class of stock and the length of the grazing season on each grazing unit. In 1947, 17,153 ranchers were permitted to graze 1,142,629 cattle and horses under paid permits. Another 3,167 had permits to graze 3,398,375 sheep and goats. About 60 percent of the holders of permits for cattle and horses grazed fewer than 40 head of stock each; only about 7 percent owned more than 200 head each. Approximately 63 percent of the permits for sheep and goats were for fewer than 1,000 animals; only about 3 percent grazed more than 4,000 head.

The forests also provide supplemental employment to many ranchers on various types of projects for improving and protecting the forests.

People living in or near the forests are especially qualified and adapted to this type of work. Because they have more than average dependence upon the resources of the forest, they have more than average interest in developing and protecting them. Those who operate small mills to supplement their ranching operations are interested in stand-improvement measures, such as thinning dense stands, pruning crop trees, and planting seedlings, and in maintaining the roads. Graziers are interested in range reseeding and construction of improvements like water developments and fences. Men who use the forest roads and trails for trailing or trucking livestock or guiding vacationists on fishing and hunting trips are anxious to maintain roads and trails.

WILLIAM L. ROBB *has been in charge of the Division of Timber Management of the Intermountain Region of the Forest Service since 1939.*

*Four scenes in the forests of Alaska—"under proper management they can be made to contribute generously to the wealth of the United States."*

# FORESTS OF ALASKA

B. FRANK HEINTZLEMAN

When the United States bought Alaska from Russia in 1867, neither party to the transaction ascribed much value to the forests embraced in the purchase, even though the best known section at the time, the southern coast, was largely clothed with a dense mantle of deep-green tree growth from the seashore to elevations of 3,000 feet.

We can understand this lack of interest in the forests, however, when we consider that there the coastal forest was merely the northern tip of a far greater timbered area, which extended down along the northwestern coast of North America to the southern boundary of Oregon, and that all the timber of this vast area was then practically untapped.

This great real estate transfer occurred only 82 years ago, but already the forest situation has changed radically. Large-scale timber industries have long since spread over the whole of the coastal forest area lying to the south of Alaska; pulp and paper manufacturers now are considering the extension of their operations to the hemlock and spruce stands of Alaska's southern coast to meet the constantly increasing demand for pulp products in the United States. Farther north, in interior Alaska, the light stands of white spruce and white birch have long been used by the small population, but increasing public interest in development there is focusing more attention on the value of those forests.

Alaska, one-fifth the size of continental United States, has many kinds of climate and many types of vegetative cover. A forester, though, divides the Territory roughly into three vegetative regions—the nontimbered Arctic and Bering Sea coast, the lightly timbered interior, and the well-timbered south coast.

The Arctic and Bering Sea coast embraces about 30 percent of the area of the Territory and includes most of the Alaska Peninsula, Aleutian Islands, the Bering Sea coastal region to an average width of about 100 miles, and the land draining into the Arctic Ocean. Generally, the region is untimbered, the climate being too severe for tree growth. Surprisingly, however, white spruce trees sufficiently large for cabin logs and narrow boards grow along the banks of the Noatak and Kobuk Rivers and some branches of the Yukon River, well north of the Arctic Circle. Much of the region is flat lowland and rounded ridges covered with a swamp and tundra vegetation of moss, lichens, sedges, dwarf willows, and other short shrubs. The more southerly lands, the Alaska Peninsula and Aleutian Islands, are mountainous and support a luxuriant growth of grass, alder, and willow.

Interior Alaska, as here considered, lies between the mountain chain, which forms the Arctic Divide on the north, and the crest of the Coastal Range, which borders the Pacific Ocean on the south. It covers about 60 percent of the area of the Territory, and comprises the watersheds of the Yukon, Kuskokwim, Copper, Susitna, and other large rivers. This is the region that meets the popular conception of Alaska. The winters are long and intensely cold. The summers are short but warm, and daylight lasts 20 hours or more of each 24 days. Much of the area has permanently frozen ground (permafrost) to within a foot or two of the surface. The annual rainfall is exceedingly light (being only 12 to 16 inches) but permafrost and the short summers prevent the development of desert conditions. Millions of acres of sparse timber give this region the classification of a forested country, but the forests occur as many scattered islands among the extensive areas of swamp and tundra vegetation on the valley floors and along the foothills. They give way entirely to shrubs, grass, and barren ground on the higher ridges and mountains.

The south coast covers about 10 percent of the area of the Territory and comprises the narrow, crescent-shaped region fronting on the Pacific Ocean from Portland Canal on the southeast to Kodiak Island on the northwest, a distance of 800 miles. Southeastern Alaska, the almost-detached section that extends southerly as a panhandle along the western side of northern British Columbia for 400 miles, makes up almost two-thirds of it. The region consists of a narrow strip of mainland extending back to the summit of the Coastal Range, numerous large and small islands, and a maze of intervening narrow waterways. The land is mountainous throughout, and rises abruptly from the water's edge to heights commonly exceeding 4,000 feet and, in many instances, 8,000 feet. A few awe-inspiring peaks extend to 15,000 and 18,000 feet above the nearby sea. The coast line of mainland and islands is highly indented, and the deep, narrow waterways, the fiords, reach far inland toward the backbone of the mountains, with the result that most of the land area is within a few miles of navigable tidewater. The lofty summit of the mountain chain on the mainland strip has great permanent icefields, from which ice is drained off by glaciers down hundreds of valleys.

The voyager along the network of narrow waterways here gains the impression of a mountain country which has been depressed about 1,000 feet, thereby transforming the former stream valleys into deep, narrow, navigable sea channels, and the summits of the high ridges into chains or elongated islands.

The south coast owes its well-timbered condition to a moist and rather warm, equable climate. A warm ocean current of the north Pacific touches the northwest coast of North America from Kodiak Island to southern Oregon along a distance of 1,800 miles and gives the intervening coastal area about the same climate throughout. The visitor from Portland feels at home in the winters of Sitka. Winds moving landward from this warm ocean water through a low barometric trough usually lying over a portion of the north Pacific, greatly modify the winter temperatures. They also produce a heavy rainfall, as much of their abundant moisture is dropped when they strike the cold, high coastal mountains.

The winters of the south-coast area are long but not severely cold. The average January temperature at sea level is 32° F., about the same as that of Washington, D. C., or Cincinnati, Ohio. A reading of zero is a rarity. The summers are cool, with an average July temperature of about 55°. The average annual precipitation is heavy. It ranges from 70 to 155 inches at sea level in different parts of the region and rapidly increases with elevation on the exposed westward slopes of the mountains. The winter precipitation near tidewater is largely in the form of rain, and the ground may be clear or nearly clear of snow for extended periods, but at elevations above 600 feet the snowfall persists throughout the winter months and accumulates to great depths. Cloudy days are common in all seasons and constitute two-thirds of the days of the year. There is no pronounced summer dry season. Harbors are not icebound, and climatic conditions at the lower elevations do not, as a rule, seriously interfere with outdoor winter activities, such as logging.

A growing season of 150 days and 16 to 18 hours of daylight are highly favorable to the growth of vegetation, especially coniferous forests, but heavy rainfall, rough topography, and thin, new soils in this part of Alaska practically rule out extensive agricultural development. Many garden crops do well if given good care.

THE LAND OF ALASKA is still almost entirely in Federal ownership. Not more than 1 percent of its 586,400 square miles has been patented to date under the homestead, mining, and other laws that permit of alienation of public lands. While considerable areas are held intact for special purposes, such as military and naval reservations and national parks, the great bulk of the land is classified as open public domain, where soil and other resources are available for occupancy and use under laws that permit patenting or leasing. This land is under the jurisdiction of the Department of the Interior.

Approximately 32,575 square miles (20,840,000 acres), or 5.5 percent of the total area of the Territory, has been designated as national forests. These national forests lie entirely in the well-timbered south-coast region and, in the main, are to be held in permanent Federal ownership for the production of successive timber crops. If tracts are found to be more valuable for such uses as mining, homesteads, homesites, water-power development, industrial sites, and resort areas, however, they are made available for those uses through land patents in some cases and a leasing system in others.

THROUGHOUT INTERIOR ALASKA, an area larger than Texas, is a mixed forest of small white spruce and Alaska white birch, with some cottonwood of various species frequently in mixture. These forests occupy the better drained soils of valley bottoms, lower slopes, and low benchlands, to an elevation of approximately 2,500 feet, but the local climatic conditions frequently hold the timber line to lower levels.

The trees sometimes reach a diameter of 18 inches, but the average diameter of mature trees is between 10 and 12 inches. The height ranges from 40 to 50 feet. The stands are fairly dense, and the volume per acre of virgin mature stands may be as high as 20 cords. Stands of trees of sawmilling size may contain from 6,000 to 8,000 board feet an acre. Ground birch, stunted alder, and willows constitute a fairly dense undergrowth, and the ground cover is a thick mat of moss. Permafrost is prevalent in the region, and because of that, and other features of a harsh climate, the rate of growth is slow.

White men started coming into this region in large numbers about 1900. Since then, extensive, devastating forest fires and, to a lesser degree, cutting operations have greatly reduced the extent of the virgin timber. Perhaps not more than 20 percent of the original white spruce-white birch stands are now intact. Reproduction after fire runs strongly to aspen.

Another forest type, which could well be classed as a brush type, consists of black spruce on wet lowlands. The trees are scattered, gnarled, and rarely more than 6 inches in diameter. Tamarack and cottonwood of stunted form are the associated tree species. Interspersed clumps of willow brush and areas of grass, peat moss, and swamp herbs occupy as much of the ground space as the black spruce and associated trees.

No one has ever made a systematic field survey and estimate of the area of the different kinds of vegetative cover in interior Alaska. A conservative guess places the area of white spruce-white birch forests, including the burned areas reproducing strongly to aspen, at 100,000 square miles, or 64 million acres. The whole type, burned and unburned, can be roughly estimated as having an average stand of 5 cords an acre, or a total volume of 320 million cords.

Interior Alaska now uses and will likely continue to need large quantities of wood products in connection with its development. Gold mining and dairy and vegetable farming are the principal local industries, although military defense projects in the past 10 years have contributed substantially to the economy.

Much of the fuel and construction material needed in mining and on the farms is cut from the local forests. Cutting operations, which have been going on since the days of the gold rushes around 1900, and the heavy losses from forest fires have led to near-depletion of the virgin timber for a score of miles around each of the larger communities. Future settlement and development of interior Alaska will continue to draw heavily on the meager local forest resources because of the distances from the outside sources of supply. Consequently, the potential value of these forests to the region is great.

Of almost equal economic importance is the use made of these forests by fur and game animals for cover and as a source of food supply. Interior Alaska is one of the better areas of the world for large wilderness game animals, and it is also an extensive producer of fur. Those resources contribute substantially to the food supply and the cash income of the native Indians and of many white settlers. The big-game animals—moose, the mountain sheep, the great brown bear, and caribou—attract hunters, wildlife photographers, and general tourists, who provide an important and constantly increasing source of income.

THE EARLY SITUATION in the forests of the Western States is being repeated in Alaska in that the interior forest area is subject to devastating fires, and the volume of timber burned is many times greater than the volume cut.

A combination of light precipitation, the long daylight hours, and the warm weather of the summer months, plus the heavy ground cover of moss, produces a serious fire hazard. Also, the vast size and the wilderness condition make effective fire-control measures difficult and costly. Another discouraging fact is the slow tree growth here, which means a slow recovery of spruce and birch on the burned-over areas. The fires in interior Alaska are largely man-made (lightning is serious in certain areas only), and until recently they have been largely due to indifference. Many settlers, hunters, prospectors, and general travelers had the attitude that the burning of an area here and there in that vast wilderness was a matter of no importance. Fires were allowed to escape from land-clearing jobs, campfires along the trails were left unextinguished, and fires were set to drive the mosquitoes from camp sites and mining operations. The past decade, however, has seen an encouraging trend away from this attitude.

The extent of individual fires is appalling to a visitor from the States, but understandable in view of the warm, dry summers and the wilderness conditions. Fires often start in the early spring and travel uninterruptedly until the fall rains extinguish them. Dozens of fires, each of 10,000 acres or more, may occur in one summer, while not uncommonly a single fire will burn from 200,000 to 400,000 acres. In 1947, at least five fires burned more than 100,000 acres each. The largest of those, on the open public domain on the west side of the Kenai Peninsula, covered approximately 250,000 acres, as determined by inspection from the air at the end of the fire season. No one knows the total area burned in interior Alaska in 1947, but it probably reached 1,150,000 acres.

The open public domain, comprising most of interior Alaska, is administered by the Bureau of Land Management (formerly the General Land Office) of the United States Department of the Interior. Before July 1, 1939, there was practically no organized forest-fire protection on these lands; but at that time an appropriation of $37,500 was made available by Congress to the General Land Office for the start of a protective unit, designated the Alaskan Fire Control Service. Up to and including the fiscal year beginning July 1, 1946, the annual appropriation had been increased to $170,000, and the organization expanded to a force of approximately 40 persons, two-thirds of them part-year employees only. The item for fire control was omitted from the Department of the Interior appropriation act for the fiscal year beginning July 1, 1947, which year proved unfortunately to be a bad fire period. That item was restored and substantially increased the next year.

The lands under the protection of the Alaskan Fire Control Service in-

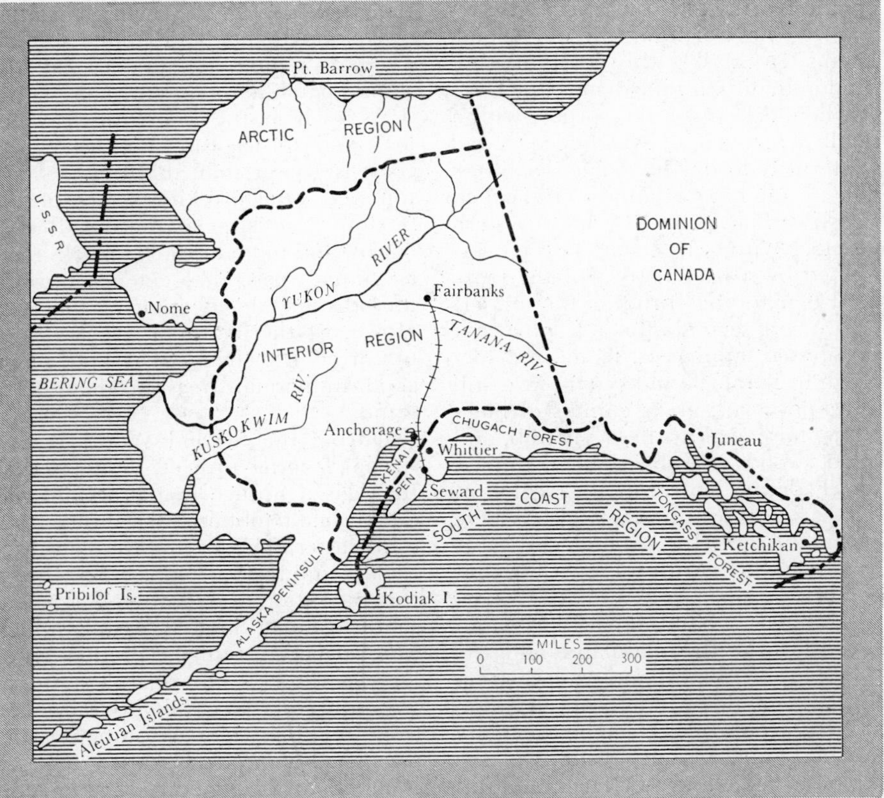


**Forest distribution in Alaska: The nontimbered Arctic slope and Bering Sea coastal region, tundra and grass; the lightly timbered interior, white spruce and white birch, which supply local construction material and fuel and provide food and cover for game and fur bearers; the heavily timbered south-coast region, extensive stands of western hemlock and Sitka spruce suitable for pulp manufacture.**

clude not only the forests of interior Alaska, but also the tundra and grasslands of interior Alaska and the Bering Sea-Arctic region, as those nonforested lands are important game and fur areas. The total area needing fire protection in Alaska is not less than 250 million acres.

Those who know the fire situation in interior Alaska estimate that an acceptable minimum of fire protection on these lands could be provided with an expenditure of $250,000 annually, supplemented at the start with $50,000 a year over a 5-year period. The supplement would provide for necessary transport equipment, such as trucks and river boats, the purchase and installation of the radio and telephone equipment, the purchase of fire-fighting equipment, and the construction of essential field stations. The $250,000 annual operating cost would be slightly more than a mill an acre. The small population of interior Alaska, and the fact that most fires are man-caused, make it possible to accomplish a great deal in fire protection at little cost by instructing the public in the need for and methods of prevention.

In the south-coast region the timberlands form a part of the coniferous forest type that occupies the so-called fog belt, usually less than 50 miles wide, along the shore line of the

Pacific Northwest from southern Oregon to the northern tip of Kodiak Island. In Alaska, this coast forest is predominantly a mixed stand of western hemlock and Sitka spruce, with a small percentage of Alaska-cedar, and western redcedar in some localities. The forest here is almost tropical in density. The main cover is western hemlock with some cedar. This is overtopped by scattered trees of the more light-demanding spruce, while underneath is a second story of somewhat suppressed saplings of the more shade-resistant hemlock and cedar. At a still lower level are great clumps of blueberry, false azalea, the devilsclub, and other woody shrubs. Fallen timber, which decays slowly in this region of all-year heavy rainfall, is everywhere abundant, and the ground surface is usually covered with a carpet of moss.

The forest occurs as a relatively narrow ribbon or band along the sinuous coast line of the mainland and the hundreds of islands, and extends from the edge of tidewater to an elevation varying from 1,000 feet in the more northerly and westerly sections of the region to 2,000 and 3,000 feet in southeastern Alaska. Because of the mountainous character of the country, the entire area of tree growth is usually within sight of tidewater and rarely extends more than 5 or 6 miles inland. Three-fourths of the commercial timber is estimated to be within 2½ miles of the coast line.

The timber stands of present merchantable quality are seldom continuous over large watersheds, but are interspersed by areas of somewhat stunted stands of the same species, designated as "scrub," and by untimbered bogs of peat moss locally known as "muskegs." The best of the Alaska forests is found in southeastern Alaska and, in general, the quality of the timber and the proportion of forested land decreases with progress northward. Thus the trees are smaller and the timber band narrower in the Prince William Sound country than in southeastern Alaska, while the trees at the very tip of the hemlock-spruce range on Afognak and Kodiak Islands are largely unmerchantable, and the stands patchlike in occurrence.

As a whole, the quality of the hemlock and spruce timber of the south coast is poorer than that of Washington and Oregon. More trees of the medium and larger sizes are affected by rot, and more of the hemlocks have a "fluted" base that extends upward into the first log section of the tree. However, there are many stands of uniformly excellent trees and many good individual trees in the poorer stands.

During the Second World War a special logging project, designated as the Alaska Spruce Log Program, was established to obtain Sitka spruce from southeastern Alaska for the construction of military airplanes. Logs from this operation were rafted 800 miles south to Puget Sound sawmills, which were specializing in the production of airplane stock. The Alaska material was fully equal in quality to that taken from the forests of Washington and Oregon. Much of the Alaska hemlock is suited to the highest uses for hemlock, such as flooring and interior trim for residences. The wood of Alaska-cedar and of western redcedar is well adapted to the manufacture of a great variety of specialty items that are in demand in the United States. A few such items are furniture parts, battery separators, wooden handles of many kinds, and rollers for window shades. Processing is ordinarily done in small plants and requires much labor. It is believed that such wood-using industries might profitably be established in the coastal towns of southern Alaska.

Most of the timber is, however, more suitable for pulp than for any of the above uses. The woods run of logs from the hemlock and spruce forests of Alaska are equal in quality to logs (No. 2 and No. 3 grade) from the Washington forests that are used by the pulp mills on Puget Sound for the highest grades of pulp.

The economy of the south-coast region, with approximately 35,000 inhabitants, is now based largely on the commercial sea fisheries, but lumber production, now approaching 100 million board feet annually, is growing in importance. When fully developed, the timber industries, including especially pulp manufacture, will likely equal and may even exceed the fisheries in value of yearly output.

THE BETTER AREAS of the coast forest lying north and west of southeastern Alaska are included in the Chugach National Forest. This forest consists principally of lands around Prince William Sound and on the eastern half of the Kenai Peninsula just north of Seward. Its area is 4.8 million acres. The timber-management plan specifies that the timber output will be used to supply the needs of localities in and around the national forest, with the excess going to the lightly timbered and nontimbered sections of Alaska farther to the north, the interior and the Arctic-Bering Sea areas.

The Chugach National Forest constitutes the nearest source of supply of large timber items for those areas, and its production capacity is not sufficient to meet their present and prospective demands. Consequently, sales of timber from the Chugach National Forest are not made to concerns that contemplate shipping their principal products out of the Territory.

The chief local demand for Chugach products is and likely will continue to be lumber, heavy sawn timbers, and piling. A sawmill with a capacity of 60,000 board feet a day, located at Whittier on Prince William Sound, a gateway of the Alaska Railroad into interior Alaska, is the largest mill on the Chugach National Forest. A few smaller mills, ranging up to 10,000 or 15,000 feet in daily capacity, supply part of the purely local lumber demands at Seward and other towns.

THE TONGASS NATIONAL FOREST is in southeastern Alaska. The Alaska forests that will be an important source of wood products, especially pulp and paper, for continental United States are those of southeastern Alaska. The system of sea channels there is more elaborate than in the more northerly and westerly sections of the south-coast region, and the timber is thus more accessible. Seventy percent of the area and most of the commercial timberlands of southeastern Alaska are included in the Tongass National Forest. In addition to suitable timber, southeastern Alaska has that second requisite for pulp manufacture—power. The heavy rainfall and the availability of many high mountain lakes for storage reservoirs, give this section good water-power resources. Detailed studies show that approximately 200 of the better undeveloped power sites have a total yearlong capacity of 800 thousand horsepower.

This national forest has a total area of 16,040,000 acres, of which 10 million acres is within the altitudinal limits of tree growth. Approximately 4 million acres carries timber of present commercial quality; another 1 million acres has timber of marginal quality; and still another 1 million acres has timber of such low quality that it is

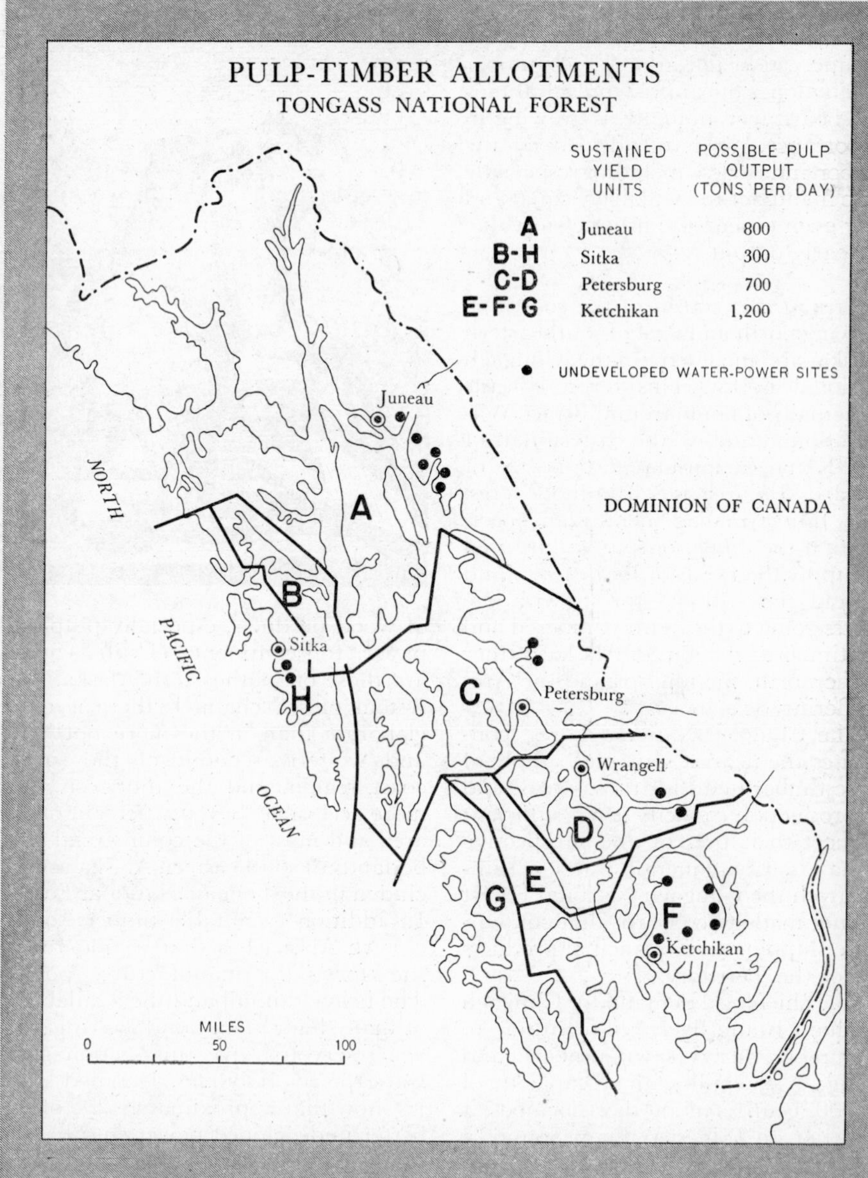


Four sustained-yield units (composed of pulp-timber allotments A, B–H, C–D, and E–F–G) have been tentatively established on the Tongass National Forest as a basis for effecting a full, orderly, and economic development of the pulp and paper industry now in prospect for Southeast Alaska. Within each unit intensive forestry will be practiced on the timberlands, and the annual cut will be limited to the estimated annual growth.

wholly disregarded in all timber-management planning. The remaining 4 million acres within the limits of the timbered zone is barren rock or is covered with muskeg, brush, or icefields.

The estimated volume of commercial timber now on the Tongass Forest is 78,500 million board feet, of which about 74 percent is western hemlock, 20 percent Sitka spruce, and 6 percent western redcedar and Alaska-cedar. The average stand on an acre of commercial timber is approximately 20,000 board feet, but individual logging units with 40,000 board feet or more are not uncommon.

The prevailing timber type of the Tongass Forest consists of a mixture of the species named previously. It is designated as the western hemlock type. Mature hemlock trees average between 3 and 4 feet in diameter, are usually quite clean-boled and well-formed, and are sound until maturity is reached. After maturity, dead tops and butt rot develop rapidly.

Sitka spruce, the other dominant member of the western hemlock type, is a larger tree than the hemlock, reaching at maturity an average diameter of 5 feet at breast height and a maximum of 8 feet or more. It usually occurs singly or as small clumps of trees scattered throughout the hemlock stands. More light-demanding, it keeps its head above the neighboring hemlocks and cedars. Its long, slightly tapering, branch-free bole and its great size make Sitka spruce an impressive feature of the Alaska forests.

The western redcedar and Alaska-cedar usually occur in clumps in the mixed forest, but on the wetter soils. They are somewhat shorter than the hemlocks, have a heavy taper, and reach dimensions at maturity of about 4 to 5 feet in diameter.

The scrub type, consisting of the open stands of somewhat dwarfed, defective trees and dense undergrowth, occupies soils of poorer drainage than the hemlock type but better drained than those occupied by muskegs. This type covers most of the million acres of timber of marginal value previously mentioned, plus additional great areas that offer only a remote possibility of attaining future commercial value. The marginal stands of scrub may have from 5 to 10 cords or even more of pulpwood an acre over large areas, but the amount of the wood defect to be eliminated and the dense underbrush and moist ground to be encountered in logging give the material a distinctly negative stumpage value at present. The muskeg, with a tree growth limited to a few scattered and gnarled hemlocks and cedars, is definitely a nontimber type. Any future economic value of Alaska muskegs lies in their peat deposits and not in their timber.

The main objective in the management of the Tongass National Forest is to bring all resources of the forest land into use and to make them contribute in the greatest possible degree to the needs of the Nation and the development and maintenance of the economy of southeastern Alaska. First, the timber resource is to be made the basis for permanent forest industries to be established in the region. Second, full use of all other resources, including recreational features, the water-power sites, minerals, and potential agricultural lands, is to be encouraged.

The timber inventories and studies of tree growth that have been made on this forest to date indicate that a rotation of 80 to 85 years will produce the most wood of good quality per acre per year and that removing the present virgin stand over that period of time will permit the cutting of approximately one billion board feet of timber a year. This volume is sufficient to make at least a million tons of chemical pulp, plus considerable quantities of high-grade lumber and plywood.

Western hemlock and Sitka spruce form an excellent forest type for the production of pulpwood. The hemlock is shade enduring and the spruce light demanding, a combination which results in a dense stand per acre. Both are fair to rapid growers and produce high total yields, and both woods have good pulping qualities. The hemlock-spruce forests, except in a few small areas, do not lend themselves to the practice of selective logging, the system of cutting under which trees of all ages are grown in one stand and individual trees are selected and removed as they reach maturity. Both the hemlock and

802062°—49——25

the spruce are shallow-rooted, and the heavy winds of this region cause serious windfall to the remaining trees if the stands are opened up by selective cutting. Consequently, the forest manager has to clear-cut the forest and, to insure natural reseeding, leave seed trees in the form of large patches of undisturbed timber spotted over the cutting area. The areas that have been cut over in this region show abundant natural reproduction under this clear-cutting, grouped seed-tree system. Selective cutting is also impracticable on most areas here from a logging standpoint. Because of the large size of the timber, the dense brush, and moist soils, powerful donkey engines and heavy wire cables must be used to pull the logs from the woods, and if individual trees were left standing throughout the logging area they could not be protected from destruction or injury by the logging equipment and machinery.

The common practice in the Pacific Northwest of broadcast burning of slash left in logging as a fire-prevention measure is unnecessary here because of the heavy rainfall. This is distinctly advantageous to the Alaska forester, as the logging areas usually have much advance reproduction of young hemlock and spruce that can be saved to provide a fine start toward the next timber crop.

THIS IS A PROSPECTIVE PULP- AND PAPER-MAKING region. The Tongass National Forest, with an extensive stand of fine pulp timber, excellent water-power resources, its cheap tidewater transportation, and mild winter climate, offers good possibilities for the development of a large, prosperous, and permanent regional pulp industry based on a system of timber cropping and the sale of the output in the general markets of the United States. If fully developed, the industry could support, directly and indirectly, a total of 30,000 persons in southeastern Alaska.

Pulp manufacturers would have the obviously very great advantage here of being able to obtain an assured supply of timber for a long term of years on a basis of paying for this material as cutting proceeds. Other favorable features include low logging costs because of the ready accessibility of the timber stands to tidewater, cheap log towing to the mills along the protected seaways, a mild winter climate, which permits of practically yearlong logging and offers no handicap to mill operation, and ocean transportation for the product direct from the mill to the general markets. In view of those features, men in the Forest Service believe that the development of this industry, which can contribute so substantially to the pulp and paper needs of the United States and to the permanent development of Alaska, will not be long delayed.

The first promising prospects for pulp and paper mills on the Tongass Forest developed in the late 1920's. At that time a large Pacific coast paper manufacturer and a combination of Pacific coast newspaper publishers applied for and received awards of timber and of water-power sites for the establishment of two large newsprint mills. Substantial sums were spent by these prospective operators on surveys and plans over a period of 3 years, but the depression that began in 1929 blocked further progress, and in 1933 the projects were definitely dropped. Subsequently, until the start of the Second World War, a number of manufacturers and users of pulp and paper made preliminary investigations of the possibilities, but financial and market conditions in those years did not encourage them to go further. In no case did interest during that period reach the point where timber- and power-site awards were applied for. Since the close of the war there has been a resurgence in interest.

The timber-management policies provide that the timber resources of the Tongass Forest shall be used for the upbuilding and the support of permanent, modern communities throughout southeastern Alaska. In line with this policy the forest has been divided into pulp-timber allotments, that in turn have been tentatively grouped into four sustained-yield units. Each unit has sufficient timberland to support one or more pulp mills of economic operating size in perpetuity. Suitable water powers that can be developed for mill and domestic use and a good plant location or locations are found in each unit. In all but one unit, plants can be located adjacent to an existing town. Sustained-yield units and the location of the better power sites are shown in the diagram on page 368. The diagram also shows the estimated maximum output of timber products in the form of tons of chemical pulp per day which the unit can maintain indefinitely. The volumes of the sustained output and the boundaries of the units may be changed somewhat as more information on timber growth is obtained.

As a result of present interest, the Forest Service in 1948 offered for sale by competitive bidding and awarded the cutting rights on a large pulp-timber unit for a proposed plant at Ketchikan, Alaska. The contract period is 50 years and sufficient timber is provided for this period to supply a chemical pulp mill of 525 tons daily capacity, plus approximately 75,000 board feet a day of lumber or plywood, to be made from high-grade logs that will come out of the woods in the pulpwood logging operations. The land is not to be sold with the timber, but is to be held indefinitely by the Federal Government for the production of successive timber crops. All cutting is to be done in accordance with specified forestry practices and under the field inspection of the Forest Service officers. Standards of utilization are provided to prevent unreasonable waste of merchantable material in logging. Timber is to be paid for as cutting proceeds on the basis of a scale of the cut material by Forest Service scalers. The prices to be paid to the Government for the material taken during the first 10 years of operation are those offered by the successful bidder. They coincide with the minimum acceptable rates named in the sale advertisement. Plant construction is expected to start in 1949 and pulp manufacture early in 1952.

At the end of the initial 10-year period, and at 5-year intervals thereafter throughout the life of the contract, the prices to be paid for stumpage, the utilization standards, and other important contract provisions are subject to readjustment to make them conform to changing conditions. Such readjustments are necessary to safeguard the interest of the public in this federally owned timber, but the contract also contains provisions designed to protect the pulp-timber purchaser against arbitrary action by Forest Service officers throughout the 50-year sale period. It establishes guides to be followed by the Government in setting new stumpage prices and making other contract changes at the specified intervals, and provides a right of appeal by the contract holder to the Secretary of Agriculture. This appeal includes the right of the contractor to have a board of specialists review the cutting-area boundaries and stumpage-price adjustments as determined periodically by the Forest Service, and advise the Secretary of Agriculture on action to be taken by him in the matter.

The protection of salmon fisheries and scenic features is provided for. The development of large pulp and paper projects on the Tongass Forest will not be permitted to jeopardize the highly important salmon fisheries of southeastern Alaska. The national forest contains hundreds of streams to which salmon return from the open sea to spawn, and the productivity of the fisheries would be seriously impaired by improper logging methods and practices in the valleys of those streams. The Secretary of Agriculture has authority to require that logging operations conform to instructions for preservation of natural conditions on salmon streams, and all pulp-timber cutting contracts will state that the logging operator must abide by such instructions as are set up for that purpose. The standard practice will be to issue the instructions for a given stream when the plans for the logging of its watershed are drafted. Arrangements have been made for cooperation of the United States Fish and Wildlife Service in determining what should be done to protect salmon-spawning streams.

Alaska's fine scenery is also to be considered when the lands to be logged are designated. Large areas of great scenic value are not to be included within the exterior boundaries of the pulp-timber sales. Small scenic areas that cannot be readily excluded from a sale will be reserved from cutting when the logging plans for that locality are drafted. In general, narrow, navigable sea channels, highways, and the recreation sites having special scenic values will be protected by reserved strips or blocks of timber to screen the logged-off land.

THE RECREATIONAL FEATURES of the Tongass National Forest possess an esthetic and an economic value that rates them high in the resource-management plans of the forest.

The many miles of narrow, navigable waterways flanked with forest-covered slopes, snow-capped mountains, and high waterfalls appeal to the cruising enthusiasm and scenery lover.

Mountain goats on the high ranges of the mainland, deer on all of the islands, and the famous Alaska brown bear of Baranof, Chichagof, and Admiralty Islands make this a good hunting country.

Persons interested in nature studies are attracted here by tidewater glaciers that discharge into the sea, the exposed geologic formations along the almost-vertical walls of the fiords, the changing types of flora between sea level and the summits of the high mountains, and the varied marine life that is uncovered on the beaches at low water by the 12-foot to 20-foot tides.

These important resources—timber stands, the commercial salmon fisheries, scenery, and recreational features—are either of a renewable or nonwasting nature. In this region practically all are now publicly owned and can be safeguarded as necessary to insure the perpetuation of the renewable resources and the development or use of the others with adequate consideration for the public interest. Under proper management they can be made to contribute generously to the wealth of the United States and the permanent economy of the Territory.

B. FRANK HEINTZLEMAN *is regional forester for Alaska, and ex-officio Commissioner for the Department of Agriculture for Alaska, with headquarters at Juneau. A native of Pennsylvania and a graduate of the School of Forestry of Yale University, he has been associated with the Forest Service in Alaska since 1918 and has participated in many public-planning activities dealing with the settlement and development of the Territory.*

# THE ADMINISTRATION OF NATIONAL FORESTS

EARL W. LOVERIDGE

Our national forests are big, complex, varied in the services they render and the land they cover, widely distributed, and diverse in use and possibility. As pertinent as the fact that their exterior boundaries embrace nearly 230 million acres is the fact that 140 million American citizens own them. The administration of the forests has to take into account all those different factors.

The great area and distribution of the forests is one basic problem of administering them in the public interest.

The other is the dual purpose for which the forests were established and are being managed. The purpose includes service to the Nation and to the local economy and welfare.

The same dual purpose controls the management of the national forest range resource, which is utilized by some 10 million head of livestock, owned by more than 25,000 ranchers and other nearby residents. So, too, with the recreation and wildlife resources, which attract millions of persons to the forests each year. Water that the forests produce likewise must be so managed to serve interstate and local needs and to reduce its high potential for such disasters as floods and siltation of reservoirs. Because of its supreme importance, water management must be given predominating consideration in the handling of each of the other national forest resources.

The situation gives the order. Obviously, decentralization and delegation of authority to the tree and grass roots are called for. When Gifford Pinchot, first Chief of the Forest Service, formed a decentralized type of organization and administration in 1908, he said, "Each locality should be dealt with on its own merits." Since then that has been the controlling principle. A small central office is maintained to meet the needs for coordination and leadership, for essential facilitating and control services, and for the work with the board of directors—Congress. Of the total employment during a normal field season, less than 2 percent is in the central office in Washington.

Administration of the national forests is one of three main responsibilities of the Forest Service. The other two and research and State and private forestry cooperation. In charge of each of the three major lines of activity is an assistant chief, who with other assistant chiefs comprise the staff of the Chief of the Forest Service in dealing with matters of national importance.

The assistant chief in charge of national forest administration, acting for the Chief of the Forest Service, has full operating responsibility for planning, coordinating, staffing, organizing, and directing all national forest functions and activities. He in turn delegates to division chiefs in his office responsibility for particular functions. This functional organization is made up of the divisions of timber management, range management, wildlife management, recreation and land use, watershed management, fire control, and such service units as engineering, information and education, finance, as well as personnel.

Territorially the United States is divided into regions, each region into national forests, and each national forest into ranger districts.

The line of authority runs from the Chief of the Forest Service to the assistant chief in charge of national forests, to the regional forester, to the forest supervisor, to the district ranger.

The functional organization in the Chief's office, however, is extended to the field. In Washington, for example, a Division of Timber Management is responsible for over-all direction of timber management. In the region there is likewise a timber management division. At the national forest level there is a functional-staff man for timber management, and in the ranger district as many men are stationed as are needed to do the work.

Here then we have a secondary organizational line parallel to the primary lines of authority, and, like it, running from top to bottom. There are as many of these secondary lines as there are functions. The purpose of the first line, that is, the so-called line of authority, is primarily that of coordinating the work of the functional divisions, although it has other important duties, as will be seen later. The various functional lines must be kept in balance and held within their proper fields.

The relationship between the line of authority and the functional lines is important. Briefly stated, the relationship is this: General policies are issued down the line of authority, and only down that line. Within the framework of those established policies, a functional chief in Washington may issue instructions to the regional forester. The same practice holds as between the regional office and the forest supervisor's office.

THE REGIONAL FORESTER is in a key position.

While ordinarily there is thus an open channel of communication down the functional lines, it is to be understood that all functional officials in the region are responsible to the regional forester, and not to the Washington functional chiefs. They are employees of the region (not of the corresponding functional divisions in Washington), and the regional forester, who is responsible only to the Chief, is their immediate supervisor. Upon the regional forester rests ultimate responsibility for the needed correlation between functions and for the success or failure of all national forest operations in his region.

With this picture in mind—a group of functional lines paralleling a controlling coordinating line—we are now ready to consider field relationships in greater detail. While the assistant chief has full responsibility for national forest operations, he and his division heads in Washington exercise control only at the over-all, Nation-wide level. That is, within the mandates of Congress and the Secretary of Agriculture, the assistant chief and his Washington staff formulate objectives, determine policies, develop plans, establish standards, and check the accomplishments. These objectives, plans, policies, and standards must apply to the Nation as a whole and must be general enough and broad enough to cover all possible conditions.

A significant feature of the organization is the small size of the functional divisions in the central office that are responsible for national forest activities. An example is the Division of Fire Control. The extent of its responsibilities is indicated by the fact that each year there are some 11,000 fires in the national forests, and as many as 20,000 fire-control workers are employed at times. Fire-control expenditures amounted to more than 12 million dollars during each of the past several years. But there are only three staff-level employees in this Division and two clerical assistants.

The United States is divided into 10 national forest regions. The average region includes about 20 million acres of national forest land and an average of 15 national forests. Those are rounded-off averages that do not apply to any one region. They do, however, indicate the general framework of the organization at this level. The person versed in administrative matters will be interested in knowing that the average "span-of-control" in the territorial organization for a regional forester and his staff of functional division chiefs is 15 forest supervisors, in contrast to the generally considered maximum "span" of 3 to 7 supervisory or other important subordinate positions that an administrator can handle effectively. That the regional forester can handle such a broad span of control is due partly to the parallel functional organization line I have described.

The assistant chief in charge of national forest administration delegates to each regional forester control over all operations within his own region, subject to the requirement that he must operate within the framework of the policies, plans, and standards established for the country as a whole. The regional forester, with his staff of functional division chiefs, then sets the objectives for his region. He establishes regional policies, makes regional plans, establishes regional standards, and, of course, makes certain of compliance by field inspection and otherwise. That is necessary because each region is different. Conditions in the Southeast, say, differ materially from conditions in the Pacific Northwest—the timber, the types of recreation, and the wildlife are different, and so on. Each region makes its own plans and carries on its own activities. It does whatever is necessary to make the national forests of greatest value in the social and economic life of the region. The only restriction is that everything done must contribute to the national objective, must come within national policy, and must be up to national standards.

The field, then, stands on its own feet. There are some exceptions, although it will be seen that even those are, in reality, applications of the general principle that the Washington staff should confine itself to national matters. Sometimes an operation, even though it is located entirely within a region, is of national importance. It then must be considered on a national basis and by the Washington office. For example, a small timber sale is of only local significance, but a large one affects national markets and has national economic importance. It is difficult to say exactly where the dividing line may be, but now it is estimated to be around 30 million feet in some regions, 50 million feet in others. If a sale involves more than that amount, it must be approved by the Washington office; if it is less than that amount, it may be approved within the region without reference to the Washington office. The same general rule applies in all other functional activities.

The regional office, which is organized for national forest work on the same general pattern as the Chief's office, is likewise manned on a skeletonized basis, with certain differences. Although each main function is represented in the Chief's office by a separate division, frequently several functions are grouped within one division at the regional level, depending on the work load. In addition, the regional office provides project and other service to individual national forests as needed, where the national forest concerned does not have enough work of that type to require the full time of specialists attached directly to the staff of the forest supervisor.

For example, the logging engineer and his assistants who are attached to the regional office will provide their specialized type of service for short periods each year as needed on the national forests that do not have a full-time logging engineer. Range- and timber-survey crews, bridge-construction experts, and central equipment and machine shops headquartered at the regional office are other examples of special services available for limited periods to all the national forests in the region. In other words, there are two general classes of personnel attached to each regional office. One is of the supervisory, or overhead, class. The other is made up of project workers engaged in direct operations in the woods and on the range. They normally have headquarters at the regional office merely as a convenient turning and base point for a succession of work assignments to different points in the field.

The constant effort to decentralize and delegate authority closer to the tree and grass roots results in rather limited authority at the regional office level. Most of the responsibility for national forest work is delegated down to the forest supervisors and the forest rangers. As has been stated, only rarely does the regional forester refer a timber sale to the Chief's office for approval. Likewise at the field level, only the larger sales are referred by the forest supervisor to the regional forester for consideration and approval. In the field of range management, too, practically none of the operating activities is administered directly from the regional office. Even a catastrophic forest fire is handled directly by the local forest supervisor, with participation from the regional office usually limited to advice and facilitating services. Such decentralization reserves for the regional office the responsibility and time needed for providing effective regional leadership and over-all services.

The national forest supervisor has great responsibility. The average national forest contains more than 1,500,000 acres within its boundaries—an area larger than the State of Delaware and 35 times larger than the District of Columbia.

The protection, development, and the utilization of the natural resources within this area is the direct responsibility of the local forest supervisor. Decentralized and delegated to him, under broad national and regional policies, are all the authorities needed normally to meet this responsibility. He has authority to enter into contracts for the sale of the timber resource, up to certain size limits. The size of this authorization depends mainly on the volume of timber available for sale and his qualifications. Some of these authorizations are for as much as 10 million board feet a year for any one sale, but with no limit to the number of such sales authorized, except as imposed by the sustained-yield productive capacity of the forest or other controlling factors prescribed in the management plan for the working circle involved.

The duties of the forest supervisor are mainly coordinating and supervisory in character. He must see that all functions are given their share of attention according to plan, and that the range work, for example, is not crowded out by a growing demand for timber. He must determine the local forest objectives, and plan and direct the work of his forest. His plans must, of course, lie within the framework of the regional plan. As the regional forester provides special project assistance to the supervisor, so, too, does the supervisor help his ranger force with facilitating services in the form of specialized assistants on types of work that do not occur in sufficient volume to justify manning each ranger district with such specialists. Handled in this manner are such types of work as timber and range appraisals, major construction projects, special recreational plans, and development of special wildlife-management plans in cooperation with State authorities. Other facilitating services provided his field forces by the supervisor include much of the clerical work involved in procurement, pay rolls, as well as in personnel procedure.

The average forest supervisor has some 6 ranger districts under his supervision. Because of geographical, work load, and other controlling factors, the actual number may vary from 4 to 11 ranger districts.

THE RANGER is the local manager of a forest property. He is in direct contact with the public. He meets the timberman, the stockman, the hunter, the camper face to face. He supervises sales, measures products sold, issues permits, protects the resources against fire, erosion, insects, and disease, carries on planting programs, and in many other ways serves as local manager of property worth from half a million to several million dollars.

The average area within the boundaries of the 765 ranger districts into which the national forests are subdivided is 300,000 acres. The actual size of the individual districts depends mainly on the work load. Where timber sales and other intensive resource-management activities are heavy, the ranger districts may be as small as 50,000 acres. The other extreme is in the thinly forested and remote back country, and especially in Alaska, where there is as yet no active market for much of the timber or other need for intensive forest management. Here the work is primarily custodial in character, and consequently the ranger districts are as large as a half million to a million and more acres in size.

In order to handle the work effectively, the district ranger in his turn must set objectives and devise a plan of operations. He has broad planning and executive authority. The ranger does the ultimate planning. Usually he is the one who decides which area and which trees are to be cut first. To make such decisions, he must know the timber and the local community. He must fit the timber business into the life and needs of the community. He works with the community and plans with it, and sees that the forest is looked on as a local enterprise and community asset.

The ranger does all this within the framework of national, regional, and forest objectives. He is checked closely against policies and regulations and must conform, but because it is a fundamental national policy that the forest take its place locally as a contributor to community prosperity, the Chief of the Forest Service insures that the ranger's authority is protected and that no one above him sabotages his planning or action. In other words, he has his job and is protected in it; his authority has limits, however. But the ranger not only makes plans; he is a distinctive part of the organization because he also puts the plans into effect.

The district ranger is responsible only to his forest supervisor. He may meet the functional chiefs, in his district or in their offices, and discuss his plans and theirs, but he receives orders only from his immediate superior, the forest supervisor.

Effective ranger district administration is based on two key points. First is sufficient delegation of authority to the district ranger so that his protection and management duties, including dealings with local settlers and communities, may be handled with effectiveness and dispatch. To that end, the ranger is authorized, for example, to make any number of timber sales of from some 50,000 to 100,000 board feet to each purchaser, subject only to the timber-management plan for the district. He also may employ lookouts and other members of his seasonal protection and improvement crews, subject only to over-all requirements, and otherwise handle the more pressing business on his district without constantly referring matters to his supervisor for prior approval.

The ranger district approaches the ultimate in territorial form of organization. That is the second rather distinctive feature of ranger-district administration.

Under the set-up, all the various responsibilities and types of work to be done within his territory—his district—are under the control of one man, the district ranger. That has been found to be more effective than the functional method of administration, under which there is a specialist reporting directly to the forest supervisor to handle each major functional activity—a specialist for timber management, a specialist for range management, other specialists for recreation management, forest protection, construction and maintenance work, and so on.

Such functionalization might mean that more expert attention is given to each activity. But with supplementary help from functional specialists on the supervisor's and the regional forester's staffs, adequately expert attention to all activities is provided in ranger-district work through the territorial form of administration. In addition, better integration of all activities is possible with less waste of time in travel, because one trip can accomplish several purposes. And of controlling importance is the fact that the local settlers and other users deal with only one forest officer instead of several.

On districts where the work is heavy, the ranger has one or more yearlong assistants. During the field season, fire-control assistants, improvement foremen, log scalers, and other aides as needed are employed to supplement the regular force. All are under the direct control of the district ranger.

The large volume of business and the technical work involved in the management of a ranger district on a multiple-use basis calls for technical competence, experience, and managerial ability. Accordingly, rangers are usually chosen from among junior foresters and range examiners who are graduates of a recognized college or university, have passed a professional examination, and have demonstrated their ability in technical work and as an assistant ranger. The rangers provide the pool of trained and tested men from which supervisors and others in higher positions are usually chosen.

Studies in organization and management have been carried on repeatedly. In 1912, F. A. Silcox, then regional forester of the Northern Rocky Mountain region, had a study made of the organization and operation of the Savenac Forest Nursery. That was the first reported use in the Forest Service of the Frederick Winslow Taylor approach to the study of the work practices and organization, which later became a primary factor in the broader field of scientific management. As is commonly known, this way of studying and performing work has been of help to American industry in attaining its high place in the markets of the world, because of the resulting combination of high-quality products and relatively low cost.

The general principles of scientific management gradually were applied elsewhere in the Forest Service. That was especially so in the California region under Roy Headley, as chief of operation and acting regional forester. Subsequently, when he became assistant chief of the Forest Service in Washington, he and Peter Keplinger, staff adviser on administrative management, gave impetus to studying and organizing national forest activities in this manner. The scientific approach was more sharply defined under his direction, beginning some 20 years ago with the development and application of "job-load analysis and planning" to the rangers' and supervisors' work and to other national forest activities.

Job-load analysis serves as a controlling basis for the manning of administrative units, for organization set-ups, for the allocation of funds, and for administrative, including the financial, controls. It parallels in considerable part the use of scientific management in American industry. Among its several aims are two principal ones: To get the work done with as high standards of quality, quantity, and economy as practicable, and to do so with unfailing regard for the men who are to perform the work. Included among the corollary aims is a meeting of minds between the supervisor and the worker and a determination of the needs for specialized training for each specific assignment to each employee.

The job-load analysis method as applied to studying, organizing, and administering national forest work consists of five main steps.

First, the objective sought in each field is clearly established. Many of the objectives are already available in resource-management plans, manuals, handbooks, and work programs. All subsequent steps in the analysis are aimed toward reaching this specific goal. Proper and sharp definition of objectives provides a stimulating incentive to distinguished effort. It also serves as a helpful shield against diverting proposals.

The second step is to break each activity down into the component jobs that must be performed to attain the objective.

The third step is to determine and establish standards for each of the component jobs; that is, the standards of quality, quantity, frequency, methods, and other practices needed to do the work as it should be done.

That is a job analysis up to this stage. To develop it into a job-load analysis, the fourth step is taken. That calls for determining the unit-time requirements for doing each job as it should be done.

The fifth step calls for grouping the separate jobs into the months in which they can be done, as controlled by the work requirements, the climatic conditions, available time, and other factors. A main purpose of this step is to redistribute peak loads to the less busy periods of the year, to the extent practicable, and thus strive for a well-balanced program of work, yearlong.

The total of the time requirements thus developed shows, of course, the total job-load weight, in man-hours, of the ranger district, forest, or special project that is being studied.

The job-load analysis method enlists the cooperation of the entire organization. To that end the analyst, in the course of each study, seeks the points of view of the local ranger, of his supervisor, and of the functional experts in each field of work. Such joint consideration establishes, clarifies, and defines in specific form both the major and minor duties of the employee. It results in widespread education and training on the part of all the participants. It promotes a common understanding of the work between subordinate and supervisor. It disentangles misunderstandings which, otherwise, are almost certain to develop from the long-distance supervision inherent in national forest work. This result has become recognized as one of the main benefits of a job-load analysis program. Nevertheless, the analyst recognizes that he must not substitute a discussion for an investigation; that five or six opinions are not necessarily better than one. All may be quite worthless. Instead, facts based on investigation and experiment, including analysis, measurement, and comparison, provide the only sound basis on which the job-load determinations can be made.

With the job-load weight and number of man-hours of work required thus arrived at, the number of employees needed is readily determined. Also, because number of hours may be readily converted to the number of dollars, the job-load analysis provides the primary base for two essentials of budget and financial management. First, it furnishes the soundest foundation possible for estimates submitted to Congress as to the amount of appropriations needed for ranger salaries, special timber-sale projects, and each of the other activities on the national forests. And, after the appropriations are made, it is the fairest basis for allocation of funds, by activities, to the regions, the national forests, ranger districts, and special projects.

An adequate cost-accounting system correlated with a primary allotment base of that type, together with systematic audits and field inspections, are key components of the financial and administrative controls, which assure expenditures of time and money as contemplated by Congress.

WORK PLANNING is done in several ways. *The National Forest Manual* contains a section devoted to each of the main functions of national forest work. Included in each section are the related regulations by the Secretary of Agriculture, based on legislative authority and supplemented by over-all instructions as approved by the Chief of the Forest Service.

Handbooks, issued by each region, localize the service-wide manual instructions. They include many local standards and some specific objectives.

Another working and planning tool is the *Program of Work* issued annually by the Chief. It includes a statement as to the activities he wishes given special emphasis in the coming year. It also contains specific objectives and programs to which each division is to give special attention. With that as a basis, each regional forester prepares a localized annual program of work. And that, in turn, is supplemented by each supervisor with a highly localized and more specific annual program of work—a real working and planning tool—for the national forest of which he is in charge. Plans are also made for the management of each of the main resources within the national forests. The need for such plans is evident when one considers that a century or more of time may be required to grow a crop of timber or build up a depleted range or watershed. Resource-management plans are also needed, because the manner in which one resource is handled may have an important effect on other resources within the same forest.

There must also be transportation plans, communication plans, fire-control plans, and other similar working tools. They all provide indispensable background material and are otherwise helpful in the job-load analysis.

The five steps in work-load analysis that I outlined determine the total time that is required to handle each job, as needed to attain the specified objective. The next step is to convert this analysis into a plan of action. A start on this is made, as previously stated, by assigning each job, or a specified part of each job, to each of the months during which it should be performed. The resulting list of jobs in each month is then assembled into an integrated plan of work.

In a ranger district, for example, the list of jobs for a month will include a great variety of work such as timber sales, inspection by fire guards, range management, and special-use administration, scattered probably over a quarter of a million acres. Travel time alone, on horseback and otherwise, may require as much as 35 percent or more of the total time devoted to all the duties on the district. Obviously, therefore, unless the work is carefully planned, travel may be unproductive and unreasonably high and it may shorten appreciably the time necessary for the actual fulfillment of duties.

EARL W. LOVERIDGE *is assistant chief of the Forest Service, in charge of administrative management and information. A native of Pennsylvania and a graduate in forestry from Pennsylvania State College, he started work with the Forest Service in Minnesota as a student assistant in 1911.*

*A juniper 3,000 years old in Cache National Forest in Utah; drawn from a photograph taken in 1924.*

# Projects of Many Uses

## OTHER FEDERAL FORESTS

F. W. GROVER

BESIDES THE NATIONAL forests, which are the most extensive of the federally owned timber and watershed lands, eight other categories of Federal lands bear large forests. Some of them are held primarily for timber production. Others, as wildlife refuges, are owned and administered for primary purposes other than the production of timber or water, but are susceptible of forestry management in correlation with the specialized uses.

THE O & C REVESTED LANDS are administered by the Bureau of Land Management of the Department of the Interior. They comprise somewhat more than 2 million acres, originally selected pursuant to grants of public lands made by Congress in 1866 and 1869 to aid in building a railroad from Portland, Oreg., to the California line and a wagon road from Coos Bay, Oreg., to Roseburg, Oreg. Violations of conditions of the grants by the grantees or their successors led in 1916 and 1919 to repossession by the Government of the unsold parts of the granted lands; these now constitute the "revested" lands. The lands are in 18 counties in western Oregon. Because only odd-numbered sections were originally granted, the predominant pattern is that of a checkerboard in squares of 640 acres, the intermingled lands being mostly private or national forest. Many of the tracts are less than a full section, however, because of disposals in the past.

Nearly all of the lands are forested; many have fine stands of old-growth conifers. The major species is Douglas-fir, and types in which it predominates cover 70 percent of the area of the timberlands. White fir, grand fir, noble fir, Pacific silver fir, western hemlock, western redcedar, Port-Orford-cedar, ponderosa pine, and sugar pine are also well represented, usually in mixtures but occasionally as dominant types. Western species of hardwoods, such as Oregon oak, bigleaf maple, red alder, madrone, and the golden chinquapin occur in limited quantities.

All but a small proportion of the

---

*A typical scene in an arboretum is shown above.*

revested lands are classed as commercial timberland. More than half of these lands still support stands of virgin timber, and most of the remainder is restocking to forest; the young trees vary from nearly merchantable second growth to seedlings and saplings in recently logged areas and burns. Some 50,000 acres, however, are in the Tillamook "burn" and are largely denuded.

By the act of August 28, 1937 (50 Stat. 874), Congress provided for the permanent management of the revested lands valuable for timber production. The act specifies that such lands shall be managed for permanent forest production and that the timber thereon shall be sold and removed in conformity with the principles of sustained yield for the purpose of producing a permanent source of timber supply, protecting watersheds, regulating stream flow, and contributing to the economic stability of local communities and industries.

The act also (1) provides that the annual productive capacity of these timberlands shall be determined and declared as promptly as possible and that until such determination be made the average annual cut of the lands shall not exceed one-half billion board feet; (2) specifies that the annual sustained capacity of the lands shall be sold each year or so much thereof as can be sold in a normal market at reasonable prices; (3) authorizes the subdivision of the lands into sustained-yield units to provide, as far as practicable, a permanent source of raw materials for support of the dependent communities and local industries of the region; (4) stipulates that timber sales from a forest unit so established shall be limited to the productive capacity of the lands in such units; (5) authorizes the Secretary of the Interior to enter into cooperative agreements with other Federal agencies, State agencies, or private forest-land owners or operators for coordinated administration of the resources of the revested lands and the other Federal, State, or private lands within the forest unit, with the objective of promoting sustained production.

To carry out the policies for the administration and use of these lands as specified by Congress, a forestry organization to make timber sales, inaugurate studies of sustained yield, make timber-management plans, and perform the numerous other tasks necessary to manage this valuable public property was established with headquarters in Portland, Oreg. Since formation of the Bureau of Land Management in 1946, by the combination of the General Land Office and the Grazing Service, forestry work on these lands, as well as on the unreserved public domain, has been under the general direction of the Division of Forestry in the office of the Director, Bureau of Land Management. A regional forester in the office of the regional administrator, Bureau of Land Management, in Portland, exercises general supervision and furnishes technical direction; on-the-ground forestry activities are performed by the staffs of five district foresters, each of whom is responsible for a prescribed area. Fire protection is performed by the Forest Service or by State or local fire-protection agencies on the basis of cooperative agreements.

The Bureau of Land Management is actively selling timber from these lands, as directed by Congress. The policies that govern timber sales call for silvicultural practices adapted to the particular site and designed to assure reforestation of the lands by the desired tree species, the protection and perpetuation of highway screen strips and lands valuable for recreation, and the safeguarding of local watersheds. Progress has been made on the long-term task of determining the sustained timber-producing capacity of the lands and in devising management plans for the utilization of the timber resources on a permanent production basis. Because of the checkerboard pattern of the revested lands, an important aspect of long-term management is the development of coordinated management of the Federal, State, and private lands within the boundaries of the revested lands. One cooperative unit has been proposed, and public hearings have been held.

During the fiscal year 1947, some 469.3 million board feet of timber, valued at about $2,197,018, was cut from the lands in commercial sales under the administration of the Bureau of Land Management. In addition, about 394,000 board feet, consisting largely of posts, cordwood, and similar products, was cut without charge by local residents. The 239 grazing leases that were issued covered 276,000 acres, receipts from which totaled $18,128.

THE UNRESERVED PUBLIC DOMAIN of the United States still includes more than 169 million acres of unappropriated and unreserved public lands, including 132 million acres in grazing districts established under the Taylor Grazing Act of 1934. There is more than 265 million acres of unreserved public lands in Alaska. Forestry activities on that land are under direction of the Bureau of Land Management, Department of the Interior.

Much of this land in continental United States is range and watershed land that bears only grass or brush or is semidesert or desert, but about 28 million acres is classed as timber or woodland, of which, according to the Bureau of Land Management, approximately 3 million acres bears commercial timber estimated at 9.5 billion board feet. These forest and woodland areas are remnants left from large grants, the establishment of national forests, parks, and other Federal reservations, and as a result of the operation of the public-land laws under which the public lands were patented to private ownership. Because they are widely dispersed throughout 20 States, a large number of the major forest types are represented, from the Douglas-fir in the Northwest, the white pine in Idaho, the lodgepole pine in Montana and Wyoming, the spruce and aspen of the Lake States, the pinyon-juniper of the Southwest, to the pine and oak-pine types of the Southeast.

Until recently, only dead, down, or damaged timber or timber threatened with damage from fire could be sold from the unreserved public domain, although timber could be taken without charge for noncommercial purposes. By the act of July 31, 1947 (61 Stat. 681), Congress authorized the sale of, among other resources, timber and timber products from these public lands, in accordance with rules and regulations of the Secretary of the Interior. Authorization is also given for free permits for use other than for industrial or commercial purposes or for sale.

Policies of the Bureau of Land Management provide for developing the timber resources of the public lands, protecting them from fire, insects, and disease, and managing them in accordance with good forestry practices with the objective of insuring continuing crops of timber and improving watershed, wildlife habitat, and recreational opportunities.

Disposal requirements are designed to provide for protection and improvement of the residual stand and for restocking of the land to desirable timber species. The forestry work is under general direction of the Division of Forestry in the office of the Director, Bureau of Land Management, and is handled locally as far as possible by the forestry personnel in the offices of the regional administrators of the Bureau. The rather wide dispersion of these lands renders supervision and management difficult.

During the fiscal year ended June 30, 1947, about 15.4 million board feet of timber, valued at $58,024, was cut from these public lands in the United States, of which about 8.9 million board feet was utilized through free permits to local residents. In Alaska an estimated 45 million board feet was sold, yielding $57,535, and additional timber products such as posts, poles, lagging, and house logs, with an estimated value of $2,158, was granted for local use without charge. Other uses of these public lands included grazing, mineral production, wildlife production, and recreation.

THE LANDS OF THE AMERICAN INDIANS, in the form of individual trust allotments, tribal lands, and Federal lands dedicated to Indian use, aggregate more than 56.5 million acres. The area comprises a large number of homestead allotments, approximately 160 acres each, on the public domain, most of which were made to individual Indians in accordance with the act of July 4, 1884 (23 Stat. 76, 96), and of reservations, several of more than a million acres, which were established in accordance with treaties with Indians and by Executive orders. A substantial part of the land within many of the reservations has been allotted to individual Indians in tracts that usually vary from 80 to 160 acres. The title to the homestead allotments and to allotments within reservations is usually held in trust by the United States for the individual owners, although, in some instances, the title to allotted lands within reservations passed to the owners but with restrictions against alienation. The basic title or fee to all unallotted tribal lands is held by the United States. Indian lands are distributed throughout 26 States, but are heavily concentrated in the West.

Of the Indian lands, more than 16 million acres is classed as forest and woodland; of that area, about 6.6 million acres (or 40 percent) is presently classed as commercial forest land capable of producing continuous crops of salable forest products. The remaining acreage is valuable for cordwood, posts, poles, nuts, fruits, and similar products for local use, and for forage, for watersheds, and as game habitat. Records of the Bureau of Indian Affairs indicate that the commercial forest land bears about 27.6 billion board feet of merchantable timber.

Because of wide geographical distribution, Indian forest lands include a variety of forest types. The hardwoods of the Appalachian Mountains, the palm and cypress of Florida, the pine-hemlock-hardwood of the Lake States, the mixed-conifer stands of the "Inland Empire," the fir, hemlock, cedar, Douglas-fir stands of the Pacific coast, and the ponderosa pine and mixed-conifer types of eastern Washington and Oregon are all represented in some degree. From the standpoint of volume and industrial use, the conifer forests of Oregon, Washington, Arizona, and Montana are by far the most important. These include an estimated 69 percent of the commercial timberland and more than 83 percent of the commercial timber volume.

The timber on the Indian lands was early recognized as a valuable asset, and logging of it became rather general after 1890. With the development of the national conservation movement at the beginning of the twentieth century, there came a demand for cutting the timber on a conservative basis to assure its perpetuation. In 1909, Congress provided for forestry work on Indian reservations, and, by the act of June 25, 1910 (36 Stat. 855), gave comprehensive authority, under regulations of the Secretary of the Interior, for sale of timber from Indian reservations, and provided that proceeds from such sales should be used for the benefit of the Indians on the reservation.

Authority was also granted for sale of timber from allotments under trust patents with the consent of the Secretary of the Interior. Pursuant to such authority and to that in section 6 of the act of 1934 (48 Stat. 984), utilization of timber from Indian lands is now carried out in accordance with conservation policies under the direction of the Forestry and Grazing Division of the Bureau of Indian Affairs, Department of the Interior.

Forests are important in the Indian economy. Only a small percentage of the Indian lands are suitable for farming, the greater part of them being chiefly valuable for forest production or grazing. The forested areas furnish fuel, logs, and lumber for houses and barns, forage for livestock, fish, game, and furs. Additionally, the commercial forests provide the Indians with substantial sources of income through sale of stumpage, through employment in industries that the timber supports, and in the protection and management of the timberlands.

The policies of the Bureau of Indian Affairs, in directing the utilization of Indian forests, therefore, have five main aspects: The maintenance of the land in a perpetually productive state through the promotion of sound forestry practices and adequate protection; regulation of the cut to insure method and order in harvesting and to promote continuous production; development, so far as is possible, of Indian forests by Indian people, so that the Indians may receive not only the value of the stumpage but also such profits as may be yielded; sale of timber not developed or used by the Indians through competitive bids; and preservation of scenic, recreational, and esthetic values and management of the forest so as to retain its beneficial effects in regulating runoff of water and minimizing erosion.

In the management of the Indian forests, however, the Bureau of Indian Affairs must recognize that these forests are part of the economic base of the Indians to whom they have been allotted or for whom they have been set aside. Forest management must be correlated with the general economy of the Indians and must occasionally be adjusted to meet the immediate needs of individuals or tribes. The large number of small allotments add greatly to management problems. To achieve the objectives and to obtain the application, so far as is possible, of sound forestry practices, professional foresters direct the utilization of the forest resources on all the larger timbered areas and give general supervision to small sales.

Indian forests have contributed substantial amounts of lumber and other products to the economy of the Nation and have added materially to the income of the Indians. From 1910 through 1947 more than 14.5 billion feet of timber, valued at $57,700,000, was cut from these lands. In the calendar year 1947, these yields (in thousand board feet) were recorded: Commercial cutting under contract, 407,822; sales for local use, 17,067; free use by Indians, 87,580. The total was 512,469 thousand board feet. The stumpage value totaled $2,501,313.

THE NATIONAL PARKS AND MONUMENTS are Federal lands set aside, reserved, and administered "to conserve the scenery and the natural and historic objects and the wildlife therein and to provide for the enjoyment of the same in such manner and by such means as will leave them unimpaired for future generations." They are intended to include not only superlative scenery but historical, geological, and biological areas of national interest and significance. Because they are comprised, in large measure, of wild lands, they contain substantial acreages of forests, and some of the parks (as the Sequoia in California and the Great Smoky Mountains in North Carolina and Tennessee) were established primarily to preserve outstanding examples of particular forest species or types.

The national parks and monuments, including historical and military parks, parkways, and similar units, as of June 30, 1947, contained 20,775,082 acres of Federal lands. Of this area, about 6,960,000 acres bear forests in the usual sense. Because of wide dispersal of the parks and monuments throughout the Nation, the forests therein vary greatly as to type and composition. Represented, among others, are the "rain forests" of the Olympic Peninsula, the mixed-conifer stands of the central Sierra region, including the giant sequoias, the pinyon-juniper types found in the arid Southwest, and the old-growth hardwood and hardwood-conifer mixtures of the Appalachian region.

802062°—49——26

Worthy of particular mention from the standpoint of the forests that they include are the Olympic National Park, in Washington, the Yosemite and Sequoia National Parks, in California, and the Great Smoky Mountains National Park, in North Carolina and Tennessee.

The Olympic National Park, in the lower valleys of its western slopes, contains extensive areas of the dense coniferous forest which has resulted from the heavy rainfall that blankets the coastal portions of the Pacific Northwest. Here Douglas-fir, western hemlock, western redcedar, Sitka spruce, and the true firs grow densely and to great size. An understory of maples, ferns, and other plants combine with the heavy stands of conifers to produce an almost junglelike density.

The Yosemite and Sequoia National Parks in the Sierra Nevada region of California contain substantial acreages of virgin conifer forests, including the sugar pine, ponderosa pine, incense-cedar, and white fir. They (especially Sequoia National Park) include also the famed groves of giant sequoias. These trees, the remnants of a once widespread genus, are native to only a narrow belt along the western slope of the central and southern Sierra Nevada. Individual specimens grow to majestic size and great age, and the parks contain several thousand that are more than 10 feet in diameter and 250 feet in height.

The Great Smoky Mountains National Park in the southern Appalachian Mountains includes one of the few remaining examples of the original forest of the Eastern States. Approximately 40 percent of its nearly half million acres is in the original forested condition. Higher elevations bear unusually dense forests of spruce, balsam, and some hemlock, while the intermediate slopes are covered with hardwoods characteristic of the Appalachian region. In this park are found 130 or more native tree species, some of which grow to record size.

By law, national parks and monuments are established for the benefit and enjoyment of the people and must be protected and retained in as nearly their natural conditions as possible. Forestry in the national parks is therefore primarily protective; its chief objective is to avoid or minimize destruction of the forest by fire, insects, disease, and unwise use by man. Commercial use, such as lumbering, is prohibited, and cutting of trees is permitted only as a method of fighting forest pests or diseases, or of reducing fire hazards.

To combat fire, the National Park Service has developed a comprehensive fire-control organization, centering about the administrative personnel in the parks and monuments. Cooperation with agencies protecting adjoining lands, whether public or private, is actively promoted. The National Park Service and the Bureaus of Entomology and Plant Quarantine and of Plant Industry, Soils, and Agricultural Engineering of the Department of Agriculture cooperate in the detection and control of insect or disease epidemics, such as bark beetle infestations and the white pine blister rust, which, next to fire, are the greatest enemies of the forests in the parks and monuments. All forestry work, including fire control, is headed by the chief forester in the office of the Director of the National Park Service. Foresters of the four administrative regions of the Park Service give on-the-ground supervision and technical advice.

Trees contribute to the inspirational and scientific values of the national parks and monuments in many ways. They form a pleasing framework for the mountains, lakes, and geological features, provide the beauty and the outdoor environment for camping, picnicking, hiking, and skiing, offer a habitat for wildlife, protect the soil in which they grow, and help to regulate the flow of streams. They offer opportunities for study of the growth and maintenance of forests under natural conditions and, where virgin forests have been included, afford examples of some of the original forest types which once covered so much of our Nation.

FEDERAL WILDLIFE REFUGES are areas of Federal lands which have been established from time to time as game or general wildlife refuges and sanctuaries under State or Federal laws concerned with preservation of our native animal and bird life. The following, however, relates only to the 3.4 million acres, more or less, of Federal land over which the Fish and Wildlife Service of the Department of the Interior has sole jurisdiction and the primary use of which is the perpetuation of indigenous species of wildlife. More specifically, most of the material relates to the 797,000 acres of such land that is forested. These wildlife refuges have been acquired by the Fish and Wildlife Service through direct purchase of private lands, through transfer of lands from other agencies of the Federal Government, and through reservation of public domain.

In assembling its system of wildlife refuges, the Fish and Wildlife Service has followed the policy of acquiring ecological units representative of broad habitat types, primarily for management to conserve and increase the native wildlife, and, secondarily, to determine practical methods of land use compatible with sustaining optimum wildlife populations. In acquisition of waterfowl refuges, for example, necessary buffer lands may include blocks of forest which, of course, may also fulfill certain needs of wildlife management. Occasionally, the forest itself is the vital element and lands are acquired specifically therefor, as in the case of the White River National Wildlife Refuge in Arkansas, where mast constitutes a principal food item of waterfowl. Large areas of forest land are also frequently desirable for upland game management. Thus the federally owned wildlife refuges include substantial acreages of forest and woodland types.

These forest lands are rather widely distributed and include a number of timber types—northern and Appalachian mixed hardwoods, bottom-land hardwoods in the Mississippi Valley, spruce, balsam, fir, the southern pines, oak, and some of the western pines. About 502,000 acres are currently considered as commercial forest land. The remaining 295,000 acres are either noncommercial in character or are set aside from commercial use because of special wildlife-management requirements, in compliance with policies on natural areas, or for recreational purposes. Included in the forested areas are some old-growth timber and some fully stocked stands of second growth. Generally, however, the timber stands tend to be understocked (because of heavy cutting before they were acquired by the United States) and consist largely of young growth.

The forest lands are administered primarily for restoration and conservation of wildlife or to test or demonstrate practical methods of game management. To the full extent consistent with these basic objectives, however, the Fish and Wildlife Service endeavors to manage the timberlands under sound forestry principles. A substantial part of the estimated 502,000 acres of commercial forest lands are under intensive forestry management. Forestry practices must necessarily be correlated with the requirements of the animals, birds, or waterfowl which populate the refuges. To this end, selective cutting on a relatively short cutting rotation is practiced in most instances, frequently on a group-selection or small-area basis to create openings. Specific needs of wildlife, such as den trees or shrubs and trees important for food production, must be taken into consideration and provided for as far as is possible. Policies also call for maintenance of buffer strips of timber along the principal roads, lakes, and streams and other places where esthetic values are dominant. The forest-management program is under the supervision of trained foresters and the field activities relative to the administration and sale of timber are handled by personnel trained in forestry work. Fire protection is accomplished by the Fish and Wildlife Service.

Between 1942 and 1947, the yearly cut from these forest lands averaged 3.2 million board feet of timber, 19,610 cords of wood, and 17,968 posts and ties. Average annual receipt for these products was $46,022. Of necessity, timber cutting must be on a moderate scale until the stands of timber are built up to the highest level consistent with wildlife production on the lands.

MILITARY RESERVATIONS of the Army, Navy, and Air Force comprise large areas of Federal land held primarily for military purposes. Much of the land is not forested, but a substantial acreage either bears forests or is capable of producing them.

The Department of the Army administers some 4 million acres, of which about 1,650,000 acres may be classed as forest land. These forest lands, of course, are widely distributed across the country and, in some instances, are only a minor proportion of the installations of which they are a part. Many Army installations, however, contain substantial blocks of productive or potentially productive forest sites. Included are southern pines, central and northern hardwoods, and the Douglas-fir type of the Pacific Northwest. The southern pine types heavily predominate.

While the primary use of these lands is necessarily military, it is the policy of the Department of the Army to conserve and maintain all of its lands, including the forests, in accordance with sound agricultural principles. In pursuance of this policy, the Army intends to develop appropriate management plans for each potentially productive forest area, and to promote timber management and timber-stand improvement as far as the dominant military use of the lands will permit.

Naval reservations, in the main, are not forested. However, some areas acquired for ordnance or training and maneuver purposes include considerable acreages of productive forest lands which are susceptible of forestry management. Efforts are being made to inaugurate forest management on certain of these areas, to the degree that such can be correlated with the necessary military use, with the cooperation of public forestry agencies.

The Department of the Air Force administers about 11.4 million acres of Federal land, a large part of which is used by the Air Force under permit or assignment from other agencies of the Government. The Air Force estimates that of this acreage approximately 495,000 acres is now forested or is capable of producing forests. Such area is distributed within nine States, but the major part is located in Florida. Forest resources are being managed, as far as is consistent with the necessary military use, in accordance with plans prepared by Federal or State forestry agencies, it being the intent of the Air Force to use and develop these resources under conservation principles to the extent possible.

LAND UTILIZATION PROJECTS were established pursuant to the National Industrial Recovery Act, the Emergency Relief Act, and, later, title III of the Bankhead-Jones Farm Tenant Act. Under such a program the Federal Government acquired about 11.3 million acres of farm, pasture, and woodland which had been abused, eroded, or otherwise so depleted as to be uneconomic for private use and in need of protection and restoration. Many of the projects have since been turned over to States for administration for forestry, wildlife, recreational, and research purposes under long-term agreements. Others have been transferred to Federal agencies for such special purposes as national forests, wildlife refuges, and Indian reservations.

Some 7,150,000 acres, however, are for the most part needed and used by farmers who occupy adjoining and intermingled privately owned land to complete desirable land use and economic adjustments. The lands are administered by the Soil Conservation Service of the Department of Agriculture in accordance with title III of the Bankhead-Jones Act (50 Stat. 522), under which the Secretary of Agriculture is authorized and directed to develop a program of land conservation and land utilization, including the retirement of lands that are submarginal or not primarily suitable for cultivation. The following relates to this last mentioned area and particularly to the forested parts thereof.

The greatest part of the 7,150,000 acres is devoted to grazing, but included in the area is approximately 500,000 acres of commercial forest land. Additional acres, of course, support woodlands or stands of pinyon and juniper which have value for local use and as watersheds. Located in 19 States, the forest lands include many of the broad forest types, such as mixed hardwoods, hardwood-pine, and southern pines, the post oak and blackjack oak types of Oklahoma and Texas, some ponderosa pine, and limited areas of aspen and spruce-fir forests in New Mexico. Hardwoods and southern pine types predominate.

Much of this land had been cut over and often repeatedly burned or heavily pastured before it was acquired by the Government. The timber stands are therefore comprised in large measure of young growth with some residual timber. When acquired, such stands were often understocked and, in the hardwoods, ran heavily to the poorer species because of persistent cutting of the more valuable trees. Fire protection in the intervening years, however, has aided in the natural restocking of many of the most depleted areas. Because much of the land was denuded or consisted of worn-out fields, a large job of artificial reforestation was, and is, necessary. Some 41,000 acres have so far been planted and nearly twice that area remains to be reforested.

The general policy of the Soil Conservation Service is to manage the forest lands under sound forestry principles to build up to a practical maximum both quantity and quality of the timber stands, with the ultimate objective of regular and sustained production of forest products. Utilization by local residents, either for domestic needs or as a means of supplementing their incomes, is encouraged.

Forestry work on the land-utilization projects, as well as other land-management activities, is under the general direction of the Land Management Division of the Soil Conservation Service. Over-all supervision of on-the-ground forestry activities is provided by a regional forester on the staff of each of the several regional conservators. The management and utilization plans are prepared by foresters, who also give training and supervision to the personnel handling sales, planting, and other forestry work.

Saw timber and a variety of forest products are sold from the timbered land each year. During the calendar year 1947, some 26.4 million board feet of saw timber, 9,200 cords of pulpwood, 3,000 cords of fuel wood, 94,000 fence posts, 5,600 poles, and other miscellaneous materials were sold for a total of $232,946. The lands also provided forage, habitat for wildlife, and recreational opportunities.

The Tennessee Valley Authority owns about 485,000 acres of land which lie above the normal full-pool levels of its series of reservoirs. Practically all of the land was acquired in connection with the reservoirs. About 340,000 acres are forested, including some 40,000 acres of plantations. Except for certain areas dedicated to forestry demonstration and investigation, the Tennessee Valley Authority retains no lands solely for timber production. It does, however, make such forestry use of the forest areas as is compatible with their primary purposes.

The forest lands of the Tennessee Valley Authority are distributed from the mountains of eastern Tennessee and western North Carolina down into northern Alabama and northward through western Tennessee and southwestern Kentucky. They therefore represent a fair cross section of the forest types of the Tennessee Valley region. Predominant types are upland hardwoods, pine-hardwoods, and oak. In general, most of the forest lands have been heavily used and abused, having in the past undergone repeated cuttings, frequent burnings, and heavy grazing. Consequently, many of them are in poor condition from the standpoint of a commercial timber production, because of the predominance of defective trees and relatively few of the more valuable species.

It is the policy of the TVA, in the management of these woodlands, that any timber cutting must be carried on in conformity with sound principles of technical forestry, with selective cutting, where such is feasible. Recognition is given in the forest-management procedures to special values such as scenic or recreational utility or to wildlife needs. Some 22,000 acres have been systematically treated with improvement cuttings. Fire protection is carried out through local or State agencies if possible, or directly by the Tennessee Valley Authority organization where it is necessary. Timber and forest products are sold on the stump, through competitive bids if the appraised value is over $250.

In 1947, more than 7.5 million feet of timber, 1,300 cords of wood, and 261,000 lineal feet of poles and posts were sold for about $79,000. Cumulative sales total more than 36 million board feet of timber, 21,600 cords of wood, and 1,050,000 lineal feet of poles and posts, with a total value of nearly $346,000.

F. W. GROVER *is chief of the Division of Land Acquisition, Forest Service, and secretary of the National Forest Reservation Commission. Mr. Grover is a graduate of the School of Forestry, University of California. He entered the Forest Service in 1930, and has served as forest ranger and as national forest and regional office staff assistant.*

# STATE FORESTS

STANLEY G. FONTANNA

State forests have six uses. They are demonstrations of good forestry practices in growing and harvesting forest products. They produce valuable forest products. They protect watersheds and wildlife. They provide places for recreation. Sometimes they are grazed.

The sixth purpose, or justification, has to do with the reason why most of them were established—public realization of the need to place under management the forest lands that otherwise would be neglected. Thus, most State forests (meaning, here, forest lands that have actually been designated State forests within the respective States and not including State-owned lands, such as game areas, forest parks, or forest lands not under any type of management) have been founded on a base of tax-reverted lands or low-value lands that were bought.

In 1885, New York began the acquisition of extensive forest land for the Adirondack and Catskill Forest Preserves. Other State forests organized at early dates were the Mont Alto in Pennsylvania in 1891, the Pillsbury in Minnesota in 1899, the Clark County in Indiana in 1903, and the Higgins Lake and Houghton Lake in Michigan in 1903. Thirty-six States now have State forests.

States have come into possession of land for State forests through grants of land by the Federal Government; tax reversion; gift, exchange, and purchase; and lease of land from the Federal Government. Federal-grant lands, the remainder of the original Federal grants to the States for schools, internal improvements, and so forth, comprise approximately 28 percent of the total acreage in State forests and, except for 1.3 million acres in Minnesota and small scattering acreages in other States, are found in the Pacific Coast and Rocky Mountain States. In Idaho, Montana, and Colorado, Federal-grant lands comprise the total acreage of the State forests.

Tax-reverted lands, titles to which have come to the States through tax delinquency, comprise approximately 31 percent of the total acreage in State forests. Except for a few thousand acres in other States, those lands are in Minnesota, Michigan, New York, and Washington.

The lands acquired by gift and exchange comprise approximately 36 percent of the total acreage in State forests. Except in Idaho, Montana, and Colorado, nearly every State that has State forests has acquired some of its lands by purchase; in many States purchase has been the only means of acquisition.

Federal-lease lands were originally acquired by the Federal Government in connection with the resettlement program of the 1930's, and have been leased to the State for forestry and other conservation purposes by the Federal Government under the administration of units of the Department of Agriculture and the Department of the Interior. As a rule, the leases are long-term and liberal; to all intents and purposes, the lands are administered as State forest lands. Lands so leased comprise but 4 percent of the total acreage in State forests. There are no lands in this category in any State west of the Mississippi; most of them are in North and South Carolina, Virginia, Florida, Tennessee, and Georgia.

Approximately 14 million of the 16.6 million acres of land in the State forests are in eight States: Michigan, 3.75 million acres; New York, 3 million acres; Minnesota, 2 million; Washington, 1.7 million; Pennsylvania, 1.67 million; Idaho, 950,000; Oregon, 570,000; Montana, 520,000 acres. The remaining 2.6 million acres are in 29 other States.

On a regional basis, 15 million of the 16.6 million acres are in these sections: The Lake States (Michigan, Wisconsin, Minnesota), 6 million acres; the Middle Atlantic States (Delaware, Pennsylvania, Maryland, New York, West Virginia, New Jersey), 5 million acres; the Pacific Coast States (Washington, Oregon, California), 2.2 million acres; the Rocky Mountain States (Idaho, Montana, Colorado), 1.8 million acres. There are only 660,000 acres in State forests in all of the Southern States; of this acreage, 450,000 acres are in lands leased from the Federal Government.

Or, in another classification of areas, the acreage is distributed thus: Saw-timber areas, 21 percent; pole-timber, 34 percent; seedling and sapling, 31 percent; poorly stocked and denuded areas, 14 percent. In the Pacific and Rocky Mountain States, the acreage in saw timber rises to an average of 33 percent; in the Eastern and Southern States, the average drops well below 21 percent.

Only five States reported estimated saw-timber volumes in excess of a billion board feet—Washington, 12 billion board feet; Idaho, 7.3 billion; Pennsylvania, 3.6 billion; Montana, 2 billion; and Colorado, 1.01 billion.

Six States reported saw-timber volumes between 100 million and 1 billion board feet: Michigan, 650 million; Colorado, 309 million; Ohio, 250 million; South Dakota, 250 million; Indiana, 150 million; and Connecticut 109 million. Oregon, New York, and Minnesota did not report saw-timber volumes, but undoubtedly the saw-timber volumes in State forests in each is more than 100 million board feet.

The State forests generally are supervised by the State forester. The agency with which the State forester is connected varies among States, however. In 21 of the 36 States that have State forests, forestry is a division of a State conservation department or a department of natural resources, with the State forester in charge of the division. In seven States, the State forester is the administrative officer of a State board or commission of forestry. In four States, he is the forestry director of the State board of forestry and parks. In Pennsylvania, he is in charge of the Bureau of Forests in the Department of Forests and Waters. In Ohio, he is in charge of the Division of Forestry under the over-all administration of the agricultural experiment station. In Montana, he works with the State Board of Land Commissioners. Direct supervision of a State forest in each State is generally exercised by a district forester or State forest supervisor, who may be responsible solely for the management of forest land or who may combine management with other duties.

In Washington, Idaho, Montana, and Colorado, administration of the State forest lands of Federal-grant origin is a joint responsibility of the State land boards and the State forestry agency. In each of those States the State land board was set up originally to dispose of Federal-grant lands; however, while a considerable acreage of forest lands in this category was still in State ownership, it was realized that the lands were an asset to the State and should properly remain in State ownership under adequate protection and administration.

Adequate management recognizes that the forests have several uses and allocates to each its proper place in the management plan. Elements of forest management that affect each of those uses are protection from fire, insects, and disease, and forest inventory.

Fire protection on State forests generally is good. Even in States that do not protect all forest lands, State forests are well looked after; in the States that have good over-all protection, State forests as a rule receive extra attention. Because most of the State forest lands are in restocking stages, good fire protection constitutes a large part of the management.

The degree of protection from insects and disease varies a great deal and depends largely on the probability of losses. In States where white pine is an important timber tree, for example, protection from the white pine blister rust is generally good. In Massachusetts, the State forestry agency carries on an active campaign against the tussock moth. In the Western States, bark beetles receive considerable attention.

The adequate management of forest lands for multiple use can only be had from a forest inventory, which classifies the lands and furnishes detailed information on timber types, volumes, and growth. Such an inventory was reported by 9 of the 36 States; several others are making an inventory.

Management for the production of forest products aims at ultimately attaining a balance of growth and drain, in well-stocked stands of desirable species. To achieve the objective, there should be adequate protection from fire, insects, and disease; harvesting of tree crops when they are ripe; improvement of the stand; and planting where necessary. Management plans based on an adequate inventory are desirable.

The type of forest management in the various States depends upon several factors, namely, a forest inventory, the condition of the forest, and available funds for forest management. Naturally, the States that have inventories of their forests have the basis for intelligent management plans and have generally followed through with such a plan.

In some States the land carries but little merchantable timber, and intensive fire protection (with perhaps some planting and improvement cuttings) constitutes the chief element of management. In Washington, Idaho, and Montana, on the contrary, there is the problem of overmature timber, and management efforts are directed toward harvesting it.

In all States the availability of funds plays a major role. The ability to inventory the forests and to hire men with adequate training and in sufficient number for management of the lands has often been in direct proportion to the amount of money that could be obtained for those purposes. In many States fire protection has been the primary interest, and State forest management has had to play a secondary role.

Practically all States maintain forest-tree nurseries, but most of the planting stock has gone to private individuals and plantings on State forest lands have not been extensive. New York and Michigan are notable examples of States with well-organized and adequately financed planting programs.

Income from the sale of forest products from State forests has not been great. That is to be expected from forests that mostly are immature. The largest returns have come from the mature forests of the Western States: Washington reported an annual income of $736,000, Montana $455,000, and Idaho $97,000. East of the Mississippi, only Pennsylvania, Ohio, Michigan, New York, and Florida reported a production of forest products whose value exceeded $50,000 annually.

On the whole, the management of State forests would rate from fair to good. Most of the States mark the timber they offer for sale and annually harvest much less than the growth. During the past few years the excellent market has afforded an opportunity for the harvesting of all species of ripe timber and for improvement cuttings.

In States in which the forestry agency is a division of a department of conservation, which also handles State fish and game affairs, the authorities are keenly aware of the relationship between forest management and game management. In Michigan, for example, cutting and planting plans for State forests require the approval of the local game manager. In New York, the plan of wildlife management has been definitely integrated with forest management.

In other States where game and fish affairs are in the hands of an independent agency, cooperation is close between that agency and the forest agency in the management of game on State forests.

Practically all States open State forest lands to public hunting. Because most of the State forests are in the restocking stages and have much young growth and many openings, hunting generally is good.

All the States have recognized the value of their forests for recreational purposes. Some of them have built camp grounds, trails, and shelters for use by the public. Roads built for fire-control purposes have made the forests accessible to recreation seekers, who have used the forests in ever-increasing numbers. Especially noteworthy are the New York Forest Preserves, some 2,400,000 acres in extent, which the State constitution requires must be "forever kept as wild forest lands." The area, developed primarily for recreational purposes, has a good system of camp sites, trails, and shelters.

Management for watershed protection is probably most important in the State forests of the Western States, where water supply is of great concern. The maintenance of forest growth on watersheds is recognized as of high priority.

In the Eastern States, the value of well-stocked forest land in the upper regions of the drainage basins is being appreciated more and more in soil conservation and flood control programs. Often the State forests are so located that the management for this purpose assumes great importance.

Management for grazing is important largely in the Western States; the State forests of Idaho and Colorado are used to some extent for that purpose. There is also some grazing on State forest lands in the South. On all of those lands, management requires that grazing be kept under control.

As to the future: Only one-third of the States have plans for future acquisition of lands for State forests.

Texas, Virginia, Missouri, Indiana, and Wisconsin anticipate small yearly additions by purchase.

Minnesota, Washington, and Oregon plan to acquire tax-reverted lands from the counties.

Massachusetts has legislative authorization for acquisition of 500,000 acres, but no appropriation for purchase.

Connecticut has a goal of 200,000 acres and is adding land by purchase at the rate of 6,000 acres a year.

Ohio's goal is 587,000 acres, and for the fiscal year 1945–46 the State appropriated $1,800,000 for land purchase.

California plans to add considerably to its State forest acreage; the legislature appropriated $2,000,000 in 1947 for the purpose.

New York's acquisition program contemplates the purchase of 20,000 to 40,000 acres annually.

Michigan spends $250,000 yearly for blocking in the present State areas, and also acquires considerable acreage annually by exchange.

Pennsylvania has a legislative appropriation for the purchase of land.

STANLEY G. FONTANNA *is the deputy director of the Michigan Department of Conservation, a post he has held since 1934. He is a graduate of the University of Michigan, a veteran of the First World War, and a former employee of several large lumber companies. He is a senior member of the Society of American Foresters, president of the Association of State Foresters, chairman of the Joint Committee of Society of American Foresters and Charles Lathrop Pack Forestry Foundation on State Forestry Administration Surveys, and a member of the Advisory Board of the Charles Lathrop Pack Forestry Foundation.*

## COMMUNITY FORESTS

GEORGE A. DUTHIE

Community forests are the woodlands that are owned by the cities and townships, school districts, counties, or another public body in a State.

They are of many types, but they are all alike in that they are maintained for the public benefit and use.

They have many purposes, but they are all an expression of the Americans' innate love for trees and belief that there is a close relationship between forests and good living.

Many kinds of communities have public forests, but they have in common a progressive citizenship that is alert and resourceful in making it a good place to live in.

The character of community forests differs according to ownership and purpose. County and township forests have about the same pattern. City and town forests, distinctive from county forests, have the greatest variations in size and type; sometimes they are large tracts that protect municipal water sources; sometimes they are only small areas, in or near a town, and were planted so as to beautify the environs. School forests are mostly used for educational purposes. Among organization forests are those maintained for the public use by churches, service clubs, the Boy Scouts, 4–H Clubs, and similar groups. In brief, community forests are public forests that are not Federal forests or State forests.

The 3,113 community forests in the United States cover 4,413,950 acres. Of the 1,121 municipal forests, about one-fourth are for watershed protection. There are 1,279 school forests. County and township forests together number 617, organization forests 96.

THE COUNTY AND TOWNSHIP FORESTS are the most extensive. They account for half of the area of all community forests. They vary in patterns and purposes; some of them are mostly for recreation; others emphasize the growing of timber.

Eleven miles south of Champaign-Urbana in Illinois is the Lake of the Woods, a 260-acre tract of woodland, open fields, and water bordering the historic Sangamon River. Here one will find a spring-fed 18-acre lake for swimming, boating, fishing, and skating; a playing field for all types of outdoor sports; picnic grounds on the lake shore; camping spots on the river; and equestrian and nature trails through the upland woods. It is Champaign County's newly organized forest preserve district. Although small in area, it has fine possibilities for expansion as more woodland areas are added along the river. The public schools are enlisted in a long-range conservation program for the forest, and the school children of the county use it in first-hand studies of the natural sciences.

The method of financing the forest is both simple and direct. Twenty-year bonds were issued to buy the land and improvements, at a cost of about $80,000. A special tax levy yields an annual fund of about $30,000, for use (during the first 5 years) to extend and develop the forest and, later, to retire the bonds. A commission of five men, who serve without compensation, manages the forest. It is under the direct supervision of a resident forester-caretaker.

There are ten such forests in densely populated Illinois. The most extensive is the Cook County Forest Preserve, which lies within the metropolitan area of Chicago.

In Wisconsin another pattern is followed. Great areas of cut-over pinelands had been abandoned after being stripped of timber; the waste land returned no taxes or revenue. In many northern counties, the productive taxable property could not support the local governments. To meet this situation, many counties availed themselves of the relief offered by the Wisconsin Forest Crop Law. Under a cooperative arrangement with the State, 10 cents is paid yearly from the general fund for each acre in the county forest to help support the local government. Another 10 cents an acre is paid annually to the county from the State forestry funds for improving and developing the forest. The State also furnishes technical supervision of the cutting of timber to insure a consistent forest policy and a uniform standard of management. In return, the State is reimbursed by a 50-percent severance tax when forest products are harvested. It is in the nature of a share-crop relationship between the county owner and the State.

Twenty-eight counties have set up crop-law forests, which have a combined area of more than 2 million acres. Some of the counties 20 years ago faced bankruptcy; under management, the forest lands now yield revenues that in time may absorb a major part of the tax burden. The annual return now is more than $150,000. The forests also furnish opportunities for public recreation.

This income is from forests that but a few years ago were waste land; a large part of the new forest cover has come from hand-planted seedlings. The future prosperity of the crop-law communities, then, seems extremely promising. The pulpwood markets are clamoring for the wood that is growing in those young trees and that will soon be ready to market.

The philosophy of government that supports a county forest program was well stated in a resolution adopted in Allegany County, N. Y., that provided for establishment of a county forest system of 2,500 acres on the following premises: Large amounts of idle land not paying taxes are not contributing to the welfare of the county; these lands are contributing to an erosion problem and costing the county large sums annually in clogged stream channels, highway maintenance, and loss of revenue; the areas are too small to be managed under the State forest program; a large industrial user of forest products will eventually be lost unless a precedent is established for the management of all forest lands in the county according to good forestry principles; the county itself is a large user of wood products for which a dependable future source must be planned; the county can supply its own needs and at the same time stabilize local employment through its forest plan; the recreational value of the Allegany County hills has been neglected; and finally, forestry is a paying proposition, and we owe it to ourselves and to our heirs to leave the county in a better and more stable position, as regards its natural resources, than we found it.

The county forests of New York constitute a State-wide system that combines a high degree of recreational development with timber production. Fifty-two of the counties have forests. From 2 million to 5 million trees have been planted by each of these counties. Some of the stands are now being thinned by the first cutting of pulpwood, fuel wood, poles, and Christmas trees. From now on they will yield a steady revenue to the counties.

There are very few counties in the United States that do not have some land that presents an administrative problem. Cut-over land, submarginal farms, spoil banks remaining from mining operations, swamps, eroding mountain slopes, deep gorges and gullies, and sand dunes are the lands that private owners cannot afford to hold, problem land that nobody wants. Such lands often become tax delinquent and a burden to the tax-paying public. In public ownership under the proper forestry management, they become an asset instead of a liability. Where they occur in very large areas, they may be incorporated into national or State forests, but small and scattered tracts are best developed into county or township forests under the administration of the local government.

Dispersal of the forest units throughout the county does not present a serious problem in county administration; from the standpoint of making recreation areas accessible to everyone, the dispersal is an advantage.

About one-third of all municipal forests are watershed forests. They are maintained on the land from which the municipalities obtain their supplies of domestic water primarily for the purpose of keeping a vegetative cover to protect it from erosion. On them, other uses—the production of timber, game protection, recreation—must be managed so as not to interfere with the main purpose. On some watershed forests the reluctance to open up the areas to public travel or to the utilization of the timber is due to danger of erosion and pollution. Construction of roads and skid trails is usually accompanied by some erosion of the cut banks, and the silt from those areas where the ground cover is broken washes down into the reservoirs. Timber cutting, therefore, does create special problems for the waterworks engineers which require special logging methods designed to prevent erosion. Likewise the construction of roads through the areas must be accompanied by special treatment of the cuts and fills to prevent silting. From the standpoint of timber production, the watershed forests have a higher potential than most other community forests.

Municipal forests that are not identified with the water system are largely managed for recreation.

On some other watershed forests, arrangements have been made for intensive human use without contamination of the domestic water.

The city of Springfield, Ill., has an intensively used municipal forest of 4,300 acres, from which the city derives water, electric power, and a revenue of more than $50,000 a year from recreational and residential use. A crop of young timber grows on a part of the fields and hillsides. There is a game preserve where wildlife is propagated.

Manchester, N. H., has a municipal

watershed forest of 5,200 acres. Its planted timber is harvested under the direction of resident foresters who know from year to year just how much timber can be taken from the stands. The timber brings in from $10,000 to $30,000 a year. The recreation areas are heavily used.

Where domestic water is not involved, the dominant uses of municipal forests usually are for recreation, timber production, education, and beautification.

Such a forest is the 10,000-acre Rocky River Forest in Cleveland, whose highways, scenic beauty, archery fields, bridle paths, walks and camp grounds and picnic places thousands of persons enjoy.

LET THE CHILDREN GROW UP WITH THE TREES is a slogan that many schools have adopted. The relation of forests to our way of life is better understood by children who have an opportunity to experience that relationship through the management of the school forest. Wherever the program of education in a school has been related to experiences in the forest, education has been benefited. The music teacher who gathered her class at the foot of tall pines in the school forest to let the children discover for themselves that there is music in the rustle in the treetops was teaching a lesson in music appreciation not soon forgotten. The children named it the song of the pines; by trying to catch its mood and meter as the teacher played the song of the pines on her violin they learned the elements of true music. The teachers of mathematics and manual arts who led their pupils in surveying a location for a shelter house on their school forest, designing the building and drawing up specification and bills of material for its construction, were teaching practical lessons that had great appeal for the boys in their classes. The girls in the domestic science classes, who worked out a practical menu that they could prepare and serve in the field to the boys who were planting trees in the school forest, were learning lessons in the art of homemaking. Such projects give point to another slogan observed on the signboards of some school forests, "Youth develops where youth builds."

The work the children do in developing the school forest property and the experiences they have in their excursions to the forest create enthusiasms that take academic drudgery out of school work and make it attractive. If the school forests had no other function than that of a laboratory for work that gives vitality to the school teaching, they would serve an important purpose. Approximately 1,300 schools have their own forests. Many more have the privilege of using municipal, county, or private forests for educational projects.

The Al Sihah Boy Scout Forest at Macon, Ga., is an example of the organization forest. In 1923 a Masonic lodge started it for the Scouts on a tract of 236 acres of cut-over woodland. Title to the property is vested in the Boy Scout Council. At the end of 16 years the stands were ready for the first improvement cutting. In the next decade, the annual cut has averaged well over 100,000 feet, which has been sold at stumpage prices up to $20 per 1,000 feet.

The profit from the sales has been used to improve a similar forest of 500 acres for Negro Scouts. It is known as Camp Benjamin Hawkins.

After the First World War, the planting of trees as memorials was very popular. Since the Second World War, the idea has increasingly found expression in the dedication of community forests as living war memorials. As a war memorial, the forest at the same time fulfills the other functions of a community forest. Its role as a memorial adds to its prestige as a public institution. It combines well the qualities that are desirable in a memorial—attractiveness, long life, usefulness, and appropriateness. The memorial forests already dedicated to those who fought in the war range from small groves to extensive forests of 64,000 acres. Public spirited citizens, chambers of commerce, and veterans, sportsmen, women's organizations, and others have sponsored or founded them. They are owned by counties, cities, towns, villages, and schools.

VALUES OF TWO TYPES accrue from the public forest—the social-economic benefits and the revenues from forest products. The social benefits are more important; they can be measured in pleasure, health, improved standards of living.

The first cash returns usually come from improvement cuttings, which consist of removal of defective trees left over from previous logging or of inferior species that have taken possession of the land. Next comes the thinning of the new stands. The first thinning may be Christmas trees, which are taken out 5 to 10 years after planting. Subsequent thinnings for pulpwood, fuel, posts, and poles come along at short intervals to release the ultimate crop trees from crowding. And so, from small beginnings, year by year, decade by decade, the forest income builds up if it is managed prudently.

The city of Oneonta, N. Y., started a municipal forest of 1,200 acres in 1911. For the first two decades the value of the cut averaged $152 a year, but in the third decade the average annual income increased to approximately $600.

The Troy town forest in Maine, started in 1938, consists of 1,000 acres of abandoned farms. Withdrawn from settlement and devoted to intensive forestry, it has yielded a net income of 89 cents an acre a year, compared to the average tax of 33 cents an acre. Six years after the forest was established, a fund of $4,000 had accumulated from the forest receipts toward a new school building.

The school forest at Minocqua, Wis., consisted of 240 acres of brush land. The first year the school fund was enriched by $400 received from an improvement cutting of aspen pulpwood.

The nature of the benefits to be derived from these public forests are such that they deserve a place in modern community planning.

*George A. Duthie is chief of the section of State and community forests in the Forest Service, which he joined in 1909. For 21 years he was employed in the administration and supervision of national forests in Colorado, Wyoming, and South Dakota. He is a graduate of the University of Michigan.*

# ARBORETUMS, PLACES OF BEAUTY AND SCIENCE

W. H. LARRIMER, ERNST J. SCHREINER

To the person who has a piece of ground, a few dollars, a love for trees and nature and beauty, a collector's instinct, and an interest in science, we should like to recommend that he start an arboretum. Few things, we think, are more worthy of effort, more productive of abiding satisfaction and accomplishment, and more enjoyable than a collection of trees of one's own.

An acre is ample for 20 or 25 specimen trees and many beautiful shrubs. Five acres is plenty for a really representative collection of trees, which can be underplanted with flowering and fruiting shrubs that will bring bird life and bird songs practically into the home. How much one pays for the trees depends on how much one wants to pay. A few pennies spent for seedlings, to which are added materials started from cuttings and gifts from neighbors, will provide the beginning.

Almost everyone collects something, and enjoyment people get out of their collection—whether trees, stamps, or first editions—derives in large measure from its completeness. And so the collector of trees and shrubs will do well to set up an objective. It might be to grow one of each of 10, 15, or 20 different species. It might be to grow rare trees, like the franklinia or the offspring of historic trees, such as the Mount Vernon Pecan or the Evangeline Oak. Or it might be to obtain a complete collection of the native trees and shrubs of his county or State. In the Northern States, such a collection will not be excessive in number of specimen plants, but farther south it will entail a great many species. If the objective were to grow all the species of one group of trees, such as pines, maples, or oaks, then the size of the collection would depend upon the group of trees one selects.

Keen enjoyment comes from the search for new specimens to add to a collection. The collector can get some specimen trees from commercial nurseries. But for many rare types—and this is one of the joys of collecting—he will have to get seeds, possibly from some public arboretum, and to grow the seedlings himself. The collector of native trees might collect seed or wild seedlings on trips through his home State, or on his travels anywhere. Some of them, gathered at a distance, will not grow, perhaps, but that is a part of the art.

An excellent example of a personal arboretum is the Hemlock Arboretum in Philadelphia. The owner, Charles F. Jenkins, aims to grow all the various growth forms of the native eastern hemlock, which are mostly slow-growing or dwarfed forms. His collection in 1948 included 190 specimens, representing 40 varieties.

Much the same, except in ownership, is the community arboretum, which deserves the consideration of garden clubs, service clubs, and other organizations interested in the enrichment of community life. Undeveloped park areas or other community property is suitable for an arboretum. A community arboretum should not be confused with a community park that is provided for physical recreation; it cannot become a dual-use area, playground and arboretum.

Sections of new parkways on the outskirts of towns and cities are excellent for arboretums. Such parkways are high-speed arteries, but arboretum areas up to several miles in length can be safely established on long and relatively narrow side strips that need tree planting. Eventually, arboretum areas should be incorporated in the plans for new highways, with provision for additional land where it is required. Visitors to such an arboretum need not interfere with traffic on the main highway; suitable parking areas can be provided in places where the aboretum strip is relatively narrow. A better arrangement for wider strips is to build a gravel side road through the arboretum, parallel to the main line of travel and wide enough to permit parking without interference to traffic.

Many people in towns undoubtedly would enjoy periodic visits to a park or parkway arboretum. School children could be brought out in busses for nature study. If the arboretum is properly identified by signs, many travelers would take time to leave the highway and drive slowly through the arboretum strip.

No arboretum should be started until a plan has been well thought out and formalized on paper. Such a plan should define the purposes to be served, which, in general, determine the space required, what and how to plant, and the costs of establishment and maintenance. The plan should indicate how the project is to be financed. Advice, when it is needed, can be had readily from nurserymen, gardeners, landscape architects, and various other specialists, professional and amateur.

The person, group, or community that establishes an arboretum follows a long and interesting tradition. The dictionary definition of an arboretum as "a botanical garden of trees" indicates that their history is part and parcel of the history of botanical gardens. Such collections of trees, arranged as specimens or in the natural groups and authentically named and maintained for educational, esthetic, reference, and research purposes, have found a place in the botanical gardens of all countries.

We have records of some ancient botanical gardens, and it is a safe assumption that trees, and thus arboretums, were an important part of at least some of these gardens.

History records that, 2,800 years before the birth of Christ, the Emperor Shen Ming had a garden in which he grew medicinal plants; and that Thotmes III, the ruler of Egypt, had a pleasure garden planned by the head gardener of the Temple of Karnak about 1500 B. C. Aristotle, the great teacher of antiquity, developed a botanic garden at Athens about 340 B. C. in which he taught his students. It would appear that these ancient gardens were established for three primary reasons—utility, pleasure, and instruction.

A wide historical gap exists between the ancient gardens and the botanical gardens of the Middle Ages. As learning returned to Europe with the close of the Dark Ages, gardens were established for the utilitarian purpose of growing and testing medicinal herbs. One such was a medicinal garden at Salerno, Italy, in 1309, which has long since disappeared. Some of the medicinal gardens eventually became botanical gardens and arboretums. In Italy, botanical gardens were started in Pisa in 1543 and in Padua and Florence in 1545. Botanical gardens were established in Germany at the University of Leipzig in 1542 and at the University of Heidelberg in 1593. A tree planted a few years after the establishment of the botanical garden at Leiden, Holland, in 1587 was still standing a few years ago. One of the oldest botanical gardens in France has been in existence at Montpellier since 1593.

The world famous Royal Botanical Gardens at Kew, London, has a particularly large collection of arboretum material. It originally comprised two royal estates, which were first combined in 1802 and became a national garden in 1841. It has been said that probably the largest number of tree and shrub species which has yet been gathered is to be found at Kew.

Tokyo had a well-established garden in 1684. A botanical garden apparently existed on the outskirts of Manila in the Philippines before 1787.

Although arboretums were usually a part of botanical gardens, some early collectors were primarily interested in trees for purposes of ornament and forestry. René du Bellay, Bishop of Mans, made a collection of trees at Touvoye, France, about the middle of the sixteenth century; the contemporary botanists called the collection the richest and the most beautiful in France, Germany, and Italy, but it has long since disappeared.

About two centuries later, Duhamel du Monceau planted approximately 1,000 species of trees and woody plants from Europe and North America in the first arboretum established for scientific purposes. His arboretum and publications led to the introduction of many exotic trees into French parks and plantations. Some of his specimens are still living.

Pierre Philippe André de Vilmorin was especially interested in the different geographical varieties of the principal timber trees of Europe. In 1825 he started an arboretum at Les Barres, France, which became one of the most important tree stations in Europe. Vilmorin planted the different races and forms of the principal European timber trees and a number of introduced species in large plantations. The property became the Arboretum National des Barres through purchase by the French Government about 1856.

An arboretum was established at Segrez, France, in 1857 by Alphonse Lavallee, which, by 1875, had become one of the largest collections of woody plants. One of the most interesting collections of the oaks of Europe and southwest Asia was started by G. Allard near Angiers, France, in 1858.

In the United States, Robert Prince, an early settler at Flushing, Long Island, started a garden and arboretum, which was called the Linnaean Botanical Garden after 1793 and became well known internationally. It was continued until 1870, by five generations of the family. Among other things, Prince is credited with planting the first Lombardy poplar in America. The fame of the garden is indicated by the fact that after the Battle of Long Island, in August of 1776, the British Gen. William Howe placed a guard around the Linnaean Garden to protect the trees and plants from the hazards of war. The Linnaean Garden had a strong influence on American horticulture and forestry.

The first botanical garden in New York City was located on Murray Hill as early as 1656. Little is known of the original garden, but in 1801 Dr. David Hosack purchased 20 acres of land in the locality and established the Elgin Botanical Garden at what is now a corner of Fifth Avenue and Forty-seventh Street. In 1810 the property became the Botanical Garden of the State of New York; it was later transferred to Columbia University and was finally abandoned as a botanical garden for lack of funds.

John Bartram, who was a Pennsylvania farmer and one of the most interesting figures among our early American botanists, is generally credited with the establishment of the first arboretum in the United States. It was Bartram who discovered in Georgia in 1760 the franklinia tree, a beautiful plant that has disappeared from the wild. Today it is to be found only in arboretums and private gardens. He was honored in his own time by appointment as botanist to the King of England for his labors in collecting and forwarding plant material to England. Bartram built a house in 1731 on the banks of the Schuylkill River at a location now the south end of Fifty-fourth Street, Philadelphia; it was there he started his arboretum. A large ginkgo, or maidenhair-tree, in this garden is said to represent one of the first trees of this species introduced into America in 1784. Bartram's Garden has been restored as a public garden after being neglected for many years.

A recent survey of public arboretums of the United States listed almost a hundred. Besides those that are more or less formally established, hundreds of small groves or plantings have specimen plants that are identified and labeled. Given time and sufficient interest, it is entirely possible that some of these "seedlings" may grow into formal arboretums. Many arboretums are started in just this way. Arboretums are not natural steps in ecological successions; to survive, they must have continuous care and attention.

Of present-day arboretums in the United States, the Arnold Arboretum in Boston has exerted great influence on our knowledge of trees and shrubs. It is devoted entirely to materials hardy in that region.

Two of the best known botanical gardens, which also include extensive arboretums, are the Missouri Botanical Garden, which dates from 1859, and the New York Botanical Garden, which was established in 1894.

The Park Department of Rochester, N. Y., has developed its arboretum in the city's Highland Park into one of the large collections of trees and shrubs in the United States. The collection of poplars at Highland Park, one of the best in the country, made possible hybridization work with poplars.

The value of living collections of plants as an aid to scientific teaching and investigation began to be recognized about the seventeenth century. Interest in the use of trees and plants for decorative purposes and landscaping, and with it the desire to possess rare and unusual forms, developed

802062°—49——27

even more slowly. It was not until the middle of the eighteenth century that this aspect had become sufficiently popular to interest men of means to become the patrons of horticultural science. Then the world was searched for new and rare species and the patrons financed the publication of some magnificently illustrated volumes. And so, as the functions of botanical gardens and arboretums were gradually multiplied, the scientific and educational aspects became more and more important.

From the writings of several men we have taken ideas on how arboretums should serve the public:

To grow a complete collection of the best hardy plants so that the public may become acquainted with their names and characteristics.

To test and introduce new plants and varieties in order to increase the productivity, economic importance, and beauty of the region.

To maintain research; to provide a laboratory for the students of botany, horticulture, forestry, as well as nature study; and to provide collections of tree species for scientific breeding.

To serve as a laboratory adjunct to the schools, garden clubs, and other organizations; to disseminate knowledge of plants and the culture of plants through lectures and publications; and to provide recreational stimulus to the public.

To conserve the native plant life of the region.

To train gardeners.

To cooperate with related institutions and agencies for the extension of knowledge.

No single arboretum can necessarily fulfill all of those functions; the functions of an arboretum depend on the available area and funds—and sometimes on the conditions under which the funds are granted.

An arboretum should never become a public park, in the sense of a recreational or picnic area where people can wander at will over the land. An arboretum should be laid out with adequate footpaths leading to speci men plants, and visitors should be re quired to stay on the paths—extensiv trampling results in packing of th soil and finally to degeneration of th trees themselves. Trees and shrub should be clearly labeled with thei name and their native habitat. Addi tional interesting information may b given for many trees, such as th offspring of historic trees or the specia uses of some trees.

Arboretums are of great importanc not only to the landscape practitione but also to the forester. Most of th forest schools and forest research insti tutions of Europe have arboretums o timber trees and, in the United State some of the forest schools and fores experiment stations also maintain such collections. The arboretum of the Cali fornia Forest and Range Experimen Station, near Placerville, Calif., is on of the largest collections of pines in the world. It was established in 192 as a breeding arboretum for the im provement of this group of timbe trees. It is a good example of a highl specialized arboretum containing spe cies of pine from all over the world

At present, the forest-tree breeding work in the eastern United States i being carried on at Philadelphia, a community that is particularly rich in blooming specimens of many tree spe cies because of its favorable climat and because of the great interest in botany of some of its prominent earl settlers. Men like Bartram made Phila delphia a center of botanical studie even before the Revolution, and th continued interest of the owners o estates has given us a heritage of na tive and exotic tree species that now makes hybridization work possible.

W. H. LARRIMER, *a forester, ha worked in the Department of Agriculture for 35 years, and has done field work in every State.*

ERNST J. SCHREINER *has done research in tree breeding since his graduation in 1924 from Syracuse University.*

# THE NATIONAL ARBORETUM

B. Y. MORRISON

The National Arboretum in the District of Columbia was established by Act of Congress approved March 4, 1927. Under this act the Secretary of Agriculture was authorized and directed to establish and maintain a National Arboretum for purposes of research and education concerning tree and plant life. Under authority of the act the Secretary of Agriculture has appointed an Advisory Council on the planning and development of the Arboretum. The Council at present consists of 15 members, representing national organizations, including nurserymen, garden clubs, educational institutions, and others interested in the aims of the Arboretum.

Since its beginning the responsibility for the development and administration of the Arboretum has been assigned to the Bureau of Plant Industry, Soils, and Agricultural Engineering.

When land purchases now in process are completed, the National Arboretum will occupy an area of about 410 acres located in the northeast section of the District of Columbia, bounded on the west by Bladensburg Road, on the south by M Street, on the east by the Anacostia Parkway, and somewhat irregularly on the north by R Street, Hickey Lane, and New York Avenue.

Its soils are somewhat varied and its terrain is so diversified that there can be found sloping sites with almost any desired exposure.

Originally composed of some forty-odd parcels, some of which had been farmed, it is now integrated into a single whole with the tree-covered mass of Mount Hamilton along the western border, the broad, inner, relatively flat, central portion diagonally traversed by Hickey Creek and its tree-covered banks, and on the eastern borders the steep and tree-covered slopes of Hickey Ridge, which overlooks the broad expanses of the Anacostia Parkway, with the Maryland hills in the distance.

The area is served by a system of roads that give access to all parts in case of fire, nuisance, and other emergency. These will be modified from their present purely functional design when the current studies are completed and several large areas now devoted actively to nurseries will be returned to their proper uses.

In the planning now under way, the Arboretum site will be organized and operated much as is the National Zoological Garden, or any one of the national museums. This will mean that there will be a major portion of the area open to the visiting public during all work hours, a smaller section devoted to the nursery and service areas in which the public would not be interested, and a large building to house scientific research, the laboratories, and collections of herbarium materials, all of which will be the concern of the technical staff and of visiting scientists and students only. These three divisions will be somewhat separated.

The Arboretum is not open to the general public at the present time, but students can arrange to work in the herbarium, which is now housed at the Plant Industry Station at Beltsville, Md., or by appointment in advance may see the living plant collections during working days. Since there is considerable active construction under way and there will be more construction for the next few years, it is hoped that the public will be understanding.

As in all proper arboretums, the major interest lies in plants themselves, with attention to woody plants only, be they tree or shrub, provided only that they are hardy and successfully grown in this climate. With species, natural forms and variations, as the base, the collections will be enlarged to include not only those variable forms worthy

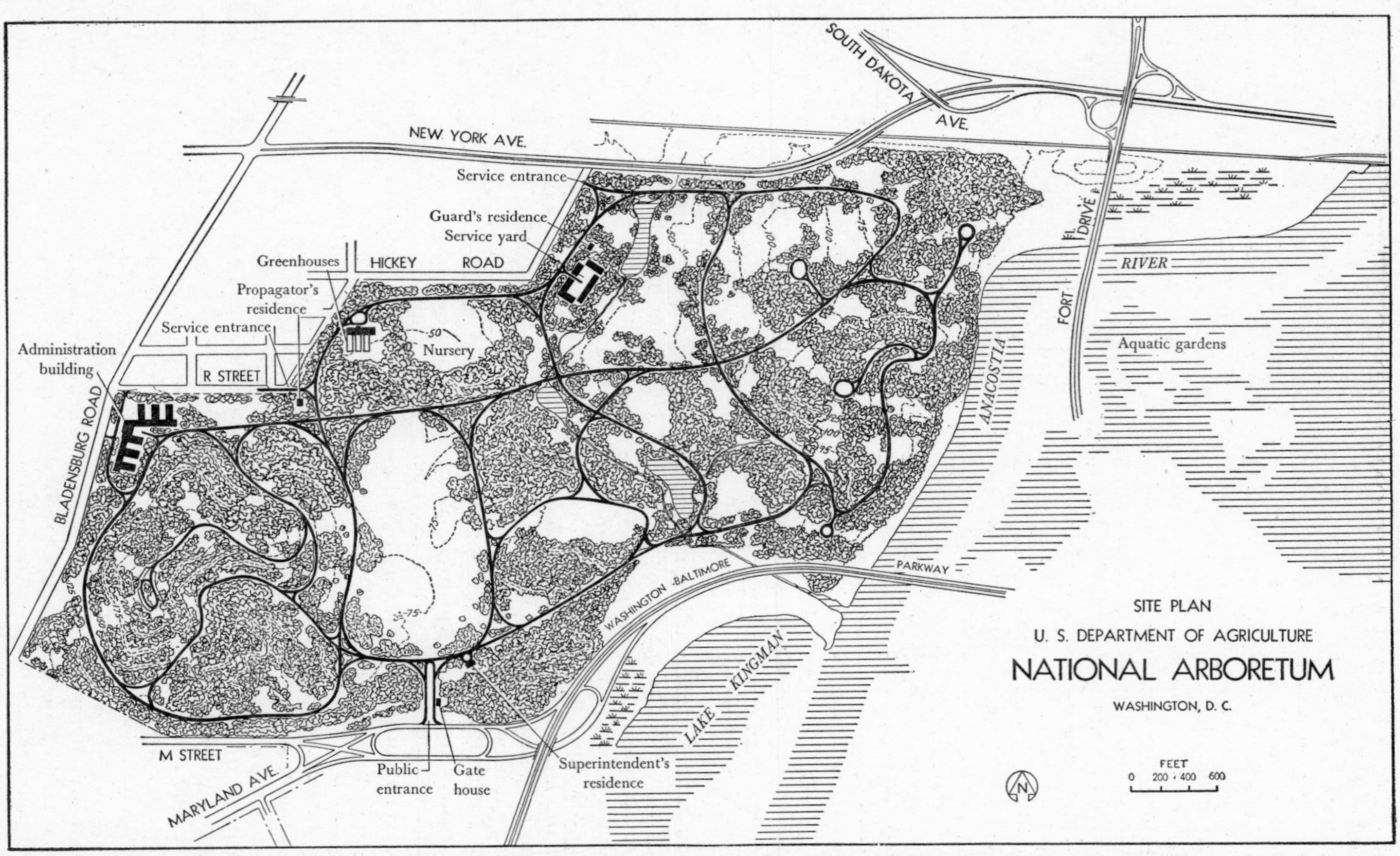
SOUTH DAKOTA AVE.
NEW YORK AVE.
Service entrance
Guard's residence
Service yard
Greenhouses
HICKEY ROAD
Propagator's residence
Service entrance
Administration building
R STREET
Nursery
BLADENSBURG ROAD
FORT DRIVE
RIVER
ANACOSTIA
Aquatic gardens
PARKWAY
WASHINGTON BALTIMORE
LAKE KINGMAN
M STREET
MARYLAND AVE.
Public entrance
Gate house
Superintendent's residence
SITE PLAN
U. S. DEPARTMENT OF AGRICULTURE
NATIONAL ARBORETUM
WASHINGTON, D. C.
FEET
0 200 400 600

of horticultural but not taxonomic rank, but as well all clonal material of hybrid or other origin. No attempt will be made to maintain varietal collections of the cultivated fruits and nuts that are maintained better elsewhere.

Because of the somewhat restricted area available for planting, it has been decided (1) that, because the Park system of the District contains larger acreages that must be kept to native trees, the Arboretum may turn its major attention to exotics; (2) that the arrangement of flowering and other materials shall be such as to throw seasonal emphasis on different parts of the Arboretum; and (3) that the planting plans shall depend for their major success on those species known to thrive in this area, with the less beautiful and those of dubious hardiness placed in secondary relationships.

In the permanent plantings that have been established, only the large azalea collection approaches the state of effective display. This, however, is still in progress, with certain alterations contemplated in the setting of the evergreen azaleas and additions to the collections of the deciduous species.

In contrast, the collections of magnolias and hollies and that of crab apples give no suggestion of what the effects will be, even in 10 years. The flank of Hickey Ridge, sloping to the south, gives a wonderful opportunity for their display, with the evergreen hollies and the evergreen magnolias the distinctive setting for the oriental magnolias that flower before their leaves, and the dark grassy meadow at the lowest level the finest base for the spring-flowering crab apples.

For the minor beauties to be found in the collections of the *Leguminosae*, little need be said, save that most visitors are surprised at the diversity of the redbuds. The maple collection is equally modest in its appeal, but some day we hope will boast a small grove of *Acer griseum*, the Chinese species with yellow bark that peels off easily.

The conifers that thoroughly enjoy our climate are not too many, but with major emphasis laid upon the juniper, the true cedars, the pines, the hemlocks, the yews, and their close relatives, one may gloss over the firs and spruces, most of them homesick for their mountains.

Whether or not the *Metasequoia glyptostroboides*, recently introduced into cultivation and represented in the Arboretum by several hundred seedlings, still in a cold greenhouse, will accept an outdoor site remains to be proved, but there is evidence that the lacebark pine, named for the famous botanist-collector, Bunge, will some day give us a fine grove with its sycamore-white trunks supporting dark-green, needle-covered crowns, not to be matched elsewhere.

There will be a small valley, looking down from Hickey Ridge, covered with cryptomerias. In their earliest years they will recall some reforested slope in Japan. Two hundred years from now, the visitor will gasp at their huge trunks as the visitor to Nikko may today. Nearby a flat-topped valley will show off the cedars from Mount Atlas, the Lebanon, and North India, with a thought perhaps for Kipling as one looks at the Deodars. Beyond these another valley for the other Indian pine, dedicated to Griffiths, another indefatigable botanist-collector, with its long, drooping needles colored like those of our own white pine, largely planted over the crown of the ridge.

These are all details. To name the 600,000 sheets of herbarium specimens and the 2,000 living species and forms is a dull business and pointless, for tomorrow and each succeeding year there will be more.

What one finds or learns at this place, as in any other collection, will depend entirely upon the visitor. No one will ask or expect the impossible.

B. Y. Morrison *is head of the Division of Plant Exploration and Introduction, Bureau of Plant Industry, Soils, and Agricultural Engineering, Beltsville, and acting director of the National Arboretum.*

*"Trees join earth and building and sky in harmony."*

# Insects, Diseases, Parasites

## INSECTS IN THE FOREST: A SURVEY

F. C. CRAIGHEAD, JOHN M. MILLER

NATURE has always used insects for her own purposes in forests. Some insects are housekeepers. Some are only incidental parts of the forest environment. Some merely prune trees. Others kill living trees, but even they do not destroy the capacity of the forest to restock and produce new stands of trees. We have convincing evidence that vast areas of mature timber were demolished in the past by insect hordes, only to regenerate after the epidemics had run their course. This was nature's way before man went into the woods. Even primitive man could not have been greatly worried by the insects that killed the forests where he got shelter and meat: Wood was plenty for all; time was plenty for young trees to grow up.

But in modern civilization those things have changed: Now the activity of destructive insects upon the trees and in the forests does matter; great areas have been cleared of forest growth for agriculture; increasing populations have increased the use of wood. Now in his search for timber stands to meet the need for sawlogs, pulp, and box shooks, the lumberman finds some areas where insects got there first and harvested the pick of the crop. For the forest resources and the commercial and esthetic values involved, we have joined battle, insects versus man, and man, for all his science and machines, is not yet the winner.

A reason why that is so is to be found in the nature of the insect infestations.

Insect populations and the timber losses they create fluctuate from year to year; only sporadically do spectacular outbreaks occur. The insects normally are present in the forests in small numbers and only occasional trees are injured or killed. A sort of natural balance seems to persist under which the processes that permit forests to reach maximum production go on uninterrupted. Then, all of a sudden, something happens to disturb this balance. A destructive insect pest appears in great numbers over wide areas and for several years its ravages may continue

*Above: Among enemies of forests are bark beetles and dwarf mistletoe.*

until a high percentage of the forest stands has been killed. Then, even more suddenly than it appeared, the epidemic subsides.

This sporadic behavior of forest-insect populations indicates that complex factors govern the abundance of certain species in the forest. Parasites, predators, unfavorable weather, resistance of the trees due to growth vigor, all tend to hold populations in check. On the other hand, conditions that will tend to weaken the trees, such as drought, preponderance of a favored food tree, failure of parasites and predators, overmaturity, and windfalls and slash, all provide favorable conditions for the destructive species to breed up in numbers. Man, himself, has at times aggravated serious insect outbreaks by his method of using the forest.

Although science has not yet been able to uncover and appraise all the factors that influence the abundance of forest-insect populations, it has shown that there are dominant conditions that must be taken into account in maintaining productive forests free from excessive losses due to insect pests. The most successful control methods that have been developed up to the present time (and no doubt those that will be used in the future) are based upon the strategy of using nature's methods as far as possible in holding down destructive insect populations.

Furthermore, the kinds of insects that attack forest trees include many species that vary widely in their habits and in the character and amount of damage they do. Some insects attack only the flowers; others the cones and seeds. The activity of these insects does not damage the tree itself, but at times so much of the seed crop is destroyed that reproduction of the forest is retarded. Sucking insects, such as scales and aphids, attack foliage and stems; they rarely kill the tree outright but gradually weaken it and slow down the growth rate. The most effective tree killers, however, are the defoliators and bark beetles, whose activities destroy vital plant organs and bring about an immediate and often fatal effect upo the growth functions of the tree. Othe insects that cause great damage are ter mites and some wood borers, whic feed only on the wood after the tree i dying or dead and destroy material tha otherwise could be put to use.

Trees are defoliated mostly by th larvae of certain moths and sawflie and to a lesser extent by both the adul and larval forms of some beetles. De foliators can kill trees by deprivin them of foliage, thus stopping the man ufacture of the plant food so that th trees slowly starve. Some of the histori defoliations of the past have been re corded not only in the chronicles of th time but also in the annual rings of sur viving trees. Outbreaks of the spruc budworm in the New England State and of the fir tussock moth in the Wes are recent examples of widespread de foliating epidemics.

Insects that feed between the bar and wood find their nutrition in th sugars and starches that are in solutio in the cells of the inner bark and cam bium. To reach these they min through the corky bark into the inne bark layer, where they introduce fun gi that develop in the sapwood an stop the flow of the sap. The leaves deprived of water, quickly wilt and th tree dies. Bark beetles make up th bulk of the destructive cambium feed ers. Certain species of bark beetles ar particularly adapted to mature stand of pine and in a number of Wester States take a heavy toll from virgi forests that are the main reserve o timber supplying the Nation's need fo high-quality soft pine. In some region during the past two decades thes insects have destroyed more merchant able timber than was cut by the saw mills and destroyed by fires, combined Characteristic of the bark beetle infes tations is their capacity to flare up int epidemics of spectacular proportions

Termites and wood borers do no kill or damage living trees and, in na ture's economy in the forest, may b of benefit in that they accelerate th deterioration and decay of dead tree ıd snags, which are thus returned to e soil. They compete with man, ›wever, when he decides to utilize e tree, and attack the wood both ıring the process of manufacture and ter it is in the finished product.

Termites and wood borers in their ›ncealed ways work along method- ally year after year. Their destruc- ›n never flares up in spectacular ·aks, but the annual attrition is none- eless disturbing and serious. Pin- ›le and worm-hole borers attacking ·een logs lower grades of lumber; ›wder-post beetles in tool handles, rniture, and flooring render quanti- ·s of finished material worthless; the d-house borer in the rafters of barns ıd houses and termites in telephone ›les and foundations of buildings aim an annual depreciation requir- g constant vigilance and replace- ent of the damaged wood products.

Estimates of the monetary val- of wood material and esthetic values at are destroyed annually by forest sects are subject to many reserva- ›ns. The money value of the forest ·oducts varies like that of other com- odities, according to demand, avail- ›ility, and the buying power of the ›llar; and the esthetic value of trees ıat are killed in parks and recrea- ›nal areas can seldom be expressed in rms of money. Although some esti- ates have been made which indi- ıte that Nation-wide timber losses ın into millions of dollars annually, ıey are based on too many assump- ›ns to be of value in this discussion. owever, if we consider only the actual ›ard feet or cubic volume of timber ıat is killed by insects, we find that ıis can be measured with consider- ›le accuracy for specific areas and eriods. Forest-insect surveys have ·en made to compute the volume of mber destroyed in many areas that ave suffered from bark beetle and de- ›liator epidemics. Such surveys have ·en made in the New England States, here the spruce budworm destroyed 50 million cords of fir and spruce, and in the Western States, where bark beetles killed 45 billion board feet of pine in recent epidemics.

All in all, these varied insect activi- ties, involving tree seeds, the natural restocking of the forests, the forest plantations, second-growth and mature stands of timber, green logs and lum- ber, telephone and telegraph poles, cross ties and buildings, create a sub- stantial loss that must more and more be reckoned with and prevented as our timber resources become smaller. This loss is often compared with that from forest fires even though all such com- parisons are difficult and incomplete.

Prevention is the starting point. If he is sufficiently interested and acts in time, man can save for his own use much of the timber that insects will otherwise destroy. There are two ways of going about it.

One approach is to initiate repres- sive measures against the insect popula- tions that are causing the losses. In the case of bark beetles, the broods are destroyed by peeling and burning the infested bark or by applying a toxic penetrative spray to the bark surface. In the case of defoliators, that usually involves spraying the trees with chemi- cals which will either kill the insects on contact or poison them through their food. These repressive measures have been termed direct control.

The second approach is to prevent the build-up of destructive insect popu- lations by preventing conditions in the forest that are favorable to their in- crease. Healthy, rapid-growing stands of timber are less susceptible to in- festations of the defoliators and bark beetles than are the slow-growing ma- ture stands. Logging out the more sus- ceptible tree species in a mixed forest, selective logging in pure stands to take out the most susceptible trees, thin- nings to encourage more rapid growth, and regulation of slash conditions to remove favorable breeding ground for the insect populations, all reduce the chances that insect populations will become destructive. These are measures that can be attained through forest management. In the case of forest products, changes in methods of manufacture and storage often completely avoid the attack of wood-boring insects. Those preventive measures have been termed indirect control.

Two of the so-called insect deadenings occurred in widely separated forests about 1895. One was in the spruce forests of West Virginia, the other in the ponderosa pine stands of the Black Hills of South Dakota. A. D. Hopkins, State entomologist of West Virginia, conducted studies in both cases and determined that two closely related species of tree-killing bark beetles were involved. He recommended the destruction of the bark beetle broods under the bark before they could develop into winged beetles and fly off to attack more green trees. The trees that contained living broods of the beetle were located, felled, and barked or burned. For every tree so treated two or three green trees were saved from attack.

Many projects have been undertaken since that time, in all costing something more than 12 million dollars up to 1949. Insect control in all cases has been the responsibility of the land-managing agencies on the land under their jurisdiction, but the many technical matters forming the basis for this control work made it necessary, particularly in the larger projects, to assign entomologists to supervise the activities. Entomologists have also assumed responsibility for detection surveys and the recommendation as to when and where and how control work should be done.

As bark beetle control increased, it became more and more evident that successful operations depended not so much on the control method used as upon a complete knowledge of the bark beetle situation on the immediate and surrounding area. A complete picture of the extent of the infestation—whether it was increasing or decreasing, the points of greatest concentration, the direction of spread—proved to be absolutely necessary. It was al necessary to have a broad gener knowledge of the insect populati throughout all susceptible timber typ so as to be able to recognize outbrea in their early stages and make recor mendations for control before the i festation was completely out of han

Such information could only be o tained by the careful surveys made skilled technicians. This unquestio ably became the function of the e tomologists. It is too bad that neith funds nor trained men have been ava able to make these surveys sufficient extensive or of the needed accurac The inadequacy of the present surv system is illustrated by the outbrea that existed during the seasons of 19 and 1948.

The adoption by Congress of th Forest Pest Control Act on June 2 1947, should mark the beginning of new era in the prevention of the exte sive losses caused each year by fore insects. This law provides authoriz tion for adequate surveys of all fore regions of the United States on bo public and private lands. This act re resents the culmination of a long effo on the part of industry, foresters, ar entomologists. It was foreseen by tho instrumental in planning and shapir this legislation that adequate surve and prompt control would gradual improve our knowledge of the inse situation so that the recurrence of suc widespread outbreaks as occurred 1947 and 1948 should be largely pr vented.

With defoliators, direct control infestations in the forest has been muc slower in its development. Such insec as caterpillars and sawflies that inju or kill trees have always been difficu for the entomologist or forester to de with. Defoliator outbreaks develop ra idly and the damage may often be com plete before the outbreak is notice Insecticidal sprays have been expensi to apply and the equipment designe for street or orchard trees was impra ical in the woods. Early attempts with irplane dusting and spraying were unatisfactory. Before the development of )DT, several attempts were made in Canada and the United States to conrol leaf feeders with the then common nsecticides—lead arsenate and calium or cryolite—by dusting from the irplane or the autogiro. Those experinents were of much technical interest ut developed little of practical value. Ve now know that those attempts ailed because of the lack of a suitable nsecticide.

THE DEVELOPMENT of DDT during he war and several more remarkable nsecticides since then—among them enzene hexachloride and chlordane—as presented an entirely new concept f the practicability of insecticidal conrol of forest insects. The toxicity of the rsenates or cryolite was so low that 15 o 30 pounds an acre was needed to btain the same degree of control as an be achieved with ½ to 1 pound of )DT. During the season of 1947, more han 500,000 acres of forest land was reated in various parts of the United States with DDT at a rate of a pound n acre. Satisfactory control resulted t costs ranging from $1 to $3 an acre. Much more remains to be done in perecting equipment and improving the echnique of application, but it seems afe to generalize that the control of lefoliator outbreaks in the future will e a sound and economical forest operation. On the average, from year to ear more than 2 million acres of forest and is defoliated annually. This enails the destruction of 10 to 75 percent f the trees in outbreaks of many different insects and in all cases a tremenlous reduction in growth in the trees ot killed outright. It does not appear oo optimistic to hope that more than ne-half of this loss can be prevented y aerial spraying with the new chemcal weapons supplied by science.

THE DIRECT METHODS of insect conrol just described are not always enirely satisfactory for several reasons: They are expensive; they are not always so effective as desired; they are strictly alleviative, that is, they do not alter the underlying causes of insect outbreaks. Dr. Hopkins fully recognized these disadvantages in his earliest efforts and again and again pointed out the advantages of adopting practices that would make conditions unfavorable for insect attack. He fully appreciated the impossibility of applying the methods that were then being developed for the control of garden- and truck-crop insects to forested areas. He made many suggestions for the control of insects affecting crude and finished forest products—practical suggestions based on operational procedures.

As early as 1913, entomologists of the Department of Agriculture pointed out that infestations of the gypsy moth in the New England States gained momentum in stands of hardwoods composed largely of "favored" species. The idea was then proposed that forests within the gypsy moth zone be managed so as to increase the proportion of unfavored host species. Similar findings, published in 1924, resulted from studies of the spruce budworm in Canada. Basic points to consider in managing the spruce-fir type to lessen the destructiveness of spruce budworm outbreaks were found to be the predilection of the spruce budworm for fir, the tendency of fir to regenerate at the expense of spruce (so that fir dominated in the cut-over stands), and the ability of younger, more vigorous trees to withstand defoliation.

In studies of pine bark beetles much research has been pointed toward finding preventive control measures. So far it is only with the western pine beetle in the ponderosa pine that any specific method of management has been found and proved to be practicable and effective. In that case it was the predilection of the beetle for certain susceptible trees in stands of ponderosa pine that served as the key to management control. Studies of the characteristics of many thousands of beetle-killed and surviving trees revealed that the mortality of pines from western pine beetle attack is closely related to growth vigor—the more vigorous the tree the less likelihood of its becoming a victim of the beetle.

Further studies showed that susceptible and resistant trees could be recognized by visible characters connected with the form and condition of the crown and that pine stands could be classified according to these characters. By using this tree classification as an index to relative resistance and susceptibility, it is now possible to log selectively the more susceptible trees and reduce greatly the hazard of western pine beetle infestations.

In wood products, the prevention of insect damage is much simpler than preventing damage in the forest itself.

Some types of damage (like defects in the standing trees) are in a sense unpreventable, but by far the greatest amount of injury to this class of material comes after the tree is felled—to the green logs, to seasoned logs, to seasoned lumber, or to the product in use, whether it be cross tie, pole, sill, flooring, rafter, or implement handle. To a great extent this type of damage can be prevented. Its occurrence is a sign of carelessness—usually insufficient precaution. Thus, if the log is attacked in the woods by borers, the simplest remedy is to get the log sawed more quickly; if injury occurs to the green lumber, more rapid seasoning is necessary. Damage that occurs to the product after it is in use (such as termite damage to cross ties and telephone poles or *Lyctus* damage to flooring or implement handles) can frequently be prevented by attention to construction details, proper storage, or by treatment with preservatives and insecticides.

Many suggestions have been made in the past three or four decades for the prevention of forest-insect outbreaks through forest management in many types of stands. They have all been made with the realization that they are more or less experimental and need the test of practical application. They are based on the known facts concerning life histories and food preferences of the insects, considered in connection with the silvicultural characteristics of the tree.

Forest-management steps so as to control species or age classes in the interest of insect protection require distribution of cutting over forest properties which heretofore has rarely been possible. An adequate system of timber-hauling roads is essential to apply such cutting measures in the places where they are necessary. In addition to affording an opportunity to place timber stands in a more resistant condition to insect epidemics, adequate road systems make it possible to salvage recently killed and highly susceptible trees before deterioration, which renders them worthless, occurs. Control of such epidemics as do occur in the incipient stage is also facilitated by adequate transportation facilities. The importance of road development for application of stand management to reduce hazards from insect epidemics, to check the spread of epidemics, and to salvage killed or infested trees is now being recognized by both public and private forest-land managers. Progress in solving insect-control problems through management practices will depend to a large degree on the extension of permanent access-road systems into national forest lands and other ownerships where forest management is being applied.

Looking back some 40 years in the practice of forest entomology—from the beginnings by Asa Fitch and A. S. Packard, through the intensive biological inquiry of Dr. Hopkins, which formed the backbone of effective bark beetle control as well as the basis for suggestions for silvicultural methods of preventing damage, to the coming of modern insecticides and airplanes—one cannot help but wonder what is ahead.

Will it be the prevention of widespread destruction of our resources by e adoption of such good forest man-gement that insects cannot develop to ijurious proportions?

Will adequate surveys so completely over all susceptible forest types that isect epidemics will be caught in their icipiency and quickly suppressed by ell-timed control measures?

Or will human nature be much the ame tomorrow as today and continue take a chance on the unseen (though omewhat predictable) future and ait for the worst to happen?

Probably some of each will prevail. ur detection system will become bet-r, good management will come to ass on more and more acreage, and iere will be plenty of opportunity for ie direct-control enthusiast. It now eems inevitable that we are going to nter an era of cheaper and more effec-ive direct control that would have eemed utter fantasy a few years ago.

Mechanical devices and versatile ower units are taking the hand labor ut of bark beetle control, and mar-elous insecticides are spread quickly ver thousands of acres by airplane at osts that are a mere fraction an acre f the values at stake. Certainly for oday the possibilities in chemical and iechanical methods of control look far righter than the possibilities for silvi-ultural methods of prevention. In the ieantime, it seems to us that more and more reliance must be placed on these direct measures of control and more effort must go into their improvement. At the same time, our detection surveys must be greatly strengthened and our research into biological and silvicultural methods of preventing damage must be pursued diligently for a more propitious future.

F. C. CRAIGHEAD *has been in charge of investigations of forest insects, in the Bureau of Entomology and Plant Quarantine of the United States Department of Agriculture, since 1923. He has been with the Department since 1912, except for 3 years spent in Canada working on forest-insect problems with the Dominion Entomological Branch. He is a native of Pennsylvania. Dr. Craighead is a graduate of Pennsylvania State College, and holds advanced degrees from George Washington University.*

JOHN M. MILLER *is a native of California and has been associated with forestry and forest-insect problems in a number of Western States since his graduation from Stanford University in 1908. He has wide experience in forest-insect control and has published numerous papers on research and control phases of his specialty. He has been with the Department of Agriculture since 1907.*

# THE KEY TO PROTECTION

S. A. ROHWER

Until research developed informa-ion on pests of our forests and devised ieans of combating them, there was ittle of immediate practical value that ould be gained from knowing where he pests occurred. Fortunately we now now procedures which can be used to ontrol many of the more common and iost destructive pests. By using these iethods we can prevent the develop-ient of outbreaks that would cause de-truction and losses over wide areas.

The key to any effort to protect our forests from these or any of the numerous insects and diseases that attack them is a knowledge of where the pest occurs and how abundant and aggressive it is. This is fundamental. It is comparable with criminal and military intelligence. All types of programs to combat common enemies employ the principle of knowledge of its whereabouts and strength. To combat successfully the forest pests we must know

ESTIMATES OF TOTAL VOLUME OF TIMBER KILLED BY PINE BARK BEETLES DURIN VARYING PERIODS UP TO 1946 (IN THOUSAND FEET BOARD MEASURE)

| *Species* | *Insect* | *Region affected* | *Period* | *Volume of timber kille* |
|---|---|---|---|---|
| Ponderosa pine | Western pine beetle | Pacific States | 1921–46 | 25,000,0 |
| Do | Black Hills beetle | Rocky Mountains | 1895–1946 | 2,500,0 |
| Do | Mountain pine beetle | do | 1910–46 | 5,500,0 |
| Sugar pine | do | California | 1921–46 | 3,500,0 |
| Western white pine | do | Pacific Northwest | 1921–46 | 750,0 |
| Do | do | Northern Rocky Mountains. | 1910–46 | 3,500,0 |
| Lodgepole pine | do | Rocky Mountains | 1910–46 | 6,000,0 |
| Do | do | Pacific coast | 1921–46 | 1,000,0 |

where they occur. Thus detection surveys are the first step in any effort to protect forests by controlling destructive insects and diseases.

The initial procedure in protecting the forest from pests is basically the same as that used to prevent destruction from fire. In many respects, however, pest control differs from fire control. It is well established that occurrence of infestation or infection on a few trees does not necessarily mean that important destructive loss will follow unless control measures are applied. It is important that this be recognized as it has a significant relation to any program of forest-pest control and survey designed to provide a basis for action. It emphasizes the essential role of the entomologist and pathologist in the survey program. Facts assembled on the occurrence of forest pests must be appraised on the basis of knowledge of their behavior and development.

Such appraisal is the second essential step in any program to combat injurious forest insects and diseases. It provides the basis for any decision to combat the pest. It has an important bearing on the type of data the survey should develop.

DETECTION AND APPRAISAL METHODS differ with the pests. The wide differences in habits and appearance of the numerous kinds of insects and diseases destructive to forests make it impossible to use any single or simple procedure in carrying out inspection to detect their presence and determin the significance of their occurrenc Methods used in making surveys wi also differ in various sections of th country. Practices will necessarily di fer with the objective sought.

TO PROTECT WHITE PINE from th destructive introduced disease—whit pine blister rust—the detection of th disease organism is secondary to th location of the currant and gooseberr bushes on which the disease must spen part of its life. The spores of the diseas produced on white pine are hardy an remain viable much longer, even whe carried long distances. Protectin white pines from the disease is largel a matter of detecting and destroyin currant and gooseberry bushes tha grow among or adjacent to the pin trees. Hence, surveys for currants an gooseberries are a part of white pin blister rust control.

IN THE CASE of another introduce pest—the gypsy moth—where it eradication in designated areas is th objective and the basis of preventin natural spread to new sections, inspections for the insect pest must be detailed and provide complete coverage Research has developed ways to d this effectively and without undu cost. An important feature of suc surveys includes application of knowledge that the winged free-flying male are attracted to extracts made fron ıe tip of the abdomen of the wingless :male.

It is thus possible to trap the males nd determine with reasonable ac- uracy whether the insect is present ı any area. With this knowledge, in- :nsive search for egg clusters provides ata on where and how abundant the est is.

WITH THE MORE DESTRUCTIVE NA- IVE insect pests such intensive inspec- ons are not needed. Here the objective to keep informed as to the areas here the pest is developing in num- ers sufficient to cause important loss. 'he fact that intensive inspections to ›cate all infestations are not required oes not mean, however, that the task is mple. Restricting surveys to the forest ests of known importance still re- uires many observations and the use f much technical knowledge.

THERE ARE MANY DIFFERENT KINDS f important pests, and the habits and ıethod of attack of these are widely aried. The habits of the various tree- illing bark beetles, although similar s to general pattern, cause different ymptoms. The fading, browning, and eddening of the foliage of injured rees provide a valuable index of the resence of many forms, such as the leadly western pine beetle. Attacks f the equally destructive Engelmann pruce beetle, however, are not fol- owed by the browning and reddening f foliage. A group of red-top trees illed by the mountain pine beetle in lodgepole forest is often the sign of he beginning of an outbreak. Grouped ed-top trees killed by the western pine eetle in a ponderosa pine forest in Colorado may indicate the subsidence f an outbreak. Only the trained, ex- perienced entomologist can distin- uish the potential difference between roups of like superficial appearance.

Many species of insects defoliate rees and here the significance of an nfestation may depend on the kind f insect and the type of forest. Where nore than one species of insect is present, and this frequently occurs, the proportion of each in the mixture may have an important bearing on the potential damage of the infestation.

IN ALL KINDS OF INSECT INFESTATIONS, and especially those where leaf feeders occur, observations on the presence of natural enemies need to be recorded. The presence and abundance of parasites, predators, and disease often have an important relation to the development of the primary pest.

Illustrations of this nature could be multiplied but would only give added emphasis to the various matters which need to be considered and made part of a survey program to determine the presence and status of forest pests. To secure facts on new and little-known insects and diseases which are or may be injurious to our forests requires an even greater use of specialized information. The importance of obtaining data on the presence of lesser known species must not be overlooked. No one can forecast when another blight, as destructive as the one which killed the chestnut, may appear. Nor should we fail to be alert to the presence and development of infestations of species which in themselves may be of only secondary importance, yet when present with other organisms have a primary place as forest pests.

THE RELATION BETWEEN BARK BEETLES and the Dutch elm disease illustrates how the combinations of pests change the significance of each. The smaller of two well-known bark beetles native to Europe has been known to be established in the United States since 1910, long before the Dutch elm disease was found here. Although it fed on elm shoots and developed in the branches, it was not of any particular significance, since it lived in dead and dying branches. When the disease was introduced, the habits of living in branches and feeding on young shoots provided a ready means of carrying disease from the infected to healthy trees. The two pests combined make formidable enemies to our elms, and control of the beetle becomes of first importance.

SURVEYS TO SECURE DATA on specific pests are always less complex. Where the plant is an annual one, as is the case with many of our agricultural crops, data needed may require fewer observations. Even here there is need for specialized technique and sampling.

When the many kinds of trees and numerous kinds of pests are involved, however, the problem increases in complexity. It is therefore necessary to simplify the task as much as possible. In planning, organizing, and executing procedures we should emphasize the known importance of the pests. Pests of first importance should have first attention. This principle has been the basis of the surveys on native forest pests that have been carried out. It should be followed in the future.

ESSENTIAL TO ALL FOREST-PEST SURVEYS are on-the-ground observations. These provide data on the presence of numbers of the pest and the environmental factors that affect its development. This calls for a system of collecting and recording the observations made by those who frequent the forests and are interested in and concerned with their protection. Survey programs are designed to receive and record their observations. Rangers, timber cruisers, and spotters provide useful and important records. The data they supply have been of material help. What they have done, however, has not been as extensive as needed; for many sections and areas there are few observers, and the means of assembling the records are inadequate. Ways should be devised to encourage and improve such reports.

To examine each year, even in a casual way, all forest areas for the occurrence and development of infestations of just the known injurious forest pests is a large order—an objective it is scarcely practical to attain now. Fortunately it is not yet necessary to do this to obtain data needed to secure reasonable protection of our fores from pests. Many factors influence tl behavior and development of the na tive insects and diseases injurious our forests. Even the weather plays a important part. Entomologists an pathologists use their knowledge an understanding of these numerous fa tors in planning surveys.

THEY CONSIDER also the compos tion, age, value, and location of tl forests. It has been discovered that f at least certain forest types the fore area may be classified into units of d gree of hazard; for example, the larg area in eastern California and Orego covered by the predominant yello pine forest type. Such discoveries an the classification of the forest types i units have made it possible to dete mine with reasonable accuracy the fr quency of surveys needed to apprais the status of the principal pests.

Research in several areas of differ ent forest types has established tha frequent inspections of sample area provide information on trends of d velopment of infestations applicabl to large areas. Thus an intensive su vey of limited sections may suffice fo extensive forest areas, except durin periods when outbreaks of the pest ar beginning to develop.

DEVELOPMENTS IN AVIATION hav supplied a new means for making r connaissance surveys to secure prelim nary data on the occurrence an development of outbreaks of insec pests, and perhaps for a few disease Observers familiar with the sympton caused by injurious insects and diseas can, in a short time and at relativel low cost, secure valuable data on pe conditions that occur over wide area

A few well-timed flights over area infested and threatened by the recer outbreak of the tussock moth in th Idaho area aided greatly in locatin and appraising the extent and intensit of infestation. Extensive, inaccessibl areas of lodgepole pine have bee quickly examined to locate red top the telltale indication of bark beetle infestations. There is still much to be learned concerning the place that the recent developments in aircraft and aerial photography will have in forest-pest surveys of the future. The timing and frequency of the flights will be important.

Current experience suggests aircraft and aerial photography will prove to be a valuable adjunct to the survey technique and that for certain of the important pests they make it possible to detect the presence and accurately estimate the extent of infestation more promptly. It is reasonable to assume, however, that detailed on-the-ground inspections will still be required to secure exact data needed to appraise the potential significance of the infestation.

Helpful as all known procedures are, it is clear that the practices of detecting infestations and infections of insects and diseases injurious to our forests need to be improved. More than this, we must use to a much greater extent the knowledge we now have if the destructive importance of the pests are detected in stages of incipiency. Early discovery of a potentially destructive infestation permits action that will prevent important loss and greatly reduce the cost of control.

S. A. Rohwer *is assistant chief of the Bureau of Entomology and Plant Quarantine in the Department of Agriculture.*

# FOUR BILLION FEET OF BEETLE-KILLED SPRUCE

N. D. WYGANT, ARTHUR L. NELSON

Ten years or so ago the Engelmann spruce forests in the higher Rocky Mountains of Colorado were a sight to behold. They were a reservoir of unexploited virgin timber, the summer homes and playground of thousands of people who love the mountains. Tall, green, silent, majestic, these forests were a gift of God, an important asset to our natural wealth and welfare.

Today, on much of that ground stand millions of dead trees—graceless, lifeless, valueless. They will stand there 20 years more, ghost forests and tragic evidence of how fast and silently a tiny insect can do its damage when once a combination of favorable factors brings about a sudden increase in its numbers.

The insect is the Engelmann spruce beetle, the *Dendroctonus engelmanni* Hopk. Without the spectacular features of smoke or fire or explosion, but as devastatingly, the beetle built up its population, mostly in the inner bark of living trees, where it fed and bred. Those trees died; then new beetles emerged and attacked other trees. No person even suspected what was happening until the outbreak was well under way and approaching its peak. Then it was too late to do much: Between 1942 and 1948, 4 billion board feet of stumpage had been killed.

Four billion board feet can furnish lumber for 400,000 five-room frame houses. The value in standing trees is estimated at 8 million dollars. It might someday have been made into products valued at 200 million dollars. The insects were more destructive than forest fires—in the 6 years, 16 times more timber was destroyed than was killed by fire in the past 30 years in the Rocky Mountain region.

And to those who love the mountains and the trees there was another kind of heartbreaking loss: Damaged for a generation were parts of our most beautiful National Forests, the White River, Grand Mesa, Routt, Arapaho, Uncompahgre, San Juan, and Dixie. On a large part of the White River National Forest, nearly all spruce of

802062°—49——28

saw-timber size—2,900 million board feet of it—was killed.

In its adult stage, the Engelmann spruce beetle is a small, cylindrical, hard-shelled beetle, about one-fourth inch in length, about the size of an ordinary housefly. When the adults leave the dead trees and start to fly in June and July, they are reddish brown to black in color. They soon settle on recently felled or standing green trees and bore through the outer bark into the living inner bark. This attack extends over most of the lower main stem of the tree.

The beetles work in pairs of male and female, each pair raising separate broods. The female makes the entrance, followed by the male, and bores a tunnel between the bark and wood, which usually extends in a vertical direction and parallels the grain of the wood. This tunnel is known as the egg gallery. The eggs are laid in alternate groups along the sides of the gallery, and the galleries are packed with boring dust mixed with pitch. There are usually 3 to 4 groups of eggs and a total of about 125 eggs in each gallery. On the average there are from 6 to 8 such egg galleries for each square foot of bark.

When the eggs hatch in 3 or 4 weeks, the larvae feed on the succulent inner bark and cut mines that run at right angles to the egg gallery. This larval feeding continues through the late summer and fall. When winter arrives they are still in the inner bark, where they become dormant.

The following spring the larvae resume feeding. As summer advances they become mature, transform to pupae, and then into adult beetles. This new adult stage is reached by midsummer, and the beetles first start feeding on the inner bark of the tree in which they were reared. By August or September they appear to be mature. Then some of the beetles emerge and congregate under the bark around the base of the tree. Others remain under the bark where they developed. In both cases they rest quietly during the second winter, and when warm weather returns the following spring they are ready to take flight and attack other living trees.

While the development of the insect is going on, the trees that have been attacked die, usually by the end of the first season of the attack. Death of the trees is caused by the girdling action of the egg galleries and the larval mines and by a blue-staining fungus that permeates the sapwood and stops sap conduction in the tree. This fungus is carried by the beetles and is always found in trees that are successfully attacked by the insects. The foliage of Engelmann spruce does not change color until about a year after the trees are attacked; then it fades to a yellowish green and the needles drop within a short period.

In nature many forces operate to keep beetle populations at a low level over long periods. There is always a high mortality during the brood-development period from eggs to new adults. The number that reach the full-grown larval stage has been found to average from 215 to 360 to the square foot of bark. By the time the new adult stage is reached and the beetles emerge, this average has been reduced to about 150 to the square foot. These averages vary widely. The larger trees tend to produce heavier emergence than smaller trees. Then, when the beetles take flight, they are exposed to all sorts of hazards from wind, weather, and birds.

The factors that tend to limit beetle populations are parasitic and predatory insects that feed on the broods while they are developing in the inner bark; woodpeckers, which locate the infested trees and chip off the outer bark to feed on the broods that are thus exposed; and good growth conditions in the spruce stands where young and vigorous trees predominate. Woodpeckers are especially effective; when they are abundant they destroy 45 to 98 percent of the brood.

Among the conditions that favor

multiplication of beetle populations are windfalls and overmaturity of the spruce stands, since the insects prefer to attack the larger mature trees and produce heavier broods in them. Large bodies of windthrown timber provide highly favorable conditions for the build-up of beetle populations, because green trees that have been blown over have been seriously disturbed in their crown and root functions and can offer little resistance to the attacks of the insects. After strong populations have developed, they will attack green stands of spruce regardless of their condition, and heavy losses usually continue until natural control factors again gain the upper hand.

PREVIOUS OUTBREAKS of the Engelmann spruce beetle occurred in the Rocky Mountain region, but most of them were so long ago that their exact extent is not known. In 1907, A. D. Hopkins, of the Department of Agriculture, found evidence on the White River National Forest of an outbreak that occurred 20 to 25 years earlier. He also estimated that severe outbreaks occurred on the Pike National Forest about 1855 and on the Lincoln National Forest in New Mexico about 1890. An outbreak that killed nearly 100 percent of the spruce volume swept over the Aquarius Plateau in Utah between 1918 and 1928. A localized outbreak was reported in the northwestern part of Yellowstone National Park in 1937. Apparently none of these earlier outbreaks even approached in intensity and total volume of destruction the one that started in Colorado in 1942.

Circumstances beyond the control of foresters and entomologists caused this spectacular outbreak. Several factors made conditions favorable. In June 1939 a severe windstorm swept from the southwestern corner of Colorado, in a northeasterly direction, across the mesa-type plateaus in the State. On thousands of acres many of the shallow-rooted Engelmann spruce blew over. Many of the roots on the down side remained in the soil to keep the trees alive for several years or until the beetles made their attack. As a native species, the Engelmann spruce beetle was present in small numbers in decadent trees in the forest. Those down trees proved to be a fertile breeding place for them.

By 1942, this breeding material had been consumed and the beetles had built up great populations. With a previously unknown reproductive force, coupled with an apparent lack of activity of natural control factors, the beetles invaded the standing spruce. By 1943, when the infestation was first discovered, the number of infested trees was so great that control by destroying the insects with fire or insecticides was economically and physically impossible. The problem then became one of determining the extent and severity of the outbreak so as to prevent its spread into other spruce forests, salvaging the dead timber, and studying the life history and habits of the beetle as a basis for development of control measures.

PLANS WERE MADE in 1943 for a survey of the spruce type in Colorado to determine the extent of the outbreaks and their progress, what action should be taken, and whether spread of the insect into nonaffected areas could be prevented.

A person who has not visited the high Rockies in Colorado can hardly realize the difficulties of making a survey and carrying out control measures in the spruce forests. Engelmann spruce grows at elevations of 9,500 to 11,500 feet, generally in rugged terrain—except for the forests on plateaus—and in places where few roads have been made. Many of the areas can be reached only by a trail, and then often with as much as a full day's travel on pack animals from the end of a road. An attempt was made in 1944 to use an airplane to scout the forests and locate the incipient outbreaks, but the infestations could not be detected from above because of lack of foliage discoloration. Nor could incipient outbreaks be detected from lookouts and vantage points.

The technique finally developed to detect the infested and killed trees required sample lines to be run through the various areas and the trees viewed at close range. Such a survey has been made annually since 1944, with a crew of three to six men. In addition, a close watch for infestation has been kept by the forest rangers during their summer travels. Although coverage has not been so complete and thorough as one would like, a fairly accurate picture has been obtained of the progress of the outbreaks.

The spruce losses have been phenomenal for such a short period. The end of the losses on the White River, Routt, and Arapaho National Forests is not yet in sight. The surveys indicate a serious flight of beetles from the center of the White River National Forest outbreak to the east across the Colorado River into extensive spruce stands. The outbreak on the Gore Range on the Routt and Arapaho National Forests is rapidly moving northward. The outbreak on these two forests has gained much of its momentum from flights of beetles across the Yampa River Valley.

A large beetle population remains on the White River National Forest, however, and the continuation of a mass flight there is still not beyond possibility. In 1946, at the end of the attack period, 77 percent of the spruce was killed on that forest north of the Colorado River. Nearly all the remaining trees were killed in 1947. The beetles have exhausted their food supply on the White River National Forest, and whether they will perish within the infested area or fly to new areas remains to be seen.

The outbreaks on the part of the White River National Forest that lies south of the Colorado River, and on the Uncompahgre, Gunnison, and San Juan National Forests in Colorado, and the Dixie National Forest in Utah started to decline in 1946. They reached an endemic status in 1947, even though ample host material re mained for the insects to attacl Natural control factors, aided by arti ficial control on the Dixie and Gun nison National Forests, reduced th outbreaks faster than they arose.

Active outbreaks continued in 194 on the Grand Mesa National Fores and on the Gore Range on the Rout and Arapaho National Forests. Log ging of the infested trees and burnin of the infested slabs at the mill pre vented the Grand Mesa infestatio from becoming more severe. A simila plan was applied to the Arapaho an Routt infestations.

It was evident in 1943 that cuttin must be immediate if this beetle-kille timber was to be used for lumber, sinc it was doubtful if it would remai usable for that purpose for longer tha 3 or 4 years after attack. Every appli cation to purchase beetle-killed spruc was granted. An aggressive campaig was started to interest more operators Small operators soon began cutting i most of the accessible areas. Lack o capital and the difficulty of obtainin proper equipment and labor kept pro duction low.

Results have been disappointin when weighed against the large volum of killed timber. It was estimated tha by January 1949 about 100 millior board feet had actually been salvaged or less than 5 percent of the operabl volume of insect-killed timber.

The 4-billion-board-foot loss of tim ber represents better than 20 percen of the Engelmann spruce timber i Colorado. The rough mountain terrai and distance to railheads and market make about half of this timber inac cessible and nonoperable from an eco nomic standpoint. Much of the 2 billion board feet considered operabl actually requires the construction o roads to make it accessible for salvage

Sparse populations, limited funds and the ruggedness of this mountai country have governed the location o routes of travel between communities Few roads have been built to open u resources, and much of the timber remains out of reach. Roads are needed to harvest the dead spruce and also much of the ripe green timber.

During the war, some so-called timber-access roads were built, including the 14 miles to open up Clinetop Mesa. A 20-mile, 16-foot surfaced road has since been built that opens up 150 million board feet of spruce timber on Coffee Pot Mesa. Surfacing of forest-development roads also has been undertaken, permitting salvage of more and more of the bug-killed spruce.

The primary need in the insect-killed area is for more timber-hauling roads. It is estimated that a million cords of pulpwood can be made accessible on the White River National Forest alone by an expenditure of $750,000 for access roads.

The insect-killed timber can be used for lumber if salvaged within 3 or 4 years after being attacked. The tree dries and cracks open up the stem. Where the woodpeckers have removed some of the bark, the cracking or checking process is speeded up on the time during which the timber can be salvaged for lumber is reduced.

Dead timber no longer suitable for sawed products has been proved to be usable for making paper. Sample carloads have been tested by some of the mills in the Lake States. The reports are that the dead spruce is entirely satisfactory if minor changes are made in processing. Since there is no pulp or paper industry in the central Rocky Mountain region, it is logical that this spruce should be used to help alleviate the shortage of pulpwood in the Lake States. Many of these pulp and paper companies are looking forward to the day when their own forests will sustain their plants. In the meantime, the next 10 to 15 years is the critical period, and if the dead Engelmann spruce can help a part of the industry over this trying period, it will have served a useful purpose.

Insect-killed spruce is expected to remain usable for pulpwood for 15 years or more. The development of a pulpwood-logging industry in Colorado is now in the early stages. Small operators are trying their hand at it. One Wisconsin pulp and paper company has sent in its own crews and equipment to test the feasibility of logging and shipping the dead spruce to its Wisconsin plant. Another has purchased 43,000 cords of which about 6,000 cords were cut by the end of 1948. One of the difficulties in getting local operators to cut pulpwood was their lack of experience and proper equipment to handle 100-inch pulpwood sticks. Also, as long as the dead timber could be made into sawed products, there was more profit in such products than in producing pulpwood. Except in limited areas of recent attack, the latter is no longer the case, and with experience and more specialized equipment available the production of pulpwood by local operators should increase, provided the selling price permits a profitable operation.

Freight rates from Colorado points adjacent to the bug-killed timber to mills in Wisconsin have been established at $15.12 a cord for a minimum carload of 24 cords or more. This makes for high-priced raw material when the cost of production ($15 to $16 a cord) is added. An added difficulty is a marked scarcity of gondolas large enough to carry the minimum load of 24 cords. Railroad officials are not too optimistic about relief from this situation and, so far, changes in the freight rate to cover lower minimum carloading have not been favored.

A permanent industry can hardly be built on the basis of salvaging insect-killed timber alone. Perhaps local industries might be established which could use the dead wood that is salvageable, then continue to operate on green timber. Felt-pulp plants for making roofing paper have been suggested. Other possibilities for better utilization include chipping in the woods and shipping baled chips to pulp or chemical conversion plants. So far, the most promising and practical outlet seems to be the shipment, as wood, to existing pulp mills. The practicability of a pulp mill in Colorado using dead and green wood is being explored.

SEVERAL LESSONS have been well learned. Underlying the rapid development of this outbreak was the great windfall of 1939. This sort of disaster is something that can neither be foreseen nor prevented, and it may happen again. The aftermath of heavy bark beetle losses can be prevented, however, if measures can be taken in time to prevent the build-up of populations. Where it is feasible, the salvage of all windthrown timber within 2 years after it is blown down will deprive the beetles of their favorite breeding material.

Direct-control measures applied before an infestation becomes general over a large area should prove effective. We know that the insect can be destroyed by peeling and burning the infested bark, by burning the infested logs, or by the application of toxic penetrating sprays. For example, a mixture of oil and orthodichlorobenzene has proved to be effective when applied to the bark of infested trees or logs. Further research may develop new methods and insecticides which can be applied from the air so as to reduce costs and permit their use over difficult terrain.

Basic to any use of direct-control methods is a well-organized system of surveys that will detect the local centers of infestation and present a comprehensive picture of the infestation before heavy increases occur.

Research may also point the way to forest-management practices based on an adequate knowledge of the ecology of Engelmann spruce stands and the role of the beetle in their natural rotation. There is a good possibility that the Engelmann spruce beetle can be held in check by indirect methods. Indications are that in healthy growing forests severe epidemics are less apt to occur. More access roads will permit cutting to take place in the most overmature and decadent timber. Sanitation cuts apparently must first be made without too much consideration of a sustained-yield policy for management of the species.

Until we know more about the forces that bring these sudden uprisings of bark beetle populations and can devise either direct or indirect methods of dealing with them, Engelmann spruce stands will continue to be subject to the hazards of devastating beetle-caused losses. In this most recent outbreak in Colorado, the best we can do now is to accept what the beetles have left us in the forest and strive for better ways of controlling the beetles next time.

N. D. WYGANT *is an entomologist in charge of the Forest Insect Laboratory in Fort Collins, Colo., in the Division of Forest Insect Investigations, Bureau of Entomology and Plant Quarantine. A graduate of Purdue University and New York State College of Forestry, Dr. Wygant joined the Department in 1935. He has worked on insect problems affecting shelterbelts in the Great Plains and the bark beetle and other forest-insect problems in California and the central and southern Rocky Mountain region.*

ARTHUR L. NELSON *is assistant regional forester in charge of the Division of Timber Management, State and Private Forestry, Forest Service, Denver. After graduation from the University of Minnesota, he entered the Forest Service in 1923 and was assigned to timber-survey work on the Bighorn National Forest in Wyoming. He worked on the Black Hills, Routt, and Roosevelt National Forests; subsequently he was supervisor of the old Leadville Forest and the Nebraska, Rio Grande, and Ouachita National Forests. From 1941 to 1944 he was assistant chief of the Division of Timber Management in Washington, D. C.*

*For further information about research, the reader is referred to other articles in this chapter, Insects, Diseases, Parasites, and to the chapters on Company Forests and The National Forests.*

# THE SPRUCE BUDWORM

R. C. BROWN, H. J. MAC ALONEY, P. B. DOWDEN

The spruce budworm is a small, foliage-feeding caterpillar that periodically kills an immense amount of spruce and balsam fir in the Eastern States and Canada. It is serious in jack pine in the Lake States, and in Douglas-fir, alpine fir, white fir, Engelmann spruce, blue spruce, lodgepole pine, and ponderosa pine in the West.

It is native to North America. Records of its ravages in the East date from about 1805. It appeared again in epidemic proportions about 1880.

The first outbreak to be studied carefully began in Quebec in 1909, appeared in Maine in 1910 and in New Brunswick and Minnesota in 1913, continued for nearly a decade, and destroyed more than 250 million cords of spruce and fir pulpwood. About 30 million cords were killed in Maine; in Minnesota, more than 20 million cords were destroyed.

But all that devastation, all that destruction may be nothing compared to a current outbreak in Canada that began to assume epidemic proportions in 1935. By 1944, it was estimated, 125 million acres in Ontario were infested. In 1945, an official of a Canadian pulp and paper company said, the insect killed enough timber to supply all Canadian pulp mills for 3 years. By 1947 most of the mature fir and a considerable part of the white spruce on an estimated 20,000 square miles had been killed, with less intense damage over a much larger area. The dead trees have created a tremendous fire hazard; large areas affected by the budworm already have been burned.

The memory of the previous outbreak in Maine and the present situation in Canada have caused great alarm among owners of timberland and officials of the pulp and paper industry in the Northeast. At stake in the region are nearly 19 million acres of spruce-fir and more than 100 million cords of pulpwood. On that timber supply depend more than 90 mills, which have an annual capacity of 3½ million cords, employ more than 55,000 workers, and manufacture goods worth more than 300 million dollars annually.

Because of the serious threat to the pulp and paper industry, the timberland owners asked Congress for funds to find ways to control the insect and to prevent widespread damage such as had occurred in Canada. The funds were voted, and in July 1944, two units of the Department of Agriculture, the Bureau of Entomology and Plant Quarantine and the Forest Service, began a program to study the problem in all its phases and develop a plan of action for the Northeast. Surveys in which the States cooperated indicated that few specimens of the spruce budworm were present then in New England forests.

But in 1945 we discovered an infestation in the Adirondacks of New York. The next year we found many more, and an outbreak seemed imminent. In 1947 and 1948, however, the population of spruce budworm dropped markedly. Over most of the area, defoliation was not severe enough to cause appreciable damage to spruce and fir. During 1945, 1946, and 1947, the insect remained at an extremely low population level in Vermont, New Hampshire, and Maine. The 1948 survey showed a low degree of abundance in Vermont and New Hampshire but a definite increase in Maine. No report of unusual abundance of the budworm has been received from the Lake States. Extensive outbreaks were in progress in 1948 in the southern, central, and northern Rocky Mountain regions and in Oregon and Washington.

From 1945 to 1948 intensive studies in biological and natural control of the insect were conducted in New York.

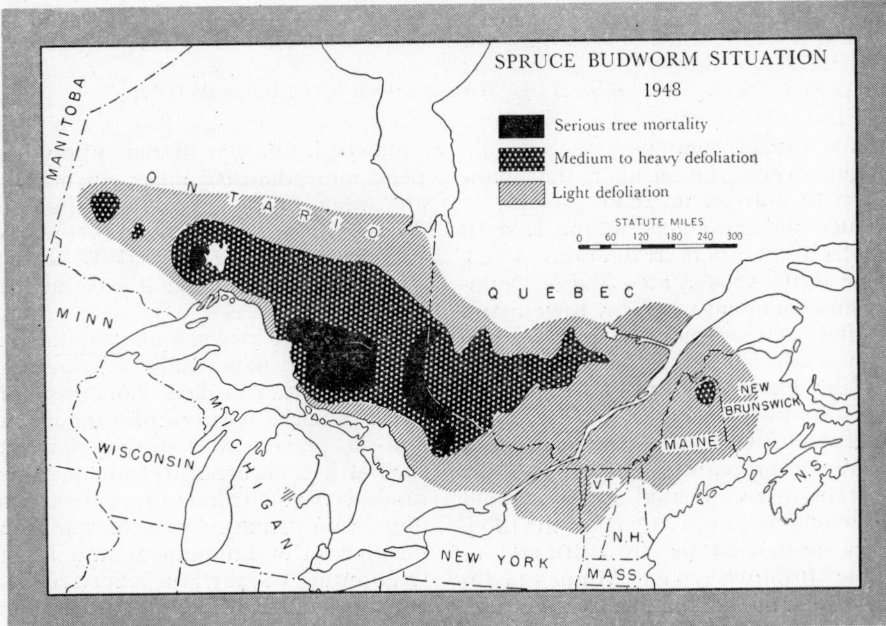


Plots and experimental areas were established in the Northeast to determine the degree of defoliation and damage caused under different forest conditions. In the Rocky Mountains there are several species of parasites of the budworm that do not occur in the East; several colonies of those parasites were obtained and released in eastern forests in the hope that they would become established.

The spruce-fir stands in the Adirondacks, relatively small in area, usually are surrounded by hardwoods. Such stands seem particularly favorable for natural control. Winter mortality during 1946–47 was approximately 75 percent. Aggregate parasitization by insect enemies ranged from 64 to 86 percent in different area. The total aggregate mortality from winterkill and parasites ranged from 83 to 98 percent. Insectivorous birds also destroyed large numbers of budworm larvae and pupae. Certainly those factors of natural control contributed tremendously in bringing about the decline in budworm infestation in 1947 in New York.

The seasonal history of a pest must be known before control measures can be undertaken.

The adult of the spruce budworm is a small moth with a wing spread of seven-eighths of an inch. Its general color is grayish with brown markings.

In the Northeastern States the moths start emerging from their pupal cases about July 1. The females deposit their pale-green eggs on the foliage in masses of 10 to 50 or more, where they overlap like the scales of a fish. One female may lay several of these egg masses and on the average produces about 175 eggs. The incubation period lasts about 10 days.

After the eggs hatch, the young caterpillars crawl about until they find suitable places under bark or bud scales to spin silken weblike coverings, or hibernacula, under which they spend the following fall and winter. These tiny larvae do not feed until they become active in late April or early May and leave their hibernacula. At first they are an orange yellow; later they turn brownish. They mine the old needles first; then they enter the opening buds, where they feed on the tender young needles which are just starting growth. They also feed on spruce and fir pollen. As the new shoots elongate, the larvae tie the needles together with silken threads and thus form shelters within which they feed. By late June they are full-grown, reddish brown in color, and start forming the pupal cases, which are attached to the twigs. The pupal period lasts 7 to 10 days, after which the moths emerge and start laying eggs—a new generation is under way.

The spruce budworm may spread over long distances to new areas by flights of the moths. Records of the 1910–19 outbreak show that in July 1911 swarms of moths appeared in Philadelphia and in 1912 and 1913 they were abundant in Connecticut. Those localities are outside the general spruce-fir range, so the presence of the moths there had significance only in showing how far they travel.

The regions where extensive tree mortality has already occurred in the present outbreak and the extent of the active infestations are shown on the accompanying map. There is no record of a flight of moths in 1944 from Canada that might have caused the outbreak conditions discovered in New York in 1945. Apparently, though, a heavy infestation arose simultaneously over an area of approximately 3,000 square miles, and careful study of the area in 1945 pointed strongly to the possibility of a widespread flight of moths in 1944.

During an outbreak period, a heavily infested tree may harbor thousands of caterpillars. Except when the young caterpillars first resume activity in the spring and form mines in the old needles, the new foliage is the preferred food and it is entirely devoured before the old foliage is eaten.

In heavy infestations the trees first exhibit a scorched appearance. Later they turn grayish as the foliage disappears. Finally dead tops become evident. A heavy defoliation for several years will reduce the volume of foliage to a degree where many of the caterpillars die from starvation and the budworm population declines, but in the meantime many of the trees will have died. Following the decline of the insect in a particular area, the loss of trees continues for several years, because secondary insects and fungi have a part in killing weakened trees.

The feeding habits of the spruce budworm determine to a large measure the damage in various types of stands.

The caterpillars show a definite preference for fir in that they develop readily on both old and current growth. Although the budworm feeds readily and develops rapidly on pollen from fir trees, the presence or absence of abundant staminate flowers has little effect on the budworm population in the forest. The lack of synchronism between budworm development and opening of buds and the poor survival on old foliage of red and black spruce indicate that these two species are less favorable food plants than balsam fir. This fundamental information on the biology and feeding habits of the spruce budworm and the fact that mortality in all species of attacked trees is directly proportional to the lack of vigor at the time of defoliation give us a basis for formulating methods for the silvicultural control of this insect.

Investigations made during and after the disastrous outbreak of 1910–19 in New Brunswick and Maine indicated that the greatest mortality of trees occurred in the red spruce-balsam fir type, particularly where the fir predominated and was overmature.

Little damage occurred in the mixed hardwood-spruce fir stands, where the hardwoods overtopped the conifers.

White and black spruce appeared to suffer less from attack than red spruce and fir.

The results of the earlier studies and the intensive work of Canadian and American entomologists during the present outbreak point the way toward a possible solution.

To view the problem in perspective, one might well review some of the factors that have brought about the present condition of the spruce-fir forests.

Because spruce is far more valuable for lumber and pulp than balsam fir, it has been cut more heavily in logging and pulpwood operations and its proportion in the forests has thus been reduced. Balsam is far more aggressive than spruce in seeding-in after a cutting operation, fire, or wind damage. Foresters repeatedly have observed that after a serious budworm outbreak the succeeding stand invariably contains a higher proportion of balsam. Man's activity and the spruce budworm, therefore, have often contributed to a gradual conversion from a forest containing a high percentage of spruce to one in which balsam predominates and which is far more favorable for the budworm.

In view of such points, then, what can be done through silvicultural practices to increase the resistance of the forest to spruce budworm attack?

There appear to be three general procedures: To clear cut mature and over-mature balsam stands; to operate balsam stands on a short rotation; to try to increase the proportion of spruce in the stand.

The first and second would be aimed at keeping existing stands of fir as young and vigorous as possible. Mature and overmature balsam fir trees suffer most during an outbreak. It is not because their foliage is more palatable to budworm caterpillars than the leaves of more vigorous trees, but because they are low in vigor and cannot survive severe defoliation. The clear cutting of such stands should be given first priority in a plan of action.

In a long-range program to build up the resistance to future budworm outbreaks, consideration needs to be given to two major types of stands, those that are predominantly balsam fir and those that contain an appreciable proportion of spruce.

In a stand that is mostly balsam, cutting on a rotation of 30 or preferably 20 years will help to maintain the stand in a condition of high vigor. Such a stand may harbor a heavy population of budworms, but it will suffer much less than a stand of low vigor. The operation of such a stand on short rotation will at the same time greatly increase the ultimate yield.

Where spruce occupies an appreciable proportion of the stand, every effort should be made through cutting operations to increase the proportion of spruce and at the same time save only the balsam firs that are very vigorous.

In order to demonstrate these cutting methods, experimental areas are being established jointly by the Forest Service, the Bureau of Entomology and Plant Quarantine, the States, and the owners of timberland in the Northeast. The areas are cruised and marked by the Federal agencies and operated by industry. They are located in several parts of the region, so that the influences and different site and stand conditions can be observed.

In these silvicultural operations, the latest findings from the biological studies are put into practice. We hope that the experimental areas will become a pattern for future commercial operations so that resistant forests eventually will be established all over the Northeast.

In sum, then, we know that each new epidemic is far more disastrous than the last, and that now the spruce-fir resources of this country and Canada are in jeopardy.

Aerial applications of insecticides offer new possibilities for controlling defoliators like the spruce budworm; further attempts to control the insect over extensive areas by aerial spraying are now in progress and will be continued during the present outbreak.

But all studies and observations by entomologists and foresters suggest that the ultimate solution lies in managing the forest so as to maintain high vigor in balsam fir stands and, where conditions permit, to increase the proportion of spruce. Every effort should be made to obtain the basic biological information useful in developing silvicultural practices that will create conditions unfavorable for the development of outbreaks or minimize damage during an outbreak.

R. C. BROWN *is an entomologist in the Bureau of Entomology and Plant Quarantine. He was graduated from the University of New Hampshire in 1922 and has been in the Bureau since 1925. In 1935 he was put in charge of the Division of Forest Insect Investigations laboratory in New Haven.*

H. J. MACALONEY *assists Mr. Brown at New Haven and has charge of studies in the application of biological information as it affects silvicultural practices. He was graduated from the New York State College of Forestry at Syracuse University in 1923 and has been in the Division of Forest Insect Investigations since 1925.*

P. B. DOWDEN *also assists Mr. Brown. He was graduated from Massachusetts State College in 1923 and has been with the Bureau of Entomology and Plant Quarantine since that time. He is in charge of the biological-control investigations on forest insects conducted at the New Haven laboratory in Connecticut.*

# PINE BARK BEETLES

F. P. KEEN

Pine bark beetles are small, dark-colored, hard-shelled insects of the size of a grain of rice or a medium-sized bean. They bore under the bark of various pines and dig egg tunnels, mostly in the inner bark, which cut the cambium layer—a tree's most vital tissue. Eggs laid along the sides of these tunnels hatch into small, white, legless grubs. Under the bark also the attacking beetles introduce fungi, blue stains, and yeasts, which penetrate the sapwood and plug the sap stream from roots to foliage. The tree is hurt in the same way that an animal would be injured or killed if worms were to bore into it and stop up all veins and arteries.

When the larvae complete their feeding in the inner bark, they change into pupae, the resting stage, then to new adults. These adults later emerge from the bark and fly off to attack other pines. Thus they perpetuate their species and continue their destructive course. The new adults may attack the green trees nearby, or they may fly several miles to find trees to attack.

A great many different kinds of beetles work into and under the bark of pines. The most destructive bark beetle enemies of American forest trees are the so-called pine beetles (*Dendroctonus* spp.), which attack primarily the more mature trees, and engraver beetles (*Ips* spp.), which prefer young trees or the tops of older ones. Species of *Dendroctonus* and *Ips* are found throughout North America.

The more important species of *Dendroctonus* that attack pine are the western pine beetle (*D. brevicomis* Lec.), which attacks ponderosa pine and Coulter pine in the Pacific States, Idaho, Montana, and British Columbia; the southern pine beetle (*D. frontalis* Zimm.), which attacks all species of pines and spruce from Pennsylvania south to Florida and west to Arkansas and Texas; the mountain pine beetle (*D. monticolae* Hopk.), which attacks lodgepole pine, western white pine, sugar pine, and other pines in the Pacific States and northern Rocky Mountain regions; the Black Hills beetle (*D. ponderosae* Hopk.), which attacks ponderosa and lodgepole pines in the southern and central Rocky Mountain regions and in the Black Hills of South Dakota; the Jeffrey pine beetle (*D. jeffreyi* Hopk.), which attacks Jeffrey pine in California; and the turpentine beetles (*D.*

*valens* Lec. and *D. terebrans* Oliv.), which attack all species of pines but usually can overcome only weakened and injured trees.

The engraver beetles (*Ips* spp.) attack all species of pines, breed readily in the tops of recently felled trees and in slash, usually develop large populations, and then move into the tops of living pines, frequently killing trees in large groups. Various species are found in different parts of the country, but they all have similar habits.

Forestry was young in America when it was discovered that pine bark beetles were forest destroyers of the first magnitude. In the first official report on forestry, submitted to Congress in 1877, Franklin B. Hough, the first Government forest officer in the United States, directed attention to the considerable injury done to the pines of South Carolina by bark beetles, and referred to an occurrence of their activity as early as 1802. Again, during the first survey and classification of lands of the newly created Forest Reserves by the United States Geological Survey in 1898, H. B. Ayres reported serious damage caused by pine beetles to the white pine stands in Montana. In 1900 the first field organization of foresters, working under Gifford Pinchot, found bark beetles killing thousands of trees in the Black Hills. As a result of this epidemic, which killed more than a billion board feet of pine timber, Dr. A. D. Hopkins, State entomologist of West Virginia, was called on to investigate and recommend measures of control for this and other forest pests.

So began in the United States a problem in forest protection that ever since has challenged the ingenuity of entomologists and foresters. For it quickly became evident that these were not isolated cases of insect damage but typical examples of what a group of insect enemies could do in many forest stands. Over a long period, the havoc that bark beetles have wrought has resulted in a greater total drain of commercial pine timber than has been sustained from any other destructive agency.

In primitive, unmanaged forests, pine bark beetles act as nature's forest managers and loggers. Young stands that have become too crowded and suffer from competition and stagnation are frequently thinned by outbreaks of engraver beetles. In the older stands, the weak, intermediate, and suppressed trees are cut out by pine beetles. And as growing forests reach maturity, the old trees that have escaped fire and storm are harvested by pine bark beetles, and young trees then come up to replace them.

In the development of forest succession, pine beetles often have a prominent part. When fir-hemlock stands of the Cascade Mountain Range are wiped out by fire, for example, lodgepole or western white pine come in as temporary species to reestablish a forest cover. When these stands get to be about 100 years old, the more tolerant fir and hemlock again become established under them. Then the mountain pine beetle appears to act as nature's forester. An epidemic conveniently eliminates about 95 percent of the pine overstory and thus aids the process of reestablishing the fir-hemlock climax.

On the other hand, the western pine beetle in ponderosa pine makes a selection cutting of certain intermediate, suppressed, and codominant trees that are growing too slowly. In the forest, group killings make holes, which are filled in by young seedlings. This process tends toward the development and maintenance of uneven-aged stands.

The trouble is that beetles are crude forest managers. Often they go too far in thinning and eliminating competing trees. They kill and waste much sound lumber. Holes left in the forest stand may take many years to fill. If we are to maintain and utilize our forest resources, we cannot afford to allow these natural processes to run their course, and yet we are often responsible for starting and encouraging them through forest mismanagement.

BECAUSE BARK BEETLES are constantly at work in pine forests—thinning, harvesting, and wiping out entire stands of timber to make room for new ones—they destroy on the whole a vast amount of commercially valuable timber. In the long run they are no threat to forest perpetuation, but they do take a tremendous toll of wood that we need badly. In some pine areas, this loss occurs as a slow but steady annual drain of merchantable trees spread over a long period of years. In other areas, the losses are more spectacular because they result from epidemic infestations that kill a fairly high percentage of the stand in just a few years. But regardless of the rate at which they occur, these beetle-caused losses affect directly the potential lumber output of pine-producing areas and indirectly the taxable wealth and pay rolls of entire communities. Estimates based on surveys in the major pine regions of the Western States are that during the period from 1926 to 1946 the western pine beetle, the Black Hills beetle, and the mountain pine beetle killed over 50 million board feet of pine.

Just as important is the damage the beetles cause to scenic and property values in our parks and summer-home areas. Mainly for that reason do people lament the extensive outbreaks of mountain pine beetle in lodgepole pine and white pine stands of Yosemite, Crater Lake, Mount Rainier, Glacier, and Yellowstone National Parks.

True, those forests will be replaced in time by other forests of the same or different types, but for many years these ghost forests of white snags are gaunt lessons of forest destruction rather than forest preservation.

Another bad feature is that the snags left by the beetles increase fire hazards. Vast areas of beetle-killed lodgepole pine are a particularly critical fire menace; some of the worst forest fires on record have occurred in these bug-killed localities.

THE CAUSES of epidemics of pine bark beetles we do not fully understand—any more than we understand the reasons for grasshopper plagues or influenza epidemics. We do know that bark beetles can increase their populations at a lightning rate—10, 20, even 500 to 1 in a single generation—but usually natural factors like parasites, predators, unfavorable weather, or the lack of suitable food keep them from doing so. When susceptible host material is abundant, however, and natural controls are ineffective, then beetles reproduce to capacity, and an outbreak occurs.

Probably the most important factor in building up beetle populations to epidemic numbers is an abundance of suitable breeding material. Just a forest of pine trees is not enough. The beetles prefer certain trees that are in a susceptible condition for attack. Such trees are the ones that are making poor growth or those that are injured and weakened by fire, windstorms, and by other causes. Recently felled trees are especially attractive to the beetles. Weakened trees can offer little resistance by pitch flow when the beetles attack and bore through to the inner bark. When their populations are low, the beetles continually select and thrive in those weak trees; when the beetles find many such trees, they usually multiply rapidly. Either natural causes or disturbances of forest conditions brought about by man's activities can cause an abundance of this susceptible host material in pine forests.

Fire-weakened trees are often favored as breeding ground by certain bark beetles, which then turn out large populations that threaten surrounding forests. To the extent that man fails to control or is responsible for forest fires, he can be charged also with the pine bark beetle damage.

Drought frequently weakens pine trees and makes them susceptible to attack. Defoliating insects also slow tree growth, reduce vigor, and make trees an easy prey to the beetles. Most pine stands also become more susceptible as they reach maturity.

In any pine forest a rapid increase of bark beetles may develop in any of these various types of favored food material. When the supply of susceptible trees becomes exhausted, the beetles are forced to turn to healthy and vigorous trees, which they overcome by sheer force of numbers. Bark beetle epidemics, once they develop, continue until brought under control by natural forces or by artificial-control measures.

THE NATURAL-CONTROL FACTORS keep some in check. Besides the limitations of food supply, disease, and unfavorable weather that restrict the populations of bark beetles, they have a number of insect enemies. Parasites and predators feed upon and destroy the bark beetles. Also, many species of birds catch beetles when they are in flight. Certain species of woodpeckers go after beetle larvae which are in or under the bark.

Bark beetles can stand heat up to about 120° F. and so they are rarely killed by hot weather, unless on the top side of a log fully exposed to the sun. But they cannot stand subzero temperatures, unless they have had time to acclimatize themselves. Overwintering broods of western pine beetle start to die at about 5° and are hard-hit at −20°.

And so it is that while the vigorous broods, free from too many parasitic insects, predators, and woodpeckers, are necessary for an outbreak, they must also have ample breeding grounds of slash, windfalls, drought-stricken trees, or susceptible stands. If both sets of conditions are favorable, a major epidemic is inevitable, and much timber will be sacrificed to the hungry hordes.

Fifty years of research has brought real progress in our ability to deal with the infestations. Many control methods have been tried. Some have been effective. Newer methods have been found and put to good use. Most significant of all advances is the growing interest and activity of private and public owners of pine forests in bark beetle control as a conservation measure.

THE FIRST OFFENSIVES against the beetle infestations were designed to destroy the beetle populations in infested trees and thus to prevent them from emerging and attacking more trees. The strategy was based on the concept that dead beetles cannot kill trees. On an area to be protected, infested trees were located in the fall, winter, and spring when the beetles and their broods were dormant. Then the insects were destroyed, usually by felling the dead trees and burning the bark.

Beginning with the relatively small project to control the Black Hills beetle in 1905, a long series of control campaigns have been carried on. The work has involved nearly all species of pine beetles and pine-producing regions. Some of the work has consisted of small routine control jobs, undertaken and completed by local forest officers or owners of summer homes; others have been large cooperative projects over thousands of acres, made possible by many individual ownerships. During the period of the Civilian Conservation Corps, the battle was carried on as part of the forest-conservation program wherever serious infestations were encountered. Recent outbreaks of mountain pine beetles and Black Hills beetles in the northern Rocky Mountains have again led to the initiation of large-scale projects.

In their unceasing effort to find new and better ways of disposing of the beetles, entomologists have explored all possibilities—from the simple expedient of hitting the beetles with an ax to radio waves and complicated electrical traps, from burning the infested bark to hauling infested trees out of the forest area and dunking them in millponds.

Toxic oils sprayed on infested bark have been used to avoid the costs and fire hazards of peeling and burning it. Fuel-oil solutions of naphthalene, orthodichlorobenzene, and of paradichlorobenzene have proved effective against the mountain pine beetle, the Black Hills beetle, and *Ips* in lodgepole pine and other thin-barked trees. New insecticides, especially DDT, have greatly increased the effectiveness of oil-spray formulas. Burning unpeeled infested trees with the aid of cheap fuel oils, and even with "goop," developed for use in incendiary bombs in the Second World War, also has been tried. Infested lodgepole pines have been burned while still standing by spraying the trunks with fuel oil, igniting it, and following up with more oil until the bark was thoroughly charred. Where conditions permitted, power saws and bulldozers have been used to fell, move, and prepare trees for burning. Mechanized equipment has been used to haul infested trees to the sawmill where the infested bark was destroyed and the logs converted into lumber. All these methods have limitations. No one method has been developed that can be used under all conditions.

INDIRECT CONTROL can help. About 1924, entomologists and foresters began working on a different approach. They studied the characteristics of trees that were attacked by the western pine beetle and found that the beetles preferred to attack slow growers and trees below normal in growth functions. Such trees could be distinguished easily from healthy, vigorous trees in the form, density, and thrift of the crowns. An off color of the needles and dieback of twigs, limbs, and tops further indicated susceptibility. The entomologists learned from their studies and experimental selective-logging operations that losses could be lessened by removing part or all of these susceptible trees from the stand. The term "sanitation salvage" has come into use to designate this new type of control. Timber companies, which were quick to try it, found that the practice could pay its way through the sale of lumber products from sound but vulnerable trees that otherwise would be killed by beetles and left to rot in the woods.

Sanitation salvage has given excellent results in controlling western pine beetles. Areas so salvaged a decade ago still show a substantial differential between the number of trees attacked and the losses on untreated areas. This 10-year period, however, does not include any test of the method during an epidemic infestation. What will happen then remains to be demonstrated.

So far, the criteria by which high-risk trees can be distinguished have been developed only for the ponderosa and Jeffrey pines found in forests east of the Sierra Nevada and Cascade Mountains. Studies are under way to develop similar criteria for indirect control of bark beetles affecting other pine types, which for the present can only be controlled through the application of direct-control measures. A method similar to sanitation salvage has been developed and is being put into practice for western white pine stands in Idaho, where selective logging of low-vigor trees reduces the amount of timber killed by the mountain pine beetle.

The continuing search for new and better methods to control the pine bark beetles seeks to keep pace with the development of sound forest-management practices and is in the direction of improving methods of surveys to detect outbreaks in their early stages and to determine the susceptibility or bark beetle hazard of various pine stands, developing better methods of direct control, particularly through the use of the newer insecticides, and developing forest-management practices adjusted to avoiding or limiting bark beetle outbreaks.

Use of the airplane in the surveys is a new development that will make possible the detection of small outbreaks in inaccessible areas before they develop into large ones. Surveys from the ground will always be necessary to follow up aerial observations.

Of greatest value to the entire survey system is the study and classification of pine areas according to expectation of bark beetle infestations. This classification of pine stands, known as a hazard survey, has been carried out only for a small part of the ponderosa pine region. This work is basic to plans for control through management and is needed throughout much of the western pine region.

The possibilities for finding better chemical methods for destroying bark beetles have by no means been exhausted. During the war, many new insecticides came into prominence, among them DDT, benzene hexachloride, and chlordane. They are now being tested in forests, and it is probable that a place will be found for some of them in the control of bark beetles.

But the greatest hope lies in better forest management. Pine silviculture must take into account the habits of the beetles themselves; by studying this behavior, we should obtain a better understanding of nature's methods of thinning, pruning, and harvesting. Then, by "beating the beetles to it" and imitating nature at her best, we should be able to develop sound silvicultural practices which will avoid further destruction from these small insects.

F. P. Keen, *a graduate of the University of California, is senior entomologist of the Bureau of Entomology and Plant Quarantine in charge of the Forest Insect Investigations Laboratory at Berkeley, Calif. His experience with bark beetle problems in the western pine region covers 34 years. He is author of a number of technical papers and bulletins on forest insects. In 1947 he received the Department's Superior Service Award for his development of a ponderosa pine tree classification, which is used as an index to the susceptibility of pine stands to bark beetle damage and as a guide to tree selection on timber sales.*

# INSECTS IN WOOD PRODUCTS

THOMAS E. SNYDER

Insects attack the forest tree in all stages of its life, from seed to maturity. The log that is cut from the tree also is vulnerable in all its stages to attack by other kinds of wood-boring insects—while it is still in the woods, while it is green or seasoned lumber at the mill, or is being stored, or, indeed, after it has been put to use in a house, barn, or a manufactured item.

The insects that bore into lumber cause losses of many kinds and degrees. Sometimes much of the wood is riddled by holes. Sometimes it is entirely pulverized so as to be completely unusable. Sometimes only the quality of the wood is lowered by the holes so that the grade is reduced. Certain stain fungi, carried by bark beetles and borers, discolor the logs and lumber; they do not affect performance, but the wood becomes unsuitable for outside and decorative purposes. After the lumber, pole, or other wood product is in use, insect damage is even more serious, because then the loss includes the costs of production, seasoning, storage, and replacement.

Two types of insects are primarily responsible. One requires wet wood; the other dry wood. Sometimes the injury is one caused by the adult beetles which fly to the log or lumber and bore directly into the wood. At other times the damage is caused by the young hatching from eggs laid under the bark or in the wood.

Adult ambrosia beetles—so-called because they require green or moist wood within which they raise fungi for food—rapidly penetrate green logs and lumber. The males may assist the females in forming new colonies, and the fungus is raised for the young to eat. They have the beginning of a social life, but do not develop different forms or castes as do the true social insects, the termites, ants, and bees. The holes, not more than one-sixteenth of an inch in diameter, are made by the adult beetles. They riddle the wood, and near them the wood is stained black. Serious losses to tight cooperage or barrel stock and balsa wood for marine life rafts and a lowering in grade of valuable lumber for veneer to be used in houses, boats, or airplanes result from their boring and staining.

Larger holes—more than one-fourth of an inch in diameter—are caused by the young of large beetles. These young are called sawyers because their borings in green logs result in piles of sawdust, as if the wood had been sawed by man. Their gnawing can be heard, and their activity is so conspicuous that it is hard to convince a tree owner that it was not this insect that killed his pines. Actually, it was the small, grain-sized bark beetles, often associated with a stain fungus, that girdled the inner bark and shut off the food and moisture supply of the tree and caused its death, thus preparing it for the larger borers.

Some types of insects need dry wood for their food. Among them are many kinds, sizes, and shapes of powder-post beetles, which pulverize wood and have other odd habits. One kind specializes in boring into wine and whiskey barrels. Another drills into and around lead-sheathed cables, unmindful of the short circuits that result when moisture penetrates the insulation. Some years ago one kind, like a weevil, damaged the trusses in the roof of the White House. An odd lot, indeed.

An extremely destructive kind is the *Lyctus* powder-post beetles, small, winged beetles that lay their elongate eggs in the pores of the sapwood of certain large-pored hardwoods but do not attack the heartwood. They go after dry or seasoned sapwood of such hardwoods as hickory, ash, oak, and walnut lumber; manufactured products like tool handles, gun stocks, tent stakes, wooden artillery wheels, wagon spokes, oars, and other products stored for long periods; and, sometimes, furniture, woodwork, flooring, and timber in homes. The young reduce the wood fibers to a powder from which all strength is gone. The presence of these insects is usually betrayed by small piles of fine powder expelled from the burrows by the young. These beetles relish items like dry ax handles because they find the wood rich in starch and quite suitable for raising their families.

But the ones that give householders the most gray hairs and sleepless nights are termites, the most destructive of all. In the United States they are of two main types. The subterranean kind, which is the worse, requires much moisture and attacks wood indirectly from the moist soil. The dry-wood termites directly attack dry wood. They are injurious only in southern California and Florida and normally do not occur in the Northern States. Termites damage buildings of all types, various kinds of stored materials, poles, posts, derricks, mine props, and many another. By their boring, also, they riddle or corrode with their moist excrement many materials that they cannot eat. Often, however, termites can be easily and cheaply controlled.

PRECAUTIONARY MEASURES in handling the green wood and lumber can eliminate much of the damage by the insects that prefer them. The measures are rapid moving, seasoning, sorting, and periodic inspection.

The logs should be handled quickly, with a minimum of delay between felling the log and stacking the lumber for drying. Drying the lumber, in the air or in a kiln, will stop the insects from boring. Any damage that has been done to the wood usually will not affect its strength. It is termed "sound wormy grade."

As for the beetles that prefer seasoned wood: Because only the sapwood is susceptible to them, sapwood and part sapwood should be sorted and piled separately from the heartwood. The stacks of sapwood then should be

802062°—49——29

dated so that the oldest or longest seasoned wood can be used first. The drier the wood, the more appetizing it is to the powder-post beetles.

Further protection can be gained by periodic inspections of the stock so that infested material can be removed for burning or treatment. This is a live-worm defect, and the insects will continue to bore until the product is destroyed or they are controlled.

Some woods have chemicals in their cells that protect them from insects, and heartwood is more resistant than sapwood. So, because insects are ready to pounce even after the wood is safely through storage and has been put to use, it is sensible to select carefully the species and grades that fit exactly the purpose at hand.

Whenever possible, one should use the heartwood of the more naturally durable or insect-resistant and rot-resistant woods instead of the perishable woods. Resistant woods like foundation-grade redwood, the southern tidewater red cypress, and the mahogany contain alcohols, alkaloids, gums, resins, or bitter essences that makes them distasteful to boring insects. Some kinds of wood that are not subject to attack by certain wood borers but are adapted for the same use should be substituted for susceptible kinds. For example, yellow pine or Douglas-fir can be used instead of oak for storage pallets to prevent losses by *Lyctus* powder-post beetles.

The relative termite resistance of certain native and exotic—particularly tropical American—untreated timbers has been determined by long-time service tests conducted in the United States and in the Canal Zone.

Among those commercially available in the United States are close-grained heartwood foundation-grade California redwood, southern tidewater red cypress, and very pitchy southern longleaf pine. The information from the long-time service tests also permits the recommendation of naturally resistant woods for use in building or bridge construction where chemically impregnated timber is not locally available, especially in the various tropical regions of the world. Greenheart, manbarklak, and guayacan of the Americas, teak and sal of India, molave and ipil of the Philippines, and cypress-pine, brush-box, and turpentine wood of New South Wales are a few of the woods found to be termite-resistant.

Termite-proof foundations can be constructed—on the basis of field research on the habits of termites and their control. The research, including studies of proper drainage of building sites, grading necessary to secure sufficient clearance between construction timbers and the earth in which termites live, the role of wood debris in the soil, soil moisture, temperature and humidity in the building of earthlike shelter tubes by termites over foundations, and measurements and exact location of ventilation openings, has led to safe construction.

Sound foundations can be constructed by the use of proper grades of mortar for masonry units and impenetrable coal-tar pitches for sealing expansion joints and vertical piping that project through concrete.

Porches, steps, and the like that have an earthen fill can be sealed off or separated from the main structure. On the basis of tests of mortars, expansion-joint seals, and barriers, specifications for termite-proof foundations have been written for various government agencies charged with housing construction. The measures recommended will protect structures from attack by termites for a slight additional cost. Advice given on the job to Federal housing officials proved particularly useful before and during the Second World War and resulted in more durable buildings than those erected at the time of the First World War.

New building materials were tested for the Housing and Home Finance Agency in an effort to speed postwar construction. Many proved to be more or less susceptible to termite attack. In accelerated laboratory tests, the research men discovered the susceptibility to termite attack of light wall panels made of paper honeycomb, impregnated with a synthetic resin and covered with thin sheets of aluminum; fiberboard made from palmetto; and wall panel made of pressed excelsior, bonded with an inorganic cement. Such materials need not be considered unsuitable for construction, but they do need further chemical protection or should be used in buildings for which termite-proof construction has been provided. Some of the honeycomb panels apparently become weakened more rapidly than untreated wood.

Sometimes chemicals must be used—sprays, dips, wood preservatives, soil poisons, poison dusts, or toxic fumigants. Chemicals suitable for preserving structural timbers have been available for years, but only recently were effective and lasting chemicals discovered for use as sprays or dips to protect green logs as well as green and seasoning lumber from borer attack.

DDT and benzene hexachloride in oil solutions are effective in preventing attack by bark beetles, sawyers, and ambrosia beetles in green logs and lumber.

Benzene hexachloride is better than DDT against ambrosia beetles.

Borax and microfine sulfur in water solution or suspension have been recommended to the Army for use as protective dips against *Lyctus* powder-post beetles for unseasoned implement handle stock.

For seasoned tool handles, pentachlorphenol in oil solution has been specified as a preventive dip.

Solutions of DDT are effective in protecting bamboo and tool handles, but such preventive dips do not stop rot or decay. The pentachlorphenol protects against both insects and decay.

Powder-post beetles infesting buildings or furniture can be controlled by pentachlorphenol sprays.

Tests in this country and in the Tropics of new chemical wood preservatives disclosed that copper naphthenate and pentachlorphenol protect ammunition boxes, crates, pallets, and the like from attack by wood-boring insects.

The arsenicals and pentachlorphenol give effective protection against termites when used as integral treatments during manufacture for fiberboards.

Poisoning the soil about the foundation of buildings is useful as a supplementary treatment against termites where structural insulation is not practicable. Suitable for such a purpose are arsenicals, chlorinated phenols, chlorinated benzenes, DDT-in-oil solution, and many other chemicals. Different types of soil and moisture conditions, types of construction, and cost determine which to use. Only odorless soil poisons should be used in places where food is near or in enclosed areas that are poorly ventilated.

Government research men and members of the National Pest Control Association have written standard specifications for the control of termites in buildings. Included were structural and chemical methods of protection, somewhat as outlined here.

The specifications have helped the industry and the public—all hands except the termites.

In southern California members of the pest-control industry recently conducted cooperative tests with the Bureau of Entomology and Plant Quarantine to discover more effective liquid chemical sprays or dusts for the control of dry-wood or nonsubterranean termites. During these experiments it was shown that isolated buildings tightly sealed with heavy paper can be rid of the dry-wood termites or powder-post beetles by fumigation with heavy dosages of hydrocyanic acid gas or methyl bromide. Fairly long periods of fumigation and forced aeration are required. *This is dangerous work that should be done only by professional fumigators.* Special precautions must be taken to protect the building, material stored therein, and human life.

Even though this method requires professional assistance, it is more effective, practicable, and cheaper in destroying heavy, hidden, deep-seated infestations than the use of liquid chemicals or poison dusts or the replacement of infested areas with chemically impregnated wood. Fumigation will not prevent reinfestation.

THOMAS E. SNYDER, *a senior entomologist in the Division of Forest Insect Investigations, Bureau of Entomology and Plant Quarantine, has devoted 40 years to the study of insects that attack forest products and ways to control them. He has published numerous articles on termites, powder-post beetles, ambrosia beetles, and the chemical wood preservatives. Dr. Snyder is an authority on the classification of termites. He has degrees from Columbia, Yale, and George Washington Universities.*

# CONTROLLING THE TUSSOCK MOTH

PAUL H. ROBERTS, JAMES C. EVENDEN

In the field headquarters at Moscow, Idaho, a tense group of men were waiting for the signal that was to start the greatest of all airplane offensives against an insect. It was 3 o'clock on the morning of May 22, 1947. The sun had not yet limned the mountain majesty of northern Idaho and neighboring Washington or the desolation wrought in the forests by the tussock moth. The report came: Weather clear; wind velocity 5 miles an hour. It was relayed to the Laird Park airstrip and the municipal airport at Moscow, the seat of the University of Idaho, and nearby Pullman, the seat of Washington State College.

At 3:20 a. m. the big C–47 trundled onto the runway, roared through a short take-off, then rose and turned toward the rough terrain of Moscow Mountain to spread 1,000 gallons of DDT spray over 1,000 acres of infested fir timber. The Ford trimotors followed. Simultaneously the small planes at the Laird Park airstrip went out, one at a time.

They were after the Douglas-fir tussock moth (*Hemerocampa pseudotsugata* McD.), which early in 1946 appeared in epidemic proportions throughout a large forest area near Moscow, Idaho. A native of northwestern United States and southeastern Canada, the small insect can kill its preferred hosts, Douglas-fir and the true firs, in a year if it destroys all the foliage; partial defoliation may result in serious top killing and the death of trees if it continues for several years.

In its life cycle this insect produces but one generation each year. Eggs are laid in August and September and hatch the following spring in late May. The tiny caterpillars are active and will travel relatively long distances in search of food. They become full-grown by late August, pupate, and transform to new adults in about 2 weeks. As the female moths are wingless, eggs are usually laid on or near the pupal case from which the moths have emerged. Any widespread distribution of an infestation must be by means other than the flight of adult moths. It is known that the young, hairy caterpillars are carried long distances by air currents. When disturbed, they drop from the limbs and hang suspended on a fine silken thread often 5 feet or more in length, which they spin as they fall. This thread and the body hairs of the caterpillar offer considerable wind resistance, and air currents of about 10 miles an hour will carry them away.

By early summer of 1946 whole mountainsides appeared brown from defoliation of trees by the insect. In the Idaho territory these brown areas intensified public concern as to remedies. On July 15 the Moscow Chamber of Commerce called a meeting for a discussion of the situation. Owners of timberland, private citizens, and representatives of lumber companies, the Idaho State Forestry Department, University of Idaho, the State Extension Service, the Forest Service, and the Bureau of Entomology and Plant Quarantine attended. They decided that it was too late to attempt control action in 1946 and that a survey should be made of the situation by the Forest Service and Bureau of Entomology and Plant Quarantine.

The two agencies gave a joint report at the annual meeting of the North Idaho Chamber of Commerce in Moscow on November 21. The primary facts disclosed were: (1) Within a gross area of about 500,000 acres, 350,000 acres with an estimated stand of 1,518,000 thousand board feet of the Douglas-fir and white fir timber were infested and an additional 1,182,000 thousand board feet were threatened; (2) the economic values involved (including, but not limited to, stumpage, lumber, pay rolls, and taxes) were more than 100 million dollars; (3) aerial spraying with a DDT solution was the only feasible means of control on the rugged terrain; (4) the estimated cost of control was $1.70 an acre; (5) to hold down losses the operations would have to be accomplished between May 20 and June 30, 1947—May 20 because it was about the date of general hatching of the tussock moth caterpillars from the egg masses, and June 30 because after that date defoliation of trees would occur to a degree that would perforce kill much of the timber stand.

The report contained many other details, including a description of the fir tussock moth; estimates of flying altitudes above timber for different types of planes; need for aerial photographic maps; estimated days of flying weather and hours of flying weather per day between May 20 and June 30; and the need for supplementary airstrips.

The meeting heartily approved the recommendations for action. This was the first of a series of steps that presented an inspiring example of varied interests that were quickly knit together and acted on decisively, forcibly, and in complete unity for the accomplishment of an objective.

The report was presented to Department of Agriculture officials in Washington on December 6 and to other groups in December and January. It was presented to the Idaho State Cooperative Board of Forestry, which recommended that the State cooperate with the private timberland owners and the Federal Government in control of the infestation. Idaho Senate Bill No. 118, enacted on February 18, cleared the way for cooperative action by the State and Federal Governments. The Idaho State Legislature on March 4 appropriated $210,000 for cooperative forest-insect and pest control. The directors of the Potlatch Timber Protective Association decided unanimously that the Association should carry its share of the costs. Congress appropriated $395,000 for the work.

The essential preparatory measures were many and varied. The nature of the task required administration by one agency; the major timberland owners agreed that the Department of Agriculture should be the one. Accordingly, the Forest Service and the Bureau of Entomology and Plant Quarantine proceeded within their means and existing authorities. The Forest Service delegated responsibility for the administration of the project to the regional forester of the Northern Region at Missoula, Mont. The Bureau of Entomology and Plant Quarantine delegated responsibility for the entomological phases to their regional forest entomologist at Coeur d'Alene, Idaho.

The regional forester designated a project leader for the Forest Service. All preparatory action was carried on by the project leader and one assistant and the leader for the Bureau of Entomology and Plant Quarantine, with the help of the regional divisions of the

Forest Service and those of the Bureau of Entomology and Plant Quarantine.

Most of the area in need of treatment was in Idaho. An area of about 4,000 acres just over the line in southeastern Washington also had to be treated because otherwise the prevailing winds would make it a source of reinfestation in Idaho. An area of about 14,000 acres in the Blue Mountains in Oregon was listed for treatment if funds were sufficient.

Cooperative agreements with all the States concerned were essential to set up authorities and responsibilities for various phases. A formal agreement with the State forester and the Land Board of Idaho was signed on April 17, 1947. The most important items of the agreement were: The regional forester at Missoula was designated as agent of the State of Idaho to conduct all phases of the control operations; the Bureau of Entomology and Plant Quarantine was to be responsible for the entomological phases; the State was made responsible for collections of contributions of funds for control from private landowners; the United States was relieved of any public liabilities arising from application of spray on State and private lands; a general formula was set up for sharing costs among private landowners, the State, and the Federal Government; and the spray formula was established as "not more than 1 pound of technical DDT in solvent and fuel oil to make 1 gallon of spray, to be applied at the rate of 1 gallon per acre."

Less detailed agreements were made with the State foresters of Washington and Oregon.

Aerial maps were essential for use of the pilots, for the delineation of infested areas, and for various other controls. Contact prints scaled to about 3½ inches to the mile and enlargements to 6 inches to the mile were assembled and prepared for use. Their value was increased by adding section lines.

Surveys to determine suitability and location of temporary airstrips were made, and seven such strips were constructed by the Division of Engineering in the Forest Service. The surveys and construction work were hampered by snow and wet ground. The last of the strips was completed shortly after spraying operations began.

The award on bids for aerial-spraying contracts had to be made far enough in advance of the scheduled date of initial spraying operations to allow the flying contractors time to construct and install the spraying equipment. The preparation of bids was difficult because there were no previous contracts to serve as a guide and no definite specifications for spray apparatus for such a job existed. The invitation to bid stipulated that the spray apparatus must regulate application to 1 gallon to the acre and would be subject to flight tests before the start of control operations. Bids were opened on April 14, but were not finally accepted until immediately after the appropriation of the Federal funds. The contractors, despite the short period available for construction and installation of spray apparatus, were ready to fly on May 20.

Procurements of DDT and the finished insecticide were handled by the Washington offices of the Bureau of Entomology and Plant Quarantine and the Forest Service. The quantities of insecticide (350,000 gallons) and the time limit heavily taxed available supplies of DDT and the capacity of the mixing equipment of the contractors. Arrangements were made with traffic managers of the railroad companies to red-tag manifest the spray tank cars and deliver the spray on a schedule which would minimize loss of the limited flying time.

Truck tractors and tank trailers for delivery of spray from the railhead to the airfields were essential. The only source from which these were obtainable was the Army Air Force, which lent the equipment it had at the Spokane Army Airfield.

Arrangements were made with the Weather Bureau to establish a 24-hour weather service at field headquarters in Moscow. June is a month of uncertain weather conditions in this area.

Weather records over a period of years were analyzed and used as a basis for the over-all plans. Even so, there was uncertainty. Abnormal rains and wind occurrence and velocity would seriously reduce favorable flying time.

A detailed survey of the general area of infestation was necessary in advance of spraying to delineate the areas to be sprayed on aerial maps for use of the pilots, to subdivide the infested areas into spray-application units, and to determine accurately the acreage to be sprayed. Because of snow and impassable roads, this precontrol survey was not completed until June 20.

Arrangements were made with the University of Idaho for a field headquarters in the university buildings. Office space and sleeping quarters were provided in one building.

Selections were made of administrative and operations personnel to be detailed from the national forests and the Bureau of Entomology and Plant Quarantine to the project a short time in advance of spraying operations. All transportation and office equipment and supplies, radios, tents, bedding, and other equipment were obtained from Forest Service and Bureau of Entomology and Plant Quarantine stocks. Purchases were then made of a small amount of special items, such as glass plates for spray checking, cleaning solvent for the glass plates, and small amounts of lumber for tent platforms.

During this preparatory period and the course of control work, the Idaho State Forestry Department assembled data on landownership and collected funds from the timberland owners.

The organization of the Federal administrative and control forces presented some new problems. Two major decisions, made early in the preparation stages, materially simplified this task. The first was that the Forest Service and Bureau of Entomology and Plant Quarantine would not handle any phase of the operations which dealt directly with flying. The delivery of spray by tank truck from the railhead to the airfields was a responsibility of the contractor. Spray-material contracts provided for delivery of the finished insecticide in tank cars so that there would be no need for mixing the DDT in solvent with the fuel oil at the project delivery point. The second decision was that artificial marking of flight lines would not be attempted.

These decisions left four primary activities upon which the Federal administrative and control organization would be based:

(1) General administration and supervision, including, but not limited to, facilitating delivery of insecticide on schedule and keeping records of all shipments, deliveries, and use; daily record of expenditures and obligations; daily progress record of acreage sprayed; the maintenance of radio and other noncontract equipment; pay rolls and payments to flying contractors and others.

(2) Information and public contacts, including cooperation with representatives of the State forestry department, extension service, and others in the organization of meetings of timberland owners in connection with collection of contributions; furnishing information to representatives of newspapers and periodicals, newsreel companies, independent writers; investigation of complaints; and other details.

(3) Checking spray application and completeness of coverage in accordance with the terms of the flying contract; also checking the tussock moth kill success.

(4) Weather predictions.

The Federal agencies' organization for those purposes required the services of 35 persons at the peak of operations.

These preparatory actions were the most critical phases of the control job and were essential to its success.

Forest Service and Bureau of Entomology and Plant Quarantine personnel moved into field headquarters and outlying field stations on May 10, set up offices and other temporary quarters,

NUMBER AND TYPE OF PLANE, THEIR ASSIGNED FLYING SPEEDS, SWATH WIDTHS, AND SPRAY-LOAD CAPACITY, AND MAXIMUM FLYING HEIGHT ABOVE TREETOPS

| *Type of plane* | *Planes* | *Speed* | *Spray load* | *Spray Swath* | *Delivery* | *Height above treetops* |
|---|---|---|---|---|---|---|
| | *Number* | *Miles per hour* | *Gallons* | *Feet* | *Gallons per minute* | *Feet* |
| Douglas C-47 | 1 | 140 | 1,000 | 400 | 112 | 100-150 |
| Ford Trimotor | 2 | 90 | 400 | 300 | 54 | 100-150 |
| Fairchild | 1 | 90 | 300 | 200 | 36 | 50-100 |
| Travelair | 2 | 90 | 200 | 200 | 36 | 50-100 |
| Stinson SM7A | 1 | 85 | 150 | 175 | 32 | 50-100 |
| Stearman | 4 | 80 | 75 | 100 | 16 | 50-100 |

and went through a training period, as planned.

The flying contractors arrived on May 19.

Insecticide was on hand. Test flights were made on May 19 and 20 to check spray apparatus and to establish swath widths for the various types of planes flying at specified speeds and heights above treetops.

Flying-weather controls were established as follows:

(1) Planes would fly only on weather clearance by the Bureau of Entomology and Plant Quarantine leader. They would stop flying on order when wind velocity reached 8 miles an hour or on their own judgment when thermal activity caused dangerous air turbulence.

(2) Spraying would stop an hour before rain and not resume until foliage was dry.

Assigned flying speeds, swath widths, and maximum flying height above treetops are shown in the table above, with the number and type of planes used and their spray-load capacity.

This was dangerous flying. Only skilled pilots familiar with the tricky air currents of rough, mountainous terrain, flying at low altitude, could lay down spray in narrow parallel swaths while following ground-level features as guides. There would be no time or clearance to parachute from a crippled plane under such conditions. Great credit is due the flying contractors for their meticulous preparation and constant care of equipment and to the esprit de corps of the flying groups, from ground crews to the contractors. They were determined to make the job a success. Only three accidents occurred out of more than 2,100 individual flights; one man got a broken nose and another a cracked ankle bone.

All-out spraying commenced on May 22. From then on the objective of both the contractors and the Federal agencies was to utilize every hour of flying weather and complete the job by June 30 or before. On 2 or 3 days the spray coverage was as high as 25,000 acres.

The pattern of flying was worked out during the first few days. With the help of aerial photographs, forest maps, and reconnaissance flights, the area was divided into flying units of 1,000 to 3,000 acres. Topographic features usually provided the boundaries. Units were assigned to individual pilots. Usually the pilot responsible for a unit would make dry runs over the area and plan his flight pattern before spraying. Then he would make the spray-application runs until the unit was completed. This was the only practical method of obtaining efficient application of spray in this rugged area. The acreage of each unit was checked against volume of spray used, which gave a relatively simple alternative method of checking application. Most of the spraying was done from about 3:30 a. m. to 9 a. m., when the air was calm and cool. Only a few times was spraying continued after 9 a. m. Seldom could spraying be done during the evening hours. After 9 a. m., thermal activity usually made flying dangerous or wind velocities became too high for satisfactory application. The ground crews worked with high efficiency; they could fill spray tanks usually in 4 to 5 minutes or less.

Work hours of the crews were those required to meet the job. They slept when they could and caught up on sleep when there was no flying weather or no spray. The first morning weather reports were made from field stations at 2:30 a. m. If the weather report was clear for flying, liaison men at the airstrips were called to notify the representatives of the flying contractors. Checkers were called and they hit for the hills to lay out their glass plates on areas designated the previous evening. Theirs was a tough job of mountain climbing. Much of the area had no roads and could be reached only by foot through heavy forests, down timber, and undergrowth. They had no means of communicating with the spray planes, so after putting out their plates they waited until they were sure flying had stopped for the day; then they retraced their route of travel, picked up the plates, and came in to headquarters. There the plates were examined for spray deposition and were washed and packed for the next flying period. The washing job was hard and hazardous: The spray particles adhered tenaciously to the plates, and highly volatile xylene had to be used for washing fluid. No accidents occurred.

When flying was over for the day, the pilots finished their coverage maps, which were delivered to the liaison men and sent in to headquarters, where the area covered was transferred to a large daily progress map. This task was completed each day, regardless of time requirements. Among other things the map provided for an over-all check on acreage covered and spray used. This detail was highly important in limiting orders for additional insecticide toward the close of the project. Several thousand dollars in freight and insecticide costs were thus saved. The periodic vouchering of payments to contractors was based on this control.

Unloading of insecticide tank cars was done whenever cars were spotted on the railroad siding. If cars were spotted at night, the contractors were notified and unloading of tank cars and transfer of insecticide to the airfields by the ground crews proceeded until planes and stand-by tank trailers were filled.

A continuous cumulative record was maintained by individual tank-car numbers of the date of shipments from St. Louis, Michigan, and Chicago of deliveries at Moscow and, as far as possible, of the daily location and progress of tank cars en route. When any stranding of cars occurred, the traffic managers were called to break the jam. Even though the railroads put the tank cars under red-tag manifest, it was not possible to maintain complete en route schedules from the point of origin of shipments to Moscow. This resulted in some lost flying time because of no spray, but most of the lost time was due to faster spraying coverage during good flying weather than was allowed as a safe estimate in the basic planning.

A close daily financial control was maintained throughout the spraying operations. There were several special reasons for this, aside from just good financial management of a large, short-period job. These were: (1) The project was planned on a coverage of 350,000 acres. It was apparent soon after the spraying was started from the precontrol survey data that the infested area would approach 400,000 acres. (2) There were about 14,000 acres in Oregon which should be sprayed if funds could be stretched to cover the cost. (3) The amount of contributions from small-timberland owners was uncertain. (4) An isolated outbreak on about 6,000 acres, discovered during the course of the operations, needed to be covered. Incomplete coverage of the Idaho outbreak might threaten the success of the entire operation.

The project aroused widespread

public interest. Many visitors—public officials, newsreel photographers, writers, and others—came to see the operations. People were very friendly and many commented on the efficiency and effectiveness of the spraying. Some farmers asked to have their infested yard trees sprayed, and we did so when they could be reached on the regular spray runs. A number of farms were sprayed under a special arrangement between the Forest Service, the farmers, and the flying contractors.

A few complaints were received, and each one was immediately investigated. The most serious complaint involved the alleged sickness of a child from eating garden vegetables that had received a light application of spray. Project officials were not concerned as to spray being the cause; they were extremely worried because no doctor had been called and they thought that the symptoms described by the father indicated tick paralysis.

The case was investigated with the view to having the child taken to a doctor for diagnosis and proper attention. When the investigator arrived at the farmstead, the child was romping with the neighbor's children. The investigator partook with relish of the strawberries which showed spray spots, and the fears of the complainant were promptly dispelled.

All spraying operations were completed on July 2. A total of 413,469 acres of fir timberland was covered and 390,878 gallons of spray was applied. The actual application was within approximately 5 percent of the first estimates—thanks to the contractors' engineers and the entomologists.

No live tussock moth caterpillars were found a week after the spraying; the infestation was stopped in its tracks. The cost of the project was just under $1.57 an acre, or about 13 cents less than the estimated cost.

People had been concerned about the possible effects of the spraying on apiaries and forest fauna. Arrangements had been made with the Fish and Wildlife Service of the Department of the Interior to conduct investigations on these aspects of the work and farmers had been warned to cover apiaries ahead of the spraying. Since the fields used by the bees were not sprayed, the covering provided adequate protection. No serious effects of the spray on birds and mammals were discovered. Some suckers and bullheads were killed, but trout were not directly affected. The supply of fish-food organisms was markedly reduced, but probably not enough to cause permanent damage.

The project demonstrated the feasibility and practicability of controlling by aerial spraying what could easily have been a disastrous insect infestation. It showed that inaccessible mountainous forest areas could be economically treated. It provided valuable technical and administrative experience and established a general pattern for the conduct of similar projects should they be necessary.

But such projects are expensive. They are hazardous to human life and to costly flying equipment. It is much better to try to make them unnecessary—to use a stitch in time by early detection and prompt suppression while the areas of infestation are small. Prevention is better than cure.

Paul H. Roberts, *assistant regional forester in the Forest Service, has worked in the Northern and Southwestern Forest Service Regions. He has also served as director of the Prairie States Forestry Project and as associate director and director of the Emergency Rubber Project. Mr. Roberts was project leader for the Forest Service of the Tussock Moth Spraying Project. He is a graduate of the University of Nebraska.*

James C. Evenden *is in charge of the Forest Insect Laboratory of the Bureau of Entomology and Plant Quarantine at Coeur d'Alene, Idaho. He served as the field technical leader on the Tussock Moth Spraying Project. He is a graduate of Oregon State College.*

# DISEASES AND THE FOREST

L. M. HUTCHINS

Trees, no less than other large forms of life, are subject to diseases that reduce their growth, destroy their usefulness, or bring death. The threat of disease is ever present, from the time that a tree emerges as a seedling to the end of its useful life.

In the virgin forests this threat was lessened because through centuries of interaction a certain degree of natural balance between the trees and their disease enemies had been achieved. Man, in his need for land, shelter, fuel, and communication, however, upset this balance by cutting, clearing, burning, and planting. He brought in exotic tree species from foreign lands, too, and otherwise so changed the forests from their original, natural state that over most of the country the once-stabilized relations no longer exist and the danger of disease has increased.

With the new tree species or their products from abroad came new diseases, which have found here a more congenial environment than in their native habitats. Thus, chestnut blight was brought in from Asia; white pine blister rust on infected pine seedlings and the Dutch elm disease and its insect carriers on elm burl logs were brought in from Europe. For our native chestnut, the results have been disastrous. Our white pines have been saved only by the development of an effective method of control. Losses in American elm from the Dutch elm disease have been heavy, and the future of the species is still in doubt, despite progress in means of control.

Losses from presumably native diseases that have become epidemic are also assuming serious proportions in several places. A highly destructive virus disease, known as phloem necrosis, has killed thousands of elms in several midwestern cities. Littleleaf, a disease whose cause we do not yet know, is making heavy inroads into stands of shortleaf pine in the southern Piedmont. Another disease of undetermined cause, provisionally named pole blight, is spreading in second-growth western white pine stands in Idaho, Montana, and Washington. Altogether, since the turn of the century, more than 25 new forest-tree diseases, introduced or apparently native, have been discovered in this country. Not all have proved equally important, but the aggregate loss of trees from them has been tremendous.

Most of the losses, however, are not from diseases of the spectacular epidemic type, but rather from the many relatively inconspicuous diseases at work always in our forests in and on leaves, bark, wood, roots, seedlings, saplings, old trees. Best estimates place the annual saw-timber loss from heart rots in the forests of the United States at 1½ billion board feet. It is these everyday insidious losses, as well as those from the spectacular epidemic diseases, that must be guarded against if our forests are to continue to supply the wood we need.

Everybody knows how necessary it is to protect farm and orchard crops—cotton, tobacco, vegetables, grains, and fruits—against disease. Even more important is the protection of forest trees, which occupy the land many years before they are harvested.

TREE DISEASES are of two main types, parasitic and nonparasitic. The parasitic or infectious diseases are frequently highly contagious. They are caused mainly by low forms of life, such as bacteria and fungi, by viruses, by microscopic eel worms or the nematodes, and by seed plants such as mistletoes and dodders.

Among the nonparasitic diseases are such disorders as the sunscald, winter injury, drought injury, root drowning or suffocation, nutritional excesses and deficiencies, and injury from gases, smoke, and fumes.

FUNGI cause most of the major losses from disease in forest trees and are the chief destroyers or deteriorating agents of forest products. They produce leaf spots and defoliation, wilts, blights, cankers, galls, heart rots, and root diseases. Trees that are weakened by fungi often are more susceptible to windthrow and to attack by insects. In forest products, other fungi cause stains, molds, and decays that are responsible for much deterioration and loss in lumber, posts, poles, buildings, containers, and in wood used for other purposes.

Not all of the fungi in the forests are harmful: Many fungi contribute to the health and growth of trees by converting the fallen leaves, twigs, and other forest debris into humus, an important constituent of forest soils and a source of nutrient elements for tree growth. Others combine intimately with the tiny feeding roots on some trees to form special absorbing bodies, called mycorrhizae, which are believed to enable the trees to take up nutrients from the soil more effectively than they would otherwise be able to do. Through the production of humus, fungi also tend to create a soil reaction that is unfavorable to the disease fungi that attack the roots of seedlings and young trees. A few fungi attack disease-producing fungi directly.

Diseases and fungi causing deterioration are commonly spread by wind, water, insects, and bird life. Soil fungi causing root rots and wilts may be carried on the wheels of vehicles or the feet of men or animals. The fungus causing canker stain of the planetree is carried on pruning tools and equipment. Virus diseases, such as the phloem necrosis of elm, are almost invariably spread by insects, as also are some stain and decay fungi.

THE EFFECTIVE CONTROL of forest diseases must be based on a sound knowledge of them and of the forest environments under which they occur. Both direct and indirect methods are employed. Direct methods include the use of sprays, dusts, and soil treatments, the removal and destruction of affected trees or parts, the prescribed use of fire, and the removal of alternate hosts. Sprays and soil treatments are used in the nurseries to protect the seedling trees against diseases, and sprays and dusts to destroy the insect carriers of diseases of shade trees, such as the Dutch elm disease and the elm phloem necrosis. Eradication is particularly important where a dangerous disease has been accidentally introduced into a locality and is known to be of limited distribution. This was the case when the European larch canker was discovered in a limited area in Massachusetts. Thorough eradication was undertaken immediately, and the disease apparently has been eliminated.

FIRE IN THE FOREST ordinarily does more harm than good, but against the brown spot disease of longleaf pine in the Southern States it has a sanitary effect when properly timed.

The white pine blister rust offers an example of a disease that can be controlled through the removal of the alternate hosts, currants and gooseberries. The rust cannot spread directly from pine to pine, but the spores from the rust on pine are carried by the wind and are able to infect currants and gooseberries. Spores from the rust developed on these are, in turn, capable of infecting white pines. The removal of the currant and gooseberry bushes to a safe distance from white pines effectively protects the pines from the rust.

If a disease has become widespread and well-established, eradication is usually impracticable, and we may have to learn to live with it and to reduce losses through indirect methods of control. This applies to most of our native diseases.

The red rot of the ponderosa pine in the Western States is an example. The causal fungus enters the trunk through naturally occurring lower dead branches and it results in an average loss of about one-fourth of the total timber volume. It rarely enters through branches less than an inch in diameter, however. Control of the disease is possible either by pruning off the lower branches before they die or by growing the trees so closely together that the lower branches are shaded out before they become large enough to support the fungus.

Fire wounds are important places of entry for decay fungi, and the prevention of fire in the woods therefore is an effective indirect means of reducing losses from timber decays.

Other indirect methods involve the proper timing of cutting, the control of stand composition to give mixtures of tree species instead of pure stands, and the development and use of disease-resistant varieties.

VARIETIES RESISTANT to disease have been successful in field and fruit crops; there is every reason to expect that they should prove equally valuable in our future forest- and shade-tree plantings. Although work along this line has scarcely more than begun, an American elm resistant to the Dutch elm disease and others resistant to phloem necrosis, strains of mimosa resistant to the mimosa wilt, and white pine resistant to blister rust have been selected and tested. These resistant trees are now being propagated and soon will be available. Although the use of resistant varieties will not save the present susceptible stands of trees, it does offer a promise of future safety in their replacement.

The prevention of deterioration, such as from stain and decay, in forest products is an effective way of extending our national timber supply. It requires different methods from those that can be used on living trees. The young-growth timber now coming into use is less resistant to decay than the wood from the older stands. Modern chemical treatments and more careful drying and storage practices make it possible to avoid damage to lumber, logs, pulpwood, and similar products, however, and are lengthening the useful life of posts, poles, railway ties, and other wood used in contact with the ground. The prompt salvage of timber that is killed by fire, insects, and disease is saving for use much timber that was formerly left to rot.

IN BUILDINGS AND OTHER CONSTRUCTION, the chances of decay is reduced by drainage of sites, use of seasoned lumber, elimination of direct contacts of wood with soil, care to keep rain from entering joints, ventilation or soil coverage under basementless houses, the judicious placing of vapor seals, and the use of preservatives.

With the ever-quickening disappearance of accessible stands of old-growth timber and with world-wide timber shortages brought on by war, the importance of disease in its effect on the future timber crop is rapidly increasing. Losses that formerly passed almost unnoticed can no longer be tolerated—from the standpoint of solvency of the timber owner no less than from the public interest. We must be able to grow good wood and grow it profitably. That can be done only if disease losses are held to a reasonable minimum.

The field to be covered by the specialist in forest diseases is immense. More than 100 tree species of commercial importance occur in the forests of the United States; each presents an individual disease problem. When account is taken of the fact that our forest industry ranks fourth in importance in the Nation, the investigative effort devoted to diseases affecting this resource up to the present does not seem proportionate to the values at stake.

L. M. HUTCHINS *is head pathologist in charge of the Division of Forest Pathology, Bureau of Plant Industry, Soils, and Agricultural Engineering. He is known for his extensive investigations of virus diseases of trees.*

# INTRODUCED TREE DISEASES AND INSECTS

G. F. GRAVATT, D. E. PARKER

Many people now are asking: Are there more insects and diseases than before? How does it happen that in a few years we have suffered scourges of gypsy moths and Japanese beetles and many others that were not here before?

The answer is that we are plagued by more insects and diseases and more destructive ones than our grandfathers were. The reason is easy to find.

Some of our present-day kinds of trees (as indicated by fossil remains) flourished in North America millions of years ago; trees and their parasites must have fluctuated in abundance long before the coming of the white man. Then, as now, periodic epidemics must have caused extensive losses—but when the trees were attacked they usually could maintain themselves against borer and beetle.

This natural balance was upset by a new factor: The early settlers, who brought in new diseases and new insects along with their new plants. Some tree pests now considered native no doubt originated in foreign countries. Many serious diseases and insects are known to have come from abroad during the past 60 years, the entire span of any real study of the diseases and insects of tree species in North America. The end of such invasions is not in sight. All over the world disease-producing organisms and insects are lurking, ready to hitchhike to this country and pounce on our important forest and shade trees.

Before the enactment of our plant-quarantine laws, the gypsy moth, chestnut blight, and white pine blister rust were introduced. Since the enactment of the laws, the so-called Dutch elm disease has sneaked in. Other less well-known foreign diseases and insects also have been introduced and are attacking various kinds of trees.

In their native homes, many insects are kept under partial control by their parasites and other natural enemies, but when they are introduced into some other area they usually leave these enemies behind. For example, when the Japanese beetle and the gypsy moth reached this country, they multiplied rapidly, partly because of a lack of natural enemies. Insect, fungus, bacterial and virus parasites of these introduced insects now are being imported, but the parasites are valuable only when the environment favors their development. Unlike insects, the organisms causing our introduced diseases do not have any important parasites that directly affect them, although parasites may be used to reduce the populations of the insects that transmit certain of those diseases.

THE GYPSY MOTH illustrates the serious consequences of the introduction of a forest insect from Europe. In 1869 a number of egg clusters of the gypsy moth were brought from France to Medford, Mass., by a French mathematician and astronomer who hoped to develop a hardy silk-producing insect by crossing gypsy moths with silkworm moths. During his experiments some of the insects escaped. Some 20 years later the population of the gypsy moth had increased to a point where the damage was severe enough to attract general notice. At that time about 360 square miles was found to be infested. Within another 5 years, the infested area had increased to 2,200 square miles. Now the gypsy moth, which defoliates both deciduous and evergreen trees, is prevalent in New England, in an extensive area in eastern New York, and in an isolated area in Pennsylvania.

At least 65 million dollars have been spent by the Federal Government and various States, chiefly during the past 40 years, in fighting the gypsy moth. The main objective of the Federal control work, conducted in cooperation with the States, is to prevent the westward and southward spread of the insect. The discovery of the extreme toxicity of DDT to the gypsy moth and the development of airplane spraying of forested areas have furnished effective means of control to aid in the program. Timely applications of DDT by airplane will kill the gypsy moth, and prevent defoliation, subsequent growth retardation, and possible death of trees.

CHESTNUT BLIGHT has caused the complete destruction of our commercial chestnut from Canada to the Gulf States. This record is not approached by that of any other disease or insect. First reported in New York City in 1904, the disease spread rapidly.

For many years roots of killed trees continue to send up sprouts, but these sprouts are usually killed before they are more than a few inches in diameter. Unfortunately, search for 40 years has not resulted in the discovery of a single American chestnut tree with sufficient resistance to be of practical value. Blight has reduced millions of acres of forest land to a lower productive status for an indefinite period, because the native tree species replacing the chestnut are usually less valuable. It also has deprived us of cherished tasty nuts and has taken from wildlife a food.

Experimental plantings with blight-resistant Asiatic chestnuts and with hybrids of these and the American chestnut indicate that on suitable sites they will produce small telephone poles and abundant sweet nuts. Most of these resistant selections, however, are less straight-stemmed, less frost-resistant, and more particular in their soil requirements than the American chestnut. Some State forestry and game departments are beginning to grow resistant Chinese chestnuts for planting in farm wood lots.

Chestnut blight was found in commercial orchards and in ornamental chestnut plantings of the Pacific coast. Prompt eradication measures by State and Federal agencies almost completely eliminated the disease. The susceptible orchards of the West, however, are not safe, because of the danger of shipment of infected chestnut trees from the East.

Chestnut blight illustrates how an introduced pest can upset a phase of the national economy. The American chestnut has been the main source of our domestic tannin used in the manufacture of leather, and dead trees still are extensively used. Tannin, a strategic material especially vital in time of war, is extracted from the chipped-up chestnut wood. The chips are then used for paper or board pulp. This extensive industry, at present supplying most of our domestic tannin, faces its end when the supply of dead trees gives out.

The chestnut blight fungus is also seriously damaging the post oak, a widely distributed tree in the eastern half of the country with a forest stand of about 5 billion board feet. It kills some trees rather slowly but has not damaged others that have been exposed for long periods. So far no other kind of oak has been seriously damaged by the chestnut blight fungus.

THE SMALLER EUROPEAN ELM BARK BEETLE is an example of an introduced insect that was of little importance until it became associated with the introduced so-called Dutch elm disease fungus. That insect is known to have been established near Boston as early as 1904. It did little damage and was not considered a primary pest for about a quarter of a century. About 1930, when the Dutch elm disease fungus reached this country, the importance of the European elm bark beetle changed; it proved to be a carrier and transmitter of the fungus. The relationship worked to the advantage of the bark beetle. American elms inoculated by contaminated beetles develop disease symptoms, are partially or completely killed by the disease, and provide suitable breeding material on which increasing populations of beetles develop.

A vicious circle thus has resulted from the relationship between the fungus and the insect.

The elm beetle unquestionably was introduced through different ports. It and the fungus were present in burl elm logs imported for veneer manufacture before quarantines prohibited the movement of elm wood into this country. Beetles and larvae have been found in elm wood used in certain types of crates received from Europe. A larger species of beetle, also a carrier of the Dutch elm disease fungus in Europe, has been introduced into this country in burl logs, but apparently it has not been successful in establishing itself here.

It is practicable to protect valuable trees from the Dutch elm disease where control measures are applied energetically, but losses are heavy in parts of New York, New Jersey, Pennsylvania, and Connecticut, and spot infections are known as far west as Denver. We may expect that these two pests and phloem necrosis, a virus disease, eventually will kill most of the elm forest growth in the northeastern quarter of the country.

The death of shade and ornamental elms is even more tragic. It is disheartening to all of us to see the large elm trees, so characteristic of New England and New York, decline and die. Sometime in the not too distant future, when the total value of the elms killed and the annual costs of removing dead trees and of spray and other control measures for those still alive are totaled, a loss figure of hundreds of millions of dollars is not unlikely.

A European-Asiatic fungus that causes white pine blister rust entered the country some 50 years ago on imported white pine seedlings. Although this fungus cannot spread from pine to pine but must first attack an alternate host—in this case currants and gooseberries—it found plenty of the hosts here. Thus it was able to complete its life cycle and spread widely. Its dependence on currants and gooseberries, however, proved its partial undoing, because spread of the disease can be stopped by removal of the plants within 900 feet of white pine.

Whitebark pine, a picturesque member of the white pine group that grows at high altitudes in the West, usually does not have sufficient commercial and esthetic value to justify the cost of removing the numerous wild currants and gooseberries near them. Thus, most of the trees of this species will be killed by the rust and many park and wilderness areas will become less interesting. Several other high-altitude species of white pine may be largely killed in the future.

Other introduced insects damage our forest and shade trees. Among them are the brown-tail moth, satin moth, European pine shoot moth, elm leaf beetle, European pine sawfly, and the European spruce sawfly.

Various other diseases also have been introduced or are suspected of having been introduced. Not all introduced diseases become established. The European larch canker, for example, was introduced into Massachusetts, but it spread slowly and was successfully eradicated. We do not know how it would act in the main larch stands of this country.

A canker disease from Asia and a scab from Europe are causing serious damage to some kinds of willows, especially in New England. Twig and leaf diseases do not excite so much interest, but their action is a perpetual drain on the productivity of the affected trees.

Insects and disease-producing organisms may work as partners. As we mentioned in connection with the Dutch elm disease, an imported fungus can make a destructive insect out of one that is relatively harmless. It seems possible, therefore, that introduced insect carriers could similarly make disastrous the two fungi that now are destructive to the London planetree and sugar maple.

Sometimes an insect and a fungus together are deadly, even though either alone is of little importance. An example is the partnership of a fungus, *Nectria* sp., and an imported European scale on beech. The fungus, which enters through the scale injuries, is a killer. The partnership has already caused the death of much of the beech growth in eastern Canada and Maine. The partners are increasing in the other New England States and threaten widely distributed beech growth elsewhere unless climatic factors limit their spread.

Hundreds of diseases and insects that have not yet been introduced are known in foreign countries to attack oaks, poplars, and other tree genera that also grow here. In addition, there undoubtedly are in the various parts of the world numerous undescribed diseases and insects that could attack our trees if they gained entrance.

Asia is the principal source of danger, because many kinds of trees native to that continent also grow here. Furthermore, those species have had little or no pathological study. Insect and disease parasites from Europe constitute the second threat, even though its flora is less varied than that of Asia. It is not wise to ignore the possibility that other Old World strains of parasites may be introduced and prove more virulent than the strains already here.

Despite our inspection service, accelerated travel gives parasites a better chance than ever before to reach this country in a living condition.

Airplane traffic alone offers a problem. During the year that ended July 1, 1948, officials of the Division of Foreign Plant Quarantines listed the arrival of 57,756 airplanes at 47 ports of entry. Planes from as far away as Cairo, Egypt, regularly arrive in Chicago as the first port of entry. Airplane traffic is still increasing. When usual ports of entry are closed because of unfavorable weather, commercial and private airplanes may land where there are insufficient inspection services. Illegal flights are not inspected at all. New areas of the world are being rapidly opened up by airplane travel. In 1948, prohibited material was found on 26 percent of the planes, and 3,500 interceptions of insects and plant diseases were made during that year.

During the same period, 44,300 inspections were made of ships arriving at ports in the United States and in 24 percent of the inspections prohibited materials were found. A special survey during 1943–45 for insect pests and plant diseases near ports of entry revealed at least 41 insects and 17 plant pathogens that had never before been recorded from the United States.

The relatively few examples of introduced pests here reported, and many unlisted ones, have caused enormous losses to our trees. A more critical situation will arise as more and more pests enter. Once established, they are with us for an indefinite time, each cutting down our forest production.

Usually the best practice is to plant tree species that originally grew on the area, but additional pests may force a change to resistant tree strains or different species. The length of time a tree must grow in place before it is ready for harvest is a serious factor in combatting introduced pests. An agronomist, troubled by a new disease one year, plants a resistant variety or another kind of crop plant the next year. Foresters often have to wait a hundred years, until the trees mature, before they can change the tree crop to another kind. Such factors emphasize the vital importance of preventing new pests from becoming established.

In reducing further introductions of pests, of first importance is a stricter regulation of the importation of seeds, cions, and plants. Seeds are by far the least dangerous form in which to make new introductions, as clean seeds after surface treatment and fumigation carry very few disease-producing organisms and insects. Because cions and plants cannot be satisfactorily inspected for virus and some

802062°—49——30

fungus and bacterial diseases, the growing of limited quantities in quarantine is the only practical method of handling such introductions. Some virus diseases have a number of widely different hosts. Some ornamental plant, for example, may be the means by which a destructive forest-tree virus might gain entrance.

Diseases and insects do not respect the boundaries between the United States and Mexico and Canada. Flying beetles or migrating birds that carry spores on their feet cannot be inspected. So all three countries have a joint interest in preventing new insects and diseases from becoming established in North America. Most tropical-tree pests fortunately do not thrive in our more northern climate, with its different tree species, but the pines in the high mountains of Guatemala, for example, may have parasites that are not present here.

A strengthening of the inspection and quarantine force to handle more adequately the importations coming into this country is needed. The increasing number of airplane flights and the volume of commerce in veneer logs and packing material pose difficult problems.

We have no method of forecasting whether an introduced insect or disease will be more or less destructive in this country than it is in its native home. Foreign pests generally become well established in this country before their presence is discovered. Much more information is needed on forest diseases and insects, both in our own country and abroad. Definite surveys, such as those called for under the Forest Pest Control Act, will build up our information so that (at least when a new local outbreak shows up) a decision can be made as to whether it is something new to this country. Study of foreign disease reports is helpful. Few of our American tree species are grown in foreign countries, and advance information on their parasites, therefore, is not available.

The systematic planting of our important American trees in different foreign regions is needed as a basis for determining the diseases and insects of those areas that may be destructive to our trees and need to be guarded against. There are some such plantings in foreign countries and these should be studied. Such information is valuable in preventing potentially dangerous diseases and insects from entering this country. This same information would be helpful in promptly handling an outbreak, if the disease or insect should get a start in this country.

Many plantings of American trees can be made at forest schools and forest experiment stations in foreign countries at no cost other than supplying the seed. Some information can be obtained on their diseases and insects from foreign scientists, but occasional inspections by American scientists will be needed. As an incentive to this project, arrangements might well be made in this country to plant foreign trees and make reports to the foreign scientists on their growth, diseases, and insect pests.

As our American forests become less productive on account of new disease and insect attacks, we will have urgent need for new species of trees for planting and hybridization. So these systematic plantings of the exotics in forest blocks will prove a most valuable addition to our own forestry as well as give our foreign cooperators information on diseases and insect pests of their native trees.

G. F. Gravatt, *a graduate of Virginia Polytechnic Institute, is a forest pathologist in the Bureau of Plant Industry, Soils, and Agricultural Engineering. He is the leader of the program for the development and distribution of blight-resistant chestnuts and has studied other introduced diseases. He has long recognized the danger to American forests from the introduced epidemic diseases and has consistently advocated the necessity for stronger protective measures to exclude them from the United States.*

D. E. Parker *is an assistant division leader of the Division of Forest Insect Investigations, Bureau of Entomology and Plant Quarantine. A graduate of the University of Massachusetts, Mr. Parker joined the Department in 1925. After 9 years in Massachusetts, where he worked on biological control of forest insects, he began studying the relation of insects to tree diseases, particularly Dutch elm disease and elm phloem necrosis. In this connection Mr. Parker spent three years studying the Dutch elm disease in Europe.*

# DUTCH ELM DISEASE

R. U. SWINGLE, R. R. WHITTEN, E. G. BREWER

The Dutch elm disease is caused by the fungus *Ceratostomella ulmi*. The disease was discovered in the Netherlands 30 years ago and it spread rapidly in Europe. It was found in the United States in 1930; it had been brought here in elm burl logs imported for the veneer industry.

Native elms of the United States are dangerously susceptible to the fungus. Despite vigorous efforts to suppress it, the disease has become established in plantations and natural stands of the principal elm shade-tree areas of this country from Boston as far westward as Indiana and Kentucky and southward to Virginia. It has been found in Tennessee. An isolated outbreak was discovered in Colorado.

Dutch elm disease produces a wilting or yellowing of leaves on one or several branches. Thereupon the leaves fall. Later in the season or in following years, the disease may spread to other parts of the tree until the entire top is affected and the tree dies. In more acute cases, the entire tree may suddenly wilt and die with or without pronounced yellowing of foliage. In all cases of Dutch elm disease, a discoloration of the sapwood occurs in affected branches, trunk, and roots. If Dutch elm disease is present, a diagonal cut through branches with wilted or yellowing leaves will show brown spots, an arc, or a complete brown circle in one or more annual rings of the wood.

Because two other common diseases of the elm produce similar symptoms, positive identification of the Dutch elm disease depends upon laboratory tests that involve identification of the fungus that may grow from the discolored wood. Without these tests, the Dutch elm disease cannot be distinguished with certainty from other wilt diseases of elm. A laboratory to which specimens may be sent for identification of Dutch elm disease is maintained by the Bureau of Entomology and Plant Quarantine of the Department of Agriculture.

*Ceratostomella ulmi* develops in living trees as a parasite and in dead elm wood as a saprophyte. In living trees, the fungus occurs in water-conducting vessels of the wood. It produces yeastlike spores that are carried through these vessels in the flow of sap. The toxins the fungus produces and the brown, gumlike deposits in the water-conducting vessels cause wilt and the death of the tree or its affected branches. After its host dies, the fungus, still growing on the wood as a saprophyte, produces spores under the loosened bark and in insect galleries formed between the bark and wood.

Occasionally the fungus spreads through linkage of diseased and healthy trees by natural root grafts, which frequently occur in dense elm stands and crowded street plantings. Normally, though, the fungus is borne from diseased trees to healthy trees by two kinds of bark beetles, the native elm bark beetle, *Hylurgopinus rufipes*

(Eichh.), and the smaller European elm bark beetle, *Scolytus multistriatus* (Marsh.). The latter is the more important. The beetles, widespread in the eastern half of the United States, are present in many places where the Dutch elm disease is not yet known to occur—an ominous warning.

The adult beetles feed in parts of living elm trees, but they breed only in recently cut, dead, or dying elms. Living elm trees are seldom injured by only the feeding of the adult, but when the beetles are contaminated with the disease organism they become of economic importance. When the Dutch elm disease fungus occurs in elm material in which these insects breed, the fungus may stick to the beetles and be carried to healthy elms or other breeding material.

The adults of the smaller European elm bark beetle emerge from infested wood and fly to nearby living elm trees, where they feed in the smaller twig crotches. The adults of the native elm bark beetle hibernate in the outer bark of living elm trees. In the spring they bore into the bark and feed on it. When the feeding injuries penetrate through the bark to the wood, the disease organism may be introduced into the vascular system of healthy elm trees. Beetles of both species may fly several miles in search of suitable breeding places, and thus may transport the disease organism from one locality to another.

All the elms commonly planted as shade trees are susceptible to Dutch elm disease. The degree of susceptibility varies both within and between species, however. The American elm, which predominates in many shade-tree plantings, is among the more susceptible species. The Chinese elm (*Ulmus parvifolia*) and the Siberian elm (*Ulmus pumila*) resist Dutch elm disease, but they have undesirable characteristics that limit their use in shade-tree plantings.

The variation in susceptibility of different species and varieties has stimulated attempts in Europe and the United States to breed and select superior types of elms that are resistant to the fungus. Scientists in Europe discovered the Christine Buisman elm, a selection of *Ulmus carpinifolia,* which has proved highly resistant in both Europe and America. After inoculating thousands of American elm seedlings, American scientists have found two resistant American elms. Other recent selections and hybrids seem promising, and elms that combine resistance to the disease and high quality should be available soon through commercial nurseries.

Because the Dutch elm disease organism is spread by insects, the loss of elm trees from this disease can be prevented by controlling the insect carriers. This can be done by the prevention of breeding in recently cut, dead, or dying elm trees and by the prevention of feeding on living elm trees.

Breeding may be prevented by burning or spraying all infested or likely-to-be infested elm wood. If a spray is to be used, the entire bark surface must be thoroughly covered with No. 2 fuel oil containing 1 percent of DDT. This spray is for dead material only, because it will injure living trees.

Feeding by bark beetles in living trees can be controlled by completely covering the bark surface with an emulsion-type spray containing 2 percent of DDT. Such sprays have produced residues that remained effective for more than 3 months. This method of control can be applied to individual trees. Further experimentation with these DDT sprays is necessary before we can make recommendations for their general use.

R. U. Swingle *is a senior pathologist in the Division of Forest Pathology, Bureau of Plant Industry, Soils, and Agricultural Engineering.*

R. R. Whitten *is a senior entomologist in the Division of Forest Insect Investigations, Bureau of Entomology and Plant Quarantine.*

E. G. Brewer *is in charge of Dutch elm disease control, Bureau of Entomology and Plant Quarantine.*

# BLISTER RUST ON WHITE PINE

J. F. MARTIN, PERLEY SPAULDING

White pine blister rust is a fungus that attacks and destroys the highly valued white, or five-needled, pines. It spreads to pines from its alternate hosts, currants and gooseberries, without which the fungus cannot infect white pines. Thus the disease is controlled by removing the alternate host plants, commonly called ribes, in the vicinity of white pines.

A point to note is that white pine blister rust is an introduced disease, not a native. Most native tree diseases are curbed by natural conditions, so that in a given outbreak they are fatal only to individuals or groups of individuals. But introduced diseases are free from the natural controls of their native habitat; in their new environment, if the conditions are unusually favorable, they sometimes become epidemic and destructive, although the existence of an entire tree species is rarely endangered.

White pine blister rust was first found in North America at Geneva, N. Y., in 1906. It occurred on cultivated ribes, and the bushes were promptly destroyed. The disease was found again in 1909 in new plantations of eastern white pines, large numbers of which had just been imported from Europe to fill a heavy demand for forest planting stock. The shipments went to most of the Northeastern and Lake States, and to eastern Canada. Many of them contained infected trees, and so the disease was widely distributed within the native range of eastern white pine. The State officials concerned immediately agreed on concerted action to find and destroy all infected pines and remove all ribes within 500 feet of the diseased plantations. They hoped thus to eradicate the fungus. The action delayed the spread of the disease, but in 1913 it became evident that infection had spread to the native white pines. By 1915 all hope of eradicating the fungus from North America was abandoned. Efforts then were concentrated on local control to prevent serious damage in stands of eastern white pine.

In 1921 the disease was found near Vancouver and in northwestern Washington on western white pine. The origin of that outbreak was a shipment of white pine nursery stock made directly from France to Vancouver in 1910.

Out of experiences with white pine blister rust, chestnut blight, and some forest insects that were known to have been imported from abroad came the enactment in 1912 of a Federal Plant Quarantine Act. The first quarantine under it prohibited further importation of white pines. Later the interstate movement of white pines and ribes was regulated to prevent spread of the disease by shipment of infected host plants. The affected States also enacted laws to control the blister rust or promulgated quarantines and regulations under established pest control laws pertaining to control of blister rust. Such action has been taken by 32 States. In 1917 a Federal embargo was placed on the movement of white pines and ribes from the Eastern States to points west of the Great Plains to prevent westward extension of the disease through the shipment of infected host plants. This embargo was lifted in 1926 after it became evident the disease had become widely scattered in western white pine forests. Adjustments were made in the Federal white pine blister rust quarantine from time to time to take care of problems created by the natural spread of the rust into uninfected territory and the removal of ribes in control areas.

White pines are among our most valuable and desirable forest trees.

Of the eight native species, three are among our leading timber species. They are the eastern white pine, which grows from Georgia to Maine and west to Minnesota; the western white pine, which is found chiefly in the Panhandle of Idaho and nearby parts of Montana and Washington; and the sugar pine of Oregon and California. They are a forest resource of great commercial importance. They are adaptable to a wide range of site conditions, they make rapid growth, and they lend themselves to forest management. Their timber, as it stands in the forest, is worth several hundred million dollars; its manufactured value is much greater. The younger growth is the timber crop of tomorrow. Both eastern and western white pine are used for reforestation. The eastern white pine also is used extensively in landscaping homes, parks, buildings, memorials, and like places.

Numerous logging, milling, and manufacturing industries that employ thousands of people and form the economic basis of many communities depend on the three species for raw material. The wood is soft, durable, fine-grained, easy to work, and excellent for patterns, matches, doors, window sashes, toys, and many other products. In northern Idaho and nearby parts of Washington and Montana, forest industries are a main support of the economic and social life. These industries, in turn, depend on western white pine, which represents about three-fourths the value of the forest products of the region. Without the white pine, the harvesting and utilization of associated trees would not be profitable.

The other five species grow at high elevations along the mountain ranges west of the Great Plains. They produce little timber, but they have considerable value in other ways—in protecting water supplies, preventing soil erosion, and making scenic and recreational areas.

Now all eight native species of white pines are endangered by blister rust. To save them will take united and sustained action by public and private agencies to bring the disease under control and keep it suppressed in pine-production areas.

Already the disease is established and is spreading in all commercial white pine belts. It is present throughout the range of eastern white pine except in the extreme southern fringe. In the West it has invaded the entire range of western white pine and of sugar pine as far south as Eldorado County in California—about 210 miles south of the Oregon border.

Further, the disease acts relentlessly and insidiously. The fungus destroys pines by girdling the limbs and trunk. Young seedlings are girdled in a short time. They die and disappear and leave no evidence that they ever existed. Diseased saplings may live several years before they succumb. Infected mature trees survive 20 years or more; if the disease is detected in time, most of them can be salvaged. No hope exists, however, for adequate future supplies of white pine if the young reproduction is killed or excessively thinned by the disease.

Ribes appear during the early formation of the forest stands. They reach maximum development in about 20 years. Then they decline. They grow from seeds, sprouts, and layered stems. Ribes usually are absent or sparse on light, sandy soils. They vary from few to many on the heavier soils. They persist indefinitely in places in the forest that are permanently open. They are suppressed by shade and root competition in fully stocked stands. Ribes are carried over from one forest generation to the next by viable seed stored beneath the litter on the forest floor. When this debris is disturbed by logging, fire, or other causes that expose the stored seed and increase the intensity of light, conditions become generally favorable for seed germination and growth of the ribes. Under those conditions, young ribes begin to produce seed in 3 to 5 years and seed storage begins anew. Ribes usually develop in abundance from seed following single light burns in forests.

In young stands, the crowns of the old ribes that are still alive may produce sprouts that grow rapidly. Double burns and severe single burns destroy the seed and crowns, and create ribes-free conditions except in wet and rocky places where they may survive the fire. The production and longevity of ribes seed, disturbances of the forest floor, shade, plant competition, and fire are factors in ribes suppression that receive careful consideration in planning control operations and forest-management practices.

Spores, the reproductive bodies of fungi, serve the same purpose for fungi that seeds do for ordinary crop plants. The blister rust spores are minute, dustlike particles that are easily carried by the wind. One kind of spore, produced in the diseased bark of white pines in the spring, cannot infect pines; they infect only ribes.

On ribes leaves, two kinds of spores are produced, an early- and a late-summer form. The early form can infect ribes leaves but not white pines. It is a repeating form, producing several generations in a season and causing local disease intensification on ribes. The late form infects white pine needles but not ribes. The fungus grows in the needles until it reaches the bark. There it causes spindle-shaped diseased areas called cankers. From 2 to 5 years after infection of the needles, spores begin to develop in the diseased bark. Thereafter each spring a new crop of spores is produced; they infect ribes and again start the life cycle of the fungus.

Blister rust may reach new localities by shipment and planting of infected white pine or ribes and by wind-borne spores from infected pines. Distance is not a limiting factor in the spread of the disease by shipment of infected host plants. Investigations in western North America showed that the disease was spread by wind-borne spores from infected pines to ribes over distances of several hundred miles. From infected ribes to the pines, however, the spread usually does not exceed 900 feet. Under especially favorable weather and topographic conditions, the spread sometimes extends for a mile or more. The amount of pine infection rapidly lessens as the distance from diseased ribes increases.

The different native white pines are highly susceptible, although there is some evidence of resistant trees among species. Native ribes species vary widely in their reaction to the rust. Some are highly susceptible, while others seldom take the disease. That fact, however, has had no significant effect on the spread or control of the disease, because susceptible ribes species are well distributed throughout the range of the white pines.

In new localities the disease follows a definite course. It starts as a single infection or several scattered infections on ribes and is transmitted to nearby white pine. Two to five years later the diseased pine produces spores that infect nearby ribes. In turn, the local pine infection increases. After this situation has developed in several spots, a favorable rust year causes abundant and widespread infection on the ribes and pines, and many pines die.

The white pines would be doomed within a few years were it not that the rate of spread of the fungus depends on the simultaneous occurrence of several factors: Widespread infection on ribes, abundant production of pine-infecting spores, and a favorable combination of temperature and moisture conditions. The integration of such conditions over extensive areas fortunately are infrequent, and new infection of pine is light in most years. Only in an occasional year is it so general as to cause widespread damage.

The control of blister rust and similar epidemic diseases, we believe, is largely a public problem because of their effect on national welfare, their interstate distribution, and the need for coordinated effort in their control. The forest resources attacked by blister rust are spread over many States and involve lands in Federal, State, and private ownership. Ribes must be removed over extensive areas regardless of land ownership. Like other trees, the white pines require years of growth to produce a crop of timber. Many young stands cannot be harvested within the lifetime of the present owners. Under such conditions, only the support of all citizens can effect the coordination and cooperation required to control the disease.

Areas selected for blister rust protection total about 28 million acres. This control area is made up of the better white pine growing sites which were selected to supply our present white pine lumber requirements. However, the range of the white pines extends over large areas outside the selected control acreage. Some of this land is good white pine site, and whenever more favorable economic conditions justify such action, it can be brought into production by ribes eradication and by pine planting to supplement natural reproduction from surviving seed trees.

Practical control of blister rust was begun by the Department of Agriculture as a Federal-aid program in cooperation with the Northeastern States. As the disease spread, other States and the Federal land-managing agencies of the Department of Agriculture and the Department of the Interior joined in the control program. Responsibility for general leadership, coordination, and technical direction of the program is assigned to the Bureau of Entomology and Plant Quarantine. This avoids duplication of effort and provides a single basis for the coordination of field work in white pine areas. In this capacity the Bureau performs the overall activities that have a common application to the work of all cooperating agencies, such as the development of control methods for cheaper and better ways of destroying ribes. The results benefit all cooperating agencies and are made available for their use.

The Bureau is jointly responsible with landowners for control of the disease on white pine areas in State and private ownership. Besides the 32 States participating in control work, many counties, townships, lumber companies, timber-protective associations, and individuals cooperate in the work. Control operations on State and private lands are financed jointly with Federal and State funds, supplemented by county, township, and local contributions and services. Control work on federally owned lands is financed by Federal appropriations.

The Forest Service is responsible for control operations on national forest lands. In the Department of the Interior, the National Park Service is responsible for work on national parks, the Office of Indian Affairs for work on Indian reservations, and the Bureau of Land Management for the revested Oregon and California railroad grant lands. This cooperation develops a mutual interest, understanding, and purpose that has resulted in effective operation of the control program. The Division of Forest Pathology in the Bureau of Plant Industry, Soils, and Agricultural Engineering had charge of the research and field work during the early years of the control program and now performs the research on the fungus.

Ribes are removed from the control areas by hand, mechanical, and chemical methods.

Crews of one to five men systematically search selected white pine areas and uproot the ribes by hand or with picks. The method is in general use.

For use in places where hand methods are not practicable, the bulldozer is adapted for clearing concentrations of ribes from brushy bottom lands. Equipped with a brush-rake blade, it uproots the brush and ribes and pushes them into windrows for burning. The cleared area is seeded to forage crops and made into permanent meadows. Bulldozers with a winch rear-mounted to drag a five-toothed grapple can uproot large clumps of upland ribes.

In the western white pine forests of northern Idaho, sprays of sodium chlorate in water were used against the western black currant (*Ribes petio-*

*lare*), whose roots are often so tangled with those of other plants that hand-pulling is difficult and costly. A complete kill was had with one application of the spray to foliage and stems; about a pound of chemical was used in a gallon of water. Equally good results were obtained on this species with ammonium sulfamate and with dichlorophenoxyacetic acid, commonly called 2,4-D.

Ribes with roots extending under logs, between rocks, or in places where it is hard to dig are cut off at the crown; the freshly exposed surface is treated with equal parts of salt and borax, saturated ammonium sulfamate, or with concentrates of aqueous amine or ester in oil formulations of 2,4-D. When so applied, small amounts of the chemicals kill the crowns and roots of several species of ribes.

Intensive forest management is important in blister rust control areas as an aid in the suppression of ribes. Also, it helps keep the stands in vigorous condition and will result in the highest possible returns from the timber crop.

After the white pine crop is harvested, the viable ribes seed stored in the forest-floor mantle germinate. This exhausts the old seed, and removal of the new ribes before they produce seed prevents formation of another seed-storage problem and leaves the area essentially free of ribes. Thus, in the next crop cycle the suppression of ribes and management of pine stands for blister rust protection will be greatly simplified.

Progress is being made in the work. The blister rust control area totals about 28 million acres. The rust is under control on nearly 12 million acres, or 42 percent of the area. In the future only a low-cost maintenance program is needed to keep this acreage safe for the production of white pine. The initial phases of control have been applied to an additional 11 million acres, or 40 percent, of the control area. The acreage comprising this part of the control area is still in a critical condition with respect to the disease. The follow-up phases of suppression work must be properly timed and applied to bring control to where future needs can be met by a small maintenance program.

On the remaining 5 million acres, there is great need for initial removal of ribes. The disease is well distributed and ready to intensify and cause severe damage to pine when favorable infection conditions occur. In many areas the pine already has been abandoned to the rust because most of the trees are fatally infected. However, only a small amount of this untreated acreage can be worked annually with present facilities because first priority must be given to the necessary follow-up work on areas where the initial phases of control have been completed.

Control operations began in 1922 in cooperation with the Northeastern States. They were extended to the North Central, Southern Appalachian, Northwestern, and Pacific coast regions as they were invaded by the disease, but 11 years elapsed before control work was well under way in all commercial white pine regions. One of the first steps in controlling the rust in each region was to delay its natural spread as much as possible by removing the cultivated European black currant (*Ribes nigrum*). This plant is highly susceptible and one of the chief agents in the long-distance spread and establishment of the disease in new localities. Its early removal was an important factor in retarding the advance of the disease.

Extensive acreages were cleared of ribes between 1933 and 1941, first with members of the Civilian Conservation Corps and later with workers paid from unemployment-relief funds. When the Second World War began, it was impossible to maintain control of the disease in all protected areas because of labor shortages, increased costs, and other war-made conditions. Only a holding program on the better white pine areas was practicable then. Some of the progress already made was lost because partly protected areas could not be reworked at the proper time to keep the disease under control. A further set-back resulted from accelerated cutting of white pine that produced about 11 billion board feet of lumber for war use. The logging changed the status of a large acreage from mature stands to cut-over lands, much of which now supports white pine reproduction and ribes. Viable ribes seed stored in the forest-floor mantle during the early formation of the mature stands were released by the logging disturbance and produced bushes which must be removed to prevent loss of the young pine crop.

Thus at the end of the war came the need for a large rework program and for the removal of ribes from a large unworked acreage. Because the annual pine losses continue where ribes are present, much of the work is urgent, particularly in the younger stands. The longer it is delayed, the greater the loss. We think the most economical procedure is to establish the work on a stable basis that would provide for all the rework as it comes due each year and for extending initial work to unprotected stands as rapidly as possible.

The blister rust fungus cannot be eradicated but it can be controlled. We must pay the cost of saving the white pines. Past work and continuance of the control program will assure white pine production on a large part of the control area. In other parts, the existing white pines will be lost to the disease unless the areas are put in condition to grow white pines by removing the ribes. The selected acreage can be enlarged by planting good sites where ribes are absent or so few that they can be easily eradicated. Increasing application of forest-management practices in the production of white pine will help suppress ribes. The prospect is good for finding a cheap chemical for killing ribes that are resistant to 2,4-D. Cooperating public and private agencies and individuals are striving to control blister rust and there is an active public interest in the problem. Thus, the outlook is favorable for ultimately controlling the disease in selected white pine forest areas.

J. F. Martin *is head of the Division of Plant Disease Control, Bureau of Entomology and Plant Quarantine, and directs the cooperative programs for control of white pine blister rust and stem rust of small grains.*

Perley Spaulding *is a pathologist in the Division of Forest Pathology, Bureau of Plant Industry, Soils, and Agricultural Engineering. He performed much of the early investigational work and research on the white pine blister rust fungus.*

# DWARF MISTLETOES

LAKE S. GILL, JESS L. BEDWELL

The dwarf mistletoes are serious pests of western coniferous forests. The losses they inflict in volume of timber and quality of lumber have never been accurately evaluated but are believed to be exceeded only by the damage done by heart rots.

The dwarf mistletoes belong to the genus *Arceuthobium* (it is also called *Razoumofskya*), a group of the family *Loranthaceae,* of which all mistletoes and some other parasitic plants are members. Among their next of kin, in the genus *Phoradendron,* are the familiar Christmas mistletoes, which attack mostly deciduous trees and junipers. In North America the junipers and their relatives are immune to dwarf mistletoes, although the generic name, *Arceuthobium,* is derived from Greek words meaning "juniper living," because juniper is the most common host in the Mediterranean region, where these plants were first described. They have also been reported from China and constitute a problem in forest management in the Himalaya Mountains of India. The dwarf species attack only conifers and are not used for decorative or symbolic purposes.

Five species are recognized in North America. One of them, *A. pusillum,* is found only from the Great Lakes region east, mainly on spruce. The other four, typically western, range from Canada and Alaska to Mexico. Of these four, one (*A. americanum*) is confined to the ranges of lodgepole and jack pine, another (*A. douglasii*) to the range of inland Douglas-fir. Of the others, *A. vaginatum* is restricted to three-needled pines, notably *Pinus ponderosa* var. *scopulorum* in the southwestern United States and Mexico, and *A. campylopodum* attacks pine, spruce, fir, hemlock, and larch from Alaska to Arizona and, probably, Mexico.

The dwarf mistletoes have been reported in Arizona, California, Colorado, Connecticut, Idaho, Maine, Massachusetts, Michigan, Minnesota, Montana, Nevada, New Hampshire, New Jersey, New Mexico, New York, Oregon, Pennsylvania, Rhode Island, Texas (the northwestern part), Utah, Vermont, Washington, Wisconsin, and Wyoming. Although the list indicates widespread occurrence from east to west, it should be pointed out that none has been found in the island of ponderosa pine covering the Black Hills of South Dakota or in the great Douglas-fir forests on the west side of the Cascade Range north of the Umpqua-Willamette Divide. It is also notable that they do not attack the high-producing forests of the South. In Texas they are restricted to isolated mountain ranges in the northwestern part of the State, where the timber values are negligible.

THE DWARF MISTLETOES are leafless, flowering plants. They are dioecious—that is, the staminate, or male, flowers are borne on separate plants from those producing the seed. The root system of these parasites has developed into an absorption system, which can invade and maintain itself in both the wood and the bark of its host.

From the host it derives nutrients and water. The absorption system has been known to live for many years within the tissues of the host plant without producing aerial shoots. The shoots are segmented stems, which may or may not branch. In *A. pusillum* they attain a height of about an inch and are unbranched. In *A. campylopodum* and *A. vaginatum* they may become several inches long and are usually branched. The primary (if not the sole) function of the shoots is to produce flowers and fruits. Most of the *Phoradendrons,* on the other hand, appear capable of producing most of their own food and are believed to rob their host primarily of water and dissolved minerals.

In all species except *A. pusillum,* the fruits mature the second season after pollination. They are berrylike structures that vary in color from light green to blue green or even brown. In size and shape they resemble a grain of wheat.

The outside casing, or skin, of the fruit is a tough and elastic sac. At maturity the sac contains the seed and a hygroscopic material called viscin. As the viscin absorbs water, pressure against the elastic wall of the casing is increased. When the seed is ripe the casing is ruptured from its base, leaving one end of the sac open. Simultaneously, the wall of the casing contracts, and the seed is forcibly ejected into the air. The stems, or pedicels, supporting the ripe fruit curl downward in such a way that the base of the fruit points skyward at the time of the explosion and the expelled seed then follows a trajectory like a mortar shell. Seed that are shot from 20 or more feet above ground and allowed to follow their course without obstruction will usually travel from 20 to 40 feet horizontally—sometimes more than 60 feet.

The seed carries with it a small amount of the sticky viscin, which serves the double purpose of holding it fast to the medium on which it alights and of gathering and holding moisture for the protection of the primary root upon germination. With proper conditions of moisture and temperature, mistletoe seed will germinate on practically any substratum, but only those that happen to be on the young, tender branchlets of suitable host plants can survive. The primary rootlet then forces its way into the tender bark and from there establishes an absorption system inside the host; after 2 years or more it may produce many crops of aerial shoots.

The explosive nature of the seed dispersal tends to intensify the mistletoe on a tree once it is infected and leads also to a slow but steady encroachment of the parasite into the forest once it is established on a single tree. In that respect it differs fundamentally from the leafy or Christmas mistletoes, which are spread only by birds, with the result that trees are seldom infected until they are large enough to provide attractive roosting places. The distribution of the dwarf mistletoes indicates that they, too, may be carried long distances, presumably by birds.

THE ECONOMIC IMPORTANCE is great. Damage by mistletoe in the forest is of four general categories: Increased mortality, the lower timber quality, reduced increment, and predisposition to other diseases or insect attack.

Mistletoe is not a killing parasite in the sense that great numbers of trees may suddenly die from it. Except in the case of young seedlings that become infected, death due to the parasite is gradual. Nevertheless, infected merchantable trees do have a lower life expectancy than healthy ones. In an investigation that continued 30 years, it was concluded that mistletoe was the greatest single cause of loss in ponderosa pine in the Southwest.

Probably greater than mortality is the loss from degrade or cull in logs caused by mistletoe. Long-standing infections of the parasite frequently result in witches'-brooms and trunk cankers which either directly, or through the aid of secondary organisms, render a part of the stem useless or less valuable for lumber. Excessively large knots are commonly associated with mistletoe infection and in the case of old trunk infections the wood itself is brash, weak, and often discolored or pitch-soaked.

Mistletoe-infected trees. are poor seed producers. Stands that are attacked by the parasite therefore do not reproduce so abundantly as healthy ones. Besides, mistletoe retards the growth of its host tree. A number of studies in Western States indicated that mistletoe may reduce the lumber production of a tree by 30 to 50 percent.

Besides those direct losses from mistletoe, the parasite tends to weaken its host physiologically. Bark beetle outbreaks may easily originate in infected trees. Heart-rotting fungi find favorable ports of attack through the exposed wood in cankers or through the excessively large branches that are associated with infection. Root diseases that healthy trees could withstand frequently kill mistletoe-weakened trees.

THE ONLY EFFECTIVE METHOD known so far for controlling mistletoe is to prune it out and thereby eliminate the absorption system and the sources of reinfection. In the case of *A. vaginatum,* if an infected branch is cut 18 inches or more behind the mistletoe shoots the entire mistletoe plant is usually removed from the tree. Where shoots appear on a branch within 18 inches of the trunk, the chances are rather high that the absorption system will have invaded the trunk and that shoots will develop on it after pruning, usually at the cut. There is no satisfactory method of eliminating mistletoe from the trunk once it becomes established there. Young infections, where the shoots appear only on 3- to 4-year-old wood, can be safely cut less than 18 inches from the trunk.

Several pruning operations are usually required to eliminate mistletoe from the branches of a tree. That is because often a lag of several years occurs between the time infection takes place and the time the first shoots appear. These latent infections will be missed at the initial pruning. Because the seeds require 2 years to mature, the interval between pruning can be 2 years without danger of self-infection. Assuming that the trunk is not infected, one should be able to prune out all mistletoe at 2-year intervals in a period of 8 years or less. It is doubtful if heavily infected trees should be pruned even though the trunk has not been invaded. If the control operation requires the removal of more than one-third to one-half of the crown, one must consider the adverse effect of pruning alone on the physiology of the tree.

IN MANAGED FORESTS, in the case of infected stands subject to their first cut, mistletoed trees are marked for cutting wherever possible. Where such trees are not merchantable, they should be eliminated as a sanitary precaution, a practice that tends to reduce the source of mistletoe seed and thus protect the oncoming young trees from infection to some degree. It is most effective in lightly infected stands where practically all mistletoe trees can be cut without sacrificing other silvicultural principles.

In more heavily infected stands, where only the worst cases can be cut and a large number of lightly mistletoed trees remain, less protection is offered to the residual stand. Increased light and the stimulating effects of release tend to favor the production of mistletoe shoots; the result is that there is likely to be heavy self-infection and spread to the younger stories of the stand.

With more intensive management than is possible in virgin stands, mistletoe will demand more drastic control measures in order to attain maximum yields of wood.

Eradication of the parasite in second growth through a series of weeding, pruning, and thinning operations appears to be one effective method. Another would be to establish barrier zones around heavily infected centers in an effort to protect surrounding uninfected timber and keep the mistletoe confined to a small area, possibly until such time as it could be clear-cut and, if necessary, planted. In the case of *A. vaginatum,* recent studies indicate that a pine-free strip 60 feet wide should keep the parasite confined.

As the problem appears today, there is a need for developing more effective direct-control methods than the present one of physically removing the parasite by pruning and cutting. A selective substance that would kill it without deleterious effects on the host would be highly desirable if it could be produced and applied economically. Also needed is more knowledge of the behavior of the dwarf mistletoes in order that the best silvicultural-management practices can be developed in forests where the parasite is taking its annual toll of wood substance and tree life.

LAKE S. GILL *is in charge of the field headquarters of the Division of Forest Pathology in Albuquerque, N. Mex. He has studied the problem of mistletoe infestation for more than a decade and has developed much basic information on its development and spread. In cooperation with the Forest Service, Dr. Gill has also conducted experiments on the control of mistletoe in ponderosa pine in the Southwest.*

JESS L. BEDWELL *is in charge of the field headquarters of the Division of Forest Pathology in Portland, Oreg.*

*For further information on dwarf mistletoes and other diseases, insects, and parasites of forest and shade trees, the reader may consult publications listed in the later section, "For Further Reference." The publications are generally available in libraries; some of the bulletins listed can be obtained from the Office of Information, the United States Department of Agriculture.*

# HEART ROT

GEORGE H. HEPTING, JAMES W. KIMMEY

Heart rots, which are caused by fungi that attack the wood of living trees, are to blame for an estimated annual loss of 1.5 billion board feet in our commercial forests. In money, the loss lies somewhere between the approximately 10 million dollar value given the cull as stumpage and the 47 million dollar value given it as logs.

Every timber species in the United States is subject to attack by one or more species of the fungi, but fortunately a large part of the losses can be prevented by proper management.

In trees that have a clearly defined heartwood—oak, ash, and most conifers, for example—the heart rots are usually confined to the true heartwood. In many other hardwoods, normal heartwood forms irregularly, and decay of the inner sapwood is also called heart rot. The term "sap rot" is used for the decay of dead or dying sapwood.

When a fungus that is decaying the heartwood of a tree has developed for a number of years, it often produces a spore-bearing structure like a mushroom or a bracket-shaped conk. Each year one such structure can produce millions of tiny spores, which are carried about by air currents. When a spore comes to rest upon exposed wood and conditions are suitable, it germinates and sends fungus filaments into the wood. By means of these threads the fungus spreads through the tree, feeding upon and rotting the heartwood as it goes. Some fungi, which cause some of our common root and butt decays, rarely produce spores, but spread largely by growth through the soil.

Entrance points for rot fungi are usually provided by the exposure of heartwood when the trunk, top, limbs, or roots are wounded by fire, logging, or storms. Butt rot in sprout hardwoods usually is transmitted from the rotting stump to the attached sprout. Some of the most important heartwood destroyers gain entrance through branch stubs or branches killed by natural suppression.

THE HIGH DECAY CULL in many eastern hardwoods reflects mostly fire-scarring, ice damage, and abandonment of defective trees in past logging. Decay cull in most eastern softwoods and in the southern pines now has reached a small percentage because their cutting ages have been reduced. Improved timber management probably will keep the losses from decay at a low figure for those species.

The basic problem of timber management in the West now is to bring hitherto unmanaged forest land into maximum production. The two principal problem types are forest lands that have been cut-over or burned (on them new growth is inadequate) and stagnated virgin stands of overmature old-growth timber. Heart rots are involved in the management of both types. Through good forest practices, heart rots in future timber stands of the West may be kept at a minimum if the factors leading to heart rot are fully understood.

Decay factors affect silvicultural practices throughout the country in seven important ways: In the determination of the cutting age; in the system of harvest cutting; in the choice of trees to be cut in partial-cutting systems; in requiring special salvage cuts in timber burned or otherwise damaged; in managing mistletoe-damaged stands; in requiring the early treatment of hardwood stump sprouts; and in pruning and similar operations. Each is discussed here.

In most of our eastern and southern species, the age at which the trees will be cut (based upon the rate of return from the land) will be lower than the age at which decay ordinarily becomes a critical factor. This is true, for example, of the southern pines, white oak, yellow-poplar, sugar maple, and many other species. But in some species decay definitely limits the desired cutting age. In aspen in the Northeast and the Lake States, stands much older than 50 years are likely to be badly decayed. Decay should limit the cutting age of balsam fir to about 70 years. Most of the oaks will pass 150 years without major decay losses but decay cull usually results in the serious break-up of scarlet oak stands over 80 years old.

In the West, the thrifty, uninjured young forest trees are generally free from heart rots. After the virgin stands have been replaced by second growth, the most profitable cutting age occurs before heart rots become serious.

FREQUENT LIGHT CUTS in the large-crowned hardwoods result in a maximum of logging damage. Clear cutting in strips or blocks or adopting a minimum number of cuts per rotation consistent with good silviculture will cause the least logging injury and the lowest subsequent decay. Logging injuries provide good opportunities for the entrance of heart rot fungi. Careless felling and frequent cutting can cause considerable breaking of the tops and branches of residual trees. Wounds exposing only sapwood in resinous species often become covered with pitch so that fungi are largely excluded. Such wounds in nonresinous species, however, readily permit the establishment of sapwood fungi, and the subsequent checking and sloughing of the decayed sapwood exposes the heartwood beneath to heartwood destroyers.

Selective logging with heavy tractors often causes extensive wounding of residual trees unless special precaution is taken. All forms of damage, including branch and top breakage, felling scars, and butt injury from skidding and yarding, increase as the frequency of cutting in a given stand increases. Heavy partial cuts in old spruce and fir result in wind breakage to the remaining stand, because these old trees are commonly heavily butt-rotted. Under such conditions some form of clear cutting should be considered in place of partial cutting.

Where partial cuts are made, the forester always aims to retain the trees that are increasing the most in volume. He marks for cutting the heavily defective trees, particularly those that are losing more wood from decay than they are adding through growth. Aids are available for estimating internal defect from external signs in some eastern and western species. The timber marker who can estimate the decay situation in a given tree can greatly enhance the net growth in selection systems of silviculture by eliminating defective trees in the earliest cuts.

Heart rots in the overmature stands of the West present a major problem in forest management. Whether such stands are clear-cut or selectively cut, all highly defective trees should be cut whether they are merchantable or not, unless it is necessary to leave them for seed trees to restock the area. In some stands there are so many cull trees that the sound timber available will not pay for their cutting and still leave a profit for the operator. Even if all were felled, considerable damage would be done to young trees and other timber left standing on the area, new young growth would be obstructed, and a serious fire hazard would develop. If they are left standing, they occupy a large percentage of the area that should be taken over by vigorous young trees.

How to dispose of the obviously worthless trees under these circumstances is a challenging problem. This same problem arises in connection with large areas of high-graded timberland in both the East and West. On these areas only the best trees were removed, leaving a considerable stand of near-worthless timber. The systematic elimination of these trees, most of which are badly decayed, is now a prominent phase of the forest land-improvement operations in many sections of the country.

The heart rots that develop through naturally suppressed branches and branch stubs are the most prevalent in western conifers. Some fungi enter almost entirely through dead branches that contain heartwood and that are nearly always an inch or more in diameter. Others enter through branch stubs that contain heartwood. Management of forests to maintain a high density in the young stands, so that branches do not form heartwood before being shaded out, and artificial pruning in more open young stands will reduce the incidence of such decay. Ground fires, insect epidemics, and heavy partial cuts that heavily thin stands and thereby stimulate the formation of large branches on the surviving trees are important factors in providing favorable places of entrance for these fungi.

A stand of timber badly burned or damaged by wind or ice should be salvaged promptly or heavy losses from decay may ruin the merchantability of a high proportion of the volume. Prompt salvage cuts of this type require knowledge on the part of timber managers of the high toll that decays can take in badly broken or heavily fire-scarred stands.

Many timber stands have been repeatedly burned by ground fires so that practically all old trees have scars at their butts. Fungi entering through these scars account for a large proportion of the heart rot in older stands. The so-called butt rots are usually confined to the roots, stump, and basal 16-foot log, but occasionally extend much farther. Other rots known as trunk rots, which may enter through butt scars or any wound or dead stub on the trunk, usually are more extensive and often cause entire trees to be culled. The resinous pines are not so subject to butt rot following injury as the nonresinous conifers and hardwoods.

The dwarf mistletoes of western conifers cause enlarged branches and burls on the trunk that provide points of entrance for heart rot fungi in old trees. Dead areas on these burls, stubs of swollen branches, holes in the stem where enlarged branches have been pulled out, and broken tops offer major rot hazards from mistletoe infections. In western hemlock in the Northwest, heart rots established through mistletoed knots and burls account for more decay than from any other cause. Silvicultural methods to prevent serious mistletoe infections in future timber stands are now being developed.

In the East, oak stump sprouts that arise more than a couple of inches high on the parent stumps are very likely to become butt-rotted from the old stump. Ground-level sprouts seldom contract rot from a parent stump. One cleaning operation made in a sprout stand at about 15 years of age can eliminate the decay-susceptible high-origin sprouts and provide single-stemmed crop trees rather than sprout clumps. Two defects can thus be minimized by a timely cleaning. In the case of scarlet oak, a pruning at 15 to 20 years will eliminate many of the future rot pockets and holes at the bases of dead branches, so common in this poorly self-pruning species.

Decay reduction and silviculture are also linked in pruning, through decreasing decay where small branches are pruned or possibly increasing it where large branches are cut. The removal of trees with spore-shedding conks, where practicable, is good silviculture. A number of common heart rot fungi may enter the trunk through the roots, either through root wounds, root grafts, or contact with decayed roots of other trees. These rots are controllable mainly through the knowledge of the age at which they become important and arrangement of the cutting schedules accordingly.

Major losses from heart rot can definitely be prevented. A certain amount of decay is bound to occur in any timber stand, but we already have the means of keeping such losses to low levels. For many species that can be achieved by adjusting downward the cutting age when necessary, by eliminating fire, reducing felling and skidding injuries, favoring low-origin sprouts in hardwood cleanings, cutting defective trees in partial-cutting operations, controlling dwarf mistletoe, and by making prompt salvage in stands that have been heavily damaged by fire, wind, or ice.

By maintaining suitable density in stands until the lower tree trunks are cleared of branches, or by artificial pruning in the more open stands, the incidence of heart rot attacks that develop through dead branches and branch stubs can be considerably reduced in young stands of a number of important western conifers. Defects can also be reduced in eastern white pine and scarlet oak by early pruning.

In eastern and southern softwoods, a cutting age up to 80 years will avoid serious rot losses unless the stands are badly damaged. If fire-scarred pines or otherwise defective pines are removed during partial cuts, even longer rotations would be fairly safe from the decay standpoint for this group. In most eastern hardwoods that are not stump sprouts, cutting ages can be raised to more than 100 years with little loss from decay where the stands are undamaged. Many of the western conifers can be grown to even greater ages without serious decay.

The heart rots that develop through the roots, as in the case of many of the spruce, fir, and pine butt rots, will never be entirely eliminated. Where they are known to be common in a stand, however, cutting can be done early enough to minimize the loss, and in such a way that the residual stand will not suffer undue breakage or windthrow as a result of the decay.

George H. Hepting, *senior pathologist of the Division of Forest Pathology, Bureau of Plant Industry, Soils, and Agricultural Engineering, has been engaged in the study of diseases of forest and shade trees and forest products for more than 20 years. He has been stationed from time to time in the Northeast, the Middle Atlantic States, and the Deep South, and is now in charge of the work of his Division in the Southeast, with headquarters at Asheville, N. C.*

James W. Kimmey, *pathologist in the same Division, has for the past 20 years conducted research in forest pathology in the West. His territory has included the entire area west of the Rocky Mountains, and some investigations have taken him into western Canada as well. Dr. Kimmey is a graduate in forestry of Oregon State College and Yale University.*

# BREEDING AND SELECTING PEST-RESISTANT TREES

RUSSELL B. CLAPPER, JOHN M. MILLER

Genetics has given us a good new tool to use against the diseases and insects of trees—the selection and breeding of trees for resistance to pests. It is a long job. The time that a tree crop takes to produce seed and to mature exceeds the span of a human generation. Natural forces, aided now and then by man, have determined through the ages which forest species should survive, and these are the species with which the forester, the geneticist, and the forest pathologist now work.

Epidemics of introduced parasitic fungi stimulated interest in the development of healthier trees. Forty years ago the Department of Agriculture employed Walter Van Fleet to breed chestnut trees that would resist the introduced blight fungus. Since then several agencies have taken up the work of breeding and selection, for the most part to obtain vigorous, fast-growing specimens for lumber and other products. More recently, greater emphasis has been placed on develop-

802062°—49——31

ing trees resistant to particular fungus and virus diseases. The development of new forms resistant to insect enemies, however, has scarcely made a beginning.

The need for the work is clear enough. Besides the losses we have incurred, in some regions of the United States forest planting is coming into use as the surest and quickest method of reproducing the desired wood crops. Planting makes it possible to control the kind and variety of tree that occupies the site and gives special emphasis to the need for careful selection of the planting stock. It costs no more to plant the resistant trees, if they are available, than to plant ordinary stock.

In the development of trees resistant to a particular disease or insect enemy, the same principles of selection and genetics apply that are employed in the development of new, vigorous, and fast-growing tree forms. The tree breeder, however, usually desires both resistance and vigor in his final selection, but when the laws of heredity decree differently, the breeder faces a difficult problem. The solution of such problems requires knowledge of several sciences, especially genetics, plant pathology, entomology, and forestry.

The breeder first attempts to select trees that show resistance to the particular pest under study. Resistant selections are propagated by grafting or by cuttings. Seed from such selections is collected and thousands of seedlings are grown in nurseries where they may be tested against the pest, or the seedlings may be transplanted to testing plots where they can be tested at a more suitable age.

Sometimes selection results indicate that no individuals of the particular species or of related species are resistant. It is then necessary to import seed of foreign species for testing. The related foreign species, however, may possess no worthy characteristic other than that of resistance. The breeder must combine this character of resistance with the desirable characters of the susceptible species. The first step to bring about this combination is to produce a hybrid by crossing a resistant tree with a susceptible tree.

Hybrids obtained from the first crossing of two varieties or species are known as first filial ($F_1$) generation hybrids. If an $F_1$ tree sets seed by its own pollen (selfing), or if two or more $F_1$ trees are crossed with one another (sib-mating), the resulting hybrids belong to the second ($F_2$) generation. The $F_2$ and subsequent generations are called the segregating generations because all the characters, visible and invisible, that were present in the $F_1$ trees segregate out among the various trees of the later generations.

RESISTANCE to a pest may be inherited in one of three ways. If resistance is inherited as a dominant character, all the $F_1$ trees will be dominantly resistant and most of the $F_2$ trees will be similarly resistant. Resistance may be inherited as an incomplete dominant, in which instance the $F_1$ trees will be more or less intermediate in their resistance to the pest. The $F_1$ trees as a group will not show the resistance of the resistant parent nor the susceptibility of the other parent. In this type of inheritance the second and subsequent generations will produce a lower proportion of resistant trees than the first type of inheritance produces. If the breeder meets either one of these types of inheritance, he will have comparatively little difficulty in obtaining trees with a satisfactory degree of resistance. But susceptibility may be inherited as a dominant character. The first-generation trees will be susceptible and will have no value except for further breeding to obtain second-generation trees. The second generation in this instance must consist of large numbers of trees because the proportion of resistant specimens will be exceedingly small.

In agricultural crop breeding, the breeder usually fixes the type by inbreeding so that it reproduces more or less true from seed. The tree breeder cannot afford to fix his hybrid types

Tree hybrids usually lose vigor when inbred, and the process of inbreeding trees requires too long a time. When the tree breeder obtains maximum resistance in his hybrids in combination with other desirable characters, he is ready to plant them on appropriate sites for final testing. Since his hybrids, in general, will not breed true, the question arises as to the nature of the progeny from these hybrids when they are planted in the wood lot and in the forest. Part of the progeny may be resistant but not vigorous, another part may be vigorous but susceptible, and another part may be both vigorous and resistant. The tree breeder can determine the theoretical proportions of these progeny types because he knows the way in which characters are inherited in the species with which he works.

Each tree-breeding project presents problems of its own. Examples of experimental work will be described to illustrate various methods of testing trees for resistance to particular pests, and to indicate the progress that has been attained. However, most of the selecting and breeding of trees for resistance to pests is still exploratory—in only a few instances hybrids have been developed to the stage that permits planting them as replacements for their inferior parents.

White pines resistant to blister rust: A. J. Riker and associates at the University of Wisconsin, in cooperation with the Department of Agriculture, have tested selections of eastern white pine against the blister rust. One thousand grafts were made from 163 trees selected for their resistance to heavy natural infection for more than 15 years or for other special properties. Most of the grafts resisted artificial infections of the blister rust fungus. However, when 10,000 seedlings from the selected trees and commercial seedlings were subjected to natural and artificial infections, a high percentage of the seedlings were infected with stem cankers within a year. Ray R. Hirt of the New York State College of Forestry, in cooperation with the U. S. Department of Agriculture, observed eastern white pines of various ages in the period of 1927–47 for resistance to the rust. He found varying degrees of rust resistance in a small percentage of the total pines observed. Those trees showing greatest resistance to rust are being propagated by grafting and cuttings so that more extensive tests for resistance can be made. The low percentage of rust-resistant seedlings reported by Riker and Hirt indicates that rust resistance is not inherited as a dominant character.

The white pine blister rust fungus also attacks other five-needle species of pine. Forest pathologists are keenly interested in determining the relative susceptibility of native and exotic species of pine to the fungus. Seven species of pine were tested against rust by Ray R. Hirt, of the New York State College of Forestry; in the Northwest, nine species were tested by Thomas W. Childs and Jess L. Bedwell, of the Division of Forest Pathology.

The species of pine that showed resistance to blister rust were: *Pinus cembra* var. *helvetica, P. armandi, P. griffithii,* and *P. koraiensis*—all are foreign species but are not known to have any timber value. Those showing susceptibility in increasing degrees were: *P. aristata, P. peuce, P. ayacahuite, P. flexilis, P. monticola, P. albicaulis,* and *P. lambertiana.* Several trees of the latter species, commonly called sugar pine, have withstood infections from blister rust for 14 years and will be used as breeding and propagating material.

Resin midge: In the blister rust experiments, inherent resistance of selected pines was determined by inoculation tests. In the case of an insect parasite, the resin midge, we find that an external characteristic of the trees—new shoots with dry, smooth bark—is an indicator of resistance. The problem was approached by selecting for this particular character.

Resin midge resistance studies were carried on from 1930 to 1940 at the Institute of Forest Genetics, near Placerville, California. This undescribed species of resin midge (*Retinidiplosis* sp.) caused considerable damage to young planted ponderosa pines at the Institute and to natural reproduction throughout much of the western pine region during this period. The feeding habits of the larvae cause resin-filled pits in the thin bark of the stems and twigs, and these pits result in growth deformities and dwarfing of the trees. In time the heavily injured trees die.

A study of the stem characteristics of many trees revealed that the heavily infested trees were those that produced new shoots covered with a sticky, resinous film, a growth character of certain trees. Noninfested trees were those that produced new shoots with dry, smooth bark. The data collected showed that only 11.2 percent of the sticky-stemmed trees escaped injury, while 93.4 percent of the smooth-stemmed trees escaped injury entirely or were only lightly attacked. The next phase of these investigations will be to determine whether dry, smooth bark is inheritable and, if so, to produce trees with this characteristic for reforestation purposes.

RESISTANCE TO WEEVIL: Resistance in pine to another parasitic insect, a weevil, was obtained by crossing a resistant with a susceptible species. The insect (*Cylindrocopturus eatoni*) is the most important enemy of young planted pines in the brush fields of northern California where, in some areas, it killed 90 percent of the trees within 10 years after planting. It also killed natural reproduction that was restocking burned-over pine areas. The trees are killed by the larval mines that extend through the phloem and cambium areas and later into the wood. In nature, the weevil's preferred hosts are ponderosa pine and Jeffrey pine. A number of other species of pines, such as Coulter pine and sugar pine, appear to be immune to its attacks.

Studies were begun at the Institute of Forest Genetics in 1946 to determine whether a resistant variety of pine could be developed that would have the same desirable wood qualities as ponderosa and Jeffrey and at the same time survive weevil infestations during the early years of growth. A number of species, hybrids, and varieties of pines were tested by forcing the attacks of the weevil on them under cage control. Among the trees tested was a new hybrid pine first produced by geneticists at the Institute in 1939 by crossing Jeffrey pine with a natural hybrid of Coulter pine.

The tests confirmed field observations that ponderosa and Jeffrey pines were generally susceptible to the weevil although some trees proved to be resistant. The Coulter pine was uniformly resistant as was also the Jeffrey-Coulter hybrid. Here we have indications of resistance to insect attack being inherited as a dominant character, not only in the first generation hybrid but also in the backcross of this hybrid on the susceptible Jeffrey pine.

ELMS RESISTANT TO THE DUTCH ELM DISEASE: The Dutch elm disease, which was discovered in this country in 1930, now threatens all native and European elm species in the United States. Elm bark beetles spread the disease.

Efforts to control the disease include destruction of infected trees, pruning infected limbs, and destroying, debarking, or spraying elm logs.

The American elm is an important forest and shade tree, native to parts of all States from the Great Plains eastward to the Atlantic coast. Two minor species, also native, are the rock elm and the slippery elm, both susceptible to the Dutch elm disease. The Siberian elm is resistant.

In 1937, scientists in the Division of Forest Pathology began breeding and selecting elms for resistance to the Dutch elm disease. Thirty-five thousand elm seedlings, collected in the Great Plains and Northeastern and

Central States, were grown in test nurseries. The seedlings were inoculated with the Dutch elm disease fungus, with the result that only two seedlings withstood inoculations in three consecutive seasons.

The American, Siberian, and rock elms bloom in the early spring, and low temperatures and strong winds are not conducive to delicate manipulations of the flowers or favorable to pollination and seed setting. A difference in chromosome numbers leads to further difficulties in obtaining progeny in large numbers. From about 20,000 controlled American-Siberian elm crosses, fewer than 100 seed were obtained, and only a fraction of those germinated. Of the hybrids obtained, one has resisted repeated inoculations with the Dutch elm disease fungus.

In 1939 some specimens of a European elm, selected for their resistance to the disease, were imported. They have retained their high degree of resistance but have failed to grow as rapidly as American elms nearby, and they do not have the characteristic shape of the American.

CHESTNUT TREES RESISTANT TO BLIGHT: The chestnut blight was discovered in New York City in 1904, and within 40 years all American chestnut stands from Maine to northern Georgia and westward to Ohio, Kentucky, and Tennessee were killed.

So far as the American chestnut is concerned, there is no control for the blight. This chestnut apparently is completely susceptible to the blight fungus. Even today there are few seedlings or sprouts that appear to be resistant.

Large-scale introductions of blight-resistant species of chestnuts from the Orient were necessary for an effective breeding program. The early breeding work of Walter Van Fleet was limited to a few introductions of the Chinese and Japanese chestnuts. Hybrids of these and the American chestnut usually died from the blight a few years after bearing.

In the breeding program, continued since 1925 by Russell B. Clapper, the present objective is to obtain the maximum vigor and resistance to blight in the first-generation trees derived from crossing the American chestnut with proved selections of Chinese chestnut. One lot of first-generation trees in Maryland grow an average of 2¾ feet a year and have considerable blight resistance. New combinations of American and Chinese chestnut are being produced for testing. Natural-crossing plots, where the American will cross naturally with a proved Chinese chestnut, will be established for the production of hybrid seed in quantity.

A number of the Chinese-American chestnut hybrids have been backcrossed to the resistant Chinese parent trees. The resulting backcross generation shows somewhat less vigor and, in some instances, poor stem form, when compared with the first-generation trees. They have practically the same degree of blight resistance, however, as the Chinese parent trees.

The Brooklyn Botanic Garden, in cooperation with the Department of Agriculture, began breeding chestnuts in 1930. Arthur H. Graves has headed the project. His objective also is to obtain a superior blight-resistant forest tree to replace the American chestnut. Promising hybrids, some with genes from the Japanese chestnut, some with genes from the Chinese chestnut, and others with genes from both species, are being tested on the same forest sites along with hybrids produced by the Division of Forest Pathology.

From about 1930, seedlings of the Chinese and Japanese chestnuts were available in large numbers, and experimental forest plantings were established under many varied site, soil, and climatic conditions, with varying degrees of success. With few exceptions, the Chinese chestnut appears to be superior to the Japanese chestnut in blight resistance, rate of growth, and stem form. Planted in the most favorable environments, the Chinese chestnut shows promise of making a fair timber tree.

The Division of Forest Pathology now is establishing the best strains of Chinese chestnut on the best types of sites, so that there will be permanent sources of seed for dissemination and distribution. Cooperators' plantings already are furnishing valuable seed for these plantings.

OTHER BREEDING AND SELECTION WORK: From 1930 to 1941 studies by R. C. Hall and others of the Forest Insect Laboratory at Columbus, Ohio, revealed that two recognized varieties of black locust were resistant to attacks of the locust borer, *Megacyllene robiniae* (Forst.). This borer has caused widespread damage to black locusts in the eastern part of the United States. From eggs deposited in bark crevices, the young larvae mine the inner bark and cambium. Later the mines are extended into the sapwood and eventually into the heartwood. Tests made on one of the resistant varieties, the Higbee locust of southern Indiana, showed that about 95 percent of the larvae planted in the bark crevices started mines in the inner bark, but only about 20 percent reached the wood and matured there. In susceptible locust varieties, practically all the planted larvae mined the inner bark and lived to the adult stage.

In 1924 the Oxford Paper Company, in cooperation with the New York Botanical Garden, began a poplar-breeding project. Approximately 13,000 hybrids were produced by crossing 34 different types of poplars. A number of plantations have been established in the eastern part of the country and the poplars are being observed for their reactions to various diseases. A. J. Riker, of the University of Wisconsin, is also testing hybrid poplars and selections of the native poplars for their qualities, including resistance to various diseases. The Division of Forest Pathology is inoculating various poplar hybrids in an attempt to obtain one that is resistant to Septoria canker and other diseases.

The mimosa is an important shade and ornamental tree in the South. A wilt disease was discovered on mimosas in 1935; since then the disease has killed entire plantings and threatens many more. Search for resistant trees started in 1939. Hundreds of seedlings, grown from seed collected from Maryland to Louisiana, were inoculated with the wilt fungus, with the result that 20 seedlings remained wilt-free. These will be crossed with one another in an attempt to get better and more resistant mimosas.

Selections of elms are being investigated by Roger U. Swingle, of the Division of Forest Pathology at Columbus, Ohio, for resistance to the virus disease, phloem necrosis. From an area where the disease has occurred for more than 50 years, about 2,000 trees that were selected from open-pollinated stock have shown high resistance to the virus. The more resistant trees are being propagated by root cuttings.

Workers in the Arnold Arboretum, Jamaica Plain, Mass., are breeding species of pines for timber purposes and are selecting from first- and second-generation hybrids for resistance to insects and diseases. They are also crossing two Oriental species of elm, *Ulmus japonica* and *U. wilsoniana*. Hybrids of those species are resistant to the elm leaf beetle.

FEDERAL, STATE, AND PUBLIC PARKS nurserymen each year plant millions of tree seedlings. The seedlings are derived from seed that came mostly from trees that are susceptible to attacks of various insects, fungi, and viruses. The planted trees will likewise be subject to attacks of these pests, resulting in the partial or total loss of time and effort of many years. One prime objective of the tree breeder is to develop forms resistant to pest attacks and to multiply those forms so that they will be available in quantities for distribution and planting. Both phases of this objective usually require many years of work. Although nature successfully replants tree species generation after generation, man is learning more and more about how to do the job with better trees.

RUSSELL B. CLAPPER *is an associate pathologist in the Bureau of Plant Industry, Soils, and Agricultural Engineering. Since 1925 he has been making all types of crosses between the Oriental chestnuts, the American chestnut, and native chinquapins to determine the resistance of the new hybrids to the blight and to find out how various other characters are inherited.*

JOHN M. MILLER, *a senior entomologist, conducts research and control investigations in the Forest Insect Division, Bureau of Entomology and Plant Quarantine. He has been with the Department of Agriculture since 1910. Since 1945 he has been conducting studies dealing with the resistance of new pine hybrids at the Institute of Forest Genetics, near Placerville, Calif.*

# THE AIRPLANE IN FOREST-PEST CONTROL

J. S. YUILL, C. B. EATON

The airplane has become a new weapon in the never-ending battle against destructive forest insects. As in military operations, it is bringing about radical changes in strategy. Aircraft are serving two purposes in this phase of forest protection: For detection surveys to locate serious insect outbreaks and for the application of insecticides to control dangerous infestations.

The extent to which those operations can be carried on from the ground is seriously limited because the areas involved are often large and remote, and because the cost of ground operations in forests is high, even under the most favorable conditions. Many outbreaks of insects in the past consequently have had to be allowed to run their natural course until eventually they were checked by exhaustion of the food supply, changes in weather conditions, increase in the abundance of natural enemies, or other factors. But, in contrast to ground equipment, airplanes can cover large and isolated areas quickly and in most cases at a reasonable cost. Although improvements must be made in equipment and procedures to develop aerial methods for extensive general use, the progress since the Second World War has been encouraging.

Finding the enemy, estimating the numbers, and determining the rate of movement are as essential in combating insect outbreaks as in conducting a successful military campaign. The Bureau of Entomology and Plant Quarantine, in cooperation with various Federal, State, and private agencies, carries on extensive surveys each year to obtain such information for planning control operations. The work commonly includes cruising representative sample plots; reconnaissance inspections by truck, horseback, or foot; and visual examination from mountaintops or other vantage points. Obviously, the surveys are limited by the relatively small proportion of total forested area that can be covered in a season. In the search for better and faster methods, the idea was advanced that if the observer could use a moving observation point—an airplane—instead of a mountaintop he could cover much more territory in a day.

THE FIRST AIR SURVEYS of defoliating insects were conducted in Canada in 1922 and 1923. In a week, air-borne observers mapped several thousand square miles seriously defoliated by the spruce budworm; by ground methods, that work would have taken 3 to 4 months. In following years, limited air surveys were made in both Eastern and Western States to detect and map several other insect outbreaks. The disadvantage in all these attempts was that only the severe infestations could be detected; the lightly infested areas could not be distinguished, with the equipment of that time, from the areas that were uninfested.

From 1925 until the outbreak of the Second World War, periodic attempts were also made to use air surveys in connection with bark beetle control. Flights made over western forests were disappointing. Dying trees could be seen from the air, but equipment had not been developed for mapping accurately their location or determining the type and size of trees attacked. In the Eastern States, air surveys were most successful for locating trees infected with Dutch elm disease, which is transmitted by elm bark beetles. Observers flying at slow speeds in an autogiro could easily detect trees showing symptoms of the disease and could pin-point their location on a base map.

MORE RECENTLY, the depletion of forest resources during the war, the greater need for more adequate control of forest insects, and the wartime improvement in the aerial observation methods gave further impetus to surveys from the air.

Three methods are used: Sketch mapping, ocular estimating or strip counting, and photographic sampling.

The first is a "look-see" method similar to that employed in the early defoliator surveys. The area is covered in a systematic pattern and observers sketch in the boundaries of infested areas on previously prepared maps. Estimates of the extent of damage are made as the mapping progresses. In the Pacific Northwest an outbreak covering more than 700,000 acres was surveyed in this manner in 1947 at a cost of about one-tenth of a cent an acre. The method is still inadequate for detecting very light defoliator infestations, but recent improvements have made it a good way to get a quick, rough estimate of the insect conditions over a large area.

Ocular estimating is being used primarily for the bark beetle surveys in western forests. In this method the plane is flown along predetermined lines over the forest. The observer watches the ground through a port in the bottom of the fuselage and counts the number of dying trees in the sample strip traversed. The estimates obtained are then checked by limited ground surveys at various points within the forest area covered from the air.

In photographic sampling, representative localities within the forest are photographed with a special aerial camera. By taking pictures that overlap, stereoscopic methods can be used to pick out the dying trees and to estimate their size and crown characters.

These new improvements have already widened the scope of forest-insect surveys. Although the air surveys still supplement rather than replace ground methods, we expect that further improvements, particularly those in aerial photography, will make it possible to do more and more of the work from above the forest instead of in it.

INSECTICIDES were first applied from the air in 1921, when a small infestation of catalpa sphinx in Ohio was controlled by dusting lead arsenate from an open-cockpit biplane.

Soon afterwards, dust applications were made in the United States and Canada against the hemlock looper, spruce budworm, and gypsy moth, and in Europe against the nun moth, pine looper, cockchafer, and other pests. The results varied. The insecticide dusts killed most of the different insects, but the method of application had three shortcomings: The dust was frequently carried away by air currents after release from the plane; the dust particles did not stick to the tree foliage and were quickly removed by strong wind or rain; and, with any of the insecticides known at that time, the quantity of dust required made treating costs high—about $7 an acre.

Later, concentrated arsenical and fluorine sprays were developed to replace dusts. The sprays were less affected by wind and adhered to foliage much better, but the quantity of insecticide needed was still too high for economical application by airplane in this country. Aerial distribution of both sprays and dusts continued to be used to some extent in European forests because of the higher values at stake.

THE DISCOVERY of the astounding insecticidal properties of DDT in 1943 revolutionized airplane spraying. Here was a chemical that by previous standards was unbelievably toxic to many insects and was therefore just what was needed to make aerial application practical. Soon the military forces were spraying entire islands in the Pacific to kill mosquitoes and other disease-bearing insects, and when DDT and other new organic insecticides became available for civilian use, airplane applications were tried on crops and forests. The results of the trials in forest spraying were so encouraging that the insecticides have been put to a wider use each succeeding year.

Much of the forest spraying has been limited to applications covering fewer than 1,000 acres, although in 1947 413,000 acres of western forest land were successfully treated for control of the Douglas-fir tussock moth and in 1948 more than 200,000 acres of eastern woodland were likewise treated for gypsy moth. DDT sprays have been so effective against those insects that airplane spraying has become the standard method of control.

In experimental tests, good results also have been obtained in controlling the spruce budworm, hemlock looper, pine sawflies, and the Saratoga spittlebug, but with bark beetles and certain other insects control has been unsatisfactory. Thus, airplane spraying does not solve all forest-insect problems, primarily because of the difficulty of obtaining a uniform deposit on all trees and on all parts of a tree.

The method is most effective for the foliage-feeding species that actively move about in the tree crowns; with them, a uniform deposit is not necessary, because their normal activities eventually bring them in contact with a lethal dose of insecticide. The less active defoliators and those in protected, situations can probably be controlled, but higher dosages or multiple applications may be required to compensate for the uneven distribution of the insecticide.

It has not been possible to obtain an efficient deposit of DDT sprays on tree trunks or other vertical surfaces with aerial application.

THE SPRAY MIXTURE most commonly used in forests is a solution of DDT in No. 2 fuel oil. The DDT is first dissolved in a naphthenic hydrocarbon solvent and then diluted to the desired volume with the fuel oil. The usual dosage rate is 1 pound of DDT in 1 gallon of liquid an acre, although under favorable conditions dosages as low as ¼ pound in 1 gallon or less an acre have been effective for some insects. In spraying watersheds where fuel oil might impart an objectionable taste or odor to domestic water supplies, xylene is used as a solvent and kerosene substituted for fuel oil.

Emulsions and suspensions have been used to a limited degree in experimental work. The former are prepared by first dissolving the DDT in a solvent as in preparing oil solutions, then adding an emulsifying agent and diluting with water. Emulsions have two serious disadvantages: They cannot be exposed to freezing temperatures and they are more toxic to fish and other aquatic animals. Suspensions are made by dispersing wettable powders or so-called colloidal preparations in water. Wettable powders have not been satisfactory, because the suspended material tends to settle rapidly after mixing, clogging the equipment. The colloidal dispersions have not been adequately evaluated.

THE AIRPLANES most commonly used in 1948 to apply sprays were military biplane trainer-type aircraft

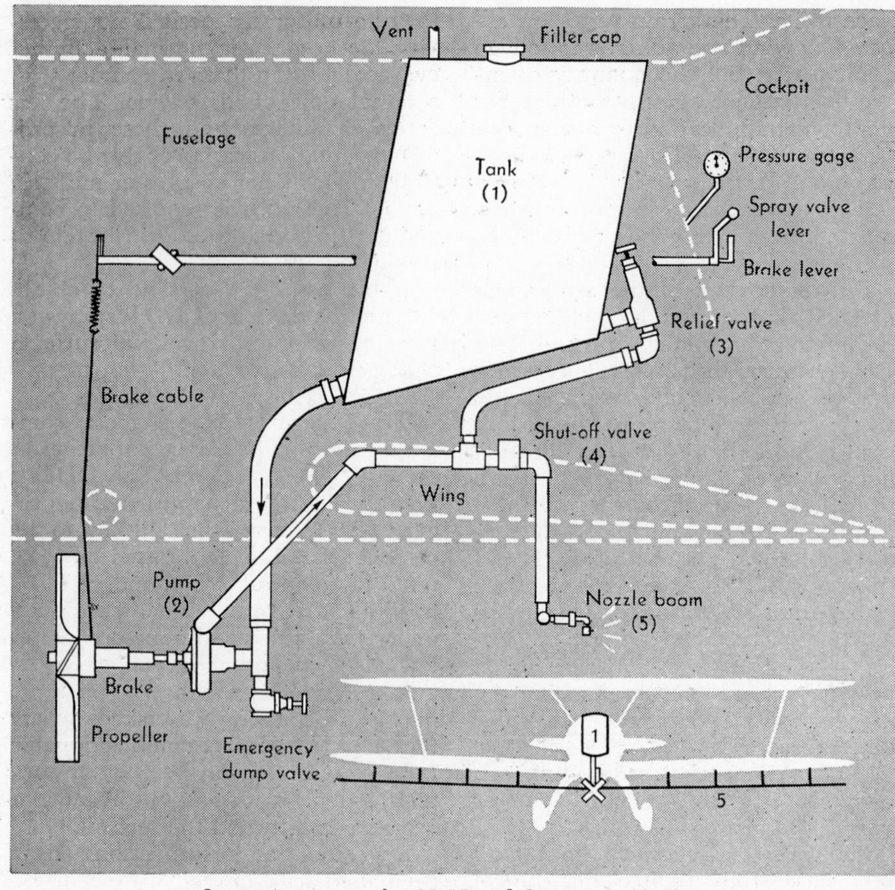


**Spray Apparatus for N3N and Stearman Airplane**

**1—Tank 70 to 80 gallons capacity, sloping bottom to provide positive drainage.**
**2—1¼- by 1-inch centrifugal pump will handle solutions, emulsions, or suspensions.**
**3—Relief valve, water type, adjustable, set for 25 psi; must have adequate capacity to maintain constant spray output at varying air speed.**
**4—Shut-off or control valve, quick acting cam type.**
**5—Nozzle boom, not less than 1 inch o. d. tubing, mounted beneath lower wing; fittings provided for 60 nozzles.**

(N3N and Stearman PT–17), which can carry about 80 gallons of spray and operate at 75 to 90 miles an hour. They are not ideal for the purpose, but they perform reasonably well, and, being war-surplus items, their initial cost is much less than that of many nonmilitary models.

Several other types of planes also have been employed—the light, high-wing monoplanes that fly at 60 miles an hour and carry only 25 gallons of spray, up to multiengine transports that fly at 150 miles an hour and carry 1,000 gallons of spray.

Helicopters, tested in experimental work, may prove useful in specialized operations because of their ability to fly low and slowly and to maneuver in small areas.

Spraying apparatus—because aerial spraying is such a new and rapidly expanding field—has not been standardized. A wide variety of distributing devices is used, such as rotating disks and brushes, venturis, nozzles, jets, and combinations of them.

For general forest spraying, the type of spray equipment shown in the diagram has been fairly satisfactory for light planes—it is simple to make, and the quantity of liquid applied and the atomization can be varied by changing the size and number of nozzles on the boom.

On the biplanes the tank is placed in the front cockpit, the pump is mounted on the landing-gear assembly, and the nozzle boom is suspended on brackets beneath the lower wing. The same type of apparatus can be adapted for larger planes, but even simpler equipment often has given fairly good performance, because the higher speed of large planes makes it possible to obtain adequate atomization of the liquid when it is discharged through straight pipes or horizontal tubes placed in the air stream beneath the fuselage.

Several types of spray apparatus have been reasonably satisfactory, but a great deal of improvement is still needed for more efficient distribution. Much remains to be learned about the type of outlets and their placement on the aircraft to obtain wider and more uniform deposit of the spray under different forest conditions. The spray apparatus in use today is patterned after ground equipment, but as our knowledge of the aerodynamics involved in spray dispersal increases, radically different sprayers may be developed.

The procedures in applying aerial sprays over forests are necessarily different from those employed in treating agricultural crops because of the larger areas involved, the irregular terrain, and uneven heights of trees.

Ordinarily, the area to be treated is first divided into blocks, using watercourses, ridges, and other features of the terrain as boundaries. If the ground is relatively flat, the pilot flies a grid pattern back and forth across the area, spacing the flight lines at a width previously determined to give satisfactory coverage of the area. This spacing, or swath width, ranges from about 60 to 400 feet, depending on the type of aircraft and the spray apparatus; for the biplane trainers the effective swath is 100 to 150 feet. Where the terrain is steep and irregular, as in many of the western forests, a grid flight pattern is unsafe, so the pilot must fly along the contours or down slope.

One of the most serious difficulties in forest spraying is to maintain the proper spacing of the flight lines. It is impossible for even the most expert pilot to estimate accurately the distance of successive swaths from the air, especially when spraying mountainous areas. Therefore small captive balloons, small wind socks, flags, or other markers often are placed in the treetops at intervals along the boundaries of the treated blocks to aid the pilot in maintaining an even pattern.

But where the area to be treated is large or inaccessible, the placing of markers by ground crews has been too time-consuming to be practical. Attempts have been made to drop markers from the air and to incorporate dyes or other materials in the spray liquid in order to make the spray deposit visible to the pilot. None of these devices have been successful, however, and considerably more developmental work will be needed to improve this phase of the operation.

In contrast to crop spraying, which is done 5 to 10 feet above the fields, the minimum safe altitude for forest spraying is 50 feet above the treetops. Over rough terrain or with the larger, less maneuverable planes, the altitude must be increased.

Wind and convection currents—the warm air rising from the ground—often carry the spray away from the area being treated or keep the spray cloud suspended above the treetops. For that reason spraying is usually confined to the early morning and evening hours, when air movement is at a minimum. Generally no spraying is done when the wind velocity is more than 10 miles an hour or when there is enough turbulence to make the air bumpy.

ARE FISH AND WILDLIFE harmed by insecticides? The use of DDT at the rate of a pound or less an acre has produced no serious effects on birds or mammals. This dosage can, under certain conditions, cause considerable injury to aquatic life. Game fish are little affected by 1 pound per acre applications, but the forms providing the bulk of fish food are sometimes sharply depleted. High dosages, on the other hand, can be very injurious. Therefore, with DDT or other new insecticides, the application rate should be held to the minimum necessary for effective control of the insect and, where extensive areas are to be treated, the work should be done under expert guidance.

THE COST of applying DDT sprays to forests has ranged from $1 to $3 or more an acre, depending on the type of terrain, size of the area to be treated, distance from the landing strip, dosage rate, and other conditions.

Such expenditures are not excessive for the protection of most forest areas when one takes into account the actual value of merchantable timber, the added fire-protection costs that may result from standing dead timber following an insect epidemic, the effect of loss of timber on the economy of the community, and the indirect losses such as erosion of watersheds.

Undoubtedly costs will decline as improvements are made in equipment, spray mixtures, and application procedures, with the result that more use will be made of aircraft for combating forest insects in the future.

It seems probable that those improvements will make it possible to locate outbreaks while they are in their initial stages and to apply insecticides before the infestations spread over large areas. Future trends are expected to be toward development of more sensitive photographic methods for early detection of insect damage, the use of larger aircraft for greater range of operation, the development of more efficient spray equipment designed on aerodynamic principles, and the application of various new insecticides.

J. S. YUILL *attended the University of Arizona and the University of California. He has been employed as an entomologist in the Division of Forest Insect Investigations, Bureau of Entomology and Plant Quarantine, since 1935. Until 1942 he was stationed at Berkeley, Calif., where he carried on research on various forest-insect problems of the California region. During the Second World War he served as a malaria control officer in the Navy. Since the war he has been engaged in the development of aerial spraying for control of forest insects at the Agricultural Research Center, Beltsville, Md.*

C. B. EATON, *a native of Massachusetts, is an entomologist in the Division of Forest Insect Investigations, Bureau of Entomology and Plant Quarantine. He was graduated from Syracuse University in 1934, and has been in forest insect research at various field stations since that time, except for 3½ years as entomologist in the Army Sanitary Corps. Since 1946 he has been at the Agricultural Research Center, working on the development of aerial spraying for forest-insect control.*

# Fire, Friend and Enemy

## PROGRESS, BUT STILL A PROBLEM

A. A. BROWN

IN 1947, in all parts of the United States, 200,799 forest fires burned over 23,226,000 acres—an area the size of Indiana—and caused tangible damage amounting to more than 55 million dollars to timber, farm homes, barns, towns, schoolhouses, places where men and women make their living and children have their being.

The damage to young tree growth, soil, watersheds, recreation areas, and wildlife cannot be converted readily into dollars, but it could easily add an equal amount to the loss we suffered from wild-land fires in just one year. Besides that, the work of controlling the fires to keep the damage from amounting to a more disastrous total cost landowners and taxpayers nearly 35 million dollars.

The record for 1947 is enough to show that fire on our wild lands is a big and important problem. Yet for the country as a whole the 1947 record was not unusual; in many past years it has been much worse.

---

*The drawing above, based on photographs, shows one terrifying aspect of forest fires.*

Forest fires remain a problem despite the great progress in dealing with them. It is a complex problem, because man-caused fires result from people's activities and habits: The man from the city, for instance, does not easily change his smoking habits when he goes into the woods. So, changing people's smoking habits becomes a part of the task.

It is complex, too, because the inflammability of forest fuels varies with weather and seasons from conditions where it takes great skill to get a campfire to burn, to conditions where a single spark explodes, as in a powder keg. So, prediction of fire danger and understanding of weather and forest fuel has become a part of forest fire-control activity.

It is complex because the value of our public forests depends on public use; as the desirable uses increase, the liability from fires generally increases. So, skillful regulation of public use also becomes a fire job.

It is particularly complex because successful fire fighting calls for quick action, yet forest fires usually start in places far from fire hydrants and paved streets.

Finally, it is complex because of the nature and behavior of uncontrolled fire. Many aspects of fire behavior are not yet fully understood, and big fires continue to defy man's efforts to control them at will by even the best of the methods that have been developed.

THE HISTORY of forest fires varies in detail from one part of the United States to another, and it is closely interwoven with our history of development. In most of our forest country it was an unhappy aspect of the conquest of the wilderness.

It is enough in this introductory survey merely to point to the use of fire to clear land when this country was young, to the big and intense fires that followed the early logging operations on millions of acres and held back a new timber crop, the awakening of citizens of half a century ago to the destruction to forest wealth that was taking place, the creation of the national forests and the enactment of many State laws designed to prevent fires and protect forest lands, and the banding together of responsible timberland owners into forest fire-protective associations in the West.

From such points of history two facts emerge: Despite a general change in attitudes about fires, the careless use of fire still persists among habits in parts of the country and remains a constant threat to the forests. Also, wherever forest lands exist, there has been a history of forest fires that have influenced the present-day forest. To the initiated, some of the things that past fires have done are clearly evident in every neglected forest tract. A forest fire may be small and it may be forgotten next year, but its effect on trees may persist for a long time. The continuing effect of fire in the forests is probably the most important single reason that forest fires, even small fires, concern everybody.

Fires such as those that occurred in 1910 in Idaho, which wiped out several million acres of virgin timber in a fe days, have not since been repeate thanks to the progress made in pro tecting forests since that time. But bi and destructive fires are still possibl even though not on so vast a scale— remember the 245,000-acre Tillamoo fire in Oregon in 1933, or the fires i Maine in 1947, when a thousand hom were destroyed.

SYSTEMATIC FOREST-FIRE CONTRO as we know it now, began in the We about a half century ago, when th possibility of controlling fire damag seemed almost like trying to contr storms and floods and the other gre forces in nature. Nevertheless, peopl realized that every fire started as small fire and that if action could b taken quickly enough it need not tur into a ruthless giant. Earlier, the chie concern in fighting forest fires had bee to protect human life and property systematic forest-fire control concen trated on the problem of protecting th forest itself.

From the start the forest fire fighte has needed equipment to make hi efforts count. At first he depended en tirely on the simple tools at hand o improvised with such things as a pin branch or a wet burlap sack. Generall he could not depend on using water Much of the story of progress in con trolling forest fires is the story of th development of more and more effec tive fire-fighting tools and of increasin mechanization of the slow and strenu ous hand work that fire fighting ha always called for.

The old problem of how to get to fire soon enough has been solved in th back country through the use of air planes and parachute jumpers; else where better roads and faster moto equipment now play a decisive role We also have portable pumps and tan trucks, which can apply water quickl to small fires within reach of any road way; radio communication, which enables a widely dispersed fire organiza tion to work together as a team; plow and bulldozers, which can establish uickly a fire line or furrow a barrier trip around the fire.

The application of systematic planing and scientific methods, described n succeeding articles, is reflected in the ecords for the national forests. The nnual area burned has decreased from nore than 5 million acres in 1910 and ½ million acres in 1919 to a level of million acres in the equally bad fire ears of 1926 and 1929. Then, following the organization of the Civilian Conservation Corps, the burn resulting rom the extreme drought years of 1931 nd 1934 was held to half that amount. n 1947 the burn on the national forests vas recorded at 475,000 acres, only lightly below those years, but with an verage since 1935 of less than 300,000 cres. Of significance too is size of the rea burned by each fire. Before 1930, he average was more than 100 acres; etween 1931 and 1940, it dropped to bout 40 acres; since 1940, the average as been 31 acres.

Such results would have been regarded as highly successful and satisfactory as late as 1930. But needs and alues have been changing rapidly; the ommercial value of the national forest roperties and the income they produce has more than doubled since 1930. The public importance of adequate protection of all forests from fire has increased similarly. No longer can even a destructive 5,000-acre forest fire (which would be far too small to be recalled in the forest history of 20 years ago) be regarded as anything short of a disaster.

In short, no longer have we any place in America where a big forest fire is not immediately destructive of some more of the wealth on which this country has been built.

A. A. BROWN, *a Kansan, was graduated in forestry from the University of Michigan. He entered the Forest Service in 1922 in Montana as a forest assistant. He later served on the Coeur d'Alene National Forest in Idaho, and as assistant forest supervisor on the Helena and Jefferson National Forests in Montana. In 1935 he was placed in charge of a forest fire-control planning project for all the California forests and in 1937 was made chief of fire control in Colorado, Kansas, Nebraska, South Dakota, and Wyoming. He was made chief of the Division of Fire Control in Washington in 1947.*

# BAD BUSINESS; YOUR BUSINESS

R. F. HAMMATT

On suitable areas and under well-planned use and control programs, ire may be a good tool in sound, long-erm management of land and resources. H. H. Chapman, professor meritus of the Yale University School f Forestry, declared that the proper se of fire, and not complete fire prevention, is the only solution of the problem of future forestry in the South. R. Merton Love and Burle J. Jones, of he California Agricultural Experiment Station, say that if governed urning is followed by revegetation nd controlled grazing, some California brushlands can be converted into grasslands that produce more meat, hides, and wool.

But those statements do not hold for wildfires. Wildfires are bad, a scourge to man and beast.

Consider what happened in Maine, for instance: In four fateful days in the fall of 1947 some 50 small wildfires, fanned by strong winds, seared a quarter of a million acres and took 16 lives.

Another instance: In the decade that ended in 1940, more than 2,100,000 wildfires swept forests and fields in the United States. That was at the rate of 575 each day. Those fires blackened an area more than seven times the size of Maine and all the other New England States. According to estimates made several years ago by the Association of American Railroads, the total amount of labor it took to put out those fires could maintain a right-of-way wide enough and long enough for nine trains to travel abreast from New York to San Francisco.

Destroyed by wildfires in those 10 years were billions of little trees that might have become forests when forests may be more sorely needed—10, 20, 50 years hence. Killed were enough big trees to keep all our daily and Sunday papers in newsprint for 11 years; or enough large trees, if made into 5-room houses, to wipe out the entire 1947 housing shortage of the United States, as estimated by the National Housing and Home Finance Agency, and leave some left over.

Trees hoary with age offer evidence that wildfires also occurred centuries ago. In *Great Forest Fires of America*, John D. Guthrie tells of basal scars that record conflagrations in California's big tree forests as far back as A. D. 245. Venerable Engelmann spruces still bear scars from fires that swept Colorado's mountain slopes in 1676, 1707, and 1781, he reports, and white spruce trees register wildfires that must have covered around 200 square miles in Maine 2 years before the frigate Old Ironsides was launched at Boston.

As calamities, great wildfires rank with floods, famines, and earthquakes. Such calamities may not have been so important when Indians formed the only—and a sparse—population in America, when they used fire as an aid in collecting acorns and grasshoppers for food, and when forests seemed inexhaustible. But many conditions have changed since then, and chronicles of the nineteenth and twentieth centuries reveal what seems to be ample justification for the statement.

Those chronicles tell us, for example, that 160 lives were lost when the Miramichi fire of 1825 roared across 3 million acres in New Brunswick, and that 1,500 people were killed by flam and smoke and crashing trees when th Peshtigo wildfire of 1871 wiped ou whole settlements as it ravaged a mi lion and a quarter acres in Wisconsi

Headstones in a forest-fringed cem tery at St. Maries, Idaho, tell of th death of 74 fire fighters who we trapped and burned in northern Idah and western Montana by raging wal of flame that jumped wide rive and laid waste a strip of mountai country 20 to 35 miles wide and 12 miles long. That was in 1910, aft wearied men had brought 90 larg wildfires and 3,000 small ones und control, despite months of high ten peratures and low humidities. The came sudden winds—and catastroph

High temperatures, low humiditie and sudden winds also set the stage f the Tillamook wildfire of August 193 In 11 days it roared through 267,00 acres of the finest virgin forests i Oregon, and burned timber equal i amount to the entire lumber cut of th United States in 1932.

But the damages wildfires do a not confined to the timber killed an the homes destroyed. Pocketbooks als suffer.

The 1947 Pellegrin fire, for instanc was in a mixture of brush and gra that may have seemed quite worthle to the casual passerby. But the burnin of this range forced ranchers to fin other feed for 500 cattle for 6 month And it threatened heavy winter loss among a herd of deer that for years ha attracted hunters—and their dollars— to California communities.

Farmers who manage their woodlan for maximum returns on a long-tim basis, and who like to go huntin now and then, know that even surfac fires often weaken cash-crop trees s they are more easily thrown by th wind. They know, too, that those fir can kill young trees and destroy co erts and nests of game birds and smal game animals.

Fishermen report that wood ashes i streams sometimes kill large numbe of trout. Sportsmen say it is not ur common for whole coveys of bewildered quail to turn back into fires from which they have just fled, then drop in the waves of heat and gas before being touched by the flames. Fire fighters tell of rabbits that have been blinded and of deer with feet so badly burned in hot ashes that they were easy prey for varmints.

There are many more small wildfires than big ones. Many people think small fires do no damage, but they are mistaken. Even small wildfires generally set in motion events that are often more far reaching and of greater importance than the immediate and direct damage done by their flames.

One such event was the destructive flood that occurred in Salt Lake City on August 19, 1945.

George W. Craddock, of the Intermountain Forest and Range Experiment Station, says this flood came during the night. From a city cemetery, he adds, it washed out more than 300 tombstones and many bodies. It spread debris, silt, gravel, and mud over streets and sidewalks. It clogged storm sewers, invaded garages and basements, cracked foundations, soaked food and furniture.

It was a man-caused wildfire that pulled the trigger on that flood. It burned only about 600 acres in grass-and-brush-covered foothill drainages north of the city. It was put out 11 months before the flood came. But by destroying the cover and impairing the power of the watershed to retain moisture, Craddock believes, it was definitely responsible for damage estimated at $347,000.

Studies by M. W. Talbot and C. J. Kraebel, of the California Forest and Range Experiment Station, reveal that water furnished by brush- and forest-covered mountains is essential in irrigating more than a million acres of high-value croplands in southern California, and in meeting domestic and industrial needs of some 4 million persons.

With about 50 percent of the population of the State, they say, southern California has only 2 percent of the water supply in California. Despite this shortage, however, they point out that it has serious flood problems. Kraebel recently said that many reservoirs in the south coastal basin of California have lost approximately a fourth of their capacity because of siltation, and some of them have been completely filled with debris. Because of this situation, he added, flood-control agencies that operate in Los Angeles County have already spent upwards of 200 million dollars for flood-control works and estimate that 100 million dollars more is necessary.

These works are designed to cope with heavy storm run-off that is greatly accelerated when wildfires burn steep brush-covered slopes.

The need for works of this nature—and for more help in stopping man-caused wildfires before they can get started—is illustrated by what has happened in many places at different times. Typical on a small scale is the aftermath of the Frankish Canyon wildfire of September 16, 1935.

Only 225 acres were burned in that canyon then, but foresters believed trouble would come to the San Antonio section, near the city of Upland. So the burn was sowed with wild mustard. The possible courses of floods were traced by Clark H. Gleason, Jr., who made a survey of potential flood hazards. Warnings were issued. When those went unheeded, the Forest Service built a small emergency basin to catch at least some of the expected debris.

Winter rains started before the mustard cover crop had grown enough to retard much run-off. The rains were ordinary in both amount and intensity, but they rolled down Frankish Canyon in three mud-and-boulder-laden floods. The floods wrecked homes, garages, pipelines, lawns, and trees. Neil F. Meadowcroft and Gleason estimated damage caused by this fire-induced flood at 47 thousand dollars, and expressed the opinion that it would have been much greater had it not been for

802062°—49——32

the 10,000 cubic yards of debris caught by the hastily built catchment basin.

Fires can start in many ways. According to official records, a bay horse feeding under a power line in a mountain meadow switched his tail into a slack wire at 1:14 p. m.

The resulting shock killed the horse and at the same time set his mane and tail on fire. This ignited the dry grass and spread over 55 acres of timber before the fire was brought under control. The reason the horse came in contact with the power line was that an insulator had been broken and the crossarm burned off, so that the line sagged within a few feet of the ground. Because the insulator had been reported to the power company as defective more than a year earlier, the fire was listed in the records as a wildfire due to man's negligence.

This listing was in line with two long-time Nation-wide averages. First: Although lightning starts 10 percent of wildfires, 9 out of 10 are man-caused. (The figure is higher in some parts of the West but lower in most of the South.) Second: Of every 9 man-caused wildfires, negligence and carelessness are responsible for 7, all of which could have been prevented if everybody had been careful.

Loggers say that the sun started one fire they put out. Smoke began to curl upward, they say, when the rays of the sun were focused by a bottle of kerosene (used to clean saws) onto a punky log. That is the only authenticated case of its kind I have found to date.

It is a matter of record, however, that friction of a steel cable wound around a stump started the disastrous Tillamook fire; that many wildfires are maliciously set—to satisfy pet peeves, to draw crowds and create excitement, to make jobs during depressions; others are started in misguided attempts to kill chiggers, spiders, and snakes.

Incendiarists start close to 28 percent of all man-caused wildfires, but farmers and ranchers are largely responsible for 16 percent.

It is not that farmers and ranchers set fires maliciously. They are too often careless about spark arrestors on machines like the combines and threshers. Or, not realizing what flames and live coals can do when abetted by high winds and low humidities, they neglect to keep complete control of the fires started to clear land, burn sedge or grass or debris, make berry patches and swamps more accessible, "green up" the woods for livestock, or smoke out bees.

Incendiarists are haled into court and prosecuted. As a preventive measure, so are people who are careless with outdoor fires—there are many more of these. Who are the careless people, who, in the aggregate, are responsible for most of our wildfires?

Among them are the people away from home who, in cars or on saddle horses or afoot, flip glowing matches or drop burning cigarettes and cigars, with no regard as to whether they roll into dry grass, brown pine needles, or dry leaves; logging bosses who fail to keep patrols on the job and to make frequent inspections of equipment and tools during fire weather; trainmen who dump hot ashes from dining-cars on railroad rights-of-way; hunters, campers, fishermen, and picnickers who, besides being careless with matches and cigarettes, forget—or do not know how—to put campfires completely out—dead out. In brief, these people are average Americans—the otherwise law-abiding citizens who visit or travel through forests and fields, who live in or near them, or who make their living in them.

Shortly after Pearl Harbor the armed forces called for intensified efforts to stop man-made wildfires before they started. Their reasons are worth repeating for the persons who, when they think of forests and fields at all, think of them only as pleasant places to visit:

1. Conservation of wood for wartime needs. (More wood than steel was used in war activities in 1942.)

2. Conservation of manpower for raising food and for war industries. (Records show that almost a million man-days of labor were being drawn yearly from farms and factories to put out man-made—and therefore preventable—wildfires.)

3. Conservation of grass and stubble (food for cattle and sheep) on ranges and farms.

4. Removal of threats by fires to uninterrupted use of vital railroads, truck lines, and war plants and cantonments that were in or near forest and range areas.

5. Prevention of "black days" that interrupted training schedules for airplane pilots and gunners. (Smoke from Wisconsin wildfires in 1894 was so dense over the Great Lakes as to interfere with the movement of vessels, according to John D. Guthrie. He also states that smoke from wildfires in Washington and Oregon interfered for 10 days in 1910 with nautical observations 500 miles at sea.)

Many methods for preventing the start of man-caused wildfires were intensified during the war. Three that seem to offer promise for the years ahead were:

1. Personal appeals by forestry representatives to key people among lumbermen, ranchers, resort owners.

2. Cooperation of State and Federal forestry and highway departments with counties, railroads, and industries in locating and then fireproofing the most hazardous stretches along roads and railroads and at sawmills and industrial plants.

3. Law enforcement—including arrest and vigorous prosecution if necessary—against incendiarists and individuals and organizations guilty of carelessness with outdoor fires.

Those methods helped to reduce the number of man-caused wildfires during the 4 years from 1942 through 1945. Also helpful were gas rationing and the Wartime Forest Fire Prevention Campaign, which was started in 1942.

The Wartime Forest Fire Prevention Campaign was (and still is, under the name of Cooperative Forest Fire Prevention Campaign) a Nation-wide educational program planned by the Advertising Council, which charted drives like those to save food and buy bonds. The campaign, a cooperative effort by State and Federal foresters, helped by winning support among national as well as local merchandisers and advertisers; by laying a ground work on which State and local campaigns might build; and by enlisting active cooperation among such national organizations as the American Red Cross, which continues to urge its chapters to help prevent wildfires because they so often bring disasters to families and communities.

This campaign helped, but it did not take the place of the measures previously mentioned—planned personal contacts by forest officers with key people, law enforcement, or fireproofing of selected high hazards.

It was all of those methods, rather than any one or two, that reduced by 18 percent the average number of man-caused wildfires during the 4 war years in comparison with the average number during the 4 years immediately before the war. This 18 percent is the Nation-wide figure for all forest and grassland in all ownerships and under organized fire protection in the United States, except Hawaii. It is derived from data furnished by State foresters and Federal agencies. In the 4 war years, also, the number of fires caused by campers dropped 50 percent from the number in the 4 prewar years; those caused by smokers dropped 29 percent; by burners of brush, 15 percent; by incendiarists, 13 percent; by lumber operations, 18 percent; and unknown, 8 percent. Only the number caused by railroads went up, by 38 percent.

The increase in railroad fires probably was due in large part to the overloading of equipment and shortage of skilled workers during the war. It is interesting to note, however, that although a comparable situation prevailed in the lumber industry, wildfires for which it was responsible—which made up 2 percent of the same prewar total—dropped 18 percent.

It is encouraging to see such Nation-wide decreases as 50 percent in the number of wildfires started during the war by careless campers and 29 percent in the number for which smokers were responsible. Encouraging, too, are the wartime records of States like Washington and Virginia, particularly when compared with what happened in California, for instance. In California an increase of 23 percent in civilian population was accompanied by an increase of 4 percent in the number of man-caused wildfires. But in Washington and Virginia, increases of 18 and 5 percent, respectively, in civilian population were accompanied by wildfire decreases of 22 and 39 percent.

The war ended. The fighters returned. Tanks could be filled with gasoline again. Once more the open road beckoned. The trek to fields and forests was in full swing by the summer of 1946. Before the snow fell, the number of man-made wildfires again had started to climb. The climb was only 2 percent Nation-wide, to be sure, but enough to be an ominous warning of what can happen if we are careless.

WE KNOW THE HEART of the problem is that 90 percent of all wildfires are still caused by people; that most of these wildfires are due to carelessness; that they are started by travelers, smokers, campers, hunters, fishermen, farmers—men, women, and children, average Americans who live in or near forests and fields, who work in or near them, or who visit them—*by all of us.*

We also know that these fires can be stopped before they start if each one of us does his part instead of leaving the job to the other fellow.

It was in that frame of mind that citizens of California approached their wildfire problem in the early spring of 1947. And although both population and the number of man-made outdoor fires had gone higher in 1946 than the wartime average for the State, progress was made before rains began in the fall of 1947, and continued through 1948.

According to State Forester DeWitt Nelson, Californians achieved a 28-percent drop from the 1946 number in their man-made wildfires. Even more noteworthy was a reduction of 50 percent in one county, Sonoma, where 498 active fire-prevention volunteers were recruited by the Central Sonoma County Chapter of the American Red Cross, acting in response to requests from officials of the State Division of Forestry.

What was done in Sonoma County indicates some of the things that may be done in other years and other places. Here are highlights from a report to the Chapter Chairman telling who the volunteers were and what they did.

Every volunteer, says the report, is a busy businessman or woman whose name is listed in classified sections of local telephone directories. Among these volunteers—who gave willingly of their time through a desire to help their own communities and their own county—were agricultural-implement dealers and auto-court owners; workers in banks and building and loan associations; barbers and book sellers; librarians; employees of public utilities, service stations, and sporting-goods stores; and members of women's clubs.

Among the outstanding volunteers, the report cites bank managers who enclosed "Smokey Bear" bookmarks with monthly statements to depositors; managers of sporting-goods stores who attached to each hunting and fishing license they issued a card with pithy suggestions about careful use and disposal of matches, cigarettes, and campfires; and owners of auto courts who kept fire-prevention blotters on desks or tables in each unit, and displayed posters on back walls of garages where they were in plain view of arriving and departing motorists.

It seems improbable that an educational set-up like the one in Sonoma County can do the whole job of preventing man-made wildfires. Also necessary will be such measures as law enforcement, planned personal contacts, and fireproofing of high-hazard rights-of-way and industrial sites.

Primary responsibility for jobs like these may logically be considered to lie with representatives of State and Federal forestry and conservation agencies and public utilities, industries, and the like. But programs like that put on by the American Red Cross in Sonoma County afford wonderful opportunities for each of us to redeem part of our wildfire responsibilities.

But only a part. The rest of our wildfire responsibilities can best be redeemed by being careful—eternally careful.

R. F. HAMMATT, *a graduate of the Harvard University School of Forestry, worked with the Forest Service from 1906 until his retirement in 1946, except for 10 years as manager of the California Redwood Association. At various times during the 30 years with Forest Service, he served as forest assistant, deputy forest supervisor, and forest supervisor of the Shasta National Forest; as chief of occupancy, assistant chief of operations, forest examiner, assistant regional forester, and assistant to the Chief of the Forest Service.*

# BUILDING A FIRE ORGANIZATION

EARL S. PEIRCE, CARL A. GUSTAFSON

Early discovery of a fire—whether in forest or city—and speed and strength in attacking it are the cornerstones on which a fire-control organization is built. The structure of the organization itself begins with the fire fighters, but involves much more than that. It includes facilities for detecting and reporting fires, transportation, fire-fighting equipment, the supervisory personnel, and well-trained forces for the initial attack. Comprehensive preliminary plans are needed; so are means for carrying them out.

Because about one-third of the total area of the continental United States is forest land, which requires organized protection against fire and which varies widely in most of the many elements related to forest fires and their control, three prerequisites are necessary to develop a forest-fire organization for any particular area: To know the local fire problem, to determine the major objectives that the efforts for protection should reach, and to define the measures needed to attain the desired goal.

Of approximately 653 million acres of forest lands in the 48 States that need some protection against wildfires, about two-thirds belongs to private owners. The other third is publicly owned. All the public land and three-fourths of the private areas are under some degree of fire control, but 107 million acres of private forest lands are still without organized protection.

In 1947, of 80,370 fires on protected lands, 8,928 occurred on Federal property and 71,442 on areas belonging to States and private owners. Fires burned 318,074 acres, or 0.15 percent, of the area protected on Federal lands, and 2,814,381 acres, or 0.86 percent, on State and private lands. The tangible losses were estimated at $2,972,786 and $21,378,477, respectively.

We have no reliable comparable figures for the lands without organized protection, but we estimate that about 15 percent of those tracts burn over each year.

In classifying forest fires by causes, eight categories are generally used: Lightning, railroads, campers, smokers, debris burners, incendiarists, lumbering, and miscellaneous.

Lightning, incendiarists, and smokers, in that order, are responsible for most fires on Federal lands. On State and private holdings, the relative major causes are different, being incendiarists, smokers, and debris burners. Lightning is a major problem on the more mountainous national forests, but it is not so important a factor in private fire-control management except in a few localities.

Complete exclusion of forest fires is rarely attainable. The degree of protection that is necessary depends on the purposes of management and the damage that fires may be expected to cause in a given area. A theoretical guide is that it is desirable to keep the total annual cost for all fire-control measures plus annual fire losses to a minimum figure. In other words, the economic objective is to secure adequate protection at least cost. The problem is the same for State, county, municipal, and Federal agencies, and the index of justifiable protection—the goal of "least cost plus damage"—might also apply to private protection agencies even though they are answerable to a board of directors rather than to the public.

EFFECTIVE FIRE CONTROL requires a careful analysis of all important factors related to the fire problem and the preparation of specific action plans for each major part of the protection job.

The completed plans in combination are termed "presuppression plans." Their primary objective is a fire-control organization that is capable and well-trained, adequately equipped, and properly supervised—one that will reduce the number of man-caused fires and can handle the worst fire situation that is likely to arise.

The elements in the planning are:

1. The major causes of fires and the measures needed to prevent or reduce those that are man-caused.

2. Occurrence of fires—past occurrence and location, segregated by major causes, seasonal periods, and times of day.

3. Fuels—kinds, density, and their relative inflammability and resistance to control measures.

4. Topography—whether flat, rolling, or rough; steepness of slopes; and other features affecting fire behavior.

5. Accessibility—relative difficulty in reaching a fire with suppression forces and the additional facilities needed with transportation available.

6. Visibility—distance in miles a fire observer may normally be expected to see an incipient fire. For example, in the usually clear atmosphere of the West, a small fire 15 miles away can be readily detected, but in the Coastal Plains of the Southeast the visibility distance is about 6 miles.

7. Meteorological factors: the wind, temperature, relative humidity, dryness of fuels, precipitation, thunderstorm activity, length of fire seasons, and the like.

8. Production in fire-control measures per unit of manpower or machine.

Besides these basic factual surveys, consideration needs to be given to other features more closely related to the operational phases of the protection plan. These we shall mention later.

The significance and effects of all pertinent factors must be correlated and definite conclusions must be reached and reflected in a "master" presuppression plan. The master plan is really not a single document; it is a term applied to the coordinated preparation and use of a number or series of specific plans that cover each major phase of action.

Different methods have been developed and used to prepare presuppression plans, but nearly all have the same objectives and fundamental factors. A good way to depict a plan of the usual type is to assume that we have the task of preparing one for an area of several million acres—a typical tract that consists of wild, remote, rugged forest lands on which fires have been bad and losses high.

THE BEST POINT AT WHICH TO BEGIN is with the precept that the best fire control is to prevent fires from starting. Nine of every ten forest fires in the United States result from man's carelessness in his use of fire; all of them can be prevented. Our major objectives, then, are:

1. To prevent or reduce man-caused fires.

2. To lessen the probability that fires will start or spread by eliminating or reducing the amount of inflammable material—the brush and grass, logging slash, and other fuels that at times become highly inflammable.

To reach these objectives, the plan must be based on a thorough analysis of the principal reasons why fires occur on the area and how the fires can be prevented or reduced. The analysis should include:

1. Study of risk.

Analyze fires by causes for the preceding 5 years. To the extent possible, the reason why each fire started should be determined.

Map the location of fires, by major causes, for the same 5-year period. This is to earmark the areas of high fire occurrence or "risk."

Classify the high-risk areas and determine the fire-starting potential of each area.

2. Study of special hazards.

Delineate dangerous areas from the standpoint of potential fuels, or hazard, such as slash, the highly inflammable brush, debris along railroads and highways and around sawmills, and so forth.

3. Correlation of the risk and hazard factors, with a relative composite rating for each problem area.

4. Determination of remedial prevention measures needed.

A general principle to be considered in preparing a fire-prevention action plan is to recognize that forest fuels and fire risks are the two controlling indices. Where critical fuels are exposed to human risks, the prevention effort must be aimed at reducing either the fire risk or the fuel hazard, or at minimizing the potentials of each. Often it is possible to eliminate or reduce abnormal fire hazards, but where that is not feasible the main effort must be directed toward lowering their exposure to unnecessary risks.

Many devices and methods have been used to reduce human risk from high-hazard fire areas at critical times. They fall into two general categories, education and restriction. The educational efforts, a wide range of activities, try to change the attitudes and careless habits of individuals and the general public. Country-wide fire-prevention programs are helpful, but the over-all educational campaigns need to be supplemented by particularized efforts that are aimed directly at the specific local needs. Personal contacts often are the most effective.

Few prevention plans can, however, depend on education alone. High-hazard fuel areas may require the restricted use of the area by people—forbidding smoking except at specified safe places, for example, or limiting the campfires, or fixing the hours and places for burning debris. Some hazardous areas might even have to be closed entirely to all use during critical periods.

The fire-prevention plan must meet the specific needs. It must be workable. It must be kept up to date. It must outline a definite course of action as to what is to be done and by whom, where and how it will be accomplished, and the period during which it will be carried out. An effective program also requires qualified and trained personnel. Respected local residents are frequently the best.

To DETECT FOREST FIRES, vigilance must be eternal. Time is of the essence. Adequate facilities and personnel are required to assure that all fires are discovered when they start. That generally demands a network of lookout points, manned by competent observers or detectors during the fire season. Patrolling by foot, car, or airplane also is sometimes necessary.

The first step in preparing a detection plan is to designate on a map all fires in the previous 5 years, grouped by major causes and zones as to frequency. This is known as the fire-occurrence business map, and it represents the number of fires that experience has shown must, on an average, be detected in a 5-year period. Fire occurrence is usually indicated by a number of broad classes representing the anticipated number of fires per unit of area. In this way the entire tract to be protected is segregated into zones of relative fire risk.

A survey is then made to select the best observation points. The original selection usually includes at least twice the number of lookouts needed and finally chosen. From each potential lookout point a map is made that shows the territory within which a small fire could be readily seen from that location. A profile tracing is made of each of these "seen area maps." By comparing and superimposing these tracings over the fire-occurrence business map, one can determine the relative value of each lookout point. All potential points can be given a comparative rating. Selection of the approved lookouts can then proceed in a businesslike manner and towers or observatories be constructed in priority order.

Generally it is not economically feasible in rough country to construct and maintain a detection system that will quickly pick up all fires that start. That would require complete ground coverage of all fire-occurrence zones. On the national forests, for example, it is considered that from 65 to 85 percent of full coverage will provide the degree of detection that is necessary and justified.

During the original field survey for lookout points, other useful data can be gathered: The needed height of towers, character of structures, timber to be felled, and the situations and requirements of transportation and communication.

THE COMMUNICATION PLAN IS NEXT. In general, it does no good to discover a fire unless the information is passed on to those responsible for putting it out. Detectors must therefore have some means of rapid communication. Usually this is to a dispatching center, which in turn transmits the information to the appropriate initial-attacking forces with any needed directions for action. Consequently, dependable communications are necessary; these, as a rule, include an independent telephone system, supplemented by the radio. Commercial telephone facilities are usually relied upon for outside calls, as when a fire escapes initial attack and additional forces from a distance are needed.

The communication plan should fulfill the following minimum requirements:

1. Immediate communication between:

Detectors and dispatching center;

Dispatching center and initial-attack forces;

Dispatching center and the ground command;

Dispatching center and selected cooperators;

Dispatching center and work crews under the jurisdiction of the protection agency.

2. Connection with other facilities:

Dispatching center and commercial facilities;

Dispatching center and centers of supply for the reinforcements—woods crews, towns, mills, mines, schools, and the like;

Dispatching centers and adjoining protection agencies—State, other national forests, private protection agencies.

After the survey is made to determine the type of communication best suited to the needs of the area, the existing and proposed telephone lines and the other communication facilities are shown on a map, with appropriate symbols. The map, kept always up to date, is the communication plan for the area.

QUICK ACTION is necessary in applying control measures after a fire has been observed and reported. Action too late or too little often means large fires. The answer is an immediately available and well-trained, adequately equipped, and properly supervised fire-suppression force that can promptly reach the fire, hit it hard, and bring it under control quickly.

An area that has a large number of fires each year may require small suppression crews strategically located and in sufficient strength to assure rapid control under normal conditions. The location and strength of initial-attack forces must be determined and arranged for in advance.

Weather, fuels, and the efficiency of personnel and equipment determine the speed and strength of initial attack needed for any fire. Planning the initial attack is primarily concerned with the manpower and equipment that should be readily available under different degrees of fire peril.

Climatic conditions, especially relative humidity and wind velocity, greatly affect fire behavior. Atmospheric measurements and forecasts and various devices for measuring dryness of fuels are therefore valuable tools in forest-fire control. However, weather factors are too variable to be given much consideration in planning an organization for initial attack. Rather, they are used to alert the entire organization and often influence the temporary strength and placement of initial-attack forces.

Under a given set of weather conditions, fire travels much faster in some forest fuels than in others. The speed with which a fire burns in a specified type of fuel under normal circumstances is called the "rate of spread." Also, different fuels may vary widely in the relative ease or difficulty of constructing fire lines or otherwise fighting a fire. "Resistance to control" is the term applied to it. Forest fuels are, therefore, rated according to those two basic factors.

Different methods can be used for classifying major fuel types on the basis of the two factors.

One is to determine and assign a composite rating for each important type of fuel. For example, dead grass would be designated "LE" indicating "low" resistance to control and "extreme" rate of spread.

Another method designates the major fuel types as I, II, III, and IV, which represent in relative order the greatest spread plus highest resistance to control.

Regardless of the system used, the first step in the development of the initial-attack plan is the mapping of the major fuels and the rating of combined effects of their respective resistance to control and rate of spread.

The second step is to set up standards for the time allowed the nearest suppression force to reach a fire in each major fuel-type zone. This is called "travel" time. It must be fast enough to permit effective attack on the front of the fire before it becomes too difficult to handle.

Increasing the strength of the initial force by adding more men or mobile equipment, such as tank trucks, will provide more time to reach the fire. In other words, the greater the strength of initial attack, the slower the travel time might be.

The third step is to determine the needed strength of the initial-attack forces. The guide here is the anticipated size or perimeter of the fire in the particular zone at the time the fire is reached. That is determined by multiplying the rate of the spread by the travel-time standard, both of which have already been established. Even on active, small fires not more than half of the calculated perimeter requires immediate action, because if the front of the fire is controlled the less active parts can be handled later. The forces required to construct and hold a fire line along the critical perimeter can be determined from a study of initial-control measures on previous fires in the zone. For small fires in certain areas, this theoretical calculation of the number of men needed will probably be larger than can be economically justified. Other means should be explored in such cases to reduce the size of the crews. The solution may be tank trucks, small tractor-drawn plows, or other machines that will reduce the needed manpower.

Planned crew strength is based on the need under average burning conditions, and can be raised or lowered to conform to changing fire danger. Fire-danger rating systems, which are based mainly on weather conditions, show the current relative fire danger for the area. This information, supplemented by weather forecasts, indicates what temporary changes are needed with respect to the size and movement of initial forces.

The fourth step concerns the location of initial-attack forces. Obviously, it would be economically unsound to place suppression crews where history has shown fires do not normally occur or could do little or no damage. Also, it would be poor business to locate fire fighters at points from which travel time is too slow.

Here again the fire-occurrence and the fuel-type maps are helpful. As in detection planning, a field survey is made to select temporarily the best locations for initial-attack forces. Silhouettes are prepared to show travel-time coverage along existing roads and trails. By superimposing these profiles over the maps which show fire occurrence, fire business, and fuel types, and also taking into consideration travel-time standards, one can get an index value for each potential location, in much the same manner as in the final selection of lookouts. Stations can then be chosen and improved on the basis of their relative value and to the extent required—up to the point of diminishing returns. The potential fire business in many areas will not justify complete initial-attack coverage within the travel-time standards. In mountainous and inaccessible country it may prove to be cheaper and more effective to use airplane smokejumpers or mobile ground fire-fighting units, rather than to station suppression crews at set locations.

A FINAL PHASE of initial-attack planning is to prepare a table showing for each station the location, number of men, fire-fighting tools, special equipment, and the season during which the station should be occupied in order to provide adequate protection for the area under average weather conditions. The tabulation should further outline how the strength at each station should vary in accordance with ratings from the fire-danger rating system established for the area.

Even after these initial-attack plans are worked out, it is more than likely that there will be some important areas which still will not be well covered.

PLANNING FOR TRANSPORTATION is the next step.

Accessibility is important. Without the degree of accessibility set up by the travel-time standards, many fires will escape the initial attack and may cause great damage. Systematic planning for an adequate transportation system therefore is essential. It should be done simultaneously with the preparation of the initial-attack plan.

The general procedure is:

1. A road study to determine how existing roads will meet the requirements of the initial-attack plan from the standpoint of allowable travel time. This can be done by making a road-log survey of each existing road in the area. Speedometer readings are shown on a map for all intersections and important points, and travel time to such points is computed, based on safe traveling speeds for initial-attack vehicles.

2. A map is then prepared showing areas which can be reached within the time requirements.

3. Comparing this map with the initial-attack plan will show the extent to which existing roads are adequate and where additional transportation facilities are needed.

This determination, however, is only one segment of the transportation picture. Improvement of existing routes of travel is not only a job of filling in the gaps for each individual locality; it must also be a part of and conform to an over-all, balanced transportation system for the area.

The decision as to which new roads are required and can be economically justified is difficult. In rough country the desired accessibility by road is often not feasible because of high construction costs. The final road plan is usually a compromise of many conflicting factors, but it should make possible the maximum coverage which can be defended economically. Often roads will be used for purposes other than protection—to remove wood products, for example—so the total cost of road construction and maintenance frequently need not all be charged against protection.

In country where road building is very expensive or in areas where the fire hazard is low and the speed of the initial attack need not be great, roads may not be needed at all. Trails may be the only means of transportation that can be justified. Planning for trails would follow the same general procedure as that for roads.

The final transportation plan should show on a map of the area all existing and proposed roads and trails by descriptive symbols. In addition, information (in atlas form) is desirable, giving the name of the road or trail, its length, termination, and number in the transportation system. It may contain also data on specifications, cost, and date of completion.

The dispatching plan comes next. Any organization dealing with conditions subject to rapid change, as in fire control, must be flexible and ready to handle emergencies that demand quick action. Every fire that starts is the beginning of a potential emergency; hence, in a fire organization a means must be provided to enable quick activation of the fire-fighting forces and equipment. If the initial attack fails, a plan of follow-up action must be ready. It is much like a field army in action.

No fire organization would be complete without a key individual whose job is to receive and evaluate reports from lookouts and dispatch initial-attack forces and equipment to fires. In emergencies he must quickly arrange for sufficient additional help in the form of fire fighters, equipment, and supervisory personnel. He is known as the dispatcher. He should be capable and familiar with the country and fire fighting; in large measure he is the sparkplug of the whole fire-control organization.

Essentials of a dispatching plan are:

1. Proper location of the dispatching center. This is usually controlled by communication facilities because the dispatcher must be stationed where he has rapid communication with both the lookouts and his initial-attack forces. Where it is feasible, he should also be able to get in contact quickly with nearby work crews. Commercial communication facilities must be available in the event it is necessary to obtain additional outside help from cooperators, the neighboring protection agencies, or other sources.
2. A list containing the names and locations of all detectors and the location and strength of all initial-attack forces.
3. A fire-danger rating system that gives daily information on the fire danger in the area.
4. Fire-weather forecasts.
5. A manning plan for each detector or initial-attack station showing when and under what conditions they will be manned and the strength to be maintained as fire danger decreases or increases.
6. Information on the availability of all additional fire fighters in or near the area; the location, the quantity, and the kinds of equipment available; food, camp cooks, cooking equipment, bedding, and such.
7. Information on wage rates and contracts for hire of private equipment.
8. Information on the availability of additional fire-control supervisory personnel.

The tools and equipment used in fire fighting are different in different sections of the country. What is most effective in one section may be useless in another. The types of hand tools and heavy equipment needed depend mainly upon the kind of fuel, character of the country, soils, and the availability of water.

The equipment plan should show the kinds and numbers of tools and equipment to be furnished each initial-attack station and also specify the types and number of tools to be kept at strategic caches throughout the area. It should likewise designate the best locations for heavy-equipment depots and should include information on the location and availability of suitable tools and equipment belonging to other nearby protection agencies and private companies.

The equipment inventory should be kept up to date so that the protection forces will not be hampered by deficiencies, as to kind or quantity.

Men assigned fire-control responsibilities must be carefully selected for special physical and mental qualifications of strength, alertness, perseverance, initiative. They are the backbone of the organization. They should be employed for specific periods and, whenever possible, for the entire fire season.

When fires escape the efforts of the initial-attacking force, large numbers of temporary fire fighters must sometimes be employed to cope successfully with a bad situation. The job of supervising these men falls to a few key individuals in the regular protection organization. Selection and employment of manpower of the right kind for both regular and temporary employment requires a carefully considered plan for recruitment.

Accomplishment in controlling forest fire depends largely on the ability and efficiency of the protection forces. Many individuals are employed for such diversified positions as lookout, suppression crew foreman, fire fighter, patrolman, the radio operator, clerk, packer, truck driver, tractor operator, cook, telephone lineman, supervisory officer, and many others. Usually it is not possible to get individuals who are experienced in these lines of work. Thorough training in all the phases of their jobs is essential.

The training plan usually outlines the duties of each fire-control position and provides for a type of instruction that will qualify the individual for the responsibility and the work to which he is assigned.

Proper supervision of the entire fire organization for a specific area is needed. Even the best prepared plans and their execution sometimes fail to control fires in their early stage. Some fires have needlessly become disastrous conflagrations. When situations develop that are too much for the initial-protection forces to handle, a directing head or ground command must be available. On the national forests, the district rangers usually have this responsibility. On non-Federal lands, the State rangers or the company fire chief is the ground command. Regardless of the title, provision for a ground command should be made in planning protection for an area.

Even after the main requisites in fire-control planning have been carefully worked out, there still is the intangible human element which materially influences the effectiveness of a fire organization.

Suitable living accommodations and food must be planned for and provided in order to care for the men properly, maintain morale, and obtain maximum efficiency.

Loyalty and esprit de corps of the personnel is important and must not be overlooked. Every key individual must feel that he is an important cog in the machine and that his best effort is needed to keep it going. Lookouts must feel that the entire organization is depending upon them to detect all fires while they are still small. Initial-attack men must believe that their failure to control small fires will result in disastrous conflagrations. Maintenance men must realize that the condition of roads and telephone lines will mean success or failure in the control of fires.

Dispatchers must recognize and accept their positive responsibility for quick thinking and sound judgment. All members of the fire-control team must be ready and willing to take the initiative and responsibility.

No specific formula can be given that will achieve automatically such elements of morale and loyalty to the work. They are compounded of mutual respect, a high regard for each other's ability, honesty in dealing with others, leadership, and many another quality of dignity and virility.

On the shoulders of the fire manager or fire chief rests probably the heaviest responsibility of all. It is he who must direct and supervise all fire-control activities, not the least of which is to keep everyone in the organization pulling together—and constantly on the alert.

EARL S. PEIRCE, *who has been chief of the Division of Cooperative Forest Protection, Forest Service, since 1935, is a graduate of Yale University and the Yale Forest School. He joined the Forest Service in 1910, and has held various positions in Wyoming, Colorado, South Dakota, Wisconsin, and in Washington, D. C.*

CARL A. GUSTAFSON *is chief of the Division of Fire Control in the Forest Service. He began work with the Forest Service in 1921 on the Nezperce National Forest; subsequent assignments were on the Wasatch, Sierra, Klamath, and Plumas National Forests and as fire staff officer in the California Regional Office.*

# FOREST FIRE DANGER

G. LLOYD HAYES

The 0.62 inch of rain that fell September 22, 1947, in southern Maine was the last most residents were to see in 47 days. Before the next rain came, the headlines told a sad story: *Boats Evacuate Blazing Bar Harbor,* on October 24; *Maine Fires Uncontrolled, 11 Dead, Damage $6,000,000,* on October 25; and *President Orders Aid to Maine,* on October 26. Damage and distress were great also in New York, Rhode Island, Pennsylvania, New Hampshire, and Massachusetts. In November, rain finally ended one of the most catastrophic periods of forest fires in history.

The fires came after the fire season was officially ended; October 15 ordinarily marks the end of serious fire weather. But fire seasons do not follow the calendar. Fire fighting cannot be scheduled the way operations in farming and manufacturing can be scheduled. Fires must be fought when they occur.

Foresters learned many years ago that the only way to avoid catastrophic losses on bad fire days was to have large numbers of men and large amounts of fire-fighting equipment available for instant use. At the same time they recognized that it would be inefficient and even impossible without unlimited funds to retain so many men on the pay rolls during the many easy days when they would not be needed. Besides, highly variable conditions complicate the work of controlling forest fires. One day a combination of factors might mean only a few fires that spread slowly and are easily controlled. The next day fearsome numbers of fires, which spread rapidly and violently and which are controlled only with large-scale effort and cost, might break out.

The variation in the number of fires from day to day in the Eastern States is shown by the records for April 8–14, 1943, in Connecticut. On those 7 days there were 8, 25, 34, 71, 11, 12, and 3 fires, respectively. The 3 fires on April 14 were put out with an equivalent of 34 man-hours of labor, but the 71 fires on April 11 required nearly 1,000. In another case, on the Kaniksu National Forest in northern Idaho, which usually averages about 1 fire a day from man's carelessness, lightning set 207 fires on July 12 and 13, 1926.

Such conditions made foresters realize that their goal should be to employ each day all the men they needed to handle all the fires that might occur that day—but no more. Even before a start could be made toward the goal, however, some means had to be developed that would indicate the approximate number of fires that would be fought each day and how much work would have to be done to suppress them. Consequently, methods of rating the danger of forest fire were developed to be used to guide fire-control action before fires start.

Eleven different systems for rating fire danger are now in use in the United States, each one having been adapted for specific conditions of weather and fuel in different parts of the country.

The systems have five advantages. They are based on scientific measurements of the key factors that create fire danger, and they eliminate such indefinite opinions and guesses as "high danger," "very bad conditions," "low danger," and "not so bad."

They focus attention on the really important factors that influence fire danger.

They point out the small changes in burning conditions that are frequently overlooked but that may mean big savings in men, money, equipment, and area burned.

They prevent men from getting caught in the off-season let-down or in peak danger conditions—something that might happen even to experienced men.

They provide indexes that can be translated into decisive preparedness and action toward suppression.

THE DIFFERENT SYSTEMS all recognize certain key factors that have to do with the chances of fires starting and the speed with which they will spread. Foremost are wind and fuel moisture. Other factors are condition of vegetation, the relative humidity, days since last rain, amount of last rain, air temperature, and time of year.

Wind velocity, the amount of moisture in the forest fuels, and condition of vegetation are the most important variables.

Strong winds cause some of the most dangerous conditions because they spread fire rapidly and make control difficult.

Green vegetation retards fire. Dead or dry vegetation spreads fire and increases the likelihood that fires will start: The degree of dryness of the forest fuels, more than any other item, determines whether fires will start and burn at all. But forest fuels are complex. They vary from fine material (such as dead grasses and pine needles, which dry rapidly) to the slow-drying fuels, like dead trees.

Most systems use either direct measurements of the moisture content of a representative kind of fine fuel on the surface or measurements of the relative humidity and temperature of the air, to which fuel moisture is closely related. Some systems supplement measurements of fine-fuel moisture with humidity and other measurements. Some recognize the dryness of the larger, more slowly drying fuels by including the amount of the last rain, days since last rain, and time of year.

Time of year also has other important effects because the length of the dry part of the day and the intensity of the heat from the sun change from month to month.

The several components of fire danger are measured at stations that are placed in strategic locations. A typical station has various instruments, among them an anemometer for determining the velocity of the wind, a rain gage, and basswood or ponderosa pine sticks, which are carefully weathered and calibrated and placed a few inches above the forest floor, where they respond to the same weather which determines the wetness or dryness of the natural forest fuels. Sensitive scales are

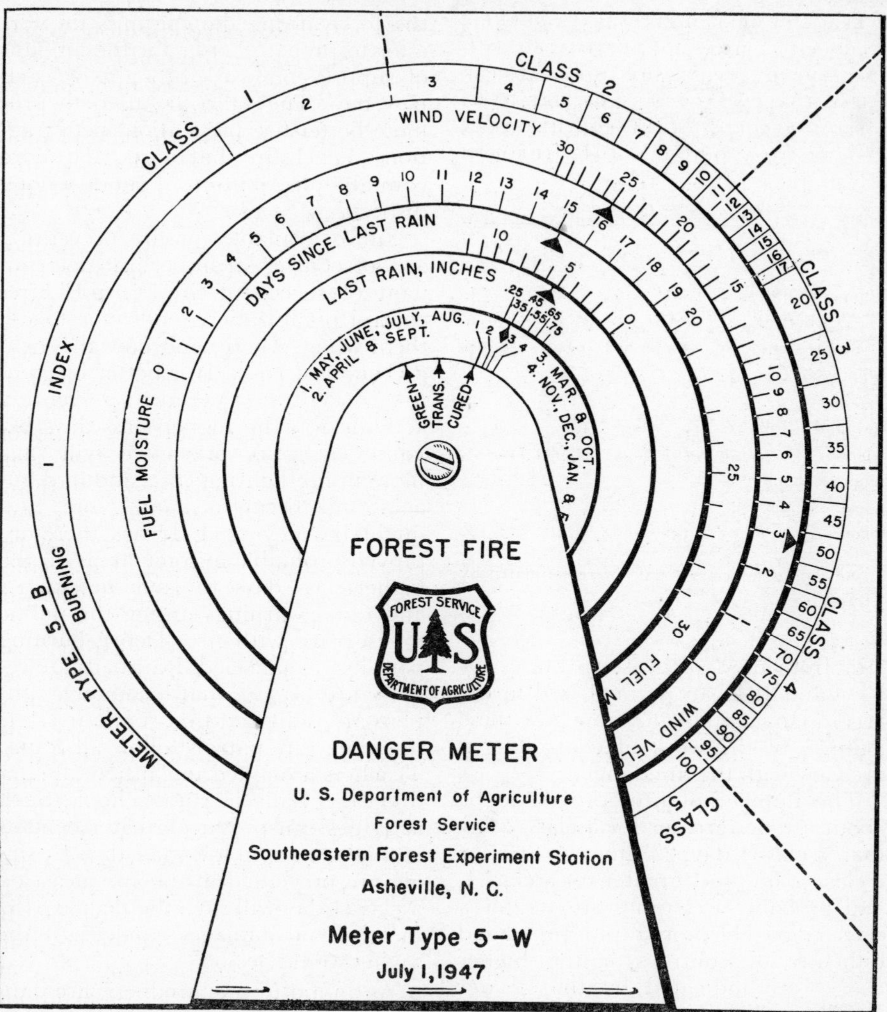


used to weigh the sticks to detect changes in moisture accurately. The measurements are integrated by a device called a fire-danger meter into a single numerical rating. In the eastern part of the United States, five danger classes are recognized, in which class 1 represents the lowest, and class 5 the highest.

Although the discussion to follow is based on these classes, the meter has recently been converted to one with 100 classes. The conversion permits more detailed expression of gradations in fire danger and a more precise evaluation of it. The chart illustrates how this new danger meter works, and shows the relation between the five danger classes and the newer 100-class scale.

A scale of fire danger is much like the Fahrenheit scale of temperature. Many phenomena are related to temperature, such as the freezing and boiling points of water and the melting points of the different metals. Likewise, many of the most significant fire phenomena are related to fire danger: The likelihood that fires will start, their rate of spread, the cost of suppression, the damage they cause, and the amount of work needed to suppress them. Rec-

AVERAGE NUMBER OF FIRES, AREA BURNED, COST OF SUPPRESSION, ESTIMATED DAMAGE, AND SUPPRESSION-JOB-LOAD PER DAY FOR FIVE CLASSES OF FIRE DAYS. FROM RECORDS OF 14 NORTHEASTERN STATES FOR OCTOBER 1942 THROUGH DECEMBER 1944

| *Item* | *Class of day* | | | | |
|---|---|---|---|---|---|
| | *1* | *2* | *3* | *4* | *5* [1] |
| Number of fires | 4 | 21 | 94 | 266 | 530 |
| Area burned (acres) | 49 | 300 | 1,852 | 9,490 | 34,500 |
| Suppression cost (dollars) | 77 | 738 | 3,293 | 11,877 | 33,000 |
| Damage (dollars) | 158 | 1,596 | 8,947 | 37,663 | 110,000 |
| Suppression-job-load (man-hours) | 13 | 133 | 894 | 3,463 | 8,100 |

[1] All figures for class 5 days were estimated by extrapolation.

ords from the Northeastern States for 1943 and 1944 are summarized in the accompanying table to show how these features of the work of controlling a fire vary with the fire danger.

The number of fires proved to be about 5 times greater for a class 2 day than a class 1 day, 23 times greater for a class 3, 66 times greater for a class 4, and probably 132 times greater for a class 5 day. The more rapid spread and difficulty of control for the higher classes are indicated by the greater area burned, despite the better advance preparation and stronger control action usually taken. The acres burned averaged 6, 38, 194, and 704 times greater for class 2, 3, 4, and 5 days, respectively, than for class 1. Suppression costs, damages, and job-load varied in a similar way.

This type of information enables the forester to interpret fire-danger classes in terms of his fire-control job and permits him to prepare more nearly for each new day with enough but not too many men, and with adequate fire equipment.

New uses for danger ratings are still being discovered. They extend beyond the forewarning that permits the forester to prepare better for the amount of suppression work brought by each new day. They also are used to promote better fire prevention, better action on each fire that starts, and more equitable distribution of funds among districts.

Funds available for fire prevention are, of course, an important determinant of successful fire control. Fire-control organizations endeavor to use them when, where, and how they will do the most good. It is better business to concentrate certain prevention activities on the higher-class days because each fire prevented will save more in fire-fighting costs and in damages and because many more fires might be prevented. It has therefore proved profitable in some areas on the higher-class days to issue newspaper and radio warnings urging the public to use care with fire. Debris-burning permits are canceled. Railroads are required to be sure that locomotive ashpans are tight and that spark arresters function. Fire patrols follow all trains. Teachers are asked to caution all children, especially in rural schools. Such activities can produce greater benefits on high- than on low-class days. A single fire prevented in the Northeast on a class 4 day will save the people $187 in costs and damages; for class 1 the saving would be $58.

As an aid to preparedness, fire-danger ratings, combined with weather forecasts, make possible advance preparation for bad days and savings on easy days. On the national forests of the West, where a relatively large force of men is employed throughout the summer, the whole force may be held in readiness for fire duty on bad days. But on class 1 and 2 days it is a justifiable risk to use the men for other necessary work like repairing telephone lines and roads. Fire-control organizations in the East typically have a smaller regular organization, which is enlarged for bad fire days by hiring farmers and other cooperators who have been trained to work in well-

AVERAGE COSTS AND DAMAGES PER FIRE FOR EACH CLASS OF DAY

| Item | *Class of day* | | | | |
|---|---|---|---|---|---|
| | *1* | *2* | *3* | *4* | *5* |
| Suppression costs.... | $19 | $35 | $35 | $45 | $62 |
| Damages.......... | 39 | 77 | 95 | 142 | 208 |
| Total......... | 58 | 112 | 130 | 187 | 270 |

organized crews under fire wardens. On bad days, these trained men leave their regular businesses to strengthen the fire-control force; when they are not needed, they return to their usual work.

By considering fire danger and other factors that affect the speed with which a fire will spread, the forester or fire dispatcher can determine the number of men and amount of equipment it will take to suppress the fire edge faster than it will grow, and thereby bring it under control. It may be calamitous to send too few men, but more than the bare minimum frequently cannot be spared—especially on bad days when numerous fires may tax the capacity of the control organization to provide crews for all. Each fire on a class 2, 3, 4, or 5 day in the Northeast in its initial stages has been found to require an average of approximately 2, 3, 4, and 5 times more work, respectively, than a fire on a class 1 day.

The danger measurements are used again in rating the size of the seasonal job-loads on different protection districts. Administrators can then distribute available funds more equitably among the fire-control districts according to the needs of each.

Another practical value of danger measurements was recognized in 1942, when smoke from forest fires blanketed the Atlantic coast and so permitted enemy submarines to roam in comparative safety. Over the land, the smoke on some days made flying unsafe and halted pilot training. The Army asked help to remove the smoke obstacle. All State and Federal forest fire-control organizations responded. One of their first steps was to revise a network of approximately 150 fire-danger measuring stations from Virginia and Kentucky to Maine. Forty two stations were moved to critical areas to measure the severity of burning conditions in all parts of the coastal States. Stations were operated by 14 States, 6 national forests, 9 units of the National Park Service, the Army, and the Marine Corps. With the ratings obtained from the stations, the State and Federal foresters were better able to recognize dangerous days and intensify fire-prevention and control activities. Consequently, smoke density has been reduced since 1942.

FIRE-DANGER RATINGS can be computed either from measurements or from forecasts of the contributing variables. For determining how many men to send to each new fire or for rating seasonal job-loads, ratings based on actual measurements are used. In preparing for a bad day, however, the forester must arrange in advance for such fire-prevention activities as radio and newspaper warnings, and mobilize in advance the men and equipment that will be needed. For those purposes the severity of danger is rated a day in advance by use of the special weather forecasts now issued by the Weather Bureau, as a regular service.

As early as 1911, the Forest Service in the West turned to the Weather Bureau for general weather forecasts. But these did not consider specifically enough the weather conditions that affect fires. Accordingly, starting in 1913, fire-weather warnings were issued when bad fire-weather threatened. In 1924, regular fire-weather forecasts, localized by use of weather measurements from the forests themselves, were started and in 1926 the modern fire-weather service was born. Reports now include a forecast of the weather (degree of cloudiness, fog, smoke), precipitation, wind direction and velocity, temperature, relative humidity, visibility, and the extent, direction, and progress of lightning storms.

802062°—49——33

Such forecasts cover three of the eight factors that are used in rating fire danger, plus lightning, which is the primary fire starter in the West, and the likelihood of rain, which is the best fire extinguisher everywhere. Of the other factors, condition of vegetation is determined by observation and the amount of rain and number of days since the last rain from local records. It is rare that a fire watcher is so isolated as to be ignorant of the date. This leaves only fuel moisture to be predicted, and it can be estimated with sufficient accuracy by consideration of today's fuel moisture, tomorrow's weather forecast, and correlations that have been developed between the two. Tomorrow's fire danger can then be computed by any fire-danger meter.

G. LLOYD HAYES *is leader of the Cascade-Siskiyou Research Center, Forest Service, at Roseburg, Oreg. He was graduated from the University of Idaho in 1934, and took graduate work in forestry at Yale University and the University of California.*

# THE FIRE ON CEDAR CREEK

FRANK J. JEFFERSON

*(Except for the names, this is a true account of how a forest fire started and was stopped. It is the composite of the experiences of a man who has fought fires in the West for 38 years. He changed the names of places and men so that he could bring in details and facts that happened at one place or another, although all of them did not occur at any one place at one time.)*

The telephone at the Red River ranger station rang urgently early one Saturday afternoon in August. Hurry Earle, the district fire dispatcher, took a message from Guy Roberts, the forest ranger at the Snag Flat fire camp.

Roberts reported:

"Fire caught by bad whirlwind. More sparks and hot embers from burning snags scattered across Red River than patrolmen can put out. New fire headed up ridges both sides Cedar Creek. Fire on east ridge climbing fast in grass. Rate about mile an hour. Spreading up ridge and to east slope. Will hit timber about mile up ridge. On west side, fire moving up ridge slower. Ridge rocky with scattered fuel but bad brush field just ahead of fire. Six patrolmen on north side of river trying to prevent east and west sides of fire spreading farther up or down river. No more men can be spared from Snag Flat without taking chance of losing it and having a bad fire on both sides Red River.

"Call Swanson's 40-man logging crew with bulldozer. Have them start right away for mouth of Cedar Creek. Start full Rock Creek road crew of 25 men and 2 bulldozers for same point. Also Strawberry Flat 4-man tanker crew. Establish camp on road at mouth Cedar Creek. Send in 100-man camp outfit, including 2 backfiring outfits. Phone forest supervisor's office advising him of the situation and action taken. Make clear to him all fire-control resources of this district now called into action. Ask him to arrange for additional help as he believes needed. Tell him will use logging and road crews to try and keep fire from crossing either Ant Creek or Fly Creek. Wind southwest. Humidity is 8. Goodbye, Hurry—but hurry!"

Thus was control work on the Cedar Creek fire started.

The forest supervisor, who had taken over for his central dispatcher during the lunch hour, in turn received the call from the local Red River dispatcher. Fire-weather forecasts had been critical for several days. Years of

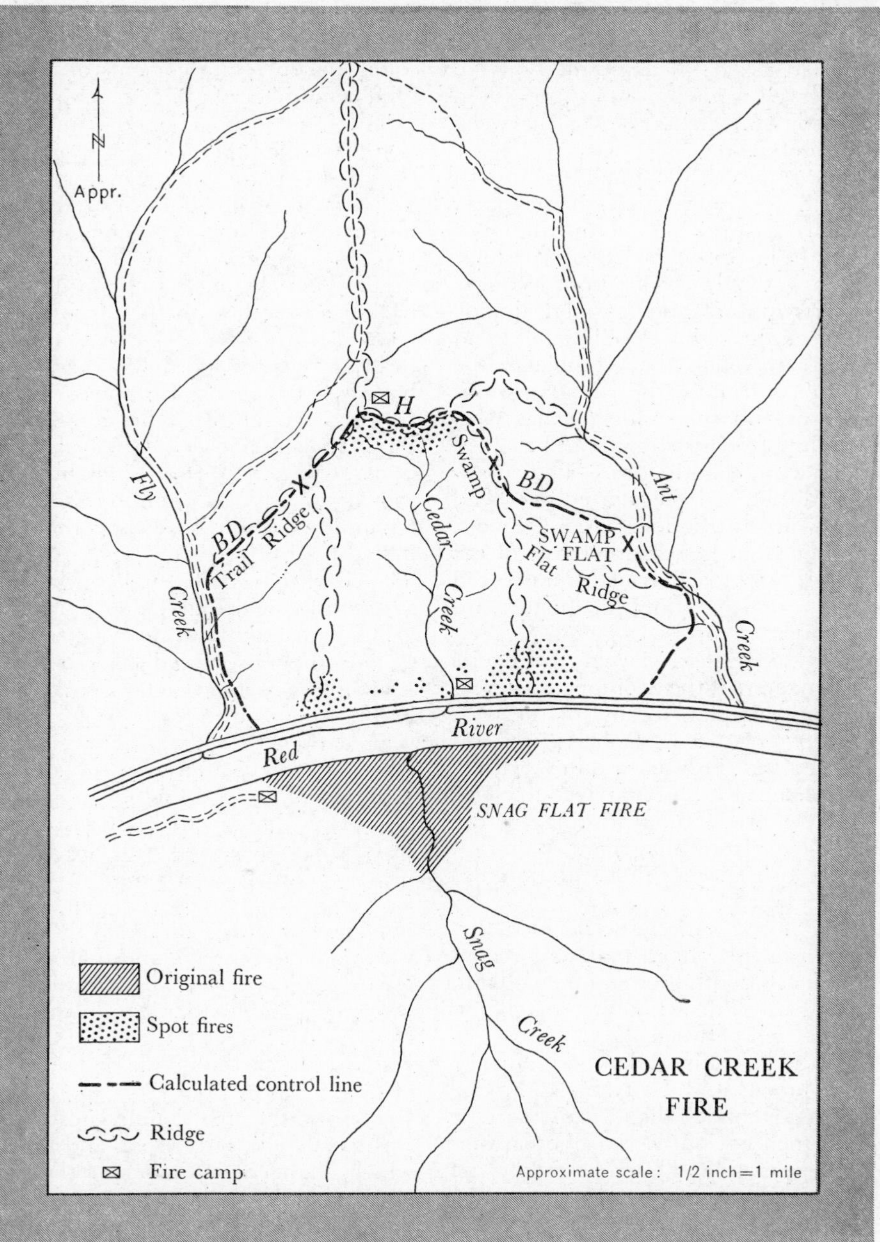


experience and observation of the explosive burning conditions that could develop by a continued alliance of dangerous degrees of wind, temperature, and humidity had given the supervisor a prescience that warned him this could be a worse Saturday afternoon than even the forecast for the day had indicated. Today, if decisions were needed, they had to be quick and sure. So he had stayed in his office this Saturday afternoon, ready for whatever might happen; he had alerted a top-flight fire-control overhead crew; he also had asked his assistant, Loitved, a man well trained in fire suppression, to be on call at home over the week end for emergency service.

The supervisor scanned a map and made his decisions. First, the new fires that were spreading across the Red River from Snag Flat should be handled as a separate operation. (Ranger Roberts himself and his men already had been through a gruelling fight and would do well if they completed the job of controlling the still dangerous main fire on their side of the river. Certainly Roberts should not be called on to handle both jobs.) The supervisor dispatched the alerted overhead crew with instructions to its fire boss, Johnson, that he was in charge of the new fire, and to call back from the Red River ranger station for further instructions.

Next, a message was sent to Roberts advising him of the decision and agreeing with his plan for use of the road and logging crew. Roberts was instructed that he was to do everything possible until Johnson arrived to check the new fire without risking further break-over from Snag Flat. A prompt report on the Snag Flat situation also was requested.

The forest supervisor decided further to have Loitved make air reconnaissance of both fires and then go into Snag Flat to do whatever correlation was needed between the two jobs.

By then, the dispatcher had returned from lunch, and Loitved, whom the supervisor had called, arrived. The three men got out aerial photographs and type maps and hurriedly conferred on a plan of action.

It was plain that one back-country fire camp out of reach of roads would have to be established quickly by airplane. The best bet for the back-country job was to obtain the specially trained 30-man crew of fire fighters, known as the "hot-shot outfit," on the adjacent Blackjack Forest, if they could be spared. Those men had been carefully chosen and trained for this sort of work and, because of their skill, could absorb reinforcements of a reasonable number of green men.

The forest dispatcher went into action. He called the nearby airport and obtained a plane equipped for cargo dropping for immediate use. He also instructed the forest warehouseman to take an air-borne camp-and-tool outfit for 50 men, including water and backfiring torches, to the airport. He requested the Lake District ranger headquarters to send three tanker outfits to Cedar Creek. He placed a call for the regional dispatcher to ask that the Blackjack hot-shot crew be sent to Cedar Creek if it were available and that he be advised promptly as to the outcome of this request and the estimated hour of arrival at Cedar Creek. The Red River dispatcher was instructed to send four saddle horses to Cedar Creek without delay.

The supervisor and his assistant, Loitved, knew that Cedar Creek itself had been logged for cedar poles many years earlier, that it was not accessible by road, and that it was full of old slash, which is good fuel for fire. They also knew that on the east a road of sorts ran 4 miles up Ant Creek, the next stream up the river from Cedar Creek, that Ant Creek was open timber interspersed with glades, that the slope was moderately steep, and that on the west a road extended about 2 miles up Fly Creek, the first stream down river from Cedar Creek. A good trail ran east from it to the divide at the head of Cedar Creek. The east side of Fly Creek, for the first 2 miles upstream, was mostly covered by oak and brush, which changed to timber at the first large easterly branch of the stream. The slope into the stream was steep and cliffy. The west side of Fly Creek and its headwaters above the trail supported a valuable stand of mature timber, as did Ant Creek. The photographs and maps showed that the divide at the head of Cedar Creek was sparsely timbered, steep, and rocky.

One conclusion the men reached

nmediately: Saving any part of Cedar Creek was out of the question—with unning fire flanking it on both sides, t was doomed. Its large volume of lried-out slash would blow up during he afternoon and scatter spot fires ino the cliffs and ravines at the headvaters of the stream. They would have o hold the fire on the two ridges, keep t out of the heads of Fly and Ant Creeks, and prevent it from crossing ither of the streams.

The surest and fastest way to do that vould be to backfire the roads up Fly Creek and Ant Creek to points from vhich effective fire lines could be built o the head of Cedar Creek. The backiring and construction of the lines vould have to be timed carefully to ivoid being flanked by either backfires or by the main fire.

From quick calculation of the probible rate of spread of the fire, based on study of the cover and topography as shown in the aerial pictures and the reported wind and humidity, it seemed ogical to the three men that lines could be constructed up side ridges from the two creeks in time to be successful. The ridge to be used from Fly Creek was designated Trail Ridge; the one from Ant Creek on the east was designated Swamp Flat Ridge. Tractors could be used on both ridges, but the ridge at the head of Cedar Creek would have to be handled by men working along the edge of the main fire after it had quieted, putting out all hot stuff found. That would be hard to do: Spot fires beyond this edge would have to be picked up later as they showed up. The country was too rough for any other sort of action. The west side of the fire would move slowly against the wind, mostly a problem of putting under control such fire spreaders as rolling logs and pine cones. The probability of spread with the wind into Ant Creek made that sector a dangerous one. First attention must focus there.

Thus the possibilities were quickly determined—more quickly than they can be explained—and Loitved announced, "Chief, I'm off to see this thing from the air. I'll phone you from Red River."

The supervisor calculated the requirements of the job ahead. If held on the lines initially planned, the fire would have a probable ultimate perimeter of 8 miles, excluding the river front facing the Snag Flat fire, which required no work except holding at both ends. Of the 8 miles, 3½ miles would be backfired road up the two creeks. The photographs showed that there should be about a mile and a half of bulldozer line in easy country, taking off from these roads along Trail Ridge and Swamp Flat Ridge, then a mile of bulldozer line in tough country, a mile of hand-work burn-out line, and a mile of control of hot spots at the head of Cedar Creek along an otherwise dormant line. There also would be an important spot-fire control job, ahead of the main fire edge, at the head of Cedar Creek and beyond.

To allow a margin of safety, he assumed that the patrolmen would fail to hold the up-and-down spread along Red River, and that closing those gaps would be the first job for the road, logging, and tanker crews, which had been ordered and part of which should be arriving shortly.

His calculations were interrupted by a call from the regional dispatcher: The hot-shot crew would arrive about 8 p. m., equipped with back-pack fire-fighting outfits; he was warned that the situation throughout the region was tough and that he would have to use local resources to the limit. No further quick help could be expected.

The supervisor proceeded with his planning, knowing the rate of production of safe fire line that could be expected from machines and men. The bulldozers, tankers, and flame-throwers that were en route apparently would be enough; their power, skillfully applied, equals the effort of many men and does some things a man cannot do. Men would be needed, however, to hold the ground gained by the machines and to go into places that machines could not reach. Fifty additional men could be used to advantage during the evening and early night to strengthen the crews now under way. Fortunately, both the logging and road crews had several men who could pinch-hit as squad leaders, or strawbosses. Given an even break, the fire should be flanked on both the Ant Creek and Fly Creek sides by night. If the plans worked, tomorrow's job should be principally to squelch the fire completely, to mop up along the backfire lines, and to clean up spot fires ahead of the solid fire edge around the head of Cedar Creek. Tomorrow morning, it appeared, he would need about 100 men with fresh bosses and strawbosses, exclusive of the hot-shot crew. If spot fires were not too numerous, the fire might be corralled before tomorrow's dangerous burning period began at about 10 a. m., an hour that has special significance to fire fighters in planning the control of big fires. It is a sort of deadline they have set for themselves, based on long experience.

The Cedarville Employment Service was called and asked to round up 50 good men to be sent immediately to Cedar Creek by bus and to send an additional 100 to arrive by 9 p. m. for the morning shift. Calls went to other ranger districts for crew bosses and strawbosses to handle the new forces. The top overhead would have to carry on through another shift without rest or sleep, but that was usual and expected in such emergencies.

Johnson, the boss of the overhead fire crew, called in. He was brought up to date on the task and the plans to meet it: Loitved would drop him a parachute message at Cedar Creek, giving the information obtained from the plane reconnaissance. Ranger Roberts' camp would have the facts on all control forces available for both the Snag Flat and Cedar Creek operations by the time of his arrival.

Loitved dropped a map and the message for Johnson, advising that the fire was rolling into Ant Creek faster than expected but that the main Ceda Creek blow-up would likely not ge out of the drainage during the after noon; that he had taken Freeman o the trip with him and that Freema would return to serve him as boss fo the spot-fire area. That was goo news—but Loitved's message also sai that, with a wind, the burning dea snags on Roberts' side of the rive could give more trouble and that, if a all possible, Johnson should assign hir a couple of saw gangs from Swanson' crew to make sure of getting all th snags cut down before morning. Johnson knew what that meant: "Look like a rough night for the boys."

A message came from Roberts camp: The road crew should be i about 2:45; the Swanson outfit abou 3. The tanker crews and Johnson an his overhead were on the job. Roberts patrolmen and the tanker crews ha cooled down the hot sectors cornerin on the Red River road. That was luck

Johnson made a quick trip up Fl and Ant Creeks to see the situatio first-hand. For the moment he woul have to depend upon the informatio in Loitved's message as to what might happen in the head of Cedar Creek. He took his fire-crew bosses, Ellsworth and Armstrong, with him on this survey because they would direct the work on the lines. The rest of the overhead crew were left to help the tanker crews on the hot sectors stemming from the Red River road.

The fire on the Fly Creek slope was found to be moving slowly downhill against the wind. The rolling, fiery pine cones and acorns as well as the red-hot rocks were the main source of spread. Fire on the Ant Creek slope was spreading downhill pretty fast with long fingers developed from rolling embers and flaming cones, but there were not many snags to be dealt with. He could probably trench around most of the snags before backfiring, and then hold fire from them with the tankers; thus he could spare two saw gangs for transfer to Roberts. If a decision had to be made between quick holding of his fire and avoiding any new breakovers at Snag Flat, the choice must be to hold Snag Flat. Even so, snags on his area, too, would have to be felled early next morning.

The fire boss rapidly made his plans. His first effort, Johnson decided, would be to hold the fire on the Ant Creek road and check its forward spread on both ridges. At first he would have to rely on the help of the wind on the Fly Creek slope and be content to control such burning stuff as might roll to the road. He would assign the Swanson crew to the job of constructing tractor and hand-built lines up Swamp Flat Ridge and backfiring and holding the Ant Creek road. The road crew would be assigned to Fly Creek to hold that road and get the tractor and hand lines constructed on Trail Ridge. As soon as the 50 emergency laborers arrived from Cedarville, he would be able to reinforce the Ant Creek crew for line-holding purposes and to start backfiring operations on Fly Creek. If no unexpected emergencies developed before the hot-shot crew arrived at 8 p. m., he would move them directly into the new camp, at the head of Cedar Creek, for which supplies had been dropped by the cargo plane. This would give them an early morning start on the hot-spotting job. If things broke badly on Ant or Fly Creek, he might have to use a few of them on the night shift and reinforce the Cedar Creek hot-shot crew in the morning with men from the expected 100-man morning shift. Since the hot-shot crew was a thoroughly competent outfit, a reasonable number of the untrained men could be paired off with the fire-trained experts.

In the meantime, planned action progressed behind the lines. Necessary supplies arrived for the Cedar Creek camp. A safe location was picked on the river flats at Cedar Creek. A volunteer group from the Red Cross arrived to handle the kitchen. The camp boss and a couple of helpers from Snag Flat came across the river to set up the new camp.

Loitved, the forest supervisor's right-hand man, had used the cargo-dropping plane for reconnaissance. On his way to the airport he had met Freeman. Freeman, the woods boss for the Lee Company, had once worked in the Forest Service and could direct many men on a fire line; he had time off over the week end, so Loitved took him along. As a result, the pilot knew precisely where the camp equipment was to be dropped; Freeman knew a lot about the spot-fire situation. Already he and two scouts with a radio set were en route by car and saddle horse to assemble the Cedar Summit camp and reconnoiter the fire on the ground. Later, one of the scouts would meet the hot-shot crew on Trail Ridge and act as a guide. The cargo dropping was to be done about 7 p. m., by two planes.

Johnson returned to Cedar Creek at 2:45. A message was waiting at the camp advising that the Swanson outfit would arrive at 5 p. m., instead of 3 o'clock, as expected. He could not defer action on Ant Creek that long. He would have to put the road crew on Ant Creek and supplement them later with part of the Swanson crew and hold up all of the proposed action on Fly Creek for the Swanson outfit. The road crew, by good timing, arrived at 2:50.

Armstrong had been assigned the Ant Creek section. Now, with his crew of a few men and one tractor with angle-dozer attachment, he was starting a control line to cut off the dangerous unburned triangle between the Red River and Ant Creek road. He sent another tractor-dozer and 10 men to Swamp Flat to start the fire-control line on Swamp Flat Ridge. The other men, with two tankers, were assigned to the backfiring job along the road on Ant Creek.

A foreman from the road outfit, who was familiar with the upper reaches of Cedar Creek, was designated to take charge of the 10 men from the Swanson crew who were to be assigned to the hot-spotting job on Swamp Flat Ridge as soon as they arrived.

The Swanson crew arrived at 5 o'clock. They were fed, and started for the lines about an hour later. Ten were sent to Armstrong for the hot-spotting job on Swamp Flat Ridge; the others were assigned to Ellsworth, who sent 15 men and a bulldozer up the Fly Creek road to start the trail-builder line on Trail Ridge. Another foreman and 10 men of his crew were scheduled for the job of building a line by hand from the end of the tractor-dozer-built line on Trail Ridge to the head of Cedar Creek. Ellsworth went along with these two crews to distribute them properly over the jobs.

Two saw gangs were immediately put across the river to Snag Flat.

The laborers from Cedarville arrived about 7. Twenty of them were assigned to Armstrong to assist in his backfiring; 20 were assigned to Ellsworth to start the backfiring job on Fly Creek; the other 10 were held in camp to augment the hot-shot crew, since a radio message from Freeman indicated that the hot-spotting job at the head of the creek would be heavier than expected.

Johnson had brought two good fire-crew bosses with him, Ellsworth and Armstrong. When Johnson had arrived at Cedar Creek, he had not anticipated additional overhead of the caliber of Freeman and had planned to handle the situation by dividing the total fire perimeter into two segments, with Ellsworth and Armstrong each in charge of a segment. The segments would be long and difficult to supervise. News of Freeman's availability therefore was most welcome. Johnson now planned to use three segments and give Freeman the entire hot-spotting and line-holding job from the ends of the tractor lines on Trail Ridge and Swamp Flat Ridge (which are indicated by the symbol X on the map). This would make three well-balanced sections and give closer supervision and better execution all along the line.

At 7:45 a radio message from one of Freeman's scouts reported that the Cedar Divide camp had been dropped all right and that all cargoes were located and retrievable—more welcome information. The fire boss' base for action was now sure. The message also advised that there were many small spot fires, that water would be essential for mopping these up, and that a plentiful supply should be dropped at camp early next morning.

Because the odds were that the area would be wholly befogged by dead smoke in the morning and that therefore operation of a plane would be impossible, Johnson placed an order for a pack train from the White resort to be at the road end on Fly Creek by morning, equipped with a full complement of water-carrying equipment, with instructions to load water at Fly Creek and proceed to the Cedar Divide camp.

Another message to Johnson said that only 75 men would arrive for the morning shift; no more were available.

Loitved arrived about 8:15 from a check-up at the Snag Flat camp. The assistant forest supervisor and Johnson made a hurried trip over the Fly Creek and Ant Creek lines to check progress and get facts upon which to base morning plans. They found that progress was satisfactory. The Ant Creek-Red River road line was completed and all inflammable material close to the line had been disposed of. The bulldozer had been moved ahead and was now being held in reserve in the event that spot fires might start from the backfiring operations. Backfiring was going to slow down soon because of increasing humidity, but the flame-throwers would be most useful—with their intense heat, they could partly overcome the effect of increasing dampness of night and safely destroy inflammable material; such an operation would be dangerous in the heat of the next day.

Loitved and Johnson met Armstrong at Swamp Flat. Armstrong, the fire-crew boss who had been assigned to the Ant Creek section, had found conditions better than expected on Swamp Flat Ridge and had been able to establish control lines directly at the 'e edge on a long section at the upper ıd. That line was done; only three en were needed to hold it. The dozer ıd the rest of the crew were now :aded down the main ridge, still on rect attack, but they were instructed change tactics and come directly ›wn the spur ridge to Swamp Flat, ıckfiring as they went if it seemed cely that fire on the lower slopes of ıe ridge could outflank them before ıey reached Swamp Flat. Armstrong ıought that the work of this crew ıd that of the road backfiring crew ıould tie together at Swamp Flat ›out 10 p. m.

Loitved and Johnson next went to ly Creek. Work there was progressing ell. The dozer and hand lines would ›nnect with the road in time for the ıckfiring operations. The tanker 'ews had done a good job of holding ıe fire at the road. While Johnson was .lking with Ellsworth, the other fire-ew boss, at the trail and road junction, ıe hot-shot crew arrived. Johnson ld the foreman to report to Freeman, ıe volunteer under whose direction : would work and who now had a ıide waiting further up the creek 'ail.

The weather forecast for next day romised unchanged wind and humid-y, with slightly lower temperatures. Johnson and Loitved then returned › Cedar Creek camp to make plans ›r the next morning. This section at ıe head of Cedar Creek was now defi-itely manned and equipped for early ıorning action. The problem of the ıoment was planning distribution of ıe 75 fresh men. It was decided to as-gn 45 of them to the Ant Creek divi-on, the rest to Fly Creek. The two ınkers would be pulled from Fly reek about 10 p. m. to give the crews chance to rest for the early morn-ıg shift. One would then be assigned › each of the two road divisions. Loit-ed felt from what he had seen on nag Flat that if the power-saw out-ts arrived, Snag Flat should be able › release the Swanson saw gangs for ıe morning shift on the Cedar Creek fire. He was going back to Snag Flat shortly to check. If the crews were available, they would be assigned to snag-falling along the two tractor lines. He would have information for Johnson as to their availability later that evening.

Johnson told Loitved that he felt things were pretty safe on the two lower divisions; that he was going by saddle horse that night to the Cedar Divide camp to be sure that work was well correlated among the three sections. He would get in touch by radio with Loitved, Ellsworth, and Armstrong early in the morning.

Just before Loitved's departure, the 75 emergency laborers arrived. They were fed at once, given the numbers of their crew units, and bedded down. During the evening contacts with Ellsworth and Armstrong, Johnson consulted with them on plans for the early morning shift and decided on the best distributions of the new men to strengthen the tractor and hand lines on Trail and Swamp Flat Ridges. A tanker and small crew would be used on each division along the road to hold backfired sections during early-morning patrol. Plans called for strengthening all along the line on both divisions at about 10:30 a. m. by utilizing all men who were released from the lines by midnight that night and the bulldozers and the remaining two tankers. Accordingly, Johnson called together the foremen and strawbosses who were on hand for morning shift, gave them their assignments for morning, and discussed the nature of the next day's job with them. Then they turned in.

Johnson, wanting to reassure himself as to the outcome of the backfiring at a treacherous angle in the Ant Creek road, went out to have a look, after gulping a cup of coffee that the Red Cross cook had given him. He found that what he had feared had happened—the fire had broken over the road. Fortunately the reserve bulldozer had arrived in time to surround and control it. Lines had been connected to Swamp Flat, and that side of the job now looked secure for the night. Armstrong told him that he planned to leave only a small holding force on after midnight; that he and the rest of his crew would be in camp at about that time. He asked that coffee and food be ready for the crew when they came in.

On return to camp, Johnson met Ellsworth, who had a similar plan. Ellsworth reported that in the dark a man had been hit by a rolling rock; several ribs had been fractured and the man had been sent to the Cedarville hospital.

Johnson then bade Ellsworth good night and success, and started his long trek to Freeman's Cedar Summit camp. The night was quiet. On his left he heard the nighttime rustles and whispers of the living forest; on his right he saw the funeral pyres of a forest's passing.

The hot-shot crew had already proceeded up Trail Ridge to the Cedar Divide camp. The meeting of Freeman and the crew foreman surprised them both. For a moment they stared speechless at each other. Then Freeman stuck out his hand.

"Ray, you old slab-sided son-of-a-gun," he exclaimed. "I have been wondering how I was going to get this fire out—and you show up! It's a cinch now."

The two men had been forest firemen together in northern Idaho 15 years earlier. Both knew the rough-and-tumble art of single-handed fire fighting and spot-fire control; each knew and respected the other's ability. The foreman told Freeman that he had 40 men with him, 30 of whom were trained fire fighters who had already worked on 15 fires this season. Freeman had studied his problem well during his evening of scouting and knew the location of critical spots for early morning attack. These he outlined on a map for the foreman.

The afternoon rush of the fire had died down when it hit the rocky cliffs, and it was necessary only to control a few hot spots to hold the main front. That would take a few competent me The big problem was the spot fires the cliffs; they carried a threat of fu ther spotting from snags and fro burning embers rolling down from o cliff to another. It was a job for ind vidual workers and a couple of strateg cally located spot-fire lookouts.

By the time this discussion was ov the crew had been bedded. Freema and the foreman likewise went to b to rest up for their 5 o'clock take-o

Johnson arrived in the camp abo midnight but he disturbed no one. H would get his facts in the mornin He rolled up in a blanket until cam activities wakened him. At 3 o'clo the noise of a butcher knife pound on a frying pan broke the mornin stillness; the cook was calling th sleeping to action.

"Roll out, roll out!" he shoute Roll out they did. Johnson, Freema and the foreman discussed the Ced Creek situation.

Johnson told Freeman the scope his section, making it clear exact what crews would be coming up th hill in the morning under compete foremen to report to him and wo these lines. Freeman and his scouts ha the Cedar Creek situation well studie The scouts could guide men to th danger spots and distribute them as h and the foreman had agreed upo Freeman's chief concern was wate but he learned that a good water sup ply was at hand in Cedar Creek abou a mile from the fire edge. With a pac train on the job, the problem of wat distribution could be solved. When tol of the pack-train assignment alread arranged, he was pleased. He apolo getically told Johnson, however, tha he was not sure that he could have a the spot fires rounded up by 10 o'cloc

Breakfast over, the hot spotte shouldered their back-pack pumps an picked up their tools. It was just break ing day. Guided by Freeman and th scouts, they proceeded to undertak the job they were there for—single handed fire fighting.

After a quick trip through the are

to size up the situation, Johnson returned to camp and radioed Loitved, asking him to make certain the new foremen coming in on both ridges were properly guided and fully instructed that their boss was Freeman and that either Freeman or Johnson would check in with them on the line shortly after their arrival. Unless something serious had developed on the lower divisions during the night, he, Johnson, wanted to spend the morning on the division of the Cedar Creek Divide because that now was the key to buttoning up the fire.

Loitved told Johnson that he had succeeded in freeing four saw gangs from Snag Flat, instead of two. Johnson asked that the two extra gangs be sent in immediately as reinforcements for the hot-shot crew.

Johnson then talked with Armstrong and Ellsworth and explained the morning situation as he saw it at Cedar Divide and on the upper end of their divisions. He asked that when the crews came on at 10:30 o'clock they send substantial strength of skilled men to those parts of their divisions. The job of putting out scattered spots of fire here was heavy and, further, Freeman might need quick support.

Work proceeded on Fly and Ant Creeks. The worth of skilled and earnest men had proved itself. The fire was checked; the principal job now was mop-up. The tankers were busy drowning out hot embers along the road. Up the slopes, small groups of men equipped with shovels, Pulaskis, and back-pack pumps were similarly engaged in watering out and destroying the fire in stumps, logs, and hot embers.

On the Cedar Creek Divide section, active war was still on, guerilla fashion. The edge of the main fire was at the moment no problem, just a job. It was quiet and had been put out on many long stretches of light fuel. It was a job that morning for the fighters who knew how to put out the hot spots remaining and test seemingly cold fire edges with their bare fingers to prove whether hot or cold. If they became careless, the hot spots would warm up and be active fire lines before noon. It was a job for experts. Ray, the foreman, assigned three of his hot-shotters to this work with two pick-up laborers apiece as helpers.

The spot fires in the cliffs were quite a different problem. They were dormant except for an occasional blazing log. The banked-in smoke cut visibility to a few yards. These fires had to be ferreted out by men who clambered around in the cliffs. The location work of the night before by Freeman and his scouts was so effective that all men were placed quickly on active fires. The scouts proceeded to search for dormant fires and at 9 o'clock two lookouts were placed to keep watch over the most doubtful areas. The pack train moved in water—and still more water—as fast as they could.

Shouts were heard: "Hey, Pete, look across the gulch; you've got a sleeper there." Two boys borrowed a rope from the packer and let themselves and water down the cliff to the spot fire.

Ray moved through the cliffs among his men, observing, encouraging, teaching. Small wonder that his crew was good. Freeman's scouts were diligent. Freeman checked the job. It looked as if Ray's boys had the job in hand. Came 9:30 o'clock, and a lifting in the smoke pall. Not an unlocated smoke finger could be seen. Ray and Freeman met, dirty and smoke-blackened, and grinned at each other. "By golly, Jingles, I believe we made it again." "Yep," said Freeman. "What did you expect? I've got to be back on the job in the morning."

Ten o'clock—the deadline hour. Johnson had checked the tractor and hand-line jobs. They looked good. The 10:30 crews could mop up, and there would be strength enough if an afternoon flare-up occurred. He met Freeman and heard his story.

Wearily, they sat down and sent a radio message to Armstrong and Ellsworth: "Lots of mop-up, but no threats to the line."

Another message went to the Cedar

Creek camp for relay to the supervisor: "Cedar Creek fire corralled 9:55 a. m.; 6,000 acres.

"All under control."

FRANK J. JEFFERSON *is assistant regional forester, in charge of the Division of Fire Control, in Region 5 (California) of the Forest Service. Since he joined the Forest Service in 1911 he has been ranger on the Lewis and Clark National Forest; assistant supervisor of the Lewis and Clark, Nezperce, and Clearwater National Forests; supervisor of the Selway and Kootenai National Forests; assistant chief of the Division of Operation in Region 1, with headquarters at Missoula, Mont.; and assistant chief of the Divisions of Engineering and Operation, Region 5.*

# FIGHTING FIRES FROM THE AIR

CLAYTON S. CROCKER

The roar of the motors faded almost to silence as the patrol plane disappeared behind a gray peak. Then it came again, its rumble a conglomerate of echoes bouncing from one canyon wall to the other. It lurched each time it crossed over the craggy divide on either side of the mile-deep canyon. Updrafts boosted it like a feather, then dropped it hundreds of feet toward the timbered country below—the Selway Wilderness Area in the Bitterroot National Forest in Montana, one of the most rugged and inaccessible areas in the United States.

Midway on the mountainside below was a small, steadily smoking fire; lightning had touched off a dry tree. In an hour it would spread through the timber and race up the steep slope, leaving devastation in its wake. No man on foot or horse could reach the blaze in less than 2 days; there are no roads near it.

The plane leveled off. It slowed almost to a stalling speed a quarter of a mile to windward and a half mile above the fire. In rapid succession three men, mere dots in that tremendously big sky and background of giant mountains, jumped out. Above each smokejumper—the minuteman of the national forest fire organization—a thin, white streamer billowed out, waved crazily for a moment, then took on the shape of a snowy umbrella.

Updrafts, downdrafts, side winds opposed each smokejumper, dangling 30 feet below his parachute, in his effort to alight on the spot he had selected. He, in turn, manipulated his chute to compensate for the contrary currents. His life and that of the forest depended upon his safe landing. He dumped the air from the chute and plummeted like a rock so as to offset too much side drift. Then, to avoid being speared by sharp-topped snags, he collapsed one side of the canopy and glided rapidly forward, falling all the while at the rate of 16 feet a second. His selected landing spot was the top of a hundred-foot green tree. With feet close together, he crashed through the branches; twigs, needles, and cones flew in all directions. Then his chute tangled amid the top branches and jerked him to a stop, his feet 70 feet above the rocky mountainside. To the trunk of the tree he quickly fastened one end of the rope he carried conveniently at his side; with it he clambered down.

Five minutes later, he and two companion smokejumpers attacked the fire. In 2 hours they had put it out, in what to them was routine fashion, a routine part of a day. Besides saving the virgin timber from devastation, they exemplified the precept that effective fire fighting depends on the fast mobilization of men and tools. Mobilization depends on transportation. Transportation now depends increasingly on aircraft, the fastest and most ffective method developed since systematic protection against forest fires egan in 1905.

That year a small group of pioneer oresters started to set up a system to educe the tremendous yearly losses in he inaccessible and priceless forest vildernesses. Transportation then was y pack horses or by pack humans. Trails were few. Fire fighters struggled foot across deep canyons and up nountain divides 12,000 feet high. They had no marked routes or dependable maps. It was hard to detect res, and many became running conflagrations before they were sighted. A fire could spread from a spark to a lisaster while the smokechaser backpacked wearily cross country 2 or 3 r 5 days to begin his attack.

The spirit of the pioneers is a glorious challenge to men of all times, a esson in courage and sacrifice—but lory puts out no fires. The odds gainst them were hopeless. The inadequacy of their system was demonstrated in the great fires of 1910, which pointed up the need for accessibility nd more speedy attack. As a result, n 1911 to 1925, a network of trails vas built, and hundreds of pack mules vere used to reduce travel time to ires. Even so, the 2½ miles an hour over the great distances within the national forests was too slow. Too nany fires still got out of hand; the osts and losses were still too heavy.

Then came the automobile and road era. Between 1926 and 1938, the levelopment of low-cost truck trails opened many forest areas to automobile transportation. Travel time was peeded up to 15 miles an hour and t became possible to put out fires that otherwise might have grown into disasters. Costs and losses were reduced naterially—further proof that speed of attack is the determining factor.

But at a certain point road transportation ceases to be economically ound; in the remote areas rugged errain makes the cost of construction prohibitive. Besides millions of acres of valuable forest remain outside the reach of road transportation. From that problem, air transport was born.

The terrible fires of 1910 left foresters desperate and willing to try anything that held any hope of solution. Airplane patrol, searching for fires, was tried in a few flights in the Lake States in 1915. The results were negative. Flying equipment was not dependable.

In 1919 the Army Air Force provided airplanes and experienced pilots for patrol work over California forests. Not much came of it. The planes available were poorly adapted to the pounding they got in the currents that rush through the mountain country. Often the downdraft was greater than the climbing ability of the planes. Pilots took tremendous risks; many had to make forced landings amid towering trees or on cliffs and rock slides.

Experiments were continued nevertheless in an attempt to make the airplane a useful tool in combating forest fires. By 1926 the airplane was accepted as an adjunct to the lookout system of the Northwest. Air patrolmen helped in observing and reporting going fires and obtaining information on the head end of fast-running fires in remote timberlands. Photographs taken from high-flying planes gave some information for maps, but equipment was poor, and cost and risk were great. Foresters were beginning to see the possibility of uses other than fire observation.

A few landing strips were built in the 1930's in central locations in the most remote forests, and fire fighters were flown to the one nearest a fire. From there they walked, and they cut hours, often days, from the time required by the old trail-travel system. Even so, the landing strips were few, and the men still had to trudge long distances and reach a fire fatigued and only partly effective. Fires still had from 4 to 36 hours to spread before the attackers could reach them.

In 1929, a bad fire season, a crew at the head of a fire was cut off from all ground transportation. They held a key point, far up on the mountainside. To maintain their stand, they required additional equipment; without it, they would lose the fire, and great tracts of valuable timber lay ahead. There was no possibility of getting pumps and other tools through by pack mule; all trails were shut off by fire. To manpack the heavy equipment over the many miles of rough, log-strewn country would have taken too many hours. The fire would not wait. The fire boss, more interested in saving the forest than in his own personal safety, suggested dropping the equipment from an airplane. That was done. Axes, shovels, and hand pumps, bundled in excelsior and blankets, were tossed out, as the little plane bounced through the churning air at treetop level. Many handles were splintered, pumps were smashed against boulders, and much of the equipment was damaged. But enough was salvaged to do the job at hand. The fire was held. That was the beginning of aerial delivery of supplies direct to fire-fighting forces.

Since then, air transportation has developed rapidly. As aircraft was improved in performance, so were techniques for dropping cargo. Pilots, the so-called bush variety, learned to maneuver planes into almost impossible spots amid spikelike peaks, into narrow rock-walled canyons, and in the difficult air currents that prevail in such country during the turbulent weather of the fire season.

In the early years of cargo dropping, bundles were released at treetop level, to fall free at the target site. Extreme accuracy was essential because an overshot of a few feet might carry the package far down into a canyon beyond the target. Breakage was severe in the free falls, and packaging to lessen that damage was costly and bulky—there was more insulation material than actual pay load. Parachutes, first used for dropping supplies in 1936, eliminated the need for bulky packaging.

The principle of the static line, or mechanical tripping of the ripcord, was discovered by a forest pilot and fire fighter in 1937. It permitted abandonment of free-fall methods and made the job more efficient and safer. By 193 much of the initial supply of foo equipment, and material necessary i the attack upon inaccessible fires w delivered by cargo chute.

A specialized use of the freight chut one that greatly simplifies fire fightin and lowers costs, is the delivery righ on the fire line of prepared hot mea for the fire fighters. The practice favored when the fire is in country s far from trails that the use of pac mules would be costly and in instanc when reliance on K-rations is imprac ticable and the nature of the job doe not warrant a field kitchen.

Air-delivered meals are prepared b restaurateurs according to a standar menu. Hot meat, vegetables, grav and other foods are packaged in ti buckets. Each 5-gallon bucket is insu lated by a kapok-stuffed canvas cove which retains the heat for severa hours. Paper plates, forks, spoons, an cups are included. Cold water in mil cans and hot coffee in insulated 5 gallon cans go along with the mea This method of feeding the crews elim inates their need for leaving the fir line for meals. Breakfast, dinner, o supper is dropped at the edge of th fire and there is no mess gear to b packed back to base after the fire.

Then came an exciting experi ment—parachuting men directly to th fire. The idea had come and gon many times, but before 1939 nobod had been willing to advocate suc seeming fantasy of sending a live ma crashing down among spearlike snags sheer precipices, ragged peaks, foam ing streams, rough underbrush, an dense stands of trees. Airmen ha smiled and walked away when the sub ject was mentioned; they thought o the vicious currents, the rarified air a high elevations, and the unpredictabl winds over the rough mountains. Bu a handful of Forest Service smoke chasers did it in the summer of 1939 They had no precedent, no informa tion about that type of parachuting Their equipment was crude accordin o present-day standards. They had assembled their protective clothing from whatever they could get—football padding, baseball masks, and such. They had only the standard emergency parachutes. So equipped, they were at the mercy of the elements.

Their first jumps were aimed at soft, grassy meadows high on the mountainside. Such sites are few in the wilderness forests, and the original concept of the possibilities of jumping was restricted to that limitation. Then, during some trial jumps, a gust of wind chanced to carry a jumper away from the meadow and slammed him down into a thicket of tall trees, the accident that all had dreaded. The jumper, swinging lightly down from the springlike branches, reported the most gentle landing he had experienced. Thereafter, jumpers attempted purposely to land in green trees, which they call "feathers."

Eleven fire seasons have passed and a war has been won since those first timber jumps. The smokejumpers, as they are now called, have had an important part in both.

From the group that pioneered the first jumps, the crew of smokejumpers has grown to an organization of 225 men, many of them college students of forestry. Stationed in squads at strategic points through the Northwest, the men perform a spectacular and dangerous task. I believe that they accomplish more actual fire protection for each dollar spent than any other department or phase of the fire-control activity in the northern Rockies.

Protective clothing has been designed to prevent injury from sharp tree limbs and rocks. Maneuverable parachutes have been invented, designed, and redesigned for maximum safety. Opening of the parachute is made automatic by use of a static-line ripcord. Slotted canopies and guide lines permit considerable control over direction and speed of descent.

A rigorous course of calisthenics, low jumps, and exercises on the ground and over hurdles and obstacles toughen their muscles, train them to be agile, and teach them how to fall, and develop the smokechasers into skilled parachutists. The smokejumpers, after they have been thoroughly trained, travel 140 miles an hour in airplanes and reach a point above a fire in the most inaccessible wilderness in a matter of minutes after it is reported. They bail out 1,500 feet above ground in numbers consistent with the need of the job to be done and land within yards of the embryo fire. Tools, rations, radio-phone, and all other necessary equipment follow by parachute. Unlike the first smokechaser who reached a fire weary from walking many miles, the jumpers are fresh and alert when they attack their fire. They have had a chance to observe the fire and surrounding area from above and have knowledge of its probable course. They know that fellow-jumpers are available as reinforcements within an hour or so.

Smokejumping is dangerous. It is no job for the timid or physically unsound. The men risk their lives with each jump, but it is a calculated risk, taken in the interest of saving an essential resource. Some accidents have occurred. Some bones have been broken, and jumpers have returned over mountain trails on stretchers carried by their comrades, but in thousands of jumps over hazardous terrain, no one has been permanently injured or killed. Jumps by squads of 2 to 100 men have been made in the most remote sections of Montana, Idaho, Oregon, Washington, California, and New Mexico.

During the war, the smokejumper organization helped the Air Force by training para-doctors and providing the specially designed jumping equipment that is essential to precision parachuting. This service helped save many lives when military craft had crashed in inaccessible locations. The cooperation with the Air Force is still active. Search and rescue specialists are being trained each year at the smokejumper base near Missoula, Mont.

A civilian physician in Helena, Mont., similarly trained, jumps with his emergency kit to the scenes of accidents on the fire line in the national forests. An injured employee, struck by a falling snag, suffering from a ruptured appendix, or bleeding from an ax wound, can thus have expert attention with less delay than would often occur had the injury been received in a large city.

Statistics on 10,000 timber jumps offer some interesting information. For instance, men older than 29 years cannot jump without high risk of injury. Nor can men weighing more than 180 pounds expect to hit the ground without broken bones. The record indicates that fewest accidents occur after the jumper has made 13 descents.

Besides smokejumping, air transportation has made other contributions to the control of forest fires. They can be illustrated by the sequence followed in suppressing a back-country fire in the Rockies, in heavily forested territory that straddles the most rugged part of the Continental Divide. It is a roadless expanse of deep, cliff-sided canyons and spectacular granite mountains up to 2 miles above sea level. The bottoms are scorching hot; the heights are chill from the air over glaciers and slides. The wind is a chaos of currents. Pack trails, which switch back steeply over the passes and skirt the precipitous walls, provide access to this wilderness of forests and wildlife. Once these trails were the tenuous supply route to the widely separated lookouts atop the peaks, and up them, when lightning started fires, the smokechaser and fire crews labored at 2 or 3 miles an hour on their slow way to the battles. They were often too late in arriving—as great burned scars, thousands of acres of ghost trees, testify.

On a few well-distributed flats along the bottom of major canyons are short landing strips, suitable for use by small, slow-flying aircraft. Larger strips are not possible because of topographic obstacles. At one of these strips is located the ranger station, which serves as a control center for air operations and in which a battery of instruments indicate current fire conditions, among them fuel moisture, humidity, and wind movement. If burning conditions are dangerous an observer in a patrol plane takes off to see if fires have broken out. His flight follows a carefully plotted course, worked out through a study of topographic profiles, the location of the most hazardous fuel bodies, the angle of the sun's rays, direction and strength of the wind, and similar factors that together tell him where and how to make the most of each minute of flying. The observer is trained in map reading, fuel identification, and fire behavior. On his analysis of conditions at a fire depends the action of the fire fighters. The pilot, too, is schooled in navigation and map reading, so that he can find any specified quarter-acre spot in a forest. He knows the air currents in all the canyons, and he also is a qualified fire observer.

The observer spots a wisp of smoke no larger than that from the chimney of a residence in a far corner of the forest. The pilot swings the plane over to investigate at close range. The observer switches on his radio and notifies the ranger station that he sees a fire. The suppression forces get the alert signal; the jumpers are readied for the take-off; a transport plane is warmed up.

The observation plane slides in over the fire at treetop level. Its exact location was plotted on the map as the approach was made; now the job is to determine just what the fire is doing and what are its potentials. This information determines the suppression action to be taken.

Within 3 minutes the observer has surveyed the situation and radios to headquarters. Calculations indicate the need for five men within the hour. Otherwise, because of the dense, highly inflammable fuels, it will become a fast-running, forest-consuming monster. It is 40 miles from the nearest road and 10 miles from the nearest trail. In 1920, or even in 1940, the situation surely would have meant a big, costly fire; now it is practically a routine affair.

Within minutes of the observer's report, the jumper plane from headquarters points its nose into the directional bearing plotted by the patrol observer. As it climbs for elevation on its direct course to the fire, five young men quickly get into their padded, white, strongly made jumping coveralls under the watchful eye of a jumpmaster or spotter. Dressing and donning their harness in the restricted space inside a plane, which is pitching in the turbulent air like a Montana bronc at a rodeo, is no simple task, but when the jumpers have done so, a complete check of rigging is made by the spotter. By that time the plane is near the fire.

The jump ship swings wide around the fire as the spotter and jumpers orient themselves as to the nearest trail on which to return, survey the geography and forest conditions around the smoke, and check on the best jumping sites. One site appears most suitable, and the pilot crosses directly over it, 1,500 feet above the trees. The spotter drops a drift chute, a 36-inch prototype of the real chutes. Its drift from a true vertical descent is recorded, and the spotter calculates the adjustments necessary in dropping his men.

The ship is maneuvered accordingly. When it is over the desired spot, the five men leap in quick succession from the door. The chutes pop like large firecrackers as the static line jerks them open. They fall rapidly in a downdraft, then catch in dead air, and perhaps drift rapidly off to the side for a moment. By that time, the jumper has checked his canopy and lines and is getting ready to land. He is confident, unafraid, because months of training have given him the skill that is essential if he is to land where he wishes and without injury. He closes one 7-foot slot in the chute and turns to face the direction he wishes to travel. If the wind is drifting him past the target, he collapses the canopy and plummets closer to the ground. If he is offside, he tips the chute and planes in the desired direction. He has selected a bushy clump of trees, and as he plows through the trees, the nylon shroud lines and canopy tangle with the topmost branches and brings him to a gentle, bouncing stop. As he swings, 40 feet above the log- and boulder-strewn ground surface, he produces a light cotton rope from a pocket in his canvas jumper suit and attaches it to the chute rigging. Detaching himself from the harness, he descends on the rope. Another minute and he is free of the jumping regalia, and with a bright yellow ribbon of crepe paper he lays out a signal that indicates in code to the plane that all is well. The plane circles low and drops packages containing complete fire-fighting equipment, radio, rations, and drinking water. Some packages hang up in tall trees but are retrieved through the use of telephone-climber spurs dropped with the jumpers.

Within 5 or 10 minutes more, the fire is being attacked by the well-trained men, who, conditioned like athletes, are free from the travel fatigue that weakened the old-time ground force before it struck the first blow.

Such action by smokejumpers has stopped, at small size and low cost, hundreds of fires, which, in the absence of aerial attack, would have raged over mountain and valley.

The location and behavior of a fire must be known by the men who plan the attack. To get the information by use of foot travel would take 4 hours, maybe 12. During that time the fire would move on, conditions would change, and the tardy reports would be inaccurate. To meet this problem, aerial scouting has been developed to a high degree of dependability.

A scout plane is put into action immediately after a fire "blows up." The plane circles the fire, and a photographer-scout takes pictures of all sides at an angle of about 45 degrees. He photographs also the area ahead of the fire.

802062°—49——34

Beside him in the seat is a small box, much like the one a doctor uses to check palpitation. It is actually a small laboratory. Its top is covered with black cloth in which are attached two sleeves, which are closed with elastic bands and through which the photographer-scout works with his hands inside the dark box. Within 15 minutes from the moment he made his last exposure, he has completed the developing and printing job. His pictures are ready to be dropped to the fire boss on the ground. The prints, still wet, are placed in a paper tube to which is attached an orange-colored ribbon 10 feet long. The tube is weighted with sand to make it fall vertically.

The orange streamer permits those on the ground to keep the falling tube in view and to find it should the landing be in dense brush or a thicket. From those photographs, the planners of the fire-fighting job obtain far more detailed information than could possibly be included in the maps and reports originally provided by ground scouts. The conditions shown by the pictures are up to date within 20 minutes. This intelligence service speeds up the action on the fire line.

Another phase of air transportation is the movement of fire-control specialists quickly to the scene of action. Sometimes several thousand men and tons of equipment and supplies are needed to control a fire. Many machines, pack trains, and fleets of motortrucks are essential in mobilizing and operating these forces under certain conditions. A small army like that requires trained organizers, planners of strategy, and crew bosses experienced in handling large numbers of men under the emergency conditions prevailing on large fires. Such specialists are few, and often must travel hundreds of miles to the fire; the airplane reduces their travel time to a few hours.

Each summer, hundreds of fire fighters are flown from work projects and employment centers across miles of mountainous country to a forest landing strip nearest the fire that has become too large for the first attack force. A few hours of walking and they arrive at the fire—a vast difference from the day 15 years ago when they would have walked 5 days to the spot.

Now we are working on procedures to fight fires with bombs containing water or chemicals. The first attempts to do so were made in 1930 by a bush pilot and an old-time fire fighter, who used a trimotored airplane. They had no bomb sights, ballistics table, or the other scientific aids that enabled the war bombardiers of 1945 to pin-point their targets; the first experiments were with a half-dozen wooden barrels filled with water and plugged tightly. The forester marked a white circle on the ground as a target and climbed in the plane. When he was over the target, he rolled a barrel out the door. Catapulted by the plane at 90 miles an hour, and falling free for only 100 feet, the barrels smashed around the target. None made direct hits, and the water, driven straight down by the force of the fall, wetted a spot little larger than the barrel itself. The result was hardly encouraging—small fires could not be hit directly, and the water covered too small an area.

Next, the same men attempted to spray fires with a hose attached to a tank of water in the plane. Water streamed out the end of the hose as it was flown back and forth over the blotters that had been laid out to check the moisture that reached the ground. Another failure. The water vaporized immediately as it left the end of the fast-moving hose, and practically none reached the ground.

Seventeen years later, more productive experiments in fire bombing became possible. Bombing techniques were improved during the Second World War, and precision instruments were developed for accurately dropping missiles of large volume and weight. The Forest Service and the Army Air Forces cooperated in comprehensive fire-bombing tests. The Air Forces made available their best equipment and personnel; the Forest Service provided the fire technicians and other facilities. The preparation and study of matériel, ballistics, and application techniques were assigned to the Proving Ground Command, and this phase of the experiment was conducted at Eglin Field, Fla.

After 18 months of study of factors such as type of bomb and plane, bomb sights, and dropping procedures, the Air Force in the summer of 1947 carried the experiments into the forests. The project was moved to Missoula, in the heart of the Rocky Mountains in Montana, where tests could be made under the greatest variety of geographic and meteorological conditions.

All that summer, a big bomber and two fighter planes, all equipped with modern devices and manned by highly competent personnel, dropped water-filled bombs on test fires. They plastered small target fires with mud and water from high altitudes, and they glide-bombed them at treetop level. Big bombs and little bombs were hurled at smokes on mountaintops 8,500 feet above sea level and in the bottoms of narrow canyons. Careful technical study was made of the effectiveness of each bomb drop on the fire.

Various types of water bomb were used. Some were designed to function through impact, like an egg thrown against the pavement. Others were exploded at varying heights above the treetops by internal burster charges. The experiments tested every reasonable suggestion that bore on an answer to the question: "Can small forest fires be retarded or put out from the air?"

The answer, according to a board of survey that comprised State foresters and members of private forest-protective associations and the Forest Service, was affirmative.

The experiments demonstrated that forest fires, if attacked by water-bombing aircraft while still small, can be retarded, and, under certain conditions, extinguished. If facilities for bombing are available, many potentially dangerous fires can be stopped or held down by bombing until smokejumpers or ground forces can reach the scene. Foresters also believe that an attack by a dozen heavy bombers upon the head of a big, running fire might well influence the rate of spread to the point where ground control can be greatly expedited.

So far, plain water appears to be a satisfactory retardant for use in bombing fires. Wetting agents, foam, and other chemicals have advantages under some circumstances and will certainly be used if fire bombing becomes a common practice.

Large-scale bombing of forest fires is not economically practicable now, if the entire operation must be paid out of funds available for forest protection—bombers are costly and their operation is expensive. I suggest, however, that the peacetime functions of the U. S. Air Force might logically include the cooperative use of bombing facilities in defense of our forests against fire.

So FAR, THE BENEFITS from airplane transportation have resulted from the speed with which aircraft can deliver fire-fighting facilities to the point of need. That same speed in conventional, fixed-wing airplanes restricts their use and, in some phases of the work, reduces their value. The conventional airplane, because of the speed required to take off and land, requires a long runway or landing strip. Sites of sufficient length are scarce in much of our western forest area, and few landing strips are available for receiving fire crews and picking up smokejumpers for the return to base. The speed of the modern airplane again lowers its value for fire protection when it is assigned to patrol duty. The observer usually must scan a strip of rapidly changing geography at least 10 miles wide; at the normal flying speed of ordinary planes, he must scan each ravine, ridge, and pocket while moving at the rate of more than 100 miles an hour. Hence, he must view more than 12,000 acres a minute. Each acre receives observation for only a small fraction of a second, and the incipient lightning fire may be making less smoke than a small campfire. Slower aircraft would afford better patrol observation.

Then, speed again operates against efficiency in such jobs as dropping supplies and jumpers. Delay by a dropper approximating the time of two heart beats can, while flying 120 miles an hour, cause loss of the vital cargo released. Just that fraction of a second could cause overshooting the target badly. Jumpers, too, must compensate for forward plane speed, and they take a terrific shock as their chutes open at 100 or 120 miles an hour—like a jump from a tall building with a 15- or 20-foot rope attached to the roof and to a person's shoulders; the jerk of the sudden stop is severe.

THE TREND in airplane design is in the direction of faster and faster craft, away from the ideal type for forest-fire operations. The helicopter, however, promises to fulfill the need for slower movement in the air.

Still in its infancy, the helicopter has already been used in fire fighting. It needs only an opening in the timber for a landing site. Its use is not restricted to costly and widely separated landing fields. It can fly slowly to permit thorough scrutiny of any spot that looks suspicious to the observer. It can almost stand still in midair while the patrolman plots the location and conditions of a fire.

During the summer of 1947, a helicopter quickly moved a large crew of fire fighters from the road end in the valley bottom to the point of critical need on a fire high up on an inaccessible mountain. There was no landing strip, only a brush-free spot on the mountain, but the task was accomplished without mishap.

Helicopters now do not carry enough pay load to make them a major factor in delivering supplies, men, or fire-extinguishing bombs, but that lack might soon be overcome. If the hovering type of aircraft is made capable of carrying a ton or more, it will be the final answer to the dreams of the fire fighters. It will follow lightning storms across the forests, hovering at treetop level to examine each strike. The patrolman can be lowered to the ground by rope ladder to extinguish any smoldering spark. He will climb back into the helicopter and proceed systematically to the next danger spot, stopping in midair here and there to scrutinize suspected areas. When a small blazing fire is discovered, the helicopter will hover directly above it, just out of reach of the heat, and water or chemical will be poured or squirted directly on the fire. Smokejumpers will be replaced with "heli-firemen," and the most dangerous and spectacular action in fire-control work will be discontinued in favor of an easier, safer, yet as effective, method of getting to the point of attack. Then, when the last spark is killed, the "heli-fireman" will not face that long, hard hike, 20 or 30 miles cross-country under a heavy back pack, to the old landing field. He will merely radio for the helicopter and climb up the rope ladder to a good comfortable ride back to the base.

He will be available for assignment to another fire hours, perhaps days, earlier than under the 1949 system of "jump to the fire and crawl back when you get her licked."

CLAYTON S. CROCKER *began seasonal work in forest-fire protection on the Selway National Forest in northern Idaho, and for 31 years has been engaged in forest-fire control activities in the Rocky Mountain country. His fire-control experience includes active participation through the eras of the pack trail, the mountain truck road, and development of aerial forestry. Since 1944 Mr. Crocker has been assistant regional forester in charge of fire control for the Northern Region of the Forest Service, and is stationed in Missoula.*

# FIRE AS A TOOL IN SOUTHERN PINE

ARTHUR W. HARTMAN

For three centuries people in the South have practiced woods burning. The custom began in the Coastal Plain flatwoods, where groups of settlers had to clear ground for farming and then for their livestock. They soon learned that late winter was a critical period for their stock—the ground had a cover of dead grass, needles, and litter, and the animals fared badly. But on a fresh winter burn new and succulent grass would spring up to tide their stock over until spring. They set fires also to clear the woods of varmints.

The settlers, observing some beneficial effects, came to believe the whole practice beneficial and, with the passage of time, the population developed customs and community procedures for burning the Coastal Plain pinelands about every second or third winter. When the people migrated inland to the rolling uplands of the Piedmont and the Appalachian, Arkansas, and Missouri Mountains, they carried with them the custom of "light burning." It became universal across the South. They had no way of knowing the extent to which the custom had grown away from beneficial application and become seriously detrimental to the then abundant timber stands.

When trained foresters carefully observed the results they concluded that light burning had been detrimental to the health, growth, and yielding capacity of the stands affected; that it was the limiting factor to good forestry practice in the Coastal Plains; and that eventually it would destroy the hardwoods and less fire-resistant pine stands of the uplands. Three figures show the magnitude of the problem in 11 Southern States: In 1947, there were 158,425 fires that burned over 21,005,581 acres in the total forest area of 185,416,000 acres.

One must not assume that a major part of a population knowingly and maliciously practices or tolerates for a long time a custom detrimental to the community. Rather, one must understand that generations of observation by the people point to some solid reasons for burning, even though application sometimes drifted into extremes.

A few early foresters investigated and concluded that all use of fire was not evil and that fire correctly used under specific conditions and for predetermined results could, in fact, be beneficial. Furthermore, they developed the thesis that the long-established and deeply ingrained custom would be broken only after foresters themselves had clearly identified and separated the helpful from the harmful application of fire and then proved the identity of the two.

Progress toward the identification of the effects to be had from fire has been under way for many years. Here and there observant landowners worked out and applied some uses of fire on their own lands. The work of such men as H. M. Wilson and William Ottmeier produced valuable lines of approach.

As far as the records reveal, the investigations of H. H. Chapman were the first attempts to identify scientifically and define woods conditions that might be bettered by fire, to measure results from actual use, to create guide lines for proper fire intensities, and to measure the influences of climatic conditions on fire behavior.

The Southern Forest Experiment Station twenty years ago began a series of studies to determine some phases of fire effects in longleaf pine stands. The studies progressed until, by 1940, there was evidence that net benefits were obtainable from fire under certain specific sets of conditions. In the meantime, pilot studies were conducted on longleaf pine lands in national forests. The sum of the evidence disclosed a need for burns to be carried out over a large area and under varied conditions.

In considering the program undertaken, certain facts and principles must be kept in view:

1. The term "prescribed burning" is meant to describe and apply only when on-the-ground examination and analysis has revealed some unsatisfactory condition that can be bettered if fire (of a specified intensity and under prescribed conditions of season, fuel moisture, wind direction and velocity) is applied at the proper time and only to the designated area.

2. Timbered land should be protected from wildfire at all times.

3. The burden of proof is on the land manager each time he uses fire as a tool. Use of fire on timber stands must be viewed as akin to surgery on a human being. It is justified only after competent diagnosis of an unsatisfactory condition indicates that opportunity for gain will be in excess of losses and cost and must presuppose acceptable skill in execution.

4. Generalizations, such as "southern pines," must be avoided; in all cases reference must be made to the tree species involved on any one area considered for treatment by fire.

5. In evolving prescribed-burning practices, it is equally as essential to determine where and when use of fire is detrimental as it is to clarify when it can be beneficial.

When the program of prescribed burning was started, available information indicated that it should be tested for its value in meeting the following situations:

1. Preparation of seedbed. Longleaf pine yields a good seed crop at intervals of 5 to 8 years. Characteristic ground cover in this timber type, 2 years or more after being burned, is a mat of dead grass and pine needles so dense that it prevents all but a small part of the seed fall from reaching mineral soil and becoming established.

2. Sanitation burning to eradicate brown spot needle disease from longleaf pine seedlings in the grass stage. Where the disease is prevalent and not cleaned off, either on the natural or planted seedlings, infected plants fail to make growth, gradually lose health and vigor, and in 5 to 8 years may suffer 90 to 100 percent mortality.

3. Subjection of healthy longleaf grass-stage seedlings to a smothering cover of grasses and overstory of brushy plants. Root competition for food and moisture, coupled with shading from sunlight, starve a seedling from starting height growth for as much as 12 years. Fire can remove the shade and reduce competition.

4. Encroachment of any undesirable growth. Edges of ponds, bays, swamps, and streams support growths of titi, gallberry, myrtle, and other commercially worthless species. Under complete fire exclusion, this growth encroaches and occupies good pine sites with thickets so dense as to exclude pine reproduction. In Florida such encroachments have taken over as much as 25 percent of the best pine sites. On the drier longleaf sites, volunteer loblolly can become an undesirable species. Fire can reclaim such areas for establishment of productive growth.

5. Protective burning. This phase of burning is full of divergent interpretations and misunderstanding and controversy. The basic idea in the investigation has nothing to do with the periodic light burning of woods as a substitute for full protection against fire. The simple fact that over Coastal Plain pinelands a wildfire will again burn rapidly within 6 months or a year after having been burned would render any such protection scheme futile.

Opportunities for protective burning are typified by the Osceola National Forest in Florida. There the ground cover is such that an intensive fire-protection organization would fail frequently and to the extent that the sum of fire losses could equal the increment of the area over a rotation period.

Fire exclusion was practiced there for 15 years. It is an area of lush and prolific growth. Longleaf and slash pine seedlings came in profusely following wildfires just previous to establishment of fire protection. Dense stands resulted, understoried by rank growths of the tolerant palmetto, gallberry, and grasses. Pine needle cast, which lasts many years without appreciable decay, drapes over the lower pine branches, bushes, and grass accumulations and creates a floor of man-high fuel heaps. By measurement, there were 25 tons of flash fuel per acre.

As the fuel accumulated, the danger of fire increased constantly. During the long dry periods in late spring and early summer, the stands reached almost explosive conditions. Whether a fire was caused by man or lightning, a moderate wind could fan it into a fast-running crown fire before a man could reach it. Then the only chance of breaking the head lay in backfiring a road that might be several miles away. Burns of thousands of acres were in prospect, particularly because the highest incidence of incendiarism in the country is found in parts of this vulnerable region.

The manager of such a forest land must calculate carefully his risks. On the one hand, can he burn out the fuel at a cost of about 15 cents an acre and the equivalent of one-half of a year's growth of his stand when a killing accumulation of fuel develops? On the other hand, should he take a chance that wildfire will not get into his stand when it is worth upwards of $20 an acre? The factors he must take into account are frequency of incendiary fires, the amount of local sentiment against having range go back to timber, the probability of accidental fires, the size and location of his investment with regard to constant surveillance, and the degree of certainty to which local fire forces can be relied upon to hold incendiary settings of fire to small size. He might also have to consider the chances of fire that exist when a plantation or an equally valuable stand of natural young growth is located in an area of high risk—near a settlement, railroad, sawmill, or a frequented fishing site.

6. Scrub oak control. Following heavy cutting on longleaf ridges, scrub oaks tend to take over the sites, producing a closed canopy that excludes pine reproduction. Some observers believe that fire can be used to thin out or even remove these scrub oak thickets.

7. Planting preparation. Burning just before planting removes the "rough," or mat of dead grasses and leaves, and facilitates planting operations. Brown spot disease is removed from whatever volunteer seedlings are present, and infection in planted stock is reduced. Also, it insures the costly plantation from destruction by wildfire during its most vulnerable period.

8. Wildlife burns. In many areas under complete fire protection, the food supply of deer, turkey, quail, and other wildlife decreases seriously and game birds lose nesting places. There is evidence that fire can be used to increase game foods and keep nesting areas open and sanitary. Sites burned for such purposes are an insignificant fraction of wooded areas, and the desired effects may often be provided by burns carried out for other purposes. However, for the guidance of those land managers who choose to practice multiple use and make some sacrifice of timber production to favor wildlife, a program of prescribed burning is obligated to test and assess methods and scope of fire use for such a purpose.

9. Exploration in the loblolly and shortleaf pine types. Indications are that fire can have a favorable effect under certain limited conditions.

The sites recently subjected to heavy cutting particularly need study. Typically, most of that ground is covered with logging debris and litter, which keeps the seed from reaching mineral soil or smothers the seedlings. Usually present are numerous shrubs, vines, and brush and worthless hardwood species, which grow vigorously and close over the site when the canopy is removed by logging. Thus they prevent most of the random pine catch from developing and from coming through.

An answer must be sought to the question as to whether fire can be used to remove the soil cover sufficiently to obtain a satisfactory natural stand of pine reproduction and at the same time kill or set back the shrubs and hardwoods to the point where the pine seedlings can successfully compete for the site.

Other areas that warrant special investigation are the extensive areas that contain few natural barriers and have nearly even-aged stands of saplings and small pole-sized growth. Conditions occur periodically in which fires spread rapidly. Unusually strong fire-fighting forces cannot stop such fires without great losses.

One solution in the past was to break up the larger vulnerable areas by clearing wide fire lanes and keeping those lanes devoid of vegetation—an expensive practice. We hope that the danger of big fires can be reduced by using a pattern of strips from which the fuel has been removed by careful burning.

Studies are under way to ascertain the amount of damage such burning would do to saplings in the strips. If the damage is low enough to allow good growth and yield on the strips, such use of fire might be cheap and quick insurance against major fire losses on any one area.

Of the 183 million wooded acres in the South, 122 million are in small ownerships. Some 100 million acres are in ownership blocks of 500 acres or less. Further, small tracts are owned by some 1,500,000 individuals. In brief, about 66 percent of the potential timber capacity of the South is in small tracts that are interspersed and integrated with many farming operations, including dairying and raising beef cattle. Some of the herds are large.

The question is: Can grazing and timber growing be adjusted to a minimum of conflicts, so that each can contribute a maximum of benefits? Broadly speaking, the factors in the problem relate to the major timber types, to the basic questions of best land use. By and large, each major timber type is a key to an entirely different combination of soil, topography, climate, species of grasses, undergrowth, and vulnerability to fire.

In late years, grazing practices have been undergoing significant changes in the mountain shortleaf pine type, the flatwoods shortleaf, mixed shortleaf-loblolly, and (to some extent) in the loblolly type. Twenty years ago most animals were of native stock and improved pastures were rare.

Usually the animals were turned loose to roam at will over any unfenced land, even in winter, when the range offered only dead grass of low nutritive value. The stock was so cheap and poor that owners could not afford other winterfeed. A late winter fire would remove the dead forage and be followed by a fresh growth of grass that could tide the animals over that critical period. At best, that type of stock industry must be classed as unstable and uneconomic. This combination of factors was the genesis of perhaps 90 percent of the incendiary woods fires in the South.

With the help of the county agricultural agents, schools and colleges of agriculture, progressive citizens, and the Department of Agriculture, a program was instituted that included elimination of the Texas fever tick, distribution of blooded bulls among the herds, and the creation of fenced, improved pastures. The program was years in the making, but now it is in practice widely, but in various degrees of application.

Over most of the shortleaf and loblolly areas, herds have been improved. Milk stock is preponderantly of good blood. Good breeding of beef stock has raised conformation and weight to a point where the product commands a high market price. The owners find it profitable to hold their cattle on improved pastures and winterfeed them. In the areas where the progress is more advanced, such as in the Ouachita Mountain shortleaf part of Arkansas, range burning has nearly disappeared. Few cattle are seen in the woods, and the conflict between grazing and timber raising has practically disappeared.

Many of the soils found in the nonmountainous belts of shortleaf, mixed shortleaf-loblolly, and loblolly favor the development of improved pastures. Many exist, and more are appearing.

This trend creates the reasonable expectation that causes of grazing fires in the shortleaf and loblolly pine types may soon disappear. There are single-purpose foresters who would deny the mixed use of the same ground for timber growing and stock grazing. That position can be granted to the few land managers who are fortunate enough to have consolidated blocks under fence or located where livestock does not have legal right-of-way. But there are owners of sizable areas of wooded land, men whose business is stock raising; timber will be produced on their lands only to the extent that they are convinced it need not seriously interfere with stock raising. In between are all degrees of mixed use. Undoubtedly there always will be some stock run in these types of woods, but such dual uses need not be considered entirely incompatible. Further, more and more people doubtless will come to the conclusion that wildfire in shortleaf and loblolly timber types is undesirable and harmful to incidental woods grazing of good cattle. With the elimination of grazing fires in the timber types I mentioned, conflict of uses will disappear.

The problem for foresters is to work out an adjusted use and through educational efforts to overcome the grazing fire. We do not foresee a relationship between planned silvicultural burning and grazing by grade cattle in the shortleaf or loblolly pine types.

The true longleaf and mixed longleaf-slash pine types (more than 22 million acres) present another problem.

The typical longleaf sites are low ridges with loose, porous, sandy soils. Humus and available mineral nutrients leach down beyond the reach of most plant life. The establishment of good pastures that contain the more nutritive grasses has been relatively rare, and experimentation has yet to prove that a general development of improved pastures on such soils will be economically feasible.

Herd improvement of range cattle in longleaf areas has lagged, partly because many experienced stockmen believe that breeds that originate in cold climates cannot thrive in a region of high temperatures, insects, and poor forage. But cattle with Brahman blood are good rustlers and can run the open range.

Under normal market conditions the sale price of native cattle will be low. Economically there can be but little winter feeding of such cattle. Yet, from the owner's viewpoint, whatever he does realize from them will be nearly all profit. Present laws in many States permit this stock to roam wherever it can without regard to landownership. Prospects are that no significant part of the vast area in this type will ever be fenced. From the viewpoint of the stock owner, winter burning of a part of the old rough to expose and speed growth of new grass is essential to this phase of animal husbandry.

Continued large numbers of woods-grazing cattle must be expected. The situation is complicated because generally the stockman owns but a small part or none of the land he is grazing. Whether or not the landowner wishes to grow timber, stock will be present and wildfires will continue.

The combination of these factors has created the outstanding concentration of woods fires in the country; the burned acreage annually exceeds the total burned by woods fires from all causes in all other parts of the United States. The situation has changed little for generations.

As a matter of firm fact, on more than 12 million acres of longleaf pine lands, the conflict right now is so acute that no organized attempt is being made to suppress the fires. The owners

of these lands have not found justification for making the business investments required to embark on good forestry practice in the face of the present certainty of heavy fire losses.

The most promising solution in sight lies in the possibilities occurring from the use of fire as a silvicultural tool. We are in no way advocating the burning of longleaf woodland for the primary purpose of grazing benefits. That is just what we must get away from.

Available experience does hold the hope that planned burning for seedbed preparation, brown spot control, removal of brush encroachments, and removal of dangerous fuel accumulations will together produce enough burned land on a managed area to meet the needs of the stock. Also, when cattlemen are informed of the burning program and pattern, and find they can depend upon its execution, much of the cause for wildfire will have disappeared.

When the program of prescribed burning began in the winter of 1943, there were approximately 3 million acres of national forest lands in the longleaf and longleaf-slash types. Reconnaissance of the lands disclosed that far more needed burning than we had facilities for. Then and since, the problem has been to select the most critical conditions for the priority of treatment.

The net areas treated in five different seasons and the costs per acre were:

| | |
|---|---|
| 1943–44: 142,677 acres | $0. 114 |
| 1944–45: 180,091 acres | . 104 |
| 1945–46: 154,617 acres | . 116 |
| 1946–47: 110,126 acres | . 155 |
| 1947–48: 216,055 acres | . 153 |

The average area burned annually represents 5.35 percent of the national forest longleaf-slash pine lands.

The main purposes for burning and the area in acres involved in each were:

| | |
|---|---|
| Seedbed preparation | 228, 000 |
| Brown spot disease control | 365, 000 |
| Longleaf seedling release | 14, 500 |
| Control of brush encroachment | 50, 000 |
| Fuel reduction | 121, 500 |
| Scrub oak control | 2, 000 |
| Planting preparation | 16, 000 |
| Wildlife burns | 3, 000 |
| Loblolly exploration | 3, 500 |

The distribution of prescribed burns by States was:

| | *Acres* |
|---|---|
| Alabama | 55, 100 |
| Florida | 333, 600 |
| Louisiana | 100, 800 |
| Mississippi | 216, 700 |
| North Carolina | 11, 100 |
| South Carolina | 41, 100 |
| Texas | 45, 100 |

The major efforts of the first year were concentrated in Florida. There (particularly on the Osceola National Forest, with its dense stands of advanced reproduction and heavy flash fuel) the burning was extremely risky, with chances of severe losses. But a force of men experienced in handling wildfires was available there; we believe that whatever the risk from burning, the risk from doing nothing was even greater. The conditions appeared to be worse there than elsewhere in the South, so that successful prescribed burning would assure solution and techniques on which to base successful operations elsewhere.

Research men currently recorded the factors present and the methods involved in each burn, measured apparent damage, and thereafter have annually remeasured the representative plots to compute delayed or slowly

appearing damage. As a result, 90,000 acres of the Osceola National Forest have been burned with a negligible amount of damage. Most of the measurable damage occurred on those burns deliberately pushed to identify safe limits of action—too early or too late in the season and too long after a rain.

Foresters who have inspected and studied the results obtained on the Osceola National Forest have concluded that the stands benefited from the treatment.

A significant fact: This 150,000-acre forest is heavily stocked with range cattle, but incendiarism has nearly disappeared, and the average area burned annually from wildfires of all causes has dropped from 3.4 to 0.033 percent of the area.

THE RESULTING CATCHES of longleaf pine seedlings on areas where the mineral soil has been exposed by burning a year or less before a seed fall have been successful. An example: On 26,000 acres in southern Alabama, burned just before the 1947 seed fall, a catch grading from satisfactory to heavy was obtained on 90 percent of the area, and at 1 percent of the cost of planting. On many burned areas following the period of seed germination, examination showed that good catches can be obtained on roughs a year old or less; that on a 2-year rough, there is some catch but not satisfactory stocking; and on roughs of 3 years or more, the catch is insignificant.

Results we obtained from seedbed burns in units of more than 300 acres in size are not in line with results from small-area experimental burns. Rodents are pretty well eliminated from the larger burns, and their damage is confined to edges. The seed-loss damage characteristic from bird concentration on small burns is reduced when they can feed over larger areas. Increased distances from brown spot infection sources delays infection of the new seedlings.

BROWN SPOT needle disease is present in varying degrees over the entire pine belt; mostly the infection on unburned grass-stage seedlings ranges from serious to epidemic. The effects are equally adverse to natural seedlings or planted stock.

Area examinations usually reveal a considerable degree of infection on 3-year-old stock. Then the disease has not seriously reduced the vitality of the plant, but if it is not overcome, it will spread rapidly, increase in severity, progressively weaken the seedlings, and destroy all but a few stragglers in the following 3 to 5 years.

A fire during the dormant period (late December through February) will control the infection if it is hot enough to defoliate the grass-stage seedlings, and has flames high enough to consume the infection-carrying needles on any reproduction up to 10 feet in height. If burned early enough, before the infection has reduced the vitality of the seedlings, the seedlings will produce a full crown of healthy needles the following growing period. The speed with which a reinfection may occur appears to be proportionate to the size of the area given a sanitary burn. A burn of 40 acres is hardly worth while. The disease left in the surrounding unburned area will reinfect to a depth of several hundred feet within a year.

Experience dictates that a burn for this purpose include at least 200 acres; results would be better on even larger units. The occurrence and virulence of brown spot disease is so variable that no time formula for treatment can be followed. In some areas the disease was not sufficiently prevalent to justify burning, while in others a dangerous degree of infection did not appear until the fifth year. Of considerable significance are indications that one fire treatment often is enough to bring the seedlings through into height growth.

Our best guide is: Never burn unless necessary; necessity must be determined by an annual reconnaissance that computes the extent of infection present and maps for treatment any areas where infection is severe.

Experience indicates that when (because of tardy treatment) only about one-quarter of the stock recovers its health, there is a net gain from reburning 2 years after the first fire. The infection must therefore be detected and burned promptly, before the disease has had time to sap the vigor of the plants.

The results from fire treatment have generally been successful. Plantations and areas of natural reproduction which were treated in time are now healthy, well-stocked stands of saplings. Even in plantations where fire was excluded so long that some mortality had set in and the remainder looked hopeless, the recovery resulted in healthy if understocked stands.

Release burning is another aspect. For reasons not yet clearly measured, longleaf seedlings not seriously diseased sometimes will remain in the grass stage and fail to start height growth for as long as 12 years. The reason probably is a combination of deficiencies in food, moisture, and sunlight, because of the competition of dense stands of grasses and shrubs. Frequently it was noted that height growth began after a wildfire had burned such areas.

To determine whether some of these lost years of growth could be saved, a program was started for burning varying age classes of the delayed-growth stands. The study, not yet completed, indicates tentatively that height growth will begin the second spring following a prescribed burn that removes the grass mat and kills back the bushes, worthless brush, and hardwood species.

Fire has been used successfully to kill back encroachments of titi, gallberry, and myrtle and permit the establishment of pine seedlings. A large area in Florida burned for this purpose now supports a good stand of slash pine seedlings.

Scrub oak thickets have been burned in all seasons and with varied intensities of flame. Usually fuel under the thickets is light and patchy; in them, high-intensity fires are impossible. Summer fires have given favorable results on small areas here and there within a large burn. We are unable yet to point to conclusive examples of successfully reducing by fire treatment the scrub oak canopy generally over commercial-size areas.

The valuable loblolly pine assumes the role of an undesirable species when it encroaches on a true longleaf pine site that has a stand of grass-stage seedlings. If it is not controlled, the loblolly takes early ascendancy and usually smothers out the longleaf. The loblolly lacks the long taproot with which nature equips the tree she designed for this site and cannot reach down through the dry topsoils to the water table. It soon loses its vigor, becomes easy prey to deforming or killing Cronartium infection, and produces an inferior stand.

Burning in loblolly sapling stands to remove fuel in strips has been under controlled tests for only one season. Preliminary findings are that the areas treated show low damage; perhaps burning techniques can be evolved that will make it practical, at low cost and low damage, to break large areas of fire-vulnerable stands into small blocks within which an intensive fire can be confined.

Loblolly areas in parts of southeastern Texas (since establishment of tight fire-protection practices) are being taken over by dense thickets of yaupon. A joint project with the Southern Forest Experiment Station is testing the possibilities of fire use to restore these areas for pine stands.

General lessons: The lowest damage to timber stands from prescribed fires occurred under the following conditions:

Burns between December 20 and February 28;

The second and third day following a rain;

Backfiring against a cold, steady north wind having a velocity of 5 to 8 miles an hour at ground level;

The area broken by clean-plowed lines at 10 to 20 chain intervals running right angles to the wind direction;

Work done during the daylight, starting about 10 a. m. and completed soon after dark;

Areas of vulnerable reproduction located, plowed around, and from which fire was excluded.

Dangerous practices:

Plowing 3 weeks or more before burning—leaves and needles drift into fire lines and they do not hold;

Burning just before a rain—winds always become shifty and create hot spots or head fires;

Using other than backfire—exception can be made and flank fire used in seedbed or planting preparation where there is little of value already on the ground; short-head fires are required to remove brush encroachments;

Burning against any but a northerly wind; others are not reliable;

Burning with no wind—the hot gases, not being dissipated by winds, rise directly upward and create high and severe needle scorch;

Burning at night—there is more probability of a calm setting in, resulting in high scorch. It affords less opportunity for good supervision; men may lose direction and make mistakes. When dew falls, the line burns unevenly, and parts of the fire go out; the fire may not burn to the control line, and conditions might be dangerous the following day;

Laying out a burning plan without first carefully reconnoitering and mapping the area;

Burning in longleaf reproduction after it has started height growth and before it exceeds 8 feet in height;

Leaving a burning job to unskilled hands;

Trying to burn even though weather conditions begin to change from those expected—it pays to put out the fire and send the crew home.

Established facts:

Fire can be backed against strong winds through our heaviest roughs, under longleaf and slash pine saplings 12 feet or more in height, and the scorch confined to the lower one-third of the needles.

Slash pine reproduction, growing over a moderate fuel accumulation, will have 90 percent survival at 6 feet in height if properly burned.

Grass-stage longleaf seedlings 2 years or more of age store sufficient reserve food in root systems to fully refoliate following a single burn.

Danger signals are these: The height of the scorch line gives a good ocular measure of the quality of a burning job. For advanced longleaf and slash pine, when the scorch involves less than the lower one-third of the live needles, no measurable slowing down of growth follows. A scorch between the lower one-third and one-half of the needles results in a loss equivalent to one year's growth. As the scorch rises into the upper half the growth loss rises rapidly, creating mortality.

Several directions and precautions can be given.

If the examination has shown a need for burning, the area involved is mapped, and a burning plan is laid out. It should set forth the desired

wind direction and velocity, temperature, number of days following rain, and the approximate dates desirable for burning.

Areas of from 300 to 500 acres in size are the most economical to handle.

The area is prepared for a day with the proper characteristics by plowing parallel lines, their ends tied into barriers or a surrounding plowed line.

Distance between interior parallel lines may be from 10 to 20 chains. Spacing distance is determined in each case by the nature and value of the stand, and the speed at which fire may be expected to back in that particular fuel.

Where fire backs at a rate of 1½ chains an hour and an 8-hour duration of burning is planned, the lines should be placed at intervals of about 12 chains.

When conditions for burning are favorable, instruct each man as to the lines he is to fire and their sequence, and, if possible, arm each with a drip torch.

As soon as test sets indicate that conditions are right, start a number of fire lines simultaneously.

Three men can fire all the lines in a 500-acre block within 50 minutes. Two safety men are needed to guard the downwind line until the fire has eaten into the point of safety.

The foreman and other men, upon completion of firing, should prowl their assigned interior and any exterior plowed lines for break-overs.

Five men are desirable to start a 500-acre burn. Two men can guard it after it is under way.

Good burning days are relatively scarce, so it is our practice to utilize them to the fullest. From the inventory of blocks planned and prepared for treatment under existing conditions, additional areas are selected and the crew fires new blocks until safety assignments absorb them.

A fire-plow unit is kept either at the scene or where it can be reached by radio in case of trouble.

When conditions are right and large blocks are available, a five-man crew can successfully burn up to 1,500 acres a day in difficult areas.

Regarding costs, we view as an error any attempt to reduce the cost of prescribed burning at the expense of quality. Rather, the objective must be a burning operation resulting in predetermined acceptable damage. Costs are then reducible to the extent that organization skill, training, and efficient supervision can eliminate excess manpower and lost motion.

Averages are misleading. Seedbed burning is done for as low as 8 cents an acre. Fuel reduction in valuable young stands often justifies as much as 25 cents an acre. Ninety percent of the burns in national forests fall within the range of 12 to 18 cents an acre.

On a typical 15-cents-an-acre longleaf burn, the costs break down about as follows: Reconnaissance and planning, 2.1 cents; plowing lines, 7.2 cents; and burning, 5.7 cents an acre.

ARTHUR W. HARTMAN *is chief of the Division of Fire Control in the Southern Region of the Forest Service. He received his early training on the Klamath, Natural Bridge, and White Mountain National Forests. He was forester for War Department lands at West Point, N. Y., until he joined the Army in the First World War. Later he was district forest ranger, timber management assistant, assistant supervisor, and supervisor on the Ouachita National Forest and the Kisatchie National Forest. He is a graduate in forestry of Pennsylvania State College.*

# MACHINES AND FIRES IN THE SOUTH

ARTHUR W. HARTMAN

After 30 years of effort by private, State, and Federal organizations to protect their forests against fire, some 97 million acres of the private wooded land in the South are under some kind of protection. An additional 15 million acres are protected by the national forest organization. More than 80 million acres of forest and potential forest land, however, receive no protection at all.

Of every 100 acres under organized protection by State forest services, an average of 1½ acres suffer burns each year. As late as 1943, when fire suppression depended mostly on men with only hand tools, fires burned 29 million acres and destroyed values estimated at 72 million dollars.

The record was not good. Several explanations, if not excuses, can be given. Because fast-spreading fires can start in flash fuels in the South a few hours after a rain any time during 8 to 12 months of the year, forest lands are in almost constant jeopardy. Combinations of low humidity and high wind often create conditions of extreme hazard, when fires may burn with an intensity beyond the ability of men to control unless they have proper machines—but, although yesterday's long lines of pick-and-shovel ditch diggers have been replaced largely by powered trenching machines operated by a few men, there are still lines of sweating, exhausted men who try to stop the fires with shovels and rakes.

For the delays in getting machines for fire fighting, one can assign several reasons. Fires occur intermittently; during times of low hazard, the fighters are scattered to perform other tasks. In periods when burning intensity is not severe, fires are handled so easily that men may lull themselves into a false security. Funds and facilities were insufficient to meet the requirements of broad-scale planning, creating, testing, experimenting, as well as developing the special equipment needed for successful fire-line performance. And, as always, there was the human resistance to change.

Nevertheless, attempts were made to adapt the available machines to the need. Foresters and an implement manufacturer in Florida, for example, made over a heavy tractor-plow, which turned out to be useful under some conditions but expensive and too big to be easily moved from one fire to another. Elsewhere farm tractors were pressed into service. Men in Arkansas developed a pusher-type plow on a crawler tractor. Fire fighters in Texas made progress with a garden-tractor plow. Others used jeeps, or any vehicle at hand, to pull light plows and haul water tanks and pumps. With such makeshifts, however, nobody was satisfied.

Then came two developments at one time. The Civilian Conservation Corps, which had supplied so many trained and vigorous men for the work, was discontinued. Then, the war drained the towns and back-country of able-bodied men. The situation left one choice: Mechanize or burn.

State, industrial, and Federal foresters, despite wartime handicaps, began to attack the problem on the scale the situation demanded. The few previous trials and errors gave them some guides and principles, but they needed information, action, and decisions on five points: Thorough knowledge of the terrain, soil, cover, and fire behavior over all forested areas from the Carolinas to Texas; reports on the design and performance of equipment that had been tried out; goals for each general timber type; specifications of units that would give the results they were after; time and funds to test new ideas.

Several other essentials complicated their problem: All designs had to assure reasonable safety to the operators. Each unit had to balance the factors of least cost, lightest weight, fastest travel and operation, dependability, the widest range of use over a major area. The designs had to use standard parts and techniques of shop procedure to facilitate repairs and maintenance. Accessories, such as backfiring devices and communications, had to be identified, selected, or developed. The size, use, and organization of crew that would be most efficient and effective had to be determined. Men had to be trained.

All that had to be done quickly—the forests and the world were burning up.

Information at hand or quickly accumulated provided several first principles: A plow-constructed, mineral soil line was superior to other types of fire lines. The multiple disk-type of plow was fastest and most efficient wherever it could be used. The middle-buster type of plow was next best on stony ground where the disks would not stand up. The crawler-type tractors were the most satisfactory power units. Multiple-drive transports were better than those with 2-wheel drives for back-country travel. The main uses of tankers in the region were to help hold the fire line at plowed lines, catch spot fires, and do mop-up.

Further investigations brought out that plows of five classes would meet most of the needs.

1. The heavy disk plow, of 2,500 pounds, for dense stands with luxuriant undergrowth of palmetto, shrubs, and grasses common to the lower Coastal Plain.

2. The medium disk, of 950 pounds, in the less dense belts of the Coastal Plain.

3. The light disk, of 475 pounds, where the fuel is principally the pine straw and grass found in the upper Coastal Plain and Piedmont.

4. The lightweight middle buster, of 475 pounds, in the stony ground of the lower hills and on Appalachian slopes of less than 25 percent grade.

5. The flyweight, cultivator type, of 125 pounds, in the open short-grass areas in the southwestern parts.

Heavy disk-type plows which would operate successfully were available commercially; the problems were to determine the lightest tractor that could ride down and pull the plow through the different densities of ground cover, and to design speedy transports that could haul the tractor and plow closer to the back-country fires. In the final assignment of locations, places were found for all sizes of tractors, from 22's to 50's. Hi-low trailers were designed in varied weights to fit their loads. They were rigged as prime movers, and ranged from 1½-ton two-wheel drives to 2½-ton 6 x 6's, according to loads and travel conditions. Eleven of these assemblies were completed in 1944 and placed in service.

Meanwhile, a lightweight unit was being tested. A key specification for it was that the tractor and plow in combination must be light enough to be transported on a 1½-ton truck. We found finally that a commercial 18-horsepower tractor, with several alterations, would fit the need. Then we designed a truck chassis to make loading and unloading easier. Seventeen of the units (called Ranger Pals) were assigned in 1944 to 10 high-fire-occurrence ranger districts. Experience with them in the field revealed opportunities to make further improvements, which we did. Twelve other lightweight units and 10 more heavy units were placed in operation in 1945. Radio receivers were installed in about half of the units. The development and field testing of a middleweight unit was under way.

Eight improved lightweight units and 10 heavy-transport units were added in 1946. Since then, 6 middleweight, 8 lightweight, and 2 fly assemblies, and nine 4 x 4 power wagon tankers have reached the fire lines. Most of them have sets for radio communication.

At the same time, several State foresters and private owners adopted some of the machines and worked to perfect others. Their difficulty, however, was that they had few pieces of equipment and large areas to protect.

Men on the national forests faced a like situation of not enough, and we had to choose between spreading the equipment generally or making some concentrations. To obtain the greatest use and protection and at the same time measure the economic aspects, we chose to favor the ranger districts that had the worst combinations of high fire occurrence and fast rates of fire spread. A number of other districts that were favorable for plow use were left without mechanical units. Because there were so many critical areas, we believed then that it was impractical to equip fully any one ranger district with what we have come to believe since is the minimum number of units.

By 1946, however, six of the worst fire districts had enough equipment to handle their situation on all but the most hazardous fire-weather days.

Meanwhile, experience produced improved tactics, increased the effectiveness of each unit, and made it possible to compare and analyze equipment, work, and trends.

One analysis brought together data for three fire seasons on seven ranger districts in Mississippi and Louisiana. The first was in 1940 (1941 records for two districts), when 315 fires were fought with muscle-power and the fire fighters were boys and men of the Civilian Conservation Corps — well trained, well organized, and readily available, and with their own fast transportation. The second season was the same months of 1946, when 526 fires were fought on those districts with mechanical suppression units in numbers adequate to permit the proper strength on the larger fires but often inadequate for prompt attacks on additional fires.

The third season was 1947, when, with added numbers of equipment units, 627 fires were controlled. It is significant that in 1947, during periods of high fire occurrence, fewer fires had to be left to burn unattended until equipment could be disengaged and dispatched from another fire and that new equipment enabled us to assign two or more suppression units to potentially bad fires. Each of these units had three men and could build as much fire line as 30 men without like equipment; furthermore, to the extent that radio sets were available for them, they could be placed at strategic travel points. The greater the danger of fire, the greater was the number of units activated; the result was that the equivalent of a strong suppression force was ready to attack a few minutes after a fire was discovered.

The results of the analysis—manpower alone in 1940, mechanized equipment in 1946, and increased mechanized equipment in 1947—are given in the table on page 531. (Not included are fires on fewer than 5 acres

802062°—49——35

COST OF EQUIPMENT—PURCHASES MADE AT DIFFERENT TIMES UNDER CHANGING MARKET CONDITIONS (ROUNDED AVERAGES)

| Item | Heavy plow unit | | Mediumweight unit | | Light plow unit | | Featherweight plow | | Tanker | |
|---|---|---|---|---|---|---|---|---|---|---|
| | *Size* | *Cost* | *Size* | *Cost* | *Size* | *Cost* | *Size* | *Cost* | *Size* | *Cost* |
| Truck | 2½-ton, 6x6 | $2,000 | 2-ton, 4x4 | $1,800 | 1½-ton | $800 | .... | .... | ¾-T, 4x4 | $1,800 |
| Hi-low trailer | ....... | 800 | ...... | 800 | ...... | ..... | ..... | ..... | ..... | ...... |
| Tractor | D-4 | 4,000 | T-6 | 2,400 | HG-Cletrac | 1,400 | .... | $315 | ..... | ...... |
| Plow | ....... | 750 | ...... | 700 | ...... | 275 | .... | 50 | ..... | ...... |
| Radio | ....... | 450 | ...... | 450 | ...... | 450 | ..... | ..... | ..... | 450 |
| Installations | ...... | ..... | ...... | ..... | ...... | ..... | ..... | ..... | ..... | 400 |
| Total | ...... | 8,000 | ...... | 6,150 | ...... | 2,925 | ..... | 365 | ..... | 2,650 |

CHARACTER OF FIRE PROTECTION ON COMMERCIAL FOREST LANDS, UNITED STATES, 1945

| Ownership class and geographic section | Commercial area | Percentage of acreage rated— Good | Fair | Poor | None |
|---|---|---|---|---|---|
| Private: | *Mil. acres* | *Percent* | *Percent* | *Percent* | *Percent* |
| North | 140 | 22 | 60 | 12 | 6 |
| South | 167 | 7 | 35 | 37 | 21 |
| West | 38 | 64 | 27 | 9 | 0 |
| Total | 345 | 19 | 44 | 24 | 13 |
| Public: | | | | | |
| North | 31 | 76 | 23 | 1 | 0 |
| South | 16 | 60 | 10 | 24 | 6 |
| West | 69 | 94 | 6 | 0 | 0 |
| Total | 116 | 85 | 10 | 4 | 1 |
| All lands: | | | | | |
| North | 171 | 32 | 53 | 10 | 5 |
| South | 183 | 11 | 33 | 36 | 20 |
| West | 107 | 83 | 13 | 4 | 0 |
| Total | 461 | 36 | 35 | 19 | 10 |

NUMBER OF FIRES, BY CAUSES, 1947

[Protected lands only]

| Land ownership | Lightning | Railroads | Campers | Smokers | Debris burning | Incendiary | Lumbering | Miscellaneous | Total |
|---|---|---|---|---|---|---|---|---|---|
| Federal | 4,502 | 117 | 481 | 1,377 | 256 | 1,521 | 86 | 588 | 8,928 |
| State and private | 1,919 | 4,701 | 2,860 | 16,430 | 12,043 | 22,172 | 1,476 | 9,841 | 71,442 |
| Total | 6,421 | 4,818 | 3,341 | 17,807 | 12,299 | 23,693 | 1,562 | 10,429 | 80,370 |

nd fires that burned from outside the ational forests and were simply held t the boundary.)

In assessing these data, it should be emembered that had manpower only een available in 1946 and 1947 the esults would have been poorer than hose of 1940. Crews then and now vould have to be recruited from disant towns, scattered farms, sawmills, nd logging camps at a greater cost of ime in reaching the fires.

The seven ranger districts covered n the analysis contain 1,133,000 proected acres. On them, an average of ,074 fires occur each year. Twentyight plow units are assigned to them, t a rate of one unit to 40,500 acres nd 38 fires. The investment in tracors, plows, transport, and radio for he units was $124,000, and the annual lepreciation of the equipment was bout $10,000.

The cost per fire, 5 acres or over in ize, fought with power equipment in 1947 was: Depreciation, $9.31; operaion and repair, $3.75; and pay of crew or suppression, mop-up, and travel ime, $13.91—or a total of $26.97.

On the basis of past experience in nanpower requirements and presentlay wages, it would have cost $52 a ire to have fought these fires with men nd hand tools alone. The direct savng by using machinery was $25.03 a ire, or $15,694 for the 627 fires.

Comparing the burned acreage reulting from like fires fought under the wo methods of suppression, we find hat if the same 1941 supply of manpower had been available and used on he 1947 fires, 65,700 more acres would have been lost than were actually ourned when machines were used. What the additional fire damage to imber and young trees would have een is speculative; our estimates show t would exceed $3 an acre, or a total of $200,000.

Less assessable values, such as the effects on water, soil, wildlife, and recreation, were not estimated. Other intangible gains from the mechanization are increased public support for

ANALYSIS OF SIZE OF FIRES ON SEVEN RANGER DISTRICTS IN THE SOUTH, UNDER VARIOUS CONTROL METHODS, 1940, 1946, 1947

| | *Average size of fires* | | | | | |
|---|---|---|---|---|---|---|
| | *Hand-tool control* | | *Plow control* | | | |
| | 1940 [1] | | 1946 [2] | | 1947 [3] | |
| *Class fire day* | *Size at beginning of attack* | *Final size* | *Size at beginning of attack* | *Final size* | *Size at beginning of attack* | *Final size* |
| | *Acres* | *Acres* | *Acres* | *Acres* | *Acres* | *Acres* |
| 3 | 23.0 | 57.2 | 14.4 | 28.7 | 11.0 | 23.2 |
| 4 | 45.6 | 93.7 | 17.7 | 36.5 | 12.9 | 27.2 |
| 5 | 49.8 | 422.2 | 22.1 | 67.9 | 16.0 | 49.5 |

[1] Based on records of 315 fires.

[2] Based on records of 526 fires.

[3] Based on records of 627 fires.

PERCENTAGE OF TOTAL FIRES REACHING CLASS D AND CLASS E SIZE

[By hand-tool and plow suppression]

| | *Class D size (100–300 acres)* | | | *Class E size (over 300 acres)* | | |
|---|---|---|---|---|---|---|
| | *Hand tools* | *Plows* | | *Hand tools* | *Plows* | |
| *Class fire day* | *1940* | *1946* | *1947* | *1940* | *1946* | *1947* |
| | *Pct.* | *Pct.* | *Pct.* | *Pct.* | *Pct.* | *Pct.* |
| 3 | 18.6 | 2.6 | 0.6 | 2.0 | ... | ... |
| 4 | 11.2 | 5.1 | 1.1 | 4.0 | 0.4 | 0.3 |
| 5 | 22.5 | 11.2 | 2.5 | 16.9 | 2.8 | 3.0 |

the work of suppressing fires and preventing wildfires, and greater confidence in the ability of the fire fighters.

As for the forest rangers, they have found that their small, compact power organization can handle any but the very worst situations. Consequently, relieved of the feeling of insecurity and dread of impending disaster, they are free to search out and remove the causes of fires. Morale has improved.

Benefits from mechanization to the 11 States (Alabama, Arkansas, Florida, Georgia, Louisiana, Mississippi, North Carolina, Oklahoma, South Carolina, Tennessee, and Texas) in the Southern region reflect generally the extent to which they have acquired equipment

ANALYSIS OF FIRE CONTROLS ON SEVEN RANGER DISTRICTS IN THE SOUTH, 1940, 1946, 1947

| | *Average time on line building* | | | *Average maximum number men per fire (including mop-up)* | | | *Average chains built line* | | |
|---|---|---|---|---|---|---|---|---|---|
| | *Hand tools* | *Plows* | | *Hand tools* | *Plows* | | *Hand tools* | *Plows* | |
| *Class fire day* | 1940 [1] | 1946 [2] | 1947 [3] | 1940 [1] | 1946 [2] | 1947 [3] | 1940 [1] | 1946 [2] | 1947 [3] |
| | *Man hours* | *Man hours* | *Man hours* | *Number of men* | *Number of men* | *Number of men* | *Chains* | *Chains* | *Chains* |
| 3.......... | 20.15 | 5.37 | 4.25 | 18.0 | 15.6 | 5.7 | 75.2 | 57.1 | 49.7 |
| 4.......... | 24.99 | 5.86 | 6.92 | 22.6 | 6.4 | 7.3 | 83.2 | 67.7 | 62.9 |
| 5.......... | 52.51 | 10.40 | 7.50 | 30.3 | 8.2 | 7.3 | 160.3 | 83.0 | 78.5 |

[1] Based on records of 315 fires. [2] Based on records of 526 fires. [3] Based on records of 627 fires.

and installed radio controls. A conclusive analysis of the benefits is not possible, but the general trend is shown in some statistics for all protected lands in the States: The fires per million acres were 572 in 1942, 601 in 1943, 328 in 1944, 317 in 1945, 382 in 1946, and 472 in 1947. The percentages of protected areas that burned were 2.72 in 1942, 3.02 in 1943, 1.24 in 1944, 1.52 in 1945, 1.45 in 1946, 1.99 in 1947.

The economic fundamentals of control of forest fires are akin to the fire insurance that an owner of other types of property would buy. The basic items are: The value of the assets that are vulnerable to fire; their intensity and duration of exposure; the value of the probable losses over the years to the owner if his lands are not protected or are protected in various degrees and the point at which the cost of protection would exceed the value of additional decrease in losses.

How do those fundamentals apply to the South?

Forested lands in the South contain stands of reproduction and merchantable stems having tangible values of $35 to $40 an acre, or about $80,000 per township. They are exposed to fire for 8 to 12 months a year. Of lands not under protection, 20 percent or more burn annually. With manpower suppression, 4.1 percent of the area studied burned annually. Of forest lands protected by mechanical equipment, 1.1 percent burned. A computation of the savings in cost of suppression and losses from fire shows that owners of timberland will make a clear financial gain by investing in a tractor-plow unit for each 25,000 acres that need protection. If the timber values on their lands vary from those used in this illustration, the justifiable area should be adjusted accordingly.

In the longleaf and slash pine belt, proper silvicultural management requires the use of fire at times to expose the soil for seed fall, to control encroachment of brush and worthless species, overcome infections of brown spot disease, release grass-stage seedlings for height growth, and (under some conditions) to reduce hazardous accumulations of fuel. To use fire safely and at reasonable cost, a plow unit is essential.

The most valuable prospect promised by these experiences is that widespread adoption of mechanical suppression methods will make it possible to give reasonable fire protection to most southern timberlands, or better than double the present protection intensity for the same average annual sum now being expended for suppression. With increased fire protection, owners of lands now idle or thinly stocked will find it a good business risk to return them to a productive condition and develop them toward their potential capacities to produce.

ARTHUR W. HARTMAN *is chief of the Division of Fire Control in the Southern Region of the Forest Service.*

# Fun in the Forests

## NEW VALUES IN THE MINDS OF MEN

L. F. KNEIPP

"RECREATION" and "recreate" mean refreshment, to give 'resh life to, reanimate, revive, divert, ımuse, gratify. The terms apply to nind and spirit and body. The ways n which the forests of the United States serve these purposes are many.

Years ago, for recreation, most peo-)le oftener went away from the forest han toward it. But as the country set-led, as industry and commerce gained ıscendancy over rural activities, as the population concentrated in cities, the orest gained increasing significance as he scene of wholesome recreation.

New living conditions modified nat-ıral forces and elements. New forms of economic activity, highly mechani-cal and monotonously repetitive, were established. New tempos of thought ınd action gave birth to new tensions ınd nervous strains. Time brought in-creasing realization that physical and spiritual well-being required periodic escape from the strains of the new modes of daily life.

*Above: A scene typical (except, perhaps, for the size of the fish) of many parts of the country.*

The qualities with which their forebears met the challenge of nature began to assume new values in the minds of men who felt a desire to revert to more primitive conditions under which such skills and qualities could be regained. A major contributing cause was probably the changes that were occurring in working standards and habits. As the average working day dropped from 12 hours to 10 and then to 8, as the average workweek dropped from 6 days to 5, as the practice of vacations ceased to be the privilege of a few, both the time and the physical energies requisite to the return to nature became increasingly available. Then automobiles overcame handicaps of distance and immobility, and many an American enthusiastically became outdoor-minded.

But while nature was regaining a hold on the minds and affections of people, it coincidentally was losing dominance over the land. Farms and fields had occupied all land suitable for such use and much that was not suitable. Hamlets grew into villages and villages into cities, and their impact on nature extended far beyond their legal limits. To link them together, networks of highways came into being, fringed, often, with garish structures that closed off the fields and woods from the roads. Within the zones tributary to roads, nature was subdued until it offers little appeal and no challenge other than the walk to the nearest filling station when one runs out of gas.

Only three major land classes had escaped even partly such modification—the shores of the oceans and lakes, the great mountain masses, and the forests. Of the three, the forests are of the greatest extent and the widest geographic distribution; they also are of the greatest variety and diversity of natural interest—the major area in which future needs of the American people for essential outdoor play can be met in properly balanced coordination with the needs of commerce, industry, and other elements of the economic structure.

Perhaps it is the influence of atavism that makes trees appeal so strongly to human emotions. The forest is the antithesis of the city, from which a respite is desired. Within the forest confines peace and calm normally prevail. The play of shadow and sunlight on majestic columns, the response of leaf, twig, branch, and trunk to the movement of the air, the complexity of the biological pattern, the myriad forms of plant, insect, bird, and animal life, the placid or turbulent flow of waters, the variations in topography and geology, all combine to stimulate, yet soothe, the senses and rid the body and mind of their adversities. In this effect lies the general charm of the forest; but beyond that is its illimitable capacity to gratify the individual interests and cravings of each visitor within its precincts.

One visitor may desire no more of the forest than to traverse it in a fast automobile over a high-speed highway, but only if his eyes can be gladdened by long tangents closely margined by stately ranks of trees or by vistas that reveal constantly changing expanses of perspectives of thrifty and beautiful tree growth against the majestic backgrounds of slope, canyon, or peak.

There is, however, a less numerous type of motorist whose greatest pleasure is in exploring areas accessible only by dim and difficult roads, that lead into distant and primitive reaches where his comforts will depend on his own skill and where his normal world temporarily is remote.

Beyond the latter class is the visitor who travels on foot or with saddle and pack horses or by canoe. He seeks quiet glades fringed with aspen or birch and watered by a trickling spring, or some little meadow where the eventide clang of horse bells will be music to his ears, or some tree-crowned point from which he can watch the golden birth of a new day or the descent of dusk and darkness upon a lake. Complete detachment from the throng is his purpose and his reward.

But most visitors to forests love nature too greatly to be content to experience it only at a speed of 60 miles an hour, but not enough to enjoy its close intimacy at a speed of 3 miles an hour. They are gregarious and have no desire to detach themselves completely from the crowds. They are comfort loving, with no inclination toward forms of subsistence, habitation, and transport that entail discomforts and deprivations. They have a love for nature in general and for the forest in particular, but they see no inconsistency in a reasonable intermixture of modern facilities and techniques.

Second in numbers are the visitors who frequent forest areas only between dawn and dusk of a single day, to lunch, play, ramble, and relax. Over the years their habits in the woods have been subject to drastic changes. Knowing more about the widespread pollution of streams and springs, they prefer locations where water of assured purity is available. With responsibility for fire damage now more rigidly attached and enforced, they see the advantage of uilding their luncheon fires in safe replaces. The more general recogni- on of the hazards of poor sanitary ractices, not only to the visitors but to ll users of the watershed, has popu- rized areas that have good sanitary cilities. Thus, this type of forest recre- tional use, once so widely diffused roughout the forest as to be a menace health and property, now largely is oncentrated, at least on those forests nder public management, in picnic nd camp grounds that are equipped nd developed to afford full protection.

Scores of thousands of lakes and onds and miles of flowing streams tersperse and thread the forests. In hem the fresh-water varieties of game sh generally are more abundant than lsewhere. Only in the forest environ- ient have game animals and some pecies of game birds been able to sur- ive in material numbers.

Despite the increasing popularity of ther types of forest recreation, large umbers of forest visitors continue to egard camping as the most enjoyable orm of summer outing. In part static, part peripatetic, its requirements in quipment, supplies, effort, and cost re not burdensome, while its compen- ations are many.

A variant is the organization camp, fixed group of structures and facili- ies, created and sponsored by a public r quasi-public agency and made avail- ble for fixed periods to associations or roups which meet all costs of opera- ion and maintenance during their oc- upancy. The primary objective of the rganization camp is to create condi- ions under which children, youths, vorkers, and other groups, for whom ummer vacations otherwise would be mpracticable or impossible, can be af- orded vacations free or at low cost.

The lakes, ponds, and pools of the orests, relatively free of industrial vastes and other major forms of pollu- ion, present pleasurable opportunities or swimming and annually attract undreds of thousands of visitors. Thousands of miles of leafy roads and rails lure the hiker and the horseback rider in corresponding numbers. A great diversity and abundance of nuts, berries, mushrooms, grapes, persimmons, barks, roots, and other edible, medicinal, or ornamental products of the forest are garnered each year by scores of thousands who find pleasure and benefit in collecting them for personal consumption or gratification.

In the forest the botanist or plant physiologist, naturalist, entomologist, ichthyologist, and geologist can find biological or geological patterns or structures or associations quite different from those with which they normally are acquainted. The person whose hobby is collecting specimens of plant, insect, bird, or animal life or of minerals or examples of early cultures can find in forest areas rich additions to their collections or can explore new fields of lore, tradition, and culture. To every visitor the forest can offer a new interest or idea or experience.

The current and growing prominence and significance of the forest as a major field for the outdoor recreational activities of the people of the United States was not inspired or promoted by foresters. To the contrary, the trend initially was regarded by many foresters as adverse, fraught with many perils to sound programs of forest management. Public carelessness with fire was a constant menace to the forest. Public indifference to good sanitation was a major hazard to the health of the populations which drew their water supplies from the forest watersheds. Public sentiment promised to be, and it frequently was, an obstacle to the harvesting of forest crops, even though such harvest might be dictated or demanded by sound principles of forest management and economy.

Besides those major considerations there were numerous minor irritations. Public camping in close proximity to springs, tanks, or troughs prevented domestic livestock grazed under permit from slaking their thirst and forced them to congest in other areas. Forest signs, erected at much effort and expense, were popular targets for the visitors' guns. Ranger or guard stations or storage buildings were subject to frequent depredation. To use the deeply rutted and high-centered wagon roads, the earlier autoists commonly filled the ruts with rocks, which teamsters, with much effort, later had to remove before the teams could move their loads. Thus, to many a forest officer the prospect of summer visitations by multiplying millions was far from a cheerful one and it seemed to him that sheer self-preservation dictated that he do all he could to reverse the trend.

But against the forces behind the movement, the views and the actions of individual forest officers were feeble and futile. The habits and practices of an entire Nation were then undergoing profound changes. New interests had been created, new desires aroused, new means to satisfy them made available. To the degree that those new interests and desires centered in the forests, they endowed the forests with purposes and functions other than the traditional ones of timber supply and stream-flow stabilization. A new era had been born, in which a tree in place as a living element of a landscape might be of immeasurably greater value than if sawed into boards. In the privately owned forest this radical change could be ignored, but in the publicly owned forest, as an expression of the public will, it had to be taken into account.

Collaterally there developed widespread realization that the combinations of natural interest that constitute the basis of forest recreation were pregnant with economic potentialities. If such an area could attract from other regions a total of a thousand people who, on an average, locally expended $25 each, the local economy would be enriched as much as by the production and shipment of several carloads of cattle, and with no appreciable diminution of natural resources. Despite its brief and transitory nature, the influx of visitors contributed to the market for labor, services, and supplies and left in the community money from outside sources which otherwise the community would never have received. Thu the recreational resources, instead o being incidental and nonprofitable, i time became definite capital assets an important factors in the economic lif of the community. In many communities, as the mines were worked out o sawmills "cut out and got out" or a depletion due to overstocking necessitated reductions in numbers of domestic livestock, the service and supply o summer visitors began to equal or eventually to surpass the other source of community support; communitie flourished which otherwise would hav dwindled or died out.

Public sentiment and economic values exert pressures, especially in publicly owned forests. It became obviou that the dominant objective of th greatest good for all involved mor than merely the production of timbe and of forage, that necessarily it mus comprehend also the conservation an orderly development of that other resource. Recognition of that fact ha motivated most of the expansion o forest recreational facilities during th past quarter-century.

In the earlier logging operations o the national forests, utilitarian considerations often dominated the estheti ones. The operation of isolated bodie of timber often entailed heavy initia expenditures for the construction o roads, railroads, camps, and other requisites. An economic cost per thousan board feet was attainable only by th removal of the maximum volume o timber. Every additional thousan board feet of timber cut increased th economic practicability of operation every thousand feet withheld from cutting reduced it. Even today, notwithstanding shorter cutting cycles an more extensive transportation systems foresters continue to be wracked by thi problem of forest economy. Some o the then most-scenic areas in the forest owed their beauty and charm mainly t blocks of trees that were mature o overmature and that represented larg monetary values; the next cutting cycl

ʼas assumed to be a half-century in ıe future, and the probability that the ʼees would live that long seemed ex-ʼemely remote. For those reasons eavy cutting seemed justified.

But the many who exalted forest eauty over forest economy rejected ıis reasoning as specious rather than ɔund. Their discovery that the stately ʼees that fringed their most cherished ıeadow or road or trail or mountain ope had been cut in a logging opera-on frequently was followed by an motional explosion. So the practice ame into force of reserving from cut-ng, or cutting only lightly, selectively, nd almost unnoticeably, the stands of ational forest timber that have defi-ite esthetic values.

Until as recently as two or three cen-ıries ago, the chief purpose of many ɔrests and many foresters in the older ɔuntries was to provide sport to the ʼealthy, the provision of fuel wood and building timber being purely incidental and subordinate purposes. It is improbable that such a narrow and illogical use of forests will ever occur in the United States, but it is not at all improbable that the provision of wholesome types of outdoor sport will be a major, if not a principal, use of many American forests.

L. F. Kneipp *entered Government service at the age of 19 by appointment as a forest ranger in the then Territory of Arizona, in April 1900. In 1904 he became acting supervisor of the Pecos River Forest Reserve in New Mexico; shortly thereafter he also assumed charge of the adjoining Jemez and Taos Forest Reserves. After several other assignments, in 1920 he became an assistant chief of the Forest Service, in charge of land activities, a position he held until his retirement from active service in 1946.*

# TRAIL RIDING IN THE WILDERNESS

SHIRLEY W. ALLEN

Because of the very inaccessibility hat gives charm and mystery to wild ·laces, few Americans in the past 40 ears have ever found themselves far rom the sound of an automobile horn. ʼewer yet, but for the foresight and ·lanning of the American Forestry ssociation, would have been able to njoy the thrills that greet the wilder-ess traveler as he rounds a bend in the rail or stream and sees before him the owering meadow, the majestic moun-ain back of it, or the wild animal which ɔoks, turns, and disappears into cover.

Not everyone will want such oppor-unities; they may be one man's meat nd another's poison. But it is safe to ay that those who crave such adven-ure would number at least a million in ur country.

Horseback trips (and to a less ex-ent, canoeing) have been available at easonable cost almost every year since 1933 to the members of this association of citizens, which serves as a rallying place for friends of forestry, whether they be trained foresters or plain public-spirited folk. It is the latter group that forms the bulk of the membership, and many of them had their introduction to the program by signing up as "Trail Riders of the Wilderness." Once exposed, they are incurable conservationists.

The idea of exploring, studying, and enjoying the wilderness country on horseback expeditions came to the American Forestry Association in 1932 from the West. The desire for such adventure had there found its best chance in terms of the small party and horseback travel. The occasion might arise as a "go-along" venture from a cattle or sheep ranch when routine work of the range had to be done. It might start with a hunting season that required saddle and pack animals to get the adventurer into back country, carrying his outfit, and bring him back with his kill. Or a planned and guided visit to wilderness country from ranch, resort, or dude ranch, with less definite objectives in mind, may have taken a family or a group of friends into one of those priceless and unspoiled parts of America, set aside to maintain their own precious values and usually located in the national forests or national parks.

In all of those early forays, from the days of Jim Bridger and the exploring expeditions in the Yellowstone to the one-night-out trip from today's most expensive resort, certain features are common.

Primitive modes of transportation; penetration of wild and infrequently visited country; camping and cooking with limited equipment and the sorts of foods that can be easily carried or that can be captured daily; sleeping under the stars; gathering in close and friendly companionship at the campfire, with the singing, the tall stories, the banter, and the long moments of dreamy silence; the flood of questions on the trail and in the camp; the grist of minor adventures with horses, storms, yellow-jackets, mountain climbing, and fishing; the amateur but serious nature study; the photographer, in the role of pest or friend; the distinctive dress; the understanding that develops between horse and rider; the color and culture of the local people who go along as guides, cooks, and wranglers—all these in the mountain trips make up the daily program, and the record in thousands of diaries, hearts, and photographic collections. Added to these, from the canoe country, may be the many ways of getting wet, the portage, the fast-water incidents, and a good bit more under the heading of "the big fish."

But left to the American Forestry Association was the development of the trail ride as an expedition of 15 to 30 persons from all parts of the country, of all ages, and of widely varying backgrounds, brought together with onl their duffel, clothing, personal effect and anticipations, to ride together wit competent guides and helpers, for 1 days to 2 weeks, deep into the wilde parts of the country. No service of sup ply, no quartermaster's departmen and no long-organized travel servic with its established connections figure in those bold ventures, which we launched in 1933.

The first trip left from Helena Mont., for the South Fork Wilderne (now a part of the Bob Marshall Wi derness area) on July 11, 1933, with 2 riders, from 10 different States and th District of Columbia. There were tw guides, two cooks, a boss packer, an four wranglers. Fifty-five horses an mules were required. The first day ride was 18 miles, and the party sper 6 days in the wilderness. They calle themselves the "Pioneers." All returne safe and enthusiastic. As their telegrar at the end reported, the venture "wa a complete success and through cour try we never dreamed existed."

The log of that trip, kept by the rep resentative of the association, is punc tuated with references to frost on th sleeping bags, seas of wild flowers, ac counts of meals that make one hungr to read, songs to banjo accompan ment, battles with wary trout, and over and over, references to the sur prise and wonderment as the journe proceeded. The second trip that yea went into the Sun River country in th same general region; it was successfu but a severe August snowstorm turne the party back short of the Great Wal its objective. It was no soft expeditio however, for only when travel becam unsafe did the members turn back. Th riders treasure not only the joys of th ride but memories of the touch of hard ship and the conquering of obstacles.

Since that year the American For estry Association has arranged and car ried out 75 expeditions, in which mor than 1,000 riders explored 19 wilder ness areas in 9 States. More than 20 of the riders have repeated the ride; score or more have been on 5 to 12 c he trips. The average party includes rom 20 to 30 riders, and requires from 60 to 70 saddle and pack animals, counting those for the guides, helpers, and cooks. A canoe trip penetrated the roadless area on the Superior National Forest in 1941; it was repeated in 1948.

Over the years a rather definite sys-em has been worked out. During the vinter the association arranges with ocal guides and packers the proposed tineraries and equipping of the trail iders for the following summer. Some-imes it has been possible for an asso-iation representative or a member of he Forest Service actually to ride the rip beforehand with the guide and to elect alternate routes. Early in the year he expeditions are announced in the *American Forests,* the monthly maga-ine of the association, a prospectus in pamphlet form is prepared, and letters are sent to former riders and inquirers. Routes, dates and costs, recommended lothing and equipment, and the ways of reaching the meeting places are ncluded.

PREPARATIONS for starting on a trail ide begin with correspondence or an nterview, in which the American For-stry Association wants to make sure hat the applicant is in good health; has some acquaintance with horses and iding; can really be counted on to stay by a decision to make the trip; under-stands that while there is no advantage n being uncomfortable the accommo-dations in general are pretty rugged; eally wants to go on the trip; and is eady to pay the moderate cost, which over the years has run from $125 to $188 for 10 days' to 2 weeks' travel. It s also important that the prospective rail rider understands that this cost s from the "jumping off place" and not from his home. Take-off points have included Ely, Minn., Asheville, N. C., Silver City, N. Mex., Kemmerer, Wyo., Glenwood Springs, Colo., Mis-oula, Mont., Sun Valley, Idaho, Se-attle, Wash., Bishop, Calif., and Lone Pine, Calif.

As the parties fill up, an association representative is selected to meet the riders, check their preparations, ar-range such things as transportation to the horses or canoes, last-minute pur-chases such as a poncho here, a western hat there, and most important, fishing tackle and fishing licenses.

How a trail rider dresses, provides himself with small comforts, and takes things which can actually be put on a pack horse or in his own small bag carried on the saddle (duffel weight must not exceed 50 pounds a person) are items that the association tries to make plain in its literature. Always, however, they have to be checked just before the trip by the representative of the association and frequently this is done in the evening after the group has gathered preparatory to the take-off the next day. Trail riding has its moments of dust, wetness, wear, and even loss of bits of equipment. So it is good to give thought to essentials of clothing, plus cameras, fishing tackle, tree, shrub, and animal identification books, and toilet articles, all of which go to make up the individual's equip-ment. Dungarees are popular for both men and women. Riding boots are worn but not recommended unless they are of the cowboy type for riding only. Some comfortable shoes for the hours around camp are needed. Bathing suits come in handy. The right kind of hats to cut down the sacrifice to the sun gods needs to be thought about and obtained. The favorite sets of spurs, the rider's own saddle, trick riding breeches, and other unusual items of costume are not recommended.

Then, with full instructions, the party assembles, the evening before taking off, for final questions, meeting local forest officers, learning each oth-ers' names, storing baggage, and de-positing valuables. Then, also, the leader extracts from each rider a prom-ise not to oversleep or hold up the take-off early the next morning. Usually there is a long stage ride to the point where the horses or canoes are to be assigned. Upon arrival, each rider is sized up by the head guide and his helpers and matched with a horse that will be his for the duration of the ride. Stirrups are adjusted, try-outs staged if there is time, and a part of the ride acomplished by the end of the first day out. There are no mantelpieces to eat from in the wilderness.

If one tried to complete a composite of the trail rider, male or female, he might come out with something like this. The woman would be in her thirties, a teacher or perhaps a stenographer who lives in a city, whose riding experience likely has been confined to the sort of horses you get out of a riding stable, who has a profound love of the out-of-doors, who systematically saves for her vacation, who is naturally friendly, and who is not so heroic that she does not occasionally ask the cook for a basin of warm water on a cool morning or perhaps hope that sometimes she may have toast instead of pancakes. The man would be a businessman, somewhat older than the woman, who is determined to get off the beaten trail, frequently is interested in fishing, is a somewhat better horseman, is given to philosophizing, and is anxious to share with his family the joy which he has experienced.

Invariably a forest officer is on hand as the journey starts, usually with his own saddle horse and pack mule, to accompany the party on the entire trip, or, if he happens to be the local ranger, to ride with the group while in his district, turning them over to the next ranger as the ride proceeds. This will also be true of the national park officers as the expeditions enter their territory. The representative of the association who leads the group may be one of its officers, or a member who may be a forestry teacher, or a well-informed individual who lives near the scene of the ride. He tries to prepare answers for all questions with the help so readily available from forest and national park officers who may accompany the party.

Nor must the medical officer be neglected. Adequate attention to health is assured by the provision for this important officer on each trail ride. Considerable study is given by him and th association to his medical kit, and he i not only a valuable friend in case c distress but an asset to the party itsel The few minor accidents have bee skillfully handled; the even fewer case where people became ill and had to b gotten out involved no serious trave troubles. Emergency messages are delivered, and sometimes even mail i received during the progress of the trip

The guides are local stockmen c people who make their living principally from the recreation industry They are good, honest, picturesque, interesting men, full of common sense good humor, and spirit-lifting bante Invariably there are natural entertainers among the packers, wranglers, and cooks, and wonders never cease at th hidden talent among the riders themselves. It is a comfort for the prospective trail rider to know that he wil be in capable hands and that resourcefulness is a commonplace among th western mountain people.

By the end of the second day's ride there may arise the rare instance of a saddle-weary or homesick rider who wants to turn back, but usually all wil have settled into the routine, staked ou claims on choice spots for that night' sleeping under the stars, insisted to th cowboy wranglers on special care fo Blackie, Old Paint, Susie, Biscuits, o another mount, and taken on that feeling of well-being that only the health tiredness of outdoor adventure ca offer.

The usual stop of the party is on night. The camp sites are selected fo beauty, convenience of terrain, goo water for camp use, bathing and fishing, and proximity to adequate fee areas, so that the saddle and pack animals can be held and recovered fo the next day's work.

The wranglers have their own trick for the latter detail, from sleeping a the pass where the animals might escape from an otherwise mountain

:ked series of meadows, to the old vice of hobbling the more influential embers of the transportation depart-ent. When feed is scant or badly scat-red, the wranglers are sometimes ithout sleep most of the night, but in-riably, although not always on exact hedule, the sound of bells and hoofs ill greet the waking campers in the orning. Often, deep in the night, one ars the far-off music of bells as the azing animals drift to the high edge the plateau where they are pastured. nd then, of course, there are times hen the bells seem to harmonize less easantly, should the four-footed embers reason that the best pasture as being slept on by their riders. Yet erybody by this time has heard the ying, "you might as well be dead as oot." So they roll over and go to sleep.

Another feature considered in select-g the camp sites is the opportunity r special adventure offered by a day's y-over. Perhaps the fishing is particu-rly good, as at Lake Imogene in the iwtooth country of Idaho or Lake In-la in the Arrowhead section of Min-sota. Or there may be a Mount hitney to climb in the high Sierra, a look into Old Mexico to capture om Magollon Baldy in the Gila River untry of New Mexico. Or in this me Gila wilderness, the party may mp near the unfrequented and un-anned cliff dwellings, where bits of ncient pottery can be seen in the avel wash at the mouth of the canyon elow the great caves. Even more ex-ting may be the chance to stalk elk id mountain goats along the Great Vall, in the Flathead-Sun River area Montana. In 1945, one day's lay-ver there gave members of the party view of more than 20 elk staging a olic on an enormous sunlit snowbank ss than a mile from a perfect ringside at; mountain goats and coyotes were en at closer range.

From these lay-over camps, large or nall groups, under safe leadership, iake their own explorations. What ill the top of that "funny-looking big ock" yield in new adventure and view? Where does this stream really start? Can that cliff actually be scaled? Who dares to take his shower under that waterfall? Did they really take gold out of that old mine where we're going? Where are the evergreen trees in the Great Smokies? Can we get enough blueberries for pie? Is the spring water really hot? Those are some of the things trail riders talk about and find out on lay-over days, unless they are fishermen, or figure that the week's laundry needs attention, or choose to reorganize the duffel after a rainy ride the previous day.

These special 2-day camps have a practical aspect, too. The head guide and his crew may take advantage of them to send out a pack string to some ranch or settlement within a half day's ride to replenish supplies. Two or three of the wranglers who are expert fisher-men may undertake to supply one meal of trout, if the riders are not doing too well. Horses and mules may need to be shod, for the trails are rough and there are no blacksmith shops in the wilder-ness. And animals need occasional rest and an extra day's grazing. As the ex-pedition passes a band of sheep (graz-ing of domestic livestock is permitted in national forest wilderness areas), a fat lamb may be purchased and a bar-becue worked out with all the cere-mony that an extra day allows.

Time for brief side-line travel and adventure is available also at single-night camps when the day's ride is not too long and the camp is reached well before suppertime.

The program normally on such a day starts with breakfast at 7 o'clock. Tents are struck, folded, and placed at a convenient packing center by 8 o'clock; meanwhile, all bedding and duffel are packed and assembled. Rid-ers do this work themselves, of course. Saddle horses are made ready and rid-ers mount well before 8 o'clock. A "lunch-mule" is packed with food for the group at noon, or each rider puts up and carries his own lunch from ma-terial set out by the cook. Or, possibly, when coffee is not to be made at noon, food for a common lunch is distributed in the saddlebags of a number of the riders. Whatever the system, there is always lunch and plenty of it.

After the riders are on the trail, with the head guide leading, experienced riders distributed in the line, and a wrangler riding behind, the remaining packers, cooks, and wranglers complete breaking camp, load the pack animals, and pass the riders while they are resting for lunch at noon. This puts the pack train into the next camp ahead of the riders. If all goes well, the latter will spot a tent fly and a curl of smoke along a stream or lake sometime between 3 and 5 o'clock and start practicing their "cowboy yells." For that is the camp. The cook has the coffee on. The duffel is off the pack animals. From then on it is a matter of riders and crew getting up sleeping tents and flies where weather or, on rare occasions, insects, make them necessary.

Mostly the "camping operations" consist of locating good spots to bed down in the open, with due attention to relative privacy, sanitary precautions, the distance that duffel must be carried, and noninterference with the "kitchen," temporary corral, and water for cooking and drinking. This takes some planning and agreement. Areas for women, for men, for families and couples have to be picked. Minimum but adequate sanitary arrangements must be located. Swampy or sloping ground must be avoided. On the 1941 canoe trip one camp was made on a small island—so small that it was most difficult to stay on it. Usually there is plenty of room. Usually the previous occupants have left the site in orderly condition. Sometimes there are old buildings, a dilapidated log cabin, or a well-maintained but unoccupied forest-guard's quarters for short-season use, or a cattle- or hunting-camp structure. Some of the riders are sure to appropriate these as camps, if the cooks do not get there first.

Available for this sort of wilderness travel are 77 established or proposed wilderness and wild areas in the n tional forests. Wilderness areas cov at least 100,000 acres each; wild are are smaller. Eight of the former co tain more than 500,000 acres eac There are large areas of wilderness most of the national parks. By far t greater number of the wilderness ar wild areas are relatively untouched. few are recaptured lands on whi lumbering or mining and prospecti was relatively active in the past. Son of them exhibit a natural conditi that would compare with those at t time of the Louisiana Purchase.

Besides the places named, the Tr Riders have penetrated, in Colorad the Maroon-Snowmass, the Flat To and the San Juan Wilderness Areas; Montana, the Spanish Peaks Wi Area; in North Carolina, the Gre Smoky Mountains National Park; Washington, the Olympic Nation Park; and, in Wyoming, the Wi River Wilderness.

Because practically all the areas, e cept the canoe country in Minnesot are high, the time when travel is sa extends only from late June to ea September. At that, the elements a not always kind. Rainstorms on t trail are uncommon, but certainly n unknown. Trail riders do not claim enjoy such weather, but it is a part the whole adventure, and they are us ally equipped with slickers or ponch that keep them reasonably dry. Alwa there is a blazing campfire in the ev ning and reasonable assurance of warm, dry night's rest.

Many of the riders' lasting memori center around the campfire convers tions, the friendly arguments, and que tionings. At those gatherings there always serious discussion, and alwa singing, with fiddle, guitar, accordio or banjo accompaniment; often speci stunts are arranged by the guides a helpers and by the riders themselves.

Anyone who plays a musical instr ment that is not too bulky or hard handle can contribute that to his duff Mouth harps, banjos, guitars, acco dions, and ukeleles are frequently tak ong. Almost always there is a theme ng for the trip that, if it does not be-me too monotonous, long after re-lls wonderful days in the mountains; is will be anything from "She's Com-g Around the Mountain" to "Only A ose," usually with only one phrase at is sung over and over.

At the campfire, the leadership may me from the head guide, one of the rangler-musicians, or from a natural-rn master of ceremonies. Sometimes e leader, representing the American restry Association, takes over. More ten the entertainment is spontane-s, with no lack of talent or of things discuss. What the day's ride has own in the way of new high-altitude ees, shrubs, and flowers, or in the way game animals, birds, rodents, or edators is sure to bring a flood of estions to the forest officer or park ficer. He may be a local cowman pe, a scientist, a practical forester, a 0-day wonder" on his first national rk assignment, a ranger-naturalist, , in rarer instances, a forest super-sor or a park superintendent or a rep-sentative from a regional office of one the two bureaus.

National forest and national park licies come in for thorough discus-n. The riders carry back to their mes and their friends such factual eanings as the real difference be-een a national forest and a national rk, the strange ends to which adap-tion can go in animal forms, the fact at the marmot actually "makes hay" his rocky fastnesses, the reasons be-nd fish and game laws, the difference tween fir trees as a group and spruce ees, the way forest fires start and are ntrolled, the age-old and little-anged procedures of burden carrying pack animals, the strange realiza-n that the amount of snowfall in e mountains the previous winter may ean water or no water in the next 2 ars for the valley below; the fact that yotes, vultures, eagles, and hawks e good sanitary officers, the economic lue of many flowering plants hereto-re considered only beautiful, the indication that plants give of soil characteristics and range condition, the inevitable use for recreation of any land that is sufficiently attractive to tempt the adventurer.

Amateur botanists and students of other nature lore find ample interests and have at their disposal some forestry or park official or the leader of the trip from whom advice and actual identification of specimens may be obtained. The photographer, amateur or professional, keeps busy and may, if too insistent on photography, find himself left behind and robbed of his subject or roundly berated, but the total collection of artistic action and even funny photographs over the years is impressive. Frequently an exchange of pictures is arranged by the Forestry Association, and black-and-white prints are sent in by various riders, labeled and priced per copy, for a round-robin circulation among members of the ride.

But all this time, the increasing consciousness of rocks, rills, woods, and templed hills has made both new and old trail riders appreciate more fully their own country and the bureaus of their Government that are responsible for managing the wild lands. Their association has put them in touch with this wilderness and made friends of them for the movement to conserve the resources which it represents.

In this day, these natural resources of solitude and life and beauty and freedom and grandeur, integrated into the one natural resource we call the wilderness, are no easy things to conserve and defend. The wilderness, with its characteristic of vastness, combined with cover which could be translated into profit, may sometimes be questioned sharply from the viewpoint of equitable distribution when it is realized that relatively few can ever make use of such sources of strength and inspiration. Moreover, if the million people who have an incurable taste for wilderness travel all decide to penetrate one wilderness at the same time, they can trample it to death. And there are those who argue that the least destructive mode of wilderness travel would be in seaplanes, that would land on interior waters and eventually take off, leaving no trace.

But wildernesses we must have, if only to dream about and cherish as saved specimens of the America we love. And many groups whose chance to see one of the great dedicated areas is remote work constantly for the idea. A "Wilderness Society" insists that wilderness is a necessary natural resource, that mechanized civilization in terms of sights and sounds must not be permitted to clash with the values of primeval environment, and that wildernesses belong to the whole people and must be defended. The Sierra Club, the Appalachian Mountain Club, and similar organizations have long cooperated with public agencies in keeping great areas inviolate. As time goes on, the need for wilderness values will increase.

Almost no additional area can now be recaptured and restored. Always the priceless opportunity for renewal and inspiration will justify the same effort at conservation that is more readily appreciated in thinking of the materi values.

As L. F. Kneipp, who was close associated with the early Forest Servi wilderness policies, has said, "It mu be an attractive and interesting sort solitude; one which enriches and stir ulates the mind, which develops th body by creating the need for physic qualities which through all histo have commanded the admiration men, qualities of hardihood, endu ance, strength, resistance to adver natural forces, combined with skill interpreting and effectively confor ing to the laws of nature."

SHIRLEY W. ALLEN *is a graduate Iowa State College. Since 1909 he h served in numerous capacities with th Forest Service and for several years the 1930's as consultant to the Nation Park Service. He was forester to th American Forestry Association fro 1924 to 1928 and since that time h been professor of forestry at the Un versity of Michigan. He has been th American Forestry Association repr sentative on eleven of its trail rides in wilderness country.*

# TREASURES OF THE NATION

## CONRAD L. WIRTH, J. H. GADSBY

Many of the great and spectacular parks in the United States are included in the national park system, which preserves for always and for everybody the outstanding scenic, historic, and scientific treasures of the Nation and provides places for unusual experiences.

The national parks had their beginning in 1872 with the establishment of the Yellowstone Park. Gradually some other areas of paramount importance, such as Yosemite, Mount Rainier, and Sequoia, were set aside by Congress to preserve areas of scenic grandeur from commercial exploitation, because their special and unique qualities made them the concern of all the people. Also established were the national mon ments—the areas of diverse size ar interest that are notable for scientif or historic reasons.

Congress recognized the need for c ordinated administration of the are in 1916 by creating the National Pa Service in the Department of the I terior. Congress then stated the ide when it enjoined the new bureau "conserve the scenery and the natur and historic objects and the wildli therein and to provide for the enjo ment of the same in such manner ar by such means as will leave them unir paired for the enjoyment of futu generations."

The requirements of this dual function, providing for protection and for human use, have been observed even through a period of total war. The principle now seems firmly established that the features that make the areas worthy of preservation should not be sacrificed, even for purposes of war, except as a last resort.

The protection of these superlative areas naturally involves certain restrictions and regulations, which at times may interfere with their untrammeled use. Precautions against destruction by fire, carelessness, or vandalism must be taken. Locations, therefore, are designated for such uses as camping, picnicking, and making fires. Rangers are assigned to guard against misuse of the public's property and to assist those who need any direction or advice. The wildlife has to be protected from visitors and the visitors from wildlife.

On the other hand, the Service maintains a staff of naturalists, historians, and other persons to explain the wonders of nature and the notable events of our history to the end that people can have full use and enjoyment of the areas. Lecturers, campfire talks, and tours are available so that visitors can get the most information in a short time. Where advisable and practicable, museums are at hand to assist in telling the story.

In most parks, foot and horse trails, suitably marked with directional and explanatory signs, lead to points of interest. Those who are physically able to take advantage of trips on the trails find them an inspiring and satisfying recreation. Then, too, fishing is excellent in many places. Inland fishing is governed by regulations to fit local conditions; in some places only fly fishing is permitted, or creel limits are set, for example. In most cases State laws apply and State licenses must be carried.

Some national parks present opportunities for swimming and boating. Where such is the case, full advantage is taken of the fact, and necessary facilities are provided. Usually bathing is of small importance, but boating facilities will be found that vary from rowboats for fishing or pleasure to fairly large excursion boats.

Hunting is prohibited in all national parks and monuments because they are wildlife sanctuaries. But the gain is great: The camera enthusiasts and the many persons who want to see the wild creatures of the forests in their natural surroundings generally are well rewarded. Frequently, also, the increase in the numbers of animals spreads beyond the park boundaries, so that hunting is better in adjacent territory.

Winter in the parks where snow falls is often the loveliest season of all. The quiet, peaceful beauty and the witchery of soft snow on trees and undergrowth, the airy creations of frozen spray from waterfalls, and the snow sculpture of the winds combine with the superb surroundings to make a breath-taking scene. It is no wonder that some of the areas, the ones that are especially adapted to winter sports, are beloved of skiers. For them, roads are kept open all winter, the ski runs are maintained where it is possible to do so without detriment to fundamental park values, and lodges are in full operation. Some parks also offer opportunities for tobogganing, skating, snowshoeing, and other winter sports.

THE PARKWAYS are a new classification of areas that has been added in recent years to the national park system. Of particular interest to motorists, they are first-class motor roads with right-of-way in the form of elongated parks. They are located so as to reach points of great historic interest (such as Mount Vernon and Yorktown), to follow historic routes (like the Natchez Trace), or to provide an outstanding scenic drive (like the Blue Ridge Parkway between the Shenandoah and the Great Smoky Mountains National Parks). Access to parkways is limited so as to promote the greatest safety and contribute to pleasure. The right-of-way is under strict control to preclude unsightly structures and damage to the growth. At appropriate locations there

802062°—49——36

are provided parking overlooks, places and facilities for picnicking, and, along the longer, remote parkways, accommodations for meals and sleeping.

The congregation of large numbers of people in the remote wilderness necessitates arrangements for housing, feeding and the maintenance of health, and a reasonable degree of comfort. Most of these services are provided by concessionaires who have invested in buildings and equipment for the purpose. The accommodations include free public camp grounds, simple cabins, housekeeping cabins, lodges, and complete modern hotel service. In nearly every park are picnic grounds maintained free to the public by the Government for the benefit of those who only have a short time to stay. Boats, fishing tackle, guide service, mountain-climbing equipment, conducted automobile tours, pack animals, riding horses, and other conveniences are offered according to the particular needs of the area.

Anyone desiring general information regarding the national park system can get it by writing to the Director, National Park Service, Washington 25, D. C. Many private enterprises, among them oil companies and several western railroads, distribute excellent literature concerning the national parks and monuments. Some will plan complete trips on request. Such agencies as the American Automobile Association are well informed on the subject and can give complete directions to their members. Information and tourist bureaus of various States gladly supply pamphlets concerning those areas within their boundaries. For the latest complete information in regard to prevailing conditions and rates in any particular area, however, it is best to address the park superintendent directly.

State parks, recreation areas, and monuments also offer opportunities for recreation.

About 80 years ago the first State park was established in the Yosemite Valley in a move to save that outstanding scenery from despoliation. For many years thereafter other State parks were set aside for similar reasons. When automobiles came into general use, the need became more urgent to seek out and preserve some of the remaining wild areas for the crowds who were beginning to travel afield in the quest for places of relaxation and recreation. The decade 1920–30 was a period of great expansion of park systems in the States that had accepted the new concept and were aware of their responsibility to meet the growing demand. It was not until the advent of the Civilian Conservation Corps and other emergency agencies, however, that many of the States found themselves financially able to inaugurate park systems. With the Federal assistance then available, the growth of physical facilities began to catch up in some measure with the needs. New areas were rapidly acquired and new facilities provided in the older parks until at present most States have some provision for out-of-door recreation in natural, forested surroundings.

In the beginning, State parks, like national parks, were created to preserve some scenic or scientific marvel, but the changed attitude brought about by transportation by automobile resulted in the selection of new areas so situated as to serve centers of heavy population. Scenic quality was a secondary consideration in many of these, but water for recreational use was a requirement. Consequently, many of the most heavily used areas represent average, rather than outstanding, segments of a State. They were chosen for accessibility and adaptability, although frequently a happy combination of scenery and recreational usefulness was attained. One of the main considerations, perhaps, was that there should be trees, at least in those regions where trees grow. The finer the trees, the more favorable is the park.

In the State parks that were established primarily for the protection of exceptional resources are some of the finest stands of remaining virgin timber. Thus are preserved some outstanding redwoods, Douglas-firs, white and southern pines, and other native trees of species that elsewhere have been so relentlessly cut to fill the needs of industry. Many other State parks are notable for some natural attraction, such as an exceptional waterfall, gorge, beach, or mountain, but usually it has also been possible to preserve or restore the forest cover.

One of the strongest contrasts between national and State parks is in the forms of recreation provided. State parks and recreation areas, being intimately associated with the locality, are heavily used by those bent on a day's outing or at least a visit of short duration. Depending on the character of the reservation and proximity to concentrations of population, they have facilities for swimming, boating, fishing, camping, picnicking, organizational camps, vacation cabins, horseback riding, hiking, small games (such as volley ball, badminton, horseshoe pitching), dancing, and winter sports. Frequently there are outdoor theaters, that are used for various celebrations or festivals, and sometimes golf courses, tennis courts, and polo fields have been provided. It is being increasingly recognized that nature study in State parks is of interest to many visitors, and the employment of naturalists and the establishment of museums for this activity is becoming common.

Overnight accommodations vary so greatly that it is possible only to mention some of the types here. One of the most popular features of many State parks is the vacation cabin, which can usually be rented at a reasonable rate, either completely equipped for housekeeping or lacking only linens and table silver. In regions where tent camping is favored, camp sites are available usually with individual outdoor cooking arrangements as well as community bathing and sanitary facilities. Closely related are areas set aside for parking trailers, where it is possible usually to plug into an electric outlet and connect to a running water system. Such conveniences, however, are not uniformly to be found in all cases. In the effort to provide for all classes and conditions of visitors, hotels and lodges have been erected in some parks where they seem warranted. Accommodations in those, while comfortable, are generally simple in character and moderate in price. Some of them are suitable for use in winter. For those who do not desire to do their own cooking and for casual visitors, many State parks have refectories or restaurants.

Where the acreage is large enough and where sufficient privacy can be had, together with an adequate swimming place, State parks and recreation areas lend themselves readily to group or organizational camping. Not infrequently the group camps are partly or wholly subsidized by one or more branches of the State Government in order to provide camping experience for crippled children or for those from families in the lower income groups. In the main, however, such groups as churches, Scouts, Y. M. C. A. or Y. W. C. A., 4–H Clubs, and Future Farmers of America are the main users of the camps. The applications of all worthy organizations receive sympathetic consideration.

The group camps are planned to take advantage of site and topography so that economy of operation and ease of control can be achieved by centralizing dining facilities, wash houses, infirmaries, and such necessities, while segregating the sleeping cabins into small, separated groups. Thus remotely located, the cabins, that ordinarily are the simplest sort of shelter for about four children each, convey the impression of being out in the woods—actually camping.

The administrators of State park and recreation areas are anxious for their visitors to enjoy themselves with a minimum of regulatory interference. However, it is always necessary to adopt a few simple rules for the protection of the areas and for the peace, comfort, and health of the visitors. The rules and regulations vary somewhat from State to State and even between areas in the same State, but they are based on the common welfare in each case. It is also necessary for the administrators to be eternally vigilant to prevent accidents or sickness as far as possible. To that end competent lifeguards are assigned to the beaches during hours that swimming is allowed; first-aid stations are maintained; water systems, swimming waters, and kitchens are given regular inspections by health authorities; every effort is made to keep buildings clean.

The States sometimes support minor forested areas (minor only in that recreation is less extensive), such as parkways and waysides, at desirable locations along highways. These are small areas of a few acres, and simple picnic facilities, water, toilets, and parking are generally all that is necessary.

It is easy for any interested person to get information about the State parks and related areas in his State or vicinity. Locations generally are shown on road maps. The central park authority, with only few exceptions, is located in the capital of the State; either he or the superintendent of any park in the State will be glad to furnish literature and information on request.

Several federal agencies, other than the National Park Service, which administer public lands, foster recreational use of areas that are suitable and where interference with the primary purpose of the areas is not serious.

The Fish and Wildlife Service of the Department of the Interior has developed limited recreational facilities for day use and overnight camping in a number of the national wildlife refuges. These are largely for local use.

Water-control projects of the Corps of Engineers and the Bureau of Reclamation often present opportunities to install various recreational facilities.

The Tennessee Valley Authority has recognized recreation as an important collateral use of its chain of lakes on the Tennessee River and its tributaries. Except for demonstration parks, however, it does not have authority to develop and operate parks and recreation areas, but cooperates with State and Government agencies by leasing lands for the purpose and by consultative assistance.

The reservoirs that are impounded by the Bureau of Reclamation and the Corps of Engineers are growing in importance in the recreation program of the country. People naturally want to use these large bodies of water for personal pleasure even though their primary function of storing water for irrigation, flood control, or power development means a fluctuation in the water level, which detracts from the ideal for recreation areas. Fortunately, the periods of greatest draw-down often do not coincide with the time of heavy recreational use. In such instances, recreational developments are included in over-all plans, their extent and importance varying greatly with such factors as accessibility, proximity to other more desirable areas, character of topography, plan of reservoir operation, and density of population within a reasonable distance. Most of these areas are of local importance only, and are or will be administered by the State or a political subdivision. In arid or semiarid sections they may loom large in the recreational picture, however. Occasionally one of the reservoirs may be so located that it is of more than local or regional significance.

The Secretary of the Interior has directed that the recreational features of reservoirs in this category that are constructed by the Bureau of Reclamation shall be administered by the National Park Service, unless they lie within the boundaries of areas under the jurisdiction of other Federal agencies, such as the Forest Service, Fish and Wildlife Service, and Bureau of Indian Affairs.

Recreational development at reservoir sites may consist of simple or elaborate facilities, depending on determination of development possibilities and probable attendance. Nothing more than a place to launch and moor boats for fishermen may be necessary or, at the other extreme, most of the facilities normally found in a State park, including group camps, may be desirable. The use of the lands surrounding reservoirs is considerably less restricted than that of national and State parks, because usually there is no compelling need to preserve the natural scenery. Consequently, after adequate provision has been made for public use, certain lands may be set aside that can be leased for summer-home sites to be constructed by the lessee—a practice not permitted in the national parks or in most State parks.

Hunting is permitted except in the heavily used parts and in parts established as wildlife refuges. It has been found that grazing and farming can be permitted when the land area is so large that such uses will not be incompatible with uses of greater priority. Because of the diversity of agencies administering these reservoir areas, there is no central agency from which to obtain information about all of them. Inquiries directed to Federal, State, or local park agencies should elicit information about any such areas under their jurisdiction.

County and metropolitan parks are transitional between State parks and municipal parks. The former have many characteristics of both of the latter. They average larger than municipal parks, and, being close to centers of dense population, have many of the same provisions for recreation that are found in the larger municipal parks. Their size and forested character, however, allow and encourage emphasis on naturalistic development and on the activities that depend on spaciousness, such as hiking, boating, horseback riding, and, to some extent, camping. Picnicking is a favorite use of these parks. Large-scale preparations have been made for it—shelters, tables and benches, and fireplaces, yet on Sundays and holidays it is well to arrive early to be sure of finding a place.

Information regarding county and metropolitan parks should be obtained from the office of the administering agency or from the superintendent of the individual area. Reference to the telephone directory will generally be sufficient for this purpose.

Special-use areas in some parks have been found desirable because of the growth of interest in and enthusiasm for winter sports, particularly skiing. From the national parks and forests down through the list of lesser areas, administrators are confronted with the demand for ski runs and other facilities wherever there are usable slopes and enough snow. It is not always possible to acquiesce in those demands where preservation of natural conditions is of primary importance. However, many such facilities do exist in all classes of parks, attendance at the most accessible ones naturally being the heaviest. Ski lifts, tows, jumps, and lodges are provided in some of the areas, but in the national parks and related areas they are limited somewhat by problems of access, safety, and likelihood of interference with other uses. Where those problems have been solved, informal skiing, ice skating, and tobogganing are encouraged. A policy of noncommercial use is followed, and no undue disfiguration of important landscapes is allowed.

In a few county and metropolitan parks, toboggan slides have been successful and popular. There are also many lakes, ponds, and artificial rinks, which are located in areas close enough to cities to be heavily patronized by skaters. Snowshoeing, it seems, is now mostly for practical purposes.

This advice to those who are novices in the use of park and recreation areas is important and will help the newcomers derive greater satisfaction and pleasure from their first outing.

By all means, choose the proper—but not necessarily expensive—clothing. Common sense prescribes light clothes for warm latitudes and heavier

ones for cool latitudes and for the higher altitudes. Strong fabrics are important. So are shoes that fit well and that are tough enough for severe use; with those specifications met, they should be as light as possible for ordinary walking. Mountain climbing and skiing call for special footgear. Socks should be of the proper size to avoid wrinkling from being too large or discomfort from being too small. Most people prefer a light wool, white sock, although some prefer cotton.

Campers would be well advised to include in their kits, in addition to the regular cooking and sleeping equipment, some form of protection against insects, such as mosquitoes, unless they have competent advice that it will not be necessary. Mosquito nets are often useful, as are the insecticides and repellents that were developed during and since the last war. In those sections of the country where chiggers, sometimes called "red bugs," are prevalent, dimethyl phthalate or benzyl benzoate will give good protection.

Fishing tackle and other gear usually can be bought in or near the parks, but if one is partial to certain types or brands he would do well to check his equipment thoroughly before leaving home. When traveling by automobile for a considerable distance, it may be of great advantage to have the best route planned in advance by someone who is familiar with that sort of thing.

Since there are usually severe restrictions on pets, it would be better to leave them behind if possible; otherwise it would be advisable either to visit an area where it has been determined by advance information that pets are allowed or to accept the fact that the animal will have to be confined or restrained on a leash.

Familiarity with all regulations will be found helpful in avoiding confusion and embarrassment and will contribute much to the enjoyment of an outing or a vacation as well as assist in the preservation of the area visited.

CONRAD L. WIRTH *is chief of the Land and Recreational Planning Division in the National Park Service. He has supervision of work related to park boundaries, land purchases, recreation studies, and cooperation with States and their political subdivisions. Mr. Wirth engaged in private practice as a landscape architect in San Francisco and New Orleans following graduation from the University of Massachusetts. He was employed by the National Capital Park and Planning Commission in 1928, and transferred to the National Park Service in 1931.*

J. H. GADSBY *is a park planner in the Land and Recreational Planning Division of the National Park Service. He holds a degree in landscape architecture from the University of Massachusetts and practiced his profession for 2 years before going into public work, first in the Park Division at Miami, Fla., and later with the South Carolina State Park Division.*

*The last section of this Yearbook contains a list of areas administered by the National Park Service, a list of national forests and their opportunities for recreation.*

*The end-paper maps show the forest areas and the main highways to them.*

# EVERYONE IS WELCOME

JOHN SIEKER

Every year Americans make 21 million visits to the national forests. They come, they say, to picnic, or (in order of preference) to fish, ski, hunt, camp, swim, hike, ride, look, and sit. They come from every State; some are tourists seeing America; others are out for a day or a weekend. Some want to do only one thing; many want to combine various of the pleasures at hand: Pitching camp in a shady spot, fishing in early morning and late afternoon, hiking in the forenoon, swimming between times, sitting around the campfire at night, and sleeping like a log in the cool of the night. But whatever they want to do, all get a sincere welcome.

The men who supervise the forests and work in them believe that recreation is a major value of the forests, that the woods and mountains should be enjoyed by their owners, the citizens of the United States, and that all have an obligation to care for the forests they have come to enjoy.

The 21 million visits a year (which aggregate 33 million days of use) create problems of sanitation, fire protection, and public welfare; because that many people could easily destroy the environment they have sought out, some regulations and preparations are necessary for the people's enjoyment and comfort and the forests' protection. In them, simplicity, appropriateness, and a minimum of rules are the keynotes. The types of recreation are encouraged that are suitable in the forest.

Simplicity of design and construction are stressed in all improvements, which generally are limited to those necessary to the health, safety, and the convenience of the users. Latrines, water systems, and fire grates have first priority. Camp and picnic tables, shelters, ski trails, and parking areas come next.

Most people who use the recreation areas appreciate the privilege of enjoying the forest, but a few destroy property and beauty and are thoughtless of the rights and privileges of others. They cost the Government—the people of the United States, including themselves—large sums each year when they destroy property. They spoil the pleasure of other people. Under Federal laws, those who destroy Government property are subject to punishment, but the supervisors of the forests prefer the precept of noblesse oblige: These national forests belong to all Americans for all Americans to enjoy; please protect your forest; please leave a camp or picnic site as clean as you would like to find it; have fun in the forest, and let others have fun in it, too.

PUBLIC RECREATION areas are found in all national forests, although some are more favorably situated than others and have more land suitable for recreation. Most forests in snow country have at least one winter-sports area.

The 4,500 camp and picnic places in the forests have 43,000 family size units. They can accommodate 280,000 persons at one time; in 1947, they received 8,780,132 visits.

All of them have safe drinking water, flyproof latrines, fire grates, and tables. Some of them, along back roads, are small and lightly used; others, along major routes of travel or near cities, are large and heavily used.

Some of these recreation areas are only for picnicking, but many of them can be used for overnight camping as well. Some are near good fishing; some are near fine hiking country; some have swimming places.

At some of the larger national forest recreation areas a small charge for camping and picnicking is made to reimburse the United States for the cost of keeping the area clean and usable. Some charge areas are operated by concessionaires who act under a special-use permit; others are operated by the Forest Service.

For those who desire free camping or picnicking, there are many areas which are equally attractive but at which there may not be regular and systematic clean-up.

Neither cabins nor tents are furnished or rented at camp and picnic areas. Campers should go prepared for the night with tents and sleeping bags or blankets. Straw is not available, and boughs may not be cut for beds. One may not cut trees for tent poles. Firewood is usually available in random lengths but must be cut up into firewood size. An ax is a necessity. Many campers find portable gasoline stoves very convenient for cooking—especially after a shower when wood is wet. Stores are seldom close by, and campers and picnickers should take their food for the day or for several days.

Some popular camp grounds are so heavily used that it is necessary to limit the length of time a camper may stay, to give more people a chance. When limits are imposed, 2 weeks is the usual time permitted; the places so restricted are conspicuously posted.

Only the largest camp and picnic areas have full-time guards or attendants, and visitors select their own sites. Camping or picnicking is prohibited between the prepared sites to avoid overcrowding the area. The sites are not reserved. It's first come, first served; late arrivals must go on to another area. Many of the camps cannot be cleaned up daily, and users are expected to leave a clean camp or picnic spot—as they would like to find it. Garbage pits or cans are always nearby. Papers should be burned in the grate.

Fires should be built only in fireplaces or stoves. Campfire permits are required (even at the improved camp grounds) in the national forests of California and some other States, but generally campfire permits are required only for camping or picnicking at unimproved areas. Campfire permits may be obtained without charge from any forest ranger. One should check with the local foresters about permits. Fires should always be built in a safe place, not against the trees or on deep duff. Fires must be thoroughly put out, with water and puddling. Heavy penalties are provided by law for leaving a campfire burning.

Everyone is urged to use the regular improved camp and picnic areas even though camping and picnicking are permitted elsewhere in the national forests except in closed areas, because of danger of forest fire and water pollution. The water in many streams and springs is not fit to drink even though it may look clear and good. It is better to be safe and drink only the water at improved camp and picnic areas. Persons who camp or picnic at other than improved areas must refrain from polluting land or water. All refuse must be buried deep.

THE 236 WINTER-SPORTS AREAS in the national forests cover 82,000 acres and received more than 2½ million visits in the 1947–48 season. It is said that 3 million Americans are skiers.

Ski areas are developed principally for the average skier. Emphasis is on the ski slope, practice slope, and intermediate trails. Expert trails and jumps are usually built by local ski clubs. Most areas have lifts and tows, operated by concessionaires. Some have separate toboggan slides, but toboggans may not be used on ski slopes or ski trails.

Most ski areas are located near highways, which the State highway departments keep cleared of snow. Many have shelters and lunchrooms.

Public shelter and parking are free, but charges are made for use of lifts and tows. The charges for lifts are around $2.50 a day; tows cost less.

Most of the winter-sport areas are in the Northern States, but some excellent ones have been developed at high elevations in New Mexico, Arizona, and southern California. Most of them in the national forests are in the Rocky Mountain area and westward in the Cascades and Sierras, but there are also some in Minnesota, Wisconsin, Michigan, New Hampshire, and Vermont. The Lake States and New England States have many winter areas on private and State land.

THE NATIONAL SKI ASSOCIATION has organized the National Ski Patrol, whose members are qualified first-aid men and expert skiers and mountaineers. They are volunteers who serve without pay, except at some larger areas where paid ski patrols are maintained.

The National Ski Association has 7 divisions and 384 member clubs from coast to coast throughout the snow belt. The Association and the National Ski Patrol have helped greatly by consulting with the Forest Service on the needs in development and administration, planning the expansion of sports centers, finding new areas, and caring for the injured.

Skiing is done under widely varying conditions. In some places the temperature may be just below freezing and storms may be rare; in others, sudden blizzards and temperatures of 20° below zero are common. Snow conditions and danger of avalanche also vary. All skiers are advised to learn about such conditions when they are in areas new to them and to be guided by the forest ranger, the National Ski Patrol, or experienced local skiers. They are advised also to be on the alert for warning signs—especially warnings of dangers of avalanches.

A good skier is a safe skier. He is not reckless. He respects the rights of other skiers. He skis only the trails he can handle and enjoy. He knows when he is tired. He saves time and money and gets more skiing by not getting hurt.

ORGANIZATION CAMPS, 65 in all, have an average capacity of 100 each. They generally include the bunkhouses, mess hall, and the recreation building. Running water and electricity are usually available. In 1947, visits that totaled 242,000 days were made to them.

The camps are rented on a noncommercial basis to organizations interested in providing a low-cost vacation to people who otherwise would not be able to have one.

Organizations using these camps must generally furnish bedding, mattresses, dishes, counsellors, and kitchen and janitor help. The Government equipment is limited to cots, stoves, icebox, light plants, and similar equipment.

All camps are located in attractive forest settings, have ample play areas, and are relatively isolated from other uses that might interfere with camp programs. Many have facilities for swimming.

All arrangements for using these camps are handled by the local forest supervisor.

WILDERNESS AND WILD AREAS, 77 in number and some 14 million acres in extent, are preserved in as primitive a condition as is consistent with their protection. The only improvements in the areas are those that are essential for fire protection. No commercial timber cutting is done.

Most wilderness areas are in high back country and above timber line where commercial timber values are small. Watershed values are tremendously important and the areas are extremely valuable for watershed protection and water production as well as for wilderness recreation. There is no conflict between water and wilderness.

These areas represent the last frontier of the United States. There will be little opportunity to increase their number or size, and it is therefore important that they be preserved as far as possible from invasion.

Wilderness areas are ideal for pack trips. The American Forestry Association conducts trail-rider trips through some of the areas each year at a cost of about $10 a person a day. Inquiries about them should be addressed to the American Forestry Association at 919

Seventeenth Street NW., Washington 6, D. C.

Many people travel the wilderness areas on their own, either afoot with back pack or with rented horses. Horses can often be rented without a guide or packer by persons competent to handle and care for them. It would be foolish for persons not familiar with horses to attempt a trip without hiring a packer. Furthermore, feed for horses is often difficult to find in wilderness areas, and, because camps must be made close to horse feed by horse parties, familiarity with the country is necessary.

Especially noteworthy is the Superior Roadless area in the Superior National Forest in Minnesota. It is in the border-lakes country along the Canadian boundary. It is accessible only by canoe, and one can travel for days through small lakes and streams without meeting another person. The surrounding country is timbered and attractive, and the fishing is excellent. Travel in the area is best after July 15, when there are fewer mosquitoes and flies. It would be unwise for nonswimmers or those not familiar with handling a canoe to plan a trip there without a guide, but persons who can handle a canoe, swim, and take care of themselves in the woods can enjoy a vacation at low cost.

Many persons travel into the wilderness areas from the western guest ranches that are in and near wild sections of the national forests. The ranches provide saddle horses, pack stock, guides, and packers for their guests. The Dude Ranchers' Association, Billings, Mont., will send information about the privately owned resorts.

The camp and picnic areas, winter-sports areas, and organization camps I have described comprise about one-hundredth of the total national forest area. The wilderness areas represent less than 8 percent.

THE 123,800 MILES OF THE FOREST HIGHWAYS and roads pass through fine forested country and mountains. Most of the roads are work roads, but many are open to pleasure drivers.

There are 144,000 miles of trails, which thousands of people enjoy each year afoot or on horseback. Some of the trails are famous, among them the Appalachian Trail from Maine to Georgia (which runs through the eastern forests), the Cascade Crest and Oregon Skyline Trail in the Pacific Northwest, and the John Muir and Sierra Trails in California. Most of them, however, were built only to enable forest rangers to get through the forest for purposes of protection and management; even so, they often pass through beautiful wild land and lead to some of the best fishing in the United States.

Forest Service maps show the locations of trails and are available from the forest supervisors. More detailed maps are available from the Appalachian Trail Conference, Washington, D. C., for the Appalachian Trail, and from the Pacific Crest Trail Conference, Green Hotel, Pasadena, Calif., for the trails through the Cascades and Sierras.

The national forests have 90,000 miles of fishing waters. Those that can be reached by car are not as good fishing, of course, as the more remote streams to which one must walk or ride.

Most of the lands are open to hunting. Big-game animals, the elk, deer, moose, antelope, mountain sheep, and grizzly bear, can be found and hunted in season. Small game and predators are abundant in places. Game birds, including pheasant, grouse, quail, and wild turkey, are common.

All game animals, game birds, and fish on the national forests are subject to State game laws. All persons who hunt or fish must observe the State laws as to license, bag limits, seasons, and so on. State wardens and forest rangers are always glad to give information on the local laws governing hunting and fishing and advice on the best places.

All persons are welcome to travel

through the national forests on the roads or highways, along the trails, or into the back country.

Some States require the nonresident hunters to hire a guide, but no one has the right to require a person to employ a guide for recreation travel over the national forests.

One should remember, however, that much of the back country is primitive. An injured person or one who is lost might die before he is found. It is unwise for inexperienced or poorly equipped persons to travel in the back country. All persons who contemplate such a trip should get the advice of the forest ranger as to routes of travel, equipment, clothing, and supplies: It can get extremely cold any month of the year at high elevations; only the foolhardy novice goes poorly shod, clothed, and equipped into the back country.

Although many public facilities are provided in recreation areas, some people want the comfort and convenience of a cabin or a hotel room. Consequently, private capital has been permitted to construct hotels, lodges, and cabin camps in national forests. The prices charged are subject to approval by the Forest Service, and the fees collected for the use of the land go to the United States Treasury.

Many persons have also been permitted to construct summer homes on Government land, in places not needed for public use. The owner of a summer home pays an annual rental to the Government.

Organizations, such as units of Boy Scouts, Y. M. C. A., Y. W. C. A., municipalities, and churches, have been permitted to construct organization camps for their own use in places where there will be no interference with more public uses. The camps perform much the same function as organization camps owned by the Government, but, being privately owned, are for the primary use of the organization that owns them.

The forest supervisors and rangers who are in charge of the individual national forests and ranger districts are the men who are intimately acquainted with local conditions; they are the men who administer the recreation areas.

Only general rules can apply to recreation areas, which extend from New Hampshire to Florida and from southern California to Minnesota. Some areas are at sea level; others are at 10,000 feet. Some are in the rain-soaked forests of the western slopes of Oregon and Washington; others are in the deserts of New Mexico and Arizona. Some recreation areas are open to the public yearlong. Others are open only in summer. Some forest areas are closed to all use during periods of high fire hazard. On some forests, campfire permits are required, even at established camp and picnic areas.

Because of all these different conditions, anyone who is planning a trip through a national forest should find out in advance what local conditions are, what facilities are available, and what equipment is recommended.

General information can be had by writing to: Regional Forester, Forest Service, United States Department of Agriculture—

Bankers Securities Building, Philadelphia 7, Pa. (For information about national forests in the New England and Eastern States as far south as Virginia.)

Madison Building, Milwaukee 3, Wis. (For information about national forests in the Lake States and States along the Ohio River and the Mississippi River as far south as Missouri.)

Glenn Building, Atlanta 3, Ga. (For information about national forests in the Southern States and Gulf States as far west as Texas and north to Arkansas.)

Federal Building, Missoula, Mont. (For information about national forests in the Inland Empire—Montana and the Panhandle of Idaho.)

Post Office Building, Denver 2, Colo. (For information about national forests in the Central Rocky Mountains—Colorado and Wyoming [east of the Continental Divide] and South Dakota.)

Forest Service Building, Ogden, Utah. (For information about national forests in the Intermountain Region—Utah, southern Idaho, Nevada, and western Wyoming.)

Post Office Building, Portland 8, Oreg. (For information about national forests in Oregon and Washington.)

630 Sansome Street, San Francisco 11, Calif. (For information about national forests in California.)

Post Office Building, Albuquerque, N. Mex. (For information about national forests in New Mexico and Arizona.)

Persons who know the national forest they plan to visit will obtain more specific information faster if they write to the supervisor of the particular forest.

The Forest Service cannot supply information as to resort, hotel, or cabin accommodations available in the national forests. Information of that kind often can be obtained from chambers of commerce in nearby towns or from an automobile association.

National forest lands are open for use unless conspicuously posted as closed. Areas are closed only when fire hazard requires it. Some forest development roads are closed when hauling is being done by heavy log trucks, because pleasure cars would be in danger.

JOHN SIEKER *is a graduate of Princeton University and the Yale School of Forestry. He entered the Forest Service in 1926 as a forest ranger. He later served as assistant forest supervisor of the Harney National Forest and as supervisor of the Shoshone National Forest. He is now chief of the Division of Recreation and Lands, a position he has held since 1938.*

# SAFETY FOR FOREST VISITORS

ROBERT S. MONAHAN

Too many forest outings have been marred, if not ruined, by faulty planning, inadequate equipment, or poor judgment. Regardless of whether the recreational travel involves a wilderness expedition or an afternoon walk in the suburbs, it should be a source of happy memories instead of a cause for regret. Those who plan carefully, equip themselves for the unexpected, and use their heads are sure to look back upon their outings with pleasure.

Many vacationists have found that one of the most enjoyable features of their trips is the fun that comes from planning them. Long before departure, itineraries are outlined (and a copy left with a responsible individual who is not making the trip), the equipment is checked, and questions are asked. Such preliminaries are not only interesting, they provide sound insurance for the enjoyment and safety.

Maps are now available for almost any area in the United States. They vary in degree of detail and reliability, but one should get the most recent editions and make the most of them. Even though you may know from previous experience the country you plan to visit, carry the maps with you—circumstances might develop that will cause you to travel in areas that you have not seen before.

Do not hesitate to ask questions, either before you leave or while you are approaching your objective. Remember that even the forest ranger generally has to request information when he visits the big city. Intelligent travelers ask questions of those qualified to give helpful answers.

A GOOD PLAN includes the route you expect to follow and alternatives in case of unfavorable weather. It lists the supplies and equipment needed to complete the journey, with a margin for safety. It anticipates the unexpected—illness, accident, and stormy weather. It is, indeed, the first essential of any trip to the hinterland.

Probably more outings have resulted in discomfort, if not disaster, from inadequate equipment than from any other cause. Again, do not hesitate to ask questions. Experience is a hard teacher; one can learn the easy way by presenting his problems to those who should know the answers.

Whether you are climbing, fishing, hunting, photographing, or enjoying any of the other pursuits that attract people into the back country, the equipment should be practicable and absolutely dependable.

Outing equipment is too varied to make possible any detailed suggestions. A few general principles apply, regardless of any particular activity: Woodswise travelers test their gear before they leave home. They make sure that their ski bindings are adjusted properly. They test the sights of their rifles. They are satisfied that their tackle box contains every inducement for whatever fish may be encountered. Most important of all, they inspect the first-aid kit to be positive that it is complete. Veteran campers check their list of items for parts needing replacement during the trip: Generators for gasoline lanterns, flashlight batteries and bulbs, bandages for first-aid kits, and matches in waterproof containers. If traveling in snake country, they make sure that the snake-bite kit is complete and that every member of the party knows how to use it. Those who are to climb mountains carefully check the condition of their ropes. If a winter expedition is contemplated, they make doubly sure that they are prepared for whatever weather may develop.

There is no substitute for good judgment when one is on his own. It can be acquired only through experience; it can be exercised only by determination to keep a cool head, regardless of circumstances.

The development of a sound judgment is one of the really worth while byproducts of back-country travel. If one cannot learn to think for himself, perhaps he should limit his outings to the fringes of civilization.

Judgment is especially important in the hunting season, whether or not one is actually hunting.

The unarmed traveler, no less than the hunter, takes his own chances in game country and should avoid any possibility of being mistaken for animals or birds. Hunters are exposed to a barrage of safety suggestions, which deserve full compliance. Above all, hunters should be positive of their target before they shoot.

THE VACATION COUNTRY is a friendly land, but there are specific dangers that should be recognized. Let us meet and get acquainted with some of them, before they surprise us.

Most mountain roads are safer than they may appear to flat-landers who are not accustomed to narrow widths, sharp turns, and heavy grades. Before attempting such roads, have your car checked, particularly the tires, brakes, lights, clutch, and cooling system. Be sure your gasoline and oil are adequate—filling stations may be few and far between. Use second or low gear while climbing or descending steep grades. Drive slowly, so that your passengers may enjoy the countryside and your car will stay in the wheel track.

Always reconnoiter a strange stream or lake before you bathe in it. Never attempt diving until you are positive the water is deep enough. Watch out for treacherous eddies, hidden holes, slippery underwater ledges and roots, broken glass, and rusty tin cans. A dip in a cool mountain lake or stream is a wonderful tonic after a hot day in the saddle or afoot, but remember that what starts as a refreshing stimulant may end in disastrous shock, if the water is especially cold and your physical condition is below par. Do not swim alone.

The least a forest visitor can do in

deference to the landowner, future vacationist, and his own conscience is to make sure that his fire is out—dead out. If local rules forbid lighting fires, there is a good reason for the regulation and for obeying it. Use plenty of water in drowning your fire; make sure that it has soaked into the ground thoroughly. Take the time to stir the water into the soil with a shovel or stout stick. Never let it be said that you found a green camp site and left it a ruin.

If there is any doubt as to the purity of the water supply, search for a reliable source, and boil the water for 15 minutes, or add one of the purifying agents available at most camping-supply stores. Take no chances with questionable drinking water.

Learn to identify poison-oak, poison-ivy, and poison sumac. Avoid them. If contact is impossible to avoid, one home remedy is to wash all exposed parts of your body with a strong laundry soap. If you set out to rid a patch of poisonous plants, wear gloves at all times; if you have to burn the plants, keep out of the smoke.

Ticks of various kinds, from mid-April to mid-August, may be a source of infection; the "sick" ticks are potential carriers of spotted fever. After a day in the woods, search for ticks that may have become attached to the skin. Check carefully under armpits and in body creases. If you find a tick, be sure that you remove his head as well as his body. Cautious forest rangers, loggers, and stockmen who work in the tick country properly respect the "sick" tick; they are inoculated before the tick season starts.

The little ones of the forests can cause great discomfort; they should be anticipated when assembling supplies for the trip. The bites of mosquitoes, punkies (midgies or no-see-ums), black flies and other biting flies, and chiggers or red bugs (mites) can be avoided by repellents, which have little or no odor and remain effective up to several hours, even when those bothersome insects assemble in large numbers. Repellents developed primarily for military use have been adopted widely for civilian purposes. Detailed information is furnished in a leaflet, *Use of Insect Repellents and Miticides,* distributed by the Bureau of Entomology and Plant Quarantine, Agricultural Research Administration, United States Department of Agriculture, Washington 25, D. C. The leaflet recommends the following mixtures of repellents as effective against a wider range of insect species and on more individuals than any one of the chemicals when used alone (all parts are by weight):

*Formula 1*

| | |
|---|---|
| Dimethyl phthalate | 3 parts |
| Indalone | 1 part |
| Rutgers 612 | 1 part |

*Formula 2*

| | |
|---|---|
| Dimethyl phthalate | 1 part |
| Indalone | 1 part |
| Rutgers 612 | 1 part |

*Formula 3*

| | |
|---|---|
| Dimethyl phthalate | 3 parts |
| Indalone | 1 part |
| Dimethyl Carbate | 1 part |

Mosquito nets often are useful.

Learn also to identify the poisonous snakes. Three of them (copperheads, water moccasins, and rattlesnakes) are easily distinguished from the harmless species by their four nostrils. If one does not care to get close enough to a questionable reptile to count his nostrils, his larger, triangular-shaped head (in contrast to the smaller, oval-shaped heads of the harmless snakes) is usually a safe distinction. The other poisonous snake, the coral snake, can be identified by its brilliant coloring. It is seldom longer than 2 feet and is encircled with alternate red, yellow, and black bands. It occurs only in the Deep South, but it is the most poisonous of all. Do not kill every snake you encounter, but you will be doing a service to mankind by dispatching the ones that have the large, triangular heads (especially those that rattle) and those in the South with brilliant coloring.

If a lightning storm overtakes you, do not seek shelter under a single tree

or any prominent lone landmark. Do not remain on a ridge or summit, and, above all, get out of the water, if you are swimming. Artificial respiration should be given a victim of lightning, as in the case of a near drowning.

Make sure your axes and knives are well-sheathed. When chopping, remove overhanging branches which might deflect your blow. Be sure that the arc of your swing does not end at your foot.

THE TRAVEL-WISE ADVENTURERS have learned the hard way that ten rules are vital. The experience of those who have disregarded them also emphasizes their importance:

1. Never travel alone, especially on overnight trips or through hazardous country. Never go into wild country without letting someone know where you are going and when to expect you back.

2. No matter how sure you may be of reaching your destination on schedule, include in your kit a powerful flashlight, dry matches, and emergency rations.

3. Wear nothing more than is necessary for comfort, but always carry extra clothing for unexpected changes in the weather. The proper clothing is not necessarily expensive clothing.

Common sense prescribes light clothes for warm latitudes and heavier ones for cool latitudes and for the higher altitudes. Strong fabrics are important.

4. An accurate compass, preferably of the floating-card type, makes no mistakes unless used near steel or iron accessories, such as a pocketknife or buckle, or near iron-ore deposits. Have faith in your compass but remember that its use is limited without a reliable map and knowledge of the terrain. Do not believe that you have an unfailing sense of direction—no one has. If fog develops or snow starts to fall, you will get turned around unless you know the country or stay on a trail—trust your compass rather than your hunch. Always keep yourself located approximately on a map. Know the major drainages in your locality and the general direction in which they flow. Have the general topography of the area in mind. Find out at what declination your compass is set and what the local declination is. Remember the compass needle points in slightly different directions in different parts of the country. There is no reliable way to tell north by the moss on trees or rocks. The only reliable way to tell direction is by the sun, the stars, or a good compass. Know the watch direction formula, and know the North Star.

5. Have plenty of rest and food before undertaking long walks or difficult climbs. Respect your age. Know your limitations. Do not think you are an experienced woodsman because you have walked along a few trails.

6. It is always better, especially in alpine travel above the timber line, to turn back and retrace your route over familiar territory than to press on into the unknown until it becomes too late to return to safety. Remember that you cannot exert yourself at high elevations as you can at sea level.

7. If in trouble, fire three shots at intervals, light three fires, or indicate your need for help by any device employing three units.

8. Maintain a slow but steady pace, rather than a fast one with frequent stops. The progress of the party is limited to the speed of its slowest mem-

ber, and if he becomes exhausted, the whole group is jeopardized. Your chances to "walk out" are slim if you break a leg. Take it easy.

9. You are just as good as your feet, and they are just as good as the shoes that protect them. Tight boots, new shoes not well broken-in, overgreased leather in cold-weather travel, and slippery soles can cause trouble. Shoes should fit well and be tough enough for severe use. Those specifications met, they should be as light as possible for ordinary walking. Mountain climbing and skiing call for special footgear. Socks should be of the proper size to avoid wrinkling (from being too large) or discomfort (from being too small).

10. If you get lost, sit down and think through your predicament. The resourceful wanderer, who remembers his bearings, follows water courses downhill to inevitable civilization, and refuses to become panicky, may be confused, but he is seldom lost. Do not fret about food—you can live for days without any food and suffer no permanent harm. So far as we know, no visitor has ever starved to death in the national forests, but some have frozen to death or died of exposure or exhaustion. Neither you nor your rescuers should ever call quits—the record is filled with cases where the lost surpassed their endurance and the rescuers found the object of their search after all hope had been abandoned. Take it easy. Do not travel at night. It might take you several days to reach civilization, but the chances are excellent that you will; you will be tired and hungry, but not harmed. Guard your matches, and keep them dry. If you smoke, do not use your matches recklessly; you may need them to build fires. One night in the cold of a high-mountain storm has finished off tough men, so look for a cave or overhanging rock early in the afternoon and gather good dry wood. Whether it is better to search for help or to wait for help depends on whether you are injured and whether you have let anyone know where you were going and when you would be back. It is useless to wait for someone to find you if no one knows about where you are. Passers-by are rare in some wild parts of the national forests.

ROBERT S. MONAHAN, *general manager of the Dartmouth Outing Club and Dartmouth College Forester, has combined his professional forestry career with leadership in recreational activities. His 15 years in the United States Forest Service took him from Maine to California and provided unusual opportunities to become well acquainted with all major forms of outdoor recreation.*

# Forests and Wildlife

## WILDLIFE IN THE SMALL WOODLAND

EDWARD H. GRAHAM

SMALL WOODLANDS are natural homes for such valuable fur bearers as the skunk, opossum, mink, raccoon, fox, and weasel. Among game animals, woodlands harbor squirrels of various kinds, woodcock, ruffed grouse, rabbit, and snipe. Fox and raccoon provide sport as well as pelts. In the woods also live flying squirrels, chipmunks, pocket gophers, mice, and other forest rodents. Song and insect-eating birds are abundant—the thrushes, warblers, woodpeckers, and nuthatches, kinglets, and whippoorwills. Predators, hawks and owls, live in the woods and feed upon insects, snakes, frogs, and small vertebrates.

Many kinds of wildlife that live in woodlands are found nowhere else. When the woodland is harmed or destroyed, these creatures become fewer or disappear. To protect the useful and beautiful wild things of the woodlands, we must first protect their woodland homes, where they get food, shelter, a place to breed and hide and live.

*Above: The bear was once a respected animal of the western range and forest country.*

The things to do to help woodland wildlife are much the same as the rules to be followed in growing the trees, for when trees are protected they make homes for wild animals.

The rules for the management of the woodland wildlife are: Protect the woodland from uncontrolled fire, protect the woodland from intensive grazing, cut the trees selectively, preserve den trees, develop woodland borders.

Wildlife usually benefits most when fire is kept out of the woodland. In the few instances in which fire is employed as a tool in forest management, it must be carefully supervised. Reckless burning destroys cover that is used by wildlife for nesting, escape from enemies, roosting, and other purposes vital to their survival. Uncontrolled fire also reduces the food supply of wildlife and may burn them to death as well. After a serious fire it may take years for the woodland trees to recover and as long to recreate the proper habitat for the birds and mammals.

The woodland that is subjected to intensive grazing is usually a poor place for wildlife. Constant trampling and

802062°—49——37

disturbance by cows, sheep, goats, or horses is especially damaging to wild animals that live on or near the ground. Severe grazing, which destroys young trees, affects the existing conditions and the future conditions under which the wildlings live.

Studies by Charles A. Dambach in Ohio disclosed that eastern woodlands that are protected from grazing have twice as many species and numbers of plants as grazed woodlands. Under protected conditions are found about twice as many kinds of birds that nest on or near the ground and nearly twice as many kinds of mammals than are found in comparable woods that are grazed.

Harvesting trees as they mature here and there throughout the woods instead of cutting the whole lot at one time is especially valuable to wildlife.

An even-aged stand of trees has less variety of wild birds and mammals than a woodland that has a mixture of mature and young trees. The more variety in the habitat, the more variety in the wildlife it supports. Furthermore, openings where trees are felled are especially valuable to certain kinds of wild creatures. In them there is a variety of herbaceous and shrubby species along with young trees, and such spots make the woodland more desirable for grouse, rabbits, and other living things.

Some of the most useful, interesting, and valuable animals of woodlands are missing when there are no trees with hollow trunks or hollow limbs. For some kinds of wildlife, a hollow tree is essential. The raccoon, for instance, is rarely found where there is not a hollow tree for a den. Another fur bearer, the opossum, also holes up in hollow trees. Flying squirrels use the holes for homes, and so do other squirrels, the wood duck, screech owl, sparrow hawk, chipmunk, nuthatch, crested flycatcher, chickadee, bluebird, purple martin, and chimney swift.

In Europe, the foresters found that the woodlands composed of even-aged stands of a single tree species supported practically no wildlife. Injurious insects were also abundant. So much damage was done by forest insects that nest boxes were finally set up to attract birds. The birds fed upon and helped to control the harmful insects. Woodlands that compose a natural community of living things give us less trouble than artificial plantings. A few scattered den trees help a great deal toward maintaining a natural balance in our small woodlands. They are especially valuable near streams or near the margins of the woodland.

At the outer margin of the small woods, where it adjoins a field or pasture, a border of shrubs is especially valuable to wildlife. It is a principle of wildlife management that there are more wild creatures in the edge of a particular type of vegetation than within the type. Counts of birds and mammals show more species, and more individuals, along the shrubby margin of a woodland than within the woodland or in the adjacent pasture or field. Protecting the woodland edge thus increases wildlife. Often fruit- and seed-bearing shrubs grow there naturally.

A simple method of producing shrub borders is to cut the trees within 20 to 30 feet of the woodland edge. Certain kinds of shrubs and other materials can be planted successfully along the margins of woodlands to improve them for wildlife.

The most valuable for the Eastern States are: Bicolor lespedeza (*Lespedeza bicolor*), bayberry (*Myrica carolinensis*), hazelnut or American filbert (*Corylus americana*), flowering dogwood (*Cornus florida*), highbush cranberry or American cranberrybush (*Viburnum trilobum*), the silky cornel or the silky dogwood (*Cornus amomum*), and the Tatarian honeysuckle (*Lonicera tatarica*).

For the Western States: Squawbush or skunkbush (*Rhus trilobata*), American plum (*Prunus americana*), chokecherry (*Prunus demissa*), the buffaloberry (*Shepherdia argentea*), tamarisk (*Tamarix gallica*), and Russian-olive (*Elaeagnus angustifolia*).

Nurserymen will be able to suggest

other shrubs and trees that are adapted to one's own locality, that can fill a double or triple purpose in woodland or, indeed, on any country place, and that have fruits that are especially appealing to the particular birds a person might want to attract. Among the suggestions might be redcedar (*Juniperus virginiana*) that is relished by more than 50 species of birds, including the bobwhite, pheasant, and the mourning dove; the sumacs, whose berries attract more than 100 birds and mammals; the elderberry, food for more than 100 birds; and snowberry, eaten by 30 species of birds.

Such shrubs need not be costly, especially if one buys them in small sizes. They are not hard to plant and care for. Or, another suggestion is that neighbors exchange cuttings, slips, or roots of shrubs. What better project can neighbors or communities or organizations—better in the enhancement of friendship, beauty, and money values—carry out than one in which groups of persons buy and exchange shrubs for woodlands, roadsides, waste places, parks?

The precepts given here will assure an abundance of wild creatures in the small woodland. The woodland wildlife has many values. It is interesting and attractive. It provides sport in the way of hunting. It yields a crop of furbearer pelts that brings cash to the landowner. Wild creatures provide a service that we often fail to appreciate because it is not obvious—they contribute to the natural balance that helps keep woodlands in condition.

A few examples illustrate this important contribution by wildlife. In northeastern forests, small mammals occur in remarkably large numbers. Studies by W. J. Hamilton, Jr., and David B. Cook show that these animals number about 100 to the acre. They eat an astonishing number of insects. Forest rodents—mice, chipmunks, and flying squirrels—have a diet that is 20 percent insects, even though they are considered to be primarily plant feeders. The food of the woodland shrews and moles runs from 50 to 75 percent insects. The insect-destroying value of such woodland mammals is high also because they are voracious creatures, many of them eating each day enough food to equal nearly one-third of their weight. Unlike most birds, they are resident creatures and are more or less active throughout the year.

In the Western States, the pandora moth attacks Jeffrey and ponderosa pines, and under some conditions it injures lodgepole pine. A large-scale attack was made upon lodgepole pine in 1937 in north-central Colorado. How much more severe the damage from the infestation might have been if wildlife had been absent is indicated by an investigation of the situation by N. D. Wygant. He found that "squirrels and bears were destroying many of the pupae . . . Bears had overturned many flat stones and the squirrels had dug cone-shaped holes in the ground in search of pupae and . . . Animal feces composed almost entirely of pandora moth eggs were found."

The value of birds in woodlands has been evident since the Department of Agriculture began its research on the food of wild animals of farm lands some 50 years ago. A large amount of food is consumed by birds, and injurious insects are among the items that compose the diet of many species. Investigators have found 5,000 ants in the stomach of a flicker, a nighthawk with a stomachful of 500 mosquitoes, and a yellow-billed cuckoo that had consumed 250 tent caterpillars.

Wildlife is a natural part of the small woodland. It belongs there just as the trees themselves, the duff on the woodland floor, and the rich soil beneath the trees. Without wildlife the small woodland is a poor place; with wildlife the small woodland is a better place for the trees, and a more productive, useful, and attractive place for people.

EDWARD H. GRAHAM *is chief of the Biology Division of the Soil Conservation Service. Before he joined the Department in 1937, Dr. Graham was for years engaged in botanical studies for the Carnegie Museum in Pittsburgh. He has written many scientific and technical papers on plant sciences and wildlife ecology, and is the author of several books, among them a treatise on the application of biological principles to the management of land, Natural Principles of Land Use.*

# FORESTS AS A WILDLIFE HABITAT

LLOYD W. SWIFT

The amount and quality of food, the difficulty in getting it, and the assurance that there will be some next winter determine many of the activities and habits of man and beast—how hard one works, where one lives, how well one is nourished. So, too, with shelter, weather, and moisture (which we sum up in the word habitat), which determine, for instance, whether a deer can live in a desert, whether a variety of corn can grow in Alabama, whether one can transplant a wild flower from its native woods to a garden. Almost any change in habitat can change the number and kind of living things in it. Wild things, wild mammals and birds, reflect more exactly than tamer creatures the conditions of their habitat, which nature and man are constantly changing.

The minute they put foot on these shores the first settlers from Europe started changing the habitat of wildlife. They (and their descendants) pursued and killed the birds and animals for food, clothing, or recreation, or because the wildlife conflicted with crops or livestock; they also caused far-reaching changes in habitat by clearing land, logging, and fires.

Originally in the eastern half of the United States, much of the cover was of hardwoods, to which many kinds of wildlife were adapted and in which the nuts or mast from oaks, hickories, chestnuts, walnuts, and beech and the fruits and berries of gum, grape, dogwood, persimmon, and other trees, vines, and shrubs gave ample food. The hardwood forests also provided small tree dens for squirrels, larger ones for raccoons, and trunk dens for big animals, like the black bear. Less favorable a habitat were the original coniferous forests in the East; the pine, hemlock, and spruce stands furnished a smaller variety and quantity of food, and dens were less frequent and satisfactory. Therefore, the animals of the conifer forests were likely to be more specialized, or at least closely associated with the more restricted food and the cover conditions found in the conifer forests.

Where the two types overlapped and made a mixture of hardwoods and conifers, or where the local climate was modified by protected and exposed sites, such as in the mountains, the variety of food and cover undoubtedly favored a greater variety of wildlife, but not necessarily a greater quantity than in the food-rich hardwood forests.

In the West, the forests were largely conifers—junipers commonly occupied the low places in the Rocky Mountains and adjacent areas, spruces the higher elevations, and pines in between. There the stands were often bisected by fingers of open grassland, meadows, or brush fields; the native forest had extensive borders or edges, a condition that is generally favorable to wildlife; the volume of nuts and fruit was not ordinarily high in the forest areas, but the forage conditions frequently favored browsing and grazing animals.

The forests on the Pacific coast, west of the crest of the Cascade Mountains, were of a closed conifer stand, which, under the influence of favorable moisture and growing conditions, were characteristically dense and tall. The ground was commonly in permanent shade. Wildlife was more restricted than in an open forest or a hardwood stand, but those forests were outstanding in the character of the fish life in the streams and the rivers, which were spawning grounds of the sea-run salmon and trout.

Thus, although the hardwood forest undoubtedly was the home of a greater variety and quantity of wildlife, all forest areas were likely to support some deer, bear, squirrels, beaver, and wolves. Some variety of grouse was native to all areas, except the forests of the Coastal Plain in the South and Southeast. Elk ranged in nearly all regions, except the South. Beaver were present in nearly all forests. Turkey were distributed from New England to Colorado and Arizona. The bighorn sheep lived in the mountains of the Western States, mountain goat in the country north of the Columbia and Snake Rivers, and moose in the north woods and northern Rocky Mountains.

Beaver were most abundant where suitable water was associated with favored food species, such as aspen, cottonwood, and the willow. The turkey range appeared to be adjusted to the availability of mast—acorns, chestnuts, and pine nuts, particularly in winter. Different species of grouse had developed rather specialized feeding habits, and could winter on the buds of conifers or hardwoods where it lived.

Similar relationships could be cited for other species, and the food preferences of some predators, such as the cougar or puma for deer, could be mentioned. Those examples are sufficient, however, to illustrate the point that the animals were distributed according to a habitat pattern, in which their basic needs for food and cover were met. In that respect, the character of the forest was paramount in determining the kind of wildlife that would fit in and how abundant it might become.

Settlement and hunting soon changed the situation. In colonial and pioneer communities, game laws were commonly thought unnecessary; the few that were passed were liberal and seldom enforced. The feeling was general that the people who settled an area or owned land were entitled to unrestricted use of the wildlife resources, a philosophy that prevailed in some sections of the country until a few years ago and that was particularly characteristic of forest communities. Further, until the present generation, many State fish and game departments were so inadequately financed that they could not maintain an adequate warden force, let alone investigate the status of the wildlife resource.

Under those circumstances, game and fur animals suffered. A few species were exterminated. Others disappeared from large sections of their native range, and only recently were reestablished through programs of restocking. In the East, the white-tailed deer had mostly disappeared by 1910; the elk were all gone by 1870. In many parts of the West, elk were killed out. One species, the Merriam elk of the Southwest, had been exterminated by 1898. Beaver were so persistently trapped that they were exterminated from large areas of the Eastern States, and became scarce in the Lake States and the Rocky Mountains. The once abundant passenger pigeon disappeared entirely.

Forest animals that came into conflict with man often became the object of eradication campaigns, which included bounties and professional hunters. They exterminated the gray timber wolf from virtually all its range except a small part of the Lake States, yet originally the timber wolf and subspecies, such as the buffalo wolf, occupied nearly all of the territory now in the United States, except California. The cougar, or mountain lion, once was associated with all forest regions; now it is found in the rougher sections of the West, but in the East is limited to a few individuals in Florida. The grizzly bear, once a respected animal of the western range and forest country, now is confined to the wilderness sections only of Montana, Idaho, and Wyoming. The last known California grizzly, the Golden Bear of the California State flag, was killed in 1922.

The clearing of forests for agriculture and the widespread cutting and burning of the remaining wooded areas profoundly affected the wildlife habitat. One important change was the increase in the borders and edges in the remaining forest and woodland areas; another was the tremendous increase in the herbaceous and shrubby cover, which favored browsing and edge animals, such as deer, bobwhites, rabbits, and grouse.

The relation of forest changes to deer management in the East and the Lake States is of particular interest. The virgin forests were not particularly well suited to deer, because openings and browse areas were limited. But after the forests were opened up by lumbermen, and further changed by fires, the browse supply became extensive. At about the same time, some States started to protect and restore the white-tailed deer. Through restocking where needed and the adoption of laws favorable to building up the herds, the deer were especially encouraged just when the food supply became most abundant.

The deer thrived beyond expectations. Instead of a few hundred or a few thousand deer, States like Pennsylvania and Michigan soon had several hundred thousand. All seemed for the best, until it was realized that the deer had exceeded the food supply. The browse shortage was intensified by the fact that under improved fire protection the forests were recapturing the land. The stems and twigs, which had been good browse for deer, had developed into pole-sized stands of second-growth forests. As the trees grew beyond the reach of the deer, they formed a closed canopy and shaded out the shrubs, vines, and herbs.

The deer and elk have made marked increases also in the western forests, but the situation has been somewhat different. There was the same public support for herd protection, but logging and fires had affected but a small proportion of the forest area. The western forests, with certain exceptions, however, were grazed by cattle and sheep. Therefore, when big-game species increased, they often did so on land that was already being grazed too heavily by domestic livestock. The situation created many problems on public and private land, and much good livestock and game range has been seriously overused. As in the East, the reduced food supply has brought about starvation of big game in localities where the hunters have not harvested the surplus.

Although the cut-over and burned forest favored deer, elk, and grouse, it was not good for species that required stands of old growth; the tree squirrels found less food and fewer dens; the marten and fisher could not exist in the new environment; the turkey also found the young, open forests unsatisfactory because they were deficient in mast.

The change in the forest cover also changed the stream conditions and fish life. Under the virgin-forest conditions, the streams were normally in a stabilized condition. And the forest cover checked the runoff; streams ran clear; flows were normal; channels tended to be stable, and water temperatures fluctuated only a little. But when watersheds were seriously disturbed by logging, fire, or grazing, the streams were subjected to flood conditions and disturbance of channels; the aquatic habitat suffered; insect life was smothered by silt or injured by abrasion; gravel spawning beds silted up; food-producing ability was lowered; and summer temperature was raised. In cases of extreme change, good trout waters became nearly barren of such fish.

When the general public realized, a generation or more ago, that the wildlife resource was so seriously impaired, there was support for wildlife protection and restoration. The first reaction was to restrict the take, often to the point of yearlong closed seasons. In extreme cases, such as the bighorn sheep, the ptarmigan, and certain other species, some States have had closed seasons for 20 years or more. Other methods of restricting the take as a measure to protect the breeding stock included refuges, short seasons, small bag limits, and restrictions on sex and age. Such forest big game as deer and elk were subjected to the "buck laws," which designated male animals with certain antler developments as legal game, providing full protection to females. Refuges became popular in the 1920's; vast areas of forest lands were included in the State game refuges, and smaller areas in Federal refuges.

The restocking of game and fish assumed a prominent place in the protection and restoration programs. Between 1910 and 1920, elk from the Northern Yellowstone and Jackson Hole herds were released in 11 Western States and in many places in the East. Most of the western plants and reestablishments were in public forest land formerly occupied by elk. Insufficient wilderness areas and conflict with farming districts prevented acceptance of elk restoration in the East.

The trapping of wild big game, mostly deer, for stocking has continued in some areas up to now. Dependence for turkey stock, however, too often has been placed upon game farms. Pen-raised birds were frequently of mixed domestic strains, and have not succeeded in the wild.

Fish hatcheries were developed by both State and Federal agencies, and in the mountain areas large numbers of trout were produced. Through indiscriminate stocking programs, the trout species were widely and, too often, unwisely mixed.

Present knowledge shows that some of these restoration programs were ill-advised; some were good at first but were continued too long. It is now generally accepted that the planting of small trout and fry, except in barren waters, is of little value. The survivals of fry to reach a fisherman's creel are extremely few, although the returns from stocking of adult trout during the fishing season are usually high.

Perhaps much of the big-game overpopulation trouble came from public pressure to retain large refuges long after the deer and elk were abundant, and from retention of the "buck law" when females should have been harvested to control or reduce the herd. The overselling of the "buck law" has probably been the major hindrance to good big-game management in the United States. Even today many big-game ranges in the Lake States as well as in the West are in a serious stage of depletion.

Game laws of the Old World have had a bearing on the legal status of wildlife in this country. The main influence came directly from England. Before the conquest by the Norman kings, landowners there were privileged to pursue wildlife on their own holdings; afterward, William the Conqueror took over forests as crown property. Hunting became the pastime of the royalty; the game became the property of the sovereign. Offenders of the King's game laws were severely punished; sometimes they paid for the offense with an eye, a hand, or even their lives. The laws were liberalized in the Magna Charta, the Charta Foresta, and other steps in the thirteenth century; a man would not lose his hands or life for killing a deer, but he could be fined and imprisoned.

The idea that game was the property

of the crown was transferred to the Colonies in a form that made wildlife the qualified property of the State. Consequently, the States, acting in a sovereign capacity for all citizens, exercised control over fish and game.

The Colonists had to learn how to hunt; in England they had had scarcely any opportunity. In the new country, wildlife was, so to speak, something which belonged to all the people. When game laws became necessary, the State replaced the crown, and all persons held an equal interest in the wildlife resources. So today all citizens are entitled to hunt and fish for resident wildlife under the laws promulgated by the States.

The game laws in the United States have created a situation wherein successful game management hinges on the cooperation of the States and the landowners, because the State, although it is responsible for the protection and restoration of wildlife, depends practically on farmers, timber owners, and other landowners for a place to produce the wildlife. The condition and use of the land has a major influence on the kind and amount of fish and game that can be supported.

THIS COORDINATION of forestry and wildlife brings us back to the all-important point of habitat.

The restrictive measures of the past to protect breeding stocks and to plant fish have turned out to be tools of wildlife management that are likely to help wildlife only if the habitat is favorable. We know now that the basic need for wildlife is a suitable habitat, one that will carry all the animals through the entire year and will vary with the species, according to their food preferences (whether browse, grass, fruits, nuts, insects, or other animals) and their cover needs (whether tree dens, thickets, brush, or weeds). If these requirements are not provided, the forest animals cannot respond to protection given them by seasons of hunting, bag limits, or other laws to perpetuate the breeding stock. The land-management practices are therefore of direct importance to the animals. What is done to the land and its cover determines how much wildlife can be produced.

In the national forests, attention has been given to the relationship between forest management and wildlife management. The method of cutting the trees is one important factor: Light selective cuttings have negligible value for wildlife because they ordinarily do little to open the forest canopy to promote reproduction and development of the shrubbery or herbaceous growth. Light cuttings to remove dead and defective trees can safeguard wildlife interests fairly well if at least one den tree is left on an acre. Heavy selective cuttings can improve wildlife conditions by creating small openings in the forest canopy; the grass, weeds, and other vegetation come in under these breaks and enhance the habitat.

Of the various cutting methods now in use, wildlife interests are best served by fairly heavy selective cutting or clear cutting in relatively small blocks. An important consideration is the cruising range of wildlife species and the length of the cutting cycle, because the advantages of the system depend on maintaining a broad range of timber-age classes within the travel range of game. If wildlife is not considered in timber-stand improvement work, food supplies may be depleted by the heavy cutting of species like beech, dogwood, sassafras, and persimmon, but appropriate consideration and planning can serve both timber management and wildlife management.

Another factor is the maintenance of the streamside forest cover. The forest canopy provides shade, which governs maintenance of water temperatures favorable to trout. Moreover, the insects that fall into the water from overhanging vegetation are food for fish. Also, the roots of trees and shrubs on stream banks bind the soil, hold the banks in place, and afford retreats for fish and habitat for aquatic life.

Another point has to do with forest

roads. If they are built too close to stream banks, erosion and damage to fishing values result. Properly located roads in forests make it possible to sell forest products in small quantities and thus to encourage variations in ages and types of vegetative cover. Forest-edge effects along roadways improve food for many forms of wildlife. A network of roads can also be important in distributing hunters.

Log-loading areas frequently provide open areas in the forest that can be retained as valuable wildlife clearings between periodic cuttings. Other small openings in the forest (5 acres or less) can be retained for their wildlife value. Plantations of conifers intermingled with hardwood stands furnish good cover.

On public forest lands, as on private lands, the greatest benefits to forest wildlife will accrue, by and large, through the coordination of wildlife needs with the timber use. But on public lands, cover is often manipulated and improvements installed directly for the benefit of the fish and game species. In the eastern half of the country, edges have been created in the solid second-growth forest stands by clearing small areas of a quarter or half acre on the better sites. Often such plots are cleared by cutting back the forest and shrub growth that invades old fields. Such steps are regarded as initial measures, because the long-time programs should be based on the development of clearings as a step in coordinating wildlife needs with sales of timber.

Although the work has been of a limited nature, both Federal and State agencies have planted shrub and tree species in forest and woodland areas to provide food and cover for the newly stocked or underpopulated wildlife species. However, on wild land such as national forests, emphasis has been on the manipulation of the native vegetation, rather than on the introduction of nonnative species.

Stream improvement has been done on many miles of streams in the national forests and on other lands. The aim has been to convert a stream of continuous riffles into a mixture of pools and riffles, so that there will be a combination of food-producing and resting areas for trout. The best results were obtained with simple log or rock dams, that looked like a natural part of the stream. Many more lakes and ponds could be created on forest lands.

Cooperative programs are a useful development. Thirty-two cooperative wildlife-management areas, nearly 2 million acres in all, have been established on the national forests in the South and the Southeast. In each of the projects, at least 30,000 acres of Federal land has good wildlife food and cover, and boundaries suitable for hunter and fisherman control are ordinarily included.

In the projects, the States and other public agencies work to build up the numbers of wildlife. The protection is intensified. The kill is adjusted to the available portion of the wildlife population; for the most part, hunting, fishing, and trapping are regulated.

Without such controls, the excessive demand would result in the overharvesting of the animals and in one season could seriously reduce the populations built up over a period of several years. But, as in timber management, it is possible to maintain a sustained yield of fish, fur, and game, so they will be available to more people in the long run than would be possible if the areas were open to unlimited hunting and fishing.

The cooperative programs also provide for carrying out work on habitat improvement. This phase has perhaps been carried further in Virginia and West Virginia than any of the other States. As in other cooperative-management areas of the East and the South, the Forest Service may provide a dwelling in the area; the State hires a man as the resident game man on the area or part of it. His responsibility is to carry out the activities related to the intensive wildlife-management program. The work is done under a plan that is prepared by the State and the Forest Service and reviewed each month by the ranger and the local State game warden or other official.

The game manager posts the boundaries, puts out salt for game, controls predators, and helps with the fish and game stocking. He checks licenses and permits for hunting and fishing, and checks the catch and kill. In places where the forest is dense and openings are needed, the manager cuts out the invading woody growth in small clearings and creates new clearings as directed. He maintains old sawmill sites, log landings, and similar openings so that these provide wildlife edges in the years between cutting operations. He plants species that are needed for cover and food, and otherwise encourages the type of growth that is helpful to turkey, deer, grouse, squirrel, and other game under management.

Land-use programs are closely coordinated with the wildlife needs. Timber sales are administered so that stream-side vegetation is maintained. Occasional den trees are left. An attempt is made to maintain a variety of forest growth, such as persimmon, grape, dogwood, and haw, for wildlife food. Some species, like white oak, black walnut, and shagbark hickory, are recognized as valuable for their wood and for the food they produce for wildlife.

Some of the work is paid for from a special fund that is collected by the States and shared with the Forest Service. The Southeastern and Southern States have enabling legislation, which is permissive rather than mandatory, for the collection of special fees. In Virginia, a State law requires that all hunters and fishermen who use the national forests possess a national forest stamp, which costs $1. The money so collected is used in cooperation with the Forest Service to finance and operate the program.

The cooperative wildlife-management programs in national forests in the Western States have usually been concerned with big game, and particularly with adjusting the herds to the yearlong food supply. Surveys have been made of the winter range conditions and the composition and vitality of the herds. Areas have been reserved for wintering deer or elk, although frequently the animals drift off the national forests in winter. All available information has been pooled to develop management plans for big game.

In some places coordination is obtained by a series of meetings, perhaps forest by forest, at which State and Federal employees review information on the abundance of game and fish, study conditions of stream and range, and discuss, among other matters, the relation of seasons to forest-fire hazards. Available data is weighed and used to prepare joint recommendations on seasons and bag limits for consideration by the State fish and game commission; management plans on restocking of fish, beaver, and other wildlife are brought up to date; and provision is made for the distribution, camping needs, and other problems that are normally associated with handling the thousands of hunters and fishermen who use the national forests.

Everywhere the land available to wildlife is being reduced through the extension of towns, cities, industries, and transportation facilities, and the burden on the forest areas grows. Although our present forests are better suited to such species as the deer and grouse (because of the irregularity of the forest cover, including openings and different age classes of trees), and there are undoubtedly more deer, bobwhites, rabbits, and opossums now than 300 years ago, the forests are less productive of the species that benefit by old-growth stands, such as tree squirrels, turkey, marten, and other true forest animals. The stream conditions generally have declined in productive capacity.

It behooves us, therefore, to give constant thought and effort to improve these all-important factors of habitat without which there would be no wildlife.

LLOYD W. SWIFT *is chief of the Division of Wildlife Management in the Forest Service. A graduate of the University of California, he has been with the Forest Service since 1929. He has worked on range management and research and wildlife management at several field stations as well as in the Washington office.*

# TREES AND FOOD FROM ACORNS

ALBERT A. DOWNS

Acorns are more valuable than many persons realize. From them, obviously enough, come oak trees. From them also (because they are rich in carbohydrate, fat, and vitamins) come feed for hogs, deer, turkeys, and squirrels, and food for humans.

Oaks produce good crops of acorns once in 3 or 4 years, on an average—unlike the red maple and the birches, which have good crops of seed almost every year, and the longleaf pine, the beech, and some other trees, which yield seed only at long intervals.

We do not know why yields vary from year to year, but weather is probably an important factor. Late frosts may kill flowers before fertilization and even the fruit when it is in the young, tender stage. Possibly oaks need more than one growing season to build up food reserves for a large crop of fruit; oaks of the white oak group (white, post, and chestnut oaks) ripen their acorns in one season, but oaks of the red oak group (northern red, scarlet, and black oaks) need 2 years to ripen their seed.

The number of acorns produced by different trees appears to depend only on the size of the crown of the tree. Because the size of the tree crown and the diameter of the trunk are correlated, diameter, which is easier to measure, is used as a guide to the productive capacity of a tree. From a 7-year study of five species of oak in northern Georgia and western North Carolina, we found that scarlet oak was the best producer, and that acorn production decreased in the larger diameters of the white oak and the northern red oak.

The production of acorns varies not only from year to year but from tree to tree of the same sizes in the same year. In 1942, a 27-inch scarlet oak produced approximately 46,000 acorns; other scarlet oaks nearby of the same size produced a fraction of that number. Very likely some trees are good producers by heredity, and some are poor producers.

In most years, oaks, except the chestnut oak, produce more small aborted acorns than well-developed ones. These small, undeveloped seeds, often unrecognizable as such, may be the result of early insect damage or bad weather.

It would seem that plenty of seed would be available to reproduce oak woodland. But that is not so. Only a small percentage of the acorns ever have the chance to germinate and grow. Studies show that at the time of seed fall 24 percent were damaged by squirrels and birds and 30 percent by insect larvae. Only 46 percent were sound. In years of small crops, the proportion damaged by insects, squirrels, and birds is greater, and in years of large crops it is less. On the ground, insects destroy many more of the sound seed, and deer, turkeys, squirrels, chipmunks, and mice feed on them.

In one place where deer were especially numerous—one deer for about 30 acres—the entire crop was eaten, except in the heavy crop years. In another area where the deer population was estimated at one deer on 2,000 acres, many acorns were eaten, but a fair surplus was left from good crops. In general, when game is plentiful, few or no seed are left to germinate except in heavy crop years.

One system of managing oak forests for timber products is by growing the trees in even-aged stands. When the trees are mature and ready to cut, there may be no small trees established, in which case the area must be reproduced by sprouts or seed.

If superior seedling reproduction is wanted, two points must be kept in mind. First, acorns, unlike pine seed, are heavy and not dispersed far from the parent tree. Thus, the number of acorns to the acre is not significant unless they are well distributed. Second, excessive drying due to long exposure to sun and wind kills acorns.

In a good seed year, 8 to 10 trees an acre, 17 inches in diameter at breast height, would produce 1,500 to 2,000 sound acorns above those destroyed by insects and animals. With 50 percent germination, there would be 500 to 1,000 seedlings to the acre. But even with the best spacing of those seed trees, some of the seedlings would be crowded under parent trees and die. Better than that, leaving 20 trees to the acre, 12 to 16 inches in diameter, would provide the same number of acorns but they would have wider distribution and more protection from drying because of shade and the cover provided by fallen leaves. This is only one method of managing oak forests and represents the minimum as far as the seed requirements are concerned. Other methods leave larger numbers of trees to the acre for growth and seed production, giving better distribution of seed and more favorable moisture conditions.

Acorns are important in the feed of deer, squirrels, and turkeys in autumn and early winter. In deciding how much game an area can support, game managers need to know the amount of food available annually. The part supplied by acorns can be computed from the table if the number of oaks to the acre, by diameter classes, is known. In the southern Appalachians, oak stands that have been cut rather heavily in the past annually produce from 100 to 150 pounds of acorns an acre.

POUNDS OF ACORNS PRODUCED IN AN AVERAGE YEAR FOR TREES OF DIFFERENT SIZES AND SPECIES

| *Diameter of trunk 4½ feet from ground* | *Chestnut oak* | *White oak* | *Northern red oak* | *Black oak* | *Scarlet oak* |
|---|---|---|---|---|---|
| *Inches* | *Pounds* | *Pounds* | *Pounds* | *Pounds* | *Pounds* |
| 10 | 0.9 | 0.7 | 0.4 | 1.1 | 2.5 |
| 12 | 3.0 | 1.4 | 2.2 | 1.7 | 3.9 |
| 14 | 5.0 | 2.8 | 5.7 | 2.3 | 5.6 |
| 16 | 6.0 | 4.5 | 10.0 | 2.8 | 8.0 |
| 18 | 8.1 | 6.7 | 14.5 | 3.4 | 12.[illegible] |
| 22 | 9.8 | 11.3 | 17.1 | 4.6 | 17.5 |
| 26 | 10.5 | 13.1 | 13.8 | 5.8 | 18.3 |
| 30 | 10.8 | 12.5 | 10.0 | 7.0 | 18.3 |

Experimental work has shown that the nutritive value of acorns for fattening hogs is fairly high. If the acorn ration is held down to one-fourth of the food eaten, acorns are in no way harmful for fattening pigs. Excessive quantities may cause constipation, soft pork, or growth below normal. As a further precaution, the protein content of the meal mixture should be increased somewhat while feeding acorn rations, because they are high in carbohydrates but low in proteins. During the finishing-off period, acorns may be withheld, in order to correct any tendency toward soft pork.

Any farmer knowing the sizes and numbers of oaks in his wood lot can determine from the table the amount of acorns he can expect annually for hog feed. If this kind of feed is worth a cent a pound, the average oak wood lot is worth $1.50 a year for each acre just for the hog feed it produces. That is about half as much as can be expected from the wood lot in timber values. In small wood lots, farmers can know their trees as individuals and weed out the poor producers when any cutting is done. In that way the yield of acorns per acre can be increased. Aside from heredity, trees with well-developed, healthy crowns are likely to produce the most acorns.

The use of acorns as food for humans is not uncommon. The Indians in California grind the acorn kernels to a fine meal or flour and leach out the bitterness with warm water. The meal is then dried and stored to be used later as a cooked mush or baked bread. In the Eastern States, the white oak and chestnut oak acorns had been used similarly by Indians. Generally, the acorns of the white oak group are sweeter than those of the black oak group, and the acorns of the swamp chestnut oak are said to be especially sweet and edible. In Europe many species of acorns are eaten, and in times of food scarcity boiled acorns are used as a substitute for bread. In Spain, acorns of the Gramont oak are regarded as superior to chestnuts.

For those interested in hunting, a good crop of acorns can attract deer, turkeys, and squirrels.

It is possible that someone with ingenuity may discover a new method of preparing acorns for human consumption—maybe even a delicacy.

ALBERT A. DOWNS *is a silviculturist at the Lake City Branch of the Southeastern Forest Experiment Station. He has done silvicultural research for 10 years in the Northeastern and Southeastern States.*

# MANAGING UTAH'S BIG-GAME CROP

D. IRVIN RASMUSSEN, DAVID M. GAUFIN

Fifteen persons of every hundred men, women, and children in Utah bought a license to hunt big game in 1948. One deer was killed by each 10 individuals in the State—all told, more than 64,000 deer and 750 elk. The management of big game, the recreation that hunting provides, and the services connected with it form a truly important business. A visitor to Utah in late October—the time of the hunting season, the time of a general exodus to the mountains from city, town, farm, and ranch in car, truck, buckboard, wagon, and pack outfit—feels in the air how general and how enthusiastic is the response there to hunting.

It was not always so. Deer have been much more abundant in recent years than at any time since white men first visited the area. We do not know exactly how all the factors and forces operated that were responsible for producing this wildlife resource, but we do know its history, which is the story of early depletion and of man's efforts and success in restoring the herds to numbers exceeding even those that the pioneers found.

The restoration of numbers has not meant the end of the big-game problem, nevertheless. Instead, situations have developed where the animals have become too abundant for their own good and have come in conflict with ranching and livestock grazing. New, almost revolutionary, programs have therefore become necessary to guarantee a continuation on a permanent basis of both the herds of big game and the production of suitable forage on the ranges.

THE FIRST WRITTEN RECORD of the native animals and plants in the territory that is now Utah is contained in the report known as *Father Escalante's Journal,* the story of the travels of a small party lead by two Franciscan friars that left Santa Fé on July 29, 1776, and returned there January 1, 1777, without having reached their objective of Monterey, in California. The party spent September and October of 1776 in the Utah country.

Father Escalante told of killing a buffalo near the present Colorado-Utah border, taking large trout with a bow and arrow in Utah streams, and seeing many grouse, waterfowl, and rabbits. He heard that buffalo roamed not far north. Utah Lake he reported as teeming with several kinds of fish, which formed a major food of the Indians. Traveling south from Utah Lake, however, the party ran out of food. They had difficulty in obtaining even small amounts of grass seeds, pinyon nuts, and fruit of the prickly-pear from the Indians, and found it necessary to kill a number of their horses for food. Once they got a small amount of dried meat of what undoubtedly was bighorn sheep. The men traveled through and around country that now is among the best big-game hunting grounds in Utah, but no mention is made of deer or elk, both of which they noted in southwestern Colorado.

The next reports were the published letters, journals, and notes of the "mountain men" and explorers in the 1820's, but from them it is difficult to determine the actual game conditions. The accounts described the western part of the State as devoid of game, but they reported its presence in the mountains, particularly in the northern part. Buffalo and antelope apparently were abundant in the northern valleys. The book, *Leonard's Narrative,* gives an account of Capt. Joseph R. Walker and a party of some 40 men who journeyed westward and reached the shores of Great Salt Lake in August of 1833. On the advice of the Indians, before starting westward they killed buffalo and antelope until "in a few days each man was provided with about 60 pounds of substantial meat, which was packed upon our horses."

On August 22, in 1826, Jedediah Strong Smith left the Great Salt Lake with 15 men for southern California. Smith's route was by Utah Lake and southward through the valley of the Sevier River in central Utah. The account of this trip is given by Harrison C. Dale in *The Ashley-Smith Explorations.* In a letter dated July 12, 1827, Smith wrote, "From this lake (Utah) I found no more signs of buffalo; there are a few antelope and mountain sheep, and an abundance of black tailed hares."

J. Cecil Alter in an article, *W. A. Ferris in Utah, 1830–1835,* quoted that trapper as follows:

"September 4, 1834, four Indians calling themselves 'Sann-pitch' came into camp bringing to my surprise, several deer skins. . . . The barrenness of their country, and scarcity of game, compel them to live by separate families, either in the mountains or in the plains. . . . Here the women and children are employed in gathering grasshoppers, crickets, ants, and various other species of insetcs which are carefully preserved for food, together with roots and grass seed. From the mountains they bring the nuts . . . of the pine, acorns from the dwarf oaks, as well as the different kinds of berries and the inner bark of the pine. . . . In the meantime, the men are actively employed in hunting small animals such as prairie dogs, squirrels, and field mice, and larger animals or birds, which fortune sometimes places within the reach of their arrows. They likewise take fish, with simple instruments of their own invention. . . ."

Ferris' camp was pitched near what is now the geographical center of the State.

The year 1847 saw the entrance of the Mormon pioneers into the valley of the Great Salt Lake and the establishment of the first white settlements. Contemporary writers recounted the hardships the pioneers endured and their difficulty in obtaining enough food to survive, but they seldom mentioned big game.

Capt. Howard Stansbury in his book, *Exploration and Survey of the Valley of the Great Salt Lake of Utah,* reported: "During the winter and spring (1847–48) the inhabitants (of Salt Lake Valley) were much straightened for food; and game being very scarce in the country, they were reduced to the necessity of digging roots from the ground, and living upon the hides of animals which they had previously made use of for roofing their cabins.

but which were now torn off for food."

It is certain, however, that the coming of civilization, with its free and its unregulated use of the ranges, with unrestricted hunting, and the establishment of ranches, towns, and cities soon reduced seriously the numbers of deer, elk, bighorn sheep, and antelope that were originally present.

With the first settlers came the first domestic livestock, which were grazed near the valley towns. In 1860, milk cows and draft oxen constituted 62 percent of the 34,000 cattle reported in the agricultural census for the Territory. After the danger of Indian depredations had ceased and the need for additional ranges developed, the cattle and sheep were moved into the canyons and onto the mountains. By 1890, suitable grazing areas of the entire State were being exploited in severe and unrestricted free use by domestic livestock. That year, 360,000 cattle and 2,000,000 sheep were reported in the Utah Territory.

At the turn of the century the mountain ranges had been depleted of much of their native forage, and numbers of big game had declined until action was necessary to save both.

THE FIRST CONSERVATION measures came in the 1890's. In 1897, the first Utah forest reserves were established. Additional areas were set aside in the next decade. The regulation of grazing by livestock was then inaugurated.

A fish and game department was established in Utah in 1894, but few regulations or restrictions were set. The open season on deer extended for 5 or 6 months. Several animals were permitted each hunter. No hunting license was required of residents until 1907.

The destruction of big game had proceeded so far that in 1908 it was deemed wise to prohibit all hunting of elk, deer, antelope, and bighorn sheep for 5 years. The people realized that immediate and drastic action was necessary to prevent a famine of game.

The legislature in 1913 enacted a "buck law" that forbade the killing of doe deer, because the female had to be protected if deer were to increase. The hunting season was shortened to 15 days in early October, and elk, antelope, and bighorn sheep were given complete protection.

The Utah Fish and Game Commissioner's tenth biennial report, which included the year 1913, said in defense of the new regulation: "The season opens generally before snowfall, which gives good protection to the deer. It assists him in escaping the aim of the huntsmen, and hampers the huntsmen in his efforts to track the game." The report also gave the first recorded estimate of the number of deer taken by hunters: "From the best information obtainable approximately six hundred deer were killed in Utah this year, yet an increase is observed." In 1916, the forest rangers reported there were some 8,400 deer on the national forests of the State.

Later, the State legislature established a series of large game preserves, which included many of the more favorable deer and elk ranges. By 1925 there were 11 State game preserves covering 940,000 acres in the national forests. Enforcement of game laws by wardens and forest rangers became more strict, and stockmen waged constant war against coyotes, wolves, bobcats, and mountain lions to protect their flocks and herds. The regulated use of the mountain ranges meant better forage and vegetative cover. Suitable conditions for big game thus were created—food, cover, control of predators, and protection.

Under the protection given them, the mule deer increased remarkably. The deer population in the national forests increased from 13,500 in 1920, to 18,500 in 1925, to 55,000 in 1930. The State game department and wildlife enthusiasts were proud of the results. An estimated 800 bucks were killed in 1920, 1,400 in 1925, and 6,400 in 1930.

But the protection apparently did not benefit the antelope and bighorn sheep. Except for one small, isolated herd, the native elk had been exterminated. Protection alone could not be depended upon to restore their numbers. An attempt was made therefore to reestablish them by importing animals. From 1912 to 1915, 155 elk from the Jackson Hole and northern Yellowstone herds were released in 6 localities. Sportsmen, ranchers, and other interested persons paid the costs of handling and shipping them.

The imported elk multiplied rapidly—so fruitful were they in their new homes that conflicts with the private property owners soon arose. By 1921 the legislature had to authorize the game commissioner to kill elk that were damaging farms or other property.

Overpopulation soon occurred. The herds of elk had grown by 1925 to the extent that some of the suitable areas were fully stocked, and competition with the domestic livestock on private and public lands was reported. The problem no longer could be solved by killing a few marauding elk.

Game wardens and forest officers learned from field investigations that the summer range in some places was fully stocked and that the winter ranges were being seriously over-browsed by too many big-game animals.

Surveys in winter disclosed hundreds of deer and elk in some localities, but townspeople, unimpressed, questioned the accuracy of the investigators and branded as heresy any suggestion of a change in the laws that, within a generation, had helped to restore the animals to the ranges. To sportsmen, any game official who made such a proposal was guilty of violating a sacred trust. The general public refused to believe that there actually could be too many big-game animals.

Thus the job of the game administrators was complex. It was one thing to recognize that overpopulations of big game did exist, and quite another to try to take corrective action without adequate authority.

The problem of administration was complicated also by the competition between big game and domestic livestock for forage on the ranges. The so-called "public-land States" in the West have a comparatively small amount of cultivated land but large areas of range land. Some of the range is privately owned, but most is administered by Federal and State agencies. Utah, for example, has 52,700,000 acres of land, of which only 3.2 percent is cultivated. Nearly all of the rest has economic value as either summer or winter grazing lands for domestic livestock. In truth, the only lands not grazed by livestock are certain barren or inaccessible sections, a comparatively small area of national parks, and some small tracts protected as city watersheds. Of the grazing land, 5,000,000 acres are in private ownership; 9,000,000 are national forests; 25,000,000 are administered by the Bureau of Land Management; 1,740,000 are Indian reservations; and 3,650,000 are owned by the State and counties.

As a rule, therefore, wherever big-game animals are present one also finds domestic livestock. Both depend on native plants. Competition for forage (sometimes real, at other times imaginary) is a factor that must be considered in any big-game-management program in the West.

The elk herd on the Nebo range in central Utah exemplifies the problems. The herd, which has passed through the cycle of early depletion, restoration, and overpopulation, ranges over a relatively small, narrow, rugged area of approximately 250,000 acres of national forest, State, and private lands. Farms, towns, and major highways surround the unit. The mountains, more than 5,000 feet above the valley floor, are bisected by the steep, timbered canyons. An unknown number of native elk were present on the ranges when the pioneers settled in the valleys below; the last ones probably disappeared about 1880.

In 1913 and 1914, 48 head obtained from the Yellowstone were released on the Nebo range. They flourished in their new environment under the watchful eyes of an interested public and sympathetic landowners. Everything went well for the next few years. Then the elk began visiting haystacks and cultivated fields at the base of the mountain. The Utah State Fish and Game Department attempted to settle for damages to haystacks and hired herders to drive the invading elk back into the hills. Neither action was satisfactory. The damage still continued. Game wardens killed 84 trespassing bull elk.

In 1924, when the 48 elk had increased to an estimated 450, it became apparent to the land administrators, landowners, and game officials that some new and drastic control measures would be necessary. Landowners and stockmen demanded reduction of the herd. Sportsmen and the general public opposed the demands at first but finally agreed to shooting bulls. The idea of killing the cows, however, was abhorrent to them.

In 1925, in the first elk hunt by sportsmen, 100 bulls were killed. The hue and cry for and against the elk arose again. Many considered killing the elk a mistake. Others contended the mistake was in planting elk in the first place, maintaining that damage to private property and range could not be avoided regardless of the number of animals. No hunt was held in 1926.

To resolve the dilemma, the Utah Legislature in the year 1927 established a supervisory committee, the State Game Refuge Committee and Board of Elk Control, whose members included representatives of sportsmen, wool growers, cattle and horse breeders, the Forest Service, the State Park Commission, and the commissioners of the county in which a particular game refuge was situated. The State Fish and Game Commissioner was chairman.

The duties of the board were to supervise the establishing, adjusting, opening, and closing of elk refuges; designating seasons and localities in which elk hunting could be done, and determining the sex and the number of animals that could be killed. Regulation of the kill was accomplished by the sale of nontransferable permits to hunt elk to sportsmen selected by public drawing.

At its first meeting in 1927 the board authorized the sale of 150 permits for bulls on the Nebo area; 100 bulls were killed. Afterwards, an argument developed as to the size of the elk population. The estimates ranged from 500 to 1,500, and it was evident that more information was necessary. In February 1928, State wardens, forest rangers, and others, taking advantage of heavy snow that had crowded the elk onto the foothills, made an actual count of 637 animals.

In the fall of 1928 there was another hunt for 150 bulls. Landowners and the stockmen maintained that the taking of surplus bulls only was not correcting the situation because there continued to be more cows with calves and the total herd was increasing. Sportsmen, however, remained adamant in their opposition to shooting cows.

Finally, in a meeting of land administrators, stockmen and farmers, and sportsmen, it was agreed that the elk population should be maintained between 500 and 600 head. That agree-

802062°—49——38

ment has been the basis of management ever since. The board has authorized the sale of permits on the basis of the best estimates of number and what the herd would produce. Experience has shown, however, that the estimates of both herd numbers and productivity have been conservative and that for several years the herd was larger than the number provided for in the agreement.

By 1929, opposition to killing cows was lessening. A hunt for 300 elk of either sex was authorized, and 140 bulls and 101 cows were killed. Since 1929, special permits have been issued regularly for elk of both sexes. There is now little or no general opposition to shooting cow elk. In places where hunters must make a choice, the demand for permits to kill cows exceeds that for permits to kill bulls.

Twenty-one special hunts have been conducted on the Nebo range since the first hunt in 1925. The areas on which the hunting has been permitted have varied. The ratio of sexes authorized to be killed has been adjusted from year to year so as to maintain a balanced and healthy herd. The success of hunters has been about 90 percent.

The outstanding result of this flexible form of management is that approximately 600 elk remain on the Nebo range—this despite the fact that 4,397 animals have been removed by sportsmen, 173 have been trapped by State officials and transplanted to new ranges, and 219 have been killed on farm by wardens to prevent damage to crops. Under such a management program over a 35-year period, the original plant of 48 elk has increased twelvefold and produced 4,789 elk.

THE MULE DEER also were creating an acute situation in the early 1930's. Efforts of the State Fish and Game Department and sportsmen for the previous two decades had been directed to the production of more deer. That there could be too many deer was as hard to comprehend as it had been to realize that there were too many elk.

Does were still legally protected under the "buck law." Killing bucks only could not regulate numbers. No one had the authority to take corrective action. The most serious result of this inaction, from the standpoint of wildlife management, was that the winter game ranges were being seriously overbrowsed and permanently damaged by the excessive number of deer. Winter losses also were becoming alarmingly heavy.

The Board of Elk Control had effectively managed the elk herds for 6 years. In March 1933, the legislature amended the law, changed its name, and extended its powers.

The new committee was designated the State Game Refuge Committee and Board of Big Game Control. It had five members—representatives of cattle and horse breeders, wool growers, sportsmen, the Forest Service, and the State Fish and Game Director, who was chairman. Their acts were to have the full force and effect of law.

The new board was authorized to define more accurately the boundaries of the game preserves and regulate travel on them; to designate additional refuges for big game; and to conduct investigations, as a basis for designating special hunting seasons and areas and the number and sex of big-game animals to be killed. Thus, adequate authority to handle the mule deer problem was provided. The exercise of this authority, however, was another matter.

Public resistance to any reduction in the deer herds became apparent at hearings of the board in 1934. After lengthy discussions, the board authorized the issuance of 1,600 special permits for antlerless deer for 3 overstocked areas. In consequence, posters and editorials all over the State pleaded, "Don't shoot the does!" Although threatened with injunctions, the board stood by its decision. But only 728 of the 1,600 permits were sold. The public had not learned that the preservation of the deer depended upon the proper harvest of the surplus.

Education as to actual conditions and the need for action had been insufficient. Sportsmen were invited to visit overbrowsed winter ranges to see for themselves that when the numbers of animals and their food supply were out of balance nature took wasteful corrective measures. The carcasses of deer under the high-lined and depleted browse convinced most of them that the winter food supply was insufficient and that something had to be done.

Some agreed that the herd had to be reduced to prevent waste of animals, preserve the food supply of the deer, and utilize the surplus. Others thought that the way out was to provide additional feed; among them were individuals who attributed most of the damage to the range to grazing by sheep and cattle. They suggested that all the forage on the winter game ranges be reserved for the deer. Still others believed "hard winters" were to blame, and the trouble could be corrected by feeding hay to carry the deer over winter.

Trained range men were convinced that the most serious grazing problem grew out of the competition of deer against deer for the limited amount of winter forage, rather than deer against livestock.

Supplemental winter-feeding programs appealed to the public as a humane and logical procedure. Game administrators started to do so on several areas, but the deer continued to die even where they were fed various kinds of hay and concentrates.

It became obvious that the program had serious faults, and an attempt was made to check on what was happening and the possibility of improving the methods or finding new and suitable foods. In a study, *Supplemental Winter Feeding of Mule Deer in Northern Utah,* it was shown that winter losses of nearly 20 percent occurred from malnutrition even during average winters, despite the intensive supplemental feeding of a variety of feeds on the crowded areas. On the other hand, heavy winter losses were shown to be abnormal among mule deer wherever enough native forage was available. On the basis of these investigations, it was recommended that hunting removals be sufficient to reduce the population to the carrying capacity of the winter range on all areas where supplemental feeding appeared necessary.

Despite some continued opposition, the board went ahead with special hunts of antlerless deer and deer of either sex on the problem areas. The special hunts have been held every year since 1934, except 1936 and 1937. Under this program, more than 150,000 deer have been taken by sportsmen, besides the regular buck kill.

At public hearings by the board, conducted annually in different parts of the State, all interested persons have opportunity to voice their opinions.

The hearings are followed by an executive session in which the problems of individual game herds and local viewpoints are considered. In the management of big game and range, the board has the help of three specialists, and representatives of the Forest Service, Bureau of Land Management, and the Utah State Fish and Game Department, who make detailed field investigations and coordinate information obtained through census and forage-utilization surveys conducted cooperatively by local game wardens, forest officers, and graziers. The board then formulates the hunting program.

The effectiveness of the program of regulated hunting is illustrated by a comparison of the Kaibab Plateau deer herd of Arizona with the Fishlake Forest deer herd of Utah. After 20 years of protection, the Kaibab herd reached an estimated peak of nearly 100,000 deer. Because of opposition, hunting was not permitted until the peak year of 1924, and then only a few hundred animals were taken. In the years immediately following 1924 thousands of deer died of starvation—the direct result of cumulative range depletion.

A similar upward trend in deer

numbers on the Fishlake Forest was largely checked by an aggressive program of controlled hunting. Even there, however, some range depletion occurred and losses from malnutrition were not entirely prevented.

Between 1920 and 1947, 34,000 deer were harvested from the Kaibab through hunting and trapping live animals for restocking purposes. This is but 16 percent of the 208,000 herd that have been removed through legal hunting from the Fishlake herd during the same period. Furthermore, the number of deer on the Fishlake in 1947 was three to four times greater than on the Kaibab. Thus, with a smaller herd in 1920 (actually one-eighth as large), the Fishlake area has produced six times as many deer for the hunters and now has nearly four times as many deer. It is believed that had the Kaibab herd been stabilized at 30,000 or so (the desirable number for the range). and the net increase removed annually through hunting, it also could have produced nearly 200,000 deer.

WHAT CAN AND CANNOT be done is shown by the experience in Utah.

Simply to protect big game from hunting will not insure a high level of production in the future. Neither can the number to be harvested be determined solely by the desires of the hunters. The number of big game that can be maintained and produced for sportsman hunting must be based upon the optimum amount of feed in the form of forage that the range will produce. To allow our game herds to build up beyond the ability of the range to supply adequate forage is a form of deficit spending. It may produce good hunting for a few years—only a few years. There must be a sustained yield of forage for the animals to guarantee a sustained yield of big game.

While we cannot crop our big-game herds as efficiently as livestock herds, the harvest can be increased if hunters keep crippling losses to a minimum, predators are controlled, and, most important of all, the number of animals is kept in balance with available food supply. The latter can only be accomplished by the removal of the surplus animals, male or female.

Although it is generally accepted that some cow elk can be hunted without reducing an elk herd, many hunters in Utah still believe that the sole objective in removing doe deer is to reduce the total number of deer. Others still believe that killing does is never justified. It is true that does must be removed if herds are to be reduced, but even in properly managed and healthy herds, removals of does are justified and necessary. The annual increase, which consists of both males and females, must be cropped by hunter harvest if the herd is to be stabilized.

Experience in Utah and Idaho has shown that healthy mule deer herds can produce annually, on a sustained-yield basis, approximately 25 animals per 100 deer in the winter population, if the kill consists of both sexes. This type of removal results in maximum returns in deer to the sportsmen, provides for perpetuation of the capital resource—the forage supply—and insures healthy and stabilized deer herds.

D. IRVIN RASMUSSEN *is in charge of wildlife management for the Intermountain Region of the Forest Service. Since 1928, he has been engaged primarily in research and management of western fish and game animals. He is a graduate of Brigham Young University and has graduate degrees from the University of Illinois.*

DAVID M. GAUFIN *holds a degree in wildlife management from Utah State Agricultural College. His first work was with the Utah Cooperative Wildlife Research Unit on sage grouse nesting and predation studies in southeastern Idaho in 1939–40. He was with the United States Corps of Engineers, 1941–46; and served as Federal-aid project leader, Utah Fish and Game Department, on big-game studies from 1946 to 1947. He is now supervisor of game management in the Utah State Fish and Game Department.*

# FORESTS AND FISH

PAUL R. NEEDHAM, FRED W. JOHNSON

Nearly all of our forest waters are trout waters, except those in the warmer localities in the Middle West and South. We do not know the full extent of fishing waters in all our forests, but in the national forests alone there are more than 90,000 miles of streams and 1.5 million acres of ponds and lakes.

Several factors determine the suitability of streams for trout. Size of stream or lake is of little moment; temperature, food, and general aquatic conditions are the items that count.

Just as our forests and other soil covers developed where soil conditions and climate permitted, fish life that we now know evolved slowly and survived through generations to fit into definite environments with interdependent patterns of habitat. It follows, then, that any misuse of these hereditary watersheds and the streams draining them will change environmental conditions favorable to trout and other life that is associated with a good forest cover.

A multitude of physical, chemical, and biological conditions affect the average trout waters: Oxygen, carbon dioxide, alkalinity of the water, food, shade, floods, ice, droughts, and temperature, among others.

The best trout waters usually range from 65° to 75° F. in the hottest times of the year. Eastern brook trout can stand short periods of exposure to temperatures close to 80°, and rainbow trout have been taken in water of 85°, but these are not good conditions. Brown trout, too, can tolerate temperatures higher than 81°; in excessively hot periods they work themselves into the gravel bottoms of pools that are cooled by upwelling water. The temperature tolerances of salmon and steelhead parallel those of rainbow trout.

Removal of shade from the margins of streams and exposure to the full heat of the sun is the principal reason why the lower reaches of many once excellent trout streams have become too warm for trout under modern conditions. Many streams (especially in the Eastern States) that used to produce good eastern brook trout fishing, by reason of high temperatures, have become better suited to brown trout. Leaving the cover strips of streamside vegetation (as now practiced by Federal agencies in logging operations) to shade watercourses of small streams from the full heat of the sun will go far toward preventing excessive stream temperatures, especially in the downstream reaches at lower elevations.

THE OXYGEN required by fish is dissolved in the water and is absorbed through the thin membranes of their gill filaments. In clean, clear, trout streams, oxygen is always present in ample quantities for fish life.

In polluted waters, however, oxygen is consumed, and carbon dioxide and other gases of decomposition are increased in the oxidation and reduction of organic or inorganic wastes. When this condition prevails, destruction of fish life may occur. Under conditions of severe pollution, all aquatic life may be destroyed. Man-caused pollution has rightly been termed our "national shame."

Natural pollution can also occur. One such is the winterkilling of fish in lakes—usually due to gradual reduction of oxygen in water under a layer of ice and snow, coupled with a great increase in carbon dioxide.

TROUT FOODS are supplied from both land and water. Insects are blown or fall into water from streamside vegetation. Analyses of stomach contents have indicated that approximately 10 percent of the food of trout is supplied from the land and 90 percent by the water itself. Riffles are the larders of streams. To stones in any normal riffle cling a myriad of immature insects of all sizes, shapes, and varieties.

Stream larders are usually well-stocked with food of many kinds. Trout waters draining granitic or rocky basins and lacking in dissolved mineral food-stuffs are usually those poorest in foods. Strongly alkaline waters that drain rich soils, either forested or farmed, are the richest in foods. The maintenance of the soil cover through good watershed management improves the capacity of streams to produce fish.

The dominant stream foods eaten by trout are the immature forms of insects such as Mayflies, stone flies, caddisflies, aquatic trueflies, beetles. The immature stages of dragonflies and damsel flies frequently bulk large in the diet of trout, as also do crayfish, hellgrammites, small snails and clams, and small fish.

The stocking of hatchery-reared fish is conducted on a large scale by the State conservation agencies, the Fish and Wildlife Service of the Department of the Interior, and the Department of Agriculture. Many millions of fish, principally trout, are annually transported in tank trucks and widely distributed in both streams and lakes. Back-country streams and lakes remote from roads are planted from pack strings of horses and mules that carry small cans of fish long distances by trails. Today, except in the most remote districts, few lakes remain barren of fish life. Without hatcheries, it would have been impossible to establish fish in many lakes and streams that were originally barren of fish life.

Although the establishment of trout populations in barren waters has provided much excellent sport, planting hatchery fish in the streams where fish were already abundant has not produced results commensurate with costs of the process. Indeed, only in recent years have we found out that in our best trout streams, nature does better work of stocking than man does. Since it was discovered in the sixteenth century that eggs of fish could be pressed by hand from fish, fertilized, and reared artificially, it has been assumed that hatcheries were the answer. No critical analysis of the survival of hatchery-reared fish was made until after the First World War. Investigations at that time caused an almost complete reversal of opinion with respect to fish hatcheries: During more than a century, millions of dollars had been spent on hatchery programs without question or test of their value.

It used to be commonly believed that there was virtually a total loss of the eggs naturally spawned by trout in streams. Several investigators have since proved that the opposite is true. A. S. Hazzard discovered that approximately 80 percent of eastern brook eggs survived through hatching in streams near Ithaca, N. Y., and D. F. Hobbs, working in New Zealand on introduced trout and salmon, found an average mortality to hatching of only 8.7 percent. He also found the efficiency of fertilization to be more than 99 percent. All the observations indicate a high survival of eggs and fish to the time they leave the gravel nests in the stream beds; after that, the losses may be heavy because of floods, predators, and other conditions.

Creel-counts on the survival of 2- to 3-inch fingerlings planted in streams have indicated extremely low survivals to anglers of usually less than 3 percent, the average being about 1 percent. Of yearling 6-inch, legal-size fish planted during open fishing seasons, 70 to 80 percent have survived to be caught. Even with fish of that size, average survivals are usually less than 25 percent in streams. In lakes, much better survivals have been obtained with legal-size fish. South Twin Lake in the Deschutes National Forest in Oregon regularly returns around 60 to 65 percent of 6- to 8-inch fish planted in it.

Research in fisheries has demonstrated that the planting of large fish just before or during angling seasons produces much better survivals than plantings in late summer or fall.

Few hatchery-reared fish can survive overwinter in streams. The wild and naturally propagated trout do suffer heavy overwinter mortalities, too, but their rates of survival are considerably higher than those of hatchery fish. Work at Convict Creek in eastern California by Paul R. Needham, J. W. Moffett, and D. W. Slater demonstrated that overwinter losses of wild brown trout of all sizes averaged 62 percent and that more than 85 percent of the fish hatched in the stream in any given year would be lost in the first 18 months of life. Variable survival conditions in any given season, rather than the number of young produced, determined the number of fish that later reached catchable size. It was also shown that over a 5-year period natural reproduction in Convict Creek contributed each year an average of 2,750 fingerlings, 3 to 4 inches long, to each mile of stream.

These facts lead to the conclusion that we badly need a critical review and revision of hatchery-rearing programs and methods to get the most out of the costly, hatchery-reared fish. We can also conclude that with hatcheries we can only supplement to a slight extent the fish produced by natural propagation.

It behooves us, therefore, to look toward stream improvement and maintenance of the stream habitat as offering a better solution of our problems than the questionable and uneconomical program of merely planting more fish. Good fishing in streams depends mainly on good forestry and land management. The streams furnish the "room and board" for fish. In turn, if their environment is maintained and improved, it will provide the long-term basis for continued and permanent good fishing in our forest waters.

Dams may be another threat to migratory fish. The large, multiple-purpose development projects under way in many major western river basins hold an ominous and uncertain future for the continued maintenance of the salmon and steelhead runs. With many high dams already constructed and many others planned or under construction, it is imperative that good forest practices be followed on the watersheds that are still open and available to migratory fish. In fact, if the main rivers are blocked by high dams, much good can be accomplished on tributaries that remain accessible for spawning purposes if our modern standards are applied in timber removal, grazing, road building, and other factors.

Our stake is heavy in sea-run fishery resources such as salmon and steelhead of the Pacific coast. The salmon and steelhead fishery of the Columbia River alone brings in approximately 17.4 million dollars annually; the entire fishery in California, Washington, and Oregon adds 50 million to 60 million dollars each year to our national economy. Every effort is being made by the Fish and Wildlife Service, as well as by conservation agencies of the States concerned, to work out feasible maintenance programs in light of the problems presented.

The Willamette River in Oregon has a fine run of large, spring chinook salmon, for which there is an intense sport fishery. This run alone produces around a million dollars annually. With such values represented, it is a basic necessity that unblocked tributaries of the lower Snake, Columbia, Willamette, and Sacramento Rivers, and other western streams that drain large forests be fully protected with the best and most modern watershed-management plans.

Fish ladders may help on low dams, but they are useless on high dams. Protection of soils and the forests on the watersheds is more important by far. Control of the lands will result in control of the rivers.

One answer to this problem would be to set aside by legislative action certain streams as fish refuges for spawning purposes on which no dams would ever be permitted. Another answer being considered is to develop lower tributaries that remain unblocked into spawning and nursery streams for salmon and steelhead. Many of the headwater tributaries lie within the boundaries of the national forests, where long-range land- and water-management plans aid these resources.

A major weakness of many of the basin-wide water-development programs is that of starting work at the wrong ends of our rivers. Water control should begin in the headwaters where the rains fall and the streams originate.

Waters of normal streams are supplied mainly by seepage from rainfall stored in soils. Denuded soils cannot efficiently hold back rainfall and melting snow. With rapid runoff from eroded lands, heavy floods occur and cause millions of dollars' damage annually. Floods often are followed by extremely low stream flows in summer, springs dry up, and ground water is reduced. Excessively high water temperatures usually accompany low flows and in both the East and the West thousands of miles of potential trout waters have been eliminated by this cause alone.

Most of us have observed that in areas where fires are controlled, where good practices are followed in grazing forest and farm lands, and where sufficient ground cover remains to hold the soil in place, the streams produce the best angling. On watersheds where good upstream management is practiced, extremes of flows in winter and summer are avoided. Where poor land management, ill-planned cutting, forest fires, or forest practices deplete the cover of headwater basins, the resulting increase in rate of discharge carries topsoil downstream in flash floods, scouring out aquatic life and reducing the productivity of streams for years to come.

Rains that follow forest fires sometimes pour large quantities of ash and other debris into streams and make them strongly alkaline so that fish are killed. Spawning beds become clogged with silt and eggs, and fish foods are destroyed. Logging debris left in the streams and piled into huge log jams by floodwaters can completely block off access by fish to their upstream spawning grounds. The clear-cutting in past years of the Douglas-fir forests in the West has harmed many trout waters, and conservation agencies are faced with a major problem in keeping migratory routes open and free from log jams.

Good watersheds are popularly associated with mature forests, but they may not necessarily be the most efficient watershed cover because trees in dense stands intercept snow and rain and much of the moisture therein may be evaporated before it can reach or enter the soil. Trees, both large and small, soil litter, herbaceous vegetation, and grasses can be manipulated by man; climate, soils, and underlying geological formations cannot.

It is good to write that forest practices initiated by several agencies in connection with logging operations on public lands are doing much to correct the poor practices we have described. The distributed cutting of small blocks of timber, leaving ample seed-tree plots, saving streamside strips, eliminating logging across or down streams, removing or burning slash, and other corrective measures are doing much to preserve our national aquatic values. Destructive logging is not universal or necessary. Our forests can be harvested in a way that works a minimum of harm to fish life.

From the standpoint of maintenance of good trout waters, it is quite possible to increase flows through proper logging and manipulation of timber stands. It is possible to have good trout waters when watersheds are conservatively used by domestic livestock in grassy and browse-covered areas. Most important is the degree of use made of these resources. Herein lies the difference between proper and exploitive use. The importance of properly maintaining our watersheds, of regulating and correlating the uses to which they are put, cannot be overemphasized.

IN THESE DAYS when evaluations are being made of all our natural resources, it would be well to consider the value of clean, productive waters to the economy of the Nation. Corn, wheat, automobiles, and percolators can all be easily evaluated, but the value of a fish in a creel is difficult to determine. Various agencies, Federal and State, and private individuals have made an effort to appraise fishery resources, but even today there is no standard method in use. The problem is extremely important in view of the irrigation, power, and flood-control programs being developed on practically all major stream systems in order to measure the benefits or damages that may result to wildlife resources from the proposed improvements.

The Oregon State Game Commission has used a figure of $5 a pound for sport-caught trout—the amount that it costs a fisherman in gasoline, oil, hotels, food, tackle, and other items to catch a pound of trout. On that basis, four popular fishing lakes in Oregon—Diamond, South Twin, East, and Paulina—in 1947 produced a total of 85,130 pounds of trout as determined from creel-census work on them. At $5 a pound, the catch was worth $425,650 to the economy of the State.

How much citizens of the State benefited in health and fun from the recreation and outdoor activity is a matter of values that are hard to measure but of great importance. If one could attach a money value to the sport, say $10 a pound for the trout, the four lakes alone would have produced close to a million dollars in a year. One can apply his own arithmetic to the other hundreds of lakes and thousands of miles of streams in Oregon that are intensively fished each year by some 265,000 persons.

But the arithmetic cannot measure the value fully. Nor should it. As every fisherman knows, "There is more to fishing than fish."

And, to summarize, good fishing is more than water. Good fishing depends on good land management.

As Dr. Ira N. Gabrielson, Director of the Wildlife Management Institute, has said, "Soil and water are the two most vital resources of this Nation and their proper management is of vital concern to every citizen. The retention and best management of the fertile soils and the greatest possible utilization of the biological productive capacity of the water is of increasing necessity to the maintenance of national health and prosperity."

PAUL R. NEEDHAM *received a doctor's degree from Cornell University in 1928. He taught in the University of Rochester for 2 years and joined the research staff of the Fish and Wildlife Service in 1931. From 1932 to 1945 he was in charge of trout and salmon work in California. In 1945 he joined the Oregon State Game Commission as director of fisheries. He resigned in late 1948 to accept a post as fishery management biologist with the Fish and Wildlife Service on the Columbia River program. He is now professor of zoology at the University of California. He is the author of the book Trout Streams and other publications dealing with fish culture, hatcheries, stream and lake stocking, and management problems.*

FRED W. JOHNSON *did undergraduate work in forest and range management at Ohio State University and graduate work at the University of California. From 1928 to 1939, he was ranger, range examiner, assistant forest supervisor, and wildlife manager in California national forests. From 1939 to 1944 he served as wildlife manager on the national forests of the Southwest and forest supervisor of the Kaibab National Forest. In 1946 he transferred to the Forest Service regional headquarters in Missoula, Mont., where he is in charge of the section of wildlife management.*

# ACTION ON THE BLUE RIDGE

THEODORE C. FEARNOW, I. T. QUINN

Two persons met by chance on the banks of a Blue Ridge Mountain stream in the George Washington National Forest one day in the early 1930's. One was the new forest ranger; the other was a local resident. They paused for a friendly exchange of words, as is the custom in the Blue Ridge country, and tarried on the banks of the clear trout stream to eat their lunches.

As they sat there, a squirrel frisked nervously in a nearby hickory tree and finally dodged into a hollow limb. The Virginian, obviously a man interested in wildlife, turned to the ranger and asked, "You foresters look after the trees, but why don't you also look after the squirrel that lives in them, the turkey that roosts in them, and the deer that browses under them?"

The ranger explained that wildlife in the national forest was "primarily the responsibility of the State" and that consequently a Federal employee could not do much about it. That was a right bad state of affairs, the Virginian remarked, pointing out that the squirrel "belonged" to the State, but the tree that gave it both food and shelter was the "property of the Federal Government," and that the poor squirrel was like the man without a country.

The ranger and the Virginian pondered the situation carefully, then and later. The ranger, A. R. Cochran, became supervisor at Roanoke of the Jefferson National Forest. The Virginian, Justus H. Cline, of Stuarts Draft, later became a director in the American Wildlife Federation and a leader in the Virginia Academy of Science. During the years that followed, both men became active in shaping a plan for cooperative wildlife management. The plan was designed to bring "the squirrel, the den tree, and the hickory nut crop" under a coordinated program of management. The meeting of those two men has come to be generally recognized as the starting point for the widely known Virginia Plan for State-Forest Service cooperation in handling the wildlife resources on 1½ million acres of national forest land in Virginia.

Up to then, the management of wildlife in the Blue Ridge had been confined mostly to a few game refuges, and the history of wildlife there was monotonously like the history of wildlife in most parts of the United States. In three centuries, from the settlement of Jamestown in 1607, the wildlife had gone from abundance to depletion.

In the haze-shrouded Blue Ridge forests of oaks, hickories, and pines, chestnut, yellow-poplar, and hemlock, sassafras, the persimmon, chinquapin, pawpaw, and wild grape lived the white-tailed deer, a staple item of food for the early Virginia settlers; it is often said that the shooting eyes that won the American Revolution owed much of their skill to experience gained in hunting this fleet-footed animal. As settlers occupied the land, the buffalo, elk, puma, and wolf were gradually exterminated. Later, mountain farming in the Blue Ridge hastened soil erosion and depletion of fertility. The struggling population, existing at a hardship level, created (as it always does) a serious threat to wildlife; hunting and fishing, relentlessly pursued with little regard to season or other restrictions, left the Blue Ridge an impoverished wildlife province by the turn of the present century. Exhaustion of the wildlife resource was in many ways indicative of the general debility brought on by abusive occupancy of the land.

When the national forest program was launched in Virginia in 1912, the Blue Ridge was known as a region of low economic status. Erosion had exposed bare red soil in many places. Forests had been logged off and burned.

Wildlife had been depleted until much of the native fauna had been exterminated and the more resistant species reduced to a mere remnant of their former numbers. Even the white-tailed deer (*Odocoileus virginianus*), named by scientists in honor of Virginia, had virtually reached the point of extinction. Agriculture had ceased to be profitable on much of the area. Small wonder that a prominent Virginian, familiar with Blue Ridge history and a resident for more than half a century, referred to it as "the most abused mountain range in America."

But now the people of the Blue Ridge have a good deal of enthusiasm as they assume an active role in the broad program of restoring the resources.

THE COOPERATIVE PROGRAM for restoring wildlife to Virginia's mountain counties is rooted in a number of important actions. In 1911, Congress passed the Weeks Law, which authorized a program of purchases of forest lands for watershed protection, under which important forest areas on the headwaters of major rivers were added to the national forest system. Scattered units in the Appalachians in Virginia have been consolidated to form two national forests, the George Washington and the Jefferson. The forests included 1,409,060 acres on June 30, 1948; approximately 40,000 acres more have been approved for purchase. The two forests follow the backbone of the Blue Ridge for several hundred miles in Virginia and extend westward and northward to the crest of the Allegheny along the Virginia-West Virginia border.

The national forest work program brought modern forest-fire protection to much of the Blue Ridge as early as 1913; besides, the Virginia Forest Service has done an effective job of fire protection for many years. This work has been an important contribution toward restoring the Blue Ridge as a satisfactory habitat for wildlife.

Establishment of the Virginia Department of Game and Inland Fisheries in 1916 marked the first Statewide administration of Virginia's wildlife. A reorganization in 1926 created the present Commission of Game and Inland Fisheries, a progressive step that placed the State in a position to work more closely with sportsmen and with other conservation agencies. Professionally trained game and fish administrators were employed. The stage was set for renewed efforts to restore wildlife, and many sportsmen in the mountain counties dipped into their own pockets to match the dollars of the struggling new Commission to buy game animals for restocking purposes.

The Emergency Conservation Program in 1933 put a new reservoir of manpower at the disposal of the national forests for the work on natural resources. The first Civilian Conservation Corps camp in the United States was constructed in the Blue Ridge foothills of Shenandoah County, in the George Washington National Forest. There followed a public demand for the use of emergency conservation funds to carry on wildlife development projects, and kindred interests brought sportsmen, the Commission, and the Forest Service into a close but informal partnership to restock and restore wildlife habitat on the national forests. That was a prelude to the cooperative wildlife program now in effect on Virginia's two notional forests.

With the launching of the cooperative wildlife program, efforts were made to spread the work over much more of the national forest acreage. A formal agreement placing both the George Washington and Jefferson National Forests under cooperative wildlife management became effective on June 13, 1938.

Legislative action by the Virginia General Assembly in 1938 provided for collection of a fee of a dollar by the Commonwealth for the privilege of hunting or fishing on national forest land and earmarked all funds so collected for wildlife restoration and management on the cooperative area. This special license, in the form of a stamp, is issued each year to cover hunting, fishing, and trapping on all national forest land in Virginia. The purchaser affixes this stamp to his regular hunting and fishing license.

One of the cardinal principles of cooperative wildlife management under the Virginia program has been the requirement that all plans and programs be jointly developed and administered under a pattern of mutual participation and assistance. The policy starts with joint preparation of each year's budget by the Director of the Commission of Game and Inland Fisheries and the forest supervisors. The budget is shaped to finance an annual work program for wildlife, which is also jointly conceived, discussed, and approved.

The diversion of a part of wildlife-license receipts to the national forests to provide funds for developing and maintaining wildlife habitat marked a new approach to wildlife restoration in Virginia. This action stemmed directly from the concept that wildlife is a product of the land and that active participation of the land manager was essential to continued production of game and fish.

The joint plans, formulated on the ground, cover stocking of game and fish, law enforcement, planting of wildlife food and cover, mowing old fields to retain them as wildlife clearings, pruning and releasing trees and shrubs of value for wildlife food and cover, control of predators, emergency feeding of game when the ground is covered by deep snows, and a score of related jobs. Periodic inspections by representatives of the Commission and the Forest Service insure adherence to the work plans and faithful compliance with job specifications.

When the cooperative program was launched, wildlife-management units ranging from 5,000 to 25,000 acres were created on many of the ranger districts. Usually these areas were chosen because of solid Government ownership and well-defined geographic boundaries. Quite commonly, an entire stream-drainage area was incorporated into a management area and a small cabin provided for the resident wildlife manager. Many of the units were originally closed to all hunting. Boundaries were clearly posted and marked with a single strand of wire drawn at waist height. An extra margin of protection and law enforcement has been provided for these areas, and they have served as centers on which to restock deer, wild turkey, and other game. Administrative units of this type are now located along the full length of the national forests for a distance of 300 miles.

Most important of all in the program was the employment and assignment of resident wildlife managers to assume direct supervision over wildlife-management areas in the national forests. Great care was given to the selection of men for the work; the usual choice was a local resident who was thoroughly familiar with the mountains and forests of his locality and interested in wildlife, one who had the respect and confidence of his neighbors. The employees were selected for intelligence, stamina, knowledge of local terrain, and familiarity with indigenous wildlife.

When large areas of national forest land were closed during the early stages of the program, the wildlife managers explained the action to nearby residents and others who had been accustomed to hunt in the area. The support of the citizens has been important in the prevention of illegal hunting and other forms of trespass on the units.

A major problem at first was the free-roaming, self-hunting dogs. The managers often captured the animals within the wildlife areas and returned them to their owners, with a courteous request that they be restrained. Sometimes sterner measures became necessary, but mostly action was prompt and complete when the people came to understand the efforts of the manager to reestablish wildlife in the mountains.

The resident wildlife manager is not a law-enforcement officer in the usual sense, but his presence day and night on the unit has strongly deterred would-be poachers. When he is confronted with a violation of game laws, he does not hesitate to summon the violator to court, but he usually sends a copy of the summons to the county game warden, who assumes responsibility for prosecuting offenders. The manager's work is related to that of the enforcement officer, but it is even more closely related to land management and animal husbandry. The tools of his profession are principally the brush hook, pruning saw, and planting hoe, rather than those of the police officer. His philosophy is that wildlife is a product of the land and that the key to wildlife restoration lies in restoration and maintenance of satisfactory habitat.

As the wildlife restoration program developed in Virginia, strong emphasis was placed on creation and maintenance of favorable wildlife habitat as a prime responsibility of the forest workers. With public interest and demand for timber, water, and other forest resources sharing with wildlife in the need for better management and utilization, the value of a well-rounded program of multiple-use forest management became clearly evident.

Shortly after the cooperative wildlife work began, a new stimulus was developed in the Pittman-Robertson Federal-aid program. Each year since 1940 Federal-aid projects have helped finance environmental improvement, including planting, pruning, and releasing game-food trees and shrubs, planting trees and shrubs for wildlife cover, creating and seeding clearings for game, and restoring old clearings, fields, orchards, and similar habitats of special value to game animals. This type of development work has brought a third agency, the Fish and Wildlife Service, into the Virginia program.

Guidance from the Cooperative Wildlife Research Unit, which was formerly maintained at Virginia Polytechnic Institute at Blacksburg, helped materially in solving the numerous problems that arose during the early years of the program. Similar assistance was later provided by the Virginia Cooperative Wildlife Station, also located at Blacksburg and supported by the Virginia Polytechnic Institute, the Commission of Game and Inland Fisheries, and the Wildlife Management Institute. More recently the United States Fish and Wildlife Service has again entered the picture and the Cooperative Wildlife Research Unit has been restored under a Federal-aid program.

One of the immediate and direct benefits of cooperative wildlife management has been an improved level of law observance in the national forests. The presence of resident wildlife managers on the major management units has gone far toward creating respect for closed seasons, bag limits, and other regulations in behalf of wildlife. The exercising of management prerogatives under the cooperative program has, of itself, brought the wildlife resource a more respected position among sportsmen and local residents.

Restocking formed an important part of early wildlife-restoration efforts under the cooperative program. An early analysis of the fragmentary deer population on the cooperative area revealed the need for numerous well-distributed spot plantings of deer on unoccupied areas of the range. By utilizing funds from national forest stamps, Pittman-Robertson contributions, and funds from the Commission of Game and Inland Fisheries, it was possible to purchase and release a total of 1,783 deer.

Wild turkeys were originally found throughout the forests but vast areas of former turkey range were no longer supporting the birds at the time the cooperative program was launched. Persistent efforts to restore this fine game bird have not been entirely successful, because of the difficulty in obtaining a strain of birds capable of retaining wild characteristics. Some flocks have been reestablished in depleted areas as a result of restocking efforts, and it is planned to continue work on the project until a solution is found.

Approximately 1,000 raccoons have been planted in the national forests and adjacent areas. Wildlife managers report a noticeable increase in the number of raccoon in recent years.

Populations of small game such as ruffed grouse and squirrel fluctuate from year to year, and it is difficult to recognize trends within a few years, but we expect an increase in their number as food supplies and other environmental factors are improved.

Some good streams that can become excellent trout waters flow from the Blue Ridge, which, as the easternmost range of the Appalachians, could provide accessible trout fishing for residents of many eastern cities. The restoration and maintenance of Blue Ridge trout streams as producing units of aquatic habitat is a major objective under the cooperative program.

The heavy demand for trout fishing in the national forest waters has required an intensive stream-stocking program. State and Federal hatcheries have supplied legal-size trout annually for the streams. To provide even more fish, an allotment of national forest stamp funds has been made to Federal hatcheries in recent years to purchase fish food. Under that arrangement, trout that would otherwise be planted as 3- and 4-inch fish are reared to 8- and 10-inch size for stocking purposes.

In the cooperative area, forest-management plans for important watersheds are being shaped to restore water-retention capacity, to stabilize stream banks, minimize soil losses through erosion, and provide shaded channels to keep water temperatures within favorable limits for the native brook trout. Already many forest streams have responded to the fire-prevention and watershed-management practices which date from 1913. Under the multiple-use concept of forest management, increased emphasis is being placed on harvesting timber in a manner that will minimize damage to fishing streams. Furthermore, man-made stream-improvement devices, including dams and other structures, have been installed to create pools and hiding places for trout. The ability of many mountain streams to provide shelter for fish has been greatly enhanced through this means and further work may be undertaken as funds become available. Stream improvement of this type often requires a heavy outlay of funds for labor, but it has proved popular with users of streams.

The growing population of deer has already demonstrated the need for planned forage production. The development of cleared areas at regular intervals throughout the forest has added materially to the forest edge, which provides improved forage conditions. Sawmill sites, log-loading areas, woods roads, and "turn arounds" have been seeded to orchardgrass and other foods for wildlife. These permanent forest openings also eliminate the need for creating a fresh disturbance to soil and forest cover with each new logging operation.

The wildlife managers were quick to recognize the value of numerous apple trees in the young, second-growth forest, particularly along old logging railroad grades where the loggers of a preceding generation had unconsciously planted them. Fruit trees around abandoned homesteads also provided a valuable source of game food; now the trees are being pruned and freed from competition. Many of them now produce annual crops of

fruit. The work has been expanded to include pruning, releasing, and planting of game-food species, such as wild raisin, persimmon, the thornapple, and wild grape.

Resident managers now make regular collections of seeds and cuttings from shrubs and trees that produce palatable game foods. The material is sent to the Forest Service nursery at Parsons, W. Va., where it is used to grow seedlings that are subsequently returned to the wildlife areas for planting under the habitat-improvement program. Clumps of conifers also are frequently planted in hardwood areas to provide roosting and escape cover; in coniferous forest areas, spot plantings of hardwoods are made.

The modern concept of forest game management relies to a great extent on manipulation of the vegetative cover to create and maintain proper environment for wildlife. While wildlife is an incidental product on practically all forest areas, the cooperative program stresses coordination of forestry and wildlife objectives as a means toward providing a stable environment that will maintain game and fish production at the highest level compatible with other land uses. Forest rangers and others engaged in selling national forest timber have been encouraged to consider the wildlife needs in shaping future plans for timber management and this field offers great promise for maintaining wildlife habitat at a favorable level.

Much of the old-growth timber in Virginia's mountain counties was cut within a short span of years, and the young, second-growth forest is therefore quite uniform in age. Old-growth stands, which provide den trees, acorns, fruits, and other mast, are not plentiful. Young browse-producing reproduction is becoming less abundant as the second-growth stand grows taller and shades the forest floor. As a result, much of the forest is now too old for browse and too young for mast production. The situation is being improved on many areas by creating small openings in the forest and retaining old fields as permanent openings for wildlife, but the final solution will involve careful planning in the field of timber management. Sustained timber production and sustained wildlife production have many requirements in common on forested areas.

The cost of clearing, planting, and otherwise developing forest areas as wildlife habitat is too great to be borne by revenue derived solely from the sale of hunting and fishing permits. For economy and effectiveness, wildlife-habitat improvement must be correlated with forest management at every step. Experimental work under the cooperative program has done much to point the way, and the close working relationship between the Commission of Game and Inland Fisheries and the United States Forest Service has developed a new consciousness of wildlife needs in the over-all program of forest management. Under the Virginia plan, 1½ million acres of forest are being carefully developed under a long-term program for wildlife production.

Meanwhile, the number of white-tailed deer on the two forests has increased from 2,400 in 1938 to 18,000

in 1947. The trend is still upward. In the same time, the population of black bear has increased from 500 to 1,200. From an estimated 2,600 in 1938, the number of wild turkeys went up to 3,400 in 1947.

Always the emphasis has been on wildlife production for public use, and the withdrawal of large acreages from hunting and fishing has been discouraged. Many closed areas have been opened to provide additional hunting grounds. The dispersal of hunting pressure over the full available land area is considered desirable, because every acre withheld from use tends to build up pressure elsewhere. Even in the Big Levels Federal refuge area of the George Washington National Forest, certain parts have been opened for deer hunting during limited periods, and the advisability of harvesting wildlife on the entire refuge is being seriously considered.

A comparison of big-game harvests shows that 40 black bear were taken on the two Virginia forests in 1938, compared to 112 in 1947. Total deer kill for 1938 was 230 animals, compared to 1,383 in 1947. Big-game animals killed on the cooperative area are tagged and examined at checking stations, so that an inventory is had each year.

Hunting, fishing, and trapping on the cooperatively managed area in Virginia has increased from 70,000 man-days a year in 1938 to more than one-half million in 1947. The sale of national forest hunting and fishing stamps increased from 11,690 in 1938 to 41,388 in 1947.

Another measure of the success of the program is the support it has among sportsmen and the general public. As evidence, several counties in the national forest area, acting through county boards of supervisors, have entered into formal agreements with the State and the Forest Service to supply additional funds for extension of wildlife management under the program.

THE LONG-BARRELED SQUIRREL RIFLE has vanished from the mountains of Virginia, along with the deerskin-jacketed pioneers. In their place have come busy farmers, businessmen, doctors, lawyers, schoolboys—not pioneers, but men and boys who get from hunting a diversion from the worries of modern life and who look to the Virginia Plan—the Blue Ridge Plan—as an assurance that the privilege of fishing and hunting will be theirs for always.

THEODORE C. FEARNOW *is a native West Virginian. He joined the Forest Service as a wildlife biologist in 1935. Previously he worked with the Division of Scientific Inquiry, United States Bureau of Fisheries. He was chief of the Division of Fisheries in the West Virginia Conservation Commission from 1927 to 1933.*

I. T. QUINN, *for 17 years, was commissioner of Conservation of Game, Fish, and Seafoods for the State of Alabama. He was president of the International Association of Game, Fish, and Conservation Commissioners from 1927 to 1928; president of the Southern Association of Game Officials from 1931 to 1939; and president of the American Fisheries Society from 1937 to 1938. During the war he worked in Washington, D. C., and returned to conservation work as executive director of the Virginia Commission of Game and Inland Fisheries in 1946.*

# Forests and Water

## TIMBER CUTTING AND WATER YIELDS

H. G. WILM

THE VALUE of forest vegetation in protecting watershed land has been so clearly demonstrated that its development and maintenance are recognized more and more as a powerful tool to control erosion and floods.

Forests are useful for this purpose in wide areas of the United States—in the Ohio River Valley, the southern Mississippi River Valley, and the Appalachian Mountains; on the rolling countrysides of New England and the rough, steep slopes of the Rocky Mountain Front Range. In all of those places and in many more, deterioration of watershed conditions due to the removal of forest cover has led to flashy, destructive stream flow and greatly increased soil erosion and sediment production. Wherever such conditions exist on land that is adapted to growing forest vegetation, the logical solution is to restore the forest by any available means.

But it is less widely recognized that the same virtues of the forest that make it valuable in the control of erosion and floods may become disadvantages in other areas, where such problems are small but water shortages are acute.

Water troubles with this different aspect can be found on long belts of high-altitude watershed land along the big backbone of the Rockies and in the upper areas of other mountain ranges: Land that produces large volumes of water and sends it down the mountain canyons to spreading plains and arid valleys below, places where almost every available drop is consumed by cities, towns, and irrigated farms.

For many years the people of dry areas like these throughout the West have worried about their water supplies. Water there is so precious that it is bought and sold by the acre-foot or even by the gallon; it is so greatly in demand that in some places existing legally established water rights exceed the highest recorded annual flow in the streams.

Under such intense pressure for water, naturally these people look to the mountain watersheds that are the

*Above: A watershed like this, a burned-over area in the Rockies, requires a careful use.*

802062°—49——39

source of their water, and they wonder whether they are getting all that might be made available. Knowing, for instance, that plants of every kind use water in considerable quantities to maintain life and produce vegetable matter, they speculate as to whether any water might be saved if watershed vegetation could be thinned or even completely removed.

This conjecture has given rise to long-standing arguments, first brought to a peak by Col. H. M. Chittenden in an article which was published in 1909. Rather significantly, Chittenden had been studying western water problems for some time and was engaged in the development of water resources for the general region east of the Rocky Mountains. He argued that forests diminish total runoff through evaporation and transpiration, and that they are not so valuable in reducing floods as had been believed. This contention was raised by others repeatedly in ensuing years and gained support by engineers and others interested in the development of water resources.

Partly as a result of such arguments, people have learned much about the true value of forest cover in watershed protection since those early days, and realize that it serves an extremely important function in stabilizing soil and in reducing floods.

But on arid western lands the need for water is sometimes so great that people are still willing to take the risk of floods and erosion in order to get it. In the unusually dry but highly developed valleys of the Southwest, men have been heard to say: "Give us the water, clean or dirty—we'll take care of the mud somehow!"

Obviously that kind of talk shows an incomplete understanding of the disastrous consequences of soil depletion and erosion—or perhaps it shows a loss of perspective, resulting from the extreme need for water in those areas. Anyway, such statements give a picture of how acute water-supply problems can be in the West and how important it is for watershed managers to get every drop that can be produce safely on mountain watershed land We dare not overlook the chance tha Chittenden and others may have ha a strong basis for their contentions— that there may be areas where vegetation can safely be removed and wate yields thereby increased.

At first glance it does look like hard problem. For any given area w have to learn whether it is necessar to maintain a complete forest cove and accept the resulting water consumption in the interest of protectio or to what extent we can relax thi requirement in order to reduce wate losses. In working on this problem w must also remember that, wherever watershed contains merchantable timber, protection may mean deprivin people of badly needed lumber an other products. We want to insure reasonable use rather than unnecessar protection.

WHAT HAPPENS TO WATER IN TH FOREST is the basis of forest management for maximum water yields unde safe conditions.

When snow or rain falls on a fores some of it is intercepted by the tre crowns and is stored for the time bein on leaves and twigs. A large par reaches the ground by dripping fror branches or running down the trunk but a part of it remains on the crowns where it is lost by evaporation afte the storm is over.

If the yearly precipitation on an area is made up of small storms separated by periods of clear weather, th evaporation from crowns is high—a much as 35 to 50 percent of the yearl total. Where storms are larger an much cloudy weather occurs, the relative amount of crown interception an loss is smaller. Interception varies als with the kind and the density of th crowns: Thick spruces catch and hol more water than thin-crowned pine while leafless cottonwoods and aspe intercept much less winter precipitation than any of the conifers. Hence i should be feasible to cut down th amount of loss from this source by thinning the forest and reducing the overall density of the canopy on a given area. Similar results might be accomplished by encouraging the growth of hardwood vegetation like aspen instead of conifers like spruce or fir.

After precipitation passes through the forest canopy, what is left piles up on the ground, if it occurred as snow, and remains there until warm weather makes it melt. When this happens, or if it fell as rain in the first place, it begins to move toward the nearest stream. In a forest it does this ordinarily by entering the litter and humus on the soil surface, then going down through porous layers of soil toward the groundwater table. If the soil was dry when melting began or the rain occurred, some of the water is held by the soil itself and may not reach the groundwater table at all. But after the soil reservoir is filled to capacity, any additional water from the rain or melting snow reaches the water table and moves through it to the stream. Because the soil is a complex body with varied layering and structures, the movement of water may be quite complicated, but this is its general course.

When water has entered the soil it is exposed to another influence of the forest on water yields: During warm weather a part of the soil water is drawn out by the trees. This draft, together with evaporation directly from the soil rather than through the roots and crowns, is what has made the soil under the forest relatively dry before rain comes or winter snows are stored on the ground. In a heavy forest, transpiration is likely to be high because of the large volume of tree crowns that are exposed to air and heat. Direct evaporation from the soil or from stored snow, on the other hand, is likely to be low because the ground is shaded, and soil evaporation is further reduced where the ground is covered with litter.

When the forest is thinned or removed entirely, transpiration is reduced or even eliminated. But evaporation goes up as the ground becomes more and more exposed to the sun through the removal of the shading canopy and the loss of organic litter. So, evaporation and transpiration tend to offset each other to some extent—if one is reduced, the other is increased. On the whole, however, it is believed that losses of water from the soil are decreased by thinning or removing forest vegetation. And when savings due to reduced interception are included, the increase in potential stream flow is likely to be substantial.

But there is a real flaw in the story as told up to this point.

It seems generally agreed that the removal of forest vegetation almost always results in some deterioration of the soil and site, and that the rate at which the soil can take in and transmit water may be lessened to a greater or smaller extent and for a varying length of time. Then the water may not all go through the soil; some of it may run off over the land surface. If it does so in any appreciable volume, it moves much faster than it can through the pores of the soil. Unless the ground is protected by a heavy sod or a deep layer of humus and litter, this water picks up soil particles as it travels. The result is a quick accumulation of muddy water in the streams—we see it in our valleys in the form of flashy, destructive floods and clouded rivers. In contrast, water that moves through the soil does so more slowly and stays free of sediment; we see the result in clear, well-regulated brooks and rivers.

Whether or not surface runoff is actually produced depends, of course, on more than just the reduction of the infiltration capacity of the soil. It requires also a rate of water application in excess of this capacity. If the peak rainfall intensity, for instance, is relatively high (say, 3 to 4 inches an hour), any reduction in the capacity of even a porous soil to take in water may result in excessive surface runoff. If, on the other hand, rates of snow-melt or rainfall intensity are quite low, reasonable reductions in infiltration capacity may do no harm; the remaining capacity may be enough to take in all the water that is applied.

As a variation of this principle, surface runoff may sometimes occur after the soil column has been saturated down to some less permeable layer, if the rate of water application exceeds the rate at which this denser layer can transmit it. Then, of course, infiltration is limited by this layer rather than by the soil above it. In such cases, the presence or absence of forest cover may have little effect on the magnitude of floods, as the peak flows may come from water that moves off the watershed rapidly by surface and subsurface flow, relatively unaffected at that stage by the infiltration and storage capacity of the forest soil.

Even under such circumstances, however, forest vegetation ordinarily does a great service in preventing soil erosion and sediment movement through the stabilizing action of its litter, humus, and roots. Those who know the high, cold spruce forests of the Rockies and elsewhere will recall the wet, boggy mountainsides toward the end of the snow-melt season. Water runs freely and rapidly down the steep slopes, but causes no erosion at all because of the thick, spongy layer of organic material on the ground. As one man remarked, "That isn't surface runoff—you're just standing up to your ankles in ground water."

These discussions on the behavior of water in the forest can be interpreted in terms of conditions that are commonly encountered. Where growing conditions for the forest are poor; where precipitation rates are high and the soil is unstable; where the effects of timber cutting are aggravated by fire, destructive logging methods, or overgrazing; or under any combination of such conditions, the removal of forest cover may be followed by severe reductions in organic matter and in the ability of the soil to take in and transmit water. The consequence is usually an accelerating cycle of flash floods and erosion. Surface runoff starts soil
movement; the eroded particles hel
clog soil pores, which in turn increas
runoff; the increased runoff intensifi
the soil movement again, and so o
Finally runoff and erosion becom
stabilized at a high rate, cutting awa
the soil and carrying large volumes c
sediment to the rivers. The result
lasting injury to the watershed, low
ered production of timber and othe
vegetation, and probably disastrou
damage to cities, farms, reservoirs, an
other installations.

Under gentle climatic condition
however, it is possible to harvest timbe
by sound silvicultural methods so as t
keep the forest producing wood an
other products, and at the same tim
benefit the water supplies. In som
cases conservative management is ac
visable, where too severe cutting migh
start the exposure of relatively un
stable soil. There the forester plans th
removal of individual trees or sma
groups of trees in light or moderat
selection cuttings. On watersheds tha
are inherently more stable, it is possibl
to apply the heavier cutting method
Where good silviculture prescribes i
even the removal of all merchantabl
trees is sometimes a sound practice, a
in the overmature, even-aged stands c
lodgepole pine at high altitudes an
on stable soil.

Where watershed conditions are un
usually safe, even forest fire has faile
in some places to cause any substantia
or permanent damage. Where the so
is stable and the climate cool, with slow
rates of snow melt and gentle summe
rains, no appreciable excesses of wate
have resulted and therefore the cycl
of erosion and floods has not occurre
In the Colorado Rockies, for instanc
many old burned-over areas provid
satisfactory and stable conditions fo
water production and there is littl
evidence of damaging past erosion. Ex
ceptions to this rule are found when
repeated fires, overgrazing, or peren
nial wood cutting and hauling hav
perpetuated and intensified any de
terioration caused by the first fire.

Thus far we have discussed wha

happens to water after it falls on the forest and what may be expected when the timber is removed. Ample experimental evidence has been obtained and published on the bad effects of unwise timber removal and destructive logging, especially in the areas that are sensitive to soil deterioration and to erosion. But what about less delicately balanced areas? Is there any evidence to show that water supplies can be increased by timber harvesting on such lands without damaging the watershed or causing serious erosion and flood production?

There is evidence on this aspect of watershed problems, though less than on erosion and flood damages caused by excessive timber use or unskillful watershed management. Several investigations have been conducted in the United States for the special purpose of showing how the forests influence stream flow and water yields and how this influence is changed by timber removal.

The first major study was started by the Forest Service and the United States Weather Bureau on the famous Wagon Wheel Gap watersheds in southern Colorado at about the time Colonel Chittenden published his report. Near the headwaters of the Rio Grande, two small watersheds were controlled by means of rain gages, stream-gaging stations, sediment basins, and other scientific equipment. After they had been studied for 8 years in their original condition—covered largely with a forest of conifers and aspen—all of the woody vegetation was removed from one of the areas. During the following 7 years, total water yields increased about 15 percent under this treatment, and yields during the snow-melt period rose about 22 percent. Even the summer and autumn stream flow was built up to some extent. Melting started a little earlier in the spring, but not enough to cause any important change in flood peaks or in the amount of water available during the irrigation season.

The increased yields seemed to be due to decreased losses from evaporation and transpiration rather than to reduced soil porosity and storage, as the augmented late-season stream flow indicated an ample supply of water to the ground-water table. Also, no appreciable erosion was caused by the complete removal of the forest cover.

Little sediment was caught, and practically all of it seemed to have come from the minor logging roads that had been built into the watershed.

Judging from those findings, timber removal obviously had a gentle effect on both water yields and erosion. There are several good reasons.

First, the climate of this area is mild from the hydrologist's viewpoint—cool, with long winters and slow melting rates of snow and with relatively low rates of summer rainfall. In those respects it resembles vast areas of forested watershed along the top of the Rockies, including 10 million acres or more from the Rio Grande to Montana.

Second, the forest cover was rather thin before treatment, so that even the removal of all the woody vegetation did not cause so drastic a change as might be expected. Because a considerable part of the forest was aspen, too, winter interception losses must have been low, and the aspen grew up rapidly after treatment so that the effects of denudation were relatively shortlived.

Finally, the soil on those areas was fairly porous and apparently did not deteriorate badly.

Thus, the quantitative results of the investigation can be applied only in a limited way to other areas. They do indicate the general effects of timber removal in a region like the backbone of the Rockies and similar mountain ranges—that timber removal may not cause damage and may even benefit water yields.

Thorough as it was, too, that experiment did not really show the influence of silviculture on water supplies, because every stick of woody vegetation was removed from the treated area. While clear cutting is a perfectly sound silvicultural method, it is not so commonly usable in watershed management as some other methods, such as selection cutting. In this way, though, the Wagon Wheel Gap studies were similar to the other watershed research that has been conducted.

Until quite recently there has been a singular dearth of studies employing practical silvicultural methods; only two seem to need mention here.

In California, Dr. Joseph Kittredge made a number of experiments to find out various aspects of forest influences. Using those experiments as a background, as early as 1936 he set up what may be considered a first-class objective of watershed management in areas where water shortages exist: "To select species of minimum foliage volume and transpiration and to maintain them by forest management at minimum sizes and densities compatible with protection of the soil."

In Idaho, Charles A. Connaughton examined the accumulation and melting of snow as they were affected by mature ponderosa pine, with and without an understory of young trees or reproduction; by reproduction stands alone; and by open land, with and without a cover of sagebrush. Taking the open areas without sagebrush as 100 percent, he found the following relative amounts of snow stored in the other cover types at the time of greatest snow accumulation in the spring: Sagebrush, 100.9 percent; pine reproduction, 94.6 percent; virgin pine without reproduction, 75.5 percent; and virgin pine with reproduction, 70.2 percent. The last snow disappeared almost simultaneously on open and brush-covered areas, about 3½ days later in the virgin forest without reproduction, and about 8 days later in the stand of reproduction alone and where it occurred under virgin timber.

Although this did not give quantitative data on factors other than snow, it did demonstrate how forest and other vegetation with different kinds of crown and densities of canopy affected interception and shading and therefore the storage and melting of snow.

It was not until Mr. Connaughton moved to Colorado in 1936 that experiments were finally started to show how selective timber cutting of high altitude conifers would influence all of the more important factors associated with water yields. In conjunction with the Division of Timber Management Research, the Division of Forest Influences in the Rocky Mountain Forest and Range Experiment Station began a series of studies with this objective in 1938. They consisted of 20 harvest-cutting plots located in a forest of mature lodgepole pine, covering a small, rugged drainage basin in the headwaters of the Colorado River near Fraser, Colo. The timber on the plots ranged in merchantable volume (including only trees larger than 9½ inches in diameter) from 7,600 board feet an acre to about 17,000 board feet, and averaged 11,900 board feet.

One of the primary objects of those plot experiments was to learn how timber cutting by selection methods affects the growth and reproduction of this type of forest. Along with the studies, however, detailed records were collected on a series of important factors involved in water production: The storage and melting of snow, the amounts of net precipitation reaching the snow or ground under the forest canopy, and the relative dryness of the soil under the forest at the end of each summer's growing period, when transpiration and evaporation had finished drawing out soil moisture.

The records were first collected in 1938 and 1939, before any timber cutting was done on the plots, to show how the various factors behaved under a virgin forest. Then 16 of the plots were cut over in 1940 by selection methods, so as to leave stands of several different densities, and 4 of them were left uncut as a check. On another set of 4, all of the merchantable timber was removed so that only trees smaller than 10 inches in diameter remained to provide a partial cover and help protect the soil. Other similar sets of plots were left with reserve stands of 2,000, and 4,000, and 6,000 board feet of merchantable timber an acre, so that a considerable variety in remaining canopy densities was provided. It should be emphasized that even the heaviest cutting by no means cleared off the plots. On the average, each acre still contained 147 trees in the diameter range between 3½ and 9½ inches, as well as a number of still smaller trees and a little underbrush.

After the plots were cut over, further records were obtained on all of the water-yield factors until 1944, when the study was temporarily discontinued. In addition to these quantitative data, observations have been made each year since 1940 to determine whether the different cuttings had damaged the plots appreciably, whether erosion was beginning, and how rapidly the plots were becoming covered again with conifer reproduction and other vegetation.

The results of all this detailed record-taking showed a decided increase in the amount of the water available for stream flow as a result of the timber cutting. Out of a total precipitation of about 24½ inches a year, about 32 percent was absorbed by canopy interception in the uncut stand, as compared to only 11 percent in the most heavily cut-over plots. This smaller amount of interception was, of course, caused by trees smaller than 9½ inches in diameter.

Additional losses due to other forms of evaporation and to transpiration averaged about 26 percent of the total precipitation on the uncut plots and about 34 percent on the heavily cut-over areas. When all forms of water consumption were combined, the remainder was only about 10⅓ inches of water available for stream flow under virgin-forest conditions as compared to about 13½ inches as a result of the heavy cutting. Thus the severe opening of the forest increased the amount of available water a full 30 percent as compared to uncut conditions. To back up those results, the other timber-cutting treatments fell in line between the two extremes: For the light, moderate, and the dense reserve stands the amounts of water available for stream flow were 11⅓, 12⅓, and about 12½ inches.

Such gains are definitely worth while. In round terms, they mean that removing merchantable timber on each 4 to 5 acres of high-altitude watershed land should make it possible to irrigate another acre of valuable land in the valleys below. Not only that, but it will increase the capital value of the watershed land itself through a treatment which ordinarily pays for itself and almost always gives a profit to the landowner and the timber operator; and it will supply wood products to western people.

That is true, of course, only if the treatment does not do damage to the land by starting an accelerating cycle of erosion and land depletion. Under the climatic conditions of the high mountain areas this is not likely to occur and is certainly not indicated by observations made since the plots were cut over. As in the Wagon Wheel Gap study, the only traces of erosion up to 1947 were small gullies cut in skid roads and trails that contribute insignificant quantities of sediment to the streams. Except in those places, almost no bare soil is exposed, and a new stand of conifer reproduction is slowly beginning to occupy areas opened on the plots; in some places aspen is beginning to come in.

Similar increases in the available water have shown up in other experiments, in which snow storage and rainfall were studied in stands of young lodgepole pine, aspen, and open areas. The last of these, several acres in extent and somewhat exposed to wind, stored a little less snow than was found in leafless aspen stands, but the smallest amounts were found under the dense cover of pine. Snow storage and rain penetration in the young pine forest have been substantially increased by thinning the stands, though enough trees were left to provide a future forest and to give partial shade and soil protection.

Still further studies have been started more recently in the spruce-fir forest type, which occupies watershed lands even higher in altitude than lodgepole pine, reaching on up to timber line. While these experiments are only well under way, the preliminary results are similar in trend to those obtained in lodgepole pine.

These influences, you may say, have been observed only on plots up to this time; perhaps things are different on a watershed. In order to test this possibility, small watersheds have been placed under experimental control at the Fraser Experimental Forest and elsewhere in the Colorado Rockies, with plans for treating one watershed at each place by desirable silvicultural methods. The results of these tests will not be available for several years.

In the meantime, however, the plot findings are fairly well supported by the Wagon Wheel Gap results and by detailed observations of soil conditions and erosion after timber cutting at a number of places in the high Rockies of Colorado and southern Wyoming. At every cut-over area visited, whether recent or old, cutting in lodgepole pine and in the spruce-fir type has not caused any serious degree of erosion or site deterioration.

Finally, although their application may be quite different, the same general influences of timber cutting on water yields seem to apply to regions other than the western mountains. In watershed studies in the southern Appalachian Mountains, C. R. Hursh and M. D. Hoover found substantial increases in total water yields following the removal of a hardwood forest. When all of the woody vegetation was cut and laid on the ground to protect the soil and reduce evaporation, annual yields were increased about 17 inches. Worth while increases in summer flow were also found to result from cutting only the vegetation on narrow strips close to the stream channels, leaving the other watershed vegetation intact.

With the research information gained up to now, we cannot supply all of the necessary answers to questions that the watershed forester must ask as he plans the management of water-producing land. Detailed studies still have to be made under a variety of conditions to show how the principles now at hand need to be altered to meet local problems. But we do have a set of basic principles on which sound but preliminary watershed-management plans can be established:

1. Forest vegetation, like all other plants, consumes water in considerable quantities through interception, transpiration, and evaporation.

2. Removing a part or all of the forest cover by timber cutting should reduce this water consumption, thus making more water available for total yields.

3. Such thinning or opening of the forest is likely to result in some site deterioration, though it may be minor in degree. But this point calls for caution and careful observation by the manager as he works with his forest.

4. If site and soil deterioration are sufficient to cause rainfall excesses (including excesses in water from melting snow) in any substantial amount, the resulting overland flow, passing over inadequately protected soil, will almost always cause soil erosion and flashy silt-laden floods. This will cause further site deterioration and the reduction of soil storage and infiltration capacities. With more water running off over the watershed surface, less will get into underground storage and the ground-water table, and, as a result, summer flow of streams will likely be lowered and springs will dry up. Together with flashy spring freshets and summer floods, this will mean a complete change of stream habits—entirely for the worse.

5. If, on the other hand, no damaging rainfall excess results from tim-

er cutting and the associated site leterioration is not serious, the opening of the forest should increase total ields of usable water, build up peak lischarges to a minor extent, and still ermit a normal supply of water to pass hrough the soil into ground water and herefore to produce sustained stream low from deep sources, such as perennial springs.

These principles are not yet completely established, and they may be xpanded or altered considerably as urther knowledge is obtained. But it s interesting to see how, even now, hey can be applied to a variety f watershed-management problems, arying from the control of erosion and loods to the production of maximum upplies of water.

Consider the first of these, for example. Where floods and sediment ause damage, the streams have too nuch water and it is concentrated too nuch in short, abrupt peaks. At the ame time they carry large amounts of terile sediment that clogs channels nd ruins farm lands. Forest vegetaion cannot do all that is necessary to emedy such conditions, but it does tabilize the soil and minimize erosion. t also intercepts and evaporates rainall and tends to dry out the soil moisure, making as much space available s possible in the great storage reservoir f the soil on watershed land.

To help solve such problems, it is dvisable to keep the forest cover as lense as possible in order to provide naximum soil protection and opporunity for the consumption of water. This may mean only the lightest and nost careful timber cutting, or perhaps o cutting at all. Then the forest will educe floods and erosion from its own rea, even though its benefits may have o be supplemented by engineering vorks and by soil and water conservaion measures on agricultural and ther nonforest land.

As a variation of this problem, perlaps our watershed may be located in n area of considerable erosion hazard, ut where there is an intense demand for water from the irrigated valleys below. A good example is provided by the cut-over, deteriorated watershed land in the ponderosa pine belt of the Rocky Mountain Front Range, with erodible soil derived from the red Pike's Peak granite. In such cases there is little question as to the proper method of watershed management. The land must be protected and erosion rates slowed down and finally controlled as much as possible, even at the cost of lowered water supplies. Again, this means building the best possible cover of forest and other vegetation and using any other measure necessary to remedy the cause. When the spiral of flash floods and erosion has been started to any serious degree, the losses due to land depletion and sedimentation far exceed the nominal benefits of augmented supplies of silt-laden water.

At the other extreme of watershed problems, suppose we are concerned with an area within the millions of acres of high mountain country that are quite safe and stable. It produces water for urban and irrigated areas, but the area itself is not susceptible to floods or erosion unless it is severely abused. Here the watershed manager can relax in comparative security, looking at clear, perennial streams with high yields but small annual variations in flow. In such an area he can design the silvicultural treatment of the forest so as to provide the best supply of all its resources, without having a constant fear of upsetting a delicate balance. His management may be varied according to the combined needs of forest and watershed benefits, from light selection cutting to clear cutting if that seems necessary. But whatever methods he deems desirable, his sound and well-planned management of this watershed will pay dividends to the people in the valleys below, through more adequate supplies of usable water.

H. G. Wilm *is a silviculturist who has specialized in research on the management and protection of mountain watershed lands. Most of the concepts presented in this article were learned while he was in charge of watershed research for the Forest Service in the Rocky Mountain Region. At present he is applying research results to flood-control problems in the South with headquarters in New Orlean. Dr. Wilm is a graduate of Colorad College and Cornell University. He ha published numerous technical an popular articles, and is an associat editor of the Journal of Forestry.*

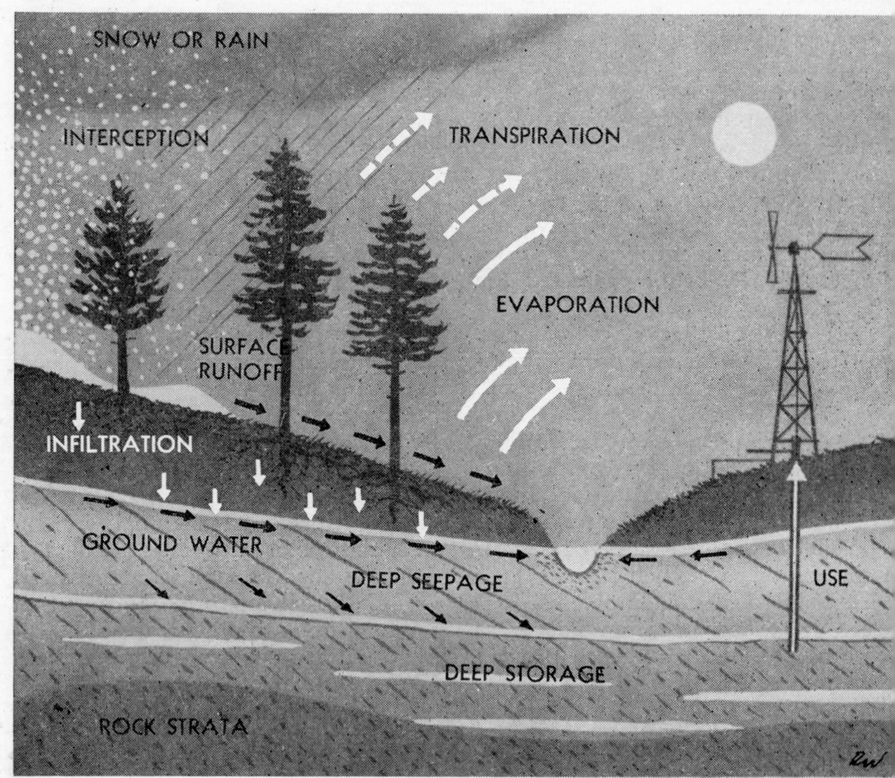


"The watershed with good plant cover, litter, and humus (made up of the decayed an decaying litter) functions like a blotter. It soaks up the water from rain or melting snow Some of this water goes back into the air later through evaporation from the groun and plants. Some enters and is stored in the soil. Part of the stored water is held in th soil for plant use; the rest slowly moves downward to feed the streams by undergroun flow. When very heavy and long rains occur, the soil may be unable to take in all th water that falls. The excess water then runs off over the surface, but at a slow rate. (From *Know Your Watersheds,* U. S. D. A. Agricultural Information Series 67.)

# WATERSHEDS AND HOW TO CARE FOR THEM

GEORGE W. CRADDOCK, CHARLES R. HURSH

A watershed is a concave or trough- haped land area in which the runoff rom rain and snow drains toward a ingle channel. A watershed may cover ess than an acre, or it may be a com- lex of many watersheds. Our entire and surface is made up of watershed nits. On them we depend for our upply of water.

Never before has our interest been reater than now in water for irriga- ion, power, industry, navigation, do- nestic use, and recreation. Most of the vater for those purposes has its source n the forest and range lands, which omprise two-thirds of the land area in he United States. Stream flow is a atural product of most of those lands, ut the usefulness of the runoff from hem hinges on their management.

Watershed management is a system f handling land resources within a lrainage primarily to achieve usable unoff. This generally involves the ame methods of husbandry that are mployed in good forest and range nanagement, but the objectives go be- ond the attainment of sustained tim- er and forage production. Watershed nanagement aims to keep the land in uch condition that there will be maxi- num yields of high-quality water.

Because watersheds have been inex- ertly handled, the water problems are ritical in all parts of the country. In he past 100 years, while population ncreased from 17 million to 140 mil- ion, the demands for water increased nanyfold. Industrial development and nunicipal expansion are now restricted n many places because of insufficient vater. The extent of destructive floods s increasing. Sediment eroded from he land is filling reservoirs, stream hannels, and harbors. Those problems vill become more serious as our popu- ations and business expand.

Through research on watersheds we re finding out how different types of land use affect runoff and water quality, how to avoid past mistakes, and how to restore and maintain our water resources in the future. Some 40 years ago two experimental watersheds near Wagon Wheel Gap in Colorado were equipped to measure the effect of clear cutting of timber on stream flow. A few years later, a pair of range watersheds near Ephraim, Utah, were similarly equipped to determine the effects of grazing herbaceous plant cover on summer storm flow and erosion. More recently, additional forest and range watershed laboratories have been established in the Rocky Mountains of Colorado and in the mountains of Idaho, Utah, Arizona, and California. The Forest Service has developed an outdoor hydrologic laboratory on the Coweeta Experimental Forest in western North Carolina. Research on runoff and erosion problems of farm lands also has expanded greatly.

EVERY ACRE of land in a drainage basin receives and disposes of precipitation and thus functions as an integral part of a whole watershed. On each acre, the plant cover and soil mantle control the reception and disposition of precipitation. The control varies from place to place, resulting in different degrees of balance between the destructive forces of the weather and the developmental processes of soil formation and plant succession.

Before man started to move soil around, the developmental processes of soil formation and plant succession were stronger than the forces of degradation on much of the forest and range lands. That is, soil had been formed on most of those lands faster than it had eroded. The naturally adjusted balances between land and weather that had been in the process of development for thousands of years, however, were disrupted by land clearing, devastation logging, overgrazing of livestock and game, and fire.

Changes took place at the ground surface that altered the manner in which precipitation entered the soil. The storage capacity of the soil was also altered. Those changes threw the original control of water and of soil stability out of balance. The result has been widespread accelerated erosion, sediment in the streams, erratic stream flow, and damaging floods. Nature's original controls were maintained by vegetation. Today, better land-management practices must be inaugurated to restore a more favorable plant cover and soil structure if we wish to maintain land and stream conditions to serve our present and future needs for usable water.

THE SOIL and the underlying rock mantle is the key to understanding the control of water on the land. Soil is capable of storing water. Some of this water is retained by the soil just as water is held behind a dam. But the soil also releases water when the mantle is filled to capacity.

Soils on forest and range lands can absorb and retain against the force of gravity from 1 to 3 inches of water per foot of mantle depth. Fine-textured soils with a high content of organic matter have a greater retention-storage capacity than coarse soils—a dry soil mantle 4 feet deep can absorb and hold from 4 to 12 inches of rain or water from melted snow without yielding a drop of runoff. This retention-storage function is the same as that performed by a dam. Removal of the soil by erosion, or otherwise, reduces the capacity of a site to retain water and so increases the chances for greater runoff and flood discharges in the same way as would the lowering of a dam.

Retention storage is only one of the storage functions of the watershed mantle. After a soil mantle is wet to its capacity to hold water against the force of gravity, it is not yet saturated. Air space still remains between the wet soil and rock particles. This additional storage space may be equivalent to a much as 2 inches a foot of mant depth. Water that enters these spac is not retained by the mantle but mov downward to the subsurface aquifer where it may replenish the groun water levels, or may emerge in channe or at springs to sustain stream flow.

The percolation of the free wat through the soil and rock mantle of watershed takes time—much longe than the escape of water over th spillway of a dam. The slowness of th percolation process is attested by th fact that streams continue to flow fo periods as long as a year after fre water disappears from the soil mantl

The delayed yield of water is one o the most important and valuable func tions of watershed lands. Communiti and industries pay millions for a sus tained yield of water and one of th major purposes of billions of dolla worth of dams is to catch spring floo and make them useful in the autum droughts. The same functions are per formed by the soil on many millions o acres of forest and range watershe lands. These natural and benefici functions of the soil must be main tained through good management.

PLANTS—herbs and shrubs, as wel as trees—are important in maintainin an efficient watershed mantle.

All who have sought shelter under tree during a rainstorm do apprecia that vegetation intercepts precipita tion in its descent to the earth. In 40-inch rainfall belt, an old-growt hardwood forest will prevent 6 or inches of rain from reaching th ground during the course of a yea This means that insofar as the soil un der the forest is concerned there i really only about 34 inches of rain in stead of 40. During individual storm the plant canopy may intercept up to 5 percent of the precipitation. The plan canopy, in other words, is an integra part of the watershed reservoir with th special function of intercepting and dis sipating a part of the precipitation be fore it reaches the soil mantle.

Plants and the plant debris on the round surface protect the soil from ne direct impact of dashing raindrops. ig drops are broken into little drops nat have less force. Tree trunks, the ems of shrubs and herbs, and dead vigs, leaves, and other trash on the round keep surface water spread out nd moving at low velocities, thus reucing the capacity to erode the soil nd retarding movement toward chanels. This favors infiltration of precipiation into the soil and rock mantle, nd the subsequent yields of water as eepage, rather than overland runoff.

Roots of plants also help in the rocess. They provide channels for the ercolation of water. They bind the urface soil against the scouring effect f storm runoff and anchor the soil nantle on steep slopes to the bedrock.

Vegetation lowers the air temperaure near the ground surface and also educes wind velocity. These influences re especially important in areas where unoff is derived mainly from snow, or they favor the accumulation of now in deep drifts and slow snownelting rates. It is not uncommon for now in the shelter of conifer trees to emain a week or two longer than in he open. This delay in snow melting n turn means a slow and prolonged ield of water.

Also to be remembered is that plants, while they produce good storage conitions, use a great deal of water. An rdinary elm tree of medium size will et rid of 15,000 pounds of water on a lear, dry, hot day. Losses of water by vaporation and transpiration on welllrained forested slopes are generally ot less than 15 inches a year and may e twice that much on sites where rainall is plentiful during the growing eason. Still greater volumes are lost y plants along streams where roots nave continuous access to water.

The ability of plants to withdraw vater from the soil may be bad or ood, depending upon the local water roblem. Where water is in high denand and the supply is limited, high osses from transpiration obviously accentuate problems of water shortage. But where flood control is important, the removal of water from the soil by transpiration maintains a greater opportunity for storing storm water.

An examination of the land, acre by acre, will show whether watershed conditions are satisfactory or unsatisfactory. Water that is not getting into the soil will accumulate and flow over the surface. Such storm runoff will leave its first traces in washed spots on the soil surface, in little rills, and small piles of leaves and debris. Later the signs are more conspicuous—severe sheet erosion and large gullies.

The management plan for the entire watershed is based on the requirements of its independent parts. Some soils can erode so easily that even the slightest change in the natural vegetation results in disastrous erosion. On them, it is good land management to prevent any possible disturbance of natural conditions; if they already have been disturbed, it is good land management to try to restore as much plant cover as conditions will support and as soon as possible.

Failure to recognize watershed deterioration in its early stages and to start remedial action toward the control of abnormal runoff and accelerated erosion is almost certain to lead to still greater deterioration and a more difficult and costly restoration job. This has happened in northern Mississippi, where 60-foot gullies are almost impossible to fill or stop.

Examination of channels and stream deposits is another approach toward determining watershed condition. Unusual deposition, channel cutting, and high watermarks may constitute direct evidence of abnormal watershed conditions. An accurate interpretation of these downstream indicators is sometimes difficult because of complex geologic and climatic factors. Even under these circumstances, however, the signs of flood runoff and siltation are the best guide toward locating the problem areas on the watershed. By indicating the source of the storm runoff and sediment, they point to the areas that need better management.

The next requirement for effective watershed restoration is the selection of the best remedial measures. These fall into several categories, depending upon the degree of deterioration and the prospects for recovery.

The first of these are measures that will aid in the natural establishment and growth of local plants. Protection from fire is important. Regulated grazing is necessary. In many sections fencing out all livestock is imperative. Seed trees must be left when the timber is harvested. In some cases all such uses must be curtailed or prohibited. These measures are applicable on areas where there has been but slight deterioration and where it is reasonable to expect rapid improvement. Chief indicators of successful natural revegetation possibilities are an abundance of seed plants and a fertile soil.

On certain areas that have been overused or damaged by fire, plants will not come in of their own accord, because seed source is inadequate. Methods of planting and seeding will differ greatly for the different regions. Planted and seeded areas must be given intensified fire protection and at least temporary protection from grazing and trampling until the new vegetation becomes well established.

Mechanical controls such as contour trenches, water spreaders, gully plugs, water drops, retaining walls, impounding dams, and debris basins constitute a third category of watershed-restoration measures. They are essential where erosion is severe and active. Mechanical measures, in nearly all instances, should be considered as methods of site preparation so as to expedite vegetation establishment.

It is of utmost importance that the need for mechanical controls be recognized. A too-optimistic judgment as to the probable success of achieving effective restoration by natural and artificial revegetation will only lead to failure and a more difficult and costly job at some future date. It is far bett to overdo the restoration work than risk failure by underestimating nee

The preservation of existing valu on a watershed is obviously a sound and cheaper course than restoration any kind. The primary objective maintenance is to preserve the wate controlling functions of the land. Th means keeping storm-flow discharg and sediment loads to a minimu Such an aim—since soil stability is t key to maintaining normal hydrolog behavior—can only be achieved wh the plant cover and soil mantle are condition to withstand damage fro occasional unusually heavy storm That is to say, a safety margin is nece sary. In countless cases it is the "usua storm that does the damage.

A high degree of fire control is t first requirement for maintaining sa isfactory watershed conditions. Th purpose of fire control in watersh management is to prevent a reducti in the density of the plant cover ar litter and in the organic-matter conte of the soil. Fires that bare the grou and lessen the water-holding capaci of the mantle almost invariably resu in accelerated erosion and increase storm-flow discharges, even on the sit where vegetation grows quickly.

Fire-control standards vary for ea drainage basin and for parts of drai age basins having different runoff ar erosion potentials. Steep watershe that are subject to rains of gre volume or high intensity obviously r quire more protection from fire tha areas on which there is a lesser risk accelerated erosion and flood runo

Fire-control plans must give ad quate consideration to the downstrea values. The presence of reservoirs, ha bors, canals, factories, farms, com munities, and other developments located downstream as to be susce tible of flood and sedimentation dam age may require a higher degree of fi control than is needed for the prote tion of the timber, forage, or oth resources on the watershed lands. some places the downstream valu nay be so great as to warrant a fire-ontrol program tight enough to pre-ent the occurrence of any man-made ire, with provision for the immediate uppression of naturally caused fires.

Construction improvements, such as oads, trails, airfields, and the like, are otentially hazardous from the stand-oint of runoff and erosion because hey uncover extensive land areas. The onstruction of such projects calls for pecial precautions.

First, roads, trails, and other clear-ngs should be located and designed so s to cause the least possible soil dis-urbance. Provision should be made for he immediate stabilization of cut and ll slopes. Because such projects in-ariably produce some runoff, experi-nce shows that adequate provision is eeded for safely passing the drainage vater to the natural channels, or for toring the runoff in the adjacent nantle by contour trenching or ter-acing the land. Provision for regular naintenance and prompt repair of cut nd fill slope stabilization works and of rainage facilities is essential. Where t is not feasible—physically or eco-omically—to meet these requirements f satisfactory watershed maintenance, he improvements should not be built.

The construction of water facilities, uch as dams, canals, and transmoun-ain diversions, present other problems. These require consideration of all pos-ible adverse effects as well as bene-icial effects on watershed conditions. All, of course, must be designed against ailure. Adequate provision should be nade in the design and operation of mpounding dams for maintaining an ffective habitat for fish and other quatic life. Transmountain diversions hould be constructed and operated so s not to cause the scouring of chan-els and consequent sedimentation in he areas to which water is diverted. Full advantage should be taken of op-ortunities to spread the store water nderground.

HARVEST CUTTINGS, timber-stand mprovement, thinnings, and the other cultural treatments of the forest and range cover offer possibilities of improving the usefulness of stream flow in two ways. Some types of treatment will result in increased, or more timely, yields of water; others, in less runoff.

Removal of trees and shrubs from along stream banks and on valley bottoms where the plant roots have continuous access to free water in the channels or valley fill is an effective means of reducing transpiration losses and thus increasing stream flow during the growing season. Conversion of a forest type to a plant cover that requires less water for growth offers another possibility of increasing water yields. It may be desirable on some western watersheds, for example, to suppress the deep-rooted aspen, which consumes up to about 20 inches of water in a growing season, and encourage a plant cover of more shallow-rooted grasses and herbs that require several inches less water for growth.

In other areas, where most of the stream flow is derived from winter snow, harvest cuttings of the conifers, which create openings for deeper accumulation of snow and decrease interception losses, offer another chance of obtaining a greater or a more prolonged yield of stream flow. Studies in Utah indicate the use of snowdrift fences may accomplish similar results on high-elevation and windswept snow fields. All such measures should be undertaken, however, only when they can be accomplished without causing accelerated erosion or a serious increase of flood discharges.

In many parts of the country the flood hazard is high because of prolonged, copious rainfall, or very high rates of rainfall and of snow melt. Flood control in such areas generally requires the maximum possible cover of vegetation and litter. Here harvest operations should be aimed at maintaining a canopy that will intercept and evaporate the greatest possible amount of precipitation before it reaches the ground. There should be a minimum of disturbance to the litter or the soil surface, so as to maintain maximum possible rates of infiltration of water into the mantle. Harvesting methods should also provide for the encouragement of the species that are capable of transpiring large quantities of water and thus maintain the greatest storage capacity in the mantle.

Logging operations can and often do cause serious watershed impairment, even though they leave the stand in satisfactory condition for natural regeneration. The chief injury is that brought about by the clearing and compaction of the soil along skid trails and haul roads. Compaction and consequent abnormally rapid surface runoff is known to persist for many years even though the land is quickly revegetated. Skid trails and similar disturbances to the soil should be held to a minimum. There should be adequate provision for the immediate stabilization of loosened soil, for the safe handling of drainage, and for the reestablishment of plant cover so as to prevent excessive runoff and accelerated erosion. Where these watershed maintenance requirements cannot be met, there should be no logging.

The most difficult of all watershed-management jobs is to maintain satisfactory watershed conditions on an area heavily grazed by livestock and big game. Many have considered this solely a western problem. But that is erroneous, for serious grazing-watershed problems exist in the Central States, in the South, and in the East.

The chief thing to avoid is overgrazing. When the livestock overcrop the herbaceous and shrubby forage, the ground surface is bared to the direct impact of the rain. This condition opens the canopy, permitting the sun's rays to hasten the disintegration of litter on the ground. Consumption of the forage, though it puts pounds on the grazing animals, robs the soil surface of its normal annual accumulation of dead grass stalks and leaves. Continued over the years, this further exposes the soil surface. In addition, the hoofs of the grazing animals compact the soil or push it down hill. All these effec lower the capacity of the land to soa up and store water and therefore favo destructive overland flow, accelerate erosion, and greater sediment loads i the streams.

Overgrazing results in progressivel serious stages of watershed deteriora tion. With each decrease in the capac ity of a site to take up and store wate less precipitation is required to caus overland flow and accelerated erosio Once the processes of deterioration ge under way, there is less and less contr of runoff and more and more soil los Thus, without any change of climat watershed impairment results in mor and larger storm flows and greate sediment loads.

The maintenance of satisfacto watershed conditions under grazing re quires extreme care in the handling c stock on the range and in the locatio and use of driveways, water develop ments, salt grounds, bed-grounds, an similar stock-control devices so as t give a minimum of soil disturbance an depletion of the plant cover. Grazin use should be avoided when the soil wet, particularly on sites that are su ceptible to compaction. In some plac satisfactory conditions can be mair tained by postponing grazing until aft the season of high-intensity storm Great care is needed to make certai that safely grazeable portions of a rang can be used without causing impai ment to adjacent lands.

Finally, there is need for adequat and frequent inspections. They shoul be made by men who can determin accurately the effect of grazing on th condition and trend of the range. The must not be limited solely to considera tion of the forage plants but must als give adequate consideration to the so and its litter surface. Inspections mu be followed by prompt remedial actio

The achievement of effective wate shed management is a big task, but is not hopeless. We have learned muc by observing the effects of unplanne exploitation of our forest and rang lands. Research in different parts of th ountry is now beginning to specify ffective management procedures. Experience and research show that effiient watershed management is usually he best possible forest and range management. Good forests, good range, ood soil, good water go together.

George W. Craddock *has worked vith the Intermountain Forest and Range Experiment Station since 1929. His work has included 4 years of reearch on spring-fall sheep range in daho and summer range in Utah, 4 ears on watershed research in Idaho, years on flood-control surveys with he Intermountain Region, and since 1946, he has been in charge of watershed management and protection research. Mr. Craddock is author and coauthor of many publications on subjects relating to his research. He holds degrees in agriculture and forestry from the University of California.*

Charles R. Hursh *is forest ecologist in charge of the Division of Forest Influences, Southeastern Forest Experiment Station. He was graduated from the University of Missouri in 1917, and received a doctor of philosophy degree from the University of Minnesota in 1923. Dr. Hursh joined the staff of the Southeastern Experiment Station in 1926.*

# TO HELP CONTROL FLOODS

GEORGE R. PHILLIPS, BERNARD FRANK

Many of our serious water problems ave their roots in the misuse of land. The same human activities that agravate water-shortage difficulties also ontribute to uncontrolled water surluses and all the misery and destrucion they bring in their wake. Basically, he flood-control program of the Deartment of Agriculture aims at more han the repair of damaged watersheds. Even more important, it seeks to help hose who now hold the land in trust o pass it on unimpaired so that the ational health and strength will be naintained.

Large acreages of our finest bottom ands lie increasingly exposed to the hreat of recurrent floods. Many farms re ruined beyond repair by the reentless cutting away of fertile fields hat border on streams. The safety and roductivity of the extensive industrial, ommunity, water-supply, and other levelopments are seriously endangered y the murky flows that so often orignate on the improperly handled crop, orest, or range lands.

Much more damage is caused anually on the average by the more frequent floods on the smaller tributaries than by the large, spectacular floods on the main streams. Flood and sedimentation damages alone now amount to well over 300 million dollars each year throughout the United States. More than 100 million dollars in losses occur on the Mississippi River system alone—damages that are mostly above and beyond the growing losses in the storage capacities of reservoirs due to filling with material carried down from eroding watersheds.

Progress has been made in the building of works on our major waterways to reduce the flood losses. Comparable progress will have to be made in treating watersheds to reduce the greater aggregate damages we find on the smaller streams and to slow down the rate at which sediment is ruining reservoirs.

Engineering developments cannot by themselves overcome the problems of floods, because they operate only after the floodwaters have concentrated in the main channels.

We must begin where the floods begin. We must retard the runoff and reduce or prevent the loss of soil from the watershed lands themselves, be-

802062°—49——40

fore they have a chance to build up to destructive potentials in the channels.

Floods are caused by the excess rain water that is not absorbed and temporarily stored in the soil or contained within defined watercourses. The damage caused by these overflows and by the sediment they carry and deposit may occur in fields adjacent to upland watercourses, in bottom lands along small tributary streams, and in the flood plains of great rivers.

Programs to improve watersheds are designed to work with nature by retarding runoff and reducing soil losses. That is accomplished by managing the soil and protective plant cover and by stabilizing gullies, watercourses, and stream banks to help control the movement of water from the time it falls as rain or snow until it enters the rivers and waterways. Such an approach builds and conserves the soil so that it will function to best advantage as a natural reservoir and at the same time become more productive.

A highly important, lasting effect of stabilizing and improving the soil and vegetation on a watershed is the gradual restoration by natural processes of a better balance between stream-channel conditions and the runoff they carry. The amount, rates, and quality of stream flow reflect the characteristics of a watershed during any given period, so any betterment in these characteristics in time brings a corresponding favorable adjustment in the habits of the stream.

Certain intense or prolonged rains produce so much water that even watersheds in the best of condition can modify the occurrence of high flood flows only to a limited extent. Proper watershed measures carefully installed and maintained can lower the frequency of floods, especially the smaller ones, greatly lessen the chances of occurrence of swift flash floods in the smaller valleys, and materially reduce the silt load that adds to both the flood volume and the amount of damage.

The natural processes whereby the soil and plant cover of a watershed operate to reduce flood flows and sedimentation are described earlier in this chapter. Let us consider briefly here the role of the land in the operation of the phase of the hydrologic cycle that pertains to flood discharges.

Watershed lands influence flood flows and sedimentation by the manner in which they dispose of rain and snow melt. Flood runoff from the land occurs when rain falls or snow melts faster than the soil can absorb it. The ability of the soil to take in and hold back water is affected in turn by the kind and condition of the vegetative cover, as well as by the structure and depth of the soil. Surface runoff is the most destructive. It is a highly important factor in sheet and gully erosion and in the rapid formation of flood peaks.

Rapid subsurface discharge from pervious shallow soils or soils with an impervious layer near the surface can also contribute to flood flows. Because the storage capacity of such soils is limited, it is soon used up, and any additional water entering the soil quickly drains off into channels. Subsurface discharge, however, is less destructive than surface runoff, in that it seldom causes erosion.

The basic principle involved in watershed flood control is to increase the ability of the soil to absorb water and temporarily keep it from entering stream channels and to control the runoff movement of water so that it causes a minimum of damage.

That is accomplished (1) by restoring and retaining a good cover of vegetation and litter to protect the soil against compaction and erosion and to increase its intake and storage capacity and (2) by stabilizing gullies, waterways, and tributary stream channels. During the growing season, vegetation, especially heavy forest growth, can also increase the storage capacity of the soil by rapid and heavy transpiration.

THE FLOOD CONTROL ACT of 1936 provides the basis for current Federal flood-control activities. It is an outgrowth of many years of an increasing realization of the importance of watersheds in control of floods and sedimentation. It reflects a growing awareness of the important interrelations between the condition of the watershed soils and vegetation and the rates of runoff.

The Flood Control Act is a historic marker in the growth of Federal legislation. It recognizes that destructive floods constitute a menace to the national welfare. It declares that flood-control investigations and improvements of rivers and other waterways and their watersheds are of general concern. It fosters local responsibility by providing that the Federal Government participate with States and their political subdivisions in the improvement of the navigable waters and their watersheds.

The act provides that Federal investigations of watersheds and measures for runoff and water-flow retardation and soil-erosion prevention on watersheds shall be undertaken under the direction of the Department of Agriculture, and that Federal investigations and improvements of rivers and other waterways for flood control and allied purposes shall be under the direction of the Chief of Engineers, Department of the Army. The two Departments work very closely together to handle the Federal responsibilities for flood control. The act also provides for appropriate correlation of such activities with investigations and river improvements incidental to reclamation projects of the Bureau of Reclamation.

Watershed flood-control activities are of two principal kinds: Investigations (preliminary examinations and surveys) of authorized watersheds, and installation of the watershed programs set forth in survey reports approved by Congress.

Preliminary examination reports contain such information as is necessary to determine whether watershed-treatment programs appear to be justified and whether surveys should be made. They are prepared largely from available data and generalized field examinations.

Survey reports describe the watersheds, their condition, flood history and flood damages, and outline remedial watershed programs and their estimated costs and benefits. They are prepared on the basis of field studies.

Both investigations and operations are conducted on a watershed or subwatershed basis. This concept is consistently followed from the initiation of the preliminary examination to the completion of the work program. The surveys develop over-all estimates of the types and quantities of remedial measures and works, their anticipated costs, and their physical and economic benefits. They do not include plans for the location or designs for the construction of specific works at specific sites. Such detailed location plans and construction designs are prepared as a part of the flood-control work plans, the first step in carrying out authorized operations on the ground.

The proposed watershed-improvement programs are recommended to Congress for flood-control operations, where the estimated total benefits to all interests concerned exceed the estimated total costs.

In developing these programs, consideration is also given to the measures and practices that will help conserve water for beneficial use, reduce pollution, and benefit fish and wildlife.

The survey reports include recommendations for public lands as well as for privately owned lands. Authorized work is initiated on the basis of agreements between the Department of Agriculture and other public agencies concerned.

In general, measures and practices installed on the lands not owned by the Federal Government are maintained by local interests. However, the Department of Agriculture has a responsibility in the public interest to see that the installed improvements on such lands are properly maintained. In the case of any major works, special consideration is given to Federal responsibility for their maintenance or for Federal supervision of their maintenance by other than a Federal agency. Survey reports indicate the proposed maintenance responsibility for the recommended types of remedial measures, together with the cost-allocation estimates.

As a means of testing effectiveness of the watershed programs and improving knowledge of watershed functioning, survey reports often provide for measuring the effects of the work upon flood flows, sedimentation, soil deterioration, and other factors in sample subwatersheds.

Watershed programs consist of such measures as the improvement of existing vegetative cover, the establishment of trees or other vegetation on denuded areas, and the protection of forests and grasslands from fire. They include the adoption of the best practices for the management of livestock and big game and of logging and forest-management practices that will maintain a good ground cover. They foster the proper use of close-growing and cover crops on tilled lands and such changes in land use and plant cover as will increase water absorption and retention in the soil and improve the soil storage capacity and crop production.

Still other measures include such soil- and water-conserving practices as contour cultivation, strip cropping, and supplemental mechanical devices or structures, like terraces, diversion ditches, check dams, small detention dams, and debris basins.

Whether the land is privately or publicly owned, the watershed-treatment programs are planned entirely by subwatersheds, with the various measures coordinated to obtain the maximum effectiveness of the work. Such measures as fire control, range reseeding, detention dams, debris basins, and stream-bank stabilization are installed only on a subwatershed basis because of the nature of the improvements and because several types and ownerships of land are often involved. However many measures (such as adjustments in use of land within farms, vegetation of farm pastures or woodlands, terraces, strip cropping, and contour farming) are installed on a farm-by-farm basis.

Altogether, the job of watershed treatment and management is one in which individuals, organizations, and local, State, and Federal Governments are concerned and from which all derive flood protection and other benefits of physical, economic, and social value.

Unless all parts of a watershed area are in good condition, damaging floods, erosion, and sedimentation may still occur. Unsatisfactory conditions on as little as 1 or 2 percent of a watershed may cause serious losses. It is of the utmost importance that the program for any watershed be considered as a whole. Although partial programs may help, the maximum possible reduction in flood and sedimentation damages and the greatest economy in expenditure can best be achieved by complete and unified application. That is the key purpose for which the program is designed, and that is the basis upon which it must be applied and maintained.

To obtain the maximum beneficial effects from a watershed-improvement program, installation should be scheduled on an orderly basis. In the case of the 11 programs already authorized by Congress, the periods specified in the survey reports vary by watersheds from 10 to 24 years. The estimated costs of installation and the expected beneficial effects of the programs outlined in the reports are geared to the specific installation periods. To the extent that delays occur in installing the programs, further watershed deterioration can be expected. Thus, the more the work is delayed, the greater will be the costs of installing the measures, and the longer it will take for them to achieve full effectiveness.

Two units of the Department of Agriculture, the Forest Service and the Soil Conservation Service, carry out the Federal responsibilities for the work programs. The preparation of the subwatershed work plans constitutes the first step in the operations phase. The work plans show what is to be done, where and how it is to be done, who will do it, what it will cost, and who will pay for it.

In preparing and carrying out the work plans, the Department cooperates closely with other public agencies. The programs contemplate local participation in installing and maintaining the various measures and practices. This involves furnishing equipment, material, labor, financial aid.

On the private lands, the Department furnishes the technical assistance and the information needed to develop the program. It lends, operates, and maintains equipment. It provides material and, sometimes, labor. It furnishes storage for materials and supplies. It cooperates with States, soil conservation districts, and the other legally acceptable organizations and individuals in carrying out the job.

Actually, many of the measures are installed by landowners and operators themselves in cooperation with soil conservation districts and with assistance from the Department of Agriculture and other Federal and State agencies. The kind and amount of assistance is based on what is needed to achieve the flood-control objectives and on the direct and indirect public benefits to be derived. The Department itself undertakes the job on lands under its administration, such as the national forests. It assists in applying flood-control measures on public lands under the administration of any other Federal or any State agency in the same manner as on privately owned lands, thus assuring proper integration of the work all over the watershed.

More than 600 watersheds have been authorized for preliminary examination and survey. The Department of Agriculture has made preliminary examinations of 164 watersheds, and completed 18 survey reports. The Congress has authorized improvement programs on 11 watersheds. Work has started on all of them.

Both the Forest Service and the Soil Conservation Service are responsible for making watershed examinations and surveys within assigned areas and for the technical and administrative determinations involved. They are also responsible for carrying on the operations called for by the approved programs.

In the Forest Service the investigations are undertaken through the forest and range experiment stations in the field and under the Division of Forest Influences Research in Washington.

The operation phases are carried out through the several administrative regional offices and under the Division of Watershed Management.

In the Soil Conservation Service, both investigations and operations are carried on through the regional offices in the field and under the Division of Water Conservation in Washington.

Policy, coordination, and other departmental responsibilities are handled by the Office of the Secretary of Agriculture.

The Department's flood-control program bears an important relation to the work of other public agencies. Cooperative arrangements are worked out and maintained from the beginning with other Federal agencies, and with State and local agencies at the field and the Washington levels. Such voluntary correlation during the development of the programs facilitates later clearance of final reports before their submission to the Congress.

Watershed programs cannot alone prevent floods nor can they alone protect the major river valleys from disastrous floods. Properly installed and steadfastly maintained, however, they will greatly lower the number of small floods and the damages to the flood plains of smaller tributaries. They will materially reduce sedimentation in reservoirs and in streams and rivers of all sizes, and modify the effects of major floods by maintaining the natural storage capacities of the watershed soils and retarding surface runoff. Only a properly designed combination of watershed and waterway treatments, encompassing all portions of a drainage basin and involving both watershed improvement and reservoirs and other necessary engineering works, can assure maximum flood protection.

Proper and continuing farm-, forest-, and range-management practices are essential to the permanent reduction of watershed damages. The repair of watersheds already damaged is only the first step. As our people understand, adopt, and demonstrate a more positive and responsible attitude toward resource conservation in all its forms, greater protection from flood and sediment damage by both land treatment and engineering activities will be realized.

GEORGE R. PHILLIPS *handles the coordination and other over-all phases of the flood-control program in the Office of the Secretary of Agriculture. Since his graduation in forestry from Michigan State College, he has worked with the Michigan Land Economic Survey and served as assistant State forester of Indiana, State forester of Oklahoma, State director for the Shelterbelt Project in Oklahoma, chief of the Division of State Forestry in the Forest Service, and chairman of the Farm Forestry Committee and the Water Facilities Board in the Department of Agriculture.*

BERNARD FRANK *is assistant chief of the Division of Forest Influences of the Forest Service, engaged in watershed management research and watershed flood-control investigations. He was graduated in forestry from Cornell University, and has done graduate work in the University of Wisconsin. He worked with the Forest Service on land-utilization problems in the southern Appalachian Mountains and in the Lake States, and served with the Tennessee Valley Authority as assistant chief forester on forest-resource investigations and planning.*

**Interception of rain and how it is stored on leaves and twigs.**

**Interception of snow and how it is stored in openings between trees.**

# Wood In Use

## THE WOOD FOR THE JOB

R. P. A. JOHNSON, CHARLES E. VAN HAGAN

BECAUSE WOOD is a part of every home and because anybody who can pull a saw or lift a hammer can work with wood, a general knowledge of its properties and uses will come in handy to every person who lives in a home.

The first point in selection of material for satisfactory performance depends on the use of the right wood for the right purpose. The man—or woman—who intends to work with wood has to determine what kind of service he expects to get from the wood. Will it be strength or hardness, or stiffness or resistance to decay, or beauty or some other property?

The use requirements usually do involve a combination of two or more, and selection involves finding the wood that has the best combination of the desired properties.

The species that have certain special properties that cost more (such as resistance to decay) should not be used unless those properties are definitely needed. For example: People often go to considerable expense to get highly decay-resistant wood for diving boards; they reason that the constant wetting and drying of the board demands it. Actually, however, the most important item in a diving board is strength, for most boards fail mechanically in a year or two if they are in continuous use, as at public beaches. The proper wood for this use, then, would be comparatively inexpensive and strong, selected with little regard to decay resistance.

Similarly, it will be wasteful to pay a premium price for wood with a beautiful grain pattern, like walnut or mahogany, for use in furniture that is to be painted. An inexpensive wood with equal or better painting characteristics but with little figure (yellow-poplar, for instance) would be a more logical choice. There is no economy in paying a high price for wood with a property that is not used.

Thus, wise use of wood in the home requires consideration of the properties needed and a basic knowledge of the main properties of the commercial

*Above: Building a prefabricated house—"The prospective buyer can learn a great deal about quality if he watches the workmen assemble a house."*

woods. The final choice of the wood may also be affected by the skill of the worker and the availability of the desired species. The farmer, for example, who wants to use wood growing on his own land has a limited selection and may not be able to choose the ideal wood for a given purpose, but with the actual demands clearly determined, he can make the most satisfactory and economical selection from the wood that he has.

The characteristics vary among species, among the individual trees of the same species, and even among pieces of wood taken from different heights of the same tree. Thus the published values for the different properties are averages and do not hold for every individual piece of wood.

One should also understand that wood does not have the same strength properties in all directions. Strength depends on the direction of the grain. When tension—pull—is applied parallel to or along the grain, for example, wood may be 300 times as strong as when the tension is applied at right angles to the grain.

The terms "hardwood" and "softwood" are used to distinguish between two general classes of wood and not to indicate the properties of the included species. Hardwood is the name given to the group of trees that are broadleaved. Softwood is the name given to trees that have needlelike or scalelike leaves and are mostly evergreen (cypress, larch, and tamarack being exceptions).

The hardwoods are not necessarily high in relative hardness; some woods classed as softwoods are actually harder than some classed as hardwoods. The softwoods are used principally in construction; the hardwoods furnish most of the wood for implements, furniture, and other industrial uses.

The weight of wood in itself has an important bearing upon the selection of a species for many uses. Weight also serves as a reliable index of the strength properties of dry wood and affords an accurate comparison between the strength properties of possible species when the degree of dryness and the actual sizes are the same. Generally speaking, the heavier a piece of dry wood, the stronger it is, regardless of the species.

Changes in temperature have little effect upon wood; they cause such small variations in size that for ordinary farm and home uses the effect of temperature can be overlooked.

Changes in moisture content, on the other hand, have a considerable effect on wood, which swells as it takes up moisture and shrinks as it dries. Difficulties may be encountered if this property is disregarded. When proper precautions are taken, however, most of the trouble due to swelling and shrinking can be avoided. The shrinking or swelling in the width of a flat-grained board is nearly twice that of a quartersawn, or edge-grained, board of the same width; the shrinkage or swelling lengthwise of the grain in both is negligible.

One can compensate for high shrinkage, if only that kind of wood is available, by using edge-grained pieces, which will prove as satisfactory as flat-grained stock of species that have lower shrinkage values. Much trouble can also be avoided by using only wood that has been dried to approximately the moisture content that the finished piece will have in service. Thorough air drying will take out about half and thorough kiln drying about two-thirds of the shrinkage of wood. That is enough for the ordinary uses.

Warping, which is the result of uneven shrinking or swelling, may occur in wood that is plain-sawed, or cross-grained, or improperly dried. It can be reduced to a minimum by the use of edge-grained, properly dried material.

Woods that are comparatively free from warping include: Northern and Atlantic white-cedar, eastern and western redcedar, cherry, chestnut, northern white pine, ponderosa pine, sugar pine, western white pine, yellow-poplar, redwood, walnut, and the eastern, Engelmann, and Sitka spruce.

THE STRENGTH PROPERTIES of wood at most concern the woodworker in-ıde bending strength, compression ength, stiffness, and toughness.

Bending strength is a measure of the ıd-carrying capacity of the members at are ordinarily used in a horizontal sition and rest on supports.

High bending strength is required in ırn rafters, girders, stringers, wagon ngues, and scaffold platforms. If the ıly available wood is low in bending ength compared with better-suited ecies, the deficiency can be overcome increasing the size of the member ed. An increase of 10 percent in the ight of a beam increases its bending rength by 21 percent. Both the vol-ne and bending strength of a beam, wever, increase in direct proportion the width is increased. Woods high bending strength for farm and home ilding include ash, beech, yellow rch, cherry, Douglas-fir, rock elm, ckory, the western larch, locust, hard aple, oak, southern yellow pine, and alnut.

Compression strength of wood is the easure of its ability to resist a load plied in such a direction that it tends crush the member, as in a post or lumn. Good compression strength is sential for members used to support ouses, garages, barns, storage bins, ıd the like, because they hold up a ad. It is not important in such items fence posts.

Low compression strength can be mpensated for in some instances by e use of proportionately larger mem-rs. In the construction of small ildings, then, the size requirements posts where the length is less than 11 mes the smallest dimension are de-rmined by bearing area, stiffness, and ability rather than by actual com-ression strength. Because these re-uirements necessitate the use of posts rge enough to carry greater actual mpressive loads than are ever placed oon them, no particular considera-on need be given to the compression rength endwise in selecting a wood r small houses. Where exceptionally heavy loads are involved, as in supports for bins or root cellars, the compression strength of the members should be considered. If the length is greater than 11 times the smallest dimension, the stiffness of the member becomes the controlling factor, and the compression strength can be disregarded. Of the woods used in farm and home building, those high in compression strength include white ash, eastern redcedar, cherry, Douglas-fir, hickory, western larch, locust, hard maple, southern yellow pine, redwood, and walnut.

Stiffness is a measure of the resistance to bending or deflection under a load. It assumes importance in floor joists of houses and in studding, where it is more important than the actual breaking strength. Lack of stiffness in these members will result in plaster cracks in ceilings and vibration of floors. Stiffness is important also in shelving, ladder rails, beams, ax handles, and long, slender columns. Construction practices can compensate for the lack of stiffness, on the one hand, or nullify the advantages of using wood with high stiffness on the other. Increasing the size of a member will increase its stiffness, but the use of wood that is not fully dry at the time of installation will result in a loss in stiffness of the structure as a whole, because the wood, as it dries, may shrink or split, so that the fastenings, bracing, and bridging will not hold so well. Woods high in comparative stiffness that are used in farm and home building include white ash, beech, yellow birch, cherry, Douglas-fir, rock elm, western hemlock, hickory, western larch, locust, hard maple, oak, southern yellow pine, the Sitka spruce, and walnut. Defects, such as knots, checks, and shakes have little effect upon stiffness. In light building construction, therefore, material of the sound, though knotty, grades may be used to good advantage for joists and studs because stiffness is more important than breaking strength in those items.

Toughness is a measure of the capacity to withstand suddenly applied loads. Tough woods, therefore, can withstand repeated shocks or blows, such as are given ax handles, wheel spokes, and wagon tongues. Because they are high in comparative toughness, the following woods are used in farm and home building when toughness is desired: Ash, beech, yellow birch, elm, hackberry, hickory, locust, hard maple, oak, and walnut. Of those woods, hickory is used most often if toughness is the main requirement.

NAILS, screws, and bolts for joining his work are a primary concern of the home woodworker, although a variety of timber connectors have been developed.

Because the strength of a unit depends on the fastenings, they merit careful consideration. The denser and harder the wood, the greater is its inherent nail-holding power. This resistance to withdrawal increases almost directly with the diameter of the nail. Thus, if the diameter of the nail is doubled, the holding power is doubled, providing the nail does not split the wood when it is driven. Nails have been treated in various ways in an effort to increase their holding power. Among such nails that are in common use, the cement-coated nail has a higher holding power than the common nail in well-seasoned wood, and the barbed nail a lower value.

The moisture content of the wood at the time of nailing strongly affects the holding power of nails driven into it. The best guarantee of good joints and high nail-holding power is to use well-seasoned wood. Nails driven into wet wood lose as much as three-fourths of their full holding power when the wood becomes dry, and such a practice can result in the loosening of siding, barn boards, fence pickets, and the like. If one has to use unseasoned wood, it is best to use barbed nails in it.

The holding power of nails is greatly reduced if the wood splits; even a slight amount of splitting results in a considerable loss in holding power. The heavy, dense woods, such as mapl oak, and hickory, split more in nailir than do the lightweight woods, such a basswood, spruce, and the true fir Woods of uneven texture, such a southern yellow pine and Douglas-fi split more than do the uniform-tex tured woods, such as eastern whi pine, sugar pine, or ponderosa pin Splitting due to nailing can be reduce by using smaller nails, but the numbe of nails must be correspondingly in creased to obtain the same holdin power. Blunt-pointed nails have smaller tendency to split wood than d sharp-pointed nails, but blunt-pointe nails have lower holding power. Th danger of splitting can be reduced b staggering the nails or by boring hol for the blunt-pointed nails.

THE SURFACE CHARACTERISTICS ( the wood affect its appearance and it strength and so should be considere when wood is selected for specific use

If maximum strength or fine appear ance is desired, the material should b chosen from the select grades, fror which most knots, pitch pockets, an the like are eliminated. The commo grades, which include those defects i greater or lesser amounts dependin upon the wood, should be used if ap pearance or high strength is not c primary importance or if knots or othe defects are desired for architectura effects, as in knotty pine trim.

A knot is the part of a branch or liml that has become embedded in the bod of a tree and subsequently has been cu through in the process of lumber man ufacture. There are various types c knots, but the distinction that th woodworker should know is the one be tween an encased knot and an inter grown knot. An encased knot is on whose rings of annual growth are no grown into those of the surroundin wood. An intergrown knot is one whos rings are completely intergrown witl those of the surrounding wood. Be cause the grain of knots is at a consid erable angle to the grain of the sur rounding wood, the knots in a flat-saw oard shrink at a faster rate than the emainder of the wood. If, as with ncased knots, the knots are not an ntegral part of the wood, they may ecome loosened even to the extent of alling out of the board.

Knots also affect both the appear-nce and the strength of a piece of ood. Except for knotty finish, they are onsidered objectionable from the tandpoint of appearance. They reduce he strength of lumber according to heir number, size, quality, and posi-ion in a piece. Strength is reduced nore by an intergrown knot than by n encased knot, or even a knot hole, ecause the wood fibers are more dis-orted.

Where painting is to be done, wood hat contains pitch—which is an ac-umulation of resin in the wood cells—hould be avoided because it does not asily retain paint or varnish. The elect grades of lumber allow only a mall amount of pitch. Pitch pockets ave a slight weakening effect on lum-er, but their chief disadvantage is that he liquid pitch sometimes runs out of he board in use. Woods that tend to ave pitch pockets can usually be de-ected by visual examination.

Wood deteriorates in use like any ther material. Iron and steel may rust pon exposure; wood may deteriorate hrough the action of fungi in damp laces. The best way to prevent decay n the wood used in homes and farms s to use only dry wood in the original vork and to keep it always dry.

Most of the wood used in homes does ot come in contact with moisture nough to cause concern. A number of he danger points, however, call for efinite precautions. Wood posts in asements should rest on concrete foot-ngs that rise about 3 inches above the loor. The same precautions should be aken where wood stairs rest on the asement floor. Points to watch outside he house include steps, siding, posts, nd framework of porches that are in ontact with the ground; basement vindow frames and siding that are near drain pipes; fence posts; and floors that are laid close to the ground over unventilated areas.

Untreated wood should be kept at least 18 inches above the ground level. When that is not practical, one should use heartwood of a decay-resistant species (sapwood of all species has low decay resistance) or wood that has been given a good preservative treatment. Wood that has been pressure-treated with a preservative gives the best service, but the life of fence posts and similar items can be extended by preservative treatment in a bath, a process the farmer or home owner can do himself.

Proper care of that kind and proper selection and use will give further evidence of the reasons why wood has been one of the foremost building materials for thousands of years.

R. P. A. Johnson *was trained in civil engineering at the Virginia Polytechnic Institute. He holds advanced degrees from the University of Wisconsin. He entered the Forest Service in 1908, serving in Montana, Arizona, New Mexico, and Arkansas. He transferred to the Forest Products Laboratory in 1918 and served in the Division of Industrial Investigations and the Division of Timber Mechanics, of which he is now the chief.*

Charles E. Van Hagan *was graduated from the University of Wisconsin as a civil engineer in 1936. After graduate work in transportation at Yale University, he was employed as an engineer by two construction firms and the Wisconsin Highway Department before joining the Forest Products Laboratory as an engineer in 1944. He is the secretary-treasurer of the Forest Products Research Society.*

*The last section of this book contains more information on the average weights of wood, characteristics and properties, and similar subjects of value to the home owner. Attention is directed to the list of some of the Forest Products Laboratory publications.*

# SEASONING OF WOOD

RAYMOND C. RIETZ

The living tree holds gallons and gallons of water in the walls and cell cavities of the fibers that make up the structure of its wood. The fibers dry out and shrink when they are exposed to air. Thus the rough products of the tree—poles, posts, ties, boards, ax-handle blanks, barrel staves—shrink as the water evaporates from the wood. This is the seasoning process—drying and shrinking.

The use to which the seasoned wood is to be put determines how much water is to be removed in drying. Lumber for a barn, which is exposed only to changing outdoor air conditions, need not be dried to as low a moisture content as hardwood boards for fine furniture, which is exposed to heated indoor air in winter. Another example: Wood for a croquet ball, which has to stay round despite knocks and dampness, must be dried and shrunk more than wood that is to be used in a rough packing crate.

Two principal seasoning processes are in common use, air drying and kiln drying, each of which is better adapted to some uses than the other.

The air drying of wood is much like drying the family washing, except that the boards cannot be so simply hung on lines or directly exposed to the sun and the wind. It consists of piling the lumber outdoors so that air currents can circulate through the pile and carry away the moisture from the surface of the wood. As the surface dries, moisture from within the board replaces it and, in turn, is carried away by the air. It is a slow process, but on the whole is quite satisfactory. For some special uses, such as hardwood furniture, flooring, and millwork, air drying in most parts of the United States does not dry wood to a low enough moisture content for satisfactory use. In such cases the hardwood lumber is usually first air-dried at the producing sawmill and then kiln-dried to a still lower moisture content at the woodworking factory.

With a little care and attention to details, lumber can be piled so that it will not warp, check excessively, or become infected with decay while air seasoning.

First, the air-drying yard should be laid out to make full use of the prevailing winds, because the greater the air movement through the pile, the quicker the lumber will be dried. The bottom of the pile should be designed to allow free movement of air underneath, and this pile should usually be arranged so that it slopes from front to rear in order that rain water will drain away readily. The slope of the pile is determined by the arrangement of the piers, those at the front being higher than those at the rear of the pile. To reduce yarding costs, some producers are experimenting with horizontal lumber piles built up from "packages" of lumber moved about with lift trucks. The pile piers are all of the same height to accommodate the handling equipment, and the built-up seasoning piles are flat.

As the pile goes up, it should have a forward pitch of about an inch to each foot of height. Over each layer of boards, narrow strips, called stickers, should be laid crosswise, about 2 to 4 feet apart, to keep the layers separated. An inch or two of space should be allowed between the edges of boards for air to move up or down through the pile. Boards should be placed carefully, so that the various air channels are unobstructed. Stickers likewise should be lined up one above the other; otherwise the boards lying on them may be bent by the weight of the boards above and warp in drying. Finally, a roof consisting of a double layer of boards, the upper layer overlapping the lower, should be put over the pile so that it will overhang the front end 1 or 2 feet and should be held about 6 inches above the top layer of boards by a few timbers laid crosswise on the pile. Piles should be built so there will be no overhanging boards at the rear.

When conditions favor too rapid drying and excessive checking, the checking can be reduced by making wider piles, narrowing the space between piles, piling the boards edge to edge, narrowing the vertical air channels, using thinner stickers, and, sometimes, by using shields around the pile for protection against wind, rain, and sun. When the season of the year reduces likelihood of checking, or the species being dried is not likely to check easily, the circulation of air through the pile can be stimulated by opening up the pile. Faster drying is thereby obtained, and stain and decay are retarded. Roof boards or pile covers prevent exposure of the boards in the top layer to the direct heat of the sun, which will invariably cause checking. At some plants, lumber of high value is air-dried in open sheds to prevent loss of quality by more direct exposure to the elements.

KILN DRYING is a process designed to hasten drying by circulating large volumes of warmed air through carefully piled lumber. Modern drying kilns equipped with blowers or fans can dry wood more thoroughly in a few days than can be done by air seasoning in months. For some kinds of lumber, kiln drying is indispensable.

In modern dry kilns, conditions can be had that favor the fastest possible drying with a minimum of drying defects. In kiln drying, as in air drying, the atmosphere is used as the medium whereby heat is conducted to the wood to evaporate the water it contains. In kiln drying, however, the atmospheric conditions of temperature and relative humidity can be controlled with a reasonable degree of accuracy. Thus, the dry kiln is independent of weather conditions.

Most modern dry kilns are of the forced-air-circulation type. Steam coils are generally used for heating air that is circulated through the loads of lumber. Recently, furnace-type dry kilns have been developed for use where it is not economical to install steam boilers. In such dry kilns, the steam-heated coils are replaced by large pipes or manifolds in which the hot gases resulting from the burning of sawdust, gas, oil, or other fuel are circulated.

Good results depend largely on good piling practices. For kiln drying, lumber is usually flat-piled on kiln trucks with an adequate number of stickers. Warping of boards is prevented by good piling, stickers used in good vertical alinement, and other mechanical devices that make better loads.

The way air circulates within the kiln determines how the loads are to be piled. Thus, in internal-fan kilns designed to move air across the loads, the lumber is piled edge to edge in each layer. In external-fan kilns designed to deliver air upward into the load from a central delivery duct, the lumber is usually stacked with an A-shaped flue in the middle of the load to distribute the delivered air. Many natural-draft kilns are still in use, however, and in such kilns the lumber is piled with spaces between the boards and usually with one or more flues. In contrast to the forced-air-circulation kiln with its edge-to-edge piled loads, the load as piled for a natural-draft kiln contains considerably less volume or footage.

Designing a lumber dry kiln requires a knowledge of mechanical heating as well as ventilation engineering. Some kilns seem to be of simple engineering arrangement, but actually the relation of the size of the room to the size of the kiln charge and the placement of fans, fan baffles, ducts, and heating coils are not simple.

The design of the heating system and the method of coupling it to the temperature-control apparatus (so as to provide uniform temperatures along the length and height of the entering-air side of the kiln charge) are particularly important if precision drying is to be done. The structural materials in the building, whether wood, concrete, brick, or tile, also have a bearing on the expected life and maintenance costs of the kiln. Manufacturers of dry kilns and engineers can provide such engineering services.

The early dry-kiln designs involving forced-air circulation with internal fans were developed at the Forest Products Laboratory, and the patents on them were dedicated to public use. The dry-kiln companies and engineers whose designs are based on those patents attest to the soundness of the design. The development by the Forest Products Laboratory of the internal-fan type of dry kiln resulted from a need for drying freshly sawn lumber quickly, cheaply, and with control of seasoning defects.

Perhaps the most important aspect of kiln operation is the changing of the conditions of temperature and relative humidity within the kiln so as to control the drying of lumber in accordance with a definite schedule. In most schedules, the initial drying conditions for lumber that is freshly sawn are mild enough to prevent seasoning defects, such as end and surface checking. For some hardwoods, the initial temperature may be 105° F.; and some softwoods can be subjected to 180°. The initial relative humidities are quite high (80 percent), but they are rapidly reduced as the stock becomes drier. As the lumber dries, the temperature is usually raised until rather high temperatures and low humidities are reached near the end of the process. Final temperatures are often near 200°, and final relative humidities as low as 15 percent.

A typical drying schedule is based on the moisture condition of the lumber, and changes in temperature and relative humidity are made when certain stages of lumber dryness are obtained. Samples in the kiln are periodically weighed to determine the moisture condition of the stock, and the rate at which the samples dry determines when the changes in temperature and relative humidity are made. Some of the softwoods, however, are dried at such high temperatures and in such short periods of time that the changes in drying conditions are placed on a time basis. In that case, freshly cut lumber is subjected to certain initial drying conditions that are changed after a certain number of hours of drying, the time of the changes having been determined by previous studies or experience.

Before any charge of lumber is removed from the dry kiln, it is desirable to operate the kiln at conditions that tend to bring all of the boards to the same moisture content. Some boards dry faster than others and the drying conditions are changed so that the dry boards will not overdry but the high moisture-content boards will continue to lose moisture. This is called the equalizing period. The time required to equalize a charge of lumber depends on the species, its thickness, and the degree of nonuniformity of its moisture content at the time the stock is ready for equalizing. After equalizing, the lumber may be subjected to a conditioning treatment to relieve stresses that develop during the drying process. If hardwood lumber, for example, is not properly conditioned after kiln drying, boards, when resawn or cut into two thinner pieces, will tend to cup toward the newly sawn faces and may not be suitable for the use intended.

Wood that has been kiln-dried to low moisture-content values that are more nearly in equilibrium with those of winter-heated homes will absorb moisture from the atmosphere if it is stored in warehouses where normal outdoor air conditions prevail.

One of two courses is recommended for lumber stocks that have been kiln-dried to low moisture-content values, such as required in the furniture industry. Either the dry lumber should be fabricated immediately and the products protected from moisture changes with finish coatings, or the stock should be stored in warehouses hat are heated sufficiently to reduce the relative humidity.

RAYMOND C. RIETZ *was trained in economics and mechanical engineering in Beloit College and the University of Wisconsin. He was employed by a producer of southern hardwood lumber in central Mississippi before he joined the Forest Products Laboratory in 1928. During the Second World War he was assistant to the chief of the Division of Matériel Containers. He directs research in the seasoning and physical properties of wood as chief of the Division of Timber Physics in the Laboratory. He has written several articles on the seasoning of wood, and has developed a method of kiln drying pine cones for seed extraction.*

# PRESERVATIVE TREATMENT OF WOOD

THOMAS R. TRUAX

Wood now in useful service is being destroyed in this country by decay and insects at the rate of several billion board feet a year—an amount approaching the normal average used annually in the construction of dwelling units. The enormous drain upon the resources of our forests can be lessened through greater use of preservative-treated wood, one piece of which may do the work of several replacements of untreated wood.

The railroads long ago found that preservative treatments save wood and money. In the early days when most railroad ties were untreated, railroads required for replacements each year approximately 450 ties to the mile; in recent years when a large percentage of all ties in service were treated, they required less than one-third as many replacements to the mile. The same order of savings also applies to telegraph and telephone poles and to poles for other public-utility lines. Ninety percent of all poles now being set in the ground are either fully treated or butt-treated.

Many other wood products that are exposed to decay and insect attack are not so extensively treated. For example, a large part of the 600 million fence posts set yearly are not treated, although it has been shown that many species of wood in post size will last from 3 to 10 times as long when well-treated as when untreated. The serviceable life of still other products would be increased by preservative treatments.

The type of preservative used and the thoroughness with which the wood is treated have much to do with the length of service rendered by the wood. Good preservatives and poor treatments or poor preservatives and good treatments are of little value. The purpose of treating wood with preservatives is to protect it against decay organisms, insects, and marine borers.

Preservatives of various kinds are used to treat various classes of wood products.

Among the wood-preserving oils, coal-tar creosote has long been effective. It has good penetrating properties and will remain in the wood for many years; it is safe to handle, harmless to wood and metal, readily available, and reasonably cheap. It is used mainly on wood that is to be in contact with the soil and water out of doors, and where its odor will be unobjectionable and painting will be unnecessary.

For wood that is used indoors or not in contact with the ground or water outdoors, water-borne preservatives are usually favored. Among these are zinc chloride, chromated zinc chloride, and several proprietary preservatives consisting of various mixtures of compounds of arsenic, chromium, copper, or fluorine, all of which leave the wood in a paintable condition.

Still other preservatives, such as

pentachlorophenol, that are soluble in volatile oils, when they are so used, provide clean, odorless, readily paintable, treated wood suitable for interior or exterior use.

Many proprietary preservatives of undisclosed composition are on the market. Some of them are good, but others have little value. A good precaution to take before accepting any proprietary preservative is to have the manufacturer state the ingredients used in his products.

Preparing the wood for treatment is necessary for satisfactory results with any treating process.

In a few methods the wood is treated green and sometimes with the bark on, but usually it should be well peeled, and, for best results with most processes, seasoned. Because preservatives will not make weak timber strong or restore the strength of timber that has been partly destroyed by decay, only sound timber should be used. The cutting, boring, and framing of the wood should be completed before treatment, if possible, to avoid the exposure of untreated surfaces that often results when cutting is delayed until after the treatment.

Wood is treated by both pressure or nonpressure processes, although the bulk of wood treated is given a pressure treatment. For most uses, wood that has been treated under pressure gives the best service. Such treatments require closed cylinders with vacuum, pressure, and heating facilities.

A number of pressure processes differ from one another in a few details, but the general principle is the same in all. The wood, placed on steel cars, is run into a long steel cylinder, which is then tightly closed and filled with preservative. The wood may be steamed or otherwise heated to reduce its moisture content and be subjected either to a vacuum or to an initial air pressure before the preservative is admitted to the cylinder. By a proper use of pressure and heat, the preservative is forced into the wood until it has absorbed the desired amount. In most kinds of wood, this results in a relatively deep penetration. This treatment, when properly made with a good preservative, should add from 20 to 30 years to the life of untreated wood for most uses. About 200 pressure-treating plants are in operation at various points in the United States.

Of the nonpressure methods, the hot-and-cold bath method is the most effective. It involves less equipment than pressure processes and is better adapted to the small commercial and home-use treatments, such as those recommended for fence posts. This method requires either one or two open treating tanks. In the one-tank method, the wood is first heated and then cooled in the same treating solution. The wood may also be heated in air, steam, or other media, and then placed in the tank of cold preservative. In the two-tank process, the wood is heated in a tank of hot preservative and then quickly transferred to the other tank, where it is submerged in cold preservative and allowed to cool. In all cases the heating and subsequent cooling creates a partial vacuum within the wood that aids penetration of the preservative. The treatment, when properly made with a good preservative, should increase the serviceable life of the wood by many years. With equal penetration and absorption of the preservative, pressure- and nonpressure-treated wood should be equal in serviceability.

Other nonpressure methods of more recent development are the cold-soaking of seasoned timbers in oil solutions of pentachlorophenol and other oil-soluble preservatives and the steeping of green or freshly cut timbers in water-borne preservatives. A single tank or container for the preservative is sufficient, but soaking treatments usually require a longer period to get the wood well-treated than when the hot-and-cold bath process is employed. When thoroughly done, these soaking methods add appreciably to the serviceable life of wood.

Brushing or spraying a preservative on wood adds only about 1 to 3 years to its serviceable life. Applied in this way, the preservative does not penetrate the wood deeply enough to form an effective barrier to wood-destroying organisms, termites, or borers, so that only a limited degree of protection can be expected.

For many years the Forest Products Laboratory has conducted tests on preservative treatments and maintained service records on treated and untreated fence posts, poles, railroad ties, and other forms of timber subject to decay and insect attack, often in cooperation with farmers, railroads, industrial concerns, experiment stations, and the national forests.

Service records have shown the good natural durability of the heartwood of such species as cedars, baldcypress, chestnut, black locust, Osage-orange, and the redwood, and the nondurable properties of the sapwood of all species, and the heartwood of many, unless protected by a preservative treatment. They have also shown differences in the value of various preservatives and methods of treatment, which provide the basis for treating specifications on which the wood-preservation industry is largely based.

THOMAS R. TRUAX *is a graduate of Iowa State College. From 1913 to 1918 he was a member of the staff of the forestry department in that institution. Since 1918 he has been engaged in research on forest products at the Forest Products Laboratory and now is chief of the Division of Wood Preservation, which conducts investigations in the preservation of wood, fireproofing, painting, glues, gluing, and veneer cutting.*

# PAINTING THE FARM AND CITY HOME

FREDERICK L. BROWNE

Painting is a good way to make wood houses attractive and to freshen or change their appearance. Paint can give wood an endless variety of colors.

The colors are important elements in design. White, or a light color, makes a small house look larger. A dark color makes a large house look smaller. Light tints emphasize attractive parts, and dark shades suppress unattractive parts of a building. Pleasantly contrasting colors can restore harmonious balance among unshapely parts of a building.

The natural color of wood after it has been exposed to the weather for a few months is dark gray, although at high altitudes it is often brown. If the gray color is satisfactory, wood buildings can remain unpainted and the cost of paint maintenance thereby be saved. Buildings unprotected by paint are by no means unusual; in fact, the two oldest frame buildings in the United States, one in Dedham, Mass., and the other in St. Augustine, Fla., have never been painted. Surviving houses of the Amana Society in Iowa still have unpainted wood siding more than three-quarters of a century old.

The decorative program for a wood building should be chosen when the building is first planned. Woodwork to be kept painted should consist of smoothly surfaced boards or plywood. Smooth wood can be painted with a third of the amount of paint and with far less effort than is required for wood with the rough surface left by sawing or splitting. The glossy paints used for house painting need smooth surfaces if the paint is to show to best advantage. On the other hand, unpainted woodwork exposed to the weather soon becomes rough; economy therefore dictates the initial choice of unsurfaced woodwork for such use.

Unpainted woodwork needs to be thicker in dimension and more firmly

802062°—49——41

fastened in place than may always be necessary for well-painted woodwork. The weather, by alternately wetting and drying the exposed surfaces of boards more rapidly than the moisture content can readjust itself within the boards, sets up severe internal stresses within the wood. The outcome is, successively, a roughening of the wood grain; wood checking; a tendency for boards to cup, to withdraw nails, and to split if they are unduly thin or short; and a tearing loose of wood fibers from the surface at such a rate that boards lose as much as one-fourth inch of thickness a century. For exposure without painting, boards should not be thinner than one-eighth their width nor shorter than four times their width; they should be kept firmly fastened with hardware that withstands corrosion without painting.

A coating of house paint on exposed wood surfaces prevents weathering by slowing down the entrance or exit of moisture enough to keep nearly equal moisture content from the center to the surface of the boards. Internal stresses are thus avoided, and the boards stay flat and keep their smooth surfaces.

With white paint, which should be renewed every 5 years, it may take 50 gallons of paint a century for each 1,000 square feet of surface to prevent the weathering away of wood. It is cheaper, of course, to omit the paint and let the wood waste away slowly, but the better appearance makes painting worth its moderate cost.

Transparent finishes sometimes are favored. The grain and color of freshly cut and smoothly surfaced wood are attractive enough to appeal to persons who like the unusual. In consequence, there is a demand for a transparent protective coating that will serve, as paint does, in preventing wood weathering and yet will not conceal the wood.

Spar varnish is one way to do it, but modernists seldom want the glossiness of a varnish finish. For that reason, linseed oil or certain proprietary oils or wood sealers, sometimes called log oils, have become popular.

The oils and sealers penetrate into the surface of wood instead of overlaying it with a coating as paint and varnish do; because the barrier against the weather is imperfect when little or no coating is interposed, the oils and sealers furnish less protection than varnish and much less than paint. Also, because the transparent finishes are less durable than paint, they must be renewed about once a year or oftener. A century's protection for 1,000 square feet of surface, therefore, may require 200 to 250 gallons of oil, sealer, or varnish, whereas 50 gallons of paint does the job more effectively. It is no wonder our thrifty ancestors preferred paint when they wanted smooth woodwork!

The transparent exterior finishes have two further disadvantages.

First, if they are allowed to go too long before renewal, the wood begins to turn gray from weathering. Once that happens, renewal of finish must begin with tedious scraping or sanding away of the weathered wood to regain a bright surface.

Second, the transparent finishes are readily attacked by fungi, which discolor the surfaces badly. The danger of fungus attack, or mildew, can be reduced greatly by putting a suitable preservative in the oil, sealer, or varnish. Proprietary sealers and varnishes containing a preservative are sold in paint stores. When linseed oil is used, the preservative, pentachlorophenol, can be dissolved in it to the extent of 5 percent by weight. If the wood contains sapwood, in which discoloring fungi grow readily if the wood becomes damp, the wood may well be treated with a commercial water-repellent preservative before the transparent finish is applied.

Rough, unsurfaced wood, which may be unduly expensive to paint, may nevertheless be colored other than the gray of weather-beaten wood. Shingle stains are inexpensive kinds of paint. They are made with pigments, linseed oil, and much volatile thinner; they are thin enough to be applied easily to rough wood, and they impart color without glossiness and without seriously obscuring the rough texture of the surface. A preservative, such as creosote or a pale distillate from creosote, is often added to shingle stain.

Although paint prevents the weathering of wood, paint cannot be relied on to prevent decay. Decay comes from the action of fungi on damp wood. Nearly always it starts on unpainted concealed surfaces and it continues usually well within the wood at a distance from the painted surface. Paint, in fact, even hastens decay if water enters the wood at unpainted joints or concealed faces and can only dry out through the painted surfaces. The paint then slows the drying and keeps the wood damp longer. Decay in buildings is prevented chiefly by taking care that masonry or other rot-resistant material is used for all contacts with damp ground or other continuing source of moisture and by seeing that all woodwork will either remain dry or dry out promptly after it is exposed to water for a short time. If wood must be used in damp places, it should be the heartwood only of naturally durable woods or wood that has been thoroughly impregnated with wood preservative.

A PAINTING PROGRAM should be planned before a house is finished—once it has been decided to build with smooth surfaced woodwork.

The principal items in a painting program are a suitable kind of paint, a reasonable schedule for repainting, and the proper amount of paint to be applied at each painting.

The ideal program is one of repair and renewal of coatings before they break up badly enough to require replacement. Over-all economy comes from anticipating and forestalling serious failures. Too often paint maintenance is left entirely unplanned, and each job is done on the spur of the moment, perhaps after the coating has come loose. The cost of repainting is therefore higher and one is prone to malign paint as being less predictable in performance than almost anything else about the house.

The most popular color for homes is white. Most wood homes are small and need the emphasis of white or a light color. For white paint of good quality, properly applied, the reasonable schedule of maintenance calls for repainting every 4 or 5 years. On some woods that are more difficult than others to paint well, special care is needed to meet that schedule.

As I described in *Wood Properties and Paint Durability,* Miscellaneous Publication No. 629 of the Department of Agriculture, the heavier softwoods, like southern yellow pine and Douglas-fir, need a carefully chosen priming paint the first time the wood is painted. Aluminum house paint is the best priming paint for the purpose. One should be sure, however, that it is aluminum house paint, not aluminum paint for some other purpose. Two coats of white paint, or paint of light color, are then needed over the aluminum paint. If the coating is then maintained by repainting before it wears away too badly, the aluminum paint need not be used again. Next best to aluminum house paint for priming the heavier softwoods are the modern house-paint primers that contain no zinc oxide and that have the property commonly called "controlled penetration." Most dealers in house paint now sell such primers.

White is popular although it is less durable than good paints of other colors. Paints of colors like cream, light yellow, light gray, buff, and tan, that are light enough to have much the same accentuating effect as white, will last a year or so longer than white paint and thus fit a schedule of repainting every 5 or 6 years. Such light colors, called tints, are made by adding very small proportions (usually less than 5 percent by weight) of colored pigments to a white paint. The added durability is remarkably great for such a slight difference in composition.

Still greater durability, one that

permits longer intervals between repaintings, can be obtained with paints made with large proportions of colored pigments and little or no white pigment. Colored-pigment paints, except for some brilliant yellows and reds, are dark paints that tend to suppress rather than to accentuate. The brilliant yellows and the reds are too gaudy for use on anything larger than minor areas of trim on buildings; besides, they make relatively expensive paints. Duller, more grayish yellows, reds, maroons, and browns, which are made from pigments containing iron oxide, are appropriate for the body color of some buildings. Paints of such colors may be moderate in cost and of exceptionally long life; with the best of them, a schedule of repainting at intervals as long as 10 years, is practicable.

Because the single-family home is usually a fairly small building, the popular choice of white or a light color to accentuate it is appropriate even though it commits the owner to more frequent repainting than might otherwise be necessary. Brightly painted homes, of course, may have the paints of dark color for contrast on trim or on parts that need toning down. The schedule of maintenance, however, is usually fixed by the requirements of the least durable paint because convenience is likely to dictate that all repainting be done at one time.

THE FARM HOME is often a small house in the midst of a group of larger buildings. The American tradition most appropriately has been to emphasize the home with white paint, but to offset the dominating size of the farm buildings by painting them dark red, relieved by contrasting touches of white trim. The home is thus made the center of the picture; the barns are reduced to supporting background; and the whole conforms to the philosophy of farming as a way of life. The scheme permits an economical painting program of once in 4 or 5 years for the house, and once in 8 or 10 years for the larger area presented by the farm buildings.

Recently a vogue has developed for painting farm buildings white. Perhaps it is to be interpreted philosophically as a shift to the concept of farming as primarily a business in which the housing of cows is more important than the housing of humans. Certainly if barns are to be accented with bright paint, they should be made architecturally more attractive than they generally have been in years past. Judging from experience, in which many farmers have been unable to keep up with the moderate 10-year program for red paint, it seems unlikely that a 5-year program with white paint will prove generally practicable. Besides, a white building badly in need of repainting calls attention to itself far more forcefully than does a modestly dark-red building in a like condition.

OF THE MANY WAYS OF MAKING PAINT, some make more durable or more reliable paint than others. No one way is superior to the others in every respect, for an improvement in one property usually necessitates some sacrifice in another. For example: Old-fashioned, pure white lead paint is more reliable in performance and wears out by a fine crumbling that makes it stand postponement of repainting longer than other white paints will, but white lead paint has the disadvantage of becoming more grimy with dirt than some other paints do. On the other hand, the more recent paints made with titanium dioxide, zinc oxide, and white lead, together with other necessary pigments and liquids, remain relatively clean and bright in appearance. They do not, however, retain color so well and, if repainting is postponed beyond the proper time, they look shabbier and are more troublesome to prepare for repainting than white lead paint.

Home owners who plan their maintenance programs carefully and stick to them can take full advantage of the newer paints, but those who may neglect their repainting would be wiser to use white lead paint.

Correct thickness of coating is necessary for reliable performance of the paint. For linseed-oil house paints, experience has shown that correct thickness is about 0.005 inch. Coatings much thinner than that wear away sooner than is necessary; coatings much thicker than that are unduly brittle and are likely to behave badly. A common mistake the first time a house is painted is to apply too little paint. Thereafter, in maintaining the coating, the tendency in towns and cities (although less often on farms) is to paint too often or with too much new paint at a time.

For painting new woodwork it takes about 3.6 gallons of prewar house paints, which are rich in linseed oil, to leave a coating 0.005 inch thick on 1,000 square feet of surface. It can be done either with three coats of about 1.2 gallons each or, if the paint is of the best quality, with two coats of 1.8 gallons each. Present paints, however, usually contain less linseed oil and more volatile thinner than the prewar paints. It therefore takes about 4.5 gallons (three coats of 1.5 gallons each) to leave the desired 0.005 inch of coating on 1,000 square feet. Two coats with such paint would require 2.25 gallons each, which is more paint than it is practicable to apply on smooth surfaces at one time.

Repainting should not be done until much of the coating has worn away, say 0.002 inch of the original 0.005 inch. The repainting should then restore the lost thickness but not much more. That can be done with 1.4 gallons of prewar paint, or 1.8 gallons of present paint, on 1,000 square feet of surface. The repainting in such cases can be done with one heavy coat or two thin ones.

The present method of selling paints by trade brands without conforming to trade standards of any kind makes it exceedingly difficult for paint users to exercise choice in selecting kinds of paint or to learn how they are best used. The manufacturers' directions for applying paint, for example, fail to indicate the important difference in the methods of applying the prewar and the present paints. The user is allowed to assume that he may properly spread the present paints over as much surface as he formerly did the prewar paints. Most responsible paint manufacturers report the composition of their paints on the labels, as the laws of some States require, but the formulas are stated in a complicated, highly technical manner. Paint users, who are able and willing to learn how, can get the needed information from the formulas by calculations. Methods of making the calculations are described in my booklet, *Classification of House and Barn Paints,* Technical Bulletin 804 of the Department of Agriculture. The bulletin points out a method of classifying paints by group, type, and grade that, if adopted by the industry, would simplify the explanation of paint to paint users and permit painting programs for buildings to be set forth in a reasonably simple manner.

This classification of native woods for relative ability to hold paint coatings may be helpful.

*Type A* are paints that wear out by checking and crumbling, such as pure white lead paint.

*Type B* are paints that wear out by cracking, curling, and flaking, such as paints containing zinc oxide mixed with other pigments.

Group 1—Woods on which paints of types *A* and *B* last longest.

*Softwoods:*

Alaska-cedar.
Incense-cedar.
Northern white-cedar.
Port-Orford-cedar.
Southern cedar.
Western redcedar.
Baldcypress.
Redwood.

Group 2—Woods on which paints of type *B* wear out faster than they do on woods of group 1, through paints of type

*A* last as long as they do on woods of group 1:

*Softwoods:*
- Eastern white pine.
- Western white pine.
- Sugar pine.

Group 3—Woods on which paints of types *A* and *B* wear out more rapidly than they do on groups 1 or 2:

*Hardwoods:*
- Aspen.
- Basswood.
- Cottonwood.
- Magnolia.
- Yellow-poplar.

*Softwoods:*
- White fir.
- Eastern hemlock.
- Western hemlock.
- Lodgepole pine.
- Ponderosa pine.
- Eastern spruce.
- Engelmann spruce.
- Sitka spruce.

Group 4—Woods on which paints of types *A* and *B* wear out more rapidly than they do on woods of group 3:

*Hardwoods:*
- Beech.
- Birch.
- Blackgum.
- Maple.
- Redgum.
- Tupelo gum.

*Softwoods:*
- Douglas-fir.
- Red pine.
- Southern yellow pine.
- Tamarack.
- Western larch.

Group 5—Woods unsuitable for conventional house painting because wood filler is required before painting to fill the large pores properly:

All hardwoods with pores larger than those in birch, as ash, chestnut, elm, hickory, oak, walnut.

FREDERICK L. BROWNE *has been in charge of work on painting and finishing of wood at the Forest Products Laboratory since 1922. He studied chemistry at Cornell University and the University of Wisconsin.*

# FUNGI AND WOOD

CARL HARTLEY

Wood is subject to several kinds of defects or blemishes that are caused by fungi and bacteria. They are forms of plant life. Many of them grow on the contents of the cells of the wood but do not attack the cell walls; their only important effect is on color. Only part of the discolorations are due to organisms and the causes of many of them have yet to be determined. Most discolorations of hardwoods are already present before the tree is cut, but sap stain or blue stain usually occurs after the lumber is sawed.

The discolorations of yellow-poplar, the tuliptree, are particularly striking. In this and several other important species most of the discolorations have been found to indicate no appreciable weakening of the wood. Browned or bleached spots or streaks, however, commonly indicate the presence of decay fungi, which dissolve the cell walls and thereby weaken or destroy the structure.

The decay fungi belong to a special group, most of which have fleshy spore-producing bodies—toadstools, mushrooms, brackets. The gills or the pores found on the under side of the fruiting bodies of most of the species have a large surface area. On these surfaces are borne a myriad of microscopic spores that are carried by wind to start new infections. The Division of Forest Pathology has about 300 species of these fungi growing in pure culture.

Wood attacked by fungi is lowered in toughness or shock resistance and (to a less degree) in bending or crushing strength before it is appreciably softened or reduced in weight. In wood to be used for paper, decay fungi reduce the quantity and quality of pulp, depending on the fungus involved and the process to be used in pulping.

Plywood is generally quite as susceptible to decay as solid wood of the species from which it is made, although some glues hinder the passing of fungi from one layer of wood to another. Wood or paper impregnated with a high content of phenolic resin (as impreg, compreg, or papreg) strongly resists decay, but impregnation with urea resins has given less consistent protection in the tests so far made.

MOST WOOD DECAY FUNGI will grow rapidly only between 60° and 90° F. They remain alive during long periods below freezing, but can be quickly killed by heat at temperatures about 150°.

The food requirements of the fungi limit many of them. The fungi that merely discolor are generally unable to attack heartwood of any species of tree because of its lack of the sugars or other readily digested food materials that they require. Some decay fungi can attack the wood of the broadleaved species only; others are limited to softwoods; some are even limited to a particular genus of trees.

Moisture is the factor most important from a practical standpoint. Fungi cannot grow in constantly air-dry wood, even in the more humid parts of the United States. Strictly speaking, there is no such thing as dry rot. Wood must contain moisture equaling more than one-fifth of the weight of the oven-dry wood before decay or staining fungi can develop in it. Decay fungi progress rarely or slowly, if ever, at moisture contents below 25 percent (oven-dry basis). The molds that grow on the sugars and other foods present in sapwood or destroy the starch or protein glues used in bonding some wood or wood-fiber products, however, can apparently work under conditions somewhat less moist than would be required for decay of wood.

Two of the decay fungi are especially dangerous to buildings because they can conduct water from moist soil or wood and thus attack wood parts of buildings that otherwise would be too dry—but they depend just as much on a source of moisture as other fungi. Fortunately these two species are not common in the United States.

The oxygen requirement becomes a limiting factor for the fungi in some situations. Wood that is completely waterlogged decays slightly, if at all. No important decay occurs in wood that is under water.

The heartwood of naturally durable species contains chemicals that limit the growth of organisms. These are nearly insoluble in cold water, but most of them can be extracted in hot water. Such woods as redwood, baldcypress, black locust, pitch-soaked pine, and several of the cedars commonly remain free from attack for decades of exposure to the conditions that favor decay. Unfortunately, the second-growth stands on which we now depend largely for lumber contain a larger proportion of sapwood, all of which is decay-susceptible. Building practices that were reasonably safe with the lumber of the past century may not be good enough with the lumber we have now.

The salt in ocean water also appears to have some importance in hindering the decay in the hulls of boats. Ammonium salts in the amounts used in wood as fire retardants have prevented the decay of wood in laboratory trials, although they favor the growth of some of the relatively harmless mold fungi.

FOR LUMBER ALREADY DISCOLORED as it comes from the tree, all that can be done at present is to distinguish colors that indicate decay from those that do not, in order to avoid discarding harmless discolorations.

To avoid discoloration from fungi that develop in logs, the best measure is to get the logs to the saw promptly. Where this cannot be done, fungi can be kept from entering through the ends of the logs and spots where the bark has been knocked off by prompt spraying or brushing of the exposed wood with solutions containing organic mercury salts or chlorophenols or phenates.

In warm weather, lumber of many species, if not kiln-dried or quickly air-dried, is commonly stained by fungi within a few days after it is sawed. This can be controlled by dipping the lumber in a toxic solution not more than 24 hours after sawing. The same fungicides are used as for logs, but at lower strengths; the cost for materials is only 15 to 20 cents a thousand board feet of lumber dipped. Such dipping, if followed by good open piling to dry the lumber, reduces to a minimum the molding and staining and also the decay that sometimes gets started during seasoning.

To prevent decay in storage or use, the most generally practicable method is to keep the wood dry all the time or for so much of it that decay fungi never have a chance to get started. Until lumber is dry, it should not be solid-piled or built into parts of structures in which further drying is slow, unless it has been dipped promptly after sawing in a stain-control chemical solution.

To avoid decay in buildings, roof leaks must be avoided. Exterior walls must be so constructed that there is a minimum chance for water to enter at joints and be trapped in the wall. Where wood is on concrete laid on soil, there should be a dampproofing layer in or on the concrete; all embedded stringers should be of a decay-resistant wood or impregnated with a preservative.

Buildings without basements are subject to a special decay risk. During cold weather, moisture evaporating from the soil under the building may condense on the cold surface of the sills and joists, and stay long enough to let decay fungi get started. This sweating can be prevented by placing ventilating openings in the foundation wall on opposite sides of the building. Under test buildings where the vents have been too few or too small to keep the wood dry, the moist condition has been relieved by simply laying a cover on the soil under the building. Heavy roll roofing (55 lbs. or more per 108 square feet) rolled out on the soil and lapped but not fastened, was very effective. A 3-inch layer of slag or gravel in the soil, though apparently somewhat less efficient, was also helpful.

Where wood must be used in contact with soil or water, it should be either heartwood of one of the highly durable species or else it should be impregnated with a good preservative. Even in the best species, the heartwood from young trees or from the central heart of old trees is likely to be rather decay-susceptible. No sapwood of any species should be used in contact with soil without thorough preservative impregnation. Treatment of sills and first-floor joists of low buildings is a desirable—although not a necessary—precaution.

Impregnation is best accomplished by pressure treatment at a commercial treating plant. Wood of ordinary lumber thickness can be reasonably well impregnated without pressure if given a hot bath followed by a cold bath. Dip or brush treatments have some place in wood members exposed to rain or occasional moisture, as in porches and window sash and frames, if it is too difficult to get impregnated lumber locally. Water and fungi enter through exposed end grain more readily than through sides; preservative treatment of ends of members is therefore especially profitable. If untreated ends are exposed, no treatment is worth much. Paint can be of value for decay prevention if it is unusually well maintained, with no cracks at the joints. If wood is painted when green, its drying out may be delayed and the decay hazard actually increased.

In the special case of boat construction, only heartwood of durable or moderately durable species should be used. These would include the woods mentioned previously; also teak and mahogany; white or chestnut oak, but ot red or black oak; and dense Doug-s-fir and dense southern pine. Sea-oned wood should be used so far as ossible. Leakage, especially of fresh ater or rain water, into the boat must e minimized. Ventilation must be pro-ided for all parts of the hull. More ttention must be paid to ventilation hen the boat is laid up than when it in use. Except for the interior trim, reservative treated wood is needed if urable wood is not used, but it is ifficult to employ with full effective-ess in boats because the cutting, fit-ng, and fairing so often expose parts f the wood that have not been pene-ated by the treatment.

Decay of wood used in aircraft is asily avoided. The cases of damage re-orted in service have nearly always een due either to failure to put drain oles at the lowest points or careless-ess in allowing them to become logged. Out-of-doors storage in crates at admit rain also caused damage.

The life of plywood bonded with rotein glue has been greatly increased in moist situations by the use of chlorophenols or phenates in the glue. The resistance of fiberboard to deterioration by molds can be increased similarly by the use of chlorophenates, which in this case must be added to the fiber during manufacture as well as to the laminating glue.

Often, when one replaces decayed members of structures, he leaves some of the old decayed material in contact with the new wood. This is an invitation to trouble. It should never be done where moist conditions may continue.

CARL HARTLEY *is a pathologist in the Division of Forest Pathology, Bureau of Plant Industry, Soils, and Agricultural Engineering. Except for 3 years of general plant-disease investigations for the Instituut voor Plantenziekten, Netherlands East Indies, Dr. Hartley has been continuously with the Department of Agriculture since 1909. His principal contributions have been on diseases of forest nursery stock and deterioration of forest products.*

# THE PREFABRICATED HOUSE

RONALD F. LUXFORD, F. A. STRENGE

The thing about a house, when a erson buys or builds one, is its perma-ence. It is probably the most durable ood a man is likely to get in his life-ime, other than the ground it is built n. Almost anything else—a car, a inder, a suit of clothes—is expected to vear out in a few years. But a man's ome, his cottage or mansion or dream ouse, is expected to survive the ages.

Into this market has come the pre-abricated house. No mystery need be ttached to the prefabricated house; he prefabricator has simply moved art of the building operations under oof and developed machinery to do hem. Presumably, this shift of opera-ions combines the advantages of ma-hine speed and accuracy with the limination of the factor of weather and lowers the cost of many building jobs otherwise done with hand tools at the house site.

According to his wishes and means, the individual prefabricator often uses some of the newer materials in his designs—moistureproof plywood, insulation, sheet-type building boards, spray-type paints and varnishes, and so on. The builder of the conventional houses also uses those materials, but the principal material for both conventional and the prefabricated houses is wood. Through economies of factory operations and more efficient engineering design, many prefabricators figure they can shave 10 to 20 percent off the cost of a conventional house of the same size and turn out a product just as good or better.

To date, however, the makers of prefabricated houses have had difficulty in convincing the buying public of the quality of their product. As these manufacturers are well aware, the buyer of a house, like any other buyer, prefers something with a proved record of service. Prefabricated houses are too new to have a long record.

Prefabrication got its real start during the 1930's but most prefabricated houses are much younger than that. Moreover, some prefabricated housing that was rushed out during the war to meet suddenly critical needs of defense workers was designed for temporary use, 5 years or less, and sometimes used inferior or substitute materials that somehow performed their emergency job but subsequently developed obvious structural ailments. The fact that some conventionally built war housing suffered similar warp, decay, and structural weakness often was not given equal consideration because conventionally built housing has a long history of durable value to offset the shortcomings of the wartime structures of its kind.

About 35,000 or more prefabricated houses were produced by some 200 companies in 1947. This was about 4 percent of the total 1947 output of the housing industry. A notable point is that a builder of conventional houses is considered relatively successful if he puts up 10 houses a year, but a number of prefabricators turn out that many or more a week, and the plant is small indeed that does not assemble the parts for at least one every workweek.

Prefabricated houses are appearing in many communities of the Nation. As these houses continue to serve their purpose through the years, public confidence in the product of house factories will be guided. Perhaps some day soon the house buyer, like the car buyer, will pick out his make and model on the basis of the maker's reputation. Meanwhile, however, the potential customer needs more specific signposts of quality on which to base his decision to buy or not to buy.

Two general kinds of prefabricated houses are being offered today. One is the semiconventional house, the parts of which—wall, ceiling, floor, and perhaps the roof sections—are of conventional size and are preassembled in a factory.

The other is the so-called stressed cover, or stressed-facing, house, the panels of which usually consist of plywood or some other sheet material bonded with glue to a framework of smaller studs, joints, and rafters. This type of construction was first developed at the Forest Products Laboratory in 1934. On the Laboratory grounds today stand two 12-year-old examples of it; they appear as sound as ever.

The panels of either kind of prefabricated house may contain insulation, vapor barriers, electrical wiring, and other installations. Between the two basic types are many modifications that result from the adaptation of new materials and production methods to one or the other type.

Perhaps the first inquiry the prospective buyer can make is whether the particular house has been approved for his locality by the Federal Housing Administration, a Government agency that requires minimum standards of construction for loan-insurance purposes. The standards are fairly uniform, but in certain respects they vary somewhat for different parts of the United States. For example, thermal insulation requirements differ according to climatic conditions of particular regions; a house needs better insulation in Minnesota than in Florida.

Further, the buyer can avail himself of certain technical guideposts that indicate the quality of materials, workmanship, and design.

The quality of a prefabricated house is compounded of good materials as well as technical skill and suitable factory conditions. An example is given by the stressed-cover, or stressed-facing house, which is manufactured by a growing number of prefabricators.

The maker of stressed-facing houses often uses plywood for his panel covers or facings. Because the strength of those panels depends largely on the plywood (as contrasted with the conventional frame house, whose strength depends primarily on the framework of studs, joists, and rafters) the quality of the plywood is important. Especially if it is used in outside walls and roofs, it must be highly water-resistant. Such plywoods are known as exterior grades, and moisture will not delaminate them.

The fact that stressed-facing panels are glued together emphasizes the need for using well-seasoned lumber and dry plywood in their manufacture. Insufficiently dried framing lumber will put excessive strains on the glue joints when it dries further, probably while in the house structure; it may even warp the panel out of shape. The good manufacturer, therefore, not only buys dry lumber and plywood, but stores it carefully at his plant in a protected indoor location. He does the same with his finished panels until they are transported to the building site. Also important is the glue that holds the facings to the panel framework. Synthetic-resin glues of the phenol, melamine, or resorcinol type are preferred. Of these, only the resorcinol glues can be cured adequately at room temperatures; when phenols or melamines are used, the panels must be put in a steam-heated or electric press or a heated curing chamber to set the glue.

Properly made panels must have well-machined, smooth, and uniformly sized framing. If two framing members meet at a corner and do not lie flush so that the plywood will be flat against both, for instance, a good glue bond cannot be made. There will be a weakening gap at this point. Too many such gaps in a number of house panels can seriously affect the structural soundness of the building. An indication of good quality in manufacture is the absence of such gaps in the glue bond between plywood and framing.

The way the plywood is attached is also to be noted. If it is nailed to the framework, the nails furnish the only pressure to hold the plywood to the framework while the glue cures. Consequently, to assure uniform pressure, they should be spaced evenly and not more than 4 to 6 inches apart. The thinner the plywood is, the closer the nails should be spaced.

Panels should have vapor barriers, usually sheets of asphalt-treated paper or aluminum sheet materials, which block passage of water vapor from the warm interiors of houses toward the outside in winter. Such vapor movement is hazardous because the vapor may be chilled inside the panel and condense as frost, which later melts and damages exterior paint and interior ceiling finish, and may even encourage decay inside the panel. For that reason, vapor barriers should always be on the warm side of wall, ceiling, roof, and floor panels; they are unnecessary in interior partitions, second-story floor panels, or first-floor panels over heated basements.

Insulation is usually installed where the climate requires it. Some types of insulation, called blanket or batt insulation, come with a paper backing that may have been treated for vapor resistance; with such insulation a separate barrier may not be needed. Reflective insulation, such as metallic foil, is a good vapor barrier. Barrier materials should be well sealed to panel framework.

The prospective buyer can learn a great deal about quality if he watches the workmen assemble a house. A look at the foundation is in order, particularly if the house has no basement. In such houses, whether prefabricated or conventional, the space underneath the floor is called a crawl space and should be at least 18 inches high between ground and subfloor. This space should be ventilated by openings resembling basement windows in the foundation walls—all such openings should be wide open at least during the spring, summer, and fall to insure ventilation. Without such openings, dangerous decay conditions can develop in the subfloor structure. Preferably, the ground of the crawl space should be covered with roofing paper and several inches of gravel.

At the building site, panels can be inspected for good workmanship to see if they are true and well-made, with continuous glue joints between framework and facings. How well they fit together while the walls, floors, ceilings, partitions, and roof are being assembled is a clue to their manufacture. Do panels join well together at room corners and at the joints where wall, floor, and ceiling meet? Small gaps here are to be expected and can be hidden with molding and other trim, but the finished job should be neat.

In most modern houses, both prefabricated and conventional, there is an unfinished attic space between ceiling and pitched roof. Insulation is laid over the ceiling. The attic space is another source of danger from moisture vapor. A vapor barrier should be laid under the insulation. The attic should also be ventilated; this is usually done by means of louvered openings in both gable ends to permit air to pass through the attic space. The openings should be ample in size; they are more likely to be too small than too large.

An inspection of the exterior of the finished house can be helpful. In particular, all the exterior joints between panels, especially the horizontal joints, should be especially well made and protected with metal flashing, drip caps over windows and doors, and similar devices for blocking the penetration of rain water. A roof with a good overhang has advantages.

The critical buyer may want to check on several other details, but he should bear in mind that the basic factors are good materials, and good workmanship, and good structural design. Each depends on the others and complements them. In building with wood, the designer keeps uppermost the fact that moisture can be his greatest enemy and he designs accordingly. With the proper safeguards, he knows that wood construction can be entirely satisfactory, safe, and economical, whether prefabricated or conventional.

RONALD F. LUXFORD *has degrees in civil engineering from the University of Minnesota and the University of Wisconsin. He has been with the Forest Products Laboratory since 1918; since 1935 he has headed the work on housing research.*

F. A. STRENGE, *a native of Chicago, was reared on a dairy farm in Wisconsin and was graduated from the University of Wisconsin. After 7 years of newspaper work, he joined the staff of the Forest Products Laboratory in 1941 as a technical writer. Since then he has written and edited various Laboratory publications, including a Manual on Wood Construction for Prefabricated Houses and a series of technical reports on housing research.*

# THE GLUING OF WOOD

DON BROUSE

Gluing, when properly done, is the strongest known means of fastening pieces of wood together. Joints made with glue are stronger than those made with nails, dowels, screws, clamps, or straps, because glue spreads in a uniform film that firmly binds together every part of the surfaces to be joined. Since its discovery, this property of glue has destined it to an intimate association with wood in the innumerable products of joinery, veneering, and cabinetmaking, for which it provides joints that can resist high stress and violent shocks and that permit the combining of wood into economical thicknesses and into useful and ornate shapes otherwise impossible.

Although the bond of all glues, except the synthetic resins, can be destroyed by prolonged wetting, with customary care in use the service value of a good glue joint is reliable, a fact that unfortunate experiences in home gluing, the result of faulty surfaces, preparation, and methods, should not obscure.

Animal glue, most of it made by cooking hides, fleshings, tendons, or bones of cattle in water, was long the world's principal wood adhesive and is still in common use.

The development of new glues began with the need of modern industry for adhesives that were cheaper or that would provide greater water resistance and thereby longer durability under the more severe service conditions of new and potential uses for its increasingly diversified products.

The first of the new glues, introduced about 1905, were vegetable or starch glues, a large part of which were derived from tropical cassava root, which easily yielded its large starch granules for the purpose. Despite their low resistance to moisture, the cheapness and prolonged workability of these glues in the cold state early recommended them for quantity manufacture of plywood and veneer products. The present production volume of vegetable glues equals or exceeds that of animal glues.

Present-day emphasis upon water resistance in glues began during the First World War, when this property became important in aircraft construction. At the end of that war, casein glue, of ancient but vague history, had won for that purpose a recognition which it still commands in such manufactures as doors, plywood, furniture, pianos, and trucks.

Casein, the dried and ground curd of milk, is relatively inexpensive. After it is dissolved in water, water resistance is commonly imparted by adding slaked lime to form with it a jelly that will set permanently and not redissolve upon wetting. Other chemicals, usually sodium salts, are added to provide satisfactory working properties. The mixture, applied cold, sets to a hard and cementlike solid, whose bonding strength approaches that of animal glue. It is commonly marketed as a dry mix that contains all essential ingredients except water.

Blood-albumin glue, which is made from blood from the packing house, was a forerunner of the resins in its requirement of a hot press to obtain proper setting and bonding of its joint. In its dry state it ranks somewhat below casein in adhesive strength, but it has better moisture resistance. It has been largely replaced by synthetic-resin adhesives.

Amid all the magic claimed for the soybean, the recent development of a practical glue from it is not surprising. Soybean glue is cheap. It can be applied cold. It has inherent water resistance comparable to casein glue, although somewhat lower in strength. Made from the meal residue of soybean-oil extraction, the glue has a rather mushy texture, but sets to a firm bond in the cold press. It has won a commanding place in the great Douglas-fir plywood industry and in other fields like wooden-box construction, because its inexpensive water-resistant joints permit mass production never before attained. Because of its relatively high alkalinity, which may cause staining, the glue is not adapted to fine veneers.

Synthetic resins, the newest adhesives, impart to the glue joint the highest water resistance yet attained. In contrast to the earlier glues that at best could withstand only a moderate amount of dampness, a first-class synthetic-resin glue appears to withstand direct and repeated wetting almost indefinitely. In tests at the Forest Products Laboratory for more than a decade, certain synthetic-resin glues did not appear to soften or hydrolyze even on continued soaking of bonded wood specimens. These glues are not attacked by molds or decay fungi and maintain their hold as long as there is any wood left to test. Thus the bond that cannot be destroyed without destroying the wood appears to have been

ADHESIVES: MIXING, APPLICATION, AND REQUIREMENTS FOR BEST USE OF GLUES IN COMMON USE

| *Glue* | *Mixing and application* | *Temperature requirements* | *Water resistance* | *Common uses* | *Available from—* |
|---|---|---|---|---|---|
| Animal | Soaked in water and melted; applied warm by hand or mechanical spreaders. | Control of temperature of glue, of room, and of wood important. | Low | Furniture, cabinet, and millwork. | Retail sources; specific grades usually obtained only from manufacturers. |
| Starch | Mixed with water and alkali usually with heat; applied cold by mechanical spreaders; too thick for hand spreading. | Used at ordinary room temperatures. | Very low | Plywood and veneered panels for furniture; not well suited to home use. | Manufacturers. |
| Casein | Mixed with water at room temperatures; applied cold by hand or mechanical spreader. | ....do | Medium | Used in gluing lumber, millwork, and plywood. | Retail sources. |
| Urea-resin: *a.* Room-temperature-setting; *b.* Heat-setting. | Powder form mixed with water at room temperatures; liquid form mixed with hardener at room temperatures. | *a.* Not recommended for use below 70° F. *b.* Requires heat for curing; hot presses commonly used. | High | *a.* Furniture, cabinet, and millwork. *b.* Plywood | *a.* Retail sources. *b.* Manufacturers. |
| Phenol-resin | Powder form mixed at room temperatures with water or water-alcohol mixtures; liquid form may require addition of hardeners; film form used as received. | Requires heat for curing; hot presses commonly used but kilns have been employed. | Very high | Plywood and laminated wood products for severe service; not well suited for home use. | Manufacturers. |
| Resorcinol-resin | Resin usually supplied in liquid form with which a powdered or liquid hardener is mixed at room temperatures. | Not recommended for use below 70° F. | ....do | Millwork and laminated wood products for severe service. | Retail sources. |
| Melamine-resins | Resin powder mixed with water at room temperature. | Requires heat for curing; hot presses commonly used. | ....do | Plywood; not well suited for home use. | Manufacturers. |

realized, although even yet the resins do not promise that their bond with wood will be spontaneous, for the production of a good joint generally requires high pressure, with or without added heat.

Phenol-formaldehyde and urea-formaldehyde are the most widely used synthetic-resin glues. Melamine and resorcinol glues, among the discoveries during the Second World War, promise good performance, the resorcinols particularly so because highly durable bonds can be obtained without hot pressing. The resins are available as powders, solutions, or prepared films. Their special advantage is that they reduce surface swelling and the other changes caused by the water in the less concentrated adhesives, particularly in furniture and other fine veneer work in which they are being adopted.

THE GLUING OF WOOD is not a simple, infallible procedure, because wood species vary chemically and physically, and glues vary in source, methods of preparation, and use.

Findings at the Forest Products Laboratory after years of research lead to five general recommendations for applying glue.

It is usually unnecessary, and often detrimental, to roughen the wood surface; in fact, the mating surfaces should be machined to a smooth, true fit.

Animal glue must not be overheated. Heating the wood is generally unnecessary or detrimental.

Glue should be thick, rather than thin, in consistency when it is pressed.

A relatively heavy pressure should be applied to bring the surfaces to be joined into firm contact until at least partial setting has occurred.

Minor details of procedure can be varied in any way that will assure a proper jellylike consistency of the glue at time of pressing.

DON BROUSE, *a native of Indiana, joined the Forest Products Laboratory in 1923 and was assigned to work on the problems connected with the application of wood-working adhesives. He is assistant to the chief of the Division of Wood Preservation at the Laboratory and has general supervision over investigations on adhesives, veneer and plywood production, and sandwich panel fabrication. Dr. Brouse has degrees from Purdue University and the University of Wisconsin.*

# CHEMICALS FROM WOOD

ALFRED J. STAMM

Chemical processing of wood, up to the present time, has been limited to (1) destructive distillation, whereby charcoal, wood alcohol, acetic acid, turpentine, and tars are produced, and (2) extraction processes with water or petroleum solvents that remove the extraneous materials, such as tannins, turpentine, rosin, and essential oils.

The destructive-distillation process in recent years has not proved to be very profitable, because many of the products formerly produced exclusively by the process are now made more cheaply by synthetic methods.

The extraction process, although highly profitable when applied to a few species, is not suitable for all woods and actually utilizes only from 1 to 20 percent of the weight of the wood.

Two rather new processing methods, hydrolysis and hydrogenation, show promise of broader application. Hydrolysis changes the cellulose and other carbohydrate material into sugars. Hydrogenation causes hydrogen gas to react with the wood components at high temperatures and pressure to form liquid products.

The new procedures, together with

the old, provide a practical approach to the chemical utilization of wood residues.

Wood residues are especially adapted for chemical processing because wood of any form or size or quality can be used. Sawdust, shavings, slabs, trimming, cordwood, and cull logs are all suitable. Further, the presence in the residue of relatively large amounts of knots, bark, and even wood in the early stages of decay does not interfere with most of the processes, although it may reduce the yield of chemical products. Even though it would usually pay to process the hardwoods (broadleaved species) separately from the softwoods (cone-bearing species) for the reason that the products and yields from those two general classes of wood differ, it is not necessary generally to separate them.

The amounts of wood residues available indicate the possible magnitude of a chemical industry based on their full utilization. Naturally, the first wood residues to be considered for such an industry would be those that occur at sawmills, veneer mills, and secondary manufacturing plants, because the material is already at hand and a large part (in the form of sawdust and shavings) is already reduced sufficiently in size for use. Some 16 million tons of such material now remain unused each year. An additional 27 million tons are burned to generate steam for plant operations. As soon as its chemical-processing value becomes greater than its fuel value, which at present averages about $4 a ton, this material, too, will be available for chemical processing.

The total mill residue is equal in weight to one-fifth of the national petroleum production. Left unused in the woods each year, because their removal is considered unprofitable, are 44 million tons more of cut wood, chiefly crooked, split, and partly decayed material unsuitable for lumber but admirably suited for chemical use. Still another 23 million tons of standing timber are killed by fire, lightning, or insects each year and left in the woods; a large part of that would also be suitable. Altogether, those residues equal in weight about half the present petroleum production. Enough wood residues are available, then, to supply a great new chemical industry.

Such a large industry would not be warranted unless its products were in sufficient demand at a price for which they could be profitably produced. The nature and uses of the products obtained by the various methods of chemically processing wood can be a measure of this demand and value.

Extraction differs from the other chemical-processing methods in that it is highly dependent upon species and alters the wood substance only slightly. The only extensive wood-extraction industry is the naval stores industry of the South, which extracts turpentine and rosin from old stumps of longleaf and slash pines from which the sapwood has decayed. Only the heartwood stumps of those species are used because of their high extractive content. The industry processes about 6,000 tons of stump wood daily to obtain 12,500,000 gallons of turpentine and 750,000 drums (520 pounds to the drum) of rosin a year. Turpentine is used chiefly as a paint thinner, a medicinal, and a raw material for making synthetic camphor and other valuable synthetic products. The rosin is used chiefly in soaps, paper size, paints, varnishes, sealing waxes, cements, and plastics. Large amounts of cymene and a rosin residue are also obtained. The latter is used in plastics and as a binder for sand in foundry cores.

Chestnut wood chips and hemlock bark are extracted to obtain tannin for tanning leather. In no case is the tannin content of wood sufficient to make extraction profitable for it alone. In the case of chestnut, the extracted chips have been used to form pulp for paper making. The chip residue might also be used for further chemical processing.

Years ago a small industry existed in the Northwestern States in which the butt logs of western larch were extracted with water to remove the large amount of water-soluble gum that they contain. The gum was chemically converted to mucic acid, which is used as the gas-liberating acid in some brands of baking powder. The process was not a financial success because the large amount of chip residue was unused.

A number of small plants scattered about the country extract essential oils, medicinals, and flavoring materials from needles, bark, roots, or wood of various species. Those plants, like all other extraction plants, could profit by chemical refining of their residues.

Destructive distillation is by far the oldest wood-chemical-processing industry. For years the charcoal residue was the only product sought. Charcoal is used as a domestic and picnic fuel; in smelting and reducing various ores; in making such chemicals as carbon bisulfide, which, in turn, is used in making viscose, rayon, and cellophane, and also sodium cyanide, a powerful disinfectant.

Now a number of valuable volatile products are also obtained by condensing the vapors from destructive distillation. In the case of hardwoods, methyl alcohol (wood alcohol), acetone, and acetic acid are obtained as a water-soluble distillate, together with the water-insoluble tars and pitches. Methyl alcohol is used as an antifreeze agent in the radiators of automobiles, for denaturing grain alcohol, as a solvent in many industries, and for making formaldehyde, which, in turn, is used as a disinfectant and in making plastics. Acetone is used as a solvent in the rayon and plastic industries, and acetic acid in making white lead paint and acetate rayon and films. Yields of methyl alcohol, acetone, and acetic acid are lower from softwoods than from hardwoods.

The pines, however, yield considerable turpentine and softwood tar. Softwood tar is used in the compounding of rubber, to some extent in manufacturing oakum for calking ships, in cordage, and also in medicinals. Both softwood and hardwood tars find use as flotation oils in mineral separation and as gasoline gum inhibitors. The heavier fractions are used as preservatives, disinfectants, and stains. The pitch finds use as a waterproofing and insulating agent and as a binder for briquets.

Although the products obtained by the two older wood-processing methods named are of considerable industrial importance and could perhaps be used in larger amounts than are now produced, a large expansion in their production does not now seem warranted. Any real increase in the chemical utilization of wood will thus have to be by the processes which produce products that are in greater demand.

Hydrolysis of wood to sugars, followed in some cases by their conversion to other products, is a most promising chemical approach to large-scale utilization of wood residues.

At the Forest Products Laboratory it was found that sugars can be produced to the extent of about half the weight of the wood by a simple process of heating wood chips or sawdust with a dilute solution of acid in water under moderate steam pressure. These sugars, which are a mixture of glucose and several different pentose sugars, would be difficult to purify and crystallize, but can be evaporated easily to a molasses that contains 50 percent sugar.

Experiments now under way are using this molasses as an animal feed. The tests have been sufficient to indicate that it is palatable to cattle and sheep. If its nutrient value proves equal to that of cane molasses, which it resembles closely, it could find extensive use as a livestock feed. Pilot-plant studies indicate that about 180 gallons of molasses can be produced from a ton of dry wood at a cost that should not exceed 10 cents a gallon. Cane molasses sold on quantity basis at 25 to 40 cents a gallon in different parts of the country in 1948. If its

802062°—49——42

price could be made as attractive as the pilot-plant studies indicate, the demand for feed molasses from wood could be tremendous. If livestock feeding could be built up to the level already demonstrated as possible with cane molasses (about 3 pounds per day per head for cows, somewhat more for beef cattle, and somewhat less for sheep), the amount of molasses used for feeding could be increased at least 75 times. In theory, such a goal could utilize the equivalent of about two-thirds of all available wood residues. Here, then, is a potential use for wood residue that could consume large quantities of it.

The sugar solution resulting from hydrolysis can also be fermented to ethyl alcohol (grain alcohol). Bark-free softwoods yield up to 60 gallons of alcohol per ton of dry wood, and hardwoods about 50 gallons. Bark may be present up to 50 percent, but its presence somewhat decreases the yield. This alcohol is suitable for many industrial purposes. A large commercial plant capable of processing 200 to 300 tons of wood residue a day in the manufacture of ethyl alcohol has been built on the Pacific coast. The short time in which it has operated has demonstrated the commercial possibilities of the process. When shortages of petroleum products occur, the ethyl alcohol produced at such plants could become one of our chief motor fuels. It can, under present conditions, be produced from wood at about one-fifth of the cost of producing it from grain.

Only the hexose sugars are used in making alcohol. The pentoses remain in the stills after distillation. They may be used for growing yeast or for conversion to furfural, which is a chemical used as a solvent in oil and rosin refining, in certain plastics, and recently as a starting material in making nylon.

Tests are under way to determine the food value of wood yeast. It is rich in riboflavin, a vitamin, and consequently should have greater food value than is indicated by its high protein content alone. The production of wood yeast thus also shows promise of developing into a sizable industry that could use up large amounts of wood residue.

Different cultures and fermentation conditions make possible the manufacture of acetic, butyric, and lactic acid from wood sugars and also acetone, butyl alcohol, and butylene glycol. Butyric acid is used in making cellulose-butyrate plastics. Lactic acid is used as a food preservative. Butyl alcohol and butylene glycol can be used in making artificial rubber. Butylene glycol would be a good antifreeze agent for use in automobile radiators.

When sugars are formed by the hydrolysis of wood, a residue of fine solid lignin remains. This material, a substance that binds the wood fibers together in a tree, has a higher fuel value than wood itself and may be burned as a fuel in the processing plant. It shows promise as a soil conditioner. When agricultural crop residues decay, the remaining humus is largely lignin, so it is natural that lignin should have soil-conditioning value. Lignin from wood hydrolysis has not shown the value in plastics found in other forms of lignin recovered from paper manufacture.

Hydrogenation has been most extensively studied on isolated lignin, but it may also be applied to all parts of wood. In the process, the lignin is suspended, or preferably dissolved, in an organic liquid that itself does not react with hydrogen and that will not decompose at the high temperatures used. Most of the work to date has been done on batch lots placed in small bombs. A metallic or metallic-oxide catalyst is used to promote the reaction. A complex mixture of liquid products and a tarlike residue are produced.

The liquid consists of a mixture of complex cyclic alcohols, phenolics, and neutral oils. The cyclic alcohols, when added to gasoline, show good antiknock properties. They are also good solvents, and some of them have toxic properties. The phenolics are a mixture of those suitable for plastics and some that are not. Means of separating them have not yet been found.

The neutral oils are of the hydrocarbon type. Part of them may prove suitable for lubricating purposes, and all as fuels.

The proportions of these three types of chemicals formed in the process may be varied with the hydrogenating conditions.

Wood may also be hydrogenated in aqueous alkaline suspension. The lignin forms compounds of the types just described. When the hydrogenation conditions are mild, the cellulose left is a pulp residue; when severe, the cellulose is broken down into sugars and glycerine. The industrial possibilities of such a glycerine-forming process must await further research.

Before the hydrogenation of either lignin or cellulose can become an industrial reality, methods for carrying on the process in continuous-flow equipment will have to be developed. The possibilities of commercial hydrogenation, however, are promising. One is to hydrogenate the lignin residue from a wood-hydrolysis ethyl-alcohol plant to obtain an optimum yield of neutral oils. Such a plant, it is estimated, could produce, by the combined methods, from a ton of dry wood about 110 gallons of liquid fuel consisting chiefly of ethyl alcohol and neutral oils, together with some methyl alcohol and furfural.

With all these possibilities, the chemical processing of wood residues may well be expected to expand rapidly in the next few years.

ALFRED J. STAMM, *a Californian, joined the Forest Products Laboratory in 1925 and at present is chief of the Division of Derived Products. He has published a number of research papers on such subjects as particle size in emulsions, capillary structure of wood, wood and cellulose-liquid relationships, swelling and its prevention, electrical properties of wood, and molecular properties of cellulose and lignin. Dr. Stamm has degrees in chemistry from the California Institute of Technology and the University of Wisconsin. In 1928 he studied in the University of Upsala, Sweden, in order to apply the ultracentrifuge technique to the study of the molecular weight of cellulose.*

# PUTTING UNUSED WOOD TO WORK

C. V. SWEET

Every time a saw chews through a log, it spits aside sawdust. Whenever a planer dresses the roughness off a board, it throws off shavings. Square-edged lumber is made only at the cost of slabs, edgings, and trims. For every log put through the sawmill a considerable tonnage of wood fiber is left in the forest. Even the digesters of pulp mills disgorge as unusable sizable quantities of the wood fed into them. And so it goes with nearly every operation concerned with harvesting and converting trees into useful things.

Those unused materials generally have been called waste, not in the sense that they signify neglect or carelessness but in the sense that they are not economically usable. If there is use for them, the margin of profit may be discouragingly narrow, the necessary investment for equipment may be prohibitive, or the expense of handling and hauling the raw material to one point may be excessive.

Theoretically, there is a use to which practically every type of unused wood is or can be put. The problem is in finding profitable ways of doing it on an adequate basis.

Only in relatively recent years have we come to regard those unused forms as important to our national economy.

Without quite yet realizing it, we have become so desperately dependent upon our forests that failure to get the maximum use from the annual timber harvest becomes increasingly vital.

Is this unused wood close to locations where it can be put to use? Just why does a waste occur? Are we making any headway in efforts to use it?

Residue occurs everywhere that wood is utilized to make things, but much of it is in remote and scattered locations. It happens for various reasons. One of the most basic is that nature did not design trees wholly, or even primarily, for man's use. Nature made them round, partially defective usually, with buttressed butts and with much of their content in branches and tops. We use only the round trunk, as a rule, and for the most part saw it into strips with squared edges to remove the bark, although veneer is peeled off like paper from a roll and the pulp-mill chippers swallow the whole barked log. But even the trunk has knots and some other defects which, for many purposes, must be cut out.

The most obvious accumulations of material discarded in processing occur at small sawmills, although back in the woods there may be even more. To the layman, the great heaps of sawdust and other scrap at the sawmills loom as an impending evil and a bad waste. The fact is, however, that those piles of refuse are in large part unavoidable even with the most efficient sawmill equipment. The finest saw inevitably chews up some of the wood as it bites through the log.

At sulfite pulp mills, only the cellulose in wood is extracted for manufacture of high-quality book and magazine paper, rayon textiles, plastics, and other chemical products. Roughly, a third of the chemical constituents of wood, known as lignin, are discarded because there is no good use for them. Lignin has thus far defied the efforts of a small army of chemists to make much profitable use of it. Not only is it unused; it pollutes the stream into which it is dumped. Some cellulose fiber is lost with the lignin.

At first glance, rotary-cut veneer, from which most softwood plywood is made, looks like an efficient way to utilize logs. Veneer bolts are mounted on a lathe that rotates them while a stationary knife cuts off a continuous ribbon of veneer. But logs are not perfect cylinders of perfect wood. A good deal of veneer has to be removed piecemeal before the log becomes a cylinder that yields a continuous sheet of veneer as it revolves against the cutter blade. Knots, cross grain, and other defects take a heavy toll, and, finally, there is the unused core of the bolt, which is too small for veneer cutting. By the time the veneer is clipped, trimmed, graded, patched, and otherwise readied for the plywood presses, some 40 to 50 percent of the log has been lost.

These and related products—including railroad ties, cooperage, mine timbers, shingles, and on down to tongue depressors and pencil slats—make up the output of the wood-using industries. In total, the discarded material from these industries bulks almost fantastically large each year.

Follow the lumber from the sawmill and you find still more loss. There are, for example, the cut-offs and degrade that result from seasoning. As lumber dries, considerable amounts are checked, warped, split, and honeycombed. Knots loosen and fall out. Some of the lumber becomes infected with decay. At the planing mill, more sawdust and shavings; at the building site, discarded ends, broken pieces, and warpage and splitting due to faulty handling and piling. In the furniture factories and millwork plants, the same processing residues occur.

A hundred million tons of unused wood each year—60 million tons of cellulose in a cellulose-hungry world—constitutes an almost untouched backlog of raw material that challenges the ingenuity of Americans.

After the piles have been out in the weather for a short time they become ractically useless except where they an be used in mixture with poisons to ontrol grasshopper plagues. Ultimate-y they may find usefulness in some reas as soil-conditioning materials to nprove the physical make-up of soils.

Sawdust fresh from the log has pres-nt and potential values as fuel for pecially designed furnaces and burn-rs. Hickory, oak, maple, and birch can requently be shipped over long dis-ances for use in smoking meats at acking plants.

If the sawdust is from dry wood cut t factories, it has a larger range of use ossibilities.

Obviously, this unused wood occurs n comparatively small rivulets all long the harvesting and production ines. But the rivulets never run into ne big reservoir that can be con-eniently tapped. There is tremendous ariation in the kind and form of the esidues that occur, and this diversity omplicates the task of utilizing them.

The task, of course, starts in the voods. More efficient harvesting meth-ds are constantly being devised. New, ast-working, labor-saving equipment or cutting, skidding, loading, and even undling has speeded forest operations o the point where it often has become rofitable to relog after primary log-ging and to salvage much cull timber or lumber and pulpwood that would ot pay its way with the ordinary log-ging equipment.

In ordinary logging, only the trunk f the tree is taken out. Tops, branches, nd stumps are left behind to be burned r eventually to decay. Sometimes the voods operators can find markets for part of this refuse. Tops of felled rees can sometimes be sold for pulp-vood along with defective trees, thin-ings, and the noncommercial species. Some refuse can be used to make char-oal where markets exist. Short logs of good material can be sawed into oards, squares, barrel staves, and nu-nerous other small products. Some hort lengths cut from between branch vhorls may be suitable for box veneer nd paper cores. Stumps, crotches, and other parts of some species provide figured veneer. Forest litter finds markets with local nurseries as mulching material. Branches can be used in such items as rustic furniture and fencing.

Everything that can be used in the form of sawed and solid wood products should be recovered first. Recovery for pulpwood and fiber products is next in order for areas near established mills.

Sawmills, too, have undergone extensive changes. In the older forest regions, many of the big stationary sawmills have shut down and have been supplanted by smaller portable mills that can be moved from one locality to another. Previously looked upon as a headache to lumbermen and foresters, portable mills are undergoing revolutionary development and are playing an increasing role in our forest economy; they require less investment, they can be moved easily, and they can operate economically where timber resources are thinner and more scattered. The design and operation of small sawmills are being studied for ways in which to make them more efficient.

Sawmills vary widely in the efficiency with which they cut up logs into lumber. Some sawdust is inevitable. Slabs, edgings, and trim wastes vary widely in quantity, however, depending on the efficiency of the mill, the type of logs being sawed, and the extent of salvage operations. The more efficient mills cut lumber accurately to size, reducing waste. With large logs, the proportion of slab and edging offal is reduced. And at some mills this slab material is cut into a great variety of secondary products and sold.

Most of the markets for sawmill refuse are specialized and either local or regional in character. In many of the larger cities, dealers handle sawdust and shavings, supplying makers of floor-sweeping compounds, the fur workers, metal finishers, toy makers, and others that use small quantities. Considerable amounts go as wood flour into linoleum, explosives, and plastics. Probably the largest use, however, is as fuel—at the sawmill to furnish power and heat, in public buildings and power plants, as well as in domestic sawdust burners. Briquets of sawdust and shavings compressed at high temperatures are a fuel product of growing interest.

A great variety of things are or can be made of slabs, edgings, and trims, depending on the species and dryness. Seasoned material has a wider market range than green wood. At the sawmill it may be cut to rough size or to finished dimensions. If softwood, such material is called "cut stock"; if hardwood, "dimension stock." Typical uses are various building materials—flooring, molding strips, sash and frame stock—and furniture flat stock, squares for bed slats, upholstery frames, chair backs and posts, core stock, core blocks, glue blocks, box and crate stock, handle squares, toys, stepladder stock, tent pegs, washboard parts, and a long list of other articles. This material is also used for fiber products, including building boards, container board, roofing felt, and even various grades of paper. Its biggest single use, however, remains as fuel, usually in mixture with sawdust but sometimes bundled or bagged for retail sale; as a processing fuel, it is used by bakers of some types of pastries and breadstuffs, in the drying of tobacco, and to heat brooders.

In the pulp and paper mills, much the same development is going on.

The enigma of lignin is being attacked by Government and privately financed research in the hope of finding uses for it. As knowledge of this complex substance grows, it is recognized as a potential source of valuable industrial chemicals. It is now used as a dispersing agent for portland cement, in the negative plates of storage batteries, and for the production of vanillin and tannins. The evaporated sulfite liquor in which it occurs is used as a binder for foundry cores, in linoleum cement, and as a road-surface binder.

As a source of valuable chemicals, wood is winning greater interest year by year. Chemists are gradually devising new methods of extracting those chemicals at economic cost levels, with their eyes trained primarily on the scrap piles now completely unused.

Sawdust can be transformed into grain alcohol, vitamin-rich yeast, and molasses for stock feed, and, along with small percentages of pulp binders, into serviceable building boards. Alcohol is being manufactured from the spent liquors of sulfite pulp mills. Molasses produced from wood residues at the Forest Products Laboratory is being fed experimentally to cattle, hogs, and chickens to establish its feed value.

But the task of utilizing wood residue does not end in the laboratory with the discovery of new ways of using it. Commercially feasible processes must be developed, financing obtained, then plants built where steady supplies are assured at practical costs, technical skills developed, and markets found. All those steps are necessary to translate research findings into commodities available for purchase and use at a profit to the manufacturers and distributors. Unless the many problems of production and distribution can also be solved, research findings are likely to remain curiosities of the laboratory.

The attack on the problem of unused wood residues has to be from many sides. It has to meet local as well as regional and national needs. A single large, centralized plant in the Pacific Northwest can perhaps make yeast, molasses, alcohol, and other industrial chemicals profitably, because of the vast supplies of raw material nearby. In the Lake States and New England, however, where supplies of wood residue are more scattered, the need is for smaller plants set up perhaps as auxiliaries to sawmills and similar primary converters.

Such small plants have a special significance for farmers, who own about 36 percent of the timber-growing land of the United States—more than is held by any other single group of owners. Much of this acreage is not producing at anything like its capacity, largely because profitable utilization and management are not practiced. If, however, new markets for low-grade timber become available—as, for example, new processing plants for fabricating, laminating, fiber processing, and converting to fodder, molasses, and yeast—farm wood lots in the locality will become more profitable.

An example of what waste-utilization measures have in store for concerns too small to run individual recovery operations is a recent step toward the organization of a wood-waste cooperative in one of the Central States. The prime movers are a number of woodworking plants in a metropolitan area. Each member company proposes to contribute capital in proportion to the weekly tonnage of scrap wood it will ship to a central conversion plant for making pressed board and other products from sawdust, shavings, and other residues. Each member will take out finished converted products for use or sale, paying to the State, as required by State law governing agricultural cooperatives, a restocking fee, in this case a fee sufficient to plant trees calculated ultimately to produce a volume of wood equal to the wood residue handled.

Regardless of whether the proposals are carried out, the plan represents a new approach to the utilization of wood wastes by means of which small concerns can do together what they cannot do alone.

C. V. Sweet *was born and educated (in forestry and wood technology) in New York State. After a period of work in industry and for the Government of India, he joined the Forest Products Laboratory 25 years ago.*

# THE FOREST PRODUCTS LABORATORY

GEORGE M. HUNT

The Forest Products Laboratory, which is maintained in Madison, Wis., as a unit of the United States Department of Agriculture, conducts research to help conserve the Nation's timber supply and make it serve more satisfactorily the needs of the people for wood products of all kinds.

For nearly 40 years the Laboratory has been doing this work. Today virtually every use of wood known to man is directly affected by it.

Hardly a day passes without visits from representatives of forest-products industries seeking information about wood: What is the correct temperature and relative humidity to use in drying magnolia for venetian blinds? Can the new resin glues be used in piano production? What is the best type of wood sheathing for house construction? What grade of plywood is best for outdoor use? How do you bag mold a plywood boat? What will happen if I apply white paint to my red barn? Am I entitled to the free use of the Laboratory's patents on the semichemical process of paper making? How does the Laboratory make molasses from wood? And many other questions about the thousands of uses to which wood is put.

Each day brings fresh batches of letters, telegrams, and telephone calls from every State—from great corporations and Government agencies, home owners, farmers, and operators of small sawmills, woodworking establishments, and factories. The questions range from the complex problems of aerodynamic design to paint peeling off a house or lumber warping in the seasoning pile. But fundamentally they are alike in that they generally involve the basic problem of wood use—an understanding of its fundamental properties, such as strength, wood-moisture relations, and the physical and chemical structure of this common but highly complex substance. It is toward a better understanding of those fundamental properties that the Laboratory has aimed its scientific inquiries, on the assumption that, if you know what wood is and why it behaves as it does, you have the information you need to solve your practical problems.

The more recent accomplishments of the Laboratory, such as transforming cull trees, sawdust, and other wood residues into sugar-rich stock feeds, or building serviceable house walls from sandwiches of veneer and paper without framing members, may appear most striking. Those and other equally solid applications of its work, however, result from its past research, which not only supplies a basis for new concepts that help make such accomplishments possible, but supplies means of constantly improving established wood uses.

The applications of this work start in the forest, where trees are cut into logs. Except for the variations in diameter, taper, and crook, all logs look much alike. Yet from early lumbering days it has been important that timber owners and mill operators be able to recognize from the outward appearance of logs the quality as well as the quantity of lumber that can be cut from them. A system of grading logs according to recognizable characteristics has become increasingly necessary so that buyers and sellers of logs, particularly from farm woodlands, can have a basis for definite and equitable dealings. Applying knowledge gathered in the woods, sawmills, veneer mills, and elsewhere, the Laboratory has developed a system of grading hardwood logs that is now followed by the Forest Service in making timber inventories and that is gradually coming into use in the commercial buying and selling of logs. When once it is firmly established, this grading system promises substantial aid in forest management.

Kiln-dried lumber has become a standard commodity throughout the United States. To assure that such lumber would be dried to the moisture content most suitable for the use to which it is to be put, the Laboratory developed schedules of temperature and relative humidity for drying lumber of various thicknesses rapidly and with a minimum of damage. It has made available such schedules for almost all native American woods and for some foreign woods. As a result, although there may be local or temporary lapses from good kiln-drying standards, the general level of excellence of wood seasoning in the United States is not equaled elsewhere in the world. The Laboratory began its work on improved kiln-drying methods in about 1913 by working out and making known the physical laws governing the rapid seasoning of wood. Its efforts continue toward development of still better technical control of the drying processes.

Most of the 5,000 or more dry kilns in use in this country have been designed by their manufacturers upon the principles of the original internal-fan kiln pioneered at the Laboratory. Those kilns, including all of the new and most of the remodeled ones, have given satisfaction of a high order.

The man who now buys lumber at a lumber yard for repairs, alterations, or new construction usually gets a product of standard dimensions and pattern that, within reasonable tolerances, will be the same as he bought for a like purpose at a previous time. This was not always true, because the lumber from different mills and areas varied widely in dimensions and pattern until some 25 years ago. About that time the Forest Products Laboratory played an important role, with the United States Department of Commerce, in standardizing lumber dimensions by assisting the manufacturers, distributors, and consumers of lumber in setting up American standards to replace the local and regional standards previously existing. Today, as a result, house flooring, siding, and other lumber can be bought in the same sizes whether made in New England, the Lake States, the South, or the West.

The bountiful supply of woods suitable for structural purposes with which the United States has been blessed has been given added value through more ntelligent use and by reliable data on he growth, structure, and strength roperties of these species. More than million tests have provided data on hich to base sound working stresses nd establish structural grades for use n design and for inclusion in building odes. The test methods developed at he Laboratory were recognized in 927 by the American Society for Testng Materials and have been adopted n many foreign countries.

More than 175 native woods, as vell as some foreign species, have been ested for strength. Companion data eeded by design engineers have been btained on such types of fastenings as ails, screws, and connectors, and tudies have been made to determine he effect of loading conditions, defects, nd moisture on strength. New contructions, such as plywood and sandvich materials, have been investigated nd the strength of these complex naterials determined both by actual ests and by means of mathematical nalyses that short-cut laborious and ime-consuming tests of individual pecimens. This information has been lepended on widely by the woodsing industries in the selection of maerial and species for specific purposes, uch as poles, structural timbers, airraft, boxes, boats, and housing.

The development of Federal specifiations for wood and fiberboard boxes has been almost entirely a responsibility of the Laboratory for the past 30 years. Although these specifications were designed for Government use, they have been widely adopted as the basis for improved commercial containers that have greatly reduced shipping costs. It has been estimated that the research on containers has effected annual peacetime savings of about 40 million dollars through reduced damage to merchandise, use of thinner lumber, and containers of lower weight and less volume.

The satisfactory service rendered by many wood products depends on the glue used as a binder for their parts. Skill in the gluing of wood has been improving for centuries, with the most striking advances taking place within recent years. Accepted standards for measuring the strength and durability of glue joints have been important in this development. To provide those standards, we devised two glue-test joints, a tension-test joint for plywood and a block-shear-test joint for heavier laminated woods, and standard methods of testing them that have been accepted by glue makers and users. The strength of new glues and their resistance to moisture, heat, and decay have been measured by their performance in these standard-type joints, both newly made and after exposure to severe conditions of service.

During the Second World War, more than 100 new commercial resin glues were tested for the Army and the Navy. The tests assisted the manufacturers in the elimination of poor glues and the rapid development of the more effective glues. These adhesives have made plywood and laminated wood joints highly durable for outdoor use. They have made practical, also, the gluing of wood to metal, plastics, and other materials that require adhesive properties not possessed by glues previously used for joining wood to wood.

In the field of wood preservation, the work here has contributed substantially to the development and to the standardization of preservatives and treating methods for a wide range of wood uses in which durability is important. An example is the work on pentachlorophenol, an oil-soluble chemical, which has come into increasing use as a wood preservative until now millions of pounds of it are produced annually for this purpose. One of its common applications is quick treatment of window sash to impart decay resistance. The development of this material as a wood preservative dates back to 1930, when we suggested to chemical manufacturers that, on the basis of observations and the theoretical poisoning effect of certain benzene compounds on decay organisms, chlorinated phenols would have special value as wood preservatives.

To broaden the source of raw materials for the pulp and paper industry, such species as the southern yellow pines and various hardwoods have been made usable by means of new pulping processes. Those species supplement the dwindling supplies of spruce and balsam that have been most favored by the industry. Research has opened the way to such new materials and processes. One entirely new process, semichemical pulping, was developed and first placed on a practical basis by the Laboratory in about 1924. This process, that is especially adapted to hardwoods, yields about 50 percent more pulp, with less costly plants, than some of the older processes. By it, nearly 500,000 tons of semichemical pulp are now being produced annually, and the amount is increasing. More recent investigations of its possibilities for the conversion of low-quality wood and wood residues are leading to increased utilization of those materials for many kinds of pulp and paper.

The painting of wood has been placed on a more scientific basis. The greater part of the knowledge on which this improvement is based has come from research and exposure tests at the Laboratory on the paint-holding capacity of American woods. As a result, the usefulness of paints for their effect on the appearance of woods (as distinguished from their protective properties) is now better understood. The common woods have been distinctly classified as to their paintability, and the causes of various types of paint failure have been determined. The disadvantages of using unlike paints in succession on the same surface, as in repainting, have become clear, and the use of special primers and control of two-coat work developed. Millions of dollars were saved by the armed forces during the war by applying the findings to the painting of military buildings.

It has been known for years that cellulose can be transformed into sugars. This knowledge was first applied in this country during the First World War and later more efficiently utilized by the Germans. In the last few years, the commercial possibilities of sugar production from wood have been developed further by reducing the treating time to one-half of that needed by the Germans and increasing the yield to about one-half ton of sugar from a ton of wood. These sugars show promise as molasses for animal feed and as the raw material for producing alcohol, yeast, and other products.

Although the Laboratory staff has been occupied largely by major research problems of the kind named, many minor problems, such as deal with a single type of use for a single species, have not been neglected. Some years ago, for example, certain western railroads were about to reject Engelmann spruce as a material for cross ties, although it was at hand in their territory, because it was difficult to treat with preservatives. The Laboratory found a means of reducing the difficulty and made possible the continued use of this wood. Similarly, a way was devised to cut southern water oak into veneer satisfactory for plywood for fruit and vegetable containers, by which a market was provided for this previously neglected species. Since then, one operator produced in 3 months a half million square feet of water oak plywood.

New wood products developed in recent years include moisture-resistant, dimensionally stable, resin-treated impreg and compreg used for aircraft propellers, knife handles, and for ship decking; the high-strength laminated paper plastic, papreg, used for table tops, truck floors, and ammunition boxes; and the dimensionally stable, resin-free, compressed wood, staypak, useful for textile spinning reels, shuttles, picker sticks, and mine guides. New uses for wood have been suggested by the unusual moisture resistance, the freedom from shrinking and swelling, the hardness, and the beautiful appearance of some of these modified woods, although their applications to use have thus far been limited by their cost.

Practical developments, such as laminated wood for ships, highly moisture-resistant plywoods, new dry-kiln schedules as well as new paper-making processes, do not come of themselves, however. Scientific progress is not, as a rule, the fruit of accidental discoveries. It is rather the result of plodding analysis of facts unearthed by painstaking research methods. The information so uncovered is then applied to so-called practical developments. The Forest Products Laboratory, therefore, keeps its sights leveled on the fundamental aspects of research, pursuing developmental work as basic findings warrant.

GEORGE M. HUNT *is the director of the Forest Products Laboratory. He has been on the staff of the Laboratory since 1913, first as a chemist specializing in the preservation of wood and later as chief of the Division of Wood Preservation. He is a native of Oregon, and a graduate of the University of California. He has been a member of the Forest Service since 1911.*

# HOW TO USE FOREST PRODUCTS LABORATORY

F. J. CHAMPION

A tremendous amount of information on matters pertaining to wood is available at the Forest Products Laboratory. About 6,000 persons and firms each month send in questions about simple matters of burning wood for fuel, the complex problems that arise in the paper and plastics industries, the precautions one should take against decay in building a house, the weight of common lumber, the wood to use in making shipping containers, and many more.

Farmers ask about simple methods for making fence posts last longer. Furniture manufacturers want to know how to avoid warping of glued-up wood panels. Lumber manufacturers ask for the latest kiln-drying schedules. Paper chemists want information on the newest discoveries on the physical properties of the wood fiber. All the inquiries are answered promptly by the staff.

For other people who do not know about the services and help that are available at the Laboratory, some suggestions are offered here.

Because the range of information available is so wide, a specific inquiry is most apt to bring the information wanted with one letter. A request like, "Send me directions for treating aspen fence posts," is easier to handle than one like, "Send me information on wood preservation."

Many inquiries can be answered satisfactorily and most cheaply with a pamphlet or bulletin. Some replies, however, require a detailed letter, based on past research or on accumulated experience and observations.

If the Laboratory does not have the information, the inquirer is so informed, and, if possible, a suggestion is given him as to where the desired information can be obtained.

It is not necessary to know anybody at the Forest Products Laboratory to place your letter in the hands of the man best qualified to answer it. Automatically all inquiries are routed to the man or men specializing in the subject matter of the letter. Letters or postal cards (which often do just as well) should be addressed: Forest Products Laboratory, Madison 5, Wis.

The Laboratory has available separate lists of publications for each major field of research, so that a person can get only the lists that are closest to his needs. One should ask for a list of publications covering wood seasoning, residential construction, forest-products manufacture, or whatever his interest may be. The list he gets includes the titles of all the other available lists, and he can go on from there should his interests broaden.

The titles of the available Forest Products Laboratory publication lists, together with a general description of the subject matter covered and some of the more popular publications mentioned in those lists, are given in the last section of this Yearbook.

Single copies of any of the available Laboratory publications are free on request.

On some subjects associated with wood, the Laboratory can offer little help. For instance, it is not the direct source of information on problems of forest management, forest protection, or general conservation—subjects that are in the province of the Forest Service headquarters in Washington and the various headquarters of the 10 Forest Service regions. The Laboratory has no body of research results on forest insects; that is taken care of by the Bureau of Entomology and Plant Quarantine in Washington, D. C., and its field staff.

On the other hand, inquiries regarding decay, stain, and mold organisms are handled at the Laboratory by the Division of Forest Pathology, maintained by the Bureau of Plant Industry, Soils, and Agricultural Engineering.

Because research on wood finishing at the Laboratory has dealt mainly with exterior finishes, little information is available on such matters as furniture finishing and refinishing.

The information to be had is principally in the field of wood properties and processing as they may affect wood utilization. Trade practices, such as carpentry and cabinet-work instructions, and details of plant woodworking machinery and its lay-out, maintenance, and operation are not covered.

The Laboratory maintains a mailing list for those who wish to keep as nearly up to date as possible with the results of its research. Every 6 months, those on the mailing list receive a brief compilation of abstracts of the reports, technical notes, and trade-journal articles published during the previous 6 months. Any publications that are of specific interest can then be requested. The mailing list is made up only of the names of people who have asked to be placed on the list.

Those who read the trade journals of a particular wood-using industry will find that a considerable amount of information from the Forest Products Laboratory appears from time to time in a number of journals in the form of signed articles by staff members.

Another important means by which the results of research at the Laboratory are acquired by users of forest products is by visiting the institution. In an ordinary year some 3,000 individuals from every part of the United States, generally representing industrial plants (such as paper mills or furniture factories) visit Madison and spend from an hour to a week ironing out production problems concerning wood, acquiring standard information on wood, or discussing new products.

A few individuals return periodically to find out at first hand about new developments in wood products and to discuss those developments with the men working on them. A visit to the Laboratory involves, for the visitor, the expenditure of travel money and, on the part of the Laboratory staff, considerable consulting time. Nevertheless, where large quantities of valuable forest products can be conserved, it is most productive of results. Although the time of the technical staff is fully engaged by the research program, visitors will find staff members easy to approach and ready to give them careful and friendly attention. There is no charge for consulting service.

The Forest Products Laboratory does no routine testing work. It is not possible, for instance, to bring stock-manufactured items of wood to the Laboratory for testing. That is a logical activity of commercial laboratories.

The nearest approach to a routine

testing activity at the Forest Products Laboratory is its wood-identification service. The Laboratory acts as Government headquarters for the identification of wood. Several thousand samples of wood products, ranging from structural timbers to antiques, are received each year and identified as to species by examination of the minute structure of the material.

In a few cases in which the Laboratory's research program, the public interest, and the needs of wood-processing groups are likely to benefit, cooperative research projects are undertaken. Although an outside agency or a commercial firm may finance such projects entirely or in part, the publication of the results of such cooperation is controlled by the Laboratory in the public interest.

A relatively new field organization, linking the Forest Products Laboratory to wood users throughout the United States for more effective service, is found in seven Forest Utilization Service units located at forest experiment stations of the Forest Service. Two or more men, trained in wood uses and prepared to serve wood users directly through expediting the handling of individual and regional problems, are located at the following stations:

California Forest Experiment Station, Berkeley 4, Calif.

Central States Forest Experiment Station, Columbus 15, Ohio.

Northeastern Forest Experiment Station, Philadelphia, Pa.

Northern Rocky Mountain Forest Experiment Station, Missoula, Mont.

Pacific Northwest Forest Experiment Station, Portland 5, Oreg.

Southeastern Forest Experiment Station, Asheville, N. C.

Southern Forest Experiment Station, New Orleans 19, La.

F. J. Champion *joined the Forest Products Laboratory in 1921 as an illustrator and since that time has engaged in a variety of activities in the Information and Educational Division. He is the author of numerous articles on the utilization of wood. He was born in Michigan.*

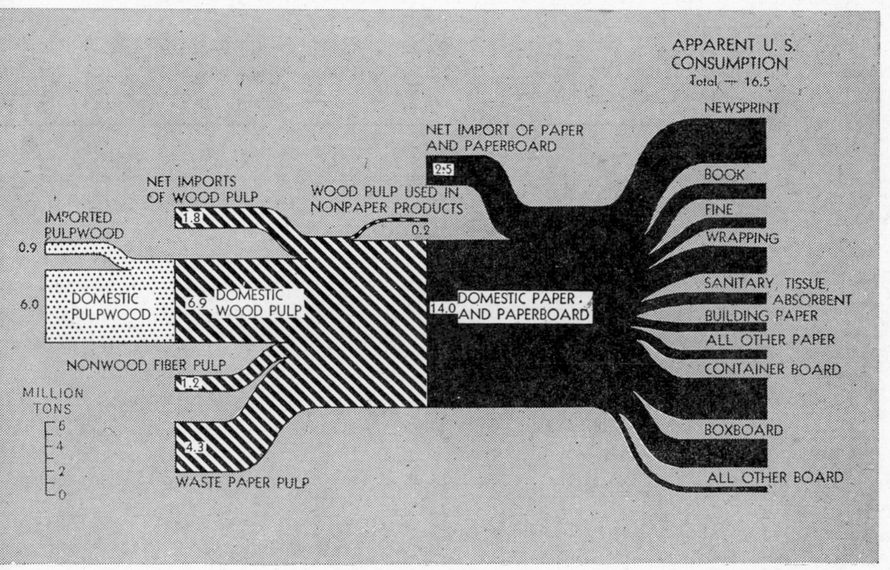


How wood as a raw material "flows" into the paper and paperboard industry is shown above.

OWNERSHIP OF SAW TIMBER ON COMMERCIAL FOREST LAND OF THE UNITED STATES BY REGION[1]

| Region | All ownerships | Federally owned or managed: Total | Federally owned or managed: National forests | Federally owned or managed: Other | State, county, and municipal | Private: Total | Private: Farm | Private: Industrial and other |
|---|---|---|---|---|---|---|---|---|
| | *Million bd. ft.* | *Million bd. ft.* | *Million bd. ft.* | *Million bd. ft.* | *Million bd. ft.* | *Million bd. ft.* | *Million bd. ft.* | *Million bd. ft.* |
| New England | 58,197 | 2,014 | 1,894 | 120 | 842 | 55,341 | 12,214 | 43,127 |
| Middle Atlantic | 62,045 | 1,863 | 1,652 | 211 | 3,877 | 56,305 | 15,855 | 40,450 |
| Lake | 50,710 | 4,300 | 3,285 | 1,015 | 5,340 | 41,070 | 10,910 | 30,160 |
| Central | 43,747 | 1,431 | 1,253 | 178 | 557 | 41,759 | 31,825 | 9,934 |
| Plains | 5,730 | 138 | 3 | 135 | 1 | 5,591 | 5,565 | 26 |
| North | 220,429 | 9,746 | 8,087 | 1,659 | 10,617 | 200,066 | 76,369 | 123,697 |
| South Atlantic | 97,141 | 6,130 | 4,316 | 1,814 | 1,427 | 89,584 | 51,847 | 37,737 |
| Southeast | 135,887 | 6,406 | 4,638 | 1,768 | 386 | 129,095 | 55,743 | 73,352 |
| West Gulf | 104,959 | 5,575 | 4,873 | 702 | 847 | 98,537 | 26,720 | 71,817 |
| South | 337,987 | 18,111 | 13,827 | 4,284 | 2,660 | 317,216 | 134,310 | 182,906 |
| Pacific Northwest: | | | | | | | | |
| Douglas-fir subregion | 504,931 | 265,641 | 208,384 | 57,257 | 35,354 | 203,936 | 8,099 | 195,837 |
| Pine subregion | 125,963 | 92,860 | 70,177 | 22,683 | 3,856 | 29,247 | 2,601 | 26,646 |
| Total | 630,894 | 358,501 | 278,561 | 79,940 | 39,210 | 233,183 | 10,700 | 222,483 |
| California | 227,565 | 104,192 | 99,770 | 4,422 | 157 | 123,216 | 15,348 | 107,868 |
| North Rocky Mountain | 127,229 | 80,541 | 73,641 | 6,900 | 10,828 | 35,860 | 5,424 | 30,436 |
| South Rocky Mountain | 56,868 | 51,183 | 44,531 | 6,652 | 954 | 4,731 | 2,180 | 2,551 |
| West | 1,042,556 | 594,417 | 496,503 | 97,914 | 51,149 | 396,990 | 33,652 | 363,338 |
| All regions | 1,600,972 | 622,274 | 518,417 | 103,857 | 64,426 | 914,272 | 244,331 | 669,941 |

[1] Prepared by Forest Service, U. S. Department of Agriculture. Status beginning of 1945. Includes trees large enough for sawlogs in accordance with the practice of the region regardless of the actual use. Volumes are on lumber-tally basis. This volume occurs on land capable of producing timber of commercial quantity and quality and available now or prospectively for commercial use.

*Minimum sizes of saw-timber trees:*

New England, Middle Atlantic: 9 inches D. B. H. for softwoods and 11 inches for hardwoods.

Lake, Plains: 9 inches D. B. H.

Central: 10 inches D. B. H.

South Atlantic, Southeast, West Gulf: 9 inches D. B. H. for pine and cypress and 13 inches for hardwoods.

Pacific Northwest (Douglas-fir subregion): 15 inches D. B. H.

Pacific Northwest (pine subregion): 11 inches D. B. H.

California: All except redwood type, 11 inches D. B. H.; redwood type, 23 inches D. B. H.

North Rocky Mountain: 11 inches D. B. H. for pine, cedar, and hardwood; 13 inches D. B. H. for other species.

South Rocky Mountain: 11 inches D. B. H.

# The Foresters' Calling

## EDUCATION IN FORESTRY

SAMUEL T. DANA

FORESTRY in the United States attained the dignity of a profession about 50 years ago, largely because of the inauguration and the rapid spread of technical training.

Two schools of forestry opened their doors in 1898, the New York State College of Forestry at Cornell University and the Biltmore Forestry School on the Vanderbilt estate near Asheville, N. C. Both were headed by men who had been trained in forestry in Germany, B. E. Fernow at Cornell, and C. A. Schenck at Biltmore. Their establishment, at a time when the opportunities for the practice of forestry were few and too far between, required vision and courage and was an essential step toward providing trained men, without whom progress would have continued to be slow and uncertain.

In 1900 were established the Yale School of Forestry and the Division of Forestry in the University of Minnesota, which are today our oldest schools in continuous existence. The school at Cornell was discontinued in 1905 as a result of legislative disapproval of the management of a tract of Adirondack forest land which had been placed at its disposal. The one at Biltmore was discontinued shortly before the outbreak of the First World War. Several other institutions, however, introduced forestry into their curricula, and by 1914 schools of forestry were in operation in all parts of the country.

*Above: A farm forester instructs a 4–H group in ways to plant and handle seedlings.*

Today 22 schools are recognized by the Society of American Foresters as providing professional training of a caliber to justify the admission of graduates to the Society without further proof of their competence.

The first three schools of forestry had different approaches to the methods of professional training. The school at Cornell was established as a State institution and comprised a 4-year undergraduate program leading to the bachelor's degree. That at Biltmore, a private enterprise, also conferred a bachelor's degree, although the course in forestry covered only a year and was devoted largely to practical work in the field. The one at Yale, a privately endowed institution, was open only to men with a bachelor's degree and offered 2 years of study leading to the degree of master of forestry.

The pattern established at Cornell has been pretty generally followed at other institutions. There are today no "master" schools similar to that at Biltmore, and only three—Yale, Duke, and Harvard—require a bachelor's degree for admission. All the others admit undergraduates and are parts of State-supported institutions. The latter fact undoubtedly reflects the belief that the importance of proper management of the forests to the permanent prosperity of the entire community is such as to warrant public support of professional training.

Several features of that training deserve special mention. Without exception, the schools require that students obtain a foundation in such subjects as biology, mathematics, physics, chemistry, geology, and economics in their first 2 years. Courses in those subjects are followed by professional instruction in the protection and harvesting, reproduction, management, and utilization of the forest and its products. Since thorough coverage of those subjects is obviously impossible in 2 years, many of the schools now offer an additional year, leading to the master's degree, in which the student's training can be broadened and intensified. Some encourage superior students to take still more intensive training for the doctor's degree. It is significant of the increasing demands being made upon foresters that more and more students are going forward to the higher degrees. The master's degree is, in fact, now commonly regarded as essential for full professional training, and the doctor's degree is becoming an increasingly valuable asset for men in teaching and research.

Forestry in the broad sense is the science, art, and business of managing forest lands for the continuous production of forest goods and services. The average practitioner must be qualified to handle most of the problems encountered in the everyday management of a forest property, whether its size is 10 acres or 100,000 acres and whether it serves primarily to produce wood, wildlife, or scenery or to prevent erosion and control stream flow, just as the ordinary doctor must be prepared to handle any disease that he is normally likely to run across. But there is also need for highly trained specialists to develop the underlying principles that the practitioner uses in his daily work and to advise on particularly difficult or unusual problems, just as there is need for specialists in the medical field.

Consequently, the schools are now graduating doctors of philosophy who are intensively trained to handle problems that deal with such matters as the determination of the contents and growth of a forest; methods of cutting to obtain satisfactory current revenues and at the same time assure the reproduction of the forest; organization of logging operations to minimize waste and maximize profits; control of the environment to provide an abundance of food and other necessary conditions for the support of the deer, muskrats, pheasants, or ducks; provision of ample forage for the production of livestock; and maintenance of a forest cover that will control the runoff of water in the interest of water users of all classes.

In all these fields—timber management, management of wildlife, range management, and watershed management—effective practice must be based on increasingly accurate and comprehensive knowledge. Education and research therefore go hand in hand; and research is being increasingly recognized as a major function of the schools.

Closely related to the production and harvesting of the forest itself is the manufacture and marketing of wood and its innumerable products. Wood technology, as this field is now commonly called, includes all matters relating to the structure and properties of wood; the processes used in its manufacture and treatment, such as kiln drying, preservation from decay and termites, treatment to render it fire-resistant, application of adhesives in the manufacture of plywood; chemical utilization; and the tools, the methods, and power required in wood-working operations of all kinds. This group of activities might be described as "timber engineering." It requires a thorough knowledge of mathematics, physics, chemistry, and their practical applications in the form of machinery and processes. Some schools now recognize the distinctive character of the training needed for their effective conduct by providing special training in which the basic and applied sciences of particular interest to the wood technologist are emphasized.

Foresters today realize that forestry as a business founded on the commercial utilization of wood will succeed only if there is a profitable market for products made from wood and that the existence of such a market, in turn, depends upon the cost and utility of the goods to the consumer. They themselves, consequently, need some knowledge of the properties and uses of woods, and they recognize the importance of the wood technologist in providing the same kind of professional competence in utilization of wood that they themselves provide in its production. Wood technologists, on the other hand, need to know something of the distribution, production, and management of the resources from which they obtain their raw material, and they recognize the importance of the forester in producing a continuous supply of the material without which the wood technologist would have nothing with which to work. Schools of forestry today are training men for both fields of endeavor and are giving each an appreciation of the other's work as a basis for effective cooperation.

Closely related to the biological and engineering aspects of forestry are its economic and social aspects. Forest policies and forest practices have to do primarily with the production and use of wealth, whether the forests to which they are applied are in private or in public ownership. The private owner is naturally most interested in obtaining a net profit in dollars and cents, while the public owner may be equally interested in services that are difficult to measure in financial terms, such as the prevention of erosion, the regulation of stream flow, the production of wildlife for fur and sport, and the provision of other recreational facilities. Private and public forests alike therefore find their ultimate justification in an economic or social return that justifies the expenditures involved.

This means that professional training in forestry now places an emphasis on the social sciences that was unusual in the early years of the century. Forestry must be practiced in a world of reality in which income (including public benefits) must justify costs, in which all operations must be conducted within the framework of existing political and social institutions, and in which the forester must be able to work with other people both as individuals and groups. Economics, political science, sociology, administration, and psychology consequently are fields with which the modern forester is expected to be familiar, in addition to such fundamental subjects as botany, zoology, chemistry, mathematics, and surveying. He also must be able to fit his own specialty of forest growing into other activities that involve the use of cultivated lands in farms and of wild lands elsewhere, so as to develop a finely integrated pattern of land utilization in which each area is devoted to the use for which it is best adapted from the combined view of the biological, engineering, and social sciences.

That forestry is now a profession that offers an attractive career to well-trained men is due largely to the effectiveness with which schools of forestry have discharged their responsibilities during the past 50 years. The profession will doubtless continue to include within its ranks many men whose training has been acquired in the woods, in the practical school of hard knocks, but as the requirements become more

802062°—49——43

rigorous and competition more keen, the advantage will increasingly lie with those who have had technical training in an academic institution.

Today these schools give the holder of an undergraduate degree in forestry a sound training in fundamentals and in the major branches of the profession. They give the man with a master's degree a somewhat broader foundation and a more thorough knowledge of some particular branch of the profession, and they give the holder of the doctor's degree a sufficiently intensive training to qualify him as a true specialist. In light of the broad scope of forestry, as it is now conceived, and of its increasing complexity, the problem is to give the general practitioner a training that will be comprehensive without being superficial, and to give the specialist a training that will be intensive without being narrow.

The successfull practice of forestry requires a knowledge and a leadership that can be supplied only by men with a professional competence which is now difficult to acquire except at a recognized school of forestry. At the same time, there are many subordinate positions that can be filled satisfactorily by men with a semiprofessional or vocational training, just as there are many positions in a hospital that can be filled satisfactorily by nurses, laboratory technicians, and orderlies. Training of this kind has long been neglected in forestry, but it is now being offered at several institutions. The probability is that it will increase in importance.

SAMUEL T. DANA *has been dean of the School of Forestry and Conservation at the University of Michigan since 1927. Before that, he served for many years in the Branch of Research in the Washington office of the Forest Service, as Forest Commissioner of Maine, and as director of the Northeastern Forest Experiment Station. He is a former president of the Society of American Foresters and for 6 years was editor in chief of its official publication, the Journal of Forestry.*

# TEACHERS AND CONSERVATION

JULIEN L. BOATMAN

More and more colleges, teacher-training institutions, and elementary schools and high schools are offering nontechnical instruction in problems and practices of forest conservation and the methods of teaching them. For rural youths and adults, forestry instruction is available through agricultural extension services and vocational agriculture courses. Several associations and foundations and similar organizations also give education in forest conservation.

Many teachers agree that a good place to start the broad field of conservation education, of which forestry is an important segment, is in the lower schools, in courses in general science and social studies.

An example is the series of illustrated bulletins published jointly by the Indiana Department of Conservation, the Department of Forestry and Conservation of Purdue University, and the State Department of Public Instruction of Indiana. The material brings out the relationships among forests, soils, water, and wildlife.

The Granite Falls School, of Granite Falls, Wash., has developed a course in practical forestry that is open to junior and senior students.

In four teaching outlines prepared by the Soil Conservation Service of the Department of Agriculture, forest conservation is emphasized in its relation to soil conservation. The outlines are designed for elementary and secondary schools. They list objectives, topics for study or discussion, classroom activities, references, as well as supplementary teaching aids, such as motion pictures, film strips, charts, and posters.

Agencies in Louisiana and South Carolina have developed forestry subject matter for the grade-school level, which has been well received.

Conservation of resource-use workshops or special courses have been conducted by several institutions of higher learning in 38 States and the District of Columbia to train teachers in general conservation. Forestry was an important segment of the instruction. Teachers of all grades attended. Sessions lasted from a few days to 8 weeks; time was allotted for field trips and the preparation of curriculum materials. In New Mexico one year all the teachers' colleges conducted conservation workshops for teachers.

In the vocational agriculture program of the United States Office of Education, forestry is often offered as a subject of classroom and field instruction for high-school students. Student participation in forest work is expected on the home farm or some other farm or school plot to give a student actual experience.

As a continuing project, the chapter of Future Farmers of America in Adrian, Ga., planted 2,500 trees 25 years ago. The trees have had constant care by succeeding members of the chapter. Several thousand farm boys in Georgia have been given practical training in tree identification, tree planting, woodland management, estimating standing timber, and the construction of firebreaks.

In Garrett County, Md., the vocational agriculture teacher arranged to teach 40 classroom hours of farm forestry. In Illinois, the State extension service and the vocational agriculture department prepared detailed subject-matter outlines and three slide films on planting farm forests, the farmstead windbreak, and improving and protecting Illinois woodlands. The material has been used by more than 350 high-school departments of vocational agriculture. In Virginia a State-wide vocational forestry program is carried on by the vocational agriculture high schools. Cooperating with the Virginia State Board of Education in the program are the State forester, the Department of Agriculture, and the forest industries.

Effective programs of providing nonresident technical and general instruction in forestry have been developed by agricultural extension services in most States. The work includes field demonstrations, group meetings, publications, and lesson materials for persons who are not attending State colleges. In the cooperative extension work, funds are provided to hire State extension foresters on the staffs of the land-grant colleges. The extension foresters carry on an educational farm-forestry program among rural people through the county agricultural agents; the educational work may include the preparation and distribution of publications, group meetings, visual aids, on-the-farm demonstrations of methods and results, and, sometimes, individual technical assistance.

The subject matter used as a basis for such nonresident instruction is founded upon the research done by Federal and State forest and agricultural experiment stations. Among rural people the education in forestry consists of tree plantings, woodland management, wood preservation, 4–H Club work, and the like. The extension forester coordinates his forestry work with other similarly employed specialists, among them specialists in livestock, dairying, horticulture, and in entomology.

As a part of the agricultural extension service educational program, 4–H forestry ranks high in conservation teaching. It has accomplished much in getting rural people to recognize the value of forestry. Through a 4–H project, a club member works out for himself the principles and theories he has been taught. The project method gives a better understanding of subject matter and develops a plan of reasoning. Not infrequently, through 4–H Club work, parents have been induced to improve their farm program.

In Nebraska, material has been prepared to make it possible for youngsters to carry 4–H forestry projects for 3 years. The first year, club members plant and care for trees and shrubs on the farm, besides studying five aspects of forestry or allied problems. The second and third years, the tree-planting and tree-study features are continued on an advanced basis, five new problems being added each year.

Nebraska once had about 10 percent of the 4–H forestry club enrollment of the Nation. Each club was under the direction of a volunteer leader, who was trained by the county agricultural agent, the State 4–H Club leaders, and the State extension forester.

Massachusetts has tree study the first year, tree planting the second year, and wood-lot practices the third year.

Often a first-year project includes tree identification or appreciation, and a club member is expected to collect, identify, and mount samples from 20 to 30 different tree species. Where farm woodlands are available, a 4–H woodland-management project is usually listed for a year's work and includes timber estimating, making a management plan for the area, and constructing firebreaks for protection.

The American Forest Products Industries, Inc., a group of several forest industries, has made available awards for outstanding achievement in 4–H forestry projects. Medals are offered winners in each State; the winner in each of four regions is awarded a trip to the National 4–H Club Congress and a college scholarship of $200.

Among other agencies that conduct educational activities is the Forest Service, which reports an increasing interest in forest conservation among educators. From their analysis of educators' problems and requests for information, supplementary reading materials, and films, men in the Forest Service find a need for three primary approaches: The training of teachers, both in-service and pre-service, in forest-conservation problems and the practices and methods of teaching them; the inclusion of forest conservation in established courses and the development of forest-conservation units; improved and simplified textbook materials and supplementary teaching aids, written and audio-visual.

Besides helping teachers, school supervisors, and administrators, the Forest Service answers many requests for assistance from organizations, agencies, and associations that cooperate with schools to encourage the study of conservation.

An example is the American Junior Red Cross, which carries on its programs through the schools. Because forest-fire disasters have been among the worst in which the Red Cross has carried on relief activities, the organization, through the junior group, cooperates in teaching principles of forest-fire prevention in schools. Its interest extends to forest conservation in general, however, because well-managed forests protect watersheds and thus help reduce the danger of floods. The American Junior Red Cross has introduced the study of forest conservation into the curriculum of its summer training centers, where outstanding high-school boys and girls are instructed in the many phases of good citizenship.

The American Forestry Association, the Charles Lathrop Pack Forestry Foundation, and the American Tree Association are national organizations dedicated to advancing the better use of American forests.

Trees for Tomorrow, an organization supported by a group of pulp and paper mills in northern Wisconsin, assists schools in preparing conservation programs, distributing forest-planting stock, and teaching proper planting methods. It also helps small landowners to make forest-management plans, and provides forestry scholarships. The Wisconsin Department of Public Instruction and the Forest Service co-

operate with Trees for Tomorrow in the training of teachers. Nine State teachers' colleges in Wisconsin sponsor a 5 weeks' summer session at a Forest Service camp that is operated under permit by Trees for Tomorrow.

The Girl Scouts and Boy Scouts offer badges for efforts that include knowledge of tree species and uses of the various trees. They offer instruction in the planting of forest trees and forest protection.

The Southern Pulpwood Conservation Association, a private organization supported by pulp and paper mills in the Southern States, gives demonstrations of good cutting practices and distributes general instructions.

The American Forest Products Industries conducts general education on forestry projects. It encourages several programs—Keep America Green, for forest-fire prevention; Tree Farming, for better timber management; and More Trees, for encouraging greater wood growth on small woodlands.

Many railroads of the country have added technical foresters to their staffs and have prepared educational materials for the forest industries and the owners of woodlands.

Federal Reserve banks disseminate materials on forestry among owners of farm woodlands.

The Forest Farmers Association represents a fairly large group of small landowners in the Southern States and distributes general information on forest management to its members.

The National Committee on Policies in Conservation Education states in its report published in 1948 that "not enough attention has been paid to education of teachers and school administrators in the importance and value of using wisely our natural resources, the assets upon which life depends. As a consequence conservation education has been sadly neglected in our public schools." This might also be said about the efforts that have been made in adult education.

The job is so big that the combined efforts of all public and private educational agencies will be required to provide each citizen with a national viewpoint and see to it that this generation and future generations have an ample supply of the products from the forests.

There are many examples in the various States where an excellent educational job in forest conservation is being done on a community or Statewide basis, but the programs so far are sketchy and do not indicate that there is a concerted drive being made to reach all the citizenry. If the timber and other natural resources are to be conserved and protected, a much greater effort will be required if the average citizen is to become conscious of the importance of doing something about one of the biggest problems confronting the United States today.

Julien L. Boatman *has been chief of the Division of Subject Matter in the Office of Extension, United States Department of Agriculture, since 1939. He has served on the Departmental Farm Forestry Committee, Tennessee Valley Correlating Committee, and National Soil Survey Committee. Previously he was State coordinator and regional agronomist with the Soil Conservation Service, and a member of the State Corn-Hog Board of Review in Iowa. In 1945–46, he was in charge of the Agricultural School at Shrivenham American University, England.*

# CONSULTING FORESTERS

NORMAN MUNSTER, ARTHUR SPILLERS

Like engineering and dentistry and other professions, forestry has opportunities for consultants, who sell advice or their services. Usually the consulting foresters are employed by landowners and industries for a short period and a specific purpose.

The number of consulting foresters is still small, but it is rapidly increasing. The Society of American Foresters estimates that 150 firms now sell professional advice or services and employ more than 200 foresters.

Forty years ago there were probably fewer than a dozen consulting foresters. Most of them did only one type of work—determining the volume of the timber on areas being traded or logged by wood-using industries. During the prosperous 1920's their number increased slowly; the depressed 1930's gave them a severe set-back, but they recovered in the late 1930's and after; as business increased, a remarkable pulpwood development started in the South and the war demanded more wood. Lately their practice has flourished with the expansion of industrial plants, the need for more forest products, and high prices for stumpage.

At the same time, the consultants are widening their field of activities. No longer do they confine themselves to timber cruising; they have branched out into many other aspects of forestry, and, as "Cap" Eldredge put it, "the forester is in a fair way of becoming a working member of the industrial family."

The skills they offer are in 21 fields of specialization, listed by the Society of American Foresters as arboriculture and tree preservation, cost and economic studies of the forest operations, forest and wood utilization, forest management and the silvicultural practices, forest protection from disease, forest protection from fire, forest protection from insects, forest taxation, game and wildlife management, logging engineering, market studies and promotion of trade (forest products), naval stores operations, the pulpwood operations, range management, surveying and mapping, timber valuation and appraisal, timber volume and quality estimates, planting of trees and reforestation (reproduction studies), preservation of wood, wood seasoning, and wood technology.

A list recently published by the Society showed that most of the consultants have seven specialties, the foremost of which are timber valuation and appraisal, forest management and silvicultural practice, and timber volume and quality estimates.

Some of the oldest consulting firms are in the Northeast; the largest ones probably are in the South and on the west coast. Most of the consultants work chiefly with the large landowners. Sometimes their services are brief consultations on specific problems, very often with the permanently employed foresters of the corporations; sometimes their work is the long-term management of forest properties. One consulting forester spends practically all his time locating sites for new industrial developments. Another concentrates on finding tropical forest products. Another specializes in appraising foreign timber investments.

Nearly all large-forest owners and industries employ consulting foresters. The usual fees vary from $20 to $200 a day. Many owners of small forests do not have enough work for consultants; many cannot afford to pay a consultant's fee or are unwilling to pay fees large enough to attract consulting foresters. An obstacle to working with small ownerships is that the expense and time involved in travel are large in proportion to the services and consequently the fees that have to be charged. Few firms of consultants have yet been able to provide a service to the small landowners at a fee that the owners are willing to pay. But because three-fourths of all privately owned commercial-quality forest land is in holdings that average 62 acres, work with the small-forest owners probably offers the greatest future opportunities for consulting foresters.

Eventually, we hope, enough consulting foresters will be available in all regions to handle all private forestry jobs for which consultants are likely to be employed. It is the policy of public agencies to encourage and assist in the development of the consulting forestry work. They recommend consulting foresters to prospective clients, distribute lists of consultants, send them the results of research, and on special problems act as "consultants to the consultants." As it is, public agencies do much to help the owners of small forests by demonstrations of good forest management, technical services in localities where there are no consultants, assistance to operations in the mill and the forest, and by showing that forestry skills can improve woodlands.

At a meeting of the Forest Farmers Association in March 1948, in Jackson, Miss., Consulting Forester John F. Kellogg, who has successfully specialized in work for small-forest owners, made the following remark: "In my consulting work with the small landowners in northern Louisiana and southern Arkansas I have done very little in direct selling of forestry to prospective customers. Most of the landowners that have turned their timber over to me for management have been sold on forestry by some of the educational programs or agencies or individual foresters prior to requesting my services. I am providing them with the means of putting into action the forestry ideals and concepts on which they have been sold."

For anyone entering the profession of consulting forester, adequate business experience and good professional training are recommended. A graduate of a forestry school generally must work for someone else for a few years before he hangs out his shingle as a consulting forester. While getting experience, he probably will find that it pays to specialize.

The most promising field now for specialization is in managerial service to small landowners. A forestry consultant should choose his territory carefully with respect to possible clients, markets, and the timber-growing possibilities. Many consultants are contracting for the long-term management of small forest properties for a percentage of the forest yields—an arrangement that the absent owner usually prefers and the consultant likes because it gives him a steady income.

Another promising opportunity for forestry consultants is with forest-products industries. Most of the 50,000 forest-products industries through the United States are small. All need technical assistance to increase their efficiency and profits. Some foresters run a portable sawmill or a small pulpwood operation and are consultants for other small firms and landowners. Cost accounting and aerial photography are growing fields for consulting foresters.

As the value of professional advice proves itself financially and demonstrates that the best way to manage timber is to do it the "forestry" way, demands for consultants will expand further. With added demands will come new specialization and standards.

NORMAN MUNSTER, *who was born and bred on a farm in Wisconsin, was educated at the University of Michigan and Harvard University. He was manager of forest properties of the University of Michigan and an employee of the Department of Agriculture before he joined the Bureau of the Budget in 1943.*

ARTHUR SPILLERS, *a graduate of the New York State College of Forestry, has worked with the Forest Service since 1929, except for short periods with the Tennessee Valley Authority, the Southern Pine Association, and as a lieutenant colonel in the Army.*

# NATIONAL FOREST PERSONNEL

H. DEAN COCHRAN

The Forest Service, in employing new personnel, seeks to hire men and women who are properly trained for the work and have high ideals and a strong desire to serve the public.

All permanent positions are in the classified Civil Service. Examinations, through which the force is largely recruited, are given for junior foresters and junior range conservationists, whose work is professional and highly technical. Academic training, equivalent to graduation from a recognized college or university, is required. Clerical and fiscal employees also must pass competitive civil-service examinations before appointment.

Most junior professional recruits are men who pass the junior professional examinations; they are first assigned to positions as assistants to district rangers in the national forests or to subordinate lines of technical work. The beginner thus supplements his academic training by field experience that should qualify him for advancement to positions such as that of district ranger, or to comparable positions in research or cooperative work.

In the early days, the forest ranger seldom had a background of technical training, nor did he carry the responsibilities that a district ranger now does. Such positions were often filled by men who passed examinations based almost solely on practical experience in woodsmanship and handling livestock. The practice has been changed with the times.

The district forest ranger today is an administrator of a quarter million acres or more and is responsible for the management of all the timber, range, wildlife, water, and recreation resources within his district. He needs both technical training and practical experience.

One line of advancement may lead the young forester or range conservationist from the post of assistant ranger to that of district ranger, then assistant forest supervisor, from which he may advance to a supervisor's position. Additional promotions may eventually take him to the regional forester's office, or even higher.

Another line of progress in national forest administration may be from technical assistant in a forest ranger's district to technician on the supervisor's staff, followed by assignment as technician for an entire region. Other lines of promotion may be in the field of research or in State and private cooperation. Varying combinations of these lines of promotion may be applied in individual cases.

Thorough technical education in advance of employment and wide training through work experience are now considered prerequisite to success in handling current activities and for advancement to the higher positions.

Training through work experience is provided in several ways. One calls for assignments at various periods during the career of the employee (especially the junior professional man) to the many kinds of work in which he needs to obtain additional technical skills and acquire broader viewpoints. The work is carried on as a part of the man's day-to-day duties under the supervision of technicians who are aware of their responsibility for training their assistants. While all supervisory officers receive instruction in the correct methods of training others, some of the district rangers are especially qualified in this respect; to them are assigned the young men who show promise of becoming rangers.

Another method is group training at special training camps and at other central points, where groups of employees, younger men, or those new in their jobs are given short periods of special training in lines of work they will be expected to perform later. At times the older employees are brought together for refresher courses. Correspondence courses, in seasons when the field-work loads are at the lowest, round out the more formal types of in-service training. In addition, annual group meetings of rangers and supervisors (together with more frequent meetings of junior members of the regional office working as a "junior staff" on study projects of interest and value to the regional forester and his immediate assistants) are an important part of the planned in-service training for technical and administrative workers.

The training of the seasonal personnel, including the fire lookouts, parachutists, the timber- and range-survey crews, and other groups, is done both on-the-job and at training camps as an indispensable part of administration.

Employees are encouraged to take special short courses in universities and colleges that relate to special subjects for the benefit of practicing foresters, graziers, and technicians in wildlife management. Technicians engaged in forest and range research are also encouraged to take suitable graduate work and to seek higher degrees.

To broaden his knowledge and experience, a forest officer may be assigned at different times to work outside the field of national forest administration in activities such as research or cooperative work. For the same reason, and often because of the stimulating effect it has on the work to be done, a man may be transferred periodically to other forests and regions. In scheduling transfers and assignments of individuals, consideration is also given the man's special aptitudes and interests, which are determined early in his career and then are developed through training.

A guiding principle in planning transfers is to try to assure sufficient length of tenure in each assignment to provide a reasonably stabilized organization in charge of each ranger district and each other national forest administrative unit. The resulting beneficial effects include an increasingly greater knowledge of the problems and needs of the forest users and other local people, continuity and development of administrative and management practices, and the welfare of the employee and his family. Normally, the minimum and maximum tenure guides (and they are guides only) vary from 4 to 8 years for the key administrative positions in the organization.

For many years civil-service regulations, in recognition of the type of work involved, called for retirement of rangers, forest supervisors, regional foresters, and other national forest employees at 62 years of age. Amendments to the Federal Retirement Act in 1942 and in 1948, however, provided (among other important and related changes) for the retirement of that group of forest officers on an optional basis beginning at age 60, after 30 years of service.

The Forest Service, for the good of the employees and for the good of the organization, has encouraged the continuation of the tradition of retirement at 62.

The career idea is carried out as above outlined by advancement as men become more proficient in their work. Forest supervisors, assistant supervisors, and regional and national officers have come up through the ranks and, in turn, will be succeeded by other men with a broad base of technical knowledge, training, and experience.

H. DEAN COCHRAN *heads the Division of Personnel Administration in the Forest Service in Washington. A native of Iowa, he entered the Forest Service in 1920. He is a graduate of Illinois College and Colorado State College. He served as technical assistant on the White River and the Routt National Forests. In 1923 he was transferred to the Forest Service regional office at Denver, where he served in various capacities, including 5 years in charge of timber management, and assignments in connection with the establishment of the shelterbelt project.*

# INDUSTRIAL FORESTRY ASSOCIATIONS

CHAPIN COLLINS

Industrial forestry is relatively new in the United States. The profession has grown, particularly since 1930, much as American citizens have grown in their awareness of the practical significance of forestry, of the forester's relationship to national economics and social welfare, of profit and loss in the forest enterprise, of the change that came about when forest industries, which once had asked only how much timber stood on an acre, began to ask how much and in how long a time timber would grow on an acre.

A forester, who earlier had been able to make little contribution to an operation that was concerned almost wholly with the harvest, became essential to an operation that was concerned with husbanding what it had and with growing more for future harvests.

Then professional foresters began to enter industry. By 1930, nearly 400 of them were regularly employed in industry. By 1940, there were 1,000. In 1949, the number of professional foresters in private employ is estimated at more than 2,500. Public employment still absorbs the majority of college-trained men of the woods, but today the most rapidly expanding field of employment is in industry.

This greater awareness of woodland management, from seedling to harvest, was given further impetus by the Copeland Report in 1933, and also by the inclusion of forestry provisions in the National Recovery Administration codes established under the National Industrial Recovery Act of 1933. Both coincided roughly with wider recognition by forest industries, which planned to stay in business, that forest acres must be kept productive and that conscious effort and investment must be made for that purpose.

The recommendations of the Copeland Report met with a mixed reception, but the report did focus attention on the opportunities and responsibilities of private ownership with respect to forest lands. Under NRA in 1934, forest industries were the first to adopt a conservation code, with provisions tending toward forest practices that would assure continuous and adequate timber crops. The committees and activities of that comprehensive program did not end with NRA in 1935. The thinking then engendered continued to influence later action, and, in many instances, machinery then set up by industries continued to operate in other forms.

A DISTINCTION is to be drawn between an industrial forestry association and the other organizations concerned with forests. In such a broad and diverse field as the forests of America, it is not surprising that the latter organizations are many and various. In general, their concern with forestry is based on broad considerations of national welfare. Some restrict their activities to individual States or regions. Others have specific objectives, in which forests play a part, such as conservation of wildlife and recreational facilities. For their membership, they look to public-spirited citizens in general. Although many of them are substantially supported by forest industries, they are not industrial forestry groups as such.

INDUSTRIAL GROUPS, in their forestry activities, are concerned chiefly with the business of growing, protecting, and harvesting trees. Their support comes from those who use wood as their raw material. With other types of associations interested in forests, the industrial group looks to permanently productive forests as its objective, but, in addition, it must consider costs and techniques. Although not all the forest industries are represented now by such groups, the major companies and possibly major production are so represented.

The typical pattern of such industrial activities can be found in trade associations.

First, such activities took the form of consulting services for association members, many of whom believed they could not afford their own forestry departments. But this activity broadened. It was obvious, for example, that forest industries could not depend exclusively upon their own lands for future supply, because collectively they own not more than 18 percent of the commercial tree-producing lands of the country. It became apparent, too, that a public unaware of tree growing as a form of agriculture could be a serious obstacle to forest management on vast areas. So, in many instances, the forestry activities of industrial groups expanded to reach other types of woodland owners and to enlist the understanding cooperation of the public.

This broadening view has given rise to two young but thriving movements in American forestry. One is the Keep America Green program. The other is the American Tree Farms system. Neither is exclusively an industrial activity now, but each had industrial origin and support. Each, in its field, is contributing to better forest protection and management, upon which so many agencies, public and private, are at work. Both function locally, but both have spread across the Nation.

Keep America Green is popular education in forest-fire prevention. Twenty-four States had organized their own Keep Green programs by the beginning of 1949, directed in most instances by State Keep Green committees, in which industry and other interests are represented.

The Tree Farm program is a means of encouraging better forest practices by woodland owners, large and small, and a method of informing the public of the practical purposes and importance of forestry. At the beginning of 1949, the Tree Farm movement was active in 23 States. Its certified tree farms totaled nearly 17 million acres. Although this acreage is not great in relation to the 344,973,000 acres of privately owned forest lands, tree-farm certifications have shown an average increase of 2 million acres a year in the first 7 years of the program. Through publicity and example, the movement helps interpret the nature of our forests to many Americans.

FOREST-FIRE ASSOCIATIONS of the West were among the early organized industrial activities relating to forests. The paramount task of controlling forest fires was assumed by such private groups, sometimes in advance of public action. Often a regional group of timberland owners would pool their holdings, meeting costs by a charge per acre. Following disastrous fires, such as the Yacolt burn in 1902, private protection agencies were formed in Washington, Oregon, California, and Idaho between 1905 and 1912.

The principle thus established of each timber owner paying the cost of protecting his own property—in a cooperative arrangement with neighboring owners—set an important precedent. The principle was incorporated into several State compulsory patrol laws. The associations were instrumental in developing Western State fire codes; they stressed practical problems first, such as adequate equipment in the field, closed burning seasons, compulsory slash disposal, and shut-downs during bad fire weather. They created a consciousness of the necessity for joint action in combating a common enemy. Such experience contributed much to the molding of the Clarke-McNary Law of 1924, which expressed the Federal policy of cooperation with States and private owners in forest protection.

THE WESTERN FORESTRY AND CONSERVATION ASSOCIATION, organized in 1909, became a sort of "grand lodge" of both private and public protection agencies in the West. It is probably senior today in the industrial forestry field. The genius of its manager, Edward T. Allen, gave western forestry far-reaching national, as well as local, leadership.

Its activities illustrate the changing emphasis resulting from changing conditions. Originally, it was to be a clearing house to promote cooperation in all private, Federal, State, and provincial forestry activities—chiefly fire—in Idaho, Washington, Oregon, Montana, California and British Columbia. In its early days it concentrated largely on forest fires, and exchanged information on fire-control problems, reports, and statistics. It sponsored and promoted State forest codes. It won quick recognition for effective work.

In the years since, the association has undertaken various educational tasks. It published a textbook on western forestry; made basic studies in forest taxation, which led to later improvements in land taxes; investigated timber insurance problems; studied pine blister rust; and provided professional foresters to help western companies get better forest production.

Today its emphasis is on education in forestry, improvement of management practices on small holdings, and other silvicultural activities that tend toward a sustained-yield program for its area. It serves as a coordinating force among private, State, Federal, and provincial agencies. Its annual meetings have become notable in its region as forums on forest subjects.

The National Lumber Manufacturers Association established a permanent forestry committee pursuant to a resolution adopted on April 20, 1920. The resolution recognized that "both national and industrial welfare demand early development of an American forest policy which shall substitute for indifference or accident an intelligent, practical, equitable, and concerted program for the perpetuation of forest supplies."

The association is a federation of regional lumber associations and represents these associations in broad national policy and action. The work of its forestry committee and conservation department has been largely informational, statistical, and legislative. The association has usually employed one or more foresters to assist in these activities.

In the field of practicing forestry, the organized efforts of the lumber industry have been concentrated in the regional groups. In the field of general education along forestry lines, the national association has given support to the American Forest Products Industries.

The Southern Pine Association created its conservation department in 1934, but its interest in forestry goes back many years before that. In 1916, it was instrumental in calling the first Southern Forestry Conference, one of whose objectives was to initiate and support State legislation to promote forestry in the South. Five Southern States had forestry departments then; the conference and subsequent activities played a part in creating such departments in all Southern States.

The organization of Southern Pine's conservation department in 1934 was further recognition of the fact that the permanent existence of the lumber industry in the Southern States depended on the continuous production of timber crops on privately owned woodlands. The conservation department has represented the southern pine lumber industry, in 12 States, in efforts to develop adequate control of forest fires, adopt sound cutting practices and equitable taxation of forest lands, strengthen State forestry organizations, and develop legislation relating to forests.

The conservation committee consists of members from each of the southern pine-producing States. Its activities are directed by a technical forester and an assistant forester.

An outstanding phase of the committee's work is the Tree Farm system in the South, in cooperation with State organizations. This program resulted in the certification, by October 1948, of

,202 tree farms, with 9,866,938 acres, ı Alabama, Arkansas, Florida, Missis- ppi, North Carolina, South Carolina, 'exas, Tennessee, and Virginia.

In general, Southern Pine Associa- on, through its conservation depart- ıent, advises members on individual ›restry problems; conducts timber- roduction meetings, which show prac- cal applications of harvesting and ›gging methods; helps to establish emonstrations of cutting practices; rovides an information service on na- onal and State activities and legisla- on affecting forest lands; and engages 1 general education on forestry, in- luding a statistical service.

The West Coast Lumbermen's ssociation, which represents leading roducers of Douglas-fir lumber, also tarted a conservation department in 934 to formulate and administer for- st-practice rules for the region under ıe National Industrial Recovery Act. 'he Pacific Northwest Loggers' Asso- iation joined this activity, and a joint ommittee on conservation was set up, ith representatives of both associa- ons, the State foresters of Washington nd Oregon, the Federal foresters of ıe region, and leaders of the two pri- ate forest-fire associations.

Although NIRA came to an end in 935, the joint committee on forest onservation has continued to function ithout interruption. It has employed p to five professional foresters. The ervices of its staff have been made vailable both to members and others.

The committee has sponsored the 'ree Farm program in the Douglas-fir egion since 1941. By October 1948, ıore than 2,744,155 acres of private ınds had been certified as tree farms. 'eriodic inspections of the areas are ıade to check forestry performance.

At the same time, and partly to nplement the Tree Farm program, he staff developed a cooperative in- ustrial nursery at Nisqually, Wash., hich supplies members with seedlings t cost. Thus, for the first time, a major ource of planting stock became available to forest industries in the area, since public nurseries were restricted by law to use their seedlings for planting on public or farmer-owned lands. By the end of 1947, the nursery had shipped more than 17 million seedlings; orders for delivery in 1948 totaled 6 million. At an average rate of 500 seedlings to the acre, nonrestocked lands replanted by the end of 1948 totaled more than 45,000 acres.

The staff performs other services, many advisory, such as: Cooperation with State forestry departments regarding fire prevention, slash disposal, fire-weather shut-downs, and similar protection activities; assistance to private operators regarding the cutting problems, restocking, partial cuttings, thinnings, and other silvicultural measures; and advice on reforestation, taxation, and public timber sales.

The committee serves also as a liaison body between private and public agencies on matters of forest policy and practice.

The Western Pine Association serves lumber manufacturers in an area roughly equal to 35 percent of continental United States. Its members manufacture about 80 percent of the lumber made in the area, chiefly from the ponderosa, Idaho white, and sugar pines. It was organized under its present name in 1931, although predecessor organizations date from 1906.

The association has been instrumental in drawing up and adopting forest-practice rules to be followed by the industry. The rules have been revised from time to time and, in 1945, were published as handbooks for each State in the region.

By that and other means, the association has encouraged the practical application of principles of conservation and sustained production of forest crops. Today's forestry staff of four members is double that of 10 years ago, and expenditures in forestry activities have tripled. Its committee on conservation formulates forestry policies.

Under this program, the association

reports substantial progress in the adoption of company programs working toward sustained yield. In 1937, 18 companies, with a production of 763,631,000 board feet a year, had adopted measures leading to that goal. Since then, 59 companies, with a yearly production of nearly 2 billion board feet, have started working toward continuous forest production. The western pine industry employs 90-some foresters.

Encouragement is given such activities by the Tree Farm program, which the association has sponsored in its region since 1942 and which has spread to 6 States in the western pine area, with 146 certified tree farms, comprising 2,643,030 acres of privately owned forest lands by October 1948. Inspection and certification of tree farms are supervised by the association staff.

In recent years, there has been a marked tendency on the part of the industry to hold and acquire forest lands to be placed under management for growing forest crops. Employees of the association have helped in the formulation of practical plans for such long-range programs.

The American Walnut Manufacturers Association, since 1944, has encouraged widespread growth of walnut trees in the area from which its members derive their raw material. The work is headed by a forester.

The association has published a booklet, *Growing Walnut for Profit.* Industrial mills help collect walnuts, which are supplied to State nurseries, which, in turn, provide stratified walnuts to farmers and others for planting. State foresters in 15 States cooperate in this program, and it is estimated that, in 1948, up to 3 million more walnuts were planted than normally would have gone into the ground. The project is promoted through newspaper and radio publicity. Buyers of wood for member mills also stress the advantages of planting walnuts for future profit.

The California Redwood Association has not established a separate forestry division, but it has helped maintain close relationships between redwood operators and agencies like the State Division of Forestry and the University of California, both relating to forest practices and to research.

The association reports definite improvement in forest practices, particularly since 1935.

The Appalachian Hardwood Manufacturers, Inc., began a forestry program in 1945. Lumber manufacturers, coal operators, railroads, and other timberland owners are members.

Directed by a forester, the program is concerned chiefly with forestry procedures for its members and with State legislation favorable to better forest practices in the Appalachian area.

The American Paper and Pulp Association appointed a forestry committee in 1938 to study the relationship of the industry to forestry, to collect and analyze data relating to forest resources and their uses, and to formulate the industry's views and recommendations with respect to any Federal forestry legislation. The formation of the committee was prompted by a special congressional committee investigation of the Nation's forest situation.

Through the years the forestry committee undertook to assemble information on forest-land ownership in the pulp and paper industry and the character of cutting programs employed by companies within the industry. The committee has always advocated a program of cooperation with Government and self-regulation by industry, as against Federal and State regulation of industrial forest lands.

To further better forestry practices on all woodlands, five regional subcommittees of the forestry committee were formed in 1947.

Pulp companies owned 14.8 million acres of commercial timberland in 1945, and, probably, through subsequent acquisitions, as much as 17 million acres in 1948. Additional acreage is owned in fee in certain Canadian 'rovinces by United States pulp mills.

Most pulp mills are cutting for con-ınuous yield on their own lands and re educating contractors and other ɹppliers to the advantages of follow-ıg good practices.

Foresters in company employ, be-ause of increased freight rates, labor osts, and other factors, are analyzing he costs of pulpwood on the basis of ransportation to varying distances. 'hose costs are being balanced against he costs of growing wood under inten-ive forest management near the mills. 'requently a large favorable balance ests with the production of wood near nills.

Under the stress of war conditions in 945, management status of pulp com-anies, with respect to forest lands, was ated by the Forest Service (in *The Management Status of Forest Lands in he United States,* Forest Service 1946, Report 3—tables 2 and 16) as follows: 4.5 million of the 14.8 million acres vere being operated with cutting prac-ices rated 82 percent fair or better. 'he ratings were high, 3 percent; good, 0 percent; and fair, 49 percent.

For comparison of various types of wnership, forests under extensive or etter management were rated as fol-ows: Pulp company forests, 69.3 per-ent; all private holdings, 23 percent; ublic forests, 72.8 percent.

The rating of the pulp companies vas three times as good as that of all rivate holdings and close to that of ublic forests, indicating that pulp and aper mills are thoroughly aware of he necessity for looking to their wood upply on a sustaining basis. The high nvestment in a pulp mill practically ompels it.

The Southern Pulpwood Con-ervation Association was organized y the pulp and paper industry in the outh in 1939. Its member companies onsume about 90 percent of all the ulpwood cut in the region. Its pur-ose was expressed thus:

"To formulate and promulgate by ducational means a practical program of utilization and conservation of the forest resources of the South, in order to assure the prevention of a timber shortage with a consequent dire effect upon the pulp and other forest industries involving the welfare of the South and of the Nation, (*a*) by voluntary application of sound principles of forest practices recognized and accepted by the membership, and (*b*) by a program of education directed to forest owners and operators and to the public."

The services of the association have been made available to independent landowners, wood suppliers, and to the general public without any distinction. The services are concerned chiefly with growing more timber, preventing fires, and cutting wisely.

The association now employs 20 field men to carry on its educational activities and demonstrations in the field. The demonstrations are for wood growers, suppliers, and labor. They show proper cutting, tree planting, and improved methods of fire fighting and prevention. In 1947, although the program was new, the 245 demonstrations were attended by more than 4,000 persons. Association employees also check pulpwood cuttings on noncompany lands to determine results of the association's cutting standards.

Forestry training camps, sponsored by the association in 8 of the 10 States of its territory, have helped train farm youth in the fundamentals of forestry. Selected boys spend a week in camp to learn how to handle a timber crop on their own woodlands.

The association reports its activities by radio and newspapers and other publications, including a periodical, *The Unit.* It has published, and keeps current, *Mechanizing Southern Forest Fire Fighting,* which contains the latest information on the subject. It also published a *Mechanization Manual.* Among the films it has produced are several on pine planting, natural pine reseedings, and forest fire. Its portable exhibits and posters have been widely used.

Trees for Tomorrow, Inc., is one of the more recent and unusual developments in industrial forestry. Its activities are confined to the Wisconsin River Valley.

An outgrowth of wartime campaigns to step up production of pulpwood, it is concerned, as its name implies, with growing tomorrow's trees. So successful was the tree-harvesting campaign in the area that a group of pulp and paper mills in the valley decided that, by somewhat similar methods, they could encourage better forest practices and planting of trees in their primary supply area of Wisconsin. So, on February 29, 1944, Trees for Tomorrow, Inc., was organized.

Its members include 10 pulp and paper mills, which own 350,000 acres of industrial forest land, on which 35 million trees have been planted. They are the Consolidated Water Power & Paper Co., Whiting Plover Paper Co., Mosinee Paper Mills Co., Marathon Corp., Wausau Paper Mills Co., Ward Paper Co., National Container Corp., Tomahawk Pulp Co., the Rhinelander Paper Co., and Flambeau Paper Co.

Its program is in two parts. The immediate phase, carried on in seven north-central Wisconsin counties, is directed to the owners of forest land. Since 1944, 2 million trees have been distributed to many private forest-land owners to plant unproductive acres. Planting sites are checked and survival count is taken to insure the best results. Since 1946, 25,000 acres of private woodlands have been mapped and management plans developed for them. A long-range program has adopted education methods, some of which are unique. Schools have been drawn into the project to the greatest possible extent. Each year, $2,500 is awarded in forestry scholarships. Help has been given to establish and manage 25 school forests. A Trees for Tomorrow conservation camp is held; in connection with it, an annual award of $200 is made to the outstanding boy in 4-H Club forestry projects.

The establishment of memorial forests is encouraged, partly to help creat a conception of forestry among citizen who do not own forest lands. Assistanc has been given to three such project totaling more than 11,000 acres. . monthly bulletin, *Tree Tips*, advanc the general educational program.

In 1947, 1,265 persons from 67 Wi consin counties and 42 States regi tered at the conservation camp, whic opened May 12 and continued unt October 24. It is operated by Trees fc Tomorrow in cooperation with th United States Forest Service.

The organizers of Trees for Tomo row, believing that Wisconsin's fore wealth can best be restored throug understanding coordination betwee industry and other agencies in the fiel have sought cooperation with repre sentatives of the Forest Service, th State conservation department, an the University of Wisconsin Extensio Service in shaping its policies and i activities. They recognize, as a majo part of the problem, the necessity o creating a practical understanding b the public of the value and possibiliti of the State's forest resources.

The Forest Industries Council a joint body, set up by various forest in dustries, to consider broad policy affec ing all those industries. Its statemen on forest policy declares:

"Permanent industries capable o producing continuous supplies of fore products are essential to the nationa welfare. The necessity for wise use o our forest resources in maintainin such industries and the communiti dependent upon them is recognize Having faith that private enterpris and initiative can provide the most ef fective management, use, and renewa of our Nation's forests, the Forest In dustries Council pledges united lead ership for betterment of America forests, and the attainment of continu ous forest production."

To further this policy, the Forest In dustries Council has approved thes objectives:

1. Extension of permanent and de

pendable protection against forest fire.

2. Adoption of forest practices, by all forest owners and operators, to insure continuous production of timber.

3. Encouragement of private ownership of forest lands that can be profitably managed, including a national land policy to include the sale and exchange of public lands in order to restore desirable lands to private ownership as well as to consolidate public holdings.

4. Encouragement of public ownership and management of forest lands incapable of producing enough wood to permit profitable private ownership.

5. Equalization of State and local taxes on forest lands.

6. Support of competent State forestry organizations to manage State-owned forest lands and to enforce State laws relating to privately owned forest lands.

7. Support of public regulation where necessary or desirable under State law.

8. Cooperation with public and private agencies to control forest insects and diseases.

9. More complete utilization of forest products.

Within the framework of the Forest Industries Council, various State committees have been formed under the name of Forest Industries Information Committees. Most of the committees, as their name implies, undertake informational work, but some have engaged in forestry promotional activities.

Among the latter are committees in Idaho, Minnesota, and Wisconsin. The Idaho committee was responsible for launching the Keep Idaho Green program by the Junior Chamber of Commerce in 1946. It has worked with 4–H Clubs to develop a tree-planting program in cooperation with the State extension service. Committee members have been active in such projects as tussock moth control and in legislative matters relating to forestry.

The Wisconsin committee initiated the Wisconsin system of industrial forests in 1944. It is somewhat similar to the Tree Farm program, but such areas are restricted to industrial holdings of 1,000 acres or more. Originally, 200,000 acres of managed lands were registered, but the acreage has increased to 411,000 acres. Most of the lands are in conifers for pulp consumption, but about 70,000 acres are in hardwoods. Most of the forestry matters of the Northern Hemlock and Hardwood Manufacturers Association are referred to the Wisconsin Forest Industries Information Committee, largely because of its broader representation.

In Minnesota, the Forest Industries Information Committee initiated the Keep Minnesota Green program, now directed by the State's Keep Green Committee. The Information Committee has conducted a continuing public forest-information program and sponsored State legislation relative to forestry subjects. Among such measures has been an act to permit the State to grow and sell forest nursery stock at cost, another to provide forestry aid to owners of small woods.

American Forest Products Industries, Inc., as an instrument of education in forest subjects, started in 1941. Although an offshoot of the National Lumber Manufacturers Association, it recognized that all forest industries, whatever their products, have trees in common, and so its program included not only lumber manufacturers but makers of pulp and paper, plywood, and other forest products. In 1946, AFPI was reorganized to give it a status independent of any single type of forest industry. Its direction is vested in trustees representing the subscribers.

AFPI began with a national survey of public opinion, which revealed some public misconceptions regarding forests and forest products. Despite rapid advances in wood utilization, large segments of the public thought of wood as an outmoded, old-fashioned product, and of the forests as something belonging to the past. There was little realization that, through man-

802062°—49——44

agement and protection, our forest lands could be made to produce abundantly forever, and that, moreover, the raw materials harvested from forests were essential to national welfare. Conservation, in the minds of many, excluded utilization.

To help counter such impressions, the program started with these objectives:

"To make the American people aware of the fact that timber is a crop which forest-products industries are endeavoring to grow and protect continuously, to keep the people accurately informed about the constructive contributions which these industries are making by creating forest products through private enterprise, products which promote the economic, social, and defense progress of the Nation.

"To stimulate, throughout the forest-products industries themselves, further and continuing improvement in forest practices which are worthy of public approval."

By general educational methods, consisting of publicity, booklets, and motion pictures, the program sought to impress the public with certain characteristics of the forest resource, with the importance of wood as an industrial raw material, and with the steps being taken to use and to conserve the forest resource.

Educational materials were furnished to schools and other interested groups throughout the country. It was not long, however, before those essentially public relations activities broadened. By 1948, in addition to its general educational program, AFPI was undertaking these projects in the field of forestry:

1. The extension of the Keep America Green movement, for popular education in forest-fire prevention on a local basis.

2. The extension of the Tree Farm program, in areas where the project was not already organized or sponsored.

3. The initiation of local More Trees projects, designed to arouse the interest of woodland owners in bette forest practices and to provide mean for informing them.

The fact that Keep Green program organized in only 3 States in 1943, ha expanded to 24 States in 1948 (wit more being organized) is evidence o the effectiveness of this phase o AFPI's work during the intervenin years. Similarly, from 1946 to 194 AFPI helped to organize Tree Farr programs in 7 other States.

In both activities, assistance is give existing programs by supplies of ma terials and by counsel. In man instances, this has resulted in the for mation of groups of interested citizen localized even to communities withi counties. Although such groups, whic include Keep Green committees, ar not industrial as such, they are largel the result of industry-sponsored pro grams for forest betterment.

A third AFPI forest program is th More Trees project. This most recen activity began in Alabama in 1948. Ad dressed primarily to owners of smal woodlands, it both sells the idea of for est management for profit and seek to bring practical fundamentals i farm forestry to woods owners.

Through an informal partnershi between the American Forest Product Industries and the Alabama Forestr Council, representing public and pri vate interests within the State, nearl every woodland owner was reache through advertising, publicity, book lets, motion pictures, and film strips One idea is stressed: Good forest man agement pays. Field demonstration and short courses in forestry are given By the end of 1948 similar project were operating in Virginia and Nev Hampshire, with others being planned

All three projects—Keep Green Tree Farms, More Trees—are collec tively described as the Trees for Amer ica program. All three have one thin in common: They work for increase forest production on a strictly loca basis. In no case does the America Forest Products Industries direct o manage them. It helps organize an ssists them whenever assistance is vanted, but each program is locally ponsored and directed. Localizing uch projects has the effect of drawing nore people into partnership for forest progress; it is education by partici- ation.

In conclusion: The contribution of these and other organized industrial roups to the forest progress of the Jnited States is doubtless larger than he size of their staffs and extent of heir expenditures would indicate. They came into the field of forest man- gement in response to a definite need. Their influence upon memberships and ssociates has been direct and constant. Many private industries have estab- ished their own forestry departments s a result of the work of the association o which they contributed financially. 'oresters in the employ of associations, n many instances, have introduced private companies to the practical ad- vantages of a forestry program.

Progress in industrial forestry has been marked. In 1933, the Copeland Report estimated that less than 5 per- cent of cutting on privately owned ands was done with provision for the enewal of the forest. Thirteen years ater, the Forest Service reported that cutting practices on all privately owned orest lands were 28 percent fair, 7 percent good, and 1 percent of high or- der. The improvement is more marked in ownerships of more than 50,000 acres, most of which are industrial for- ests. In that class of ownership, 39 per- cent of cutting is rated fair, 24 percent good, and 5 percent of high order.

Sustained-yield management had been applied to less than 1 percent of the privately owned forest area, the Copeland Report said in 1933. The 1946 report of the Forest Service con- sidered that 22.4 percent of all private holdings were under extensive manage- ment, and 0.6 percent under intensive management. In this respect industrial holdings again made a relatively better record. The management status of lum- ber company holdings is rated as 32.2 percent extensive and 3.4 percent in- tensive. The management status of pulp company holdings is rated as 66.7 percent extensive and 2.6 intensive.

A direct comparison of the most re- cent Forest Service reappraisal with the Copeland Report is not statistically possible because methods, standards, and thoroughness of the two surveys are not identical. Yet findings indicate a striking change for the better in 13 years. Many factors contributed to that progress. Among those factors, the in- fluence of industrial forestry associa- tions looms large.

Chapin Collins *is a native of Seattle. He was graduated from the University of Washington in 1921. After a year of graduate study, he worked on various daily newspapers and in 1927 bought the Montesano Vidette in Grays Harbor County, Wash. In his newspaper office, in a dis- cussion among several interested men, the Tree Farm idea was born and be- came a reality with the dedication of the nearby Clemons Tree Farm, owned by the Weyerhaeuser Timber Co. Since then, the Tree Farm project has as- sumed national proportions. After serv- ice in the Army, Mr. Collins joined the staff of the American Forest Products Industries in Washington, D. C., in 1943, and became its director in 1945. He resigned in 1948 to return to Montesano.*

CORRELATION OF GRADE OF CUTTING WITH SUSTAINED YIELD, UNITED STATES, 1945

| | *Percentage of acreage in each cutting class that was also on sustained yield* | | |
|---|---|---|---|
| *Ownership class* | *High order* | *Good* | *Fair* |
| Public: | *Percent* | *Percent* | *Percent* |
| National forests..... | 93 | 68 | 76 |
| Other Federal....... | 100 | 61 | 47 |
| State and local...... | 23 | 44 | 35 |
| Private: | | | |
| Large holdings...... | 98 | 86 | 36 |
| Medium holdings.... | 68 | 46 | 16 |

# PRESCRIPTION FOR WOODS SAFETY

SETH JACKSON

A woods crew was talking about safety.

"You think most accidents come from unsafe working conditions and unsafe acts," the logging boss said. "That may be true, but in the woods you can't do much to improve what you find in the woods. Take Joe Sablock. Joe was killed by a widow maker; it dropped on him while he was chopping an undercut. And Jim Mathews—he was killed on a fire when a rock came rolling down the mountain. Falling things kill or cripple lots of woods workers, and we can't do much about it!"

"Yes," I said, "there are reasons why the logging industry has a high injury rate. But we can do many things to improve the record."

"What are you going to do about our Joes and our Jims," he said, "or about the man whose ax slips and he cuts his foot, or the fellow who falls and breaks his leg when he's carrying a stick of pulpwood? We can't change woods conditions much. We can't be around enough to tell 'em how to swing an ax, or lift, or walk carefully."

The logging boss had put his finger on two main reasons why the rates of injury and death in the woods are five times higher than for industry as a whole. Many woods working conditions are beyond the practical control to be had in factories, and supervision is not so close.

The logging boss had also touched on another reason. That is the attitude toward safety that is found among woods workers, from top officials down. These men, working alone or in small groups, give safety little consideration compared with their factory brothers. More thought could well be given to such things as hard hats for the Joes and the Jims in danger areas; clearing limbs, brush, and vines out of the swing of hand tools; getting firm footing; providing protective devices for machin equipment.

"It's just too expensive to prever all accidents around here," said th woods superintendent. "Besides, th boys in the head office are alway pounding us for more production."

"True," I said, "accident preventio does cost money, but accidents cost lot, too. More, probably, than most c us figure. Lost-time injuries to Federa workers average $205 for direct compensation and medical payments, base on 332,289 cases. Industrial costs ar even higher, according to the Nationa Safety Council. In industry, occupational injuries average $274 each fo 232,068 cases.

"But that isn't all. The generall accepted 4 to 1 ratio for indirect cost brings the total to about a thousan dollars for each lost-time injury. Indirect costs include time lost by thos who stop work to aid or watch th injured; time lost by supervisors an others in investigating causes, preparing reports, and training replacements lost production due to upsetting othe workers; lowered efficiency of the injured person when he returns to th job; and damaged equipment or material."

One of the swampers in the crev spoke up: "You brought out the cost to the company. It sets us workers bacl plenty, too, when we get hurt. Beside our own injury, our families suffe from less money in the pay envelop while we're laid up. Compensatio payments are a lot less than our usua wages."

The logging boss asked, "I wonde just how much good accident prevention costs?"

"Some companies spend as much a $25 per employee each year," I said "but amounts as low as $2 a year, o less, will produce some results. O course, it costs more at the start be cause you have a big selling job with all workers then. An outfit with high hazards like logging must spend more than one where dangers aren't so great. Many concerns pay more for accident prevention than for accident compensation. They believe these large sums year after year are more than repaid by less direct and indirect injury costs, improved production, efficiency, and morale. The National Safety Council has recommended $4.50 to $6 per employee per year for Government operations with high hazards, such as construction and motor-vehicle operation. This includes salaries and travel expenses of all safety personnel, purchase of publications and materials. Some funds should be earmarked for protective equipment such as guards, hard hats, goggles."

"You know," said the cat operator, "when it comes right down to it, every accident we have on the job shows us that something is wrong in the outfit somewhere. Each accident is usually someone's fault—lack of skill, carelessness, poor supervision, wrong design, haywire equipment, poor job instruction, no follow-up on safety, and so forth. We all talk about a right way to do a thing. Isn't the right way the safe way; and the safe way the best way?"

Every accident is a symptom that something is wrong with men, methods, or material. It should stimulate management at all levels to do something about it. Accident prevention will pay increased dividends in the form of greater efficiency and production, better job satisfaction and morale, financial savings to both the worker and management, less loss and breakage of equipment and materials.

The source of woods accidents is something to consider. An analysis of Forest Service injuries for 1947 shows this, because its conditions of employment are widely varied—construction and maintenance of the roads, trails, bridges, telephone lines, lookout towers, buildings; planting; timber-stand improvement; and forest-fire fighting. Most of the work is done under situations found in typical logging operations—workers largely on their own or with a minimum of supervision in isolated areas far from medical help. As often as not they are in rugged, timbered country, which is treacherous underfoot.

The analysis shows that about one out of four injuries comes from hand tools, 93 percent of which are due to unskilled use. A further break-down shows that the ax is the main offender. As one would expect, most of the really serious cases come from operation of motor vehicles, tractors, and graders—machines—especially when they are operating too fast for existing conditions, even though the actual speed may be only 15 miles an hour or less. Disregard for safe practices is one of the primary causes why workers get hurt. Supervision has a direct responsibility here.

Few accidents have single causes. Consider the man who broke his leg. He tripped. Why? He was holding the load in such a way that he could not see. Why? He was carrying the load improperly. Why? He had never been told how. Why? His boss had never told him. Why? Management had not held the boss responsible for accidents. Why? Management did not require bosses to plan for safety, to train for safety, and to follow up on the job to insure that a safe job was being done. That makes seven causes so far, not considering the man's possible physical or mental defects.

A thorough investigation of all accidents is an important part of a good safety program. And before that? A prescription for safety has three parts: Policy, planning, human engineering.

The first, policy, concerns the necessity for the active and full support of the head office. This must go further than just signing directives or making safety rules. A statement on the safety policy is needed that shows the support of management and defines safety responsibilities of each individual. Management must demonstrate its interest in the safety of all workers at all levels. The worker will do a job if he knows his boss wants it done; by the same token, if the boss is in earnest about preventing accidents, the workers will work hard at it, too. This principle applies to any operation, regardless of size; aggressive interest by the persons at the top will produce results.

The second, planning, means that if one wants a good safety program, he must provide for it in advance.

What is important to keep the men safe when they work in the next drainage? Who is going to watch out for safety when the planting crew starts? Who is going to handle the safety instruction of the new felling and bucking crews? Is responsibility fixed so they will not work dangerously close together? Has provision been made for safety at the new camp location? What items should be covered there?

Most accidents come from unsafe conditions and unsafe acts. Working conditions in the woods are subject to some control, and this phase of safety should not be overlooked. Within practical limitations, plans should be laid to eliminate hazards on all jobs. Management can control roads, tools, equipment, loading and unloading sites. The workers can control, to some extent, their working areas. A disorderly place is an unsafe place to work. In the more dangerous work situations, hard hats or even lookouts will help.

There is almost no limit to what can be done to prevent unsafe acts. The drive to prevent them is the third part of the safety prescription. Human engineering means better job relations in all parts of the operation.

First, recruit only workers who are physically and mentally qualified, and put them on the jobs they can do best.

Second, instruct them in the safe, most efficient way to do their work as soon as they report for duty. A large proportion of accidents is caused by green hands during their first days or weeks on the job. A new worker will never need help more, nor be more

willing to accept help than during th first hours on the job. That is the tim to make him fully aware of the need fo safety. His support should be enliste in a thorough effort to eliminate acci dents. It is largely a question of job in struction. The pulpmaker must b shown how properly to lift a heavy ob ject. The swamper must learn how t use his ax safely. The truck driver mus be told the rules of safety on the road

Third, be sure that all work super visors make it a point to follow throug on safety in all their contacts with th workers. Do the men understand th key points of safety? Do they apply al safety instructions conscientiously? I the right man on the right job? Thes and similar questions should be raise by all inspecting officers. Many agen cies have found that most injuries coul have been prevented if supervisors ha been more alert to requirements an standards. Failure of supervision is on of the most important of all acciden causes, and supervisors are the key me in any accident-prevention program.

The Department of Labor, in a study of the pulpwood-logging industr in 1933–44, found that nearly half o all disabling injuries happened to fall ers and buckers, about 16 percent t employees loading and unloading logs and another 16 percent to those transporting logs and equipment. Injuries to legs, feet, and toes were most common. Logs, trees, hand tools, working surfaces, and vehicles were the leading injury-producing agencies. Outstanding among unsafe working conditions were rough, slippery, or obstructed working areas, and decayed or dead limbs and trees. The most common unsafe acts were the unsafe use of equipment, particularly hand tools, inattention to footing, and unsafe planning of felling.

In larger companies, a safety staff should be available to analyze facts of accidents, to show the organization how and where its efforts will produce the best results in accident prevention. One of the most important functions of a safety staff is to see to it that training in safety is followed through, that performance follows the precept. The precept is: Injuries can be prevented.

SETH JACKSON *worked in the logging camps of northern Ontario and Michigan before his graduation in forestry from Cornell University. After 2½ years with the International Paper Co. in Newfoundland, he joined the Forest Service. He now has charge of the safety program. He has held administrative positions on national forests in Wisconsin, Michigan, and in Montana.*

# PICTURING FORESTS FROM THE AIR

RAYMOND D. GARVER

Aerial photographs have many uses in forestry.

In the management of forest and range lands, aerial photographs supplement and sometimes supplant planimetric maps and ground examinations in locating roads, trails, telephone lines, firebreaks, recreation areas, and other improvements. They are used in mapping and administering timber sales and range allotments and appraising timber for sale. They provide basic reference material for forest-management plans. They are an indispensable aid in certain types of forest research, such as country-wide forest surveys. They record forest conditions at a given time and place, and supply the basis for essential measurements for classifying timber. If they are supplemented by additional study and measurements of the timber on the ground, the results rate high as a statistic in computing total forest area, volume, and growth; the kind, age, condition, and size of trees; general accessibility; areas of forest depletion by cutting, fire, and disease; and location of the timber in relation to transportation.

They were first used in a practical way during the First World War. Methods of making and applying them expanded greatly during the Second World War. Between the wars, progress was moderate, and possibly the widest application was in planimetric and topographic mapping, with forestry a secondary objective.

Aerial photography is employed in Australia, Canada, the Soviet Union, Europe, Africa, Central America, South America, and the United States, where photographs are used in appraising forests.

The techniques in the United States and probably in other countries are not yet perfected to a point where they fully meet the needs of foresters, but because increasing use is made of the photographs in forestry, study and effort to improve the technique of taking the pictures and interpreting them are going on all the time.

The first use of air photographs in the United States probably was in 1917 in mapping part of the Columbia National Forest in Washington. During the past two decades about two-thirds of the United States has been photographed from the air—often called "flown." But on at least half of the area, the pictures are more than 8 years old.

That is unsatisfactory, because forests are changing all the time. Timber stands decline in area and volume because of cutting, fire, wind, decay, insects, and other losses. On the other hand, they expand in area, size, and volume through growth. Because of the changing factors, the old photographs may not correctly show the current condition of the forests. They may, however, correctly represent old-growth timber areas and topographic features, such as streams and roads that have not changed materially. It is important to have up-to-date photographs in timber surveys and periodically—say every 5 or 10 years—to refly areas where the forest cover has changed significantly. Although old aerial photographs still have high value for engineering purposes, new pictures are preferred.

Another problem is the scale. Foresters require a larger scale for resource studies than engineers need for their work. So far, it has not been possible to agree on one scale that would be best for both kinds of work. Experienced engineers and foresters feel that (considering costs and usability) the best arrangement would be to have a special kind and scale of photographs for forestry and another for engineering purposes. Actually, that is only a part of the problem; the other part is the need for improvement in the technical aspects of taking photographs (such as the best kind of film, the scale, season of the year, focal length of camera), and concerted efforts to adapt the pictures to the major use for which they are being taken.

The scale of usable photographs in forestry work is somewhat restricted in range—from 1:12,000 to 1:22,000. A scale of 1:15,840 is commonly preferred; the figure means that 4 inches on the photograph covers 1 mile of forest on the ground. Because the scale is the factor that primarily controls the relative size of the objects that appear on the photographs, its selection is important and must be adjusted as far as possible to the purpose for which the photographs are taken and the allowable cost. Some caution in using scale to determine distances on photographs is necessary, because changes in altitude of the plane, its tip or tilt, and variations in elevation of the country being photographed may introduce errors of, say, 10 percent in area determination on individual photographs.

The two general types of aerial photographs are verticals and obliques. Vertical photographs—taken with the camera in as nearly a vertical position as one can keep it in a fast-flying airplane—are preferred for forest surveys, topographic and planimetric mapping, and on-the-ground forestry practices. Oblique photographs are taken with the camera intentionally inclined to the vertical at a given angle. They cover large areas at a low cost and are sometimes used for rough mapping.

The best type of film for forestry photographs from the air is still to be determined and perfected. Three types now used are panchromatic, infrared with various filters, and color films.

Panchromatic is most common, but fails to meet fully the foresters' needs in differentiating between forest types and species of trees. The infrared film, with a minus blue filter, has produced photographs showing an improved contrast between species and forest types in summer pictures, but needs further trial tests and experimentation. Color film has not been tried over a large area. In theory, it looks good for identifying species of trees, particularly for hardwoods in the fall when seasonal coloring of the leaves is at its height.

Besides type of film, the season best suited to bringing out forest characteristics is important in interpreting the aerial photographs in surveys or other economic and management investigations. For forest-survey purposes, spring and fall are believed to be the best seasons for photographing forests.

As a first step in interpreting the data, foresters usually examine overlapping pairs of aerial photographs under a stereoscope; the effect is about the same as if a person were suspended over a timbered area so as to be able to see the three dimensions of the objects below. From this vantage point, the forest types and stand-size classes are identified and often delineated on the contact print. The information can be plotted on a good map by a number of methods. One simple plan for flat country is to transfer the forest-type boundaries and other timber data by using a divider and a scale. Another method is to use the new radial planimetric plotter, which helps correct for differences in elevation of the area being mapped.

The area of the forest land can be determined directly from the aerial contact prints or from a forest-type map by one of several methods. One way is to measure the forest area by means of a planimeter, a mechanical device for measuring the surface area on a map by following the boundary of the forest land with a pointer attached to a tabulating indicator. To get the forest-land area, the result is multiplied by a conversion factor adjusted to the scale of the map.

Another method, called "counting dots," is to put a clear acetate sheet, on which are regularly spaced dots, over aerial photographs or a map and then count the dots that fall on and off forest land. It provides the basis for computing the percentage in forest land; the figure applied to the total acreage of the tract in question gives the area of forest land.

Another step is to classify and delineate the timber according to forest type, tree-size class, and density. For that, a code has been developed. "P5d," for example, means pine type, intermediate saw timber of good density; "A" indicates agricultural land, and "N" noncommercial forest land. The classification is usually done by examining the aerial photographs under a stereoscope. The area of the different classes is determined by one of the methods listed previously.

For rough exploratory work on new areas or for checks on previously surveyed tracts, volumes per acre are sometimes estimated from the photographs for each stand-size class of timber, such as saw-timber areas and pole-timber areas. For a more exacting timber inventory, it is considered best to measure a number of sample areas—say one-fourth acre in size—in each stand-size class on the ground to provide a factor for computing the total volume of the area under study.

The height of trees is sometimes used to separate forest areas into height classes by forest types. Several methods can be used to measure the approximate height of trees as shown on the photographs. One is to measure the length of shadows and compute the height of the corresponding trees by a rather simple formula. A solar ephemeris, time, and latitude and longitude of the tree are needed.

Another method is to use one of several stereoplotting instruments, which measure the difference in parallax between the top and the base of a tree. This factor, when it is correlated with the height of the plane above ground, the length of the air base, and the focal length of the camera, gives the height of a tree.

Still another instrument is the parallax wedge. It is a simple device that has two converging lines etched on glass or other transparent material; one of the lines has marks to indicate distance. When used with a stereoscope and overlapping pairs of photos, the lines converge into a single sloping line that makes it possible to determine the height of trees. All these methods are considered precise enough to place most timber in 10-foot height classes with reasonable consistency.

Efforts are being made to use timber height and density as controlling factors in making volume estimates. Some tests have been made with varying success. The aim is to find a method of inventorying timber from aerial photographs which requires only a minimum of costly supplemental ground work. In somewhat oversimplified terms, that means the ability to identify tree species, to measure diameter, height, and width of crown, and to determine factors of tree condition, such as soundness, quality, and thrift, on aerial photos with accuracy and adequacy. The results could then be applied to special tables to get volume, quality, defect, and possibly growth, without any on-the-ground measurements.

To summarize: We need to know much more about taking and reading aerial photographs, but present techniques are good enough to aid greatly in the Forest Survey and to meet emergency needs for a quick inventory.

An example is the inventory of the forest fire in Maine in 1947, when 220,000 acres burned over in a few days and a critical situation developed be cause it was felt that the fire-kille timber had to be utilized within a yea before insects and storms could destro it. A map and timber inventory to shov the location, kind, and volume of th timber was immediately needed to ai in the necessary salvage plans. The are was flown, maps were prepared fror the photographs, ground plots wer measured, and reports made ready i only 8 weeks.

RAYMOND D. GARVER *is director o the Nation-wide Forest Survey, Divi sion of Forest Economics, in the Fores Service. He is a graduate of the Uni versity of Nebraska and holds a mas ter's degree in forestry from Iowa Stat College. For more than 30 years he ha worked in forest research and adminis tration of national forests.*

# RAILROADS AND FORESTERS

ROBERT N. HOSKINS

Railroads have always run on wood. Wooden rails made the road over which the horse-drawn vehicles hauled brick and clay products up Beacon Hill in Boston in 1795. Three miles of wooden track was the total length of the first railroad incorporated in Massachusetts in 1826. When new frontiers opened, railroads pushed across the continent; for the 227,355 miles of track they laid, they needed wood—wood for cross ties, wood for piling, wood for switch ties, wood for a hundred other uses. Their need for wood continues in an age of steel, plastics, and glass; actually, in Class I railway track today there are 994,516,000 wooden cross ties.

The history of railroading can be told as the history of the use of wood. With mechanization, notably the steam locomotives, the use of horses for the motive power was discontinued. As heavier equipment moved greater and greater distances, the originally designed wooden rails, capped by strip of iron, became obsolete and were re placed by all-steel rails. The demand of the lusty, growing giants, the rail roads, and the expanding Nation the served and, indeed, nourished, grew a the railroads grew. To meet the neces sities of a growing Nation, our virgi forests were cut over rapidly. Th effort was little and the need small t carry on any program of conservatio to insure future operations on thos timberlands.

The real demand for action to b taken came much later. One reaso for it when the need did arise was tha durable species were declining in th volumes needed. Maintenance cost increased yearly because the material needed for operation had to come fror the less durable species like the red oal gum, and pine. To meet the risin costs, extensive studies were under taken in wood preservation. Railroads aware of their problem, which was on of constant tie replacement, naturally became one of the first organizations in the country to establish wood preservation plants whose function was to impregnate wood with chemicals which guarded them against decay, lengthened their useful life, and reduced the volume of wood needed.

The companies that supply the railroads conduct research to find better ways to use wood; the railroads themselves are continually making tests to prove or disprove the adaptability of new products, to find superior materials and to improve old methods, and further the forest-products research. A typical example of increasing the life of the forest products is that of treating cross ties with creosote.

In 1937, Class I railroads required in maintenance of their tracks 9,594,370 untreated cross ties and 35,554,782 treated cross ties. In 1946 the number of untreated ties dropped to 1,840,765, with the treated ties used for replacement totaling 35,429,179. The greater use of treated ties has had a direct bearing on replacement; within this 10-year period, 7,879,208 fewer ties were placed in service. An indication of the amount of money involved is the outlay of $64,274,000 the first 8 months of 1947 by Class I railroads for cross ties. Another example: One railroad, the Seaboard Air Line Railroad Company, in 1946 alone, purchased 997,000 cross ties, 5,083,000 board feet of treated and untreated switch ties, 12,419,000 board feet of lumber, and 337,000 feet of piling for its 4,000 miles.

Railroads, which are among the largest users of forest products, have an enormous stake in the future timber supply. No satisfactory substitute has been developed for the wood ties.

The railroads derive millions of dollars in revenue from forest products in their many forms which they transport, such as logs, lumber, shingles, lath, pulpwood, rosin and turpentine, printing paper, paper bags, wrapping paper, paperboard, pulpboard, wallboard, and wood pulp.

In the southern district (those States east of the Mississippi, and south of the Ohio and Potomac Rivers, including Virginia, North and South Carolina, Georgia, Florida, Kentucky, Tennessee, Alabama and Mississippi), Class I railroads, with a total mileage of 35,000, loaded 741,716 cars with forest products in 1944 and 823,146 cars in 1947.

In turn, the railroads spend large sums to develop equipment to facilitate the movement of this class of tonnage, to lower costs, and to provide more safely for the loads. One of the results of this endeavor is the woodrack car, which is used in hauling pulpwood. When the pulp and paper industry began its initial construction in the South, low-side gondolas, high-side gondolas, and box cars were used to move pulpwood. The woodrack car has effected cost savings in both loading and unloading pulpwood. The Seaboard Air Line Railroad has in construction enough woodrack cars to serve all paper mills along its lines. More than 2,000 such cars are in use.

Because railroads recognize the importance of forest products as a source of income and of material for operation and maintenance, they are interested in the management of forests. Some of the earliest hand-plantings of trees were made by railroads. The employment of foresters by railroads dates from the turn of the century, largely, at first, in the fields of wood utilization, preservation, and purchasing. Now railroads employ foresters to manage company-owned lands, assist landowners, youth groups, and others with their woodland problems, and to further the work of conservation of timber resources, planning in reforestation, and fire prevention.

Fourteen railroads now employ 24 foresters. They are the Atlantic Coast Line Railroad; Central of Georgia Railway Company; Chicago and North Western Railway; Erie Railroad; Gulf, Mobile and Ohio Railroad; Illinois Central Railroad; New York Central System; New York, New Haven and Hartford Railroad Company; Northern Pacific Railway; Pennsylvania Railroad; Seaboard Air Line Railroad Company; Soo Line; Southern Railway System, and the Southern Pacific Company.

The railroad foresters, in a meeting in Washington, D. C., in 1946, adopted the following program to promote better forestry practices:

To identify the railroads as one of the industries actively engaged in the perpetuation of our forests.

To encourage reforestation on forest lands not now producing revenue.

To encourage forest-fire prevention.

To promote forest conservation.

To assist actively all forest agencies in forestry education.

To encourage use of proper grades and species of wood by the railroads.

A NEW POSITION in railroading is that of the industrial forester, whose work is to encourage the development and better utilization of forest lands. To that end, he cooperates with the farm youth, the farmer, the forestry associations, State and Federal, civic organizations, State departments of education, and the States served by the railroad.

The Seaboard Air Line Railroad was the first to engage in such activity. Its lines serve six Southeastern States, which have more than 100 million acres in forest lands and in which numerous pulp and paper mills have located since 1937. The Seaboard initiated a forestry program in 1937. In cooperation with the State forest services, extension services, the United States Forest Service, and State departments of vocational agriculture, this company has conducted woodland-improvement demonstrations throughout the Southeast. The demonstrations have been well attended by adult farmers, the veterans who receive on-the-farm training, students of vocational agriculture, and representatives of wood-using industries. In them, stress is placed on the proper marking and cutting of the small farm woodlands and the use of varied types of equipment which can facilitate economic efficiency in the farm woods. Some of the equipment demonstrated includes mechanical power saws and tree planters.

The Seaboard has given full cooperation to wood industries and others in forming associations to work for improvement in cutting practices and to present facts on forestry to legislative committees. The need to protect forests from fires, a vital part of the program, is presented in exhibits, news articles, contests, and meetings with civic organizations, farm groups, and railroad maintenance forces.

The Seaboard operated a forestry train over its system in 1941. At more than fifty stops the message of better protection and improved cutting practices was brought to people in the Southeast. Menus in Seaboard dining cars have featured information about trees along the route. Radio broadcasts on aspects of this railroad's forestry activities have reached large audiences. Since 1946 a forestry bulletin has been published quarterly for 12,000 readers. It has featured articles on various activities of Federal, State, and extension forest services, departments of vocational agriculture, and other forestry associations. Outstanding work in forestry by farmers, farm youth, and others is given recognition in each issue.

In cooperation with the vocational agriculture departments of the six Southeastern States, through the State supervisors of vocational agriculture and wood-using industries, the company has carried on a program with young farmers since 1945. It includes trips, scholarships to forestry training camps, and bonds that have been awarded to representatives of the national organization—Future Farmers of America—for their work on their own home wood lots. Classroom instruction and on-the-ground assistance is a part of the plan. Plantings in Florida alone amounted to 1,000,000 seedlings during the 1947–48 planting season, and in Alabama 1,400,000 seedlings were set out by students enrolled in vocational agriculture. The anticipated result of this industry-sponsored program can be attested by the fact that participation in all Southeastern States has increased 75 to 200 percent. Some States have organized voluntary fire crews, with the assistance of the State divisions of forestry. The men in charge believe that if forestry is to develop on a progressive basis, the education of young people must receive greater support from railroads as well as from other agencies.

Other railroads are setting up similar programs in the States they serve. Their aim is the same as that of any wood industry, State or Federal forest agency—sufficient timber to meet today's and tomorrow's requirements. An integral part of the activity is on-the-ground training for students of vocational agriculture, with awards of prizes and trips to those who make the most progress. It is one of several indications that more and more railroads recognize the value of forestry programs and the importance of wood.

ROBERT N. HOSKINS *is employed as industrial forester by the Seaboard Air Line Railroad Company. After he received a bachelor's degree in forestry from Iowa State College in 1939, he was employed with the Missouri Conservation Commission and the Florida Forest Service, in Tallahassee.*

**THE CAUSES OF ACCIDENTS AMONG WOODS WORKERS**

**About one out of four injuries involves the unskilled use of hand tools. The ax is the main offender. Most of the serious accidents are due to the operation of motor vehicles, tractors, and graders at speeds too fast for existing conditions, even though the actual speed may be only 15 miles an hour or less.**

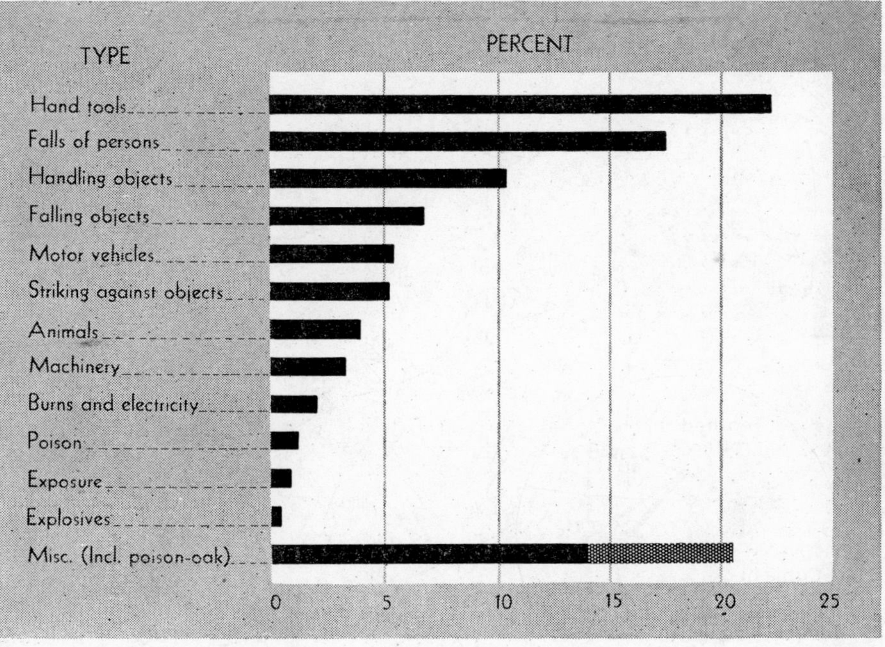

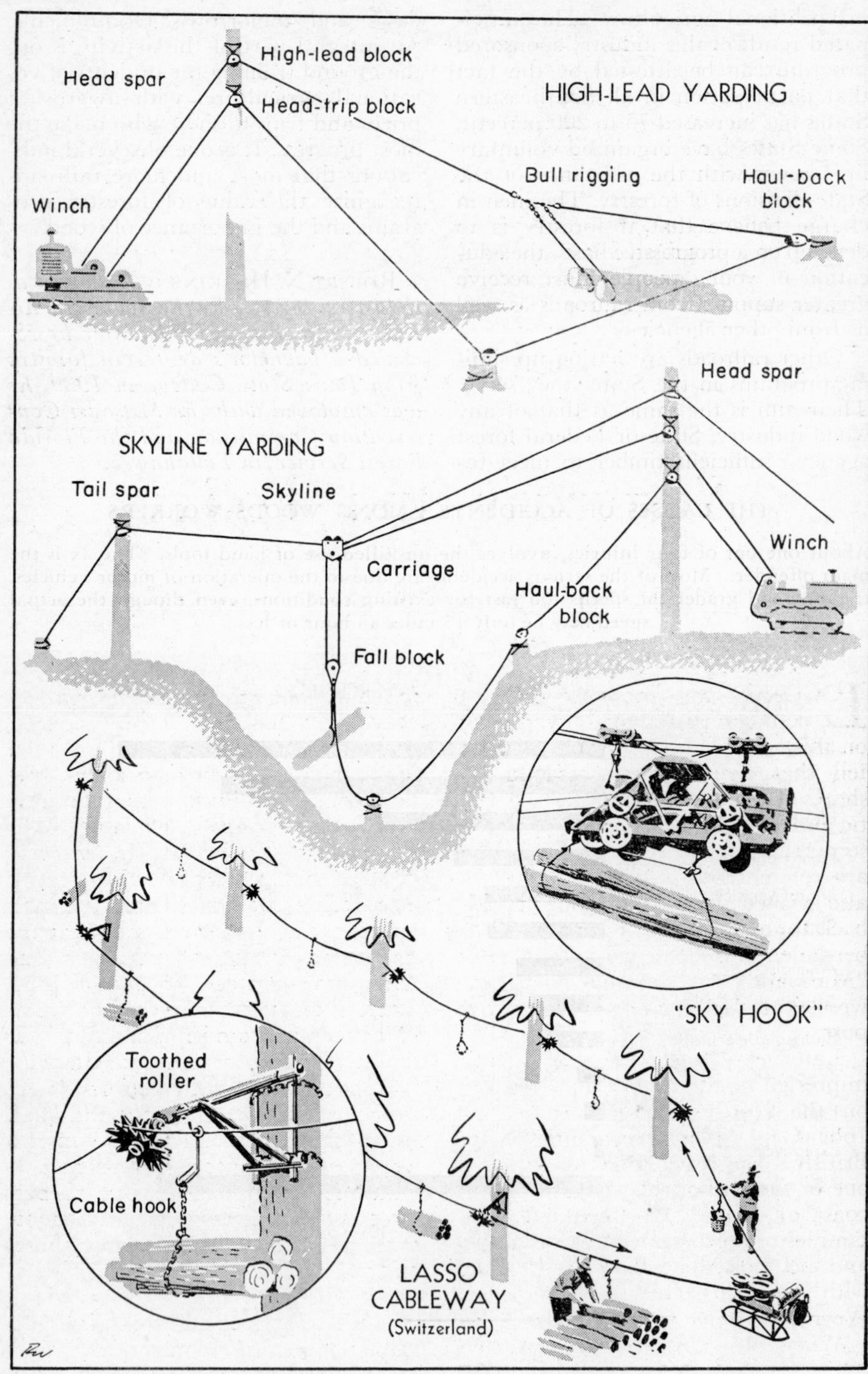


These logging machines and methods are discussed in the following chapter.

# Yesterday and Today

## SINCE THE DAYS OF LEIF ERICSON

FRED C. SIMMONS

LOGGING was probably the first commercial activity of white men on this continent. Old Norse accounts tell that Leif Ericson went to the shores of a land across the North Atlantic and brought back a cargo of timber some time about A. D. 1000. There are references to other voyagers who also visited that land and brought back timber. There is record of a timber-laden ship, homeward bound from "Markland" to Iceland, that was wrecked in 1347 just before it reached port.

Later explorers were also greatly impressed by the timber that they saw on the North American shores. In 1605 Capt. John Weymouth of the British Royal Navy nosed his ship into one of the harbors of what is now the coast of Maine. His men cut some samples of northern white pine timber and he took these back to England with him. This pine is still known as Weymouth pine in the British Isles.

When the colonists arrived they found timber growing to the water's edge. They had to cut trees to make room for their homes and for their fields. Houses, barns, stockades, and bridges were built of logs that were everywhere readily available. The small, round timbers were preferred because they could be handled easily. The date of the first sawmill is a matter of debate; some contend that the settlers in Virginia were using one some time between 1608 and 1620. There is an authentic record of a sawmill that was established in 1634 near the site of South Berwick, in Maine.

Captain Weymouth's efforts to inform his countrymen about the quality of the timber in North America were highly successful—especially with the Royal Navy. Mast timbers were soon in heavy demand. White pine from the New England shores and yellow pine from the Colonies to the south began to move to England in ships built specially for this trade. Depletion of the supply of tall trees on the Baltic shores made the English apprehensive about the preservation

*Above: A drawing after an old photograph of early big-wheel logging in the West.*

of their new-found supply. Suitable trees in the New England forests were marked with the King's broad arrow and thus reserved for the exclusive use of the Royal Navy.

The colonists used logging equipment and methods of rudimentary character. The early mills and shipping docks were mostly on tidewater. Heavy stands of timber grew on stream banks or on slopes from which logs could readily be put in water by hand and then floated to mills or shipside. Timber that was more distant from the watercourses and hardwood logs that would not float had to be skidded—either by the brute strength of men or by use of the oxen that pulled the farmers' plows. The colonists soon found that skidding could be done most easily on ice and snow, and wintertime became the traditional season for such work. Scandinavian and Dutch colonists added their skill to the more scanty experience of the English.

New methods have developed, although some of the pioneers' practices are still used throughout the country—principally on small jobs. The ax and the ox team are primitive logging tools, but they can still be found at work in the woods. The ax has been improved in design and quality of its steel. Modern metallurgy has enabled the manufacturer to make a top-grade tool every time, something not possible when axheads were forged by hand; some were good and some were poor. When a logger got hold of a really good ax he guarded it jealously—and might even take it to bed with him. The crosscut saw, introduced about 75 years ago, was at first a crude cutting tool.

The modern crosscut saw is made of excellent steel, holds its set and cutting edges well, and runs freely in the cut. The peavey, invented about 85 years ago by a blacksmith in Stillwater, Maine, has made the work of rolling logs by hand easier and safer. The pulp hook, the bow saw, the explosive wedge, and even the tractor, the power saw, and the motortruck are becoming commonplace throughout the country even on small logging jobs.

But it is in the bigger operations that revolution after revolution in logging methods has taken place. Big-time logging had its origin in Maine, where heavy stands of pine and spruce, watercourses leading to good harbors on tidewater, and long, cold winters when little else could be done provided a favorable environment. The Machias, the Penobscot, the Kennebec, and the Androscoggin watersheds were the nursery from which came a new technique of logging and a tribe of loggers that later fanned out to other timber regions across the continent.

Maine loggers developed the art of chip-chopping in felling trees and in cutting them into logs. They learned to take advantage of gravity and snow and ice in skidding the logs to watercourses. They developed the art of driving the logs down the streams to sorting booms at tidewater. Living in rough camps far back from the towns and farming country, they were a tough and hardy brood—now well celebrated in song and story.

But their very energy and efficiency in time brought about depletion of the accessible large virgin pine and spruce of that State.

The center of large-scale lumbering began to move westward—first to the headwaters of the Connecticut, then the Hudson, and then the Susquehanna and the Ohio. Rafting was developed on the more placid waters of the Susquehanna and Ohio, not only to keep the logs together but also to keep afloat the choice hardwoods that were bound into the rafts with the pine. Winter logging and stream driving were developed still further in the Lake States to keep pace with the increasing capacity of the sawmills and the ever-expanding demand for lumber. There, too, the first logging railroad came into use, and cable skidding was developed.

As the virgin timber stands of the Lake States neared depletion, the tide of the lumber-industry migration split.

Some of it moved into the flatland pine stands of the South. Some of it moved across the Rocky Mountains to the great coniferous forests of the Pacific slope. In those regions, especially in the West, the use of the cable skidder and the logging railroad reached its apogee. The volume of timber cut and moved to the mills by those methods was astounding. They were, however, destructive, wasteful, short-sighted.

Along the path of the migrations, the pioneer loggers were joined by hardy men from other parts of the country and by a large number of immigrants from abroad — Scandinavians, French Canadians, Austrians, men from the Balkans and from Russia. All contributed to the growing store of logging lore.

The French Canadians introduced the travois or dray—an idea that they had borrowed from the Indians of the Plains. The Austrians brought in the log chute and slide for use on steep slopes. The idea of cableways came from Switzerland. The English developed the crawler track, used first in the steam log-hauler in Maine.

Some of the best known lumber companies operating today on the west coast and in the South originated in Maine, in Pennsylvania, and in the Lake States.

As THE TIDE of logging advanced across the country, and then eddied back into the Rockies, the southern swamps, the Appalachians, and the wilderness areas of northern Maine and New Hampshire, there were always ingenious loggers who kept on inventing new devices and others who were ready and eager to try them out.

But there also have been loggers determined to resist any change of the methods that they knew to be tried and true. Men still living can remember, when the crosscut saw was introduced, how loggers, proud of their chip-chopping skill, left camp rather than use the new tool. In recent years the introduction of the power chain saw was met by similar resistance. Crews have been known purposely to leave a power saw where it would be smashed by a falling tree in order that they might resume the use of their familiar crosscut saws.

But still the tide of change goes on. In region after region horses replaced oxen because they are faster and more intelligent. It is interesting to watch a good woods-wise horse as he goes about his skidding job, often without reins or word of command. He comes up the skid trail, turns around in front of a log, and waits for the teamster to hook the skid chain. Then he moves away down the trail without guidance or command, swinging wide, or even squaring away on the curves to keep his load in the trail and to avoid getting it stuck on stumps and roots. Right up to the skidway he goes, stops with the load in the correct position, and waits for it to be unhooked.

As the sources of timber became more distant from the mills or from the rivers, it was necessary to increase horsepower efficiency. That was done by scoots, sleds, wagons, and bummers. The next step was the use of mechanical power, first applied in the steam log-hauler—steam engines built on the pattern of the early locomotive with the rear end on crawler tracks and the front on wheels or a sled. The man who did the steering occupied a seat in front of the boiler and directly over the front truck. Log-haulers were used to pull trains of sleds or wagons out of the woods to a landing. Later, on many operations, they were replaced by logging railroads that handled bigger loads on longer hauls.

The invention of the geared locomotive made it possible to negotiate steeper grades and sharper curves than had been possible with the conventional line-haul locomotive. Motortruck log hauling has become so efficient that it is fast replacing the logging railroad even in the heavy timber of the Pacific Northwest. This change has been greatly speeded up by improvements in motortrucks themselves, by the construction of public motor highways, and by the bulldozer,

802062°—49——45

the tractor grader, and other tools for building low-cost access roads.

Water transportation is still used. River driving remains the cheapest means for transporting large quantities of wood over long distances. Elaborate systems of dams and other works are used to provide the necessary flow of water to carry the wood down. In one famous case, Maine loggers diverted water from the St. John headwaters into those of the Penobscot and precipitated some international complications with Canada. When the drives must be taken across lakes or other bodies of still water, it is usually necessary to enclose acres of floating wood in booms of long logs chained end to end. The two ends are drawn together and this giant wood-filled purse is then pulled across the lake.

For longer voyages on big bodies of water that may be rough, various types of barges and rafts have been used. A plywood company is towing rafts of hardwood logs made buoyant by spruce frames the length of Moosehead Lake in Maine. Large quantities of pulpwood are rafted across Lake Superior from Canada to the United States. On the Pacific coast, a cigar-shaped structure bound together with cables and containing up to a million board feet of long logs is pulled by a tugboat. High-grade spruce logs needed for aircraft manufacture were recently brought from Alaska to Puget Sound by this method.

Back in the woods the methods for skidding the logs to the roads have also become more specialized. As logging pushed into the rougher and more swampy country, the horse reached the end of his road. Other skidding methods had to be found.

Various types of chutes and slides have been tried, but cable skidders have generally been more successful. The first was the cable skidder that pulled the log by a single cable reeled in on a steam-powered drum. It was soon found that the inward pull of the cable, carried through a block hung on a nearby tree, would also have a lifting action sufficient to bring the log over the stumps and other obstacles. Thus the method known as "high-lead" logging was born. Then another drum was attached to the winding engine and a lighter cable was strung through blocks out to the scene of the cutting and fastened to the end of the main dragline; in this way it was possible to have a power haul-back on the dragline. It was only a step further to the idea of a cable skyline with a carriage pulled in by the dragline and out again by the haul-back. The further development of a locking and tripping device made it possible to pick up the log at its stump, pull it up to the carriage, and bring it to the landing entirely suspended in the air. Many and varied are the adaptations of the cable systems—the North Bend, the Dunham, the Tyler, the slack line, and so forth. Each has its merits for specific localities or types of timber.

On the more favorable terrain, the arts of ground skidding developed in another direction. Loggers found that their scoots and sleds, first used for winter skidding, were effective also in the summer. In country with stony and gravel soils these devices helped to keep the logs clean and free from dirt that wrecked saws and chipper knives at the mills. Wheeled devices of various kinds came into use—carts, wagons, and bummers. Finally came the colorful high wheels, which supported the front ends of huge loads of long logs as they were dragged to the landing.

Ground skidding, however, really got its new lease on life with the development of the crawler tractor equipped with winch and arch. The arch is even more sturdy and effective than were the high wheels. The cable from the tractor winch is carried through a fair-lead at the top of the arch, and this gives some of the high-lead effect in the bunching of scattered loads of logs. The crawler tracks, or pneumatic tires, upon which the arch is mounted, provide a means for carrying the front end of the load. Other devices, such as the skidding pan, the tractor-drawn scoot, and the tractor-drawn wagon on crawler treads, have been highly successful. They have nearly supplanted cable logging except in the heaviest timber and on the steep and swampy lands.

Loading has also gone through several stages of development. First it was found that logs could be rolled up inclined skids easier than they could be lifted. The skidway or brow built out from a hillside to hold logs off the ground at about the height of the hauling vehicle was the next step in the development of loading methods. But as the logs and the volume to be handled got bigger, hand loading rapidly became obsolete. Power loading came into use. First came the cross haul, by which horses or a tractor can be used to roll logs up inclined skids onto the hauling vehicle. Next came the jammer, an inclined **A**-frame with a sheave at the apex over which the loading cable could be passed to give a lifting as well as a pulling action. Then came a variety of jib booms and cranes, some mounted on stationary spars, some on sleds, some on crawler tracks, and some on pneumatic tires. These made the loading job much faster and easier. In recent years a number of types of self-loading trucks, with cross hauls, jib booms, or flippers powered from the truck motor have been put into use on smaller jobs.

The last part of the logging job to be mechanized has been felling and bucking. Chain saws, consisting of teeth mounted on a bicyclelike chain, were introduced from Germany about 1924. The cutting chain runs around a grooved steel guide bar and is powered by a small gasoline, electric, or pneumatic motor. Recent improvements have made this a reasonably reliable tool. It is now widely used throughout the country.

In the flat, open pinelands of the South, a circular saw mounted ahead of a wheeled frame like that of a garden cultivator has proved useful. The power is provided by a small gasoline motor mounted between the shafts of the frame. The saw can be used either

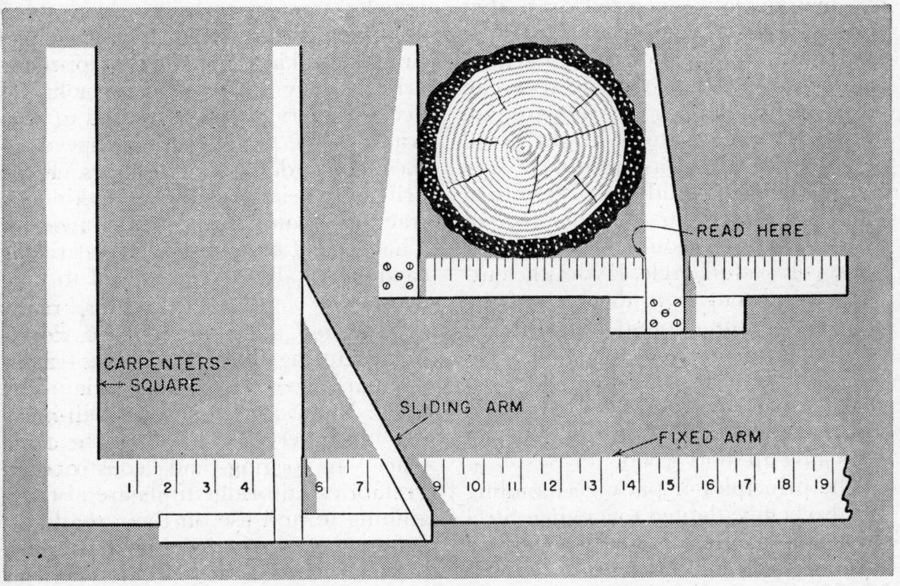


**Home-made calipers for measuring the diameters of trees. Hold breast high (4½ feet above ground) and read diameter of tree direct from the caliper.**

in the horizontal position for felling or in the vertical position for bucking. Either type of power saw, properly handled by a well-trained crew, enables the crew to cut twice as much wood per man-day as would be possible with hand tools. Portable circular slasher saws are now commonly used to cut short pulpwood and millwood bolts from tree-length second-growth poles skidded into the landing. Powered chain conveyors are in use to carry the bolts from the saw to the hauling vehicle or to a pile. Such equipment can buck up to 80 cords of 4-foot wood a day.

Several of the war-born devices, developed for other uses, are being adapted for use in the woods. Electric generators that produce alternating current of 180 to 360 cycles (the standard frequency is 60 cycles) make possible electric motors of smaller size and lighter weight for use as chain-saw power units. High-pressure hydraulic systems utilizing synthetic rubber tubing are being employed in light and extremely flexible loaders. One of these, mounted on a crawler tractor, has hydraulically operated arms that can be used to gather up a cord of wood just as a boy picks up an armful of stovewood. The hydraulic arms can push the load along on the ground, lift it into the air to a height of 12 or 15 feet, swing it around to any desired position, and drop it into a truck or railroad car. Another type of hydraulic crane, mounted on a truck, can revolve a full circle. Hydraulic outriggers push out from the base of the machine to the ground and thereby stabilize it while it is in use. The boom is extensible and the cable is pulled in by hydraulic power. It has an hydraulically operated grapple for use in picking up short wood.

The principles of package handling are also being adapted to logging. Steel straps and cables are used to bundle a cord or more of short bolts or long logs for more convenient handling during transshipments. Pallets of wood and tubular steel devices are used as packaging for short bolts. Some of them can be loaded, skidded through the woods, and pulled up a ramp onto a truck and off again at the mill.

There are also some developments in cable skidding—particularly in light, fast equipment that reduces the damage to the remaining trees. One west coast inventor has put his motive power and the operator into a carriage that rides on a skyline. A winch in the carriage hoists the bundles of logs up under the carriage; then the carriage pulls itself along the skyline to the landing. The new equipment can carry tractors and the other heavy equipment into otherwise inaccessible places.

Swiss engineers have developed several extremely light cable-logging systems to bring small logs or bundles of wood off steep slopes. One consists of an endless cable (suspended from trees), which makes a circuit from the cutting area to the landing. The cable runs through star-shaped wheels. Individual bolts of wood are hung on the line by one crew at the cutting area and taken off by another at the landing.

Rubber treads are being tried now on crawler tractors to make them more adaptable to the rocky terrain. A hydraulic braking device, developed to arrest heavy planes landing on the decks of carriers, has been used to hold trucks to a predetermined speed as they come down steep slopes. Fluid drives are being used in cable skidders, tractors, motortrucks, and sawmills. That type of transmission gives greater capacity to absorb shocks and to take overloads.

New steel alloys are utilized to improve cutting tools of all sorts—axes, circular-saw teeth, and chain-saw teeth. New explosives and earth-moving machinery are also finding their place in logging-road construction. Prefabricated bridge units are also beginning to find use on these roads.

Some of these developments have been set-backs to the development of forest-management practices. Early logging methods were not particularly harmful to the forest—generally the early loggers searched out the biggest and best trees, felled them, cut out the best parts by hand, and then skidded the logs to the mill or the water with animals. By our present-day standards those methods were wasteful, but they did leave a good stand of trees for continuing growth.

As time went on and the markets for timber became bigger and less selective, faster and faster methods of logging and more complete cuts became the style. Particularly harmful were the high-lead cable-skidding jobs that usually went with logging railroads. It was costly to put a temporary logging railroad into a timbered area, and frequently the operator believed it was necessary to cut everything merchantable in the area to repay his railroad-installation cost. Cable skidding, especially a carelessly used high-lead, frequently knocked down everything that was not cut. Skylines frequently are not so destructive, except when the line is pulled directly from one tail spar to another, mowing down everything between. Both railroads and steam-powered cable skidders were also responsible for starting many forest fires. Some of the new cable-skidding systems powered by internal-combustion motors can be operated with a minimum of damage.

Tractor and truck logging in itself is not so damaging. Truck roads frequently can be built more cheaply than railroads, and they have a lasting value, particularly for fire protection after the logging job is completed. Tractors can be operated efficiently on a selective-logging job, if proper care is taken in laying out the skid trails and in felling the trees so that they can be pulled directly into the trail without switching around. Some tractor drivers, particularly of the heavier and more powerful machines, are responsible for much unnecessary damage as a result of the way in which they plow around in the woods.

The chain saw also has been responsible for some unnecessary losses in the woods. It takes considerable experience with the chain saw to learn to fell trees as accurately as the old-time loggers do with hand tools, but it can be done. Once skill is acquired, tricks can be done with it that were impossible by hand methods. The chain saw with its faster cutting rate also makes it economical to recover sound portions from partially rotten or poorly formed trees that would not have been touched by men using hand tools.

Integrated logging is the harvest of all the trees that should be cut at a given time in one operation, and the distribution of each product obtained to the industry that can use it to the best advantage.

Too much of our logging has been one-product logging: A pulp mill would cut the spruce and fir pulpwood from a stand; a few years later a veneer mill would go into the same area to log out the high-grade hardwood veneer logs. That usually required the construction of new roads and camps or the rebuilding of old ones. Later operations in the same place might be conducted by an ash or hickory handlestock concern, a white pine or hardwood sawlog man, and finally a fuel or distillation-wood operator. Many of these operations would leave lying on the ground material that could have been used to advantage by one of the other concerns. The sum total of the logging costs would be much greater than the total of one integrated operation, recovery from the trees cut would be less, and in many cases fast-growing trees that should have been left would have been cut to help pay the overhead costs of the individual jobs.

There are many obstacles to conducting completely integrated logging. When labor is scarce, each concern wants to obtain the maximum amount of material with its force for its own needs. Different equipment is sometimes needed to log different products. Unfamiliar specifications and markets have to be learned. But advantages usually outweigh disadvantages. Pulp companies can trade high-grade veneer logs for two to three times as much wood suitable for their mills. At the same time the veneer mills can augment their dwindling and increasingly expensive supply of raw materials.

Modern logging machinery and methods make possible delivery of tree-length logs to the landing or even to the mill, where a trained crew can buck out and segregate the various qualities of material that are needed by different industries. Truck logging over public or private roads enables industries to obtain their raw material from lighter and more selective cuts over a wider area.

THE OLD RACE OF LOGGERS, proud of their skill with loggers' hand tools and contented to live a rough life, is dying out. It is almost impossible these days to find a crew that will be satisfied to live in a rough lumber camp, 20 miles back from a hard road, working from dawn to dark all winter, and then proudly bringing down the drive—"walking down the middle of the river" the old loggers used to call it—for a brief period of roistering in town in the spring. Such methods were picturesque, but they wasted timber and manpower. Mills cannot get their full quota of logs that way any more.

The introduction of modern machinery and the trend toward permanence of logging operations on tracts managed for sustained timber production are beginning to bring a new breed of loggers into the woods. Young men who once would have shunned logging now see better opportunities in woods work. Operators, alarmed by the advancing age of the old-time loggers who were willing to lead single lives in remote camps, see the need for change. In every region one can now find examples of the new logging community with comfortable homes for families, with schools, churches, electric light plants, and waterworks. Logging is still one of the most dangerous major occupations in American industry, but operators, unions, insurance companies, State industrial accident commissions, and other agencies are engaged in a concerted accident-prevention program, in which they are achieving substantial progress.

All in all, it is a new day and a better day for the loggers who want a normal home life, good working conditions, steady work, year-round employment at good wages, and modern personnel policies that pay attention to the logger's capabilities for advancement and to safety and training for the job.

FRED C. SIMMONS *is a specialist in logging and primary processing at the Northeastern Forest Experiment Station. He has worked with northeastern logging operators and wood-using industries in improvement of their practices since 1944. He is the author of The Northeastern Loggers' Handbook and numerous articles that have appeared in trade journals and technical publications. Mr. Simmons earned degrees in forestry from Cornell and Yale Universities and has been engaged in logging work since 1923, when he went to work on a primitive operation in the Adirondacks of his native New York. Since then he has worked on and around logging operations in the Pacific Northwest, Arkansas, the South, and the Northeastern States.*

# LOGGING THE PACIFIC SLOPES

NEWELL L. WRIGHT

Lumbering started on the west coast about 1850, in the days of the Gold Rush. Sawmill machinery was brought around Cape Horn from the East in sailing vessels. The first mills were for medium and small-sized timbers. Logs were furnished by farmers and land clearers from the timbered areas that adjoined navigable waters wherever it was cheaper to put them in a stream than to pile them for burning. Much of this was done with the ax, saw, and log jack, toil and sweat, grunt and groan.

The start was small but, step by step, production increased, and machinery was built to saw the larger logs. This called for more power in the woods.

Timber was abundant—much too much for the early settler, whose first thought was food and whose first problem was to find unforested areas or clear fields for farming. Fire was the great land clearer, and in the early 1850's great forests went up in smoke. Soon the timber line receded, and the ox team and skid road came into being. The big timber started moving to the crack of the bull whip and the roar of the puncher.

Horses followed the ox team; as production increased, speed as well as power was needed. The proper application of gravity was the influencing factor in logging with the ox and horse team. Grades favorable with the load were necessary, but logging shows were plentiful, and no great engineering skill was needed.

A good woodsman—usually the foreman—did the locating. Rough ground and poor timber stands were bypassed. Only the high-quality timber was cut, and only the best logs were removed. The margin between costs and recovery value was low, and low-grade material could be handled only at a loss. Fire ravaged much of the lands that were so handled; some remained in fair condition, and new growth was started; practically all reverted to the counties for nonpayment of taxes.

As the demand for lumber increased and transportation facilities (such as adequate ports for seagoing vessels and transcontinental railroads for land shipments) became available, domestic and foreign markets expanded. More production was needed. In logging this meant greater increases in speed and power. In the early eighties there was much timber near the mills, but some of it was on ground unsuitable for ox- or horse-team logging. Of the various steam-powered machines that came into use, the most successful was the donkey engine, which had a horizontal drum and a vertical-type boiler.

Because it had been a slow and laborious job to haul the felled and bucked timber to the skid roads, the first donkey engines supplanted the horses and oxen in this work. They were strong enough to pull logs out of canyons with little application of blocks, which often were necessary when horses and oxen were used. For some time the animals were still used for skid-road work and for hauling the logs to the water. The donkey engine yarded the big logs to the road and made up the turn for its trip to the water. It was soon found that a machine could do it faster, however, so roading donkeys were built. These machines were bolted to huge log sleds, which made good foundations and made the unit easily movable in the woods. The unit was moved by hanging a block some distance ahead and running the main drum line out through the block, then back to the sled; it was made fast on the sled runner. By applying steam to roll the drum, the unit would be moved toward the block. It simply pulled itself by its own power.

The roading donkey was built with huge drums, which had a great line capacity. When the roading distance got greater than the line capacity of one machine, often one and sometimes two more machines were added to relay the logs to the water. The building of donkey sleds and skid and pole roads became a craft of importance. The skid-road builder sometimes assisted the foreman in making the location. Straight roads on easy grades were most desirable.

Such logging was successful in limited areas of timber, but soon the length of haul compelled a different line of action.

The demand for lumber was good. In 1899, Douglas-fir lumber was averaging almost $9 a thousand at the mill. Eastern lumbermen were becoming interested in the big timber of the West. Large consolidations were under way. By 1905, timberland homesteads were being picked up for $5 or so an acre. At the turn of the century railroad logging was starting. The need for logging engineers was recognized. Until colleges supplied the training, some of the best logging engineers in the early days were trained woodsmen, self-educated in civil engineering. Logging railroads became the principal medium of transporting logs to the mills; it still is considered the cheapest for hauls of more than 50 miles when transportation by water is not possible.

Always original and ever a pioneer, the logger did not follow the road specifications of the regular railroad systems. Because his capital was more limited, he kept construction costs at a minimum, even at the sacrifice of operation. Seven-percent favorable grades and 20° curves were common; so there was need for the geared engine, which sounded, when traveling 15 miles an hour, like a passenger train going 60. It probably has delivered more logs to waterways at lower cost than any other piece of transportation equipment.

In the western woods this was the age of steam. Three notable western machinery builders expanded into the heavy logging-equipment field, and the competition brought about great advances in the construction of the donkey engine.

DONKEY ENGINES were generally listed by diameter of cylinder and length of stroke in inches. One of the first prize machines was a 7 by 9 inch, with a single drum. A line horse was used to pull the cable line and the choker—a length of cable with a flat hook on one end and an eye in the other to be passed around the log and fastened to the main haul line—back to the woods.

On rough ground the haul-back job became too hard for a horse, so an ingenious mechanical engineer designed the haul-back drum. A line smaller than the main line was found sufficient for this work, but it had to be more than twice as long, because it went out to a corner haul-back block at about the main-line length from the donkey engine, over to a lead haul-back block. From there it was strung to and hooked on the main line at the fair leads, on the end of the donkey sled. The haul-back line had first to be pulled out through the blocks by hand and hooked to the end of the main line. From then on, steam did the work until the line needed changing to reach more logs. Laying out the haul-back line was an arduous task and all hands were called to help. To speed up the job, an additional drum was added to the machine. This held what is called a straw line, about three-eighths inch in diameter, which was easier strung out by hand and was used to string out the haul-back line. On simple yarding donkeys this is the drum arrangement in use today.

The yarding donkey, sitting at a point near where the logs were to go in the water, on a skid road, or on cars, dragged the logs in a straight line from a distant point. Immovable objects, such as stumps and trees in the line of travel, had to be avoided, or the log rolled or kicked around them with the main line. The logger's term for these obstacles was "hang-ups." A poorly chosen skid road caused the rigging slinger to remark that he had been fighting hang-ups all day. The more hang-ups, the fewer logs hauled out. The selection of good donkey settings and skid roads greatly influenced the log production and marked the worth of the crew boss, or hook tender.

ASSEMBLING LOGS to facilitate loading on cars was important to a smooth-working operation. It was necessary to accumulate enough logs at one point so that a well-balanced carload could be formed. This was done by building inclined log-crib landings with jump-up approaches so the logs would be hauled first to the higher part of the landing and then rolled toward the front.

These landings served only the timber on one side of the tracks and the setting was half of a circle or square. The selection of landings was influenced by timber and topography. Because some of the small operators located their roads to conform with these previously chosen landings, expensive mistakes in railroading often resulted. The operators who controlled larger bodies of timber did more intensive planning of the railroad system, built main lines to more exacting specifications, and depended on spurs to reach landings that had been chosen in advance.

Loading in the west coast fir region—a region on the Pacific slopes that is representative of two distinct types—was done by the gin-pole crotch-line method. The loader was set parallel to the track facing the landing. The gin pole was set across the track from the landing and leaned toward it so that the lead block was about plumb with the outside rail. In the early set-ups, the main line was shackled to two loading straps of equal lengths, and on the end of each was an L-shaped loading hook. The loaders pulled the slack of the main line as they carried the loading hook to the ends of the log for hooking. The loading engineer placed the log as the head loader required by hoisting it and judging its swing. Soon the addition of a haul-back drum lessened the work of getting the hooks back over the log as well as regulating its placement on the car. A third drum was added for use in spotting the cars for loading when the train crew was away. A somewhat similar loading method was used in the ponderosa pine region—another Pacific slope region—although not so extensively.

It was soon found that logging by the ground-lead method resulted in less hang-up delay when the logs were pulled uphill by the donkey. The log tended to follow up the side of a stump and shear away from it. More power and speed were needed, which the machinery builders supplied when they turned out the 10- by 12-inch and 11- by 13-inch compound-geared yarders with extended firebox boilers. Noting the speed-up resulting from fewer hang-ups, a versatile logger experimented with fastening a heavy yarding block on a high stump. The idea caught on at once. By 1918, camp after camp had gone to the air, in a manner of speaking.

HIGH-LEAD LOGGING was under way, and the lay of the ground brought out various adaptations to fit the problem.

Through the years many changes have been made in loading devices in order to conform to the progress in high-lead and high-line systems of logging. Among these various methods are the McLean boom, the single tong boom, and the duplex system.

In the early 1890's logging in the pine region developed in a big way. Logs rolled out in an almost endless procession of splendidly matched four-horse teams and big wheels.

Railroad logging outfits had their logs loaded on cars with speed and precision by use of a steam jammer, and large production was maintained. The steam jammer is one of the fastest log loaders in use even today and, although in more general use in the pine region, it has also found favor among some of the heavy fir-log producers.

The greater flexibility brought about

by the use of logging trucks demanded greater flexibility in loading. The rapid movement necessary for gathering right-of-way logs brought about the converted shovel loader, and finally the more mobile rubber-tired loader of today.

Generally speaking, logging in the pine region has followed a different pattern than in the more rugged country along the coast. Some use has been made of tight-line skidders, but the small volume from an acre called for a more mobile type of equipment. The first logging trucks with hard rubber tires required hard, dry soil conditions in the woods. Because they could only be used on good roads, they did not go well with the industry. It was still necessary to have a railroad for an all-year operation. Steam logging continued to a large extent with the use of railroads. Urged by the persistence of high-ball loggers, who demanded more and more speed and power, the machinery manufacturers built enormous high-lead units, interlocking skidders, and slack-line machines. Only a railroad could transport those heavy machines, and large settings were necessary for their success. With these machines, the then loggable timber was swept from large continuous areas. Very little reserve timber was left for a seed supply, and a surge of public resentment influenced a change in cutting methods.

Near the middle 1920's, logging with steam equipment commenced to wane. Gradually gasoline and Diesel-powered drum units, tractors, and pneumatic-tired trucks came into being; they brought with them better trained and more skillful mechanics or, as the loggers said, monkey-wrench artists. Instead of words like valve oil, gear dope, donkey doctors, boiler flues, and ash-pans, we now hear terms like cycles, torque converters, hydrotarders, tolerances, sludge, and floating power.

Soon the smaller patches of timber left by the early horse loggers and ground-lead operators drew the attention of operators with little capital—the "gyppo loggers." By building truck roads and using lighter equipment, the gyppo started the era of truck logging. With the pneumatic-tired light truck, he found he could operate on fairly low-standard, cheaply built roads. His first drum units were about the size of those used on the old 7- by 9-inch steam donkey and, by sprocket and chain adaptation, connected to a farm-type tractor. The wheels were removed from the tractor and the whole unit mounted on a log sled. This was light enough to haul on a small logging truck and made a quite mobile logging unit. With this beginning—a jump from heavy steam equipment back to light, mobile, internal combustion-driven donkey engines—a great change was made in logging methods.

As the most accessible of the scattered small bodies of timber were logged, builders of machinery were again urged to turn out heavier units. Better roads, bigger trucks, rougher ground, and a fight for more production and lower costs have brought about the larger equipment of the present.

THE OPERATION least affected by change of methods and equipment probably has been the process of getting the tree down on the ground.

The tree is still being cut off at the stump and allowed to drop. The falling equipment has changed somewhat. In the early days, the single-bit pole ax was the only tool, and the trees were guided to their fall by skilled choppers. Later the ax, improved to a double-bitted falling ax, was used only in making the under cut, and the crosscut saw supplemented it. Then falling of timber became a two-man job. It is still that, but now one or two other men, called buckers, cut the tree into log lengths. In many camps, power-driven chain saws have supplanted the crosscut saw but, except for skillful control of the direction of the fall by cutting and wedging, no concerted attempts have been made to let the tree down other than allowing it to crash. Expert fallers use other trees to some extent for braking power to lessen the impact on the ground. Sometimes a nesting place of level ground or windrowed slash is prepared to receive the trees.

As the valuable, large, high-quality trees become scarcer, one can expect the development of improved timber-falling units that will cut and let timber down in places more accessible for cutting into logs and moving to yards.

Loggers have done much more ingenious things than that, and when the challenge becomes acute, they will meet it; they will perfect some device that will eliminate breakage and allow them carefully to analyze the tree, cut it to quality sections, and recover the poorer grades in sizes that are easy to handle. Our logged-over areas, covered with large-diameter broken chunks, mixed with small poles, have been and still are the eyesore and the shame of the industry and the public. Things will be changed, I am sure.

So, ALSO, must the wood-using industry be ready to welcome change, because it is affected by a growing demand for products from the forest. In this, the handling of raw products of the forest is always the challenging problem. Research in forestry has pointed the way to greater yields on forest lands; research in chemistry has enlarged the scope of utilization; next must come the economical harvesting of forest wastes. Those who preach the unfailing abundance of forest supply may have overlooked the steady increase in world population and the growing demands for products from trees.

To meet these demands and keep the lands productive, the logger is face to face with the need for more intensified harvesting of lower-quality material, on rougher ground over longer hauls. For that, he has the help of forest technicians and civil and mechanical engineers. The science of forestry must be linked more closely to the mechanics of logging if forest land is to produce its maximum growth.

Logging remains a problem in transportation, with good roads a controlling factor. The life of a road is its foundation and drainage system. For years operators have built railroads and truck roads with a view to later abandonment, because they were built only to serve the timber the operators themselves owned. Often permanent construction was unnecessary, but as public timber becomes more in demand and truck logging more universal, permanent roads will be more common and requirements of base and drainage more exacting. As hauls get longer, heavier loading is required and higher speeds demanded; therefore, heavy-surfaced roads have to be built.

Further, a well-built road system, the foundation of good forest management, makes possible the removal of overmature timber; closer utilization of low-grade material, which is a requirement of good forestry; more orderly cutting; and the seasonal harvesting of the higher-elevation timber in summer and the lower-elevation timber in winter. Species in demand can be cut when needed and the others left for future harvesting. The cutting systems necessary to the practice of good silviculture and good fire protection can then be used more successfully.

Years ago, it was found that better equipment was needed to speed up road construction. The pick and shovel and wheelbarrow were replaced by the power shovel now in common use on construction jobs. In 1925, while constructing roads on a forest project, technicians of the Portland office of the Forest Service fastened a revamped grader blade on the old tractor in such a way that they could push dirt with it. They proved that this arrangement would greatly exceed the grading work done by several horse teams working with Fresno scrapers. Their experimental piece of equipment was the forerunner of a great development in dirt-moving practice—the bulldozer, one of the most valuable pieces of logging and road-building equipment now in use.

Hand in hand with the road system is planning the method of cutting that is best for continued forest growth, a method that takes into account the ideal control of the fall and less damage to reserved trees. In the west coast fir region, damage in falling and skidding is serious, because the accompanying species are apparently more susceptible to fungus attack than is ponderosa pine. Also, the stands are so much denser in the fir region that damage is greater.

THE METHOD OF CUTTING by the operators of private timber in the west coast fir region has been to clear out the areas considered recoverable at a profit. In the early days, when no high lead was used, it was possible to remove the larger timber and leave a certain amount of smaller trees to continue growing. The remaining trees often reseeded well. Much of the land, abandoned to the counties for taxes, has since been purchased by small operators, and, in some cases, by large pulp concerns. Now the remaining large trees are being removed and the areas networked with roads so that younger growth can be logged as needed.

When the operators took to the air, so to speak, with high leads and skyline logging, they ended the system of heavy selection cutting. From 1918 to 1934, clear cutting meant taking the timber that was operable at a profit and leveling the rest in the process. One often sees logged-off land on which 10,000 board feet or more of good, sound timber an acre has been left to rot or to be burned. Timber fallers were instructed to leave timber less than 20 inches in diameter because it did not pay to handle it. Pulling in the larger logs with the high lead knocked over most of these smaller trees. Where two-storied stands were common, this waste of small timber became enormous. These smaller trees had reached an age where the annual growth layer was of high-quality material. Everyone recognized that cutting methods had to be changed.

In the pine region also, operators seemed to favor clear cutting. The initial stand per acre was small, and the operators felt it necessary to remove most of it to amortize the opening-up costs. Soon, however, it was found that high mortality losses necessitated the coverage of the area in a shorter span of time in order to remove first the trees most susceptible to this damage.

In both regions, the necessary changes in cutting methods required changes in equipment. Getting over the ground faster meant more roads of a permanent character; so the loggers turned to trucks and truck roads. The development of tractor logging got under way and at first found its greatest success in the pine region, where the timber is less dense, the slopes easier, and the ground drier.

In the fir region, tractors were first tried by smaller operators. Their use has been limited by conditions of topography and soil. Some larger operators use them on favorable shows during the drier seasons. As was the case with the donkey engine, it was soon found advantageous to have an upward pull when dragging in the log. To attain this the logging arch was designed as an attachment to the farm and industrial tractor. The logging arch is cumbersome and rather unwieldy, and its use results in considerable yarding damage to reserved trees. On steep slopes it is sometimes impossible to get the empty arch to the log, in which case the implement is unhooked and the logs are dragged on the ground behind the tractor.

Sometimes, when the logs have previously been piled at a central point, the tractor with arch is used on well-defined roads to relay the piles to loading-out points. This practice is called roading. Some operators surface these roads where the volume of logs in the piles warrants. In the pine region, the accepted cutting method is individual tree selection, and spectacular skidding on extremely rough territory is still done with horses or tractors. In the west coast fir region, the extremely rough territory is almost universally clear-cut and yarded with drum units mounted on sleds or tractors.

On national forests, various cutting methods have been tested through contractual requirements in timber sales. Individual tree selection in the ponderosa pine region, with varying degrees of cutting to meet the silvicultural requirements, has been for some time a required practice. In the west coast fir region, where silvicultural and mechanical problems are more complicated, more and more diversification is to be found. It is easier to determine the undesirable cutting practice than to determine the most desirable one to avoid the waste of timber that comes with clear cutting large acreages and leaving unused material on the ground and to avoid the loss of production if the cut forest is not restocked by planting.

To clear-cut small spots on which the trees are preponderantly overmature groups is considered good silviculture for Douglas fir, which does not tolerate shade and thrives best in open areas. When the cut spots are small, fires that start in the slash are more likely to be controlled. Small cut-over areas stand a good chance of being reseeded naturally from the closely adjacent timber. The Forest Service requires cutting by this method or the tree-selection method on its sales in the west coast fir region, depending on the silvicultural problems confronted. Many sales of both types on national forests have been processed recently.

Great strides have been made in logging equipment and cutting methods; many problems remain unsolved. One of the greatest is the salvage logging of broken chunks, decaying wood, small sizes, and stumps. Some progress is being made in removing this type of material. More progress will come when industrial plants needing wood waste become so numerous that the supply of mill waste will not keep them operating to capacity. Chemical research has made possible the converting of practically all logging waste to valuable products. The gathering, transporting, and processing of this material into clean chips is yet the job that commands the greatest effort. Costs eventually must be lowered to meet the competition of mill waste; that will require ingenuity on the part of the logger. Steps made in the advancement of transportation facilities for logging the virgin timber will, of course, greatly assist in harvesting the so-called salvage material. The equipment and knowledge required to get the material to the road at reasonable cost will follow. We can feel sure that a new era is here and that much better use of the wood on the land can soon be realized.

NEWELL L. WRIGHT *grew up on a small ranch in Northwestern Washington. He received a degree in logging engineering at the University of Washton in 1913, and worked in private industry as logging engineer and logging camp superintendent for 20 years. He joined the Forest Service as senior logging engineer in 1934 and has continued in that capacity in the North Pacific region.*

PERCENTAGE OF OPERATING ACREAGE IN PROPERTIES AND WORKING CIRCLES BEING CUT ON A SUSTAINED-YIELD BASIS, UNITED STATES, 1945

| *Ownership class* | *Total* | *Percent on sustained yield by grade of cutting* [1] *High order* | *Good* | *Fair* |
|---|---|---|---|---|
| Public: | *Pct.* | *Pct.* | *Pct.* | *Pct.* |
| National forests.... | 71 | 10 | 47 | 14 |
| Other Federal...... | 44 | 6 | 23 | 15 |
| State and local..... | 23 | 1 | 21 | 1 |
| Private: | | | | |
| Large holdings..... | 39 | 5 | 20 | 14 |
| Medium holdings... | 9 | 1 | 3 | 5 |

[1] Cutting rated poor or destructive excluded as property from the sustained-yield classification.

# THE HISTORY OF FORESTRY IN AMERICA

W. N. SPARHAWK

The history of forestry in the United States can be divided into five periods.

The first, the colonial period ending in 1776, was characterized by a gradual pushing back of the forests to make room for settlement, nearly all east of the Allegheny-Appalachian Range.

The second period, from 1776 to the beginning of forestry work in the Federal Department of Agriculture, lasted just 100 years. This was a period of forest exploitation, gradual at first, but rapidly increasing after about 1850.

The following 21 years, also a period of accelerated exploitation, was marked by the campaign of public education and propaganda that finally led to the establishment of a forestry policy for Government timberlands in 1897.

From 1897 to 1919 was the period of development of the national forest system and the establishment of a forestry profession. The movement for conservation of natural resources in general also took shape early in this period.

Finally, the period since 1919 has been marked by an increasing emphasis on private forestry, both in legislation and in the policies of the forest-land owners themselves.

Several salients stand out in the story of how forestry and the country grew up from a spoiled, wasteful childhood to rational adulthood. In its broad outline, forestry in the United States is evolving in much the same way as it did in Europe, but much faster. Forestry in America has not caught up with forestry in the more advanced European countries, but we have come a long way in our brief period as a Nation, and the progress we have made came not from slavishly copying the European pattern; American forestry, as it grows to maturity, tends more and more to become indigenous.

DURING THE COLONIAL PERIOD, wood was a necessity, but it was overabundant and free for the taking. The forests harbored Indians and wild beasts and encumbered the ground needed for crops and pastures. So the pioneers, in the words of Gifford Pinchot, "came to feel that the thing to do with the forest was to get rid of it."

Local wood shortages sometimes arose near the larger towns despite the abundant supplies, because transportation facilities were poor. This occasionally led to restrictions on cutting, until the timber farther back could be opened up. Timber export from New England began with or before the first settlement—masts and hand-made staves, clapboards, and shingles at first, and later sawn lumber, staves, and ship timbers. These commodities formed the basis of a thriving trade with the West Indies and with Europe. The English Government, anxious to insure a supply of masts for the Royal Navy and to prevent other countries from getting them, attempted to reserve all white pine trees that were suitable for masts, but succeeded only in arousing the resentment of the colonists. These and similar ordinances and regulations were essentially police measures for the protection of town and crown property, and had nothing to do with forestry.

Perhaps the best-known attempt at forest conservation during the colonial period was William Penn's provision, in 1681 or 1682, that an acre should be maintained in forest for every five cleared in lands granted by him. So far as known, this provision was not long enforced.

IN THE FIRST CENTURY of independence, settlement spread over most of the country. Transcontinental railroads were built. Wooden ships were on their last voyages. The westward migration had already caused the abandonment of many farms in the Northeast and the Southeast. Most of the old-growth white pine of New England had been cut; that in New York and Pennsylvania was going fast. Pine production in the Lake States was approaching its peak. It was still the favored species for lumber, for the sawmill output of white pine exceeded that of all other species combined.

At the beginning of the nineteenth century, concern was felt over local shortages of firewood and other timber near the cities and over the supply of ship timbers. In 1791 the Philadelphia Society for the Promotion of Agriculture offered medals for planting locust for posts and treenails. The Massachusetts Society offered premiums for growing trees, in 1804. The New York Society named a committee to study the "best mode of preserving and increasing the growth of timber." That or another committee, in a report in 1795, recommended that inferior agricultural land be devoted to trees. In 1817 the Massachusetts Legislature asked its State Department of Agriculture to encourage the growing of oaks for ship timbers; in 1837 it authorized a survey of forest conditions in the State, with the idea that the findings might induce landowners to consider the importance of "continuing, improving, and enlarging the forests of the State."

In 1799, the Congress, heeding John Jay's warning that ship timbers and masts would become scarce unless steps were taken to prevent waste and preserve the existing supplies, authorized President Adams to spend $200,000 to buy reserves of live oak on the South Carolina and Georgia coasts. That was probably the first appropriation by the Federal Government for acquisition of timberland.

It was followed several years later by acts authorizing the President to reserve public lands bearing live oak and cedar in Florida, Alabama, and Louisiana; to purchase similar lands; to conduct experiments in the planting and cultivation of live oak (probably the first Federal forestry research); and to take appropriate measures to prevent depredations and preserve live oak stands. Besides the small areas bought in Georgia, some 244,000 acres was reserved in the Gulf States. Meanwhile, stealing of timber from the reservations and other public lands went on unchecked, and the Government continued to sell oak timberland at $1.25 an acre and buy stolen oak timber for $1.50 a cubic foot. The Louisiana reservations were canceled in 1888.

In 1831 Congress prohibited cutting live oak and other trees on naval reservations or any other lands belonging to the United States. Although seldom enforced, the act remained for almost 60 years the basic and only law aimed at protecting the timber on Government lands. The Commissioner of the General Land Office attempted to enforce the law in 1851, but was dismissed for doing so. Carl Schurz tried again when he was Secretary of the Interior, but was stopped by Congress in 1880.

After the Civil War, citizens began to take more interest in forests; earlier they generally were indifferent to them. The heavy requirements for wood during the war and the extensive destruction in some areas by military operations, the rapid pace of lumbering in the Lake States and the widespread destruction by forest fires, the growing realization of the relation of forests to stream flow and water supplies—all caused people to think about future timber supplies and the importance of forest cover.

A paper by the Reverend Frederick Starr, in the report of the Department of Agriculture for 1865, is said to have had great influence on the forestry movement. He predicted a timber famine within 30 years and advocated the immediate undertaking of carefully planned research on how to manage forests and how to establish plantations. The research, he maintained, should be done by a Government-endowed private corporation in order to avoid the evils of the spoils system, frequent changes in personnel, and general corruption in the Government. That, more than likely, was the start of the movement for better forest management.

What may have been the first State commission appointed to inquire into the forest situation and recommend a forestry policy for the State was set up at the request of the Wisconsin Legislature in 1867. The resulting report, by I. A. Lapham, failed to emphasize the need for sustained-yield management of the existing forests and overstressed the need for planting, but demonstrated clearly the relation of forests to stream flow. No action was taken on the report.

Maine appointed a commission on forestry policy in 1869, but the result was some relatively unimportant laws.

A New York commission set up in 1872 investigated the question of preserving the Adirondack forest for its effect on the Hudson and other rivers and the Erie Canal. No action was taken at that time.

From 1868 on, tree planting caught the public attention and interest. A number of States enacted laws to encourage planting by offering bounties or by granting tax reductions or exemption. Arbor Day was first celebrated in Nebraska in 1872, at the instigation of J. Sterling Morton, later Secretary of Agriculture. Several railroad companies planted trees for ties and timber, mostly in the Great Plains.

The Timber Culture Act, passed by Congress in 1873, offered land free to settlers who would plant trees on 40 (later reduced to 10) acres of each 160-acre claim.

Opinions differ as to the efficacy of the measures. One estimate is that 2 million acres was planted under the act of 1873. Others report that most of those plantations were neglected and died, so that perhaps not more than 50,000 acres could be considered successful. Most of the State laws are reported to have accomplished little, though Governor Morton told the American Forestry Congress in 1885 that Nebraska had more than 700,000 acres of planted trees. B. E. Fernow, in his *History of Forestry,* suggested that Arbor Days may have retarded real forestry by centering attention on planting, to the exclusion of the proper use of existing forests, and by introducing poetry and emotional appeal instead of practical economic considerations.

The first systematic effort to arouse public interest in the preservation and conservative use of the natural forest areas— as distinct from planting of artificial forests—was instigated by Franklin B. Hough's address before the American Association for the Advancement of Science in 1873.

The speech led the Association to send to Congress and to the State legislatures, in 1874, a memorial that said:

"The preservation and growth of timber is a subject of great practical importance to the people of the United States, and is becoming every year of more and more consequence, from the increasing demand for its use; and while this rapid exhaustion is taking place, there is no effectual provision against waste or for the renewal of supply. . . . Besides the economical value of timber for construction, fuel, and the arts . . . questions of climate . . . the drying up of rivulets . . . and the growing tendency to floods and drought . . . since the cutting off of our forests are subjects of common observation. . . ."

The Association asked Congress to create the position of Federal Commissioner of Forestry, whose duties would be to ascertain (1) the amount and distribution of woodlands in the United States, the rate of consumption and waste, and measures necessary to insure adequate future supplies of timber; (2) the influence of forests on climate, especially in relation to agriculture; and (3) the methods of forestry practiced in Europe.

THE YEARS FROM 1876 TO 1897 brought a growth in national and State firest-land policies. The Agriculture appropriation bill enacted in 1876 contained a rider on the section dealing with free seed distribution, which authorized the Commissioner of Agriculture to appoint, at a salary of $2,000, "a man of approved attainments and practically well acquainted with the methods of statistical inquiry" to investigate and make a detailed report on forestry.

Dr. Hough was appointed to the new position, and his three voluminous reports, published in 1877, 1880, and 1882, contained much significant information on American forests and the forest-products industries and on European forestry.

A fourth volume was contributed in 1884 by N. H. Egleston, who succeeded Hough in 1883. At that time the Division of Forestry, which had been formally established in 1881, consisted of the Chief and three field agents, and received an appropriation of $10,000.

Both Hough and Egleston, and the Commissioners of Agriculture, were active in the work of the American Forestry Association and the American Forestry Congresses. The Association was organized in Philadelphia in 1876 for the purpose of "protection of the existing forests of the country from unnecessary waste, and the promotion of the propagation and planting of useful trees." In calling the preliminary organization meeting in 1875, John A. Warder stated as one objective of the proposed association, "The fostering of all interests of forest planting and conservation on this continent." The term "forest conservation," therefore, was in use more than 30 years before it was taken up and popularized by Gifford Pinchot and Theodore Roosevelt.

The Association was not very active, but took on new life in 1882 when it merged with the American Forestry Congress, organized earlier that year on the occasion of a visit by Baron von Steuben, a Prussian forester and descendent of the general who helped defeat Cornwallis at Yorktown.

The constitution of the merged association, drafted under the leadership of B. E. Fernow, specified as its objectives "the discussion of subjects relating to tree planting; the conservation, management, and renewal of forests; the climatic and other influences that affect their welfare; the collection of forest statistics; and the advancement of educational, legislative, or other measures tending to the promotion of these objects."

The new organization met one or more times each year and was active in drafting proposals for both State and Federal legislation. At a meeting in 1886 in Denver, two resolutions were adopted:

"That the public lands at the sources of streams, necessary for the preservation of the water supply, should be granted by the General Government to the several States, to be held and kept by such States in perpetuity, for the public use, with a view to maintaining and preserving a full supply of water in all rivers and streams."

"That fire is the most destructive enemy of the forest, and that most stringent regulations should be adopted by the National and State and Territorial governments to prevent its outbreak and spread in timber stands."

Largely through the influence and encouragement of the American Forestry Congress, several local or State associations were formed; they were responsible for the formulation and enactment of a number of State forestry policies.

Colorado was the first State to make provision for management of its forest lands. Its constitution, adopted when it was admitted to the Union in 1876, directed the legislature to provide for protection and management of State forest lands. Nothing was done until 1885, when a Forestry Commission was created, but the Commission was active for only a few years. The Colorado Constitutional Convention also asked Congress to turn over control of Federal forest lands to the States and Ter-

802062°—49——46

ritories in regions where irrigation is necessary, for the reason that the existing system of public-land disposal, if continued, would injure Colorado and "bring destruction and calamity upon the entire population of the so-called Far West." No action was taken on the recommendation.

In California, also, a State Board of Forestry, established in 1885, urged in its first report that all Federal and State timberlands not fit for agriculture be permanently reserved and put in charge of forestry officers. In 1888 a resolution of the legislature asked Congress to stop disposing of Federal forest lands in California and to preserve them permanently for protection of watersheds.

New York, in 1883, carried out the recommendations made 11 years earlier and stopped the sale of tax-reverted forest lands in the Adirondacks. In 1885 a Forestry Commission was set up, with an appropriation of $15,000, to organize a State forest-protection system and administer the State's forest reserve, the primary object of which was the protection of water supplies, not timber production. Suspicion soon arose that the Forest Commissioners were working for the interests of the lumbermen, so a constitutional amendment in 1894 prohibited the cutting of timber and required that the reserve be kept forever in a wild condition.

Pennsylvania created a Division of Forestry in its Department of Agriculture in 1895 to collect and publish information on forest resources, enforce the fire laws, give advice on forestry, compile statistics on timber production and consumption, and manage all forest lands belonging to the State. In 1897 provision was made for purchase of tax-delinquent forest lands, to establish "a forestry reservation system having in view the preservation of the water supply at the sources of the rivers of the State, and for the protection of the people of the Commonwealth and their property from destructive floods." Another law in 1897 directed the commissioner to recommend to the Governor or the legislature three forest reservations of not less than 40,000 acres each, on the headwaters of the Ohio, Delaware, and Susquehanna Rivers, to be acquired by purchase. By 1910 the State had acquired more than 900,000 acres under these acts.

At the time that Western States were urging the reservation of public lands and when the Forestry Congress proposed their transfer to the States, the Federal Government had made no move to withhold them from disposal and only occasional gestures to protect them from fires and depredation.

Carl Schurz, Secretary of the Interior from 1877 to 1881, repeatedly, but vainly, urged the reservation of all public-domain timberlands and their protection and conservative management. Numerous bills looking to this end were introduced in almost every Congress from 1876 on.

Finally, in 1891, largely on the insistence of Secretary of the Interior Noble, a rider, which Gifford Pinchot called "the most important legislation in the history of forestry in America," was attached to an act amending the land laws. It authorized the President to reserve forest lands of the public domain, whether bearing commercial timber or not, in any State or Territory having Federal land. President Harrison acted promptly and proclaimed the first reserve, the Yellowstone Park Timberland Reserve, on March 30, 1891. This was the beginning of the national forest system. More reservations followed by President Harrison and then by President Cleveland.

Congress failed to provide, however, for the protection and administration of the reserves, nor was there any legal way in which timber could be sold or forest management applied. Timber thieves and graziers continued to operate without restriction. Bills were introduced in each Congress to remedy the situation. In 1894 the McRae bill, drafted by B. E. Fernow, Chief of the Division of Forestry since 1886, was passed by both Houses but too late for agreement in conference. This bill was passed again by the House of Representatives in 1896, but not by the Senate. Meanwhile, through efforts of the American Forestry Association, Secretary of the Interior Hoke Smith in 1896 was induced to ask the National Academy of Sciences to study and report on the problem.

After a trip to look over the situation in the West, the Committee set up by the Academy, being unable to agree on recommendations for administration of the forests, merely recommended the establishment of some 21 million acres of new forest reserves. In order to act before his term expired, President Cleveland proclaimed these reservations without the customary consultation with local people and Members of Congress. His act aroused opposition throughout the West, especially because it merely locked up the resources without provision for their use, and Congress suspended temporarily all but two of the reservations.

However, the act suspending the reservations (the Sundry Civil Appropriation Act of June 4, 1897) carried an amendment by Senator Pettigrew that provided for administration and management of existing and future reserves, much as proposed in the McRae bill of 1894. This amendment is the charter on which the operation of the national forests has been based.

Among its important provisions is a statement of objectives:

"No public forest reservation shall be established except to improve and protect the forest," secure "favorable conditions of water flow," and "furnish a continuous supply of timber for the use and necessities of citizens of the United States." The principal specifications regarding administration and use of the reserves are the instructions to the Secretary of the Interior to make provision for protection against fire and trespass; to make rules and regulations for occupancy and use of the reserves and their products; to sell, after due examination and appraisal, dead and mature timber; and to allow free use of timber by bona fide settlers and others for their domestic needs.

Management of the public forests—and of private forests, too—required more than legislative authority and appropriations. Without an adequate basis of scientific knowledge (meaning research) and an adequate staff of technical foresters (meaning a forestry profession), good forest management would be impossible.

As Fernow told the American Forestry Congress in 1885:

"Generalities on forest preservation or forest destruction and forestal influences have become trite and their constant reiteration without positive data will dull the interest of listeners and readers, create suspicion and defection. We need definite, well-authenticated local observations, arrived at by well-described scientific methods; we need methodical work in establishing the conditions of growth for different species, their behavior towards the soil and towards each other in different soils, their rate of growth at different periods of life under different conditions. In fact, besides making propaganda, we should by concerted effort establish the principles upon which the forestry we advocate is to be carried on."

Unfortunately, the Division of Forestry in the Department of Agriculture, during its first 20 years, found itself unable to carry on much scientific research in the woods, because it controlled no forest land, could not get permission to use public timberlands or military reservations, and was not allowed to use the private lands for fear of criticism that public money was being used for the benefit of private individuals.

The States were repeatedly urged by Fernow and his predecessors, speaking through the forestry associations and congresses, to undertake forestry research at their land-grant colleges and experiment stations, but the result appears to have been small. The Division cooperated with the State agricultural experiment stations in a few experiments, mainly in planting, including experimental planting in the Nebraska Sand Hills and cultivation of cork oak from imported acorns. Monographs were prepared, by the botanists rather than foresters, on several important timber trees.

The greater part of the Division's activity between 1886 and 1898 was devoted to forest-products research, which Fernow believed would encourage better and more economical use of wood and reduce waste, and would make industrial and other timber owners take an interest in conservation of timber resources. Among the subjects investigated were the use of chestnut oak as a substitute for white oak railroad ties, the use of metal ties to replace wood, tannin content of chestnut and other woods, strength properties of turpentined pine (until then considered inferior to unbled timber), blue stain of southern pine and yellow-poplar lumber, and timber physics.

Regarding the need for trained foresters, Hough's paper on "Forestry Education," presented at the American Forestry Congress in St. Paul in 1883, is illuminating. He believed that lectures on the importance of forests should be given in all primary and secondary schools, but he saw no need for technical training in forestry. Noting a proposal for a Federal forestry school in St. Paul, he asked where the graduates would find employment, and said:

"Neither the general nor the State governments have any systems of forest management needing their services. There may be a few railroad companies who would employ one, but this is not certain, and as to private estates, I know of none upon which such a person would be likely to find an engagement. . . . We do not for the present, and perhaps for many years to come, require a class of persons who have been specially trained to the degree that is deemed necessary in the better class of forest schools in Europe, because such persons could not find employment either in charge of public or private forests at the present time. . . ."

It should be noted that neither Hough nor Egleston had any technical knowledge of forestry except what they may have picked up in the course of their work. Fernow was the first technically trained forester in Government service but, as he admits, he was at a disadvantage because he was "a foreigner who had first to learn the limitations of democratic government."

Partly as a result of urging by the forestry associations and the reports of State commissions of inquiry, forestry instruction was introduced into the curricula of many of the land-grant colleges beginning about 1883. There is some difference of opinion as to which was the first to include such a course, but there was one at Iowa State College in 1883, in 9 or 10 institutions by 1887, and in some 20 by 1898.

During the last two decades of the nineteenth century, there were frequent expressions of concern over depletion of timber supplies in the East. Manufacturers frequently complained of difficulties in getting supplies of ash, hickory, white oak, walnut, and high-grade white pine—the same species that we hear about in 1949. In 1883, George Loring, then Commissioner of Agriculture, stated that white pine was nearly gone in New Hampshire and New York, and going rapidly in the other Northeastern States; that only 10 to 20 years' supply remained in the Lake States, and that eastern spruce was nearly exhausted. In 1887 it was reported that shiploads of pine were coming into the United States from Russia. In 1889 Professor Prentiss of Cornell predicted that hemlock, "the most valuable tree east of the Mississippi, except white pine," would be exhausted in 20 to 30 years at the current rate of cutting. Evidently southern pine was not well thought of in the New York market at that time.

In 1890 Fernow reported to the American Forestry Congress: "While the area of forests in the United States probably does not diminish now at as rapid a rate as it used to, the value of the remaining area is very rapidly depreciating, not only by removing the accumulated supplies, but by cutting the best and leaving the inferior material, by neglecting to give attention to the reproduction of the better kinds, or even by recurring fires destroying the capacity for such reproduction."

In 1892 Fernow expressed regret that the funds were inadequate for testing all of the important woods, because there was considerable demand for tests of species which, though "still more or less unknown . . . are now being drawn upon to eke out the deficiency of supply of the better-known kinds." Those unknown species included Douglas-fir, cedars, sugar pine, and baldcypress.

As another evidence of the concern felt by some members of the industry over waning timber supplies, there may be mentioned the paper presented by H. C. Putnam, a Wisconsin lumberman, which called for action by Congress for protection against fires and protection of young trees in logging—both to insure a future timber supply and to protect stream flow.

The accomplishments of the forestry movement prior to 1898 have been criticized on the ground that there was much forestry in words but none in the woods. It is important to realize, however, that without the many years of propaganda, of learning and informing at least part of the public regarding the facts of the forest situation and the need for doing something about it, the conservation movement of the early 1900's would likely have been a dud. It is necessary to remember, also, that there were almost no trained foresters to carry forestry into the woods before 1898. The Division of Forestry and the associations not only were successful in stimulating public interest in forestry problems, but they had a large share in developing public forestry policies and in drafting basic legislation, both Federal and State. As Fernow said, in his Report upon Forestry Investigations, 1877–98:

"To have established the conception that forestry, silviculture, and forest preservation are not the planting of trees, but cutting them in such a manner that planting becomes unnecessary, is one of the most potent results of the efforts of the Division of Forestry. . . . For preservation, it must by this time have become clear, does not consist in leaving the forests unused, but in securing their reproduction."

Pointing out that by 1898 the lumber-trade journals gave respectful hearing to the advocates of forestry whom they had ridiculed as "denudatics" only 12 years before, Fernow goes on to say:

"The time has come when it [the Division] should not only more vigorously pursue technical investigations, but when it should have charge of the public timberlands, and especially the public forest reservations, which will never answer their purpose until controlled by systematic management. . . . A Division of Forestry in a government which has reserved millions of acres of forest property must logically become the manager of that forest property."

Between 1897 and 1919, the national forest policy developed.

As directed by the act of June 4, 1897, the Secretary of the Interior immediately undertook to provide for the protection and administration of the forest reserves. The task was assigned to the General Land Office, which appointed a field force of forest superintendents, rangers, and others, and an office staff in Washington. None of them had any technical knowledge of forestry, and it was not until 1902—when a tentative arrangement for the Bureau ("Division" until 1901) of Forestry in the Department of Agriculture to handle the forestry work on the reserves fell through—that the General Land Office set up its own technical forestry division. Filibert Roth was put in charge of the work. He borrowed several men from the Bureau of

Forestry, but he stayed only a year and then left to head the forestry school that was being established at the University of Michigan.

Meanwhile, Dr. Fernow had left the Government service in 1898 to organsize the school of forestry at Cornell. The only other systematic instruction in forestry at that time was the elementary instruction given at some 20 land-grant colleges and the short course offered at Biltmore, N. C., by C. A. Schenck, a German forester.

Gifford Pinchot succeeded Fernow as Chief of the Division of Forestry in 1898. He undertook to introduce better forestry methods into the operations of the private owners, large and small, by helping them make working plans and by demonstrating good practices on the ground. There were then only two technical foresters and nine other employees on the staff of the Division, and probably fewer than a dozen foresters in the country. Accordingly, a start toward building up a profession was made by recruiting student assistants who had an inclination and aptitude for forestry and who would supplement academic work with field experience in the Division. In order to provide a high grade of forest training suited to American conditions, the Pinchot family provided an endowment for a 2-year postgraduate school at Yale University. H. S. Graves and J. W. Toumey were released from the Division in 1900 to start the school. In the fall of 1900, the Cornell school had 24 students, Biltmore 9, and Yale 7. (In 1946 there were some 6,000 American-trained professional foresters.) During the next few years schools or departments of forestry were organized at the University of Michigan, Harvard, University of Nebraska, Mont Alto, Pa., Pennsylvania State College, and elsewhere.

In 1900, under Pinchot's leadership, the Society of American Foresters was founded. It had seven charter members. The objects of this professional society are: "To further the cause of forestry in America by fostering a spirit of comradeship among foresters; by creating opportunities for a free interchange of views upon forestry and allied subjects; and by disseminating a knowledge of the purpose and achievements of forestry."

In 1901 the newly christened Bureau of Forestry was given broader authority to make working plans for private owners, and much larger appropriations than had been available to the Division. The forest-products research that had been stopped shortly before Fernow left was resumed, along much the same lines as before. In 1910 the products work was centered at the Forest Products Laboratory, operated in cooperation with the University of Wisconsin at Madison. In 1902 the earlier experimental planting in the Nebraska Sand Hills was followed up by reservation of part of the area and planting on a fair scale.

The unsatisfactory situation in which the Federal forest reserves were administered, in a different department from that in which the Government's technical forestry work had been established, rapidly became a major issue. Theodore Roosevelt's first message to Congress in 1901 and the report of a commission on the organization of Government scientific work in 1903 reiterated earlier proposals that all responsibility for the reserves be transferred to the Department of Agriculture. Secretary of the Interior Hitchcock also supported the proposal. Finally, a special American Forestry Congress met in Washington in January 1905 for the specific purpose of bringing about the transfer. The meeting was sponsored by the Secretary of Agriculture, the heads of the Geological Survey, Reclamation Service, and General Land Office, the president of the National Lumber Manufacturers' Association, the presidents of the National Livestock and National Woolgrowers' Associations, the presidents of the Union Pacific and Great Northern Railroads, and the head of the Weyerhaeuser lumber companies. The resolutions adopted by the gathering no doubt helped consummate the transfer, which was made by act of Congress on February 1, 1905. The Bureau of Forestry was renamed Forest Service that year, and the forest reserves were renamed "national forests" in 1907.

In a letter to Gifford Pinchot, dated February 1, 1905, Secretary of Agriculture James Wilson laid down the guiding principles. The letter read, in part:

"In the administration of the forest reserves it must be clearly borne in mind that all land is to be devoted to its most productive use for the permanent good of the whole people, and not for the temporary benefit of individuals or companies. All the resources of forest reserves are for use, and this use must be brought about in a thoroughly prompt and businesslike manner, under such restrictions only as will insure the permanence of these resources.

"In the management of each reserve local questions will be decided upon local grounds; the dominant industry will be considered first, but with as little restriction to minor industries as may be possible; sudden changes in industrial conditions will be avoided by gradual adjustment after due notice; and where conflicting interests must be reconciled the question will always be decided from the standpoint of the greatest good of the greatest number in the long run."

Activities in 1908 and 1909 can be regarded as the culmination of the early conservation movement. The White House Conference of Governors on conservation of natural resources was conducted in 1908. It set up a National Conservation Commission which, in a three-volume report (1909), presented a survey of the status of America's natural resources, including forests. Also in 1909 was held the North American Conference on Natural Resources, which served to give an international flavor to the movement.

The first decade of the twentieth century saw the most rapid growth of the national forests, which embraced about 56 million acres in 1901, more than 100 million in 1905, and 175 million acres in 1910. After 1910 the area was gradually reduced by the elimination of almost 27 million acres that was classified as more valuable for agriculture or grazing than for forestry. This reduction was partly offset by increases through exchange with States and private owners and by acquisition of land through purchase.

Most of the forest lands reserved from the public domain were in the West, but the interest in conserving forests for protection of watersheds was almost as strong in the East, where there was little or no Federal public land. The first suggestion that the Government buy land for a forest reserve in the East was made in 1892 or 1893 by the State geologist of North Carolina. Later, an Appalachian National Park Association was formed; in 1901 it induced Congress to authorize a survey of the Southern Appalachian area proposed for a reserve. In 1900 and also in 1901 the legislatures of North Carolina, Georgia, Alabama, and Tennessee authorized the Federal Government to acquire lands for a forest reserve.

After many attempts, in which the southern interests joined forces with the advocates of a national forest in the White Mountains of New Hampshire, Congress was persuaded to enact the Weeks Law of March 1, 1911. The law provided for the purchase of forest lands on the headwaters of navigable streams, after certification by the Geological Survey that they affect navigation. The authority of this act was broadened in 1924; about 18 million acres has been purchased to date.

At the same time that the national forests were expanding in area, progress was being made in their administration and management. Six regional offices were set up in 1908 so as to bring the administration closer to the people most concerned. A systematic program of timber surveys was also adopted in 1908 to afford a basis for timber sales and management plans.

A scientific approach to forest-fire prevention and control began in 1911 as a result of the 1910 conflagrations which burned over nearly 5 million acres and destroyed more than 3 billion feet of timber. Reforestation by planting and sowing was mostly on an experimental basis before 1911 but, by 1919, more than 150,000 acres had been covered—more than half of it by sowing and not all of it successful.

A comprehensive plan of forestry research—mainly in silviculture—was formulated in 1908 by Raphael Zon and others. Several of the experiment stations proposed in this plan were set up, and in 1915 a branch of research was established, with Earle H. Clapp in charge.

Cooperation of the Federal Government with the States to encourage fire protection on the watersheds of navigable streams was authorized by the Weeks Law of 1911. Federal contributions were to be contingent upon adequate legislation and matching appropriations by the States. In 1911 the Government spent about $37,000, in cooperation with 11 States, to protect 61 million acres of State and private land. In 1919 the Federal expenditure was $100,000, with 22 States cooperating and nearly 110 million acres under organized protection. In the fiscal year 1948, with an appropriation of $9,000,000, the Federal Government cooperated with 43 States and Hawaii in protecting 328 million acres.

By 1919 many of the States had established some sort of forestry department, usually headed by a technically trained forester. Nearly all of them had legislation providing for control of forest fires, though the laws were not always effective. Several States had set aside State forests. The States have continued to expand and strengthen forestry work, and in 1948 it was reported that 38 States were administering 11.6 million acres as State forests.

In 1919, Henry S. Graves, the Forester, summed up the situation with respect to forestry on private lands in his annual report, as follows:

"In the early years of the present century it really looked as though the management of forests as permanently productive properties might be voluntarily undertaken by private owners on a very large scale. Although many obstacles were presented by the internal conditions of the lumber industry, progressive lumbermen were giving much serious attention to the possibility of engaging in the practice of forestry. The chief stimulus was furnished by the rising value of stumpage. The panic of 1907 radically changed the situation. The lumber industry entered a period of protected depression. From that time on private forestry made relatively little progress in the United States, except on farm woodlands. While public forestry has made vast strides, the forests of the country that are in private hands are being depleted with very great rapidity, and almost everywhere without effort to renew them."

Graves concluded that "the general practice of forestry on privately owned lands in the United States will not take place through unstimulated private initiative." He proposed a broad forestry policy for the Nation, to include an expanded public program of land acquisition and a program for the protection and perpetuation of forest growth on all privately owned forest land that is not better for agriculture or settlement. He proposed that the Federal Government cooperate with and work through the States in promoting private forestry.

Between 1919 and 1949, private forestry and public forestry expanded.

Graves' 1919 report marked the start of a campaign, which is still in progress, to develop a national policy for bringing about forestry on private lands.

W. B. Greeley, who became head of the Forest Service in 1920, took up the campaign where Graves left off. In 1920 the Capper Report on timber depletion, lumber prices, and forest ownership, and the report of the forestry policy committee of the Society of American Foresters, headed by Pinchot, aroused widespread interest by showing the seriousness of the situation. As a result of these reports and the ensuing discussion, two bills were introduced in Congress. The Capper bill, which was revised once or twice, proposed direct Federal control of operations on private lands, through a taxation and bounty device. The Snell bill proposed Federal assistance to States in the exercise of their police power over private lands. Both bills included cooperation for protection against forest fires. The bills were debated widely and heatedly.

The result was the appointment of a Senate committee to consider these and other proposals for legislation and to hold hearings in various sections of the country. Meanwhile, the Forest Service undertook a series of "minimum-requirements" studies to develop a clearer analysis of what might be acceptable as reasonably good forestry practices in the various forest regions and types of forest. The Senate committee's deliberation led to enactment on June 7, 1924, of the Clarke-McNary Law.

This act extended the national forest acquisition policy to lands primarily useful for timber production rather than for watershed protection and broadened the fire-protection cooperation of the Weeks Law. Small appropriations were authorized for cooperation with States in growing forest planting stock for farmers and in advising farm-forest owners.

Enactment of the McSweeney-McNary Law in 1928 provided a broad charter for forestry research. It set up a 10-year program that included a system of forest and range experiment stations, expanded research in forest products, and a Nation-wide survey of forest resources and requirements. The Knutsen-Vandenberg Act of 1930 authorized a larger national forest planting program than had been possible before. By 1947, more than 1.2 million acres had been successfully restocked.

The depressed and distressed condition of the lumber industry in the late 1920's led President Herbert Hoover in 1930 to appoint a Timber Conservation Board to study what might be done about it. One result was a temporary relaxation of efforts to sell Government timber. The study also led to the Copeland Report (A National Plan for American Forestry, S. Doc. 12, 73d Congress), an encyclopedic analysis of the forestry situation, published in 1933. The report laid greatest emphasis on acquisition of forest land by Federal, State, and local governments and increased assistance to private owners. A 20-year goal for acquisition was placed at 134 million acres for the Federal Government, and 90 million acres for State and local governments.

Good forestry practices were included in the lumber and other forest-industry codes under the National Industrial Recovery Act of 1934–35. Although this act was declared unconstitutional, work on the codes, particularly on the lumber code, was beneficial in giving the lumbermen a better understanding of what sustained-yield management means, of the advantages of selective logging, and of the nature of essential silvicultural measures.

Another depression-born activity that did much to dramatize forest conservation was the Civilian Conservation Corps. Set up as a major feature of Federal unemployment relief in 1933, almost half of the 2,600 camps operating at its peak in 1935 were engaged on forestry projects. In 9 years of existence, the Civilian Conservation Corps contributed some 730,000 man-years of work in forest protection, in construction and maintenance of improvements on public forests, in tree planting, and in timber-stand improvement. It greatly stimulated the establishment and expansion of public forests, particularly by States and communities in the East.

The Norris-Doxey Farm Forestry

Act of 1937 was aimed mainly at improving forestry practices on the many small farm woodlands. It authorized appropriations up to $2,500,000 a year to provide advice, investigation, and plants for farmers, in cooperation with the States. In the fiscal year 1948 the Forest Service cooperated in 173 farm-forestry projects, located in some 650 counties in 40 States. Besides, about 65 forestry extension specialists worked in 45 States and 2 Territories.

In March 1938, President Franklin D. Roosevelt sent a special message to Congress recommending a study of the forest situation by a joint committee of both Houses, to form a basis for policy legislation relating to cooperation of the Federal Government and the States with private forest owners. He also proposed that the committee consider the need for regulatory controls and the extension of public ownership. The committee was appointed, held hearings at various places, and produced a report in 1941. Among other things, the report recommended Federal financial assistance to the States for regulation of forestry practices, but it did not suggest additional Federal acquisition of forest land.

The Forest Service undertook to make a new reappraisal of the situation in 1945 in order to bring up to date and amplify basic information on our timber resources, to interpret this information in relation to the national economy, and to reexamine national needs in forest conservation.

This study brought out that the crux of the forestry problem now is not the large tracts owned by industries but the small holdings of farmers and other tracts of similar size.

Many of the larger owners, particularly in the South and the Northwest, have been developing an interest in forestry for a considerable period. According to the Society of American Foresters, more than 2,500 trained foresters were employed by private industries in 1948, although there had been fewer than 400 in 1930 and only about 1,000 in 1940.

Meanwhile, several States, notably Oregon in the West, Maryland in the East, and Mississippi in the South, have enacted laws that provide for some form of regulation of cutting practices on private lands—mandatory in some States, optional in others.

Summing up the situation today, it can be said that although our forests as a whole are poorer in quantity and quality than they were 30 years ago, the stage is set for a reversal of the downward trend. The basic principles of forestry are better understood by more people than ever before. More and more timberland owners seem to be acquiring a sense of stewardship—a conviction that it is their duty to leave their land at least as productive as they found it. Furthermore, people are coming to realize that if our forests are destroyed we cannot expect the rest of the world to supply us with timber.

W. N. SPARHAWK *is a native of New Hampshire and a graduate of Yale University. He joined the Forest Service in 1910. After almost 6 years on timber reconnaissance and in various research assignments in the western national forests, he was transferred to Washington, where his first assignment was a Nation-wide study of fire hazard and protection. As a forest economist, he participated in the preparation of numerous reports and bulletins that dealt with economic problems in forestry. He is joint author with Raphael Zon of the two-volume work on Forest Resources of the World, 1923. During the Second World War he was consultant to military agencies on foreign forestry. Mr. Sparhawk is a fellow of the American Association for the Advancement of Science and the Society of American Foresters, and a member of the Washington Academy of Sciences. He is editor of the forestry section of Biological Abstracts, and was associate editor of the Journal of Forestry from 1936 to 1948. Mr. Sparhawk retired from the Forest Service in 1948 and is now living in New Hampshire.*

# Today and Tomorrow

## FOREST LAND AND TIMBER RESOURCES

C. EDWARD BEHRE

ONE OF EVERY THREE ACRES in the United States is forest land. The forests are important in all regions except the Great Plains, but even there they occupy almost 10 percent of the land. After more than 300 years of settlement, three-fourths of New England is classified as forest land. Five-sixths of the Douglas-fir region, on the other side of the country, is in forest. In the South, more than half of all the land is chiefly valuable for forests.

That is enough ultimately to grow all the timber products we need, with a margin for export, new uses, and national security—if it is properly managed. But our forests are not now in condition to meet prospective needs.

The acreage of forest land is not likely to change much from the present 624 million acres. For the most part, today's forest land is that which has proved unsuited for agriculture because of roughness, stoniness, poor soils, aridity, or other circumstances.

*Above: A mill worker scales logs; just so we measure our lumber supply.*

It includes much worn-out or low-grade land that at one time or another has been cultivated. Additional acres of the poor cropland are likely to revert to forest use, but some of the better lands now in forests will be cleared for agriculture. There will also be reductions for urban development, construction of highways, and other facilities, but these will not be large.

About three-fourths of the forest land, 461 million acres, is classed as "commercial," capable now or prospectively of growing merchantable timber, and available for that use. The remainder, 163 million acres, classed as "noncommercial" because it is not suitable and not available for timber growing, is important for watershed, range, and other services. Mostly in the West and the plains of Texas and Oklahoma, it includes, for example, the open-grown mesquite and pinyon-juniper lands of the Southwest, the chaparral in southern California, and alpine mountain forests. Included also are some 13 million acres of better sites set apart for parks and game preserves.

In present or potential productiveness, the forest lands of the South and of the Douglas-fir region of the Pacific Northwest are outstanding. Climate and other factors there favor forest renewal and rapid timber growth. Those regions have 45 percent of the commercial forest.

It is too bad, but too little of the commercial forest is producing as it should. More than 75 million acres—one-sixth of the total—is denuded or is so poorly stocked with seedlings and saplings as to be unproductive for decades. In addition, 30 million acres of pole timber, too small for sawlogs, and 58 million acres of second-growth saw timber have less than 40 percent of the number of trees needed for full stocking. Most of the denuded and poorly stocked land is in the East; the southern forests are the most deficient.

The idle land contributes little to the maintenance of schools, roads, or other community services. It supports no jobs. In some regions it contributes needlessly to destructive floods and the siltation of reservoirs. Taxes, if paid, must come from some other productive enterprise.

It is reasonable to assume that the acreage of poorly stocked land will shrink as a result of improved fire protection and better cutting practices. Indeed, stocking in the South is better than it was a decade ago. Young growth is springing up on millions of acres now protected from fire—a hopeful sign. Nevertheless, the United States faces a huge job of planting to restore the less favored lands to productivity.

Character of ownership is a fundamental factor in the forest situation. Most private ownership is, properly, motivated by financial gain. Seventy-five percent of the commercial forest land, generally including the more productive and accessible, is privately owned and furnishes about 90 percent of the timber cut. In contrast, only about 40 percent of the noncommercial forest is in private ownership.

One-third of all the forest land is publicly owned or managed, but half of this is noncommercial. The national forests include the major part of the public forest land. Placing the national forests—about one-twelfth of our total land area—under intensive management has been hampered by remoteness and inaccessibility, by poorly consolidated ownership, and by inadequate funds. Yet steady progress has been made and these forests are contributing increasingly to the economy.

The nature of the ownership of the 345 million acres of private commercial forest is largely the result of national land policies that favored small-scale, fee-simple ownership. Seventy-six percent of the private commercial forest is in more than 4 million small properties that average only 62 acres each. The other 24 percent is held in properties of more than 5,000 acres each by only 3,600 owners. Even in the West more than half is in small holdings.

Wood-using industries, directly dependent on timberlands for their raw material, own a surprisingly small part of the private commercial forest. Lumber and pulp companies together hold only 15 percent, some 51 million acres in all, mostly in large holdings. On the other hand, the 139 million acres of farm woods is the largest single category of forest land.

Farm ownership generally affords a favorable setting for forestry, and public policy has long encouraged farmers to make woodland management an integral part of the farm business. Yet most farm woodlands are still mistreated, being subject to unwise cutting, pasturing, and burning. Along with other small holdings, farm woodlands are at the heart of the Nation's forest problem.

THE TIMBER RESOURCE for 300 years, particularly during the past century, has contributed richly to the development of the country. Now we can see the end of our virgin resources; a timber shortage, the impact of which has been deferred by almost 20 years of depression and war, is brought into sharp relief by the demands of the present high level of industrial activity. There is a great need for housing that will not be satisfied for many years. Wholesale prices for lumber in 1948 were three times as high as in 1940, and they have risen much faster than those of other building materials. Suitable locations for large-scale logging operations are increasingly hard to find.

No longer can timber safely be viewed as a reserve to be drawn upon without regard for replacement. Now we must rely more and more on what is grown each year.

When timber is grown as a crop, the amount that can be regularly harvested year after year depends upon the volume of growing stock or standing timber. Until the productive capacity of the land is reached, the more growing stock or forest capital there is, the greater the crop available for cutting each year. And to maintain an annual crop of merchantable timber, there must be a succession of age classes from seedlings up to full-grown timber so that as mature trees are cut new ones will take their places. Thus to sustain a high output of timber products, we must maintain a substantial volume of standing timber as forest capital. If we liquidate our forest capital, we cut down the size of the crop which accrues as interest on it. This does not apply strictly to virgin forests, because in them death and decay usually offset current growth. They do not fully meet the growing-stock concept until they have been converted to a net growing condition by removal of overmature trees.

Since the timber crop must be harvested in trees of a size and quality suitable for commercial use, and since about 80 percent of all timber products are cut from trees of saw-timber size, it is important to think of the timber crop primarily in terms of saw timber.

As of 1945, the stand of saw timber in the United States was estimated at 1,601 billion board feet, about half of which is in virgin stands. The volume of all timber 5 inches or more in diameter breast high was 470 billion cubic feet. Those are large figures. But critical examination shows that the forest capital is by no means satisfactory.

For one thing, growing stock east of the Great Plains is badly depleted. The land is generally understocked and much of the timber is of small size and inferior quality. Although fully three-fourths of the commercial forest land is in the East, the timber there, 558 billion board feet, is little more than one-third of the national total.

On the other hand, Washington, Oregon, and California have less than one-seventh of the commercial forest land, but they have more than half the saw timber in the United States. About 80 percent of the 1,043 billion board feet of saw timber in the entire West is in virgin stands. Although the average volume needed as growing stock for future crops will generally be less than in the virgin stands, the backlog of forest capital in those stands is an extremely important part of our timber supply and should be husbanded.

The occurrence of different species and the replacement of the valuable species by inferior species is another factor. Timber in the West is almost all softwood, the kind that is in greatest demand for the major industrial uses, but in the North just about three-fourths is hardwood. There is now only 15 billion board feet of white and red pines, species that once were foremost in our lumber markets. Maine is the only Northern State with more softwood than hardwood. Even in the South, noted for its vast pine forests and prolific second growth, 43 percent of the saw timber today is hardwood.

Despite some significant progress in forestry, the timber situation is, generally speaking, on the down grade. In the 15 States comprising the Pacific Northwest and Lake States regions and most of the South, for which comparable forest survey data are available, saw-timber volume declined 14 percent in a period between surveys averaging 11 years.

The decline has meant scarcity of good timber in many parts of the country. This has resulted in cutting much young timber before it is mature. Many small mills are cutting 6-inch trees. For much of the South, the average pine saw-timber tree in 1945 was 20 percent smaller than a decade earlier. In the Mississippi Delta, many hardwood mills are operating on logs one-half or one-third as large as formerly. Even in the Douglas-fir region of the Pacific Northwest, the cut of second-growth timber reached 25 percent of the total output in 1947.

In North and South, the demand for pulpwood, mine timbers, box-grade lumber, and other items that can be cut from small trees also contributes to premature cutting. In a vicious circle, all this tends to perpetuate and worsen the shortage of larger timber.

Quality also is lowered. The fine logs needed by many forest industries are no longer abundant. High grading—cutting the best trees and leaving the poor trees—destructive cutting, and fire have replaced valuable timber with inferior stands.

In southern New England and parts of the Middle Atlantic States, the deterioration of sprout hardwood forests by repeated cutting, fire, and the chestnut blight has left little timber that is attractive to lumbermen. In fact, forest management there is handicapped by the difficulty of disposing of the inferior growth that preempts so much of the land.

In the Lake States, between 1936 and 1945, the volume of white and red pine saw timber dropped 29 percent, and beech, birch, and maple together declined 16 percent; the volume of the less desirable aspen, however, increased 55 percent.

In the South, longleaf pine has been succeeded by scrub oak on more than 2 million acres, mostly in Florida. Heavy cutting in the pine-hardwood stands, taking pine to a smaller diameter than hardwood, has allowed hardwoods of increasingly inferior quality to take over. The total cubic-foot volume of softwood timber in 9 Southern States from Georgia to Texas decreased 4 percent from the early 1930's to 1945, but the hardwood volume increased 5 percent. Hardwood saw timber declined almost as fast as the pine. In the Appalachian Mountains, removal of yellow-poplar and the better oaks often reduced the remaining forest to an unmerchantable condition from which it has been slow to recover.

In the West, the utilization of white pine, ponderosa pine, and sugar pine often has left a forest in which less desirable species predominate.

Only one-fourth of the remaining acreage of virgin timber meets the high standards generally associated with that class of timber: Heavy stands of large, high-quality trees of good species with little defect. The timber on one-third of the virgin acreage is of doubtful value—long past its prime, defective, and often of inferior species.

As a result of rapid exploitation of private timber and of a conservative policy since the turn of the century in opening up the public forests—both related to economic circumstances—43 percent of the saw timber now stands on the 25 percent of the commercial forest land that is publicly owned. In the West, almost one-half the timber is in the national forests, and 15 percent is in other public ownership; less than 40 percent is privately owned. But the 397 billion board feet of private timber in the West, mostly in Washington, Oregon, and California, is generally more accessible and of better quality than the public timber. In the East, 93 percent of the timber is privately owned.

More than one-fourth of the private timber is on the farms. The farm-timber resources are indispensable to the national supply. Properly managed, they can be a more stable and better source of farm income.

Private timber in other than farm holdings is the major source of raw material for the timber industries. How much of the 670 billion board feet in this class of ownership is held by the industries themselves is not known. The lumber and pulp companies, however, own only 15 percent of the private commercial forest land. Plainly, good management of the industrial timber holdings, although essential, will not of itself provide an adequate supply of timber products.

THE CRUX of the country's forest problem is the continued shrinkage and deterioration of forest growing stock.

Annual growth of saw timber is now estimated at 35.3 billion board feet, and of all timber at 13.4 billion cubic feet. More than half of the saw-timber growth is in the South. Only one-fourth is in the North, although the North has almost as much commercial forest land as the South. The remaining one-fifth is in the West. Timber growth in the West may be expected to increase as the two-fifths of the commercial forest land still in virgin timber, making little or no net growth, is converted by cutting to effectively growing forest.

The current estimate of saw-timber growth is 3.3 billion board feet greater than the 1938 estimate. Most of the difference may be due to the nature of the estimates rather than to actual changes. As a matter of fact, only for the Lake States and the South are the estimates comparable. In the Lake States, saw-timber growth dropped 24 percent in 10 years (the decline was more acute for softwoods than hardwoods) and the total cubic-foot growth declined 13 percent.

In the South, saw-timber growth is 3 percent greater than it was 10 years ago. But the net increase of 622 million board feet is the result of an increase of 886 million board feet (12 percent) of hardwoods and a decrease of 264 million board feet (2 percent) of softwoods. Similarly, two-thirds of a 9-percent increase in the all-timber growth in the South was in hardwoods. These figures are further evidence of the replacement of the more desirable pine by hardwoods; they really reflect deterioration rather than building up.

Forest drain, or the volume taken by cutting and by fire and other destructive agents, included 53.9 billion board feet of saw timber in 1944. This was the equivalent of 80 percent of the all-timber drain of 13.7 billion cubic feet. Although domestic use of wood was sharply reduced because of the war, saw-timber drain in 1944 was more than 6 billion board feet above that in 1936, the year of the last previous comprehensive estimate. With the great industrial activity of the postwar period, lumber cut in 1947 was some 3 billion board feet more than in 1944. This would put forest drain close to the level attained in the peak war years 1941 and 1942.

In 1944, saw-timber drain from the South (25 billion board feet) was 25 percent greater than that from the West (20 billion board feet). Because of the advanced stage of depletion in the North (which limits the opportunity for timber industries) only 17 percent of the saw-timber drain came from that section.

Lumber, by far the largest item, made up about 70 percent of the saw timber and 55 percent of the cubic-foot cutting drain. Fuel wood made up 18 percent of the cutting drain, mostly in the East and about two-thirds in hardwoods. Pulpwood, a rapidly increasing element of drain, accounted for 11 percent of cut in 1944, largely because of the expansion of the pulp and paper industry in the South.

That saw-timber drain exceeds annual growth by 50 percent is perhaps the most challenging fact in our forest situation today. It is a measure of the rate at which we are overdrawing our forest bank account. If the 1944 trend were continued with no changes in forest practices for 20 years (which is highly improbable because scarcity of suitable accessible timber will make it increasingly difficult for the forest industries to sustain output at the 1944 rate) the saw-timber stand would drop 27 percent.

In the South, continuation of the 1944 cut and prevailing forest practices for 20 years would mean a decline of 117 billion board feet, or one-third of the already inadequate saw-timber growing stock. Obviously such a decline in timber volume would mean curtailment of the forest industries and drastic readjustment in dependent communities.

The greatest reduction of saw timber is taking place in the Douglas-fir region, where 20 years more at the 1944 rate of decline would bring the volume down 206 billion board feet—41 percent. Because the backlog of virgin timber is so large, this and lesser losses in other parts of the West would not reduce the growing stock there dangerously. But it would be accompanied by the closing of many established mills and the continued shift of industrial activity from one locality to another. Even with good forest practices and farsighted planning for both public and private lands, waning of the virgin timber may be accompanied by a substantial reduction of output. Certainly depletion of the Douglas-fir, ponderosa pine, western white pine, sugar pine, and redwood would force western forest industries to adapt themselves to the production and marketing of different classes of products than at present.

Because continued timber depletion is so crucial, a balance between growth and drain is often represented as the solution of the problem. But balance in itself is not an adequate goal. As a matter of fact, we have a near balance now between cubic-foot growth and drain of all timber in trees 5 inches or more in diameter.

If the balance between cubic-foot growth and drain for all timber were an adequate criterion, we would have to conclude that the forest situation in the North is satisfactory today—because cubic-foot growth is well in excess of drain there. Yet forest depletion and deterioration are more acute in the North than in other sections, and the timber industries there are, in general, at a low ebb. Many of the older wood-using plants have been forced out of business, and the shortage of good timber makes it difficult for new plants to start. Shrinkage of the timber industries has caused drain to fall far below the productive capacity of the land. And the excess of all-timber growth over drain is a reflection of the inferior quality and small size of a large part of the timber. In fact, one of the major forest problems of the North is to find markets for the small, low-grade timber, which should be got out of the way to make room for more valuable growth.

The near balance between all-timber growth and drain is deceiving in other ways also. The over-all figures mask the fact that, for softwoods, the drain is 21 percent more than growth, while for hardwoods it is 17 percent less. Furthermore, four-fifths of the drain is in saw timber, whereas much of the growth is in small, low-grade trees and inferior hardwoods. The Nation should not be satisfied with a balance based on poles and saplings when its forest industries depend so largely on saw timber. Even the pulp and paper industry, which can use trees of less than saw-timber size, obtains about three-fourths of its wood from saw-timber trees.

There is no basis for assuming that the gap between saw-timber growth and drain is being reduced. In fact, despite the increase of 3.3 billion board feet in estimate of saw-timber growth between 1936 and 1944, the disparity between saw-timber growth and drain was about 3 billion board feet greater in 1944 than in 1936—and is even greater today.

In any event, the needs of this country for timber products is considerably greater than the present cut. A careful study of long-range potentialities indicates that 65 to 72 billion board feet would be a reasonable goal of annual saw-timber growth. To double saw-timber growth, as this suggests, is a big order. But to aim for less would not be sound public policy or consistent with the responsibilities and needs of the Nation.

Adequate protection against fire, insects, and disease will reduce the losses of merchantable timber and save for future timber production millions of seedlings and saplings now destroyed each year. Planting a substantial part of the 75 million acres now denuded or only poorly stocked with seedlings and saplings would lay the foundations for additional timber growth in the future. But improved forest practices applied to the timber now standing are the surest and quickest means of increasing annual growth.

A crop of wood cannot be grown in a single year like a crop of corn. Tomorrow's wood supply is in the trees growing in the forests today. It will take decades of good forestry, going far beyond what has been accomplished in the past, to develop a well-balanced growing stock that will meet future timber needs.

C. EDWARD BEHRE *is staff consultant in the Forest Service. He was graduated from Yale with a master's degree in forestry in 1917. From 1919 to 1923 he was on the faculty of the School of Forestry at the University of Idaho. Mr. Behre joined the staff of the Northeastern Forest Experiment Station at the time of its organization in 1923 and was its director from 1929 to 1942.*

# FOREST RESOURCES AND THE NATION'S ECONOMY

EDWARD C. CRAFTS, MARTHA A. DIETZ

Natural resources and human ingenuity determine a country's wealth, security, standing among nations, and the welfare of its people.

One of the natural resources is the forest, which supplies timber, water, forage, wildlife, and spiritual strength.

So common are the products and services of the forest in everyday living that their presence often is taken for granted and their essentiality overlooked. But when one analyzes the relationship of the forest to the Nation's economy and considers all the products and services, he sees the part they have in the lives of all the people.

INDUSTRY AND TRADE, to a large degree, depend on natural resources. Such dependency is sometimes obvious, more often obscure, and rarely tied to only one resource. Nevertheless, one standard for measuring the value of any resource is the size and essentiality of that segment of industry and trade so closely tied to it that the dependency relationship is obvious. The forest supports directly dependent industries impressive both in variety and size.

The growing of timber is the most obvious function of the forest. Timber, widely adaptable, is the backbone of a large group of conversion industries. With only crude shaping, splitting, or cutting, wood can be used as it comes from the forest—for fuel wood, posts, mine props, piling, and other rough uses. With relatively little processing, it is used as sawed lumber, shingles, railroad ties, veneers, and charcoal. In further processed form, it is consumed in housing, boxes and crates, cooperage, furniture, agricultural implements, truck bodies, boats, venetian blinds, baseball bats, and pencils. It is the basic raw material in pulp, paper, rayon, and a variety of other products. Extracts used in the tanning of hides and skins are produced from wood and the bark of certain trees. In addition, the living tree itself is a production plant for pine oleoresin, which is the raw material for turpentine, rosin, and other naval stores.

Since the Second World War, the average annual gross value of all timber products is estimated at 15 to 20 billion dollars.

Harvesting and primary manufacture of most timber products is con-

802062°—49——47

ducted near the logging site, because of the bulkiness of the raw material. Consequently, the primary manufacturing industries are widely dispersed, large in number, located in or near the forest, and generally far from centers of consumption. This is in contrast to many manufacturing industries for which nearness to markets, access to plentiful and cheap power, supplies of skilled or common labor, or other considerations are more important determinants of plant location than is proximity to raw materials.

In numbers, there are some 60,000 sawmills, 650 veneer and plywood plants, 325 shingle mills, 200 to 250 pulp plants, and a large number of miscellaneous and specialty plants. By far the greater number of these are in the East.

No reliable over-all estimates of investments in forest land, timber, and timber industries are available. The 1946 market value for timber purposes of all forest land and timber in the United States, public and private, was probably between 10 and 20 billion dollars.

The total capital investment in the lumber industry alone, including land and timber as well as buildings and equipment, may approximate 3 to 4 billion dollars. In the Douglas-fir area of Washington and Oregon, where there are heavy concentrations of large timber, a rough estimate of the investment in privately owned land and timber is about 1 to 1.25 billion dollars, with at least an additional 350 million dollars invested in logging improvements, equipment, and primary manufacturing plants.

Investment in individual establishments varies greatly, both within and among industries. For example, sawmills require initial capital outlays from a few thousand to several million dollars, and pulp mills from about 750 thousand dollars up, depending on kind and capacity. Investment per employee and per dollar of sales in the pulp and paper industry ranks among the highest in American industry. Modern steam distillation plants in the naval stores industry require an investment from 50 thousand to 250 thousand dollars. Other primary timber-products industries, excepting veneer and plywood, require comparatively small plant investment.

Estimates of the output and value of rough (nonmanufactured) forest products in 1947 show that sawlogs, fuel wood, and pulpwood logs and bolts had the highest total value. Together they represented about 80 percent of the total value of nonmanufactured timber products, or about 2.4 billion dollars. In each of seven States (Oregon, Washington, Georgia, North Carolina, Alabama, Mississippi, and California) the value of nonmanufactured timber products exceeded 100 million dollars. The East produced 75 percent of the national total.

Since the Second World War, the estimated average annual value of timber products in the first stage of manufacture has been about 4.2 billion dollars. This includes sawed wood, veneer, and plywood, 3.3 billion dollars; wood pulp, 730 million dollars; and naval stores, 120 million dollars; and miscellaneous products, 100 million dollars.

Secondary manufacture of forest products is the third major step in preparing timber products for the market—the first two being harvesting the raw material and initial or primary manufacture.

Some of the secondary industries rely almost entirely on wood as raw material, such as the wooden box and crate industry, wood sash, door and other millwork, hardwood flooring, wooden furniture, and wooden handles. Many more, however, such as paper, paper products, rayon manufacture, ship and boat building, and residential and other construction, utilize wood as only one of many raw materials. The separate contribution of wood, other raw materials, labor, managerial skills, and capital to the finished product is difficult to assess. Each is needed to finish the product.

Industrial and residential construction, the largest single market for lumber, accounts for about two-thirds of all lumber used annually in the United States. Nearly every one of the 40 million dwellings in the United States contains a substantial amount of wood. From one-fourth to one-third of the cost of the average house is for wood in some form. The exterior walls of three-fourths of all dwellings are made of wood; most have a wood framework; and wood is also used extensively for interior finish and trim.

In 1947, total construction activity in the United States was 21 billion dollars, a substantial part of which represented the cost of timber products, including the cost of labor and overhead to incorporate them into the structure.

The fabricated wood products, too numerous to list, add to the Nation's real income and standard of living. The wood-furniture industry alone creates products valued annually at about 1.3 billion dollars. Among the wood-fabricating industries, it is one of the largest consumers of wood. It is exceeded only by the box and millwork industries. The total estimated use of wood in all fabricated products in 1940 was 12 billion board feet.

Annually since the Second World War the paper and paperboard industry has manufactured products valued at about 2.5 billion dollars. Paper of all sorts (news, book, wrapping, writing, tissue, and building) and paperboard for boxes and containers are the principal products of this industry. Two of the raw materials required in their manufacture are products of the forest, that is, wood pulp (made from pulpwood) and rosin, which together account for more than 80 percent of the value of all raw materials used in paper making. Converted paper products have an estimated annual value of another 2.5 billion dollars.

The rayon yarn and fiber industry, which now puts more than 750 million dollars' worth of products on the market annually, also depends largely upon wood as a raw material. About 80 percent of the fibrous material used in rayon is wood pulp. Further processing of rayon yarns into textiles and apparel broadens the Nation's industrial structure by providing employment and additional manufactured products of great value and utility.

Trade in forest products is another important activity. The rough-timber products, such as fuel wood, fence posts, mine timbers, and poles, often pass directly from producer to consumer without entering wholesale or retail distribution channels. The more important primary products, such as lumber, veneer, cooperage, and pulp and paper, however, are normally distributed by wholesalers, retailers, and other middlemen.

Before the Second World War, 50 to 55 percent of the lumber produced reached consumers through some 25,000 retail yards, whose volume of sales equaled 1.5 billion dollars in 1939, the latest year for which we have data. The sale of lumber, millwork, plywood, lath, shingles, and other building materials of wood probably represented no more than half that amount. Total commodity sales of timber products from the 1,800 wholesale lumber and millwork establishments in that year were about 475 million dollars. Of the 600-million-dollar business that the wholesale paper and paper-products trade did in 1939, about 80 percent represented sales of paper and paper products. Since 1945, the annual dollar-volume sale of the wholesale trade in both lumber and millwork and paper and paper products is estimated to have trebled the prewar level, primarily because of increases in prices.

World distribution of timber resources and rates of depletion are dominant factors in determining the pattern of foreign trade in timber products. The United States is traditionally a net exporter of lumber, primarily because of the high domestic rate of softwood production and the general world scarcity of softwoods. Naval stores produced in the United States also are prominent in the export trade.

On the other hand, large United States requirements for paper and paper products, combined with limited timber resources and plant capacity for pulp and paper making, are major reasons why about one-third of the wood going into the paper consumed in the United States comes from foreign sources. Considering all timber products, the United States has long been a net importer. For example, in 1947 timber-product imports, valued at more than 800 million dollars, were more than twice as great as exports; other years show a similar pattern.

The transportation systems of the United States use large quantities of timber products, and also depend on them for much revenue freight.

Railroad track is laid on wooden cross, switch, and bridge ties. A great deal of lumber is used in railroad cars and the construction of bridges, stations, warehouses, and other structures.

Millions of feet of piling and lumber go into wharves and jetties. Wood is used extensively for bracing and holding cargo in place. Substantial amounts are used in boat and ship building as an integral part of the structure and as scaffolding. Naval stores are also used in boat and ship construction, although not so extensively as formerly.

Highway transportation depends partly on the timber supply, because road and bridge construction, as well as truck and trailer manufacture, requires wood.

The distribution of timber products by rail, water, and truck creates millions of tons of revenue freight each year. Before reaching the consumer, many timber products may be reshipped several times from forest to primary manufacturing plant, secondary processing plant, wholesaler, retailer, and finally to consumer. Often several forms of transportation are used in these various steps.

In 1946, Class I railways carried more than 100 million tons of timber products, including paper and furniture other than metal, or nearly 8 percent of all tonnage carried. About two thirds of this tonnage was in the form of logs, pulpwood, and lumber. With an average haul of about 450 miles, timber products accounted for about 45 billion ton-miles. In 1946, Class I railways received more than 535 million dollars in revenue from timber products, or nearly 9 percent of the revenue from all commodities.

Truck transportation has become the most important means of getting raw material out of the woods for the forest-products industries. About 80 percent of all sawlogs and veneer logs produced, 90 percent of all pulpwood, and more than 90 percent of all commercial poles, posts, piling, and mine timbers are transported all or part of the way from woods to plant or market by truck. Trucks are used almost exclusively to move lumber from thousands of small mills to concentration yards and to haul about 30 percent of total lumber tonnage all or part of the way to its first destination beyond concentration yards and sawmills.

Since the Second World War about 300 million tons of timber products have been transported annually by truck. Although this is three times the volume hauled by rail, truck hauls are short compared with rail transportation and average only 10 to 15 miles. Thus, trucking of timber products accounts for about 4 billion ton-miles annually, or less than one-tenth of the ton-miles by rail.

Water transportation is also significant in the domestic movement of timber products. In 1946 about 30 million tons of logs, lumber, pulpwood, wood pulp, and paper were moved to domestic destinations through inland waterways and by coastal and intercoastal routes. Logs alone accounted for two-thirds of this tonnage, which includes logs or pulpwood floated or driven on rivers. Domestic cargo shipments of poles, piling, posts, fuel wood, naval stores, tanning materials, furniture, and other timber products provided additional substantial tonnage. In terms of ton-miles, domestic water shipments of timber products probably exceed truck shipments.

In other ways, also, timber from the forest influences industry and trade. Electric power and rapid communication depend on the 50 million poles that support telephone, telegraph, and power lines. About 8 million new poles are needed each year for replacements and additional lines.

Coal heats homes and factories, powers industry, and moves trains. Wooden mine props, ties, lagging, and cribbing are essential to mining.

The timber industries, themselves, offer a substantial market for goods and services. For example, manufacturers of logging and specialized woodworking equipment and paper and pulp machinery are wholly dependent upon the timber supply. A substantial volume of trucks, tractors, power generators, and a great variety of small tools are also consumed.

Another function of the forest, one of the most important, is to supply water by protecting watersheds. Practically all industry and trade depend, in one way or another, on a supply of water that is adequate in amount and effectively controlled.

Permanent and prosperous industries and communities need an adequate water supply. Consumption is enormous. For example, the five main urban centers from Boston to Washington consume about 3.5 billion gallons of water daily. Good management of the forest cover at headwaters is one way of protecting the source.

In many parts of the West, water shortages are potentially and actually acute. As population and per capita consumption of water increase, many cities are going greater and greater distances in search of water. San Diego, Los Angeles, and San Francisco tap sources hundreds of miles away, and spend large sums for reservoirs, aqueducts, and pumping stations. The headwaters of nearly all lakes and rivers lie in forested areas.

Supplying water to homes and industry is the largest of municipal enterprises. In 1945, operating revenue from water-supply systems in cities that have populations of 25,000 or more was 310 million dollars, or nearly 150 percent greater than operating expenses. To the extent that such water originates from forest land, municipal water systems depend upon the forest.

All but three States use power developed from streams. Manufacturing industries in most sections partly depend on hydroelectric power. In 29 States water power is also important as a source of electric current for homes and city lighting. Water is the source of nearly one-fourth of the country's electric-power capacity, yet water power still undeveloped is capable of producing electric energy greater than that now supplied by both fuel and water. Good management of forest cover on upland watersheds is vital to safeguarding power development.

Conversion of stream flow to electric energy creates a market for goods and services by providing construction contractors and producers and distributors of materials with millions of dollars' worth of business. Dams built to store water for power production rank among the Nation's great engineering feats. One of the latest, the 2,160-foot-long earth and concrete Center Hill Dam in north-central Tennessee, built for hydroelectric-power production and flood control and completed in 1948, cost the United States about 33 million dollars; the Grand Coulee Dam in Washington cost more than 110 million dollars.

Rivers and lakes of the United States are important media in the distribution of goods. Between 1938 and 1947, freight commerce on the natural waterways averaged about 200 million tons annually, more than 20 billion ton-miles. Maintenance of an adequate forest cover materially aids navigation by retarding sedimentation, lessening floods, and maintaining more stable water levels.

Another major function of the forest is to produce forage in the form of grasses, weeds, and shrubs under trees and in openings. This forest range covers 350 million acres and represents more than one-half the total forest area of the United States and more than one-third of the total range area. Roughly, 155 million acres lie west of the Great Plains, representing nearly 70 percent of the total western forest area; 142 million acres of forest range occur in the South. By supporting large numbers of domestic livestock, forest ranges contribute significantly to the Nation's meat, wool, and leather industries. The proper utilization of forest range is of primary importance in multiple-use management of the forest resource.

There is no way to isolate and measure precisely the contribution of forest range to our industry, trade, and general economy. It is enough to recognize that large numbers of western livestock summer on forest range, that a great many fat cattle and sheep are marketed directly from far western ranges, and that the rural South would be hard-pressed indeed if its forest range were not utilized by the cattle and hogs that roam the piney woods.

Wildlife and recreation are linked closely with the forests.

Varied climates and habitat conditions of the forest lands are conducive to many species of fur bearers and birds. About 95 percent of the country's big game—deer, elk, moose, bighorn sheep, mountain goat, and bear—live in the forest. Roughly one-fourth of the small game and fur bearers are associated with wooded areas.

Camping, picnicking, winter sports, sightseeing, and similar recreation constitute another major service of the forest. For hunting and fishing alone during the 1946–47 season, nearly 25 million licenses were sold. It is estimated that more than a third of the hunters and fishermen went to forested areas.

Expenditures for sporting arms and fishing tackle in 1945 exceeded 60 million dollars, and nearly equaled all other expenditures for sporting goods. Annual cost to the hunters and fishermen in the forest for travel, food, and lodging is currently placed at about 750 million dollars. At least half a million people earn all or part of their living supplying goods and services to forest recreationists.

Agriculture also is linked to the forest. No longer is the forest an enemy to be cut down, burned, and destroyed. The farmer's own wood lot and the forest cover on the more distant hills and mountains provide protection against erosion, water for irrigation, essential timber products, and forage for livestock. Local forest industries also provide an outlet for truck crops and employment in the nonfarming season.

Forests are the principal source of the irrigation water, supplying roughly 300,000 farms in the United States. Irrigation agriculture has improved 20 million to 25 million acres of low-productivity land, increasing crop yield and materially enhancing land values. In the arid valleys of the West, intensive agriculture is made possible only by harnessing and applying to the land water which originates in the forested mountains. The forest cover markedly influences water-table levels and this affects the supply of irrigation water even in those areas where water is obtained from wells.

More than 95 percent of both the number of irrigated farms and acreage irrigated are located in 17 Western States and Arkansas and Louisiana. In 1945, although less than 18 percent of the total farm acreage in these States was irrigated, 27 percent (5 billion dollars) of the value of all farm lands and buildings was on farms wholly or partly irrigated. In 1939, capital invested in irrigation enterprises in 19 Western States exceeded one billion dollars.

Timber products are essential to the operation of the 6 million American farms. Much lumber, to begin with, is used on the farm for new dwellings, barns and other service buildings, and fences and for repair and maintenance.

Lumber and veneer also are used in baskets, boxes, barrels, and crates for shipping farm products. Many agricultural implements and equipment—wagons, tool handles, and feeding troughs—are made of wood. The bulk of the posts used on farms are wood. More than three-fourths of the 330 million wooden fence posts used annually in the United States are for farms. Like everyone else, farmers consume wood in the form of paper, furniture, and in numerous miscellaneous wood products.

Most farmers still depend on wood for fuel, although such use is steadily declining. Each year between 50 million and 60 million cords of wood are burned for fuel; about half of it is used by the rural population in the form of cordwood from the forest. More than one-third is waste from wood-manufacturing industries which use it for fuel. In the aggregate, fuel wood still constitutes the second largest use of our timber supply, the first being lumber.

Of approximately 7 million farm dwellings in the United States, nearly 95 percent are of wood construction—a considerably higher proportion than of either urban or rural nonfarm dwellings. The average farmhouse requires more lumber than the average urban dwelling. The average annual replacement of nonrepairable farm dwellings following the Second World War has been about 150,000; this construction requires about 2 billion board feet of lumber. Current annual requirements for both new farm construction and maintenance and repair total between 4 billion and 5 billion board feet.

An additional 1 billion to 1.5 billion board feet of lumber is consumed annually in the manufacture of boxes, crates, barrels, and baskets, which are used for the distribution of fresh fruits, vegetables, and other farm products. Although the amount of wood used in agricultural implements, including tool handles, is declining, roughly 125 million board feet is used annually for that purpose.

Wood lots are an asset to most farms. They provide timber products for farm use, are a source of supplementary cash income, and afford protection against the elements. In 1944 farm woodlands totaled 166 million acres, or nearly 15 percent of all land in farms, and on many farms the sale of forest products comprised more than half the value of all farm products sold.

Farm woodlands are an important component of the total forest economy, comprising nearly a third of our total commercial forest area. Nearly 85 percent of the farm woodland is commercial forest actually or potentially valuable in supplying commercial timber products. Although so seriously depleted or poorly managed that they produce no more than one-third to one-half the volume of wood they are capable of producing, farm forests nevertheless supply nearly one-fourth of the total output of sawlogs, one-third of the pulpwood and gum naval stores, and the bulk of the fence posts, cordwood used for fuel, and maple syrup and maple sugar. They also furnish large quantities of railroad ties, poles, pit props, wood naval stores, and numerous other forest products.

It is estimated that in 1947 the value of nonmanufactured forest products obtained from farm woodlands (including both products sold and those for home use) was about 700 million dollars, or 29 percent of the value of such products from all forest land. Ten States, all but one of which were in the South, each produced farm timber products valued at more than 25 million dollars.

The individual benefits from the forest in many ways. Not only does it contribute to his well-being and the national standard of living but also it offers many persons a livelihood that can be both secure and challenging, advantages of residence in stable and progressive communities, and spiritual and physical welfare.

Employment and income that can be attributed to the timber resource have not been estimated authoritatively. Several incomplete and not wholly comparable estimates in the aggregate indicate reasonably well the size of forest-based employment.

According to the United States Bureau of Labor Statistics, the average number of wage and salary workers in the lumber and timber basic-products industries gradually increased from 465,000 in 1939 to 716,000 in 1947. The Forest Service estimated that, in July 1944, 356,000 workers were employed in the woods and 509,000 workers at plants that use rough timber products, such as round logs or bolts, poles, bark, crude gums.

In 1946, it is estimated, there were the equivalent of 3.3 million man-years of full employment by persons productively engaged in activities that can be traced back basically to the timber resource. If the concept of attributing to one of the basic resources a fraction of total productive employment is acceptable, approximately 6 percent of the national total man-years of full employment in 1946 may be attributed to timber-based industries and trade. By a similar analysis, timber resources contributed 6.3 billion dollars of wages and salaries to persons productively engaged in 1946. This is equal to 5.7 percent of total wages and salaries in the Nation.

The proportion of total national income attributed to timber is slightly less than corresponding proportions of persons productively engaged or wages and salaries paid; similarly, the proportion of wages and salaries paid is less than the proportion of productive employment. These facts mean that the wages and salaries paid to persons engaged in economic activity attributable to timber are slightly less than the average for all economic activity and that other components of national income also are below average in timber-based activities.

From 1939 to 1947 in the lumber and timber basic-products industries the average hourly wages increased from 48.9 to 102.7 cents; weekly earnings from $19.02 to $43.45; and weekly hours from 39 to 42.2. Great seasonal and geographical variations are known to exist in not only these items but also working conditions.

Managed forests improve communities: If the forest resource is to fulfill its potential in building and supporting a strong economic and social structure, it must be managed in the broadest sense of the term. Mismanagement of growing stock through continued utilization in excess of long-term productive capacity leads only to forest destruction and a boom-and-bust type of community.

On the other hand, an important natural resource is unnecessarily wasted if there are too few wood-using industries in a particular area or if they are not diversified enough to permit full utilization of the raw material commensurate with leaving the land reasonably productive and on its way to producing another crop.

A balance between the continuous productive capacity of the forest and the size, number, and kinds of wood-using industries in a particular area means permanent communities at a reasonably high living standard. This in turn means good schools, churches, hospitals, service businesses, public libraries, and other cultural, economic, and social advantages.

The national economy is an imprecise concept. It is a synthesis of all the factors that comprise the national life. Its goodness is tested by things that American citizens hold dear: Security, high standard of living, progress, freedom, free enterprise, opportunity. The discipline of economics is too restrictive to embrace more than a few of the standards that gage the national economy, but all too often these are taken as the total.

We have described so far some of the varied contributions of the forest resource to the national economy. Attempts to express the value of such contributions in dollars are not only impractical but also misleading and undesirable because of their inadequacy. Forest values transcend the dollar concept. How is it possible, for example, to assess in dollars the essentiality of wood in wartime, or the saving of lives by reduction of peak floods, or the restoration of health and spirit by play and rest in the forest?

Besides the contributions of the forest to industry, trade, agriculture, and the individual that have been discussed, the relation of timber resources to national security and income merits consideration.

As to national security, the essentiality of wood can be judged by the extent and character of its military uses and its importance in recovery from the effects of war.

In 1940 and 1941, the United States used about 6.5 billion feet of lumber for military purposes, or the equivalent of total military consumption in all of the First World War. During the four subsequent years (1942–45), an estimated 101 billion board feet of lumber was consumed for military purposes, as follows: 49 percent for construction; 42 percent for boxes, crating, and dunnage; and 9 percent for fabricated products. That was 70 percent of the amount of lumber consumption for all purposes, or enough to build more than 9.5 million average-sized five-room frame houses, a number equal to about one-fourth of all houses existing in the United States in 1940.

In 1942 alone, nearly 12 billion board feet of lumber was used for building cantonments and other military structures. New factories and plants, built for the manufacture of implements of war, and new houses for war workers called for additional amounts of construction lumber. The building of every Liberty ship took 350,000 board feet. The capture of a strategic point was often accompanied by heavy damage to existing facilities. For example, following the capture of Naples by Allied forces, 50 million feet of lumber was requied to put the port on a temporary operating basis.

Huge quantities of lumber in the form of boxes, crating, and dunnage were used in the shipment of supplies and material. Each 10,000-ton cargo ship took 250,000 feet to brace the cargo. For every soldier sent overseas, 300 board feet of lumber was required to box and crate his initial supplies, and nearly 50 feet of lumber per month was needed to maintain him. A crate for an airplane took about 5,000 board feet. The need for lumber for shipment of military goods reached a peak in 1944—about 10 billion feet.

Fabricated products required lumber of the highest quality and most exacting specifications for such items as aircraft, firearms, pontons, military trucks, boats and ships, tanks and vats, freight cars, tool handles, and furniture. A PT boat required 28,000 board feet of lumber; each submarine chaser 200,000 feet for decks, bulkheads, and other uses; each escort carrier a similar amount of high-grade Douglas-fir for the flight deck alone. About 50 million feet of high-quality wood was consumed for Army rifle stocks in a year.

Timber products other than lumber are equally essential. During the Second World War, plywood and veneer were used for boat hulls, life rafts, trucks, freight cars, torpedo boats, landing craft, containers, and radar equipment. One cord of pulpwood made smokeless powder for 90,000 rounds of ammunition for a Garand rifle, or 24 rounds for 16-inch naval shells, or 1,800 containers, or 4,200 waterproof packages for shipping blood plasma, or 1,480 paper parachutes for dropping supplies or flares, or 800 wadded paper vests for high-altitude flying.

Timber is a key component in the economic recovery of a nation from the debilitation of war. Although timber-import needs of the 16 countries (and western Germany) participating in the European Recovery Program represent only 4.4 percent (2.5 billion dollars) of the total value of recommended imports of all commodities, the importance of timber to European economic recovery is far greater than the proportion indicates.

Without timber, recovery would be ineffective, even if other import needs were met. For example, timber is required as pit props to make possible the restoration of coal mining, as cross ties for the reconstruction of the European railway system, for construction and rebuilding of damaged factories and homes for the agricultural population, for the new hydroelectric plants, and for poles for transmission of communications and power.

Although immediate timber needs of the participating countries are 40 percent greater than their own expected production, the long-term value of forests is so well recognized that the countries are determined, despite the immediate need, to maintain their forests on sustained-yield or its approximate equivalent, and to rehabilitate promptly those overcut or otherwise damaged during the war.

Timber resources of the United States have been so reduced by long-continued overcutting and lack of forestry measures that requirements of another emergency similar to the Second World War could be met only by extraordinary measures, and would greatly reduce growing stock and virtually exhaust high-quality material of certain species.

In terms of economic activity, the timber resource contributes an important share of national income and gross national product. National income is based on an industrial classification permitting comparison between industries, and includes such items as wages and salaries, business profits, interest and rents, dividends, and transfer and miscellaneous income payments.

Assuming that timber resources are basically responsible for certain segments of economic activity, it is estimated that in 1946 the national income attributable to timber resources was 5.4 percent of the total national income, or 9.6 billion dollars. This estimate is crude and subject to challenge because it overlooks the interdependence between different raw materials and between materials and human effort. For example, all economic activity in the lumber and timber basic-products industries is ascribed to the timber resource, even though the industries depend upon the mineral resource for machinery and other equipment. The proportions of other economic activities attributable to the timber resource vary widely and are difficult to estimate, but the over-all estimate (5.4 percent) is conservative, and other estimates have approximated 10 percent. Certainly, if other forest resources besides timber were included, the proportion of total national income attributable to all forest resources might exceed 10 percent.

It is wrong to conclude that national income would drop by 5 or 10 percent if activities based on timber or forest resources were eliminated. Theoretically, alternative activities would partly replace forest activities, but at the cost of a reduction in standards of living. Of far more import, however, and based on considerations of history, biology, and security, which override economics, is the inescapable conclusion that without forests this Nation would not long survive.

EDWARD C. CRAFTS *is chief of the Division of Forest Economics in the Forest Service.*

MARTHA A. DIETZ *is a forest economist in that Division.*

ESTIMATED PULP PRODUCTION AND PULPWOOD REQUIRED TO MEET THAT PRODUCTION, UNITED STATES, 1950–55

| *Type of pulp* | *Required pulp production* | *Conversion factor* | *Pulpwood required* |
|---|---|---|---|
| | *1,000 tons* | | *1,000 cords* |
| Ground wood | 2,294 | 1.10 | 2,085 |
| Sulfite | 2,037 | .55 | 3,704 |
| Sulfate | 8,071 | .65 | 12,417 |
| Soda | 459 | .58 | 791 |
| Other | 3,029 | 1.10 | 2,754 |
| Total | 15,890 | | 21,751 |

# FUTURE REQUIREMENTS FOR TIMBER

A. C. CLINE

When we estimate our future needs for timber, we have to be concerned with many products besides lumber—fiberboards, plastics, modified woods, alcohol, fodder yeast, and others of the exciting array that modern chemistry has given us. We must plan on meeting requirements for all kinds of pulp and paper products, the liquid fuels, wood sugars, and plywood. Perhaps, also, atomic energy will make obsolete all our ideas about heating and power. Even though great changes like these lie ahead, we cannot discard the experience that people have accumulated these thousands of years. The wisest policy is to plan on a growing population and a rising standard of living and dependence on the forest.

In this article, the country's future requirements for timber are termed "potential timber requirements"—the quantity of timber products that might be used by consumers who are afforded reasonable latitude in choice of readily available materials, including timber products, in a national economy functioning at a high level of employment and output. The definition differs from definitions of future consumption or of future demand based on whatever economic conditions happen to be at any given future time. Of course, the assumed condition of ready availability may not come to pass. It is plain that, unless the present trend toward forest depletion is reversed, the timber shortage will become more and more acute, prices will go still higher, and effective demand for timber will decline.

Emphasis is placed on requirements for trees of saw-timber size, because nearly 80 percent of all timber products are cut from such trees. Small trees from unmanaged forests might supply our future requirements for such products as pulpwood, fuel wood, fence posts, and small poles, which can be got from poorer and smaller trees, but not requirements for lumber, plywood, and other high-grade products.

In 1944 the commercial cutting of timber resulted in the removal of 49.7 billion board feet of saw timber; losses of 4.2 billion from fire, disease, insects, and so on brought the total saw-timber drain to 53.9 billion board feet. At the same time, annual saw-timber growth was 35.3 billion board feet. Thus, the excess of saw-timber drain over growth is slightly more than 50 percent.

The separate items making up the saw-timber drain in 1944 (in billion board feet) were:

| | |
|---|---|
| Lumber | 34. 4 |
| Pulpwood | 4. 8 |
| Fuel wood | 3. 9 |
| Veneer—logs and bolts | 2. 0 |
| Railroad ties—hewed | 1. 6 |
| Cooperage stock | . 7 |
| Mine timbers | . 3 |
| Shingles | . 3 |
| Other | 1. 7 |
| Losses due to fire, diseases, insects, etc | 4. 2 |
| Total | 53. 9 |

Timber products whose end use is the primary form, that is, those that require no processing in a sawmill or other type of manufacturing plant, will be taken up first. They are also called the nonmanufactured products, because they are produced in the forest principally with the use of only hand tools. They include fuel wood, poles, piling, posts, mine timbers, and railroad ties. The major products in this group account for 19.8 percent of the all-timber drain, but only 8.8 percent of the saw-timber drain. The proportions are somewhat smaller than actual, because there are a few other products whose end use is in the primary form; for example, wood poles used in shade-grown tobacco, rough wood used for dunnage in storing ship cargo, and round and split material used in rustic construction.

The requirements for fuel wood are declining. In 1880, the country consumed about 146 million cords of fuel wood, but only 62 million in 1945. The drop, despite a large increase in population, is due to the increased use of more efficient and convenient fuels, including coal, oil, gas, and electricity. The fuel-wood drain on the forest is further lessened by the fact that only one-half or less of the total quantity consumed is cut from sound, living trees, the remainder coming from cull and dead trees or industrial waste from logging and milling operations. Moreover, the cutting of sound, living trees for fuel wood can be limited largely to trees of small size or inferior species that should be removed from the forest in the course of thinnings and other cuttings made to improve the final timber harvest.

Looking into the future, it appears likely that the per capita requirements for fuel wood will decline still further. The United States has abundant supplies of coal. The present wood waste from logging and milling operations that now goes to feed boilers may find a more profitable outlet in the field of chemical utilization of wood waste. Farms and other rural buildings eventually will be supplied with electricity; it is those outlets that now consume most of the fuel wood. Atomic power may lower the cost of producing electricity for all heating purposes, thus further reducing the use of other fuels. On the other hand, should the need arise, wood can be substituted for other fuels, even to the extent of powering motorcars and motortrucks. And automatic wood-burning stoves have been invented that are a great improvement over the ordinary stove, in both convenience and efficiency.

It is estimated that fuel-wood requirements in 1950–55 will be about 60 million cords, declining to about 50 million a half century from now.

Requirements for poles—telephone, telegraph, electric light, and other utility-line poles made of wood—increased from about 3.7 million in 1909 to nearly 8 million in 1947. Nearly one-third of all the poles put in place now are for rural electrification. But there is a general trend in cities to put wires underground, and new developments in communications permit large numbers of messages to be sent without a corresponding increase in the number of lines. Ways and means will still be sought to eliminate pole lines, because they are repeatedly damaged by storms and other destructive forces, they are unsightly, and they take up space needed for other uses.

Changes are also taking place in the kind of poles used. Chestnut, northern white-cedar, and the western redcedar used to be preferred because of their durability; later, preservative treatment and a shortage of the preferred species gave first place to southern pine and Douglas-fir. In 1910 less than 20 percent of the poles produced received any preservative treatment whatever; now nearly 95 percent are treated.

The telephone and telegraph companies probably will not materially increase their use of wood poles; even now, some long-distance communications lines are going underground—especially in localities subject to severe ice storms. And eventually the rural electrification program will be largely on a maintenance basis.

For the period 1950–55, potential annual requirements for poles are estimated at about 5.7 million. Looking 50 years ahead, annual requirements may not be more than 5 million.

In 1947 the production of poles that were preservatively treated was divided among the various species as follows:

| | *Percent* |
|---|---|
| Southern pine | 74.0 |
| Douglas-fir | 9.1 |
| Western redcedar | 5.1 |
| Lodgepole pine | 6.4 |
| Northern white-cedar | 1.9 |
| Ponderosa pine | .4 |
| Mixed species | 3.1 |
| Total | 100.0 |

A large part of future pole requirements can be got from thinnings made in dense stands to relieve congestion and give the selected saw-timber crop trees more room for growth. Thus the same stand that yields saw timber can also yield poles without materially reducing the output of the former.

Wood piling ranges from about 30 feet to more than 90 feet in length and from a top diameter of 5 inches to a butt diameter of about 2 feet. The best grades of piles are suitable for heavy railway bridges and trestles, piers, and other heavy construction; the poorest grades can be used for light building foundations, cofferdams, false work, and various temporary work.

Before the Second World War, consumption of treated piling averaged about 16.5 million linear feet annually. Assuming that 60 percent were treated (the correct percentage is not known), total consumption was about 28 million. Potential annual requirements for 1950–55 have been estimated at 38 million linear feet, with a drop to about 23 million 50 years hence.

As in the case of poles, this need not be a heavy drain on the forest. Dense stands of second-growth timber will yield excellent piling through the removal of trees in thinnings made to improve the final saw-timber crop. Such trees are slender in form and have the dense wood desired in piling, because they are crowded and partially overtopped by the main crop trees.

The species used for piling that was preservatively treated in 1947 ranked as follows:

| | *Percent* |
|---|---|
| Southern pine | 74. 9 |
| Douglas-fir | 20. 8 |
| Oak | . 8 |
| Norway pine | . 3 |
| Western redcedar | . 1 |
| Jack pine | . 1 |
| Ponderosa pine | . 1 |
| All others | 2. 9 |
| Total | 100. 0 |

Fence posts are used chiefly on farms, and most of them are cut in farm wood lots. Many species are used, but the more durable and preferred ones are Osage-orange, cedar, chestnut, locust, and catalpa; they have an average life of 15 to 30 years or more. Oaks, walnut, and cherry are somewhat shorter lived; some of the pines, willow, and cottonwood are good for about 5 years.

Preservative treatment greatly increases the service life of posts, but as yet comparatively few posts are treated. In 1947, about 12 million were treated out of a total of several hundred million put in place. A survey in 1937 showed that about 460 million posts were put into use on farms in that year; that does not include posts for the highways, railroads, industrial plants, and other nonfarm uses.

The potential annual requirement for posts in 1950–55 is estimated at about 600 million, of which 80 percent would be cut from sound, living trees.

Posts can be cut from trees that need to be removed in thinnings and other cuttings in immature stands to improve the quality of later saw-timber harvests. Both fuel wood and fence posts needed on the farm can generally be got at the same time that the farm wood lot is being improved.

Mine timbers, hewed or round, include mine ties, pit props, legs and posts, horizontal cross bars (or collars), lagging and cribbing, and caps used for tightening props and legs. Certain items are used both in the sawed and in the round or hewed state.

The quantities of wood used per unit of mine output vary not only with the kind of material mined—bituminous coal, anthracite coal, iron ore, or precious metals—but also with the type of extraction, such as underground or surface mining. One of the early surveys, in 1905, showed a total consumption of 165 million cubic feet of round material and 435 million board feet of sawed. Then pine comprised one-half of the softwood round timber and one-third of the softwood sawed timber; oak was the leading hardwood species. Of course, what species are favored depends on the location of the mine. In the precious-metal mines—all in the West—western pines and Douglas-fir were favored, while in the anthracite mines of Pennsylvania, oak was way ahead and pine a poor second.

In 1935, about half of all mine timber was sawed, whereas 30 years earlier two-thirds was round, split, or hewed. But, unlike poles or railroad ties, the preservative treatment of mine timbers has showed little change. As late as 1935, only 1 percent, in volume, of mine timber was treated; also, only 14 percent of all mine material was steel and concrete. Evidently the fact that mine timbers in most cases are abandoned after a short time makes it unprofitable to resort to preservative treatment or to use the more costly materials.

As of 1935, it was estimated that requirements in the next 10 years would rise to something like 250 million cubic feet, of which some 130 million would be in the round and the rest, equivalent to 550 million board feet, sawed timber.

In 1950–55, for all mines and quarries in the United States, it is estimated that potential annual requirements for round, split, and hewed timber will approximate 220 million cubic feet, with little change 50 years hence.

Under good forest-management practices such quantities can be got without heavy drain on saw-timber growing stocks. Mine timbers can be cut chiefly from the smaller or poorer trees removed in improvement cuttings in stands being managed primarily for higher-quality products.

Railroad ties are mostly sawed, and because sawed material is classed as lumber, the requirements for railroad cross ties will be discussed later, under lumber requirements of the railroads. The latest record of tie consumption, based on the number of ties preservatively treated in 1947, showed 63 percent of all cross ties sawed and 37 percent hand-hewed, out of a total of nearly 48 million. Because at least 90 percent of all cross ties are treated, somewhat more than 50 million ties may be taken as the current annual consumption.

It is estimated that the potential annual requirement for all railroad cross ties in 1950–55 is about 52 million, of which about 22 million will be hewed—equivalent to 238 million cubic feet. Requirements for hewed ties 50 years hence are estimated to be substantially lower, in line with the generally increasing proportion of sawed timber products as compared with hewed—perhaps not more than 18 million, or 194 million cubic feet.

The heaviest drain on the forest is caused by cutting sawlogs to make lumber. Although the per capita consumption of lumber has declined from a peak of more than 500 board feet in the early 1900's to less than 300 feet at present, the growth in population compensates in a large measure for declining per capita use. Lumber production in 1947 and 1948 (about 35.5 billion board feet) was only 5 percent below the average for the decade from 1920 to 1930.

Based on estimated potential lumber requirements in 1950–55, the major fields of lumber use rank in importance as follows (in billion board feet and percentages):

| | *Billion board feet* | *Percent* |
|---|---|---|
| Construction (including railroad car lumber, flooring, and millwork) | 31.5 | 74 |
| Fabricated wood products | 5.0 | 12 |
| Shipping uses | 6.0 | 14 |
| Total | 42.5 | 100 |

Lumber is used in an endless number of structures—houses, barns, factories, business buildings, mining structures, waterfront facilities, airports, fire towers, barracks. Of greatest importance now is housing.

Housing (other than farm houses) represents nearly 35 percent of total construction requirements; farm contruction, including maintenance and epair, represents about 20 percent.

The postwar housing shortage grew rom failure during the depression ears to keep pace with the growing population and to restrictions on all inds of civilian construction during he war. In 1946, the President created he Office of the Housing Expediter, which set goals of 1,250,000 housing units to be started in 1946 and 1,500,-000 in 1947. According to the National Housing Agency, a rate of 1,250,000 new dwelling units a year needs to be maintained for at least 10 years. Such a rate has not yet been attained. It was estimated that somewhat fewer than a million units were started in 1948.

The Joint Committee on Housing of the 80th Congress recommended housing legislation to provide additional aids to housing "which are needed to reach and maintain housing production at a rate of 1,250,000 to 1,500,000 dwellings per year . . ." It also found that "a very substantial proportion of our existing supply of housing falls far below minimum standards of decency." The Committee concluded, "We should have a construction program that will produce at least 15,500,000 nonfarm housing units between now and the end of 1960. This would call for the average annual construction of not less than 1,285,000 nonfarm units."

The National Conference on Family Life also reported in May 1948: "The supply [of lumber] does not appear to be sufficient, however, to permit any increase in house building at the price levels at which any increase should occur. The upward sweep of lumber prices to new record levels month after month has been strong evidence of the affects of a heavy pressure of demand against a supply that is even now not entirely adequate."

Here is an illustration of the distinction between potential requirements and effective demand. Lumber had priced itself out of the low-income market, and thousands of families in need of housing continued to live with other families, in trailers, or in makeshift accommodations.

It has been estimated that the 1,250,000 housing units annually required would take nearly 11 billion board feet of lumber, as follows:

| *Type of unit* | *Number* | *Lumber content (million bd. ft.)* |
|---|---|---|
| One- and two-family conventional | 400, 000 | 5, 120 |
| One-family cottage type | 200, 000 | 2, 000 |
| Multiple-family conventional | 400, 000 | 2, 560 |
| Prefabricated | 250, 000 | 1, 250 |
| Total | 1, 250, 000 | 10, 930 |

The estimate makes some allowance for the increasing substitution of plywood, building boards, concrete, brick, and metals for lumber, a trend that appears likely to continue.

Housing requirements 50 years hence will depend largely on the population increase between now and then. A conservative estimate of 167 million persons has been used, or about 43 million families. With the necessary allowance for about 5 percent vacancy, and for a 40-year replacement basis, the number of housing units required annually would be about 1.1 million. Assuming 8,000 board feet as the average quantity of lumber per unit 50 years hence, the total potential requirement would be about 9 billion board feet.

FARM CONSTRUCTION, including maintenance and repair, also failed to keep pace with needs during the long period of depressed farm income in the 1930's and the years when military requirements had first call on lumber supply. The Secretary of Agriculture in a statement to the 79th Congress reported that about two-thirds of the Nation's farm families are not adequately housed and that one-third are living in houses in such poor condition that they are virtually beyond repair.

Farm housing requirements for the next decade are estimated at 150,000 units annually, with an average of 14,000 board feet of lumber per unit, or a total of 2.1 billion board feet. About 5 billion board feet is needed annually for normal replacements and repair of farm buildings, and about 1 billion for other farm uses, making a grand total of 8.1 billion board feet. If we assume that 20 percent of the lumber in the buildings torn down will be used again, the net potential annual requirement for all farm uses in 1950–55 is about 6.5 billion board feet.

Fifty years hence, even with a total population 20 percent greater than at present, the farm population is not expected to gain any; some forecasters think it will decline further. But it is generally held that the average size of farms will continue to grow, which means more or larger buildings per farm and consequently more lumber required per farm than now. Taking those various counteractive factors into consideration, requirements are estimated at about the same level as in 1950–55.

RAILROAD CONSTRUCTION AND MAINTENANCE includes requirements for sawed ties (which are classed as lumber), railroad car lumber, and all railroad maintenance. There are about 1 billion cross ties in Class I railway tracks throughout the United States and about 24,000 miles of track laid with switch and bridge ties.

Although no satisfactory substitute for the wooden cross tie has been found, many changes have taken place in its use during past years. In 1920, nearly 86 million cross ties were laid, 56 percent of them untreated. Today, the number laid is from 45 to 50 million, and the percentage preservatively treated is nearly 95. Preservative treatment has nearly doubled the service life of ties, so that a treated tie properly laid is good for 25 to 30 years.

Changes in the percentages of the different tree species used for making ties that are treated are not so striking, as shown by the following compari sons:

| *Species* | *1914 Percentage* | *1947 Percentag* |
|---|---|---|
| Oak | 37 | 36. |
| Southern pine | 24 | 18. |
| Douglas-fir | 18 | 8. |
| Gum | 2 | 8. |
| Ponderosa pine | 5 | 1. |
| Lodgepole pine | --- | 1. |
| Tamarack (larch) | 2 | 1. |
| All other | 12 | 23. |
| Total | 100 | 100. |

The source of the 1914 figures i the Division of Forest Products of th Forest Service; the 1947 figures cam from the Forest Service publication *Preliminary Wood Preservation Sta tistics,* June 1948.

As to future requirements for cros ties, the continued improvement i highways and the increased use o motortrucks is offset to some degree b the need for more tracks on many line that have an increased traffic. Demands for greater speed in transportation makes greater the needs fo multiple-track lines.

It is estimated that for 1950–55 th potential requirements for cross tie will be at the rate of 143 ties a mil (135 for replacement and 8 for new trackage) for some 365,000 miles o track, or about 52 million cross tie annually. That compares with nearl 48 million preservatively treated i 1947 (treated ties comprise nearly 95 percent of all ties). Because the average cross tie contains about 35 boar feet, the total volume required is abou 1.8 billion board feet. Assuming tha 30 million ties are sawed and 22 million hewed, the total annual requirement for ties made by sawmills would be about 1.05 billion board feet. Potential requirements for switch and bridge ties in 1950–55 are estimated at 200 million board feet annually.

As for lumber for cars, some marked changes have occurred during the past few decades. Since 1925 there has been nearly a 25 percent decrease in the number of freight cars in use; since 1928 the use of lumber in their construction and repair has been reduced by nearly one-half. Metal has displaced wood as a freight-car material. Potential requirements in the 1950–55 period, even with heavy traffic, are placed at 600 million board feet.

In the case of general railroad maintenance, the trend is also away from wooden structures and toward steel and concrete. Potential requirements for such uses in 1950–55 are estimated at 425 million board feet annually.

In summary, potential annual requirements for lumber by the railroads in millions of board feet in 1950–55 are:

| | |
|---|---|
| Cross ties (sawed only) | 1,050 |
| Bridge and switch ties | 200 |
| Freight-car lumber | 600 |
| All other maintenance | 425 |
| Total | 2,275 |

In addition to the round and hewed material, the mines also have requirements for lumber. Annual needs for sawed mine timber, of all kinds, in the period 1950–55 are estimated at 500 million board feet.

All other new construction includes such classes as commercial buildings, manufacturing and power plants, schools, hospitals, telephone and telegraph facilities, marine construction, highways, airports, water supply and sanitation, and construction distinctly military in character. Public works are an important segment of this group; it has been estimated that a backlog of 75 billion dollars of needed public works exists. It includes more than 40 billion dollars for highways and 10 billion dollars for schools.

Lumber consumption for these construction uses is determined by applying board-feet-per-dollar conversion factors to the dollar-volume of estimates made currently by Government agencies. By determining the past relationship between dollar volume of construction and gross national product (the total value of currently produced goods and services flowing to all consumers, to Government, and for purposes of gross capital formation) and estimating what the gross national product will be in the future under conditions of full employment, a basis is obtained for estimating potential requirements for lumber.

Of course, certain allowances have to be made. The changes that will take place in the board-feet-per-dollar conversion factors cannot be accurately predicted. It is to be expected that the proportion of lumber may continue to decrease somewhat in relation to that of steel, concrete, and other more durable and fireproof materials especially preferred in heavy construction.

The annual dollar volume (on a 1946 price basis) of construction in 1950–55 is estimated as 4.86 billion dollars for all private construction (commercial, industrial, and so on); 2.83 billion dollars for all private utilities construction; 2.5 billion dollars for all public construction (educational, institutional, and so on); and 5.33 billion dollars for all other public works (military, highways, airports, conservation, and so on). The indicated potential lumber requirements for all these is 8,508 million board feet.

All other maintenance and repair includes lumber requirements for maintaining and repairing all types of structures except farm buildings and those connected with the railroads and mines. As in the case of new construction, the increased use of plywood, composition wallboard, and other substitutes for lumber must be taken into account, as well as the lesser amount of upkeep and repair required where durable materials like steel and concrete are used in construction. Taking these various factors into consideration, potential annual requirements for all other maintenance and repair in 1950–55 are estimated at 2.7 billion board feet.

Requirements 50 years hence for all other new construction and maintenance and repair (all except nonfarm

802062°—49——48

residential and farm) and for railroad and mine operation will be influenced by the increased volume of construction necessitated by a larger population and the increased use of substitute materials and preservative treatment to prolong the service life of wood. Potential annual requirements 50 years hence for these uses have been estimated at 12.5 billion board feet, as compared with 14.0 billion feet in the period 1950–55.

FABRICATED PRODUCTS include thousands of different articles made of wood, many of them requiring lumber of the choicest species and highest qualities.

Furniture is the most common product in the group. Others are handles, musical instruments, caskets, vehicles, tanks, vats, boats, toys, sporting goods, military truck bodies, boats and ships, life rafts and floats, pontons, firearms, and aircraft. It is in fabricated wood products that foreign woods, such as balsa, teak, and mahogany, are in great demand for special purposes.

The domestic species used range from soft paper birch (for turning) to tough-textured white ash and hickory (for tool handles) and the fancy figured furniture made from black walnut, birdseye maple, and figured redgum. Some woods are preferred because of their physical properties, others because of pleasing appearance. The supply of some of the most highly prized woods, such as Port-Orford-cedar for battery separators, and high-quality hard maple, yellow birch, and white oak for furniture, is growing short. In certain articles, substitute materials, including metals, plastics, and plywood, find increasing use.

Consumer demand for the less-essential fabricated products bears a direct relationship to disposable income. In other cases, like caskets, matches, and pencils, the demand remains comparatively constant. The consumption of such products as pattern stock, textile machinery parts, and laundry appliances by industry rises or falls with the general level of industrial production.

Past surveys of fabricated products showed the following total quantities of lumber consumed (not including car lumber, hardwood flooring, and millwork) in million board feet:

| | |
|---|---|
| 1912 | 5, 319 |
| 1928 | 4, 319 |
| 1940 | 2, 771 |

For the period 1950–55, under the assumed high level of employment and output, it is estimated that potential annual requirements for fabricated wood products will be 5 billion feet.

FOR SHIPPING PURPOSES we use all kinds of wooden boxes and crates made from lumber; lumber is used as dunnage and blocking, pallets, skids, reels, grain doors, cleats in plywood or veneer boxes and crates, and other containers or equipment used in shipping or in handling and stowing goods for shipment.

Before the Second World War, consumption of shipping lumber reached a high point of 6.5 billion board feet in 1923 and 1927, with an average of 4.9 billion for 1920–40. During the war it rose to 15.5 billion.

The importance of an adequate supply of lumber for shipping the products of our farms and factories can scarcely be exaggerated. The increasing use of paperboard has made little change in the demand for lumber in the heavier types of containers needed for shipping machinery, aircraft parts, electrical equipment, and so forth, and lumber is also still the preferred material for shipping fresh fruits and vegetables. Of course, shifts have been made from wooden boxes to fiber cartons for many commodities, but from the standpoint of the timber resource this merely results in a reduced demand for lumber and an increased demand for paperboard—both made from trees.

On the basis of a continuing high level of production and increased foreign trade, potential requirements for shipping lumber in 1950–55 have been estimated at six billion board feet annually.

THE TOTAL ESTIMATED REQUIREMENTS for lumber for all purposes can be summarized thus (in million board feet):

| | 1950–55 | 1999 |
|---|---|---|
| Construction (total) | 31, 500 | 28, 000 |
| Housing other than farm | 11, 000 | 9, 000 |
| Farm, including maintenace and repair | 6, 500 | 6, 500 |
| Railroads | 2, 300 | |
| Mines | 500 | |
| All other new construction | 8, 500 | 12, 500 |
| All other maintenance and repair | 2, 700 | |
| Fabricated products | 5, 000 | 5, 000 |
| Shipping uses | 6, 000 | 6, 000 |
| Total | 42, 500 | 39, 000 |

THE USE OF VENEER AND PLYWOOD has grown phenomenally in recent years.

Plywood is strong and stiff in proportion to its weight and relatively free from warping and shrinking. It can be molded into various forms, including shapes with compound curves. Adding further to its versatility are developments in bonding surface plies of other materials, such as metals and plastics, to wood inner plies; and the so-called sandwich construction that employs varying combinations of materials. The famous British Mosquito bomber used in the Second World War had wing surfaces of sandwich construction with a thick, inner core of balsa wood and an outer surface of yellow birch veneer.

The main uses of veneer and plywood are in construction, containers, and fabricated products. In building construction, the use of softwood plywood has grown enormously—for paneling, sheathing, subfloors, and even siding. "Stressed skin" plywood panels are especially adaptable to prefabricated housing. Container veneer is widely used in boxes, crates, baskets, hampers, and various other types of packages—made of both softwood and hardwood. Fabricated products such as furniture, radio cabinets, and small boats require large quantities of the highest grades of plywood, much of it from woods chosen for their natural beauty.

In 1925 the production of softwood plywood was 150 million square feet. Now the industry has an annual production of about 2 billion square feet. Hardwood plywood likewise has spurted ahead—from a production of 800 million square feet just before the Second World War to nearly 1,200 million in the latter part of the war.

Potential annual requirements for veneer and plywood in 1950–55 are estimated to be 1.3 billion board feet (log scale) for construction, 600 million for containers, and 500 million for fabricated products. The total is 2.4 billion board feet.

Because veneer and plywood production requires high-grade logs, the future of the industry is linked closely with forest management, especially the extent to which high-quality trees in the larger sizes are grown. For the present, the industry is faced with a diminishing supply of the high-grade veneer logs and is gradually being forced to resort to patching defects and using less desirable species and smaller logs, other facing materials, or wood faces from imported woods.

FOR COOPERAGE STOCK—the staves and heading from which barrels, kegs, tubs, hogsheads, and similar containers are made—logs and bolts are needed. Cooperage may be either tight or slack, the former being tightly fitted to hold liquids, and both hardwoods and softwoods are required. Wood of high quality free from defects is required for tight cooperage. Large quantities of the finest white oak have been used for barrels, and the present stand of such timber is inadequate to meet potential requirements.

With the growing use of metal barrels, multiwall paper bags, plywood and fiber drums, tank-car shipments of liquids, and other substitute methods of packaging and shipping liquids and granular or powdered material, the cooperage industry has steadily declined—from 2 billion board feet log scale in 1909 to 746 million in 1939.

The potential annual requirement in 1950–55 has been estimated at 775 million board feet, with a decline to around 700 million 50 years hence.

PULPWOOD as a raw material yields thousands of different paper and paperboard products, plastics, cellulose yarns, and many other articles in everyday use.

There seems to be no end to the growing demands for pulpwood products. The production of all kinds of paper and paperboard has nearly doubled in the past 20 years. Per capita demand has grown at a faster rate than has population, as new uses for paper and pulp products constantly have been developed.

In estimating pulpwood requirements, the many uses and also the various processes by which wood is transformed into pulp must be taken into account, because the quantity of wood required to produce a unit of pulp varies with the process.

Potential annual requirements for paper and paperboard in 1950–55 are estimated at 24 million tons, divided among end products roughly as follows (figures are for thousand tons):

| | |
|---|---|
| Newsprint | 500 |
| Printing and fine paper | 4, 500 |
| Coarse and industrial papers | 3, 500 |
| Sanitary and tissue papers | 2, 000 |
| Building papers | 1, 500 |
| All papers | 12, 000 |
| Container board | 6, 000 |
| Boxboard | 3, 200 |
| Building boards | 2, 000 |
| Other paperboards | 800 |
| All paperboards | 12, 000 |
| Total | 24, 000 |

The 24 million tons of paper and paperboard is a total requirement. But the United States is an importer of pulpwood, wood pulp, and paper and paperboard, and undoubtedly will remain so. Thus, only the pulpwood required for part of domestic pulp and paper production need finally be estimated in order to determine the future drain on United States forests.

From an estimated total requirement of 17,890 thousand tons of wood pulp in 1950–55 is subtracted an estimated annual import of 2,000 thousand tons. The remainder, 15,890 thousand tons, is divided among the different types of pulp.

Finally, allowance is made for pulpwood imports, estimated at 1,500 thousand cords annually. This subtracted from 21,751 thousand cords leaves 20,251 thousand cords as a potential annual requirement in 1950–55. (See table on page 730). This amount is to be supplied from domestic forests. The equivalent of another 7,500 thousand cords will need to be imported in the form of pulp and paper.

Fortunately, pulpwood can be got from a large variety of species, both softwood and hardwood, and from trees of small size and inferior quality that under good forest management would be cut in the course of improving stands for the production of saw timber, veneer logs, and other high-quality products. And there are at present huge volumes of so-called inferior hardwoods in the forests that could go into container boards, wallboards, and similar products.

DISTILLATION converts wood into charcoal, acetic acid, methyl alcohol, and tar products. It is a declining industry, however; 1,150,000 cords were used in 1909, and 485,000 cords in 1939.

Where there is a good market for charcoal, the industry persists, but for the most part coke and carbon black are strong competitors of charcoal for the more important of the various industrial uses.

Methyl alcohol and acetic acid made by a synthetic process also have cut into the market for those products made by destructive distillation of hardwood.

It is estimated that the potential requirements for hardwood for the purpose in 1950–55 will not exceed 500,000 cords annually, and that 50 years hence the requirement will be approximately the same. Because distillation wood can be got from trees of small size and below saw-timber quality, such a requirement can easily be met without difficulty under conditions of good forest management.

Logs and bolts also are used for many other products, among them spools, dowels, and wood novelties made by the wood-turnery industry; shoe lasts, picker sticks, bobbins, and shuttles; shingles; baseball bats, and other athletic equipment made from bolts rather than lumber. In many cases, high-quality wood is required—wood that is not only free from visible defects but also is straight-grained and tough-textured. Among the species that can be used are white ash, hickory, western redcedar, paper birch, dogwood, persimmon, hard maple, yellow birch, and the other woods that have special technical properties rather than pleasing appearance.

For all such uses, the potential annual requirement in 1950–55 is estimated at 1 billion board feet (log scale), with an increase to 1.5 billion 50 years hence.

Other uses of cordwood include a wide variety of products, such as excelsior, wood for tannin extraction, composition roofing, wood poles used in raising shade-grown tobacco, rough wood used as dunnage in the storage of ship cargo, and round and slit material for rustic construction.

Potential annual requirements in 1950–55 have been estimated at 5 million cords, with an increase to 7 million cords 50 years from now. This is not an exacting requirement with respect to wood quality and could be met under conditions of good forest management with little drain on the saw-timber growing stock of the forests.

The total annual needs for saw timber in 1950–55, for the production of commodities for domestic consumption, is estimated at 61 billion board feet. Fifty years from now the requirements may be even higher, despite a continuing per capita decline in the use of lumber and certain other wood products. However, the figure of 61 billion will be used as the estimated future requirement. To this must be added allowances for (1) unavoidable losses caused by forest fires, insects and diseases, and other natural forces, (2) a margin of safety in times of emergency, when extraordinary demands are made on the forests, (3) the export of United States timber products to foreign countries, and (4) a margin for the discovery of new uses for wood as a basic material, requiring additional quantities of timber.

Future losses from destructive agencies (the so-called noncommodity drain on the forest) are estimated to be 3.2 billion board feet annually, and the margins for national security, exports, new uses, and other contingencies at 7.8 billion board feet, making a grand total of 72 billion board feet of saw timber required annually.

This quantity should be our annual growth goal. The forests of the United States should be built up to a level that would permit a drain of 72 billion board feet each year in perpetuity without depleting the saw-timber growing stock.

A. C. Cline *is foreign forestry specialist for the Forest Service. Formerly he was in charge of the industry-resource analysis section in the Division of Forest Economics in the Forest Service and was responsible for estimating the Nation's future timber requirements. During the Second World War he was vice chairman of the requirements committee of the Lumber and Lumber Products Division of the War Production Board. Before that, he was director of the Harvard Forest, Petersham, Mass.*

# THE WORLD FOREST SITUATION

STUART BEVIER SHOW

Many countries lack the wood they need in manifold forms for construction and reconstruction, for industry, for pulp and paper products, even for the specialized needs of industrial agriculture. In some other countries, if the wood is available, it is at such high prices as to be effectively beyond the reach of those who need it. In western Europe, the lack of wood is one of the deterrents to reconstruction and industrial recovery. Only few countries have more than enough for their own immediate needs. To understand the whole situation is the first step in suggesting the effective measures through which an attainable abundance of forest products can become actually available to potential users.

In 1948 the Food and Agriculture Organization of the United Nations, through its Forestry and Forest Products Division and with the cooperation of many member and nonmember governments, assembled and analyzed information on such essential points as the total productive and accessible areas of forests; their potential growth; and the output, production, consumption, and distribution of forest products. Through questionnaires dealing with forests and forest products, it was possible to draw a clearer picture than ever before.

That is not to say, however, that everything is known that should be known. Even in the United States, which for nearly 20 years has had under way a well-organized forest survey, there are still sizable regions in which forest area, volume, growth and loss, production, and use of forest products are known only through substandard estimates. Thus is it understandable that in many countries the state of forest knowledge is inaccurate. In Latin America, most of Asia and the Far East, and elsewhere, a good deal of inventory and survey work remains to be done, and the best available figures are no more than an approximation of the truth. In most of Europe, by contrast, information on forests is relatively accurate and complete. Because the Union of Soviet Socialist Republics provided no official figures on her vast forests, it is necessary in this article to use estimates that lack authority of that government.

THE TOTAL FOREST AREAS—that is, including forests suited only for the production of fuel wood—are distributed unevenly in different regions and in individual countries. Whether forest area is expressed as a percentage of total land area or as area per person, it is evident that some regions and countries are relatively wealthy in forests, others impoverished. Such extremes—as between the South American (43 percent) and Pacific Area (9 percent) regions, and between Canada (37 percent) and Syria (2 percent)—show the differences in potential availability of wood supplies, expressed as percentage of total land area. The contrast between South America (18.03 acres) and Asia (0.99) and between Canada (67.2) and Egypt (0) illustrates the great spread in forest area per person among different countries. By measures like those, the United States stands in relation to the grand average for the world as 33 to 30 percent for area, and as 4.61 to 4.20 acres per person.

A striking feature is the great contrast between countries in the same region—for example, Sweden, with 57 percent forest area and 8.65 acres per person compared to Great Britain, with 6 percent and 0.32 acre, in Europe; or Brazil, with 46 percent and 22.35 acres, compared to Uruguay, with 2 percent and 0.49 acre, in South America. The other continents show sharp contrasts as well.

DISTRIBUTION OF FOREST AREA BY REGIONS AND SELECTED COUNTRIES

| Region or country | Total area | Forest area | Percentage forest | Population | Forest area per person |
|---|---|---|---|---|---|
| | Million hectares [1] | Million hectares [1] | Percent | Millions | Hectares [1] |
| Europe (excluding Union of Soviet Socialist Republics) | 482 | 1,046 | 38 | 578 | 1.8 |
| Union of Soviet Socialist Republics | 2,255 | | | | |
| North America | 2,347 | 728 | 31 | 201 | 3.6 |
| South America | 1,755 | 755 | 43 | 103 | 7.3 |
| Africa | 3,060 | 849 | 28 | 191 | 4.4 |
| Asia (excluding Union of Soviet Socialist Republics) | 2,591 | 520 | 20 | 1,224 | .4 |
| Pacific area | 855 | 80 | 9 | 12 | 6.7 |
| Total | 13,345 | 3,978 | 30 | 2,309 | 1.7 |
| Sweden | 41.0 | 23.5 | 57 | 6.7 | 3.5 |
| Great Britain | 22.7 | 1.3 | 6 | 49.6 | .03 |
| Canada | 896.7 | 334.4 | 37 | 12.3 | 27.2 |
| United States | 771.0 | 252.5 | 33 | 141.2 | 1.8 |
| Brazil | 851.1 | 395.9 | 46 | 46.7 | 8.5 |
| Uruguay | 18.6 | .5 | 2 | 2.3 | .2 |
| Belgian Congo | 228.4 | 120.3 | 53 | 10.6 | 11.4 |
| Egypt | 100.0 | ........ | ........ | 18.6 | 0 |
| Siam | 51.3 | 32.4 | 63 | 18.1 | 1.8 |
| Syria | 18.6 | .4 | 2 | 3.0 | .1 |
| Australia | 770.4 | 30.9 | 4 | 7.5 | 4.1 |
| New Zealand | 26.4 | 6.8 | 26 | 1.8 | 3.8 |

[1] 1 hectare equals 2.47 acres.

This is one useful measure of forests, but it fails to show what kind of forests, and more particularly, the accessible and productive forest estate. In the United States, for example, large areas are classed as forest that contain thin stands of short, scrubby trees, which may be useful as sources of local fuel, but can hardly contribute to national or world demands for manufactured wood, such as sawn lumber, pulp, ties, and poles.

The same condition exists in Australia, Africa, and elsewhere along the dry southern edge of forest belts and also generally on the cold, dry northern edge of the forests of Canada, northern Europe, and the Soviet Union. So, to form a more realistic picture of the productive forest estate, it is necessary to eliminate such local-use forests. From the second table, it is evident that for the world fully 34 percent, for the African region 64 percent, and for New Zealand 72 percent of the total forest area cannot be expected, under existing economics and technology, to yield forest products other than fuel. This reduces the grand average per person from 4.20 acres to 2.72. The United States, with a reduction from 4.61 to nearly 3.46, ranks ahead of the world average. (The United States has customarily reported its forest areas as commercial and noncommercial. Certain areas in the latter category are so classed because they are reserved for recreation or other purposes, but are reported by FAO as productive forest, because they are physically capable of producing crops of usable wood.)

This is the most realistic measure of the true productive forests yet available. It shows that no continent, and relatively few countries, are fortunate

DISTRIBUTION OF PRODUCTIVE ACCESSIBLE AND INACCESSIBLE CONIFEROUS AND BROAD-LEAVED FORESTS BY REGIONS AND SELECTED COUNTRIES

| Region or country | Accessible | | | Inaccessible | | |
|---|---|---|---|---|---|---|
| | Conifers | Broad-leaved | Total | Conifers | Broad-leaved | Total |
| | Million hectares [1] | Million hectares [1] | Million hectares [1] | Million hectares [1] | Million hectares [1] | Million hectares [1] |
| Europe and Union of Soviet Socialist Republics | 316 | 108 | 424 | 212 | 91 | 103 |
| North America | 180 | 154 | 334 | 135 | 38 | 173 |
| South America | 10 | 297 | 307 | 5 | 352 | 357 |
| Africa | 2 | 148 | 150 | ........ | 156 | 156 |
| Asia (excluding Union of Soviet Socialist Republics) | 31 | 143 | 174 | 43 | 141 | 184 |
| Pacific area | 4 | 20 | 24 | 4 | 22 | 26 |
| Total | 543 | 870 | 1,413 | 399 | 800 | 1,199 |
| France | 3.0 | 8.0 | 11.0 | ........ | ........ | ........ |
| Norway | 4.5 | .7 | 5.2 | .8 | .1 | .9 |
| Canada | 72.8 | 39.8 | 112.6 | 83.0 | 15.0 | 98.0 |
| United States | 88.4 | 82.4 | 170.8 | 19.4 | 1.6 | 21.0 |
| Argentina | .1 | 17.0 | 17.1 | .1 | 5.6 | 5.7 |
| Brazil | 5.2 | 147.4 | 152.6 | 3.5 | 221.1 | 224.6 |
| French Morocco | .6 | 1.9 | 2.5 | ........ | ........ | ........ |
| French Cameroons | ........ | 2.3 | 2.3 | ........ | 16.5 | 16.5 |
| Burma | ........ | 22.7 | 22.7 | ........ | ........ | ........ |
| China | 13.5 | 3.4 | 16.9 | 34.9 | 4.5 | 39.4 |
| Australia | 1.6 | 12.1 | 13.7 | .1 | 6.5 | 6.6 |
| New Zealand | .6 | .1 | .7 | .3 | 1.0 | 1.3 |

[1] 1 hectare equals 2.47 acres.

enough to have all or nearly all the forest land in the productive category.

Of this productive forest estate as presently measured or estimated, by no means all is now yielding goods for national and world needs. Even in the advanced economy of the United States, substantial areas of productive forests (52 million acres) remain inaccessible to use and lack transportation and industrial establishments.

In many other countries and regions, even higher fractions of the productive forests are not usable at present or for the foreseeable future. Thus, 46 percent of Canada's productive forest area is inaccessible, as is 60 percent of the great forests of Brazil, 64 percent of New Zealand's, and 80 percent of the large productive forest areas of the Netherlands East Indies. By contrast, a high proportion of the productive forests in Europe (excluding the Soviet Union) is accessible.

In comparison, the area of productive and accessible forest per person for the 2.3 billion people of the world (1.48 acres) is 50 percent of that available (2.96 acres) to the 146 million people in the United States from her own forests.

It is clear that large areas of productive forest, totaling 2,862 million acres, once made accessible, are still available to contribute to national, regional, and world needs for wood. This presently unused resource represents one of the great and widespread opportunities to improve living standards. Only 54 percent of the productive forests of the world have been made accessible, and well over half of these are in Europe,

DISTRIBUTION OF PRODUCTIVE AND ACCESSIBLE FOREST AREAS BY REGIONS AND SELECTED COUNTRIES

| *Region or country* | *Total forest area* | *Productive forest area* | *Percentage productive to total forest* | *Accessible forest area* | *Percentage accessible productive to total forest* |
|---|---|---|---|---|---|
| | *Million hectares* [1] | *Million hectares* [1] | *Percent* | *Million hectares* [1] | *Percent* |
| Europe and Union Soviet Socialist Republics... | 1,046 | 727 | 70 | 424 | 41 |
| North America... | 728 | 507 | 70 | 334 | 46 |
| South America... | 755 | 664 | 88 | 307 | 41 |
| Africa... | 849 | 306 | 36 | 150 | 18 |
| Asia (excluding Union Soviet Socialist Republics). | 520 | 358 | 69 | 174 | 33 |
| Pacific area... | 80 | 50 | 63 | 24 | 30 |
| Total... | 3,978 | 2,612 | 66 | 1,413 | 35 |
| Hungary... | 1.1 | 1.1 | 100 | 1.1 | 100 |
| Norway... | 7.5 | 6.1 | 81 | 5.2 | 69 |
| Canada... | 334.4 | 210.6 | 63 | 112.6 | 34 |
| United States... | 252.5 | 191.8 | 76 | 170.8 | 68 |
| Argentina... | 48.6 | 22.9 | 47 | 17.1 | 35 |
| Brazil... | 395.9 | 377.2 | 95 | 152.6 | 38 |
| Belgian Congo... | 120.3 | 119.5 | 99 | 69.0 | 57 |
| French West Africa... | 170.0 | 50.0 | 29 | 25.0 | 15 |
| Japan... | 22.3 | 22.3 | 100 | 19.7 | 88 |
| Netherlands Indies... | 120.0 | 70.0 | 58 | 11.0 | 9 |
| Australia... | 30.9 | 20.3 | 66 | 13.7 | 44 |
| New Zealand... | 6.8 | 1.9 | 28 | .7 | 10 |

[1] 1 hectare equals 2.47 acres.

Soviet Russia, and in North America.

As to the kinds of forests, it is well known that industrially developed countries—such as the United States and those in western Europe—require large amounts of manufactured coniferous products for their economies. It is less well recognized, but equally true, that public education depends largely on the printed page, which is made of paper coming mostly from softwood trees. And advanced irrigation agriculture depends on containers for shipping, which are largely of board or paperboard made mostly from softwood trees. So it is particularly important to know the availability of softwood supplies.

The broadleaved forests, both those of the Temperate Zones and of the Tropics, have great values, but so far these have been used more for specialty woods than for the general utility woods required in industry, building, agriculture, and publishing. Hardwoods can be substituted to some degree for softwoods, but by no means generally. Relative costs are important.

In responding to our inquiry, countries classified their productive, accessible forests into two broad categories, conifers and broadleaved.

Conifers (softwoods): All trees classified botanically as Gymnospermae (that is, pine — *Pinus,* fir — *Abies,* spruce—*Picea,* larch—*Larix,* Parana pine—*Araucaria,* and ginkgo—*Ginkgo*) have been included in this category. Broadleaved species (hardwoods): All trees classified botanically as Angiospermae. The species belonging to this group are generally broadleaved (that is, oak—*Quercus,* beech—*Fagus,* maple—*Acer,* lignum

DISTRIBUTION OF FOREST COMMODITY PRODUCTION AND USE BY REGIONS AND SELECTED COUNTRIES

| Region or country | Production (1946) | Population | Use per person: Fuel wood | Use per person: Other wood | Use per person: Total |
|---|---|---|---|---|---|
| | *Million cubic meters* [1] | *Millions* | *Cubic meters* | *Cubic meters* | *Cubic meters* |
| Europe | 262 | 578 | 0.435 | 0.465 | 0.900 |
| Union of Soviet Socialist Republics | 252 | | (2) | (2) | (2) |
| North America | 352 | 201 | .440 | 1.680 | 2.120 |
| South America | 179 | 103 | .530 | .200 | .730 |
| Africa | 49 | 191 | .460 | .090 | .550 |
| Asia | 300 | 1,224 | .350 | .070 | .420 |
| Pacific area | 16 | 12 | .850 | .530 | 1.380 |
| Total | 1,410 | 2,309 | .31 | .30 | .61 |
| | | *Thousands* | | | |
| Finland | 22.4 | 3,877 | 2.700 | .81 | 3.510 |
| Greece | 3.7 | 7,400 | .420 | .11 | .530 |
| Sweden | 39.0 | 6,719 | 2.200 | 1.60 | 3.800 |
| Lebanon | .02 | 1,160 | .005 | .04 | .047 |
| Canada | 77.0 | 12,307 | 1.690 | 1.99 | 3.680 |
| United States | 258.1 | 141,229 | .390 | 1.60 | 1.990 |
| Honduras | 1.8 | 1,220 | 1.125 | .35 | 1.480 |
| Puerto Rico | 2.4 | 2,128 | 1.100 | .07 | 1.170 |
| Japan | 55.9 | 75,323 | .670 | .26 | .930 |
| French Equatorial Africa | 10.0 | 3,984 | 2.010 | .53 | 2.540 |
| French West Africa | 1.9 | 16,200 | .100 | .20 | .120 |
| Australia (1945 data) | 9.9 | 7,516 | .460 | .86 | 1.320 |
| New Zealand | 2.6 | 1,761 | .480 | 1.11 | 1.590 |

[1] Millions cubic meters roundwood equivalent.

[2] Data not available.

vitae—*Guiaicum*, ebony—*Diospyros*, balsa—*Ochroma*, poplar—*Populus*).

The really substantial softwood forest areas of the world are confined to the United States and Canada, northern Europe, and the Soviet Republic. The countries of Latin America report only 2 percent of their total productive forest area in softwoods, which is 0.25 acre per person. The relative scarcity in Australia and New Zealand is reason for their extensive softwood planting programs. Asia and Africa have extremely limited natural coniferous forests.

It seems correct to say that countries that possess relatively abundant supplies of softwood have a great competitive advantage in maintaining or developing an industrial economy and in advancing the general level of public education.

THE ESSENTIAL FACTS about the forests of the earth as a source of commodities may be summed up as follows: They are distributed unevenly in relation to total area of regions and countries and per person. Substantial parts are unproductive except for fuel. Substantial parts of the productive forests are inaccessible. The softwood forests are more unevenly distributed than are all forests. Relative to the world, the United States is in a strongly favorable position in all these respects.

THE MANAGEMENT OF FORESTS cannot be described in detail—nor is that necessary in drawing the broad picture of the world forest situation. It is first necessary to note that in most of the forest and geographic regions the same destructive practices still persist on a large scale which have been traditional throughout history. These destructive forms of land use destroyed forests and wrecked agriculture in many of the ancient countries of the Mediterranean, China, and India.

ONE MAJOR FORM of destruction of forest and land is shifting cultivation—that is, deliberate clearing of the forest to make room for annual field crops. The practice, particularly destructive on sloping land, is today widespread in many parts of Latin America, Africa, the East Indies, and elsewhere. Through erosion induced by clearing forests, the soil, agriculture, and downstream lands suffer. Associated with shifting cultivation is the use of fire for clearing land, a practice that, if unwisely used, expands and speeds up the ill effects of shifting cultivation.

Overgrazing, another widespread practice, first depletes the natural grasslands, then drives flocks and herds to seek new lands—the forest lands. Since these may not be naturally productive of forage, fire or logging is used to open them up in the first place, and firing is often repeated to make feed accessible. Great areas of Africa and Asia have been treated in that way. In Africa it is estimated that more than 60 percent of the original forest has been destroyed by shifting cultivation, overgrazing, and the associated use of fire. The process is continuing.

In countries and regions in which those practices are sanctioned, it is found that no effective effort is made to control forest fires; fire, whether deliberate or accidental, continues to be a major destructive force in most regions and many countries. In the United States, which has an advanced organization for the control of forest fires, there remain, according to the United States Forest Service, about 111 million acres of productive forest on which fire control is not applied.

In many lands, the exploitation of forests for their useful products remains on a destructive basis, in whole or in large part. The effect, whether caused by logging alone or by logging plus fire, is to prevent or delay regrowth, thereby retaining unproductive land.

The effect of any or all of these destructive forces is twofold: Regrowth is prevented or delayed or reduced in volume far below what the land could support. Further, the beneficial effects of forests in stabilizing waterflows and soils are reduced or destroyed; thereby the ill effects of alternating floods and low water stages, of erosion and deposition of unwanted soil and rock, are visited on crop lands in the lower river basins.

ALL THIS is the negative side of forest management. That there is a large continuing reduction of productive forest area and a failure to realize the potential useful growth of the productive forest lands there can be no doubt, even though statistical measures of extent are now lacking. Destructive forces and practice must, of course, be brought under control before forestry can be most effective. Information for the world as a whole is far less complete than it is for the United States.

But the other side of the story—constructive and effective forest management—needs emphasis as well. Many forest lands in Europe are handled to obtain a high percentage of their full growth capacity, and idle land is the exception. But considerable areas are only partly stocked; on them the full growth capacity is by no means utilized. Large and increasing areas of Canadian and United States forests are kept at work, though generally on a less intensive (that is, fully productive) basis than those of western Europe. A great deal of the forest areas of India, Pakistan, Burma, and of parts of the East Indies has been placed under good forest management. So, too, with parts of colonial empires in Africa.

For many other regions and countries no records are available to show what fraction of forest land is handled so as to remain a productive asset. Though available evidence is far from detailed, it seems that in Latin America and Africa, at least, the destruction of forests is outstripping the adoption of sound practices.

THE RATE OF APPLYING FOREST MANAGEMENT is, of necessity, slow.

First of all, a nation itself must have the genuine intent, expressed in forest policy and forest law, to conserve its forests for its own benefit. Then a forest organization must be established to put into effect the policy and law decided on. To build a competent organization where none has existed always involves such time-consuming steps as providing professional education and training, developing operating facilities, deciding on the form of the organization, developing leadership, and obtaining required financial support. A vital forestry program must come from within the individual country.

A true and insistent initial realization of the need for forestry seldom arises until forest products become locally or nationally scarce. Until that stage is reached, exploitation is commonly tolerated or accepted by governments and peoples. At present, the greatest continental area in which this realization is developing seems to be Latin America. Certainly the response in the Latin-American Conference on Forestry and Forest Products in April 1948, sponsored by the Food and Agriculture Organization, shows active interest. At the conference, several countries, large and small, planned for the establishment of effective forestry, spurred on by the existence of local wood shortages and by a realization of the part forests and forestry can have in the whole economy.

European countries generally are placing great emphasis on restoring forests destroyed by war and on improving the growth in overcut forests, as part of their basic recovery programs.

In several countries of Asia, new governments are taking over the forestry programs already set up by former colonial services. The United States is particularly interested in the program in the Philippines, which is continuing from the foundation work done by this country.

THE CURRENT GROWTH on productive forest lands is a measure of the effectiveness of forestry. In the countries with the most advanced practices, the actual growth is a relatively high proportion (up to 80–85 percent) of that which forest soils could produce under the best conditions.

The growth potential is realized by curbing destructive forces, such as fire, insects, and diseases; by productive use of small trees and limbs of trees for pulp, fuel wood, and so on; and by frequent working of the forest so that slow-growing trees are removed and used.

In contrast, no net current growth is obtained from forest lands when the forest is undisturbed (virgin forest) and growth is offset by natural loss and decay. That is the situation in many unworked forests—that is, the productive, inaccessible forests. Nor is net current growth obtained when restocking of productive forest soils has failed. That is the situation when destructive forces, such as fire or logging followed by fire, have destroyed forests and prevented regrowth.

The estimation of total growth of forests is complex and difficult, and it is understandable that in many countries only a general attempt to do so has been made. Indeed, valid estimates usually can be prepared only after forests have been placed under systematic management.

Even more difficult is the estimation of natural losses caused by fire, insects, and disease. Fire and insect losses tend to occur irregularly, and many losses of wood caused by disease are concealed within the boles of trees.

Nevertheless, some countries have solid estimates of both total and net growth obtained under management, so that it is possible to appraise what the productive forests of the world can produce. It must be emphasized that such an appraisal assumes reasonably good management—that is, keeping forest lands productive.

The reported present growth rates for coniferous forests in Europe range downward from 104 cubic feet per acre in Denmark to 21 for Great Britain and 23 for Poland. The figures for Great Britain and Poland reflect devastation of forests during the war. The average of the rates reported is about 31. It is fair to assume that as the forestry programs are expanded, this rate can be increased to not less than 43 cubic feet per acre.

An unofficial estimate of growth in the coniferous forests of the Soviet Union is 28 cubic feet per acre. It would be unwise to assume a higher average for the future, because of the northerly location of many of the forests.

In Canada the current rate of growth of coniferous forests is about 14 cubic feet per acre, and an attainable rate of 28 can be assumed as better management is applied.

In the United States the reported growth rate of 33 cubic feet per acre reflects the high-growth potential of many of the coniferous forest lands. It is estimated that improved management could increase the average to 57.

All in all, the accessible coniferous forests of the world, with reasonably good management, could be made to produce an average net yield of about 31 cubic feet per acre, or a total of more than 40 billion cubic feet. The present normal use of coniferous wood is estimated as about 26 billion cubic feet.

The inaccessible coniferous forests are not likely to attain rates of growth as high as are assumed for the accessible forests, because growing conditions are generally less favorable. But the 986 million acres of inaccessible coniferous forests, as put under management, should yield an annual average growth of 22 billion cubic feet.

Thus, with reasonably good management, the coniferous forests of the world could be made to yield continuously well over twice the amount of wood now normally used and lost. That result cannot be expected in a short time, and an expansion of the current rate of consumption of the coniferous wood is not safe at the present time.

About 64 percent of the total productive forest area of the world consists of broadleaved species. Of this, about 14 percent is temperate hardwoods and 50 percent tropical hardwoods.

In Europe and in North America, the present estimated growth of the temperate hardwoods is about the same as for coniferous forests. We estimate that these rates of growth can be increased substantially.

In the tropical broadleaved forests, only a few of the many species are being exploited. For the merchantable species only, annual growth rates of 7 to 21 cubic feet per acre have been estimated. Growth as high as 100 cubic feet per acre has been estimated as attainable where it is possible to use all the species, including those that are at present unused.

The future productivity of the tropical hardwood forests thus depends on finding uses for many more species, and, most important, on curbing the current rates of forest destruction through controlling the practices mentioned earlier.

The world can have a far larger supply of wood than it now uses, and can have it permanently, if the productive forests are given reasonably good management.

One over-all measure of the forest-management situation is the relation between average growth and drain on the accessible productive forests, that is, those that have been or are being worked over. Growth on all trees in the forests is one side of the balance sheet; losses from natural causes plus fellings, the other. Comprehensive world figures are not available, because by no means all countries have been able to report both growth and drain.

Sixteen European countries report in total an almost exact balance between growth and drain for all forests, both the coniferous and broadleaved. Seven have a plus balance, nine a minus balance. The Soviet Union, Germany, and Hungary are not included. On the same basis, the United States reports a drain of 2½ percent in excess of growth. The same European nations report a small excess (1.4 percent) of drain over growth for coniferous forests. The excess drain on conifers in the United States is 23.5 percent; the excess of growth over drain for broadleaved species is more than 18 percent.

In the United States, the Forest Service reports an excess of drain over growth of about 50 percent for trees of saw-timber size, a significant imbalance. Comparable figures have not been reported for the European countries, but in general the saw-timber supply seems to be fairly well kept in balance with the allowed cut. Some countries are now contemplating an attempt to offset severe overcutting during the war by reduced rate of cutting.

A large excess of drain over growth, particularly if it is in larger size trees, is a danger signal, indicating need for measures to reduce the gap. The general nature of the steps is mentioned in the latter part of this paper. The detailed measures, applicable to the specific urgent situation in the United States, have been reported by the Forest Service (*Gaging the Timber Resource of the United States,* U. S. D. A. Forest Service, 1946). Continuation of a process of taking out more than is grown can have only the effect of reducing the growing stock—the situation already reported in detail by the Forest Service.

I NOTED EARLIER that forests were unevenly distributed, both in relation to population and as a fraction of the total land area of countries and regions. It is equally true that the production and use of forest products varies enormously from country to country and from region to region.

The figures in the table on page 746 are based on responses, covering 1945–46, from 75 countries. It is known that the figures for use of wood as fuel are at best wide approximations, because detailed records are seldom kept. And since not all nations are able to report on production, exports, and imports, it has been necessary to estimate regional production and use of forest products.

The total estimated production in 1946 was nearly 50 billion cubic feet, about 6 percent less than the 53 billion, which was regarded as the prewar normal. More than 61 percent of this total came from the forests of Europe, the Soviet Union, and North America, with 47 percent of the productive forest area of the world, and about 13 percent from South America, with 25 percent of the productive forest area.

It is estimated that, as a world average, 48 percent of wood is used for construction and industrial purposes and slightly more as fuel. The best available estimates indicate that in North America about 78 percent of the total consumption is as industrial wood, whereas in South America and Asia only about 17 percent is so used, the rest going as fuel.

Thus it is clear that the industrialized regions and countries are relatively heavy users of processed wood, both as lumber and as pulp. A relatively large part of this is coniferous wood. Moreover, a relatively small part of their total use of wood is as fuel.

The great industrialized regions—Europe, the Soviet Union, and North America—have about one-third of the people of the world and use 80 percent of all the processed wood.

The great bulk of the world's population uses relatively little manufactured wood—far less per person than the industrialized nations.

The slightly industrialized regions—Asia, Africa, and South America—and countries such as Greece, Lebanon, Honduras, and French West Africa use relatively little manufactured wood. The slightly industrialized regions and countries are in two broad categories—those with little forest area per person and those with relatively much. The first group uses little wood, even for fuel. This in extreme form, as in China, India, and the Middle East, results in use of agricultural refuse and dung as fuel, materials that should be returned to the cropped soils. The second may have a relatively high per person use—mostly for fuel—as in Honduras, Puerto Rico, and French Equatorial Africa.

The per person rate of consumption for the United States is among the highest for any region or country and indicates the level toward which a vigorous and developing economy and a growing population may push the use of wood.

About half of the world's total consumption of wood is as fuel.

How SIGNIFICANT these present generalizations may be in the future will depend on future developments in various regions and countries, and these are not predictable.

But it is worth noting that the Soviet Union has changed in a few years from a net exporter to a net importer of forest products, partly because of a major program of industrial development. The United States has long been a net importer of all forest products. From 1920 to 1940 she was a net exporter of lumber, but has since become a net importer, except by a narrow margin in 1947.

On the whole, an extremely large latent demand for wood must exist in many of the present low-use countries.

Either of two developments could turn potential use into actual use. Any substantial industrial development would do so, and this could include certain forms of intensive agriculture, particularly those involving fruits and vegetables and other foods processed and packed for consumer use. Any substantial increase of living standard also could do so. A relatively small change upward in housing standards, the addition of a small weekly newspaper, or another use of pulpwood to the average family income would add greatly to the total and per person use of wood. If the nearly 1¼ billion people of Asia should raise consumption to the level now in effect in South America, an increase of more than one-third in the total drain on the world's forests would result. Even a continuation of present per person use will mean increased total demand, for population is increasing rapidly, particularly in the countries with low use of wood or with a low level of industrialization.

It is speculative whether all of this increased demand will develop. But it would appear prudent for countries, regions, and the world to act in the expectation that some increase in effective demand for wood products will develop.

The essential facts of the forestry and forest-products situation and of the trends in economic affairs indicate how possible is an increased consumption of forest products.

The essentials are:

1. Industrialization requires use of relatively large quantities of general utility softwoods. Substitution of tropical hardwoods for softwoods under existing technological and economic conditions will be slow and difficult.

2. The major sources of supply for softwoods are Canada, United States, the Soviet Union, and northern Europe. Of these, only the first is now a net exporter. The United States and northern Europe cannot supply their own net estimated needs for some time.

3. Native softwood supplies in South America, Africa, Asia, and Oceania are less than required for the long run for those regions. They are now net importers.

4. Industrial development of additional countries, such as is now apparently planned in parts of South America, Asia, and Africa, would increase competition for the already limited softwood supplies available for export.

5. The best opportunities for piecing out existing supplies of softwoods lie in four directions:

Larger recovery of products from forests and trees, which might increase supplies from 15 to 20 percent (i. e., pulp as a byproduct of lumber), and salvaging the unused material in the woods.

More efficient design in the use of wood, for example, in housing, which might reduce use in the order of 10 to 15 percent.

Substitution of other materials, for example, in housing—steel, stone, cement, brick.

Substitution of hardwoods for softwoods. The great area of tropical hardwoods offers an apparent opportunity to do so. Many such substitutions are technologically feasible and are primarily questions of economics, that is, of price levels.

But established habits and patterns change slowly and substantial changes in forms and economy of use are seldom made overnight, even under the most severe pressure of need.

THE EXISTING SHORT SUPPLY, particularly of softwoods, emphasizes the need for the installation of forestry practices everywhere, and the opening to use of inaccessible productive forests. There is little evidence that any country, great or small, can continue to depend indefinitely on readily available imports, at least to the degree that now exists. It appears, rather, that full use of native supplies, even though they are not ideal, will be forced. The opening up of unused forests, constructive management of forests now under exploitation and, for the long run, restoration of forests are all required to insure supplies as needed.

It is worthy of note that a large fraction of the productive inaccessible forests are classed as "tropical hardwoods." This generic term encompasses thousands of tree species, of which only at most a few hundred have been adequately studied to determine the use values of their woods. Most of these are now of interest to consumers only for highly special—and valuable—qualities, such as beauty, hardness, softness, durability.

THE TASK OF FINDING out what the tropical hardwoods can do to better balance the world's needs for utility woods requires a vast deal of technological research. Effective market demand and substitution of one wood for another is not apt to come about through vague generalizations. The industrialized wood-using areas of the world can potentially ease their supply problems by research programs in wood technology, regardless of where the raw material supplies may be. Supply, as well as quality, needs to be known for the thousands of presently unused tropical hardwood species. The using nations have a valid motive to take interest in forest exploration and inventory and in technological research.

The meaning of the world's forest situation as here sketched seems reasonably clear. The Food and Agriculture Organization, an international organization set up to study, analyze, advise, and help, needs to continue to do everything proper to stimulate and aid governments to apply forest management. Primary initiative must, of course, come from each nation acting in its own self-interest. A country such as the United States, which possesses a great estate of productive forest land, which has appraised its own current and prospective needs, which has estimated current and prospective forest growth, needs to keep its own balance sheets in continuous review and decide on and apply production goals for its own needs and for export. There is every reason to believe that growing industrialization of presently underdeveloped countries will add to the demand for forest products and thereby give an outlet to those countries with an exportable surplus, especially of softwoods. The danger of unwieldy surpluses is remote, in a world-wide sense, if national and regional economics recover or advance.

It is clearly impracticable to set down in detail the steps through which nations may realize the full value of their estates of forest land, lands which in most instances are unsuited to other uses. Situations vary so greatly—from the thoroughly devastated forests of many Near and Middle East countries, to the largely unknown, untouched, and inaccessible forests of the Amazon basin, to the perennially productive forests of western Europe, to the mixed situation of the United States with some elements of the ruling conditions of all continents.

The general nature of the essential steps that must be taken to establish forestry are well established by world experience:

1. To halt and control the major destructive forces and processes—shifting cultivation, overgrazing and burning, exploitative and excessive rate of utilization of productive forests.
2. To create a body of public forest policy and law and to apply it through a competent professional organization.
3. To obtain the understanding and support of affected people for the program. To estimate prospective needs for forests and their products and to determine what the forest lands of the country can produce under forestry.
4. To apply the forestry practices which may be effective and economically feasible with a forward-looking view of economics in making the forest lands productive.
5. To learn a great deal more about forests and forest products than is now known.

The information available indicates that forests will be called on to play a greater rather than a lesser part in the economies of nations and regions, and that constructive management—that is, realization of the growth of potential forest soils—will be more rather than less necessary.

802062°—49——49

Thus, it is important that each nation move aggressively to improve its own forest situation. It is equally important that nations act with full knowledge of the total and regional forest situations, that they have access to data on improved methods and techniques, and that they consult regularly with each other on questions of regional concern.

The great fact about the world's forest situation is that there is enough productive forest land to turn out continuously much more wood than at present, and thereby to raise standards of living and support increased industrialization. But this goal can be reached only if nations replace destructive exploitation by forestry. Such exploitation is no longer the problem of individual nations, to be noted with regret. It is a matter of deadly seriousness to all nations.

The unsatisfied needs for forest products are less potent than is lack of food as a cause of unrest. But all the basic requirements of food, clothing, and shelter need to be met to create a decent standard of life.

Greater attention to forests everywhere is one of the steps that must be taken to build a more solid foundation for peace.

Stuart Bevier Show *is chief of the forestry branch, Division of Forestry and Forest Products, of the Food and Agriculture Organization of the United Nations. He is a graduate of Stanford University and Yale and a life-long resident of California. Mr. Show was regional forester in charge of the California region of the Forest Service from 1926 to 1946. He is the author of numerous publications on forest management, forest planting, forest-fire control, and forest-land ownership and use.*

# THE REAL INTERESTS OF THE PEOPLE

WILLIAM GREEN

Labor has a vital interest in the forests and in what happens to them. Forests mean jobs. Forest-based industries and activities support more than 2 million workers and their families in the United States—loggers in the woods, workers in sawmills and planing mills and lumber yards, in pulp and paper and rayon mills and processing plants, in furniture factories, cooperage plants, box plants, in naval stores, and in other forest-products industries.

Indirectly, the forests contribute to the support of additional millions of workers—railroad workers, printers, factory workers. The transportation, wholesaling, and retailing of commodities made wholly or partly from forest products mean still more jobs.

The interest of organized labor in the Nation's forests, however, goes far beyond their value as a source of employment. Workers are also consumers, and they have the same interests in a steady flow of forest products as any other consumers. They want homes; they want the things forests give that make for comfortable and pleasant living. And they want these things at prices they can afford to pay.

Workers also are interested in the recreational value of the forests. The practice of vacations and holidays with pay has become almost universal throughout American industry. Hundreds of thousands of workers spend much of their vacation and holiday leisure in the forests, picnicking, camping, hiking, hunting, and fishing. As increasing production efficiency and rising living standards bring more leisure time, the need for such recreational opportunities will grow.

Most forest industries in this country grew up on the exploitation of virgin timber. As the timber was cut out in one locality, operators moved on to another. The workers had to move on, too, or else be left jobless in a community that was apt to go into rapid decline after its principal economic support had departed.

Workers in the forest industries are no different from other people in their desire for the things that make life good. They want to live in homes of their own, rather than migrate from camp to camp. They want to bring up their children in a wholesome environment. They want to have a part in the life of their community. But they cannot look forward to these things if their jobs are based on cut-out-and-get-out operations.

A STEADY FLOW of forest products can come only from steadily producing forests. Permanent employment in all the industries and trades that depend on forest products can come only from steadily producing forests. Yet the bulk of our forest land is not being managed for steady production. Official reports show that we are taking saw timber from the forests faster than it grows. A declining resource certainly is not a basis for expanding industry and employment. It cannot continue indefinitely to support even the present level of employment and production.

Building up our forest lands to full productiveness will increase the opportunities for permanent employment. Forest improvement is a capital investment. It will furnish more security for present forest industries and the people who work in them, and will build up a resource base for additional employment.

ORGANIZED LABOR has for a long time recognized the value of a comprehensive program to conserve the Nation's timberland. Almost annually, the convention of the American Federation of Labor has gone on record as favoring the development of an over-all forestry program.

The 1946 convention of the American Federation of Labor, for example, adopted a resolution, submitted by the delegate from the Montana State Federation of Labor, that said, in part:

> We favor immediate action in the development of a State and National program for all forest lands that will protect the forests from fire, insects, and disease damage; promote forestry practices that will result in full use of the productive capacity of these lands but not overuse which would bring exhaustion of usable timber at a later date; promote greater utilization of the wood products thereby eliminating waste and conserving timber supplies now available; and provide for an aggressive start on reforestation of lands now not producing anything of commercial value. . . .

Numerous State and local affiliates of the American Federation of Labor also have actively campaigned for a program that would bring an end to the destructive cutting of the Nation's forests.

Organized labor continues to have great faith that the Nation's forests can make a great contribution to the welfare of the wage earners of this country. In order to achieve this objective, labor will continue to fight for the development of a program that will manage the forest land in the real interests of the people.

William Green *is president of the American Federation of Labor.*

# LABOR LOOKS AT TREES AND CONSERVATION

PHILIP MURRAY

Never before has labor been more acutely aware than it is today of how its welfare is tied to the Nation's resources of trees and forests.

Millions of worker families find that lumber for the houses they want to buy or build costs three times what it did before the Second World War and about six times what it cost before the First World War. The pinch of wood scarcity is felt, too, by many labor unions when they shop for newsprint on which to publish union papers.

No matter where a worker is employed, moreover, he sees parts of trees put to many vital uses. All too frequently in recent years, shortage of one kind or another of tree products has been a bottleneck or stumbling block to production and to employment.

Industrially, tree products are used and needed everywhere. Wood is basic, like steel.

As a result of their heightened awareness that something must be wrong with the Nation's tree and forest resources, numerous groups within organized labor have been studying the economics of basic wood and of forestry more intensively than ever before. Those studies are making labor conscious of certain key facts about trees and forests—facts that demand action.

Labor sees that the basic wood and forest resource is renewable or exhaustible, depending wholly on how that resource is managed. It is renewable if the forests are protected from fire; if logging is done conservatively in accordance with sound forestry principles; if the wood is utilized efficiently; and if depleted and devastated areas are promptly reforested.

But the wood resource is exhaustible if forest fires are not controlled; if logging is heedless of future tree crops; if utilization is recklessly wasteful; and if depleted and devastated areas are left as idle stump and brush lands or as eroded deserts. Labor has found that the latter conditions have prevailed—and still prevail—on far too much of the Nation's forest land.

Today, moreover, as peacetime employment stands at the highest and fullest of any time in our history, labor is coming to see another resource fact more clearly than ever before. This grows out of the wartime experience which proved that our Nation's factories can produce more than most people thought was possible. It grows also out of our postwar experience which has proved that an America fully employed with anything near a decent wage has a capacity to consume the products of farm and of factory at a rate much greater than most people ever believed. For even with excessive price inflation, cruelly cutting the value of the workers' pay check and restricting to bare essentials the purchases of millions of families, we are consuming vastly more consumer goods than many people thought we could.

These experiences point sharply to the fact that natural resources—raw materials—are the number-one long-range limiting factor in the ability of America to raise the standard of living of all its people to a decent and continually rising level. Our factory technology and the skill of our labor can boost production almost unbelievably, provided we can get enough raw material to work with. But shortages of raw materials can tragically defeat this high American purpose.

As the definitely exhaustible resources, such as metals and petroleum, become scarcer, industry obviously must turn more and more to renewable resources—such as trees—for its raw materials. The broadening frontiers of forest-products research are disclosing more and more how that can be done.

Thus the forest is crucially important to labor, and to the American interest as a whole. It is so important that America can afford no longer to temporize with the excessive forest-fire losses, the destructive logging, the wasteful wood utilization, and the extremely laggard reforestation of fire-and-ax-idled forest acres.

The groups in labor who have been studying this problem are aware that its solution is not a simple one. And they want the solution to be in the progressive American way, rather than totalitarian methods. They believe that a large part of a typically American solution to the problem lies in providing technical and economic aids to the millions of farmers and other owners and operators of small forest tracts who control a huge proportion of the Nation's forests, and account for the bulk of its production of sawlogs, veneer logs, pulpwood, chemical wood, railway ties, mine props, poles, piling, posts, fuel wood, rough lumber, and other forest products.

Practical, effective ways of providing such assistance have been developed and proved through many years of fruitful and richly rewarding experience with the Nation's comprehensive farm program. There has been far too much delay already in putting that experience to work in the forests.

Labor is interested, too, in the multiple-use principle of forest management, whereby forests are developed and managed for all the many benefits which well-managed forests can yield: Wildlife, recreation, watershed protection, livestock grazing, and minor forest products as well as wood production. For that is the way to make forests contribute in fullest measure to the abundant and secure life which is labor's goal. The multiple-use principle has been splendidly demonstrated and applied on Government forests. It is time to develop ways and means of applying the same principle to private forest lands.

Labor, especially the workers in communities which depend directly on wood industries for jobs and income, is vitally interested in sustained-yield forest management for community stability and lasting prosperity. All of us, however, have a stake in that to keep woodworking communities self-supporting instead of letting them become impoverished by cut-out-and-get-out logging, and then requiring heavy expenditures for relief and rehabilitation. This is one of the many reasons why labor has called for national regulation of cutting practices on private land, for the extension of the national forest system, and for the more intensive management of public forests.

A vast majority of workers who have expressed themselves on sustained-yield forestry insist, however, that it be sought by means other than those which strengthen and spread the grip of monopoly, whether it be national monopoly or local monopolization by a few over the resources on which a community depends for jobs, income, and opportunity for its citizens. Therefore, we are opposed to sustained-yield plans that entail monopolistic control over local forest resources.

Labor is also interested in safety in the wood industry, and deplores the fact that sawmilling and logging have by far the worst accident record of any industry. Conservation of logging and lumber workers calls for action just as much as does conservation of forests.

Wilderness preservation is also desired by many people in labor, so that there may always be areas where one may find recreation and inspiration where nature is unspoiled and untouched by industrialization and commercialization. That problem calls for special attention to save remaining areas of our country that are suited and can be spared for such use and that need to be reserved in perpetuity and guarded against all encroachment.

Beyond trees and forestry as such, and overshadowing even that great movement, labor and all people of good will are deeply indebted to the men who pioneered in the practical application of forestry science in America's timberlands. It was their devotion to the public interest and their practical vision of the outdoors as a whole that gave America the conservation policy.

Under the broad conservation policy that was given to America by its pioneer foresters, the farmer's fight for security and well-being on the land, the drives for social security and liberties, the great works of conservation and development of rivers and land, and, of course, the labor movement itself, all come together as parts of one vast, inspiring panorama. It has given men a new vision of their relations with the earth, and of how science and democracy working together can and must develop fruitful harmonious relations of people with the earth and with each other. Neither can be achieved without the other.

PHILIP MURRAY *is president of the Congress of Industrial Organizations.*

# A NATIONAL PROGRAM FOR FORESTRY

LYLE F. WATTS

Our greatest tasks in forest conservation lie ahead.

The conservation idea has won general acceptance, but it has yet to be applied on the ground to most of our forest lands. The downward trend of our forests has yet to be reversed.

We need to restore millions of acres of depleted forest land to productivity.

We need to build up our growing stock of timber. We have to increase the growth rate of all timber by one-half, and double the growth of saw timber.

We need to bring about good forest management on all forest lands. Our national forests and most other public forests are or will be managed for sustained yield. The crux of the problem is the forest lands in private ownership; to them we must look for the bulk of our supply of forest products.

We will have to be on the alert to safeguard the watershed values on forest and range lands.

We shall need to check further range deterioration and build up and wisely manage wild-land ranges for permanent productivity.

We shall also wish to maintain the wildlife in forests, in balance with the natural food supply; preserve scenic values in the forests; develop opportunities and facilities for recreation.

To attain those objectives, a broad program of action is needed both on public and private forest lands. We believe 10 elements are essential in such a program.

*Extend and improve protection against fire.*

Millions of acres of forest land in the United States still lack any form of systematic fire protection. Fire-control forces and facilities on many other areas are still far from being adequate. Organized protection should be extended as rapidly as possible to all areas needing it, and strengthened wherever it is now inadequate.

*Provide more adequate protection against destructive insects and diseases.*

An effective attack on the insect and disease problem will require a detection system, with surveys and observations by competent technicians, for prompt location of potential danger centers and incipient outbreaks; a control organization equipped and ready for immediate action; and intensified studies to discover and develop the best methods of control.

*Eliminate overgrazing and other abuses of forest range lands.*

Many ranges, both public and private, have been heavily overstocked. On national forest ranges, we have attempted to bring grazing into balance with forage growth, with as little hardship as possible to holders of grazing permits who are dependent on these ranges. At least half of the national forest ranges are now in good condition. On some areas, however, further action is necessary to prevent progressive range deterioration. Similar problems exist on many other public and private ranges, and encouragement should be given to sound management of all range lands.

*Reduce forest waste.*

Of all the wood cut or destroyed in logging in the United States, it is estimated that only 43 percent winds up in useful products other than fuel. Twenty-two percent is used as fuel, much of it inefficiently; 35 percent is not used at all. More research is needed to develop new techniques for harvesting wood and making products with less waste, and new ways of utilizing what is now unused. We need also to get such improved methods into use, through increased technical assistance to woodland owners and wood processors and through encouragement of greater integration of timber-products industries. Reduction of waste can give us more wood products without increasing the drain on our forests. Of equal or even greater importance, it produces more employment and more wealth for each thousand board feet cut from the forest.

*Regulate timber cutting and related forest practices.*

An urgent need is to stop destructive cutting. The Department has recommended a Federal-State control plan, which includes: Prohibiting the stripping of every tree from the land, except under special circumstances; prohibiting the premature or wasteful cutting in young stands; providing for certain safeguards against fire, insects, and diseases; and providing for the reservation of sufficient growing stock of desirable trees to keep the lands reasonably productive.

Those five standards are aimed at protection and wise use of the forest values we still have. They would check further destructive exploitation and deterioration, and in some degree start our forest resources toward recovery.

But we need more than this. We need positive action to restore and build up the forests for full production and service.

*Public aids to private forest-land owners, especially the small owners.*

Commercial forest land in private ownership is divided among more than 4 million owners. Among the various classifications of private ownership, the highest percentage of good forest-management practice is found on lands in large industrial ownerships. Many industrial forest-land owners employ their own technical foresters or engage consulting foresters to help them develop good timber-management plans. But large ownerships (of more than 50,000 acres) cover only about 14 percent of the privately owned timberlands. Of the 345 million acres of private commercial forest land, the great bulk is in small holdings, averaging less than 62 acres each. Small holdings include 139 million acres in farms, divided among 3.2 million farmers. Another 122 million acres is held by nearly one million nonfarm owners. Many of these are absentee owners, with whom the problem of encouraging good forestry practice is especially difficult. Most of the timberlands held by farmers and other small owners are in an understocked condition; relatively few are handled with any thought of producing continuous crops of trees. Poor management is reflected in yields and financial returns that are far below potential levels.

Under the Norris-Doxey Law, the Forest Service and a number of States are cooperating in a highly successful but small-scale program of providing on-the-ground advice and technical assistance to individual farm woodland owners. Such technical assistance is resulting in greater returns to the farmer from his timberland as well as improvement in the condition of the forests. The work is now carried on in some 600 counties. But such work is needed in some 2,000 counties, on both farm and nonfarm forest lands, for an effective attack on one of the toughest phases of the Nation's forest problem—the small woodland, in which only about 4 percent of present management meets the demands of good silviculture, and in which some 71 percent of the cutting is poor or destructive.

Other cooperative aids to private owners that would help to encourage better forest management include public assistance in the establishment of cooperative forest management and marketing associations; provision for long-term credit to forest owners to facilitate sustained-yield management and encourage rehabilitation of run-down forests; provision for insurance on growing timber; and promotion of improved systems of taxation of forest lands (tax systems in some cases add to the pressure for quick liquidation of growing timber).

Such cooperative aids would help forest owners make the transition from destructive cutting to continuous production, and would encourage them to go beyond the basic standards that might be required by public regulation and work toward real sustained-yield management.

*More tree planting.*

In the national forests, some 3,200,000 acres need planting to bring the land back into productivity. In addition, about 1,500,000 acres are so understocked that fill-in planting is needed. Many more millions of acres of idle, submarginal farm land and nonproductive State and private woodland also need planting. The Forest Service is cooperating in a small way with 42 States and 2 Territories in the production of forest-tree planting stock for distribution to farmers. Other public and private agencies also carry on planting programs, but at the present rate of planting by all agencies it will take generations to cover all the depleted forest land in need of reforestation. The Forest Service has suggested an over-all planting goal, public and private, of 32 million acres in 25 years—more than a billion trees a year—as a reasonably adequate attack on the reforestation job.

*More range improvement and reseeding.*

Research has developed techniques for reseeding depleted range in several western regions. Where reseeding can be accomplished successfully it will not only check erosion and improve watershed conditions but greatly increase the grazing capacity of the range. Several million acres of national forest range need reseeding, as well as large areas of other public and private range land in the Western States. Other range improvements, such as stock-watering facilities, fences, and stock driveways, can contribute to building up deteriorated range by making possible better control and distribution of livestock grazing.

*Extension and development of public forests.*

Within the boundaries of existing national forests are about 35 million out of some 49 million acres of intermingled private land, that are suitable for forestry purposes and that should be purchased and included in the national forests to facilitate their full development. There are other lands for which public ownership—Federal, State, or community—would be the best guaranty that the lands would be developed and managed in the Nation's best interest. These include forest lands where the productivity is too low for private owners to be expected to hold them for timber growing; lands which lie in such rough or inaccessible country that they have little attraction for private enterprise; and lands so denuded as to offer no prospect of income for many decades. Also for certain areas where acute problems of watershed protection or development of scenic or recreational values or other public interests are paramount, public acquisition is indicated.

There should, of course, be adequate provision for the protection, effective administration, and full development of the public forests now existing or yet to be established. There is need for more intensive management on many of the national forests and other public timberlands and ranges; for tighter protection against fire; for more tree planting, range reseeding, and upstream engineering work; for development of recreation facilities and improvement of wildlife habitat. Present forces and facilities on the public forests are spread thinly over a large area. The public forests should be developed and managed for maximum production and service.

*More research.*

Fundamental to all action programs for the restoration and development of the forest and wild-land resources is sound, scientific knowledge. Research and experience already have produced a great deal of knowledge and ability in forestry—enough to provide a sound basis for an effective forest conservation and development program. But there are many problems in forest management, range management, and watershed management yet unsolved. There are great possibilities for improvements in wood utilization, development of new forest products, and reduction of waste. An enlarged and intensified program of research should increase our basic knowledge of forest and wild-land resources, and find new and better ways of doing things at less cost.

Deterioration of forest resources in the United States already has gone so far that we face a period of timber shortage before timber growth can be built up to the point of sustained abundance. We are already experiencing shortage in many kinds of forest products. The longer action to build up the timber resource is delayed, the longer and more acute the period of short supply will be.

The need for forest rehabilitation and improved forest management is not confined to the United States alone. It is world-wide. The Food and Agriculture Organization of the United Nations has reported: "In the face of . . . rapidly multiplying uses for wood which create ever-mounting wood needs, the world is confronted by the inescapable fact that the forests—sole source of wood—are steadily diminishing."

We have the forest land in the United States to meet our own requirements for timber eventually and to help supply other less fortunate countries. With intelligent, courageous, positive action, we can achieve permanent timber abundance. We can make trees and forests serve human welfare forever.

LYLE F. WATTS *is the Chief of the Forest Service, the United States Department of Agriculture, which he entered as a forest assistant in 1913.*

# LISTS AND OTHER AIDS

# To Know the Trees

## IMPORTANT FOREST TREES OF THE UNITED STATES

ELBERT L. LITTLE, JR.

FOR A SELECTED LIST of 165 important native forest tree species of the United States the following information is compiled here: (1) Approved common and scientific names, as well as other names of lumber and other names in use; (2) drawings, keys, and nontechnical descriptive notes for identification; (3) distribution maps showing ranges; and (4) lists of principal uses, chiefly of the wood. This summary is intended as an introduction to the forest trees, as well as a compilation of their distribution and commercial uses.

Trees are considered here as woody plants having one well-defined stem or trunk at least 2 inches in diameter at breast height, a more or less definitely formed crown of foliage, and a height of at least 10 feet. Though the division between trees and shrubs is not sharp, shrubs typically are the smaller woody plants, usually with several branches from the ground instead of one trunk.

The kinds, or species, of native trees in the United States number about 845, excluding hybrids and varieties but including smaller trees not of commercial timber size and those classed also as large shrubs. These are further grouped into about 222 genera and 69 plant families. Of the total, about 150 species belong to the single, highly variable group, or genus, of hawthorns (*Crataegus*), in which numerous other minor forms (including many shrubs) have been proposed as separate species. About 110 other native tree species are tropical or subtropical trees known in the United States only from Florida. Thus, without the hawthorns and the trees confined to Florida, there are about 585 tree species native in the United States. In addition, 90 or more foreign tree species widely planted have escaped from cultivation, and have become naturalized, so that they may be considered properly as at home here. More than a third of these exotics are tropical trees limited to Florida. Many other tree species from foreign lands have been introduced as ornamental, shade, and fruit trees.

Botanists have named and distinguished also numerous varieties and more than 85 natural hybrids and apparent hybrids among the native trees, including more than 60 hybrid oaks (*Quercus*). However, foresters distinguish only a few botanical varieties, or minor variations, by name, although they do recognize unnamed geographic races. Aside from the hawthorns, the largest groups, or genera, of native trees are the oaks, with 57 species; willows (*Salix*), with 33 species; and pines (*Pinus*), with 34 species.

Nearly three-tenths of the 585 native tree species (excluding hawthorns and the tropical trees of Florida), or 165 species, have been selected and included here primarily for the commercial importance of their woods or other products, although a few are more important for other values in forestry. These are grouped in 51 genera, the largest groups being the oaks (*Quer-*

*cus*), with 28 species, and the pines (*Pinus*), with 20 species. The species in the series of leaflets on economically important species, *American Woods,* by H. S. Betts, are represented, as are most of the 182 tree species designated as important forest trees in the check list by George B. Sudworth (*Check List of the Forest Trees of the United States,* U. S. D. A. Miscellaneous Circular 92, 1927; now out of print).

The important native tree species of Alaska and Canada are also here included, because the ranges of some species of the northern United States extend northward. These northern species are indicated by mention of Alaska or Canada (or a Canadian Province) in the notes on distribution. The 18 species of Alaska included here are more than half of the 32 native tree species of Alaska. The 89 Canadian species in this list are almost three-fifths of the 150 native tree species of Canada, excluding hawthorns (*Crataegus*), although some of these range northward only to extreme southern Ontario.

The 165 important forest tree species of the United States have been separated into two lists, eastern and western, because the tree species of the two regions are almost entirely different. The first list contains 110 species found in the eastern half of the United States (extending west to the prairie-plains), and the second list has 55 species found in the western half of the United States (from the prairie-plains westward including Alaska). The eastern list is larger than the western because there are more commercially important hardwood species in the East. Several species that have wide distribution in both East and West have been placed in one list, with a cross-reference in the other.

In the descriptive summary, the approved common and scientific names are those officially accepted and widely used. Other lumber names and common names in use in some localities and a few scientific names have been added as synonyms. A few important varieties are listed under the names.

Size is indicated as large (more than 70 feet tall), medium-sized (from 30 to 70 feet tall), or small (less than 30 feet tall).

The descriptive notes are a summary of the leading characteristics, such as bark, leaves, and fruits and flowers, if showy or distinctive. These notes, together with the drawings (by Miss Leta Hughey) of the leaves and fruits, may be used to find tree names.

The distribution maps prepared especially for this article are based largely upon data published in various State tree manuals and State floras. Thus, the geographic areas in the United States and southern Canada as well (but excluding Mexico), where each species grows wild, or is native, are summarized concisely. However, maps are subject to certain limitations and minor inaccuracies based upon incomplete knowledge of exact distribution and limits, insufficient botanical exploration in some regions, lack of compilation of numerous herbarium and published records of range extensions, and difficulties in mapping scattered and isolated stations. In order that these maps can be revised and made more accurate, additional information on distribution, including both corrections and range extensions, will be welcomed by the author.

By showing the native ranges, these maps will aid in identification of trees. Thus, when a tree specimen is compared with drawings and descriptions, the maps indicate which species are native in a particular region and which are not to be expected there. However, many species have been planted beyond their native ranges and often have spread by escaping from cultivation. A few, such as Osage-orange, black locust, and northern catalpa, have become widely naturalized.

The notes on principal uses have been compiled largely from data in the leaflets, *American Woods,* by H. S. Betts, published by the Department of Agriculture in 1945.

To assist in the identification of trees, a simplified key, based chiefly upon leaves and twigs, has been inserted in the text. This key is an outline in which trees with certain characteristics in common are grouped together. The name of a tree specimen is found by elimination through successive selection of one from a pair of groups, with descriptive characters that fit the specimen. The paired groups are designated by the same letter, single and double, beginning with "A" and "AA," at the left of the page. Under the group fitting the specimen, the elimination continues with the next paired groups indented below, such as from "AA" to "N" or "NN" and from "NN" to "O" or "OO," the pair next indented to the right, until the name is reached. Some descriptive notes applying to a genus have been inserted in the key and not repeated in the notes under each species. The key is limited to the tree species represented here and will not serve to identify other trees. Identifications, of course, may be made directly from the drawings, maps, and descriptive notes, without use of the key.

The arrangement of species in the lists of eastern and western trees is artificial, to fit the key, rather than botanical. In each list the conifers are placed first, sorted into those with needlelike leaves and those with scalelike leaves, followed by broadleaf trees. The latter are grouped into trees with paired (opposite) simple leaves, trees with paired (opposite) compound leaves, trees with single (alternate) compound leaves, and trees with single (alternate) simple leaves, with the oaks placed last. (A compound leaf is divided into leaflets, which usually are smaller than leaves and are attached on a common leafstalk that sheds with them. Also, the leaf has a developing bud at its base, while the leaflets of a compound leaf do not.)

Various handbooks, manuals, and other publications may be consulted for the identification of the trees of the United States, especially those not found here, and for additional information. A list of 30 references for identification of trees, both popular and technical, including the illustrated books on the commoner trees of the United States and books on the trees of geographic regions, will be found in the bibliography. Trees are described also in the various botanical floras and manuals, usually technical and without illustrations, which have been prepared for geographical regions, single States, or smaller areas.

The State forester can furnish information about publications on the trees of your State and how to obtain them.

To identify with certainty the numerous kinds of native trees, some of which differ but slightly, some knowledge of systematic botany or dendrology as well as of the technical terminology is desirable. Properly prepared dried and pressed botanical specimens of twigs with leaves and flowers or fruits may be submitted for identification to specialists, such as to departments of botany and schools of forestry in universities and colleges, to botanical gardens, herbaria, and museums, or to the United States Department of Agriculture. Specimens should be accompanied by notes, such as locality where found, collector's name, date, size, whether wild or planted, and other data of interest. Material for the Department of Agriculture may be sent to either of the following: Forest Service, Washington 25, D. C.; or Bureau of Plant Industry, Soils, and Agricultural Engineering, Plant Industry Station, Beltsville, Md.

On the next two pages are indexes of common and scientific names of the species discussed on pages 768–814. Thus, a reader who wishes to look up pecan finds that it has the number 41 in the index of common names. By going through the list, he finds pecan described on page 780.

Or, if he encounters the scientific name *Carya illinoensis,* he will learn from the index of scientific names that it is number 41 and described (as pecan) on page 780.

# INDEX OF COMMON NAMES BY NUMBER

*In addition to these accepted common names for the 165 species, lumber names and other common names in use are listed in the text.*

## INDEX OF SCIENTIFIC NAMES BY NUMBER

*Widely used synonyms of these accepted scientific names for the 165 species are mentioned in the text. The numbers refer to the entries on pages 768–814.*

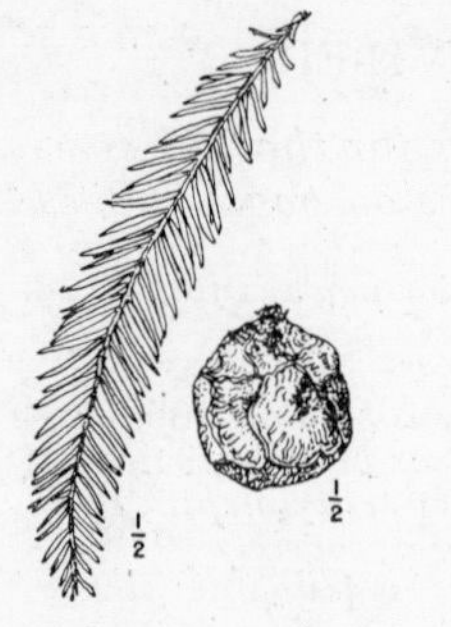


1. **Baldcypress.**

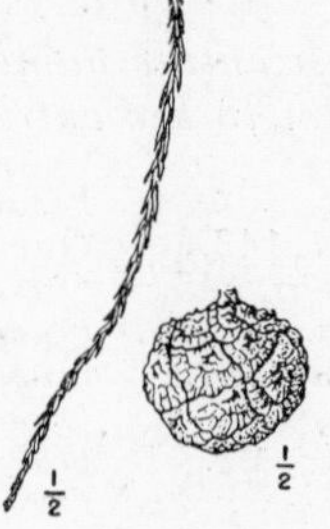


2. **Pondcypress.**

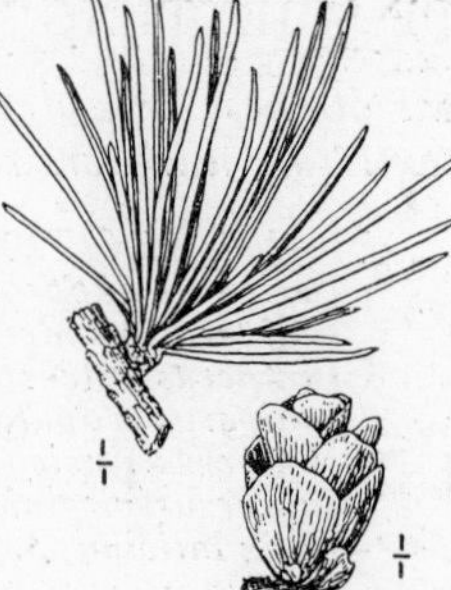


3. **Tamarack.**

4. **Eastern white pine.**

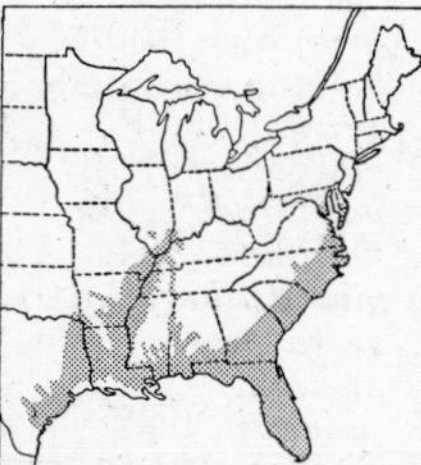

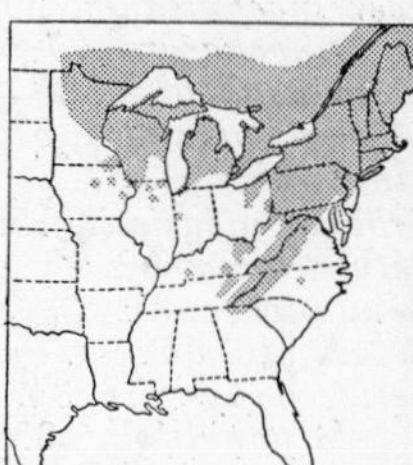

## EASTERN TREES

*Tree species Nos. 1 to 100 are native wholly or mainly in the eastern half of the United States, west to the prairie-plains. In addition, species No. 150 in the list of western trees occurs also in the eastern United States.*

### GYMNOSPERMS (CONIFERS OR SOFTWOODS)

A (AA on p. 774). Trees resinous, with leaves needlelike or scalelike, evergreen (except Nos. 1–3); seeds borne on scales of a cone (berrylike in juniper, Nos. 22, 23)—GYMNOSPERMS (conifers or softwoods, such as pines, spruces, firs).

B. Leaves shedding in fall, on slender twigs mostly shedding in fall also or on short spur branches.

C. Leaves needlelike or scalelike, on slender twigs mostly shedding in fall—BALDCYPRESS (*Taxodium*).

1. BALDCYPRESS, *Taxodium distichum* (L.) Rich. (common baldcypress, southern cypress, red cypress [lumber], yellow cypress [lumber], white cypress [lumber], tidewater red cypress, gulf cypress).

Large tree with swollen base and "knees," swamps and river banks, South Atlantic and Gulf Coastal Plains and Mississippi Valley. Bark reddish brown or gray, with long fibrous or scaly ridges. Leaves crowded featherlike in two rows on slender horizontal twigs, flat, 3/8 to 3/4 inch, long, light yellow green, or whitish beneath, shedding in fall. Cones 3/4 to 1 inch in diameter, of hard scales.

Principal uses: Chiefly for building construction and heavy construction. Boxes and crates, caskets, general millwork, and tanks. Also ships and boats, greenhouses, and railroad-car construction. Railroad ties. Ornamental.

2. PONDCYPRESS, *Taxodium ascendens* Brongn. (pond baldcypress, cypress).

Large tree with swollen base, ponds, swamps, and river banks, South Atlantic and Gulf Coastal Plains. Bark reddish brown or gray, with long fibrous or scaly ridges. Leaves nearly flat against the slender erect twigs, scalelike or needlelike, 1/8 to 3/8 inch long, light yellow green, shedding in fall. Cones 3/4 to 1 inch in diameter, of hard scales. (Perhaps only a variety of No. 1.)

Principal uses: Same as No. 1.

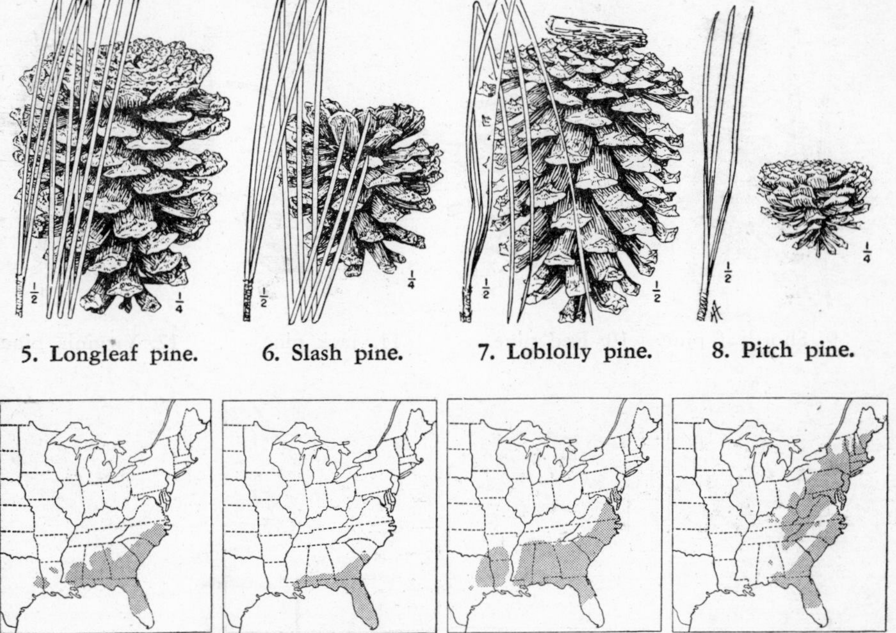

**5. Longleaf pine.** **6. Slash pine.** **7. Loblolly pine.** **8. Pitch pine.**

CC. Leaves needlelike, many in cluster on short spur branches—LARCH (or tamarack, *Larix*).

3. TAMARACK, *Larix laricina* (Du Roi) K. Koch (eastern larch, American larch, hackmatack; *L. americana* Michx.).

Medium-sized tree of wet soils in northeastern United States, and across Canada to Alaska. Bark reddish brown, scaly. Needles many in cluster on short spur branches (or single on leading twigs), 3-angled, ¾ to 1 inch long, blue green, shedding in fall. Cones upright, ¾ inch long.

Principal uses: Lumber (largely framing for houses), and railroad ties. Also ship knees in shipbuilding.

BB. Leaves evergreen, on normal twigs.
D. Leaves needlelike, more than ½ inch long (usually shorter in No. 17).
E. Needles in clusters of 2 to 5 with a sheath at base—PINE (*Pinus*).
F. Needles 5 in cluster—WHITE (SOFT) PINES.

4. EASTERN WHITE PINE, *Pinus strobus* L. (northern white pine [lumber], white pine, northern pine, soft pine, Weymouth pine).

Large tree (the largest northeastern conifer) of northeastern United States, adjacent Canada, and Appalachian Mountain region. Bark gray or purplish, deeply fissured into broad ridges. Needles 5 in cluster, slender, 2½ to 5 inches long, blue green. Cones long-stalked, long and narrow, 4 to 8 inches long, yellow brown, with thin, rounded scales.

Principal uses: Important timber species. Chiefly for boxes, formerly mostly for building construction. Also patterns for castings, millwork, caskets, and many other uses. Shade tree and ornamental. (State tree of Maine and Minnesota.)

FF. Needles 2 or 3 in a cluster—YELLOW (HARD, OR PITCH) PINES.
G. Needles 3 in cluster.
H. Needles more than 8 inches long.

5. LONGLEAF PINE, *Pinus palustris* Mill. (southern pine [lumber], longleaf yellow pine, southern yellow pine, pitch pine, hard pine, heart pine; *P. australis* Michx. f.).

Large tree of South Atlantic and Gulf Coastal Plains. Bark orange brown, coarsely scaly. Needles 3 in cluster, slender, very long, 10 to 15 inches long, dark green. Cones large, 5 to 10 inches long, dull brown, prickly.

Principal uses: A leading world producer of naval stores. Lumber for miscellaneous factory and construction purposes, flooring, railroad-car construction, shipbuilding.

802062°—49——50

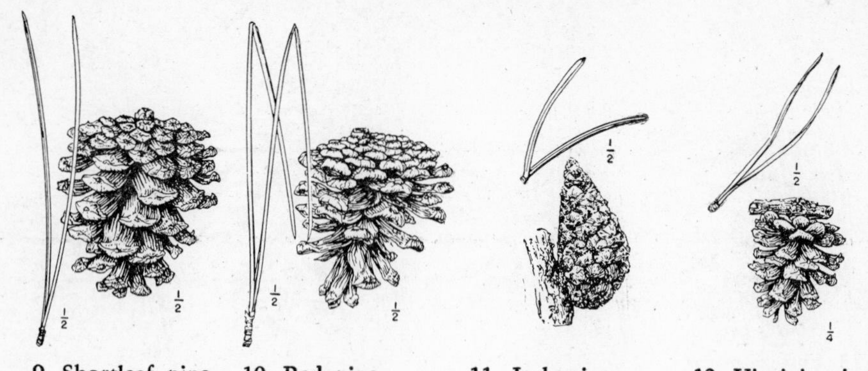


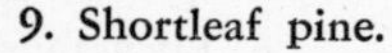

**9. Shortleaf pine.** **10. Red pine.** **11. Jack pine.** **12. Virginia pine.**

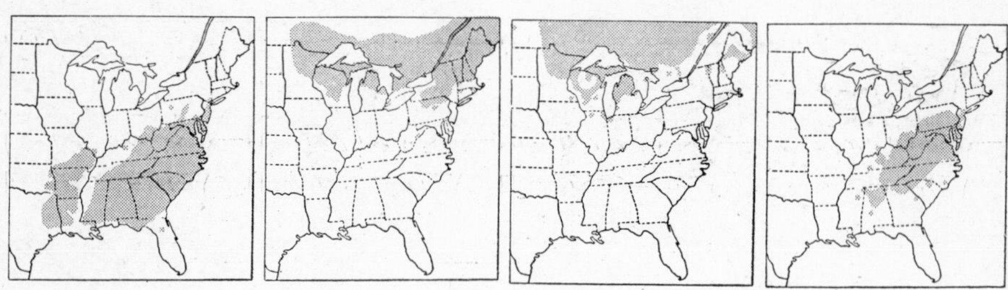

6. SLASH PINE, *Pinus caribaea* Morelet (southern pine [lumber], Cuban pine, yellow slash pine, swamp pine, pitch pine).

Large tree of South Atlantic and Gulf Coastal Plains; also in West Indies and Central America. Bark purplish brown, with large thin scales. Needles 3 (or 2 and 3) in cluster, stout, 8 to 12 inches long, dark green. Cones 3 to 6 inches long, shiny brown, with minute prickles.

Principal uses: Same as No. 5. (State tree of Alabama.)

HH. Needles mostly less than 8 inches long.

7. LOBLOLLY PINE, *Pinus taeda* L. (southern pine [lumber], North Carolina pine [lumber], Arkansas pine [lumber], oldfield pine, shortleaf pine).

Large tree of Atlantic and Gulf Coastal Plains. Bark reddish brown, deeply fissured into broad scaly plates. Needles 3 in cluster, slender, 6 to 9 inches long, pale green. Cones 3 to 5 inches long, reddish brown, with stiff, sharp prickles.

Principal uses: Important timber species. Same as No. 9.

8. PITCH PINE, *Pinus rigida* Mill. (southern pine [lumber], southern yellow pine; variety: pond pine, *P. rigida* var. *serotina* (Michx.) Loud.).

Medium-sized tree of Atlantic coast and Appalachian Mountain regions and in adjacent Canada, Needles 3 in cluster, stout, 3 to 6 inches long (6 to 8 inches in a variety, pond pine), dark yellow green. Cones short and broad, 1½ to 3 inches long, light brown, shiny, with small prickles, remaining on branches several years after opening.

Principal uses: Fuel and lumber.

GG. Needles 2 in cluster (or partly 3 in No. 9).

I. Needles more than 3 inches long.

9. SHORTLEAF PINE, *Pinus echinata* Mill. (southern pine [lumber], North Carolina pine [lumber], Arkansas pine [lumber], shortleaf yellow pine, yellow pine, southern yellow pine).

Large tree of southeastern quarter of United States north to New York. Bark reddish brown, with large, irregular, flat, scaly plates. Needles 2 or 3 in cluster, slender, 2½ to 5 inches long, dark blue green. Cones small, 1½ to 2½ inches long, dull brown, with small prickles.

Principal uses: Important timber species. Lumber chiefly for building material including millwork, also for boxes and crates, agricultural implements, motor vehicles, low-grade furniture. Veneer for containers. This and other southern pines are the leading native pulpwoods and leading woods in production of slack cooperage. Also

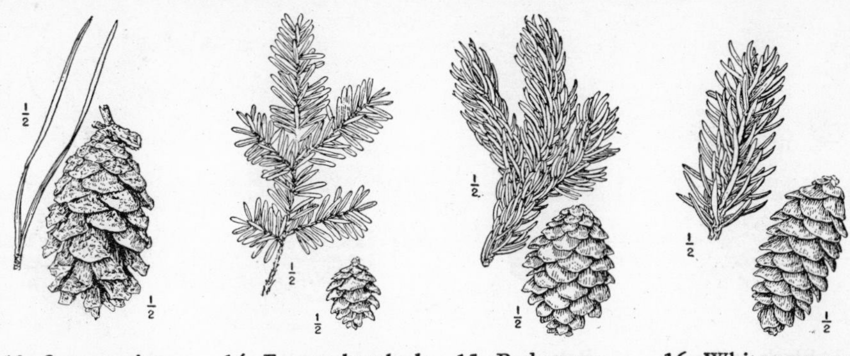


**13. Spruce pine. 14. Eastern hemlock. 15. Red spruce. 16. White spruce.**

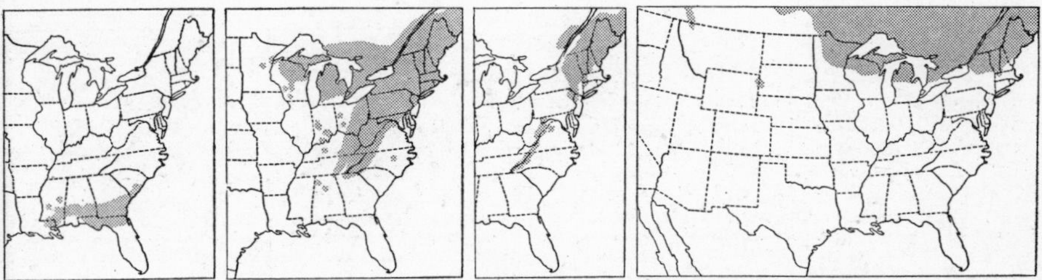

railroad ties, poles, piling, mine timbers, excelsior, and veneer. Ornamental. (Pine (*Pinus* spp.) is the State tree of Arkansas.)

10. RED PINE, *Pinus resinosa* Ait. (Norway pine [lumber]).

Medium-sized to large tree of northeastern United States and adjacent Canada. Bark reddish brown, with broad, flat, scaly plates. Needles 2 in cluster, slender, 5 to 6 inches long, dark green. Cones 2 inches long, light brown, without prickles.

Principal uses: General building construction, planing-mill products, general millwork, and boxes and crates. Pulpwood. Ornamental and shade tree.

II. Needles less than 3 inches long.

11. JACK PINE, *Pinus banksiana* Lamb. (scrub pine, gray pine, black pine).

Usually small (or medium-sized) tree of northeastern United States and nearly across Canada. Bark dark brown, with narrow scaly ridges. Needles 2 in cluster, stout, twisted, ¾ to 1½ inches long, dark green. Cones one-sided, much curved, small, 1 to 2 inches long, light yellow, without prickles, remaining closed at maturity.

Principal uses: Pulpwood, lumber for boxes and crates and rough construction, and fuel. Ornamental.

12. VIRGINIA PINE, *Pinus virginiana* Mill. (North Carolina pine [lumber], Jersey pine, scrub pine).

Usually small tree (sometimes large) of Atlantic Coastal Plain, Appalachian Mountain, and Ohio Valley regions. Bark dark brown, thin, with scaly plates. Needles 2 in cluster, stout, twisted, 2 to 3 inches long, gray green. Cones 2 inches long, reddish brown, shiny, very prickly.

Principal uses: Lumber and fuel.

13. SPRUCE PINE, *Pinus glabra* Walt. (cedar pine, southern white pine).

Medium-sized to large tree of Gulf and South Atlantic Coastal Plains. Bark on small trunks and limbs gray and smooth; bark on large trunks with flat scaly ridges. Needles 2 in cluster, slender, 1½ to 3 inches long, dark green. Cones 1 to 2 inches long, reddish brown, shiny, with minute prickles.

Principal uses: Lumber and fuel.

EE. Needles borne singly and not in clusters.

J. Twigs roughened by projecting bases of old needles; cones hanging down.

K. Needles flat, soft, blunt-pointed, with short leafstalks, appearing in 2 rows—HEMLOCK (*Tsuga*).

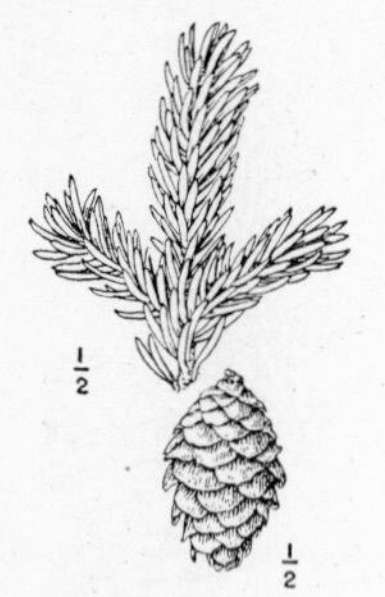


17. **Black spruce.**

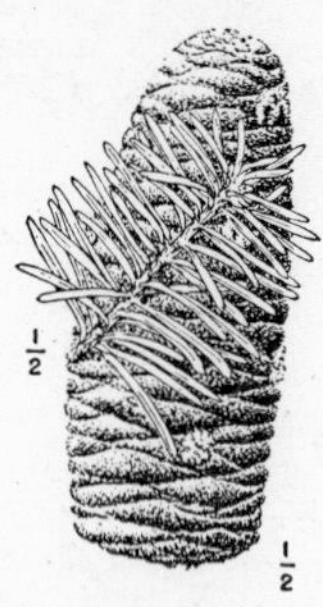


18. **Balsam fir.**

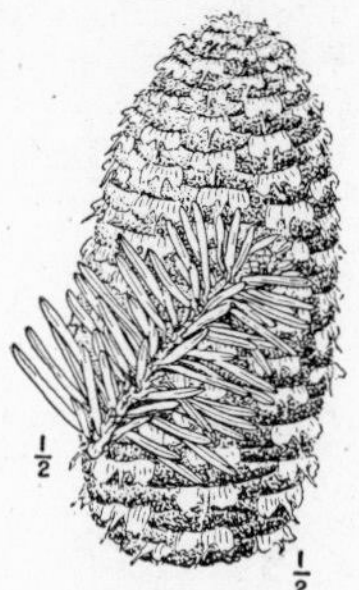


19. **Fraser fir.**

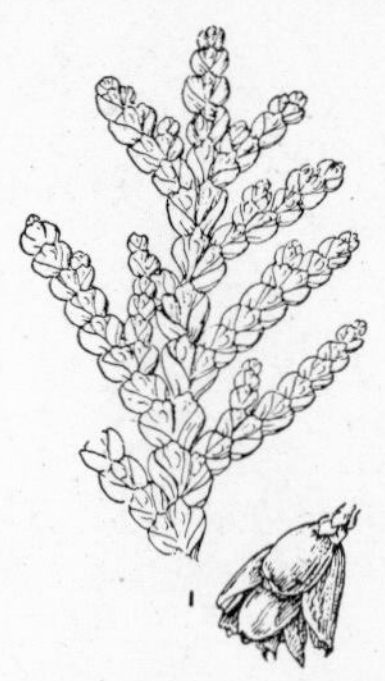


20. **Northern white-cedar.**

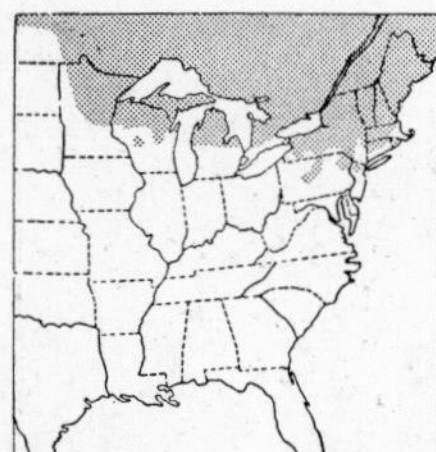

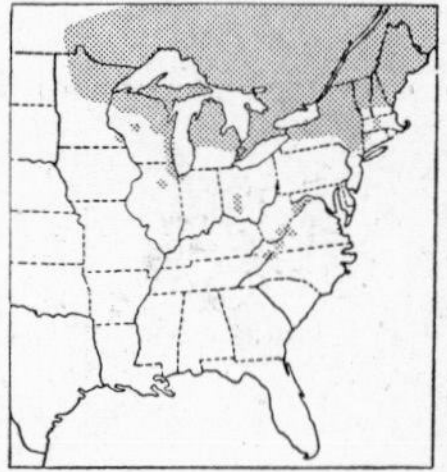

14. EASTERN HEMLOCK, *Tsuga canadensis* (L.) Carr. (Canada hemlock, hemlock spruce).

Medium-sized to large tree of northeastern United States, adjacent Canada, and Appalachian Mountain region. Bark brown or purplish, deeply furrowed into broad scaly ridges. Needles short-stalked, flat, soft, blunt-pointed, 3/8 to 5/8 inches long, shiny dark green, lighter beneath, appearing in two rows. Cones 5/8 to 3/4 inches long, brownish.

Principal uses: Building construction and boxes and crates. Pulpwood. The bark is a source of tannin. Ornamental and shade tree. (State tree of Pennsylvania.)

KK. Needles 4-angled, stiff, sharp-pointed, without leafstalk, extending out on all sides of twig—SPRUCE (*Picea*).

15. RED SPRUCE, *Picea rubens* Sarg. (eastern spruce [lumber], Canadian spruce, yellow spruce, West Virginia spruce; *P. rubra* (Du Roi) Link, not A. Dietr.).

Medium-sized to large tree of northeastern United States, adjacent Canada, and Appalachian Mountain region. Bark reddish brown, thin, scaly. Twigs hairy. Needles 4-angled, 1/2 inch long, dark green, shiny. Cones 1 1/4 to 1 1/2 inches long, light reddish brown, shiny, with scales rigid, rounded, and with edges smooth or slightly toothed.

Principal uses: Pulpwood. Boxes and crates, construction. Also furniture, millwork, ladder rails. Christmas trees. Ornamental and shade tree.

16. WHITE SPRUCE, *Picea glauca* (Moench) Voss (eastern spruce [lumber], Canadian spruce, skunk spruce, single spruce; *P. canadensis* (Mill.) B. S. P., not (Michx.) Link); variety: western white spruce, *P. glauca* var. *albertiana* (S. Brown) Sarg., Alberta white spruce).

Medium-sized tree of northeastern United States, Black Hills, and across Canada to Alaska. Bark gray or brown, thin, scaly. Twigs without hairs. Needles 4-angled, 1/2 to 3/4 inch long, blue green, of disagreeable odor when crushed. Cones slender, 1 1/2 to 2 inches long, pale brown and shiny, with scales thin, flexible, rounded, and with smooth margins.

Principal uses: Same as No. 15. Important timber species of Canada.

17. BLACK SPRUCE, *Picea mariana* (Mill.) B. S. P. (eastern spruce [lumber], bog spruce, swamp spruce).

Small to medium-sized tree of bottom lands and bogs, northeastern United States and across Canada to Alaska. Bark grayish brown, thin, scaly. Twigs hairy. Needles 4-angled, 1/4 to 5/8 inch long, pale blue green. Cones 3/4 to 1 1/2 inches long, dull gray brown, with scales rigid, rounded, and slightly toothed.

Principal uses: Same as No. 15.

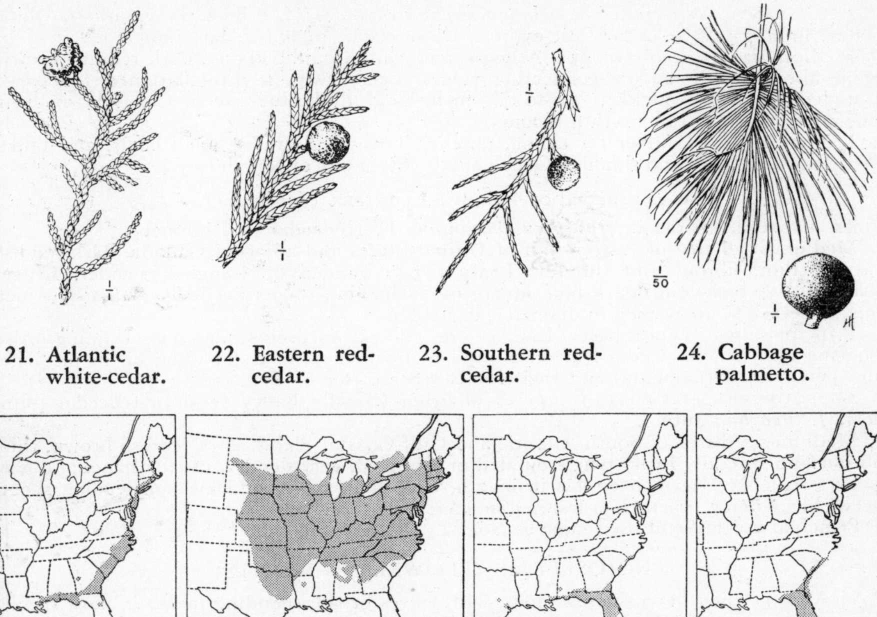

**21. Atlantic white-cedar.** **22. Eastern red-cedar.** **23. Southern red-cedar.** **24. Cabbage palmetto.**

JJ. Twigs smooth; cones upright, in top of tree—FIR (*Abies*).

18. BALSAM FIR, *Abies balsamea* (L.) Mill. (eastern fir [lumber], balsam, Canada balsam).

Medium-sized tree of northeastern United States, Appalachian Mountain region, and across Canada to Alberta. Bark gray or brown, thin, smoothish, with many resin blisters, becoming scaly. Needles flat, ½ to 1¼ inches long, dark green, usually rounded at tip. Cones upright, 2 to 3 inches long, purple, with cone scales usually covering the bracts.

Principal uses: Pulpwood. Lumber, chiefly for boxes and crates. Canada balsam (an oleoresin). Christmas trees.

19. FRASER FIR, *Abies fraseri* (Pursh) Poir. (balsam fir [lumber], eastern fir [lumber], Fraser balsam fir, southern balsam fir, balsam).

Medium-sized tree of Appalachian Mountains in Virginia, North Carolina, and Tennessee. Bark gray or brown, thin, smoothish, with many resin blisters; bark on larger trunks with thin papery scales. Needles flat, ½ to 1 inch long, dark green, usually rounded at tip. Cones upright, 1½ to 2½ inches long, purple, with yellow-green bracts partly covering the cone scales.

Principal uses: Same as No. 18.

DD. Leaves scalelike, less than ¼ inch long (or needlelike and up to ⅜ inch long on leading shoots).

L. Leafy twigs more or less flattened.

M. Twigs much flattened, about ⅛ inch broad including leaves—THUJA (*Thuja*).

20. NORTHERN WHITE-CEDAR, *Thuja occidentalis* L. (eastern arborvitae, white-cedar, swamp-cedar, arborvitae).

Medium-sized tree of northeastern United States, adjacent Canada, and Appalachian Mountain region. Bark reddish brown, thin, fibrous, with narrow connecting ridges. Twigs flattened and branching in one plane. Leaves appearing flattened in 2 rows, scalelike, 1/16 to ⅛ inch long, light yellow green, aromatic. Cones ⅜ to ½ inch long, pale brown.

Principal uses: Poles, railroad ties, and posts. Lumber for boxes, millwork, tanks, and building construction. Cedar-oil, used in medicine. Ornamental.

MM. Twigs slightly flattened, less than 1/16 inch broad including leaves—WHITE-CEDAR (*Chamaecyparis*).

21. ATLANTIC WHITE-CEDAR, *Chamaecyparis thyoides* (L.) B. S. P. (southern white-cedar [lumber], white-cedar false-cypress, white-cedar, swamp-cedar, juniper).

Medium-sized tree of swamps, Atlantic and Gulf Coastal Plains. Bark reddish brown, thin, fibrous, with narrow connecting ridges. Leafy twigs slightly flattened (or partly 4-angled). Leaves scalelike, 1/16 to 1/8 inch long, dull blue green. Cones 1/4 inch in diameter, bluish purple, with a bloom.

Principal uses: Lumber for siding, porches, boxes and crates, small boats, and tanks. Woodenware, poles, and shingles. Ornamental. (State tree of New Jersey.)

LL. Leafy twigs rounded or 4-angled—JUNIPER (*Juniperus*).

22. EASTERN REDCEDAR, *Juniperus virginiana* L. (redcedar, red juniper).

Medium-sized tree of eastern half of United States and adjacent Canada. Bark reddish brown, thin, fibrous and shreddy. Leafy twigs rounded or 4-angled, slender. Leaves scalelike, 1/16 inch long, dark blue green, or on leading shoots needlelike, up to 3/8 inch long. "Berry" 1/4 to 3/8 inch in diameter, dark blue.

Principal uses: Fence posts. Lumber for chests, wardrobes, and closet lining. Also flooring and pencils. Cedar-leaf oil is used in medicine and cedar-wood oil in medicine and perfumes. Ornamental and shelterbelts. (State tree of Tennessee.)

23. SOUTHERN REDCEDAR, *Juniperus silicicola* (Small) Bailey (eastern redcedar [lumber]; *J. lucayana* auth.).

Medium-sized tree of South Atlantic and Gulf Coastal Plains. Bark reddish brown, thin, fibrous and shreddy. Leafy twigs rounded or 4-angled, very slender, usually hanging down. Leaves scalelike, 1/16 inch or less in length, dark blue green, or leaves on leading shoots needlelike. "Berry" 3/16 inch or less in diameter, dark blue.

Principal uses: Wood used same as No. 22. Ornamental.

## ANGIOSPERMS (FLOWERING PLANTS)

AA (A on p. 768). Trees nonresinous, with leaves broad, shedding in fall in most species (evergreen in palmetto, holly, magnolia, live oak, etc.); seeds enclosed in a fruit—ANGIOSPERMS (flowering plants).

## MONOCOTYLEDONS

N. Leaves parallel-veined, evergreen, clustered at top of trunk or large branches; trunk with woody portions irregularly distributed, without clear distinction of bark and wood, and without annual rings—MONOCOTYLEDONS (palms, yuccas, etc.).

24. CABBAGE PALMETTO, *Sabal palmetto* (Walt.) Lodd. (palmetto, cabbage-palm).

Medium-sized palm tree of south Atlantic and Gulf coasts from North Carolina to Florida. Trunk stout and unbranched, grayish brown, roughened or ridged, with a cluster of large leaves at the top. Leaves evergreen, coarse, fan-shaped, 4 to 7 feet long, thick and leathery, much folded and divided into narrow segments with threadlike fibers hanging between. Leafstalks 5 to 8 feet long. Fruits in a much branched cluster about 7 feet long, numerous, 3/8 to 1/2 inch in diameter, black, 1-seeded.

Principal uses: Trunks are used for wharf pilings, docks, and poles. Brushes and whiskbrooms are made from the young leafstalk fibers; baskets, mats, hats, brooms and thatch are made from the leaves. Ornamental. (State tree of Florida and South Carolina.)

## DICOTYLEDONS (BROADLEAF TREES OR HARDWOODS)

NN. Leaves net-veined; trunk with bark and wood distinct and with annual rings in wood—DICOTYLEDONS (broadleaf trees, or hardwoods, such as oaks, poplars, ashes, maples).

O (OO on p. 779). Leaves and usually branches in pairs (opposite; or in threes in No. 25).

P. Leaves not divided into leaflets (simple).

Q. Leaf edges smooth, not lobed.

R. Leaves heart-shaped, large, more than 6 inches long, in threes or pairs—CATALPA (*Catalpa*).

25. NORTHERN CATALPA, *Catalpa speciosa* Warder (western catalpa, hardy catalpa, cigartree).

Medium-sized to large tree of lower Ohio Valley and central Mississippi Valley, naturalized elsewhere in eastern United States. Bark reddish brown, with flat, scaly ridges. Leaves in threes or paired, large, heart-shaped, 6 to 12 inches long, long-pointed, edges smooth, thick, dark green above, hairy beneath. Leafstalk 4 to 6 inches long. Flowers large and showy, about 2 inches long, whitish and purple spotted, in few-flowered clusters in late spring. Fruiting capsule cigarlike, long and narrow, 8 to 18 inches long and 5/8 inch thick, dark brown, with many winged seeds.

Principal uses: Fence posts. Shade tree and ornamental. Shelterbelts.

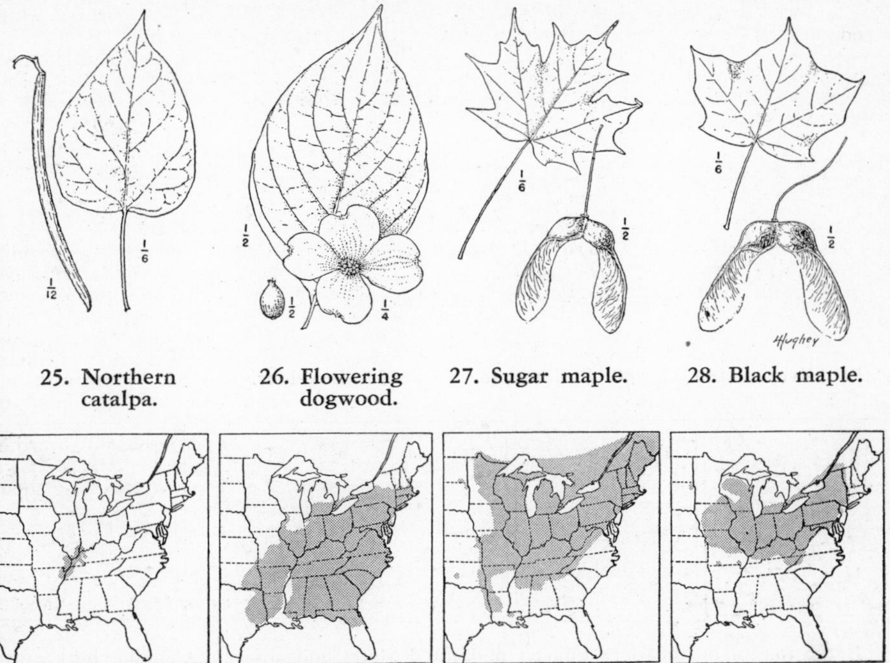


**25. Northern catalpa.** **26. Flowering dogwood.** **27. Sugar maple.** **28. Black maple.**

RR. Leaves elliptical, less than 6 inches long—DOGWOOD (*Cornus*).

26. FLOWERING DOGWOOD, *Cornus florida* L. (dogwood, boxwood; *Cynoxylon floridum* (L.) Raf.).

Small tree of eastern half of United States; also in southern Ontario and a variety in northeastern Mexico. Bark dark reddish brown, broken into small square or rounded blocks. Leaves paired, elliptical or oval, 3 to 6 inches long, short-pointed, edges appearing smooth but minutely toothed, lateral veins curved, bright green and nearly smooth above, whitish and slightly hairy beneath, turning bright scarlet above in fall. Flowers greenish yellow, in a dense head with 4 showy, white, petallike bracts 2¼ to 4 inches in diameter, in early spring. Fruits egg-shaped, ⅜ inch long, bright scarlet, shiny, fleshy, 1- or 2-seeded.

Principal uses: Important ornamental tree. The outstanding wood for shuttles (used in textile weaving). (Dogwood is the State tree of North Carolina and Virginia.)

QQ. Leaf edges toothed, deeply 3- or 5-lobed (fruit of paired, long-winged "keys")—MAPLE (*Acer*).

S. Teeth of leaves few and blunt—HARD MAPLES.

27. SUGAR MAPLE, *Acer saccharum* Marsh. (hard maple [lumber], rock maple; *A. saccharophorum* K. Koch).

Large tree of eastern half of United States and adjacent Canada. Bark gray, furrowed into irregular ridges or scales. Leaves paired, heart-shaped, 3 to 5½ inches in diameter, 3- or 5-lobed with the lobes long-pointed and sparingly coarsely toothed with few blunt teeth, dark green above, light green or pale and usually smooth beneath, turning yellow, orange, or scarlet in fall. Key fruits 1 to 1¼ inches long, maturing in fall.

Principal uses: As a group, the maples rank third in production of hardwood lumber, next to oak and sweetgum, and are among the leading furniture woods. Sugar maple is used for flooring, furniture, boxes and crates, shoe lasts, handles, woodenware and novelties, spools and bobbins, and motor-vehicle parts. Also distillation products, veneer, railroad ties, and pulpwood. Sugar maple is the outstanding wood for flooring under heavy use and is the commercial source of maple sugar and sirup. Much planted as a shade tree. (State tree of New York and Vermont. Maple (*Acer* spp.) is the State tree of Rhode Island and Wisconsin.)

28. BLACK MAPLE, *Acer nigrum* Michx. f. (hard maple [lumber], black sugar maple, sugar maple; *A. saccharum* var. *nigrum* (Michx. f.) Britton).

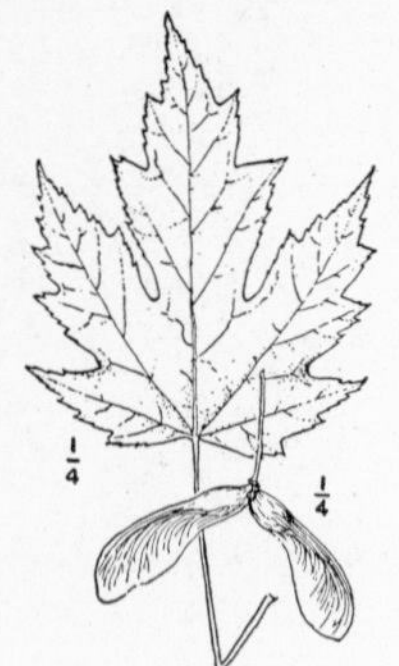


29. **Silver maple.**

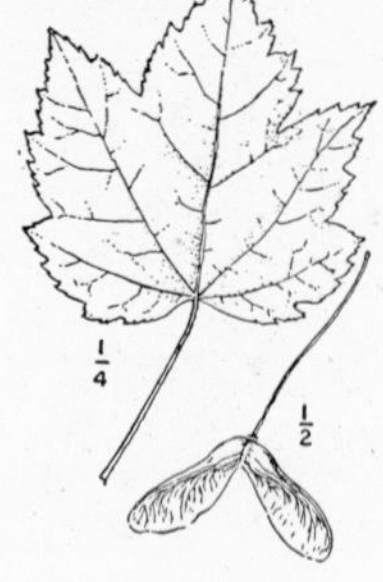


30. **Red maple.**

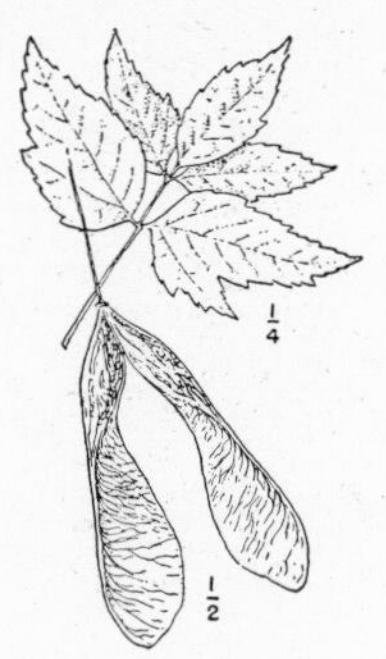


31. **Boxelder.**

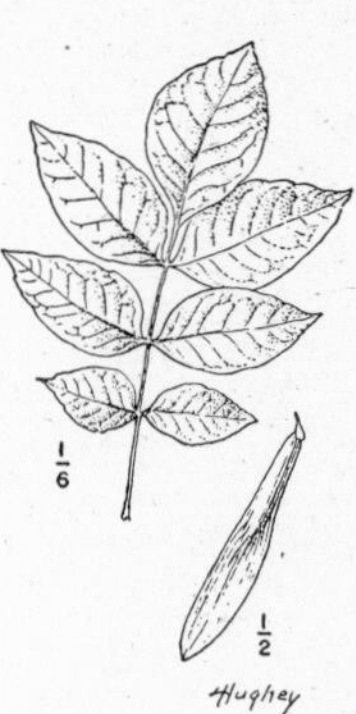


32. **White ash.**

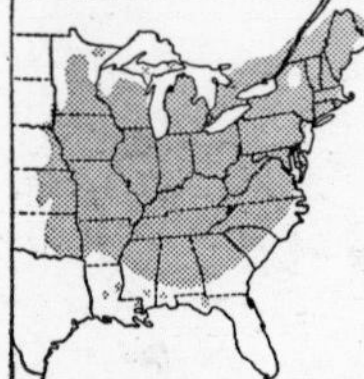

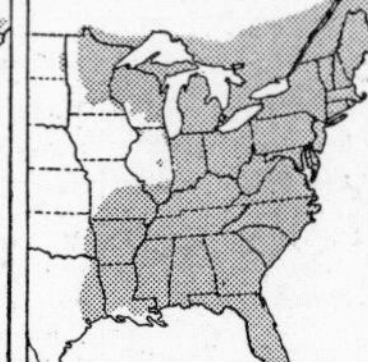

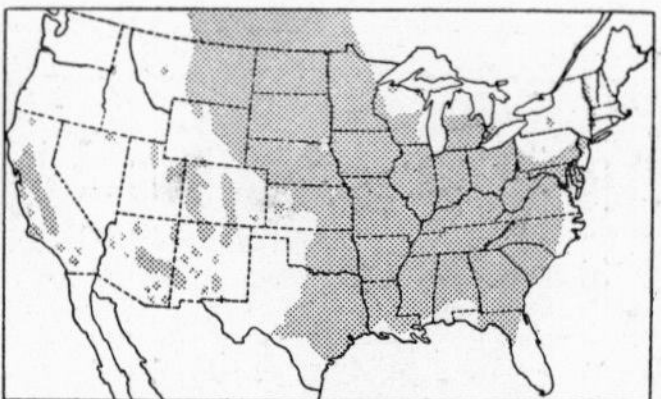

Large tree of northeastern quarter of United States and adjacent Canada. Bark gray, becoming deeply furrowed. Leaves paired, heart-shaped, 4 to 5½ inches in diameter, 3-lobed or occasionally 5-lobed, lobes short-pointed and sparingly coarsely toothed with blunt teeth, the sides drooping, dull green above, yellowish green and hairy beneath, turning yellow in fall. Key fruits 1 to 1¼ inches long, maturing in fall. (Perhaps only a variety of No. 27.)

Principal uses: Same as No. 27.

SS. Teeth of leaves many and sharp—SOFT MAPLES.

29. SILVER MAPLE, *Acer saccharinum* L. (soft maple [lumber], white maple, river maple, water maple, swamp maple).

Large tree of eastern half of United States and adjacent Canada. Bark gray, thin, smooth, on large trunks broken into long, thin scales. Leaves paired, slight heart-shaped, 3 to 6 inches long, deeply 5-lobed, lobes long-pointed, deeply, sharply, and irregularly toothed, bright green above, silvery white beneath, turning yellow in fall. Key fruits 1½ to 2½ inches long, maturing in spring.

Principal uses: Furniture, boxes and crates, handles, woodenware and novelties, and spools and bobbins. Also distillation products, railroad ties, and pulpwood. Shade tree. Shelterbelts.

30. RED MAPLE, *Acer rubrum* L. (soft maple [lumber], water maple, scarlet maple, white maple, swamp maple).

Large tree of eastern half of United States and adjacent Canada. Bark gray, thin, smooth, on large trunks broken into long, thin scales. Twigs reddish. Leaves paired, heart-shaped, 2½ to 4 inches long, 3- or 5-lobed, lobes short-pointed, irregularly and sharply toothed, dark green and shiny above, whitish and slightly hairy beneath, turning scarlet or yellow in fall. Key fruits ¾ inch long, maturing in spring.

Principal uses: Same as No. 29.

PP. Leaves divided into 3 to 11 leaflets (compound).
T. Leaflets attached along the extended leafstalk (pinnate).
U. Leaflets 3 to 7, sharply toothed, with veins extending to the teeth (fruits paired, clustered, long-winged "kels")—BOXELDER (*Acer negundo*).

31. BOXELDER, *Acer negundo* L. (ash-leaf maple, three-leaf maple; *Negundo aceroides* Moench).

Medium-sized tree, including its varieties widely distributed across the United States and adjacent Canada. Bark gray or brown, thin, with narrow ridges and fissures. Twigs green. Leaves paired, compound, with usually 3 or 5, rarely 7 or 9, oval or lance-oblong

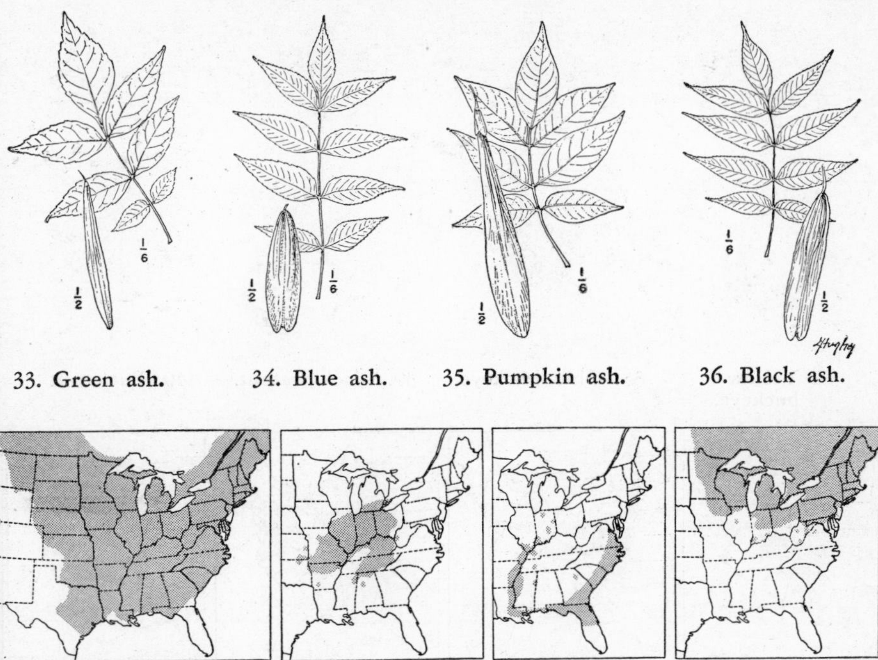


**33. Green ash.** **34. Blue ash.** **35. Pumpkin ash.** **36. Black ash.**

eaflets 2 to 4 inches long, long-pointed, coarsely and sharply toothed, bright green, nearly mooth or hairy. Key fruits 1 to 1½ inches long, paired and in clusters, maturing in fall.

Principal uses: Same as No. 29.

UU. Leaflets 5 to 11, bluntly toothed or without teeth, with veins curved within the edges (fruits clustered but not in pairs, long-winged "keys")—ASH (*Fraxinus*).

V. Leaflets with stalks.

32. WHITE ASH, *Fraxinus americana* L. (American ash, Biltmore ash; *F. biltmoreana* Beadle).

Large tree of eastern half of United States and adjacent Canada. Bark gray, with deep, diamond-shaped fissures and narrow, forking ridges. Leaves paired, compound, 8 to 12 inches long, with 5 to 9, usually 7, stalked, oval or broadly lance-shaped leaflets 2½ to 5 inches long, long- or short-pointed, edges usually smooth or slightly toothed, smooth or hairy beneath. Key fruits 1 to 2 inches long and ¼ inch wide, with wing at end.

Principal uses: Handles, cooperage, furniture, motor-vehicle parts, boxes, baskets, and crates, and sporting and athletic goods. Also railroad ties, veneer, and fuel. Shade tree.

33. GREEN ASH, *Fraxinus pennsylvanica* Marsh. (red ash is the typical variety; green ash is *F. pennsylvanica* var. *lanceolata* (Borkh.) Sarg., white ash, swamp ash, water ash; *F. viridis* Michx.).

Medium-sized tree of eastern half of United States and adjacent Canada west to Montana and Texas. Bark gray, fissured. Leaves paired, compound, 10 to 12 inches long, with 7 or 9, stalked, oval or lance-shaped leaflets 2 to 6 inches long, long-pointed, slightly toothed, smooth or hairy beneath. Key fruits 1¼ to 2¼ inches long, ¼ inch or more in width, with wing extending nearly to base.

Principal uses: Same as No. 32. Also shelterbelts and shade tree. (Green ash is the State tree of North Dakota.)

34. BLUE ASH, *Fraxinus quadrangulata* Michx.

Medium-sized to large tree of Central States, chiefly Ohio and Mississippi Valley regions; also in southern Ontario. Bark gray, fissured, with scaly and shaggy plates. Twigs 4-angled and more or less winged. Leaves paired, compound, 8 to 12 inches long, with 7 to 11, short-stalked, oval or lance-shaped leaflets 2½ to 5 inches long, long-pointed, toothed. Key fruits 1¼ to 2 inches long, ⅜ to ½ inch wide, oblong, with wing extending to base.

Principal uses: Same as No. 32.

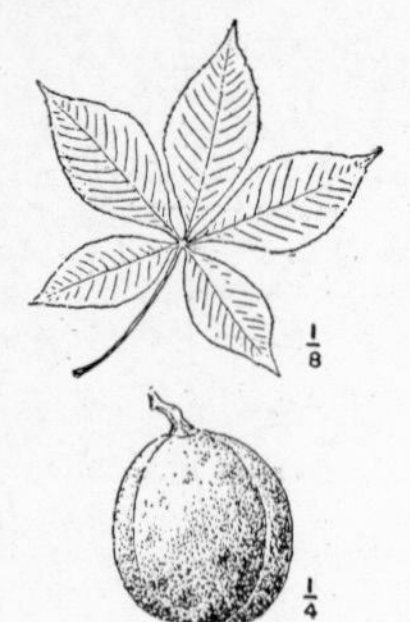


37. **Yellow buckeye.**

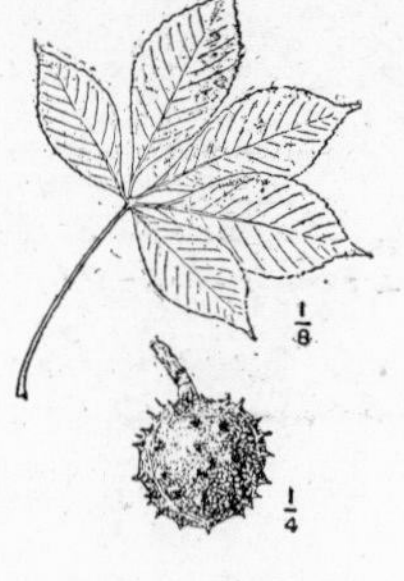


38. **Ohio buckeye.**

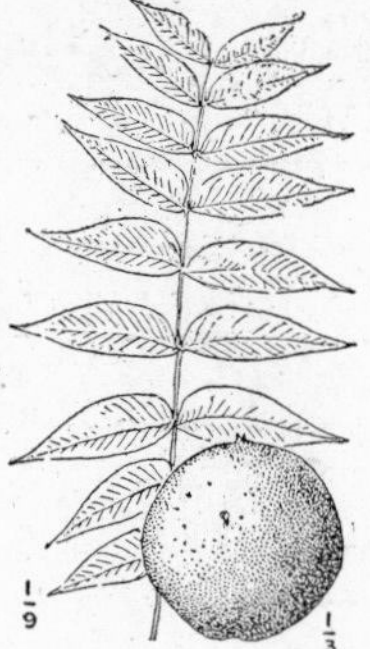


39. **Black walnut.**

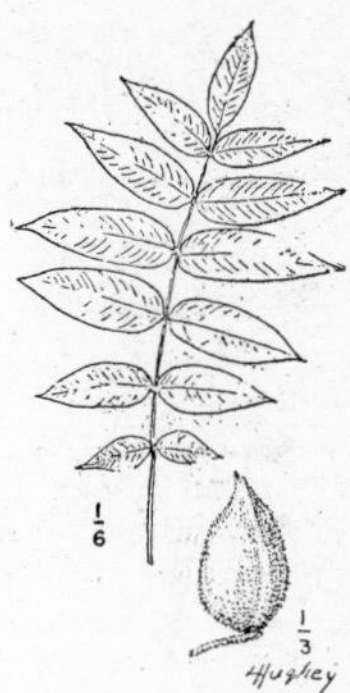


40. **Butternut.**

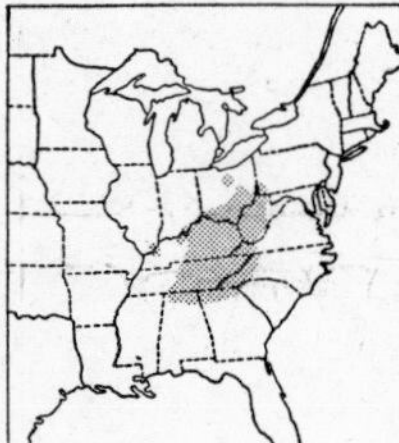

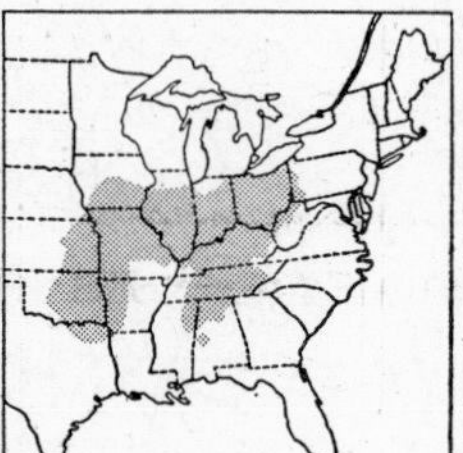

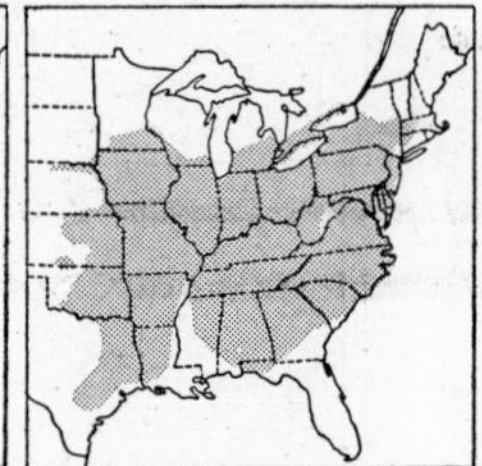

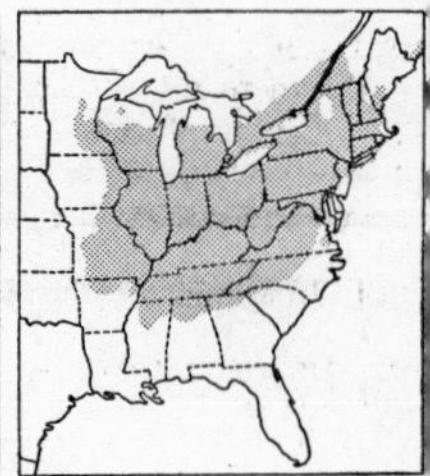

35. PUMPKIN ASH, *Fraxinus tomentosa* Michx. f. (*F. profunda* (Bush) (Bush).

Large tree with swollen base, wet soils in Mississippi Valley and coastal plain regions. Bark gray, fissured. Twigs and leafstalks hairy. Leaves paired, compound, 9 to 18 inches long, with 7 to 9, stalked, elliptical or lance-shaped leaflets 4 to 10 inches long, long-pointed, with edges smooth or slightly toothed, soft hairy beneath. Key fruits 2 to 3 inches long and 3/8 to 1/2 inch wide, with large broad wing.

Principal uses: Cooperage, furniture, and boxes, baskets, and crates. Also railroad ties, veneer, and fuel.

VV. Leaflets without stalks.

36. BLACK ASH, *Fraxinus nigra* Marsh. (brown ash, hoop ash, basket ash, swamp ash, water ash).

Medium-sized to large tree of wet soils in northeastern quarter of United States and adjacent Canada. Bark gray, scaly or fissured. Leaves paired, compound, 12 to 16 inches long, with 7 to 11, stalkless, oblong or broadly lance-shaped leaflets 3 to 5 inches long, long-pointed, finely toothed, with tufted hairs beneath. Key fruits 1 to 1 1/2 inches long, 3/8 inch wide, flat, with wing extending to base.

Principal uses: Same as No. 35.

TT. Leaflets 5 (or 7), all attached at end of leafstalk and spreading fingerlike (palmate)—BUCKEYE (*Aesculus*).

37. YELLOW BUCKEYE, *Aesculus octandra* Marsh. (sweet buckeye, large buckeye).

Medium-sized tree of Central States, chiefly Ohio Valley and Appalachian regions. Bark gray, separating into thin scales. Leaves paired, compound, with leafstalks 4 to 6 inches long. Leaflets 5, oblong or elliptical, 4 to 6 inches long, long-pointed, narrowed at base, finely toothed. Flowers in branched clusters 4 to 6 inches long, showy, 1 1/4 inches long, yellow, with petals unequal in length. Fruiting capsule 2 to 2 1/2 inches in diameter, smooth, with 2 poisonous seeds 1 1/2 to 1 3/4 inches wide.

Principal uses: Furniture, boxes and crates, and caskets. Also artificial limbs. Ornamental.

38. OHIO BUCKEYE, *Aesculus glabra* Willd. (fetid buckeye, stinking buckeye, American horsechestnut).

Small tree (or shrubby to medium-sized) of Central States, chiefly Ohio and Mississippi Valley regions. Bark gray, much furrowed and broken into scaly plates. Leaves paired, compound, with leafstalks 4 to 6 inches long. Leaflets 5 (5 to 7 in shrubby varieties),

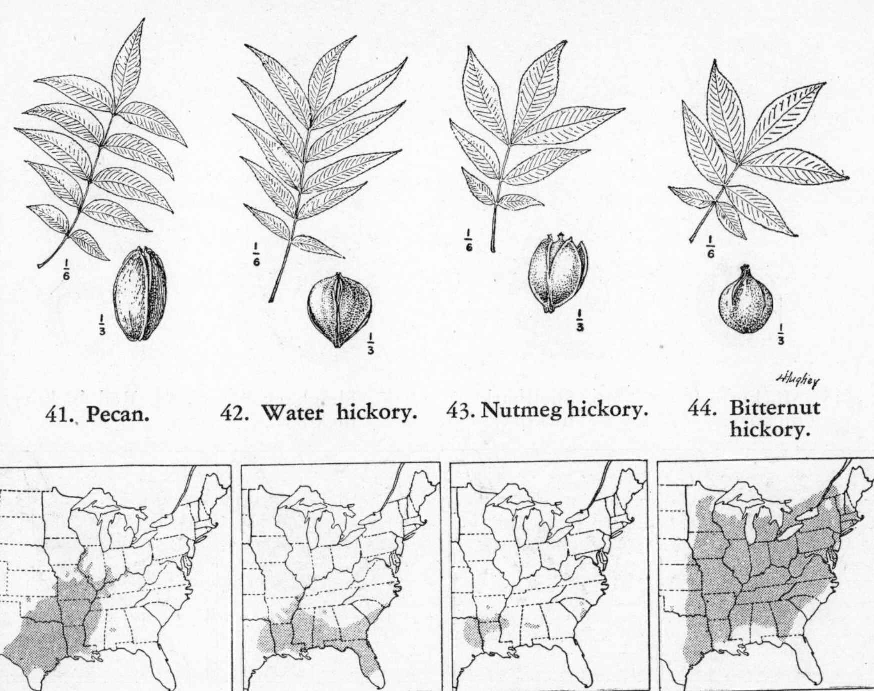

41. **Pecan.** 42. **Water hickory.** 43. **Nutmeg hickory.** 44. **Bitternut hickory.**

elliptical, 3 to 5 inches long, long-pointed, narrowed at base, finely toothed. Flowers in branched clusters 4 to 6 inches long, showy, ¾ to 1¼ inches long, pale greenish yellow, with petals nearly equal in length. Fruiting capsule 1¼ to 2 inches in diameter, prickly, with 1 or 2 poisonous seeds 1 to 1½ inches wide.

Principal uses: Same as No. 37. (State tree of Ohio.)

OO (O on p. 774). Leaves and usually branches borne singly (alternate).

W (WW on p. 782). Leaves divided into leaflets (compound), attached along the extended leafstalk (pinnate).

X. Leaflets long-pointed; twigs not spiny; fruit rounded or egg-shaped.

Y. Leaflets finely toothed, shedding in fall; fruit a nut with a husk.

Z. Leaflets 11 to 23; pith of twigs in plates; husk of nut not splitting off—WALNUT (*Juglans*).

39. BLACK WALNUT, *Juglans nigra* L. (eastern black walnut, American walnut, walnut).

Large tree of eastern half of United States and southern Ontario. Bark dark brown to black, thick, with deep furrows and narrow, forking ridges. Compound leaves 12 to 24 inches long. Leaflets 15 to 23, without stalks, broadly lance-shaped, 2½ to 5 inches long, long-pointed, finely toothed, nearly smooth above, soft hairy beneath. Nuts single or paired, 1½ to 2½ inches in diameter including the thick husk, nearly spherical, irregularly ridged, thick-shelled, sweet and edible, known as walnuts.

Principal uses: Valuable furniture wood, solid and as veneer. Also for radio and phonograph cabinets, sewing machines, and interior finish. The leading wood for gunstocks. Edible walnuts. Shade tree. Shelterbelts. (State tree of Iowa.)

40. BUTTERNUT, *Juglans cinerea* L. (white walnut, oilnut).

Medium-sized to large tree of northeastern quarter of United States and adjacent Canada. Bark light gray, furrowed into broad, flat ridges. Compound leaves 15 to 30 inches long. Leaflets 11 to 19, without stalks, broadly lance-shaped, 2 to 4½ inches long, long- or short-pointed, finely toothed, slightly hairy above, soft hairy beneath. Nuts 3 to 5 in drooping clusters, 1½ to 2½ inches long including the thick husk, egg-shaped, pointed, irregularly ridged, thick-shelled, sweet and oily, known as butternuts.

Principal uses: Furniture. Shade tree. Edible butternuts.

ZZ. Leaflets 5 to 11 (11 to 17 in No. 41); pith of twigs solid; husk of nut splitting off—HICKORY (*Carya;* formerly known also as *Hicoria*).

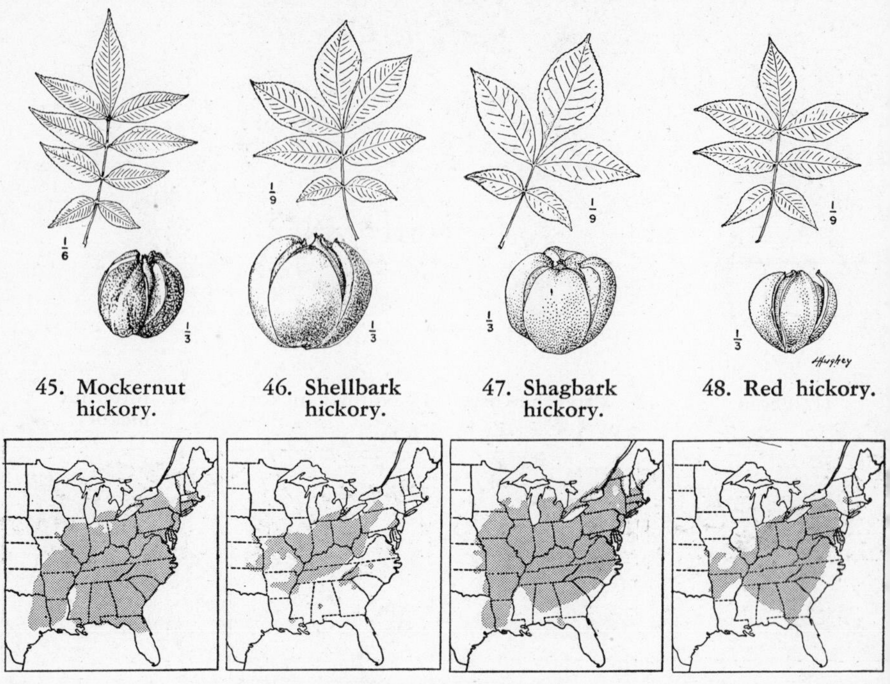


45. Mockernut hickory. 46. Shellbark hickory. 47. Shagbark hickory. 48. Red hickory.

a. Leaflets lance-shaped and often slightly sickle-shaped; winter buds with 4 to 6 scales, fitting at edges and not overlapping; nuts thin-shelled (except No. 43), husks usually 4-winged—PECAN HICKORIES.

41. PECAN, *Carya illinoensis* (Wangenh.) K. Koch (sweet pecan; *C. pecan* (Marsh.) Engl. & Graebn., *Hicoria pecan* (Marsh.) Britton).

Large tree of Mississippi Valley region; also in Mexico. Bark light brown or gray, deeply and irregularly furrowed and cracked. Compound leaves 12 to 20 inches long. Leaflets 11 to 17, short-stalked, lance-shaped and slightly sickle-shaped, 2 to 7 inches long, long-pointed, finely toothed, smooth or slightly hairy. Nuts 1 to 2 inches long including the slightly 4-winged, thin husk, oblong, pointed, thin-shelled, sweet and edible, known as pecans.

Principal uses: Boxes and crates, motor vehicles, furniture, and flooring. Fuel and for smoking meats. Pecan nuts from wild and cultivated trees. Shade tree. (State tree of Texas.)

42. WATER HICKORY, *Carya aquatica* (Michx. f.) Nutt. (pecan [lumber], bitter pecan, swamp hickory; *Hicoria aquatica* (Michx. f.) Britton).

Medium-sized or large tree of wet soils in South Atlantic coast, Gulf coast, and Mississippi Valley regions. Bark light brown, fissured, with long, thin scales. Compound leaves 9 to 15 inches long. Leaflets 7 to 13, stalkless or short-stalked, lance-shaped, 2 to 5 inches long, long-pointed, finely toothed, dark green above, brownish and hairy or smooth beneath. Nuts 1 to 1½ inches long including the pointed, 4-winged, thin husk, nearly spherical, flattened, angled, and wrinkled, thin-shelled, bitter.

Principal uses: Wood used same as No. 41.

43. NUTMEG HICKORY, *Carya myristicaeformis* (Michx. f.) Nutt. (pecan [lumber], bitter water hickory, swamp hickory; *Hicoria myristicaeformis* (Michx. f.) Britton).

Large tree of South Atlantic coast and Gulf coast regions; also in Mexico. Bark dark brown, fissured, with small, thin scales. Compound leaves 7 to 14 inches long. Leaflets 5 to 9, short-stalked, broadly lance-shaped or oblong, 2 to 5 inches long, long-pointed, finely toothed, dark green above, more or less hairy or smooth and whitish beneath. Nuts 1¼ to 1½ inches long including the pointed, 4-winged, thin husk, nearly spherical but longer than broad, thick-shelled, sweet and edible.

Principal uses: Wood used same as No. 41. Edible hickory nuts.

44. BITTERNUT HICKORY, *Carya cordiformis* (Wangenh.) K. Koch (pecan [lumber], bitternut, pignut, swamp hickory; *Hicoria cordiformis* (Wangenh.) Britton).

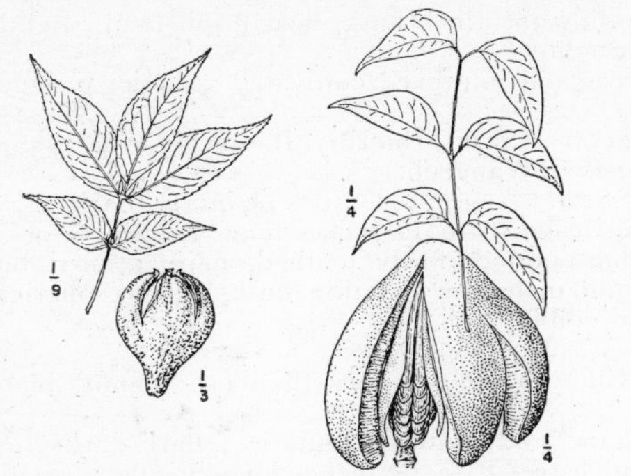

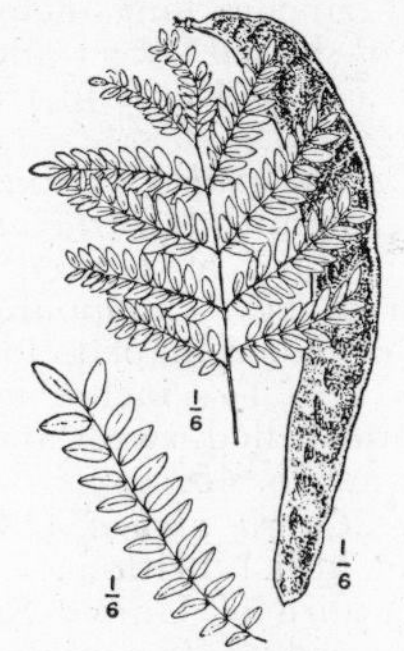

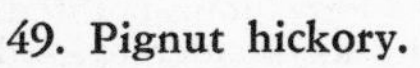

**49. Pignut hickory.** **50. West Indies mahogany.** **51. Honeylocust.** **52. Black locust.**

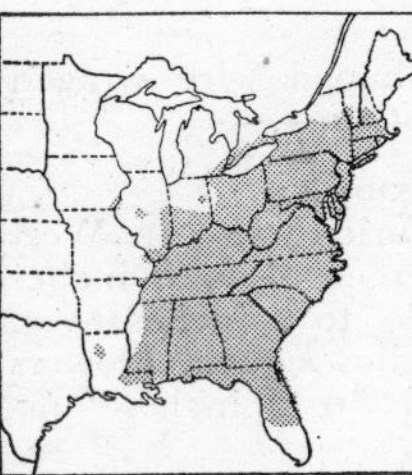

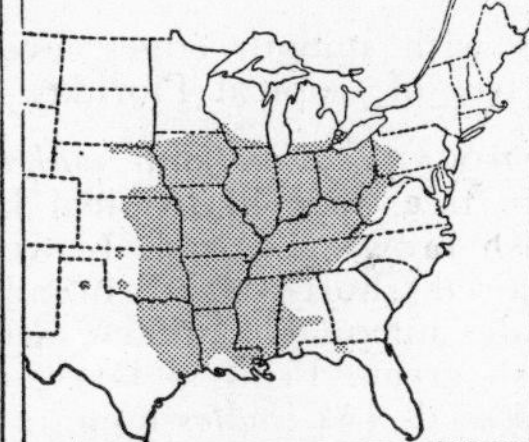
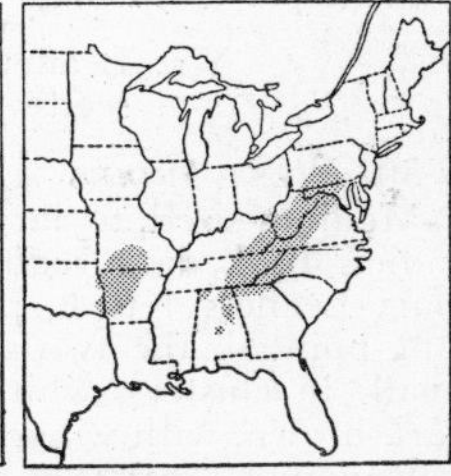

Medium-sized to large tree of eastern half of United States and adjacent Canada. Bark light brown, shallowly furrowed, with narrow, forking ridges or thin scales. Compound leaves 6 to 10 inches long. Leaflets 5 to 9, without stalks, lance-shaped, 2 to 6 inches long, long-pointed, finely toothed, more or less hairy beneath. Winter buds bright yellow. Nuts ¾ to 1¼ inches long including the 4-winged, yellowish, thin husk, nearly spherical, slightly flattened, short-pointed, thin-shelled, bitter.

Principal uses: Wood used same as No. 41.

aa. Leaflets oblong to broadly lance-shaped; winter buds with more than 6 overlapping scales; nuts thick-shelled (except Nos. 47 and 48), husks without wings—TRUE HICKORIES.

45. MOCKERNUT HICKORY, *Carya tomentosa* Nutt. (hickory [lumber], mockernut, whiteheart hickory, bullnut, hognut, white hickory; *C. alba* auth., *Hicoria alba* auth.).

Medium-sized to large tree of eastern half of United States except northern border; also in southern Ontario. Bark gray, irregularly furrowed into flat ridges. Compound leaves 8 to 20 inches long. Leaflets 7 or 9, without stalks, oblong or broadly lance-shaped, 2 to 8 inches long, long-pointed, finely toothed, dark yellow green and shiny above, pale and densely hairy beneath. Nuts 1½ to 2 inches long including the thick husk, nearly spherical, slightly flattened and angled, thick-shelled, sweet and edible.

Principal uses: Hickory, including several species, is the world's foremost wood for tool handles. Also for vehicle parts, fuel, and smoking meat. Hickory nuts.

46. SHELLBARK HICKORY, *Carya laciniosa* (Michx. f.) Loud. (hickory [lumber], bigleaf shagbark hickory, big shellbark, western shellbark, thick shellbark, bottom shellbark, kingnut; *Hicoria laciniosa* (Michx. f.) Sarg.).

Large tree of Ohio and Mississippi Valley regions. Bark gray, shaggy with long, thin, straight plates. Compound leaves 15 to 22 inches long. Leaflets usually 7, without stalks or short-stalked, broadly lance-shaped, 2 to 8 inches long, long-pointed, finely toothed, dark green and shiny above, pale and soft-hairy beneath. Nuts 1¾ to 2½ inches long including the thick husk, nearly spherical, slightly flattened and angled, pointed at ends, thick-shelled, sweet and edible.

Principal uses: Same as No. 45. Hickory nuts of commerce.

47. SHAGBARK HICKORY, *Carya ovata* (Mill.) K. Koch (hickory [lumber], shagbark, shellbark hickory, scalybark hickory, upland hickory; *Hicoria ovata* (Mill.) Britton).

Large tree of eastern half of United States and adjacent Canada. Bark gray, shaggy with long, thin, curved plates. Compound leaves 8 to 14 inches long. Leaflets usually 5, without stalks, elliptical or broadly lance-shaped, 3 to 7 inches long, long-pointed, finely toothed. Nuts 1¼ to 2½ inches long including the thick husk, nearly spherical, slightly flattened and angled, thin-shelled, sweet and edible.

Principal uses: Same as No. 45. Wild trees and improved cultivated varieties produce hickory nuts of commerce.

48. RED HICKORY, *Carya ovalis* (Wangenh.) Sarg. (hickory [lumber], oval pignut hickory, pignut hickory, pignut; *Hicoria ovalis* (Wangenh.) Ashe).

Large tree of eastern third of United States (except coastal plains). Bark gray, furrowed, often scaly or shaggy. Compound leaves 6 to 12 inches long. Leaflets 7 or 5, without stalks, oblong or lance-shaped, long-pointed, finely toothed, hairy at first but becoming smooth. Nuts 1 to 1¼ inches long including the thin husk, nearly spherical but variable in shape, thin-shelled, sweet and edible.

Principal uses: Same as No. 45.

49. PIGNUT HICKORY, *Carya glabra* (Mill.) Sweet (hickory [lumber], pignut, black hickory; *Hicoria glabra* (Mill.) Britton).

Large tree of eastern third of United States and southern Ontario. Bark dark gray, with furrows and forking ridges. Compound leaves 8 to 12 inches long. Leaflets usually 5, or 5 and 7, without stalks, oblong or lance-shaped, 3 to 6 inches long, long-pointed, finely toothed. Nuts 1 to 2 inches long including the thin or thick husk, broader toward apex and usually not angled, thick-shelled, usually bitter.

Principal uses: Same as No. 45.

YY. Leaflets with smooth edges, evergreen; fruit egg-shaped with winged seeds (tree of tropical Florida)—MAHOGANY (*Swietenia*).

50. WEST INDIES MAHOGANY, *Swietenia mahagoni* Jacq. (mahogany).

Medium-sized to large tree, rare in tropical keys of southern Florida; also in West Indies. Bark dark reddish brown, fissured. Leaves compound, evergreen, 4 to 6 inches long. Leaflets 4 to 8, paired, short-stalked, broadly lance-shaped, 1½ to 3 inches long, long-pointed, the two sides unequal, leathery, with edges smooth, yellow green. Flowers small, in clusters, whitish green. Fruit, a large, egg-shaped capsule 3 to 5 inches long, dark brown, with winged seeds 1¾ inches long.

Principal uses: Not of commercial importance in Florida because of its rarity. Mahogany, including other species, is the world's foremost cabinetwood and the most valuable timber tree in tropical America. Planted as an ornamental and shade tree in Florida.

XX. Leaflets rounded or blunt-pointed; twigs spiny; fruit a flat beanlike pod.

b. Leaflets with inconspicuous rounded teeth—HONEYLOCUST (*Gleditsia*).

51. HONEYLOCUST, *Gleditsia triacanthos* L. (common honeylocust, sweet-locust, thorny locust).

Large tree of Appalachian Mountain and Mississippi Valley regions, naturalized elsewhere in eastern half of United States; also in southern Ontario. Bark grayish brown or black, fissured into long, narrow, scaly ridges. Trunk and branches with large, stout, usually branched spines, rarely absent. Leaves once or twice divided (compound), 4 to 8 inches long. Leaflets numerous in pairs, elliptical, ⅜ to 1¼ inches long, blunt-pointed or rounded at apex, with inconspicuous rounded teeth, shiny dark green and smooth above, yellow green and nearly smooth beneath. Flowers small, greenish or whitish, in narrow clusters 2 to 2½ inches long, in late spring. Pods 12 to 18 inches long and 1 to 1¼ inches wide, flat, dark brown, hairy, slightly curved and twisted.

Principal uses: Wood used locally for fence posts, construction, furniture, and railroad ties. Shade tree. Shelterbelts. The sweetish pods are eaten by livestock and wildlife.

bb. Leaflets not toothed—LOCUST (*Robinia*).

52. BLACK LOCUST, *Robinia pseudoacacia* L. (locust, yellow locust, shipmast locust).

Medium-sized tree, native in Appalachian Mountain and Ozark regions and widely naturalized in eastern half of United States and southern Canada. Bark brown, thick, deeply furrowed, with rough, forked ridges. Twigs with a pair of spines about ½ inch long developing at base of each leaf. Compound leaves 8 to 14 inches long. Leaflets 7 to 19, oval, 1 to 2 inches long, usually rounded at apex, with smooth edges, dark blue green and smooth above, pale and smooth or nearly so beneath. Flowers white and very fragrant, ⅝ to ¾ inch long, in clusters 4 to 8 inches long, in spring. Pods 2 to 4 inches long and ½ inch wide, flat, brown.

Principal uses: Fence posts, mine timbers, poles, railroad ties, stakes, and fuel. The principal wood for insulator pins. Also lumber for rough construction. Planted for ornament and shade, shelterbelts, and erosion control.

WW (W on p. 779). Leaves not divided into leaflets (simple).

c. Leaves aromatic when bruised, edges smooth or 2- or 3-lobed; twigs bright green—SASSAFRAS (*Sassafras*).

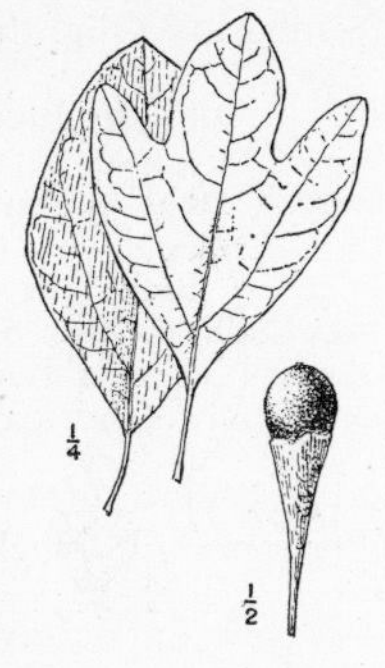


53. Sassafras.

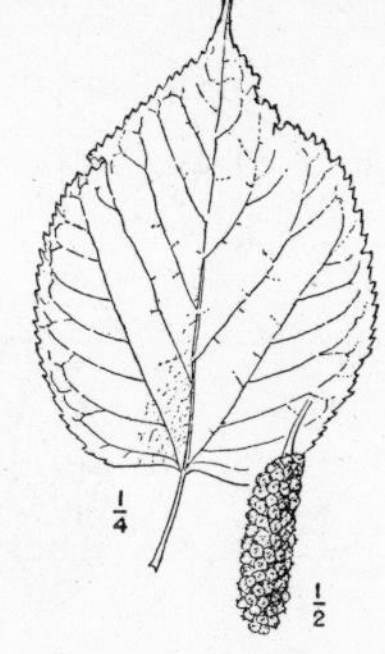


54. Red mulberry.

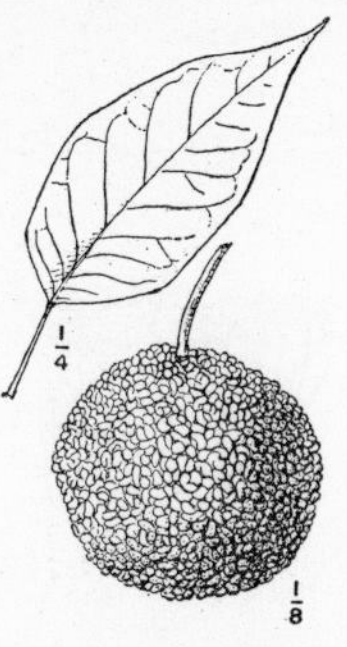


55. Osage-orange.

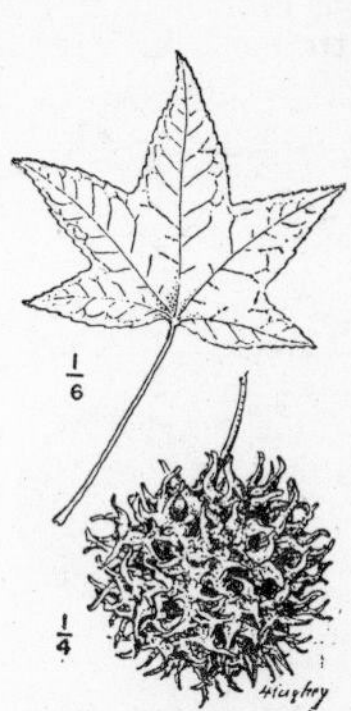


56. Sweetgum.

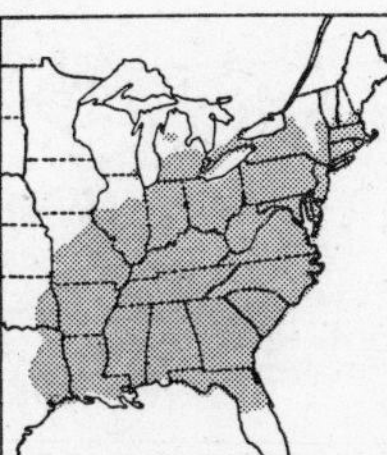

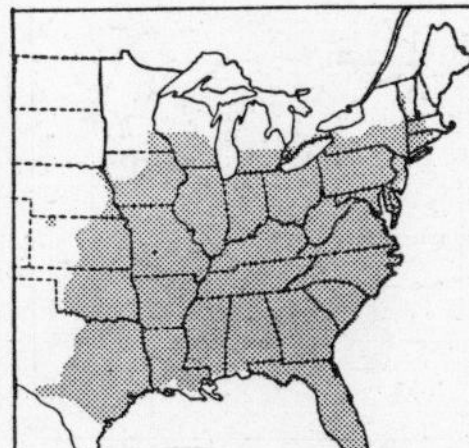

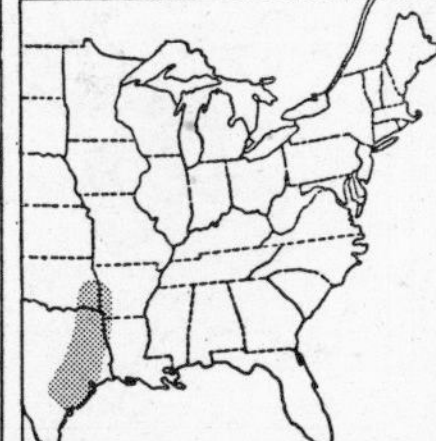

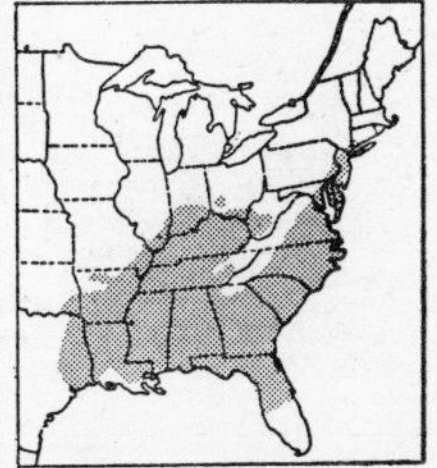

53. SASSAFRAS, *Sassafras albidum* (Nutt.) Nees (common sassafras; *S. officinale* Nees & Eberm., *S. variifolium* (Salisb.) Ktze.).

Medium-sized tree (sometimes large) with aromatic odor and taste, eastern half of United States and southern Ontario. Bark reddish brown, deeply furrowed. Leaves oval or elliptical, 3 to 5 inches long, blunt-pointed, often 2- or 3-lobed, with smooth edges, bright green above, paler and smooth or hairy beneath, turning orange or scarlet in fall. Flowers about 3/8 inch long, yellow, in small clusters in early spring. Fruits egg-shaped, 3/8 inch long, dark blue, with fleshy red stalk.

Principal uses: Fence posts. Lumber occasionally mixed with that of black ash (No. 36). Sassafras tea and oil of sassafras, used to perfume soap, are prepared from roots and root bark. Shade tree and ornamental.

cc. Leaves not aromatic, edges smooth, toothed, or lobed; twigs brown or gray.
d. Juice milky.
e. Leaves toothed, sometimes 2- or 3-lobed; twigs not spiny—MULBERRY (*Morus*).

54. RED MULBERRY, *Morus rubra* L. (mulberry).

Medium-sized tree of eastern half of United States and southern Ontario. Bark dark brown, fissured and scaly. Leaves broadly oval or heart-shaped, 3 to 7 inches long, abruptly long-pointed, coarsely toothed, sometimes 2- or 3-lobed, rough above, soft-hairy beneath. Fruits 1 inch long, dark purple or black, sweet, juicy, and edible, known as mulberries.

Principal uses: Wood used locally for fence posts, furniture, interior finish, agricultural implements, and cooperage. Shade tree. Edible mulberries, eaten also by domestic animals and wildlife.

ee. Leaves with smooth edges; twigs spiny—OSAGE-ORANGE (*Maclura*).

55. OSAGE-ORANGE, *Maclura pomifera* (Raf.) Schneid. (bodark, mockorange, bowwood, hedge; *Toxylon pomiferum* Raf.).

Medium-sized tree with milky juice, native of Arkansas, Oklahoma, Louisiana, and Texas but naturalized in eastern half of United States except northern border. Bark orange brown, deeply furrowed. Twigs with stout straight spines 3/8 to 1 inch long. Leaves oval or narrowly oval, 2 to 5 inches long, long-pointed, with smooth edges, shiny dark green above and paler beneath. Fruit a yellowish ball 4 to 5 inches in diameter.

Principal uses: Extensively planted for shelterbelts, hedges, ornament, and shade. The

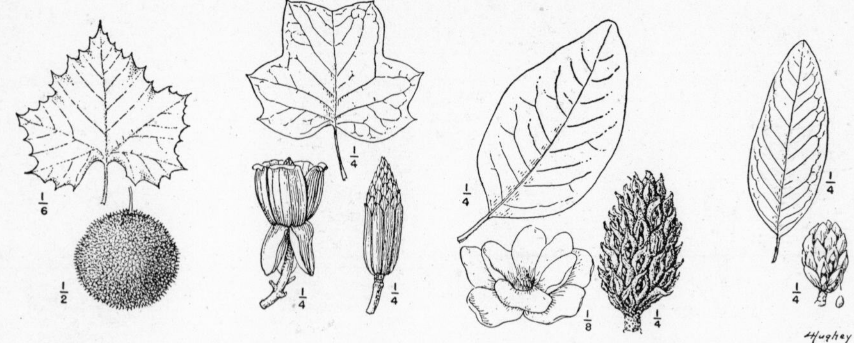

57. American sycamore. 58. Yellow-poplar. 59. Southern magnolia. 60. Sweetbay.

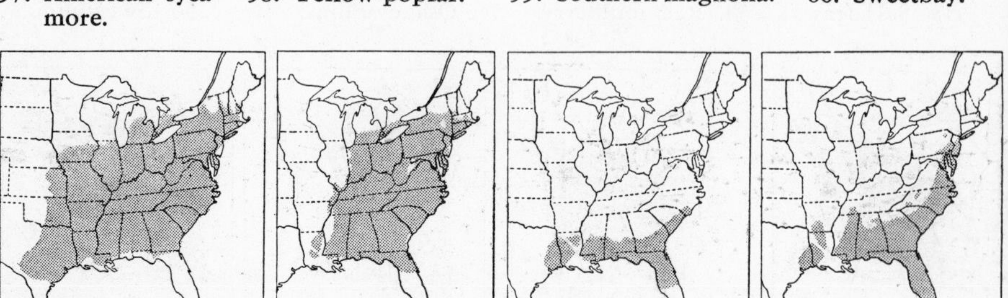

wood is used chiefly for fence posts and for fuel and has been used for archery bows and as a source of a yellow dye.

dd. Juice watery.
f (ff on p. 793). Winter buds 1 or none at tip of twig; pith of twigs round or nearly so in cross section (star-shaped in Nos. 77 to 80 and 90); fruit not an acorn.
g. Leaves with 3 to 6 lobes.
h. Leaves with pointed apex and 3 or 5 lobes.
i. Leaves star-shaped, deeply 5-lobed—SWEETGUM (*Liquidambar*).

56. SWEETGUM, *Liquidambar styrciflua* L. (redgum [lumber], sapgum [lumber], American sweetgum, starleaf-gum, bilsted).

Large tree of eastern third of United States, except northern border; also in Mexico and Central America south to Nicaragua. Bark gray, deeply furrowed. Twigs reddish brown, developing corky ridges. Leaves maplelike, star-shaped, 3 to 7 inches long and wide, with 5 long-pointed, finely toothed lobes, shiny dark green above, paler beneath, slightly aromatic, turning deep crimson in fall. Fruit a brownish, spiny ball 1 to 1¼ inches in diameter.

Principal uses: Important timber tree in United States, second in production among the hardwoods, the leading furniture wood, and second in veneer production. Also boxes and crates, radio and phonograph cabinets, interior trim and millwork, woodenware and novelties, and slack barrels. Shade tree. The gum, "sweetgum" or storax, is used in perfumes and drugs.

ii. Leaves heart-shaped, slightly 3-lobed—SYCAMORE (*Platanus*).

57. AMERICAN SYCAMORE, *Platanus occidentalis* L. (American planetree, sycamore, buttonwood, planetree, buttonball-tree).

A very large tree (the largest eastern hardwood in trunk diameter) of wet soils in eastern half of United States and southern Ontario. Bark of branches whitish, thin, smooth; bark of trunk peeling off in large flakes, smoothish, with patches of brown, green, and gray. Leaves heart-shaped, 4 to 8 inches long and wide, slightly 3- or 5-lobed, the shallow, pointed lobes coarsely toothed with long-pointed teeth, with 3 main veins from base, bright green and smooth above, paler and slightly hairy beneath. Fruit a ball 1 inch in diameter.

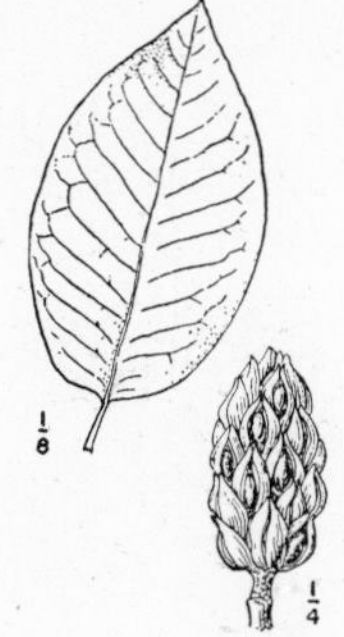


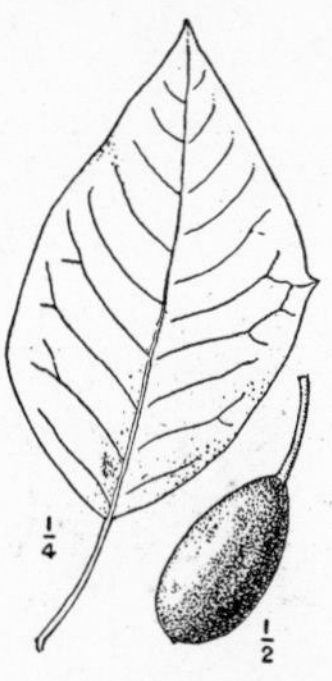


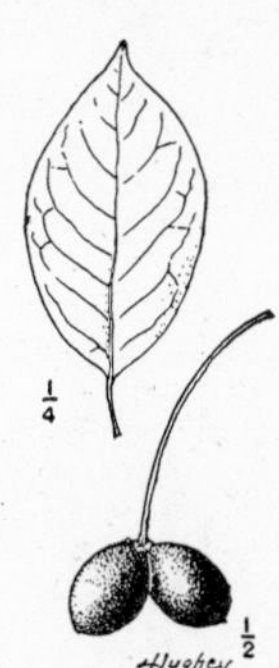


61. Cucumbertree. 62. Common persimmon. 63. Water tupelo. 64. Black tupelo.

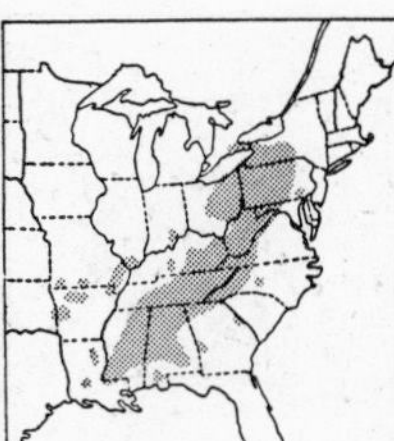

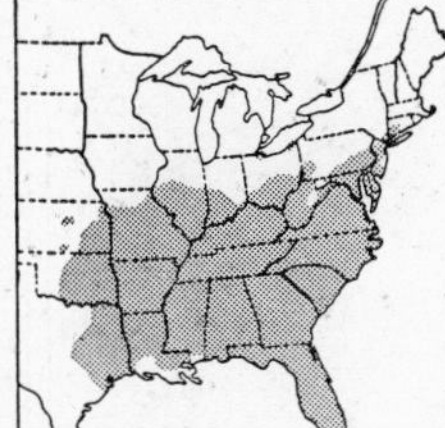

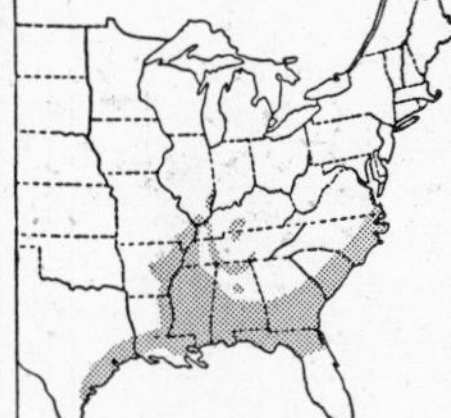

Principal uses: Furniture and boxes and crates (mostly small food containers). Also railroad ties, cooperage, fence posts, and fuel. Shade tree.

hh. Leaves with broad, slightly notched apex and 4 or 6 lobes—YELLOW-POPLAR (*Liriodendron*).

58. YELLOW-POPLAR, *Liriodendron tulipifera* L. (tuliptree, whitewood, white-poplar, tulipwood, hickory-poplar, poplar).

Large tree (the tallest eastern hardwood) of eastern third of United States and southern Ontario. Bark brown, becoming thick and deeply furrowed. Leaves of unusual squarish shape with broad, slightly notched or nearly straight apex and 2 or 3 lobes on each side, 3 to 6 inches long, long and broad, shiny dark green above and pale green beneath. Flowers large and showy, tulip-shaped, 1½ to 2 inches in diameter, greenish and orange, in spring. Fruit conelike, 2½ to 3 inches long, ½ inch thick.

Principal uses: Furniture (solid and veneer), boxes and crates, interior finish, siding, fixtures, radio cabinets, musical instruments, and caskets. Pulpwood. Ornamental and shade tree. (State tree of Indiana and Kentucky.)

gg. Leaves with edges smooth or toothed but without lobes.

j. Leaf edges smooth (see also No. 76).

k. Twigs with faint ring at base of each leaf—MAGNOLIA (*Magnolia*).

59. SOUTHERN MAGNOLIA, *Magnolia grandiflora* L. (magnolia [lumber], evergreen magnolia).

Medium-sized to large tree of South Atlantic and Gulf Coastal Plains. Bark gray or light brown, broken into small, thin scales. Leaves evergreen, oblong or elliptical, 5 to 8 inches long, short-pointed, edges smooth, leathery, shiny bright green and smooth above, rusty-hairy beneath. Flowers cup-shaped, very large, 6 to 8 inches across, white, fragrant, spring and summer. Fruit conelike, 3 to 4 inches long, 1½ to 2½ inches thick, rusty-hairy.

Principal uses: Furniture, boxes, and venetian blinds. Ornamental and shade tree. (State tree and State flower of Louisiana and Mississippi.)

60. SWEETBAY, *Magnolia virginiana* L. (magnolia [lumber], sweetbay magnolia, swamp-bay, swamp magnolia).

Small to medium-sized tree of Atlantic and Gulf Coastal Plains. Bark brownish gray, smoothish. Leaves shedding in winter or almost evergreen in the South, elliptical or narrowly oval, 3 to 5 inches long, short-pointed, wedge-shaped at base, edges smooth, thick, shiny bright green and smooth above, whitish and nearly smooth beneath. Flowers cup-

65. Ogeechee tupelo.

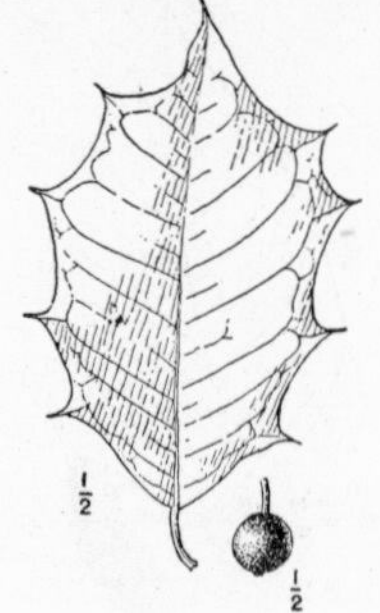


66. American holly.

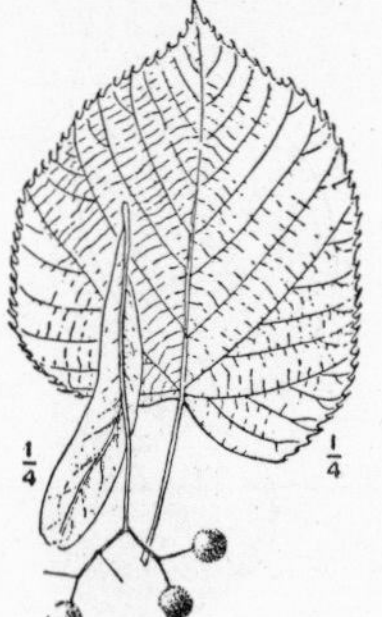


67. American basswood.

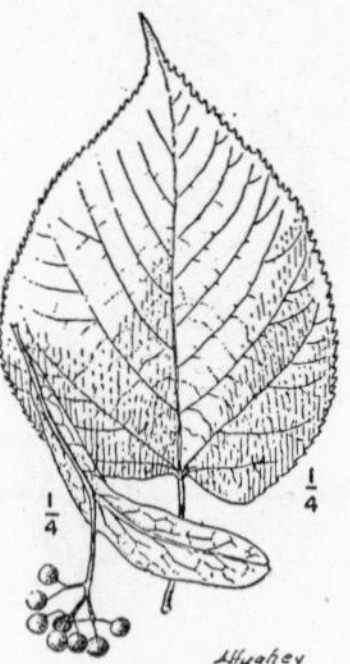


68. White basswood.

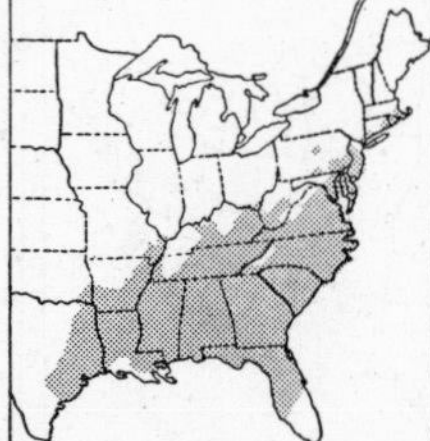

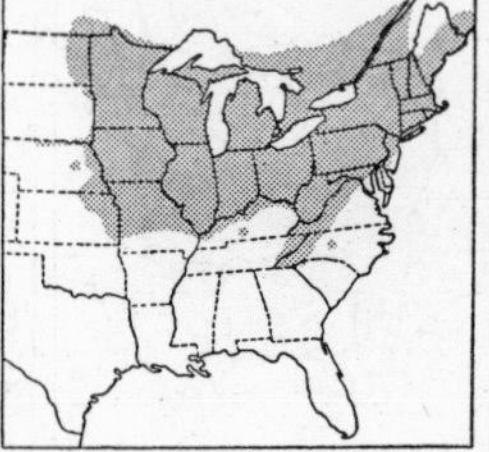

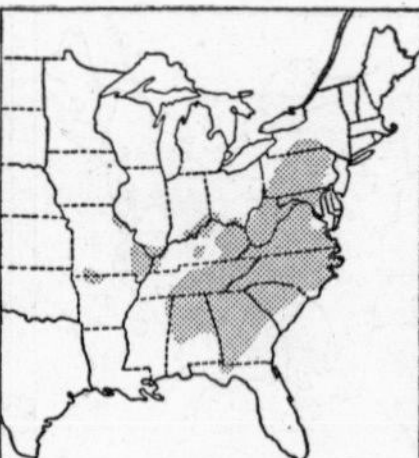

shaped, 2 to 2½ inches across, white, fragrant, spring and early summer. Fruit conelike, 1½ to 2 inches long and ½ inch thick, dark red, smooth.

Principal uses: Furniture, boxes, and venetian blinds. Ornamental.

61. CUCUMBERTREE, *Magnolia acuminata* L. (cucumbertree magnolia, mountain magnolia).

Large tree of Appalachian Mountain and Ozark regions and intervening portions of Ohio and Mississippi Valleys; also in southern Ontario. Bark dark brown, furrowed, with narrow, scaly, forking ridges. Leaves shedding in fall, elliptical or oval, 5 to 10 inches long, short-pointed, yellow green and smooth above, light green and soft-hairy or nearly smooth beneath. Flowers bell-shaped, greenish yellow, 2½ to 3½ inches long. Fruit conelike, 2 to 3 inches long and 1 inch thick, red.

Principal uses: Wood used same as yellow-poplar, No. 58. Ornamental and shade tree.

kk. Twigs without rings.

l. Leaves broadest below middle—PERSIMMON (*Diospyros*).

62. COMMON PERSIMMON, *Diospyros virginiana* L. (persimmon).

Medium-sized tree of eastern half of United States except northern border. Bark dark brown, thick, deeply divided into small, square, scaly blocks. Leaves oval or elliptical, 2½ to 6 inches long, long-pointed, rounded at base, shiny dark green above, pale green and smooth or hairy beneath. Male and female flowers on different trees in spring, ⅜ to ⅝ inch long, whitish, in angles of leaves. Fruits ¾ to 1¼ inches in diameter, yellow or pale orange, maturing in fall, fleshy, sweet, and edible, known as persimmons.

Principal uses: Shuttles (used in textile weaving) and golf-club heads. Sometimes planted for the edible persimmon fruits and for ornament.

ll. Leaves broadest above middle—TUPELO (*Nyssa*).

63. WATER TUPELO, *Nyssa aquatica* L. (tupelo, tupelo-gum, swamp tupelo, cotton-gum, sour-gum).

Large tree with swollen base, swamps of South Atlantic Coastal Plain, Gulf Coastal Plain, and lower Mississippi Valley. Bark dark brown, thin, rough, with scaly ridges. Leaves oval or oblong, 4 to 6 inches long, short- or long-pointed, edges smooth or with a few teeth, shiny dark green above, pale and soft-hairy beneath. Fruits oblong, 1 inch long, fleshy, purple, acid, 1-seeded.

Principal uses: Furniture, boxes, crates, and baskets, and pulpwood. Also railroad ties and cooperage.

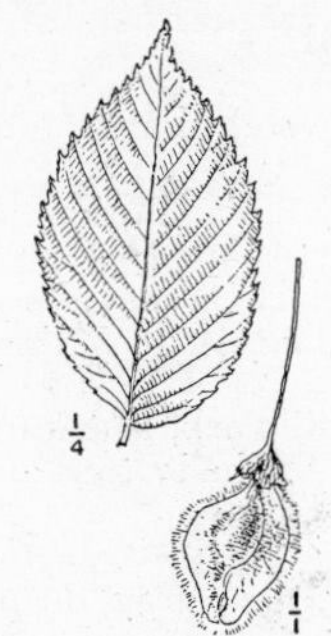

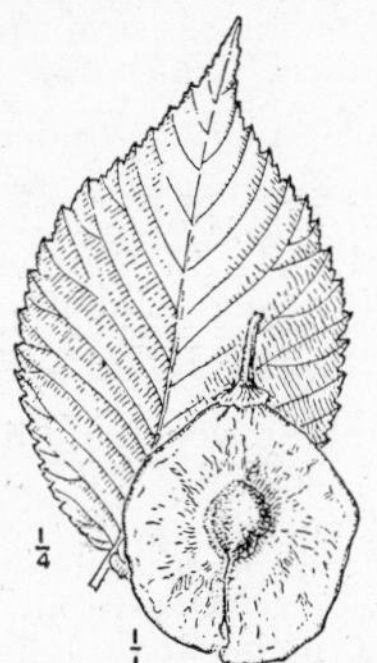

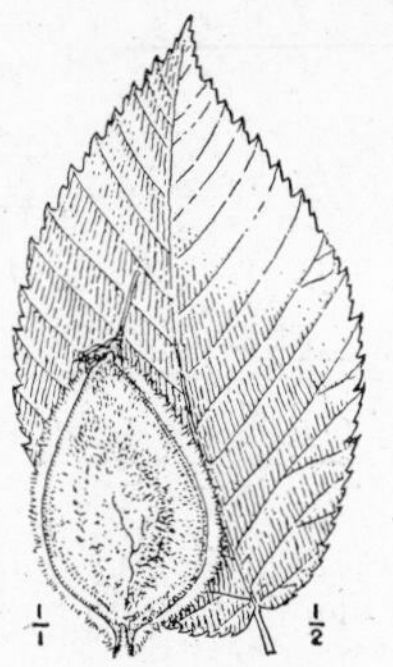

69. American elm. 70. Slippery elm. 71. Rock elm. 72. Winged elm.

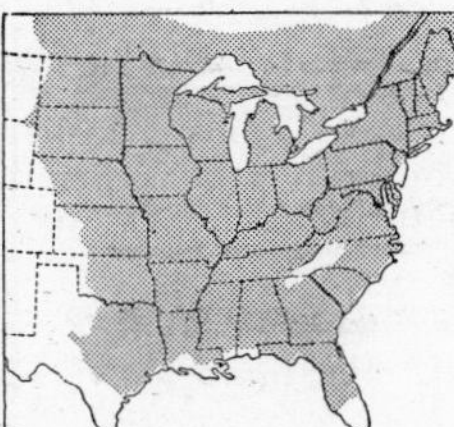
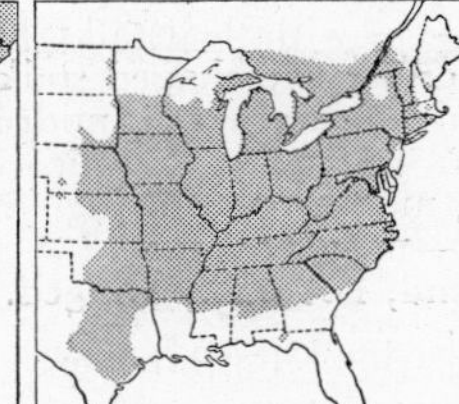

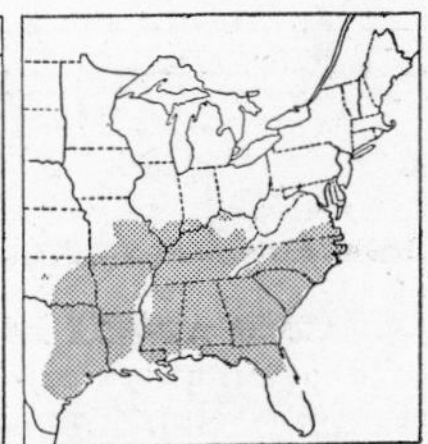

64. BLACK TUPELO, *Nyssa sylvatica* Marsh. (blackgum, sour-gum, tupelo, pepperidge, tupelo-gum; variety: swamp tupelo, *N. sylvatica* var. *biflora* (Walt.) Sarg., blackgum, swamp blackgum, swamp black tupelo).

Large tree of eastern third of United States; also in southern Ontario and Mexico. Bark reddish brown, deeply fissured into irregular and block-shaped ridges. Leaves elliptical or oblong, 2 to 5 inches long, short- or blunt-pointed, wedge-shaped or rounded at base, edges smooth, shiny dark green above, pale and often hairy beneath, turning bright scarlet in fall. Fruits egg-shaped, 3/8 to 1/2 inch long, fleshy, blue black, bitter, 1-seeded.

Principal uses: Boxes, crates, and baskets, furniture, and pulpwood. Also railroad ties and cooperage. Ornamental and shade tree.

65. OGEECHEE TUPELO, *Nyssa ogeche* Bartr. (sour tupelo-gum, sour tupelo, Ogeechee-lime, limetree).

Small to medium-sized tree, local in swamps of Coastal Plain in South Carolina, Georgia, and Florida. Bark dark brown, thin, irregularly fissured. Leaves elliptical, 4 to 6 inches long, short- or blunt-pointed, wedge-shaped at base, edges smooth, thick, shiny dark green and slightly hairy above, pale and hairy beneath. Fruits 1 to 1 1/2 inches long, fleshy, red, sour, 1-seeded.

Principal uses: A preserve, Ogeechee-lime, is made from the fruit. The wood is of little importance commercially.

jj. Leaf edges toothed (see also No. 63).

m. Leaves with few large spiny teeth, evergreen—HOLLY (*Ilex*).

66. AMERICAN HOLLY, *Ilex opaca* Ait. (holly, white holly, evergreen holly, boxwood).

Medium-sized to large tree of Atlantic coast, Gulf coast, and Mississippi Valley regions. Bark light gray, thin, smoothish, with wartlike projections. Leaves evergreen, elliptical, 2 to 4 inches long, spine-pointed and coarsely spiny-toothed, stiff and leathery, shiny green above and yellowish green beneath. Male and female flowers on different trees, small, greenish white. Berrylike fruit spherical, 1/4 to 3/8 inch in diameter, red.

Principal uses: Christmas decorations. The wood is used for scientific and musical instruments, toy boats, furniture inlays, and sporting and athletic goods. Ornamental and shade tree. (State tree of Delaware.)

mm. Leaves with many small teeth, shedding in fall.

n. Leaves with the 2 sides unequal and 1 side larger at base, in 2 rows on twig.

o. Leaves broad, heart-shaped, with leafstalks more than 1 1/4 inches long (the fragrant, pale yellow flowers and round, nutlike fruits borne on a strap-shaped greenish stalk)—BASSWOOD (or linden, *Tilia*).

67. AMERICAN BASSWOOD, *Tilia americana* L. (American linden, basswood, linden, linn, beetree, limetree; *T. glabra* Vent.).

Large tree of northeastern quarter of United States and adjacent Canada. Bark gray, deeply furrowed into narrow, scaly ridges. Leaves in 2 rows, heart-shaped, 4 to 8 inches long, long-pointed, coarsely toothed with long-pointed teeth, dark green above, light green beneath with tufts of hair in angles of main veins. Fruits nutlike, 3/8 to 1/2 inch in diameter.

Principal uses: Boxes (especially food containers), venetian blinds, millwork, furniture, apiary supplies, and woodenware. Also veneer, excelsior, and cooperage. Shade tree and important honey plant.

68. WHITE BASSWOOD, *Tilia heterophylla* Vent. (beetree linden).

Large tree of Appalachian Mountain region west to Mississippi Valley. Bark gray, deeply furrowed. Leaves in 2 rows, heart-shaped, 3 to 6 inches long, long-pointed, the 2 sides unequal at base, finely toothed, shiny dark green and smooth above, beneath white or brownish with dense hairy coat. Fruits nutlike, 1/4 to 3/8 inch in diameter.

Principal uses: Same as No. 67.

oo. Leaves narrower, with leafstalks less than 1/2 inch long (flowers not on a strap-shaped stalk).

p. Leaves with 1 main vein (midrib) and many parallel lateral veins; fruits flat, elliptical or rounded, bordered with a wing, maturing in spring (maturing in fall in Nos. 73 and 74)—ELM (*Ulmus*).

q. Twigs round, not corky winged.

69. AMERICAN ELM, *Ulmus americana* L. (white elm [lumber], soft elm [lumber], water elm, gray elm, swamp elm).

Large spreading tree of eastern half of United States and adjacent Canada, now threatened in the Northeast by the Dutch elm disease. Bark gray, deeply furrowed, with broad, forking, scaly ridges. Twigs soft-hairy, becoming smooth, not corky winged. Leaves in 2 rows, elliptical, 3 to 6 inches long, long-pointed, the 2 sides unequal, coarsely and doubly toothed with unequal teeth, thin, dark green and smooth or slightly rough above, pale and usually soft-hairy beneath. Fruits elliptical, flat, 3/8 to 1/2 inch long.

Principal uses: Containers (boxes, baskets, crates, and barrels), furniture, dairy, poultry, and apiary supplies, caskets, and vehicle parts. American elm is extensively planted as a shade tree across the United States. Shelterbelts. (State tree of Massachusetts.)

70. SLIPPERY ELM, *Ulmus rubra* Muhl. (soft elm [lumber], red elm, gray elm; *U. fulva* Michx.).

Medium-sized tree of eastern half of United States and adjacent Canada. Bark dark brown, deeply furrowed; inner bark mucilaginous. Twigs hairy and rough, not corky winged. Leaves in 2 rows, elliptical, 4 to 8 inches long, long-pointed, the 2 sides unequal, coarsely and doubly toothed with unequal teeth, thick, dark green and very rough above, densely soft-hairy beneath. Fruit rounded, flat, 1/2 to 3/4 inch long.

Principal uses: Wood used same as No. 69.

qq. Twigs usually becoming corky winged.

71. ROCK ELM, *Ulmus thomasi* Sarg. (cork elm, hickory elm; *U. racemosa* Thomas, not Borkh.).

Medium-sized to large tree of northeastern quarter of United States and adjacent Canada. Bark gray, deeply furrowed. Twigs often corky winged. Leaves in 2 rows, elliptical, 2 to 4 inches long, short-pointed, the 2 sides unequal, coarsely and doubly toothed with unequal teeth, thick, shiny dark green and smooth above, pale and soft-hairy beneath. Fruit elliptical, flat, 5/8 to 3/4 inch long.

Principal uses: Wood used same as No. 69. Shade tree.

72. WINGED ELM, *Ulmus alata* Michx. (wahoo, cork elm).

Medium-sized tree of southeastern quarter of United States. Bark light brown, thin, irregularly fissured. Twigs usually becoming corky winged. Leaves in 2 rows, oblong, 1 1/4 to 2 1/2 inches long, short-pointed, the 2 sides unequal, coarsely and doubly toothed with unequal teeth, thick, dark green and smooth above, pale and soft-hairy beneath. Fruit elliptical, flat, 3/8 inch long.

Principal uses: Wood used same as No. 69. Shade tree.

73. SEPTEMBER ELM, *Ulmus serotina* Sarg. (red elm).

Medium-sized tree of Mississippi Valley region from Illinois to Georgia and Oklahoma. Bark light brown, thin, fissured. Twigs often corky winged. Leaves in 2 rows, oblong, 2 to 3 inches long, long-pointed, the 2 sides unequal, coarsely and doubly toothed with

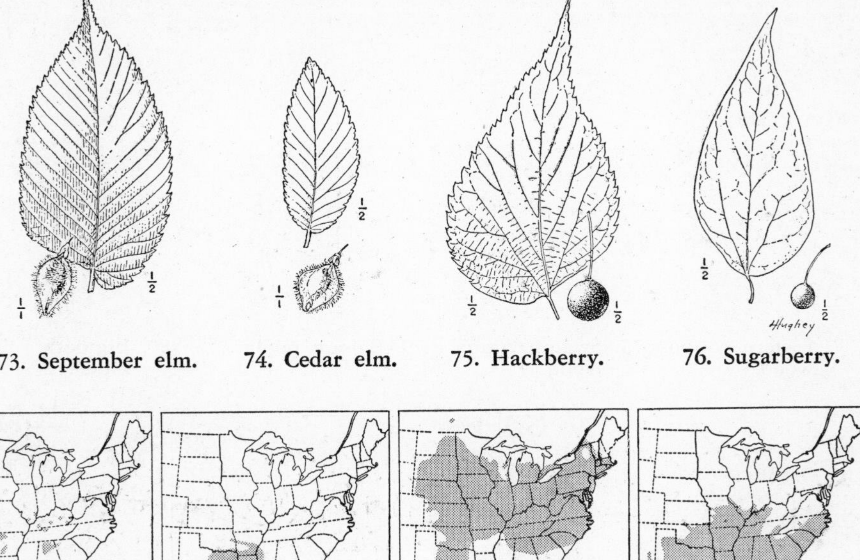


73. **September elm.** 74. **Cedar elm.** 75. **Hackberry.** 76. **Sugarberry.**

unequal teeth, shiny yellow green and smooth above, pale and slightly hairy beneath. Flowering in fall. Fruit elliptical, ½ inch long, flat.

Principal uses: Wood used same as No. 69.

74. CEDAR ELM, *Ulmus crassifolia* Nutt. (red elm, basket elm, southern rock elm).

Large tree of lower Mississippi Valley to Texas and adjacent Mexico. Bark light brown, fissured. Twigs usually becoming corky winged. Leaves in 2 rows, elliptical, 1 to 2 inches long, short-pointed or rounded, the 2 sides unequal, coarsely and doubly toothed with unequal teeth, thick, shiny dark green and rough above, soft-hairy beneath. Flowering in late summer or fall. Fruit oblong, ⅜ to ½ inch long, flat.

Principal uses: Wood used same as No. 69.

pp. Leaves with 3 main veins from base; fruits round, wingless, maturing in fall—HACKBERRY (*Celtis*).

75. HACKBERRY, *Celtis occidentalis* L. (common hackberry, sugarberry).

Medium-sized to large tree of eastern half of United States except southern border; also in adjacent Canada. Bark light brown to gray, with corky warts or ridges becoming scaly. Leaves in 2 rows, oval 2 to 4½ inches long, usually long-pointed, the 2 sides unequal, sharply toothed except in lower part, with 3 main veins from base, bright green and smooth or sometimes rough above, paler and nearly smooth beneath. Fruits ¼ to ⅜ inch in diameter, dark purple, 1-seeded.

Principal uses: Furniture and boxes and baskets. Shelterbelts and shade tree.

76. SUGARBERRY, *Celtis laevigata* Willd. (sugar hackberry, hackberry, Mississippi hackberry, southern hackberry; *C. mississippiensis* Spach).

Medium-sized to large tree of southeastern quarter of United States, with a variety west to New Mexico and northeastern Mexico. Bark gray, smoothish, with prominent corky warts. Leaves in 2 rows, broadly lance-shaped, 1½ to 4 inches long, long-pointed, the 2 sides unequal, edges smooth or sometimes with a few teeth, with 3 main veins from base, dark green and smooth or sometimes rough above, paler and usually smooth beneath. Fruits ¼ inch in diameter, orange red, or purple, 1-seeded.

Principal uses: Furniture and boxes and baskets. Shelterbelts and shade tree.

nn. Leaves with both sides equal, spreading around twig (in 2 rows in No. 89).

r. Leafstalks more than 1½ inches long, slender; seeds cottony, in long-clustered capsules—POPLAR (*Populus;* see also Nos. 150 and 151).

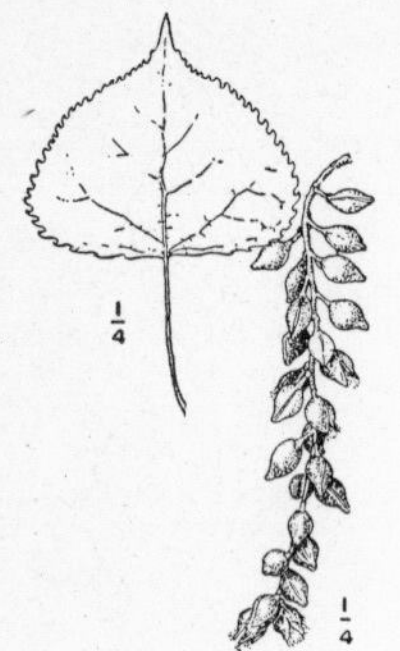


77. Eastern cottonwood.

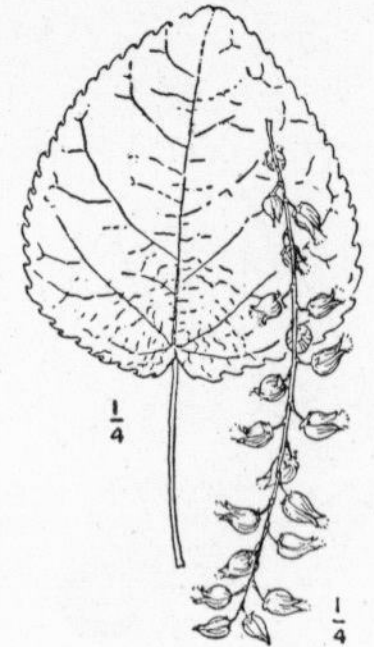


78. Swamp cottonwood.

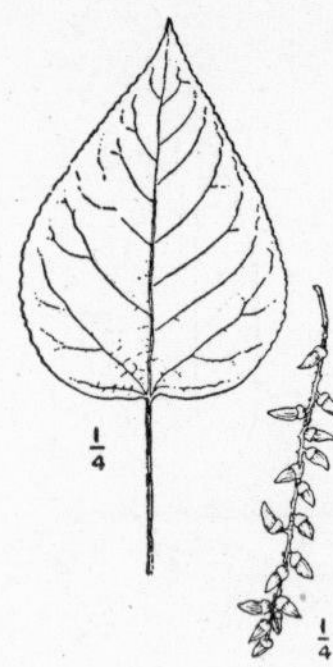


79. Balsam poplar.

80. Bigtooth aspen.

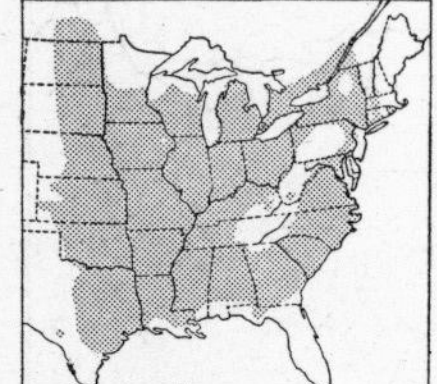

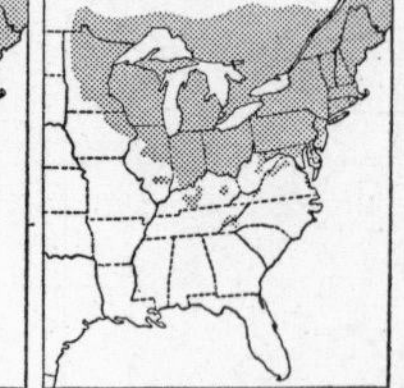

77. EASTERN COTTONWOOD, *Populus deltoides* Bartr. (cottonwood, eastern poplar, Carolina poplar, necklace poplar; *P. balsamifera* auth.).

Large tree of eastern half of United States and adjacent Canada. Bark at first yellowish green and smooth, becoming gray and deeply furrowed. Leaves triangular, 3 to 6 inches long and wide, long-pointed, coarsely toothed with curved teeth, smooth, light green and shiny. Leafstalks flat.

Principal uses: Lumber and veneer, used principally for boxes and crates but also for furniture, dairy and poultry supplies, etc. Also pulpwood, excelsior, and fuel. Shade tree and shelterbelts. (Cottonwood (*Populus* spp.) is the State tree of Kansas, Nebraska, and South Dakota.)

78. SWAMP COTTONWOOD, *Populus heterophylla* L. (cottonwood, swamp poplar, black cottonwood, river cottonwood).

Medium-sized to large tree of Atlantic coast, Gulf coast, and Mississippi Valley regions. Bark grayish brown, furrowed into scaly ridges. Leaves heart-shaped, 4 to 7 inches long and nearly as wide, short-pointed or rounded at apex, finely toothed with small, curved teeth, hairy when unfolding but becoming smooth or remaining woolly beneath, dark green above, paler beneath. Leafstalks round.

Principal uses: Wood used same as No. 77.

79. BALSAM POPLAR, *Populus tacamahaca* Mill. (tacamahac, tacamahac poplar, balm-of-Gilead, balm-of-Gilead poplar, balsam, cottonwood, poplar; *P. balsamifera* auth.).

Large tree widely distributed in northeastern border of United States, northern Rocky Mountain region, and across Canada to Alaska. Bark at first reddish brown and smooth, becoming gray, furrowed, with flat, scaly ridges. Winter buds resinous and fragrant. Leaves oval or broadly lance-shaped, 3 to 5 inches long, short-pointed, finely toothed with rounded teeth, smooth or nearly so, shiny dark green above, pale green beneath. Leafstalks round.

Principal uses: Boxes and crates and pulpwood. Balm-of-Gilead, derived from the buds, is used in cough medicine. Ornamental.

80. BIGTOOTH ASPEN, *Populus grandidentata* Michx. (largetooth aspen, aspen, poplar, popple).

Medium-sized tree of northeastern quarter of United States and adjacent Canada. Bark greenish, smooth, thin, becoming dark brown, irregularly fissured, with flat ridges. Leaves elliptical or nearly round, 2½ to 4 inches long, coarsely toothed with curved teeth. Leafstalks flat.

Principal uses: Pulpwood, boxes and crates, excelsior, and matches.

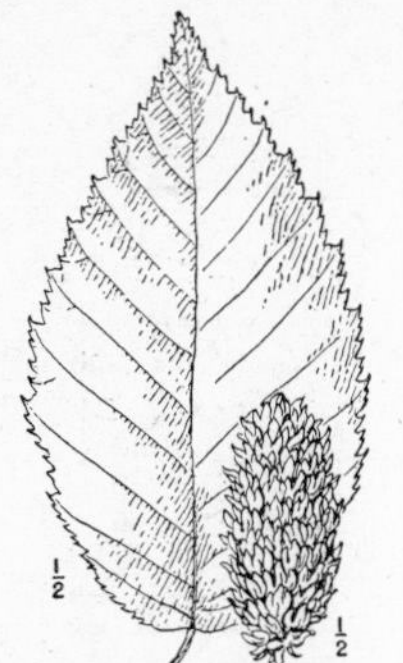

**81. Yellow birch.**

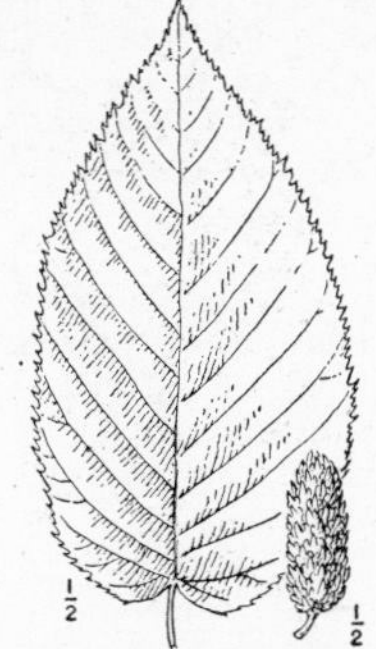

**82. Sweet birch.**

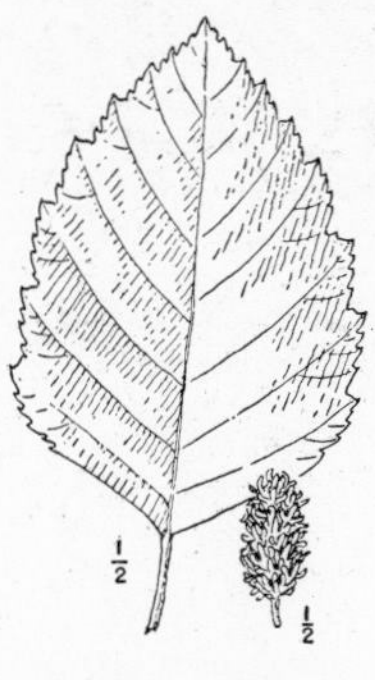

**83. River birch.**

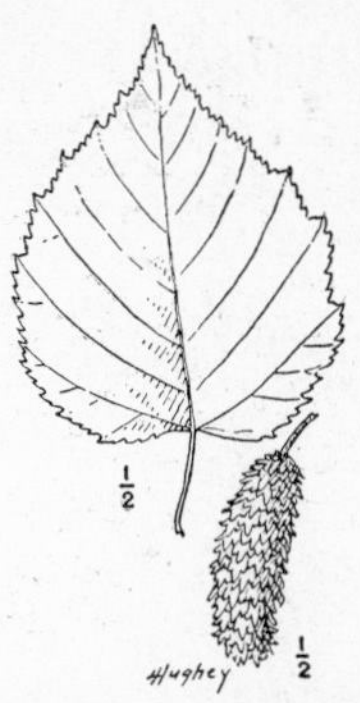

**84. Paper birch.**

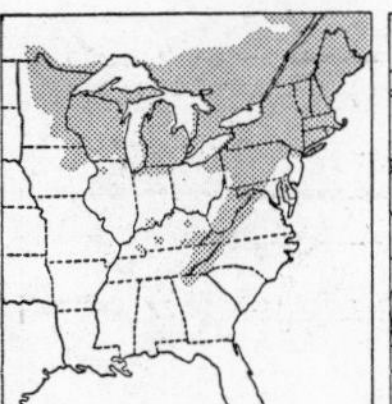

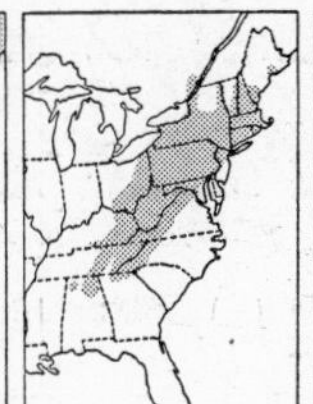

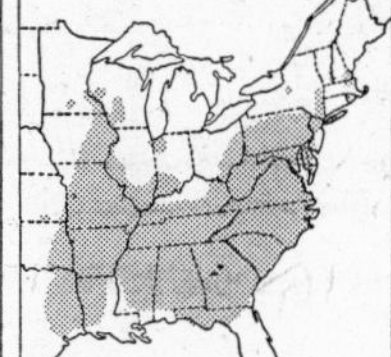

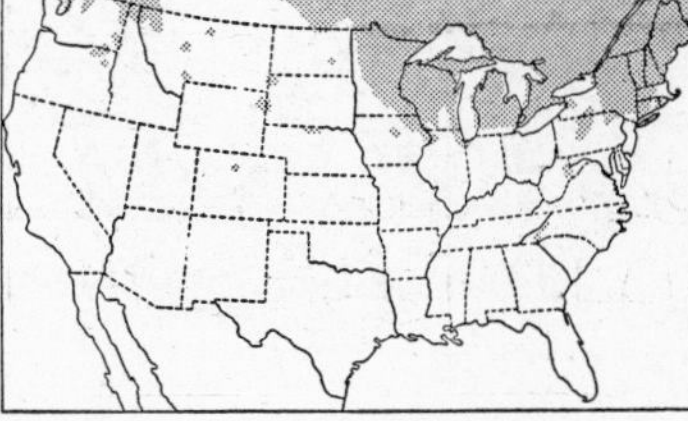

rr. Leafstalks less than 1 inch long; seeds not hairy (except Nos. 86 and 87).

s. Leaf edges with teeth of 2 sizes and slightly irregular; fruit a cone, upright in Nos. 81–83, hanging down in Nos. 84 and 85—BIRCH (*Betula*).

t. Leaves mostly with 9 to 11 main veins on each side.

81. YELLOW BIRCH, *Betula lutea* Michx. f. (birch [lumber], gray birch, silver birch, swamp birch).

Large tree of northeastern United States and adjacent Canada and Appalachian Mountain region. Bark (aromatic on young branches) yellowish or silvery gray, shiny, separating into papery, curly strips; on old trunks reddish brown. Leaves oval, 3 to 5 inches long, long- or short-pointed, sharply and doubly toothed, mostly with 9 to 11 main veins on each side, nearly smooth, dull dark green above, yellow green below. Cones ¾ to 1¼ inches long.

Principal uses: Birches are among the leading furniture woods. Also boxes, baskets, crates, woodenware, handles, spools and bobbins, millwork, flooring, distillation products, railroad ties, and fuel. Yellow birch plywood is used in airplane construction. Shade tree. (State tree of New Hampshire.)

82. SWEET BIRCH, *Betula lenta* L. (birch [lumber], black birch, cherry birch).

Medium-sized to large tree of Appalachian Mountain region and adjacent Canada. Bark aromatic on young branches, dark reddish brown, smooth, shiny; on large trunks fissured into scaly plates. Leaves oval, 2½ to 5 inches long, long-pointed, sharply and doubly toothed, mostly with 9 to 11 main veins on each side, silky-hairy beneath when young but becoming nearly smooth, dark dull green above, light yellow green beneath. Cones ¾ to 1½ inches long.

Principal uses: Same as No. 81.

tt. Leaves mostly with 4 to 9 main veins on each side.

83. RIVER BIRCH, *Betula nigra* L. (red birch).

Medium-sized to large tree of wet soil in eastern half of United States. Bark reddish brown or silvery gray, shiny, becoming fissured and separating into papery scales. Leaves oval, 1½ to 3 inches long, short-pointed, wedge-shaped at base, doubly toothed, mostly with 7 to 9 main veins on each side, shiny dark green above, whitish and usually hairy beneath. Cones 1 to 1½ inches long.

Principal uses: Ornamental and for erosion control.

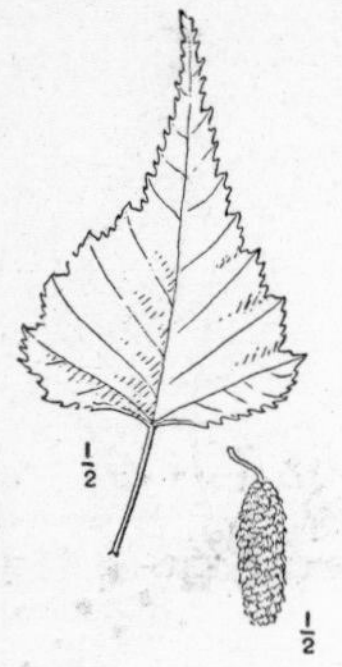


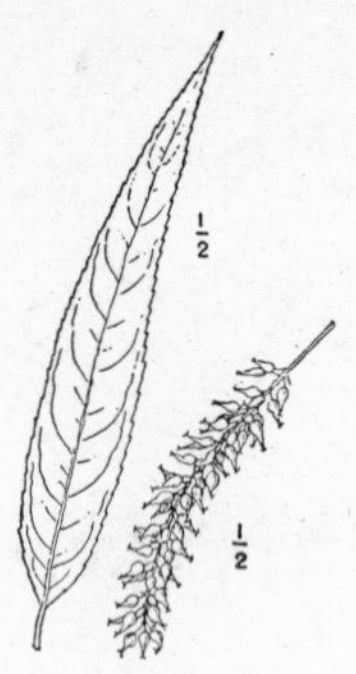


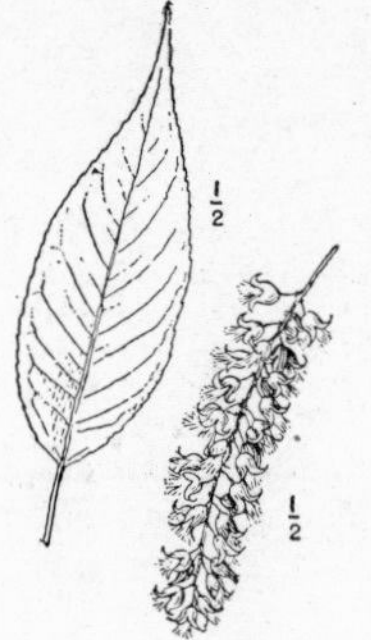


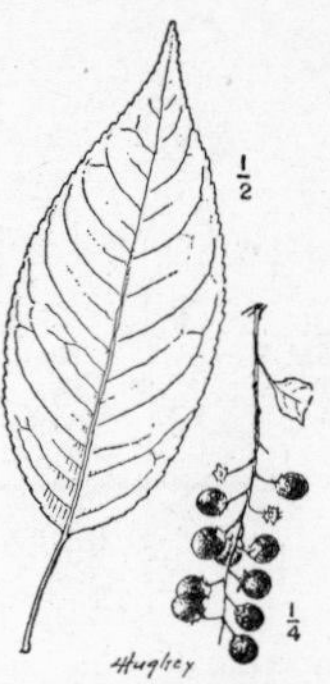


**85. Gray birch. 86. Black willow. 87. Peachleaf willow. 88. Black cherry.**

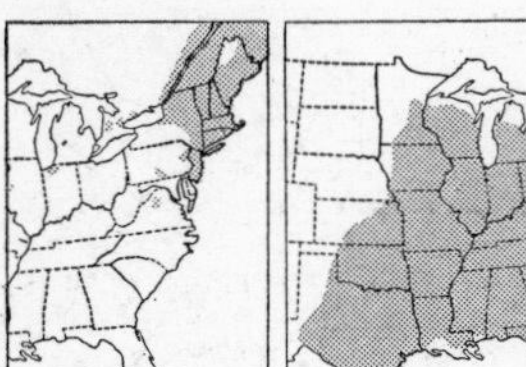

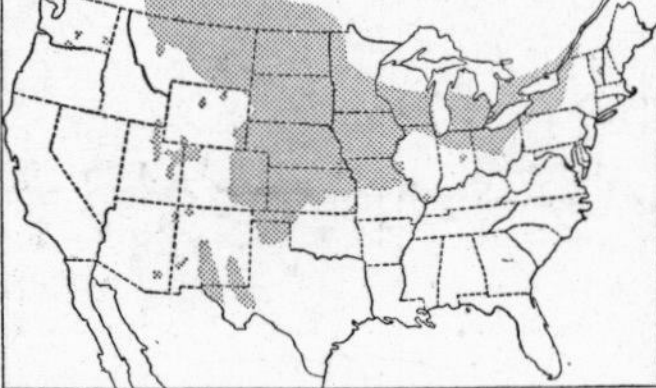

84. PAPER BIRCH, *Betula papyrifera* Marsh. (white birch, canoe birch, silver birch).

Medium-sized to large tree, including its varieties widely distributed in northeastern border of United States, northern Rocky Mountain region, and across Canada to Alaska. Bark white, smooth, thin, separating into papery strips. Leaves oval, 2 to 4 inches long, long-pointed, wedge-shaped or rounded at base, coarsely and usually doubly toothed, mostly with 5 to 9 main veins on each side, dull dark green and smooth above, light yellow green and smooth or slightly hairy beneath. Cones narrow, 1½ to 2 inches long and ⅜ inch wide, slender-stalked and hanging down.

Principal uses: Spools and other turned articles. Toothpicks. Ornamental and shade tree. Bark used by Indians for canoes and small articles.

85. GRAY BIRCH, *Betula populifolia* Marsh. (white birch).

Small tree of northeastern United States and adjacent Canada. Bark grayish white, smooth, thin; on larger trunks darker and fissured. Leaves triangular, 2 to 3 inches long, long-pointed, sharply and doubly toothed, mostly with 4 to 8 main veins on each side, dark green and shiny above, paler beneath. Cones ¾ to 1 inch long, slender-stalked and hanging down.

Principal uses: Spools and other turned articles. Fuel.

ss. Leaf edges with uniform teeth; fruit not a cone.
u. Leaves finely toothed, with curved lateral veins.
v. Leaves narrow, more than three times as long as wide (seeds hairy, in long-clustered capsules)—WILLOW (*Salix*).

86. BLACK WILLOW, *Salix nigra* Marsh. (swamp willow, willow).

Medium-sized to large tree of wet soil, eastern half of United States and adjacent Canada. Bark dark brown or blackish, deeply furrowed, with scaly, forking ridges. Leaves lance-shaped, 2½ to 5 inches long, long-pointed, finely toothed, green on both sides, shiny above and pale beneath. Male and female flowers on different trees in early spring, minute, yellowish or greenish, many in narrow clusters 1½ to 3 inches long.

Principal uses: Boxes and baskets, furniture, and caskets. A special use is for artificial limbs. Erosion control. Shade tree.

87. PEACHLEAF WILLOW, *Salix amygdaloides* Anderss. (peach willow, almond willow).

Small to medium-sized tree of wet soil, nearly across northern United States and adjacent Canada, south to Texas and Arizona. Bark brown, irregularly fissured into flat ridges. Leaves lance-shaped, 2½ to 5 inches long, long-pointed, finely toothed, shiny green above and pale beneath. Male and female flowers on different trees in early spring, minute, yellowish or greenish, many in narrow clusters 2 to 3 inches long.

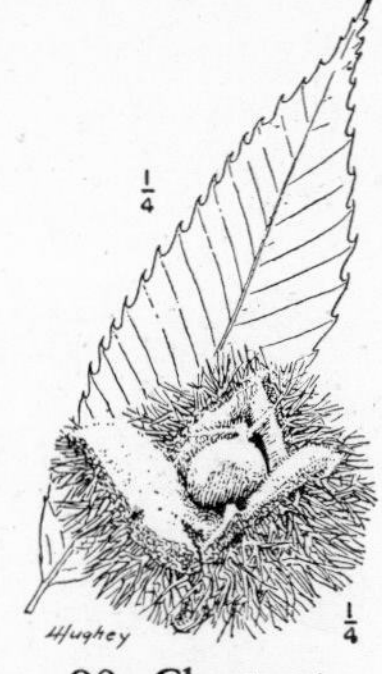


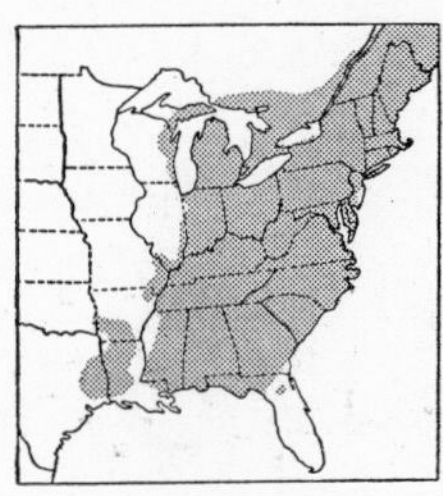

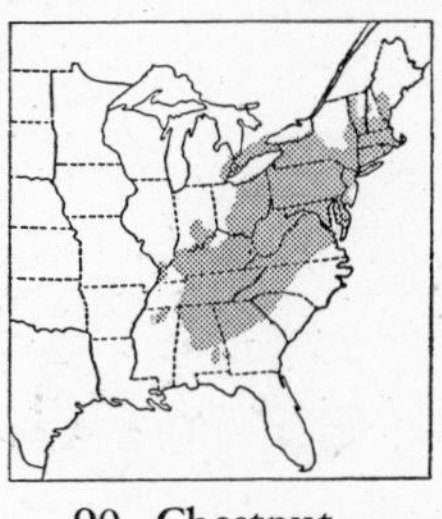

**89. Beech.** **90. Chestnut.** **89. Beech.** **90. Chestnut.**

Principal uses: Same as No. 86.

vv. Leaves less than three times as long as wide—CHERRY (*Prunus*).

88. BLACK CHERRY, *Prunus serotina* Ehrh. (wild black cherry, wild cherry, rum cherry, cherry; *Padus virginiana* auth.).

Medium-sized to large tree of eastern half of United States and adjacent Canada. Bark dark reddish brown, smooth at first, becoming irregularly fissured and scaly. Leaves oblong, 2 to 5 inches long, long-pointed, finely toothed, shiny dark green above, light green beneath. Flowers white, ¼ inch long, in spring. Fruits edible cherries ⅜ inch in diameter, black.

Principal uses: Furniture and printers' blocks for mounting electrotype plates. Shade tree. Edible wild cherries.

uu. Leaves coarsely toothed, with parallel lateral veins; fruit a spiny bur with edible nuts.

w. Leaves about twice as long as wide—BEECH (*Fagus*).

89. BEECH, *Fagus grandifolia* Ehrh. (American beech; *F. americana* Sweet, *F. ferruginea* Ait.)

Large tree of eastern third of United States and adjacent Canada. Bark blue gray, thin, smooth. Leaves in 2 rows, oval, 2½ to 5 inches long, long-pointed, coarsely toothed, the lateral veins parallel, dark blue green above and light green beneath, usually smooth or nearly so. Fruit a shiny bur ¾ inch long containing 2 or 3 triangular, edible nuts ½ to ¾ inch long, known as beechnuts.

Principal uses: Food containers, chairs and other furniture, handles, flooring, woodenware and novelties, laundry appliances, etc. Also distillation products, railroad ties, veneer, pulpwood, cooperage, and fuel. Beechnuts. Shade tree.

ww. Leaves about three times as long as wide—CHESTNUT (*Castanea*).

90. CHESTNUT, *Castanea dentata* (Marsh.) Borkh. (American chestnut).

Large tree of Appalachian Mountain and Ohio Valley regions; also in southern Ontario; now almost exterminated by the chestnut blight. Bark dark brown, irregularly fissured into broad, flat ridges. Leaves narrowly oblong, 5 to 9 inches long and 1½ to 3 inches wide, long-pointed, coarsely toothed with slightly curved teeth, many parallel lateral veins, yellow green, smooth. Fruit a spiny bur 2 to 2½ inches in diameter, containing 2 or 3 broad, flattened, edible nuts ½ to 1 inch wide, known as chestnuts.

Principal uses: The wood, largely from blight-killed trees, is the main domestic source of tannin. Lumber for construction and for manufacture of furniture, caskets, and boxes and crates. Pulpwood. Chestnuts. The leaves are an official drug.

ff (f on p. 784). Winter buds 3 or more in cluster at tip of twig; pith of twigs star-shaped in cross section; fruit an acorn—OAK (*Quercus*).

Twenty species of eastern oaks included here have commercially important wood.

Principal uses: Oaks are the most important hardwood timbers of the United States. Oak is used principally for lumber, fuel (including charcoal), and cooperage (white oak group), and is the leading wood for railroad ties and mine timbers. Besides the lumber used in building construction, much is manufactured into flooring (oak is the principal flooring wood), boxes and crates, furniture, railroad-car construction, vehicle parts, general millwork, ships and boats, agricultural implements, caskets, fixtures, woodenware and

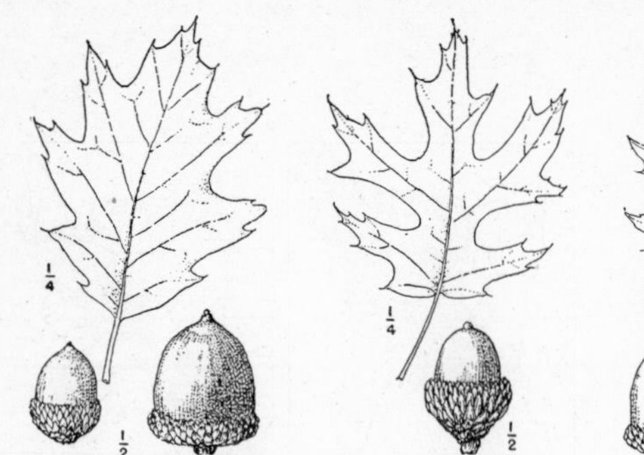
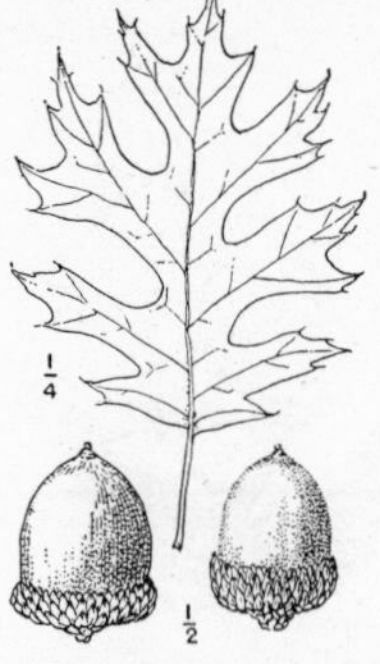

91. Northern red oak. 92. Scarlet oak. 93. Shumard oak. 94. Pin oak.

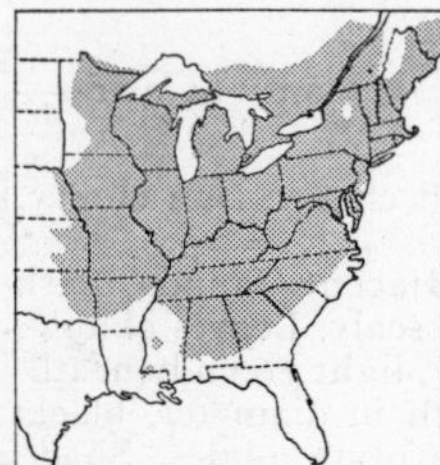

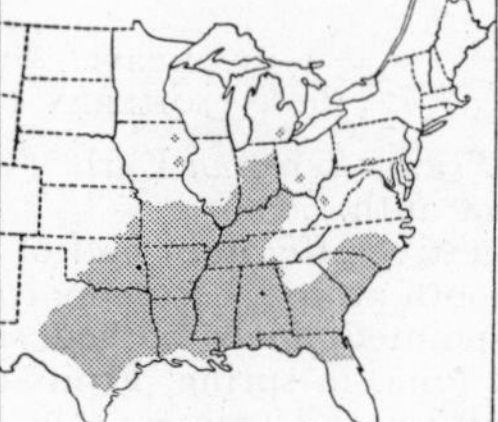
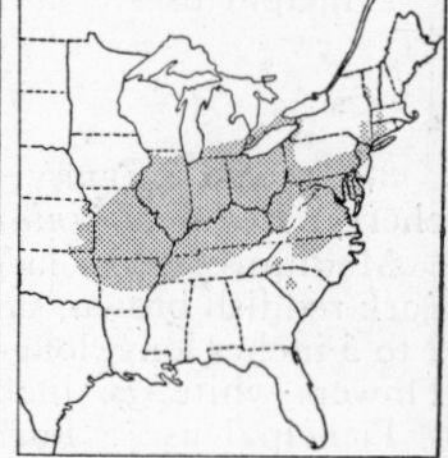

novelties, and handles. Also fence posts, piling, veneer, and distillation products. Some species are important shade trees. The acorns are eaten by wildlife and livestock. ("Native oak" (*Quercus* spp.) is the State tree of Illinois.)

x. Leaves and their lobes, if present, bristle-tipped; acorns maturing in second year—BLACK OAKS (or red oaks, the lumber of most species included here usually sold as red oak).

y. Leaves broad, more than 2 inches wide, the margins distinctly lobed and with bristle-pointed teeth.

z. Under surface of leaves green and nearly smooth.

91. NORTHERN RED OAK, *Quercus borealis* Michx. f. (red oak [lumber], eastern red oak; *Q. rubra* auth.).

Large tree of eastern half of United States except southern border and in adjacent Canada. Bark dark brown, fissured into broad, flat ridges. Leaves oblong, 5 to 9 inches long, 7- to 11-lobed less than halfway to middle, the lobes with a few irregular bristle-pointed teeth, dull dark green above, beneath pale yellow green, smooth or nearly so, usually turning red in fall. Acorns ⅝ to 1⅛ inches long, with deep or shallow cup.

Principal uses: The most important lumber tree of the red oak group. Shade tree.

92. SCARLET OAK, *Quercus coccinea* Muenchh. (red oak [lumber]).

Large tree of eastern third of United States except southern border; also in southern Ontario. Bark dark brown or gray, fissured into irregular, scaly ridges. Leaves oblong or elliptical, 3 to 6 inches long, deeply 7-lobed nearly to middle, the lobes broader toward the tip and with a few bristle-pointed teeth, edges rounded between the lobes, bright green, shiny, and smooth above, paler and nearly smooth beneath, turning scarlet in fall. Acorns ½ to ¾ inch long, a third to half enclosed by the deep cup.

Principal uses: Red oak lumber. Shade tree.

93. SHUMARD OAK, *Quercus shumardii* Buckl. (red oak [lumber], Shumard red oak, Schneck oak, Texas oak, southern red oak).

Large tree of eastern United States, chiefly in Atlantic coast, Gulf coast, and Mississippi Valley regions. Bark gray or reddish brown, fissured into scaly plates. Leaves oval or elliptical, 3 to 7 inches long, 5- to 9-lobed more than halfway to middle, the lobes with a few bristle-pointed teeth, edges rounded or pointed between the lobes, dark green and shiny above, beneath light green with tufts of hairs along midrib. Acorns ⅝ to 1⅛ inches long, with shallow or deep cup.

Principal uses: Important timber tree for red oak lumber. Furniture, cabinet work, and veneer. Shade tree.

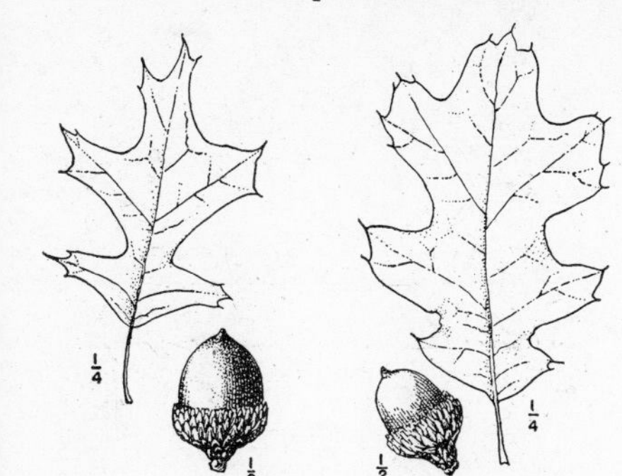

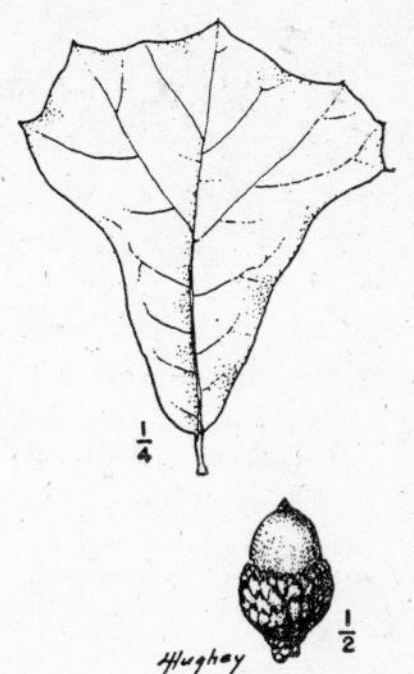


**95. Nuttall oak. 96. Black oak. 97. Southern red oak. 98. Blackjack oak.**

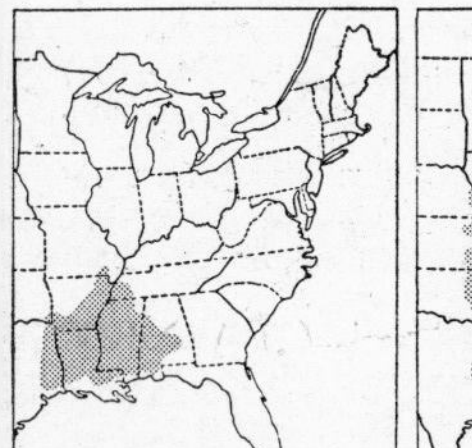
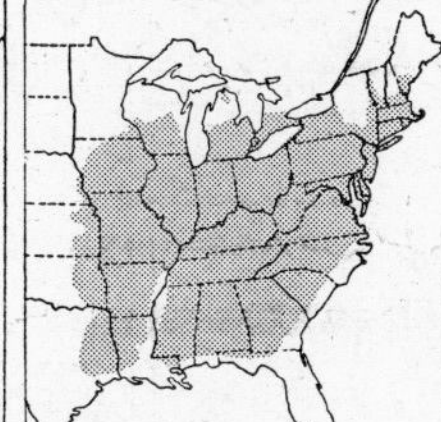
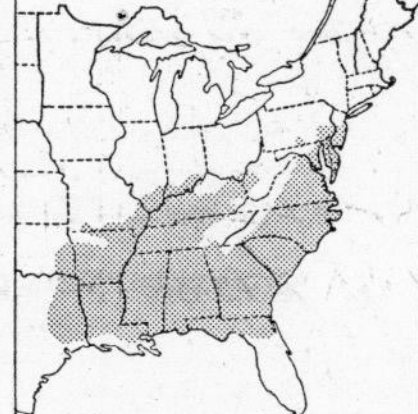
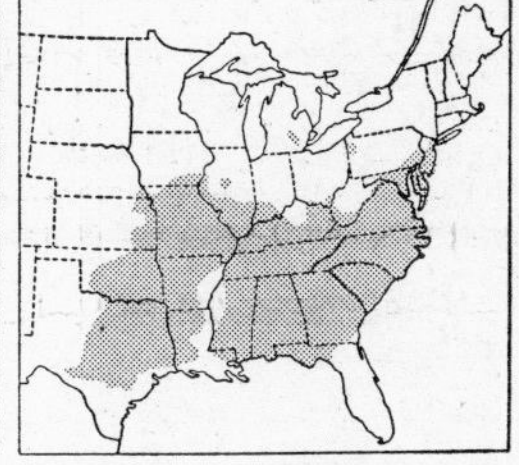

94. PIN OAK, *Quercus palustris* Muenchh. (swamp oak).

Large tree of northeastern quarter of United States except northern border; also in southern Ontario. Bark grayish brown, smooth, becoming fissured with low, scaly ridges. Leaves elliptical, 3 to 5 inches long, deeply 5- to 7-lobed nearly to middle, the lobes with a few bristle-pointed teeth, dark green and very shiny above, light green and nearly smooth beneath. Acorns rounded, about ½ inch in diameter, with shallow cup.

Principal uses: Fuel wood, charcoal, and distillation products. Shade tree.

95. NUTTALL OAK, *Quercus nuttallii* Palmer (red oak [lumber]).

Large tree of lower Mississippi Valley and Gulf Coastal Plain regions from Alabama to Missouri and Texas. Bark dark brownish gray, slightly fissured. Leaves oblong or elliptical, 4 to 8 inches long, deeply 5- or 7-lobed, the narrow lobes with a few bristle-pointed teeth, dark green above, paler and nearly smooh beneath. Acorns oblong, ¾ to 1¼ inches long, enclosed one-third to one-half by the deep cup.

Principal uses: Red oak lumber.

zz. Under surface of leaves with brownish or gray hairy coat.

96. BLACK OAK, *Quercus velutina* Lam. (red oak [lumber]), yellow oak, quercitron oak).

Large tree of eastern half of United States and southern Ontario. Bark blackish, thick, deeply furrowed, with blocklike ridges; inner bark yellow. Leaves oval or oblong, 4 to 10 inches long, 7- to 9-lobed about halfway to middle, the lobes broad and with a few bristle-pointed teeth, shiny dark green above, usually brown-hairy beneath, turning dull red or brown in fall. Acorns ⅝ to ¾ inch long, half enclosed by the deep cup.

Principal uses: Red oak lumber. The bark is a source of tannin. Fuel. Shade tree.

97. SOUTHERN RED OAK, *Quercus falcata* Michx. (red oak [lumber], Spanish oak; *Q. rubra* auth.; variety: swamp red oak, *Q. falcata* var. *pagodaefolia* Ell., cherrybark oak).

Large tree of Atlantic coast, Gulf coast, and Mississippi Valley regions. Bark dark brown, thick, fissured into narrow ridges. Leaves elliptical or oval, 3 to 8 inches long, deeply 3- to 7-lobed nearly to middle or slightly 3-lobed near broad apex (less deeply 5- to 11-lobed in the variety, swamp red oak), the lobes with 1 to 3 bristle-pointed teeth, dark green, smooth, and shiny above, rusty or grayish hairy beneath, turning brown or orange in fall. Acorns rounded, about ½ inch in diameter, with shallow cup.

Principal uses: Important timber tree for red oak lumber. Shade tree.

98. BLACKJACK OAK, *Quercus marilandica* Muenchh. (blackjack, jack oak, black oak).

Small tree of eastern half of United States except northern border. Bark blackish, thick and rough, divided into small squarish blocks. Leaves oval, 3 to 7 inches long, broadest and 3-lobed at apex, the lobes shallow and broad with 1 or few bristle-pointed teeth, dark green, smooth, and shiny above, brownish or rusty-hairy beneath, turning

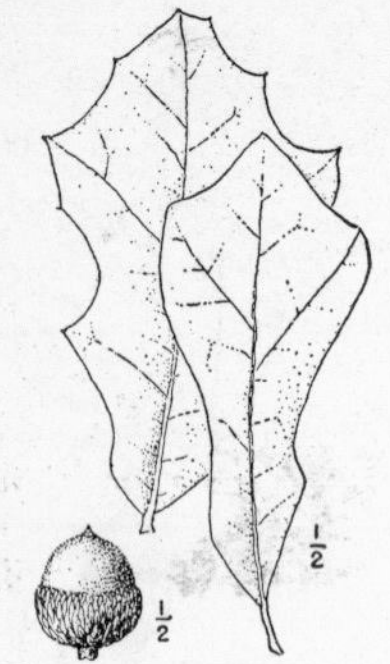

99. Water oak.

100. Laurel oak.

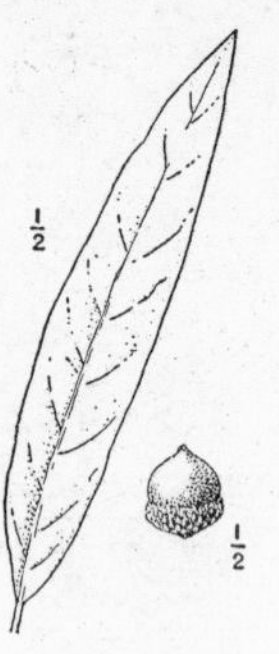

101. Willow oak.

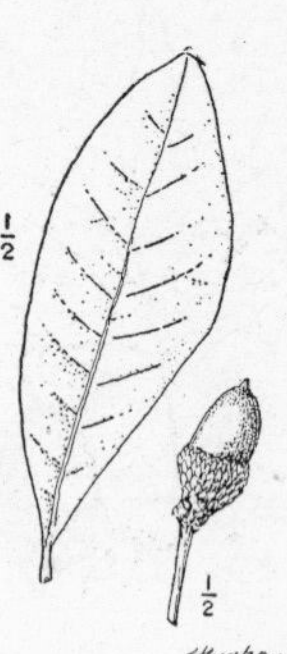

102. Live oak.

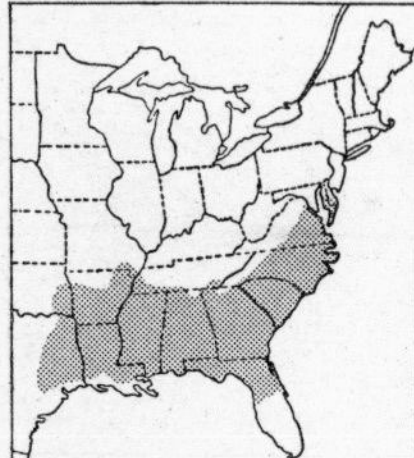

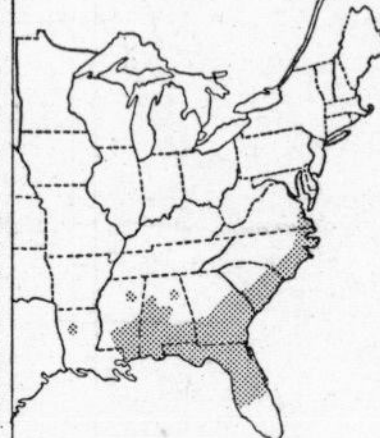

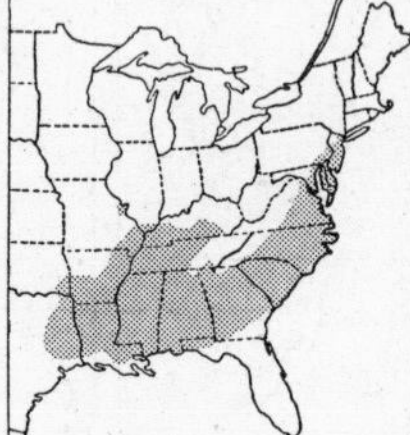

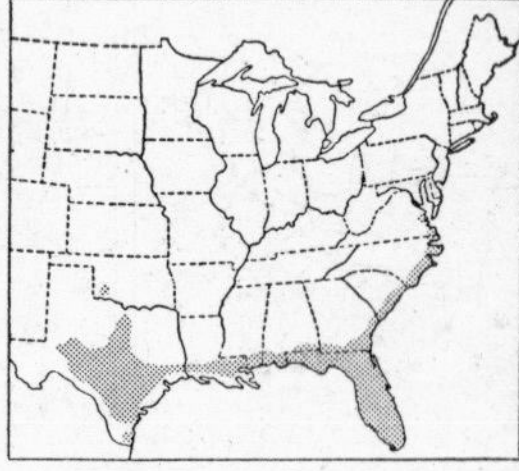

brown or yellow in fall. Acorns ¾ inch long, about half enclosed by the deep cup.

Principal uses: Fuel wood, charcoal, and distillation products.

yy. Leaves narrow, less than 2 inches broad, with edges smooth or slightly 3-lobed.

99. WATER OAK, *Quercus nigra* L. (red oak [lumber]).

Large tree of Atlantic coast, Gulf coast, and Mississippi Valley regions. Bark gray, fissured into irregular, scaly ridges. Leaves oval, 1½ to 5 inches long, broadest at the 3-lobed or smooth apex or sometimes with several lobes, dull blue green, paler beneath, becoming smooth except for tufts of hairs along axis, turning yellow in fall and shedding in winter. Acorns rounded, ⅜ to ⅝ inch in diameter, with shallow cup.

Principal uses: Red oak lumber. Fuel. Shade tree.

100. LAUREL OAK, *Quercus laurifolia* Michx.

Large tree of South Atlantic and Gulf Coastal Plains. Bark dark brown, smoothish, on large trunks becoming deeply furrowed, with broad ridges. Leaves oblong, 2 to 5½ inches long, short-pointed with smooth or sometimes slightly lobed edges, shiny dark green above, light green beneath, smooth, nearly evergreen but shedding in early spring. Acorns rounded, about ½ inch in diameter, with shallow cup.

Principal uses: Fuel wood, charcoal, and distillation products. Shade tree.

101. WILLOW OAK, *Quercus phellos* L. (red oak [lumber]).

Large tree of Atlantic coast, Gulf coast, and Mississippi Valley regions. Bark gray or brown, smoothish, on large trunks becoming fissured into scaly ridges. Leaves very narrowly oblong or lance-shaped, 2 to 4 inches long and ⅜ to ¾ inch broad, short-pointed with smooth or slightly wavy edges, light green and shiny above, beneath dull and slightly hairy or nearly smooth, turning pale yellow in fall. Acorns small, rounded, ⅜ inch in diameter, with shallow cup.

Principal uses: Red oak lumber. Shade tree.

xx. Leaves and their lobes not bristle-tipped; acorns maturing in first year—WHITE OAKS (the lumber of most species sold as white oak).

A. Leaves with edges usually smooth and rolled under, evergreen.

102. LIVE OAK, *Quercus virginiana* Mill.

Medium-sized, widespreading tree of South Atlantic coast and Gulf coast regions. Bark dark brown, furrowed and slightly scaly. Leaves evergreen, elliptical or oblong, 2 to 5

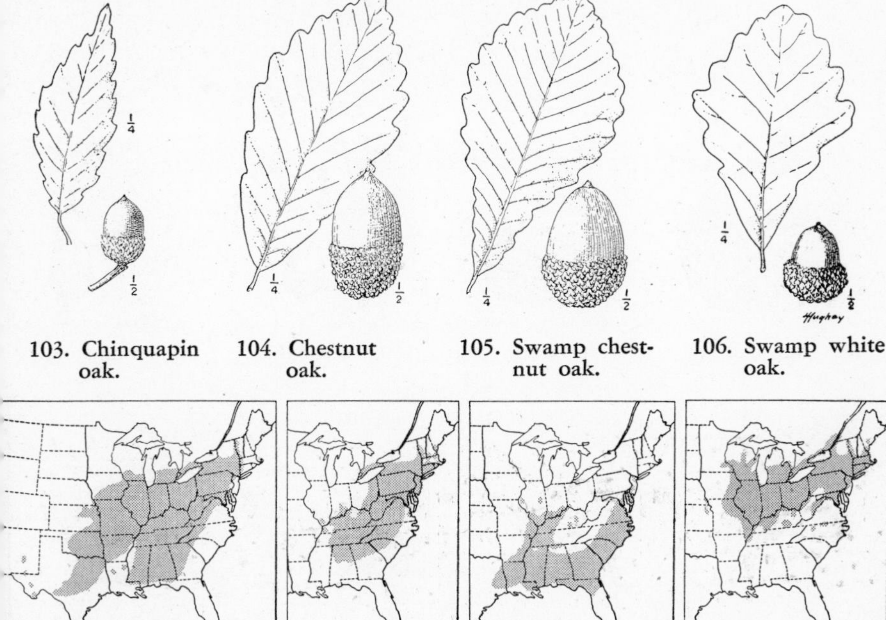


103. Chinquapin oak. 104. Chestnut oak. 105. Swamp chestnut oak. 106. Swamp white oak.

inches long, usually rounded at apex, edges usually smooth and rolled under, shiny dark green above, whitish hairy beneath. Acorns 1 to 5 on stalks ½ to 3 inches long, ¾ to 1 inch long, narrow, with deep cup.

Principal uses: Shade tree. Formerly used in shipbuilding. (State tree of Georgia.)

AA. Leaves with edges lobed or toothed, shedding in fall.

B. Leaf edges wavy with uniform, rounded teeth (CHESTNUT OAKS).

103. CHINQUAPIN OAK, *Quercus muehlenbergii* Engelm. (chestnut oak, yellow oak).

Large tree of eastern half of United States and local in New Mexico; also in southern Ontario. Bark light gray, thin, fissured, and flaky. Leaves oblong or broadly lance-shaped, 4 to 6 inches long, short- or long-pointed, usually rounded at base, edges wavy with coarse, slightly curved teeth, dark or yellowish green above, whitish hairy beneath, turning orange and scarlet in fall. Acorns ½ to ¾ inch long, rounded, half enclosed by the deep cup.

Principal uses: Railroad ties and construction timbers.

104. CHESTNUT OAK, *Quercus montana* Willd. (white oak [lumber], rock chestnut oak, rock oak; *Q. prinus* auth.).

Large tree of Appalachian Mountain and Ohio Valley regions; also in southern Ontario. Bark brown or blackish; on large trunks becoming deeply furrowed into broad ridges. Leaves oblong, 5 to 8 inches long, short- or long-pointed, narrowed and pointed or rounded at base, edges wavy with rounded teeth, shiny yellow green above, paler and hairy or nearly smooth beneath, turning dull orange in fall. Acorns large, 1 to 1½ inches long, one-third to one-half enclosed by the thin, deep, warty cup.

Principal uses: White oak lumber and railroad ties. The bark is a source of tannin.

105. SWAMP CHESTNUT OAK, *Quercus prinus* L. (white oak [lumber], basket oak, cow oak; *Q. michauxii* Nutt.).

Large tree of Atlantic coast, Gulf coast, and Mississippi Valley regions. Bark light gray, fissured and scaly. Leaves oblong, 4 to 8 inches long, short- or long-pointed, wedge-shaped or rounded at base, edges wavy with rounded teeth, shiny dark green above, grayish hairy beneath, turning crimson in fall. Acorns large, 1 to 1½ inches long, one-third or more enclosed by the thick, deep cup composed of many distinct scales.

Principal uses: White oak lumber.

106. SWAMP WHITE OAK, *Quercus bicolor* Willd. (white oak [lumber]).

Large tree of northeastern quarter of United States and adjacent Canada. Bark brown, scaly; on old trunks becoming furrowed into long, scaly ridges. Leaves oblong, 4 to 6 inches long, gradually narrowed toward base, broadest above middle, edges wavy with rounded teeth or lobes, dark green and shiny above, whitish hairy beneath, turning yellow

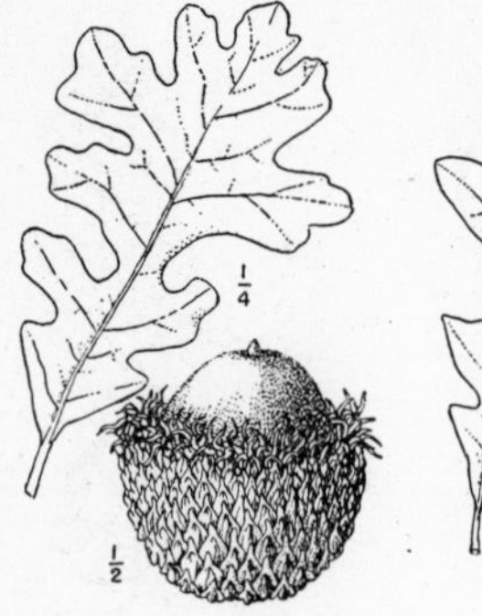


**107. Bur oak.**

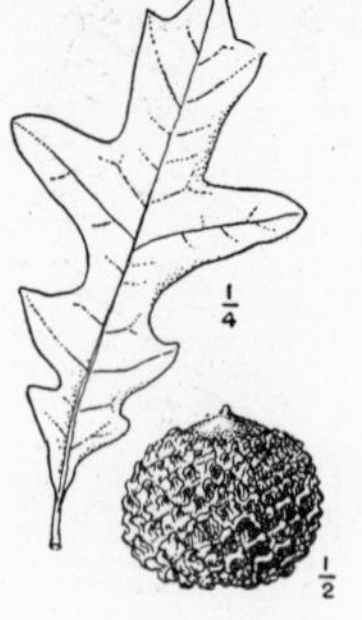


**108. Overcup oak.**

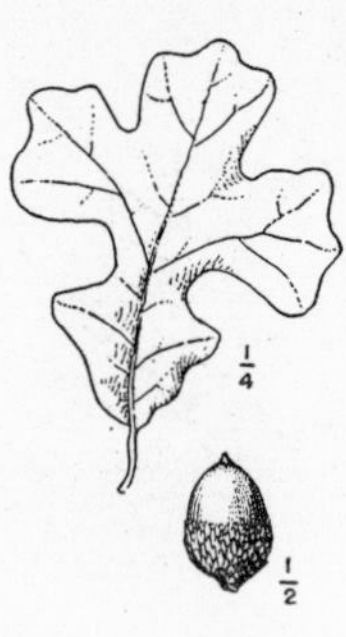


**109. Post oak.**

**110. White oak.**

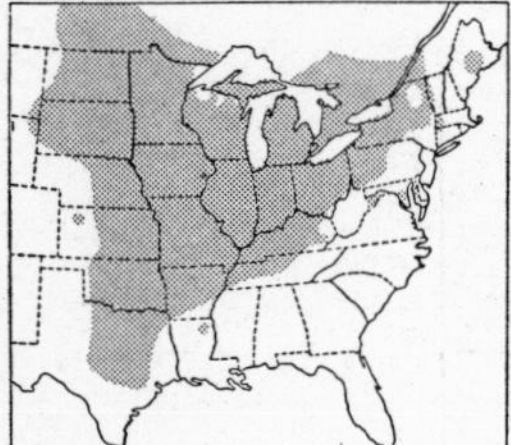

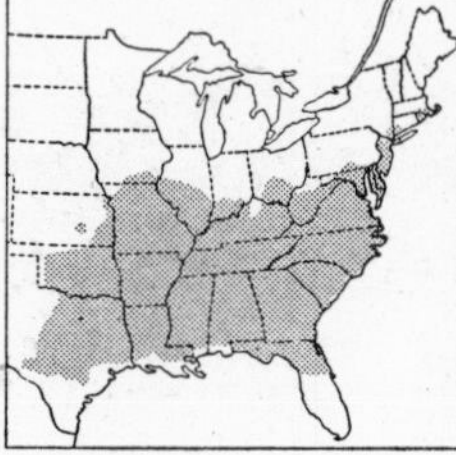

brown, orange, or red in fall. Acorns usually in pairs on stalks 1½ to 3 inches long, ¾ to 1¼ inches long, one-third enclosed by the deep cup.

Principal uses: White oak lumber.

BB. Leaf edges deeply lobed.

107. BUR OAK, *Quercus macrocarpa* Michx. (mossycup oak).

Large tree of eastern half of United States west to Montana and in adjacent Canada west to Saskatchewan. Bark light brown, deeply furrowed into scaly ridges. Leaves oblong, 4 to 10 inches long, wedge-shaped at base, broadest above middle, the lower part deeply lobed nearly to middle and the upper half with shallow lobes, dark green and usually shiny above, grayish or whitish hairy beneath, turning yellow or brown in fall. Acorns usually large, ¾ to 2 inches long, broad, half enclosed by the large cup with fringelike border.

Principal uses: Lumber and railroad ties. Shelterbelts. Shade tree and ornamental.

108. OVERCUP OAK, *Quercus lyrata* Walt. (swamp white oak; white oak [lumber]).

Medium-sized to large tree of Atlantic coast, Gulf coast, and Mississippi Valley regions. Bark brownish gray, fissured into large irregular, scaly ridges. Leaves oblong, 6 to 8 inches long, wedge-shaped at base, deeply lobed nearly to middle with 7 to 9 rounded or pointed lobes, the 2 lowest lobes on each side much smaller, dark green and smooth above, white hairy beneath, turning yellowish, orange, or scarlet in fall. Acorns ½ to 1 inch long, nearly enclosed by the spherical deep cup with ragged edge.

Principal uses: White oak lumber.

109. POST OAK, *Quercus stellata* Wangenh.

Small to medium-sized (rarely large) tree of eastern half of United States except northern border. Bark reddish brown, fissured into broad, scaly ridges. Leaves oblong, 4 to 8 inches long, usually wedge-shaped at base, deeply 5- to 7-lobed (3-lobed in a variety), the lobes broad and middle lobes largest, dark green and rough above, grayish hairy beneath, turning brown in fall. Acorns ½ to 1 inch long, nearly half enclosed by the deep cup.

Principal uses: Railroad ties and construction timbers.

110. WHITE OAK, *Quercus alba* L.

Large tree of eastern half of United States and adjacent Canada. Bark light gray, fissured into scaly ridges. Leaves oblong, 4 to 9 inches long, deeply or shallowly 5- to 9-lobed, smooth, bright green above, pale or whitish beneath, turning deep red in fall. Acorns ¾ to 1 inch long, with shallow cup.

Principal uses: The most important lumber tree of the white oak group and one of the best oaks with high-grade all-purpose wood. The outstanding wood for tight barrels. Shade tree. (State tree of Connecticut, Maryland, and West Virginia.)

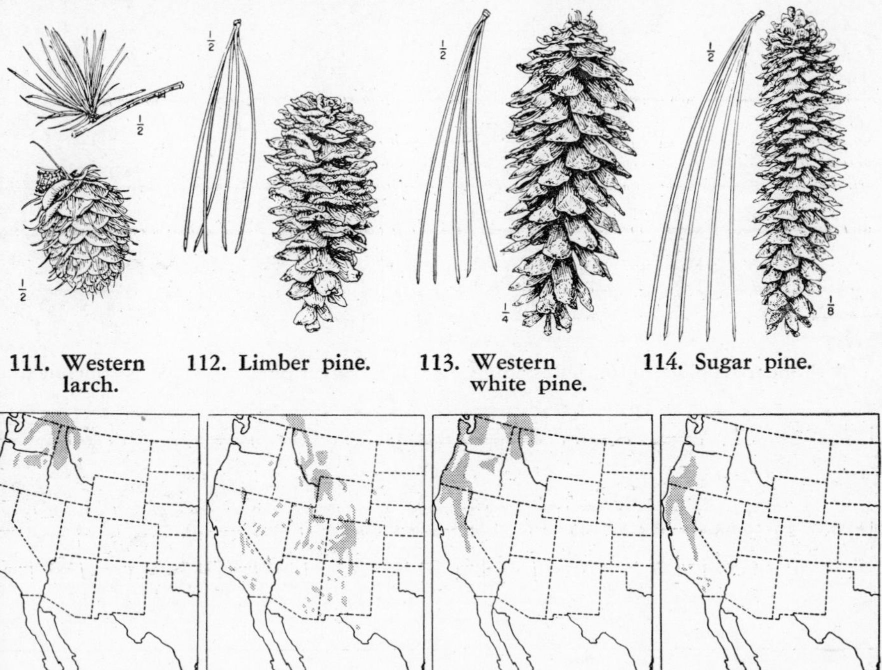

111. Western larch. 112. Limber pine. 113. Western white pine. 114. Sugar pine.

## WESTERN TREES

*Tree species Nos. 111 to 165 are native in the western half of the United States, west of the prairie-plains. In addition, the following 9 species in the list of eastern trees occur also in western United States: Nos. 16, 31, 33, 76, 79, 84, 87, 103, and 107. Also, Nos. 11, 17, and 18 extend to western Canada though not to western United States. The 18 important tree species of Alaska, mostly in the list of western trees, are: Nos. 3, 16, 17, 79, 84, 119, 122, 123, 124, 127, 130, 131, 138, 140, 147, 150, 152, and 153.*

### GYMNOSPERMS (CONIFERS OR SOFTWOODS)

A (*AA* on p. 808). Trees resinous, with leaves needlelike or scalelike, evergreen (except larch, No. 111); seeds borne on scales of a cone (berrylike in juniper, Nos. 142 to 145, or seeds single in a fleshy scarlet disk in yew, No. 122)—GYMNOSPERMS (conifers or softwoods, such as pines, spruces, firs).

*B.* Leaves shedding in fall, needlelike, many in cluster on short, spur branches—LARCH (*Larix;* see also No. 3).

111. WESTERN LARCH, *Larix occidentalis* Nutt. (larch, western tamarack, tamarack, mountain larch, Montana larch, hackmatack).

Large tree of mountains of northwestern United States and southeastern British Columbia. Bark reddish brown, scaly, becoming deeply furrowed into flat ridges with many overlapping plates. Needles many in cluster on short, spur branches (or single on leading twigs), 3-angled, 1 to 1¼ inches long, light pale green, shedding in fall. Cones upright, 1 to 1½ inches long, with long, pointed bracts.

Principal uses: Lumber for building construction, also interior finish, flooring, and millwork. Railroad ties, mine timbers, fuel. The gum (galactin) can be used in manufacture of baking powder. Ornamental.

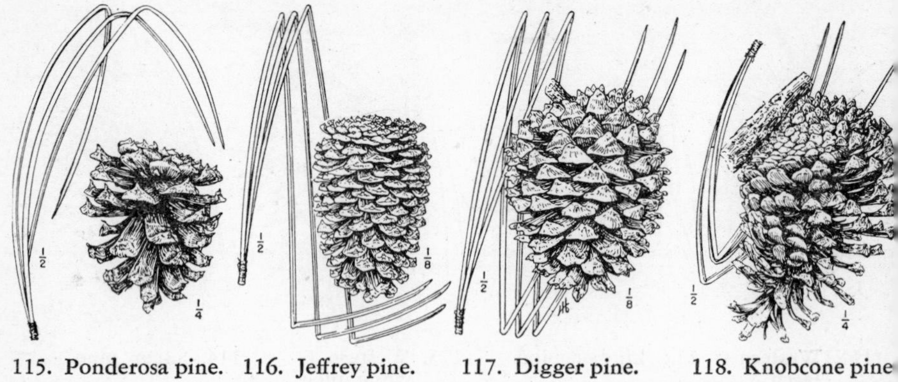

115. **Ponderosa pine.** 116. **Jeffrey pine.** 117. **Digger pine.** 118. **Knobcone pine**

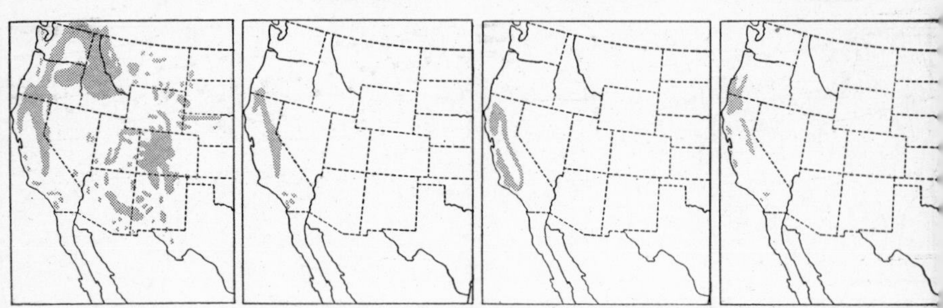

*BB*. Leaves evergreen, needlelike or scalelike, single or not more than 5 in a cluster
*C*. Leaves with a sheath at base, in clusters of 2 to 5 (or 1 in No. 121) needlelike—PINE (*Pinus*).
*D*. Needles 5 in a cluster—WHITE (SOFT) PINES.

112. LIMBER PINE, *Pinus flexilis* James (Rocky Mountain white pine, white pine; variety: *P. flexilis* var. *reflexa* Engelm., *P. strobiformis* auth.).

Medium-sized tree of Rocky Mountain region, including adjacent Canada and Mexico Bark dark brown, furrowed into rectangular, scaly plates. Needles 5 in cluster, slender 2 to 3½ inches long, dark green. Cones short-stalked, 3 to 6 inches long, yellow brown with thick, rounded scales and large seeds ⅜ to ½ inch long.

Principal uses: Lumber (mostly for rough construction and occasionally for boxes) mine timbers, railroad ties, poles, and fuel.

113. WESTERN WHITE PINE, *Pinus monticola* Dougl. (Idaho white pine [lumber], white pine).

Large tree of northern Rocky Mountain and Pacific coast regions, including southern British Columbia. Bark gray, thin, smoothish, becoming fissured into rectangular, scaly plates. Needles 5 in cluster, stout, 2 to 4 inches long, blue green. Cones long-stalked, 5 to 12 inches long, yellow brown, with thin, rounded scales.

Principal uses: Important timber tree. Lumber for building construction, matches (the leading match wood), boxes, and millwork. (State tree of Idaho.)

114. SUGAR PINE, *Pinus lambertiana* Dougl. (California sugar pine).

Large tree (largest of the pines) of Pacific coast region from Oregon to Lower California. Bark brown, furrowed into irregular, scaly ridges. Needles 5 in cluster, stout 3 to 4 inches long, blue green. Cones long-stalked, very large, 12 to 18 inches long, yellow brown, with thin, rounded scales.

Principal uses: Lumber for building construction, boxes and crates, millwork, and foundry patterns.

*DD*. Needles 3 or fewer in a cluster—YELLOW (HARD) PINES (Nos. 115 to 119) and PINYONS (or nut pines, Nos. 120 and 121).
*E*. Needles more than 4 inches long.

115. PONDEROSA PINE, *Pinus ponderosa* Laws. (western yellow pine, pondosa pine western soft pine, yellow pine; variety: *P. Ponderosa* var. *scopulorum* Engeim, Rocky Mountain ponderosa pine).

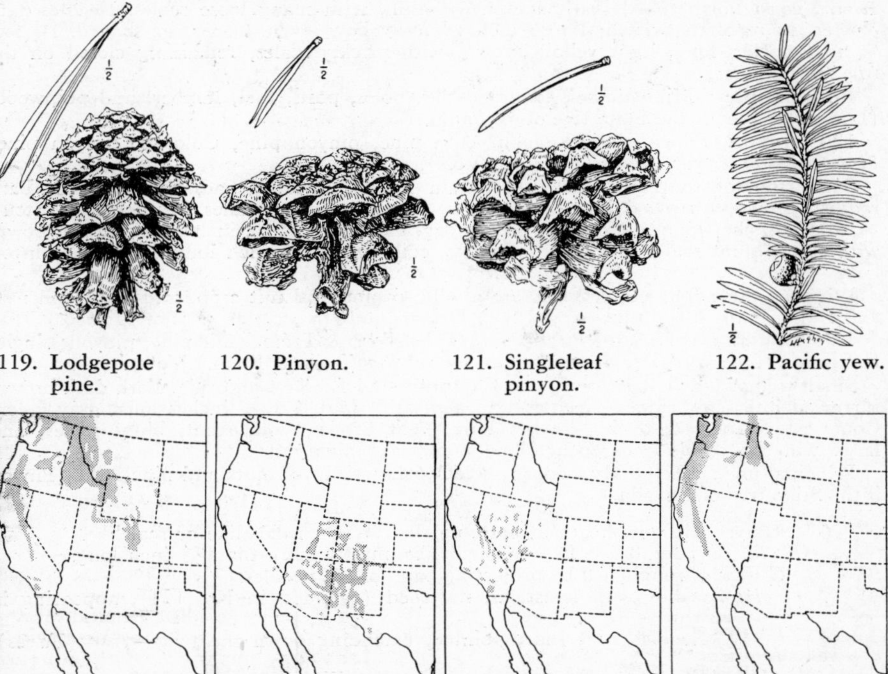

119. Lodgepole pine. 120. Pinyon. 121. Singleleaf pinyon. 122. Pacific yew.

Large tree of Rocky Mountain and Pacific coast regions, including adjacent Canada. Bark brown or blackish, furrowed into ridges; on older trunks becoming yellow brown and irregularly fissured into large, flat, scaly plates. Needles 3 or 2 and 3 in cluster, stout, 4 to 7 inches long, dark green. Cones short-stalked, 3 to 6 inches long, light reddish brown, the scales with prickles.

Principal uses: Important timber tree, the most important western pine, and second to Douglas-fir in total stand in United States. Lumber for many uses, such as building construction, boxes and crates, and millwork; also caskets, furniture, toys. Piling, poles, posts, mine timbers, veneer, railroad ties, and fuel. Shelterbelts and ornamental. (State tree of Montana.)

116. JEFFREY PINE, *Pinus jeffreyi* Grev. & Balf. (western yellow pine).

Large tree of Pacific coast region from Oregon to Lower California. Bark purplish brown, becoming fissured into large plates. Needles 3 in cluster, stout, 5 to 10 inches long, blue green. Cones short-stalked, 5 to 10 inches long, light brown, the scales with prickles.

Principal uses: Lumber sold as ponderosa pine (No. 115) and has similar uses.

117. DIGGER PINE, *Pinus sabiniana* Dougl. (gray pine, bull pine).

Medium-sized tree of California foothills. Bark dark brown, irregularly furrowed into broad, irregular, scaly ridges. Needles 3 in cluster, slender and drooping, 8 to 12 inches long, pale blue green. Cones long-stalked, 6 to 10 inches long, red brown, with stout scales ending in curved spines. Seeds ¾ to ⅞ inch long, edible.

Principal uses; Fuel. Shelterbelts.

118. KNOBCONE PINE, *Pinus attenuata* Lemm.

Small to medium-sized tree of southwestern Oregon and California. Bark brown, thin, fissured into large, scaly ridges. Needles 3 in cluster, slender, 3 to 7 inches long, yellowish green. Cones usually clustered and abundant, 1-sided, 3 to 6 inches long, light yellow brown, with prickly scales, remaining closed on the tree indefinitely.

Principal uses: Fuel. Shelterbelts.

*EE.* Needles less than 3 inches long.

119. LODGEPOLE PINE, *Pinus contorta* Dougl. (shore pine, knotty pine, black pine, spruce pine, jack pine; *P. contorta* var. *latifolia* Engelm.).

Medium-sized to large tree of Rocky Mountain and Pacific coast regions including adjacent Canada and Lower California; the typical variety shore pine, a small tree of

802062°—49——52

Pacific coast north to Alaska. Bark brown, thin, with many loose scales. Needles 2 in cluster, stout, often twisted, 1 to 3 inches long, yellow green. Cones egg-shaped, 1-sided ¾ to 2 inches long, light yellow brown, with prickly scales, remaining closed on the tree many years.

Principal uses: Mine timbers, railroad ties, poles, posts, fuel, lumber, and pulpwood. (Lodgepole pine is the State tree of Wyoming.)

120. PINYON, *Pinus edulis* Engelm. (nut pine, pinyon pine, Colorado pinyon pine *Pinus cembroides* var. *edulis* (Engelm.) Voss).

Small tree of southern Rocky Mountain region, including adjacent Mexico. Bark reddish brown, furrowed into scaly ridges. Needles 2 (sometimes 3) in cluster, stout ¾ to 1½ inches long, dark green. Cones egg-shaped, 1½ to 2 inches long, light brown with stout, blunt scales and large, wingless, edible seeds ½ inch long, known as pinyon nuts.

Principal uses: The edible seeds are a wild, commercial nut crop, sold as pinyon nuts and Indian nuts. Mine timbers and fuel. Ornamental. (State tree of New Mexico.)

121. SINGLELEAF PINYON, *Pinus monophylla* Torr. & Frém. (nut pine, pinyon; single-leaf pinyon pine; *Pinus cembroides* var. *monophylla* (Torr. & Frém.) Voss).

Small tree of Great Basin region to California and Lower California. Bark dark brown, furrowed into scaly ridges. Needles 1 in a sheath, stout, 1 to 2 inches long, gray green. Cones egg-shaped, 2 to 2½ inches long, light brown, with stout, blunt scales, and large, wingless, edible seeds ¾ inch long, known as pinyon nuts.

Principal uses: The edible seeds are sold locally as pinyon nuts and pine nuts. (Pinyon is the State tree of Nevada.)

*CC.* Leaves without sheath at base, not in clusters, needlelike or scalelike.

*F* (*FF* on page 805), Leaves needlelike, mostly more than ½ inch long.

*G.* Twigs roughened by projecting bases of old needles.

*H.* Needles with leafstalks, flattened (rounded in No. 124), appearing in 2 rows.

*I.* Needles stiff, sharp-pointed, extending down the twig—YEW (*Taxus*).

122. PACIFIC YEW, *Taxus brevifolia* Nutt. (western yew, yew).

Small to medium-sized tree of Pacific Coast and northern Rocky Mountain regions north to Canada and Alaska. Bark purplish brown, very thin, smoothish, with papery scales. Needles in 2 rows, flat, slightly curved, paler beneath, stiff, sharp-pointed, ½ to 1 inch long, dark yellow green, the leafstalks extending down the twigs. Seeds single, ⅜ inch long, exposed at apex but partly surrounded by a thick, fleshy, scarlet, cuplike disk.

Principal uses: Of limited use because of its scarcity. Poles, canoe paddles, bows, and small cabinet work. Ornamental.

*II.* Needles soft, blunt-pointed, not extending down the twig—HEMLOCK (*Tsuga*).

123. WESTERN HEMLOCK, *Tsuga heterophylla* (Raf.) Sarg. (west coast hemlock [lumber], Pacific hemlock, hemlock; formerly *Tsuga mertensiana* auth.).

Large tree of Pacific coast and northern Rocky Mountain regions north to Canada and Alaska. Bark reddish brown, deeply furrowed into broad, flat ridges. Needles short-stalked, flat, ¼ to ¾ inch long, shiny dark green, lighter beneath. Cones ¾ to 1 inch long, brownish.

Principal uses: Important timber tree. Pulpwood, and lumber for building material, boxes and crates, and flooring. The bark is a potential source of tannin. Ornamental. (State tree of Washington.)

124. MOUNTAIN HEMLOCK, *Tsuga mertensiana* (Bong.) Carr. (black hemlock, alpine hemlock).

Large tree of timber line, Pacific coast and northern Rocky Mountain regions north to Canada and Alaska. Bark reddish brown, deeply furrowed into narrow ridges. Needles short-stalked, rounded or angled, ¼ to 1 inch long, blue green. Cones long, 1 to 3 inches long, usually purplish but turning brown.

Principal uses: Ornamental.

*HH.* Needles without leafstalks, 4-angled (flat in No. 127), sharp-pointed, extending out on all sides of twig—SPRUCE (*Picea;* see also Nos. 16 and 17).

125. ENGELMANN SPRUCE, *Picea engelmanni* Parry (white spruce, mountain spruce, silver spruce).

Large tree of high altitudes, Rocky Mountain and Pacific coast regions, including adjacent Canada. Bark grayish or purplish brown, thin, with loosely attached scales. Needles 4-angled, ⅝ to 1⅛ inches long, dark or pale blue green, of disagreeable odor

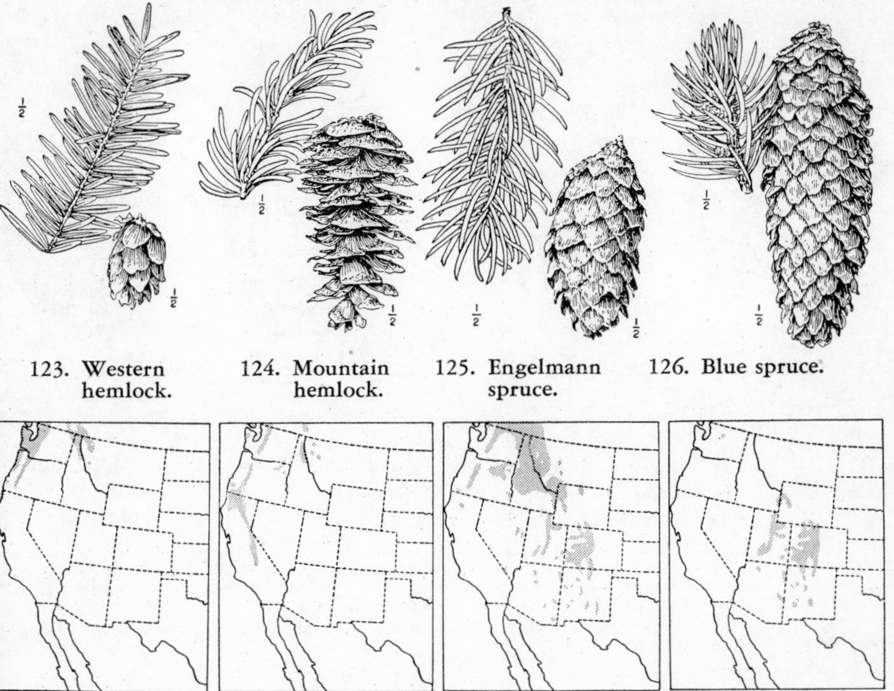

123. Western hemlock. 124. Mountain hemlock. 125. Engelmann spruce. 126. Blue spruce.

when crushed. Cones 1½ to 2½ inches long, light brown, with long, thin, flexible scales irregularly toothed and more or less pointed.

Principal uses: Lumber for building construction and boxes. Also mine timbers, railroad ties, and poles. Ornamental.

126. BLUE SPRUCE, *Picea pungens* Engelm. (Colorado blue spruce, Colorado spruce, silver spruce).

Large tree of Rocky Mountain region. Bark gray or brown, furrowed into scaly ridges. Needles 4-angled, ¾ to 1⅛ inch long, dull blue green. Cones 2½ to 4 inches long, light brown, with long, thin, flexible scales irregularly toothed and more or less pointed.

Principal uses: Ornamental and shelterbelts. Posts, poles, and fuel. (State tree of Colorado and Utah.)

127. SITKA SPRUCE, *Picea sitchensis* (Bong.) Carr. (yellow spruce, tideland spruce, western spruce, silver spruce, coast spruce).

Large to very large tree of Pacific coast region north to Canada and Alaska. Bark reddish brown, thin, with loosely attached scales. Needles flat, ⅝ to 1 inch long, dark green. Cones 2 to 3½ inches long, light orange brown, with long, stiff scales, rounded and irregularly toothed.

Principal uses: Lumber for boxes and crates, furniture, planing-mill products, millwork, ladders, and construction. Pulpwood and cooperage. The most important wood for aircraft construction. Ornamental.

*GG.* Twigs smooth or nearly so.

*J.* Needles with short leafstalks; cones hanging down—DOUGLAS-FIR (*Pseudotsuga*).

128. DOUGLAS-FIR, *Pseudotsuga taxifolia* (Poir.) Britton (Douglas-spruce, red fir, yellow fir, Oregon pine, common Douglas-fir; *Ps. douglasii* (Sabine) Carr., *Ps. mucronata* (Raf.) Sudw.; variety: *Ps. taxifolia* var. *glauca* (Mayr) Sudw.).

Large tree (next to giant sequoia and redwood in size) of Pacific coast and Rocky Mountain regions, including Canada and Mexico. Bark reddish brown, thick, deeply furrowed into broad ridges. Needles short-stalked, flat, ¾ to 1¼ inches long, dark yellow green or blue green. Cones 2 to 4 inches long, light brown, with thin, rounded scales and long, 3-toothed bracts.

Principal uses: Important timber tree, first in United States in total stand, lumber production, and production of veneer for plywood. Used principally for building construc-

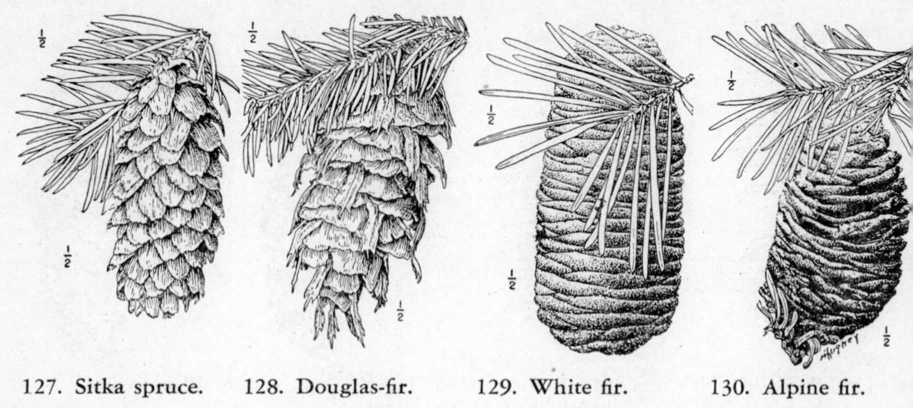


127. Sitka spruce. 128. Douglas-fir. 129. White fir. 130. Alpine fir.

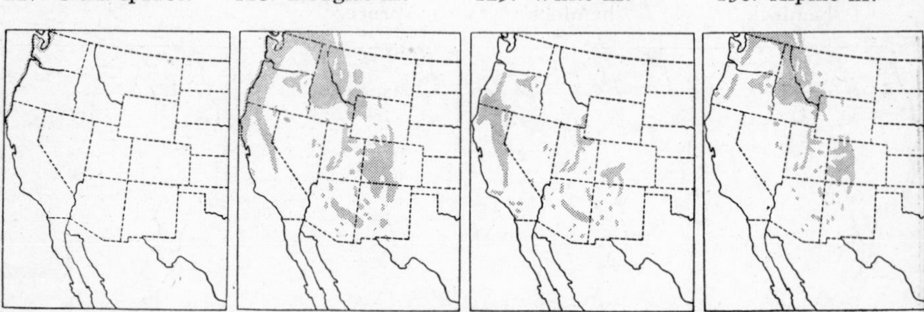

tion as lumber, timbers, piling, and plywood. Also fuel, railroad ties, cooperage, mine timbers, and fencing. Lumber manufactured into millwork, railroad-car construction, boxes and crates, flooring, furniture, ships and boats, ladders. Storage battery separators. Also shade tree, ornamental, and shelterbelts. (State tree of Oregon.)

*JJ*. Needles without leafstalks; cones upright, in top of tree—FIR (*Abies;* see also No. 18).

*K*. Needles flat.

129. WHITE FIR, *Abies concolor* (Gord. & Glend.) Hoopes (balsam fir, silver fir, white balsam).

Large tree of Rocky Mountain and Pacific coast regions, south to Lower California. Bark gray, smoothish, becoming thick, deeply furrowed into scaly ridges. Needles flat, 1½ to 2½ inches long, pale blue green. Cones upright, 3 to 5 inches long, greenish, purple, or yellow.

Principal uses: Lumber for building construction, chiefly in houses, boxes and crates, planing-mill products, and general millwork. Pulpwood. Ornamental and shade tree.

130. ALPINE FIR, *Abies lasiocarpa* (Hook.) Nutt. (white fir [lumber], balsam, white balsam).

Large tree of high altitudes, Rocky Mountain region north to Canada and Alaska. Bark gray, smoothish, becoming fissured. Needles flat, 1 to 1¾ inches long, blue green. Cones upright, 2½ to 4 inches long, purple.

Principal uses: Same as No. 129.

131. PACIFIC SILVER FIR, *Abies amabilis* (Dougl.) Forb. (silver fir [lumber], white fir [lumber], Cascades fir, red fir, lovely fir).

Large tree of Pacific coast region from Oregon north to Canada and Alaska. Bark gray, smoothish. Needles flat, ¾ to 1¼ inches long, dark green and shiny, silvery white beneath. Cones upright, 3 to 6 inches long, purple.

Principal uses: Same as No. 129.

132. GRAND FIR, *Abies grandis* (Dougl.) Lindl. (white fir [lumber], lowland white fir, balsam fir, lowland fir, silver fir, yellow fir).

Large tree of northern Rocky Mountain and Pacific coast regions, including southern British Columbia. Bark reddish brown, becoming deeply furrowed into narrow ridges. Needles flat, 1 to 2 inches long, dark green and shiny, silvery white beneath. Cones upright, 2 to 4 inches long, green.

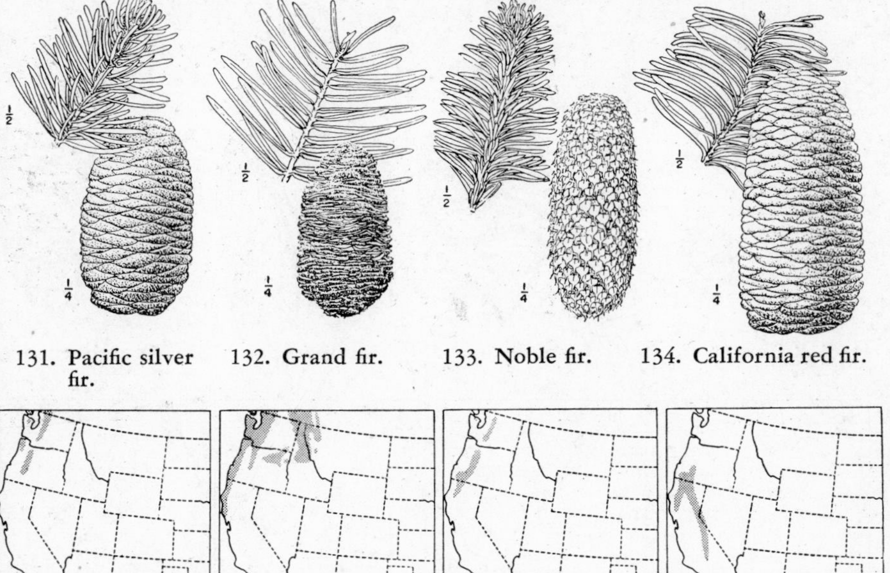


131. Pacific silver fir. 132. Grand fir. 133. Noble fir. 134. California red fir.

Principal uses: Same as No. 129.

*KK.* Needles 4-angled, or both 4-angled and flat.

133. NOBLE FIR, *Abies procera* Rehd. (white fir [lumber], red fir; *A. nobilis* (Dougl.) Lindl., not A. Dietr.).

Large tree of Northwest Pacific coast region. Bark gray brown, smoothish, becoming furrowed and broken into irregular scaly plates. Needles of lower branches flat and of top branches 4-angled, 1 to 1½ inches long, blue green. Cones upright, 4 to 6 inches long, purplish brown, with long greenish bracts covering the cone scales.

Principal uses: Lumber for interior finish, moldings, sidings, and millwork, aircraft construction, venetian blinds, ladder rails, and boxes. Pulpwood. Ornamental.

134. CALIFORNIA RED FIR, *Abies magnifica* A. Murr. (golden fir [lumber], white fir [lumber], red fir).

Large tree (the largest native true fir) of Oregon and California. Bark reddish brown, thick, deeply furrowed into narrow ridges. Needles 4-angled, ¾ to 1½ inches long, blue green. Cones upright, 6 to 9 inches long, purplish brown.

Principal uses: Same as No. 129.

*FF* (*F* on p. 802). Leaves scalelike, less than ¼ inch long, or both scalelike and needlelike (to ¾ inch long).

*L.* Leaves single—SEQUOIA (*Sequoia*).

135. REDWOOD, *Sequoia sempervirens* (D. Don) Endl. (coast redwood, California redwood).

Large tree (the world's tallest tree species) of Pacific coast in California and southwestern Oregon. Bark reddish brown, thick, deeply furrowed, fibrous. Leaves both scalelike and needlelike, flat, slightly curved, unequal in length, ¼ to ¾ inch long, dark green, spreading in 2 rows. Cones ¾ to 1 inch long, reddish brown, maturing the first year.

Principal uses: Important timber tree. Largely for building construction and bridges and other heavy construction. Also boxes and crates, planing-mill products, general millwork, paneling, tanks, caskets, greenhouse construction. Insulating material is made from the bark. Ornamental. (State tree of California.)

136. GIANT SEQUOIA, *Sequoia gigantea* (Lindl.) Decne. (bigtree, Sierra redwood; *S. wellingtonia* Seem.).

Large tree (including the world's largest and oldest) with swollen base, Sierra Nevada,

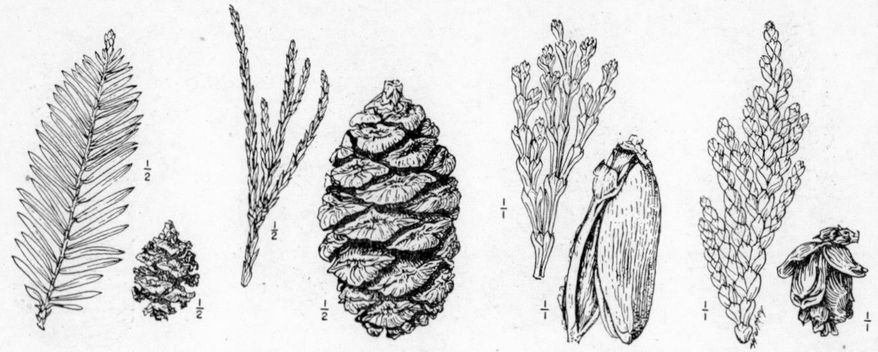

135. Redwood. 136. Giant sequoia. 137. Incense-cedar. 138. Western redcedar.

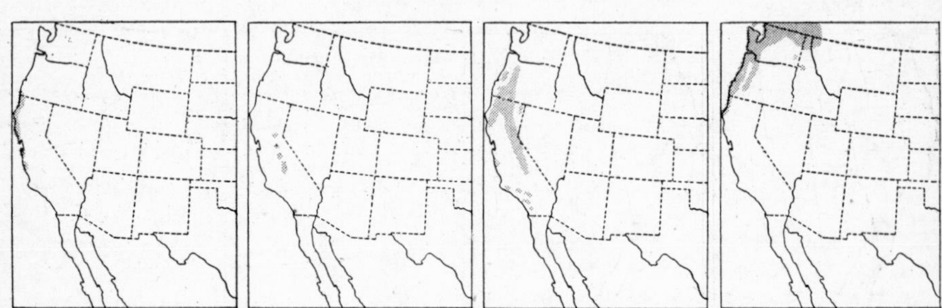

California. Bark reddish brown, thick, deeply furrowed, fibrous. Leaves scalelike, 1/8 to 1/4 inch long or on leading shoots 1/2 inch long, blue green, sharp-pointed, growing all around the twig and overlapping. Cones 1 3/4 to 2 3/4 inches long, reddish brown, maturing the second year.

Principal uses: The largest trees are preserved in national parks and national forests. Formerly lumbered for the same uses as No. 135.

*LL.* Leaves in pairs, threes, or fours, scalelike.

*M.* Leafy twigs more or less flattened.

*N.* Twigs much flattened, more than 1/16 inch broad including leaves.

*O.* Joints of leafy twigs distinctly longer than broad—INCENSE-CEDAR (*Libocedrus*).

137. INCENSE-CEDAR, *Libocedrus decurrens* Torr. (California incense-cedar).

Large tree of Pacific coast region from Oregon to Lower California. Bark reddish brown, thick, deeply and irregularly furrowed into shreddy ridges. Twigs flattened, the internodes wedge-shaped, 1/8 to 1/2 inch long, bright green, with scale leaves 1/16 to 1/8 inch long, their bases extending down the twigs. Cones 3/4 to 1 inch long, reddish brown.

Principal uses: The leading wood for pencils. Venetian blinds, lumber for rough construction, fence posts, and railroad ties. Ornamental and shade tree.

*OO.* Joints of leafy twigs about as long as broad—THUJA (*Thuja*).

138. WESTERN REDCEDAR, *Thuja plicata* Donn (giant arborvitae, canoe cedar, arbovitae, shinglewood, gigantic cedar, Pacific redcedar).

Large to very large tree of Pacific coast and northern Rocky Mountain regions north to Canada and Alaska. Bark reddish brown, thin, fibrous. Twigs flattened and branching in one plane. Leaves scalelike, 1/16 to 1/8 inch long, shiny, dark green. Cones 1/2 inch long, pale brown, with leathery scales.

Principal uses: The chief wood for shingles. Lumber used largely in construction such as siding. Also a leading wood for poles and widely used for posts.

*NN.* Twigs slightly flattened, less than 1/16 inch broad including leaves—WHITE-CEDAR (*Chamaecyparis*).

139. PORT-ORFORD-CEDAR, *Chamaecyparis lawsoniana* (A. Murr.) Parl. (Port-Orford white-cedar, Lawson falsecypress, Oregon cedar, Lawson cypress).

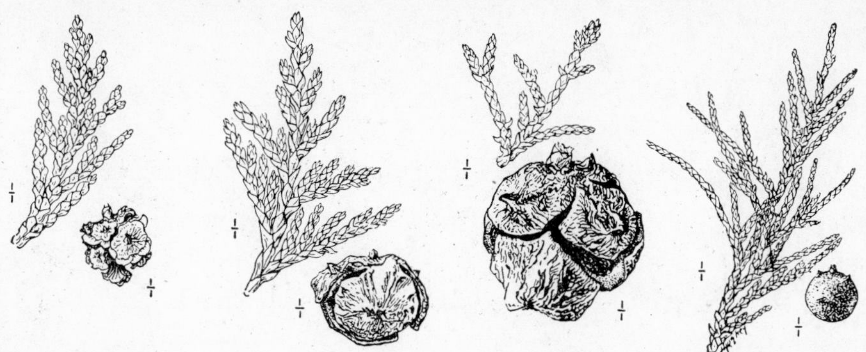

139. Port-Orford-cedar. 140. Alaska-cedar. 141. Arizona cypress. 142. Rocky Mountain juniper.

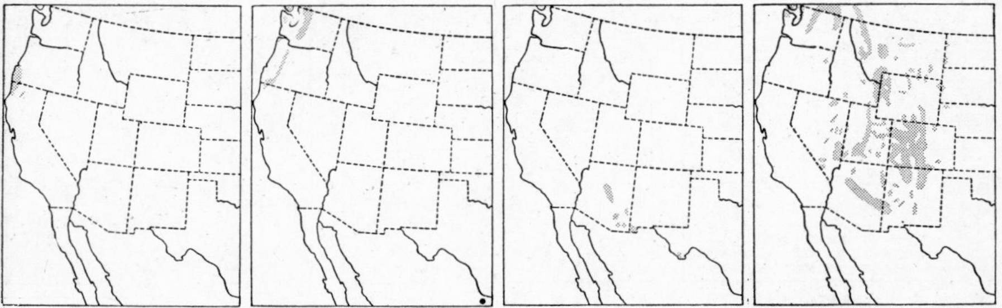

Large to very large tree of Pacific coast in southwestern Oregon and northwestern California. Bark reddish brown, very thick, deeply furrowed into large, fibrous ridges. Twigs slender, flattened. Leaves 1/16 inch long, or 1/8 to 1/4 inch long on leading shoots, bright green or pale beneath, glandular on the back. Cones about 3/8 inch in diameter.

Principal uses: The principal wood for storage battery separators. Venetian blinds. Lumber for construction and other uses. Shade tree, ornamental, and shelterbelts.

140. Alaska-cedar, *Chamaecyparis nootkatensis* (D. Don) Spach (Alaska yellow-cedar, Nootka falsecypress, yellow-cedar, Sitka cypress, yellow cypress).

Large tree of Northwest Pacific coast region north to Canada and Alaska. Bark grayish brown, thin, irregularly fissured, fibrous and scaly. Twigs stout, 4-angled or slightly flattened. Leaves 1/8 inch long, or 1/4 inch long on leading shoots, dark green, usually without glands. Cones nearly 1/2 inch in diameter.

Principal uses: Interior finish, cabinet work, small boats, furniture, and novelties. Ornamental.

*MM*. Leafy twigs rounded or 4-angled.

*P*. Leafy twigs regularly branched almost at right angles; seeds in a hard cone—cypress (*Cupressus*).

141. Arizona cypress, *Cupressus arizonica* Greene (smooth cypress; *C. glabra* Sudw.).

Medium-sized tree of southwestern United States and adjacent Mexico. Bark gray, rough, furrowed and fibrous, or checkered, or smoothish and shedding in thin scales. Leaves scalelike, 1/16 inch long, pale blue green. Cones 3/4 to 1 1/4 inches in diameter, on stout stalks 1/4 to 1/2 inch long and remaining attached several years.

Principal uses: Fence posts, ornamental, and shelterbelts.

*PP*. Leafy twigs irregularly branched at small angles; seeds in a "berry"—juniper (*Juniperus*).

142. Rocky Mountain juniper, *Juniperus scopulorum* Sarg. (western juniper [lumber], Rocky Mountain redcedar, redcedar).

Small to medium-sized tree of Rocky Mountain region, including adjacent Canada. Bark reddish brown, thin, fibrous and shreddy. Leafy twigs slender, about 1/32 inch in diameter. Leaves scalelike, 1/16 inch long, usually gray green, or on leading shoots needle-like, up to 1/4 inch long. "Berry" 1/4 inch in diameter, bright blue, bloomy, usually 2-seeded, maturing the second year.

143. Alligator juniper.

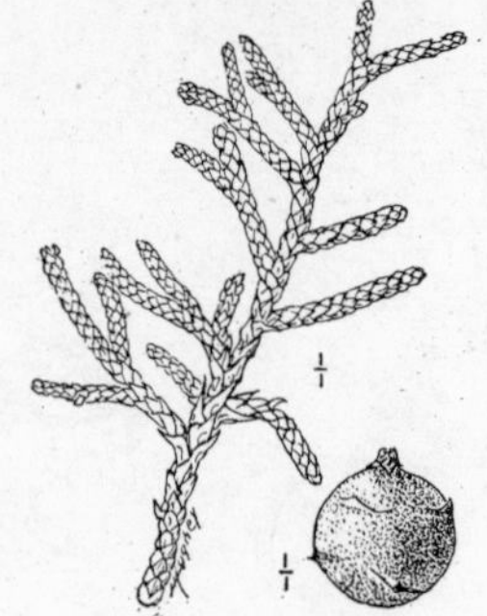

144. Utah juniper.

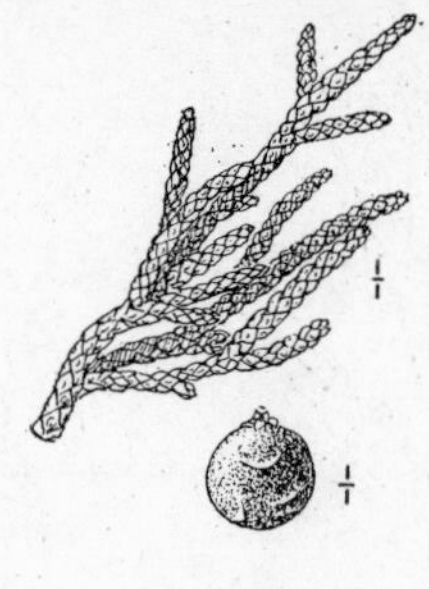

145. Western juniper.

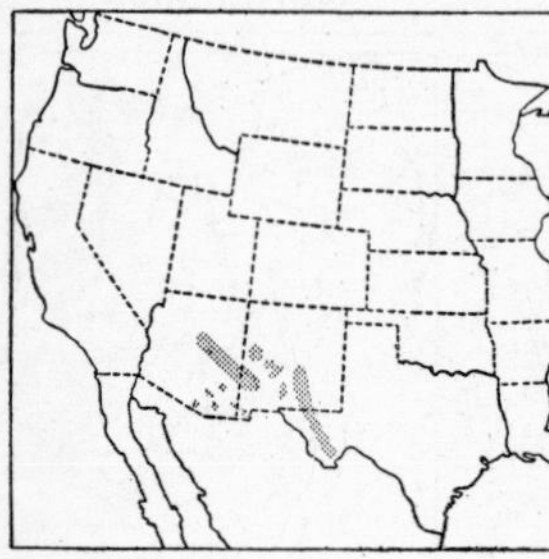

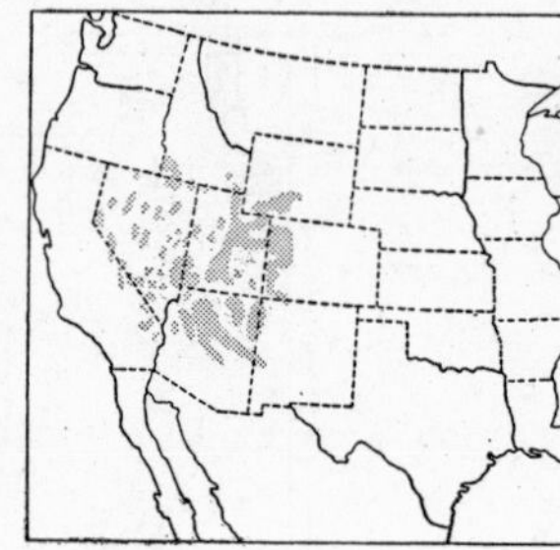

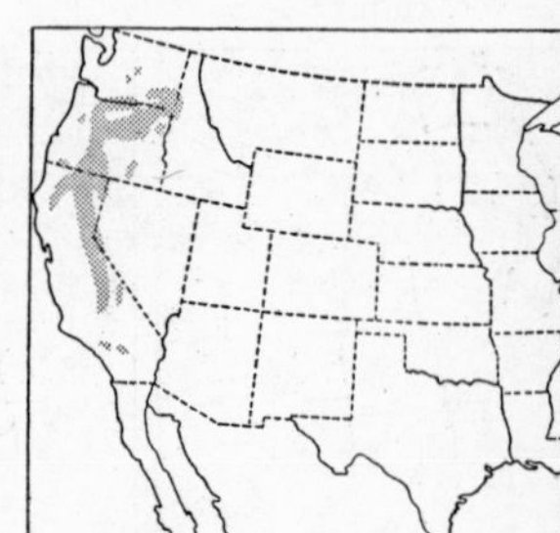

Principal uses: Fence posts, fuel, lumber. Shelterbelts and ornamental.

143. ALLIGATOR JUNIPER, *Juniperus deppeana* Steud. (western juniper [lumber]; *J. pachyphloea* Torr.).

Medium-sized tree of southwestern United States and Mexico. Bark gray, thick, deeply furrowed into checkered or square plates. Leafy twigs 1/32 to 1/16 inch in diameter. Leaves scalelike, 1/16 inch long, blue green, glandular, often with whitish drops of resin, or on leading shoots needlelike, up to 1/4 inch long, pale or whitish. "Berry" 1/2 inch in diameter, bluish or brownish, bloomy, 4-seeded, maturing the second year.

Principal uses: Fuel and fence posts.

144. UTAH JUNIPER, *Juniperus osteosperma* (Torr.) Little (western juniper [lumber]; *J. utahensis* (Engelm.) Lemm.).

Small tree of Great Basin and Rocky Mountain regions. Bark gray, fibrous and shreddy. Leafy twigs stout, about 1/16 inch or less in diameter. Leaves 1/16 inch or more in length, yellow green. "Berry" 1/4 to 1/2 inch in diameter, brownish, bloomy, with 1 or 2 seeds.

Principal uses: Fence posts, fuel, and interior finish.

145. WESTERN JUNIPER, *Juniperus occidentalis* Hook. (western juniper [lumber], Sierra juniper).

Small to medium-sized tree of Pacific coast region. Bark reddish brown, furrowed and shreddy. Leafy twigs stout, 1/16 inch or more in diameter. Leaves scalelike, 1/16 inch or more in length, glandular. "Berry" 1/4 inch in diameter, bluish black, with 2 or 3 seeds.

Principal uses: Fence posts, fuel, pencils.

## ANGIOSPERMS (FLOWERING PLANTS)

*AA* (*A* on p. 799). Trees nonresinous, with leaves broad, shedding in fall in most species (evergreen in some oaks, tanoak, golden chinquapin, California-laurel, palms, etc.); seeds enclosed in a fruit—ANGIOSPERMS (flowering plants).

*Q*. Leaves parallel-veined, evergreen, clustered at top of trunk or large branches; trunk with woody portions irregularly distributed, without clear distinction of bark and wood, and without annual rings—MONOCOTYLEDONS (palms, yuccas, etc.; omitted here).

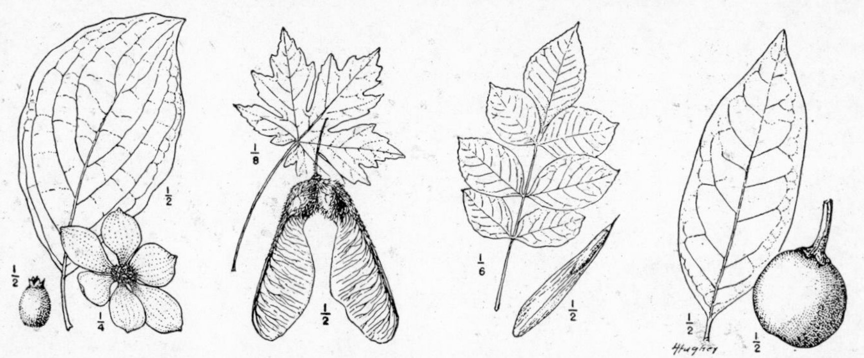

**146. Pacific dogwood. 147. Bigleaf maple. 148. Oregon ash. 149. California-laurel.**

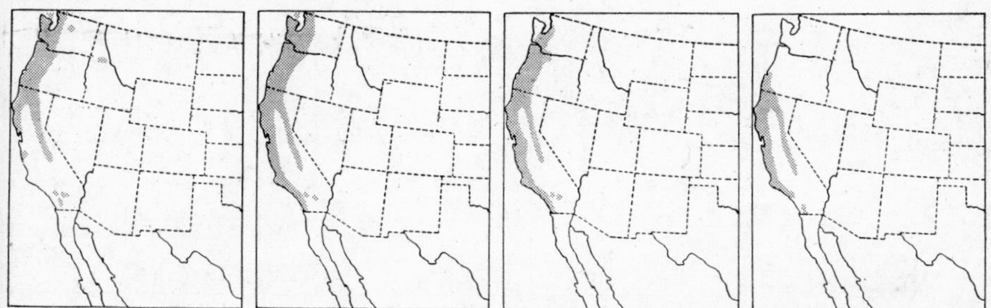

## DICOTYLEDONS (BROADLEAF TREES OR HARDWOODS)

*QQ*. Leaves net-veined; trunk with bark and wood distinct and with annual rings in wood—DICOTYLEDONS (broadleaf trees, or hardwoods, such as oaks, poplars, ashes, maples).

*R*. Leaves and usually branches in pairs (opposite).

*S*. Leaves not divided into leaflets (simple).

*T*. Leaf edges smooth, not lobed—DOGWOOD (*Cornus*).

146. PACIFIC DOGWOOD, *Cornus nuttalli* Audubon (western dogwood, dogwood).

Small to medium-sized tree of Pacific coast region north to British Columbia. Bark reddish brown, thin, smoothish. Leaves paired, oval, 3 to 5 inches long, short-pointed, edges appearing smooth but minutely toothed, lateral veins curved, bright green and nearly smooth above, whitish and hairy beneath, turning orange and scarlet in fall. Flowers greenish yellow, in a dense head with 4 to 6 (usually 6) showy, white, petallike bracts 3 to 5 inches in diameter, in early spring. Fruits egg-shaped, 3/8 to 1/2 inch long, bright red or orange.

Principal uses: Shuttles (used in textile weaving). Ornamental.

*TT*. Leaf edges toothed, deeply 3- or 5-lobed—MAPLE (*Acer*).

147. BIGLEAF MAPLE, *Acer macrophyllum* Pursh (Oregon maple, broadleaf maple).

Large tree of Pacific coast region north to Canada and Alaska. Bark gray brown, thin, smoothish, becoming deeply furrowed. Leaves paired, heart-shaped, very large, 6 to 12 inches in diameter, deeply 3- or 5-lobed with additional smaller lobes, dark green and shiny above, pale green below, turning bright orange in fall. Leafstalks long and stout, 10 to 12 inches long. Key fruits 1 1/4 to 2 inches long, long-winged, paired and in clusters.

Principal uses: Veneer, furniture, handles and fixtures, and woodenware and novelties. Shade tree.

*SS*. Leaves subdivided into 5 to 9 leaflets (compound)—ASH (*Fraxinus;* see also Nos. 31 and 33).

148. OREGON ASH, *Fraxinus oregona* Nutt.

Medium-sized to large tree of Pacific coast region, including British Columbia. Bark dark gray or brown, with diamond-shaped fissures and forking ridges. Leaves paired, compound, 5 to 14 inches long. Leaflets usually 7 or 5, usually without stalks, elliptical, 2 to 5 inches long, short-pointed, edges smooth or slightly toothed, light green, nearly

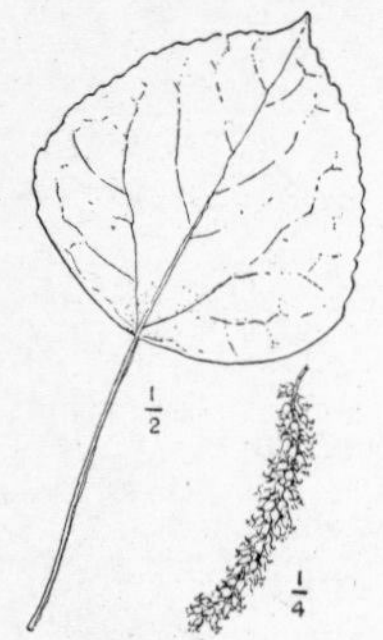

150. Quaking aspen.

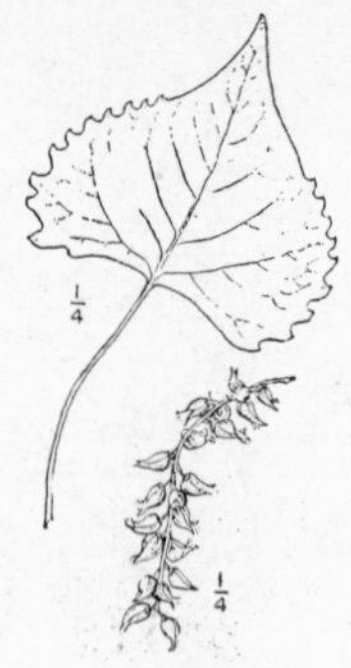

151. Plains cottonwood.

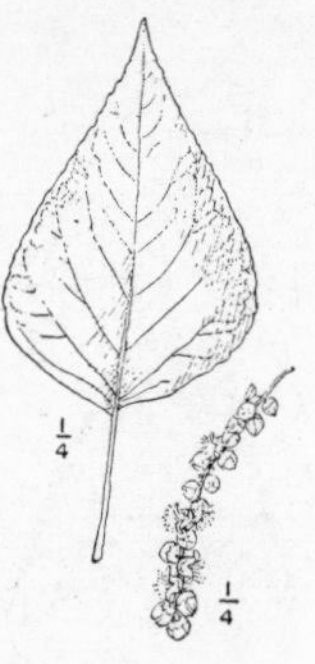

152. Black cottonwood.

153. Red alder.

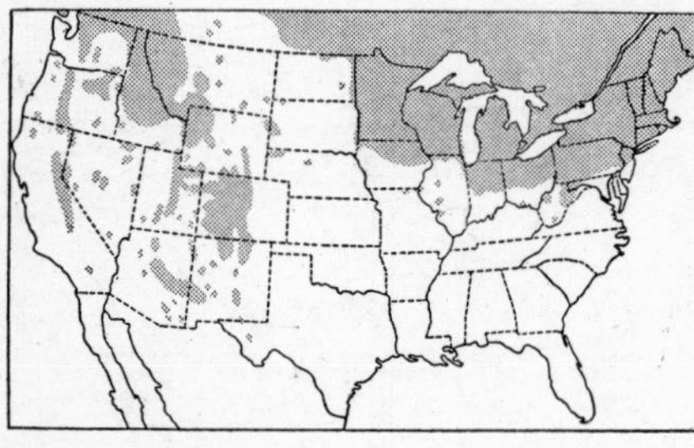

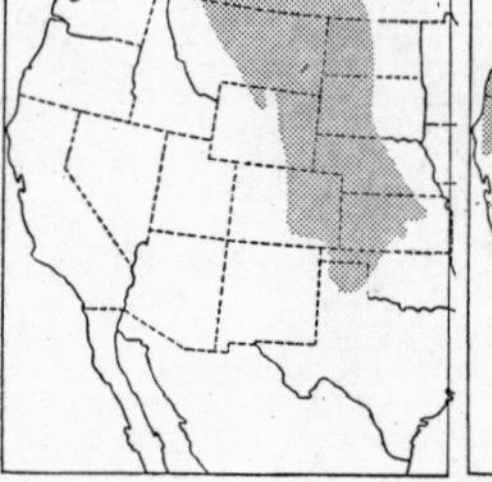

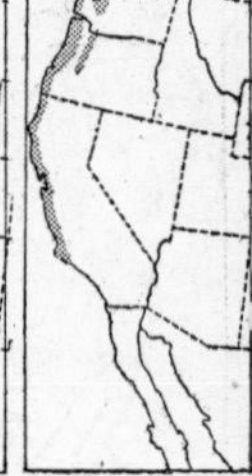

smooth above, finely hairy beneath. Key fruits in crowded clusters, 1 to 2 inches long, with wing at end.

Principal uses: Handles, cooperage, and furniture. Shade tree.

*RR.* Leaves and usually branches borne singly (alternate).

*U.* Leaves aromatic when bruised—CALIFORNIA-LAUREL (*Umbellularia*).

149. CALIFORNIA-LAUREL, *Umbellularia californica* (Hook. & Arn.) Nutt. (Oregon-myrtle, mountain-laurel, spice-tree).

Medium-sized to large tree of Oregon and California. Bark dark reddish brown, thin, with flat scales. Leaves aromatic, evergreen, elliptical or lance-shaped, 2 to 5 inches long, short-stalked, wedge-shaped at base, short-pointed, with smooth edges, leathery, shiny dark green above, dull beneath. Flowers yellowish green, 3/16 inch long, in clusters. Fruits rounded, 1 inch in diameter, greenish or purplish.

Principal uses: Veneer for furniture and paneling. Novelties and woodenware, cabinet work, and interior trim. Ornamental.

*UU.* Leaves not aromatic.

*V.* Winter buds 1 or none at tip of twig; fruit not an acorn.

*W.* Leaves thin, with edges toothed, shedding in fall.

*X.* Leafstalks more than 1½ inches long, slender, leaves more or less triangular, rounded at base and pointed at apex; seeds cottony, in long-clustered capsules—POPLAR (*Populus;* see also No. 79).

150. QUAKING ASPEN, *Populus tremuloides* Michx. (aspen, quaking asp, trembling poplar, poplar, popple, golden aspen, mountain aspen).

Small to medium-sized tree, widely distributed in Northeastern, Rocky Mountain, and Pacific coast regions and across Canada to Alaska. Bark yellowish green or whitish, smooth, thin; on large trunks becoming black, thick, with furrows and flat ridges. Leaves nearly round, 1¼ to 3 inches long, short-pointed, finely toothed, smooth, shiny green above, dull green beneath. Leafstalks flat. Seeds rarely produced in the West.

Principal uses: Pulpwood, boxes and crates, excelsior, and matches.

151. PLAINS COTTONWOOD, *Populus sargentii* Dode (cottonwood, plains poplar).

Large tree of Great Plains and eastern border of Rocky Mountains north into Canada. Bark gray, deeply furrowed. Leaves broadly oval, often wider than long, 3 to 4 inches long and wide, long-pointed, coarsely toothed with curved teeth, smooth, light green, shiny. Leafstalks flat.

Principal uses: Fuel. Shade tree. Shelterbelts.

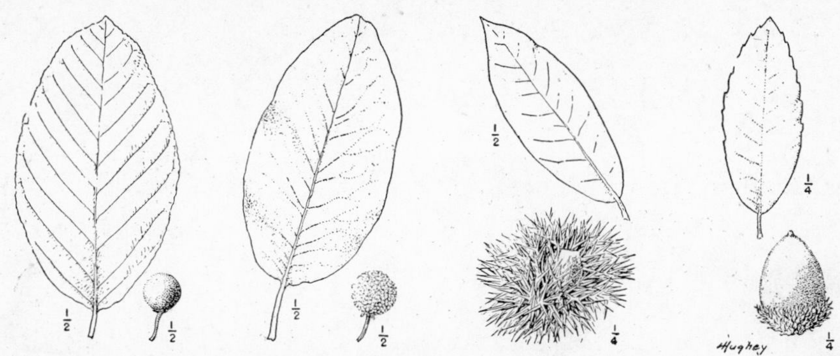


**154. Cascara buckthorn. 155. Pacific madrone. 156. Golden chinquapin. 157. Tanoak.**

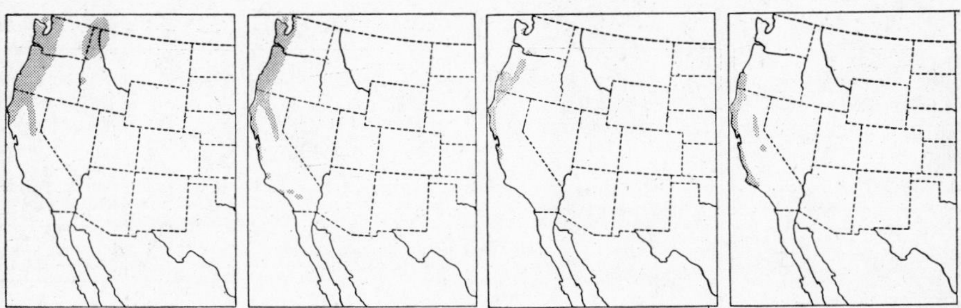

152. BLACK COTTONWOOD, *Populus trichocarpa* Torr. & Gray (California poplar, cottonwood, balsam cottonwood, western balsam poplar; variety: *P. trichocarpa* var. *hastata* (Dode) Henry, Pacific poplar).

Large tree (the tallest western broadleaf tree) of northern Rocky Mountain and Pacific coast regions north to Canada and Alaska. Bark gray, smooth at first, becoming deeply furrowed with flat ridges. Leaves broadly oval, 3 to 7 inches long, short- or long-pointed, finely toothed, smooth or slightly hairy, dark shiny green above, whitish or rusty beneath. Leafstalks round.

Principal uses: Boxes and crates, pulpwood, and excelsior.

*XX*. Leafstalks less than 1 inch long, leaves elliptical or oval; seeds not hairy.
*Y*. Leaf edges with teeth of 2 sizes and slightly irregular—ALDER (*Alnus;* see also No. 84).

153. RED ALDER, *Alnus rubra* Bong. (alder, Oregon alder, western alder).

Medium-sized to large tree of Pacific coast region north to Canada and Alaska. Bark mottled light gray to whitish, smooth, thin. Leaves oval or elliptical, 3 to 6 inches long, short-pointed, both coarsely and finely toothed, dark green and nearly smooth above, grayish green or rusty beneath. Cones ½ to 1 inch long.

Principal uses: The leading hardwood in the Pacific Northwest. Furniture.

*YY*. Leaf edges with uniform, small teeth—BUCKTHORN (*Rhamnus;* see also Nos. 76 and 87).

154. CASCARA BUCKTHORN, *Rhamnus purshiana* DC. (cascara sagrada, cascara).

Small tree or shrub of northwest Pacific coast and northern Rocky Mountain regions north to British Columbia. Bark brown or gray, thin, scaly. Leaves elliptical, 2 to 6 inches long, blunt-pointed or rounded, finely toothed, dark green above, lighter and slightly hairy beneath. Fruits berrylike, ⅜ to ½ inch in diameter, purplish black, with 2 or 3 seeds.

Principal uses: The bark is the source of the drug Cascara Sagrada. Wood is used locally for fuel and fence posts. Ornamental.

*WW*. Leaves thick, with edges mostly smooth, evergreen.
*Z*. Leaves pale or whitish beneath—MADRONE (*Arbutus*).

155. PACIFIC MADRONE, *Arbutus menziesii* Pursh (madroño, madrona).

Small to large tree of Pacific coast region north to British Columbia. Bark of limbs and

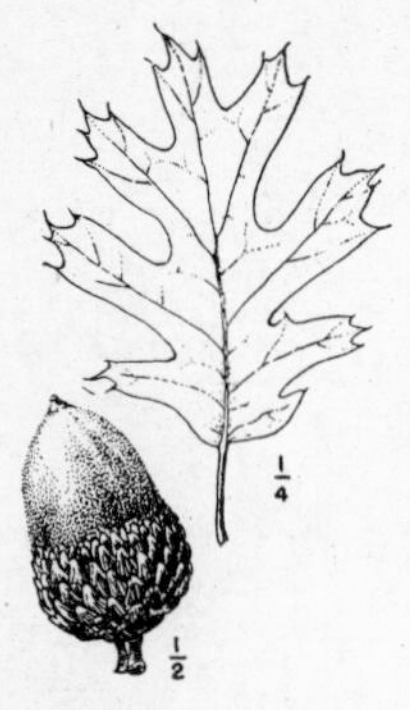


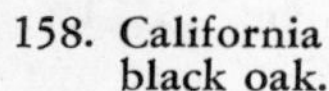

**158. California black oak.**

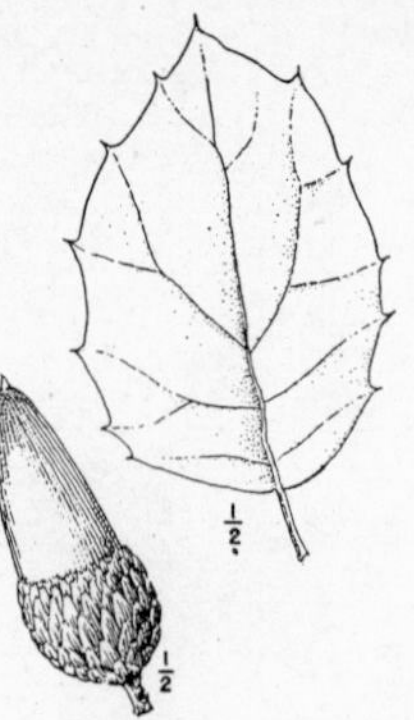


**159. California live oak.**

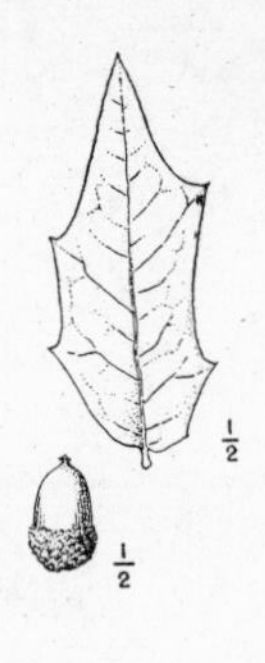


**160. Emory oak.**

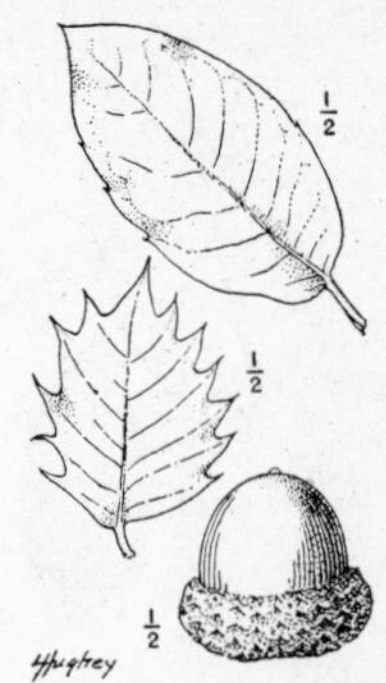


**161. Canyon live oak.**

twigs bright red, smooth and peeling off; bark of larger trunks dark reddish brown, fissured and scaly. Leaves evergreen, oval, 3 to 5 inches long, blunt-pointed, thick and leathery, edges smooth or sometimes toothed, dark green and shiny above, whitish beneath. Flowers small, white, clustered, 3/8 inch long. Fruits 1/2 inch in diameter, orange red.

Principal uses: Fuel. Shuttles (used in textile weaving). Ornamental.

*ZZ.* Leaves with coat of golden yellow scales beneath—CHINQUAPIN (*Castanopsis*).

156. GOLDEN CHINQUAPIN, *Castanopsis chrysophylla* (Dougl.) A. DC. (giant evergreen-chinkapin, chinquapin, golden-leaf chestnut).

Medium-sized to large tree (a variety is shrubby) of Pacific coast region. Bark reddish brown, becoming furrowed into thick plates. Leaves evergreen, oblong to lance-shaped, 2 to 6 inches long, narrowed and tapering at both ends, with smooth edges, leathery, dark green and shiny above, coated beneath with golden yellow scales. Fruits golden spiny burs 1 to 1 1/2 inches in diameter with 1 or sometimes 2 edible nuts 5/8 inch long, maturing the second year.

Principal uses: Furniture. Ornamental.

*VV.* Winter buds 3 or more in cluster at tip of twig; fruit an acorn.

*a.* Leaves with many parallel lateral veins less than 1/4 inch apart, evergreen; scales of acorn cup slender, spreading, curved, more than 1/8 inch long—TANOAK (*Lithocarpus*).

157. TANOAK, *Lithocarpus densiflorus* (Hook. & Arn.) Rehd. (tanbark-oak, chestnut-oak).

Large tree (a variety is shrubby) of Oregon and California. Bark reddish brown, deeply fissured into squarish plates. Leaves evergreen, oblong, 3 to 5 inches long, short-pointed, toothed, with many parallel lateral veins less than 1/4 inch apart, leathery, pale green, shiny and nearly smooth above, rustry-hairy or whitish beneath. Acorns 3/4 to 1 1/4 inches long, rounded, the shallow cup with spreading light-brown scales 1/8 to 3/16 inch long, maturing the second year.

Principal uses: The bark is a source of tannin. Wood used locally for fuel, furniture, and mine timbers. Ornamental.

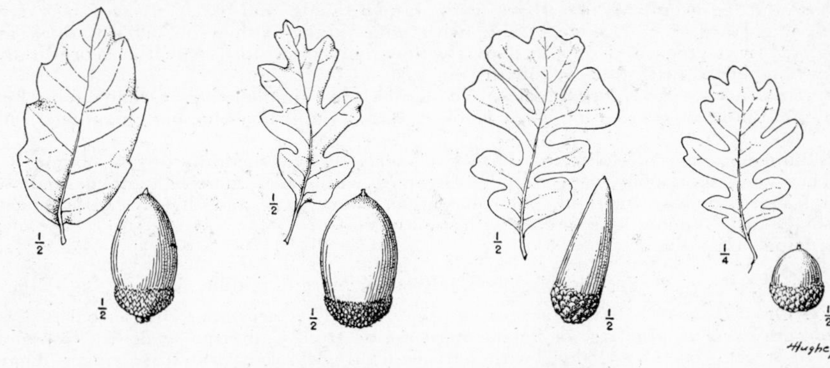
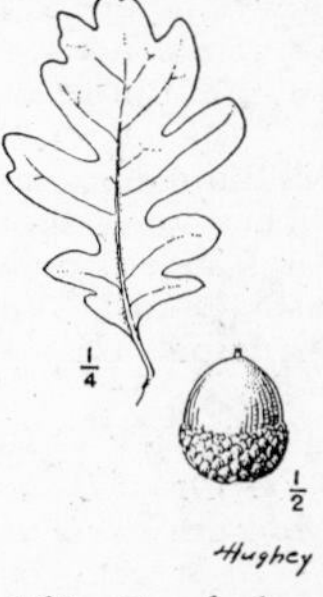


162. Blue oak. 163. Oregon white oak. 164. California white oak. 165. Gambel oak.

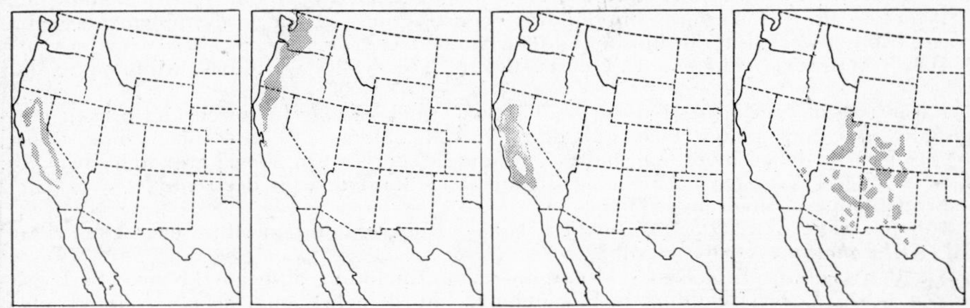

*aa.* Leaves with lateral veins not parallel (except in No. 161), falling in autumn or evergreen; scales of acorn cup small and inconspicuous—OAK (*Quercus*).

*b.* Leaves with bristle-tipped teeth; acorns maturing the second year (first year in No. 159)—BLACK OAKS.

158. CALIFORNIA BLACK OAK, *Quercus kelloggii* Newb. (black oak; *Q. californica* (Torr.) Coop.).

Large tree of Oregon and California. Bark dark brown, furrowed into irregular plates and ridges. Leaves falling in autumn, oblong, 4 to 10 inches long, usually 7-lobed about halfway to middle, each lobe with a few bristle-pointed teeth, thick, dark yellow green and smooth above, light yellow green and smooth or hairy beneath. Acorns 1 to 1½ inches long, rounded, with deep cup.

Principal uses: Fuel.

159. CALIFORNIA LIVE OAK, *Quercus agrifolia* Née (coast live oak).

Large tree of California and Lower California. Bark dark brown, thick, deeply furrowed. Leaves evergreen, elliptical to oblong. ¾ to 3 inches long, short-pointed or rounded at tip, spiny-toothed, thick and stiff, dark green above, beneath paler, shiny, and smooth or hairy. Acorns long, ¾ to 1½ inches long, pointed, with deep cup.

Principal uses: Fuel. Shade tree and ornamental.

*bb.* Leaves lobed, toothed, or entire but not bristle-tipped; acorns maturing the first year (second year in No. 161)—WHITE OAK (see also Nos. 103 and 107).

*c.* Leaves not lobed or only shallowly lobed.

160. EMORY OAK, *Quercus emoryi* Torr. (black oak).

Medium-sized tree of Southwestern region and adjacent Mexico. Bark blackish, divided into thin plates. Leaves evergreen, broadly lance-shaped, 1 to 2½ inches long, short-pointed, with a few short teeth, thick, stiff, leathery, flat, shiny dark green on both sides, nearly smooth. Acorns ½ to ¾ inch long, rounded, edible.

Principal uses: Fuel.

161. CANYON LIVE OAK, *Quercus chrysolepis* Liebm. (live oak, maul oak; variety: Palmer oak, *Q. chrysolepis* var. *palmeri* (Engelm.) Sarg.).

Medium-sized to large tree (a variety is shrubby) of Pacific coast and Southwestern regions and adjacent Mexico. Bark gray brown, scaly and flaky. Leaves evergreen, elliptical or oval, 1 to 3 inches long, with edges spiny-toothed or smooth, thick and leathery, bright green and smooth above, yellow-hairy or whitish beneath. Acorns 1 to 2 inches long, broad, with thick yellowish cup.

Principal uses: Parts of vehicles and agricultural implements. Ornamental. Fuel.

162. BLUE OAK, *Quercus douglasii* Hook. & Arn. (California blue oak, mountain white oak).

Medium-sized tree of California. Bark gray, scaly. Leaves shedding in fall, oblong, 1 to 3 inches long, short-pointed or rounded at apex, with edges coarsely toothed, shallowly 4- or 5-lobed, or smooth, rigid, pale blue green above, pale and slightly hairy beneath. Acorns ¾ to 1½ inches long, broad, with shallow cup.

Principal uses: Fuel.

*cc.* Leaves deeply lobed halfway or more to middle.

163. OREGON WHITE OAK, *Quercus garryana* Dougl. (Garry oak, Oregon oak).

Medium-sized to large tree of Pacific coast region from California to British Columbia. Bark light gray or brown, thin, with narrow fissures, broken into scaly ridges. Leaves shedding in fall, oblong, 3 to 6 inches long, deeply 5- to 9-lobed halfway or more to middle with blunt-pointed or slightly toothed lobes, dark green above, light green and usually hairy beneath. Acorns 1 to 1¼ inches long, broad and rounded, with shallow cup.

Principal uses: Furniture, shipbuilding, construction, agricultural implements, cooperage, cabinet work, interior finish, and fuel. Shade tree.

164. CALIFORNIA WHITE OAK, *Quercus lobata* Née (valley white oak, white oak, valley oak).

Large tree of California. Bark gray or brown, thick, deeply furrowed and broken horizontally into thick plates. Leaves shedding in fall, oblong, 2½ to 4 inches long, broad, deeply 7- to 11-lobed more than halfway to middle, dark green above, gray-hairy beneath. Acorns long, 1¼ to 2¼ inches long, slender and pointed, with deep cup.

Principal uses: Shade tree. Fuel.

165. GAMBEL OAK, *Quercus gambelii* Nutt. (Rocky Mountain white oak, Utah white oak; *Q. utahensis* (A. DC.) Rydb.).

Small tree or shrub of Rocky Mountain region, including adjacent Mexico. Bark gray brown, scaly. Leaves shedding in fall, oblong, 4 to 8 inches long, deeply 7- to 11-lobed halfway or more to middle, dark green above, light green and soft-hairy beneath. Acorns ⅝ to ¾ inch long, broad and rounded, with deep cup.

Principal uses: Fence posts and fuel.

ELBERT L. LITTLE, JR., *dendrologist in the Division of Dendrology and Range Forage Investigations, Forest Service, in Washington, D. C., has been in research work with the Forest Service since 1934. He has published papers on names of trees of the United States and various botanical subjects. During the Second World War he made forestry and botanical surveys in Latin American countries. Dr. Little holds degrees from the Universities of Oklahoma and Chicago.*

# FIFTY TREES FROM FOREIGN LANDS

ELBERT L. LITTLE, JR.

Since ancient times mankind has sought out from distant parts of the earth new and better farm crops, garden plants, and trees. Many of these strange trees, introduced from seeds brought back by explorers and travelers through the years, have been highly successful for shade, ornament, fruits and nuts, shelterbelts, lumber, and other uses where the conditions for growth are not too different from those in their native lands. Discovery of the New World made possible great interchange of trees and other plants between East and West. Much of the early botanical exploration of North America was made by horticultural collectors who were hunting new plants for European gardens.

With settlement of the climatically diverse portions of the United States came introduction of trees from far away. Naturally the colonists from Europe brought their familiar shade trees, most of which succeeded also in eastern United States where the climate is similar. Examples are Norway spruce, white poplar, European white birch, and sycamore maple. The Yankee Clippers and afterwards botanical explorers brought back from temperate portions of Asia other kinds, such as ginkgo, Chinese scholartree, particled goldenrain-tree, and royal paulownia. The subtropical regions of Florida, southern Texas, southern Arizona, and California have obtained a wealth of exotic trees from tropical lands throughout the world.

After some years of testing, the good points and limitations of these introduced trees, such as their degree of hardiness to winter temperatures, soil and moisture requirements, drought resistance, tolerance to city smoke and dust, and susceptibility to insects and disease, have become known. Indeed, some of these exotics have been so successful that they have escaped from cultivation and have become naturalized, propagating themselves in waste places, roadsides, and woods as if wild. However, the native trees in any locality, having become adapted through the ages, usually are preferable to untested exotics.

At present more than a thousand kinds, or species, of foreign trees, not counting their numerous horticultural forms, are grown in the United States for shade and ornament. Additional thousands not yet popular have been introduced in arboretums and botanical gardens or have been planted infrequently as specimen trees. For their size, the subtropical regions from Florida to California have more different kinds of exotic trees than do any of the temperate regions of the United States. Because of the richness of tropical floras over the earth, many hundred kinds of trees have become available to these warmer regions.

Home owners in all parts of the United States now have wide selections of foreign trees for planting. The less familiar exotics command attention in contrast to the common native shade trees. Improved horticultural varieties, such as those with drooping branches, columnar crown, odd-tinted or cutleaf foliage, or distinctively colored flowers, are available. Aristocratic trees rich in history and legend may be planted. Among these is the ginkgo, a peculiar living fossil from China saved from extinction by plantings around temples through the ages. The cedar-of-Lebanon, so closely associated with the Holy Land and the source of the beautiful wood used in King Solomon's Temple, deserves to be planted more but is not hardy in the far North. The Italian cypress, the classical cypress of the ancient Greeks and the Romans, whose columnar shape is displayed in formal gardens, can be grown in Southern and Pacific States.

For a tropical atmosphere, hardy trees that are representative of their relatives from warmer lands can be grown northward. Examples are silk-tree ("mimosa"), with its fernlike foliage and pink, ball-like blossoms; ailanthus, with its coarse, compound leaves; and royal paulownia, with its big leaves and striking clusters of large violet flowers. Certain nut trees and fruit trees can serve a double purpose for shade or ornament also.

For forestry purposes, such as in reforestation of large areas through establishment of plantations, native trees generally have been more satisfactory than introduced trees. Scotch pine and Norway spruce, the most popular foreign forest trees, have been planted chiefly in the Northeastern States. California has its plantations of eucalyptus from Australia. In the prairie-plains shelterbelts, several exotic trees, such as the following, have been successful: Siberian elm, Chinese elm, Russian-olive, Russian mulberry, Austrian pine, white willow, and ailanthus.

In this article 50 species of the commonest and most popular trees from foreign lands are described briefly and illustrated, primarily for their identification. Though emphasis has been given to the trees widely planted for shade and ornament in temperate regions of the United States, about a fourth of the species selected are tropical trees restricted to the subtropical regions along the southern border from Florida to California.

Several are no longer widely recommended, because of objectionable features or susceptibility to disease or insects or because some better kinds are available, though they may be suitable for special purposes. Nevertheless, they have been planted so frequently that they merit inclusion in a list used for identification purposes. Nearly half of these 50 species have already become naturalized and grow in their adopted home as if native.

The description of each tree species contains the approved common and scientific names as well as other names frequently used. Size is stated as large (more than 70 feet tall), or medium-sized (30 to 70 feet tall), or small (less than 30 feet tall). Leading characteristics useful in identification, such as form of the tree, bark, leaves, flowers, and fruits, are briefly described in nontechnical terms. However, some horticultural varieties with unusual or extreme characteristics may differ from the general descriptions. Though many trees reveal their geographic origin in their names, the native home is stated along with the regions in the United States where the species is grown.

Notes on special uses and desirable qualities as well as objectionable points are included. The drawings of leaves and fruits by Leta Hughey, botanical artist, Forest Service, will aid in naming trees or specimens.

The degree of hardiness of introduced trees and shrubs to cold weather in winter is expressed by division of the United States into hardiness zones, climatic zones based upon average annual minimum temperatures (U. S. D. A., *Atlas of American Agriculture*, Climate, page 9, figure 1928). Alfred Rehder (*Manual of Cultivated Trees and Shrubs*, edition 1, 1927; edition 2, 1940), Donald Wyman (*Hedges, Screens, and Windbreaks*, 1938), and other authors on horticultural subjects have adopted these hardiness zones, citing the northernmost zone where each species can be grown.

On the next page is a revised map of hardiness zones of the United States, based upon the map of average annual minimum temperature for the 40-year period from 1899 to 1938 (U. S. D. A., *Climate and Man*, Yearbook of Agriculture, page 707. 1941).

Ten zones for North America have been designated by number, beginning with zone 1, with average annual minimum temperature exceeding −50° F. and representing the treeless zone of northern Canada and Alaska. The nine zones of the United States with their limits of average annual minimum temperature (Fahrenheit) are, from north to south: Zone 2, −50° to

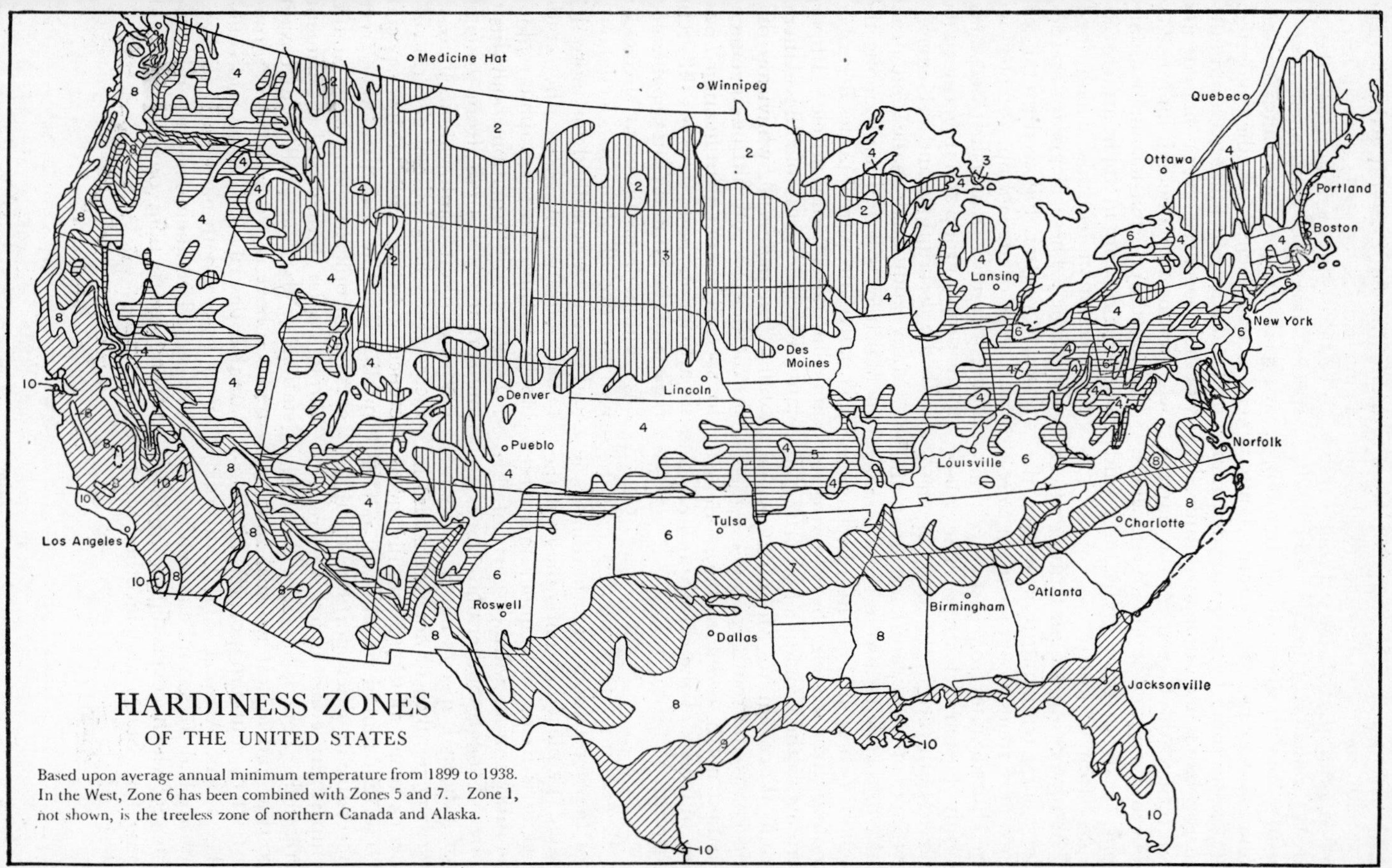


HARDINESS ZONES
OF THE UNITED STATES

Based upon average annual minimum temperature from 1899 to 1938. In the West, Zone 6 has been combined with Zones 5 and 7. Zone 1, not shown, is the treeless zone of northern Canada and Alaska.

802062°—49——53

−35°; zone 3, −35° to −20°; zone 4, −20° to −10°; zone 5, −10° to −5°; zone 6, −5° to 5°; zone 7, 5° to 10°; zone 8, 10° to 20°; zone 9, 20° to 30°; zone 10, above 30°. In mountainous regions of western United States the zones become crowded into narrow bands according to altitude. To conform to the base map, the narrow zone 6 is omitted in the West, where zone 5 extends from −10° to 0° and zone 7 from 0° to 10°.

As factors other than latitude affect the coldest temperature in winter, the hardiness zones do not extend across the United States from east to west uniformly in parallel strips. The zones curve southward in the interior, where extremes of temperature are great, and shift to the south also in mountainous regions, where higher altitudes have a cooling effect. Zone 2, the coldest, is restricted to the Canadian border region from Wisconsin to Montana. Along the coasts the southern zones project farthest north, owing to the moderating influence of the oceans and ocean currents.

For each foreign tree species the northernmost zone of hardiness is stated, or placed in parentheses if the species is hardy only under favorable conditions or in warmer parts of this zone. Though southernmost zones are not indicated, species hardy in the far north generally will not thrive also in the extreme south. Naturally many trees from humid regions will not be successful in drier portions of these temperature zones unless watered or irrigated. Zone 10 includes the nearly frostless and almost tropical zones of restricted, southern portions of Florida, Texas, Arizona, and California. Subtropical trees can be grown also in zone 9, which covers larger areas in these four States and in other States along the Gulf, South Atlantic, and Pacific coasts.

To assist in identification, the 50 species have been combined into 11 artificial groups according to leaf characters, such as whether evergreen or deciduous (shedding leaves in fall), whether borne singly or paired, and whether or not divided into leaflets (leaflets differ from leaves in usually smaller size and in their attachment on a common leafstalk which sheds with them). These 11 groups are designated by letter, followed by the leaf characters of the group. A specimen being identified should first be placed in the proper group and then compared with the descriptions and drawings.

Many additional shade and ornamental trees will be found among the 165 native forest tree species described and illustrated in the article, "Important Forest Trees of the United States," on page 763, which also has instructions for submitting specimens to specialists for identification. The six articles on shade trees for different regions of the United States (pages 48–85) contain notes on other species as well as nearly all of the 50 selected here and should be consulted for more detailed information about the kinds best suited to each geographic region.

For further information about shade and ornamental trees from foreign lands and their identification, there is included a selected list of general references together with a few special publications on the distinctive trees of the subtropical regions. Most States, through their agricultural experiment stations or the State college extension services, have issued bulletins or circulars that describe the shade and ornamental trees, both native and foreign, best suited to their regions and containing instructions on planting and care.

## INDEX OF COMMON NAMES BY NUMBER

*The 50 species are listed here by accepted common names. Other common names in use are mentioned with the descriptions.*

*The numbers refer to the descriptions of the species on pages 820–832.*



## INDEX OF SCIENTIFIC NAMES BY NUMBER

*Additional scientific names in use for some of these 50 species are cited as synonyms with the descriptions.*

A. Evergreens (subtropical and warm temperate), leaves scalelike, Nos. 1 to 3.

1. HORSETAIL CASUARINA, *Casuarina equisetifolia* L. (horsetail beefwood, Australian-pine). Large evergreen tree resembling conifers, with thin crown of drooping branches and with leaves reduced to scales. Bark smoothish. Twigs wiry, pale green, jointed and grooved, with rings 1/4 inch apart consisting of 6 to 8 brownish scale leaves 1/16 inch long. Male flowers in narrow clusters 1/2 inch long and female flowers in short clusters 1/8 inch in diameter. Fruiting cones 1/2 inch in diameter, light brown. Native of tropical Asia and Australia. Planted in subtropical regions of Florida, southern Texas, southern Arizona, and California. Extensively naturalized in southern Florida. Used for windbreaks and planting on sand dunes as well as a street tree and ornamental. Rapidly growing and adapted to dry, sandy, alkaline, and saline soils. Zone (9).

2. ATHEL TAMARISK, *Tamarix aphylla* (L.) Karst. (athel, evergreen athel, evergreen tamarisk; *T. articulata* Vahl). Small to medium-sized evergreen tree with many spreading branches and dense rounded crown. Twigs wiry, gray green, jointed, the joints composed of scale leaves 1/16 inch long each circling the twig and ending in a minute point. Flowers very small, pink, less than 1/16 inch long, in slender branched clusters in summer. Fruit a small capsule. Native of northeastern Africa and western Asia. Planted in subtropical regions in southern Texas, southern Arizona, and California. Rapidly growing tree used for shade and windbreaks. Drought-resistant and tolerant of alkaline and saline soils. Zone (9).

3. ITALIAN CYPRESS, *Cupressus sempervirens* L. (Mediterranean cypress). Tall, medium-sized, cone-bearing evergreen tree (conifer) with erect or horizontal branches and narrow, columnar crown. Bark thin, gray, smooth or slightly fissured. Leaves scalelike, 1/24 inch long, blunt-pointed, dark green, crowded and forming 4-angled twigs. Cones 1 inch in diameter, gray, with a short knob or point on each scale. Native of southern Europe and western Asia. The classical cypress of the ancient Greeks and Romans, much planted in formal gardens in southern Europe. Hardy in subtropical and warm temperate climates in the Pacific, Gulf, and South Atlantic States. Common in California. Zone (7).

B. Evergreens, leaves needlelike (cone-bearing, or conifers), Nos. 4 to 8.

4. CEDAR-OF-LEBANON, *Cedrus libani* Loud. (*C. libanotica* Link). Large cone-bearing evergreen tree with irregular spreading crown of horizontal branches. Bark dark gray, becoming fissured and scaly. Twigs smooth or slightly hairy. Needles many in cluster on short spur branches (or single on leading twigs), 3-angled, short, 3/4 to 1 1/4 inches long, dark or bright green. Cones 3 to 4 inches long, reddish brown, upright. Native of Asia Minor and Syria. Adapted to warm temperate and subtropical climates in Atlantic, Gulf, and Pacific regions but not hardy in far North. Beautiful ornamental tree of special interest because of its association with the Bible and the Holy Land. Zone 5.

5. DEODAR CEDAR, *Cedrus deodara* (Roxb.) Loud. (Deodar). Large cone-bearing evergreen tree with regular pyramidal shape and graceful drooping branches down to base. Bark dark gray, becoming fissured and scaly. Twigs densely hairy. Needles many in cluster on short spur branches (or single on leading twigs), 3-angled, short, 1 to 2 inches long, dark blue green. Cones 3 to 5 inches long, reddish brown, upright. Native of Himalaya. Adapted to subtropical climates of Gulf, Mexican border, and Pacific regions and especially popular in California. Zone 7.

6. SCOTCH PINE, *Pinus sylvestris* L. (Scots pine). Large cone-bearing evergreen tree with irregular crown, spreading branches, and blue green foliage. Bark reddish brown, on older trunks becoming grayish and fissured into scaly plates. Needles 2 in cluster, 1 1/2 to 3 inches long, blue green, usually twisted. Cones 1 1/2 to 2 1/2 inches long, yellow brown, with minute prickles. Native and widely distributed across Europe and northern Asia and one of the most important timber trees of Europe. Hardy across the United States. In the Northeast and in adjacent Canada extensively planted in forestry plantations, shelterbelts, and for ornament, and spreading and becoming naturalized. However, native pines are usually superior for forestry purposes. Thrives on poorer, sandy soils as well as on better loams. Resistant to city smoke. Zone 2.

7. AUSTRIAN PINE, *Pinus nigra* Arnold (*P. austriaca* Hoess, *P. laricio* Poir.). Medium-sized to large pyramidal cone-bearing evergreen tree with spreading branches and dense, dark-green foliage. Bark dark gray, fissured into irregular, scaly plates. Needles 2 in cluster, 3 1/2 to 6 inches long, dark green, stiff. Cones 2 to 3 inches long, yellow brown, shiny, usually with short prickles. Several geographic varieties and garden forms are distinguished. Native of central and southern Europe and Asia Minor and a valuable timber tree there.

→

**1. Horsetail casuarina. 2. Athel tamarisk. 3. Italian cypress. 4. Cedar-of-Lebanon. 5. Deodar cedar. 6. Scotch pine. 7. Austrian pine. 8. Norway spruce. 9. English holly. 10. Cajeput-tree. 11. Red-ironbark eucalyptus. 12. Longbeak eucalyptus. 13. Tasmanian blue eucalyptus.**

1
1x
5x
2
1x
5x
3
5x
1x
4
½x
5
½x
6
½x
7
½x
8
½x
9
½x
10
½x
11
½x
12
½x
13
½x

Across the United States one of the commoner foreign ornamental trees. Used also in shelterbelts. Hardy in East extending north to southern New England and in west except coldest, hottest, and driest regions. Grows in sandy, loam, and clay soils. Tolerant of city dust and smoke. Zone 4.

8. NORWAY SPRUCE, *Picea abies* (L.) Karst. (*P. excelsa* Link). Large conical cone-bearing evergreen tree with spreading branches and drooping twigs. Bark reddish brown, scaly. Needles 4-angled, 3/8 to 1 inch long, dark green. Cones 4 to 6 inches long, light brown, with thin, slightly pointed, irregularly toothed scales. There are numerous horticultural forms. Native of northern and central Europe, where it is the common spruce and used for paper pulp and lumber. Adapted to cool moist climates of northeastern United States, Rocky Mountains, and Pacific coast. Widely planted for ornament, shelterbelts, and forestry plantations, and occasionally escaping from cultivation. Best suited to well-drained loam but successful on most other soils. Zone 2.

C. Broadleaf evergreens (subtropical, except No. 9), leaves not divided into leaflets (simple), Nos. 9 to 15.

9. ENGLISH HOLLY, *Ilex aquifolium* L. Small to medium-sized evergreen tree with short, spreading branches and dense pyramidal crown. Leaves oval, 1 1/2 to 3 inches long, stiff and leathery, the wavy edges with large spiny teeth, shiny dark green, lighter beneath. Flowers male and female on different trees, white, small, less than 1/4-inch long, fragrant, in late spring. Fruits 1/4 to 3/8 inch in diameter, berrylike, bright red, shiny, usually clustered, remaining on tree in winter. There are numerous horticultural forms. Native from western and southern Europe and northern Africa to western Asia and China. Planted in Atlantic, Southern, and Pacific States for the ornamental evergreen foliage and red fruits. Zone 6.

10. CAJEPUT-TREE, *Melaleuca leucadendron* (L.) L. (punk-tree, bottlebrush). Medium-sized to large, slender tree with drooping, smooth or silky twigs. Bark thick and spongy or corky, whitish, peeling off in many thin layers. Leaves evergreen, narrowly elliptical or lance-shaped, 2 to 4 inches long, pointed at base and apex, with parallel veins, thick, pale green on both sides. Flowers creamy white, 3/4 inch long, stalkless, in many-flowered clusters 2 to 4 inches long, suggesting a bottle-brush, in summer and fall. Fruiting capsules less than 1/4 inch in diameter, the clusters remaining on the tree. Native of Australia. Subtropical tree planted in Florida, where it has become naturalized, and in southern California and southern Texas. Fast growing and resistant to wind, drought, fires, and salt water. Suitable for windbreaks and beach planting as well as for ornament and shade. The bark is used for packing fruits and for roofs and boats. Cajeput oil of medicine is obtained from the leaves. Zone (9).

11. RED-IRONBARK EUCALYPTUS, *Eucalyptus sideroxylon* Cunn. (red ironbark, mulga ironbark eucalyptus, mugga). Medium-sized slender evergreen tree. Bark rough, deeply furrowed, blackish. Leaves lance-shaped, 3 to 6 inches long, often curved, gray green on both sides. Flowers showy, white to pink to red in different varieties, about 3/4 inch broad, numerous in clusters in winter and spring. Fruiting capsules oval, 1/4 to 3/8 inch in diameter. Native of Australia. Subtropical tree planted in southern California, where it is hardy, drought-resistant, and moderately tolerant of alkali. Zone (9).

12. LONGBEAK EUCALYPTUS, *Eucalyptus camaldulensis* Dehnh. (redgum; *E. rostrata* Schlecht., not Cav.). Tall evergreen tree with slender symmetrical crown and slender, slightly drooping branches. Bark dark gray, rough and furrowed near base, smooth and peeling off above. Leaves lance-shaped, 4 to 6 inches long, leathery, long-pointed, with smooth edges, green on both sides. Flowers whitish, 3/4 inch broad, clustered. Fruiting capsules 1/4 inch in diameter. Native of Australia. Planted in subtropical regions of California, southern Arizona, southern Texas, and Florida. One of the hardiest species of eucalyptus in resistance to drought, frost, heat, and alkali. Thrives in good moist soils. Zone (9).

13. TASMANIAN BLUE EUCALYPTUS, *Eucalyptus globulus* Labill. (Tasmanian bluegum, bluegum). Very tall evergreen tree with straight trunk and narrow crown. Bark peeling off in long thin strips, becoming smooth and grayish. Leaves lance-shaped, slightly curved, 6 to 12 inches long, leathery, long-pointed, with smooth edges, green on both sides, aromatic; leaves of young plants and young shoots paired, stalkless, broad and oval, bluish, covered with a bloom. Flowers whitish, 1 1/2 inches broad, scattered, in winter and spring. Fruiting capsules 4-angled, 3/4 to 1 inch broad, warty, bluish white. Native of Tasmania. Subtropical species, the most commonly cultivated eucalyptus in the world. Common in California, where it grows very rapidly. Used also for plantations and windbreaks. Adapted to a wide range of conditions and alkali-tolerant but thrives in good, moist soil. Objectionable because the roots penetrate defective sewers. Zone (9).

14. CAMPHOR-TREE, *Cinnamomum camphora* (L.) Nees & Eberm. (*Camphora camphora* (L.) Karst.). Small to medium-sized evergreen tree with enlarged base and dense oval crown. Leaves long-stalked, elliptical, 2 to 5 inches long, long-pointed, with 2 or more

prominent side veins, pinkish when young, shiny green above and grayish white beneath, with odor of camphor when crushed. Flowers yellowish, small, ⅛ inch long, in clusters 2 to 3 inches long. Fruit a berry ⅜ inch in diameter, black, 1-seeded. Native of tropical Asia and Malaya to China and Japan. In the United States extensively planted as an ornamental in subtropical and warm temperate regions in Florida, along the Gulf, and in southern California. Also escaped from cultivation in the South. Alkali-tolerant. Camphor is obtained from the wood and leaves. Zone 9.

15. INDIA-RUBBER FIG, *Ficus elastica* Nois. (India rubber-plant, Indian rubber-tree). Large, much branched evergreen tree with enlarged or buttressed base, broad crown, and milky juice. Leaves large, oblong or elliptical, 4 to 12 inches long, short-pointed, leathery, smooth, shiny green, lighter beneath. Fruits paired, stalkless, oblong, ½ inch long, greenish yellow. Native of tropical Asia. Cultivated and naturalized in subtropical Florida and planted also in southern California. This is the familiar rubber-plant grown indoors in the North. The milky latex has been used as a source of rubber. Zone 10.

D. Broadleaf evergreens (subtropical), leaves divided into leaflets (compound), Nos. 16 to 19.

16. PEPPERTREE, *Schinus molle* L. (California peppertree, Peruvian mastic-tree, Peruvian peppertree). Medium-sized spreading evergreen tree with rounded crown, graceful drooping branches, and fine foliage. Leaves compound, 6 to 12 inches long, drooping, with milky juice. Leaflets about 20 to 40, narrowly lance-shaped, 1 to 2 inches long, short-pointed, with edges smooth or slightly toothed, light green. Flowers male and female on different trees, yellowish white, small, ⅛ inch long, numerous in clusters 4 to 6 inches long. Fruits many, beadlike, 3/16 inch in diameter, reddish, remaining on tree in winter. Native of Peru. Subtropical tree extensively planted in California, where it has become naturalized, and in southern Arizona. Adapted to a wide range of soils, alkali-tolerant, and drought-resistant. Subject to black scale and root rot. Zone (9).

17. SILK-OAK, *Grevillea robusta* A. Cunn. (silk-oak grevillea, Australian-ferntree). Large, graceful tree with many branches and evergreen fernlike foliage. Leaves 4 to 12 inches long, twice divided or very deeply lobed into narrow, pointed divisions with edges rolled under, deep green above and white silky beneath. Flowers orange or yellow, ¼ inch long, long-stalked, in clusters 3 to 5 inches long, numerous on the trunk and main branches in spring and early summer. Pods ¾ inch long, broad, curved, black, 1- or 2-seeded. Native of Australia. Planted in subtropical regions of Florida, southern Texas, southern Arizona, and California and indoors northward as a fernlike ornamental potted plant. Naturalized in southern Florida. Drought-resistant. The brittle branches break easily. Zone (9).

18. CAROB, *Ceratonia siliqua* L. (St. Johns-bread, algarroba). Small to medium-sized spreading evergreen tree. Bark dark, reddish brown. Leaves compound, 4 to 8 inches long, with 4 to 8 oval leaflets 1 to 2 inches long, rounded, shiny dark green above, paler beneath. Flowers male and female, small, red, in clusters 1 to 2 inches long. Pods large, 4 to 12 inches long, thick and flattened, leathery, dark brown, with sugary edible pulp, used for forage and human food. Native probably of Asia Minor and Syria but long cultivated in the Mediterranean Basin and elsewhere as a forage crop for the edible pods. In the United States limited to subtropical regions of Florida, southern Texas, southern Arizona, and California. Grown both as a shade tree and for forage. Adapted to hot dry climates and to a variety of soils including alkali, thriving in heavy soils. The name St. Johns-bread is from the mistaken belief that the seeds and sugary pulp were the locusts and wild honey which St. John the Baptist found in the wilderness. The pods were the "husks" in the parable of the Prodigal Son. Zone (9).

19. GREENWATTLE ACACIA, *Acacia decurrens* Willd. (green wattle; blackgreen-wattle acacia, or black wattle, and silvergreen-wattle acacia, or silver wattle, are varieties). Small to medium-sized evergreen tree with rounded crown. Leaves finely divided, twice compound, 3 to 6 inches long, with 15 to 30 feathery forks, each with 30 to 80 very narrow leaflets ⅛ to ⅜ inch long, grayish green or dark green. Flowers crowded in many yellow balls ¼ inch in diameter in spring. Pods 2 to 4 inches long and ¼ inch wide, reddish. Native of Australia. Subtropical tree extensively planted in California. Adapted to a wide range of soils. Zone (9).

E. Deciduous, leaves fan-shaped, mostly clustered on short spur branches, No. 20.

20. GINKGO, *Ginkgo biloba* L. (maidenhair-tree). Medium-sized to tall resinous tree with few branches and conical crown. Bark gray, irregularly fissured or furrowed. Leaves 3 to 5 in a cluster on short spur branches or single, with leafstalks 1 to 2 inches long. Leaf blades oddly fan-shaped, 1 to 2 inches long and 1½ to 3 inches broad, often 2-lobed, with parallel veins, leathery, bright to dull green, turning yellow and shedding in fall. Pollen and seeds on different trees. Seeds single or paired, stalked, plumlike, 1 inch long,

yellowish, with an ill-smelling thin outer coat and large edible nut. Ginkgo is a living fossil from China related to conifers and the sole survivor of its family, not found wild but long perpetuated in cultivation in China and Japan around temples. Adapted to moist temperate regions in eastern United States and Pacific coast. Especially suited as a street tree because it is resistant to smoke, dust, wind, and ice, and free from insect injury. Male trees are preferred, because of the disagreeable fruits of the female. Zone 4.

F. Deciduous, leaves paired (opposite), not divided into leaflets (simple), Nos. 21–23.

21. ROYAL PAULOWNIA, *Paulownia tomentosa* (Thunb.) Steud. (paulownia, princess-tree). Small to medium-sized, widely spreading tree with stout branches. Bark gray brown with shallow fissures. Leaves paired, resembling those of catalpa, with leafstalks 3 to 8 inches long and large heart-shaped leaf blades 5 to 16 inches long, with edges smooth or slightly 3-lobed, light green, slightly hairy above and densely hairy beneath. Flowers large and very showy, violet, about 2 inches long, fragrant, borne in dense upright clusters 6 to 10 inches long in spring before the leaves appear. Fruiting capsules egg-shaped, pointed, 1 to 1½ inches long, brown, remaining on tree in winter. Native of China. Planted as an ornamental for the showy violet flowers and large leaves in eastern United States north to New York but not hardy where the winters are severe. Grown also in Pacific States. Thrives in rich moist soil and naturalized as a "weed" tree in waste places in Eastern States. Zone (5).

22. NORWAY MAPLE, *Acer platanoides* L. (Schwedler maple is a variety). Medium-sized to large spreading tree with rounded symmetrical crown of dense foliage. Bark dark, with narrow ridges and furrows. Leafstalks about 3 inches long, with milky juice. Leaves paired, heart-shaped, 3 to 7 inches in diameter, 5-lobed, with few pointed teeth, smooth, bright green, turning yellow in fall. Flowers yellowish green, abundant in many-flowered clusters in spring before the leaves develop. Key fruits paired, long-winged, 1½ to 2 inches long, spreading horizontally. Native across Europe from Norway to Caucasus. Widely planted in eastern United States and in Pacific and Rocky Mountain regions. Fast growing, tolerant of city smoke and dust, and relatively free from insect pests and diseases. The popular variety Schwedler maple has bright red leaves when young, changing to dark green. Zone 3.

23. PLANETREE MAPLE, *Acer pseudoplatanus* L. (sycamore maple, "sycamore" in Europe). Large spreading tree with rounded crown. Bark with broad flaky scales. Leafstalks 3 to 4 inches long. Leaves paired, heart-shaped at base, 3 to 6 inches in diameter, 5-lobed with the lobes pointed and coarsely toothed, dark green above, pale and smooth or slightly hairy beneath. Flowers yellowish green, distinctive, hanging in long, narrow clusters 3 to 7 inches long in spring. Key fruits paired, long-winged, 1¼ to 2 inches long. Native of Europe and western Asia, where it is an important timber and shade tree. Planted as a shade tree in Pacific States and in Eastern States except coldest regions, but not as hardy as Norway maple. Rapidly growing and suited to exposed situations. Zone 5.

G. Deciduous, leaves paired (opposite), divided into leaflets (compound), Nos. 24 and 25.

24. AMUR CORKTREE, *Phellodendron amurense* Rupr. Large, aromatic tree with low, spreading branches and rounded crown. Bark light gray, corky, deeply fissured, conspicuous in winter. Twigs yellowish gray. Leaves paired, compound, 6 to 12 inches long. Leaflets 5 to 13, oval, 2 to 4 inches long, long-pointed, with minute dots, shiny dark green above, light green and smooth or hairy beneath, turning yellow in fall. Flowers small, yellowish green, ¼ inch long, in clusters 2 to 8 inches long in early summer. Fruit ⅜ inch in diameter, black, 5-seeded, ornamental, with odor of turpentine. Native of northern China and Manchuria. Hardy in most temperate regions of United States. Tolerant of city conditions and relatively free from insects and disease. Zone 3.

25. HORSECHESTNUT, *Aesculus hippocastanum* L. (common horsechestnut). Medium-sized to large spreading tree with rounded crown. Bark brownish, thin, fissured and scaly. Leaves paired, compound, with leafstalks 3 to 7 inches long. Leaflets 5 to 7, spreading fingerlike (palmate), elliptical, 4 to 10 inches long, wedge-shaped at base and broader toward the abrupt point, toothed, dark green above, paler beneath. Flowers white with red spots, about ¾ inch long, in large showy upright clusters. Fruiting capsule 2 to 2½ inches in diameter, spiny, with 1 or 2 large inedible seeds. Native of Balkan Peninsula. Widely planted across the United States and escaped from cultivation in the Northeast. The showy flowers and large palmate leaves have made this species a popular ornamental

→

**14. Camphor-tree. 15. India-rubber fig. 16. Peppertree. 17. Silk-oak. 18. Carob. 19. Greenwattle acacia. 20. Ginkgo. 21. Royal paulownia. 22. Norway maple. 23. Planetree maple.**

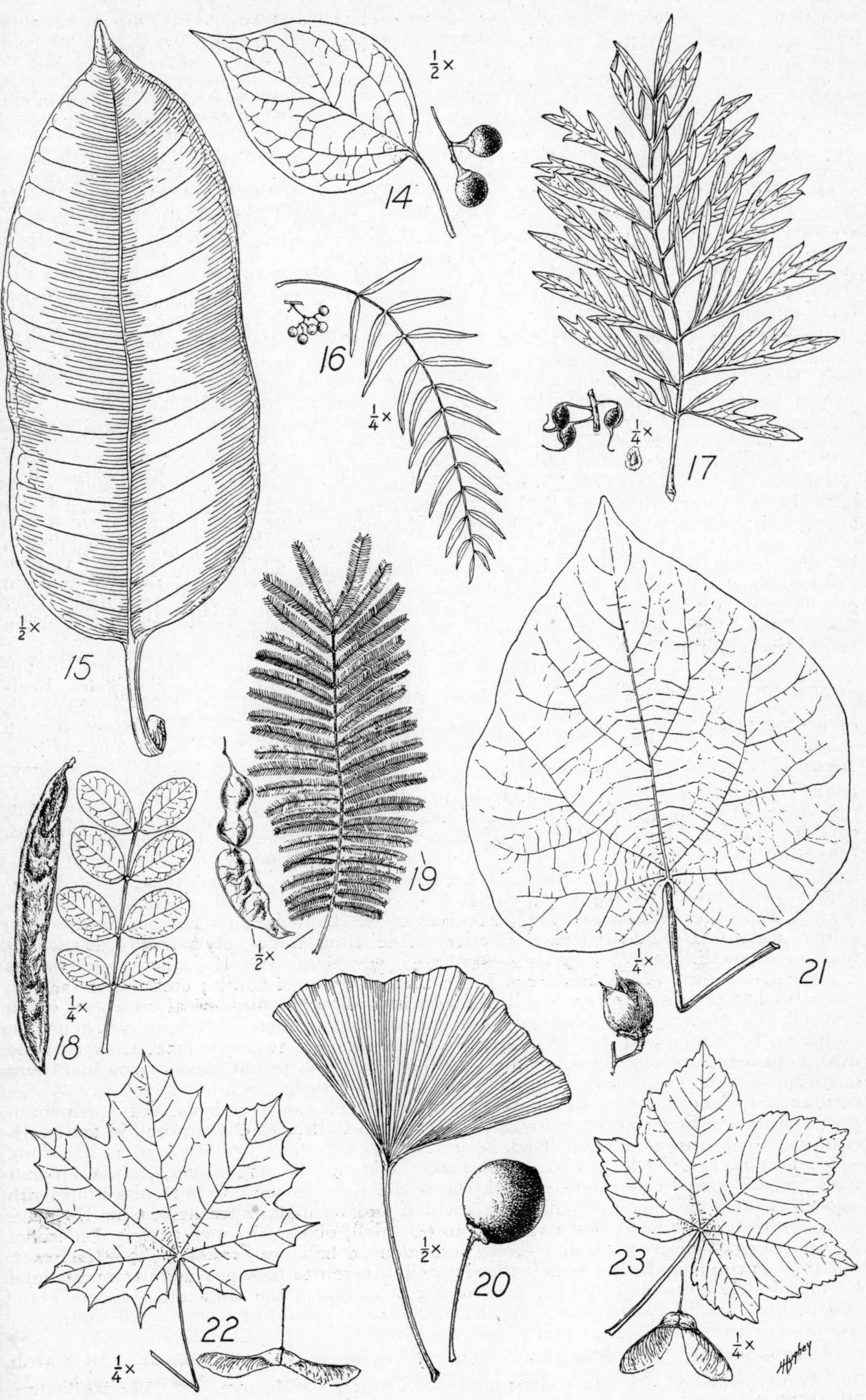

½×
14
16
¼×
¼×
17
½×
15
19
½×
¼×
21
¼×
18
½×
20
23
22
¼×
¼×

and shade tree. Tolerant of city smoke but subject to insect attacks and disease. Zone 3.

H. Deciduous, leaves borne singly (alternate), divided into leaflets (compound), Nos. 26 to 32.

26. CHINESE SCHOLARTREE, *Sophora japonica* L. (Japanese pagoda-tree). Medium-sized tree with spreading branches and dense rounded crown. Bark gray, fissured. Twigs dark green, smooth or nearly so. Leaves 6 to 10 inches long, compound. Leaflets 7 to 17, narrowly oval, 1 to 2 inches long, short-pointed, with smooth edges, shiny dark green above, pale and finely hairy beneath. Flowers yellowish white, ½ inch long, beanlike, in loose showy clusters 6 to 12 inches long in late summer. Pods 2 to 3 inches long and ⅜ inch in diameter, narrowed between the seeds. Native of China and Korea and cultivated around temples in Japan. Planted in the southern half of the United States and hardy north to New York. Especially suitable as a street tree because of its tolerance of city fumes, but slow growing. Relatively free from insect pests and diseases. Zone 4.

27. PERSIAN WALNUT, *Juglans regia* L. (English walnut). Medium-sized tree with spreading branches and rounded crown. Bark smooth, silvery gray. Compound leaves 8 to 16 inches long. Leaflets usually 5 to 9, oblong, 2 to 5 inches long, pointed, with edges usually smooth, bright green, nearly smooth. Male flowers in narrow clusters 2 to 4 inches long. Nuts 1½ inches in diameter including the green husk, thin-shelled, sweet and edible, known as English walnuts. Native from southeastern Europe to Himalaya and China. Planted as a nut tree in warmer parts of United States, especially in the Pacific States and also in Southeastern States. Useful also as a shade tree. Zone (5).

28. AILANTHUS, *Ailanthus altissima* (Mill.) Swingle (tree-of-Heaven ailanthus, tree-of-Heaven; *A. glandulosa* Desf.). Medium-sized, coarsely branched tree with smooth, striped bark. Leaves large, compound, 1½ to 2½ feet long, with 13 to 25 leaflets, short-stalked and mostly paired, broadly lance-shaped, 3 to 5 inches long, long-pointed, with 2 to 4 teeth near base, each tooth with a gland beneath. Flowers small, greenish, ¼ inch long, in large clusters 6 to 10 inches long in summer, the male flowers with disageeable odor. Fruits winged, 1½ inches long, reddish brown, showy in fall. Native of China but widely planted and naturalized as a "weed" tree in waste places in eastern United States, southern Rocky Mountains, and Pacific States. Rapid growing, with handsome coarse foliage. Not among the more desirable trees but successful in crowded city and smoky factory districts where most other kinds will not thrive. Planted also in shelterbelts. Objectionable about drains, springs, and wells, as the roots get into drains and both roots and leaves are poisonous. Grows on a variety of soils from sand to clay and spreads rapidly by suckers. Only seed-bearing plants should be propagated, because of the ill-scented male flowers. Zone 4.

29. PANICLED GOLDENRAIN-TREE, *Koelreuteria paniculata* Laxm. (China-tree, pride-of-India, varnish-tree). Small, sparingly branched tree with rounded open crown. Leaves once or twice compound, 6 to 15 inches long. Leaflets 7 to 15, oval, 1 to 3 inches long, coarsely and irregularly toothed, dark green and smooth above, paler and slightly hairy beneath. Flowers bright yellow, small, ½ inch long, in broad, showy clusters 8 to 14 inches long in summer. Pods showy, bladderlike, egg-shaped, 1½ to 2 inches long, pointed, with papery walls, brown. Native of China, Korea, and Japan. Planted in Atlantic, southern, central, Rocky Mountain, and Pacific regions of the United States but not hardy in the colder regions. Drought-resistant, relatively free from insect pests and diseases, and tolerant of alkali. Zone 5.

30. CHINABERRY, *Melia azedarach* L. (chinatree, pride-of-China; umbrella chinaberry or umbrella-tree is a variety). Small tree with spreading, hemispherical crown or, in the umbrella chinaberry, with crowded branches forming a dense, flattened crown like an umbrella. Bark furrowed. Leaves large, twice compound, 1 to 2 feet long. Leaflets many, oval, 1 to 3 inches long, sharp-pointed, toothed or lobed, bright green, smooth. Flowers purplish, ⅝ inch across, fragrant, in open clusters 4 to 8 inches long in spring. Fruit ⅝ inch in diameter, yellow, 1-seeded. Native of Himalaya, Planted for shade and ornament in southern United States north to Virginia and west to California. Naturalized in the Southeast. Rapidly growing but short-lived. Zone 7.

31. SILKTREE, *Albizia julibrissin* Durazz. (silktree albizia, "mimosa," powder-puff-tree). Small, widely branched tree with spreading, flattened crown. Bark blackish, nearly smooth. Leaves twice compound, finely divided and fernlike or feathery, 6 to 15 inches long, with 10 to 24 forks, each with 30 to 60 small, oblong, pointed, pale-green leaflets ⅜ inch long. Flowers pink and showy, crowded in ball-like clusters 1 to 2 inches in diameter in summer. Pods 4 to 6 inches long, flat, green to brown. Native from Persia to China. Widely cultivated and escaped from cultivation in the Gulf and Atlantic States and planted also in Pacific States. As the hardiest of a group of tropical and subtropical leguminous trees, this ornamental is reminiscent of warmer regions. Zone 7 (5).

➔

**24. Amur corktree. 25. Horsechestnut. 26. Chinese scholartree. 27. Persian walnut. 28. Ailanthus.**

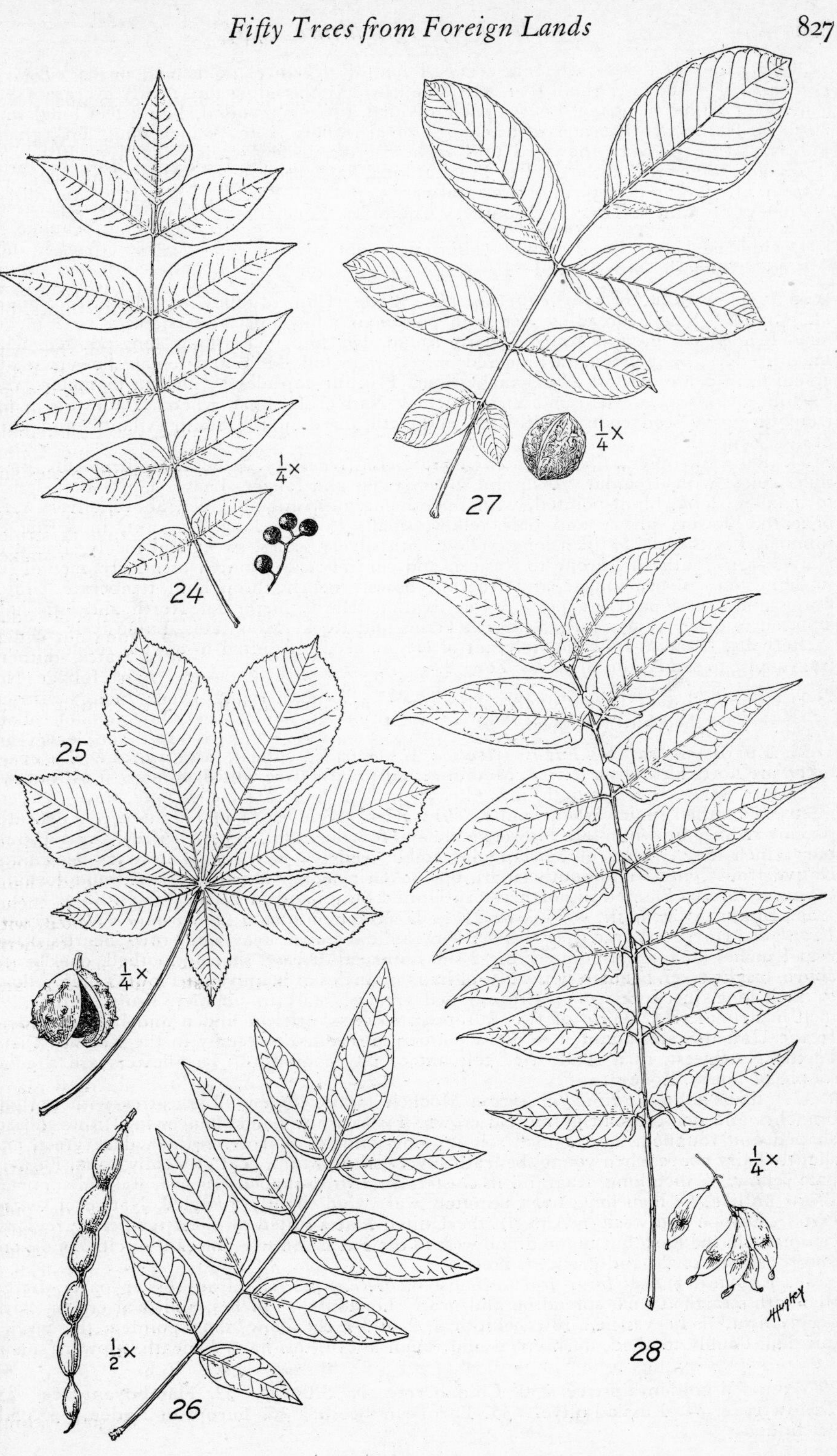
24
1/4×
27
1/4×
25
1/4×
26
1/2×
28
1/4×
Hughes

32. FLAMBOYANT-TREE, *Delonix regia* (Bojer) Raf. (royal poinciana, peacock-flower; *Poinciana regia* Bojer). Small tree with broad, widely spreading top, nearly evergreen but leafless for a time in spring. Leaves finely divided, twice compound, 1 to 2 feet long, with 20 to 50 feathery forks, each with 30 to 70 oval leaflets ¼ to ½ inch long, dark green. Flowers large and very showy, 3 to 4 inches across, bright scarlet, in large clusters in spring and summer. Pods large, 1 to 1½ feet long, flat, dark brown. Native of Madagascar. A brilliantly flowered tropical ornamental very popular in Florida, where it is naturalized. Planted also southern Texas and southern California. Zone 10.

I. Deciduous, leaves borne singly (alternate), not divided into leaflets (simple), leaf edges smooth, Nos. 33 and 34.

33. TALLOWTREE, *Sapium sebiferum* (L.) Roxb. (Chinese tallowtree; *Triadica sebifera* (L.) Small). Small spreading tree with poisonous milky juice. Leafstalks 1 to 2 inches long. Leaf blades broadly oval or nearly round, 1½ to 3 inches long, long-pointed, with smooth edges, light green, turning red or yellow in fall. Male and female flowers small, greenish, in dense clusters 2 to 4 inches long. Fruiting capsules ½ inch in diameter, with 3 white, oval, waxy seeds remaining attached. Native of China, where candles are made from the waxy seed coats. Cultivated and naturalized in the South Atlantic and Gulf States. Zone 7.

34. RUSSIAN-OLIVE, *Elaeagnus angustifolia* L. (oleaster). Small tree or shrub, sometimes spiny, with irregular crown and silvery twigs and foliage. Leaves lance-shaped, 1½ to 3 inches long, blunt-pointed, with smooth margins, grayish green above, silvery scaly beneath. Flowers silvery and pale yellow, small, ⅜ inch long, fragrant, in spring or summer. Fruits oval, ⅜ inch long, yellow with silvery scales, sweet and mealy, 1-seeded. Native from southern Europe to western and central Asia. Planted as an ornamental for its handsome silvery foliage and fragrant flowers nearly throughout temperate United States and occasionally escapes from cultivation. Hardy in the far North and especially adapted to drier regions, such as Great Plains and Rocky Mountains. Extensively used in shelterbelts. Drought-resistant, tolerant of city smoke, and suited to a wide range of soils from moist to sandy and alkaline. Zone 2.

J. Deciduous, leaves borne singly (alternate), not divided into leaflets (simple), leaf edges toothed but not lobed, Nos. 35 to 44.

35. EUROPEAN BEECH, *Fagus sylvatica* L. (purple, cutleaf, and weeping European beech are horticultural varieties). Medium-sized to large tree with symmetrical oval crown and dense foliage. Bark smooth, gray. Leaves in 2 rows, 2 to 4 inches long, short-pointed, minutely toothed, hairy when young, shiny dark green above and light green beneath, turning reddish brown in fall. Flowers male and female, small, in early spring. Fruit a spiny bur 1 inch long, with 2 or 3 triangular edible seeds ¾ inch long known as beechnuts. Native from central and southern Europe to Crimea, an important hardwood forming extensive forests. Planted in northeastern United States and in Pacific States. Zone 4.

36. EUROPEAN LINDEN, ×*Tilia europaea* L. (common linden; *T. cordata*×*platyphyllos*, *T. vulgaris* Hayne). Large tree with dense pyramidal crown. Leaves in 2 rows, heart-shaped, 2 to 4 inches long, short-pointed, the 2 sides unequal at base, sharply toothed, dark green above, bright green beneath with tufts of hairs in angles of main veins. Flowers pale yellow, ¼ inch long, in clusters on a strap-shaped greenish stalk in summer. Fruits nutlike, ¼ inch in diameter. A hybrid of two European species, littleleaf linden and bigleaf linden. In the United States adapted to moist temperate regions, especially in the Northeast and Pacific Northwest, as a shade tree tolerant of city conditions. The flowers are a good source of honey. Zone 3.

37. SILVER LINDEN, *Tilia tomentosa* Moench (white linden). Large tree with upright branches and dense broad pyramidal crown. Twigs white hairy. Leaves in 2 rows, heart-shaped and rounded, 2 to 5 inches long, long-pointed, sharply toothed, dark green and slightly hairy above when young, beneath silvery white with a coat of woolly hairs. Flowers pale yellow, ⅜ inch long, fragrant, in clusters on a strap-shaped greenish stalk in summer. Fruits nutlike, ⅜ inch long, oval, minutely warty and slightly 5-angled. Native of southeastern Europe and western Asia. In the United States suited to moist temperate regions, especially in the East, but planted also west to the Pacific States. Tolerant of city conditions and resistant to heat and drought. Zone 4.

38. ENGLISH ELM, *Ulmus procera* Salisb. ("*U. campestris*" of authors in part). Large tree with straight trunk, spreading and nearly horizontal branches, and oval crown. Bark deeply fissured. Leaves in 2 rows, elliptical, 2 to 3 inches long, short-pointed, the 2 sides unequal, doubly toothed, dark green and rough above, soft-hairy beneath. Flowers small, →

**29. Panicled goldenrain-tree. 30. Chinaberry. 31. Silktree. 32. Flamboyant-tree. 33. Tallowtree. 34. Russian-olive. 35. European beech. 36. European linden. 37. Silver linden.**

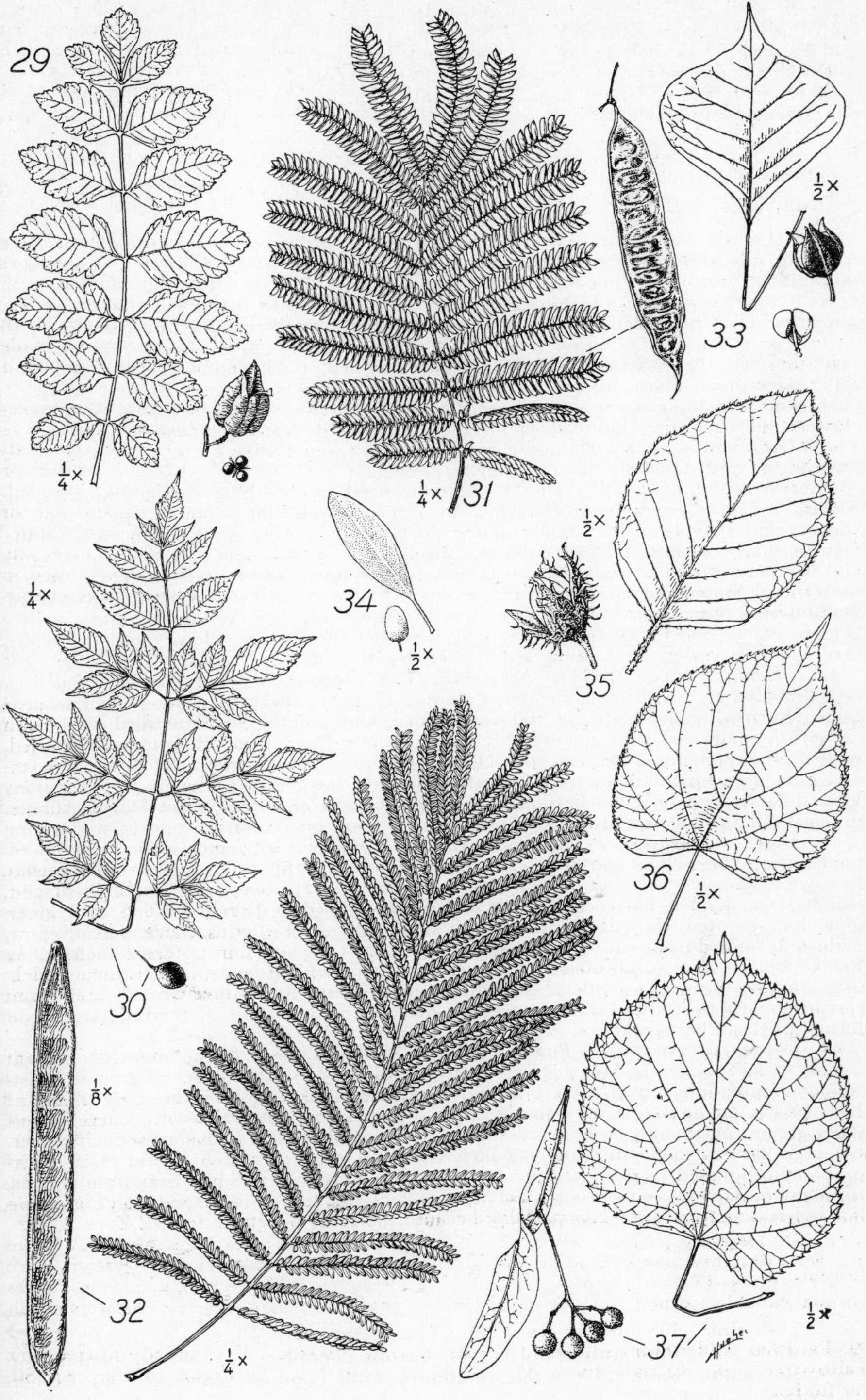
29
1/4×
1/4×
30
1/8×
32
31
1/4×
34
1/2×
1/4×
33
1/2×
1/2×
35
36
1/2×
37
1/2×

greenish, in clusters in early spring. Fruits flattened, ½ inch in diameter. Native of western and southern Europe. In the United States planted in moist temperate regions of Pacific and Eastern States. Tolerant of city smoke but produces undesirable root sprouts. Subject to Dutch elm disease and attacked by elm leaf beetle. Zone 5.

39. SIBERIAN ELM, *Ulmus pumila* L. (Asiatic elm, Pekin elm, dwarf elm, dwarf Asiatic elm; erroneously called Chinese elm, which is *U. parvifolia* Jacq., No. 40). Small to medium-sized tree with rounded crown and rough bark. Twigs hairy when young. Leaves in 2 rows, narrowly elliptical, small, ¾ to 2 inches long, short-pointed, the two sides almost equal, toothed, thick, smooth and dark green above, becoming smooth beneath. Flowers small, greenish, in clusters in early spring. Fruits flattened, ½ inch in diameter. Native from Turkestan to eastern Siberia and northern China. Widely grown in central and western United States for shade and shelterbelts. Hardy in dry regions and drought resistant, tolerates city smoke and poor soils, and grows rapidly. Subject to cotton root rot and canker disease. Zone 4.

40. CHINESE ELM, *Ulmus parvifolia* Jacq. Small tree with broad rounded crown and spreading branches, shedding leaves in fall or half-evergreen in warm climates. Bark smooth or rough. Twigs hairy. Leaves in 2 rows, elliptical, small, ¾ to 2 inches long, short-pointed, the two sides slightly unequal, toothed, thick and leathery, smooth and shiny dark green above, paler and becoming nearly smooth beneath, turning to red or purple or remaining green into winter in warm climates. Flowers small, greenish, in clusters in fall. Fruits elliptical, ⅜ inch long, flattened. Native of northern and central China, Korea, and Japan. Planted especially in Gulf and Pacific States but hardy northward in the East. Used also for shelterbelts. Zone 5.

41. WHITE WILLOW, *Salix alba* L. Medium-sized tree with spreading branches and whitish foliage. Leaves lance-shaped, 2 to 4 inches long, long-pointed, finely toothed, whitish and silky beneath. Male and female flowers on different trees in early spring, minute, many in clusters 2 inches long. Capsules with cottony seeds. Native from Europe and northern Africa to central Asia. Grown for ornament in moist temperate regions of the United States and adjacent Canada, where it has become naturalized. A commonly planted variety or hybrid of this species with yellow branches (yellowstem white willow, golden willow; var. *vitellina* (L.) Stokes) is one of the basket willows. Both the typical form and this variety have been used in shelterbelts in the North. Zone 2.

42. WEEPING WILLOW, *Salix babylonica* L. (Babylon weeping willow). Small to medium-sized tree with long, slender, drooping branches. Bark gray, rough and fissured. Leaves narrowly lance-shaped, 2 to 6 inches long, long-pointed, finely toothed, dark green above and paler beneath, smooth. Male and female flowers on different trees in early spring, minute, many in clusters ¾ to 1½ inches long. Capsules with cottony seeds. Native of China. Long planted for its weeping foliage as a lawn and landscape tree in eastern United States, where it has become naturalized. Grown also in Western States. Adapted to moist soil and tolerant of city smoke. Zone (5).

43. LOMBARDY POPLAR, *Populus nigra* L. (black poplar is the typical variety; Lombardy poplar is a hybrid clone known as var. *italica* Muenchh.). Medium-sized to tall columnar tree with narrow crown of upright branches. Bark gray, furrowed. Leafstalks 1 to 2 inches long, slender, flattened. Leaf blades wedge-shaped or triangular, 1½ to 3 inches long, long-pointed, the edges with curved teeth, smooth or slightly hairy. The trees are male only and do not produce seeds, the male flowers many in clusters 2 inches long. Black poplar is native of Europe and western Asia. Lombardy poplar, distinguished by its columnar crown, is widely cultivated almost throughout the United States and spreads by root-sprouts. Grown especially in rows for shelterbelts, roadside trees, and formal effects. Short-lived and subject to European canker disease. Zone 2.

44. CAROLINA POPLAR, ×*Populus eugenei* Simon-Louis (*P. deltoides*×*nigra* var. *italica*, ×*P. canadensis* Moench var. *eugenei* (Simon-Louis) Schelle). Large tree with rounded, spreading crown. Bark gray, furrowed. Leafstalks 1 to 2 inches long, flattened. Leaf blades triangular, 3 to 4 inches long, long-pointed, the edges with curved teeth, shiny green and smooth on both sides. The trees are male only and not producing seeds, the male flowers many in clusters 3 inches long in early spring. A hybrid clone which probably originated in Europe. Extensively planted across the United States and spreads from cultivation by root-sprouts. Tolerant of city smoke and dust and quick growing, but not recommended for city planting because the roots penetrate sewers. Zone 4.

→

38. English elm. 39. Siberian elm. 40. Chinese elm. 41. White willow. 42. Weeping willow. 43. Lombardy poplar. 44. Carolina poplar. 45. White poplar. 46. European white birch. 47. White mulberry. 48. London planetree. 49. Chinese parasoltree. 50. English oak.

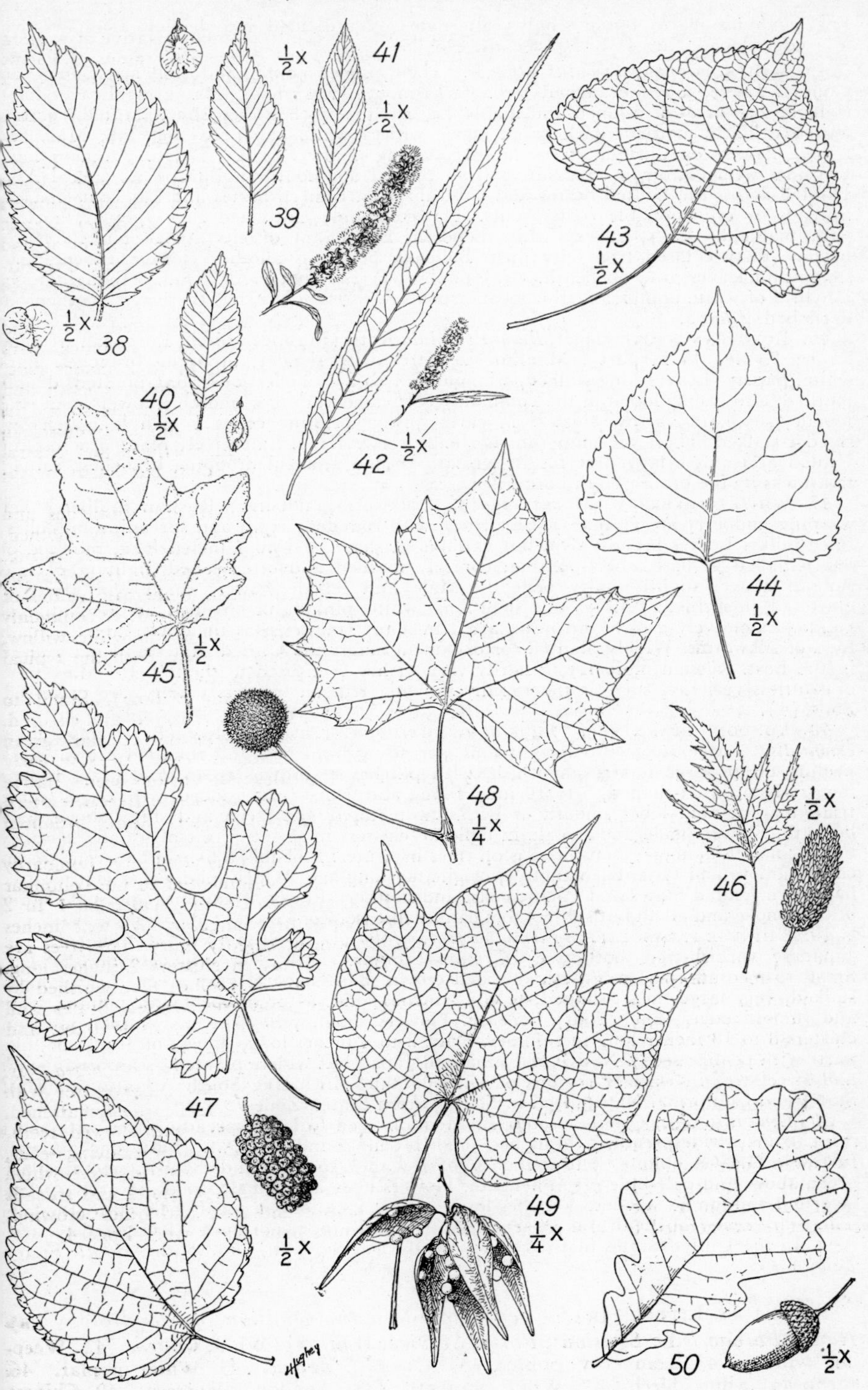

38
½ x
39
½ x
40
½ x
41
½ x
42
½ x
43
½ x
44
½ x
45
½ x
46
½ x
47
½ x
48
¼ x
49
¼ x
50
½ x

K. Deciduous leaves borne singly (alternate), not divided into leaflets (simple), lea edges lobed, Nos. 45 to 50 (see also No. 35).

45. WHITE POPLAR, *Populus alba* L. (ebele; silver poplar and Bolleana poplar ar clones). Large, much branched tree. Bark smooth, whitish or light gray. Leaves long stalked, oval or 3- or 5-lobed and maplelike, 2½ to 4 inches long, short-pointed, coarsel and irregularly toothed, dark green above with a white hairy coat beneath. Male an female flowers on different trees in early spring, many in clusters 2 to 3 inches long Capsules with cottony seeds. Native from central and southern Europe to central Asia Planted across the United States and naturalized in Eastern States and adjacent Canada Spreads by objectionable root-sprouts. The commonly cultivated silver poplar, a clon with maplelike leaves silvery white beneath, is tolerant of city smoke but its leave become dirty colored from city dust. Bolleana poplar is another clone with columna shape and leaves green beneath. Gray poplar (*P. canescens* (Ait.) Sm.), thought to b a hybrid of white poplar and European aspen (*P. tremula* L.), has the leaves toothed bu not lobed. Zone 3.

46. EUROPEAN WHITE BIRCH, *Betula pendula* Roth (European birch, European weepin birch; *B. alba* L. in part). Medium-sized tree with slender, drooping branches. Bar white, papery. Leaves long-stalked, triangular, 1 to 2½ inches long, long-pointed, doubl toothed, also deeply lobed in the commonly cultivated varieties, smooth. Flowers male an female, small, in narrow clusters in early spring. Fruiting cones 1 inch long, narrow slender-stalked. There are numerous horticultural varieties. Extensively planted across th United States as a lawn tree for its white bark and graceful drooping branches. Subjec to attacks by the bronze birch borer. Zone 2.

47. WHITE MULBERRY, *Morus alba* L. (silkworm mulberry; Russian mulberry an weeping mulberry are varieties). Small tree with rounded crown and spreading branches juice milky. Leaves broadly oval but variable in shape, 2½ to 7 inches long, rounded o heart-shaped at base, short-pointed, coarsely toothed and often lobed, light green and smooth above, slightly hairy beneath. Male and female flowers small and greenish, clustered, in spring. Fruits ⅜ to 1 inch long, white, pinkish, or purplish, edible. Native o China. Extensively grown and naturalized in many countries, as the leaves are the main food of silkworms. Widely planted for ornament across the United States and naturalized in the East. Russian mulberry, a hardy variety, has been used in shelterbelts. Male trees or fruitless varieties, such as the rapidly growing Kingan fruitless variety, are preferred Zone (4).

48. LONDON PLANETREE, ×*Platanus acerifolia* (Ait.) Willd. (*P. occidentalis*× *orientalis*). Large tree with upright axis, spreading branches, and rounded crown. Bark peeling off in large flakes, smoothish, with patches of brown, green, and gray. Leaves long-stalked, heart-shaped, 5 to 10 inches long and wide, 3- or 5-lobed, with edges of the triangular pointed lobes smooth or with few teeth, bright green and shiny above, pale beneath. Flowers male and female in ball-like clusters in spring. Fruit of usually 2 bristly balls 1 inch in diameter, conspicuous on trees in winter. Probably a hybrid between American sycamore and Oriental planetree, originated long ago. Widely planted as a street tree in eastern United States and Pacific coast and southern Rocky Mountain regions. Tolerant of city smoke and alkali but subject to a canker disease. Zone 5.

49. CHINESE PARASOLTREE, *Firmiana platanifolia* (L. f.) Schott & Endl. (Phoenix-tree, Japanese varnish-tree, bottletree; *Firmiana simplex* auth., *Sterculia platanifolia* L.). Small to medium-sized tree with rounded crown. Bark smooth, gray green. Leaves long-stalked, very large, heart-shaped, 6 to 12 inches long, 3- or 5-lobed with pointed lobes and smooth edges, finely hairy beneath. Flowers small, yellow green, ½ inch long, in clusters 8 to 18 inches long in summer. Fruit 2 to 4 inches long, showy, of 4 or 5 podlike parts with pealike seeds. Native of China and Japan but widely planted as an ornamental and street tree in warmer regions of United States, including South Atlantic and Gulf States and California. Naturalized in Southeastern States. Zone 7.

50. ENGLISH OAK, *Quercus robur* L. Medium-sized to large spreading tree with short stout trunk, widespreading branches, and broad rounded crown. Bark dark, deeply furrowed. Leaves oblong, 2 to 5 inches long, with 7 to 15 rounded lobes, smooth, dark green above and pale blue green beneath. Flowers male and female, small, in early spring. Acorns 1 to 5 on a stalk 1 to 3 inches long, ⅝ to 1 inch long, a third enclosed by the cup. There are many horticultural varieties. Native of Europe, northern Africa, and western Asia. In the United States planted chiefly in the Pacific, Gulf, and South Atlantic States. Zone 4.

ELBERT L. LITTLE, JR., *is dendrologist in the Division of Dendrology and Range Forage Investigations, Forest Service, Washington, D. C.*

# KEY FOR THE IDENTIFICATION OF WOODS WITHOUT THE AID OF A HAND LENS OR MICROSCOPE[1]

## HARDWOODS

Pores visible as minute rounded openings on smoothly cut end grain and as fine grooves on planed side-grain surfaces.

A. Ring-porous; that is, the pores at the beginning for each annual ring (springwood) are comparatively large, forming a distinct porous ring, and decrease in size more or less abruptly in the outer part of each annual ring (summerwood) where they are not visible without magnification.

1. Summerwood figured with light and dark irregular V-shaped radial patches.
   (a) Many rays broad and conspicuous. Wood heavy to very heavy.
   The OAKS
   ($a_1$) Many usually without reddish tinge. The large pores of the heartwood mostly closed (exception, chestnut oak).
   The WHITE OAK GROUP:
   WHITE OAK
   SWAMP WHITE OAK
   BUR OAK
   POST OAK
   CHINQUAPIN OAK
   SWAMP CHESTNUT OAK
   OVERCUP OAK
   CHESTNUT OAK
   OREGON WHITE OAK
   CALIFORNIA WHITE OAK
   ($b_1$) Wood with reddish tinge, especially near knots. The large pores of the heartwood mostly open (exception, blackjack oak).
   The RED OAK GROUP:
   NORTHERN RED OAK
   EASTERN RED OAK
   SOUTHERN RED OAK
   SWAMP RED OAK
   BLACK OAK
   SCARLET OAK
   PIN OAK
   WATER OAK
   WILLOW OAK
   LAUREL OAK
   BLACKJACK OAK
   CALIFORNIA BLACK OAK
   (b) Rays not noticeable. Color grayish brown. Wood moderately light.
   AMERICAN CHESTNUT
2. Summerwood figured with short or long wavy tangential lines or brands, in some woods (elms, hackberry, sugarberry, and mulberry) throughout the summerwood, in others more pronounced toward the outer part of the summerwood.
   (a) Heartwood bright cherry red. Pores in springwood mostly open and very distinct.
   ($a_1$) Rays plainly visible. Tangential bands in summerwood usually distinct, except in narrow rings. Pith small, commonly size of lead in ordinary pencil. Sapwood usually more than three-fourths inch wide. Wood very heavy.
   HONEYLOCUST
   ($b_1$) Rays not plainly visible. Tangential bands in summerwood obscure. Pith large, 0.2 to 0.3 inch in diameter. Sapwood usually less than three-fourths inch wide. Wood heavy.
   KENTUCKY COFFEETREE

---

[1] Unless otherwise directed, all observations as to structure should be made on the end surface of rings of average width, cut smoothly with a very sharp knife; and all observations as to color should be made on a freshly cut longitudinal surface of the heartwood. A reading glass will help to see some of the structural features more distinctly but should not be used in judging visibility with the unaided eye. Odor can best be determined on freshly cut surfaces of the heartwood.

The Key was prepared by Arthur Koehler, chief of the Division of Silvicultural Relations, Forest Products Laboratory, Madison, Wis.

802062°—49——54

(b) Heartwood brown with reddish tinge.

($a_1$) Tangential bands long and very conspicuous throughout the summerwoc

($a_2$) The porous ring of the springwood from 2 to 4 pores wide. Sapwo mostly less than 1 inch wide. Heartwood with characteristic odor slippery elm bark. Wood moderately heavy.

SLIPPERY EL

($b_2$) The porous ring of the springwood only one pore wide, except in ve wide rings. Sapwood mostly more than 1 inch in width.

($a_3$) Pores in springwood fairly conspicuous, open, and close togeth Wood moderately heavy.

AMERICAN EL

($b_3$) Pores in springwood inconspicuous because comparatively small, close and not close together. Wood heavy.

ROCK EL
CEDAR EL
WINGED EL

($b_1$) Tangential bands short, inconspicuous, and limited to outer summerwoo Springwood zone several pores wide. Sapwood more than 1 inch, usual several inches wide. Wood heavy.

WHITE AS
GREEN AS
OREGON AS

(c) Heartwood yellowish or golden brown becoming dark brown on exposu Pores in heartwood completely closed. Sapwood less than three-fourths in wide.

($a_1$) Wood heavy. Tangential bands uniformly distributed throughout the su merwood. Rays distinct.

RED MULBERR

($b_1$) Wood very heavy to very, very heavy. Tangential bands confined to, or mo pronounced in, the outer portion of the summerwood. Rays not distinct.

OSAGE-ORANGE

(d) Heartwood greenish brown. Pores in heartwood completely closed. Rays n distinct. Sapwood less than three-fourths inch wide. Woods very heavy to ver very heavy.

BLACK LOCUST

(e) Heartwood silvery brown, with spicy odor and taste. Rays not distinct. Sa wood less than three-fourths inch wide. Wood moderately heavy.

SASSAFRA

(f) Heartwood grayish brown with lavender tinge, after prolonged exposu resembling butternut or black walnut in color. Sapwood narrow, rarely mo than three-fourths inch wide. Wood moderately light.

NORTHERN CATALP

(g) Heartwood yellowish or light greenish gray, not distinct from the sapwoo Tangential bands long and very conspicuous throughout the summerwoc (resembling slippery elm except for color). Rays fairly distinct. Wood mo erately heavy.

HACKBERR
SUGARBERR

3. Summerwood not figured with radial or tangential patterns visible without a len

(a) Heartwood reddish brown. Sapwood more than 1 inch wide.

($a_1$) Pores decreasing in size abruptly from springwood to summerwood. Woo heavy to very heavy.

TRUE HICKORIES
SHAGBARK HICKORY
SHELLBARK HICKOR
MOCKERNUT HICKOF
PIGNUT HICKORY

($b_1$) Pores decreasing in size more or less gradually from springwood to sun merwood. Wood heavy.

PECA
WATER HICKOR

[2] Osage-orange sometimes is difficult to distinguish from black locust wood, but whe put on a wet cloth or blotter, Osage-orange heartwood gives off a distinct yellow color i a few minutes, whereas black locust does so only faintly or not at all. Dry black locus heartwood fluoresces brilliant yellow in ultra violet light; Osage-orange does not fluoresc when dry.

(b) Heartwood light cherry red. Sapwood usually less than three-fourths inch wide. Wood heavy.

KENTUCKY COFFEETREE

(c) Heartwood grayish brown. Sapwood usually less than three-fourths inch wide. Wood moderately heavy.

BLACK ASH

**B.** Diffuse-porous; that is, no ring of large pores is formed at the beginning of each annual ring, the pores being uniform in size or gradually decreasing in size from the inner to the outer part of each annual ring.

1. Individual pores plainly visible on end grain and side grain, gradually decreasing in size from inner to outer part of each annual ring.

(a) Some rays broad and conspicuous, fully as wide as the largest pores. Pores arranged in radial groups extending across the annual rings.

($a_1$) Southern species. Wood exceedingly heavy.

LIVE OAK

($b_1$) Western species. Wood very heavy.

CANYON LIVE OAK

(b) All rays smaller than the largest pores. The pores not arranged in radial groups extending across the rings.

($a_1$) Tangential surface marked with very fine bands which run across the grain and are due to the storied arrangement of the rays. Heartwood black, or brownish black (usually very small). Sapwood wide, white or pale gray. Wood very, very heavy.

COMMON PERSIMMON

($b_1$) Tangential surface not marked with fine cross bands.

($a_2$) Heartwood reddish brown. Sapwood wide. Wood heavy.

WATER HICKORY

($b_2$) Heartwood chocolate or purplish brown. Sapwood narrow to moderate in width. Wood heavy.

BLACK WALNUT

($c_2$) Heartwood light chestnut brown, frequently with dark springwood and pinkish-brown summerwood. Sapwood narrow. Wood moderately light.

BUTTERNUT

**2.** Individual pores barely visible under conditions of good light and a very smoothly cut surface, fairly uniform in size throughout each annual ring.

(a) Pores not crowded on end surface. Heartwood reddish brown.

($a_1$) Wood heavy to very heavy. Pith flecks very rare.

YELLOW BIRCH
SWEET BIRCH

($b_1$) Wood moderately heavy. Pith flecks common.

PAPER BIRCH
RIVER BIRCH

(b) Pores crowded on end surface. Wood light.

($a_1$) Heartwood grayish.

COTTONWOOD

($b_1$) Heartwood dark reddish brown.

BLACK WILLOW

($c_1$) Heartwood light reddish brown.

WHITE WILLOW

**[illegible].** Pores not visible.

A. Rays comparatively broad and conspicuous. Color of heartwood in various shades of light reddish brown.

1. The rays crowded on end grain; up to three-sixteenths inch high on radial and tangential surfaces, producing pronounced, crowded, "flakes" when quarter-sawed. No denser and darker band of summerwood noticeable. Wood usually has interlocked grain; moderately heavy.

SYCAMORE

2. The broad rays not crowded; up to one-eighth inch high on radial and tangential surfaces, producing scattered "flakes" when quarter-sawed. A distinct, denser, and darker band of summerwood present. Wood usually fairly straight-grained; heavy.

BEECH

B. Rays not conspicuous but distinctly visible.

1. Heartwood deep, rich, reddish brown. Sapwood narrow, usually less than 1 inch wide. Annual rings clearly defined. Rays very distinct. Wood moderately heavy.

BLACK CHERRY

2. Heartwood dingy, reddish brown, often with darker streaks. Sapwood moderate wide, usually more than 1 inch. Annual rings not clearly defined. Rays relative not very distinct. Wood moderately heavy.

SWEETGU

3. Heartwood light grayish brown with reddish tinge. Sapwood more than 1 in wide. Annual rings clearly defined by a thin, darker reddish-brown layer. Ra very distinct.

(a) Wood heavy; difficult to cut across the grain. Pith flecks very rare.

SUGAR MAPI
BLACK MAPI

(b) Wood moderately heavy; rather easy to cut across the grain. Pith flecks oft abundant.

SILVER MAPI
RED MAPI
BIGLEAF MAPL

4. Heartwood light yellowish brown with greenish tinge, occasionally purplish. Sa wood usually more than 1 inch wide. Annual rings clearly defined. Rays fair distinct. Wood moderately light to moderately heavy.

YELLOW-POPLA
CUCUMBERTRI
SOUTHERN MAGNOLI

5. Heartwood creamy brown. Sapwood wide and not sharply defined from t heartwood. Rays fairly distinct. Wood light.

BASSWOO

C. Rays not distinctly visible.

1. Annual rings not clearly divided into a band of soft springwood and denser ar darker band of summerwood and, therefore, not conspicuous.

(a) The heartwood distinctly darker than the sapwood.

($a_1$) Heartwood reddish brown. Wood not cross-grained.

($a_2$) Wood heavy to very heavy. Pith flecks very rare.

YELLOW BIRC
SWEET BIRC

($b_2$) Wood moderately heavy. Pith flecks common.

PAPER BIRC
RIVER BIRC

($c_2$) Wood light.

($a_3$) Heartwood dark reddish brown.

BLACK WILLO

($b_3$) Heartwood light reddish brown.

WHITE WILLO

($b_1$) Heartwood grayish brown.

($a_2$) Wood cross-grained; moderately light to moderately heavy.

BLACK TUPELO (BLACKGUM
WATER TUPEL

($b_2$) Wood fairly straight-grained; light.

COTTONWOO

(b) The heartwood light-colored, not distinctly darker than the sapwood.

($a_1$) Wood light in weight; odorless and tasteless.

($a_2$) Color yellowish white.

YELLOW BUCKEY
OHIO BUCKEY

($b_2$) Color plain white, sometimes partly discolored to pale salmon brow near center of tree or around knots.

QUAKING ASPE
BIGTOOTH ASPE

## SOFTWOODS

($b_1$) Wood moderately light. Odor of heartwood spicy; color pale brown.

PORT-ORFORD-CEDA

($c_1$) Wood moderately heavy. Odor of heartwood pungently disagreeable, n spicy; color light canary yellow.

ALASKA-CEDA

2. Annual rings clearly divided into a band of soft springwood and a denser an darker band of summerwood. Although the summerwood may not be pronounce yet the annual rings are always clearly defined by it.

(a) Wood resinous, as indicated by exudations of resin, or pitch, especially whe heated, the presence of occasional pitch pockets or pitch streaks, or th presence on longitudinal surfaces of brownish lines (resin ducts) from a fraction of an inch to several inches long.

($a_1$) Heartwood darker than the sapwood.

($a_2$) Heartwood reddish brown or orange brown. Resin ducts abundant. Heartwood with "piney" odor.

($a_3$) The summerwood inconspicuous and not much darker or harder than the springwood. Wood light to moderately light.

The SOFT PINES:

($a_4$) Eastern species.

EASTERN WHITE PINE

($b_4$) Western species.

WESTERN WHITE PINE
SUGAR PINE

($b_3$) The summerwood conspicuously darker and harder than the springwood.

The HARD PINES:

($a_4$) Wood moderately light.

($a_5$) Western species.

($a_6$) Heartwood not much darker than sapwood. Tangential surface slightly dimpled, as if hit lightly with coarse shot. Sapwood usually less than 2 inches wide.

LODGEPOLE PINE

($b_6$) Heartwood distinctly darker than sapwood after exposure to air and light. Tangential surface not dimpled, or only in narrow-ringed wood. Sapwood usually more than 2 inches wide.

PONDEROSA PINE

($b_5$) Northeastern species.

JACK PINE
RED PINE

($b_4$) Wood moderately heavy to very heavy. Eastern and southern species.

VIRGINIA PINE
PITCH PINE
SHORTLEAF PINE
LOBLOLLY PINE
POND PINE
LONGLEAF PINE
SLASH PINE

($b_2$) Heartwood light orange red to cherry red. Resin ducts scarce. Tangential surface not dimpled. Heartwood with characteristic, but not "piney," odor.

DOUGLAS-FIR

($c_2$) Heartwood pinkish to pale reddish brown. Resin ducts scarce. Tangential surface slightly dimpled, as if lightly hit with coarse shot, except in wide-ringed wood. Wood without distinct odor.

SITKA SPRUCE

($b_1$) Heartwood not appreciably darker than the sapwood. Resin ducts present but scarce and inconspicuous. Wood without distinct odor.

WHITE SPRUCE
RED SPRUCE
ENGELMANN SPRUCE

(b) Wood not resinous.

($a_1$) Heartwood decidedly darker than the sapwood.

($a_2$) Heartwood medium to dark reddish brown.

($a_3$) Heartwood without odor or taste. Wood moderately light.

REDWOOD

($b_3$) Heartwood with spicy odor and taste (like cedar shingles). Wood light.

WESTERN REDCEDAR

($c_3$) Heartwood with aromatic odor and taste. Wood moderately heavy.

EASTERN REDCEDAR

($b_2$) Heartwood light brown, with spicy odor and taste. Wood light.

NORTHERN WHITE-CEDAR

($c_2$) Heartwood light pinkish brown, with aromatic odor. Wood light.

ATLANTIC WHITE-CEDAR

($d_2$) Heartwood variable from pale brown to dark brown, with rancid odor but without taste. Wood variable from moderately light to moderately heavy.

BALDCYPRESS

(b₁) Heartwood only slightly darker than sapwood.

(a₂) Heartwood light canary yellow, odor not spicy or aromatic, somewha disagreeable. Wood moderately heavy.

ALASKA-CEDA

(b₂) Heartwood pale brown, odor pungently spicy. Wood moderately ligh

PORT-ORFORD-CEDA

(c₁) Heartwood not appreciably darker than sapwood when dry.

(a₂) Springwood white, summerwood light brown with lavender tinge.

WHITE FI
GRAND FI

(b₂) Springwood and summerwood pale reddish brown.

(a₃) Heartwood with disagreeable odor, especially when moist.

NOBLE FI
CALIFORNIA RED FI

(b₃) Heartwood without disagreeable odor.

EASTERN HEMLOC
WESTERN HEMLOC

---

ESTIMATED OUTPUT AND VALUE OF NONMANUFACTURED FOREST PRODUCTS IN TH UNITED STATES, 1947

| *Product* | | *Output, units cut* | *Total value at mill or local point of delivery* |
|---|---|---|---|
| | | *Number* | *Million dollars* |
| Sawlogs | billion board feet [1] | 35.5 | 1, 2 |
| Veneer logs and bolts | do | 2.3 | 1 |
| Cooperage logs and bolts | million standard cords | 1.4 | 3 |
| Pulpwood logs | billion board feet [1] | 1.8 | 5 |
| Pulpwood bolts | million standard cords | 14.4 | 20 |
| Other logs | billion board feet [1] | .4 | 1 |
| Other bolts | million standard cords | 1.1 | 2 |
| Fuel wood from live timber | do | 27.8 | 30 |
| Other fuel wood | do | 27.9 | 19 |
| Chemical wood | do | .4 | |
| Piling | million linear feet | 34.4 | 1 |
| Poles | million pieces | 7.5 | 3 |
| Mine timbers (not sawed) | do | 68.9 | 2 |
| Hewn ties | do | 23.6 | 2 |
| Posts | do | 234.7 | 6 |
| Crude gum for naval stores | | ........ | 3 |
| Pine distillation wood (naval stores) | million tons | 2.3 | 1 |
| Christmas trees | million trees | 21.4 | [2] |
| Maple sirup and sugar | | ........ | [3] 1 |
| Miscellaneous | | ........ | |
| Total | | ........ | 2, 41 |

[1] International ¼-inch rule. [2] 1946 data. [3] Bureau of Agricultural Economics data.

## AVERAGE WEIGHTS OF COMMERCIALLY IMPORTANT WOODS

| *Species* | *Weight per cubic foot in sawed form air-dry (12-percent moisture content)* | *Weight per 1,000 board feet (nominal size air-dry (12-percent moisture content)* |
|---|---|---|
| | *Pounds* | *Pounds* |
| Alaska-cedar | 31 | 2,580 |
| Alder, red | 28 | 2,330 |
| Ash, black | 34 | 2,830 |
| Ash, commercial white [1] | 41 | 3,420 |
| Ash, Oregon | 38 | 3,160 |
| spen | 26 | 2,170 |
| Baldcypress | 32 | 2,670 |
| Basswood | 26 | 2,170 |
| Beech | 45 | 3,750 |
| Birch [2] | 44 | 3,670 |
| Birch, paper | 38 | 3,160 |
| Butternut | 27 | 2,250 |
| Cherry, black | 35 | 2,930 |
| Chestnut | 30 | 2,500 |
| Cottonwood, eastern | 28 | 2,330 |
| Cottonwood, northern black | 24 | 2,000 |
| Douglas-fir (coast region) | 34 | 2,830 |
| Douglas-fir ("Inland Empire" region) | 31 | 2,580 |
| Douglas-fir (Rocky Mountain region) | 30 | 2,500 |
| lm, American | 35 | 2,920 |
| lm, rock | 44 | 3,670 |
| lm, slippery | 37 | 3,080 |
| ir, balsam | 25 | 2,080 |
| ir, commercial white [3] | 27 | 2,250 |
| Gum, black | 35 | 2,920 |
| Gum, tupelo | 35 | 2,920 |
| Hackberry | 37 | 3,080 |
| Hemlock, eastern | 28 | 2,330 |
| Hemlock, western | 29 | 2,420 |
| Hickory, pecan [4] | 45 | 3,750 |
| ickory, true [5] | 51 | 4,250 |
| oneylocust | ........ | ........ |
| ncense-cedar | ........ | ........ |

| *Species* | *Weight per cubic foot in sawed form air-dry (12-percent moisture content)* | *Weight per 1,000 board feet (nominal size) air-dry (12-percent moisture content)* |
|---|---|---|
| | *Pounds* | *Pounds* |
| Larch, western | 36 | 3,000 |
| Locust, black | 48 | 4,000 |
| Magnolia, cucumber | 33 | 2,750 |
| Magnolia, evergreen | 35 | 2,920 |
| Maple, bigleaf | 34 | 2,830 |
| Maple, black | 40 | 3,330 |
| Maple, red | 38 | 3,170 |
| Maple, silver | 33 | 2,750 |
| Maple, sugar | 44 | 3,670 |
| Oak, red [6] | 44 | 3,670 |
| Oak, white [7] | 47 | 3,920 |
| Pine, lodgepole | 29 | 2,420 |
| Pine, eastern white | 25 | 2,080 |
| Pine, red | 34 | 2,830 |
| Pine, ponderosa | 28 | 2,330 |
| Pines, southern yellow: | | |
| Loblolly | 36 | 3,000 |
| Longleaf | 41 | 3,420 |
| Shortleaf | 36 | 3,000 |
| Pine, sugar | 25 | 2,080 |
| Pine, western white | 27 | 2,250 |
| Port-Orford-cedar | 29 | 2,420 |
| Redcedar, eastern | 33 | 2,750 |
| Redcedar, western | 23 | 1,920 |
| Redwood | 28 | 2,330 |
| Redgum | 34 | 2,830 |
| Spruce, eastern [8] | 28 | 2,330 |
| Spruce, Engelmann | 23 | 1,920 |
| Spruce, Sitka | 28 | 2,330 |
| Sugarberry | 36 | 3,000 |
| Sycamore | 34 | 2,830 |
| Tamarack | 37 | 3,080 |
| Walnut, black | 38 | 3,170 |
| White-cedar, northern | 22 | 1,830 |
| White-cedar, southern | 23 | 1,920 |
| Yellow-poplar | 28 | 2,330 |

[1] Average of Biltmore white ash, blue ash, green ash, and white ash.

[2] Average of sweet birch and yellow birch.

[3] Average of lowland white fir and white fir.

[4] Average of bitternut hickory, nutmeg hickory, water hickory, and pecan.

[5] Average of bigleaf shagbark hickory, mockernut hickory, pignut hickory, and shagbark hickory.

[6] Average of black oak, laurel oak, pin oak, red oak, scarlet oak, southern red oak, swamp red oak, water oak, and willow oak.

[7] Average of bur oak, chestnut oak, post oak, swamp chestnut oak, swamp white oak, and white oak.

[8] Average of black spruce, red spruce, and white spruce.

## BROAD CLASSIFICATION OF WOODS ACCORDING TO CHARACTERISTICS

[A, among the woods relatively high in the particular respect listed; B, among the woods intermediate in the particular respect listed; C, among the woods relatively low in the particular respect listed]

| Kind of wood | *Working and behavior characteristics* | | | | | | | | | | | *Strength properties* | | | | *Surface characteristics of common grades* | | | | | | *Distinctive uses* | |
|---|---|---|---|---|---|---|---|---|---|---|---|---|---|---|---|---|---|---|---|---|---|---|---|
| *Kind of wood* | *Hardness* | *Weight, dry* | *Freedom from shrinkage* | *Freedom from warping* | *Ease of working* | *Paint holding* | *Nail holding* | *Decay resistance of heartwood* | *Proportion[1] of heartwood* | *Amount of figure* | *Freedom from odor and taste (dry)* | *Bending strength* | *Stiffness* | *Strength as a post* | *Toughness* | *Number of knots* | *Size of knots* | *Number of pitch defects* | *Size of pitch defects* | *Number of other defects* | *Size of other defects* | *Farm* | *Commercial* |
| 1 | 2 | 3 | 4 | 5 | 6 | 7 | 8 | 9 | 10 | 11 | 12 | 13 | 14 | 15 | 16 | 17 | 18 | 19 | 20 | 21 | 22 | 23 | 24 |
| Ash: Black | A | B | C | B | C | ... | ... | C | C | A | ... | B | B | C | A | C | B | None | ... | B | B | Implements | |
| Ash: White | A | A | B | B | C | ... | A | C | C | A | A | A | A | A | A | C | B | None | ... | B | B | Handles, implements | Handles, vehicle. |
| Baldcypress | B | B | B | B | B | A | B | A | B | A | B | B | B | B | B | C | B | None | ... | B | B | Silos, tanks, construction. | Greenhouses, tanks, construction. |
| Basswood | C | C | C | B | A | ... | C | C | C | C | A | C | B | C | C | C | B | None | ... | C | C | Woodenware | Fixtures, furniture parts. |
| Beech | A | A | C | C | C | ... | A | C | B | B | A | A | A | B | A | B | B | None | ... | A | A | Woodenware, containers, fuel. | Woodenware, flooring, furniture. |
| Birch, yellow | A | A | C | B | C | ... | A | C | C | B | A | A | A | B | A | C | B | None | ... | B | B | Millwork, furniture. | Millwork, furniture. |
| Cherry | A | B | B | A | C | ... | ... | ... | B | B | B | A | A | A | B | C | B | None | ... | ... | ... | Furniture | Electrotype blocks. |
| Chestnut | B | B | B | A | B | ... | B | A | A | A | B | C | C | C | B | C | A | None | ... | A | B | Poles, posts, trim | Caskets, poles, core stock. |
| Cottonwood | C | B | C | C | B | ... | C | C | C | C | B | C | B | C | B | C | C | None | ... | C | C | Wagon boxes, containers. | Boxes, cases, furniture parts. |
| Douglas-fir | B | B | B | B | C | C | B | B | A | A | C | A | A | A | B | B | B | B | B | B | B | Construction | Construction. |
| Elm: Rock | A | A | C | B | C | ... | ... | B | B | A | A | A | A | B | A | B | B | None | ... | B | B | Implements | Cooperage. |
| Elm: Soft | A | A | C | C | C | ... | A | B | B | A | A | B | B | B | A | B | B | None | ... | A | A | Cheese boxes | Containers. |
| Fir: Balsam | C | C | B | B | B | B | ... | C | B | B | A | C | C | C | C | A | C | None | ... | B | B | Light construction | Pulpwood. |
| Fir: White | C | C | B | B | B | B | C | C | C | B | A | B | B | B | C | B | B | None | ... | B | A | do | Light construction, pulpwood. |
| Hackberry | A | A | C | B | C | ... | ... | ... | C | A | A | B | C | C | A | C | A | None | ... | B | B | Furniture | Automobile bodies. |
| Hemlock: | | | | | | | | | | | | | | | | | | | | | | | |
| Eastern | B | B | B | B | B | B | B | C | B | B | A | B | B | B | B | B | B | None | ... | A | A | Construction | Construction. |
| Western | B | B | B | B | B | B | B | C | B | B | A | B | A | B | B | B | B | None | ... | B | B | do | Do. |
| Hickory: Pecan | A | A | C | B | C | ... | ... | C | B | B | ... | A | A | A | A | C | A | None | ... | A | A | Wagon and buggy parts. | Furniture, automobile bodies. |

| | | | | | | | | | | | | | | | | | | | | | | | |
|---|---|---|---|---|---|---|---|---|---|---|---|---|---|---|---|---|---|---|---|---|---|---|---|
| Larch, western | A | A | B | B | C | C | A | B | A | A | C | A | A | A | B | A | C | C | C | A | C | Construction | Construction |
| Locust, black | A | A | B | B | C | ... | A | A | A | A | B | A | A | A | A | B | B | None | | B | B | Fence posts | Insulator pins. |
| Maple: Hard | A | A | C | B | C | ... | A | C | C | B | A | A | A | A | A | B | B | None | | B | B | Implements, flooring. | Flooring, furniture, machine parts. |
| Maple: Soft | A | A | B | B | C | ... | A | C | C | B | A | C | C | C | C | C | B | None | | C | C | Fuel | Furniture. |
| Oak: Red | A | A | C | B | C | ... | A | C | B | A | ....... | A | A | B | A | C | A | None | | B | B | Implement parts, construction. | Furniture, flooring. |
| Oak: White | A | A | C | B | C | ... | A | A | B | A | ....... | A | A | B | A | C | A | None | | B | B | Implement parts, posts, building. | Cooperage, furniture, flooring. |
| Pine: | | | | | | | | | | | | | | | | | | | | | | | |
| Eastern white | C | C | A | A | A | A | B | (2) | B | C | C | C | C | C | C | A | C | C | C | B | B | Millwork, siding | Millwork, planing-mill products, etc. |
| Ponderosa | C | B | B | A | A | B | B | (2) | C | C | C | C | C | C | C | B | B | B | B | B | B | Millwork, light construction. | Millwork, planing-mill products, etc. |
| Southern yellow | A | A | B | B | C | C | A | B | C | A | C | A | A | A | B | C | A | A | A | B | B | Construction | Construction. |
| Sugar | C | C | A | A | A | A | ... | (2) | B | C | C | C | C | C | C | A | B | C | C | B | C | Millwork | Patterns, millwork. |
| Western white | C | B | B | A | A | A | B | (2) | B | C | C | B | B | B | B | A | C | C | C | A | C | Millwork, siding | Millwork, etc. |
| Redcedar: | | | | | | | | | | | | | | | | | | | | | | | |
| Eastern | A | A | A | A | B | ...... | | A | B | B | C | B | C | A | B | A | C | None | | C | C | Posts | Chests, pencils. |
| Western | C | C | A | A | A | A | C | A | A | B | C | C | C | B | C | C | A | None | | C | C | Posts, shingles, siding, and poles. | Poles, shingles, siding. |
| Redwood | B | B | A | A | B | A | B | A | A | B | ...... | B | B | A | B | C | A | None | | C | B | Silos, tanks, construction. | Tanks, planing-mill products, etc. |
| Spruce: | | | | | | | | | | | | | | | | | | | | | | | |
| Eastern | C | B | B | A | B | B | B | C | C | B | A | B | B | B | B | A | C | C | C | B | B | Construction | Pulpwood, musical instruments. |
| Sitka | C | B | B | A | B | B | ... | C | C | B | A | B | A | B | B | B | B | C | B | B | B | Ladders, building. | Airplanes, building. |
| Sweetgum | B | B | C | C | B | ... | B | B | B | B | B | B | B | B | B | C | B | None | | C | C | Boxes for food. | Furniture, boxes. |
| Sycamore | A | A | C | C | C | ... | A | C | B | B | ....... | B | B | B | B | C | B | None | | B | B | Baskets and boxes. | Boxes, millwork. |
| Tupelo | A | A | B | C | C | ... | A | C | C | C | A | B | B | B | B | C | C | None | | C | C | Fruit and vegetable boxes. | Factory flooring, boxes and crates. |
| Walnut | A | A | B | A | B | ...... | | A | B | B | ...... | A | A | A | A | C | B | None | | C | C | Furniture | Furniture, millwork. |
| White-cedar: | | | | | | | | | | | | | | | | | | | | | | | |
| Atlantic | C | C | A | A | A | A | ... | A | A | C | C | C | C | C | C | ........ | | None | | | | Posts, poles, shingles. | Boat and tank stock poles. |
| Northern | C | C | A | A | A | A | C | A | A | C | C | C | C | C | C | A | C | None | | C | C | Posts, shingles | Posts, poles, boats. |
| Yellow-poplar | C | B | B | A | A | ... | B | C | B | B | A | B | B | C | C | C | B | None | | C | C | Millwork | Millwork, furniture. |

[1] Exclusive of the all-heartwood grades available on special order in birch, cedar, baldcypress, Douglas-fir, sweetgum, southern yellow pine, redwood, walnut.

[2] Conflicting opinion and absence of adequate test data preclude a definite rating; one should not rely on high decay resistance when this wood is used untreated.

## COMPARATIVE STATEMENT OF MATERIAL TREATED IN THE UNITED STATES, VARIOUS YEARS*

[Quantity—cubic feet]

| Preservative | Year | Cross ties | Switch ties[1] | Piles | Poles[2] | Wood blocks | Cross arms | Construction timbers | Miscellaneous material | Total |
|---|---|---|---|---|---|---|---|---|---|---|
| Creosote[3] | 1910 | 44,525,229 | ........... | 5,219,254 | 255,597 | 4,692,453 | 88,069 | 7,801,272 | 2,687,713 | 65,269,587 |
| | 1930 | 117,179,841 | 10,685,378 | 16,570,876 | 70,498,226 | 5,002,733 | 1,115,944 | 16,646,617 | 7,977,750 | 245,677,365 |
| | 1940 | 70,184,412 | 5,253,407 | 15,249,088 | 72,029,690 | 2,729,228 | 650,799 | 9,315,869 | 13,189,445 | 188,601,938 |
| | 1942 | 98,406,987 | 10,125,804 | 27,291,087 | 49,480,446 | 10,686,937 | 703,567 | 10,698,130 | 18,815,171 | 226,208,129 |
| | 1944 | 94,416,927 | 7,850,606 | 18,077,871 | 51,632,874 | 2,445,602 | 1,440,327 | 7,380,483 | 14,662,834 | 197,907,524 |
| | 1946 | 82,203,660 | 5,122,373 | 8,217,620 | 55,636,893 | 3,082,606 | 631,484 | 4,542,763 | 9,521,200 | 168,958,599 |
| Creosote-petroleum[4] | 1935 | 36,760,266 | 2,744,975 | 448,676 | 29,920 | ........... | ......... | 1,405,727 | 146,270 | 41,535,834 |
| | 1940 | 55,064,619 | 3,523,771 | 393,316 | 117,339 | 793 | 19,280 | 2,346,351 | 615,051 | 62,080,520 |
| | 1942 | 60,899,574 | 3,716,649 | 759,392 | 218,328 | 533 | 4,202 | 3,012,167 | 1,696,480 | 70,307,325 |
| | 1944 | 63,497,232 | 3,136,396 | 267,244 | 10,349 | 19,351 | ......... | 2,177,344 | 1,477,689 | 70,585,605 |
| | 1946 | 49,417,914 | 2,212,803 | 833,526 | 17,497,964 | 788,770 | 159,185 | 2,412,877 | 3,248,642 | 76,571,681 |
| Creosote-petroleum-copper-naphthenate[5] | 1946 | 4,379,124 | 151,757 | 178,568 | 12,159,066 | ........... | 6,601 | 11,941 | 647,639 | 17,534,696 |
| Zinc creosote[6] | 1920 | 7,414,866 | ........... | 79,354 | .......... | .......... | ......... | 484,123 | 5,231 | 7,983,574 |
| | 1930 | 4,034,838 | 296,481 | .......... | .......... | .......... | ......... | ........... | 54,312 | 4,385,631 |
| Zinc chloride | 1920 | 87,398,160 | ........... | .......... | .......... | .......... | ......... | 1,823,437 | 94,151 | 89,315,748 |
| | 1930 | 19,278,987 | 854,415 | .......... | .......... | .......... | ......... | 93,758 | 912,405 | 21,139,565 |
| | 1940 | 1,808,928 | 57,755 | .......... | 2,447 | .......... | ......... | 17,119 | 423,697 | 2,309,946 |
| | 1942 | 1,289,979 | 44,615 | .......... | .......... | .......... | ......... | 39,594 | 159,752 | 1,533,940 |
| | 1945 | 1,386 | 876 | 2,010 | .......... | .......... | ......... | 179,289 | 274,899 | 458,460 |
| | 1946 | 538,212 | ........... | .......... | .......... | .......... | ......... | ........... | 109,669 | 650,740 |
| | 1940 | 484,818 | 1,367 | 1,777 | 885,315 | .......... | ......... | 663,837 | 3,968,155 | 6,005,269 |
| Chromated zinc chloride | 1942 | 766,647 | 24,504 | 32,778 | 64,821 | ........... | 47 | 1,579,704 | 2,629,902 | 5,098,403 |
| | 1945 | 4,443 | 16,374 | .......... | 15,752 | 24 | 10,914 | 135,243 | 2,080,434 | 2,263,184 |
| | 1946 | 62,937 | 2,859 | 2,381 | 103,646 | ........... | 107,667 | 246,813 | [illegible] | [illegible] |

| | | | | | | | | | | |
|---|---|---|---|---|---|---|---|---|---|---|
| | 1945 | 233,265 | 16,441 | 8,423 | 8,360 | ........ | ........ | 177,056 | 1,733,581 | 2,177,126 |
| | 1946 | 3,000 | ........ | ........ | 8,184 | ........ | 6,585 | 235,260 | 5,529,126 | 5,782,155 |
| Zinc meta arsenite...... | 1940 | 215,289 | ........ | ........ | 65,067 | ........ | 4,847 | 76,474 | 163,903 | 525,580 |
| | 1942 | 329,619 | ........ | ........ | 122,214 | ........ | 1,911 | 182,503 | 161,582 | 797,829 |
| | 1945 | ........ | ........ | ........ | 1,056 | ........ | ........ | 15,592 | 10,723 | 27,371 |
| Celcure............... | 1942 | ........ | ........ | ........ | ........ | ........ | ........ | ........ | 433,573 | 433,573 |
| | 1945 | ........ | ........ | ........ | ........ | ........ | ........ | ........ | 217,895 | 217,895 |
| | 1946 | ........ | ........ | ........ | 1,690 | ........ | 417 | ........ | 196,449 | 198,556 |
| Pentachlorophenol [7]..... | 1945 | 13,866 | 1,659 | ........ | 338,342 | ........ | 3,349 | 38,197 | 305,871 | 701,284 |
| Creosote-petroleum-pentachlorophenol........ | 1946 | 54,495 | 2,322 | 831,002 | 26,426,835 | 18,606 | 259,086 | 62,083 | 1,801,004 | 29,455,433 |
| Petroleum pentachlorophenol............... | 1946 | 347,658 | 29,302 | 24,945 | 2,437,983 | ........ | 13,855 | 14,525 | 231,664 | 3,099,932 |
| Miscellaneous [8]......... | 1935 | 330,210 | 1,120 | 15,389 | 422,206 | ........ | 109 | 1,176,300 | 979,079 | 2,924,413 |
| | 1940 | 190,080 | 12,432 | ........ | 102,168 | ........ | ........ | 28,743 | 343,220 | 676,643 |
| | 1942 | 444,072 | 11,799 | 388,664 | 700,322 | ........ | ........ | 174,768 | 1,882,513 | 3,602,138 |
| | 1945 | 32,907 | 1,286 | 60,917 | 81,963 | ........ | ........ | 126,178 | 830,761 | 1,134,012 |
| | 1946 | 66,531 | 1,004 | 8,150 | 137,949 | ........ | ........ | 34,834 | 1,395,391 | 1,643,859 |
| All preservatives, ...... | 1910 | 78,467,031 | ........ | 5,257,646 | 255,597 | 4,692,453 | 88,069 | 8,523,929 | 2,789,419 | 100,074,144 |
| | 1915 | 111,256,755 | ........ | 6,295,284 | 2,512,780 | 7,707,971 | 90,627 | 11,834,087 | 1,161,459 | 140,858,963 |
| | 1920 | 134,962,596 | ........ | 8,092,546 | 10,309,746 | 6,741,410 | 318,707 | 11,645,811 | 1,238,689 | 173,309,505 |
| | 1925 | 187,691,733 | 13,616,760 | 9,636,747 | 42,204,413 | 3,408,489 | 621,705 | 14,375,693 | 2,918,999 | 274,474,539 |

*For footnotes, see end of table.

## COMPARATIVE STATEMENT OF MATERIAL TREATED IN THE UNITED STATES, VARIOUS YEARS—continued

[Quantity—cubit feet]

| *Preservative* | *Year* | *Cross ties* | *Switch ties* | *Piles* | *Poles* | *Wood blocks* | *Cross arms* | *Construction timbers* | *Miscellaneous material* | *Total* |
|---|---|---|---|---|---|---|---|---|---|---|
| All preservatives...... | 1930 | 189, 801, 321 | 14, 622, 713 | 17, 027, 153 | 75, 258, 146 | 5, 012, 445 | 1, 299, 246 | 19, 013, 369 | 10, 284, 184 | 332, 318, 577 |
| | 1935 | 103, 509, 441 | 7, 836, 488 | 8, 574, 542 | 35, 793, 120 | 1, 483, 810 | 351, 476 | 15, 683, 306 | 6, 206, 787 | 179, 438, 970 |
| | 1940 | 127, 999, 794 | 8, 859, 145 | 15, 659, 660 | 74, 129, 493 | 2, 730, 021 | 674, 988 | 12, 496, 453 | 22, 923, 595 | 265, 473, 149 |
| | 1942 | 162, 526, 140 | 13, 948, 134 | 28, 525, 800 | 50, 606, 142 | 10, 687, 470 | 710, 763 | 16, 778, 072 | 29, 152, 100 | 312, 934, 621 |
| | 1943 | 144, 687, 201 | 11, 583, 243 | 20, 688, 032 | 35, 696, 742 | 7, 984, 287 | 868, 691 | 13, 478, 044 | 26, 152, 740 | 261, 138, 980 |
| | 1944 | 159, 133, 794 | 11, 022, 845 | 18, 366, 084 | 52, 691, 285 | 2, 465, 200 | 1, 440, 327 | 10, 404, 609 | 22, 162, 583 | 277, 686, 727 |
| | 1945 | 140, 205, 531 | 9, 898, 799 | 20, 524, 583 | 74, 391, 434 | 3, 293, 955 | 1, 469, 390 | 9, 802, 809 | 19, 863, 433 | 279, 449, 934 |
| | 1946 | 137, 073, 531 | 7, 522, 420 | 10, 096, 192 | 114, 410, 210 | 3, 889, 982 | 1, 184, 880 | 7, 561, 096 | 25, 975, 289 | 307, 713, 600 |

[1] Included in construction timbers prior to 1925.

[2] Includes both full-length pressure-treated poles and nonpressure (butt-treated) poles.

[3] Includes distillate coal-tar creosote, solutions of creosote and coal tar, water-gas tar, and water-gas-tar solutions.

[4] Includes various-percentage solutions of creosote and petroleum.

[5] Not shown prior to 1946.

[6] Use of zinc-creosote solutions for the preservative treatment of wood discontinued by the industry in 1933.

[7] Not shown for years previous to 1945. Entries under poles treated with creosote and with creosote-petroleum solutions include poles given butt treatment with these preservatives followed by full-length dip treatment in pentachlorophenol solution.

[8] Not shown for years prior to 1912.

Notes. For years not shown see previous annual reports. Entries under construction timbers and miscellaneous material treated with chromated zinc chloride and miscellaneous preservatives in 1942, 1943, 1944, 1945, and 1946 include material given fire-retardant treatment during those years.

Converting factors:

To obtain the number of cross ties treated, divide the figures shown by 3.

To obtain the number of board feet of switch ties, multiply the figures shown by 12.

To obtain the number of linear feet of piles treated, divide the figures shown by .6763.

To obtain the number of square yards of wood blocks, divide the figures shown by 2.625.

To obtain the number of board feet of construction timbers, multiply the figures shown by 12.

To obtain the number of board feet of miscellaneous material, multiply the figures shown by 12.

To obtain the number of poles, divide the figures shown by 17.6 for years prior to 1946. For 1946 a conversion factor of 17.6 was used for 6,424,687 poles and 11.0 for 121,429 poles.

To obtain the number of cross arms, divide the figures shown by .6198.

*Taken from: Wood Preservation Statistics—1946, by Henry B. Steer (Quantity of Wood Treated and Preservatives Used in the United States in 1946), Forest Service, U. S. Department of Agriculture, in cooperation with the American

# TREES BEST ADAPTED FOR SPECIAL PURPOSES

## NORTHEASTERN UNITED STATES

Shade trees for suburban homes:
- Evergreen:
  - Canada hemlock
  - Colorado blue spruce
  - Eastern white pine
  - Nikko fir
  - White fir
  - In northern part only—
  - Balsam fir
  - White spruce
- Deciduous:
  - American hornbeam
  - American mountain-ash
  - American yellowwood
  - European beech
  - European linden
  - Littleleaf linden
  - Norway maple
  - Panicled goldenrain-tree
  - Pin oak
  - Scarlet oak
  - Schwedler maple
  - Silver linden
  - Sugar maple
  - Sweetgum
  - Tuliptree
  - White oak

Roadside, boulevard, and avenue trees:
- Evergreen:
  - Canada hemlock
  - Eastern white pine
  - Red pine
- Deciduous:
  - American linden
  - American yellowwood
  - Black tupelo
  - Common hackberry
  - Ginkgo (staminate form)
  - London planetree
  - Northern red oak
  - Norway maple
  - Pin oak
  - Red maple
  - Scarlet oak
  - Silver linden
  - Schwedler maple
  - Sugar maple
  - Sweetgum
  - Tuliptree

Street trees:
- Evergreen:
  - None
- Deciduous:
  - Ailanthus (pistillate form)
  - Amur corktree
  - Ginkgo (staminate form)
  - London planetree
  - Norway maple
  - Pin oak
  - Thornless common honeylocust
  - Tuliptree

Park and garden trees (*see also* Shade and Roadside trees):
- Evergreen:
  - Common Douglas-fir
  - Oriental spruce
  - Red pine
- Deciduous:
  - Amur corktree
  - Bolleana poplar
  - Common horsechestnut
  - Cutleaf weeping birch
  - Eastern black walnut
  - English elm
  - Golden weeping willow
  - Japanese pagodatree
  - Kentucky coffeetree
  - Paper birch
  - Rock elm
  - Scotch elm
  - Silverpendent linden
  - Weeping silverpendent linden
  - White ash
  - White oak

Trees with autumn color:
- American hornbeam (orange, scarlet)
- American yellowwood (yellow)
- Black tupelo (scarlet)
- Ginkgo (yellow)
- Northern red oak (red)
- Norway maple (yellow)
- Pin oak (scarlet, dark red)
- Red maple (orange, red, scarlet)
- Scarlet oak (scarlet, dark red)
- Sugar maple (yellow, orange, scarlet)
- Sweetgum (red, scarlet)
- Tuliptree (yellow)

Trees with conspicuous flowers:
- American mountain-ash (white)
- American yellowwood (white)
- Common horsechestnut (pinkish white)
- Japanese pagodatree (yellowish white)
- Panicled goldenrain-tree (yellow)
- Red maple (red)
- Sugar maple (yellowish green)
- Tuliptree (greenish yellow)

## PLAINS AREA

Shade and park trees:
- Throughout Plains Area:
  - Deciduous:
    - American elm
    - Bur oak
    - Cottonwood
    - Green ash
    - Hackberry
    - Honeylocust
    - Russian-olive
  - Evergreens:
    - Austrian pine
    - Eastern redcedar
    - Ponderosa pine
    - Rocky Mountain cedar

Nebraska northward:
- Deciduous:
  - Boxelder
  - Hawthorn
  - Maples
  - Willows
- Evergreens:
  - Douglas-fir
  - Scotch pine
  - Spruce
  - White fir

Nebraska southward:
- Deciduous:
  - Ailanthus
  - American sycamore
  - Black locust
  - Black walnut
  - Catalpa
  - Russian mulberry

Oklahoma and Texas:
- Deciduous:
  - Chinese elm
  - Desertwillow
  - Kentucky coffeetree
  - Soapberry
- Evergreen:
  - Arizona cypress (Texas)
  - Loblolly pine
  - Shortleaf pine

Street trees:
- Deciduous:
  - American elm
  - American sycamore
  - Boxelder
  - Bur oak
  - Green ash
  - Hackberry
  - Maples
  - Russian mulberry
  - Siberian elm
- Evergreens:
  - Austrian pine
  - Ponderosa pine

Trees with showy flowers:
- Black locust
- Catalpa
- Desertwillow
- Hawthorn
- Honeylocust

Trees with showy foliage in autumn:
- Cottonwood (yellow)
- Green ash (golden yellow)
- Maple (gold and red)
- Oak (yellow to red)
- Sycamore (clear yellow)

Trees suitable for use on phymatotrichum root rot infected soil:
- Deciduous:
  - Ailanthus
  - Desertwillow
  - Hackberry
  - Mulberry
  - Soapberry
- Evergreens:
  - Eastern redcedar
  - Rocky Mountain cedar

## SOUTHEASTERN AREA

Shade and roadside trees:
- Deciduous:
  - American beech
  - American elm
  - American sycamore
  - Laurel oak
  - Pecan
  - Sugarberry
  - Sweetgum
  - Water oak
  - Weeping willow
  - White oak
  - Willow oak
  - Winged elm
  - Yellow-poplar
- Evergreen:
  - Live oak
  - Southern magnolia

Street trees:
- Deciduous:
  - American elm
  - American sycamore
  - Cabbage palmetto
  - Common crapemyrtle
  - Laurel oak
  - Sugarberry
  - Sweetgum
  - Water oak
  - White oak
  - Willow oak
  - Winged elm
- Evergreen:
  - Camphor-tree
  - Live oak
  - Southern magnolia

Park and lawn trees:
- Deciduous:
  - American beech
  - American elm
  - American sycamore
  - Common crapemyrtle
  - Eastern redbud
  - Flowering dogwood
  - Laurel oak
  - Mimosa
  - Panicled goldenrain-tree
  - Pecan
  - Red maple
  - Sugarberry
  - Sweetgum
  - Water oak
  - Weeping willow
  - White oak
  - Willow oak
  - Winged elm
  - Yellow-poplar
- Evergreen:
  - American holly
  - Camphor-tree
  - Canary date
  - Carolina laurel-cherry
  - Eastern arborvitae
  - Eastern redcedar
  - Live oak
  - Southern magnolia

Trees with autumn color:
- Deciduous:
  - Flowering dogwood
  - Pin oak
  - Red maple
  - Scarlet oak
  - Sweetgum
  - Yellow-poplar

Trees with conspicuous flowers or fruits:
- Deciduous:
  - Common crapemyrtle
  - Eastern redbud
  - Flowering dogwood
  - Mimosa
  - Panicled goldenrain-tree
  - Red maple
- Evergreen:
  - American holly
  - Southern magnolia

## SOUTHERN ROCKY MOUNTAIN REGION

Street trees:
- Deciduous:
  - Green ash
  - Lanceleaf poplar
  - Linden
  - London planetree
  - Narrowleaf poplar
  - Northern catalpa
  - Norway maple
  - Siberian elm
  - Velvet ash
  - White ash

Roadside trees (*see also* Street trees):
- Deciduous:
  - Black locust
  - Lombardy poplar
- Evergreen:
  - Arizona cypress
  - Eucalyptus
  - Ponderosa pine

Shade trees (*see also* Street and Roadside trees):
- Deciduous:
  - American elm
  - Boxelder
  - Plains poplar
  - Red mulberry
  - White mulberry

Park and garden trees (*see also* Street, Roadside, and Shade trees):
- Deciduous:
  - Common hackberry
  - Russian-olive
  - Tamarisk
  - Thornless honeylocust
  - Tree-of-Heaven ailanthus
- Evergreen:
  - Aleppo pine
  - Austrian pine
  - Colorado pinyon pine
  - Colorado spruce
  - Engelmann spruce
  - Rocky Mountain juniper
  - Scotch pine

Trees for difficult sites:
- Deciduous:
  - Black locust
  - Boxelder
  - Common hackberry
  - Russian-olive
  - Siberian elm
  - Tamarisk
  - Thornless honeylocust
  - Tree-of-Heaven ailanthus
  - Velvet ash

Trees with conspicuous flowers:
- Deciduous:
  - Black locust
  - Northern catalpa
- Evergreen:
  - Eucalyptus

Trees with autumn color:
- Deciduous:
  - Lanceleaf poplar
  - Lombardy poplar
  - Narrowleaf poplar
  - Norway maple
  - Plains poplar

## NORTH PACIFIC COAST AREA

Street trees:
- American yellowwood
- Common hackberry
- European linden
- Pin oak

Lawn trees:
- American yellowwood
- Atlas-cedar (conifer)
- Common hackberry
- European linden
- Himalayan pine (conifer)
- Oregon white oak
- Pacific madrone (broadleaf evergreen)
- Pin oak
- Sweetgum
- Tuliptree

Trees with showy fall foliage:
- American yellowwood
- Pin oak
- Sweetgum

Trees with showy or fragrant flowers:
- American yellowwood
- European linden
- Pacific madrone

A SELECTED LIST OF TREES AND SHRUBS FOR PLANTING WINDBREAKS AND SHELTERBELTS IN THE GREAT PLAINS

[Results to be expected: G—Good; F—Fair only; X—Not recommended]

| *Common names of trees* | *North Dakota and northwestern Minnesota* | *South Dakota, southwestern Minnesota, and northwestern Iowa* | *Nebraska and southwestern Iowa* | *East-central Kansas* | *Western Kansas and eastern Colorado* | *Eastern Wyoming* | *Eastern Montana* | *Central and western Oklahoma* | *Central Texas* |
|---|---|---|---|---|---|---|---|---|---|
| CONIFERS | | | | | | | | | |
| Eastern redcedar | G | G | G | G | G | G | G | G | G |
| Rocky Mountain juniper | G | G | G | G | G | G | G | X | X |
| One-seed juniper | X | X | X | X | X | X | X | G | G |
| Limber pine | X | X | [4] G | X | F | G | X | X | X |
| Ponderosa pine | G | G | G | G | G | G | G | F | F |
| Austrian pine | X | [2] G | G | G | F | F | X | X | X |
| Shortleaf pine | X | X | X | [2] G | X | X | X | G | G |
| Black Hills spruce | G | G | [5] G | X | X | F | F | X | X |
| Blue spruce | G | G | G | X | F | F | F | X | X |
| Douglas-fir | F | F | G | F | X | F | G | X | X |
| Arizona cypress | X | X | X | X | X | X | X | [2] F | G |
| SHRUBS | | | | | | | | | |
| Caragana (on dry sites) | G | G | F | X | X | F | G | X | X |
| Cotoneaster | G | G | G | G | G | G | G | G | G |
| Buckthorn | G | G | G | G | G | G | G | G | G |
| Tatarian honeysuckle | G | G | G | G | G | G | G | F | F |
| American wild plum | G | G | G | G | G | G | G | X | X |
| Chickasaw plum | X | X | X | X | X | X | X | G | G |
| Western chokecherry | G | G | G | G | G | G | G | F | F |
| Nanking cherry [6] | G | G | G | G | G | [6] ? | [6] ? | [6] ? | [6] ? |
| Golden currant | G | G | G | G | G | G | G | F | F |
| Buffaloberry | G | G | G | F | G | G | G | X | X |
| Lilac | G | G | G | G | G | G | G | G | G |
| Multiflora rose [6] | [6] ? | G | G | G | [6] ? | [6] ? | [6] ? | [6] ? | [6] ? |
| Redbud | X | G | G | G | F | X | X | G | G |
| Soapberry | X | X | X | G | F | X | X | G | G |
| LOW TREES | | | | | | | | | |
| Russian-olive | G | G | G | G | G | G | G | G | G |
| Diamond willow | G | G | G | G | F | G | G | X | X |
| Boxelder | G | G | G | G | F | F | F | X | X |
| Siberian crab | F | F | G | G | F | X | X | X | X |
| Seedling apricot | X | X | [2] F | G | G | X | X | X | X |
| Desertwillow | X | X | X | G | F | X | X | G | G |
| Mulberry | X | X | [2] F | G | F | X | X | G | G |

See footnotes at end of table.

A SELECTED LIST OF TREES AND SHRUBS FOR PLANTING WINDBREAKS AND SHELTERBELTS IN THE GREAT PLAINS—continued

| *Common names of trees* | *North Dakota and northwestern Minnesota* | *South Dakota, southwestern Minnesota, and northwestern Iowa* | *Nebraska and southwestern Iowa* | *East-central Kansas* | *Western Kansas and eastern Colorado* | *Eastern Wyoming* | *Eastern Montana* | *Central and western Oklahoma* | *Central Texas* |
|---|---|---|---|---|---|---|---|---|---|
| MEDIUM TREES | | | | | | | | | |
| Green ash | G | G | G | G | G | G | G | F | F |
| Bur oak | G | G | G | G | G | F | F | X | X |
| American elm | G | G | G | G | G | G | G | G | G |
| Red elm | X | X | G | G | X | X | X | X | X |
| Black walnut | X | [2] F | G | G | [1] F | X | X | F | F |
| Pecan | X | X | X | [2] G | X | X | X | G | G |
| Texas walnut | X | X | X | X | X | X | X | G | G |
| Osage-orange | X | X | [2] F | G | G | X | X | G | G |
| Crack willow | [1] G | [1] G | [1] G | [1] G | [1] G | [1] G | [1] G | [1] G | [1] G |
| TALL HARDY TREES | | | | | | | | | |
| Hackberry | G | G | G | G | G | G | G | G | G |
| Honeylocust (thornless) | [2] G | [2] F | G | G | G | G | X | G | G |
| Kentucky coffeetree | X | F | G | G | X | X | X | G | G |
| Red oak | X | X | G | G | X | X | X | G | X |
| Black locust | X | [2] F | [3] G | G | X | X | X | G | F |
| TALL FAST-GROWING TREES | | | | | | | | | |
| Cottonwood | [1] G | [1] G | [1] G | [1] G | [1] G | [1] G | [1] G | [1] G | [1] G |
| Chinese elm | G | G | G | G | G | G | G | G | G |
| Sycamore | X | X | [1,3] G | [1] G | X | X | X | [1] G | G |
| White willow | [1] G | [1] G | [1] G | [1] G | [1] G | [1] G | [1] G | [1] G | [1] G |
| Golden willow | [1] G | [1] G | [1] F | [1] G | [1] G | X | [1] G | [1] G | [1] G |
| Silver maple | X | X | [1] G | [1] G | [1] G | [1] G | X | [1] G | [1] G |
| Catalpa | X | X | [1] G | [1] G | X | X | X | F | [1] F |

[1] Does best where there is a good supply of moisture.

[2] Southern part only.

[3] Not recommended for western Nebraska.

[4] Western Nebraska only.

[5] Eastern Nebraska and western Iowa only.

[6] A new species that has not been thoroughly tried.

ESTIMATED VALUE OF NONMANUFACTURED FOREST PRODUCTS IN THE UNITED STATES BY REGIONS AND PORTION OBTAINED FROM FARM WOODLANDS, 1947 (See page 721)

| *Region* [1] | *Total value* | *Obtained from farm woodlands* *Value* | *Proportion of total* |
|---|---|---|---|
| | *Million dollars* | *Million dollars* | *Percent* |
| New England | 153 | 36 | 23 |
| Middle Atlantic | 172 | 50 | 29 |
| Lake | 171 | 65 | 38 |
| Central and Prairie | 202 | 133 | 66 |
| South Atlantic | 303 | 152 | 50 |
| Southern | 751 | 240 | 32 |
| East, total | 1,752 | 676 | 39 |
| North Pacific | 469 | 12 | 3 |
| South Pacific | 111 | 2 | 2 |
| North Rocky Mountain | 47 | 2 | 5 |
| South Rocky Mountain | 40 | 7 | 17 |
| West, total | 667 | 23 | 3 |
| United States, total | 2,419 | 699 | 29 |

[1] *New England:* Connecticut, Maine, Massachusetts, New Hampshire, Rhode Island, Vermont; *Middle Atlantic:* Delaware, Maryland, New Jersey, New York, Pennsylvania, West Virgina; *Lake:* Michigan, Minnesota, Wisconsin; *Central:* Illinois, Indiana, Kentucky, Missouri, Ohio, Tennessee; *Prairie:* Iowa, Kansas, Nebraska; *South Atlantic:* North Carolina, South Carolina, Virginia; *Southern:* Alabama, Arkansas, Florida, Georgia, Louisiana, Mississippi, Oklahoma, Texas; *North Pacific:* Oregon, Washington; *South Pacific:* California, Nevada; *North Rocky Mountain:* Idaho, Montana; *South Rocky Mountain:* Arizona, Colorado, New Mexico, South Dakota, Utah, Wyoming.

A CLASSIFICATION OF TIMBER PRODUCTS AND THEIR RELATIVE IMPORTANCE [1]

| *Product* | *Percent of total forest drain* [2] *All timber* [3] | *Saw timber* [4] |
|---|---|---|
| Major timber products utilized in primary form: | | |
| Fuel wood | 12.6 | 5.0 |
| Poles | .6 | .5 |
| Piling | .2 | .2 |
| Fence posts | 3.3 | .8 |
| Mine timbers, hewed or round | 1.5 | .5 |
| Railroad ties, hewed | 1.6 | 1.8 |
| Total | 19.8 | 8.8 |
| Major timber products that are further processed: | | |
| In the manufacture of wooden products— | | |
| Saw logs for lumber | 59.4 | 72.7 |
| Logs and bolts for veneer | 3.9 | 4.6 |
| Cooperage stock | 1.3 | 1.5 |
| Total | 64.6 | 78.8 |
| In the manufacture of chemical products— | | |
| Pulpwood | 11.4 | 9.5 |
| Wood for hardwood distillation | .2 | .1 |
| Total | 11.6 | 9.6 |
| Logs and bolts for all other purposes | 1.6 | 2.0 |
| Cordwood for all other purposes | 2.4 | .8 |
| Total | 100.0 | 100.0 |

[1] Based on estimated forest drain to meet potential requirements in the United States, 1950–55.

[2] Drain refers to the volume of timber cut annually to supply requirements for commodities.

[3] Includes all trees 5 inches and larger in diameter at breast height.

[4] Includes trees large enough to produce saw logs; minimum diameter varies by regions and species, but in no case less than 9 inches in diameter at breast height. (See page 731.)

# MEASURING TIMBER

AMOUNT OF SAW TIMBER IN TREES, BY DIAMETER AND MERCHANTABLE HEIGHT
INTERNATIONAL ¼-INCH RULE

| Diameter of tree, breast-high | Volume, according to number of usable 16-foot logs | | | | | | | | | | |
|---|---|---|---|---|---|---|---|---|---|---|---|
| | 1 | 1½ | 2 | 2½ | 3 | 3½ | 4 | 4½ | 5 | 5½ | 6 |
| *Inches* | *Bd. ft.* | *Bd. ft.* | *Bd. ft.* | *Bd. ft.* | *Bd. ft.* | *Bd. ft.* | *Bd. ft.* | *Bd. ft.* | *Bd. ft.* | *Bd. ft.* | *Bd. ft.* |
| 10 | 39 | 51 | 63 | 72 | 80 | ..... | ..... | ..... | ..... | ..... | ..... |
| 11 | 49 | 64 | 80 | 92 | 104 | ..... | ..... | ..... | ..... | ..... | ..... |
| 12 | 59 | 78 | 98 | 112 | 127 | 136 | 146 | ..... | ..... | ..... | ..... |
| 13 | 71 | 96 | 120 | 138 | 156 | 168 | 181 | ..... | ..... | ..... | ..... |
| 14 | 83 | 112 | 141 | 164 | 186 | 201 | 216 | ..... | ..... | ..... | ..... |
| 15 | 98 | 132 | 166 | 194 | 221 | 240 | 260 | ..... | ..... | ..... | ..... |
| 16 | 112 | 151 | 190 | 223 | 256 | 280 | 305 | ..... | ..... | ..... | ..... |
| 17 | 128 | 174 | 219 | 258 | 296 | 325 | 354 | ..... | ..... | ..... | ..... |
| 18 | 144 | 196 | 248 | 292 | 336 | 369 | 402 | ..... | ..... | ..... | ..... |
| 19 | 162 | 222 | 281 | 332 | 382 | 420 | 457 | ..... | ..... | ..... | ..... |
| 20 | 181 | 248 | 314 | 370 | 427 | 470 | 512 | 546 | 580 | ..... | ..... |
| 21 | 201 | 276 | 350 | 414 | 478 | 526 | 575 | 616 | 656 | ..... | ..... |
| 22 | 221 | 304 | 387 | 458 | 528 | 583 | 638 | 685 | 732 | ..... | ..... |
| 23 | 244 | 336 | 428 | 507 | 586 | 646 | 706 | 761 | 816 | ..... | ..... |
| 24 | 266 | 368 | 469 | 556 | 644 | 708 | 773 | 836 | 899 | ..... | ..... |
| 25 | 290 | 402 | 514 | 610 | 706 | 779 | 852 | 922 | 992 | ..... | ..... |
| 26 | 315 | 436 | 558 | 662 | 767 | 849 | 931 | 1,008 | 1,086 | ..... | ..... |
| 27 | 341 | 474 | 606 | 721 | 836 | 925 | 1,014 | 1,100 | 1,185 | ..... | ..... |
| 28 | 367 | 510 | 654 | 779 | 904 | 1,000 | 1,096 | 1,190 | 1,284 | 1,368 | 1,453 |
| 29 | 396 | 551 | 706 | 842 | 977 | 1,080 | 1,184 | 1,289 | 1,394 | 1,491 | 1,588 |
| 30 | 424 | 591 | 758 | 904 | 1,050 | 1,161 | 1,272 | 1,388 | 1,503 | 1,613 | 1,723 |
| 31 | 454 | 634 | 814 | 973 | 1,132 | 1,254 | 1,376 | 1,497 | 1,618 | 1,740 | 1,862 |
| 32 | 485 | 678 | 870 | 1,042 | 1,213 | 1,346 | 1,480 | 1,606 | 1,733 | 1,867 | 2,001 |
| 33 | 518 | 724 | 930 | 1,114 | 1,298 | 1,442 | 1,586 | 1,722 | 1,858 | 2,005 | 2,152 |
| 34 | 550 | 770 | 989 | 1,186 | 1,383 | 1,537 | 1,691 | 1,838 | 1,984 | 2,144 | 2,304 |
| 35 | 585 | 820 | 1,055 | 1,266 | 1,477 | 1,642 | 1,806 | 1,965 | 2,124 | 2,291 | 2,458 |
| 36 | 620 | 870 | 1,121 | 1,346 | 1,571 | 1,746 | 1,922 | 2,093 | 2,264 | 2,438 | 2,612 |
| 37 | 656 | 922 | 1,188 | 1,430 | 1,672 | 1,858 | 2,044 | 2,230 | 2,416 | 2,600 | 2,783 |
| 38 | 693 | 974 | 1,256 | 1,514 | 1,772 | 1,970 | 2,167 | 2,368 | 2,568 | 2,761 | 2,954 |
| 39 | 732 | 1,031 | 1,330 | 1,602 | 1,874 | 2,087 | 2,300 | 2,507 | 2,714 | 2,920 | 3,127 |
| 40 | 770 | 1,086 | 1,403 | 1,690 | 1,977 | 2,204 | 2,432 | 2,646 | 2,860 | 3,080 | 3,300 |

AMOUNT OF SAW TIMBER IN TREES, BY DIAMETER AND MERCHANTABLE HEIGHT

DOYLE LOG RULE

| Diameter of tree, breast-high | Volume, according to number of usable 16-foot logs | | | | | | | | | | |
|---|---|---|---|---|---|---|---|---|---|---|---|
| | 1 | 1½ | 2 | 2½ | 3 | 3½ | 4 | 4½ | 5 | 5½ | 6 |
| *Inches* | *Bd. ft.* | *Bd. ft.* | *Bd. ft.* | *Bd. ft.* | *Bd. ft.* | *Bd. ft.* | *Bd. ft.* | *Bd. ft.* | *Bd. ft.* | *Bd. ft.* | *Bd. ft.* |
| 10 | 16 | 20 | 23 | 24 | 26 | ..... | ..... | ..... | ..... | ..... | ..... |
| 11 | 24 | 30 | 35 | 38 | 42 | ..... | ..... | ..... | ..... | ..... | ..... |
| 12 | 31 | 39 | 47 | 52 | 57 | 60 | 62 | ..... | ..... | ..... | ..... |
| 13 | 42 | 53 | 64 | 72 | 80 | 84 | 88 | ..... | ..... | ..... | ..... |
| 14 | 52 | 67 | 82 | 93 | 104 | 109 | 114 | ..... | ..... | ..... | ..... |
| 15 | 64 | 84 | 104 | 118 | 132 | 141 | 150 | ..... | ..... | ..... | ..... |
| 16 | 77 | 101 | 125 | 143 | 161 | 174 | 186 | ..... | ..... | ..... | ..... |
| 17 | 92 | 122 | 152 | 175 | 198 | 214 | 230 | ..... | ..... | ..... | ..... |
| 18 | 108 | 144 | 179 | 206 | 234 | 254 | 273 | ..... | ..... | ..... | ..... |
| 19 | 126 | 168 | 210 | 244 | 278 | 301 | 324 | ..... | ..... | ..... | ..... |
| 20 | 144 | 193 | 242 | 282 | 321 | 348 | 374 | 396 | 417 | ..... | ..... |
| 21 | 164 | 221 | 278 | 324 | 370 | 403 | 436 | 462 | 489 | ..... | ..... |
| 22 | 185 | 250 | 315 | 368 | 420 | 458 | 497 | 529 | 561 | ..... | ..... |
| 23 | 208 | 282 | 356 | 417 | 478 | 521 | 564 | 604 | 643 | ..... | ..... |
| 24 | 231 | 314 | 397 | 466 | 536 | 583 | 630 | 678 | 725 | ..... | ..... |
| 25 | 256 | 350 | 443 | 522 | 600 | 655 | 710 | 764 | 818 | ..... | ..... |
| 26 | 282 | 386 | 489 | 576 | 663 | 727 | 791 | 852 | 912 | ..... | ..... |
| 27 | 310 | 425 | 540 | 638 | 735 | 806 | 877 | 946 | 1,015 | ..... | ..... |
| 28 | 339 | 466 | 592 | 700 | 807 | 885 | 963 | 1,040 | 1,118 | 1,188 | 1,258 |
| 29 | 370 | 509 | 648 | 766 | 884 | 970 | 1,056 | 1,144 | 1,232 | 1,315 | 1,398 |
| 30 | 400 | 552 | 703 | 832 | 961 | 1,055 | 1,149 | 1,248 | 1,346 | 1,442 | 1,537 |
| 31 | 434 | 599 | 764 | 906 | 1,049 | 1,154 | 1,260 | 1,364 | 1,469 | 1,576 | 1,684 |
| 32 | 467 | 646 | 824 | 980 | 1,137 | 1,254 | 1,370 | 1,481 | 1,592 | 1,712 | 1,831 |
| 33 | 502 | 696 | 889 | 1,060 | 1,230 | 1,356 | 1,483 | 1,604 | 1,726 | 1,860 | 1,994 |
| 34 | 538 | 746 | 954 | 1,138 | 1,322 | 1,459 | 1,596 | 1,728 | 1,861 | 2,008 | 2,156 |
| 35 | 576 | 801 | 1,026 | 1,225 | 1,424 | 1,573 | 1,722 | 1,867 | 2,012 | 2,167 | 2,322 |
| 36 | 615 | 857 | 1,099 | 1,312 | 1,526 | 1,688 | 1,849 | 2,006 | 2,163 | 2,326 | 2,488 |
| 37 | 656 | 915 | 1,174 | 1,406 | 1,638 | 1,811 | 1,984 | 2,157 | 2,330 | 2,502 | 2,675 |
| 38 | 697 | 973 | 1,249 | 1,499 | 1,749 | 1,934 | 2,119 | 2,308 | 2,496 | 2,679 | 2,862 |
| 39 | 740 | 1,036 | 1,332 | 1,598 | 1,864 | 2,065 | 2,266 | 2,462 | 2,658 | 2,855 | 3,052 |
| 40 | 784 | 1,099 | 1,414 | 1,696 | 1,979 | 2,196 | 2,413 | 2,616 | 2,819 | 3,030 | 3,241 |

Data from Mesavage and Girard, tables for estimating board-foot volume of timber. (Form class 80.) U. S. Department of Agriculture, Forest Service. 1946.

For exceptionally tall, slender trees add 10 percent.

For exceptionally short, stubby trees deduct 10 percent.

THE CONTENTS OF LOGS, IN BOARD FEET, BY THE DOYLE LOG RULE [1]

| *Diameter of log small end, inside bark* | *Contents, according to length of log in feet* | | | | | | | | | | | | |
|---|---|---|---|---|---|---|---|---|---|---|---|---|---|
| | 6 | 7 | 8 | 9 | 10 | 11 | 12 | 13 | 14 | 15 | 16 | 17 | 18 |
| *Inches* | *Bd. ft.* | *Bd. ft.* | *Bd. ft.* | *Bd. ft.* | *Bd. ft.* | *Bd. ft.* | *Bd. ft.* | *Bd. ft.* | *Bd. ft.* | *Bd. ft.* | *Bd. ft.* | *Bd. ft.* | *Bd. ft.* |
| 6......... | 1 | 2 | 2 | 2 | 2 | 3 | 3 | 3 | 3 | 4 | 4 | 4 | 4 |
| 7......... | 3 | 4 | 4 | 5 | 5 | 6 | 7 | 7 | 8 | 8 | 9 | 10 | 10 |
| 8......... | 6 | 7 | 8 | 9 | 10 | 11 | 12 | 13 | 14 | 15 | 16 | 17 | 18 |
| 9......... | 9 | 11 | 12 | 14 | 16 | 17 | 19 | 20 | 22 | 23 | 25 | 27 | 28 |
| 10........ | 13 | 16 | 18 | 20 | 22 | 25 | 27 | 29 | 31 | 34 | 36 | 38 | 40 |
| 11........ | 18 | 21 | 24 | 28 | 31 | 34 | 37 | 40 | 43 | 46 | 46 | 52 | 55 |
| 12........ | 24 | 28 | 32 | 36 | 40 | 44 | 48 | 52 | 56 | 60 | 64 | 68 | 72 |
| 13........ | 30 | 35 | 40 | 46 | 51 | 56 | 61 | 66 | 71 | 76 | 81 | 86 | 91 |
| 14........ | 37 | 44 | 50 | 56 | 62 | 69 | 75 | 81 | 87 | 94 | 100 | 106 | 112 |
| 15........ | 45 | 53 | 60 | 68 | 76 | 83 | 91 | 98 | 106 | 113 | 121 | 129 | 136 |
| 16........ | 54 | 63 | 72 | 81 | 90 | 99 | 108 | 117 | 126 | 135 | 144 | 153 | 162 |
| 17........ | 63 | 74 | 84 | 95 | 106 | 116 | 127 | 137 | 148 | 158 | 169 | 180 | 190 |
| 18........ | 73 | 86 | 98 | 110 | 122 | 135 | 147 | 159 | 171 | 184 | 196 | 208 | 220 |
| 19........ | 84 | 98 | 112 | 127 | 141 | 155 | 169 | 183 | 197 | 211 | 225 | 239 | 253 |
| 20........ | 96 | 112 | 128 | 144 | 160 | 176 | 192 | 208 | 224 | 240 | 256 | 272 | 288 |
| 21........ | 108 | 126 | 144 | 163 | 181 | 199 | 217 | 235 | 253 | 271 | 289 | 307 | 325 |
| 22........ | 121 | 142 | 162 | 182 | 202 | 223 | 243 | 263 | 283 | 304 | 324 | 344 | 364 |
| 23........ | 135 | 158 | 180 | 203 | 226 | 248 | 271 | 293 | 316 | 338 | 361 | 384 | 406 |
| 24........ | 150 | 175 | 200 | 225 | 250 | 275 | 300 | 325 | 350 | 375 | 400 | 425 | 450 |
| 25........ | 165 | 193 | 220 | 248 | 276 | 303 | 331 | 358 | 386 | 413 | 441 | 469 | 496 |
| 26........ | 181 | 212 | 242 | 272 | 302 | 333 | 363 | 393 | 423 | 454 | 484 | 514 | 544 |
| 27........ | 198 | 231 | 264 | 298 | 331 | 364 | 397 | 430 | 463 | 496 | 529 | 562 | 595 |
| 28........ | 216 | 252 | 288 | 324 | 360 | 396 | 432 | 468 | 504 | 540 | 576 | 612 | 648 |
| 29........ | 234 | 273 | 312 | 352 | 391 | 430 | 469 | 508 | 547 | 586 | 625 | 664 | 702 |
| 30........ | 253 | 296 | 338 | 380 | 422 | 465 | 507 | 549 | 591 | 634 | 676 | 718 | 760 |
| 31........ | 273 | 319 | 364 | 410 | 456 | 501 | 547 | 592 | 638 | 683 | 729 | 775 | 820 |
| 32........ | 294 | 343 | 392 | 441 | 490 | 539 | 588 | 636 | 686 | 735 | 784 | 833 | 882 |
| 33........ | 315 | 368 | 420 | 473 | 526 | 578 | 631 | 683 | 736 | 788 | 841 | 894 | 946 |
| 34........ | 337 | 394 | 450 | 506 | 562 | 619 | 675 | 731 | 787 | 844 | 900 | 956 | 1,012 |
| 35........ | 360 | 420 | 480 | 541 | 601 | 661 | 721 | 781 | 841 | 901 | 961 | 1,021 | 1,081 |
| 36........ | 384 | 448 | 512 | 576 | 640 | 704 | 768 | 832 | 896 | 960 | 1,024 | 1,088 | 1,152 |
| 37........ | 408 | 476 | 544 | 613 | 681 | 749 | 817 | 885 | 953 | 1,021 | 1,089 | 1,157 | 1,225 |
| 38........ | 433 | 506 | 578 | 650 | 722 | 795 | 867 | 939 | 1,011 | 1,084 | 1,156 | 1,228 | 1,300 |
| 39........ | 459 | 536 | 612 | 689 | 766 | 842 | 919 | 995 | 1,072 | 1,148 | 1,225 | 1,302 | 1,378 |
| 40........ | 486 | 567 | 648 | 729 | 810 | 891 | 972 | 1,053 | 1,134 | 1,215 | 1,296 | 1,377 | 1,458 |

[1] To find the number of board feet in a 16-foot log according to the Doyle scale, subtract 4 from the diameter (in inches) of the small end of the log. Multiply the remainder by itself. This gives the contents of the log (in board feet). An 8-foot log would have half as many board feet, a 12-foot log three-fourths as many.

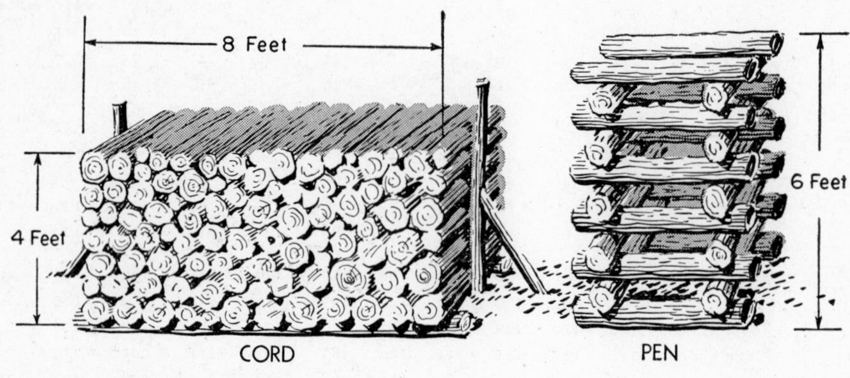
PILING PULPWOOD for measuring
8 Feet
4 Feet
6 Feet
CORD
PEN

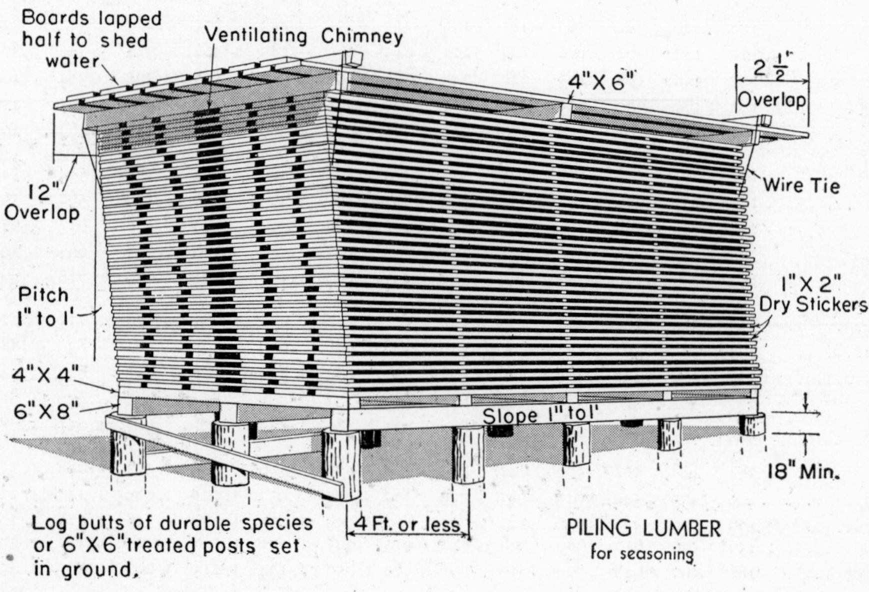
Boards lapped half to shed water
Ventilating Chimney
4"X 6"
2 1/2" Overlap
12" Overlap
Wire Tie
Pitch 1" to 1'
1" X 2" Dry Stickers
4" X 4"
6" X 8"
Slope 1" to 1'
18" Min.
Log butts of durable species or 6"X 6" treated posts set in ground.
4 Ft. or less
PILING LUMBER for seasoning

# A Vacation Guide

## NATIONAL FORESTS

### ALABAMA

WILLIAM B. BANKHEAD NATIONAL FOREST

Headquarters at Montgomery, reached by U. S. Highways 31, 43. (Ranger Headquarters at Haleyville.)

*Special features:* Limestone gorges; Clear Creek Falls; two natural bridges; wildlife refuge and management area. *Recreation resources:* Managed deer, turkey, and squirrel hunting. Bass and bream fishing in Brushy Lake. Improved picnic area on Sipsey River. Commercial accommodations at Haleyville, Russellville, Decatur, Cullman, and Jasper. *Acres:* 177,976.

CONECUH NATIONAL FOREST

Headquarters at Montgomery, reached by U. S. Highway 29. (Ranger Headquarters at Andalusia.)

*Special features:* Large, clear ponds. *Recreation resources:* Bass and bream fishing. Deer, turkey, and small-game hunting. Improved picnic and swimming area at Open Pond. Commercial accommodations at Andalusia. *Acres:* 83,866.

TALLADEGA NATIONAL FOREST

Headquarters at Montgomery, reached by U. S. Highways 78, 241, State Highway 6. (Ranger Headquarters at Centerville, Heflin, and Talladega.)

*Special features:* Payne Lake Wildlife Management Area; Skyway scenic drive; Mount Cheaha, 2,407 feet elevation, highest point in Alabama; Lake Chinnabee. *Recreation resources:* Deer, turkey, duck, and squirrel hunting. Bass, bream, and perch fishing. Swimming at Cheaha State Park. Picnic grounds at Payne Lake and Horn and Horseblock towers. Resort hotel and cabins at Cheaha State Park. Commercial accommodations at Centerville, Marion, Tuscaloosa, Selma, Talladega, Sylacauga, Anniston, and Heflin. *Acres:* 356,794.

### ALASKA

CHUGACH NATIONAL FOREST

Headquarters at Juneau, direct plane service to Juneau. (Ranger Headquarters at Cordova and Seward.)

*Special features:* Tidewater, Hanging and Piedmont Glaciers. Aleut villages, picturesque old Russian churches, native bidarkas. Shrimp, crab, clam, and salmon canneries. Alaska Railroad. Mountains of the Kenai; scenic fiords of Port Wells. *Recreation resources:* Rainbow trout fishing in Russian River. Moose, sheep, goat, and brown bear hunting. Duck, grouse, and ptarmigan hunting. Hiking along scenic trails; 140 miles of roads, 285 miles of trails. Regarding accommodations, inquire at Cordova, Seward, and Juneau offices. Plane and boat services to these towns. Two improved public forest camps. Rail service Anchorage to Seward. *Acres:* 4,801,902.

TONGASS NATIONAL FOREST

Headquarters at Juneau, direct plane service to Ketchikan and Juneau. (Ranger Headquarters at Ketchikan, Petersburg, Craig, and Sitka.)

*Special features:* Salmon canneries. Totems, territorial museum, and Indian villages; gateway to Canadian hinterland and Yukon, "Trail of '98," gold mines. Fur farms; glaciers; fiords; Alaska Highway from Haines; "Ice Cap" back of Juneau; fiords of Tracy Arm and Rudyerd Bay. Observatories where bear can be watched fishing for salmon. Ward Lake, Auke Village, Admiralty Island. *Recreation resources:* Trout fishing, salt-water fishing for salmon and halibut. Alaskan brown and grizzly bear, goat, and deer hunting. Boating on lakes and inland waterways. Hiking scenic wilderness trails. Mountain climbing; 210 miles of roads, 780 miles of trails. Eighteen improved forest camp grounds. Inquire concerning public camps and hotels at Juneau office. Hotel accommodations in all southeastern Alaska towns, all of which are served by boat and plane. *Acres:* 16,045,753.

### ARIZONA

APACHE NATIONAL FOREST

Headquarters at Springerville, reached by U. S. Highways 60, 260, 666.

*Special features:* Scenic Coronado Trail and other drives through spruce and mountain-meadow country. Prehistoric Blue River cliff dwellings. Big and Crescent Lakes. Blue Range and Mount Baldy Wilderness Areas. (Forest lies partly in New Mexico.) *Recreation resources:* Lake and stream trout fishing. Big-game hunting, including elk, deer, bear; turkey hunting. Horseback riding, pack trips. Thirty-three public camp and picnic areas. Resorts, lodges, cabins. Nearby towns: Greer and Alpine, Ariz.; Luna and Reserve, N. Mex. *Acres:* 1,567,210.

COCONINO NATIONAL FOREST

Headquarters at Flagstaff, reached by U. S. Highways 66, 89, 89–A.

*Special features:* Mormon Lake, largest natural lake in Arizona; San Francisco peaks, 12,611 feet, highest in Arizona; near Grand Canyon National Park; nearby National Monuments are Sunset Crater, Walnut Canyon (cliff dwellings), Wupatki (ancient ruins), and Montezuma Castle. Lowell Astronomical Observatory. Sycamore Canyon Wild Area. More than 1,000 miles of scenic drives through timbered country. *Recreation resources:* Hunting, including deer, elk, and mountain lion. Horseback riding. Eleven public camp and picnic areas; Arizona Snow Bowl winter-sports area. Resorts, towns, camps, and dude ranches. Nearby towns: Williams, Sedona, Clarkdale, Cottonwood, Camp Verde, and Winslow. *Acres:* 1,751,001.

CORONADO NATIONAL FOREST

Headquarters at Tucson, reached by U. S. Highways 80, 84, 89.

*Special features:* Rugged mountains rising abruptly from surrounding desert; cactus to pines and swimming to skiing in an hour's time and 40 miles apart. Madera and Sabino Canyons; Chiricahua Wild Area. Colossal Cave State Park; Saguaro and Chiricahua National Monuments. (Forest lies partly in New Mexico.) *Recreation resources:* Deer and javelina hunting. Scenic drives and horseback trails in the rugged Santa Catalina, Chiricahua, Santa Rita, and Huachuca Mountains. Many forms of bird life, including the trogon; rare species of plants such as Chihuahua pine, chilicote, and madrona; and rare species of animals, including coati-mundi, Chiricahua squirrel, and javelina. Thirty-three camp and picnic grounds; southernmost winter-sports area in the United States. Many dude ranches, resorts, and hotels. Adjacent towns are Nogales and Douglas on the Mexican border; Tucson, Benson, Patagonia, Tombstone (the town "too tough to die"), Willcox, Bisbee, Bowie, San Simon, and Fort Huachuca. *Acres:* 1,385,561.

CROOK NATIONAL FOREST

Headquarters at Safford, reached by U. S. Highways 60, 70, 666, State Highways 77, 78, 88.

*Special features:* Semidesert to alpine country, elevations from 3,500 to 10,700 feet; Mogollon Rim and Pinaleno Ranges. Parts of the Gila and Superstition Wilderness Areas; Galiuro Wild Area. Coolidge and Roosevelt Dams; Indian reservations. *Recreation resources:* Hunting, including bear, mountain lion, deer, elk, peccary, turkey, and quail. Scenic drives: U. S. Highway 60, Pinal Mountain, Swift Trail, and Coronado Trail. Nineteen public camp and picnic areas. Four dude ranches near or within the boundary; hotels and auto courts. Nearby towns: Safford, Clifton, Duncan, Globe, Superior, and Miami. *Acres:* 1,422,629.

KAIBAB NATIONAL FOREST

Headquarters at Williams, reached by U. S. Highways 66, 89, 64, 67.

*Special features:* Grand Canyon National Game Preserve with the famous Kaibab forest deer herd; wild buffalo herd; only habitat of the Kaibab squirrel. Access to both North and South Rims of Grand Canyon and Supai Indian village in Havasu Canyon. East Rim; North Canyon; Thunder River; Bill Williams Mountain; White Horse Lake; Sycamore Canyon Wild Area. *Recreation resources:* Hunting, including deer and elk, antelope, bear, mountain lion, turkey, and buffalo. Wilderness trips, scenic drives, winter sports, fishing, riding and pack trips. Unlimited photographic opportunities in vivid coloring and geological formations. Thirteen public camp and picnic areas; Bill Williams Winter-sports Area. Hotels, resorts, cottage courts, guest ranches, hunting camps. Nearby towns: Williams, Grand Canyon, Flagstaff, Jerome, Ashfork, Fredonia, and Cottonwood, Ariz.; Kanab, Utah. *Acres:* 1,793,577.

PRESCOTT NATIONAL FOREST

Headquarters at Prescott, reached by U. S. Highway 89.

*Special features:* Rugged back country in the high mountains. Granite Basin Lake with rugged Granite Mountain overlooking the lake; Sycamore Canyon and Pine Mountain Wild Areas. Jerome "billion dollar copper camp." Prescott is known as "Cowboy Capital of the World." *Recreation resources:* Deer hunting. Some fishing. Many horseback-riding trails. Scenic drives. Ten public camp grounds and picnic areas; two winter-sports areas. Resorts, hotels, cabins, and dude ranches. Nearby towns: Prescott, Mayer, Jerome, Clarkdale, and Cottonwood. *Acres:* 1,252,168.

SITGREAVES NATIONAL FOREST

Headquarters at Holbrook, reached by U. S. Highway 60, State Highways 77, 173.

*Special features:* Scenic Mogollon Rim drive; Pueblo ruins. Large elk herd. *Recreation resources:* Limited hunting, including deer, turkey, antelope, bear. Saddle and pack trips. Three forest camping grounds. Resorts, hotels, cabins, and guest ranches. Nearby towns: Winslow, Show Low, Lakeside, and Pinetop. *Acres:* 805,167.

TONTO NATIONAL FOREST

Headquarters at Phoenix, reached by U. S. Highways 60, 70, 80, 89.

*Special features:* Famous Tonto Basin; Superstition Mountains; Mogollon Rim; Superstition Mountain and Mazatzal Wilderness Areas; Sierra Ancha Wild Area. A small band of Mexican bighorn sheep in the Superstition Mountains. Apache, Canyon, and Stewart Mountain Lakes on the Salt River; Bartlett and Horseshoe Lakes on the Verde River. Many remains of prehistoric occupancy, including Tonto National Monument and the Pueblo Canyon ruins. Unusually varied and colored topography. Semidesert to ponderosa pine forests. *Recreation resources:* Lake and warm-water stream fishing; fair trout fishing. Quail hunting; deer, elk, bear, and mountain lion hunting. Saddle and pack trips. Winter photographic possibilities. Scenic drives: Apache Trail and forest highway from Payson to Mogollon Rim, by way of Colcord Mountain. Fourteen public camp and picnic areas. Resorts, dude ranches, cabins, hot mineral baths, boats with or without motor, winter and summer open playgrounds. Nearby towns: Payson, Pine, Young, Roosevelt, and Mesa. *Acres:* 2,410,529.

## ARKANSAS

OUACHITA NATIONAL FOREST

Headquarters at Hot Springs National Park, reached by U. S. Highways 70, 71, 270, 271.

*Special features:* Ouachita, Kiamichi, and Winding Stair Mountains. Four major lakes and many smaller artificial lakes in or near forest. Caddo Gap, where De Soto fought Indians; explored by LaSalle and De Tonti, accounting for the many French names. Crystal Cave; Little Missouri Falls. Four game refuges; medicinal springs. (Forest lies partly in Oklahoma.) *Recreation resources:* Bass fishing. Deer, quail, squirrel hunting. Scenic drives, hiking, and swimming. Fourteen improved forest camp and picnic grounds, with overnight shelters at four areas. Commercial hotels, resorts, and cabin camps in and near the forest. Nearby towns: Hot Springs and Mena, Ark.; Poteau, Okla. *Acres:* 1,485,902.

OZARK NATIONAL FOREST

Headquarters at Russellville, reached by U. S. Highways 64, 71, State Highways 22, 7.

*Special features:* Inviting summer climate; oak forests; scenic drives; five game refuges; three recreational lakes. Mount Magazine. *Recreation resources:* Stream and lake fishing. Deer and small-game hunting. Swimming. Thirteen improved camp and picnic areas. Mount Magazine Lodge and cabins, White Rock Mountain cabins, commercial cabins nearby. Nearby towns: Fort Smith, Fayetteville, Ozark, Clarksville, and Harrison. *Acres:* 991,196.

## CALIFORNIA

ANGELES NATIONAL FOREST

Headquarters at Los Angeles, reached by U. S. Highways 6, 66, 99.

*Special features:* Steep, rugged mountains adjoining Los Angeles metropolitan area; Old Baldy, 10,000 feet. Chiefly a chaparral forest, which serves as a watershed for the Los Angeles area and as an easily reached mountain playground for the inhabitants. Devil Canyon; Bear Canyon Wilderness Area. *Recreation resources:* Scenic drives with wonderful views, especially of city lights at night. Riding and hiking trails, winter sports, fishing, hunting, some swimming and boating. Fifty-two camp and picnic areas; four winter-sports areas, ski lifts and tows. Resorts, cabins, pack and riding stables. Hotels and motor courts in Los Angeles and foothill towns. *Acres:* 646,823.

CLEVELAND NATIONAL FOREST

Headquarters at San Diego, reached by U. S. Highways 101, 395, 80, State Highways 78, 94.

*Special features:* Primarily a watershed forest with an unusually mild climate, between the desert and the sea. Agua Tibia Wilderness Area. The world's largest telescope at the Palomar Observatory. *Recreation resources:* Camping. Warm-water fishing and duck hunting on the impounded lakes of the water systems. Big-game hunting is confined to a deer season of one month during which there is heavy competition; pigeon and quail hunting. The first day's ride of the Mexico to Oregon Trail crosses the forest. Twenty-four public camp and picnic areas; one winter playground. Three resorts with cabins, and dude ranches nearby. The cities of San Diego and Santa Ana are less than 2 hours' drive from the forest. *Acres:* 381,694.

ELDORADO NATIONAL FOREST

Headquarters at Placerville, reached by U. S. Highways 50, 88.

*Special features:* Rugged mountains in Sierra Nevadas. Hundreds of mountain lakes; includes south end of Lake Tahoe, 23 miles long, 13 miles wide, elevation 6,225 feet. Famous early-day mining communities, including Coloma, site of Sutter's mill where discovery of gold started the rush of 1849. (Forest lies partly in Nevada.) *Recreation resources:* Lake and stream fishing. Deer and bear hunting. Scenic drives: Highway 50 to Lake Tahoe; Carson Pass Highway 88, famous for Fremont expedition in 1844 led by Kit Carson; Georgetown to Wentworth Springs. Riding trails, wilderness trips. Twenty-seven public camp and picnic areas; three winter-sports areas. Resorts, hotels, cabins, and dude ranches. Nearby towns: Sacramento, Calif., and Reno, Nev. *Acres:* 624,357.

INYO NATIONAL FOREST

Headquarters at Bishop, reached by U. S. Highways 6, 395.

*Special features:* High Sierra Wilderness Area and Mount Dana-Minarets Wild Area. Palisade Glacier, southernmost glacier in the United States and largest in Sierra Nevadas. Mount Whitney, highest point in continental United States; rugged and spectacular back country, with many peaks more than 14,000 feet elevation. (Forest lies partly in Nevada.) *Recreation resources:* Lake and stream fishing. Deer hunting. Wilderness trips. Many natural lakes, some accessible by paved road up to 9,700 feet elevation. Mammoth Lakes and June Lake-Silver Lake recreation areas. Forty-two public camp and picnic areas; eight winter-sports areas. Resorts, cabins. Nearby towns: Lone Pine, Independence, Bigpine, Bishop, and Leevining. *Acres:* 1,777,478.

KLAMATH NATIONAL FOREST

Headquarters at Yreka, reached by U. S. Highway 99.

*Special features:* Klamath River and tributaries, famous for salmon and steelhead trout. Marble Mountain and Salmon-Trinity Alps Wilderness Areas. High mountain lakes and streams. (Forest lies partly in Oregon.) *Recreation resources:* Steelhead and salmon fishing. Deer hunting. Hiking, riding, and pack trips. Forty improved forest camp and picnic grounds. Commercial cabin camps, resorts, and dude ranches. *Acres:* 1,310,548.

LASSEN NATIONAL FOREST

Headquarters at Susanville, reached by U. S. Highway 395, State Highways 36, 89.

*Special features:* Caribou Peak and Thousand Lakes Wilderness Areas. Many lakes; southern end of Cascade Wonderland; volcanic laval flows and craters; ice caves, lava flow tubes, hot springs, mud pots. Indian pictographs and hieroglyphics. Old emigrant trails. *Recreation resources:* Lake and stream fishing for rainbow, Lochleven, and steelhead trout. Deer and bear hunting. Riding and hiking trails. Scenic road over Mount Lassen crosses through Lassen National Park. Fifty public camp and picnic areas; trailer space. Privately operated resorts, hotels, cabins. Nearby towns: Susanville, Westwood, Chester, Chico, Red Bluff, Redding, Burney, Fall River Mills, McArthur, and Stirling City. *Acres:* 962,500.

LOS PADRES NATIONAL FOREST

Headquarters at Santa Barbara, reached by U. S. Highways 101, 99, 399, State Highways 1, 166, 150.

*Special features:* Primitive forest, varying from coast redwood to semidesert; home of the California condor. Ventana and San Rafael Wild Areas. Snow-capped peaks. *Recreation resources:* Quail and pigeon hunting; some deer and wild boar hunting. Trout fishing. Scenic drives, wilderness trips. Sixty-seven public camp and picnic areas on roads; numerous other trail camps. Kern County Ski Lodge. Hotels, cabins, and a limited number of dude ranches. Nearby towns: Santa Barbara, Ojai, Taft, Santa Maria, San Luis Obispo, Carmel, King City, Monterey, Atascadero, Paso Robles and Ventura. *Acres:* 1,767,196.

MENDOCINO NATIONAL FOREST

Headquarters at Willows, reached by U. S. Highway 99W.

*Special features:* Middle Eel-Yolla Bolly Wilderness Area. Columbian black-tailed deer. *Recreation resources:* Hunting, fishing, hiking, saddle and pack trips. Forty public camps. Local commercial dude ranches and cabin camps. *Acres:* 839,088.

MODOC NATIONAL FOREST

Headquarters at Alturas, reached by U. S. Highways 299, 395, State Highway 139.

*Special features:* South Warner Wilderness Area. Glass Mountain lava flows. Scene of Modoc Indian wars. Winter range of interstate deer herd. Clear Lake Reservoir bird refuge. *Recreation resources:* Stream and lake fishing. Mule deer and waterfowl hunting. Scenic rides, summit trail through South Warner Wilderness Area, wilderness trips. Thirteen public camps; one winter-sports area. Hotels, cabins, and hunters' camps during deer season. Nearby towns: Alturas, Cedarville, Canby, Adin, and Tulelake. *Acres:* 1,609,812.

PLUMAS NATIONAL FOREST

Headquarters at Quincy, reached by State Highways 89, 24.

*Special features:* Feather River country; Feather Falls, one of the highest and most picturesque falls in the United States. Historic gold-mining areas of La Porte, Johnsville, and Rich Bar; largest lumbering industry in California; extensive hydroelectric developments. Limestone caves; large, beautiful mountain valleys: Indian, American, Mohawk, and Sierra. Historic winter-sports areas of La Porte and Johnsville. *Recreation resources:* Lake and stream fishing. Mule and black-tailed deer, bear, duck, geese, quail, and dove hunting. Scenic drives include Feather River Canyon, Lake Almanor, Bucks Lake, Bald Rock Canyon, Quincy-La Porte, Lakes Basin Recreational Area, and Little Last Chance Creek. State riding and hiking trail. Sixteen improved public camp and picnic areas; one winter-sports area at Johnsville. Resorts, hotels, and cabins. Nearby towns: Marysville,

Oroville, Chico, Chester, Susanville, and Sierraville. *Acres:* 1,230,649.

SAN BERNARDINO NATIONAL FOREST

Headquarters at San Bernardino, reached by U. S. Highways 18, 66, 74, 99.

*Special features:* Highest mountains in southern California (San Gorgonio, 11,485 feet, six others of more than 10,000 feet). San Jacinto, San Gorgonia, and Cucamonga Wild Areas. Historical landmarks: Big Bear and Arrowhead Lakes; Mount Jacinto. *Recreation resources:* Lake and stream fishing. Deer hunting. Good sites for municipal and organization youth camps. Camping and pack trips, winter sports. Forty-five public camp and picnic areas with space for trailers; seven winter-sports areas. Resorts, hotels, auto courts, cabins at Arrowhead and Big Bear Lakes. *Acres:* 604,191.

SEQUOIA NATIONAL FOREST

Headquarters at Porterville, reached by State Highways 65, 180, 178, 190.

*Special features:* High Sierra Wilderness Area, with 200 peaks more than 11,000 feet. Mineral King Recreation Area; parts of John Muir Trail; Kings River Canyon; Hume Lake; Kern River Canyon; Boydens Cave; Sequoias; Sequoia National Game Refuge. *Recreation resources:* High mountain lakes and stream fishing. Big-game hunting includes the California mule deer and bear. Scenic drives: Kern River Canyon, Kings River Canyon. Riding trails in wilderness area, hiking, swimming, boating. Sixty public camp and picnic areas; one winter-sports area. Resorts, hotel, cabins. Nearby towns: Fresno, Sanger, Visalia, Porterville, and Bakersfield. *Acres:* 1,114,932.

SHASTA NATIONAL FOREST

Headquarters at Mount Shasta, reached by U. S. Highways 99, 97, 299.

*Special features:* Mount Shasta, 14,161 feet; five living glaciers; Shasta Lake, 365 miles mountain shore line; Trinity Alps Wilderness Area; lava beds; Glass Mountain; Castle Crags. *Recreation resources:* Lake and stream fishing, home of Dolly Varden trout. Waterfowl, upland birds, deer, bear, small-game hunting. Prehistoric limestone caves, lava caves and chimneys. Riding trails in wilderness area. Twenty-nine public camp and picnic areas; two winter-sports areas. Resorts, hotels, motels, and guest ranches. Nearby towns: Dunsmuir, Weed, McCloud, Redding, Callahan, Etna, Trinity Center. and Dorris. *Acres:* 1,264,120.

SIERRA NATIONAL FOREST

Headquarters at North Fork (Madera County), reached by U. S. Highway 99, State Highways 41, 168.

*Special features:* Huntington, Florence, and Shaver Lakes; Dinkey Creek; Bass Lake Recreation Areas. Nelder and McKinley Groves of Big Trees; Central Sierra section of the John Muir Trail. High Sierra Wilderness Area and Mount Dana-Minarets Wild Area. Devils Post Pile National Monument and Rainbow Falls in the Reds Meadow Area. Watershed of the San Joaquin and Kings Rivers. *Recreation resources:* Lake and stream fishing. Deer, bear, and quail hunting. Boating, mountain climbing, pack and saddle trips, numerous swimming areas, winter sports. One hundred and twelve improved forest camp and picnic areas. Commercial cabin camps, hotels, resorts, and dude ranches. Mono Hot Springs, improved mineral water and mud baths. *Acres:* 1,343,184.

SIX RIVERS NATIONAL FOREST

Headquarters at Eureka, reached by U. S. Highways 101, 199, 299.

*Special features:* Giant redwood and fir forests. Klamath, Smith, Eel, and Mad Rivers. Mild, cool climate yearlong; rugged back country. *Recreation resources:* Trout fishing, spring and summer; steelhead and salmon fishing, fall and winter in six rivers. Deer and bear hunting. Wilderness-trip riding trails. Scenic drives. Sixty-eight public camp and picnic areas; one winter-sports area; three organization camps. Resorts, hotels, cabins. Nearby towns: Crescent City, Klamath, Orick, Trinidad, Arcata, Eureka, Fortuna, and Orleans. *Acres:* 926,105.

STANISLAUS NATIONAL FOREST

Headquarters at Sonora, reached by State Highways 4, 108, 120.

*Special features:* Nearest mountain country to San Francisco Bay region and portion of San Joaquin Valley, elevations from 1,100 to 11,575 feet. Deep canyons cut by Merced, Tuolumne, Stanislaus, and Mokelumne Rivers. Fine timber stands. Emigrant Basin Wild Area. Routes of early-day pioneers. Sonora and Ebbets Pass. *Recreation resources:* Fishing in lakes and 715 miles of streams. Big-game hunting for deer and bear. Camping and picnicking, organization camping, scenic drives, hiking, saddle and pack trips, winter sports. Twenty-six public camp and picnic areas; sixteen organization camps; two winter-sports areas. Resorts, cabins, stores, boating areas, packer stations. Nearby towns: Sonora, Jamestown, Columbia, Angels Camp, San Andreas, and Groveland. *Acres:* 897,198.

TAHOE NATIONAL FOREST

Headquarters at Nevada City, reached by U. S. Highway 40, State Highways 20, 49, 89.

*Special features:* Attractive lakes and streams, including shore line of famous Lake Tahoe. Historic Donner Monument and Trail of Forty-niners; mother lode country and scene of much of the California gold-rush history. *Recreation resources:* Excellent terrain and snow conditions for winter sports. Lake and stream fishing. Big-game hunting for deer and bear. Riding and hiking trails. Scenic drives through historic gold-mining towns. Thirty-three public forest camp and picnic areas. Summer resorts, cabins, hotels, and private-club accommodations. Nearby towns: Nevada City, Grass Valley, Truckee, Downieville, Sierra City, Sierraville. *Acres:* 630,490.

#### TRINITY NATIONAL FOREST

Headquarters at Weaverville, reached by U. S. Highway 299, State Highway 36.

*Special features:* Extensive stands of virgin timber. Trinity River drainage. Salmon-Trinity Alps and Yolla Bolly-Middle Eel Wilderness Areas. *Recreation resources:* Deer hunting. Lake and stream fishing, including steelhead and salmon on the Trinity River. Scenic drives, riding trails, wilderness trips. Twenty-three public camp and picnic areas. Resorts, hotels, and cabins. *Acres:* 1,037,579.

### COLORADO

#### ARAPAHO NATIONAL FOREST

Headquarters at Idaho Springs, reached by U. S. Highways 6, 40.

*Special features:* Mount Evans. Gold, silver mining; ghost towns. Gore Range-Eagle Nest Wild Area. *Recreation resources:* Lake and stream fishing. Big-game hunting for elk, deer, and bear, and some small-game hunting. Scenic high mountain routes: Mount Evans, Loveland and Berthoud Passes, Peak to Peak Highway. Riding trails, wilderness-area trips. Forty-nine public camp and picnic grounds; seven winter-sports areas. Resorts, hotels, cabin camps, dude ranches. Nearby towns: Idaho Springs, Dillon, Hot Sulphur Springs, Granby, Grand Lake, and Kremmling. *Acres:* 1,013,523.

#### GRAND MESA NATIONAL FOREST

Headquarters at Grand Junction, reached by U. S. Highways 24, 50.

*Special features:* Grand Mesa Plateau, 10,500 feet high; 250 lakes and reservoirs. Cliffs, canyons, waterfalls, wild flowers. *Recreation resources:* Lake and stream fishing. Deer, bear, duck hunting. Scenic drives, saddle trips, winter sports. Twenty-one public camp and picnic grounds; one winter-sports area. Commercial cabin camps, resorts in and near forest. Nearby towns: Grand Junction, Delta, Palisade, and Rifle. *Acres:* 651,061.

#### GUNNISON NATIONAL FOREST

Headquarters at Gunnison, reached by U. S. Highway 50.

*Special features:* One thousand miles trout fishing streams; many high lakes. Twenty-seven mountain peaks more than 12,000 feet; Ruby Range; Taylor Park reservoir and valley; ghost towns. West Elk and Maroon Bells-Snowmass Wilderness Areas. *Recreation resources:* Fishing. Elk, deer, mountain sheep, bear hunting. Hiking, saddle trips, wilderness-area trips. Twenty-one public camp and picnic grounds; one winter-sports area. Resorts and cabin camps in and near forest. *Acres:* 1,472,335.

#### PIKE NATIONAL FOREST

Headquarters at Colorado Springs, reached by U. S. Highways 24, 85, 285.

*Special features:* Pikes Peak with highway to summit; historic Cripple Creek and Alma gold camps; scenic Rampart Range Road; Devil's Head Forest Fire Lookout; Monument Forest Nursery; Manitou Forest Experiment Station. Platte and Arkansas River watersheds. *Recreation resources:* Hunting, fishing, camping, picnicking, hiking, saddle trips, scenic drives, winter sports. Thirty-six public camp and picnic grounds; Pikes Peak winter-sports area. Commercial hotels, resorts, cabin camps in and near forest. Nearby towns: Colorado Springs and Cripple Creek. *Acres:* 1,078,762.

#### RIO GRANDE NATIONAL FOREST

Headquarters at Monte Vista, reached by U. S. Highways 160, 285.

*Special features:* Mountain lakes and trout streams; Wolf Creek Pass; rugged mountains; Wheeler National Monument; Upper Rio Grande and La Garita-Sheep Mountain Wilderness Areas; active mining camps. *Recreation resources:* Trout fishing. Deer, elk, and duck hunting. Saddle and pack trips, hiking, and scenic drives. Eighteen improved public camp and picnic areas; one winter-sport area. Commercial cabin camps in and near the forest. Nearby towns: Monte Vista, Creede, Saguache, Alamosa, and Antonito. *Acres:* 1,765,123.

#### ROOSEVELT NATIONAL FOREST

Headquarters at Fort Collins, reached by U. S. Highway 287.

*Special features:* Arapaho, Isabelle, and South St. Vrain Glaciers; rugged Continental Divide with many alpine lakes; Poudre and Big Thompson Canyons; Rawah Wild Area. *Recreation resources:* Trout fishing. Deer, bear, mountain lion, grouse, and duck hunting. Saddle and pack trips, hiking, scenic drives. Thirty-three improved public camp and picnic areas; winter-sports areas. Commercial cabin camps and dude ranches in and near the forest. Nearby towns: Fort Collins, Denver, Loveland, Longmont, Boulder, and Estes Park. *Acres:* 782,920.

#### ROUTT NATIONAL FOREST

Headquarters at Steamboat Springs, reached by U. S. Highway 40.

*Special features:* Continental Divide with

perpetual ice and snow; trout streams and alpine lakes. Mount Zirkel-Dome Peak Wild Area; Big Creek Lakes Recreation Area. *Recreation resources:* Trout fishing. Deer, elk, grouse, and duck hunting. Scenic drives, pack and saddle trips, hiking. Thirty-five improved public camp and picnic areas; winter-sports areas. Commercial cabin camps in and near the forest. Nearby towns: Steamboat Springs, Yampa, Hayden, Craig, Walden, and Kremmling. *Acres:* 956,370.

SAN ISABEL NATIONAL FOREST

Headquarters at Pueblo, reached by U. S. Highways 24, 50, 85, 87.

*Special features:* Highest average elevation of any national forest in the United States; Sangre de Cristo Range; 12 peaks more than 14,000 feet, Mount Elbert, second highest in the United States. More than 40 timber-line lakes; Snow Angel on Mount Shavano; Molybdenum mines; Lake Isabel Recreation Area. *Recreation resources:* Lake and stream trout fishing. Deer, elk, bear, mountain lion, and small-game bird hunting. Scenic drives, pack and saddle trips. Twenty-nine improved public camp and picnic areas; three winter-sports areas. Commercial cabin camps and dude ranches in and near the forest. Nearby towns: Pueblo, Canon City, Salida, Walsenburg, and Leadville. *Acres:* 1,153,401.

SAN JUAN NATIONAL FOREST

Headquarters at Durango, reached by U. S. Highways 160, 550.

*Special features:* Alpine lakes; Mount Wilson, 14,250 feet; canyons, waterfalls, cataracts, peculiar geologic formations. Archaeological ruins; historic mines. San Juan and Wilson Mountain Wilderness Areas. *Recreation resources:* Trout fishing. Deer, elk, bear, mountain lion, grouse, and duck hunting. Scenic drives, hiking, saddle and pack trips. Twenty-four improved public camp and picnic areas; winter-sports areas. Commercial cabin camps and dude ranches in and near the forest. Nearby towns: Durango, Pagosa Springs, Mancos, Cortez, Rico, Dolores, and Silverton. *Acres:* 1,848,707.

UNCOMPAHGRE NATIONAL FOREST

Headquarters at Delta, reached by U. S. Highways 50, 550.

*Special features:* Many mountain peaks more than 13,000 feet; Uncompahgre Plateau; gold mines; Uncompahgre Wild Area and Ouray Scenic Area. *Recreation resources:* Trout fishing streams and lakes. Deer, elk, bear, mountain lion, and grouse hunting. Scenic drives, saddle and pack trips. Nine improved public camp and picnic areas; winter-sports areas. Commercial cabin camps and dude ranches in and near the forest. Nearby towns: Delta, Montrose, Silverton, and Ouray. *Acres:* 946,897.

WHITE RIVER NATIONAL FOREST

Headquarters at Glenwood Springs, reached by U. S. Highway 24.

*Special features:* Spectacular Glenwood Canyon; Hanging Lake; Bridal Veil Falls; mineral hot springs; caves; alpine lakes. Zinc and silver mines; source of marble for Lincoln Memorial and Tomb of the Unknown Soldier. Maroon Bells-Snowmass, Flat Tops, and Gore Range-Eagle Nest Wilderness Areas. *Recreation resources:* Trout fishing. Elk, deer, and bear hunting. Hiking, saddle and pack trips, scenic drives. Fifty-five improved public camp and picnic areas; winter-sports areas. Commercial cabin camps and dude ranches in and near the forest. Nearby towns: Glenwood Springs, Aspen, Leadville, Eagle, Gypsum, Rifle, New Castle, Meeker, Hayden, Craig, Yampa, and Steamboat Springs. *Acres:* 1,984,558.

## FLORIDA

APALACHICOLA NATIONAL FOREST

Headquarters at Tallahassee, reached by U. S. Highways 90, 98. (Ranger Headquarters at Tallahassee and Wilma.)

*Special features:* Southern forest in process of development for sustained timber production. Bottom-land hardwood swamps along large rivers contain trees whose natural habitat is far to the north; rare Florida yew and stinking cedar. Old Fort Gadsden, State game refuge. *Recreation resources:* Three rivers and their tributaries with many miles of fishing waters—bass, bream, perch. Quail hunting; deer and bear hunting. Numerous lakes and ponds provide boating and swimming. Five organization camps; one camp and picnic ground. Commercial accommodations near forest. *Acres:* 553,517.

OCALA NATIONAL FOREST

Headquarters at Tallahassee, reached by U. S. Highways 17, 41. (Ranger Headquarters at Ocala.)

*Special features:* Juniper Springs—flows 8 million gallons fresh water daily; lakes. Subtropical palms, hardwoods, and scrub pine. National game refuge. *Recreation resources:* Numerous lakes, streams, and ponds with fishing and camping sites. Annual deer hunt. Three organization camps, eleven improved forest camps and picnic grounds. Cabins at Juniper Springs. Commercial accommodations near forest. *Acres:* 352,869.

OSCEOLA NATIONAL FOREST

Headquarters at Tallahassee, reached by U. S. Highways 41, 90. (Ranger Headquarters at Lake City.)

*Special features:* Extremely flat country, dotted with numerous ponds and cypress swamps; in center of naval stores production area. Olustee Experimental Forest;

State game-breeding ground. *Recreation resources:* Bass, perch, and bream fishing. Deer, turkey, quail, and dove hunting. Swimming and boating at Ocean Pond. Recreation residence site on Ocean Pond. *Acres:* 157,200.

## GEORGIA

### CHATTAHOOCHEE NATIONAL FOREST

Headquarters at Gainesville, reached by U. S. Highways 19, 23, 27, 41, 76.

*Special features:* Brasstown Bald, 4,768 feet, highest point in Georgia; Blue Ridge Mountains; lakes; Tallulah Gorge; waterfalls. Appalachian Trail. *Recreation resources:* Deer and small-game hunting; bow-and-arrow hunt for deer. Trout and bass fishing. Swimming, boating. Sixteen improved forest camp and picnic grounds. *Acres:* 650,635.

## IDAHO

### BOISE NATIONAL FOREST

Headquarters at Boise, reached by U. S. Highways 20, 30, 95, State Highways 15, 16, 17, 21, 22, 52.

*Special features:* Active placer, hydraulic, and shaft mining and dredging in historic gold-rush areas of early days; ghost towns. Rugged back country; beautiful virgin stands of ponderosa pine. Scenes of early Indian camps and massacres. Arrowrock and Anderson Ranch Dams. *Recreation resources:* Lake and stream fishing for trout and salmon. Big-game hunting, including bear, elk, and deer. Scenic drives include spectacular Payette River Canyon, Boise Ridge, and the edge of the Sawtooth Wilderness Area. One hundred and twenty-two public camp and picnic areas; one winter-sports area. Resorts, hotels, cabins, and dude ranches, with horses, boats, and other facilities. Nearby towns: Boise, Emmett, Mountain Home, Cascade, Idaho City, and Horse Shoe Bend. *Acres:* 2,616,608.

### CARIBOU NATIONAL FOREST

Headquarters at Pocatello, reached by U. S. Highways 91, 191, 30.

*Special features:* Generally high plateau topography spotted with beautiful valleys divided by narrow mountain ranges with towering peaks. Includes the world's largest known phosphate reserve containing almost one-third of the world's supply. Historic markers and trails, natural soda springs; beautiful streams and waterfalls. (Forest lies partly in Utah and Wyoming.) *Recreation resources:* Stream fishing; game birds, deer and bear hunting. Scenic drives: Mink Creek to Scout Mountain, Skyline Road, Snake River-McCoy Road along the south bank of the south fork of Snake River, Georgetown Canyon-Diamond Creek and Snowslide-Crow Creek Roads. Numerous riding trails into wilderness areas. Seventeen public camp and picnic areas; two winter-sports areas. Resort, hotel, and cabin accommodations in nearby Idaho Falls, Ririe, Swan Valley, Montpelier, Soda Springs, Lava Hot Springs, and Malad City, Idaho; and Afton, Wyo. *Acres:* 980,508.

### CHALLIS NATIONAL FOREST

Headquarters at Challis, reached by U. S. Highways 20, 93, 93A.

*Special features:* Mt. Borah, elevation 12,655 feet, in Lost River Range, the highest peak in Idaho. Majestic Sawtooth Primitive Area and Stanley Basin; Middle Fork of the Salmon River in the Idaho Wilderness Area. Lemhi, Lost River, and White Cloud Peaks; Salmon River and White Knob mountain ranges, headwaters of the Salmon River. *Recreation resources:* Stream and lake trout and salmon fishing. Big-game species include deer, elk, mountain goat, mountain sheep, antelope, and bear. Stanley Basin scenic drive, riding and hiking trails, wilderness boating and pack trips. Ten public camp and picnic areas. Resorts, hotels, cabins, dude ranches; commercial packers and guides. Nearby towns: Challis, Mackay, Salmon, and Stanley. *Acres:* 2,447,999.

### CLEARWATER NATIONAL FOREST

Headquarters at Orofino, reached by State Highways 9, 11.

*Special features:* Lewis and Clark Route (Lolo Trail Road); Selway-Bitterroot Wilderness Area. Spring log drive on Clearwater and North Fork; large stands of virgin white pine. *Recreation resources:* Trout and salmon fishing in back country. Big-game hunting for elk and bear; deer hunting on part of forest. Scenic drives: North Fork, Lolo Trail, and Lochsa Road. Six improved public camp areas; numerous camping spots. Commercial cabins, camps, and dude ranches. *Acres:* 1,102,855.

### COEUR D'ALENE NATIONAL FOREST

Headquarters at Coeur d'Alene, reached by U. S. Highways 10, 95.

*Special features:* Rich Coeur d'Alene mining district, great producer of zinc, lead, and silver; several large sawmills. Mullan tree on U. S. Highway 10; Cataldo Mission, built in 1846. *Recreation resources:* Many miles of fishing streams. Big-game hunting for deer. Six hundred miles of scenic forest roads. Adjacent to beautiful Coeur d'Alene Lake with 104 miles of shore line. Ten public camp areas; one winter-sports area on U. S. Highway 10. Resort hotels, cabins in Coeur d'Alene, Hayden Lake, Wallace, Kellogg, Mullan, and nearby towns of Spirit Lake and Twin Lakes. *Acres:* 724,285.

### KANIKSU NATIONAL FOREST

Headquarters at Sandpoint, reached by U. S. Highways 95, 195, 10A, 2, 6.

*Special features:* Rugged back country; Selkirk Mountain Range. Pend Oreille Lake (Lake Loop Drive, 107 miles); Priest Lake; Sullivan Lake. Kullyspell House, Clark Fork Area; Roosevelt Ancient Grove of Cedars; Chimney Rock. (Forest lies partly in Montana and Washington.) *Recreation resources:* Lake and stream fishing. Big-game, grouse, and duck hunting. Boating, swimming, scenic drives, wilderness trips. Thirty-three public camp and picnic areas; winter-sports areas. Resorts, hotels, lodges, cabins. Nearby towns: Sandpoint, Bonners Ferry, Priest River, Clark Fork, and Hope. *Acres:* 1,411,318.

MINIDOKA NATIONAL FOREST

Headquarters at Burley, reached by U. S. Highway 30.

*Special features:* "Silent City of Rocks"—fantastic wind- and water-worn rocks. Cleveland, Independence, and smaller alpine lakes; exceptional panoramic views of Snake River Valley. (Forest lies partly in Utah.) *Recreation resources:* Small-stream fishing. Big-game hunting for deer. Scenic drives: Rock Creek-Bostetter-Oakley and Howell Canyon-Lake Cleveland, City of Rocks; riding and hiking trails. Twenty-seven public camp and picnic areas; two winter-sports areas. Nearby towns having hotel and tourist-cabin accommodations: Twin Falls, Kimberly, Hansen, and Burley. *Acres:* 600,632.

NEZPERCE NATIONAL FOREST

Headquarters at Grangeville, reached by U. S. Highway 95, State Highways 9, 13, 14.

*Special features:* Selway-Bitterroot Wilderness Area; Seven Devils Range between Salmon and Snake Rivers; Hells Canyon on the Snake River; Red River Hot Springs. Historic Elk City. *Recreation resources:* Big-game hunting, including elk, deer, and bear. Lake and stream fishing. Horse trails, wilderness trips. Scenic drives: Selway River, Lochsa River, Salmon River. Eighteen public camp and picnic areas; one winter-sports area. Resorts, hotels, cabins. Nearby towns: Grangeville, Stites, Kooskia, Kamiah, Riggins, and White Bird. *Acres:* 1,931,193.

PAYETTE NATIONAL FOREST

Headquarters at McCall, reached by U. S. Highways 95, 15.

*Special features:* Idaho Wilderness Area, Grand Canyon of Snake River, Payette Lakes Vacation Land, Seven Devils Mountains. *Recreation resources:* Fishing for trout and salmon (154 fishing lakes, 1,530 miles fishing streams). Big-game hunting for deer, elk, goats, sheep, bear. Scenic drives; wilderness trips. Thirty improved camps; one winter-sports area. Dude ranches. Nearby towns: McCall, Council, and New Meadows. *Acres:* 2,307,708.

ST. JOE NATIONAL FOREST

Headquarters at Saint Maries, reached by U. S. Highway 95A.

*Special features:* Rugged Bitterroot Range of Idaho-Montana divide; St. Joe River drainage; St. Maries River Valley; canyon areas of Little North Fork of Clearwater River; Clearwater-St. Joe divide, Palouse River area; virgin white pine timber stands. *Recreation resources:* Big-game hunting, including elk, deer, bear, and mountain goat. Lake and stream fishing. Scenic drives along St. Joe River from mouth to source. Thirty public camp ground and picnic areas; two winter-sports areas accessible by highway and trail. One dude ranch; Spring Creek cabins on St. Joe River. Nearby towns: Moscow, Potlatch, Saint Maries, Avery, and Clarkia. *Acres:* 864,291.

SALMON NATIONAL FOREST

Headquarters at Salmon, reached by U. S. Highway 93, State Highways 27, 28.

*Special features:* Idaho Wilderness Area, Big Horn Crags, Lewis and Clark Trail, Salmon River Canyon. *Recreation resources:* Fishing. Big-game hunting, including deer, elk, sheep, goats, bear, cougar, and antelope. Salmon River and Panther Creek forest roads; boat trips on "River of No Return" and Middlefork. Five improved forest camp and picnic grounds, winter-sports areas. Dude ranches. Nearby towns: Salmon and Leadore. *Acres:* 2,049,046.

SAWTOOTH NATIONAL FOREST

Headquarters at Hailey, reached by U. S. Highways 22, 93.

*Special features:* Sawtooth, Pioneer, and Smily Ranges; Sawtooth Wilderness Area; numerous glacial lakes, 1 to 1,500 acres in size. *Recreation resources:* Lake and stream fishing. Big-game hunting, including deer, elk, bear. Scenic drives: Warm Springs Creek, South Boise River, Wood River, Salmon River, Alturas and Red Fish Lakes. Riding trails, wilderness trips, boating, hot springs, mountain climbing. Twenty-eight public camp and picnic areas; two winter-sports areas, including internationally famous Sun Valley with 5 miles of ski lifts. Resorts, hotels, cabins, and dude ranches. Nearby towns: Hailey, Ketchum, Fairfield, and Stanley. *Acres:* 1,202,242.

TARGHEE NATIONAL FOREST

Headquarters at Saint Anthony, reached by U. S. Highways 91, 191, State Highways 22, 29, 31.

*Special features:* Island Park country, lakes and streams; Grand Canyon of the Snake River; Grand Teton Peaks; Big Falls; North Fork of Snake River; Cave Falls; Falls River. (Forest lies partly in Wyoming.) *Recreation resources:* Lake and stream fishing. Big-game hunting, including black and brown bear, deer, elk, and moose. Many riding and hiking trails into semiwilderness areas. Twenty improved camp and picnic areas; three winter-sports areas. Resorts, cabins, dude ranches, boating facilities, pack outfits for hunting parties, and one boys' dude ranch. Nearby towns: Idaho Falls, Rexburg, Rigby, Saint Anthony, Ashton, Driggs, Victor, and Dubois. *Acres:* 1,367,109.

## ILLINOIS

### SHAWNEE NATIONAL FOREST

Headquarters at Harrisburg, reached by U. S. Highways 34, 51, State Highways 1, 3, 34, 127, 144, 145, 146, 151.

*Special features:* Prehistoric stone forts and Indian mounds; interesting rock formations; confluence of the Ohio and Mississippi Rivers at Cairo. *Recreation resources:* Fishing in larger streams. Hunting for quail, migratory waterfowl, squirrel, rabbits, fox, and raccoon. Artificial lakes in and adjacent to forest provide fishing, boating, and swimming. Sixteen State and Forest Service camp and picnic areas. Hotels and cabins at nearby towns of Cairo, Metropolis, Harrisburg, and Marion. *Acres:* 198,510.

## INDIANA

### HOOSIER PURCHASE UNITS

Headquarters at Bedford, reached by U. S. Highways 50, 150.

*Special features:* Pioneer Mothers Memorial Forest containing Nation's outstanding specimen of black walnut. Final outlet of Lost River; Ten O'Clock Indian Boundary Line crosses the forest. Old trail of migrating buffalo between Western Plains and French Lick. *Recreation resources:* Squirrel, fox, and quail hunting. Fishing in the Ohio, Lost, Patoka, and East Fork of the White Rivers and Salt Creek for catfish, bass, and blue gill. Scenic drives for spring flowers (dogwood and redbud) and fall coloring. One public camp and picnic area, with 3-acre lake for swimming and fishing. Commercial hotels and cabin camps. Nearby towns: Evansville, Jasper, and Bedford. *Acres:* 87,861.

## KENTUCKY

### CUMBERLAND NATIONAL FOREST

Headquarters at Winchester, reached by U. S. Highways 25, 27, 60.

*Special features:* Western rim of Cumberland Plateau; sandstone cliffs 100 feet or more high; Red River Gorge; natural rock arches; numerous limestone caves and mineral springs. Cumberland Falls and Natural Bridge State Parks nearby. *Recreation resources:* Bass and pike fishing in larger streams. Red River Gorge drive. Hiking. Two picnic areas. Hotel and cabins at Cumberland Falls State Park and other places near forest. *Acres:* 433,030.

## LOUISIANA

### KISATCHIE NATIONAL FOREST

Headquarters at Alexandria, reached by U. S. Highways 71, 165, 167, 84, State Highways 19, 21.

*Special features:* Colonial homes; Natchitoches, oldest town in Louisiana on Old San Antonio Trail; Stuart Nursery, one of the largest pine nurseries in the world. Extensive plantations of longleaf, loblolly, and slash pines; stand of virgin pine (privately owned), one of few remaining in South. Many bayous and lakes screened with Spanish moss. *Recreation resources:* Fishing in lakes and bayous. Hunting for deer, quail, and migratory birds. Boating, swimming, picnicking, camping, scenic drives. Two artificial lakes; public recreational areas for picnicking and swimming at Valentine Lake, 20 miles west of Alexandria, and Gum Springs, 10 miles west of Winnfield. Commercial hotels and cabin camps nearby. *Acres:* 524,338.

## MICHIGAN

### LOWER MICHIGAN—HURON NATIONAL FOREST

Headquarters at Cadillac, reached by U. S. Highways 23, 27.

*Special features:* Lumbermen's Monument. Forest easily accessible for the large population of southern Michigan, northern Ohio, Indiana, and Illinois. *Recreation resources:* Trout fishing in the AuSable River and smaller streams. Deer, small-game, and bird hunting. Lake Huron with excellent beaches on eastern side. Eighteen public camp and picnic areas; one winter-sports area. A large number of resorts, hotels, and cabins. Towns within and near the forest: East Tawas, Tawas City, Oscoda, Harrisville, Grayling, Roscommon, West Branch, Rose City, and Mio. *Acres:* 378,213.

### LOWER MICHIGAN—MANISTEE NATIONAL FOREST

Headquarters at Cadillac, reached by U. S. Highways 10, 31, 131.

*Special features:* Easily accessible for the large population of southern Michigan, northern Illinois, Indiana, and Ohio. *Recreation resources:* Many lakes and streams provide fishing. Deer and small-game hunting. Good skiing conditions on northern part of forest. Many of the lakes, including Lake Michigan, have beaches for swimming. Canoeing. Sixteen public camp and picnic areas; one winter-sports area. A large number of resorts, hotels, and cabins. Towns within and near the forest: Manistee, Ludington, Scottville, Whitehall, Fremont, Newaygo, White Cloud, Big Rapids, Reed City, Baldwin, Wellston, Brethren. *Acres:* 352,012.

OTTAWA NATIONAL FOREST

Headquarters at Ironwood, reached by U. S. Highways 2, 45, State Highways 28, 35, 64.

*Special features:* Numerous easily accessible lakes and streams: Bond, Agate, Sturgeon, Conglomerate, Gorge, Sandstone, and Rainbow Falls. Victoria Dam; James Toumey Nursery; State Fish Hatchery; forest plantations. *Recreation resources:* Lake and stream fishing; deep-sea trolling in Lake Superior. Deer and bear hunting. Many scenic drives. Fifty-one Federal, State, and county camp and picnic areas; two winter-sports areas. Numerous hotels and cabins. Nearby towns: Ironwood, Wakefield, Bessemer, Iron River, Ontonagon, Watersmeet, Kenton, Marenisco, and Trout Creek. *Acres:* 723,421.

UPPER MICHIGAN—HIAWATHA AND MARQUETTE NATIONAL FORESTS

Headquarters at Escanaba, reached by U. S. Highways 2, 41, State Highways 28, 77, 94.

*Special features:* Lakes Huron, Michigan, and Superior; Pictured Rocks on Lake Superior; Mackinac Island; scenic automobile drives; waterfalls. *Recreation resources:* Lake and stream fishing for trout, bass, northern and walleyed pike, perch; smelt dipping. Deer, black bear, ruffed and sharp-tailed grouse hunting. Canoeing. Twenty-five public camp and picnic areas; two winter-sports areas. Resorts, hotels, many cabins. Nearby well-equipped State parks. Adjacent towns: Rapid River, Gladstone, Escanaba, Munising, Manistique, Saint Ignace, and Sault Sainte Marie. *Acres:* 781,972.

## MINNESOTA

CHIPPEWA NATIONAL FOREST

Headquarters at Cass Lake, reached by U. S. Highways 2, 71, 371.

*Special features:* Headwaters of the Mississippi River; Leech Lake, Lake Winnibigoshish, Cass Lake, and hundreds of smaller lakes; stands of virgin red pine. Home and present headquarters of the Chippewa Indians. *Recreation resources:* Lake fishing for walleyed and northern pike, and pan fish. Waterfowl and upland game-bird hunting; big-game hunting, including deer and black bear. Hundreds of miles of good roads and scenic drives, swimming, boating, and water sports. Winter sports, including skiing, tobogganing, snowshoeing, and ice fishing. Eighteen public camp and picnic areas; one winter-sports area. Three hundred resorts in and adjacent to the forest. Hotels, cabins, organization camps, boys' and girls' camps. Nearby towns: Cass Lake, Walker, Deer River, Grand Rapids, Remer, Bemidji, and Blackduck. *Acres:* 586,701.

802062°—49——56

SUPERIOR NATIONAL FOREST

Headquarters at Duluth, reached by U. S. Highways 1, 53, 61.

*Special features:* Five thousand lakes, rugged shore lines, picturesque islands, sand beaches; million acres of virgin forest. Superior and Little Indian Sioux Roadless Areas, outstanding for canoe trips; historic water route to northwest. *Recreation resources:* Lake and stream fishing. Deer hunting. Scenic drives: Gunflint, Ely-Buyck, Sawbill, and Honeymoon Trails. Sixteen unusual canoe routes. Twenty public camp and picnic grounds. Resorts, hotels, and cabins. Nearby towns: Duluth, Virginia, International Falls, Ely, Two Harbors, and Grand Marais. *Acres:* 1,807,085.

## MISSISSIPPI

BIENVILLE NATIONAL FOREST

Headquarters at Jackson, reached by U. S. Highway 80, State Highway 35. (Ranger Headquarters at Forest.)

*Special features:* Coastal plain, second-growth pine and hardwood forest; numerous forest-management demonstration areas; 80 acres of virgin loblolly pine surrounding Bienville Ranger Station. *Recreation resources:* Quail hunting. Fishing. Swimming. One improved forest camp and picnic ground. *Acres:* 175,375.

DELTA PURCHASE UNIT

Headquarters at Jackson, reached by U. S. Highway 61. (Ranger Headquarters at Rolling Fork.)

*Special features:* Extensive areas of virgin bottom-land hardwood. *Recreation resources:* Deer hunting. Fishing. No improved campgrounds. *Acres:* 59,152.

DE SOTO NATIONAL FOREST

Headquarters at Jackson, reached by U. S. Highways 11, 90. (Ranger Headquarters at Gulfport, Laurel, and Hattiesburg.)

*Special features:* Ashe Forest Nursery; Harrison Experimental Forest; site of South Mississippi Gun and Dog Club field trials. *Recreation resources:* Quail hunting. Fishing. Bathing and boating. Three improved forest camp and picnic grounds. *Acres:* 498,079.

HOLLY SPRINGS NATIONAL FOREST

Headquarters at Jackson, reached by U. S. Highways 72, 78. (Ranger Headquarters at Holly Springs.)

*Special features:* Area contains some of the largest erosion gullies known; intensive erosion-control projects. Annual bird-dog field trials at Holly Springs. *Recreation resources:* Quail and small-game hunting. No improved forest camp or picnic grounds. *Acres:* 123,066.

HOMOCHITTO NATIONAL FOREST

Headquarters at Jackson, reached by U. S. Highways 61, 84. (Ranger Headquarters at Meadville.)

*Special features:* One of finest natural timber-growing sites in the United States with numerous forest-management demonstration areas. Picturesque eroded loess country near Natchez. *Recreation resources:* Fishing, swimming, picnicking, and camping, with trailer facilities at Clear Springs Recreation Area. One improved forest camp and picnic area. *Acres:* 188,974.

## MISSOURI

CLARK NATIONAL FOREST

Headquarters at Rolla, reached by U. S. Highways 8, 19, 21, 60, 67.

*Special features:* Big springs; clear fast-flowing streams; Ozark Mountains covered with oak and pine forests; spring bloom of redbud and dogwood and brilliant fall coloring. *Recreation resources:* Small-mouthed bass and other fishing. Squirrel and fox hunting. Hundreds of miles of streams for "John-boat" float trips. Thirteen public camp and picnic grounds. Nearby towns: Doniphan, Poplar Bluff, Van Buren, Ironton, Steelville, Salem, and Eminence. *Acres:* 865,464.

MARK TWAIN NATIONAL FOREST

Headquarters at Springfield, reached by U. S. Highways 63, 66.

*Special features:* Ozark Mountains; numerous coves, rock cairns, and springs. *Recreation resources:* Clear streams with fishing for pan fish, bass, and pike. Quail hunting. Scenic drives. Two roadside campgrounds and one developed camping, picnic, and swimming area. Resorts and hotels in nearby towns of Branson, Hollister, Cassville, Forsyth, Rolla, Willow Springs, and West Plains. *Acres:* 427,209.

## MONTANA

BEAVERHEAD NATIONAL FOREST

Headquarters at Dillon, reached by U. S. Highway 91, State Highways 1, 41, 34, 36, 43.

*Special features:* Anaconda-Pintlar Wilderness Area; Big Hole Battlefield Monument; Sacajawea Memorial Area; first capital of Montana. Tobacco Root, Madison, Gravelly, Snowcrest, and Continental Divide Ranges; Madison, Ruby, Beaverhead, and Big Hole Rivers; alpine lakes. *Recreation resources:* Fishing. Deer, elk, moose, antelope, and bear hunting. Wilderness trips, scenic drives. Hot springs. Twenty-six public camp and picnic areas; winter-sports areas. Resorts, hotels, and cabins in and near forest. Nearby towns: Dillon, Wisdom, Jackson, Lima, Ennis, Virginia City, and Sheridan. *Acres:* 2,131,323.

BITTERROOT NATIONAL FOREST

Headquarters at Hamilton, reached by U. S. Highway 93.

*Special features:* Bitterroot Valley and spectacular Bitterroot Mountains; scores of mountain lakes and hot springs. Ancient Indian hieroglyphics. Saint Mary's Mission and Fort Owen. Selway-Bitterroot Wilderness Area, largest in United States; Anaconda-Pintlar Wilderness Area. (Forest lies partly in Idaho.) *Recreation resources:* Lake and stream fishing. Big-game hunting for elk, deer, bear, and goats. Bitterroot Valley scenic drive, riding trails, wilderness trips. Ten public camp and picnic areas, one winter-sports area. Resorts, hotels, cabins, and dude ranches. Nearby towns: Darby, Hamilton, Corvallis, Stevensville, and Missoula. *Acres:* 1,917,466.

CABINET NATIONAL FOREST

Headquarters at Thompson Falls, reached by U. S. Highways 10, 10A, State Highway 28.

*Special features:* Cabinet Mountains Wild Area; rugged mountain ranges; numerous highland lakes and mountain streams. One hundred miles of Clark Fork River Valley combining agricultural lands, forested areas, and picturesque mountain grandeur. *Recreation resources:* Mountain lake, stream, and river fishing. Big-game hunting, including bear, elk, black- and white-tailed deer. Numerous scenic drives; primitive area and trail riding trips; huckleberrying. Fifteen developed public camp and picnic areas; Lookout Pass winter-sports area on U. S. Highway 10. Limited resort, hotel, cabin, and dude ranch facilities. Nearby towns: Thompson Falls, Plains, Hot Springs, Paradise, Saint Regis, Noxon, Saltese, and Trout Creek. *Acres:* 1,133,417.

CUSTER NATIONAL FOREST

Headquarters at Billings, reached by U. S. Highways 10, 12.

*Special features:* Spectacular Red Lodge-Cooke City highway; snow-clad peaks and alpine plateaus; Granite Peak, 12,962 feet, highest point in Montana; hundreds of lakes; Woodbine Falls, 900 feet; glaciers and ice caverns. Rich fossil beds; Indian hieroglyphics and burial grounds. Beartooth Wilderness Area. (Forest lies partly in South Dakota.) *Recreation resources:* Trout fishing. Big-game hunting. Saddle and pack trips. Thirty public camp and picnic areas; one winter-sports area. Resorts, hotels, cabins, and dude ranches. Nearby towns: Red Lodge, Laurel, and Billings. *Acres:* 1,171,909.

DEERLODGE NATIONAL FOREST

Headquarters at Butte, reached by U. S. Highways 10S, 10A, 91, State Highway 38.

*Special features:* Anaconda-Pintlar Wilderness Area; Tobacco Root Mountains; Mount Powell and Flint Creek Range;

numerous alpine lakes. *Recreation resources:* Lake and stream fishing. Big-game hunting, including bear, deer, elk, and special moose seasons. Riding trails, wilderness trips. Twenty-five public camp areas; five winter-sports areas. Resorts, hotels, cabins, and dude ranches. Nearby towns: Whitehall, Butte, Boulder, Anaconda, Philipsburg, and Deer Lodge. *Acres:* 1,134,709.

FLATHEAD NATIONAL FOREST

Headquarters at Kalispell, reached by U. S. Highways 2, 93, State Highways 35, 37.

*Special features:* Spectacular geological formations, including massive Chinese Wall and jagged Mission Mountains; hanging valleys; glaciers and scores of glacial lakes. Mission Mountains Wild Area; Bob Marshall Wilderness Area. *Recreation resources:* Fishing. Hunting big game, including elk, deer, moose, bear, mountain sheep and goats. Picnicking, boating, camping, canoeing, hiking, and riding. Scenic drives around Flathead Lake; wilderness trips. Twelve public camp and picnic areas; two winter-sports areas, including Big Mountain ski course. Resorts, hotels, cabins, and dude ranches. Nearby towns: Whitefish, Columbia Falls, Coram, Belton, and Bigfork. *Acres:* 2,230,517.

GALLATIN NATIONAL FOREST

Headquarters at Bozeman, reached by U. S. Highways 191, 10, 89.

*Special features:* Great Gallatin Valley; Crazy Mountains; canyons, snow-clad peaks; 11 outstanding waterfalls; more than 200 lakes and thousands of miles of trout streams. Spanish Peaks and Absaroka Wild Areas. *Recreation resources:* Lake and stream fishing. Big-game hunting, including bear, moose, elk, and deer. Scenic drives: Gallatin Canyon, Boulder Canyon, and Yankee Jim Canyon. Trail riding and wilderness trips. Thirty-eight public camp and picnic areas; three winter-sports areas. Resorts, hotels, cabins, and dude ranches. Nearby towns: Bozeman, West Yellowstone, Livingston, Bigtimber, and Gardiner. *Acres:* 1,695,638.

HELENA NATIONAL FOREST

Headquarters at Helena, reached by U. S. Highways 10N, 91.

*Special features:* Continental Divide; Big Belt and Elkhorn Mountain Ranges. Boat trip to Gates of Mountains on Missouri River; old Fort Logan original blockhouse; ghost towns: Diamond City, Marysville, Crow Creek Falls. Gates of the Mountains Wild Area. *Recreation resources:* Lake and stream fishing. Elk and deer hunting. Scenic drives: Trout and Beaver Creek Canyons. Riding trails, wilderness trips. Five public camp and picnic areas; one winter-sports area. Resorts, hotels, cabins, and dude ranches. Nearby towns: Helena, Townsend, Lincoln, and White Sulphur Springs. *Acres:* 964,230.

KOOTENAI NATIONAL FOREST

Headquarters at Libby, reached by U. S. Highway 2, State Highway 37.

*Special features:* Cabinet Mountains Wild Area; Whitefish Range; Yaak River; Kootenai Canyon; Fisher River. (Forest lies partly in Idaho.) *Recreation resources:* Lake and stream fishing. Big-game hunting, including black bear and deer. Scenic drives: Yaak River, Kootenai Canyon, Fisher River. Riding trails. Ten public camp and picnic areas; one winter-sports area. Hotels, cabins, and dude ranch facilities. Nearby towns: Libby, Troy, and Eureka. *Acres:* 1,803,934.

LEWIS AND CLARK NATIONAL FOREST

Headquarters at Great Falls, reached by U. S. Highways 87, 89, 91, State Highway 29.

*Special features:* Bob Marshall Wilderness Area; Chinese Wall and Continental Divide; scenic limestone canyons and rolling mountains with many open parks; Little Belt Mountains. *Recreation resources:* Stream and lake fishing. Big-game hunting for deer, elk, grizzly and black bear, and antelope. Wilderness trips, riding trails. Numerous scenic drives: Kings Hill, Judith River, Crystal Lake, Sun River, and Teton River. Twenty camp and picnic areas; one winter-sports area. Many resorts, cabins, and dude ranches. Nearby towns: Great Falls and Lewistown. *Acres:* 1,861,674.

LOLO NATIONAL FOREST

Headquarters at Missoula, reached by U. S. Highways 10, 93, State Highway 20.

*Special features:* Bob Marshall and Selway-Bitterroot Wilderness Areas; Mission, Bitterroot, and Swan Ranges; Continental Divide; Lewis and Clark Trail; junction Clark Fork and Bitterroot Rivers. (Forest lies partly in Idaho.) *Recreation resources:* Stream and lake fishing. Hunting for native grouse, Chinese pheasant, elk, deer, and bear. Wilderness pack trips. Scenic drives: Lolo Trail, Lochsa River, Seeley Lake, Buffalo Park, Rock Creek. Mountain saddle trails, foot trails to a hundred lakes and peaks. Twenty-nine public camp grounds; Pattee Canyon picnic area. Resorts, dude ranches. Nearby towns: Missoula, Ovando, Superior, Alberton, and Drummond. *Acres:* 1,718,707.

## NEBRASKA

NEBRASKA NATIONAL FOREST

Headquarters at Halsey, reached by U. S. Highway 20.

*Special features:* Bessey Nursery; extensive sand-hill forest plantations; largest herd of mule deer in Nebraska; entire forest in game refuge; nesting grounds of great blue heron, grouse, and prairie chicken. *Recreation resources:* Pheasant, migratory bird, and small-game hunting in season outside the forest boundaries. Fishing. Swimming. One improved public camp and picnic ground. Hotel accommodations at Broken Bow and Valentine. *Acres:* 206,028.

## NEVADA

### HUMBOLDT NATIONAL FOREST

Headquarters at Elko, reached by U. S. Highways 18, 40.

*Special features:* Wildhorse Reservoir; Owyhee River Canyon; Humboldt, Independence, and Ruby Mountains. Thriving livestock industry in the Northfork and Mountain City areas. *Recreation resources:* Fishing in streams and Wildhorse Reservoir. Deer hunting. Saddle and pack trips. No forest camp grounds. Resort and dude ranch at Wildhorse Reservoir. Hotel facilities at Elko and Mountain City. *Acres:* 1,056,878.

### NEVADA NATIONAL FOREST

Headquarters at Ely, reached by U. S. Highways 6, 50, 93, State Highway 39.

*Special features:* Mount Wheeler, 13,061 feet, is the highest peak wholly in Nevada. The Charleston Division is famous because of its large pine trees and cool climate in the midst of hot desert country. Lehman Caves National Monument. *Recreation resources:* Deer hunting; Nevada's only elk herd. Scenic trails on Snake Division and Charleston Mountain. Twenty public camp, picnic, and trailer-camp areas; two winter-sports areas. Nearby towns: Las Vegas, Ely, McGill, Ruth, and Kimberly. *Acres:* 1,238,566.

### TOIYABE NATIONAL FOREST

Headquarters at Reno, reached by U. S. Highways 395, 50, 40, 6, 88, 108, 95, California State Highway 4, Nevada State Highways 8A, 88, 3, 22.

*Special features:* Sierra Nevada, Toiyabe, Santa Rosa Ranges; alpine lakes; Virginia Creek, Green Creek, and Twin Lakes; Hoover Wild Area. (Forest lies partly in California.) *Recreation resources:* Lake and stream fishing, golden and Piute trout. Black-tailed and mule deer, antelope hunting. Scenic drives: Mount Rose, Lake Tahoe, Ebbetts and Sonora Passes. Riding trails, wilderness trips. Twenty-three public camp and picnic areas; two winter-sports areas. Resorts, hotels, cabins, and dude ranches. Nearby towns: Reno, Carson City, Minden, Austin, Tonopah, and Winnemucca. *Acres:* 3,299,844.

## NEW HAMPSHIRE

### WHITE MOUNTAIN NATIONAL FOREST

Headquarters at Laconia, reached by U. S. Highways 2, 3, 302.

*Special features:* Embraces a major portion of the White Mountains. Mount Washington, 6,288 feet, highest point in New England; Presidential Range; Tuckerman Ravine; Glen Ellis Falls; Lakes of the Clouds. (Forest lies partly in Maine.) *Recreation resources:* Mountain-stream fishing. Deer hunting, bear hunting. Scenic drives through famous notches. Winter and spring skiing; mountain climbing and hiking, more than 1,000 miles of foot trails; swimming. Sixteen public camp and picnic grounds, including popular Dolly Copp Area. High-country cabins. Nearby hotels and cabins. *Acres:* 704,538.

## NEW MEXICO

### CARSON NATIONAL FOREST

Headquarters at Taos, reached by U. S. Highway 64, State Highways 3, 75, 38.

*Special features:* Home and burial place of Kit Carson; well-known art colony; Taos Indian pueblo. Sangre de Cristo Mountains, including Wheeler Peak, 13,123 feet; trout streams, lakes, and hot springs; Harwood Foundation. *Recreation resources:* Lake and stream trout fishing. Hunting, including turkey and brown bear. Scenic drives; saddle and pack trips. Thirty public camp and picnic grounds; two winter-sports areas. Nearby towns: Taos, Sante Fe, and Raton. *Acres:* 1,114,329.

### CIBOLA NATIONAL FOREST

Headquarters at Albuquerque, reached by U. S. Highways 85, 66, 60.

*Special features:* Mount Taylor, 11,389 feet, and Sandia Crest, 10,800 feet, accessible by auto. Antelope herds. Pueblo Indian villages; prehistoric ruins; ancient "sky city" of Acoma. *Recreation resources:* Deer and antelope hunting. Limited fishing. Scenic drives. Thirty-four public camp and picnic areas; two winter-sports areas. Resorts, hotels, cabins, and dude ranches. Nearby towns: Albuquerque, Mountainair, Belen, Socorro, Hot Springs, Grants, and Gallup. *Acres:* 1,711,100.

### GILA NATIONAL FOREST

Headquarters at Silver City, reached by U. S. Highway 260, State Highways 180, 52, 78, 185, 186.

*Special features:* Abundant game. Gila and Black Range Wilderness Areas; Mogollon, Black, Pinos Altos, and Diablo Mountain Ranges. Gila Cliff Dwelling National Monument; prehistoric ruins. *Recreation resources:* Stream fishing. Big-game hunting, including black bear, mule deer, white-tailed deer, antelope, and mountain lion, and turkey hunting. Scenic drives: Outer Loop, Inner Loop. Riding and hiking trails; wilderness trips. Eighteen public camp and picnic areas. Private cabins, lodge resorts, and dude ranches. Nearby towns: Silver City, Glenwood, Deming, Lordsburg, and Hot Springs. *Acres:* 2,394,763.

LINCOLN NATIONAL FOREST

Headquarters at Alamogordo, reached by U. S. Highways 54, 70, 380, State Highway 83.

*Special features:* White Mountain, 12,000 feet; extensive ponderosa pine and fir stands. Scene of Lincoln County range war. White Mountain Wild Area. Adjoins Carlsbad Caverns National Park and White Sands National Monument. *Recreation resources:* Fishing. Big-game hunting. Winter sports, scenic drives, saddle and pack trips. Golfing at Ruidoso and Cloudcroft, highest golf course in the world. Eight public camp and picnic areas; two winter-sports areas. Resort hotels, lodges, cabins, dude ranches, and organization camps. Nearby towns: Ruidoso, Cloudcroft, Alamogordo, Carlsbad, Artesia, and Roswell. *Acres:* 1,178,910.

SANTA FE NATIONAL FOREST

Headquarters at Santa Fe, reached by U. S. Highways 285, 85, 64, 84.

*Special features:* Sangre de Cristo Range, including Truchas Peaks, 13,306 feet, highest in New Mexico; Pecos and Jemez Rivers; mountain streams and lakes. San Pedro Parks Wild Area; Pecos Wilderness Area. Indian villages; ancient pueblo and Spanish mission ruins; cliff dwellings. *Recreation resources:* Lakes and streams furnish much of the clear water for trout fishing in State. Turkey, elk, deer, and bear hunting. Wilderness trips. Thirty-one public camp and picnic areas; one winter-sports area. Commercial resorts, hotels, and cabin camps on Pecos and Jemez Rivers, in vicinity of Santa Fe, Las Vegas, and Jemez Springs. Nearby towns: Santa Fe, Las Vegas, Pecos, Espanola, and Bernalillo. *Acres:* 1,253,719.

## NORTH CAROLINA

CROATAN NATIONAL FOREST

Headquarters at Asheville, reached by U. S. Highways 17, 70. (Ranger Headquarters at New Bern.)

*Special features:* Historic New Bern, founded 1710; Civil War breastworks. Five large lakes; pine and swamp hardwoods, 3 miles from Atlantic Ocean. *Recreation resources:* Deer, bear, turkey, quail, and migratory bird hunting. Fishing. Boating, swimming. Two improved forest camp and picnic grounds. Commercial resorts and cabin camps in and near forest. *Acres:* 146,831.

NANTAHALA NATIONAL FOREST

Headquarters at Franklin, reached by U. S. Highways 19, 64, 129, 23.

*Special features:* Fontana, Hiwassee, Santeetlah, Aquone, Cheoah, Glenville, and Apalachia Lakes; Fontana Dam; Cullasaja, White Water River, Bridal Veil, Toxaway, and Dry Falls. Joyce Kilmer Memorial Forest; 80 miles of Appalachian Trail. Southern Appalachian Mountains famous for azaleas and rhododendrons. *Recreation resources:* Lake and stream fishing for bass and trout. European wild boar, deer, bear, turkey, and bird hunting. Hiking, swimming, and boating. Eight improved forest camp and picnic grounds. Swimming at Cliffside Lake and Arrowood; Van Hook Glade trailer camp. Tourist and cabin accommodations in and near forest. *Acres:* 386,161.

PISGAH NATIONAL FOREST

Headquarters at Asheville, reached by U. S. Highways 19, 23, 25, 64, 70, 221, 276, 321, and Blue Ridge Parkway.

*Special features:* Mount Mitchell, 6,684 feet; Linville Falls and Gorge. Pisgah National Game Refuge; Boone, Mount Mitchell, and Sherwood Cooperative Game Management Areas, with annual big-game hunts. Craggy Gardens and Roan Mountain famous for purple rhododendron; Appalachian Trail. *Recreation resources:* Trout, bass, and perch fishing. Deer, bear, and small-game hunting. Hiking, horseback riding, swimming. Eighteen improved forest camp and picnic grounds. Commercial resorts and cabin camps in and near forest. Nearby towns: Hot Springs, Lenoir, Marion, and Pisgah Forest. *Acres:* 467,016.

## OHIO

WAYNE PURCHASE UNITS

Headquarters at Columbus, reached by U. S. Highways 21, 23, 33, 35, 50, 52.

*Special features:* Particularly beautiful fall coloring of hardwoods. Nearby points of interest include historic Marietta, Gallipolis, Blennerhasset's Island, and Amesville "Coonskin Library." Iron and old charcoal furnaces. *Recreation resources:* Small-game hunting. Fishing on numerous streams and lakes. Hiking, horseback riding, automobile tours, scenic lookout points. Lake Vesuvius Recreation Area and five other developed areas. Overnight accommodations at numerous cabin camps, tourist homes, and hotels along the main highways and at the larger towns throughout the area. *Acres:* 82,784.

## OREGON

DESCHUTES NATIONAL FOREST

Headquarters at Bend, reached by U. S. Highways 28, 97.

*Special features:* Snow-clad peaks, ice caves, waterfalls, and scores of beautiful mountain lakes; lava caves; Deschutes River; Newberry Crater; "Century Drive." Mount Jefferson Wild Area and Three Sisters Wilderness Area. *Recreation resources:* Rainbow trout fishing. Deer hunting. Scenic drives, saddle and pack trips, winter sports. Thirty-eight improved forest camp and picnic grounds; one winter-sports area. Commercial dude ranches, cabin camps, and resorts in and near forest. Nearby towns: Sisters, Redmond, Bend, and Crescent. *Acres:* 1,644,125.

FREMONT NATIONAL FOREST

Headquarters at Lakeview, reached by U. S. Highway 395.

*Special features:* Abert fault east of Lake Abert, second-largest vertical fault in world. Indian paintings and writings. Protected herds of antelope. Oregon Desert; Gearhart Mountain Wild Area. *Recreation resources:* Deer hunting. Thirteen improved forest camp and picnic grounds. Commercial cabin camps in and near forest. Nearby towns: Lakeview, Bly, Paisley, Crescent, and Klamath Falls. *Acres:* 1,252,280.

MALHEUR NATIONAL FOREST

Headquarters at John Day, reached by U. S. Highways 28, 395.

*Special features:* Cabin of Joaquin Miller. Mountains; miles of fishing streams; archers' hunting reserve; fossil beds of prehistoric plants and animals; extensive stand of ponderosa pine forest. Strawberry Mountain Wild Area. *Recreation resources:* Stream trout fishing. Elk and deer hunting. Scenic drives, saddle and pack trips. Eleven improved forest and camp and picnic grounds. Commercial cabin camps in and near forest. Nearby towns: John Day, Burns, and Prairie City. *Acres:* 1,180,615.

MOUNT HOOD NATIONAL FOREST

Headquarters at Portland, reached by U. S. Highways 30, 99.

*Special features:* World-famous scenic drives; hot springs; renowned Timberline Lodge; Multnomah Falls; glaciers, lakes, and flower-filled alpine meadows. Mount Hood and Mount Jefferson Wild Areas. On Oregon Trail route. *Recreation resources:* Stream and lake fishing. Swimming, winter sports, saddle and pack trips, spectacular auto tours. Fifty-five improved forest camp and picnic grounds; four winter-sports areas. Timberline Lodge and other commercial resorts in and near forest. Nearby towns: Portland, Hood River, Gresham, Estacada, Sandy, and Maupin. *Acres:* 1,107,305.

OCHOCO NATIONAL FOREST

Headquarters at Prineville, reached by U. S. Highways 28, 97.

*Special features:* Parklike ponderosa pine forests; many beaver colonies. Frontier-day Army post; scene of early-day range wars. *Recreation resources:* Trout fishing. Deer hunting. Scenic drives. Five improved forest camp and picnic grounds. Commercial cabin camps in and near forest. Nearby towns: Prineville and Dayville. *Acres:* 836,847.

ROGUE RIVER NATIONAL FOREST

Headquarters at Medford, reached by U. S. Highway 99.

*Special features:* Table Rock, site o[f] bloody war with Rogue River Indians Rogue River; lakes, trout streams, and waterfalls; extensive sugar pine and Douglas fir forests. Mountain Lakes Wild Area (Forest lies partly in California.) *Recreation resources:* Rainbow and steelhead trout fishing. Deer and migratory bird hunting Scenic drives; saddle trips and pack trips Twenty-four improved forest camp and picnic grounds. Commercial cabin camps in and near forest. Nearby towns: Medford, Ashland, Grants Pass, Klamath Falls, and Crescent. *Acres:* 896,284.

SISKIYOU NATIONAL FOREST

Headquarters at Grants Pass, reached by U. S. Highways 99, 101, 199.

*Special features:* Famous fishing grounds in lower Rogue River gorge; early-day gold camps. Home of Port-Orford-cedar and Oregon-myrtle; profuse growths of wild lilac, rhododendron, azaleas, and pitcher plants; Brewer weeping spruce; Saddler oak. Kalmiopsis Wild Area. (Forest lies partly in California.) *Recreation resources:* Cut-throat and steelhead trout and salmon fishing. Deer, bear, and cougar hunting. Boat trips, saddle and pack trips, scenic drives. Seventeen improved forest camp and picnic grounds. Commercial resorts, outfitters, and cabin camps in and near forest. Nearby towns: Grants Pass, Powers, Gold Beach, and Brookings. *Acres:* 1,079,451.

SIUSLAW NATIONAL FOREST

Headquarters at Corvallis, reached by U. S. Highways 20, 99, 101.

*Special features:* Heavy stands Sitka spruce, western hemlock, cedar, and Douglar-fir; pitcher plants, rhododendron, and azaleas. Bordered by Pacific Ocean. Cape Perpetua; sand dunes. Cascade Head Experimental Forest. *Recreation resources:* Ocean, lake, and stream fishing. Deer, bear, cougar, and migratory-bird hunting. Swimming, boating, clam digging, saddle and pack trips, scenic drives. Nineteen improved forest camp and picnic grounds. Commercial cabin camps and resorts in and near forest. Nearby towns: Corvallis, Eugene, Newport, Mapleton, Florence, Waldport, and Taft. *Acres:* 597,696.

UMATILLA NATIONAL FOREST

Headquarters at Pendleton, reached by U. S. Highways 30, 395.

*Special features:* On old Oregon Trail route; famous "Pendleton Roundup." Blue Mountains; hot sulphur springs; Starkey Experimental Forest and Range. (Forest lies partly in Washington.) *Recreation resources:* Elk, deer, pheasant hunting. Saddle trips and scenic drives, winter sports. Seventeen improved forest camp and picnic grounds; one winter-sports area. Commercial hostelries in and near forest. Nearby towns: Pendleton and La Grande, Oreg.; Walla Walla, Wash. *Acres:* 1,385,235.

UMPQUA NATIONAL FOREST

Headquarters at Roseburg, reached by U. S. Highway 99.

*Special features:* Spectacular North Umpqua Cataracts; Toketee and Lemolo Falls; Umpqua River; Diamond Lake; Mount Thielsen. *Recreation resources:* Steelhead and rainbow trout fishing. Deer, bear, cougar hunting. Scenic drives, saddle and pack trips. Twenty-three improved forest camp and picnic grounds. Commercial resorts and cabin camps near forest. *Acres:* 979,845.

WALLOWA NATIONAL FOREST

Headquarters at Enterprise, reached by U. S. Highway 30.

*Special features:* Snow-capped peaks; Wallowa and many other lakes; glaciers; alpine meadows and rare wild flowers; Minam River, famous fishing stream. Grand spectacle of Snake River and Imnaha Canyons from Grizzly Ridge Road. Eagle Cap Wilderness Area. *Recreation resources:* Stream and lake trout fishing. Elk, deer, bear hunting. Saddle and pack trips, scenic drives. Sixteen improved forest camp and picnic grounds. Commercial resorts and cabin camps in and near forest. Nearby towns: Enterprise, Wallowa, and Joseph. *Acres:* 979,264.

WHITMAN NATIONAL FOREST

Headquarters at Baker, reached by U. S. Highways 28, 395, 30.

*Special features:* Blue and Wallowa Mountains; Anthony Lakes; Eagle Cap Wilderness Area. *Recreation resources:* Stream and lake fishing. Deer, bear, elk hunting. Scenic drives, saddle and pack trips. Eight improved forest camp and picnic grounds; one winter-sports area. Commercial cabin camps and dude ranches in and near forest. Nearby towns: Baker, La Grande, Union, and Prairie City. *Acres:* 1,483,303.

WILLAMETTE NATIONAL FOREST

Headquarters at Eugene, reached by U. S. Highways 20, 28, 54, 99.

*Special features:* Most heavily timbered national forest in United States. Snow-capped peaks, lakes, waterfalls, and hot springs; McKenzie Pass Highway. Three Sisters Wilderness Area, including extraordinary volcanic formations; Mount Jefferson Wild Area. *Recreation resources:* Stream and lake fishing. Deer and bear hunting. Scenic drives, saddle and pack trips. Fifty-one improved forest camp and picnic grounds; two winter-sports areas. Commercial cabin camps and pack-trip outfitters in and near forest. Nearby towns: Eugene, Albany, Salem, and Lebanon. *Acres:* 1,666,998.

## PENNSYLVANIA

ALLEGHENY NATIONAL FOREST

Headquarters at Warren, reached by U. S. Highways 6, 62, State Highway 59.

*Special features:* Allegheny Mountains; oil field; Watermill Race ski trail; Chief Cornplanter Indian Reservation. Hearts Content and Tionesta Natural Areas, virgin timber stands; 300 miles of trout streams. Beaver Meadows Waterfowl Refuge. *Recreation resources:* Trout and bass fishing. Hunting for bear and deer. Scenic drives. Eight public camp and picnic areas; two swimming areas; two organization camps. Hotels, cabins. Nearby towns: Kane, Bradford, Marienville, Sheffield, Tionesta, Ridgway, and Tidioute. *Acres:* 463,179.

## PUERTO RICO

CARRIBEAN NATIONAL FOREST

Headquarters at Rio Piedras, reached by plane: 5 hours from New York, 4 hours from Miami. By car from Rio Piedras: 1 hour to Luquillo Division, 2 hours to Toro Negro Division.

*Special features:* Tropical rain forests, air conditioned 2,000 feet above the humid lowlands; climatic relief due to difference in elevation. Breath-taking panoramic views of palm-covered mountain slopes, timbered valleys, rocky gorges, cliffs, and waterfalls. *Recreation resources:* For the nature lover, more than 300 tree species, 21 different orchids, 500 varieties of graceful ferns have been identified. Forests abound with wild parrots, foot and horseback trails, observation points on mountaintops. Scenic mountain drives over excellent highways; vivid comparison between heavy rainfall and arid sides of Island. La Mina Recreation Area on the Luquillo Division—500 acres of highly developed picnic areas, restaurant, rental cabins, swimming pools. Dona Juana Recreation Area on the Toro Negro Division, with equal facilities. Nearby towns offer resort and hotel accommodations, with ocean beaches, surf bathing, and trips to sugar centrals, pineapple plantations, and canning factories. *Acres:* 21,137.

## SOUTH CAROLINA

FRANCIS MARION NATIONAL FOREST

Headquarters at Columbia, reached by U. S. Highways 17, 52. (Ranger Headquarters at Moncks Corner and McClellanville.)

*Special features:* Ruins and remnants of early colonial settlements and plantations. Many "meteor bays;" picturesque moss-hung oaks, flowering yucca, dogwood, and holly. *Recreation resources:* Bass and other fishing. Alligator, deer, turkey, and quail hunting. Boating, bathing, scenic drives; one improved forest picnic ground. Commercial hostelries nearby. *Acres:* 245,438.

SUMTER NATIONAL FOREST

Headquarters at Columbia, reached by U. S. Highways 25, 76, 176. (Ranger Headquarters at Newberry, Walhalla, and Greenwood.)

*Special features:* Piedmont and Blue Ridge Mountains; rank growth of rhododendron and other flowering shrubs; Walhalla Trout Hatchery. *Recreation resources:* Trout and some bass fishing. Quail hunting. Scenic drives. Four improved forest picnic grounds. Commercial hostelries near forest. *Acres:* 321,334.

## SOUTH DAKOTA

BLACK HILLS NATIONAL FOREST

Headquarters at Deadwood, reached by U. S. Highways 14, 85.

*Special features:* Spectacular canyons and waterfalls; crystal caves. Historic gold-rush area, where famous early-day characters lived and were buried, including Calamity Jane, Wild Bill Hickok, Deadwood Dick, and Preacher Smith; famous and fabulous Homestake Mine; logging and lumbering operations. (Forest lies partly in Wyoming.) *Recreation resources:* Fishing. Deer and migratory-bird hunting. Swimming, hiking, saddle trips. Scenic drives. Twenty-four improved public camp and picnic areas. Numerous commercial cabin camps and dude ranches in and near the forest. Nearby towns: Deadwood, Rapid City, Belle Fourche, Custer, and Hot Springs, S. Dak.; Sundance and Newcastle, Wyo. *Acres:* 665,780.

HARNEY NATIONAL FOREST

Headquarters at Custer, reached by U. S. Highways 16, 85.

*Special features:* Harney Peak, highest point east of Rockies. Mount Rushmore National Memorial. Logging and lumbering operations; gold, silver, and feldspar mining. (Forest lies partly in Wyoming.) *Recreation resources:* Lake and stream trout fishing. Deer and elk hunting. Swimming, boating, hiking, saddle trips, scenic drives. Twenty-three improved public camp and picnic areas. Commercial cabin camps and dude ranches in and near the forest. Nearby towns: Custer, Rapid City, Belle Fourche, Hot Springs, and Edgemont, S. Dak., Newcastle, Wyo. *Acres:* 547,810.

## TENNESSEE

CHEROKEE NATIONAL FOREST

Headquarters at Cleveland, reached by U. S. Highways 421, 19E, 19W, 25, 64, State Highways 68, 67, 70.

*Special features:* Rugged mountain country cut by river gorges. Ducktown Copper Basin—one of the South's outstanding examples of deforestation and erosion. Three game-management areas. (Forest lies partly in North Carolina.) *Recreation resources:* Lake and stream fishing, including rainbow and brook trout. Small- and large-game hunting, including wild boar. Hiking, boating, swimming. Eighteen public camp and picnic areas. Hotels and tourist cabins. Nearby towns: Bristol, Johnson City, Mountain City, Elizabethton, Erwin, Greenville, Newport, Madisonville, Tellico Plains, Etowah, Benton, and Cleveland. *Acres:* 566,718.

## TEXAS

ANGELINA NATIONAL FOREST

Headquarters at Lufkin, reached by U. S. Highways 59, 69.

*Special features:* Flat to rolling sandy hills and with longleaf pine; hardwood forests along river bottom. Angelina River and many overflow lakes; Boykin Lake. *Recreation resources:* Bass and cat fishing in rivers and lakes. Quail and dove hunting. Swimming and picnicking. One improved picnic and camping area and 12-acre lake. *Acres:* 154,324.

DAVY CROCKETT NATIONAL FOREST

Headquarters at Lufkin, reached by U. S. Highway 287, State Highways 94, 103. (Ranger Headquarters at Crockett and Groveton.)

*Special features:* Flat, shortleaf-loblolly pine woods; hardwoods in bottoms; timber-management demonstration area. *Recreation resources:* Bass and cat fishing in rivers and lakes. Some deer hunting. Swimming, camping, and picnicking. One improved recreation area and 80-acre lake. *Acres:* 161,481.

SABINE NATIONAL FOREST

Headquarters at Lufkin, reached by U. S. Highway 96, State Highway 21. (Ranger Headquarters at San Augustine.)

*Special features:* Southern pine and hardwood forests; Sabine River and overflow lakes; Boles Field Fox Hunt Area. *Recreation resources:* Bass and cat fishing in river and lakes. Fox hunting. Swimming, camping, and picnicking. One improved recreation area and 17-acre lake. *Acres:* 184,138.

SAM HOUSTON NATIONAL FOREST

Headquarters at Lufkin, reached by U. S. Highway 75, State Highway 190. (Ranger Headquarters at Huntsville.)

*Special features:* Flat, shortleaf-loblolly pine woods; hardwoods in bottoms; numerous lakes and small streams; part of the "Big Thicket" area. *Recreation resources:* Bass and cat fishing in rivers and lakes. Swimming, camping, and picnicking. One improved recreation area and 30-acre lake. *Acres:* 158,155.

## UTAH

ASHLEY NATIONAL FOREST

Headquarters at Vernal, reached by U. S. Highways 30, 40, State Highway 44.

*Special features:* East half of Uinta Mountain Range, highest range in United States extending east and west; Kings Peak, 13,498 feet; Red Gorge of the Green River, 1,500 feet deep; exposed geological formations a billion years old; High Uintas Wilderness Area, mostly above 10,000 feet; numerous scenic gorges, natural erosion formations. (Forest lies partly in Wyoming.) *Recreation resources:* Lake and stream fishing. Big-game hunting, including deer, elk, and antelope. Riding trails; wilderness area pack trips. Twenty public camp and picnic areas. Five resorts; cabins, and dude ranches. Nearby towns: Mountainview and Green River, Wyo.; Manila, Vernal, Duchesne, and Roosevelt, Utah. *Acres:* 1,079,260.

CACHE NATIONAL FOREST

Headquarters at Logan, reached by U. S. Highways 30S, 89, 91, State Highway 39.

*Special features:* Rugged mountains; Bear River and Wasatch Ranges; Minnetonka Cave; Logan and Ogden Canyons; Monte Christo Mountain; Snow Basin winter sports. (Forest lies partly in Idaho.) *Recreation resources:* Trout fishing. Deer and elk hunting. Scenic drives, riding and hiking trails. Forty-six camp and picnic areas; two winter-sports areas. Nearby towns: Ogden, Brigham, and Logan, Utah; Preston, Soda Springs, and Paris, Idaho. *Acres:* 632,881.

DIXIE NATIONAL FOREST

Headquarters at Cedar City, reached by U. S. Highways 91, 89.

*Special features:* Red Canyon, Panguitch and Navajo Lakes, Pine Valley Mountains, Boulder Top Plateau and its many lakes not accessible by road. Table Cliff Point from where peaks in four States (Colorado, Arizona, Nevada, and Utah) can be observed on a clear day. Spectacular, colored cliffs. *Recreation resources:* Deer, elk, and cougar hunting. Fishing in lakes and streams. Twenty-five public camp and picnic areas; one winter-sports area. Resorts, hotels, dude ranches, and cabins. Nearby towns: Cedar City, Parowan, Saint George, Panguitch, Enterprise, Escalante, Boulder, Teasdale. *Acres:* 1,838,991.

FISHLAKE NATIONAL FOREST

Headquarters at Richfield, reached by U. S. Highways 89, 91.

*Special features:* Tushar Mountains, Thousand Lake Mountain Scenic Area, Petrified Wood Scenic Area tributary to Wayne Wonderland. *Recreation resources:* Lake and stream fishing. Big-game hunting, including deer and elk. Scenic drives: Beaver Canyon, Wayne Wonderland, Fishlake-Salina, and others. Twenty public camp and picnic areas. Resorts, hotels, and cabins. Nearby towns: Richfield, Salina, Monroe, Loa, Bicknell, Koosharem, Beaver, Kanosh, and Fillmore. *Acres:* 1,416,234.

MANTI NATIONAL FOREST

Headquarters at Ephraim, reached by U. S. Highways 89, 50, State Highways 10, 29, 31.

*Special features:* Wasatch Plateau; Skyline Drive penetrates high alpine meadows and sylvan glades; colorful canyons; unique geology, east part of forest widely underlain with coal. Great Basin Forest Research Center. Indian writings and battlefields. *Recreation resources:* Trout fishing. Deer, elk, cougar hunting. Hiking, saddle trips. Eleven major, thirty-one smaller camp and picnic areas. Nearby towns: Manti, Ephraim, Mount Pleasant, Price, Huntington, and Ferron. *Acres:* 727,612.

UINTA NATIONAL FOREST

Headquarters at Provo, reached by U. S. Highways 40, 50, 91, 189.

*Special features:* Wasatch upthrust limestone strata of particular interest to geologists. Near Provo deep canyons and waterfalls bisect the formation. Balance of forest has more moderate terrain, open range mixed with oak, maple, aspen, spruce, and fir. *Recreation resources:* Rocky Mountain mule deer hunting, limited number of elk. Nineteen public camp and picnic areas; four valley-view and overlook points. Hotels and cabins at nearby towns: Provo, Spanish Fork, Nephi, Heber, Moab, and Monticello. *Acres:* 930,773.

WASATCH NATIONAL FOREST

Headquarters at Salt Lake City, reached by U. S. Highways 91, 40, 530, 30S, 50, 303, State Highways 152, 210, 65, 239, 168, 35.

*Special features:* Rugged back country; Wasatch, Uinta, Stansbury, Onaqui Ranges and High Uintas Wilderness Area. Alpine Scenic Highway; Timpanogas Cave; Mirror Lake; Grandaddy Lakes. Alta and Brighton Skiing Areas. *Recreation resources:* Lake and stream fishing. Deer and elk hunting. Boating, swimming, picnicking, camping. Riding and hiking trails, wilderness trips, skiing, skating, and mountain climbing. Seventy-eight public camps and picnic areas; three winter-sports areas. Numerous resorts, hotels, cabins, and dude ranches. Nearby towns: Salt Lake City, Provo, Ogden, Murray, Heber, and Kamas, Utah; Evanston, Wyo. *Acres:* 867,978.

## VERMONT

GREEN MOUNTAIN NATIONAL FOREST

Headquarters at Rutland, reached by U. S. Highways 4, 7.

*Special features:* Rugged mountains, scenery, picturesque valleys, quaint New England villages. Green Mountain Range traversed by the "Long Trail", Champlain Valley and points of historic interest, such as famous battlegrounds of Revolutionary and French and Indian Wars. *Recreation resources:* Lake and stream fishing. Bird shooting and big-game hunting for deer and bear. Bridle trails and hiking, scenic drives. Four improved forest picnic areas, ten high-country cabins, two camp areas; famous ski areas. Summer resorts and famous New England inns; hotels and cabins. Nearby towns: Burlington, Rutland, Manchester, Middlebury, Brandon, and Rochester. *Acres:* 168,139.

## VIRGINIA

### GEORGE WASHINGTON NATIONAL FOREST

Headquarters at Harrisonburg, reached by U. S. Highways 11, 33, State Highways 42, 260.

*Special features:* Rugged country, elevations up to 4,500 feet; Blue Ridge, Shenandoah, Allegheny, and Massanutten Ranges. Crabtree Falls; limestone caverns; Ramsey's Draft Natural Area; Duncan, Bald, High, Reddish, and Elliott Knobs; Shenandoah and Warm Springs Valleys. Part of a forest originally surveyed by George Washington. (Forest lies partly in West Virginia.) *Recreation resources:* Trout and bass fishing. Bear, deer, turkey, and grouse hunting. Panoramic vistas, 500 miles of scenic drives, Blue Ridge Parkway, 1,000 miles of foot trails. Swimming, camping. Sherando Lake Recreation Area with 20-acre lake; six smaller recreation areas. Hotels, resorts, and numerous cabin camps near forest. Nearby towns of Waynesboro, Staunton, Buena Vista, Harrisonburg, Covington, Clifton Forge, and Hot Springs, Va.; Franklin, W. Va. *Acres:* 919,769.

### JEFFERSON NATIONAL FOREST

Headquarters at Roanoke, reached by U. S. Highways 11, 220, 21, 52, 23, 58.

*Special features:* Blue Ridge Mountains; Mount Rogers, 5,719 feet, highest point in Virginia. Transitional zone northern and southern flora; rhododendrons. Glenwood Furnace; Appalachian Trail; Blue Ridge Parkway. *Recreation resources:* Big-game hunting (white-tailed deer). Network of good secondary roads supplementing main highways. Seven public camp and picnic areas. Resorts, hotels, cabins. Nearby towns: Lexington, Roanoke, Radford, Bluefield, Wytheville, Marion, Abingdon, Bristol. *Acres:* 551,312.

## WASHINGTON

### CHELAN NATIONAL FOREST

Headquarters at Okanogan, reached by U. S. Highway 97.

*Special features:* Lake Chelan 55 miles long, between precipitous ranges; alpine meadows, snow peaks, and glaciers. North Cascade Wilderness Area. *Recreation resources:* Lake and stream fishing. Boating, saddle and pack trips, mountain climbing. Forty improved forest camp and picnic grounds. Commercial dude ranches and cabin camps in and near forest. Nearby towns: Okanogan, Tonasket, Chelan, and Twisp. *Acres:* 2,041,366.

### COLUMBIA NATIONAL FOREST

Headquarters at Vancouver, reached by U. S. Highways 99, 830.

*Special features:* Mount Adams, 12,300 feet, reached by scenic Evergreen Highway; Spirit Lake and many others; snow-capped peaks; Mineral Springs. Wind River forest nursery. Goat Rocks and Mount Adams Wild Areas. *Recreation resources:* Lake and stream trout fishing. Deer and bear hunting. Spectacular auto tours, saddle and pack trips, mountain climbing. Forty improved forest camp and picnic grounds. Commercial cabin camps and resorts in and near forest. Nearby towns: Vancouver, Stevenson, Randle, Castle Rock, and White Salmon. *Acres:* 1,263,329.

### COLVILLE NATIONAL FOREST

Headquarters at Colville, reached by U. S. Highway 395.

*Special features:* Roosevelt Lake is 151 miles in length and covers an area or 82,000 acres, impounded by Grand Coulee Dam, the most massive man-made masonry structure in the world. Mountain lakes; scenic drive along Roosevelt Lake. Greatest mineral-producing area in the State of Washington. Old mission near Kettle Falls constructed without the use of nails in 1845. *Recreation resources:* Hunting and fishing—noted for large mule deer with a record weight of 440 pounds. Water transportation from Roosevelt Lake to Arrowhead Lakes in Canada. Huckleberries and mushrooms. One winter-sports area near Chewelah. Three developed camp grounds, located at Lake Thomas, Swan Lake, and 10-Mile on U. S. Highway 44; five campgrounds with minor developments. Four resorts and cabins at Curlew Lake; one resort at Lake Thomas. Nearby towns: Chewelah and Republic, Wash.; and Grand Forks, British Columbia, Canada. *Acres:* 690,687.

### MOUNT BAKER NATIONAL FOREST

Headquarters at Bellingham, reached by U. S. Highway 99.

*Special features:* Superlative mountain scenery; snow-capped peaks, glaciers, and alpine lakes; heavy stands of giant Douglas-fir. North Cascade Wilderness Area. *Recreation resources:* Trout fishing. Deer and bear hunting. Winter sports, saddle and pack trips, mountain climbing. Thirty improved forest camp and picnic grounds; one winter-sports area. Commercial cabin camps, hotels, and resorts, and experienced guides nearby. Nearby towns: Bellingham, Everett, Darrington, and Granite Falls. *Acres:* 1,818,163.

OLYMPIC NATIONAL FOREST

Headquarters at Olympia, reached by U. S. Highways 99, 401, 101.

*Special features:* Dense forests of big trees; spectacular snow peaks; scores of lakes and fishing streams. *Recreation resources:* Stream and lake fishing. Deer, bear, cougar, and elk hunting. Winter sports, scenic drives, saddle and pack trips. Twenty-eight improved forest camp and picnic grounds. Commercial resorts, cabin camps, and dude ranches. Nearby towns: Olympia, Port Angeles, Shelton, and Quilcene. *Acres:* 627,610.

SNOQUALMIE NATIONAL FOREST

Headquarters at Seattle, reached by U. S. Highways 10, 410.

*Special features:* Snoqualmie Falls, 250 feet high; Naches Pass, featured by pillars of the Dalles; largest known Douglas-fir tree; snow peaks, lakes, and miles of fishing streams. Mather Memorial Parkway; Goat Rocks Wild Area. *Recreation resources:* Stream and lake fishing, including steelhead trout. Black-tailed and mule deer, bear, and elk hunting. Scenic drives, saddle and pack trips. Forty-three improved forest camp and picnic grounds; one winter-sports area. Commercial cabin camps and outfitters available locally. Nearby towns: Seattle, Everett, Tacoma, Yakima, and Cle Elum. *Acres:* 1,197,480.

WENATCHEE NATIONAL FOREST

Headquarters at Wenatchee, reached by U. S. Highways 10, 97.

*Special features:* Many snow-capped peaks, lakes, alpine meadows, and rare wild flowers; many miles of fishing streams; Lake Wenatchee. *Recreation resources:* Stream and lake trout fishing. Deer and bear hunting. Scenic drives, saddle and pack trips. Thirty-two improved forest camp and picnic grounds; two winter-sports areas. Commercial cabin camps and dude ranches in and near forest. Nearby towns: Wenatchee, Leavenworth, Cashmere, and Cle Elum. *Acres:* 1,194,333.

## WEST VIRGINIA

MONONGAHELA NATIONAL FOREST

Headquarters at Elkins, reached by U. S. Highways 33, 219, 220, 250.

*Special features:* Southern Appalachian and Allegheny Mountains; Spruce Knob, highest point in State; Blackwater Canyon and 60-foot falls; spectacular Seneca Rocks on historic Seneca Indian Trail. Botanically curious Cranberry Glades; rhododendrons in July; eleven wildlife-management areas; unexplored limestone caves; beaver colonies. Parsons Forest Nursery; Smoke Hole mountain settlement. *Recreation resources:* Trout and bass fishing. Deer, bear, grouse, turkey, and small-game hunting. Swimming, hiking, horseback riding, scenic drives. Eight improved forest camp and picnic grounds. Commercial tourist homes and highway cabins in and near forest. *Acres:* 805,911.

## WISCONSIN

CHEQUAMEGON NATIONAL FOREST

Headquarters at Park Falls, reached by U. S. Highway 2, State Highways 13, 63 64, 70, 77.

*Special features:* Hundreds of large and small lakes. Pine, spruce, and balsam forests; extensive jack pine plantations. *Recreation resources:* Lake and stream fishing, particularly for muskellunge. Deer and small-game hunting. Canoe travel on Flambeau and Chippewa Rivers. Twenty-six public forest camp and picnic grounds; two winter-sports areas. An organization camp, resorts, and cabins. Nearby towns: Medford, Park Falls, Ashland, Washburn, and Hayward. *Acres:* 812,356.

NICOLET NATIONAL FOREST

Headquarters at Rhinelander, reached by U. S. Highways 17, 32, 55, 64, 70, 139.

*Special features:* Northern Wisconsin Lake region; trout streams and scenic rivers. Pine, spruce-balsam, hardwood, and cedar-spruce swamp forests. *Recreation resources:* Lake and stream fishing for muskellunge, pike, bass, and trout. Deer, bear, grouse, and duck hunting. Swimming, boating, canoe trips, nature hikes, snowshoeing, and skiing. Sixteen public camp and picnic grounds, five of which have swimming beaches; one ski area. Numerous resorts and cabins are located on private lands within and near the forest. *Acres:* 622,499.

## WYOMING

BIGHORN NATIONAL FOREST

Headquarters at Sheridan, reached by U. S. Highways 14, 16, 87.

*Special features:* Bighorn Mountains; snow-capped peaks; glaciers; 300-odd lakes. Curious prehistoric Indian Medicine Wheel on Medicine Mountain; Indian battlefields. Cloud Peak Wild Area. *Recreation resources:* Trout fishing. Elk, deer, bear, and duck hunting. Saddle and pack trips, scenic drives. Seventy-seven public camp and picnic areas; winter-sports areas. Commercial cabin camps and dude ranches in and near forest. Nearby towns: Sheridan, Buffalo, Lovell, Greybull, and Worland. *Acres:* 1,113,517.

BRIDGER NATIONAL FOREST

Headquarters at Kemmerer, reached by U. S. Highways 89, 189, 187.

*Special features:* Wind River Mountain Range; live glaciers; Bridger Wilderness Area. *Recreation resources:* Lake and stream fishing. Big-game hunting, including bear, moose, elk, mountain sheep, and deer.

Scenic drives: Pinedale Skyline Drive, Greys River Road. Wilderness trips. Twenty-five improved public camp and picnic areas; two winter-sports areas. Resorts, hotels, cabins, and dude ranches. Nearby towns: Pinedale and Afton. *Acres:* 1,699,098.

MEDICINE BOW NATIONAL FOREST

Headquarters at Laramie, reached by U. S. Highway 50.

*Special features:* Medicine Bow, Sierra Madre, Laramie, and Pole Mountains; Snowy Range Natural Area; many lakes and fishing streams; numerous beaver colonies. *Recreation resources:* Fishing and deer hunting. Saddle and pack trips. Scenic drives. Thirty-five improved public camp and picnic areas; two winter-sports areas. Commercial cabin camps and dude ranches in and near the forest. Nearby towns: Laramie, Cheyenne, and Encampment. *Acres:* 1,063,521.

SHOSHONE NATIONAL FOREST

Headquarters at Cody, reached by U. S. Highways 14, 20, 287.

*Special features:* Rugged Asbsaroka Mountains and Beartooth Plateau with perpetual snow; Gannett Peak, 13,785 feet, highest point in Wyoming; largest glaciers in Rocky Mountains; hundreds of lakes. North and South Absaroka, Glacier, Stratified Wilderness Areas; Popo Agie Wild Area. *Recreation resources:* Good fishing. Mountain sheep, elk, moose, deer, bear, and game-bird hunting. Saddle and pack trips, scenic drives. Fifty-five public camp and picnic grounds. Commercial cabin camps and dude ranches in and near the forest. Nearby towns: Cody, Lander, and DuBois, Wyo.; Red Lodge, Mont. *Acres:* 2,430,028.

TETON NATIONAL FOREST

Headquarters at Jackson, reached by U. S. Highways 89, 187, 287, State Highway 22.

*Special features:* Unspoiled scenic back country famous for big-game herds. Gros Ventre Slide, Gros Ventre, Teton, and Wind River Ranges, Continental Divide. Teton Wilderness Area; famous Jackson Hole country. *Recreation resources:* Stream and lake fishing. Big-game hunting, including moose, elk, deer, mountain sheep, grizzly bear. Scenic drives: Hoback Canyon, Wind River Highway. Eleven public camp and picnic areas; warm swimming pool; winter-sports area. Resorts, dude ranches, cabins. *Acres:* 1,700,302.

# WILDERNESS AND WILD AREAS

In the national forests are many of the last remaining parts of the country that are still in much the same primitive state as when the first settlers reached their vicinity. They include many of the mountain ranges and peaks that the pioneers saw as landmarks and as spiritual symbols of a new world and a new life.

Most of the Nation's wild areas have been tamed by highways, automobiles, and the other devices of a mechanical civilization. But as modern developments continue, the interests of recreation, public education, and science have made it increasingly desirable to preserve representative areas of our original wilderness.

To contribute toward the satisfaction of this need, 77 areas have been designated to be preserved as wilderness. They cover 14 million acres on 73 national forests in 11 States. Of the 77 established areas, 28 exceed 100,000 acres and are known as wilderness areas. Forty-six, containing at least 5,000 acres, are called wild areas. Three, on which restriction of commercial use is less rigid, are known as roadless areas.

Their uses are limited to those consistent with their values. Most are still classified under regulation L–20 as primitive areas; other are classified under the later wilderness and wild area regulations (U–1 and U–2), established by the Secretary of Agriculture in 1939. For convenience, all areas, whether actually classified as primitive or wilderness, are now referred to as wilderness or wild areas, because their management is identical in nearly all instances.

The total acreage reserved is approximately 8 percent of that of the national forests. The areas are usually the least productive of commercially valuable timber; considerable portions are above the timber line or have only noncommercial timber growth. Most of the timber stands on the remaining parts are inaccessible because of location. The public is thus assured of preservation of the wilderness without material sacrifice of usable timber or of other values important to the economic welfare of the region.

Many of the areas have outstanding scenic values, but they were established for another reason. They were selected as typical of the Rockies, Sierras, Cascades, and other regions where people can enjoy unspoiled and unmodified nature. Similar tracts exist in the East, but they are too small to be formally classified as wild or wilderness areas. A number of these smaller remnants of primitive forests are in the Appalachians, Alleghenies, and in the Presidential Range of the White Mountains.

Wilderness areas are designated by the Secretary of Agriculture upon recommendation of the Chief of the Forest Service. To come under this category, the lands must have no roads or other provision for motorized transportation, no commercial timber cutting, and no occupancy under special-use permit for hotels, stores, resorts, summer homes, organization camps, or for hunting and fishing lodges.

Grazing of domestic livestock and improvements necessary for fire protection may be permitted on wilderness areas, subject to restrictions made by the Chief of the Forest Service. Within designated wildernesses, the landing of airplanes on national forest land or water and the use of motorboats on national forest waters are prohibited, except where such use has already become well established or is required for administrative needs and emergencies.

Regulations further provide that wilderness areas will not be modified or eliminated except by order of the Secretary of Agriculture. Notice of every proposed establishment, modification, or elimination will be published or publicly posted by the Forest Service for at least 90 days before the approval of the contemplated order; if there is any demand for a public hearing, the regional forester will hold a hearing and report fully on it to the Chief of the Forest Service, who will submit it with his recommendation to the Secretary. It is the policy of the Department of Agriculture to allow modifications of established wilderness areas only when it is clearly in the public interest to sacrifice wilderness values in favor of other public needs.

Similar regulations apply to the establishment and maintenance of the smaller wild areas, except that decision is by the Chief of the Forest Service instead of the Secretary of Agriculture.

Wilderness areas are open to the public without restrictions except those essential for protection from fire. Hunting and fishing are permitted in wilderness areas in accordance with State laws.

The canoe country of the Superior Roadless Areas in Minnesota is unique. Many lakes and miles of connecting rivers make a canoe country without parallel. The canoe camper, the wilderness enthusiast, or the fisherman can spend weeks exploring its many bays and islands or can travel from lake to lake by connecting streams or by short, well-marked portages. The timbered shores offer excellent camp sites. Vacation trips in this area may be made at low cost—$1.50 a day for a canoe is the whole cost except for food. Only persons physically unable to paddle or unable to swim need a guide and most parties go without one.

In the western mountain wilderness areas travel is by foot, horseback, or burro. Anyone accustomed to the woods can travel the trails with safety, but handling horses and pack animals is a job only for experienced persons. A packer is needed by most wilderness travelers. Packer-guides may be hired and riding horses and pack animals may be rented in the vicinity of most of the wilderness areas.

Trail travel with back pack or with camp outfit on a single burro is quite popular, especially along the Cascades and Sierras. Long, continuous trips can be made through Washington, Oregon, and California, along well-maintained trails, such as the Cascade Crest, the Oregon Skyline, Tahoe-Yosemite, Sierra, and John Muir trails. The Federation of Western Outdoor Clubs and the Pacific Trail Conference are local organizations that sponsor trail travel. In the East, the Appalachian Trail stretches from Maine to Georgia, traversing a number of national forests and passes through the wildest remaining parts of the Appalachians.

Dude ranches operate near many of the wilderness areas in the West, and feature trips for their guests. Information on dude ranches can be obtained from railroad companies, chambers of commerce, or from the Dude Ranchers' Association, 21½ Broadway, Billings, Mont.

The Trail Riders of the Wilderness, organized in 1933 by the American Forestry Association, 919 Seventeenth Street NW., Washington, D. C., conducts expeditions each summer to several western wilderness areas.

### WILDERNESS AREAS AND WILD AREAS IN THE NATIONAL FORESTS

#### Arizona

| *Name* | *National forest and headquarters* | *Special features* |
|---|---|---|
| Blue Range, Wilderness Area (218,164 acres). | Apache (Springerville).<br>Crook (Safford). | Largest remaining wilderness in Arizona. Traversed by Mogollon Rim, with spruce and fir above and broken country below in ponderosa pine. Big game is abundant. |
| Mazatsal, Wilderness Area (205,346 acres). | Tonto (Phoenix). | Of precipitous topography containing many geologic formations. |
| Superstition, Wilderness Area (131,820 acres). | Crook (Safford).<br>Tonto (Phoenix). | A land of desert and mountain brush types with occasional prominent peaks. Has been called "a land of enchantment." |
| Chiricahua, Wild Area (18,000 acres). | Coronado (Tucson). | Located on crest of Chiricahua Mountain Range. Scenic attractions and rock formations similar to Chiricahua National Monument. Among game species is the Chiricahua squirrel, apparently found only in these mountains. |
| Galiuro, Wild Area (55,000 acres). | Crook (Safford). | Knifelike mountains jutting out of the Arizona plain. Average slope is probably in excess of 85 percent. Good hunting for experienced mountain hunters. |
| Mount Baldy, Wild Area (7,400 acres). | Apache (Springerville). | On the northeast slope of Mount Baldy at the head of the West Fork of the Little Colorado River. Elevation to 11,496 feet. |
| Pine Mountain, Wild Area (17,500 acres). | Prescott (Prescott).<br>Tonto (Phoenix). | Moderately rough terrain along the Verde Rim. Included in a State game refuge. |
| Sierra Ancha, Wild Area (34,000 acres). | Tonto (Phoenix). | Precipitous mountains including prehistoric cliff dwellings. Large game abundant. |
| Sycamore Canyon, Wild Area (47,230 acres). | Coconino (Flagstaff).<br>Kaibab (Williams).<br>Prescott (Prescott). | Includes a good representation of the canyon types of flora and fauna of northern Arizona. |

#### California

| *Name* | *National forest and headquarters* | *Special features* |
|---|---|---|
| High Sierra, Wilderness Area (393,945 acres). | Inyo (Bishop).<br>Sierra (Northfork).<br>Sequoia (Porterville). | Extends to an elevation of 12,200 feet on Goat Mountain, with timber ranging from Jeffrey pine to alpine types. |

WILDERNESS AREAS AND WILD AREAS IN THE NATIONAL FORESTS—continued

CALIFORNIA—Continued

| *Name* | *National forest and headquarters* | *Special features* |
|---|---|---|
| Marble Mountain, Wilderness Area (237,527 acres). | Klamath (Yreka). . | Supports a wide variety of timber types and species including the rare Brewer's spruce. |
| Middle Eel-Yolla Bolly, Wilderness Area (143,426 acres). | Mendocino (Willows).<br>Trinity (Weaverville) | Large variety of natural rugged scenery. Wildlife abundant with some good fishing in early part of the season. |
| Salmon Trinity Alps, Wilderness Area (285,432 acres). | Klamath (Yreka).<br>Shasta (Mt. Shasta)<br>Trinity (Weaverville). | A region of scenic beauty, including granite peaks, many alpine lakes, and numerous streams teeming with trout. |
| Agua Tibia, Wild Area (35,116 acres). | Cleveland (San Diego). | Includes some of the most scenic country in southern California. |
| Caribou Peak, Wild Area (16,443 acres). | Lassen (Susanville). | A gentle, rolling, forested plateau adjoining Silver Lake in northern California. |
| Cucamonga, Wild Area (5,000 acres). | San Bernardino (San Bernardino). | Gentle to rugged topography, reaching a maximum altitude of 9,000 feet. |
| Desolation Valley, Wild Area (41, 380 acres). | Eldorado (Placerville). | Extremely rough, rugged, and alpine in every respect. Elevations are from 6,500 to 10,020. |
| Devil Canyon-Bear Canyon, Wild Area (36,200 acres). | Angeles (Los Angeles). | An area of deep canyons; 40 miles by road from Los Angeles. |
| Emigrant Basin, Wild Area (98,043 acres). | Stanislaus (Sonora). . | Includes many lakes, fine fishing; high granite topography. |
| Hoover, Wild Area (20,540 acres). | Toiyabe (Reno, Nev.).<br>Inyo (Bishop). | Adjacent to Yosemite National Park. Granite peaks approach 13,000 feet elevation. Heavy snows and glaciers occur. |
| Mount Dana-Minarets, Wild Area (82,376 acres). | Inyo (Bishop).<br>Sierra (Northfork). . | Highest mountain range in southern California. Adjacent to Yosemite National Park. |
| San Gorgonio, Wild Area (19,083 acres). | San Bernardino (San Bernardino). | San Gorgonio Peak, 11,485 feet; desert to alpine scenery and vegetation. |
| San Jacinto, Wild Area (33,291 acres). | San Bernardino (San Bernardino). | Level flats to precipitous cliffs. |
| San Rafael, Wild Area (74,990 acres). | Los Padres (Santa Barbara). | Embraces the main range of the San Rafael Mountains. |
| South Warner, Wild Area (70,682 acres). | Modoc (Alturas). . . | Contains a 15-mile ridge mostly over 9,000 feet in elevation, numerous noted peaks, many small meadows and lakes. |
| Thousand Lake Valley, Wild Area (16,335 acres). | Lassen (Susanville). | Of varying topography, including the level Thousand Lake Valley of about 200 acres. |
| Ventana, Wild Area (55,884 acres). | Los Padres (Santa Barbara). | An area of low elevation but rugged terrain. |

COLORADO

| *Name* | *National forest and headquarters* | *Special features* |
|---|---|---|
| Flat Tops, Wilderness Area (117,880 acres). | White River (Glenwood Springs). | Unique wilderness with attractions including excellent fishing and hunting. Has numerous ideal camping places. |
| San Juan, Wilderness Area (240,000 acres). | San Juan (Durango). | Includes virgin forests and rugged mountains with extensive and varied timber-line areas. |
| Gore Range-Eagle Nest, Wild Area (61,275 acres). | Arapaho (Idaho Springs).<br>White River (Glenwood Springs). | One of the most rugged, picturesque mountain ranges in Colorado. |

WILDERNESS AREAS AND WILD AREAS IN THE NATIONAL FORESTS—continued

COLORADO—Continued

| *Name* | *National forest and headquarters* | *Special features* |
|---|---|---|
| La Garita-Sheep Mountain, Wild Area (38,030 acres). | Gunnison (Gunnison). Rio Grande (Monte Vista). San Isabel (Pueblo). | Considerable portion above timber line. Within a game refuge, it affords unusual opportunity for observation, especially of mountain sheep and elk. |
| Maroon-Snowmass, Wild Area (64,600 acres). | White River (Glenwood Springs). | This awe-inspiring area includes Snowmass Lake, Maroon Bells, and Pyramid Peak. Mountain sheep summer and winter at Conundrum Hot Springs. |
| Mount Zirkel-Dome Peak, Wild Area (43,120 acres). | Routt (Steamboat Springs). | Includes several high rugged peaks, beautiful fishing lakes, and protection stands of lodgepole pine and Engelmann spruce. |
| Rawah, Wild Area (25,720 acres). | Roosevelt (Fort Collins). | In Medicine Bow Range. Includes a small glacier and numerous glacial lakes. Part of area is exceptionally rugged. |
| Uncompahgre, Wild Area (69,253 acres). | Uncompahgre (Delta). | A region of extremely rugged mountains, lakes, and waterfalls. Wildlife is abundant. |
| Upper Rio Grande, Wild Area (56,600 acres). | Rio Grande (Monte Vista). | A mountainous area where wildlife is plentiful and fishing is the major recreational activity. |
| West Elk, Wild Area (52,000 acres). | Gunnison (Gunnison). | Embraces parts of several high mountain ranges, open park ranges, lakes, and rushing streams. Part of a game refuge. |
| Wilson Mountains, Wild Area (27,347 acres). | San Juan (Durango). | Includes five mountains and two major peaks of the Wilson Range. Large and small game are found in considerable numbers. |

IDAHO

| *Name* | *National forest and headquarters* | *Special features* |
|---|---|---|
| Idaho, Wilderness Area (1,232,744 acres). | Challis (Challis). Salmon (Salmon). Payette (McCall). | Rough, mountainous country with many large open areas and some small lakes. Fishing in some of the lakes and in Salmon River and its tributaries is excellent. |
| Sawtooth, Wilderness Area (200,942 acres). | Boise (Boise). Challis (Challis). Sawtooth (Hailey). | Of abruptly rising, broken topography with camping places along lakes and streams. Interesting fishing and much small game. |
| Selway-Bitterroot [1] Wilderness Area (1,581,210 acres). | Clearwater (Orofino) Nezperce (Grangeville). Lolo (Missoula, Mont.) Bitterroot (Hamilton, Mont.) | Mountainous, wooded area lying mostly west of the Bitterroot Range. Wildlife of great variety and abundance. |

MINNESOTA

| *Name* | *National forest and headquarters* | *Special features* |
|---|---|---|
| Caribou, Roadless Area (45,750 acres). | Superior (Duluth). | The first canoe country in America; has hundreds of lakes ideal for canoeing. Excellent fishing in more remote regions. Largest wilderness east of the Rockies. |
| Little Indian Sioux, Roadless Area (103,018 acres). | Superior (Duluth). | |
| Superior, Roadless Area (889,975 acres). | Superior (Duluth). | |

[1] Also located in Montana.

WILDERNESS AREAS AND WILD AREAS IN THE NATIONAL FORESTS—continued

MONTANA

| *Name* | *National forest and headquarters* | *Special features* |
|---|---|---|
| Anaconda-Pintlar, Wilderness Area (145,000 acres). | Beaverhead (Dillon). Bitterroot (Hamilton). Deerlodge (Butte). . | Rough mountain territory distinguished by a chain of barren, precipitous peaks, from which drop long forested slopes. |
| Beartooth, Wilderness Area (230,000 acres). | Custer (Billings) . . . | Rugged high mountain area. Includes Granite Peak, highest in Montana; Grasshopper Glacier. |
| Bob Marshall, Wilderness Area (950,000 acres). | Flathead (Kalispell). Lewis & Clark (Great Falls). | High mountainous area noted for good hunting and fishing, remoteness from commercial activity, and historic and geologic interest. |
| Selway-Bitterroot,[2] Wilderness Area (291,085 acres). | Bitterroot (Hamilton). | Mountainous, wooded area lying mostly west of the Bitterroot Range. Exclusive wildlife. |
| Absaroka, Wild Area (64,000 acres). | Gallatin (Bozeman) | High mountain area, mainly wooded, typical peaks. Good fishing; fair hunting; moose. |
| Cabinet Mountains, Wild Area (90,000 acres). | Cabinet (Thompson Falls). Kootenai (Libby) . . | A lofty, peak-studded area of scenic grandeur. Big game and wild flowers in abundance. |
| Gates of the Mountains, Wild Area (28,562 acres). | Helena (Helena) . . . | Spectacular limestone cliffs and Indian writings. |
| Mission Mountains, Wild Area (75,500 acres). | Flathead (Kalispell). | High mountainous area of alpine lakes, glaciers, and peaks, and containing unique glacial evidence. Grizzly bear and mountain goats. |
| Spanish Peaks, Wild Area (50,000 acres). | Gallatin (Bozeman). | Wild, but not too rough topography. Fishing is outstanding. |

NEW MEXICO

| *Name* | *National forest and headquarters* | *Special features* |
|---|---|---|
| Black Range, Wilderness Area (169,984 acres). | Gila (Silver City) . . | Rough, forested terrain providing good trout fishing; good deer and bear hunting. |
| Gila, Wilderness Area (567,054 acres). | Gila (Silver City) . . . | Topography is rough to precipitous, with many deep box canyons. Hunting and trout fishing. |
| Pecos Division, Wilderness Area (137,820 acres). | Santa Fe (Santa Fe). | High back country adjoining an area of high recreational use. |
| San Pedro Parks, Wild Area (41,132 acres). | Santa Fe (Santa Fe). | A high plateau containing numerous old pueblos, cliff dwellings, and other evidence of historic and prehistoric Indian occupancy. |
| White Mountain, Wild Area (24,000 acres). | Lincoln (Alamogordo). | A variety of mountain scenery and forest cover types is represented. Elevation 6,000 to 11,000. |

OREGON

| *Name* | *National forest and headquarters* | *Special features* |
|---|---|---|
| Eagle Cap, Wilderness Area (220,280 acres). | Wallowa (Enterprise). Whitman (Baker) . . | Embraces some of the highest peaks (to 10,000 feet) and includes some of the best fishing waters in eastern Oregon. |
| Three Sisters, Wilderness Area (246,728 acres). | Deschutes (Bend) . . Willamette (Eugene). | Includes the Three Sisters Mountains and numerous peaks and glaciers, among them Collier Glacier, Oregon's largest. |
| Gearhart Mountain, Wild Area (18,709 acres). | Fremont (Lakeview). | 300 foot "Gearhart Notch" near top of mountain; good deer hunting. |
| Kalmiopsis, Wild Area (78,850 acres). | Siskiyou (Grants Pass). | In the Port-Orford-cedar region; 17 species of conifers. |

[2] Also located in Idaho.

802062°—49——57

WILDERNESS AREAS AND WILD AREAS IN THE NATIONAL FORESTS—continued

OREGON—Continued

| *Name* | *National forest and headquarters* | *Special features* |
|---|---|---|
| Mount Hood, Wild Area (14,160 acres). | Mount Hood (Portland). | Occupies the high country north and west of the summit of famous Mount Hood, with two outstanding examples of alpine meadows. |
| Mount Jefferson, Wild Area (86,700 acres). | Deschutes (Bend). Mount Hood (Portland). Willamette (Eugene). | Snow-capped Mount Jefferson, with perpetual glaciers is main feature. Second highest peak in Oregon. |
| Mountain Lakes, Wild Area (23,071 acres). | Rogue River (Medford). | A rugged area, 80 percent of which is between 6,000 and 7,000 feet elevation. |
| Strawberry Mountain, Wild Area (34,080 acres). | Malheur (John Day). | Bow-and-arrow deer hunting; good fishing in alpine lakes. |
| **UTAH** | | |
| High Uintas, Wilderness Area (240,717 acres). | Ashley (Vernal). Wasatch (Salt Lake City). | A wild picturesque region in the Uinta Range, the highest in Utah and the only prominent east-west range in the United States. Rich in scenic, geological, and biological interest. |
| **WASHINGTON** | | |
| North Cascade, Wilderness Area (801,000 acres). | Chelan (Okanogan). Mount Baker (Bellingham). | An area to satisfy the most ardent wilderness traveler; he can travel for months without retracing his steps. |
| Goat Rocks, Wild Area (82,680 acres). | Columbia (Vancouver). Snoqualmie (Seattle) | Extremely precipitous peaks; glaciers; several large lakes; great profusion of mountain flora. Mountain goats are abundant. |
| Mount Adams, Wild Area (42,411 acres). | Columbia (Vancouver). | Largely above timber line; spectacular "Around the Mountain" trail. |
| **WYOMING** | | |
| Bridger, Wilderness Area (383,000 acres). | Bridger (Kemmerer). | Includes barren, grassland, water, and timbered areas; rises to 13,785 feet at the summit of Gannett Peak, the highest in Wyoming. |
| Glacier, Wilderness Area (177,000 acres). | Shoshone (Cody) | Of extremely rugged topography, including Fremont Peak, innumerable alpine lakes, and some of the largest living glaciers in the Nation. |
| North Absaroka, Wilderness Area (379,460 acres). | Shoshone (Cody) | Includes glaciers, natural bridge, standing petrified trees. Excellent hunting, fishing, camping. |
| South Absaroka, Wilderness Area (614,216 acres). | Shoshone (Cody) | Fishhawk Glacier; deep, straight-walled canyons; back country pack horse trips. |
| Stratified, Wilderness Area (147,000 acres). | Shoshone (Cody) | A region of narrow valleys and broad flat-topped mountains, built up of lava flow. Rich in petrified forest remains and abounds in game. |
| Teton, Wilderness Area (565,291 acres). | Teton (Jackson) | Outstanding in the amount of big game. An area of high plateaus, large valleys, and mountain meadows. |
| Cloud Peak, Wild Area (94,000 acres). | Bighorn (Sheridan). | Rugged, precipitous country rising to 13,165 feet. |
| Popo Agie, Wild Area (70,000 acres). | Shoshone (Cody) | Extremely rough topography along the Continental Divide. Contains 75 lakes. |

# NATURAL AREAS

*(Natural areas are areas representative of one or more forest or range types set aside to be permanently preserved in an unmodified condition, so that the characteristic plant and animal life and soil conditions of each type and the factors influencing its biological make-up are available for purposes of scientific study, research, and education.)*

ARIZONA

| *Name* | *Administrative unit* | *Vegetative types preserved* | *Area Acres* |
|---|---|---|---|
| Butterfly Peak | Coronado National Forest | Interior ponderosa pine | 420 |
| | | Interior Douglas-fir | 100 |
| | | Pinyon—juniper | 80 |
| | | Nonforested: Brush | 400 |
| | | | 1,000 |
| Chiminea Canyon | Saguaro National Monument in Coronado National Forest. | Cactus, mesquite, paloverde (a desert-shrub association). | 160 |
| Oak Creek Canyon | Coconino National Forest | Interior ponderosa pine | 900 |
| | | Interior Douglas-fir | 40 |
| | | | 940 |
| Pole Bridge Canyon | Coronado National Forest | Interior ponderosa pine | 320 |
| San Francisco Peaks | Coconino National Forest | Interior Douglas-fir | 350 |
| | | Engelmann spruce | 350 |
| | | Aspen | 100 |
| | | Nonforested: Alpine | 80 |
| | | | 880 |
| Santa Catalina | Coronado National Forest | Interior ponderosa pine | 3,160 |
| | | Interior Douglas-fir | 40 |
| | | Nonforested: Brush | 1,264 |
| | | | 4,464 |

CALIFORNIA

| *Name* | *Administrative unit* | *Vegetative types preserved* | *Area Acres* |
|---|---|---|---|
| Devil's Garden | Modoc National Forest | Sierra juniper | 1,600 |
| Harvey Munroe Hall | Inyo National Forest | Lodgepole pine | 800 |
| | | Whitebark pine | 475 |
| | | Nonforested: Rocks and glaciers | 2,975 |
| | | | 4,250 |
| Indiana Summit | Inyo National Forest | Jeffrey pine | 1,000 |
| San Joaquin | San Joaquin Experimental Range. | Digger pine—oak | 50 |

COLORADO

| Name | Administrative unit | Vegetative types preserved | Area Acres |
|---|---|---|---|
| Gothic | Gunnison National Forest | Engelmann spruce | 509 |
| | | Nonforested: Brush, grass, barren | 395 |
| | | | 904 |
| Hurricane Canyon | Pike National Forest | Interior Douglas-fir | 354 |
| | | Interior ponderosa pine | 101 |
| | | Engelmann spruce | 30 |
| | | Nonforested: Brush and barren | 35 |
| | | | 520 |
| Narraguinnep | San Juan National Forest | Interior ponderosa pine | 891 |
| | | Pinyon—Juniper | 715 |
| | | Aspen | 114 |
| | | Nonforested: Brush | 1,080 |
| | | | 2,800 |

FLORIDA

| Name | Administrative unit | Vegetative types preserved | Area Acres |
|---|---|---|---|
| Osceola | Osceola National Forest | Tupelo gum | 341 |
| | | Longleaf pine—slash pine | 323 |
| | | Slash pine | 207 |
| | | Southern cypress | 109 |
| | | Pond pine | 18 |
| | | | 998 |

IDAHO

| Name | Administrative unit | Vegetative types preserved | Area Acres |
|---|---|---|---|
| Canyon Creek | Priest River Experimental Forest in Kaniksu National Forest. | Engelmann spruce—alpine fir | 379 |
| | | Western white pine | 313 |
| | | Western hemlock | 129 |
| | | Whitebark pine | 50 |
| | | Lodgepole pine | 47 |
| | | Interior Douglas-fir | 14 |
| | | Larch—Douglas-fir | 12 |
| | | Western redcedar | 9 |
| | | Nonforested: | |
| | | Barren (rock slides) | 56 |
| | | Grass and brush | 25 |
| | | | 1,034 |
| Montford Creek | Deception Creek Experimental Forest in Coeur d'Alene National Forest. | Western white pine | 299 |
| | | Western hemlock | 29 |
| | | Larch—Douglas-fir | 6 |
| | | Lodgepole pine | 1 |
| | | | 335 |
| Teepee Creek | Kaniksu National Forest | Western white pine | 746 |

INDIANA

| Name | Administrative unit | Vegetative types preserved | Area Acres |
|---|---|---|---|
| Indiana Pioneer Mothers' Memorial. | Hoosier Purchase Unit | Yellow-poplar—White oak—red oak | 62 |
| | | Beech—sugar maple | 26 |
| | | | 88 |

KENTUCKY

| Name | Administrative unit | Vegetative types preserved | Area Acres |
|---|---|---|---|
| Rock Creek | Cumberland National Forest. | Hemlock | 176 |
| | | Shortleaf pine | 13 |
| | | | 189 |

MINNESOTA

| Name | Administrative unit | Vegetative types preserved | Area Acres |
|---|---|---|---|
| Keeley Creek | Superior National Forest | Jack pine | 420 |
| | | Black spruce | 146 |
| | | Tamarack | 20 |
| | | Nonforested: Nonproductive swamp | 54 |
| | | | 640 |
| Lac La Croix | Superior National Forest | White pine | 232 |
| | | Aspen | 214 |
| | | Norway pine | 208 |
| | | Black spruce | 39 |
| | | Balsam fir | 36 |
| | | Jack pine | 28 |
| | | Nonforested: | |
| | | Brush | 20 |
| | | Water | 196 |
| | | | 973 |
| Pine Point | Chippewa National Forest. | Aspen | 310 |
| | | Norway pine | 261 |
| | | White pine | 42 |
| | | Black spruce | 18 |
| | | Tamarack | 15 |
| | | Oak | 13 |
| | | Nonforested: | |
| | | Meadow and unproductive swamp | 493 |
| | | Water | 24 |
| | | | 1,176 |

MISSISSIPPI

| Name | Administrative unit | Vegetative types preserved | Area Acres |
|---|---|---|---|
| Delta Purchase Unit | Mississippi National Forest | Overcup oak—water hickory | 100 |
| | | Redgum | 40 |
| | | | 140 |

| Name | Administrative unit | Vegetative types preserved | Area |
|---|---|---|---|
| | | | Acres |
| **Montana** | | | |
| Coram | Coram Experimental Forest in Flathead National Forest. | Larch—Douglas-fir | 605 |
| | | Interior Douglas-fir | 175 |
| | | Western white pine | 21 |
| | | Engelmann spruce—alpine fir | 8 |
| | | Nonforested: Marsh | 2 |
| | | | 811 |
| **North Carolina** | | | |
| Black Mountain | Pisgah National Forest | Red spruce—southern balsam fir | 542 |
| | | Chestnut | 419 |
| | | Chestnut oak | 229 |
| | | Sugar maple—beech—yellow birch | 126 |
| | | Pin cherry | 13 |
| | | Nonforested: Old fields and balds | 76 |
| | | | 1,405 |
| **Nevada** | | | |
| Sweetwater | Toiyabe National Forest | Pinyon—juniper | 2,012 |
| | | Sagebrush | 223 |
| | | | 2,235 |
| **New Hampshire** | | | |
| The Bowl | White Mountain National Forest. | Red spruce | 220 |
| | | Yellow birch—red spruce | 123 |
| | | Sugar maple—beech—yellow birch | 92 |
| | | Red spruce—sugar maple—beech | 20 |
| | | Nonforested: Subalpine | 55 |
| | | | 510 |
| **New Mexico** | | | |
| Monument Canyon | Sante Fe National Forest. | Interior ponderosa pine | 580 |
| | | Interior Douglas-fir | 60 |
| | | | 640 |
| **Oregon** | | | |
| Abbot Creek | Rouge River National Forest. | Ponderosa pine—sugar pine—fir | 2,055 |
| | | Nonforested: Brush, grass, barren | 605 |
| | | | 2,660 |
| Coquille River Falls | Siskiyou National Forest | Port-Orford-cedar—Douglas-fir | 500 |
| Goodlow Mountain | Fremont National Forest | Interior ponderosa pine | 1,081 |
| | | Sierra juniper | 100 |
| | | Nonforested: Sagebrush and grass | 79 |
| | | | 1,260 |

OREGON—Continued

| Name | Administrative unit | Vegetative types preserved | Area Acres |
|---|---|---|---|
| Lobster Creek | Siskiyou National Forest | Port-Orford-cedar—Douglas-fir | 1,205 |
| | | Oak—madrone | 135 |
| | | | 1,340 |
| Metolius | Deschutes National Forest | Interior ponderosa pine | 1,315 |
| | | Grand fir—larch—Douglas-fir | 125 |
| | | | 1,440 |
| Neskowin Crest | Siuslaw National Forest | Western hemlock | 305 |
| | | Sitka spruce—western hemlock | 260 |
| | | Sitka spruce | 127 |
| | | | 692 |
| Ochoco Divide | Ochoco National Forest | Interior ponderosa pine | 968 |
| | | Larch—Douglas-fir | 907 |
| | | Nonforested: Grass | 45 |
| | | | 1,920 |
| Persia M. Robinson | Mount Hood National Forest. | Ponderosa pine—larch—Douglas-fir | 640 |
| Port-Orford-Cedar | Siskiyou National Forest | Port-Orford-cedar—Douglas-fir | 811 |
| | | Pacific Douglas-fir | 322 |
| | | | 1,133 |
| Pringle Falls | Deschutes National Forest. | Lodgepole pine | 563 |
| | | Ponderosa—lodgepole pine | 353 |
| | | Interior ponderosa pine | 196 |
| | | Ponderosa pine—sugar pine—fir | 48 |
| | | | 1,160 |

PENNSYLVANIA

| Name | Administrative unit | Vegetative types preserved | Area Acres |
|---|---|---|---|
| Tionesta | Allegheny National Forest. | Hemlock (—beech) | 2,113 |

SOUTH DAKOTA

| Name | Administrative unit | Vegetative types preserved | Area Acres |
|---|---|---|---|
| Upper Pine Creek | Harney National Forest | Interior ponderosa pine | 1,070 |
| | | Nonforested: Barren | 120 |
| | | | 1,190 |

VIRGINIA

| Name | Administrative unit | Vegetative types preserved | Area Acres |
|---|---|---|---|
| Little Laurel Run | George Washington National Forest. | Chestnut oak | 1,769 |
| | | Hemlock | 127 |
| | | Pitch pine | 89 |
| | | Yellow-poplar—hemlock | 62 |
| | | White pine | 45 |
| | | | 2,092 |

VIRGINIA—Continued

| *Name* | *Administrative unit* | *Vegetative types preserved* | *Area* *Acres* |
|---|---|---|---|
| Ramsey's Draft | George Washington National Forest. | Chestnut | 883 |
| | | Chestnut oak | 368 |
| | | Pitch pine | 210 |
| | | Hemlock | 179 |
| | | White pine | 85 |
| | | Red oak—basswood—white ash | 53 |
| | | Bear oak | 16 |
| | | | 1,794 |

WASHINGTON

| *Name* | *Administrative unit* | *Vegetative types preserved* | *Area* *Acres* |
|---|---|---|---|
| Cedar Flats | Columbia National Forest. | Pacific Douglas-fir | 400 |
| | | Western redcedar | 220 |
| | | Nonforested: Swamp | 60 |
| | | | 680 |
| Lake 22 | Mount Baker National Forest. | Western redcedar—western hemlock | 455 |
| | | Pacific silver fir—hemlock | 80 |
| | | Western redcedar | 40 |
| | | Red alder | 15 |
| | | Black cottonwood—willow | 10 |
| | | Nonforested: Barren and lake area | 190 |
| | | | 790 |
| Long Creek | Mount Baker National Forest. | Western redcedar—western hemlock | 240 |
| | | Western hemlock | 200 |
| | | Pacific silver fir—hemlock | 120 |
| | | Douglas-fir—western hemlock | 40 |
| | | Nonforested: Barren | 40 |
| | | | 640 |
| Meeks Table | Snoqualmie National Forest. | Interior ponderosa pine | 77 |
| | | Nonforested: Grass | 9 |
| | | | 86 |
| North Fork Nooksack | Mount Baker National Forest. | Pacific Douglas-fir | 482 |
| | | Western redcedar—western hemlock | 437 |
| | | Douglas-fir—western hemlock | 296 |
| | | Black cottonwood—willow | 4 |
| | | Nonforested: Burns and grass | 133 |
| | | | 1,352 |
| Quinault | Olympic National Forest | Western hemlock | 495 |
| | | Sitka spruce | 360 |
| | | Sitka spruce—western hemlock | 280 |
| | | Western redcedar—western hemlock | 240 |
| | | Pacific Douglas-fir | 60 |
| | | | 1,435 |

WASHINGTON—Continued

| *Name* | *Administrative unit* | *Vegetative types preserved* | *Area* |
|---|---|---|---|
| | | | *Acres* |
| Wind River | Columbia National Forest | Douglas-fir—western hemlock | 695 |
| | | Pacific Douglas-fir | 365 |
| | | Western redcedar | 40 |
| | | | 1,100 |

WISCONSIN

| | | | |
|---|---|---|---|
| Moquah | Chequamegon National Forest. | Nonforested: Upland brush and grass (originally supported a heavy stand of Norway pine with some white pine. Set aside "to determine what will naturally take place on this area if it is afforded fire protection only") | 640 |

WYOMING

| | | | |
|---|---|---|---|
| Snowy Range | Medicine Bow National Forest. | Engelmann spruce | 739 |
| | | Nonforrested: | |
| | | Brush and grass | 20 |
| | | Lakes | 12 |
| | | | 771 |

## AREAS ADMINISTERED BY THE NATIONAL PARK SERVICE

A list of the areas and of officials to whom requests for information should be addressed.

*Key to abbreviations:* NP—National Park; NHP—National Historical Park; NMP—National Military Park; NM—National Monument; NHS—National Historic Site; NBP—National Battlefield Park; NMem—National Memorial; NMemP—National Memorial Park; RDA—Recreation Demonstration Area; RA—Recreational Area.

| *Area* | *Address* |
|---|---|
| Abraham Lincoln NHP | Custodian, RFD 1, Hodgenville, Ky. |
| Acadia NP | Superintendent, Bar Harbor, Maine. |
| Ackia Battleground NM | Superintendent, Natchez Trace Parkway, Tupelo, Miss. |
| Adams Mansion NHS | Superintendent, Salem Maritime NHS, Custom House, Derby Street, Salem, Mass. |
| Andrew Johnson NM | Custodian, Greeneville, Tenn. |
| Antietam NBS | Custodian, Sharpsburg, Md. |
| Appomattox Court House NM | Custodian, Box 28, Appomattox, Va. |
| Arches NM | Custodian, Moab, Utah. |
| Atlanta Campaign NHS | Superintendent, Chickamauga-Chattanooga NMP, Fort Oglethorpe, Ga. |
| Aztec Ruins NM | Custodian, Aztec, N. Mex. |
| Badlands NM | Custodian, Interior, S. Dak. |
| Bandelier NM | Custodian, Los Alamos, Star Route, Santa Fe, N. Mex. |
| Big Bend NM | Superintendent, Marathon, Tex. |
| Big Hole Battlefield NM | Superintendent, Yellowstone NP, Yellowstone Park, Wyo. |
| Black Canyon of the Gunnison NM. | Superintendent, Mesa Verde NP, Colo. |
| Blue Ridge Parkway | Superintendent, Box 1710, Roanoke, Va. |
| Brices Cross Roads NBS | Superintendent, Natchez Trace Parkway, Tupelo, Miss. |
| Bryce Canyon NP | Superintendent, Springdale, Utah. |
| Cabrillo NM | Superintendent, Sequoia NP, Three Rivers, Calif. |
| Canyon de Chelly NM | Custodian, Box 8, Chinle, Ariz. |

| *Area* | *Address* |
|---|---|
| Capitol Reef NM | Superintendent, Zion NP, Springdale, Utah. |
| Capulin Mountain NM | Custodian, Capulin, N. Mex. |
| Carlsbad Caverns NP | Superintendent, Carlsbad, N. Mex. |
| Casa Grande NM | Custodian, Coolidge, Ariz. |
| Castillo de San Marcos NM | Superintendent, P. O. Box 1431, St. Augustine, Fla. |
| Castle Pinckney NM | Superintendent, Castillo de San Marcos NM, Box 1431, St. Augustine, Fla. |
| Catoctin RDA | Custodian, Thurmont, Md. |
| Cedar Breaks NM | Superintendent, Zion NP, Springdale, Utah. |
| Chaco Canyon NM | Custodian, c/o Blanco Trading Post, Bloomfield, N. Mex. |
| Chalmette NHP | Custodian, Box 125, Arabi 16, La. |
| Channel Islands NM | Superintendent, Sequoia NP, Three Rivers, Calif. |
| Chesapeake & Ohio Canal | Superintendent, National Capital Parks, 1229 Interior Building, Washington 25, D. C. |
| Chickamauga and Chattanooga NMP. | Superintendent, Fort Oglethorpe, Ga. |
| Chiricahua NM | Custodian, Dos Cabezos, Ariz. |
| Colonial NHP | Superintendent, Yorktown, Va. |
| Colorado NM | Custodian, Fruita, Colo. |
| Coulee Dam RA | Superintendent, Coulee Dam, Wash. |
| Cowpens NBS | Superintendent, Kings Mountain NMP, Kings Creek, S. C. |
| Crater Lake NP | Superintendent, Crater Lake, Oreg. |
| Craters of the Moon NM | Custodian, Arco, Idaho. |
| Custer Battlefield NM | Superintendent, Crow Agency, Mont. |
| Death Valley NM | Superintendent, Trona, Calif. |
| Devil Postpile NM | Superintendent, Yosemite National Park, Calif. |
| Devils Tower NM | Custodian, Devils Tower, Wyo. |
| Dinosaur NM | Superintendent, Rocky Mountain NP, Estes Park, Colo. |
| El Morro NM | Custodian, Ramah, N. Mex. |
| Everglades NP | Superintendent, Box 275, Homestead, Fla. |
| Father Millet Cross NM | Superintendent, Morristown NHP, Morristown, N. J. |
| Federal Hall Memorial NHS | Superintendent, Morristown NHP, Morristown, N. J. |
| Fort Donelson NMP | Superintendent, Dover, Tenn. |
| Fort Frederica NM | Superintendent, Castillo de San Marcos NM, Box 1431, St. Augustine, Fla. |
| Fort Jefferson NM | Custodian, Key West, Fla. |
| Fort Laramie NM | Custodian, Fort Laramie, Wyo. |
| Fort Matanzas NM | Custodian, St. Augustine, Fla. |
| Fort McHenry NM | Custodian, Baltimore 30, Md. |
| Fort Necessity NBS | Custodian, Farmington, Pa. |
| Fort Pulaski NM | Custodian, Box 204, Savannah Beach, Ga. |
| Fort Raleigh NHS | Custodian, Mateo, N. C. |
| Fort Sumter NM | Superintendent, Charleston, S. C. |
| Fossil Cycad NM | Superintendent, Wind Cave NP, Hot Springs, S. Dak. |
| Fredericksburg & Spotsylvania County Battlefields Memorial NMP. | Superintendent, Box 679, Fredericksburg, Va. |
| George Washington Birthplace NM. | Superintendent, Washington's Birthplace, Westmoreland County, Va. |
| Gettysburg NMP | Superintendent, Gettysburg, Pa. |
| Gila Cliff Dwellings NM | Custodian, Silver City, N. Mex. |
| Glacier Bay NM | Regional Director, 180 New Montgomery Street, San Francisco 5, Calif. |
| Glacier NP | Superintendent, Belton, Mont. |
| Gran Quivira NM | Custodian, Gran Quivira, N. Mex. |
| Grand Canyon NM | Superintendent, Grand Canyon NP, Grand Canyon, Ariz. |
| Grand Canyon NP | Superintendent, Grand Canyon, Ariz. |
| Grand Teton NP | Superintendent, Moose, Teton County, Wyo. |
| Great Sand Dunes NM | Custodian, Mosca, Colo. |
| Great Smoky Mountains NP | Superintendent, Gatlinburg, Tenn. |
| Guilford Courthouse NMP | Custodian, RFD #2, Greensboro, N. C. |

| *Area* | *Address* |
|---|---|
| Hampton NHS | Custodian, Fort McHenry NM, Baltimore 30, Md. |
| Hawaii NP | Superintendent, Hawaii NP, Hawaii, Territory of Hawaii. |
| Holy Cross NM | Superintendent, Rocky Mountain NP, Estes Park, Colo. |
| Home of Franklin D. Roosevelt NHS. | Superintendent, Vanderbilt Mansion NHS, Hyde Park, N. Y. |
| Homestead NM | Custodian, Beatrice, Nebr. |
| Hopewell Village NHS | Custodian, Birdsboro, Pa. |
| Hot Springs NP | Superintendent, Hot Springs NP, Ark. |
| Hovenweep NM | Superintendent, Mesa Verde NP, Colo. |
| Isle Royale NP | Superintendent, via Duluth, Minn. |
| Jackson Hole NM | Superintendent, Grand Teton NP, Moose, Teton County, Wyo. |
| Jefferson National Expansion Memorial NHS. | Superintendent, Old Courthouse, 415 Market Street. St. Louis 2, Mo. |
| Jewel Cave NM | Superintendent, Wind Cave NP, Hot Springs, S. Dak. |
| Joshua Tree NM | Custodian, Box 289, Twentynine Palms, Calif. |
| Katmai NM | Superintendent, Mount McKinley NP, McKinley Park, Alaska. |
| Kennesaw Mountain NBP | Custodian, Marietta, Ga. |
| Kill Devil Hill National Memorial NM. | Custodian, Kill Devil Hills, N. C. |
| Kings Mountain NMP | Custodian, Kings Creek, S. C. |
| Lake Mead RA | Superintendent, Box 755, Boulder City, Nev. |
| Lake Texoma RA | Superintendent, Box 694, Denison, Tex. |
| Lassen Volcanic NP | Superintendent, Mineral, Calif. |
| Lava Beds NM | Custodian, Tulelake, Calif. |
| Lee Mansion NMem | Superintendent, National Capital Parks, 1229 Interior Building, Washington 25, D. C. |
| Lehman Caves NM | Superintendent, Lake Mead RA, Box 755, Boulder City, Nev. |
| Lincoln Memorial | Superintendent, National Capital Parks, 1229 Interior Building, Washington 25, D. C. |
| Lincoln Museum NMem | Superintendent, National Capital Parks, 1229 Interior Building, Washington 25, D. C. |
| Mammoth Cave NP | Superintendent, Mammoth Cave, Ky. |
| Manassas National Battlefield Park NHS. | Custodian, Manassas, Va. |
| Meriwether Lewis NM | Custodian, Hohenwald, Tenn. |
| Mesa Verde NP | Superintendent, Mesa Verde NP, Colo. |
| Millerton Lake RA | Custodian, Friant, Calif. |
| Montezuma Castle NM | Custodian, Camp Verde, Ariz. |
| Moores Creek NMP | Custodian, Currie, Pender County, N. C. |
| Morristown NHP | Superintendent, Box 759, Morristown, N. J. |
| Mound City Group NM | Custodian, Chillicothe, Ohio. |
| Mount McKinley NP | Supeintendent, McKinley Park, Alaska. |
| Mount Rainier NP | Superintendent, McKinley Park, Alaska. |
| Mount Rushmore NMem | Superintendent, Wind Cave NP, Hot Springs, S. Dak. |
| Muir Woods NM | Custodian, Mill Valley, Calif. |
| Natchez Trace Parkway | Superintendent, Tupelo, Miss. |
| Natural Bridges NM | Regional Director, Region Three Office, Box 1728, Santa Fe, N. Mex. |
| Navajo NM | Custodian, Tonalea, Ariz. |
| New Echota Marker NMem | Superintendent, Chickamauga and Chattanooga NMP, Fort Oglethorpe, Ga. |
| Ocmulgee NM | Custodian, Box 936, Macon, Ga. |
| Old Kasaan NM | Regional Director, 180 New Montgomery Street, San Francisco 5, Calif. |
| Old Philadelphia Custom House NHS. | Superintendent, Morristown NHP, Morristown, N. J. |
| Olympic NP | Superintendent, Port Angeles, Wash. |

| *Area* | *Address* |
|---|---|
| Oregon Caves NM | Superintendent, Crater Lake NP, Medford, Oreg. |
| Oregon Pipe Cactus NM | Custodian, Ajo, Ariz. |
| Perry's Victory and International Peace Memorial NM. | Custodian, Put-in-Bay, Ohio. |
| Petersburg NMP | Superintendent, Petersburg, Va. |
| Petrified Forest NM | Superintendent, Holbrook, Ariz. |
| Pinnacles NM | Custodian, Pinnacles, Calif. |
| Pipe Spring NM | Custodian, Moccasin, Ariz. |
| Pipestone NM | Custodian, Box 371, Pipestone, Minn. |
| Platt NP | Superintendent, Sulphur, Okla. |
| Prince William Forest Park RDA. | Superintendent, National Capital Parks, 1229 Interior Building, Washington 25, D. C. |
| Rainbow Bridge NM | Regional Director, Region Three Office, Box 1728, Santa Fe, N. Mex. |
| Richmond NBP | Custodian, RFD #14, Box 140, Richmond 23, Va. |
| Rocky Mountain NP | Superintendent, Estes Park, Colo. |
| Saguaro NM | Custodian, Route 2, Box 544, Tucson, Ariz. |
| Salem Maritime NHS | Superintendent, Custom House, Derby Street, Salem, Mass. |
| Saratoga NHP | Custodian, RFD #1, Stillwater, N. Y. |
| Scotts Bluff NM | Custodian, Gering, Nebr. |
| Sequoia-Kings Canyon NP | Superintendent, Three Rivers, Calif. |
| Shenandoah NP | Superintendent, Luray, Va. |
| Shiloh NMP | Superintendent, Pittsburg Landing, Tenn. |
| Shoshone Cavern NM | Superintendent, Yellowstone NP, Yellowstone Park, Wyo. |
| Sitka NM | Custodian, Sitka, Alaska. |
| Statue of Liberty NM | Superintendent, Bedloe's Island, New York 4, N. Y. |
| Stones River NMP | Superintendent, Chickamauga and Chattanooga NMP, Fort Oglethorpe, Ga. |
| Sunset Crater NM | In Charge, Tuba Star Route, Wupatki NM, Flagstaff, Ariz. |
| Theodore Roosevelt NMemP | Superintendent, Medora, N. Dak. |
| Timpanogos Cave NM | Custodian, Pleasant Grove, Utah. |
| Thomas Jefferson NMem | Superintendent, National Capital Parks, 1229 Interior Building, Washington 25, D. C. |
| Tonto NM | Custodian, Roosevelt, Ariz. |
| Tumacacori NM | Custodian, Tumacacori, Ariz. |
| Tupelo NBS | Superintendent, Natchez Trace Parkway, Tupelo, Miss. |
| Tuzigoot NM | Custodian, Box 36, Clarkdale, Ariz. |
| Vanderbilt Mansion NHS | Superintendent, Hyde Park, N. Y. |
| Verendrye NM | Custodian, Sanish, N. Dak. |
| Vicksburg NMP | Superintendent, Box 349, Vicksburg, Miss. |
| Walnut Canyon NM | Custodian, Box 400, RFD #1, Flagstaff, Ariz. |
| Washington Monument | Superintendent, National Capital Parks, 1229 Interior Building, Washington 25, D. C. |
| Wheeler NM | Regional Director, Region Three Office, Box 1728, Santa Fe, N. Mex. |
| White Plains NBS | Superintendent, Statue of Liberty NM, Bedloe's Island, New York 4, N. Y. |
| White Sands NM | Custodian, Box 231, Alamogordo, N. Mex. |
| Whitman NM | Superintendent, Mt. Rainier NP, Longmire, Wash. |
| Wind Cave NP | Superintendent, Hot Springs, S. Dak. |
| Wupatki NM | Custodian, Tuba Star Route, Flagstaff, Ariz. |
| Yellowstone NP | Superintendent, Yellowstone Park, Wyo. |
| Yosemite NP | Superintendent, Yosemite NP, Calif. |
| Yucca House NM | Superintendent, Mesa Verde NP, Colo. |
| Zion NM | Superintendent, Zion NP, Springdale, Utah. |
| Zion NP | Superintendent, Springdale, Utah. |

# PUBLIC FOREST-TREE NURSERIES

## FOREST SERVICE

*Region 1.*—Montana, northeastern Washington, northern Idaho, northwestern South Dakota.
Savenac Nursery, Saltese, Mont.

*Region 2.*—Colorado, Kansas, Nebraska, South Dakota, eastern Wyoming.
Monument Nursery, Monument, Colo.
Bessey Nursery, Bessey, Nebr.

*Region 5.*—California.
Durbin Nursery, Susanville, Calif.

*Region 6.*—Washington, Oregon.
Bend Nursery, Bend, Oreg.
Wind River Nursery, Carson, Wash.

*Region 7.*—Maine, New Hampshire, Vermont, Massachusetts, Connecticut, Rhode Island, New York, Pennsylvania, New Jersey, Delaware, Maryland, West Virginia, Virginia, Kentucky.
Parsons Nursery, Parsons, W. Va.

*Region 8.*—Alabama, Arkansas, Florida, Georgia, Louisiana, Mississippi, North Carolina, Oklahoma, South Carolina, Tennessee, Texas.
R. Y. Stuart Nursery, Pollock, La.
W. W. Ashe Nursery, Brooklyn, Miss.

*Region 9.*—Illinois, Indiana, Iowa, Michigan, Minnesota, Missouri, North Dakota, Ohio, Wisconsin.
Vallonia Nursery, Vallonia, Ind.
Chittenden Nursery, Wellston, Mich.
J. W. Tourney Nursery, Watersmeet, Mich.
Eveleth Nursery, Eveleth, Minn.
Hugo Sauer Nursery, Rhinelander, Wis.

*Tennessee Valley Authority.*—Norris, Tenn.
Clinton Nursery, Clinton, Tenn.
Muscle Shoals Nursery, Florence, Ala.

## SOIL CONSERVATION SERVICE

*Region 1.*—Connecticut, Delaware, Maine, Maryland, Massachusetts, New Hampshire, New Jersey, New York, Pennsylvania, Rhode Island, Vermont, West Virginia.
Beltsville, Md.
Big Flats, N. Y.

*Region 2.*—Alabama, Florida, Georgia Kentucky, Mississippi, North Carolina, South Carolina, Tennessee, Virginia, Puerto Rico, Virgin Islands.
Thorsby, Ala.
Brooksville, Fla.
Americus, Ga.
Paducah, Ky.
Chapel Hill, N. C.
Rock Hill, S. C.
Sandy Level Nursery, Gretna, Va.

*Region 3.*—Illinois, Indiana, Iowa, Michigan, Minnesota, Missouri, Ohio, Wisconsin.
Winona, Minn.
Elsberry, Mo.
Zanesville, Ohio.

*Region 4.*—Arkansas, Louisiana, Oklahoma, Texas.
Minden, La.
San Antonio, Tex.

*Region 5.*—Kansas, Montana, Nebraska, North Dakota, South Dakota, Wyoming.
Manhattan, Kans.
Two Rivers Nursery, Waterloo, Nebr.
Mandan, N. Dak.

*Region 6.*—Arizona, Colorado, New Mexico, Utah.
Tucson, Ariz.
Albuquerque, N. Mex.

*Region 7.*—California, Idaho, Nevada, Oregon, Washington, Hawaii.
Little Rock, Calif.; Pleasanton, Calif.; San Fernando, Calif; Warrenton, Oregon.; Bellingham, Wash.; Pullman, Wash.

STATE FOREST NURSERIES COOPERATING IN FEDERAL-STATE TREE DISTRIBUTING PROGRAM, 1948

| State | Name and location | Approximate capacity In thousands |
|---|---|---|
| Alabama | Autaugaville Nursery, Autaugaville, Ala | 20,000 |
| Arkansas | Arkansas State Nursery, Bluff City, Ark | 10,000 |
| Connecticut | Peoples Forest Nursery, Pleasant Valley, Conn | 400 |
| | Nye-Holman Nursery, West Willington, Conn | 100 |
| Delaware | State Forest Tree Nursery, c/o State Forest Ranger Station, Georgetown, Del. | 1,000 |
| Florida | Florida Forest Service Nursery, Olustee, Fla | 10,000 |
| | Munson Nursery, Munson, Fla | 25,000 |
| Georgia | Herty Nursery, Albany, Ga | 20,000 |
| | Flowery Branch Nursery, Flowery Branch, Ga | 5,000 |
| | Davisboro Nursery, Davisboro, Ga | 25,000 |
| Idaho (N) | School of Forestry Nursery, Moscow, Idaho | 500 |
| Illinois | Mason Tree Nursery, Topeka, Ill | 3,000 |
| | Union Tree Nursery, Jonesboro, Ill | 5,000 |
| Indiana | Clarke State Nursery, Henryville, Ind | 1,000 |
| | Jackson State Nursery, Vallonia, Ind | 5,000 |
| | Jasper-Pulaski State Nursery, Medaryville, Ind | 2,000 |
| Iowa | Iowa State Conservation Commission, Des Moines, Iowa | 500 |
| Kansas | State Forest Nursery, Hays, Kans | 500 |
| Kentucky | Division of Forestry Nursery, Louisville, Ky | 1,100 |
| | Pennyrile Nursery, Dawson Springs, Ky | 500 |
| Louisiana | Oberlin State Nursery, Oberlin, La | 10,000 |
| | Sibley State Nursery, Sibley, La | 15,000 |
| Maine | University of Maine Forest Nursery, Orono, Maine | 125 |
| Maryland | Beltsville Nursery, Beltsville, Md | 100 |
| | State Forest Nursery, Berwyn, Md | 1,250 |
| Massachusetts | Amherst State Nursery, Amherst, Mass | 500 |
| | Clinton State Nursery, Clinton, Mass | 1,000 |
| | Bridgewater State Nursery, Bridgewater, Mass | 500 |
| | Erving Nursery, Erving, Mass | 100 |
| Michigan | Bogue Nursery, East Lansing, Mich | 5,000 |
| | Dunbar Nursery, Sault Ste. Marie, Mich | 800 |
| | Higgins Lake State Nursery, Roscommon, Mich | 10,000 |
| | Hardwood State Nursery, Boyne Falls, Mich | 1,500 |
| Minnesota | Badoura Nursery, Akeley, Minn | 750 |
| | Gen. C. C. Andrews Nursery, Willow River, Minn | 2,000 |
| Mississippi | Covington County State Nursery, Mount Olive, Miss | 20,000 |
| | Winona Nursery, Winona, Miss | 5,000 |
| Missouri | Meramec Nursery, Sullivan, Mo | 2,200 |
| | Licking Nursery, Licking, Mo | 5,000 |
| Montana | Forest Nursery, Montana State University, Missoula, Mont | 1,000 |
| New Hampshire | State Forest Nursery, Gerrish, N. H | 1,000 |
| New Jersey | Washington Crossing Forest Nursery, Washington Crossing, N. J | 700 |
| | Green Bank Forest Nursery, Green Bank, N. J | 300 |
| New York | Saratoga Nursery, Saratoga Springs, N. Y | 20,000 |
| | Lowville Nursery, Lowville, N. Y | 15,000 |
| North Carolina | Crab Creek Nursery, Penrose, N. C | 500 |
| | Clayton Nursery, Clayton, N. C | 10,000 |
| North Dakota | North Dakota School of Forestry Nursery, Bottineau, N. Dak | 550 |

STATE FOREST NURSERIES COOPERATING IN FEDERAL-STATE TREE DISTRIBUTING PROGRAM, 1948—Continued

| *State* | *Name and location* | *Approximate capacity In thousands* |
|---|---|---|
| Ohio | Marietta Nursery, Marietta, Ohio | 4,000 |
| | Green Springs, Green Springs, Ohio | 6,000 |
| Oklahoma | Goldsby Field Nursery, Route 1, Norman, Okla | 5,000 |
| Oregon | Oregon Forest Nursery, R. F. D. 1, Corvallis, Oreg | 1,500 |
| Pennsylvania | Clearfield Nursery, Clearfield, Pa | 1,550 |
| | Greenwood Furnace Nursery, Petersburg, Pa | 1,000 |
| | Mont Alto Nursery, Fayetteville, Pa | 2,020 |
| | Penn Nursery, Milroy, Pa | 1,000 |
| South Carolina | Horace L. Tilghman State Forest Nursery, Wedgefield, S. C | 25,000 |
| Tennessee | Marietta Nursery, Pinson, Tenn | 4,000 |
| Texas | Indian Mound Nursery, Alto, Tex | 20,000 |
| Utah | Utah Clarke-McNary Nursery, Logan, Utah | 110 |
| Vermont | State Forestry Nursery, Essex Junction, Vt | 1,000 |
| Virginia | Virginia State Forest Tree Nursery, Charlottesville, Va | 2,500 |
| | Peary Nursery, York County, Va | 1,250 |
| Washington | Federal State Forest Tree Nursery, Pullman, Wash | 150 |
| | Capitol State Forest Nursery, Olympia, Wash | 3,200 |
| West Virginia | West Virginia State Forest Nursery, LeSage, W. Va | 2,000 |
| Wisconsin | Griffith State Nursery, Wisconsin Rapids, Wis | 20,000 |
| | Gordon State Nursery, Gordon, Wis | 6,000 |
| | Trout Lake State Nursery, Trout Lake, Wis | 10,000 |
| | Hayward Nursery, Hayward, Wis | 10,000 |
| Wyoming | Torrington State Experiment Farm, Torrington, Wyo | 2.5 |
| | Total | 392,757.5 |
| Hawaii | Haiku Nursery, Haiku, Maui | 50 |
| | Hilo Nursery, Hilo, T. H. | 60 |
| | Lihue Nursery, Lihue, Kauai | 35 |
| | Makiki Nursery, Honolulu, T. H. | 90 |
| | Molokau Nursery, Kaunakakai, Molokai | 40 |
| | Olinda Nursery, Makawao, Maui | 100 |
| Puerto Rico | Catalina Nursery, Palmer, P. R. | 2,000 |
| | Mayaguez Nursery, Mayaguez, P. R. | 500 |
| | Rio Piedras Nursery, Rio Piedras, P. R. | 1,000 |
| | Toa Nursery, Toa Baja, P. R. | 10,000 |
| | Total | 13,875 |
| | 40 States, 71 nurseries, total capacity | 392,757.5 |
| | 2 Territories, 10 nurseries, total capacity | 13,875.0 |
| | Grand total (81 nurseries) | 406,632.5 |

## STATE FORESTRY AGENCIES

| *State* | *State administering agency* | *Mail address of administrative official* |
|---|---|---|
| Alabama | Department of Conservation, Division of Forestry. | State Forester<br>5 North Bainbridge St.<br>Montgomery 4, Ala. |
| Arizona | State Land Commission | State Land Commissioner<br>Phoenix, Ariz. |
| Arkansas | Arkansas Resources and Development Commission, Division of Forestry and Parks. | Director, Division of Forestry and Parks<br>Post Office Box 1940<br>Little Rock, Ark. |
| California | Department of Natural Resources, Division of Forestry. | State Forester<br>Sacramento, Calif. |
| Colorado | State Board of Forestry | State Forester<br>124 Capitol Bldg.<br>Denver 2, Colo. |
| Connecticut | State Park and Forest Commission | State Forester<br>165 Capitol Ave.<br>Hartford, Conn. |
| Delaware | State Forestry Department | State Forester<br>State House<br>Dover, Del. |
| Florida | Florida Board of Forestry and Parks, Florida Forest Service. | State Forester<br>Post Office Box 1200<br>Tallahassee, Fla. |
| Georgia | Division of Conservation, Department of Forestry. | Director, Department of Forestry<br>435 State Capitol<br>Atlanta 3, Ga. |
| Hawaii | Board of Commissioners of Agriculture and Forestry. | Territorial Forester<br>Post Office Box 3319<br>Honolulu, T. H. |
| Idaho | State Board of Land Commissioners | State Forester<br>801 Capitol Blvd.<br>Boise, Idaho. |
| Illinois | Department of Conservation, Division of Forestry. | State Forester<br>301½ East Monroe St.<br>Springfield, Ill. |
| Indiana | Department of Conservation, Division of Forestry. | State Forester<br>Indianapolis, Ind. |
| Iowa | Iowa Conservation Commission | Forestry Department<br>Iowa State College<br>Ames, Iowa. |
| Kansas | State Board of Administration, Department of Forestry and Floriculture. | Extension Forester<br>Kansas State College<br>Manhattan, Kans. |

STATE FORESTRY AGENCIES—Continued

| *State* | *State administering agency* | *Mail address of administrative official* |
|---|---|---|
| Kentucky | Conservation Department | Director, Division of Forestry<br>Frankfort, Ky. |
| Louisiana | Louisiana Forestry Commission | State Forester<br>Post Office Box 1269<br>Baton Rouge, La. |
| Maine | Maine Forest Service | Forest Commissioner<br>Augusta, Maine. |
| Maryland | Maryland Department of State Forests and Parks | State Forester<br>State Office Bldg.<br>Annapolis, Md. |
| Massachusetts | Department of Conservation | Commissioner of Conservation<br>15 Ashburton Pl.<br>Boston, Mass. |
| Michigan | Department of Conservation | Director, Department of Conservation<br>Lansing, Mich. |
| Minnesota | Department of Conservation | Director, Division of Forestry<br>State Office Bldg.<br>St. Paul, Minn. |
| Mississippi | Mississippi Forest and Park Service | State Forester<br>First Federal Savings and Loan Bldg.<br>Jackson 105, Miss. |
| Missouri | Missouri Conservation Commission | State Forester<br>Jefferson City, Mo. |
| Montana | State Forest Department | State Forester<br>Missoula, Mont. |
| Nebraska | University of Nebraska, College of Agriculture. | Extension Forester<br>College of Agriculture<br>Lincoln, Nebr. |
| Nevada | State of Nevada | State Forester-Fire Warden<br>Carson City, Nev. |
| New Hampshire | Forestry and Recreation Department. | State Forester<br>Concord, N. H. |
| New Jersey | Department of Conservation, Division of Forestry, Geology, Parks, and Historic Sites. | Director, Division of Forestry, Geology, Parks, and Historic Sites<br>State House Annex<br>Trenton, N. J. |
| New Mexico | State Land Commissioner | Commissioner of Public Lands<br>Santa Fe, N. Mex. |
| New York | New York Conservation Department, Division of Lands and Forests. | Director, Division of Lands and Forests<br>Albany, N. Y. |
| North Carolina | Department of Conservation and Development, Division of Forestry and Parks. | State Forester<br>204 State Education Bldg.<br>Raleigh, N. C. |

802062°—49——58

STATE FORESTRY AGENCIES—Continued

| *State* | *State administering agency* | *Mail address of administrative official* |
|---|---|---|
| North Dakota | State School of Forestry | State Forester<br>Bottineau, N. Dak. |
| Ohio | Agricultural Experiment Station, Department of Forestry. | State Forester<br>Wooster, Ohio. |
| Oklahoma | Oklahoma Planning and Resources Board, Division of Forestry. | Director, Division of Forestry<br>536 State Capitol<br>Oklahoma City 5, Okla. |
| Oregon | State Board of Forestry | State Forester<br>Salem, Oreg. |
| Pennsylvania | Department of Forests and Waters | Chief, Bureau of Forests<br>Harrisburg, Pa. |
| Puerto Rico | Department of Agriculture and Commerce, Forest Service. | Director, Forest Service<br>Post Office Box 577<br>Rio Piedras, P. R. |
| Rhode Island | State Department of Agriculture and Conservation, Office of Forests and Parks. | Chief Forester, Office of Forests and Parks<br>18 State House<br>Providence, R. I. |
| South Carolina | State Commission of Forestry | State Forester<br>506 Calhoun Office Bldg.<br>Columbia B, S. C. |
| South Dakota | Department of School and Public Lands and Commission of Game, Fish, and Parks. | State Forester<br>Pierre, S. Dak. |
| Tennessee | Department of Conservation, Division of Forestry. | State Forester<br>309 New State Office Bldg.<br>Nashville 3, Tenn. |
| Texas | Texas Forest Service | Texas Forest Service<br>Agricultural and Mechanical College<br>College Station 5, Tex. |
| Utah | Utah State Department of Agriculture, Board of Forestry and Fire Control. | Chief Forester-Fire Warden<br>School of Forestry<br>Logan, Utah. |
| Vermont | Vermont Forest Service | State Forester<br>Montpelier, Vt. |
| Virginia | Virginia Conservation Commission | State Forester<br>University Station<br>Charlottesville, Va. |
| Washington | Department of Conservation and Development, Division of Forestry. | State Supervisor of Forestry<br>Olympia, Wash. |
| West Virginia | Conservation Commission | State Forester<br>Charleston, W. Va. |
| Wisconsin | Wisconsin Conservation Department | Director of Conservation<br>Madison, Wis. |
| Wyoming | University of Wyoming | Extension Forester<br>University of Wyoming<br>Laramie, Wyo. |

# PUBLICATIONS OF THE FOREST PRODUCTS LABORATORY

## 1. PUBLICATION LISTS

(*Fields of investigation for which lists of publications have been prepared are printed below. Requests for the lists should specify the subject or subjects in which one is interested, and should be addressed to the Director, Forest Products Laboratory, North Walnut Street, Madison 5, Wis.*)

*Boxing and Crating.*—Strength and serviceability of shipping containers, methods of packing.

*Building Construction Subjects.*—Partial list of Government publications of interest to architects, builders, engineers, and retail lumbermen.

*Chemistry of Wood and Derived Products.*—Chemical properties and uses of wood and chemical wood products, such as turpentine, alcohol, and acetic acid.

*Fungus Defects in Forest Products.*—Pathology in cooperation with the Bureau of Plant Industry, Soils, and Agricultural Engineering—heart rots of trees; decay, molds, and stains in timber, in buildings, and in wood products; antiseptic properties of wood preservatives.

*Glue and Plywood.*—Development of waterproof glues, preparation, and application of various glues, plywood-manufacturing problems.

*Growth, Structure, and Identification of Wood.*—Structure and identification of wood; the effect of cellular structure of wood on its strength, shrinkage, permeability, and other properties; the influence of environmental factors, such as light, soil, moisture, and fire, on the quality of wood produced; and secretions of economic value produced by trees and their exploitation.

*Logging, Manufacturing, and Utilization of Timber, Lumber, and Other Wooden Products.*—Methods and practices in the lumber-producing and wood-consuming industries; standard lumber grades, sizes, and nomenclature; production and use of small dimension stock; specifications for small wooden products; uses for little-used species and commercial woods, and low-grade and wood-waste surveys.

*Mechanical Properties of Timber.*—Strength of timber and factors affecting strength; design of wooden articles or parts where strength or resistance to external forces is of importance.

*Pulp and Paper.*—Suitability of various woods for pulp and paper; fundamental principles underlying the pulping and bleaching processes; methods of technical control of these processes; relationship of the chemical and physical properties of pulps and the relation of these properties to the paper-making qualities of the pulps; waste in the industry, for example, decay in wood and pulp, utilization of bark, white water losses, etc.

*Seasoning of Wood.*—Experimental and applied kiln drying, physical properties, air drying, steam bending.

*Use of Wood in Aircraft Construction.*—Strength, selection, and character of aircraft wood and plywood; fabrication and assembly problems; methods of calculating the strength of wooden parts; structure of wood in relation to its properties and identification.

*Wood Finishing Subjects.*—Effect of coatings in preventing moisture absorption; painting characteristics of different woods and weathering of wood.

*Wood Preservation.*—Preservative materials and methods of application; durability and service records of treated and untreated wood in various forms.

## 2. A SELECTED LIST OF FOREST PRODUCTS LABORATORY PUBLICATIONS

| *No.* | *Title* |
|---|---|
| TN B–10 | The nailing of boxes. |
| TN 164 | Common styles of boxes. |
| TN 134 | The crate corner. |
| TN 237 | Metal straps on boxes. |
| R1666–9 | Wood flour. |
| R13 | Seventeen fallacies about wood. |
| R1432 | Microstructure of cellulose fibers. |
| R1189 | Exploring the labyrinth of cellulose and lignin. |
| R1236 | Utilization of waste lignin. |
| R1171 | Research on wood, cellulose, and lignin. |
| R911 | Microstructure of a wood pulp. |
| R1617 | The Madison wood-sugar process. |
| R1438 | Wood and paper-base plastics. |
| R1268 | Resin-treated, laminated, compressed wood. |
| TN 251 | Prevention and control of decay in dwellings. |
| R982 | Making log cabins endure. |
| TN F–2 | Strength of commercial liquid glues. |
| TN F–4 | Water-resistant glues. |
| TN 131 | Properties of ordinary wood compared with plywood. |
| TN 197 | Veneered and solid furniture. |

| *No.* | *Title* |
|---|---|
| TN 207 | Glues for use with wood. |
| R543 | Notes on the manufacture of plywood. |
| 1336 | Synthetic-resin glues. |
| R1624 | Fluid pressure molding of plywood. |
| R1635 | Manual on the laminating of timber products by gluing. |
| R285 | Manufacture of veneer. |
| TN 189 | Differences between heartwood and sapwood. |
| TN 209 | The structure of a softwood. |
| TN 210 | The structure of a hardwood. |
| TN 116 | How to tell birch, beech, and maple apart. |
| TN 214 | Southern yellow pine. |
| TN 215 | The white pine group. |
| R1585 | Guide to determining the slope of grain in lumber and veneer. |
| TN 153 | "Virgin growth" and "second growth." |
| TN 171 | Red hickory as strong as white hickory. |
| 1387 | A rapid method of determining the specific gravity of veneer. |
| R1637–1 | Equipment survey notes. |
| R899 and | Small sawmill improvement. |
| R1666 | General recommendations regarding methods for wood waste utilization. |
| R1479 | Some reference books on domestic and foreign woods. |
| TN 218 | Weights of various woods grown in the United States. |
| TN 101 | Comparative value of timber cut from live and dead trees. |
| TN 236 | Nail-holding power of American woods. |
| TN B–11 | Method of determining the moisture content of wood. |
| TN B–14 | Method of determining the specific gravity of wood. |
| TN 180 | Comparative strength of air-dried and kiln-dried wood. |
| R1687 | Tests of glued laminated wood beams and columns and development of principles of design. |
| TN 242 | Pictured good and poor practice in frame house construction. |
| TN 245 | Suitability of woods for use in the frame house. |
| TN 246 | Suitability of woods for use in barns and other farm structures. |
| R896 | The rigidity and strength of frame walls. |
| R1421 | How to minimize condensation in unheated rooms. |
| R991 | Practical suggestions on frame house construction. |
| R1196 | Condensation problems in modern buildings. |
| R1025 | Plywood as a structural covering for frame walls and wall units. |
| R1026 | Stressed plywood for floor panels. |
| TN 196 | Identification of pulpwoods. |
| TN 229 | Comparative decay resistance of heartwood of different native species. |
| R1677 | Insulation board, wallboard, and hardboard. |
| R1461 | Pulp-reinforced plastics. |
| 1319 | Strength and related properties of Forest Products Laboratory laminated paper plastics (papreg) at normal temperature. |
| TN 235 | Chemical analysis of wood. |
| TN 204 | Commercial processes of pulping woods for paper. |
| TN 212 | American woods for paper making. |
| TN 220 | Use of fibrous plants for paper manufacture. |
| TN 179 | The reuse of waste paper. |
| TN 241 | Shrinkage table for softwood lumber. |
| R966 | Wood bending. |
| R1650 | Shrinkage of wood. |
| TN 180 | Comparative strength of air-dried and kiln-dried wood. |
| TN 181 | Coatings for minimizing changes in the moisture content of wood. |
| R1657 | Air seasoning of lumber. |
| R1435 | Coatings for the prevention of end checks in logs and lumber. |
| TN 175 | Hardwood and softwood drying schedules. |
| R1661 | Types of lumber dry kilns. |
| R1655 | Moisture content of wood in use. |
| R962 | When and how to paint homes and farm buildings. |
| TN 221 | Weathering and decay. |
| R1053 | Behavior of paints on different woods. |
| R1118 | Experiments in fireproofing wood. |
| R1280 | Fire-retardant coatings. |
| R149 | Wood preservatives. |
| R761 | Preservative treatment and staining of shingles. |
| R154 | Methods of applying wood preservatives. |
| R1468 | Selecting a suitable method for treating fence posts. |
| TN 177 | Properties of a good wood preservative. |
| TN 165 | When preservative treatment of wood is an economy. |

# For Further Reference


A TREE IS A LIVING THING
(Page 1)

Büsgen, Moritz, and Münch, E.: *The Structure and Life of Forest Trees,* translated by Thomas Thomson, 436 pages, John Wiley and Sons, New York. 1931.

Meyer, Bernard S., and Anderson, Donald B.: *Plant Physiology,* 696 pages, D. Van Nostrand Company, New York. 1939.

SHADE TREES FOR NORTHEAST
(Page 48)

Swingle, Roger U.: *Phloem Necrosis, a Virus Disease of the American Elm,* U. S. D. A. Circular 640, 8 pages. 1942.

Walter, J. M., May, Curtis, and Collins, C. W.: *Dutch Elm Disease and Its Control,* U. S. D. A. Circular 677, 12 pages. 1943.

POINTERS ON PLANTING
(Page 85)

Bailey, L. H., editor: *The Standard Cyclopedia of Horticulture,* volume 3, pages 2656–2706, The Macmillan Company, New York. 1928.

Levison, J. J.: *The Home Book of Trees and Shrubs,* 424 pages, Simon and Schuster, New York. 1940.

Mulford, F. L.: *Transplanting Trees and Shrubs,* U. S. D. A. Farmers' Bulletin 1591, 34 pages. 1929.

Thompson, A. Robert: *Transplanting Trees and Other Woody Plants,* U. S. National Park Service, Tree Preservation Bulletin 9, 59 pages. 1940.

*Transplanting of Trees and Shrubs in the Northeastern and North Central United States,* Combined Proceedings of the Nineteenth National Shade Tree Conference and the Tenth Western Shade Tree Conference, pages 70–146. 1943.

KEEP SHADE TREES HEALTHY
(Page 91)

*Care of Damaged Shade Trees,* U. S. D. A. Farmers' Bulletin No. 1896, 34 pages. 1942.

*Common Diseases of Important Shade Trees,* U. S. D. A. Farmers' Bulletin 1987, 53 pages. 1948.

*Reducing Damage to Trees from Construction Work,* U. S. D. A. Farmers' Bulletin 1967, 26 pages. 1945.

PROTECTING SHADE TREES
(Page 97)

Fowler, M. E., Gravatt, George F., and Thompson, A. Robert: *Reducing Damage to Trees From Construction Work,* U. S. D. A. Farmers' Bulletin 1967, 26 pages. 1945.

THE COMMUNITY OF TREES
(Page 103)

Baker, Frederick S.: *Theory and Practice of Silviculture,* 502 pages, McGraw-Hill Book Company, Inc., New York. 1934.

Platt, Rutherford H.: *Our Flowering World,* 278 pages, Dodd, Mead & Company, New York. 1947.

Zon, Raphael: *Climate and the Nation's Forests,* Yearbook of Agriculture 1941 (Climate and Man), pages 477–498.

FOREST TYPES, UNITED STATES
(Page 109)

Bates, Carlos G.: *Forest Types in the Central Rocky Mountains as Affected by Climate and Soil,* U. S. D. A. Bulletin 1233, 152 pages. 1924.

Cajander, Aimo K.: *The Theory of Forest Types,* 108 pages, Finnish Literary Society, Helsinki. 1926.

Carpenter, J. Richard: *An Ecological Glossary,* 306 pages, University of Oklahoma Press, Norman. 1938.

Clements, Frederic E.: *Plant Formations and Forest Types,* Proceedings of the Society of American Foresters, volume 4, number 1, pages 50–63, Washington, D. C. 1909.

Cooper, J. G.: *On the Distribution of the Forests and Trees of North America, with Notes on Its Physical Geography,* Annual Report of the Board of Regents of the Smithsonian Institution for the year 1858, pages 246–280. 1859.

Cotta, Heinrich von: *Systematische Anleitung zur Taxation der Waldungen,* 2 volumes, Berlin. 1804.

Dice, Lee R.: *The Biotic Provinces of North America,* 78 pages, University of Michigan Press, Ann Arbor. 1943.

*Forest Cover Types of the Eastern United States,* 39 pages, Society of American Foresters, Washington, D. C. 1940.

*Forest Cover Types of Western North America,* 35 pages, Society of American Foresters, Washington, D. C. 1945.

*Forestry Terminology,* 84 pages, Society of American Foresters, Washington, D. C. 1944.

Graves, Henry Solon: *Practical Forestry in the Adirondacks,* U. S. Division of Forestry Bulletin 26, 85 pages. 1899.

Harshberger, John W.: *Phytogeographic Survey of North America,* 790 pages, G. E. Stechert and Company, New York. 1911.

*Instructions for Making Timber Surveys in the National Forests,* 45 pages, U. S. Forest Service. 1925.

Kruedener, Arthur A. von: *Waldtypen,* volume 1, 122 pages, J. Neumann, Neudamm, Germany. 1927.

Mowry, Jesse B.: *The Nature and Development of Forest Types,* 18 pages, Gloucester, R. I. 1920.

Pearson, Gustaf A.: *Forest Types in the Southwest as Determined by Climate and Soil,* U. S. D. A. Technical Bulletin 247, 144 pages. 1931.

Sampson, Arthur W.: *The Stability of Aspen as a Type,* Proceedings of the Society of American Foresters, volume 11, number 1, pages 86–87, Washington, D. C. 1916.

Shantz, H. L., and Zon, Raphael: *Natural Vegetation,* U. S. D. A. Atlas of American Agriculture, 29 pages. 1924.

Schütze, W.: *Beziehungen zwischen Chemischer Zusammensetzung und Ertragsfähigkeit des Waldbodens,* Zeitschrift für Forst- und Jagdwesen, volume 3, pages 367–390, Berlin. 1871.

Westveld, Marinus: *Type Definitions Based on Statistics of Stand Composition,* U. S. Forest Service, Northeastern Forest Experiment Station Technical Note 15, 1 page, New Haven, Conn. 1934.

Zon, Raphael: *Principles Involved in Determining Forest Types,* Proceedings of the Society of American Foresters, volume 1, number 3, pages 179–189, Washington, D. C. 1906.

## FORESTS AND SOILS

(Page 114)

Auten, John T.: *Forests for Old Fields,* Yearbook of Agriculture 1943–1947 (Science in Farming), pages 473–480. 1947.

Coile, Theodore S.: *Relation of Soil Characteristics to Site Index of Loblolly and Shortleaf Pines in the Lower Piedmont Region of North Carolina,* Duke University School of Forestry Bulletin 13, 78 pages, Durham, N. C. 1948.

Dreibelbis, F. R., and Post, F. A.: *An Inventory of Soil Water Relationships on Woodland, Pasture, and Cultivated Soils,* Proceedings of the Soil Science Society of America, volume 6, pages 462–473. 1941.

Heiberg, S. O., and Chandler, R. F., Jr.: *A Revised Nomenclature of Forest Humus Layers for the Northeastern United States,* Soil Science, volume 52, pages 87–99. August 1941.

Hill, W. W., Arnst, Albert, and Bond, R. M.: *Method of Correlating Soils with Douglas-fir Site Quality,* Journal of Forestry, volume 46, pages 835–841. November 1948

Holtby, B. E.: *Soil Texture as a Site Indicator in the Ponderosa Pine Stands of Southeastern Washington,* Journal of Forestry, volume 45, pages 824–825. November 1947.

Rommel, L. G., and Heiberg, S. O.: *Types of Humus Layer in the Forests of the Northeastern United States,* Ecology, volume 12, pages 567–608. July 1931.

## FOREST RENEWAL

(Page 120)

Burns, George P.: *Studies in Tolerance of New England Forest Trees, Part 4, Minimum Light Requirement Referred to a Definite Standard,* Vermont Agricultural Experiment Station Bulletin 235, 32 pages. 1923.

Haig, I. T.: *Factors Controlling Initial Establishment of Western White Pine and Associated Species,* Yale University, School of Forestry Bulletin 41, 149 pages, New Haven, Conn. 1936.

Kramer, Paul J., and Decker, John P.: *Relation Between Light Intensity and Rate of Photosynthesis of Loblolly Pine and Certain Hardwoods,* Plant Physiology, volume 19, pages 350–358. April 1944.

Schwappach, Adam: *Forestry,* translated by F. Story and E. A. Nobbs, 158 pages, J. M. Dent & Company, London. 1904.

Shirley, Hardy L.: *Reproduction of Upland Conifers in the Lake States as Affected by Root Competition and Light,* American Midland Naturalist, volume 33, pages 537–612. May 1945.

## THE SEED, THEN THE TREE

(Page 127)

Baldwin, Henry Ives: *Forest Tree Seed of the North Temperate Regions with Special Reference to North America,* 240 pages, Chronica Botanica Company, Waltham, Mass. 1942.

Engstrom, H. E., and Stoeckeler, J. H.: *Nursery Practices for Trees and Shrubs, Suitable for Planting on the Prairie-Plains,* U. S. D. A. Miscellaneous Publication 434, 159 pages. 1941.

Toumey, J. W., and Korstian, C. F.: *Seeding and Planting in the Practice of Forestry,* 520 pages, John Wiley & Sons, Inc., New York. 1942.

## DIRECT SEEDING OF TREES
(Page 136)

McQuilkin, W. E.: *Tests of Direct Seeding with Pines in the Piedmont Region,* Journal of Agricultural Research, volume 73, pages 113–136. August 15, 1946.

Minckler, Leon S., and Downs, Albert A.: *Machine and Hand Direct Seeding of Pine and Cedar in the Piedmont,* U. S. Forest Service, Southeastern Forest Experiment Station Technical Note 67, 10 pages, Asheville, N. C. 1946.

Priaulx, Arthur W.: *Direct Seeding Tool,* American Forests, volume 52, pages 472–473. October 1946.

Schopmeyer, C. S., and Helmers, Austin E.: *Seeding as a Means of Reforestation in the Northern Rocky Mountain Region,* U. S. D. A. Circular 722, 31 pages. 1947.

Shirley, Hardy L.: *Direct Seeding in the Lake States,* Journal of Forestry, volume 35, pages 379–387. April 1937.

Smith, C. F., and Aldous, S. E.: *The Influence of Mammals and Birds in Retarding Artificial and Natural Reseeding of Coniferous Forests in the United States,* Journal of Forestry, volume 45, pages 361–369. May 1947.

Stoeckeler, J. H., and Sump, A. W.: *Successful Direct Seeding of Northern Conifers on Shallow-Water-Table Areas,* Journal of Forestry, volume 38, pages 572–577. July 1940.

## PINE BREEDING, UNITED STATES
(Page 147)

Richens, R. H.: *Forest Tree Breeding and Genetics,* Imperial Agricultural Bureaux Joint Publication 8, 79 pages, London. 1945.

Riker, A. J., Kouba, T. F., Brener, W. H., and Byam, L. E.: *White Pine Selections Tested for Resistance to Blister Rust,* Journal of Forestry, volume 41, pages 753–760, October 1943.

Stockwell, Palmer, and Righter, F. I.: *Hybrid Forest Trees,* Yearbook of Agriculture 1943–1947 (Science in Farming), pages 465–472. 1947.

Syrach-Larsen, C.: *The Estimation of the Genotype in Forest Trees,* Royal Veterinary and Agricultural College Yearbook, pages 87–128, Copenhagen, Denmark. 1947.

*Tree Breeding at the Institute of Forest Genetics,* U. S. D. A. Miscellaneous Publication 659, 14 pages. 1948.

## POPLARS CAN BE BRED
(Page 153)

Schreiner, E. J.: *Creative Forestry,* Paper Industry and Paper World, volume 20, pages 302–307. June 1938.

Schreiner, E. J.: *How Sod Affects Establishment of Hybrid Poplar Plantations,* Journal of Forestry, volume 43, pages 412–427. June 1945.

Schreiner, E. J.: *Improvement of Forest Trees,* Yearbook of Agriculture 1937, pages 1242–1279.

Schreiner, E. J.: *Inhibiting Effect of Sod on the Growth of Hybrid Poplar,* U. S. Forest Service, Northeastern Forest Experiment Station Occasional Paper 8, 10 pages, New Haven, Conn. 1940.

Schreiner, E. J.: *Possibilities of Improving Pulping Characteristics of Pulpwoods by Controlled Hybridization of Forest Trees,* Paper Trade Journal, volume 100, number 8, pages 105–109. February 21, 1935.

Schreiner, E. J.: *The Role of Disease in the Growing of Poplar,* Journal of Forestry, volume 29, pages 79–82. January 1931.

Schreiner, E. J.: *Silvicultural Methods for Reforestation with Hybrid Poplars,* Paper Industry and Paper World, volume 19, pages 156–163. May 1937.

Schreiner, E. J.: *Tree Breeding for Desirable Qualities and Disease Resistance,* National Shade Tree Conference Proceedings, volume 22, pages 56–59. 1946.

Schreiner, E. J.: *Two Species of Valsa Causing Disease in Populus,* American Journal of Botany, volume 18, pages 1–29. January 1931.

Schreiner, E. J.: *Variation Between Two Hybrid Poplars in Susceptibility to the Inhibiting Effect of Grass and Weeds,* Journal of Forestry, volume 43, pages 669–672. September 1945.

Schreiner, E. J., and Stout, A. B.: *Descriptions of Ten New Hybrid Poplars,* Bulletin 61 of the Torrey Botanical Club, pages 449–460. November 1934.

Stout, A. B., McKee, R. H., and Schreiner, E. J.: *The Breeding of Forest Trees for Pulpwood,* Journal of the New York Botanical Garden, volume 28, pages 49–63. March 1927.

Stout, A. B., and Schreiner, E. J.: *Hybrids Between the Necklace Cottonwood and the Large-Leaved Aspen,* Journal of the New York Botanical Garden, volume 35, pages 140–143. June 1934.

Stout, A. B., and Schreiner, E. J.: *Results of a Project in Hybridizing Poplars,* Journal of Heredity, volume 24, pages 216–229. June 1933.

## WINDBREAKS AND SHELTERBELTS
(Page 191)

Bates, C. G.: *The Windbreak as a Farm Asset,* U. S. D. A. Farmers' Bulletin 1405, 22 pages. 1944.

Den Uyl, Daniel: *Windbreaks for Protecting Muck Soils and Crops,* Indiana Agricultural Experiment Station Circular 287, 12 pages. 1943.

Furnas, R. W.: *Tree Planting and Growing on the Plains,* U. S. D. A. Miscellaneous Special Report 2, pages 202–206. 1883.

Lillard, Richard G.: *The Great Forest,* 399 pages, A. A. Knopf, New York. 1947.

Munns, E. N., and Stoeckeler, J. H.: *How are the Great Plains Shelterbelts?* Journal of Forestry, volume 44, pages 237–257. April 1946.

Stoeckeler, J. H.: *Narrow Shelterbelts for the Southern Great Plains,* Soil Conservation, volume 11, pages 16–20. July 1945.

Thompson, H. M.: *Plan of Forest Planting for the Great Plains of North America,* American Journal of Forestry, volume 1, Pages 226–232. February 1883.

Ware, E. R.: *Forests of South Dakota, Their Economic Importance and Possibilities,* 27 pages, U. S. Forest Service, Lake States Forest Experiment Station and South Dakota State Planning Board, St. Paul, Minn. 1939.

Ware, E. R., and Smith, L. F.: *Woodlands of Kansas,* Kansas Agricultural Experiment Station Bulletin 285, 42 pages. 1939.

GROWING BETTER TIMBER

(Page 200)

Paul, Benson H.: *The Application of Silviculture in Controlling the Specific Gravity of Wood,* U. S. D. A. Technical Bulletin 168, 19 pages. 1930.

Paul, Benson H.: *Knots in Second-growth Pine and the Desirability of Pruning,* U. S. D. A. Miscellaneous Publication 307, 35 pages. 1938.

Pillow, M. Y., and Luxford, R. F.: *Structure, Occurrence, and Properties of Compression Wood,* U. S. D. A. Technical Bulletin 546, 32 pages. 1937.

CHRISTMAS TREES

(Page 251)

Barraclough, K. E.: *Christmas Trees, A Cash Crop,* New Hampshire Extension Circular 278, 15 pages. 1946.

Cope, J. A.: *Christmas-Tree Farming,* New York State College of Agriculture at Cornell University, Extension Bulletin 704, 32 pages. 1946.

Fenton, Richard H., and Callward, Floyd M.: *Home-Grown Christmas Trees for Connecticut,* Connecticut University, College of Agriculture Extension Bulletin 409, 16 pages. 1948.

Murphey, F. T.: *Christmas Tree Farming in Pennsylvania,* Pennsylvania State College Extension Circular 284, 24 pages. 1945.

MANAGEMENT ON CHIPPEWA

(Page 311)

Ayres, H. B.: *Timber Conditions of the Pine Region of Minnesota,* U. S. Geological Survey, Twenty-First Annual Report, 1899–1900, Part 5, pages 673–689.

Chapman, H. H.: *The Chippewa National Forest,* American Forests, volume 35, pages 561–565. September 1929.

*Endorsement of Minnesota Forest Reserve,* Forestry and Irrigation, pages 73–77. February 1906.

Eyre, Francis H., and Zehngraff, Paul J.: *Red Pine Management in Minnesota,* U. S. D. A. Circular 778, 70 pages. 1948.

*Forest Management in Minnesota,* Forestry and Irrigation, volume 10, pages 580–582. December 1904.

Kittredge, Joseph, Jr.: *Thinning Red Pine,* Journal of Forestry, volume 25, pages 555–559. May 1927.

Shirley, Hardy L.: *Improving Seedbed Conditions in a Norway Pine Forest,* Journal of Forestry, volume 31, pages 322–328. March 1933.

Woolsey, T. S., and Chapman, H. H.: *Norway Pine in the Lake States,* U. S. D. A. Bulletin 139, 42 pages. 1914.

Zon, Raphael: *Results of Cutting on the Minnesota National Forest Under the Morris Act of 1902,* Proceedings of the Society of American Foresters, volume 7, pages 100–105. 1912.

TAMING A WILD FOREST

(Page 326)

Andrews, H. J., and Cowlin, R. W.: *Forest Resources of the Douglas-Fir Region,* U. S. D. A. Miscellaneous Publication 389, 169 pages. 1940.

Kirkland, Burt P.: *Forest Resources of the Douglas-Fir Region,* 74 pages, Joint Committee on Forest Conservation of the Pacific Northwest Loggers Association and the West Coast Lumbermen's Association, Portland, Oreg. 1946.

Langille, H. D., Plummer, F. G., Dodwell, A., Rixon, T. F., and others: *Forest Conditions in the Cascade Range Forest Reserve, Oregon,* U. S. Geological Survey Professional Paper 9, 298 pages. 1903.

Munger, T. T., and Matthews, D. N.: *Slash Disposal and Forest Management After Clear Cutting in the Douglas-Fir Region,* U. S. D. A. Circular 586, 56 pages. 1941.

*National Forest Areas,* 15 pages, U. S. Forest Service. 1947.

Nelson, Milton N., and Colver, Carol: *The Economic Base for Power Markets in Linn County, Oregon,* 46 pages, U. S. Department of the Interior, Bonneville Power Administration. 1946.

Smith, Warren D., Ballaine, Wesley C., and Goldhammer, B.: *The Economic Base for Power Markets in Lane County, Oregon,* 52 pages, U. S. Department of the Interior, Bonneville Power Administration. 1946.

## PINYON-JUNIPER IN SOUTHWEST

(Page 342)

Bolton, Herbert Eugene, editor: *Spanish Exploration in the Southwest, 1542–1706,* 487 pages, Charles Scribner's Sons, New York. 1916.

Hough, Walter: *Antiquities of the Upper Gila and Salt River Valleys of Arizona and New Mexico,* Smithsonian Institution, Bureau of American Ethnology Bulletin 35, 96 pages. 1907.

Kidder, Alfred Vincent, and Guernsey, Samuel J.: *Archeological Explorations in Northeastern Arizona,* Smithsonian Institution, Bureau of American Ethnology Bulletin 65, 228 pages. 1919.

Pearson, G. A.: *Forest Types in the Southwest as Determined by Climate and Soil,* U. S. D. A. Technical Bulletin 247, 143 pages. 1931.

*Spanish Explorers in the Southern United States, 1528–1543,* 411 pages, Charles Scribner's Sons, New York. 1907.

## BEETLE-KILLED SPRUCE

(Page 417)

Hopkins, A. D.: *Bark Beetles of the Genus Dendroctonus,* U. S. Bureau of Entomology Bulletin 83, Part 1, 169 pages. 1909.

## INSECTS IN WOOD PRODUCTS

(Page 432)

*Decay and Termite Damage in Houses,* U. S. D. A. Farmers' Bulletin 1993, 20 pages. 1948.

*Powder-Post Beetles,* U. S. Bureau of Entomology and Plant Quarantine, Insects in Relation to National Defense Circular 6, 16 pages. 1941.

*Preventing Damage To Buildings by Subterranean Termites and Their Control,* U. S. D. A. Farmers' Bulletin 1911, 37 pages. 1942.

Snyder, T. E.: *Defects in Timber Caused by Insects,* U. S. D. A. Department Bulletin 1490, 46 pages. 1927.

Snyder, T. E.: *Our Enemy the Termite,* 257 pages, Comstock Publishing Company, Ithaca, N. Y. 1948.

Snyder, T. E.: *Powder-Post Beetles and Their Control,* Pests, volume 12, number 4, pages 8, 27, 31. April 1944.

Snyder, T. E., and Zetek, J.: *Effectiveness of Wood Preservatives in Preventing Attack by Termites,* U. S. D. A. Circular 683, 24 pages. 1943.

Wilford, B. H.: *Chemical Impregnation of Trees and Poles for Wood Preservation,* U. S. D. A. Circular 717, 30 pages. 1944.

## BLISTER RUST ON WHITE PINE

(Page 453)

Buchanan, T. S.: *Blister Rust Damage to Merchantable Western White Pine,* Journal of Forestry, volume 36, pages 321–328. March 1938.

Clinton, G. P., and McCormick, Florence A.: *Infection Experiments of Pinus Strobus with Cronartium Ribicola,* Connecticut Agricultural Experiment Station Bulletin 214, pages 428–459. 1919.

Davis, Kenneth P., and Moss, Virgil D.: *Blister Rust Control in the Management of Western White Pine,* U. S. Forest Service, Northern Rocky Mountain Forest and Range Experiment Station, Station Paper 3, 34 pages, Missoula, Mont. 1940.

Filler, E. C.: *Blister Rust Damage to Northern White Pine at Waterford, Vt.,* Journal of Agricultural Research, volume 47, pages 297–313. September 1, 1933.

Fulling, E. H.: *Plant Life and the Law of Man, Part 4, Barberry, Currant and Gooseberry, and Cedar Control,* Botanical Review, volume 9, pages 483–592. October 1943.

Hirt, Ray R.: *The Relation of Certain Meteorological Factors to the Infection of Eastern White Pine by the Blister-Rust Fungus,* New York State College of Forestry Technical Publication 59, 65 pages, Syracuse. 1942.

Lachmund, H. G.: *Damage to Pinus Monticola by Cronartium Ribicola at Garibaldi, British Columbia,* Journal of Agricultural Research, volume 49, pages 239–249. August 1, 1934.

Martin, J. F.: *Eradication of the Cultivated Black Currant in White Pine Regions,* U. S. D. A. Leaflet 175, 8 pages. 1939.

Martin, J. F., and Gravatt, G. F.: *Treatment of White Pines Infected with Blister Rust,* U. S. D. A. Farmers' Bulletin 1885, 28 pages. 1942.

Mielke, J. L.: *White Pine Blister Rust in Western North America,* Yale University, School of Forestry Bulletin 52, 155 pages, New Haven, Conn. 1943.

Offord, H. R.: *The Chemical Eradication of Ribes,* U. S. D. A. Technical Bulletin 240, 24 pages. 1931.

Offord, H. R., Van Atta, G. R., and Swanson, H. E.: *Chemical and Mechanical Methods of Ribes Eradication in the White Pine Areas of the Western States,* U. S. D. A. Technical Bulletin 692, 49 pages. 1940.

Snell, Walter H.: *Blister Rust in the Adirondacks,* Journal of Forestry, volume 26, pages 472–486. April 1928.

Snell, Walter H.: *Forest Damage and the White Pine Blister Rust,* Journal of Forestry, volume 29, pages 68–78. January 1931.

Spaulding, Perley: *The Blister Rust of White Pine,* U. S. Bureau of Plant Industry Bulletin 206, 78 pages. 1911.

Spaulding, Perley: *Investigations of the White-Pine Blister Rust,* U. S. D. A. Bulletin 957, 100 pages. 1922.

Spaulding, Perley: *Longevity of the Teliospores and Accompanying Uredospores of Cronartium Ribicola Fischer in 1923,* Journal of Agricultural Research, volume 31, pages 901–916. November 15, 1925.

Spaulding, Perley: *White Pine Blister Rust: A Comparison of European with North American Conditions,* U. S. D. A. Technical Bulletin 87, 58 pages. 1929.

Spaulding, Perley, and Rathbun-Gravatt, A.: *The Influence of Physical Factors on the Viability of Sporidia of Cronartium Ribicola Fischer,* Journal of Agricultural Research, volume 33, pages 397–433. September 1, 1926.


## PROGRESS, BUT STILL A PROBLEM

(Page 477)


Holbrook, Stewart Hall: *Burning an Empire,* 229 pages, The Macmillan Company, New York. 1943.


## BAD BUSINESS; YOUR BUSINESS

(Page 479)


Chapman, H. H.: *Prescribed Burning Versus Public Forest Fire Services,* Journal of Forestry, volume 45, pages 804–808. November 1947.

Craddock, George W.: *Salt Lake City Flood, 1945,* Proceedings of the Utah Academy of Sciences, Arts, and Letters, volume 23, pages 51–61. 1945–1946.

*Forest Fires and How You Can Prevent Them,* 11 pages, U. S. Forest Service. 1945.

*Forest Fire Statistics, 1936–1945,* U. S. Forest Service.

Guthrie, John D.: *Great Forest Fires of America,* 9 pages, U. S. Forest Service. 1936.

Hall, A. G.: *Four Flaming Days,* American Forests, volume 53, pages 540–542, 569–570. December 1947.

Love, R. M., and Jones, Burle J.: *Improving California Brush Ranges,* California Agricultural Experiment Station Circular 371, 31 pages. 1947.

Talbot, M. W., and Kraebel, C. J.: *Relation of Forest Lands to Agriculture, Industry, and People in Southern California,* U. S. Forest Service, California Forest and Range Experiment Station, Forest Research Note 39, 5 pages. 1944.

*Wartime Forest Fire Prevention Program,* 10 pages, U. S. Forest Service. 1945.


## FIRE AS TOOL IN PINES

(Page 517)


Siggers, Paul V.: *The Brown Spot Needle Blight of Pine Seedlings,* U. S. D. A. Technical Bulletin 870, 36 pages. 1944.


## TRAIL RIDING IN WILDERNESS

(Page 537)


*Aircraft Use in Wilderness Areas,* U. S. National Research Council, Division of Biology and Agriculture, Bimonthly Report, volume 5, pages 38–55. 1947.

Allen, Shirley W.: *Wilderness Trails by Canoe,* American Forests, volume 47, pages 416–419, 441. September 1941.

Kneipp, L. F.: *Enriching and Stimulating Solitude,* Living Wilderness, volume 3, number 3, page 4. December 1937.

Lord, Russell, editor: *Forest Outings,* 311 pages, U. S. Forest Service. 1940.

*The Pioneer Trail Riders,* American Forests, volume 39, pages 401–404, 424. September 1933.


## TREASURES OF THE NATION

(Page 544)


*A Study of the Park and Recreation Problem of the United States,* 279 pages, U. S. National Park Service. 1941.

Butcher, Devereaux: *Exploring our National Parks and Monuments,* 160 pages, Oxford University Press, New York. 1947.

*Glimpses of Our National Parks,* 107 pages, U. S. National Park Service. 1941.

James, Harlean: *Romance of the National Parks,* 240 pages, The Macmillan Company, New York. 1939.

Merriam, John C.: *Parks: National and State,* Published Papers and Addresses of John Campbell Merriam, volume 4, pages 2256–2264, Carnegie Institution, Washington, D. C. 1938.

*Municipal and County Parks in the United States,* 173 pages, National Recreation Association, New York. 1940.

*Portfolio on the National Park and Monument System,* 4 volumes, American Planning and Civic Association, Washington, D. C. 1938.

*The National Parks Portfolio,* 274 pages, U. S. National Park Service. 1931.

*1946 Yearbook, Park and Recreation Progress,* 122 pages, National Conference on State Parks, Washington, D. C.


## WILDLIFE IN SMALL WOODLAND

(Page 561)


Dambach, Charles A.: *A Ten-Year Ecological Study of Adjoining Grazed and Ungrazed Woodlands in Northeastern Ohio,* Ecological Monographs, volume 14, pages 255–270. July 1944.

Graham, Edward H.: *The Land and Wildlife,* 232 pages, Oxford University Press, New York. 1947.

Hamilton, W. J., Jr., and Cook, David B.: *Small Mammals and the Forest,* Journal of Forestry, volume 38, pages 468–473. June 1940.

Wygant, N. D.: *An Infestation of the Pandora Moth, Coloradia Pandora Blake, in Lodgepole Pine in Colorado,* Journal of Economic Entomology, volume 34, pages 697–702. October 1941.

FORESTS AS WILDLIFE HABITAT
(Page 564)

Gabrielson, Ira N.: *Wildlife Conservation,* 250 pages, The Macmillan Company, New York. 1941.

Graham, Edward H.: *The Land and Wildlife,* 232 pages, Oxford University Press, New York. 1947.

Leopold, Aldo: *Game Management,* 481 pages, Charles Scribner's Sons, New York. 1933.

TREES AND FOOD FROM ACORNS
(Page 571)

Merriam, C. Hart: *The Acorn, a Possibly Neglected Source of Food,* National Geographic Magazine, volume 34, pages 129–137. August 1918.

Morris, Robert T.: *Edible Acorns as Food for Man, Livestock, and Fowls,* Northern Nut Growers Association Report, volume 18, pages 35–43. 1927.

MANAGING UTAH'S BIG GAME
(Page 573)

Alter, J. Cecil: *W. A. Ferris in Utah, 1830–1835,* Utah Historical Quarterly, Salt Lake City, volume 9, pages 81–108. 1941.

Auerbach, Herbert S., editor: *Father Escalante's Journal,* 142 pages, Utah Historical Quarterly, Salt Lake City, volume 11. 1943.

*Biennial Report,* Utah State Fish and Game Commissioner: 10th, 1913–1914; 12th, 1917–1918.

Dale, Harrison Clifford: *The Ashley-Smith Explorations and the Discovery of a Central Route to the Pacific, 1822–1829,* 352 pages, The Arthur H. Clark Company, Cleveland. 1918.

Doman, Everett R., and Rasmussen, D. I.: *Supplemental Winter Feeding of Mule Deer in Northern Utah,* Journal of Wildlife Management, volume 8, pages 317–338. October 1944.

Stansbury, Howard: *Exploration and Survey of the Valley of the Great Salt Lake of Utah,* 487 pages, Lippincott, Grambo and Company, Philadelphia. 1852.

Wagner, W. F., editor: *Leonard's Narrative; Adventures of Zenas Leonard; Fur Trader and Traveler, 1831–1836;* Reprinted from the rare original of 1839, 317 pages, The Burrows Brothers Company, Cleveland. 1904.

FORESTS AND FISH
(Page 581)

Gabrielson, Ira N.: *Prescription for Wildlife,* Oregon State Game Commission Bulletin, volume 3, number 3, page 3. March 1948.

Hazzard, A. S.: *Some Phases of the Life History of Eastern Brook Trout, Salvelinus fontinalis Mitchell,* Transactions of the American Fisheries Society, volume 62, pages 344–350. 1932.

Hobbs, D. F.: *Natural Reproduction of Trout in New Zealand and Its Relation to Density of Populations,* New Zealand Marine Department Fisheries Bulletin 8, 93 pages. 1940.

Needham, P. R., Moffett, James W., and Slater, Daniel W.: *Fluctuations in Wild Brown Trout Populations in Convict Creek, California,* Journal of Wildlife Management, volume 9, pages 9–25. January 1945.

Watts, Lyle F.: *Forests and the Nation's Water Resource,* Report of the Chief of the Forest Service, 48 pages. 1947.

TIMBER CUTTING AND WATER
(Page 593)

Bates, C. G., and Henry, A. J.: *Forest and Streamflow Experiment at Wagon Wheel Gap, Colorado,* Monthly Weather Review Supplement 30, 79 pages. 1928.

Chittenden, H. M.: *Forests and Reservoirs in Their Relation to Streamflow, with Particular Reference to Navigable Rivers,* Transactions of the American Society of Civil Engineers, volume 62, pages 245–546. 1909.

Connaughton, Charles A.: *The Accumulation and Rate of Melting of Snow as Influenced by Vegetation,* Journal of Forestry, volume 33, pages 564–569. June 1935.

Connaughton, Charles A., and Wilm, H. G.: *Post-War Management of Western Forested Watershed-Lands for Water-Yield,* Transactions of the American Geophysical Union, Part 1, pages 36–40. 1944.

Dunford, E. G., and Niederhof, C. H.: *Influence of Aspen, Young Lodgepole Pine, and Open Grassland Types Upon Factors Affecting Water Yield,* Journal of Forestry, volume 42, pages 673–677. September 1944.

Frank, Bernard, and Betts, Clifford A.: *Water and Our Forests,* U. S. D. A. Miscellaneous Publication 600, 29 pages. 1946.

Hoover, M. D.: *Effect of Removal of Forest Vegetation Upon Water-Yields,* Transactions of the American Geophysical Union, Part 6, pages 969–977. 1944.

Hoyt, W. G., and Troxell, H. C.: *Forests and Streamflow,* Proceedings of the American Society of Civil Engineers, volume 58, pages 1037–1066. 1932.

Kittredge, Joseph, Jr.: *Forests and Water Aspects Which Have Received Little Attention,* Journal of Forestry, volume 34, pages 417–419. April 1936.

Munns, E. N., and others: *Watershed and Other Related Influences, and a Watershed Protective Program,* 73d Congress, 1st session, Senate Document 12, Separate 5, pages 299–461, 1509–1536. 1933.

Niederhof, C. H., and Wilm, H. G.: *The Effect of Cutting Mature Lodgepole-Pine Stands on Rainfall Interception,* Journal of Forestry, volume 41, pages 57–61. January 1943.

Wilm, H. G.: *Mountain Water for Thirsty Lands,* American Forests, volume 51, pages 536–537. November 1945.

Zon, Raphael: *Forests and Water in the Light of Scientific Investigation,* 62d Congress, 2d session, Senate Document 469, 106 pages. 1912.

## PAINTING FARM AND CITY HOME

(Page 625)

Browne, F. L.: *Classification of House and Barn Paints,* U. S. D. A. Technical Bulletin 804, 36 pages. 1942.

Browne, F. L.: *Wood Properties and Paint Durability,* U. S. D. A. Miscellaneous Publication 629, 10 pages. 1947.

## FUNGI AND WOOD

(Page 630)

Cartwright, K. St. G., and Findlay, W. P. K.: *Decay of Timber and Its Prevention,* 294 pages, His Majesty's Stationery Office, London. 1946.

*Cause and Prevention of Blue Stain in Wood,* U. S. Forest Service, Forest Products Laboratory Technical Note 225, 4 pages. 1941.

*Decay and Termite Damage in Houses,* U. S. D. A. Farmers' Bulletin 1993, 21 pages. 1948.

Diller, Jesse D.: *Decay a Hazard in Basementless Houses on Wet Sites,* American Builder, volume 68, number 7, pages 92, 122, 124. July 1946.

Hartley, Carl: *Fungi in Forest Products,* Yearbook of Agriculture 1943–1947 (Science in Farming), pages 883–889. 1947.

Hartley, Carl, and May, Curtis: *Decay of Wood in Boats,* Motor Boat, volume 23, number 12, pages 34, 36, 38, 40, 42, 44. December 1946.

Hepting, George H.: *Preventing Decay in Wood Aircraft,* Aero Digest, volume 44, pages 126, 128, 142, 213. February 15, 1944.

Scheffer, T. C.: *Diagnostic Features of Some Discolorations Common to Aircraft Hardwoods,* U. S. Bureau of Plant Industry, Soils, and Agricultural Engineering, Forest Pathology Special Release 19, 5 pages, Madison, Wis. 1944.

Scheffer, T. C.: *Progressive Effects of Polyporus Versicolor on the Physical and Chemical Properties of Red Gum Sapwood,* U. S. D. A. Technical Bulletin 527, 45 pages. 1936.

## PRESCRIPTION, WOODS SAFETY

(Page 676)

*Accident Facts,* 96 pages, National Safety Council, Chicago. 1947.

## HISTORY OF FORESTRY

(Page 702)

*A National Plan for American Forestry,* U. S. Forest Service, 73d Congress, 1st session, Senate Document 12, 2 volumes. 1933.

Fernow, Bernhard E.: *A Brief History of Forestry,* 506 pages, University Press, Toronto, and Forestry Quarterly, Cambridge, Mass. 1911.

Fernow, Bernhard E., editor: *Forestry Bulletin,* numbers 1, 2, 3. May, September 1884; January 1885.

Fernow, Bernhard E.: *Report upon the Forestry Investigations of the U. S. Department of Agriculture, 1877–1898,* 55th Congress, 3d session, House Document 181, 401 pages. 1899.

Lillard, Richard G.: *The Great Forest,* 399 pages, Alfred A. Knopf, New York. 1947.

Pinchot, Gifford: *Breaking New Ground,* 522 pages, Harcourt, Brace and Company, New York. 1947.

*Proceedings of the American Forestry Congress,* 1882–1889.

*Proceedings of the American Forestry Association,* 1890–1893.

*Report of the Forester,* 1910–1934; *Report of the Chief,* 1935–1947, U. S. Forest Service. 1910–1947.

*Report of the Secretary, 1892, 1893,* 2 volumes, U. S. Department of Agriculture. 1893, 1894.

Smith, Herbert A.: *The Early Forestry Movement in the United States,* Agricultural History, volume 12, pages 326–346. October 1938.

## FUTURE TIMBER REQUIREMENTS

(Page 731)

Behre, C. Edward, and Hutchison, S. B.: *Gaging the Timber Resource of the United States,* U. S. Forest Service Reappraisal Report 1, 62 pages. 1946.

*General Housing Act of 1945,* Senate Committee on Banking and Currency, 79th Congress, 1st session, Hearings on S. 1592, Revised, Part 1, 538 pages. 1946.

*Housing Study and Investigation, Final Majority Report,* Joint Committee on Housing, 80th Congress, 2d session, House Report 1564, 2 parts. 1948.

Rettie, J. C., and Hallauer, F. J.: *Potential Requirements for Timber Products in the United States,* U. S. Forest Service Reappraisal Report 2, 70 pages. 1946.

## THE WORLD FOREST SITUATION

(Page 742)


Behre, C. Edward, and Hutchison, S. B.: *Gaging the Timber Resource of the United States,* U. S. Forest Service Reappraisal Report 1, 62 pages. 1946.

*Forest Resources of the World,* Unasylva, volume 2, pages 161–182. July-August 1948.

*Yearbook of Forest Products Statistics, 1947,* 209 pages, Food and Agriculture Organization of the United Nations, Washington, D. C. 1948.


## IMPORTANT FOREST TREES

(Page 763)


Benson, Lyman, and Darrow, Robert A.: *A Manual of Southwestern Desert Trees and Shrubs,* University of Arizona Biological Science Bulletin 6, 411 pages, Tucson. 1945.

Blakeslee, A. F., and Jarvis, C. D.: *Trees in Winter,* 292 pages, The Macmillan Company, New York. 1931.

Britton, Nathaniel Lord, and Shafer, John Adolph: *North American Trees,* 894 pages, Henry Holt and Company, New York. 1908.

Brown, H. P.: *Trees of Northeastern United States,* 490 pages, Christopher Publishing House, Boston. 1938.

Coker, William Chambers, and Totten, Henry Roland: *Trees of the Southeastern States,* 419 pages, University of North Carolina Press, Chapel Hill. 1945.

Collingwood, G. Harris, and Brush, Warren D.: *Knowing Your Trees,* 312 pages, American Forestry Association, Washington, D. C. 1947.

Curtis, Carlton C., and Bausor, S. C.: *The Complete Guide to North American Trees,* 337 pages, New Home Library, New York. 1943.

Eliot, Willard Ayres, and McLean, G. B.: *Forest Trees of the Pacific Coast,* 565 pages, G. P. Putnam's Sons, New York. 1938.

Emerson, Arthur I., and Weed, Clarence M.: *Our Trees, How to Know Them,* 295 pages, Garden City Publishing Company, Garden City, N. Y. 1946.

Green, Charlotte Hilton: *Trees of the South,* 551 pages, University of North Carolina Press, Chapel Hill. 1939.

Harlow, William M.: *Trees of the Eastern United States and Canada, Their Woodcraft and Wildlife Uses,* 288 pages, McGraw-Hill Book Company, Inc., New York. 1942.

Harlow, William M., and Harrar, Ellwood S.: *Textbook of Dendrology,* 542 pages, McGraw-Hill Book Company, Inc., New York. 1941.

Harrar, Ellwood S., and Harrar, J. George: *Guide to Southern Trees,* 712 pages, McGraw-Hill Book Company, Inc., New York. 1946.

Hough, Romeyn Beck: *Handbook of the Trees of the Northern States and Canada East of the Rocky Mountains,* 470 pages, The Macmillan Company, New York. 1947.

Illick, Joseph S.: *Tree Habits; How To Know the Hardwoods,* 337 pages, American Nature Association, Washington, D. C. 1924.

Jaques, H. E.: *How To Know the Trees,* 166 pages, W. C. Brown Company, Dubuque, Iowa. 1946.

Keeler, Harriet L.: *Our Native Trees and How To Identify Them,* 533 pages, Charles Scribner's Sons, New York. 1929.

Kirkwood, J. E.: *Northern Rocky Mountain Trees and Shrubs,* 340 pages, Stanford University Press, Stanford University, Calif. 1930.

Leavitt, Robert Greenleaf: *The Forest Trees of New England,* 179 pages, Arnold Arboretum, Jamaica Plain, Mass. 1933.

Longyear, Burton O.: *Trees and Shrubs of the Rocky Mountain Region,* 244 pages, G. P. Putnam's Sons, New York. 1927.

McMinn, Howard E., and Maino, Evelyn: *An Illustrated Manual of Pacific Coast Trees,* 409 pages, University of California Press, Berkeley. 1946.

Mathews, F. Schuyler: *Field Book of American Trees and Shrubs,* 465 pages, G. P. Putnam's Sons, New York. 1915.

*Native Trees of Canada,* Canada Forest Service Bulletin 61, 210 pages, Ottawa. 1939.

Preston, Richard J., Jr.: *Rocky Mountain Trees,* 285 pages, Iowa State College Press, Ames. 1947.

Rehder, Alfred: *Manual of Cultivated Trees and Shrubs Hardy in North America,* 996 pages, The Macmillian Company, New York. 1940.

Rogers, Julia Ellen: *The Tree Book,* 565 pages, Doubleday, Doran and Company, Garden City, N. Y. 1935.

Sargent, Charles Sprague: *Manual of the Trees of North America,* 910 pages, Houghton Mifflin Company, Boston. 1933.

Sudworth, George B.: *Forest Trees of the Pacific Slope,* 441 pages, U. S. Forest Service. 1908.

Taylor, Raymond F.: *Pocket Guide to Alaska Trees,* U. S. D. A. Miscellaneous Publication 55, 39 pages. 1929.

Trelease, William: *Winter Botany,* 396 pages, Urbana, Ill. 1925.


## TREES FROM FOREIGN LANDS

(Page 815)


Bailey, L. H.: *The Cultivated Conifers in North America,* 404 pages, The Macmillan Company, New York. 1933.

Bailey, L. H., editor: *The Standard Cyclopedia of Horticulture,* 3 volumes, The Macmillan Company, New York. 1930.

Bailey, L. H., and Bailey, Ethel Zoe, compilers: *Hortus Second,* 778 pages, The Macmillan Company, New York. 1941.

Felt, Ephraim Porter: *Shelter Trees in War and Peace,* 320 pages, Orange Judd Publishing Company, New York. 1943.

Friend, W. H.: *Plants of Ornamental Value for the Rio Grande Valley of Texas,* Texas Agricultural Experiment Station Bulletin 609, 156 pages, College Station. 1942.

Grant, John A., and Grant, Carol L.: *Trees and Shrubs for Pacific Northwest Gardens,* 335 pages, F. McCaffrey, Seattle, Wash. 1943.

Hottes, Alfred Carl: *The Book of Trees,* 440 pages, A. T. De La Mare Company, New York. 1942.

Hoyt, Roland Stewart: *Check Lists for the Ornamental Plants of Subtropical Regions,* 383 pages, Livingston Press, Los Angeles, Calif. 1938.

Kumlien, L. L.: *The Friendly Evergreens,* 237 pages, D. Hill Nursery Company, Dundee, Ill. 1946.

McMinn, Howard E., and Maino, Evelyn: *An Illustrated Manual of Pacific Coast Trees,* 409 pages, University of California Press, Berkeley. 1946.

Mowry, Harold: *Ornamental Trees,* Florida Agricultural Experiment Station Bulletin 261, 134 pages, Gainesville. 1933.

Mulford, Furman Lloyd: *Trees for Roadside Planting,* U. S. D. A. Farmers' Bulletin 1482, 50 pages. 1928.

Mulford, Furman Lloyd: *Trees for Town and City Streets,* U. S. D. A. Farmers' Bulletin 1208, 30 pages. 1927.

Rehder, Alfred: *Manual of Cultivated Trees and Shrubs Hardy in North America,* 996 pages, The Macmillan Company, New York. 1940.

Sturrock, David, and Menninger, Edwin A.: *Shade and Ornamental Trees for South Florida and Cuba,* 172 pages, Stuart Daily News, Stuart, Fla. 1946.

Wilson, Ernest H.: *Aristocrats of the Trees,* 279 pages, Stratford Company, Boston. 1930.

# Some Words Woodsmen Use

ABSCISSION The natural separation of parts of a plant (such as flowers, bark, fruit, leaves, or branches) by the breakdown of the absciss layer, which is a layer of cells across the base of a branch or embedded in the bark through which the leaf or branch or other part breaks off.

ACCESS ROAD A road built into isolated stands of commercial timber so they can be reached by loggers, fire fighters, and others.

ACID WOOD Wood cut for use in plants that manufacture charcoal, acetic acid, and methanol by destructive distillation. It is sometimes called distillation wood or chemical wood.

ARBORICULTURE The science and art of growing trees, especially as ornamental or shade trees. Distinguished from silviculture or forestry (the science and art of growing trees as a forest or for lumber) and from tree horticulture or pomology (growing trees for fruit, nuts, etc.).

ASSOCIATION As used in botany: An assemblage of plants, usually over a wide area, that has one or more dominant species from which it derives a definite aspect.

BACKFIRE A fire intentionally set along the inner edge of a control line located ahead of an advancing fire, for the purpose of facilitating control by a widening of the control line and the removal of intervening combustible materials.

BALL-HOOTER A slang term loggers use for a man who rolls or slides logs down a hillside.

BARBER CHAIR In loggers' slang, a stump on which is left standing a slab that splintered off the tree as it fell. Generally it indicates careless felling.

BLAZE A mark made on the trunk of a standing tree by painting or chipping off a spot of bark with an ax. It is used to indicate a trail, boundary, location for a road, trees to be cut, and so on.

BOLE The stem or trunk of a tree, usually the lower, usable or merchantable portion of the tree trunk.

BOOM (1) Logs or timbers fastened together end to end and used to hold floating logs. The term includes also the logs enclosed. There are many varieties depending on construction and use, such as bag, barge, bracket, catch, fender, fin, glancing, holding, limber, pocket, receiving, round, rudder, shear, sorting, storage. (2) Projecting arm of a log-loading machine, which supports the log during loading. May be either of the swinging or the rigid type.

BROADLEAF A tree with two cotyledons, or seed leaves; it usually is deciduous—that is, it sheds all its leaves annually. The broadleaved trees, such as maple and oak, have relatively broad, flat leaves, as contrasted with the conifers, such as pine, which have narrow leaves, or needles.

BUCK To saw felled trees into logs or bolts; to bring or carry, as to "buck" water.

BURL A hard, woody growth on a tree trunk or on roots, more or less rounded in form. It is usually the result of entwined growth of a cluster of buds. In lumber, a burl produces a distorted and unusual (but often attractive) grain.

BURNS Areas in which fires have injured the forest.

CAMBIUM A soft layer, strip, or cylinder of living cells, one row thick, between the living bark and living wood of a tree. During the growing season its cells divide continuously, giving origin to the wood tissues and the bark tissues.

CAMP INSPECTOR To loggers, a man who drifts from camp to camp, trying out the food and living accommodations but working as little as possible.

CANOPY In a forest, the cover of green leaves and branches formed by the crowns of all the individual trees. Its density is ordinarily expressed as the amount (or percentage) of the ground that would be completely shaded by the forest if the sun were straight overhead.

CELLULOSE A complex, threadlike material, the molecules of which are made up of hundreds or thousands of sugar residues present in all plant materials. Wood, cotton, flax, and hemp fibers, and similar fibers, are the main sources of cellulose. It is the raw material for making paper, films, artificial silk, cellulose lacquers.

CHORE BOY To loggers, one who cleans the sleeping quarters, cuts firewood, builds fires, and carries wood. Synonyms: Flunky, buck, bull cook, barroom man.

CLEAR CUTTING A method of cutting that removes all merchantable trees on the area in one cut.

CLIMAX A plant community that does not change unless there is a change in the climate. It is the culminating stage in natural plant succession. The plants in a climax community are favored by the environment which they themselves create, and so are in balance with it.

CLONE The aggregate of plants derived from a single seeding by means of vegetative propagation such as the rooting of cuttings or slips, budding, or grafting. Every member of a clone has the same heredity, so that under uniform environment a group of plants from a single clone is quite uniform. Well-known tree clones are the Lombardy poplar, Koster's blue spruce, the Irish yew, and the named varieties of fruits and nuts.

CORDUROY ROAD A road built of logs or poles laid side by side across the roadway, usually in low or swampy places.

CROWN The upper part of a tree, including the branches with their foliage.

CRUISE A survey of forest lands to locate and estimate volume and grades of standing timber; also, the estimate obtained in such a survey. ("Scaling" is the measurement of the volumes of individual logs after the trees have been felled.)

CULL (1) A tree or log of merchantable size that is unmerchantable because of defects. (2) The deduction from gross volume made to adjust for defect. (3) To cut a small portion of a stand by selecting one or a few of the best trees. (4) To reject a tree, log, or board in scaling or grading.

CUT The yield, during a specified period, of products that are cut, as of grain, timber, or, in sawmilling, lumber.

DEADMAN (1) A timber to which the end of a hawser or cable is secured. (2) A log buried in the ground, by which a guy line is anchored.

DEFOLIATE To shed leaves; to lose leaves; to cause a tree to lose its leaves.

DIAMETER LIMIT A specified diameter at breast height (4½ feet above the ground) above which all trees are cut, under a diameter-limit cutting agreement.

DINGLE (1) The roofed-over space or "alley") between the kitchen and sleeping quarters of an old-style logging camp, commonly used as a storeroom. (2) The shedlike structure for storing food supplies in the newer type camps.

DINKEY A small logging locomotive.

DONKEY DOCTOR One who maintains and repairs donkey engines, which are portable steam engines equipped with drum and cable, used in cable logging, or gasoline or Diesel engines similarly equipped.

DRIVE Logs or timbers that are being floated on a stream from the forest to a mill or shipping point. It is also a verb.

DRUPE A simple, fleshy, or pulpy fruit; a stone fruit, as peach, plum, and cherry.

DRY-KI Trees killed by flooding. Often found in areas flooded by beaver dams.

ECOLOGY The study of the effect of environment on plants and animals, and of their influence on the environment.

ENDEMIC Indigenous or native in a restricted locality; confined naturally to a certain limited area or region, in contrast to epidemic.

ENVIRONMENT All the external conditions that affect the life and growth of a plant or animal. Air, sunlight, rain, wind, and the resultant temperature and moisture are parts of the environment of plants.

ENZYME An organic catalyst (or stimulator) produced by an animal or plant organism. It accelerates such chemical reactions as splitting starch into sugar. Almost all vital processes involve enzyme action. Animal and plant enzymes are much alike.

EXOTICS Nonnative or foreign species, introduced to a continent or geographic region from outside its natural range. Scots pine, Norway spruce, Siberian elm, and Russian mulberry are examples of exotic tree species.

FIREBREAK An existing barrier, or one constructed before a fire occurs, from which all or most of the inflammable materials have been removed; designed to stop or check creeping or running but not spot fires, or to serve as a line from which to work and to facilitate the movement of men and equipment in fire suppression.

FIRE EDGE The line, usually irregular, to which a fire has burned at a given moment; the boundary of a fire at a given moment.

FUNGUS (*singular*); FUNGI (*plural*) A low form of plant life having no chlorophyll, reproducing by spores, having a mycelium, and living as a parasite or saprophyte on organic matter. The fungi are numerous on and in soil where they aid in breaking down organic debris to humus.

GENETICS The science that seeks to explain resemblances and differences between plants or animals related by descent.

GIRDLING The act of encircling the stem of a living tree with cuts that completely sever bark and cambium and often are carried well into the outer sapwood.

GO-DEVIL A small, short sled without a tongue, used in skidding logs.

GRAFTING Act or process of inserting a cion, less strictly a bud, of a specified variety into a stem, root, or branch of another plant so that a permanent union is effected, especially for purposes of propagation.

GROUND WATER Water that stands or flows beneath the ground surface in soil or rock material which is thoroughly saturated. The upper surface of this saturated zone is called the water table.

GUM As applied to naval stores products: The raw product (oleoresin) which exudes from the wood of a living pine tree when a wound is made through the bark into the living tissues.

HABITAT The kind of place where a plant or animal naturally grows or lives.

HAYWIRE OUTFIT A logging operation that has poor equipment; originally, makeshift repairs in harness.

HEAD (of a fire) The hottest, most active forepart of a blaze.

HEARTWOOD The central portion of the trunks of trees, entirely dead and without function; usually darker and more durable in service than the outer portion or sapwood.

HEREDITARY Transmitted from parents to offspring. Properly, only factors may be so described, but we commonly speak of hereditary size or shape. Used to distinguish characteristics of an animal or plant derived from its parents from those predominantly controlled by the environment, although the distinction cannot be pushed too far, because all characteristics are the result of interaction between heredity and environment.

HOT-LOGGING A logging operation in which logs go from the stump to the mill without pause.

HOVEL A stable for logging teams.

HYBRID The offspring resulting from mating two plants or animals that differ in one or more hereditary factors. This is the narrowest—the geneticist's—use of the term. A hybrid is more commonly understood to be the plant resulting from crossing two plants that are so distantly related as to belong to different races, varieties, species, or even genera. For precision, we may speak of interracial or interspecies hybrids.

INITIAL ATTACK (1) The first suppression effort at control of a fire. (2) The first attack by an insect.

INTEGRATED LOGGING A method of logging designed to make the best use of all timber products. It removes in one cutting all timber that should be cut, and distributes the various timber products to the industries that can use them to best advantage.

JACK POT (1) An unskillful piece of logging work. (2) A bad slash. (3) As a verb, to "jack-pot" is to pile trees or logs crisscross, without regard for orderliness.

LIGNIN A complex substance that serves as the cementing material between fibers in woody plants. It is the part of wood that is insoluble in strong mineral acids. A group of organic substances that, with cellulose, form wood.

LOBBY The place in a logging camp where the men wash and wait before mealtime.

LUMBERJACK One who works at log-

802062°—49——59

ging. Synonyms: Timber beast, woodhick, logger, shantyman.

Lunch in A noon meal served in the dining quarters of the logging camp.

Mast The accumulated fruits (nuts) found on the forest floor. The major contributors are such species of trees as oaks, beeches, chestnuts, and some pines. Usually thought of and used when referring to its property as a food for hogs, deer, turkeys, or other wildlife.

Monoecious Pertaining to a plant in which stamens and pistils are produced in separate flowers, both of which are borne on the same plant. The word means "one house." When staminate and pistillate flowers, respectively, are produced on separate plants (two houses), the condition is said to be dioecious. Most flowers as we know them produce both stamens and pistils (the plant's reproductive organs)—which condition is said to be *perfect*.

Mutation A sudden variation in which the offspring differs from its parents in some well-marked character or characters as distinguished from a gradual variation, in which the new characters become highly developed only in the course of many generations.

Necrosis A localized or general death of plant tissue caused by low temperatures, fungi, and such (plant pathology). A disease quite often caused by a virus which is characterized by black dead plant tissue.

Ovule A rudimentary seed occurring in the ovary. A young seed in course of development. The cells that contain the embryo sac which develops into the seed after it is fertilized.

Peavy A stout wooden lever for rolling logs. A curvey metal hook is hinged to the lower part of the handle, and the tip is armed with a sharp steel spike.

Peeler (1) Usually one who removes bark from timber cut in the spring months when bark "slips." (2) A log used in the manufacture of rotary-cut veneer.

Periodicity Quality or state of being periodical, or regularly recurrent. In plant physiology, the tendency of a plant to exhibit rhythmical changes in vital functions.

Petiole A leafstalk; the slender stalk by which the blade of a leaf is attached to the stem.

pH (acidity) An index of the acidity or alkalinity of a material based on a logarithmic scale. A pH of 7.0 represents neutrality, 7.0 to 14.0 increasing alkalinity, and 7 to 0 increasing acidity.

Phloem A complex tissue in higher plants, which consists typically of sieve tubes and companion cells (although the companion cells are sometimes lacking, as in gymnosperms) and usually in addition various kinds of parenchyma and fiber cells, stone cells, etc.; bast tissue. In a narrow sense, the term is used as applying to the sieve tissue only.

Photoperiod Length of daylight hours. Photoperiodism is a physiological response of a plant to a different length of daylight hours. Discovered in 1920 by W. W. Garner and H. A. Allard, of the United States Department of Agriculture.

Photosynthesis A complicated physiological process of plant life in which an organic substance (sugar) is made from the carbon dioxide of the air combined with water. This process utilizes energy of light through the agency of chlorophyll.

Plywood An assembled product constructed of three or more layers of veneer joined with glue and usually laid with the grain of adjoining plies at right angles. Almost always an odd number of plies are used to secure balanced construction.

Pollen The fertilizing dustlike powder produced by stamens; functionally the same as the male sperm in animal reproduction. (Pollinate and pollenize are verb forms.)

Porosity The aggregate space between soil particles. The degree to which the soil is permeated with pores or cavities, expressed in percent of the volume of the soil unoccupied by solid particles.

Predator An animal or plant that preys upon another; especially one that obtains its food by killing and eating other animals. Also applies to insects. A predator usually destroys several hosts, as distinct from a parasite, which lives on one.

Progeny test A nursery or plantation test of the progeny or offspring of individual tagged seed trees to determine their inherent characteristics. This term may also be applied to any tests conducted on seedlings.

Pulp Wood or other vegetable matter

reduced to its component fibers. It is used to make paper or synthetic fabrics. Pulp is produced in various degrees of refinement. Alpha pulp is almost pure alpha cellulose. Other pulps have various percentages of hemi cellulose and even lignin.

Regeneration The reproduction or regrowth of a part which has been lost or destroyed; reestablishment on a better basis. Renewal by self-sown seeds, sprouts, rhizomes, and such.

Release cutting A cutting of larger individual trees that are overtopping young trees, for the purpose of freeing the young trees to permit them to make good growth.

Reproduction In forestry, the young trees that start from self-sown seed of the older trees in a stand.

Resistance The ability of a plant to develop and function normally despite adverse environmental conditions or the attacks of disease or insects.

Ring (in trees) Annual growth; the growth layer put on in a single growth year.

Road monkey A man who inspects and repairs a logging road.

Rosin A hard, brittle, natural resin obtained from the oleoresin exudate of certain resinous trees. Rosin is a particular kind of resin. Rosin is obtained either from gum that exudes from the living pine tree or from wood by extraction. Wood rosin and gum rosin are kinds of resins.

Sapling A young tree, usually one that is between 2 and 4 inches thick.

Sapwood The outer wood of trees in which certain of the cells are still alive and serve to conduct water from the roots to the leaves.

Saprophyte Any organism that lives on dead or decaying organic matter. Most of the higher fungi (like mushrooms and toadstools), various orchids, as the coralroot, and certain families, as the *Monotropaceae,* are saprophytes.

Saw timber Trees of a size and quality that will make logs suitable for sawing into lumber; trees suitable for production of sawlogs. Timber that will make lumber.

Scalping The removal of turf or other vegetation in the small area where a tree is to be planted.

Second-growth forest Forest growth which comes up after removal of the old stand by cutting, fire, or other cause. In lumberman's parlance, the smaller trees left after lumbering or the trees available for a second logging.

Seedling Generally speaking, any tree that originates from a seed is called a seedling, in contrast with those originating as a sprout, a root sucker, or from a cutting. In applied forestry, the term is restricted to such trees under 6 feet in height, while in forest-nursery practice, a seedling is a tree that is grown from seed and that has not been transplanted to secure a better developed root system.

Selection Picking out, or culling; the choosing of the best of a group. Any process, natural or artificial, which results or tends to result in preventing certain individuals or groups of organisms from surviving and propagating and in allowing others to do so, with the result that the particular traits of the latter are given pronounced expression.

Selective logging or cutting The removal of selected mature, large, or diseased trees as single, scattered trees or in small groups of trees. Young trees start in the openings thus made; the result of this type of cutting is an uneven-aged forest.

Shake (1) A wood shingle made by splitting flat strips from a bolt. (2) A crack or fissure in the stem of a tree, usually caused by frost or excessive bending in a strong wind. Shake usually follows the annual rings, while checks are radial, that is, extend across the annual rings.

Shelterwood A system of cutting in which the trees are removed in two or more cuts, the young trees coming in under the shelter of the remaining large trees.

Slash Branches, bark, top, chunks, cull logs, uprooted stumps, and broken or uprooted trees left in the ground after logging of timber is completed; also, large accumulation of debris after wind or fire.

Snags A stump or base of a branch that has been lopped off; also, a rough branch broken off. A tree from which the top has been broken; a rampike, especially one tall enough to be an extra fire hazard.

Soiling (of crops) The action of spreading or filling with soil, dirt, or manure.

Species A group of individuals (plants or animals) with so many common characteristics as to indicate a high relationship as well as common origin and descent. It is the unit of plant and animal classification.

STEM The main axis, trunk, or body of a tree or other plant.

STOMATA (*plural*); STOMA (*singular*) Minute openings, chiefly on the surface of the leaves of plants, through which water is evaporated and through which gaseous exchange takes place. Stomata are physiologically regulated by the plant.

STRATIFICATION The operation or method of burying seeds to keep them fresh and to soften their coverings, or to expose them without injury to cold temperatures that they may be more readily germinated, that is, for storage or to overcome dormancy.

STUMPAGE The value of timber as it stands uncut in the woods; in a general sense, the standing timber itself.

SUCCESSION The process of replacement of one plant community by another until the climax is reached. Each community in turn changes the temperature, moisture, and other factors of the environment; these new conditions hinder the community that brought them about and favor a new one, which becomes the next step in the succession.

THINNING A cutting made in an immature stand for the purpose of increasing the rate of growth and improving the form (or quality) of the trees that remain and increasing the total production of the stand.

TOLERANCE The ability of a tree to withstand extreme conditions of shade, disease, or other hazards.

TRANSPIRATION The process by which trees or other plants remove water from the soil and pass it through their roots, upward through the trunks and branches, and then out through the leaves into the air. Transpiration is a physiological process regulated by a living organism; evaporation is a physical process—such as evaporation of water from the surface of a lake.

UNDERSTORY That portion of the trees in a forest that is below the level of the main canopy; also, the trees forming such a layer.

VAN The small store in a logging camp in which clothing, tobacco, and medicine are kept to supply the crew. A portable van is also used, particularly on long river drives.

VASCULAR Of or pertaining to a vessel or vessels for the conveyance of a fluid, especially (in animals) a nutritive fluid, as blood or lymph, or (in plants) the sap; designating, or pertaining to, the entire system of vessels having this function.

VEGETATIVE Applied to propagation of plants by rooting cuttings or slips, budding, or grafting. This type of propagation leads to the formation of a clone if all the cuttings, buds, or cions are taken from the same seedling, and is to be distinguished from sexual or seed propagation. For this reason, the term asexual propagation is sometimes used.

VENEER A thin sheet of wood produced by rotating a log or bolt against a knife in a lathe or by sawing or slicing.

VIRGIN (of forests) A mature or overmature forest growth essentially uninfluenced by human activity. Virgin forests are also referred to as "old-growth" forests, as contrasted to newer or "second-growth" forests. In Douglas-fir, trees more than 200 years old are generally considered to be "old growth."

WATER TABLE When water occupies a zone of saturation beneath the ground, the upper edge of this zone is called the water table. If the table is tilted, the water moves toward the low side in an effort to make the surface level. When the water table intersects the land surface, as in a valley bottom, the ground water is drained by means of surface stream. See GROUND WATER.

WIDOW MAKER A broken limb hanging loose in the top of a tree, or a chunk or limb knocked loose by a falling tree.

WINDFALL A tree knocked down by the wind. An area of such trees. Synonym: Blow-down.

WOODPECKER A poor chopper. Synonym: Beaver.

WORKING CIRCLE A unit of forest land that is handled in accordance with a specific plan of management for the timber resources of that area.

WOLF TREE A forest tree whose size and position cause it to prevent the growth of many small trees around it by usurping their space, light, and nourishment.

WEED TREE A tree that has little or no commercial value.

# Index[1]



[1] *In this index, approved common names of trees are printed in ordinary type; the scientific names and certain names that are in common, but not approved, use are italicized.*
*The abbreviation* N. F. *stands for national forest.*

802062°—49——60

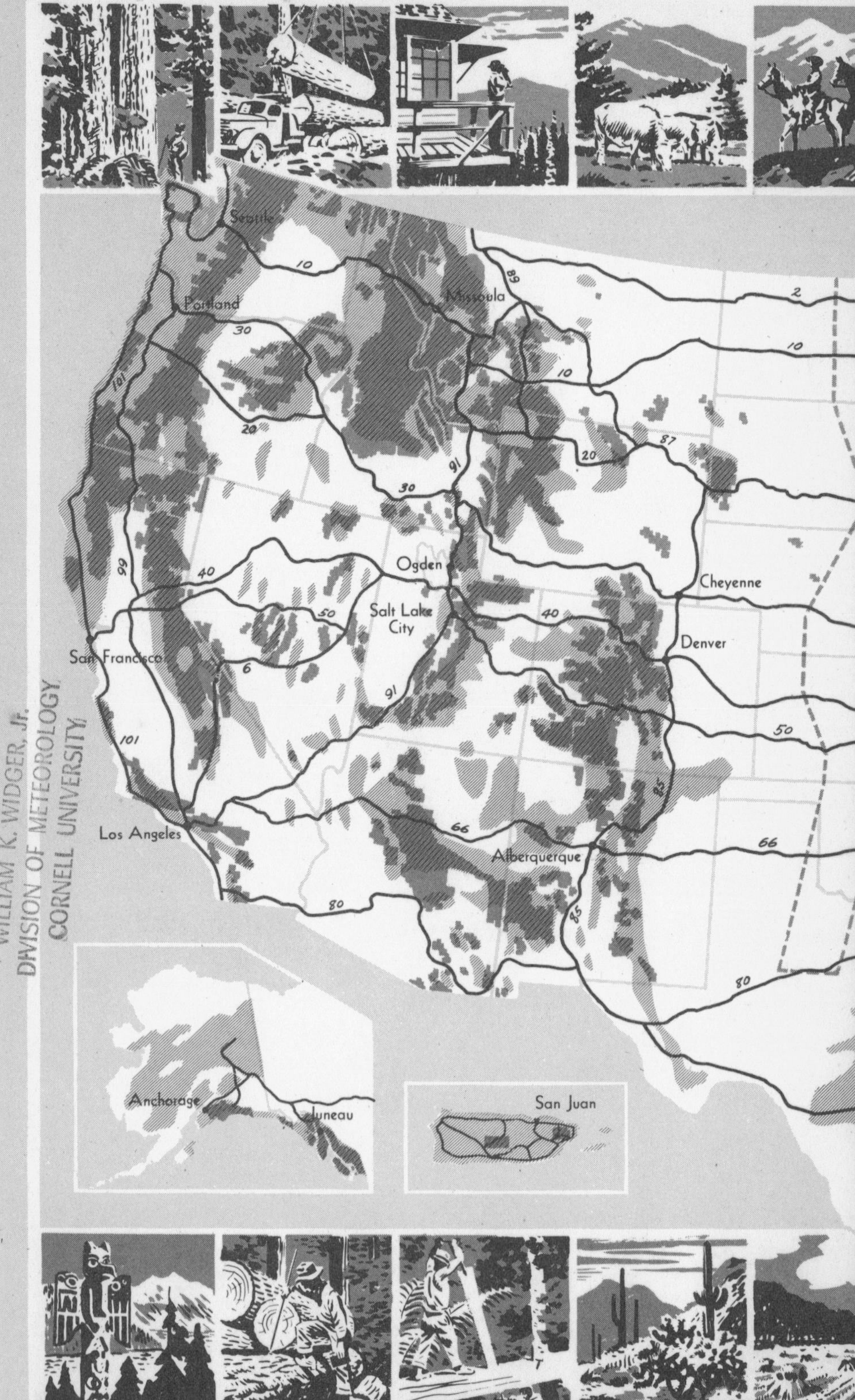

Seattle
Portland
Missoula
Ogden
Salt Lake City
Cheyenne
Denver
San Francisco
Los Angeles
Alberquerque
Anchorage
Juneau
San Juan
10
2
30
20
101
99
40
50
6
91
89
87
85
66
80